BUILDINGS AND STRUCTURES

OF

AMERICAN RAILROADS.

A REFERENCE BOOK

FOR

Railroad Managers, Superintendents, Master Mechanics, Engineers, Architects, and Students.

BY

WALTER G. BERG, C.E.,

PRINCIPAL ASSISTANT ENGINEER, LEHIGH VALLEY RAILROAD.

NEW YORK:
JOHN WILEY & SONS,
53 East Tenth Street.
1893.

FERRIS BROS.,
Printers,
326 Pearl Street,
New York.

ROBERT DRUMMOND,
Electrotyper,
444 & 446 Pearl Street,
New York.

PREFACE.

THIS work is intended to serve as a reference book for Railroad Managers, Superintendents, Master Mechanics, Engineers, Architects, Students, and others connected with the various departments of railroading or kindred interests, who are desirous of obtaining data as to the existing practice on American railroads relating to any of the subjects discussed in the book. Extracts from the first sixteen chapters were previously published in serial form in the *Railroad Gazette*, and met with favorable and encouraging comments.

It is hardly necessary to call attention to the scarcity of American literature on buildings and similar structures connected with the station service, maintenance of way and operating departments of railroads. With the exception of isolated articles to be found in technical periodicals or in the publications of professional societies, accurate and exhaustive data relating to existing railroad structures can only be obtained by personal inspection or by addressing the proper department official in charge of the work in question. The purpose of this book is to obviate to a large extent the necessity of railroad men and others in search of such information having to resort to tedious investigations and personal inquiries. Attention is also called to the fact that most of the subjects embraced in this book have never before been discussed in print in a systematic and thorough manner.

The aim of the author has been to present a collection embodying the best practice for each particular class of structure, whether cheap or expensive, and showing the sundry variations caused by individual views or local conditions in different sections of the country. Particular attention has been paid to the smaller buildings connected with the roadway and operating departments. The cheap and simple structures in use in the thinly settled sections of the country have been considered of as much importance as those of the most elaborate and artistic design.

Each subject is discussed in a general manner at the beginning of the corresponding chapter, so that inexperienced persons can gain information on the salient points and controlling features for each class of structures, while others more conversant with the subject will find these general discussions convenient for reference. The second part of each chapter is devoted to detail descriptions and illustrations of structures in use on American railroads.

The extensive territory covered is shown by the fact that over *five hundred* different buildings and structures are described, illustrated, or referred to, while there are nearly *seven hundred* illustrations accompanying the text, of which over *six hundred* have been specially prepared for this work. The illustrations, which range from the simple details, general plans, sections, and elevations of structures, to elaborate and artistic half-tone cuts of exteriors and interiors, are inserted throughout the book in their proper places opposite the text.

The collection and selection of the necessary data and the preparation for publication of such a large number of illustrations have been accomplished only by great assiduity and considerable expense. The intrinsic merit of the book is enhanced by the fact that Engineers, Architects, and Railroad Men from all parts of the country have placed valuable plans and important information at the disposal of the author which otherwise would be very difficult to obtain.

The author desires to express his thanks to all who have so generously and kindly assisted him in the preparation of this book. It has been his aim to give credit throughout the book to the originators or contributors of designs or data. Where the designers or persons in charge of work are not mentioned, it is because they were unknown to the author, and not through any desire to suppress their names.

While it is obviously difficult to mention all persons who have personally, directly or indirectly, furnished data or information utilized in the preparation and compilation of this book, the author feels bound to place on record the valuable assistance furnished by the following railroad men, engineers, and architects:

L. M. Allen, General Passenger Agent, New York & Northern Railway.
M. J. Becker, Chief Engineer, Pennsylvania Lines West of Pittsburg.
V. G. Bogue, Chief Engineer, Union Pacific Railway.
Geo. W. Boyd, Assistant General Passenger Agent, Pennsylvania Railroad.
W. W. Boyington, Architect, Chicago, Ill.
E. F. Brooks, Engineer Maintenance of Way, New York Division, Pennsylvania Railroad.
E. D. B. Brown, Architect and Civil Engineer, New York, N. Y.
Wm. H. Brown, Chief Engineer, Pennsylvania Railroad.
C. W. Buchholz, Chief Engineer, New York, Lake Erie & Western Railroad.
R. Caffrey, Supervisor, Eastern Division, Philadelphia & Reading Railroad (formerly General Roadmaster, Lehigh Valley Railroad).
H. E. Chamberlin, Superintendent, Concord Railroad.
F. A. Chase, Master Mechanic, Kansas City, St. Joseph & Council Bluffs Railroad.
S. French Collins, Car Department, Lehigh Valley Railroad.
P. H. Conradson, formerly Chemist, New York & New England Railroad.
F. S. Curtis, Chief Engineer, New York, New Haven & Hartford Railroad.
Philip H. Dewitt, Assistant Engineer, Lehigh Valley Railroad.
Charles B. Dudley, Chemist, Pennsylvania Railroad.
H. T. Douglass, Chief Engineer, Baltimore & Ohio Railway.
Cyrus L. W. Eidlitz, Architect, New York, N. Y.
H. Fernstrom, Chief Engineer, Minnesota & Northwestern Railroad and Chicago, St. Paul & Kansas City Railroad.
L. Focht, Assistant Engineer, Lehigh Valley Railroad.
William Forsyth, Mechanical Engineer, Chicago, Burlington & Quincy Railroad.
Wolcott C. Foster, Civil Engineer, New York, N. Y.
J. D. Fouquet, Assistant Chief Engineer, New York Central & Hudson River Railroad.
F. W. Fratt, Chief Engineer, Wisconsin Central Railway.
Geo. H. Frost, Managing Editor, *Engineering News*, New York, N. Y.
C. C. Genung, Chief Engineer, Ohio Valley Railway.
George Gibbs, Mechanical Engineer, Chicago, Milwaukee & St. Paul Railway.
T. H. Grant, Assistant Engineer, Central Railroad of New Jersey.
Bradford L. Gilbert, Architect, New York, N. Y.
Walter D. Gregory, formerly Chemist, New York, Lake Erie & Western Railroad.
A. Griggs, Superintendent of Motive Power, New York & New England Railroad.

Charles Hansel, formerly Resident Engineer, Wabash, St. Louis & Pacific Railway.
S. B. Haupt, Superintendent Motive Power, Norfolk & Western Railroad.
Edwin A. Hill, Chief Engineer, Indianapolis, Decatur & Springfield Railway.
Hawthorne Hill, Managing Editor, *The Engineering Magazine*, New York, N. Y.
Julius G. Hocke, Assistant Engineer, Lehigh Valley Railroad.
W. B. W. Howe, Jr., Chief Engineer, Savannah, Florida & Western Railroad.
F. W. Johnstone, Superintendent, Mexican Central Railroad.
J. M. Jones, Station Master, Concord Railroad, Concord N. H.
W. S. Jones, Chief Engineer, Chicago & Northern Pacific Railroad.
Walter Katté, Chief Engineer, New York Central & Hudson River Railroad.
J. W. Kendrick, Chief Engineer, Northern Pacific Railroad.
John S. Lentz, Superintendent Car Department, Philadelphia & Reading Railroad, formerly Superintendent Car Department, Lehigh Valley Railroad.
Chas. F. Loweth, Civil Engineer, St. Paul, Minn.
S. D. Mason, Principal Assistant Engineer, Northern Pacific Railroad.
Wm. McIlvaine, Civil Engineer, Philadelphia, Pa.
J. M. Meade, Resident Engineer, Atchinson, Topeka & Santa Fe Railroad.
Alex. Mitchel, Superintendent of Motive Power, Philadelphia & Reading Railroad, formerly Superintendent, Lehigh Valley Railroad.
R. Montford, Chief Engineer, Louisville & Nashville Railroad.
H. K. Nichol, Chief Engineer, Philadelphia & Reading Railroad.
C. B. Nicholson, Chief Engineer, Cincinnati, New Orleans & Texas Pacific Railroad and Alabama Great Southern Railroad.
W. Barclay Parsons, Jr., Civil Engineer, author of "Track," New York, N. Y.
W. F. Pascoe, Superintendent Bridges and Buildings, Lehigh Valley Railroad.
Wm. H. Peddle, Division Superintendent and Engineer, Central Railroad of New Jersey.
H. G. Prout, Editor, *Railroad Gazette*, New York, N. Y.
L. S. Randolph, Engineer of Tests, Baltimore & Ohio Railroad.
A. L. Reed, Chief Engineer, Port Huron & Northwestern Railway.
C. A. Reed, Supervising Architect, Minnesota & Northwestern Railroad and Chicago, St. Paul & Kansas City Railroad, St. Paul, Minn.
C. Rosenberg, General Foreman, Lehigh Valley Creosoting Works (formerly Master Carpenter, New Jersey Division, Lehigh Valley Railroad).
F. E. Schall, Assistant Engineer, Lehigh Valley Railroad.
F. M. Slater, Chief Engineer, National Docks Railway.
E. F. Smith, Engineer in Charge, Philadelphia & Reading Terminal, Philadelphia, Pa.
A. W. Stedman, Chief Engineer, Lehigh Valley Railroad.
C. B. Talbot, Civil Engineer, Northern Pacific Railroad, Tacoma, Wash.
J. F. Wallace, Chief Engineer, Illinois Central Railroad.
H. F. White, Chief Engineer, Burlington, Cedar Rapids & Northern Railroad.
Wilson Brothers & Co., Civil Engineers and Architects, Philadelphia, Pa.
H. Wolters, Architect, Louisville, Ky.

The technical journals and publications have been carefully examined in order to furnish desirable references to matter previously published. The author takes pleasure in acknowledging the uniform courtesy extended to him by the editors of the technical press and the liberal spirit manifested in according permission to quote from their files. The publications thus utilized are as follows: *American Architect and Building News; Engineering News and American Railway Journal; Railroad Gazette; Railroad Topics; The Engineering Magazine; The Engineering Record* (*Building Record and The Sanitary Engineer*); *The Inland Architect and News Record; The Railroad and Engineering Journal; The Railway News; The Railway Review;* and others.

The preparation of this work has extended over several years, not through any lack of enthusiasm on the part of the author, but owing to the fact that the book had to be written in such hours that could be spared from the exacting demands of an extensive professional practice. The author trusts, therefore, that any omissions or deficiencies found in the book will not be too severely criticised, and that " Buildings and Structures of American Railroads " will be accepted as a valuable contribution to the technical literature of the day and take its place among standard reference books in the libraries of Railroad Men, Engineers, Architects Students, and others interested in the subject.

NEW YORK, N. Y., December, 1st, 1892.

TABLE OF CONTENTS.

* Illustrated.

CHAPTER IV. DWELLING-HOUSES FOR EMPLOYÉS.

CHAPTER V. SLEEPING QUARTERS, READING-ROOMS, AND CLUB-HOUSES FOR EMPLOYÉS

CHAPTER VI. SNOW-SHEDS AND PROTECTION-SHEDS FOR MOUNTAIN-SLIDES.

CHAPTER VII. SIGNAL-TOWERS.

CHAPTER VIII. CAR-SHEDS AND CAR-CLEANING YARDS.

CHAPTER IX. ASHPITS.

CHAPTER X. ICE-HOUSES.

CHAPTER XI. SAND HOUSES.

CHAPTER XII. OIL-STORAGE HOUSES.

CHAPTER XIII. OIL-MIXING HOUSES.

CHAPTER XIV. WATER STATIONS.

CHAPTER XV. COALING STATIONS FOR LOCOMOTIVES.

CHAPTER XVI. ENGINE-HOUSES.

CHAPTER XVII. FREIGHT-HOUSES.

CHAPTER XVII. PLATFORMS, PLATFORM-SHEDS, AND SHELTERS.

CHAPTER XIX. COMBINATION DEPOTS.

CHAPTER XX. FLAG-DEPOTS.

CHAPTER XXI. LOCAL PASSENGER DEPOTS.

CHAPTER XXII. TERMINAL PASSENGER DEPOTS.

APPENDIX.

SPECIFICATIONS.

LIST OF ILLUSTRATIONS.

CHAPTER I. WATCHMAN'S SHANTIES.

CHAPTER II. SECTION TOOL-HOUSES.

CHAPTER III. SECTION HOUSES.

CHAPTER IV. DWELLING-HOUSES FOR EMPLOYÉS.

CHAPTER V. SLEEPING QUARTERS, READING-ROOMS, AND CLUB-HOUSES FOR EMPLOYÉS.

CHAPTER VI. SNOWSHEDS AND PROTECTION-SHEDS FOR MOUNTAIN-SLIDES.

CHAPTER VII. SIGNAL-TOWERS.

CHAPTER VIII. CAR-SHEDS AND CAR-CLEANING YARDS.

CHAPTER IX. ASHPITS.

CHAPTER X. ICE-HOUSES.

CHAPTER XI. SAND-HOUSES.

CHAPTER XIV. WATER STATIONS.

CHAPTER XV. COALING STATIONS FOR LOCOMOTIVES.

CHAPTER XVI. ENGINE-HOUSES.

CHAPTER XVII. FREIGHT-HOUSES.

CHAPTER XVIII. PLATFORMS, PLATFORM-SHEDS, AND SHELTERS.

CHAPTER XIX. COMBINATION DEPOTS.

CHAPTER XX. FLAG-DEPOTS.

CHAPTER XXI. LOCAL PASSENGER DEPOTS.

CHAPTER XXII. TERMINAL PASSENGER DEPOTS.

BUILDINGS AND STRUCTURES OF AMERICAN RAILROADS.

CHAPTER I.

WATCHMAN'S SHANTIES.

WATCHMAN'S, flagman's, or switch-tender's shanties (frequently called flag-houses, switch-houses, or watch-boxes) are used along railroads at exposed points, as crossings, drawbridges, sharp curves, dangerous cuts, or at yard systems, crossovers and leaders, where regular switch-tenders are required. Owing to the large number of buildings of this kind necessarily in use on a railroad, the adoption of a standard or of a series of standard alternate designs becomes a matter of prime importance, either to satisfy the varying requirements at different sites, or to avoid sameness of design over the entire road. While the building is small and the design not difficult, the importance of studying the details carefully, so as to satisfy all requirements with the least expenditure of material and labor, is very apparent.

Where a standard design exists, the several parts of the building are generally turned out in large numbers at one of the shops of the road, and kept in stock. When a house is to be built, the finished material for it is shipped from stock and put together at site. If the size of the building permits shipment in sections or in one piece, then most of the framing and fitting is done at the shop, reducing the work at the site to a minimum. In this manner great economy and uniformity can be attained. Monotony of design need not necessarily follow, as the varying localities and r·quirements will call for several standards, while each design can receive certain modifications in the finish of the exterior, as the details of the panels, scroll-work, finial, ridge-roll, chimney-top, etc., sufficient to relieve the eye without in reality changing the important features of the plan.

The framework of these structures is in all cases wood, sheathed on the outside either with vertical boards and battens, or with plain or ornamental horizontal weather-boarding, or with narrow tongued and grooved boards, or with corrugated iron. The roofing is generally tarred roofing-felt, tin, fancy shingles, slate, or corrugated iron. On some railroads corrugated iron for the roof and sides of the building, covering a light framework of wood, is very much in favor, as it is cheap, light, and to a certain extent fire-proof.

The general requirements for the buildings under discussion vary according to the exact purpose for which they are intended. Usually the size is limited owing to the location of the building among tracks or between tracks and the edge of the right of way. Inside the building there should be sufficient space for a small stove, a bench adapted for a man to lie down on, a locker and places for keeping signal-flags, lamps, oil, waste, coal, etc. The windows should be so arranged as to command a good view of the tracks and other points that the watchman or switchman is expected to keep in sight.

The shape of the building can be either square, octagonal, or oblong. The square building is generally made about 5 ft. in the clear inside. The octagonal shape is especially serviceable where a large territory has to be controlled by the watchman, as small windows are easily introduced on all sides; its minimum size is about 5 ft. inside. A very usual size for oblong buildings is 5 ft. × 7 ft. inside; the least size known to be in use is 3 ft. 3 in. × 7 ft. 7 in. inside. The oblong style of building is capable of enlargement to any desired size for the accommodation of a larger number of men.

Buildings for car-inspectors, car-checkers, yardmen, trainmen, weighers, etc., are usually built very similar to oblong watchman's shanties, except that the size of the building, interior arrangements, and the spacing of doors and windows are varied to suit each case. For this latter class of buildings the Lehigh Valley Railroad and other roads are largely adopting frame structures, covered on sides and roof with light corrugated iron.

Following are descriptions of watchman's shanties actually in use in this country.

Square Watchman's Shanty, Richmond & Alleghany Railroad.—The watchman's shanty of the Richmond & Alleghany Railroad, shown in Figs. 1 to 3, can serve as an example of a cheap, un-

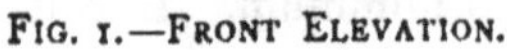

FIG. 1.—FRONT ELEVATION.

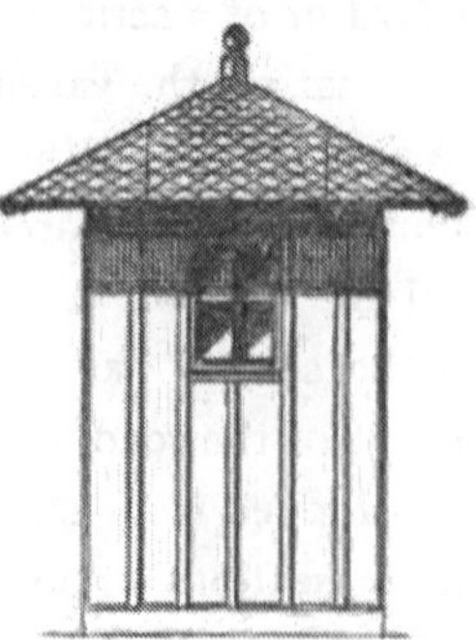

FIG. 2.—SIDE ELEVATION.

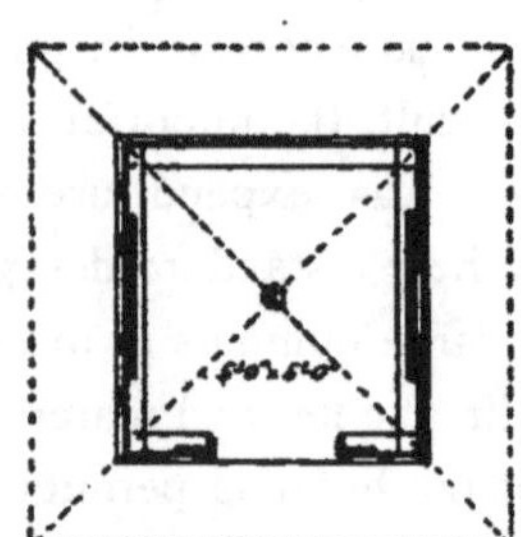

FIG. 3.—GROUND-PLAN.

pretending standard for a watchman's or switch-tender's house, much used on roads where a low first cost is of greater consideration than a pleasing exterior. The box is 5 ft. square in the clear inside, with a 2-ft. door in front and small hinged windows on the sides. The frame is covered on the outside with upright boards and battens. The inside is not ceiled, which in colder climates, however, would be essential. The hip roof is covered with tin or tarred roofing-felt. The height of frame from bottom of mud-sill to top of plate is 7 ft. 6 in. The dimensions of the principal timbers used are as follows: mud-sills, 8 in. × 10 in., laid flat; sills, 3 in. × 4 in.; plates, 2 in. × 2½ in.; nailer under plate, 1½ in. × 10 in.; nailer at half height of frame, 1½ in. × 6 in.; door-posts, 1½ in. × 6 in.; rafters, 2 in. × 4 in.; outside boarding and roof-boards, ⅞ in.

Octagonal Watchman's Shanty, Richmond & Alleghany Railroad.—The octagonal watchman's shanty of the Richmond & Alleghany Railroad, shown in Figs. 4 and 5, offers more room and commands a better view of the surroundings than the square standard does. Although of cheap and plain construction, its general appearance is very neat. The squaring off of one side of the octagon to a full square forms a convenient place for a stove or for a bench long enough for a man to lie down on. Where these features are not essential, a regular octagon can be used just as well. The box is 6 ft. wide in the clear between parallel sides of the octagon. The frame, boarding, and roofing are similar to the square standard of the same railroad, described above, except that the building is, in addition, ceiled on the inside. The dimensions of the principal timbers used are as follows: mud-sills, 6 in. × 8 in.; sills and plates, 2 in. × 2½ in.; rafters, 2 in. × 4 in.; outside sheathing, 1 in.; inside ceiling, ⅞-in. tongued and grooved boards; roof-boards, 1 in., rough; floor, 2 in.

FIG. 4.—FRONT ELEVATION.

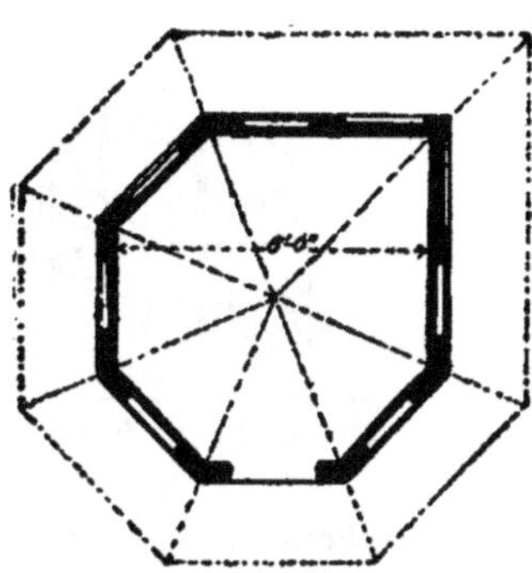

FIG. 5.—GROUND-PLAN.

Watchman's Shanty, Alleghany Valley Railroad.—A watchman's shanty observed by the author on the Alleghany Valley Railroad, in the suburbs of Pittsburgh, presents certain features in common with a large number of structures of the kind in question throughout the country. The building is oblong, 6 ft. × 8 ft. inside, with a double-pitched gable roof. The frame is covered on the outside with horizontal, bevelled weather-boarding. There is a door on the gable end facing the track, 2 ft. 6 in. × 6 ft. 6 in., made in two sections, one over the other, so-called halved doors. The windows on each of the long sides of the room are placed near the front end of the building, the advantage being that a man standing just inside of the door is also opposite the windows on each side. The height of frame from sill to plate is 8 ft. The principal timbers used are as follows: sills, 4 in. × 6 in.; corner-posts, 3 in. × 3 in.; studding, 2 in. × 3 in.; plates, 3 in. × 4 in.; rafters, 2 in. × 3 in., spaced 16 in. centres; door, ⅞-in. boards; sides, ⅞-in. bevelled weather-boarding; roof, 1-in. boards, covered with tin.

Watchman's Shanty, Philadelphia & Reading Railroad.—The watchman's shanty of the Philadelphia & Reading Railroad, shown in Figs. 6 to 8, offers a very handsome and attractive appearance. This is one of a number of standard alternate designs, which vary in the style of the

FIG. 6.—FRONT ELEVATION.

FIG. 7.—SIDE ELEVATION.

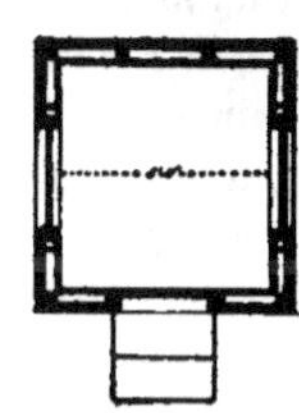

FIG. 8.—GROUND-PLAN.

roof and the detail of the panels and scroll-work on the outside, being otherwise all alike so far as the frame and the general features are concerned. The building is 5 ft. square in the clear, ceiled inside and outside with narrow tongued and grooved boards. There is a 26-in. door on the front, and windows are provided on each side. The roof is covered either with ornamental shingles or slate, and is finished off with a heavy galvanized-iron ridge cresting and ornamental chimney-top.

Watchman's Shanty, Lehigh Valley Railroad.—The watchman's shanty of the Lehigh Valley Railroad, shown in Figs. 9 and 10, is an octagonal frame structure with one side of the octagon on

FIG. 9.—FRONT ELEVATION.

FIG. 10.—SIDE ELEVATION.

the rear of the house squared off to a full square, similar to the standard of the Richmond & Alleghany Railroad, shown in Figs. 4 and 5. The finish of the roof is neat, and the building presents a very pleasing appearance.

Watchman's Shanty of Limited Width, New York Division, Pennsylvania Railroad.—The Pennsylvania Railroad, in passing through Jersey City, Newark, and other cities, where its right of way is limited in width, is frequently forced to locate a watchman's shanty between tracks. To meet this emergency the standard narrow watchman's shanty, shown in Figs. 11 to 13, was designed, and

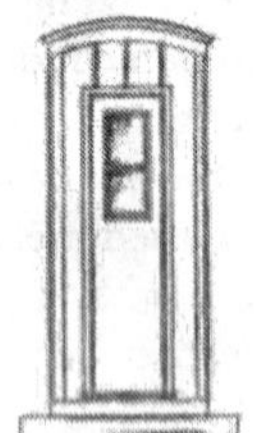

FIG. 11.—FRONT ELEVATION.

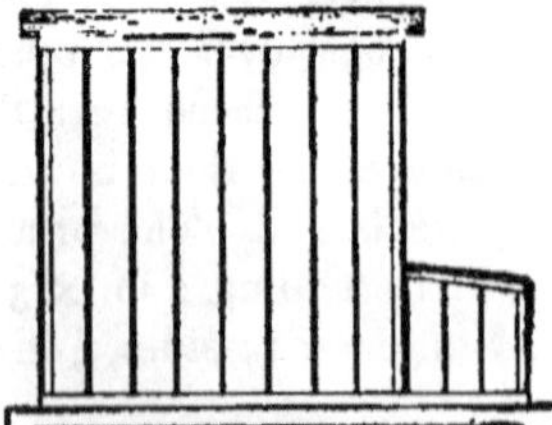

FIG. 12.—SIDE ELEVATION.

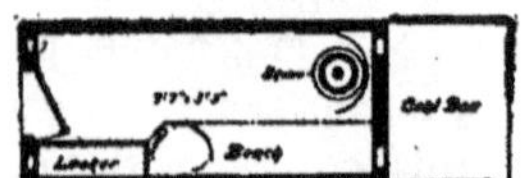

FIG. 13.—GROUND-PLAN.

has been found by the writer to have been successfully used with tracks as close as 15 ft. 9 in., centre to centre, or about 10 ft. 8 in. between the outside of the nearest rail-heads.

This narrow standard could no doubt be used with comparative safety where the tracks are even 6 in. or 9 in. closer than the figures given above, but the clearance would be very scant, and this reduced spacing, therefore, is not to be recommended. The building is 3 ft. 7 in. wide, out to out, and 8 ft. 3 in. long, out to out, with a coal-box on the rear 2 ft. 9 in. long. The height of the eaves above top of rails is 8 ft. When the building is located between a main track and a side track, the side facing the main track is placed 4 ft. in the clear from the gauge face of the nearest rail, while the side facing the side track is placed 3 ft. 6 in. in the clear from the nearest gauge face. The room is 3 ft. 3 in. wide, 7 ft. 7 in. long, and 7 ft. 6 in. high inside, in the clear. The door-opening is only 19 in. wide in the clear; the door is 6 ft. 6 in. high, with a fixed sash in upper panel.

There is one window, 18 in. × 3 ft. 6 in., in the rear end. The room is provided with a small cast-iron stove, taking up about 18 in. of floor-space; a bench, 14 in. wide by 4 ft. long; and a locker, 9 in. deep and 2 ft. 6 in. wide, extending from floor to ceiling. A small stool or chair completes the interior outfit. The building is ceiled inside with narrow tongued and grooved boards, and sheathed on the outside with upright boards and battens. No studding whatever is used on the long sides of the building, parallel with the tracks, the inside ceiling being nailed directly against the outside boarding. At the ends of the building studs 2 in. thick are used at the corners and on each side of the door and rear window. The roof is slightly curved, made of tongued and grooved boards laid lengthwise with the building, and covered with tin.

Standard Watchman's Shanty, Pennsylvania Railroad.—The standard watchman's shanty of the Pennsylvania Railroad, illustrated and described in the issue of the *Railroad Gazette* of November 12, 1880, is an oblong frame structure, 5 ft. × 7 ft. inside, with a plain double-pitched gable roof. There is a 2 ft. × 6 ft. 3 in. door in front, and on each side of the room are large windows. A stove occupies one of the rear corners of the building, while the opposite side of the room is provided with a long bench. The roof projects about 18 in. on all sides, and is covered either with tin or tarred roofing-felt. The building is ceiled on the inside only, the frame showing on the outside, arranged so as to produce a pleasing effect.

Watchman's Shanty, Norfolk & Western Railroad.—The watchman's shanty of the Norfolk & Western Railroad, shown in Figs. 14 to 16, is an oblong frame structure, 5 ft. × 7 ft., with a plain

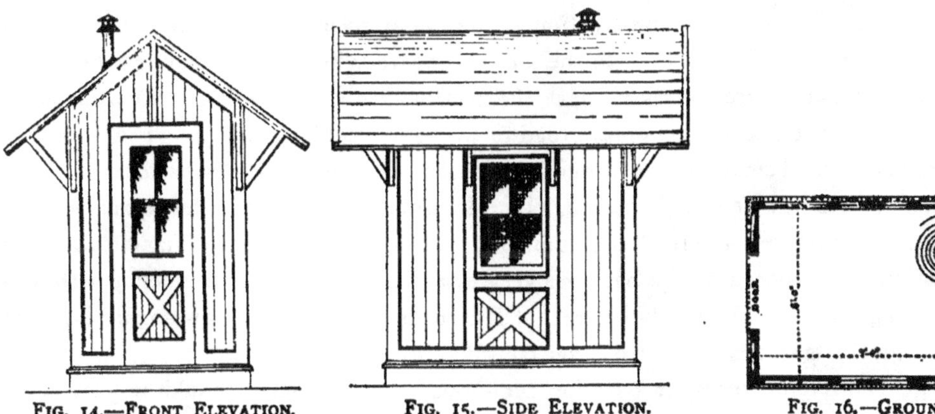

FIG. 14.—FRONT ELEVATION. FIG. 15.—SIDE ELEVATION. FIG. 16.—GROUND-PLAN.

double-pitched gable roof covered with tin. The building is ceiled on the inside only, the frame showing on the outside. The details of this design are practically the same as the standard watchman's shanty of the Pennsylvania Railroad, illustrated in the issue of the *Railroad Gazette* of November 12, 1880, as mentioned above.

Design for a Watchman's Shanty, by W. B. Parsons, Jr.—Mr. W. B. Parsons, Jr., presents in his book on "Track" a design for a watchman's shanty. The building is oblong, 5 ft. × 7 ft. inside, with a double-pitched gable roof covered with No. 24 galvanized corrugated iron. The outside is covered with upright boards and battens, but the inside is not ceiled. There is a 2 ft. 6 in. × 6 ft. 6 in. door in front with a fixed 12 in. × 12 in. light in the upper panel. On all sides of the room are small windows. The dimensions of the principal timbers used are as follows: sills, 3 in. × 6 in.; floor-joists, 2 in. × 3 in.; corner-posts, 3 in. × 3 in.; plates, 3 in. × 6 in.; door-studs, 2 in. × 3 in.; horizontal studding, 2 in. × 3 in.; rafters, 2 in. × 4 in., spaced 27 in. centres; purlins at eaves and at ridge, 1 in. × 4 in.; eaves-board, 2 in. × 5 in.; window and door casings, 4 in. × 1 in.; door, 1-in. boards; frame covered with 1-in. boards and 2-in. chamfered battens; floor, 2-in. plank.

CHAPTER II.

SECTION TOOL-HOUSES.

SECTION tool-houses or hand-car houses are used for storing hand-cars, tools, and supplies required in connection with the construction or the maintenance of the track and roadbed on a railroad. They also afford shelter to the men during very heavy or prolonged storms and are, to a limited extent, frequently used as the section-master's workshop. There is usually one house for every track section of the road or for every regular track gang; in yards or at large terminals several small houses or one large tool-house are frequently used.

Section houses will be found located, as a rule, from three to ten miles apart, according to the local conditions on each road, the number of tracks, and other controlling circumstances. The adoption of a standard design becomes very essential, owing to the frequency with which these buildings occur. Hence there are but few roads that cannot show something in this line, although the methods employed differ considerably.

The general requirements for a section tool-house are that space should be provided for the hand-car and tools used by the gang on the track, in addition to which provision should be made for the storage of lamps, signal appliances, oil-cans, and, to a limited extent, such supplies as rope, spikes, nails, track-bolts, fishbars, etc., without seriously blocking the floor-space. Boxes, shelves, and racks for storing tools, lamps, oil-cans, bar iron, tool steel, etc., conveniently arranged, aid materially in keeping everything well assorted and yet confined to the least space. A small locker for the section foreman to keep blank reports, time books, and other papers, and a short work-bench, to be used at odd times for making light repairs to the outfit, will about complete the furniture. On some roads the tool-house only serves for storing the hand-car and the few tools in daily use, in which case a building slightly larger than the hand-car suffices without any further inside fixtures.

The location of the building should be alongside of a track. The most desirable site is at the head of a siding opposite the stopping-post near the switch leading off the main track, the advantage being that the section men can dodge in and out of the main track between trains with greater ease and less risk than if they had to lift the hand-car on and off the main track. In yards or at stations this feature is preserved by locating the tool-house near the head of the yard.

These buildings, with probably few exceptions, are frame structures, sheathed only on the outside and roofed with tin, shingles, or corrugated iron. The designs in use differ mainly in the location of the large door and the position the hand-car track occupies inside of the house. In all cases provision must be made to enable a hand-car to be placed outside of the house without obstructing any tracks. Whether to place the door in the gable end or in the side of the building is a much-disputed question, which the width of the right of way available outside of the tracks will frequently determine. With a very limited right of way width the design with the door in the gable end and the building placed lengthwise with the track and close to it will be the proper standard to adopt, as it takes up the least space crosswise of the right of way. The disadvantage is that the hand-car must be turned on the platform in front of the house instead of running directly into the house after being lifted off the track.

If the house is small, the placing of the door to either side of the central line of the building is a good method to adopt, as otherwise the hand-car, when in the house, seriously narrows the floor-space on both sides. The best location for the door is near one end of the long side of the building. There should be, however, sufficient space left between the hand-car and the nearest gable end for a man to pass, and also to allow the wall-space along the gable to be used for racks to hold extra tools and sundry supplies. At the opposite gable end, tool-boxes, shelves, lockers, and a short work-bench could be located, leaving ample floor-space for the men to move around freely and for the storage of miscellaneous supplies in small quantities.

One or more small windows, closed either with a board shutter or sliding board sash, are useful for the admission of sufficient light to allow of the selection and assorting of materials, the cleaning of lamps and repairing of tools, etc., without having to depend on the open door for light, which would be objectionable in stormy weather. A floor of cinders or fine ballast serves for all purposes as well as a wooden floor, provided the location of the building will admit of good drainage.

While quite cheap in design, the Pennsylvania Railroad's tool-house presents a very neat appearance. The Philadelphia & Reading Railroad's tool-house ranks well in point of appearance, but it is hardly to be recommended for tool-houses generally, except on sections of a railroad with heavy passenger travel. The tool-house of the Union Pacific Railway is one of the best buildings for the purpose, unless a gable-end standard is required owing to limited width of right of way. The general style of the tool-house presented by W. B. Parsons, Jr., in his book on "Track," and the standard of the Atchison, Topeka & Santa Fe Railroad, are very similar to the design of the Union Pacific Railway. In the Cincinnati Southern Railway's tool-house, where the track enters on one side of the gable end, the floor-space is not utilized as well as in the Union Pacific Railway's design. The Northern Pacific Railroad's plans belong to the cheapest structures shown; they are not intended for carrying much material or many extra tools in store, and are, therefore, small.

Relative to the size of these structures, the Pennsylvania Railroad has three standards, respectively 16 ft. 2 in. × 30 ft. 2 in., 16 ft. 2 in. × 20 ft. 2 in., and 12 ft. 2 in. × 14 ft. 2 in.; the Cincinnati Southern Railway, 12 ft. × 16 ft. 8 in.; the Union Pacific Railway, 10 ft. × 14 ft.; the Atchison, Topeka & Santa Fe Railroad, 12 ft. × 16 ft.; design by W. B. Parsons, Jr., 12 ft. × 18 ft.; the Philadelphia & Reading Railroad, 10 ft. × 13 ft.; the Northern Pacific Railroad, 10 ft. × 14 ft.; the single hand-car house on the Northern Pacific Railroad, 9 ft. × 12 ft.; the Lehigh Valley Railroad, 16 ft. × 20 ft.

Descriptions and plans of the following tool-houses are presented illustrative of the subject discussed in this chapter.

Standard Section Tool-house, Pennsylvania Railroad.—The standard section or foreman's tool-house of the Pennsylvania Railroad, shown in Figs. 17 to 21, published in the ***Railroad Gazette*** of November 12, 1880, is an oblong frame building with a double-pitched gable roof; the sides are sheathed on the outside with upright boards and battens, the roof being covered with tin. There

FIG. 17.—FRONT ELEVATION.

FIG. 18.—GROUND-PLAN.

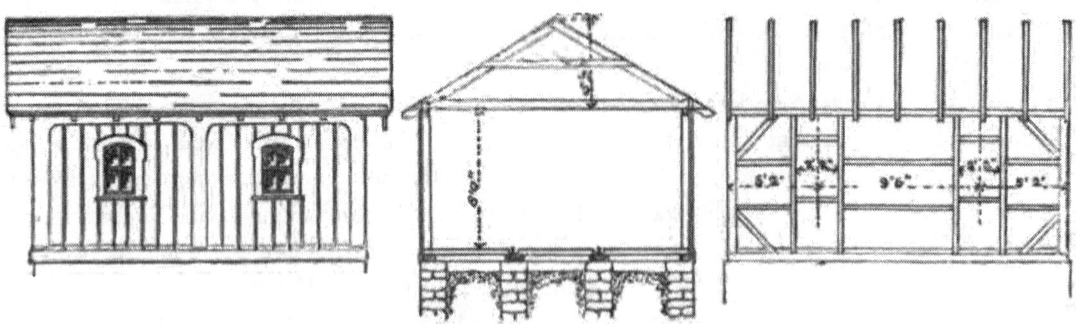

FIG. 19.—SIDE ELEVATION.

FIG. 20.—SECTION.

FIG. 21.—ELEVATION OF FRAME.

are three standard sizes in use, viz.: size "A," 16 ft. 2 in. × 30 ft. 2 in.; size "B," 16 ft. 2 in. × 20 ft. 2 in.; size "C," 12 ft. 2 in. × 14 ft. 2 in. The building is placed either with the gable end or the side facing the tracks, according to the space available between the outside track and the right of way line. In all cases a large door for admitting a hand-car is provided at the centre of the gable end. The details of the door and window casings, corner-boards, cornices, and gables are simple but very neat.

Size "B" is shown on the plans mentioned. Size "A" is substantially similar in design, except that a third window is added on each of the long sides. The buildings are generally placed on a stone foundation-wall, which is, however, omitted on branch roads. There are stone walls under the rails forming the hand-car track inside the house, which walls serve also to support the floor-joists. The principal dimensions are as follows: track-stringers, 5 in. × 12 in.; floor-joists, 5 in. × 8 in.; 2-in. floor, top of floor flush with top of rail; sills, 5 in. × 8 in.; corner-posts, 5 in. × 6 in.; door and window studs, 3 in. × 5 in.; plates, 4 in. × 6 in.; rafters, 3 in. × 6 in., spaced 30 in. between centres; collar, 2 in. × 4 in.; tie-beam, 2 in. × 6 in.; windows, four lights, each 10 in. × 16 in., with shutters; door, 7 ft. × 7 ft., in two sections, hung on rollers; height from top of floor to bottom of tie-beam, 8 ft. There are two lines of nailing-pieces between the upright studs, and also angle-braces at the corners of the frame.

In size C there is only one window on a side, and the door is single, hinged, 3 ft. 6 in. wide. The floor is made of 2-in. plank, laid on regular floor-joists crosswise of the building, 3 in. × 12 in., and spaced 15 in. between centres. This standard is only used where a hand-car need not be housed.

Standard Section Tool-house, Union Pacific Railway.—The standard section tool and hand-car house of the Union Pacific Railway, shown in Figs. 22 to 24, is a frame building, 10 ft. × 14 ft., with a double-pitched gable roof. The building is sheathed on the outside with vertical boards and battens; the roof is covered with shingles. The large door, 6 ft. × 6 ft., for the hand-car is situated at one end of the long side of the house facing the track. At each gable end of the building there is one window, 2 ft. × 3 ft. 7 in., without sash, but closed with a board shutter hinged on the outside of the building. The height of frame from top of sill to top of plate is 6 ft. 9 in.

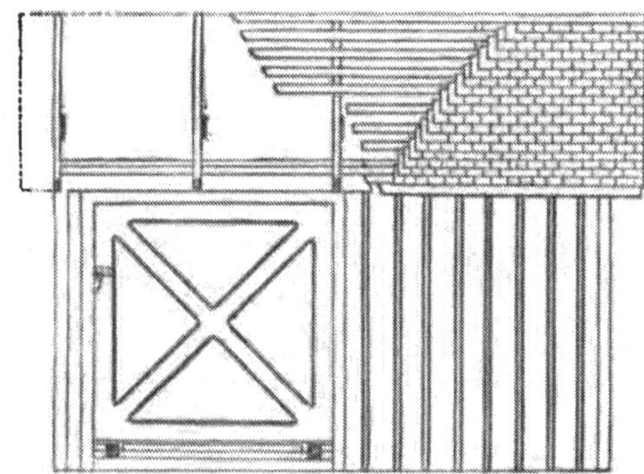

FIG. 22.—FRONT ELEVATION.

The principal sizes are as follows: sills, 4 in. × 4 in.; plates, 2 in. × 4 in., double; corner-posts, 4 in. × 4 in.; studs, 2 in. × 4 in.; door-studs, 2 in. × 4 in., double; nailing-pieces, 2 in. × 4 in.; rafters, 2 in. × 4 in., spaced 42 in. between centres; collars, 1 in. × 6 in.; roof-boards, 1 in. × 6 in., laid open; sub-sills, 2 in. × 6 in.; rails for hand-car track, 4 in. × 4 in., laid on the ground; corner-boards, ⅞ in. × 4 in.; frieze, ⅞ in. × 10 in.; door-rails, 2 in. × 6 in.; door-styles, 2 in. × 8 in.

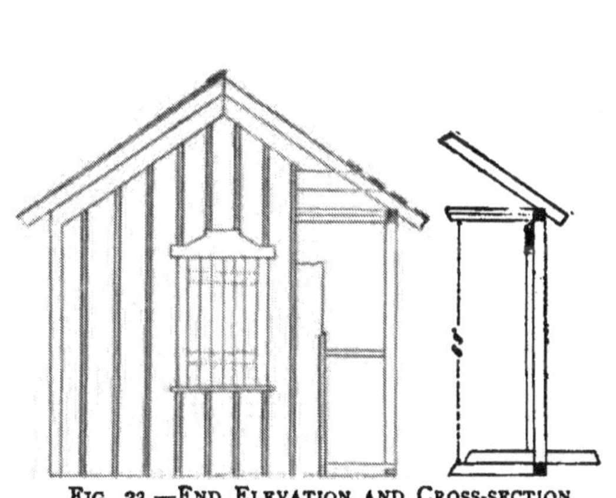

FIG. 23.—END ELEVATION AND CROSS-SECTION.

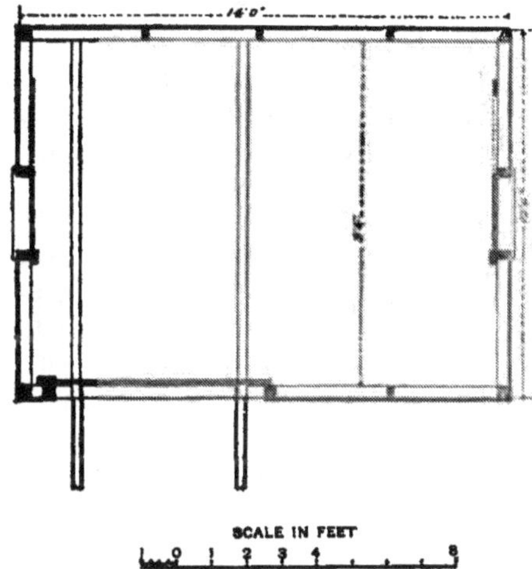

FIG. 24.—GROUND-PLAN.

Standard Hand-car and Tool-house, Cincinnati Southern Railway.—The standard hand-car and tool-house of the Cincinnati Southern Railway, shown in Figs. 25 to 27, is a frame building, 12 ft. × 16 ft. 8 in., with a double-pitched gable roof. The building is sheathed on the outside with vertical boards and battens, and roofed with shingles. The door for the hand-car is located on one side of one of the gable ends of the building; its size is 7 ft. × 7 ft., in one piece, and hinged on one side. There are no windows whatever in the building. The height of frame from top of floor to bottom of tie-beam is 7 ft. 2 in. The hand-car track, entering on one side of one of the gable ends of the building, remains on that side in the building, while the rest of the floor and wall space on the opposite side is reserved for storage of tools, lanterns, and sundry materials. For this purpose there are two boxes, each 6 ft. long, 2 ft. 6 in. wide, and 2 ft. 6 in. high, and a set of shelves.

The principal sizes used are as follows: foundation-posts, 8 in. × 8 in.; sills, 4 in. × 4 in.; corner-posts, 4 in. × 4 in.; door-studs, 4 in. × 4 in.; intermediate studs on long sides, 2 in. × 4 in.;

plates, 2 in. × 4 in., double; rafters, 2 in. × 4 in., spaced 24 in. between centres; ridge-piece, 2 in. × 6 in.; tie-beams at every other set of rafters, 2 in. × 4 in.; roof-boards, 1 in., laid close; angle-braces at top and bottom corners of frame, 2 in. × 4 in.; outside boarding, 9 in. × 1 in.; battens, 3 in. × 1 in.; board at end of rafters, 8 in. × 1 in.; door, 1-in. boards; door-rails, door-styles, and angle-

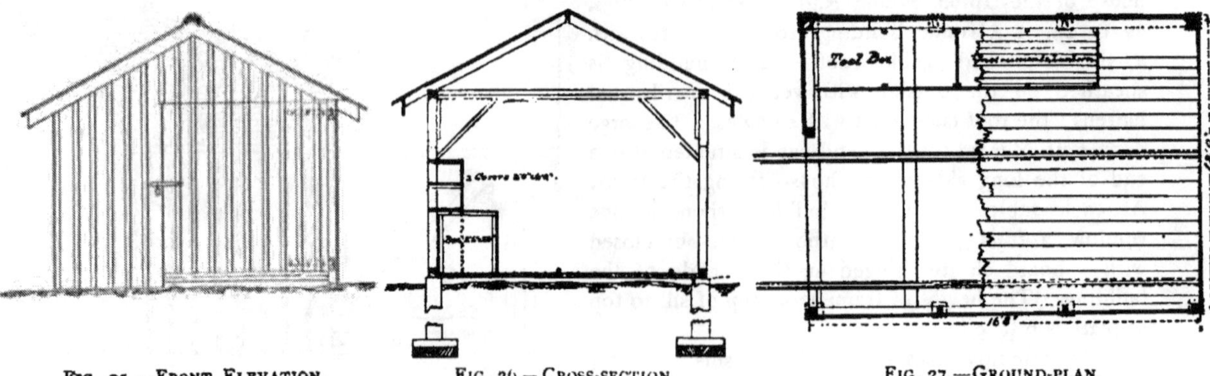

FIG. 25.—FRONT ELEVATION. FIG. 26.—CROSS-SECTION. FIG. 27.—GROUND-PLAN.

brace of door, 8 in. × 1½ in.; barge-board, 7 in. × 1 in.; floor, 2-in. oak. The floor and the rails for the hand-car track rest on 6 in. × 4 in. mud-sills, laid on the ground, 4 ft. apart. The top of the rail is 2 in. above the top of floor.

The contract price for these standard tool-houses, erected complete in place, was $75—at the time the Cincinnati Southern Railway was built, about 1878 to 1880.

The specification for this building will be found included in the *General Specifications* of the Cincinnati Southern Railway, printed in the Appendix at the back of this book.

Standard Tool-house, Atchison, Topeka & Santa Fe Railroad.—The standard tool-house of the Atchison, Topeka & Santa Fe Railroad is a frame building, 12 ft. × 16 ft., with a double-pitched gable roof. The outside is sheathed with upright boards and battens; the roof is covered with tin. The door for the hand-car, 6 ft. × 6 ft., hung on rollers, is located at one end of the long side of the house facing the track, similar to the design for the tool-house of the Union Pacific Railway, shown in Figs. 22 to 24. In each gable end there is one window-opening, 2 ft. 6 in. × 2 ft. 6 in., closed by a sliding board sash. The height of frame from the bottom of sill to the top of plate is 8 ft.; the top of floor is one foot above the bottom of sill and consists of boards laid on joists. There is no special track in the house or outside of it for the hand-car. The long side of the building is placed parallel with the track, 12 ft. distant from the nearest rail. The standard plan shows pile foundations, three lines with four piles each; one line under each gable and one line across the middle of the building. The space between the front of the building and the nearest track-rail, 12 ft. wide and 16 ft. long, is covered by a platform having a fall from the building toward the track.

The principal sizes are as follows: sills, 4 in. × 4 in.; corner-posts, 2 in. × 4 in., double; studs, 2 in. × 4 in.; plates, 2 in. × 4 in.; nailing-pieces, 2 in. × 4 in.; rafters, 2 in. × 4 in., spaced 27 in. between centres; tie-beams, 6 in. × 1 in.; angle-braces at top and bottom corners of frame, 2 in. × 6 in.; joists, 2 in. × 6 in., spaced 20 in. between centres, spanning 8 ft.; floor, 2-in. boards. Pitch of roof ¼.

Standard Tool-house, Philadelphia & Reading Railroad.—The standard tool-house of the Philadelphia & Reading Railroad is a frame structure, 13 ft. × 10 ft., shown in ground-plan in Fig. 28. There are quite a number of alternative designs for the exterior of these buildings adopted as standards, so as to avoid sameness of design along the road; the general features and the ground-plan, however, remain the same in all cases. One of these alternatives, shown in Figs. 29 and 30, has a double-pitched gable roof with a false front and shed-roof extension over the large door. Another design has a hip roof, as shown in Figs. 31 and 32. The buildings in all cases are sheathed on the outside with narrow tongued and grooved boards, put on diagonally, vertically, or horizontally, which feature, in connection with the corner-boards, base-boards, frieze-boards, and panel-boards, causes the exteriors of these buildings to present a very striking and tasteful appearance. The inside of the building is ceiled close. There are no windows at all. The door is located at the middle of the long side next to the track, and it is 6 ft. wide, in two sections, hung from above and sliding sideways. The floor is formed of boards on joists. The roof-covering is tin or slate, frequently laid, or painted,

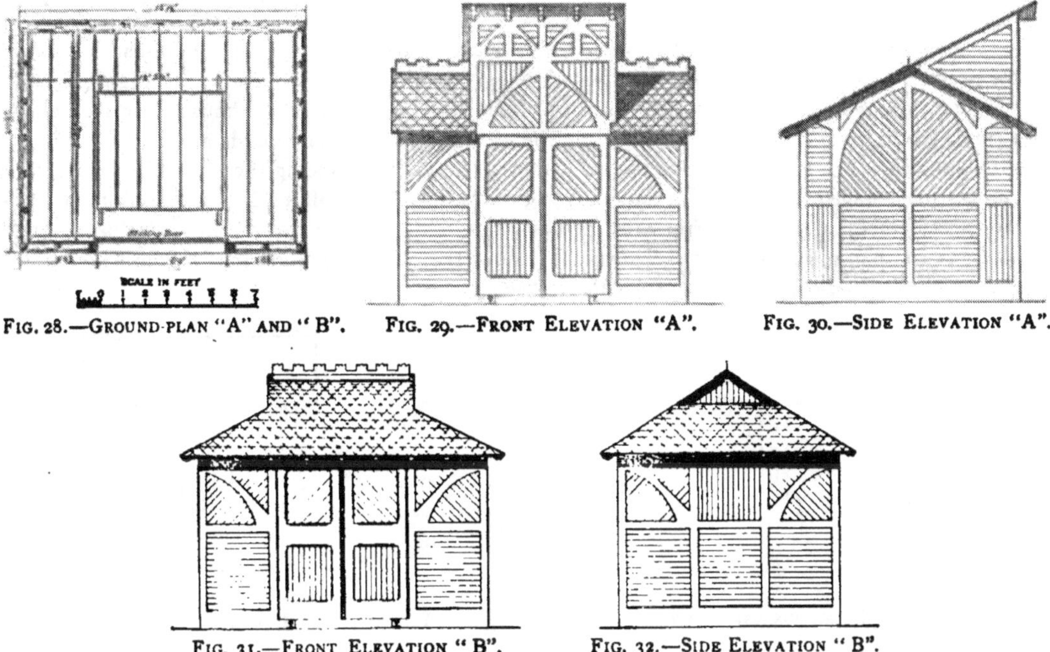

FIG. 28.—GROUND-PLAN "A" AND "B". FIG. 29.—FRONT ELEVATION "A". FIG. 30.—SIDE ELEVATION "A".

FIG. 31.—FRONT ELEVATION "B". FIG. 32.—SIDE ELEVATION "B".

according to an ornamental design, and finished off with galvanized-iron cornices, ridge-rolls, and finials.

Section Tool-house, Northern Pacific Railroad.—The standard section tool-house of the Northern Pacific Railroad, shown in Figs. 33 to 35, is a frame structure, 10 ft. × 14 ft., with a double-pitched gable roof, sheathed on the outside with horizontal weather-boarding, and roofed with

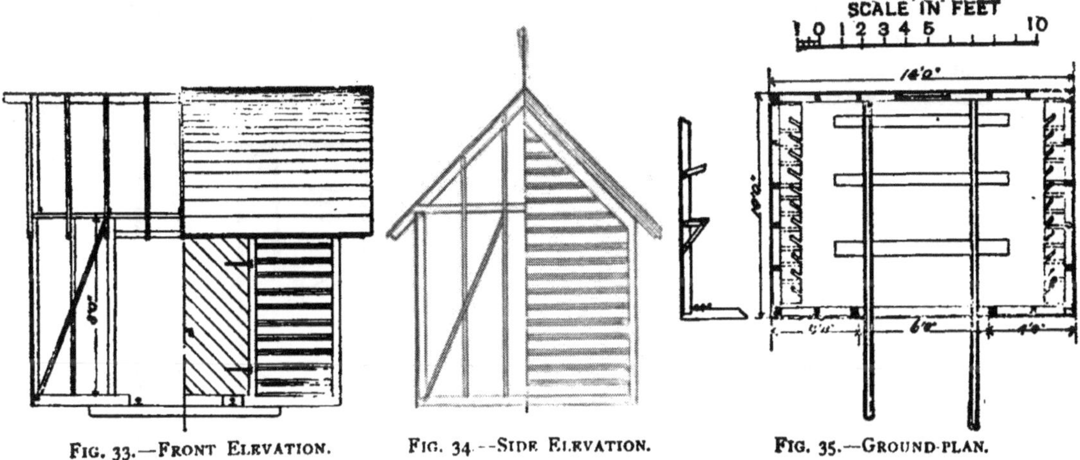

FIG. 33.—FRONT ELEVATION. FIG. 34.—SIDE ELEVATION. FIG. 35.—GROUND-PLAN.

shingles. The large door for the hand-car is situated in the centre of the long side of the building facing the track; it is 6 ft. wide, in two sections, hinged on the outside of the building. There is one window in the house opposite the entrance. The height from the top of sill to the bottom of plate is 8 ft.

The hand-car track inside of the house is formed of rails on cross-ties. Along each gable end of the house there are racks and shelves for stocking tools.

The principal sizes used are as follows: sub-sills, 6 in. × 8 in.; sills, 6 in. × 6 in.; door-studs, 4 in. × 4 in.; braces, 2 in. × 4 in.; studs, 2 in. × 4 in.; plates, 2 in. × 4 in.; ceiling-joists, 2 in. × 4 in.; rafters, 2 in. × 4 in.

Single Hand-car House, Northern Pacific Railroad.—The standard single hand-car house of the Northern Pacific Railroad, with accommodations for one hand-car, shown in Figs. 36 and 37, adopted on some sections of the road in place of the standard section tool-house, described above, is a frame structure, 9 ft. × 12 ft., sheathed on the outside with vertical boards and battens and roofed with shingles. The large door is at the gable end of the building facing the track; it is 6 ft. wide, in two sections, hinged on the outside and swinging outward. The building is placed with the gable end facing the track, 15 ft. distant from the nearest rail. This space is covered by a platform, the same width as the house, and sloping down toward the track. The height of frame from floor to top of plate is 7 ft. There are no windows in the house.

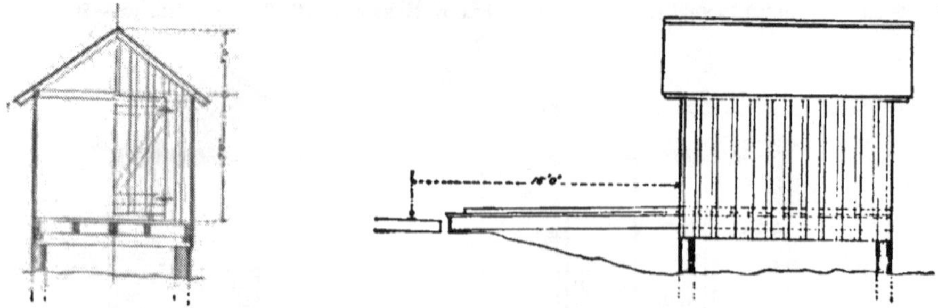

FIG. 36.—FRONT ELEVATION AND CROSS-SECTION. FIG. 37.—SIDE ELEVATION.

The principal sizes used are as follows: sills, 6 in. × 6 in.; floor-joists, 4 in. × 8 in., spaced 27 in. between centres, spanning 12 ft.; plates, 2 in. × 4 in., upright; rafters, 2 in. × 4 in.; floor, 2 in.; joists under platform, 2 in. × 8 in., spaced 27 in. between centres, spanning 12 ft.; hand-car track rails, 2 in. × 3 in., nailed on top of flooring.

Double Hand-car House, Northern Pacific Railroad.—The standard double hand-car house of the Northern Pacific Railroad is practically composed of two single houses, the same as shown in Figs. 36 and 37, placed side by side with one roof over both of them. This standard can be used with certain advantages, wherever several gangs are located at the same place and it is desirable to separate the tools and equipment of each gang, while keeping the general stock and supplies under the same roof.

Section Tool-house, Lehigh Valley Railroad.—The tool-house of the Lehigh Valley Railroad,

FIG. 38.—FRONT ELEVATION.

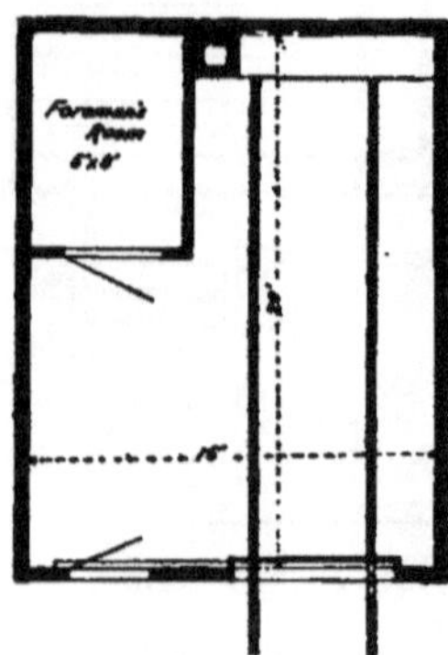

FIG. 39.—GROUND-PLAN.

in use on the New Jersey Division, shown in Figs. 38 and 39, designed by Mr. C. Rosenberg, Master Carpenter, New Jersey Division, L. V. R. R., is a frame structure, 16 ft. × 20 ft., ceiled on the inside with 1-in. boards, sheathed on the outside with bevelled weather-boarding, and roofed with slate on boards. Inside there is a small space, 8 ft. × 6 ft., partitioned off for the foreman. In the front gable end there is a small door and a large sliding door for hand-cars. On each of the sides of the building there are two windows. At the back of the room there is a brick flue and a small work-bench. This building can accommodate several hand-cars and push-cars, and offers storage space for a considerable quantity of track tools and miscellaneous supplies. The design does not offer any particularly new features, excepting the special inclosure for the use of the foreman, which is to be recommended wherever foremen are expected to do considerable clerical work in connection with reports, etc. It also affords an opportunity to lock up special supplies and more costly articles, keeping them thus distinct from the general stock that all the men have access to.

Tool-house Design by W. B. Parsons, Jr.—Mr. W. B. Parsons, Jr., gives in his book on "Track" a design for a tool-house, the characteristic features of which are described below. The building is a frame structure, 12 ft. × 18 ft., sheathed on the outside with vertical boards and battens, and roofed with a double-pitched gable roof covered with No. 24 galvanized corrugated iron. The large door for the hand-car, 6 ft. 9 in. square, hung on rollers, is situated at one end of the long side of the building facing the track, similar to the arrangement on the Union Pacific Railway and the Atchison, Topeka & Santa Fe Railroad. In each gable end and on the side of the house away from the track there is a window with a sliding sash, four lights, each 10 in. × 12 in. There is no special track or set of stringers for a hand-car inside of the house. The floor is laid on joists. The height of frame from top of floor to bottom of plate is 6 ft. 10 in. There is a 2-ft. work-bench and a locker located at the gable end of the building away from the door.

The principal materials and sizes used are as follows: sills, 6 in. × 6 in; corner-posts, 4 in. × 6 in.; studs at centre of long sides, 4 in. × 6 in.; plates, 4 in. × 6 in.; nailing-pieces, 4 in. × 6 in.; door-studs, 2 in. × 5 in.; rafters, 2 in. × 4 in., spaced 24 in. between centres; collars, 6 in. × 1 in.; floor, 2 in.; floor-joists, 3 in. × 8 in., spaced 21 in. between centres, notched 3 in. onto sills; barge-boards, 2 in. × 1½ in.; door-frame, 5 in. × 1 in.; door, 1-in. boards; top, middle, and bottom door-rails, 9 in. × 1 in.; door hung with two No. 4 barn-door hangers, 4-in. wheels; board at ends of rafters, 5 in. × 1 in. The corrugated iron roofing rests on three boards, 4 in. × 1 in., laid on the rafters, one at the ridge, one at the eaves, and one at the centre of each rafter.

Section Tool-house, Macon & Birmingham Railroad.—The standard section tool-house of the Macon & Birmingham Railroad is illustrated in the issue of *Engineering News* of May 26, 1892.

CHAPTER III.

SECTION HOUSES.

THE name "section house" on a railroad generally applies to the dwelling-houses supplied by the railroad company for the use of the men employed, more particularly on the track, as foremen or track hands. It is very essential that the men employed on track-work live on their section, or as close to it as feasible, so as to be always on hand in case of emergencies and to avoid loss of time in going to and from their work. Where the route of a railroad does not pass through thickly-settled districts, a railroad company is forced, for the reasons mentioned, to build special houses, known as "section houses." The distinction between these and "dwelling-houses for employés" lies mainly in the different styles and sizes of the two, the section houses being usually much smaller and built on a cheaper scale than the dwelling-houses proper. The latter will be grouped under the heading of "Dwelling-houses for Employés."

The general requirements for a section house are that it be cheap and built to suit the local climatic conditions. There are two kinds in use, namely, one for the accommodation of one or more families and the other for a number of men. The section foreman and the married hands who have their families with them generally live in the first-mentioned style of house, while the single men or men without their families are expected to club together under one roof.

Section houses, probably in all cases, are frame structures, roofed with shingles or tin, and sheathed on the outside with upright boards or horizontal weather-boarding. According to the importance and the locality the exterior is more or less elaborate. The designs vary in the different sections of the country, and the influence of the prevailing types of farm-house architecture on the designs adopted for different localities is clearly perceptible. According to the fuel, large, old-fashioned chimneys for wood fires or brick and iron flues are used.

In the Northeastern States the country is generally so thickly settled that the railroad companies have not paid much attention to adopting standard section-house plans. Where buildings of that character are required at a few isolated points along the line, it is very easy to build a small dwelling-house similar in its principal features to the general style of country houses in vogue at each place. In the Western sections of the country the standard designs, while practical and economical, are as plain and as cheap as possible. In the Southeastern States the designs indicate a tendency to finish the buildings more comfortably and neatly.

This difference can probably be traced to the character of the employés to be accommodated. In the West the class of the employés on a section is of a more roving nature than in the Eastern States, where the men attach themselves more permanently to a railroad and where there is, hence, more of a disposition on the part of the railroad management to provide pleasant homes for them.

The changes of design caused by the climatic conditions are clearly shown by comparing the standards of the Northern Pacific Railroad, where everything tends to keep the cold out, with the standard of the Savannah, Florida & Western Railroad, which introduces all possible means to obtain good ventilation in and around the building.

It would be impossible to undertake to prescribe any particular style or certain structural methods as the best, as the local conditions and circumstances in each particular case preclude all possibility of drawing summary conclusions.

Descriptions of the following section houses are presented as illustrative of the subject.

Two-room Section House, East Tennessee, Virginia & Georgia Railroad.—The standard two-room section house of the East Tennessee, Virginia & Georgia Railroad, shown in Figs. 40 to 43, is a one-story frame building, 41 ft. × 16 ft., with a double-pitched roof and a small entrance-porch. This standard is intended more for the accommodation of a number of men than for a section foreman or a man with a family. The ground-plan consists simply of two rooms, each about 15 ft. × 18 ft. There is one common chimney at the centre of the house leading up from large fireplaces in each room. The rooms have each an entrance-door from the front porch; otherwise there are no doors in the building.

FIG. 40.—FRONT ELEVATION.

FIG. 41.—END ELEVATION.

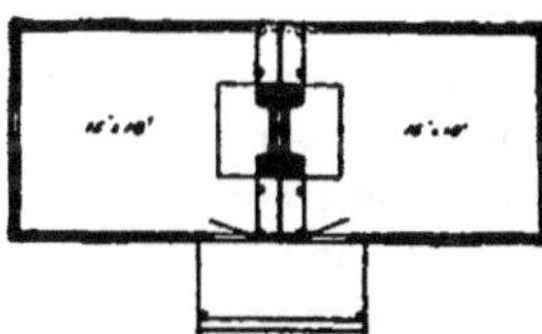

FIG. 42.—GROUND-PLAN.

FIG. 43.—CROSS-SECTION.

The building is roofed with shingles or tin, and sheathed on the outside with upright boards and battens. It is not ceiled on the inside. The height of the frame is 10 ft. from sill to plate.

The principal timbers used are as follows: sills, 6 in. × 8 in.; corner-posts, 6 in. × 6 in.; door and window studs, 3 in. × 6 in.; nailers, 3 in. × 6 in.; plates, 4 in. × 6 in.; rafters, 2 in. × 6 in., spaced 24 in. centres; ridge-plate, 1½ in. × 8 in.; tie-beams, 2 in. × 8 in.; roof-boards, 1 in.; outside sheathing, 1 in. × 10 in., with ⅞ in. × 2½ in. battens; floor-joists, 2½ in. × 12 in., spaced 18 in. centres, spanning 15 ft.; flooring, 1 in., tongued and grooved boards; windows, double sash, each sash six lights, 10 in. × 12 in.; doors, 3 ft. × 7 ft.

Two room Section House, Cincinnati, New Orleans & Texas Pacific Railroad.—The standard section house, known as plan No. 2, of the Cincinnati, New Orleans & Texas Pacific Railroad, is similar in general design to the standard two-room section house of the East Tennessee, Virginia & Georgia Railroad, shown in Figs. 40 to 43, with exception of the porch-roof, which is a single-pitch shed-roof in place of the high gable-roof, shown in the illustrations mentioned. The standard plan shows the building to be 16 ft. wide × 32 ft. long, although it can be built to any desired length.

Three-room Section House, East Tennessee, Virginia & Georgia Railroad.—The three-room section house of the East Tennessee, Virginia & Georgia Railroad, shown in Figs. 44 to 47, designed

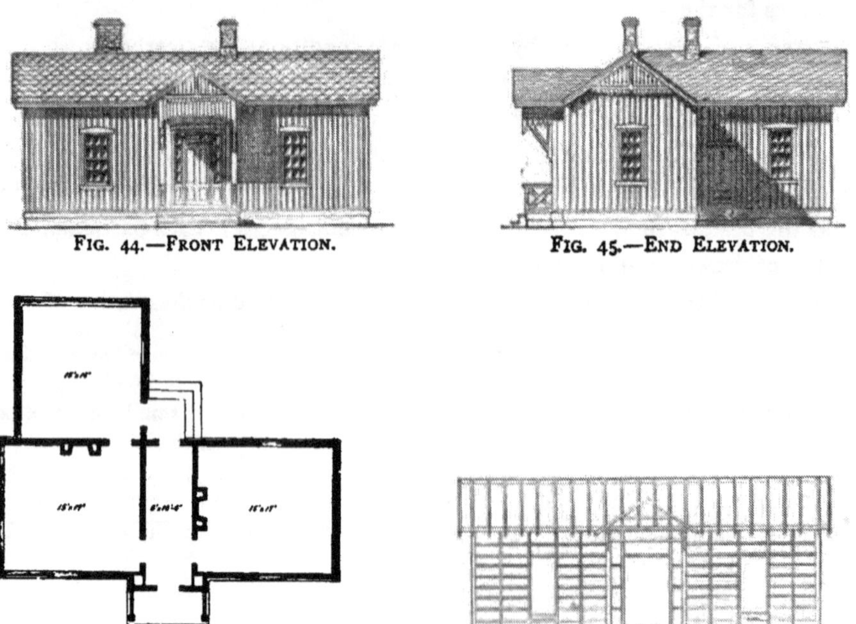

FIG. 44.—FRONT ELEVATION.

FIG. 45.—END ELEVATION.

FIG. 46.—GROUND-PLAN.

FIG. 47.—ELEVATION OF FRAME.

by Mr. William Hunter, is a one-story L-shaped frame building, 42 ft. × 16 ft., the wing being 16 ft. × 16 ft. It has a front and a rear porch with a hallway connecting them through the centre of the house, which feature is quite a consideration in a southern climate. On each side of the hallway is a room, 17 ft. × 15 ft., the wing having a third room, 15 ft. × 16 ft., suitable for a kitchen.

The building is roofed with tin or shingles, and covered outside with upright boards and battens; the building is ceiled or plastered. The height of frame from sill to plate is 13 ft.

The principal timbers used are as follows: sills, 6 in. × 6 in.; corner-posts, 6 in. × 6 in.; door and window studs, 4 in. × 5 in.; intermediate studding, 2 in. × 5 in.; nailers, 2 in. × 5 in., spaced 16 in.; angle-braces, 4 in. × 4 in.; plates, 4 in. × 4 in.; rafters, 4 in. × 4 in., spaced 24 in. centres; floor-joists, 2 in. × 12 in.; windows, double sash, each sash six lights, 10 in. × 16 in.; doors, 2 ft. 10 in. × 6 ft. 10 in.

Three-room Section House, Chesapeake & Ohio Railway.—The three-room section house of the

FIG. 48.—FRONT ELEVATION.

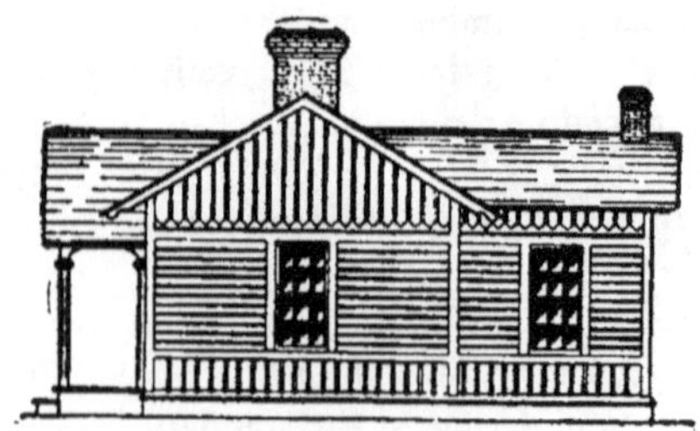

FIG. 49.—END ELEVATION.

Chesapeake & Ohio Railway, shown in Figs. 48 to 50, is a one-story L-shaped frame building, 33 ft. × 17 ft., the wing being 10 ft. 6 in. × 11 ft. It has a front and a rear porch, two front rooms, respectively 18 ft. × 16 ft. and 13 ft. 6 in. × 16 ft., and a kitchen, 10 ft. × 10 ft.

The building is roofed with tin or shingles, covered outside partly with upright boards and battens and partly with bevelled weather-boards, which arrangement, in connection with the corner, base, and string boards, adds materially to the appearance of the building. The inside is plastered. The height of the frame is 11 ft. from sill to plate.

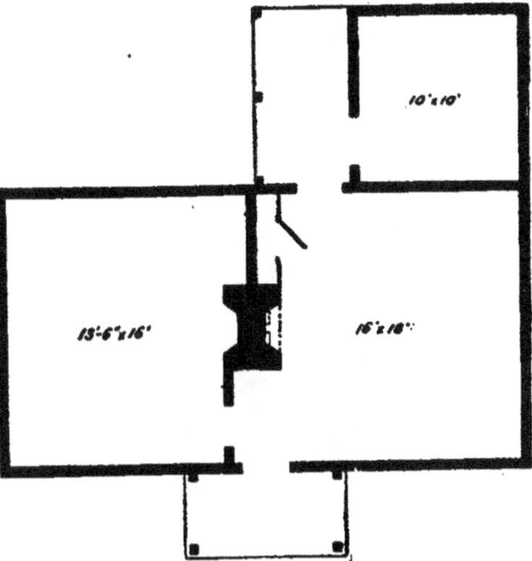

FIG. 50.—GROUND-PLAN.

The principal timbers used are as follows: sills, 6 in. × 8 in.; corner-posts, 4 in. × 4 in.; studding, 2 in. × 4 in.; nailers, 2 in. × 4 in.; plates, 3 in. × 4 in.; rafters, 2 in. × 6 in., spaced 24 in.; ridge-plate, 2 in. × 8 in.; ceiling-joists, 2 in. × 10 in.; floor-joists, 2 in. × 12 in., spaced 18 in. centres and spanning 16 ft.; flooring, 1 in., tongued and grooved boards; windows, double sash, each sash six lights, 10 in. × 16 in.; doors, 3 ft. × 7 ft.

The cost of this building is stated to be about $800.

Three-room Section House, New Orleans & North Eastern Railroad.—The standard three-room section house of the New Orleans & North Eastern Railroad, a part of the Cincinnati, New Orleans & Texas Pacific Railway system, shown in Figs. 51 and 52, is very similar in the general

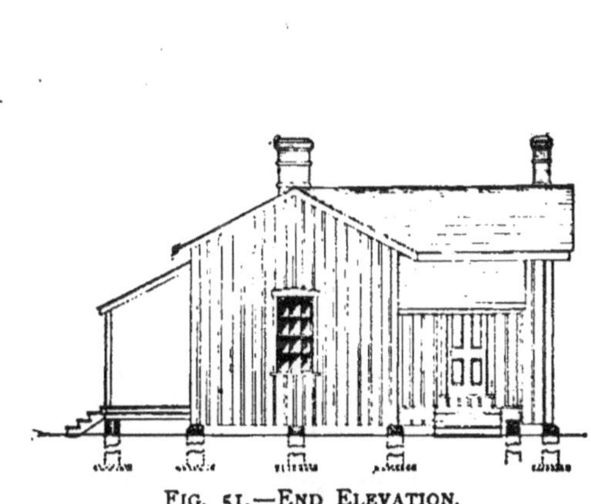
FIG. 51.—END ELEVATION.

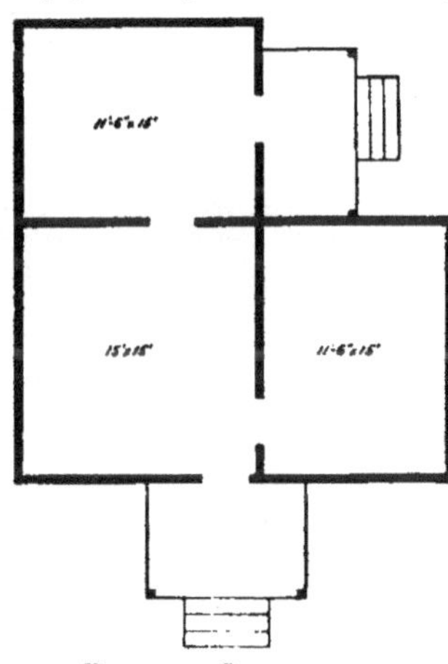
FIG. 52.—GROUND-PLAN.

lay-out to the design of the Chesapeake & Ohio Railway, just described; but it is a much cheaper building and less importance is given to the exterior. The design shows a one-story L-shaped frame building, 28 ft. × 16 ft., the wing being 16 ft. × 12 ft. The building has a front and a rear porch; two front rooms, respectively 15 ft. × 15 ft. and 15 ft. × 11 ft. 6 in., and a kitchen 15 ft. × 11 ft. 6 ins.

The roof is covered with tin or shingles. The outside sheathing consists of upright boards and battens. The interior is ceiled or plastered according to circumstances. The height of the frame is 12 ft. from sill to plate. The brick flues rest on the ceiling-joists.

The principal timbers used are as follows: sills, 6 in. × 10 in.; corner-posts, 4 in. ×4 in.; door and window studs, 3 in. × 4 in.; studs, 2 in. × 4 in.; nailers, 2 in. × 4 in.; angle-braces, 4 in. × 4 in.; plates, 3 in. × 4 in.; rafters, 2 in. × 6 in., spaced 18 in. centres, ceiling-joists, 2 in. × 6 in.; ridge-plate, 2 in. × 6 in.; floor-joists, 2 in. × 12 in., spaced 16 in. centres, spanning 15 ft., and stayed with 2 in. × 3 in. double bridging.

Section House, Atchison, Topeka & Santa Fe Railroad.—The standard section house of the Atchison, Topeka & Santa Fe Railroad, known as Class No. 4, shown in Figs. 53 to 55, is a very plain but practical and economical design. It is a one-story T-shaped frame building, 14 ft. × 31 ft., with a wing, 14 ft. × 14 ft. No covered porches are provided, but there is a platform on the rear with a washing-shelf. The front door leads into a room 18 ft. × 13 ft., with two bunks in it, each bunk 6 ft. 6 in. × 4 ft. 3 in. At the end of the main portion of the building is a room, 11 ft. 6 in. × 13 ft., connected only with the kitchen. The kitchen on the rear is 13 ft. × 13 ft. A cellar under the kitchen is entered by a small trap-door in the floor of the kitchen.

The building is roofed with shingles and sheathed outside with ⅞-in. drop siding; the interior is plastered with two coats, the second or brown coat being trowelled smooth. The walls are wainscoted 3 ft. high from the floor. The standard plan shows a foundation of round logs set on mud-sills and buried in the ground. The height of frame from sill to plate is 10 ft.

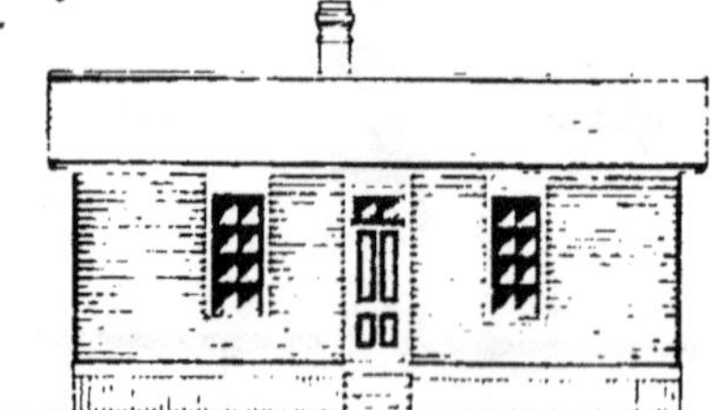

FIG. 53.—FRONT ELEVATION.

The principal timbers are as follows: sills, 2 in. × 6 in., flat; floor-joists, 2 in. × 8 in., spaced 16 in. and spanning 13 ft.; studding, 2 in. × 4 in.; plates, 2 in. × 4 in.; rafters, 2 in. × 4 in., spaced 24 in. centres; ceiling-joists, 2 in. × 4 in., spaced 16 in. centres.

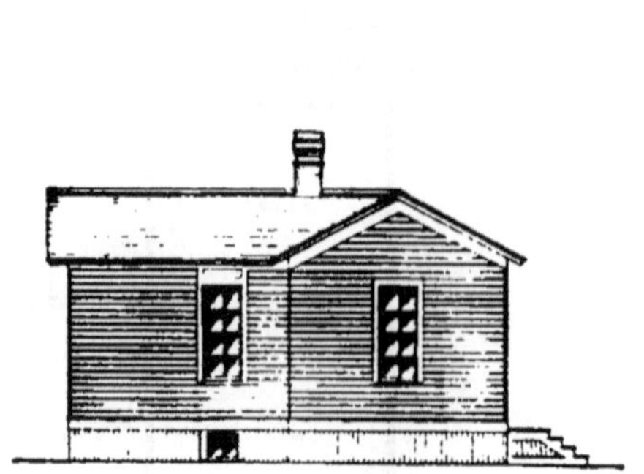

FIG. 54.—END ELEVATION.

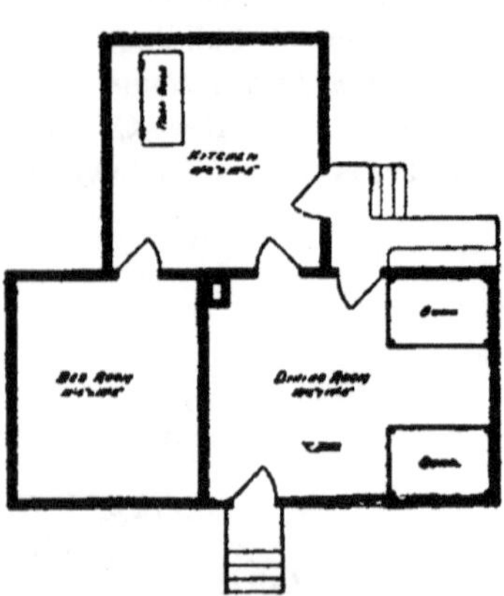

FIG. 55.—GROUND-PLAN.

White Men's Section House, Northern Pacific Railroad.—The white men's section house of the Northern Pacific Railroad, designed by Mr. C. B. Talbot, shown in Fig. 56, is a very cheap one-story frame building without any studding. The standard plan shows it to be 18 ft. × 24 ft., without any porches or platforms around it. There are four rooms, namely, a living-room, 11 ft. × 12 ft., two bedrooms, each 7 ft. × 12 ft. and a kitchen, 11 ft. × 12 ft.

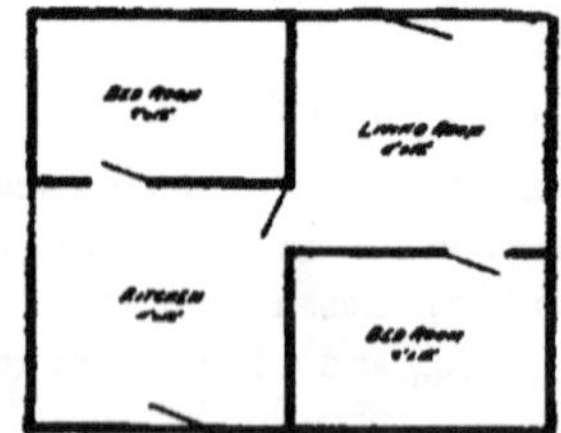

FIG. 56.—GROUND-PLAN.

The building is roofed with cedar shingles on boards and sheathed outside with two layers of boards, laid close, with building-paper between them. The interior of the rooms is ceiled with 1 in. boards, with a layer of building-paper between the boards and the ceiling-joists. The flooring is double, with building-paper between the two layers. The clear height of the rooms is 8 ft. 8 in.

The principal timbers used are as follows: sills, 6 in × 8 in.; plates, 2 in. × 6 in., upright and nailed against the boarding; rafters, 2 in. × 6 in., spaced 24 in. centres; floor-joists, 2 in. × 8 in., spaced 16 in. centres and spanning 9 ft.; ceiling-joists, 2 in. × 6 in., spaced 24 in. centres; doors, 2 ft. 6 in. × 6 ft. 6 in.; windows, double sash, each sash four lights, 12 in. × 14 in. There is no studding in this design, the double boarding outside connecting the plate and sill.

Two-story Section House, Northern Pacific Railroad.—The standard two-story section house of the Northern Pacific Railroad, shown in Figs. 57 to 60, is a plain two-story frame building

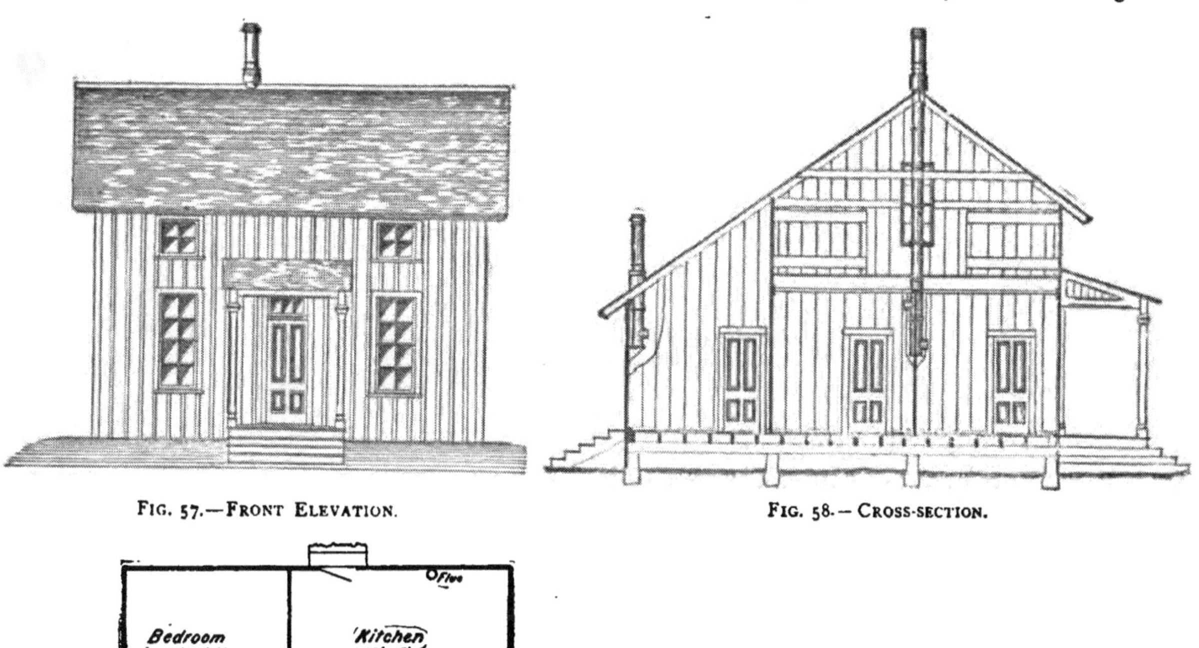

Fig. 57.—Front Elevation.

Fig. 58.—Cross-section.

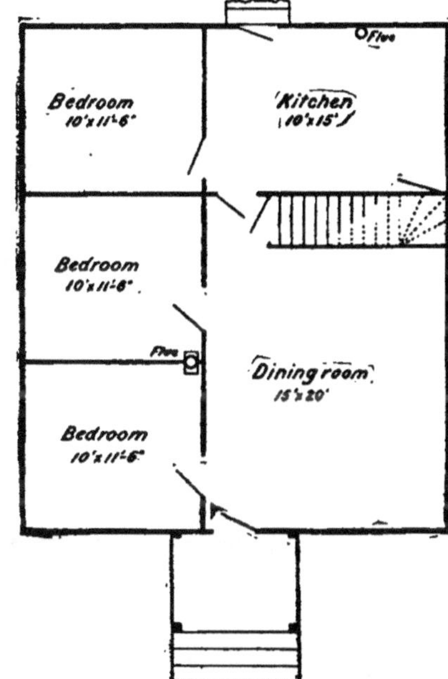

Fig. 59.—Ground-plan.

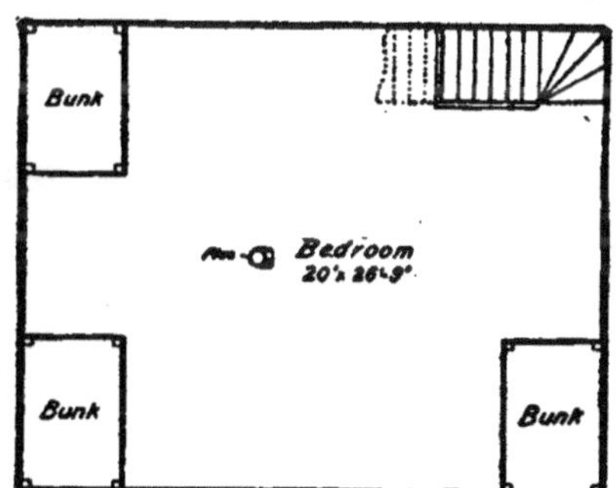

Fig. 60.—Second-floor Plan.

without studding; the main portion of the house is 26 ft. × 20 ft., with a kitchen annex, 26 ft. × 10 ft. There are five rooms on the ground-floor, namely, a dining-room, three bedrooms, and a kitchen. The second floor forms one large common bedroom with a number of double bunks, 6 ft. 6 in. × 4 ft. 6 in. Where desired, this second floor can be divided into rooms by appropriate partitions.

The building is roofed with shingles on boards, and sheathed outside with two layers of boards with building-paper between them. Earth is packed against the foot of the building to exclude the cold, so far as possible, from getting under the floor.

The principal timbers used are as follows: sills, 6 in. × 8 in.; inter-ties, 2 in. × 8 in., upright; plates, 2 in. × 6 in., upright; rafters, 2 in. × 6 in.; ties, 1 in. × 6 in.; floor-joists of ground-floor, 2 in. × 8 in., spaced 24 in. centres and spanning 13 ft.; floor-joists of second floor, 2 in. × 10 in., spaced 20 in. centres; inside partitions, double 1 in. boards; inside doors, 2 ft. 6 in. × 6 ft. 6 in.; outside doors, 2 ft. 8 in. × 7 ft.

Section House, Savannah, Florida & Western Railroad.—The standard section house of the Savannah, Florida & Western Railroad and of the Charleston & Savannah Railroad, shown in Figs. 61 to 63, is particularly well suited for southern climates; in fact, the design is practically

FIG. 61.—SIDE ELEVATION.

FIG. 62.—FRONT ELEVATION.

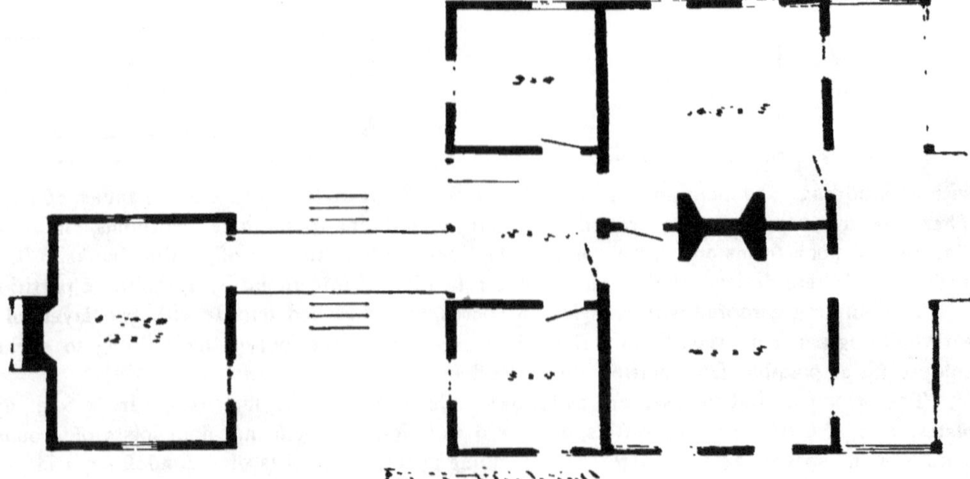

FIG. 63.—GROUND-PLAN.

copied from a similar type of southern farm-houses. The house is a one-story frame building with a high garret well ventilated at the gable ends with louvres. A large porch extends along the entire front of the house. The kitchen is in a separate building, 15 ft. distant from the rear of the main building, the two being connected by a covered walk.

The house and kitchen are set on brick or stone pillars. The space below the floor is left open to give ventilation; several strands of barbed wire are stretched from pillar to pillar around the buildings, to prevent animals from getting under the building.

The main building is 33 ft. 6 in. × 31 ft. in size and has five rooms. The kitchen is 13 ft. × 16 ft.

Two-story Section House, Louisville & Nashville Railroad.—The two-story section house of the Louisville & Nashville Railroad, shown in Figs. 64 to 66, is a frame building, 32 ft. × 15 ft. 10 in., with a 6-ft. porch extending along the entire front, and a kitchen annex, 12 ft. × 12 ft. 6 in.

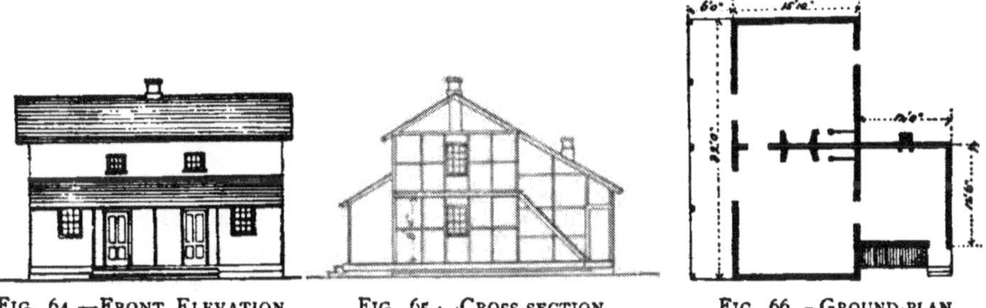

FIG. 64.—FRONT ELEVATION. FIG. 65.—CROSS-SECTION. FIG 66.—GROUND-PLAN.

The ground-floor has two rooms, each 15 ft. × 15 ft., and a kitchen, 12 ft. × 12 ft. The upper story is reached by steps leading up from the kitchen at the rear of the house.

Design for a Section House by W. B. Parsons, Jr.—Mr. W. B. Parsons, Jr., presents in his book on "Track" a design for a section house or "dwelling-shanty," shown in Figs. 67 and 68, which

FIG. 67.—FRONT ELEVATION. FIG. 68.—GROUND-PLAN.

is a two-story frame building with a kitchen annex. On the ground-floor there are two bedrooms, a large sitting-room, and a kitchen. The second floor can be divided by partitions, or left as one large room. The stairs start inside the sitting-room, the space underneath them being utilized for a closet and for a passageway from the sitting-room to the kitchen.

For further details and data see the book referred to above, as also the issue of *Engineering News and American Contract Journal* of August 15, 1885.

Standard Section House, Gulf, Colorado & Santa Fe Railroad.—The standard section house of the Gulf, Colorado & Santa Fe Railroad, now part of the Atchison, Topeka & Santa Fe Railroad system, shown in Figs. 69 and 70, designed by Mr. W. J. Sherman, Chief Engineer, G., C. & S. F. R. R., is a single-story frame structure, 59 ft. × 18 ft., with a kitchen annex, 14 ft. × 18 ft. This structure deserves attention, as it represents practically the class of section houses in general use in the southwest sections of the country, and, owing to the great simplicity of the design and cheapness of the construction, it is particularly adapted to pioneer roads or wherever cheapness of first cost is an important consideration. The building is divided into a sleeping-room, 18 ft. × 30 ft., with eight bunks; a dining-room, 15 ft. × 18 ft.; a family room, 14 ft. × 18 ft.; and a kitchen, 14 ft. × 18 ft.

There is a 6-ft. platform running along the front and the rear of the main building. The kitchen is a separate building adjoining the back platform. A feature in this design is the use of a water-tub, 8 ft. diameter by 9 ft. high, placed on blocking near the buildings to serve as a cistern to catch rain-water from the roofs, which are carefully guttered and provided with leaders to the cistern. This feature is an essential one in connection with buildings in sections of the country like Texas, where the water-supply is frequently limited.

The foundations are round timber blocks of cedar or live oak, 12 to 15 in. in diameter, set in

FIG. 69.—END ELEVATION AND CROSS-SECTION.

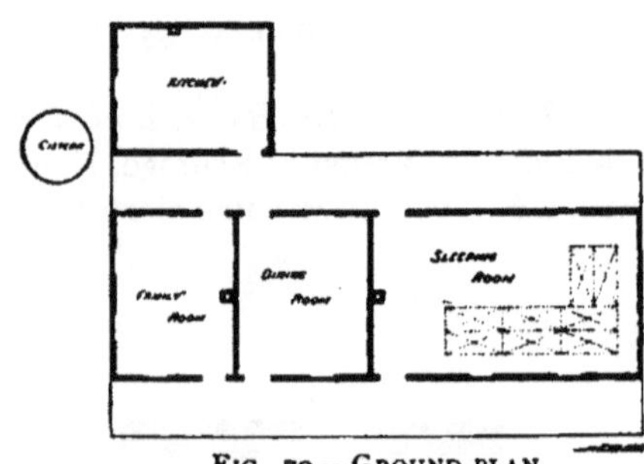

FIG. 70.—GROUND-PLAN.

the ground. The building has a 4-in. frame and is sheathed on the outside with upright boards and battens without any attempt at ornamentation. The interior is ceiled with 1-in. tongued and grooved boards, and the roof is covered with shingles on 1-in. × 4-in. sheeting. There are two 16-in. square brick flues hung in the roof of the main building, and one flue in the kitchen. The principal materials used are: sills, 3 in. × 12 in., notched onto the foundation-blocks; joists, 2 in. × 10 in.; plates, 4 in. × 4 in.; corner, door, and window studs, 4 in. × 4 in.; intermediate and partition studs, 2 in. × 4 in.; nailers, 2 in. × 4 in.; rafters, 2 in. × 4 in., spaced 24 in. centres; ceiling-joists, 2 in. × 6 in.; tie-plate for ceiling-joists, 1 in. × 6 in.; roof-brackets, 2 in. × 4 in.; outside sheathing, 1 in. × 12 in., with O. G. battens; interior ceiling, 1-in. tongued and grooved third-class boards, well seasoned, one side dressed; flooring, 1-in. tongued and grooved second-class boards, one side dressed; roof-sheeting, 1 in. × 4 in. The doors are 3 ft. × 7 ft. × $1\frac{5}{8}$ in. The windows are 2 ft. 10 in. × 5 ft. 10 in., glazed with twelve lights, each 10 in. × 16 in. The remainder of the building materials consists of mouldings, facia-boards, cornice-boards, 6-in. tin gutter, 3-in. tin-pipe leaders, shingles, brick for chimney, nails, spikes, etc. The building is painted a light brown with dark trimmings.

Standard Section Houses, Macon & Birmingham Railroad.—A number of designs for two-room and three-room standard section houses of the Macon & Birmingham Railroad are illustrated in the issue of *Engineering News* of May 26, 1892.

CHAPTER IV.

DWELLING-HOUSES FOR EMPLOYÉS.

SPECIAL dwelling-houses have frequently to be built by railroad companies for the use of their employés, wherever their roads pass through sparsely settled districts, or where, for other reasons, it is desirable to have the men live at certain localities selected by the railroad company. Apartments for the accommodation of agents are frequently furnished in the depot buildings, and trackmen are given "section houses" to live in; but there are numerous other employés to be provided for, especially at points where shops or junction stations are located at some distance from settlements.

While the principles governing the design of a dwelling for railroad men do not differ from those for other persons under similar conditions, it will prove interesting to present a few standard designs for dwelling-houses as actually adopted and in use on several railroads at the present time. There is considerable material to select from, but, as the subject is not distinctly a railroad specialty, it does not warrant devoting too much space to it.

A cottage in use on the Northern Pacific system (designed by Mr. C. B. Talbot) illustrates the practice on Northwestern roads. Designs for cottages of the Chesapeake & Ohio Railroad (designed by Mr. H. Jacob, Engineer and Architect, Richmond, Va.), and plans of a dwelling or section house on the Atchison, Topeka & Santa Fe Railroad, will serve to present the practice on southern systems.

The following descriptions of a number of buildings are presented as illustrative of the subject under discussion.

Agent's Dwelling, Northern Pacific Railroad System.—The standard plan for an agent's dwelling of the Spokane & Palouse Railway, connected with the Northern Pacific Railroad system, shown in

FIG. 71.—FRONT ELEVATION.

FIG. 72.—END ELEVATION.

Figs. 71 to 73, designed by Mr. C. B. Talbot, is intended to meet the conditions to be encountered in a northern climate. It is a one-story frame building, 24 ft. × 24 ft., with a small front porch and a woodshed annex. There are four rooms in the house, as follows: a sitting-room, 11 ft. 6 in. × 13 ft. 6 in.; a kitchen, 11 ft. 6 in. × 13 ft. 6 in.; and two bedrooms, each 9 ft. × 11 ft. 6 in. The woodshed adjoins the kitchen, so that in winter fuel and other supplies are close at hand.

The foundations are either posts set in the ground in three rows, each row with five posts, or blocking, according to the local circumstances in each case. The sills are 6 in. × 8 in.; floor-joists, 3 in. × 8 in., spaced 2 ft. centres and spanning 12 ft. The frame is of the usual style and

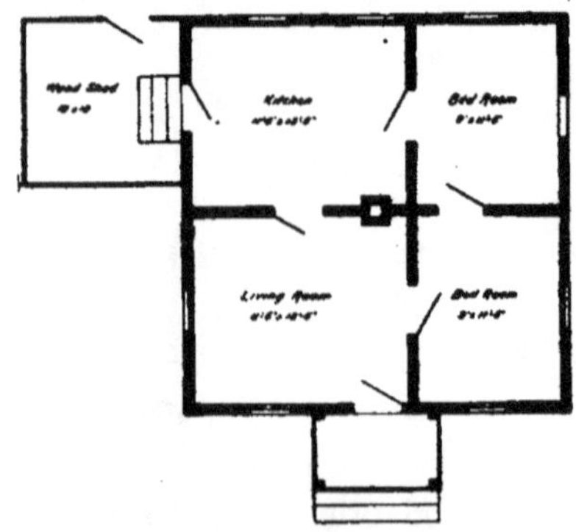

FIG. 73.—GROUND-PLAN.

dimensions, covered on the outside with V rustic sheathing and roofed with cedar shingles on boards or otherwise, according to circumstances. The shed annex is sheathed with rough boards and battens.

Five-room Cottage "K," Chesapeake & Ohio Railway.—Plans for a five-room cottage on the Chesapeake & Ohio Railway, known as plan "K," designed by Mr. H. Jacob, are shown in Figs. 74 to

FIG. 74.—PERSPECTIVE.

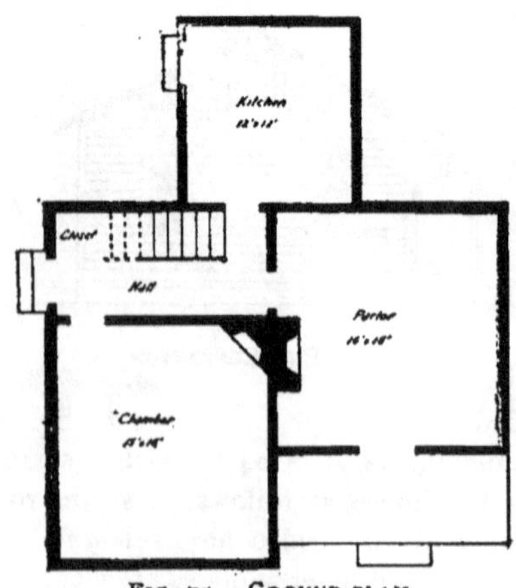

FIG. 75.—GROUND-PLAN.

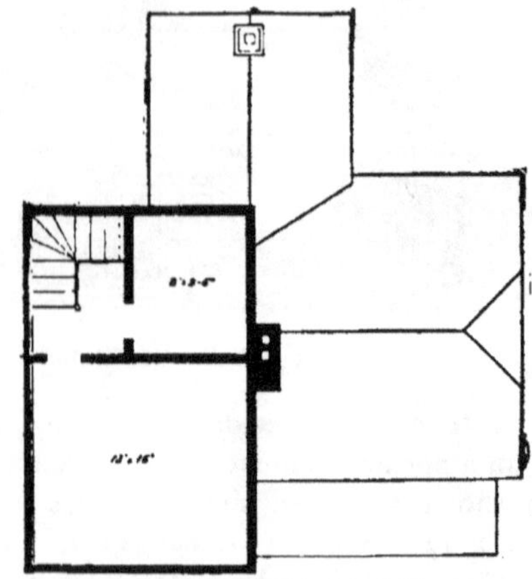

FIG. 76.—SECOND-FLOOR PLAN.

76. The building is a frame structure, 32 ft. 6 in. × 24 ft. 6 in., with a kitchen annex, 12 ft. 6 in. × 13 ft. The ground-floor has a veranda; a parlor, 16 ft. × 16 ft.; a chamber, 15 ft. × 16 ft.; and a kitchen, 12 ft. × 12 ft. The second floor has two rooms, respectively 13 ft. × 16 ft. and 8 ft. × 9 ft. 6 in.

Five-room Cottage "L," Chesapeake & Ohio Railway.—The plans for a five-room cottage of the Chesapeake & Ohio Railway, known as plan "L," designed by Mr. H. Jacob, are shown in Figs. 77 to 79. The structure is a frame building, L-shaped, the main section 23 ft. × 35 ft. 6 in., with an annex for a kitchen, 16 ft. × 12 ft. 6 in., and an annex for a chamber, 17 ft. × 17 ft.

The ground-floor has two verandas or porch-entrances; a parlor, 16 ft. × 16 ft.; a dining-room, 15 ft. × 16 ft.; a chamber, 16 ft. × 16 ft.; and a kitchen, 12 ft. × 15 ft. The second floor has one room, 16 ft. × 16 ft.

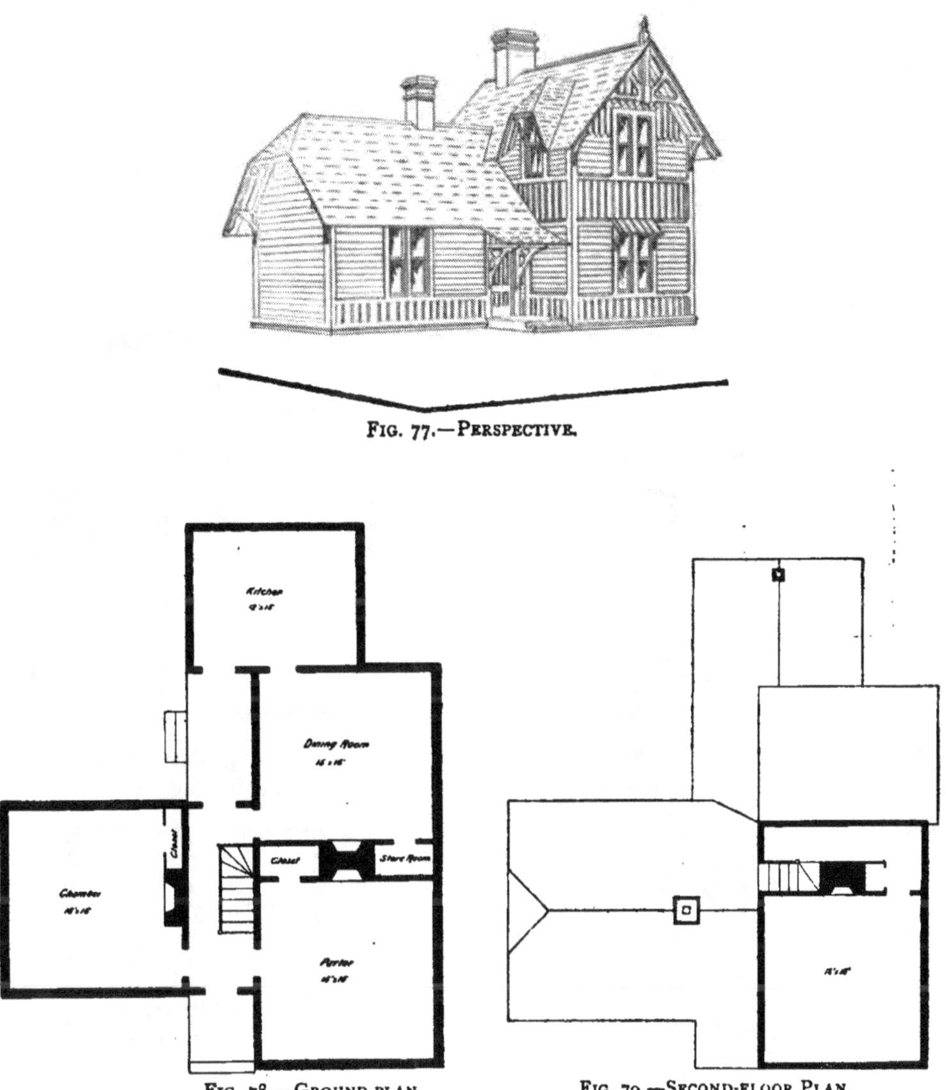

FIG. 77.—PERSPECTIVE.

FIG. 78.—GROUND-PLAN. FIG. 79.—SECOND-FLOOR PLAN.

Seven-room Cottage, Chesapeake & Ohio Railway.—The plans for a seven-room cottage of the Chesapeake & Ohio Railway, designed by Mr. H. Jacob, are shown in Figs. 80 to 82. The structure is a two-story frame building throughout, excepting a small single-story kitchen annex. The ground-floor has a front veranda and a back porch ; a parlor, 13 ft. × 16 ft.; a dining-room, 15 ft. × 18 ft. 6 in.; a chamber, 15 ft. × 18 ft.; and a kitchen, 12 ft. × 12 ft. The second floor has three rooms, respectively 15 ft. × 18 ft., 13 ft. × 16 ft., and 11 ft. 6 in. × 18 ft. 6 in.

FIG. 80.—PERSPECTIVE.

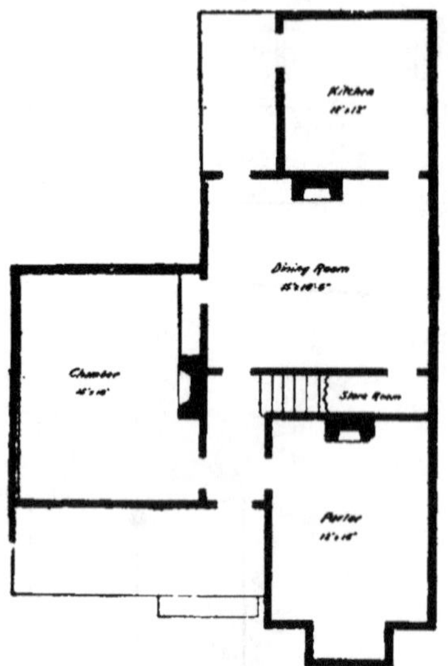

FIG. 81.—GROUND-PLAN.

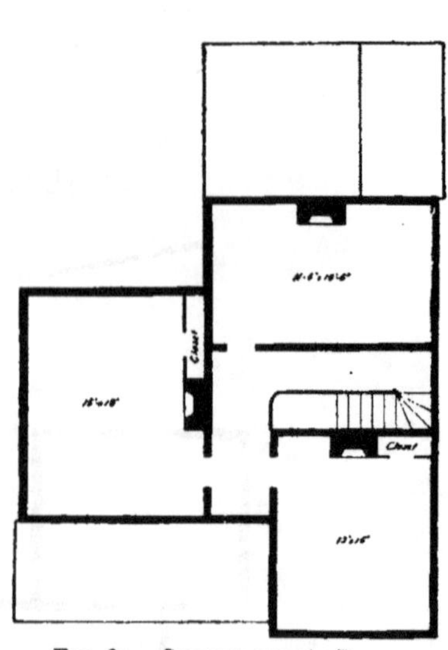

FIG. 82.—SECOND-FLOOR PLAN.

Dwelling-house, Union Pacific Railway.—The design for a dwelling-house of the Union Pacific Railway, shown in Figs. 83 and 84, consists of a two-story frame cottage, the general style of

FIG. 83.—FRONT ELEVATION.

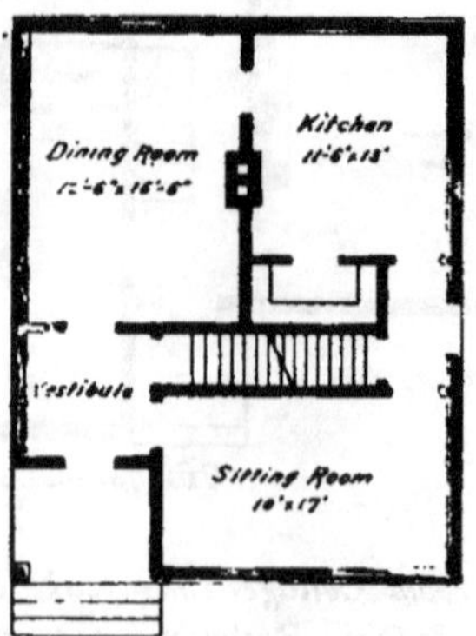

FIG. 84.—GROUND-PLAN.

which resembles a town residence. There is a cellar under the front part of the house. The ground-floor has a front-entrance porch, a vestibule, a sitting-room, a dining-room, and a kitchen. The second floor has three bedrooms and a large closet.

Dwelling-house, Atchison, Topeka & Santa Fe Railroad.—The Atchison, Topeka & Santa Fe Railroad has three classes of standard dwelling-houses, known respectively as section houses Nos. 1, 2, and 3. In Figs. 85 to 87 the standard plan No. 2 is shown. The other standards do not differ materially from the one illustrated, except in size and minor details. In general the designs show a two-story plain frame building, sheathed on the outside with upright boards and battens, and the whole built very cheaply and without any attempt at display.

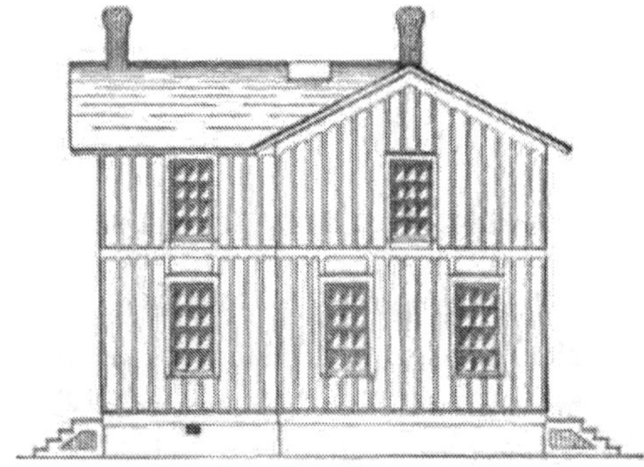

FIG. 85.—SIDE ELEVATION.

Standard No. 2 shows a building occupying a ground-space of 30 × 30 ft. There is a cellar under the house. The ground-floor has a living-room, 12 ft. × 17 ft.; two bedrooms, each 8 ft. × 12 ft.; a kitchen, 12 ft. × 14 ft.; and a large pantry. The second floor has three bedrooms, each about 12 ft. × 17 ft.

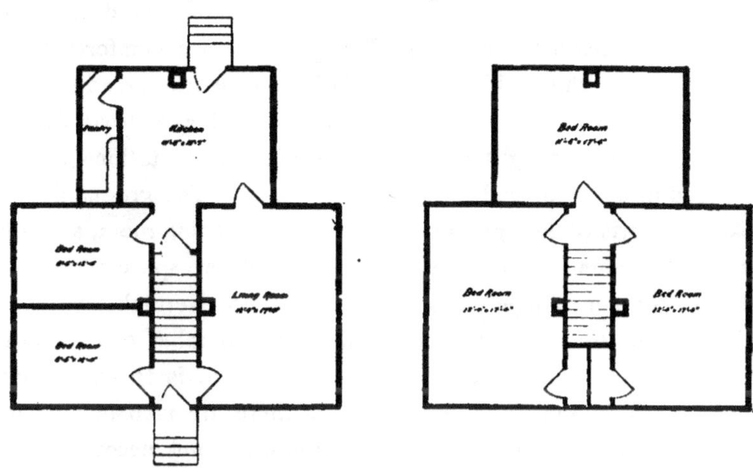

FIG. 86.—GROUND-PLAN. FIG. 87.—SECOND-FLOOR PLAN.

Employés' Homes of Westinghouse Air-brake Co., Wilmerding, Pa.—A model system of homes for employés, as built by the Westinghouse Air-brake Company at Wilmerding, Pa., will be found described and illustrated in the *Railroad Gazette* of March 14, 1890. There are three distinct types of dwellings furnished, namely: Class A, eight rooms, cellar, bath, and range, costing $3550; Class B, six rooms, cellar, bath, and range, costing $2700; Class C, five rooms, costing $2000.

CHAPTER V.

SLEEPING QUARTERS, READING-ROOMS, AND CLUB-HOUSES FOR EMPLOYÉS.

MOST of the large railroads of the country at their main termini or junction points have special rooms or small buildings set apart for the use of employés who are forced to spend more or less time at such stations. The accommodations consist either of rooms for making up reports, for lounging, and for changing clothes, or of reading-rooms, or regular sleeping quarters. The Union Pacific Railway is the only road which, to the author's knowledge, has a special design for a reading-room for use at points along its lines. In order to meet with general favor in providing quarters for employés, the principal conditions to be observed consist in removing all unnecessary restrictions and in offering the men a comfortable set of rooms to sleep or lounge about in, with suitable accommodations for writing, reading, smoking, talking, or playing games. Any two-story frame dwelling-house, such as railroad companies are often compelled to buy in acquiring right of way in the vicinity of stations, can, at a very small expense, be changed into a comfortable home for the men. The ground-floor should have a room for preparing reports (if not provided elsewhere), a reading-room, a smoking-room, and also a sitting-room with lounges and comfortable chairs, if the space permit. Upstairs there should be bedrooms for men obliged to stay at the station overnight whose regular homes are at other places along the line, and a room with a large number of cots on which men can rest for a few hours between runs. A yet better arrangement is to have a large number of smaller rooms each with the same number of cots as there are men in a train-crew, so that when a crew is called the rest of the men in the house are not necessarily disturbed. The usual toilet- and bath-room facilities would complete the list. A house of this kind, with a janitor to look after it, would contain all that the employés of a railroad could desire in this line.

The Railroad Branch of the Young Men's Christian Association has done much toward furnishing proper accommodations for railroad men at a number of the principal termini of the country, where railroad managements through false economy or a lack of forethought have been careless about securing to trainmen a place for the much-needed rest between runs and the proper kind of recreation when off duty.

As mentioned above, any small frame building, or floor in a larger building, can generally, with very little expense and trouble, be fitted up for trainmen's quarters, and it is a very short-sighted management that cannot appreciate the numerous advantages to be derived from furnishing the men with comfortable quarters and suitable accommodations.

Below will be found several descriptions of employés' reading or club rooms and sleeping quarters which will prove of additional interest in connection with this subject.

Bunk-house at Jersey City, N. J., Lehigh Valley Railroad.—The bunk-house for trainmen of the Lehigh Valley Railroad at Jersey City, N. J., shown in Figs. 88 and 89, consists of an old two-story frame dwelling-house, which the railroad company obtained in buying certain terminal lands, remodelled to suit the new purposes to which the building is devoted. The house is 18 ft. 6 in. × 25 ft. 6 in., and has accommodations for twenty men. A single-story annex, 18 ft. 6 in.×7 ft. 6 in., is built on to the building and serves for wash-room and toilet-room. The entrance to the building is through this annex. The building is heated by steam from an adjacent boiler system.

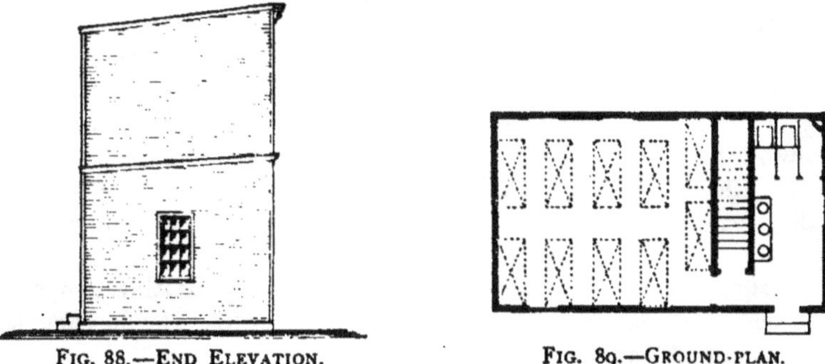

FIG. 88.—END ELEVATION. FIG. 89.—GROUND-PLAN.

Bunk-house at Perth Amboy, N. J., Lehigh Valley Railroad.—The bunk-house of the Lehigh Valley Railroad at Perth Amboy, N. J., designed by Mr. Charles Rosenberg, Master Carpenter, L. V. R. R., shown in Figs. 90 to 92, is a two-story frame building, 33 ft. 6 in. × 38 ft., with high

FIG. 90.—FRONT ELEVATION.

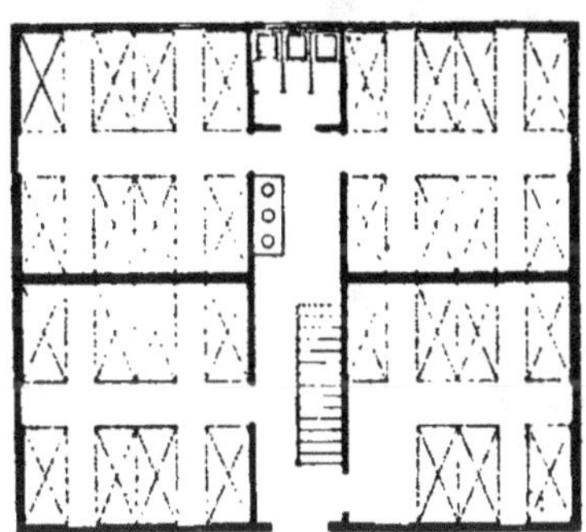

FIG. 91.—GROUND-PLAN.

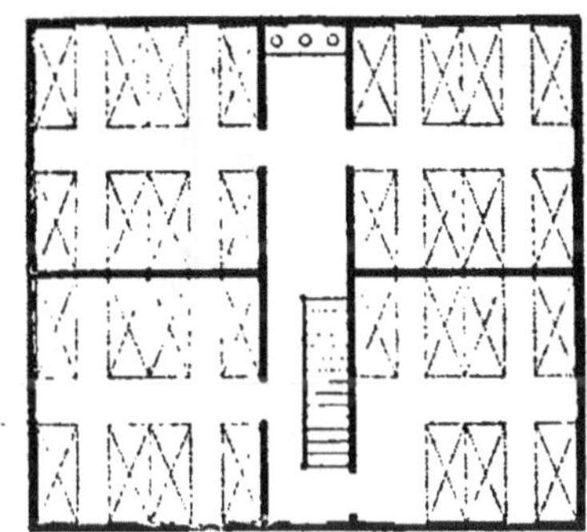

FIG. 92.—SECOND-FLOOR PLAN.

attic, sheathed on the outside with horizontal weather-boarding and roofed with tin. The building is finished in the interior the same as an ordinary dwelling, the walls being plastered throughout, so as to avoid using wood on the inside as much as possible to promote cleanliness and prevent the house being overrun with vermin. The building is intended to accommodate 76 men, 31 on the first floor, 31 on the second floor, and 14 on the attic floor. The interior is divided into rooms, each accommodating not over eight men, which is done not only for hygienic reasons, but also to prevent other men being disturbed when any particular train-crew or set of men are called out. The necessary wash-basins and water-closets are placed in convenient places and provided with running water. The location of the house is in the vicinity of a round-house and boiler-house of a shop system, so that the building is heated by steam and hot water easily obtained. The bedsteads are of iron and are 2 ft. 9 in. wide and 6 ft. 3 in. long, furnished with a woven wire spring, a husk mattress with cotton top, one pair of woollen blankets, and one feather pillow, costing complete $10.90 per bed.

The specification for the building is in general as follows: frame to be of hemlock; joists, 3 in. × 8 in.; sills, 6 in. × 8 in.; studs, 2 in. × 4 in., spaced 16 in. centres; door and window studs, 3 in. × 4 in.; plates, 4 in. × 6 in.; rafters, 2 in. × 6 in.; partitions, 4 in. Outside sheathing, pine bevelled siding; flooring, $1\frac{1}{4}$-in. yellow pine. Inside finish of walls, three coats of plastering. Slate roof. All woodwork painted two coats of paint. Panelled doors throughout, outside 2 in. and inside $1\frac{1}{2}$ in. thick. All sash, twelve lights, 10 in. × 14 in.

This building cost erected complete, fully equipped with beds and bedding, including all plumbing, $3300.

The same design can be utilized for a smaller house accommodating 37 men, by cutting off the building on one side of the hallway, leaving it 33 ft. 6 in. × 23 ft. The first and second floors would accommodate 15 men each and the attic 7 men more.

Reading-room, Union Pacific Railway.—The design for a reading-room of the Union Pacific Railway, designed in 1886, in the Resident Engineer's office at Omaha, shown in Figs. 93 to 95

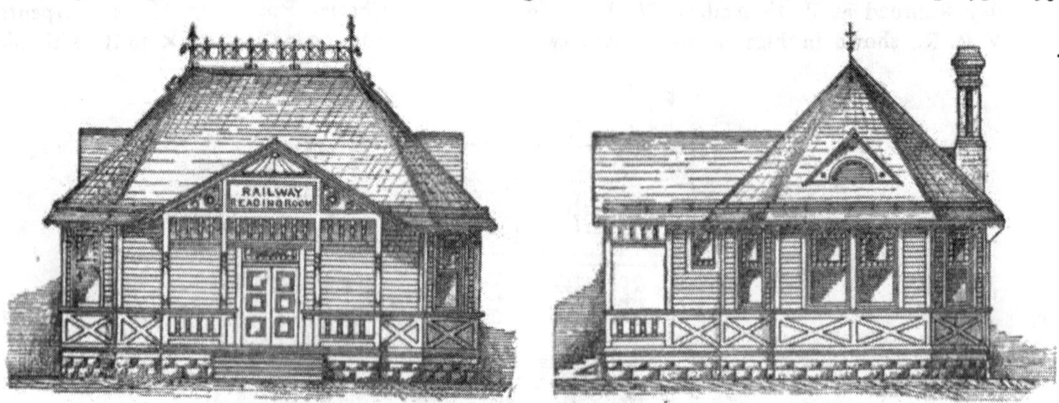

FIG. 93.—FRONT ELEVATION.

FIG. 94.—SIDE ELEVATION.

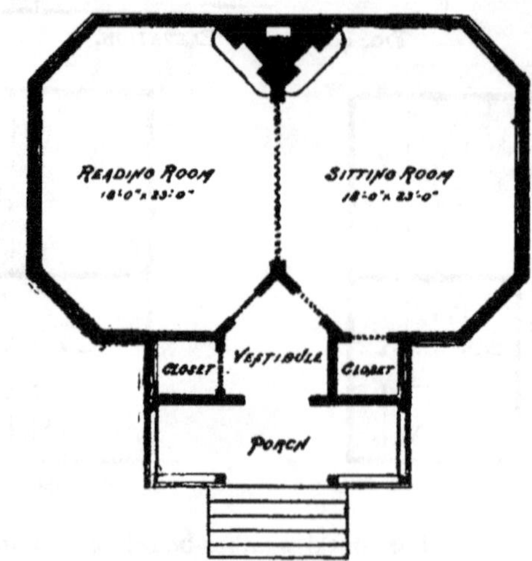

FIG. 95.—GROUND-PLAN.

presents a very pretty and original design for the purpose. It is a small one-story frame cottage, 24 ft. × 38 ft., with a large front porch 20 ft. wide. The interior is divided into two octagonal rooms, which serve respectively as reading-room and sitting-room. They are connected by a pair of large doors, which can be thrown open, when desired, to make one large room of the interior. A vestibule with closets on both sides leads from the porch to the inner rooms. The foundations of the building are shown to be stone. Besides the ordinary furniture each room is provided with large ornamental bookcases.

This design, however, while very tasteful, does not cover all the requirements that can be made of such a building and is, in addition, too elaborate to be recommended as a standard for general adoption. Structures were built according to these plans at a number of points along the line of the Union Pacific, but the design adopted within recent years for similar structures offers decided improvements over the older design, being more practical in construction and giving better facilities for the men.

Railroad Branch Building, Young Men's Christian Association, at East Buffalo, N. Y.—As a well-arranged and interesting design, the plans of the Railroad Branch Building, Y. M. C. A., at East Buffalo, N. Y., shown in Figs. 96 to 99, as published in the *Railway Review*, October 6, 1888, are presented. This building is a substantial structure, three-story and high attic, 75 ft. × 36 ft., with stone and brick walls, the interior being appropriately fitted up. The arrangement of the interior is shown on the plans, and the following description of the building is taken from the publication mentioned:

The basement, which is high and light, will contain a dining-room, lunch-counter, kitchen, pantry, barber-shop, shower and sponge baths, and toilet accommodations, as indicated in the plan, fitted up neatly and with all modern improvements. The woodwork will be of hard wood.

The first floor will contain a reading-room and library. A room devoted to different games adjoins the main hall, as does the office lobby, into which the general secretary's room will open. Across the hall, as shown in the plan, are two light, airy rooms which will be used for a hospital. A third ward and the nurses' room of the hospital are on the second floor, as are the dormitory, two class-rooms, which can be easily turned into one large parlor, and necessary storerooms.

The second floor will be fitted up for the use of the janitor and with additional sleeping-rooms. A wing, not shown in the illustration, will be devoted to a gymnasium, that much-appreciated portion of every well-planned association building.

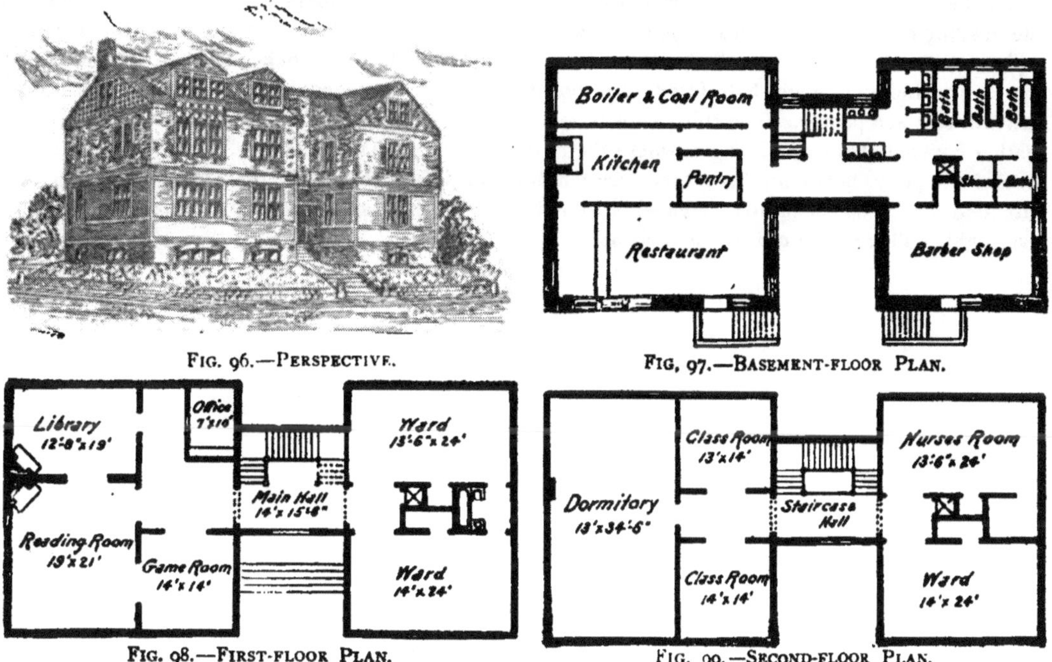

FIG. 96.—PERSPECTIVE.

FIG. 97.—BASEMENT-FLOOR PLAN.

FIG. 98.—FIRST-FLOOR PLAN.

FIG. 99.—SECOND-FLOOR PLAN.

Employés' Club-house, Chicago, Burlington & Northern Railroad.—The employés' club-house of the Chicago, Burlington & Northern Railroad is a handsome brick building with hard-wood finish, fitted up and supplied with all modern and essential appointments. On the first floor are a reading-room, smoking-room, billiard-room, and toilet; on the second are twelve large bedrooms, two bathrooms, and a large toilet-room. Every room is heated by steam, lighted by gas, and ventilated in the best manner.

Railroad Branch Building, Young Men's Christian Association, New York Central & Hudson River Railroad, New York, N. Y.—The Railroad Branch building of the Young Men's Christian Association at the shops of the New York Central & Hudson River Railroad at Seventy-second Street and North River, New York City, is a two-story building appropriately arranged, the interior being plastered and wainscoted in natural wood; the ground-floor has three large rooms, a kitchen, two bathrooms, and the secretary's office. The upper story is provided with twenty comfortable, well warmed and ventilated sleeping-rooms, arranged about a gallery, similar to the second tier of state-rooms on a steamboat. The rooms are intended for railroad employés who live at distant points and are forced to lay over between runs at the New York end of the road.

Railroad Men's Club-house, New York Central & Hudson River Railroad, New York, N. Y.—A very extensive and handsome club-house for the use of the employés of the New York Central & Hudson River Railroad and associated companies using the Grand Central Station at Forty-second Street, New York City, was formally opened on October 3, 1887, by Mr. Cornelius Vanderbilt, at whose expense the building was erected. The building is controlled by a board of trustees, composed of directors and officers of the interested railroads, and the detail management is under the direction of the Railroad Young Men's Christian Association.

The building is described in the issue of the *Railroad Gazette* of October 7, 1887, as follows: The building has been designed with thorough consideration for its uses. It stands at the corner of Madison Avenue and Forty-fifth Street, adjacent to the yard of the Grand Central Station. It is built of brick and terra cotta, and is two stories high, with a tower running up two stories higher. There are a gymnasium, bowling-alleys, and bathrooms in the basement, and a plunge-bath 6 ft. deep, 9½ ft. wide, and 13½ ft. long. The bathtubs are porcelain, the ceiling and walls of glazed brick and tiles. The partitions in the basement are of marble, set in a framework of solid bronze, and the plumbing work is nickel and brass. On the main floor is a library with 6000 volumes on its shelves. Then there are a reading-room, a social room, a general secretary's room, and committee room. In the reading-room there are files of 95 daily, weekly, and monthly papers. In the social room there is a piano. The floors here are tiled, and the walls are panelled in dark oak. On the second floor is the lecture and amusement hall, fitted up in polished oak and frescoed in light, pleasing tints. This hall will seat 400 people. The third floor is occupied by a thoroughly comfortable room, filled with leather-covered chairs and lounges, where the railroad men can have luncheon. Hot coffee is served free of charge. On the top floor there are ten bedrooms, furnished with brass bedsteads, which are intended for the use of railroad men who, by reason of long runs, are compelled to stay in the city overnight. There is no charge for their use.

CHAPTER VI.

SNOWSHEDS AND PROTECTION-SHEDS FOR MOUNTAIN-SLIDES.

SNOWSHEDS are in extensive use on the Northwestern and Canadian railroads to protect the track and keep it clear in winter wherever the snowfall is heavy or bad slides are to be expected. While the use of these structures is more immediately confined to a limited section of the country, the plans adopted to overcome the difficulties encountered are of interest to a larger group of railroads, as indicative of the best general methods that can be adopted to protect a line along side hills, where slides or heavy stones rolling down the steep mountain-slopes endanger the safety of trains.

While snowsheds are more particularly employed and essentially necessary in deep cuts and dangerous side-hill sections of the railroads mentioned, they are also used on level ground to protect the track against heavy vertical snowfalls, which might, in the absence of such protection, cause serious blockades. We thus obtain two distinctive forms of snowsheds, namely, sheds adapted for use in through or side-hill cuts, where drifts and slides might occur, and known as "valley sheds" or "gallery sheds," and sheds on level ground for protection against heavy snowfalls, known as "level-fall sheds." Valley sheds are used where avalanches could strike the shed on both sides, and gallery sheds where avalanches can only come down on one side of the track.

The weight of compressed snow in a slide varies from 25 to 45 lbs. per cubic foot, and it is generally discharged in balls of varying sizes, according to the state of the weather and the condition of the snow.

Dry snow descends with great velocity, and its impact upon a structure is severe. Wet snow, on the contrary, though heavier, descends more slowly, and hence is not as destructive in its effects. Snowsheds on level ground are not exposed to slides or large masses of moving snow, and have, therefore, only the vertical snow-pressure to resist. As wet snow is heavier than dry snow, the standards of the railroads vary according to the nature of the snow to be guarded against. On the Selkirk range, Canadian Pacific Railway, the snow frequently lies 20 ft. deep on the level, requiring miles of snowsheds to be built on level ground, in addition to the usual protection in deep through and side-hill cuts.

Snow sheds on level ground can be compared to wooden tunnels or galleries, having side walls of round or square timbers, sheathed with plank, and covered by a double-pitched roof, with proper bracing for lateral stiffness and suitable openings for ventilation. The clear width is 16 ft., and the clear height above top of rail is 18 to 21 ft. The bents are usually spaced from 6 to 10 ft. apart. The standards in use for level-fall sheds do not differ materially.

For deep through or heavy side-hill cuts, where slides and drifts are to be encountered, a large number of standard designs exists to meet the varying conditions in different localities.

As a rule, the construction consists of square or round timber bents, from 4 to 6 ft. apart, provided with heavy timber bracing or anchored with tie-rods to the rock, the whole covered with a plank roof pitched according to the slopes of the adjoining hillside. Log cribs filled with stones or earth are frequently used to aid in resisting the impact of the sliding masses of snow.

The most extensively adopted design on the Canadian Pacific Railway is that of a crib built up to the level of the top of the slope on the hillside of the track, the space between the hill and the crib being filled with earth. On the other side of the track there is a framework of timbers resting on mud-sills, piles, or toe-cribs. A properly constructed roof spans the track. Where the top of the cut does not reach up to the top of the shed, heavy embankments are thrown against the side of the shed. Descending slides on striking the embankment are deflected from their course, and pass over the shed without subjecting the timbers to serious strains.

Proper ventilation in these long wooden galleries or tunnels is secured by leaving suitable openings in the side planking and by providing louvred lanterns and air-shafts where feasible. In the summer season part of the side planking is taken off, or hinged panels are thrown open, for the admission of air and light. In some cases special summer tracks are maintained outside of the sheds.

For protection against the spread of fires, the wooden siding is replaced at intervals by galvanized iron, or several sections of the shed are cut out completely. To guard against drifts or slides, split fences or glance fences are built opposite the opening, which divert the snow to the shedded sections. Special fire-service trains are kept constantly in readiness in connection with an organized fire patrol and telegraphic signal-boxes along the route. In addition, pipe lines inside the sheds, with tanks, hydrants, and hose-reels at proper intervals, serve to complete the system.

The cost of snowsheds is placed as follows by Mr. C. A. Stoess, Resident Engineer, Pacific Division, Central Pacific Railway: The sheds protecting the track against snow-slides cost from $25 to $70 per lineal foot of shed, according to location; the sheds for use on the level cost from $8 to $10 per lineal foot of shed. Mr. Thomas C. Keefer, in his paper on the Canadian Pacific Railway, read at the annual convention of the American Society of Civil Engineers in 1888, states that the typical type of snowshed in the Selkirk region, namely, a solid rock-filled crib on the mountain-side and a strongly braced framework for its outer side, costs $40 to $70 per lineal foot; a gallery shed, without cribwork, but with roof extended against the mountain-side, used where the impact of the snow is not severe, costs $15 to $40 per lineal foot; a combination of the typical and the gallery sheds, called "toe-crib and gallery shed," where cribwork is used as a foot-wall on the mountain side, costs $27 to $54 per lineal foot.

Below will be found descriptions and plans of a number of standard designs of snowsheds, as also a description of a protection-shed for mountain slides, in actual use in this country.

Snowshed on Level Ground, Central Pacific Railroad.—The standard snowshed on level ground of the Central Pacific Railroad, shown in Figs. 100 to 102, is formed of heavy timber bents, spaced generally about 8 ft. between centres. The outside is sheathed with horizontal boards, with suitable openings for ventilation. The roof is double-pitched and covered with rough boards. Louvred lanterns or air-shafts are provided at intervals.

The sheds are 16 ft. wide in the clear, and 18 ft. high in the clear above top of rail. The principal timbers used are as follows: posts, 8 in. × 10 in.; principal rafters, 6 in. × 10 in.; intermediate rafters, 6 in. × 8 in.; collar-beams, 8 in. × 3 in.; brace-posts, 8 in. × 10 in.

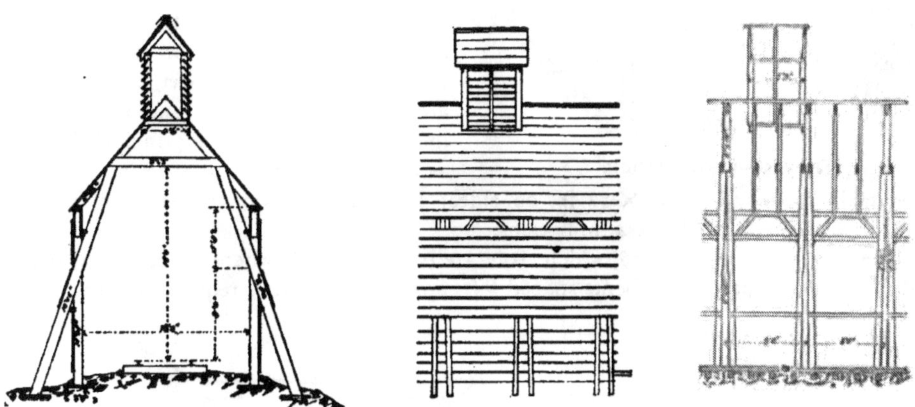

FIG. 100.—CROSS-SECTION. FIG. 101.—ELEVATION. FIG. 102.—LONGITUDINAL SECTION.

Snowshed on Level Ground, Northern Pacific Railroad.—The standard snowshed on level ground of the Northern Pacific Railroad, shown in Figs. 103 and 104, is formed of heavy timber bents spaced for wet snow from 6 to 8 ft. apart, and for dry snow from 6 to 10 ft. apart. The outside is sheathed with upright boards and battens. The roof is double-pitched and covered with rough boards and battens. The sheds are 16 ft. wide in the clear, and 19 ft. high in the clear above top of rail. There are two standards, one for wet and one for dry snow.

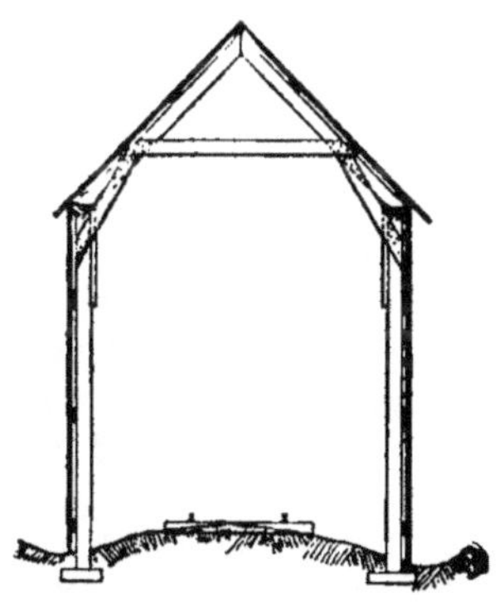

FIG. 103.—CROSS-SECTION.

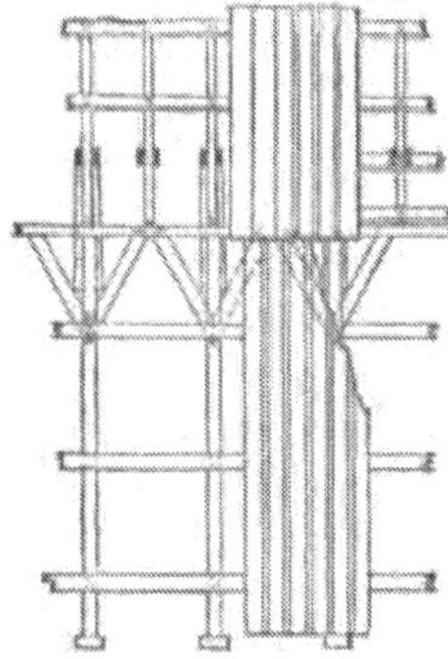

FIG. 104.—ELEVATION.

In the wet-snow standard the principal timbers used are as follows: posts, 8 in. × 10 in.; rafters, 4 in. × 10 in.; collar-beams, 2 in. × 10 in.; plates, 4 in. × 12 in.; horizontal studding, 4 in. × 10 in.; siding and roofing, 2-in. boards.

In the dry-snow standard the principal timbers used are as follows: posts, 8 in. × 8 in.; rafters, 4 in. × 8 in.; collar-beams, 2 in. × 8 in.; plates, 4 in. × 11 in.; horizontal studding, 2 in. × 8 in.; siding and roofing, 1-in. boards.

For bents spaced 6 ft. apart the wet-snow standard requires 304 ft. B. M. lumber and 13.3 lbs. of iron per lineal foot of shed, and the dry-snow standard requires 211 ft. B. M. lumber and 5.2 lbs. of iron per lineal foot of shed.

Snowsheds over Cuts or on Side Hills, Northern Pacific Railroad.—The Northern Pacific Railroad has a large number of standards for snowsheds over cuts or on side hills to suit the varying circumstances, two of which are shown in Figs. 105 and 106 from designs of Mr. C. B. Talbot.

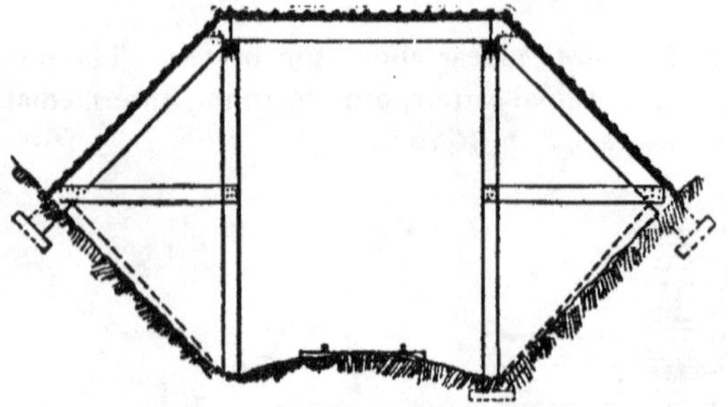

Fig. 105.—Cross-section.

The style of shed shown in Fig. 105 is more particularly applicable in through cuts. The bents are spaced 6 ft. apart, or as may be necessary. For bents spaced 6 ft. apart, the materials required are 484 ft. B. M. lumber and 14.0 lbs. of iron per lineal foot of shed. The principal timbers used are as follows: posts, 10 in. × 12 in.; caps, 10 in. × 16 in. over main span, and 10 in. × 14 in. on sides; brace-plank, two pieces, 3 in. × 12 in.; roof-plank, 4 in. × 12 in., and 1 in. × 4 in. battens.

In the case shown in Fig. 106, which structure is for side hills where slides occur, the bents are spaced 4 ft. to 6 ft. apart. For bents spaced 6 ft. apart, the materials required are 634 ft. B. M. lumber and 9.3 lbs. of iron per lineal foot of shed. The principal timbers used are as follows: posts, 10 in. × 12 in.; caps, 10 in. × 16 in. over main span, and 10 in. × 12 in. on sides; bank sill on outside at foot of posts, 10 in. × 12 in., continuous from bent to bent; mud-sill up slope of side hill, 10 in. × 12 in.; brace plank, two pieces, 3 in. × 12 in.; roof-plank, 4 in. × 12 in., and 1 in. × 4 in. battens.

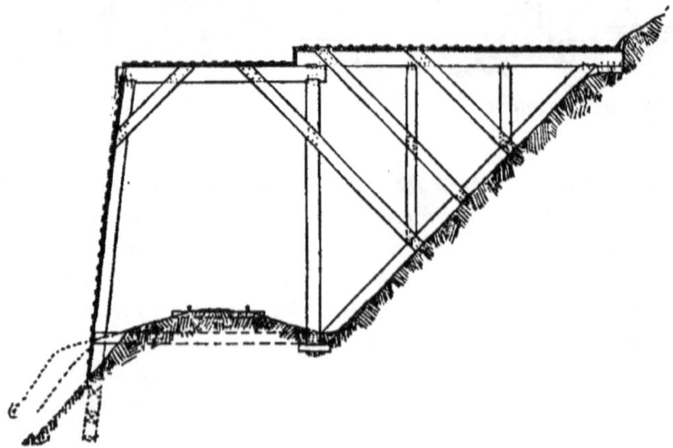

Fig. 106.—Cross-section.

The space left for the track is in all cases 16 ft. wide in the clear, and 19 ft. high in the clear above top of rail.

Snowsheds, Canadian Pacific Railway.—The Canadian Pacific Railway has a very large number of snowshed standards, as built at different times under varying conditions. Four of these standards are shown in Figs. 107 to 110, the last of which has been most extensively employed. The clear space left for the trains in all the standards of the road is 16 ft. wide and 22 ft. high above the grade line.

The design shown in Fig. 107 is for use in through cuts, and for protection against level fall. The bents are spaced 8 ft. apart. The principal timbers used are as follows: posts, of round timbers; plates, 8 in. × 10 in.; rafters, 9 in. × 12 in.; brace-posts, 6 in. × 8 in.; roof-plank, 3 in.

In Fig. 108 a design is shown for use in through or side-hill cuts. The bents are 8 ft. apart. The principal timbers used are as follows: posts, of round timbers; plates, 10 in. × 10 in.; caps, over main span, 12 in. × 15 in., and on sides, 12 in. × 12 in.; roof-plank, 4 in.

Fig. 109 shows a design for use in through and side-hill cuts. The spacing of the bents and the general sizes of the timbers are similar to those in the last-described design.

The standard, shown in Fig. 110, deserves more than passing attention, as it is the type of snowshed at present in favor on the Canadian Pacific Railway for use on side-hill and through cuts where heavy slides can be expected. A crib is built up to full height of the top of the cut on the hill side of the track, the space between the crib and the hill being filled with earth. On the lower side of the track a framework of 12 in. × 12 in. timbers or round logs, resting on sills, piles, or a toe-crib, supports the lower end of the roof over the track. The crib is formed of 12 in. × 12 in. or 10 in. × 12 in. front logs and round back logs, spaced with 3-in. openings. The front and back logs are connected by 8 in. × 8 in. square, or by round log ties, spaced 5 ft. apart, dovetailed to the front logs

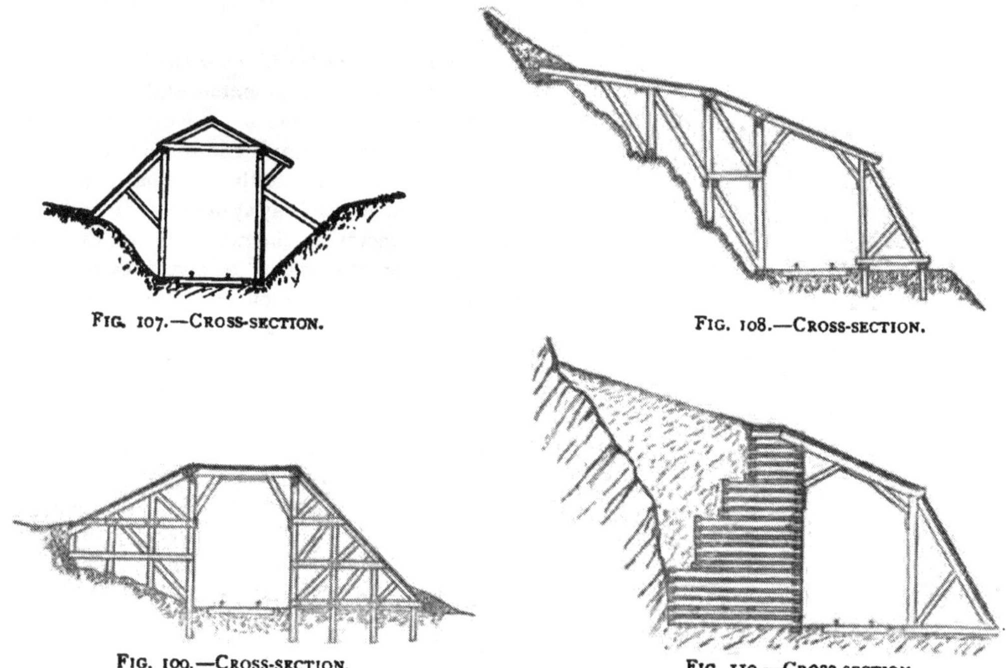

FIG. 107.—CROSS-SECTION.

FIG. 108.—CROSS-SECTION.

FIG. 109.—CROSS-SECTION.

FIG. 110.—CROSS-SECTION.

and saddled or dovetailed into the flatted back logs. The roof-plank is 6 in. thick. The timberwork throughout is only drift-bolted or dowelled together; no mortises or tenons are used.

For additional standards and data see the *Railroad Gazette*, issue of July 6, 1888; the *Engineering News*, issues of January 21, 1888, and December 14, 1889; the *Railway Review*, issues of July 21, December 8, and December 22, 1888; and Transactions of the American Society of Civil Engineers, August, 1888, with paper on the Canadian Pacific Railway, by Thomas C. Keefer, president of the society.

Snowshed over Cuts or on Side Hills, Central Pacific Railroad.—The snowshed of the Central Pacific Railroad, shown in Fig. 111, is for use in through or side-hill cuts. It forms a roof over the

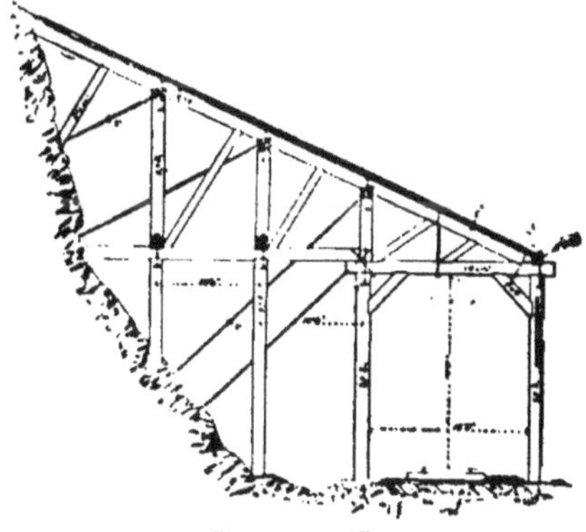

FIG. 111.—CROSS-SECTION.

track which carries any material coming down the hillside safely over the road. The bents are spaced from 4 to 6 feet apart, according to circumstances. The design shows the structure anchored to the rock in the side cut with a number of 2-inch rods. Where this is not feasible, appropriate bracing has to be introduced.

The clear space for the track is 15 ft. 9 in. wide and 18 ft. high above top of rails. The principal timbers used are as follows: main posts, 12 in. × 14 in.; side posts, 12 in. × 12 in.; caps, 12 in. × 14 in. over main span, and all others 12 in. × 12 in.; braces, 8 in. × 12 in.; roof-plank, 5 in.; side planks, 2 in.

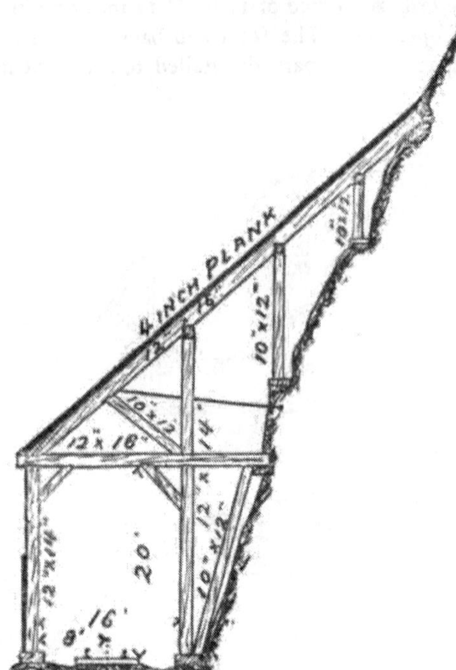

FIG. 112.—CROSS-SECTION.

Protection-shed for Mountain-slides, Oregon & California Railroad.—A mountain-slide of large proportions and under unusual conditions occurred in March, 1890, at the north end of tunnel No. 9 on the Oregon & California Railroad, connected with the Southern Pacific Railway system. The methods employed for removing the materials and the construction of a protection-shed to divert earth or rocks, that might come down on the track, were described and illustrated in a paper prepared by Mr. W. G. Curtis and read before the American Society of Civil Engineers, which paper was published in the Transactions of the Society for 1890. In Fig. 112, reproduced from the publication mentioned, a section is shown of the protection-shed adopted and built after the slide had been removed. This shed has proved to be sufficiently strong to divert earth and rocks which have fallen down from the mountain since the construction of the shed. The length of the slide measured 200 ft. along the track, the height of rock slope is about 100 ft., and the vertical height from the grade to the top of the slide about 300 ft. This structure illustrates clearly the application that is made in practice of the general principles governing the construction of snowsheds on side hills to structures intended to protect a railroad from mountain-slides or boulders liable to fall down on the track.

CHAPTER VII.

SIGNAL-TOWERS.

SIGNAL-TOWERS are used on railroads where it is necessary to station a watchman, signalman, gateman, switch-tender, or operator, at a sufficient elevation above the railroad to enable him to command a good view of the tracks and surroundings, or to allow the signalman or his signals to be readily seen from approaching trains, vehicles, or other signal stations. There are two classes of signal-towers, namely, those intended to protect exposed points on the line, and those forming part of a block-signaling system.

The former are, as a rule, simply watchman's houses set on trestles, and are used to afford protection at railroad and highway grade crossings, tunnels, sharp curves, dangerous points of the line where the view is obstructed, and at the head of or connected with switch and yard systems. Signals are given by hand, lamps, flags, vanes, targets, balls, movable arms, or other appropriate means.

The second class, namely, block-station signal-towers, form part of a more or less extensive signaling system by which the road is divided into sections or "blocks" of a length dependent on the varying conditions and necessities of the traffic. A signal-tower, equipped with the requisite signaling apparatus and connected with the neighboring towers by wire, is located at the end of each block or section. The control of the trains on each block or section is thus completely in the hands of the signalmen or operators in the towers at each end of the block.

Where there is an interlocking switch system, or switches worked by levers from a distance, it is customary, if feasible, to locate the working levers in the signal room of a signal-tower, so that one man can control the switches and the movement of trains. Signal-towers with switch levers are usually to be found at terminal yards, stations, junction points, and cross-over systems.

Most railroads have block signals at their regular stations or stopping-places, even where the regular block system is not employed between stations, in which case the regular operator at the station performs the duties of signalman. Station buildings, in which the operator is located in a small tower or extended gable front above the ground-floor, have been quite extensively introduced, enabling the operator to obtain a better view of the road and lessening the possibility of being interrupted by passengers or others. This combination of signal tower and station building is advisable, however, only where, in addition to the station agent and other help, a special operator is employed. Where one or two men are required to perform all the duties connected with the station and the signaling apparatus, it is objectionable to have part of the work located in the upper story.

Descriptions and plans of a number of signal-towers are presented below as illustrative of the different types in actual use.

Octagonal Signal-tower, Philadelphia & Reading Railroad.—The octagonal signal-tower shown in Fig. 113 represents a style of tower much in use on the Philadelphia & Reading Railroad at dangerous places or where the view is obstructed. This form of tower is in reality an elevated watchman's house, the signals being under the control of a special watchman or signalman. These towers are sometimes connected with neighboring towers by wires, as, for instance, at tunnels, in which case they become in a certain sense block-signal stations. As a rule, however, they are too small for the modern block-signal system, which requires more space in the tower than offered in the design under discussion, especially when connected with interlocking switch systems.

FIG. 113.
FRONT ELEVATION.

These signal-towers are frame structures, from 30 ft. to 50 ft. high, and built in the shape of an octagonal pyramid, thus giving much stability against wind and side pressures of any kind. The entrance is on the ground-floor, and a ladder inside the building leads up to the watchman's room. The signaling apparatus, shown on top of the tower, consists of two vanes, each vane having three faces, and each face being painted a different color, signifying, respectively, danger, caution, and safety. The vanes are illuminated at night by lanterns, which are lighted in the room below and hoisted into place by pulleys. The vanes are separated by a blackboard, against which the lights and colors are clearly seen, and are turned by levers working upon round tables in the watchman's room, upon which are painted colors corresponding with the colors of the vanes, so that the lever being locked upon any color on the table, the same color upon the vane is known to be facing the approaching train.

At railroad grade crossings the towers are set in the angle of intersection of the two roads, and have one vane with four faces and two colors, so arranged that one road is always blocked when the other is open.

The signals displayed from these towers need not necessarily be vanes, arranged as just described, but can be flags, movable arms, balls, targets, or revolving cylinders, worked by levers or other suitable appliances.

The framework of the lower story of the tower can be left open, if no reasons exist for inclosing it ; but, as a rule, it will prove convenient to inclose it to permit of its use as a store or tool room.

Square Signal-tower, Philadelphia & Reading Railroad.—The square signal-tower of the Philadelphia & Reading Railroad is only a slight modification of the octagonal tower just described, and is used under the same circumstances and conditions as the latter. The square tower is built in the shape of a square in place of an octagonal pyramid.

Signal Station, Philadelphia, Wilmington & Baltimore Railroad.—A signal station on the Philadelphia, Wilmington & Baltimore Railroad, designed by Mr. S. T. Fuller, Chief Engineer, is described and illustrated in the issue of the *Railroad Gazette* of January 9, 1880. The upper story is used for the signalman and signal apparatus, while the ground-floor is intended to be utilized for passengers or for other business of the railroad company. The design is quite elaborate, and the building presents a fine appearance.

Elevated Gate-house at Whitehaven, Pa., Lehigh Valley Railroad.—The gate-house of the Lehigh Valley Railroad at Whitehaven, Pa., designed by Mr. W. F. Pascoe, Superintendent of Bridges, L. V. R. R., shown in Fig. 114, is a good type of an elevated gate-tender's house at important grade crossings, where a system of gates is in use and the clear view from the level of the railroad is liable to be obstructed. The design presented is rather elaborate for use at an open country road or turnpike crossing outside of settlements, but it is well adapted for crossings in towns and at important thoroughfares where the neat appearance of all railroad structures is considered desirable.

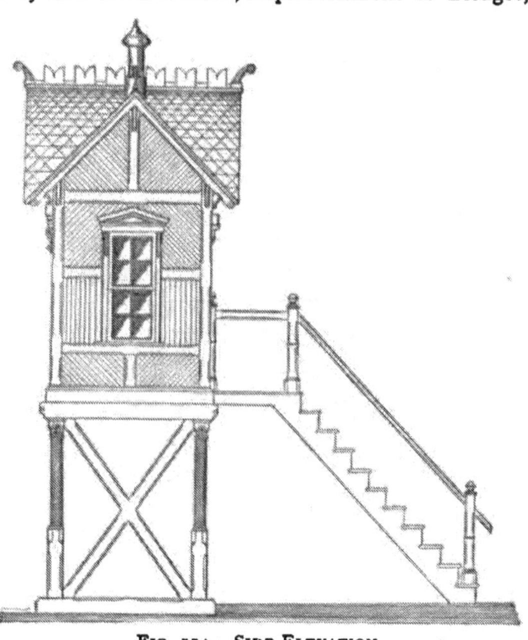

Fig. 114.—Side Elevation.

The building is a frame structure, 7 ft. square on the outside, set on trestles, the floor of the building about 10 ft. above the track rail. The height of frame is 8 ft. from the sill to the plate. The sides of the building are sheathed on the outside and inside with narrow tongued and grooved boards; the roof is covered with tin or slate, laid on 1-in. boards.

The principal timbers used are as follows: sills, 4 in. × 6 in.; plates, 2 in. × 4 in.; corner-studs, 4 in. × 4 in.; door and window studs, 3 in.

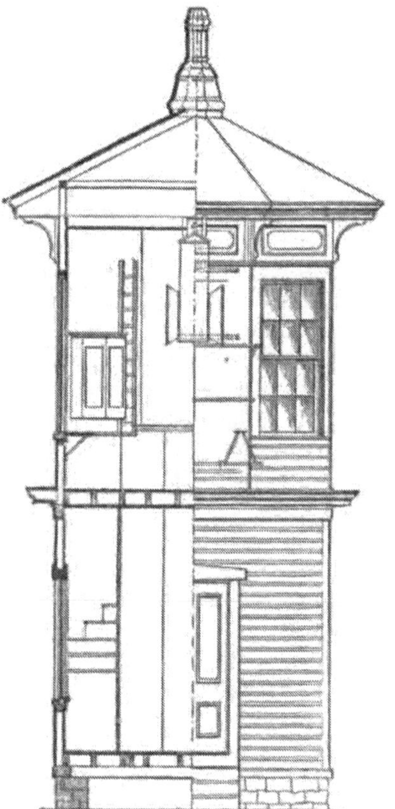

Fig. 115.—Cross-section and Front Elevation.

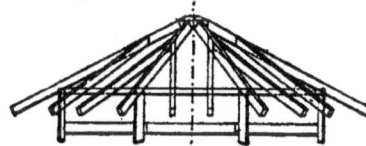

Fig. 116.—Elevation of Frame.

× 4 in.; rafters, 3 in. × 4 in.; floor-joists, 3 in. × 6 in., spaced 18 in.; windows, double sash, each sash four lights, 10 × 12; door, 2 ft. 9 in. × 6 ft. 4 in.; trestle-legs, 8 in. × 8 in.; trestle X-bracing, 6 in. × 6 in.; trestle sills and caps, 10 in. × 10 in.

Standard Signal-tower, Pennsylvania Railroad.—The standard block-station signal-tower of the Pennsylvania Railroad, shown in Figs. 115 to 118, is a two-story frame structure, the lower part being square, and the upper part octagonal in shape. The lower story is about 12 ft. square and about 15 ft. high, and is used for keeping sundry signal and road supplies. Steps inside the tower lead to the upper floor or the signal-room, in which the operator or signalman is stationed, surrounded by the necessary signaling and telegraphic apparatus. The general design of this tower is very ornamental and attractive, while the details are carefully arranged to secure the best results in all respects without prejudice to economy. A large part of the structure is usually framed and put together in the shop before being shipped to the site.

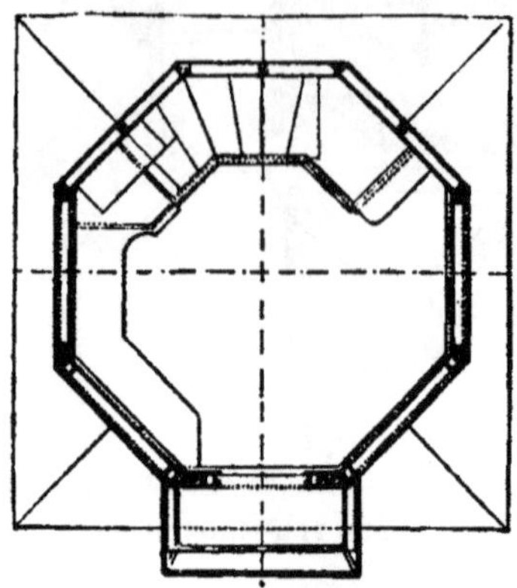

FIG. 117.—SECOND-FLOOR PLAN.

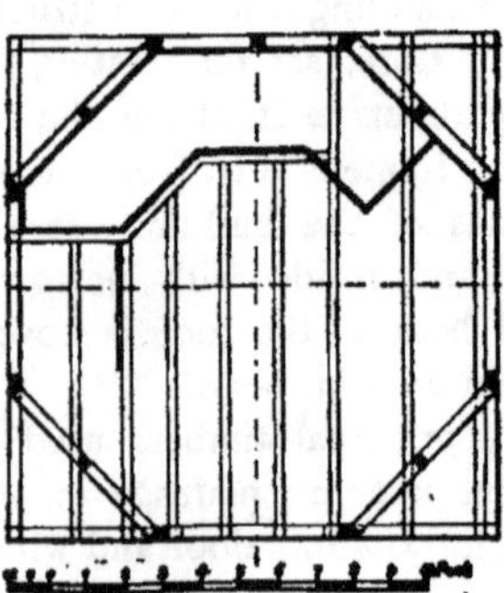

FIG. 118.—SECOND-FLOOR FRAMING PLAN.

Where an extensive and complicated switch system is connected with a block station, the space offered by the building under discussion is too small for the accommodation of the switch levers, and another standard is used, namely, an oblong, two-story frame building, the length of which is varied to suit the requirements of each case. The general features and style of the two standards are otherwise similar.

The kinds of signals controlled by the signalman are numerous. The signals at the tower are frequently located on a light bridge thrown over the tracks or else on arms or brackets attached to the building. In addition there are usually "home" and "distant" signals connected with the tower, consisting of lamps, balls, targets, semaphores, or other appliances, all of which are controlled and operated with great ease and certainty from the signal-room of the tower.

Signal-tower on Depot Building, Richmond & Alleghany Railroad.—In Fig. 119 is shown a signal tower or room on top of a depot building, designed for use on the Richmond & Alleghany Railroad, which design illustrates the method of establishing a block-signal station in the upper story of a depot. The building itself is very plain and cheaply built, representing in its general style a class of structures in extensive use for local depots at small settlements in the South and Southwest.

Signal-tower at Jutland, N. J., Lehigh Valley Railroad.—The signal-tower of the Lehigh Valley Railroad, at Jutland, N. J., shown in Fig. 120, designed by Mr. C. Rosenberg, Master Carpenter, L. V. R. R., is used at the grade crossing of an important county road, where the view of the railroad from the level of the road is obstructed, making it necessary to station the gate-tender or signalman at some height above the ground so as to see approaching trains.

The house proper is a small frame watch-box of the usual style, 8 ft. × 8 ft. outside dimensions, height of frame about 8 ft., with large windows on all sides. This building is placed on a trestle about 14 ft. above the track, with steps leading up to the house. The trestle is built of the following timbers: posts, 6 in. × 8 in.; horizontal ties, 6 in. × 8 in.; X-bracing, 6 in. × 6 in.

Signal-tower at Hillsboro, N. J., Lehigh Valley Railroad.—The signal-tower of the Lehigh Valley Railroad at Hillsboro, N. J., shown in Figs. 121 and 122, designed by Mr. C. Rosenberg,

Master Carpenter, L. V. R. R., is a two-story frame tower structure, 10 ft. × 10 ft. outside dimensions and 19 ft. high from ground to eaves. The first story is 9 ft. high in the clear, the second one 8 ft.

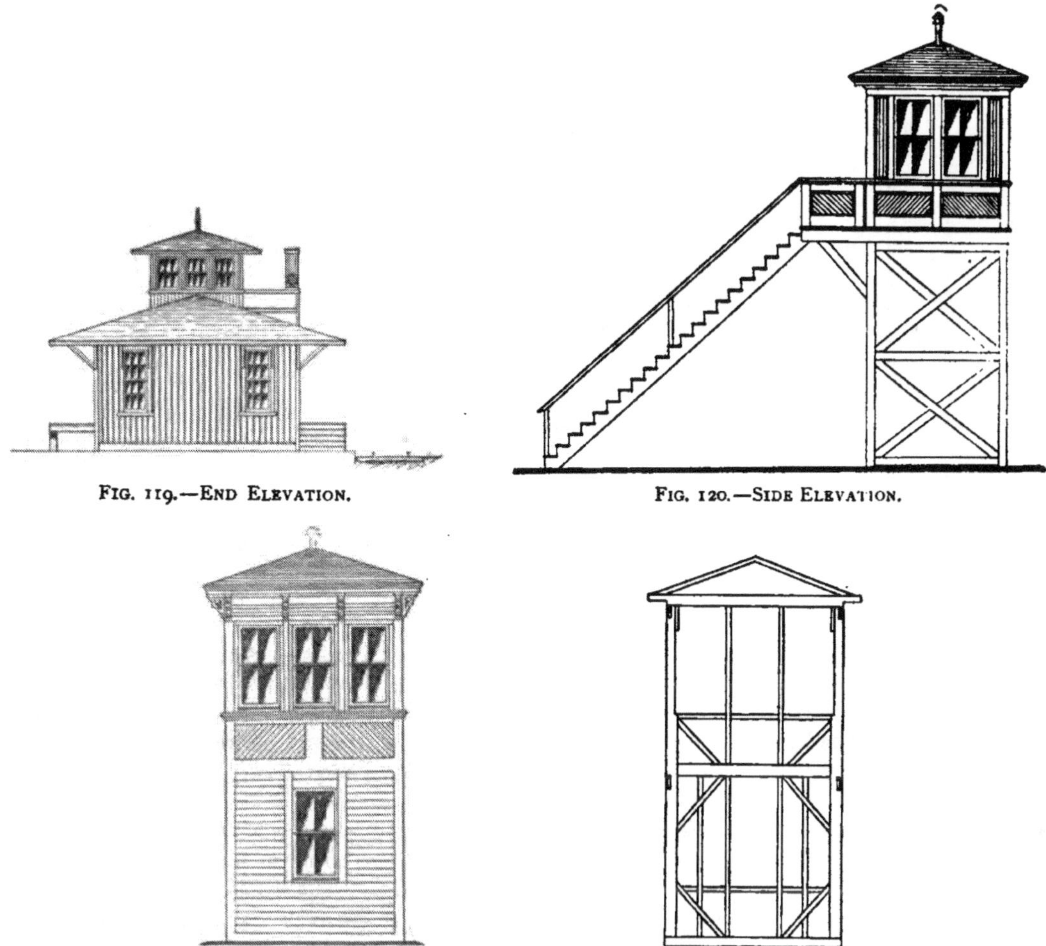

FIG. 119.—END ELEVATION.

FIG. 120.—SIDE ELEVATION.

FIG. 121.—FRONT ELEVATION.

FIG. 122.—ELEVATION OF FRAME.

9 in. high in the clear. Steps on the outside of the building lead to the upper story, which is used for the signalman and the signaling apparatus. The lower story has three windows and a door, and is used for storing various supplies.

The principal timbers used are: sills, 6 in. × 8 in.; interties, 4 in. × 8 in.; plates, 4 in. × 8 in.; corner-posts, 4 in. × 8 in.; studs, 3 in. × 4 in.; angle-braces, 3 in. × 4 in.; rafters, 3 in. × 4 in. The inside is lined with tongued and grooved boards; the outside is covered with bevel siding; the roof consists of tin on 1-in. boards; the windows in the upper story have 13-in. × 34-in. lights, and those of the lower story 13-in. × 26-in. lights.

Signal-tower at Jersey City, N. J., Lehigh Valley Railroad.—The signal-tower of the Lehigh Valley Railroad at Jersey City, N. J., also designed by Mr. C. Rosenberg, Master Carpenter, L. V. R. R., shown in Figs. 123 and 124, is a two-story frame tower structure, 12 ft. × 29 ft. outside dimensions and 21 ft. high from ground to eaves.

This tower is located at the centre of a large terminal yard, and the upper story serves for signaling purposes and as an office for the yardmaster and his clerks. The elevation admits of an unobstructed view over the entire yard system, thus assisting materially in keeping track of the general movement of the cars and the trains in the yard. The ground-floor is divided into two rooms, one for trainmen and yardmen to occupy when not engaged in actual work around the yard, and the other for use as a lamp, oil, and waste room, and for storage of sundry small supplies connected with the train operations.

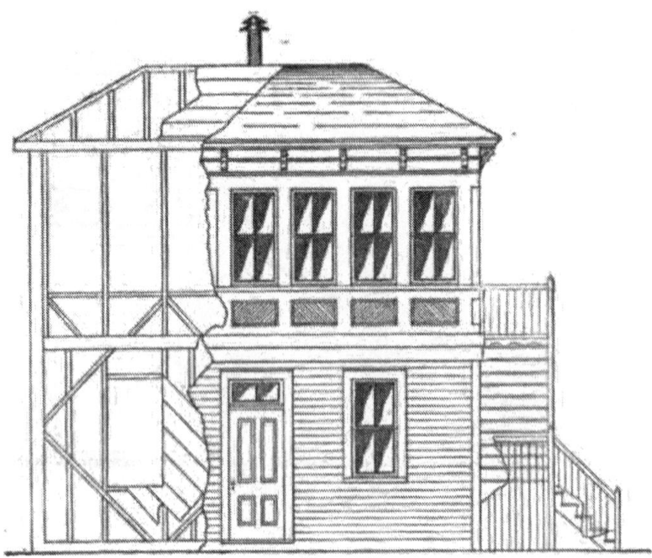

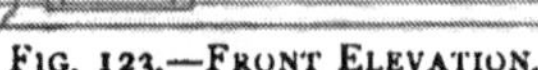
FIG. 123.—FRONT ELEVATION.

FIG. 124.—SIDE ELEVATION.

The principal timbers used are as follows: sills, 6 in. × 8 in.; floor-joists, 3 in. × 8 in.; ceiling-joists, 2 in. × 8 in.; interties, 4 in. × 6 in.; plates, 4 in. × 6 in.; corner-posts, 6 in. × 8 in.; studs, 3 in. × 4 in.; angle-braces, 3 in. × 4 in.; rafters, 3 in. × 6 in. The outside is sheathed with 1-in. rough hemlock boards, covered with white pine weather-boards; the roof is covered with tin on 1-in. hemlock boards. The lights of the windows in the upper story are 13 in. × 18 in., four lights per window; and those of the lower story 13 in. × 28 in., four lights per window. Stairs on the outside of the building lead to the upper story. The interior is finished in wood.

Two-legged Signal-tower at Newark, N. J., Pennsylvania Railroad.—The signal-tower shown in Fig. 125 represents a form of tower or elevated watchman's house in use on the Pennsylvania Railroad at Newark, N. J., and other places along their line where the ground space available for a tower is limited. The illustration shows the general style of the construction, the two posts or legs being 12-in. × 12-in. sticks. The door on the side toward the track is to enable the watchman to give the proper hand or flag signals to trains.

FIG. 125.—PERSPECTIVE.

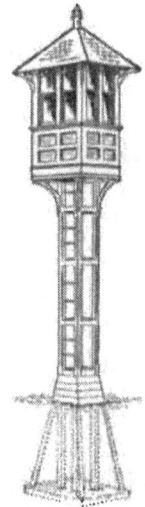

One-legged Signal-tower at Chicago, Ill., Atchison, Topeka & Santa Fe Railroad.—In Fig. 126 a perspective view is shown of a signal-tower in the terminal yard of the Atchison, Topeka & Santa Fe Railroad at Chicago, Ill. This building is about 6 ft. square and rests on four posts, each 6 in. × 6 in., which are fastened to a framework bedded in the ground. The four posts mentioned form a square, that only takes up 24 in. of ground space. Iron rungs fastened to the posts on one side of the square form a ladder leading up to the house, the entrance being through a trap-door in the floor. A number of switch and signal levers are located in the house, the connecting-rods down to the ground being placed inside the square formed by the posts.

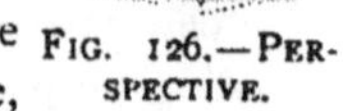
FIG. 126.—PERSPECTIVE.

Signal-tower at Jersey City, N. J., Central Railroad of New Jersey.—In Fig. 127 is shown a perspective of the large signal-tower of the Central Railroad of New Jersey, connected with the extensive interlocking switch and signal system in their terminal yard at Jersey City, N. J.

FIG. 127.—PERSPECTIVE.

Signal-tower and Bridge, New York Central & Hudson River Railroad.—The standard signal-tower and signal-bridge adopted by the New York Central & Hudson River Railroad for block-signal stations on its four-track roadbed are described and illustrated in detail in the issue of the *Railroad Gazette* of May 13, 1892. There is a tower on the ground and also one on the bridge. The bridge, which has a span of 56 ft., and 20 ft. clearance over the rails, is of iron on iron columns, and is equipped with the necessary semaphore and lamp signals.

CHAPTER VIII.

CAR-SHEDS AND CAR-CLEANING YARDS.

CAR-SHEDS are provided on railroads to protect expensive passenger or private cars, when not running, from the weather, and also, as a rule, to allow the cars to be cleaned under cover. In southern sections of the country car-sheds are frequently used as a protection against the injurious effects of the sun on the varnish and paint of the exterior of the cars. Car-sheds are usually located at terminal or junction points, where passenger cars are side-tracked, when not in use, or the cleaning has to be done prior to starting the cars on a new trip.

Car-sheds are not in universal use in this country, so that there is no general standard or system recognized as the best for the purpose. Local circumstances and individual requirements determine the leading features and the choice of the style of the structure. Where new buildings are erected for the storage of surplus cars during slack seasons, or for the cleaning of cars between runs, brick and frame buildings will be found in use. Frequently an abandoned shop, engine house, freight-house, or train-shed is pressed into service as a car-shed after its usefulness for other purposes has ceased. Thus, the Pennsylvania Railroad has utilized its former terminal train-shed at West Philadelphia for a car-shed, since the opening of the new Broad Street station in Philadelphia and the practical abandonment of the West Philadelphia terminus. A great many roads make no provision whatever for the storage of passenger cars under cover, and allow expensive cars to stand on side tracks for long periods exposed to the weather and the heat of the sun. More attention should be paid to the comparative cheapness of temporary car-sheds, as described more fully below, and to the advantage of using them, where funds are not on hand at the time for a more elaborate structure, or the final location of a car-shed in connection with a terminal or shop lay-out cannot be definitely determined.

The essential requirements for a car-shed, in which car cleaning is to be done, are good light, a convenient water-supply, and ample space between the tracks, and between the side of the building and the nearest track, to allow the exterior of the cars to be properly cleaned. It is customary to keep minor car supplies and fixtures in the same building, and to provide space for cleaning carpets, car-seats, etc., outside of the cars. In northern climates it is desirable to heat the house slightly in very severe weather.

The illustrations presented below show car-sheds with only one or two tracks. Where the length of a building is limited by local circumstances, or the number of cars to be stored is very large, a building with more than two tracks is employed, usually with a light frame roof set on posts between the tracks. For cleaning cars between runs, they are, as a rule, not placed under cover, but switched to so-called car-cleaning tracks or yards, where the car-cleaners are stationed and platforms, racks, wire nets for cleaning carpets, water-supply, etc., are provided. In connection with car-sheds or cleaning tracks the palace- and sleeping-car companies have frequently at the terminals of their routes special buildings for the storage of the sundry supplies connected with the service, including facilities for mending and repairing the interior fixtures, furniture, bedding, etc.

The following detail descriptions of car-sheds refer to structures actually in use in this country.

Brick Car-shed at Mauch Chunk, Pa., Lehigh Valley Railroad.—The brick car-shed of the Lehigh Valley Railroad at Mauch Chunk, Pa., shown in Figs. 128 to 131, was built to accommodate the

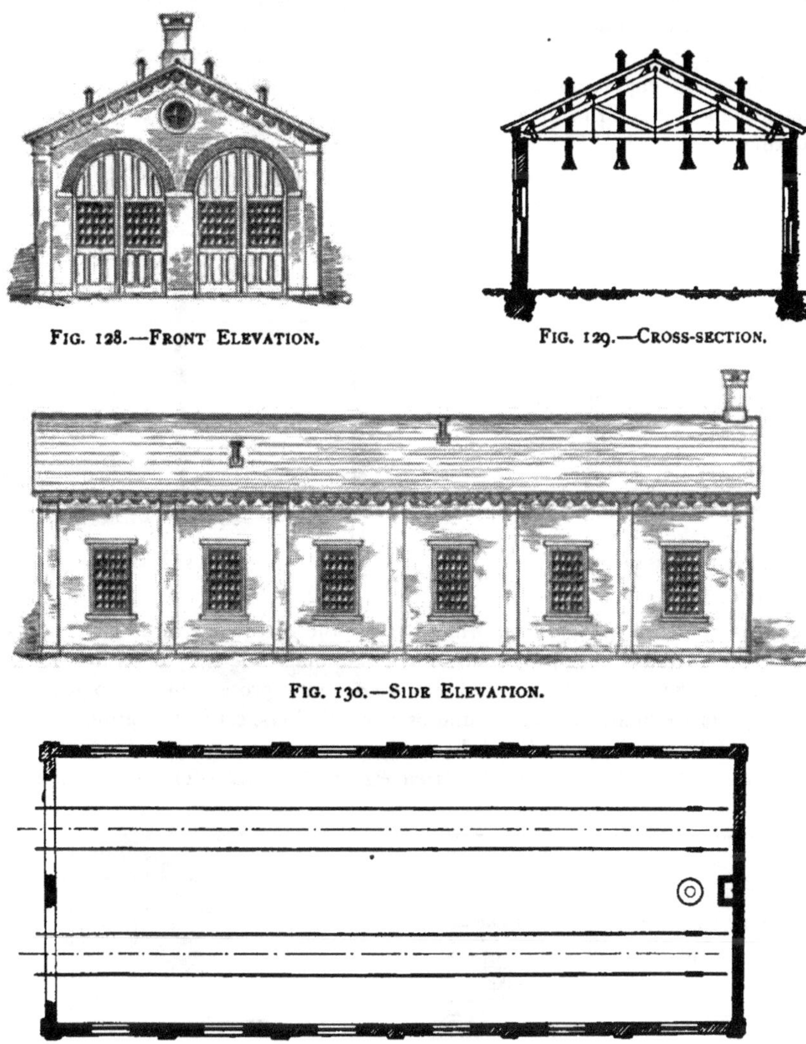

FIG. 128.—FRONT ELEVATION.

FIG. 129.—CROSS-SECTION.

FIG. 130.—SIDE ELEVATION.

FIG. 131.—GROUND-PLAN.

president's car and the pay car of that road, the former being one of the finest private cars in the country, and hence desirable to house it when not in use. The building is 34 ft. 2 in. wide, 85 ft.

long, and 17 ft. 8 in. high from the floor to the bottom of the tie-beams. The walls are brick, 13 in. thick in the panels and 17 in. thick at the pilasters, base and frieze courses. Two tracks, spaced 14 ft. 10 in. centres, enter the house, the clear width of the house being 31 ft. There are two pair of large, circle-top engine-doors at one gable end of the house, the width of the door opening being 11 ft. 1 in. in the clear, and 17 ft. 4 in. high in the clear above the top of the rails over the centre of the track. One of the engine-doors has a small wicket-door inserted in it. The roof-trusses are spaced 14 ft. centres, the dimensions of the principal roof members being as follows: tie-beams, 6 in. × 10 in.; principal rafters, 6 in. × 8 in.; truss-braces, 6 in. × 6 in.; tie-rod at centre, 1⅛ in. diam.; tie-rods on sides, ⅞ in. diam.; purlins, 4 in. × 8 in., spaced 3 ft. 10 in.; rafters, 2 in. × 4 in., spaced 18 in.; roof-boards, 1¼ in., covered with slate.

There are small funnels over each track, as shown on plans, suspended from the roof so as to correspond to the position of the stove-pipes on the cars mentioned, and thus avoid smoke in the house from the car-stoves. A stove connecting with the brick flue at the end of the house serves to heat the house in winter. The tracks have patented iron stop-blocks on each rail at the rear of the house. The rails are laid on ordinary ties bedded in the cinder forming the floor.

This design can be recommended wherever it is desired to have a substantial brick house to be used for a car-shed or an engine-house. It could be used to good advantage also as a small paint-shop for cars, or small repair-shop, if made a little wider, so as to give more space between cars and side walls for working.

Temporary Car-sheds, Richmond & Alleghany Railroad.—The designs for car-sheds, shown in Figs. 132 and 133, illustrate a type of temporary sheds used on the Richmond & Alleghany Railroad

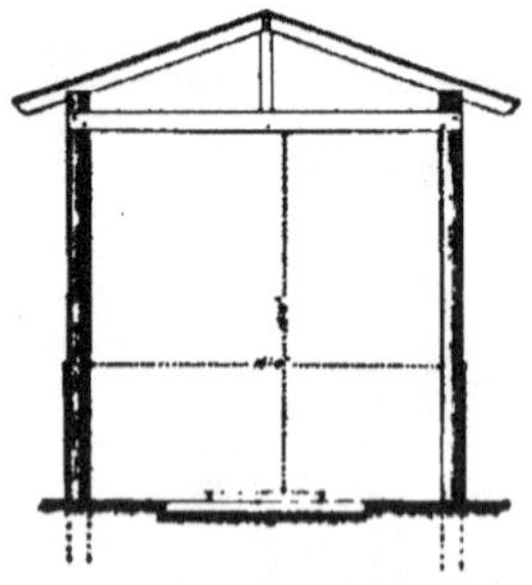

FIG. 132.—CROSS SECTION.

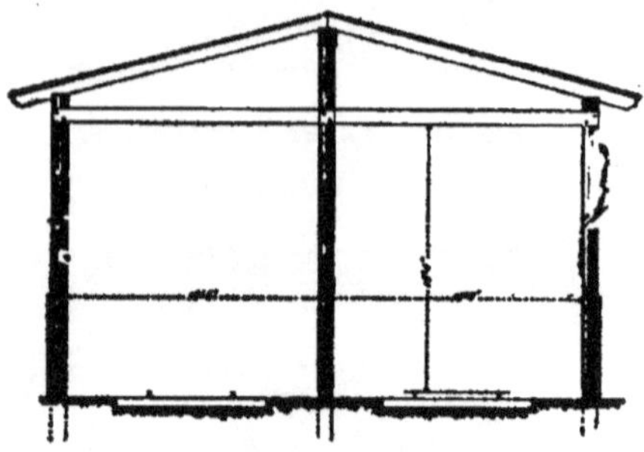

FIG. 133.—CROSS-SECTION.

for the protection of their passenger-cars, while part of the road was still under construction and the final lay-out of the yards and shop systems at the terminals not fully determined. The plans are self-explanatory, and show how cheaply and easily adequate protection for expensive cars can be provided. The posts are made of rough round or hewn timbers, set in the ground, and tied together and roofed with plank, scantlings, and boards, as shown.

Frame Car-shed at Wallula, Wash., Northern Pacific Railroad.—The car-shed of the Northern

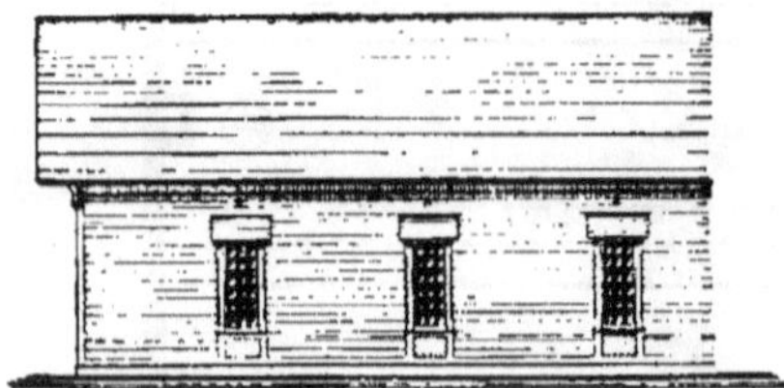

FIG. 134.—SIDE ELEVATION.

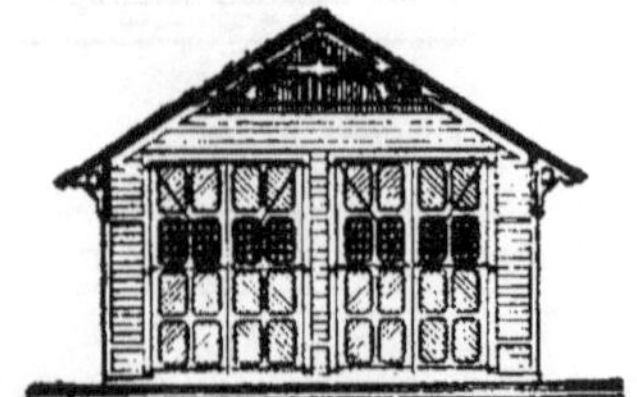

FIG. 135.—FRONT ELEVATION.

Pacific Railroad at Wallula, Wash., shown in Figs 134 to 136, is a frame structure 40 ft. × 200 ft. out to out, and about 20 ft. height of frame. There are two tracks, spaced 17 ft. centres, running through the house, which enter at each gable end through two pairs of large square engine-doors, the door openings being 14 ft. wide in the clear and 18 ft. high in the clear above the top of the rails. The roof-trusses are spaced 20 ft. centres. The windows have two sash, each 8 lights, 12 in. × 16 in.

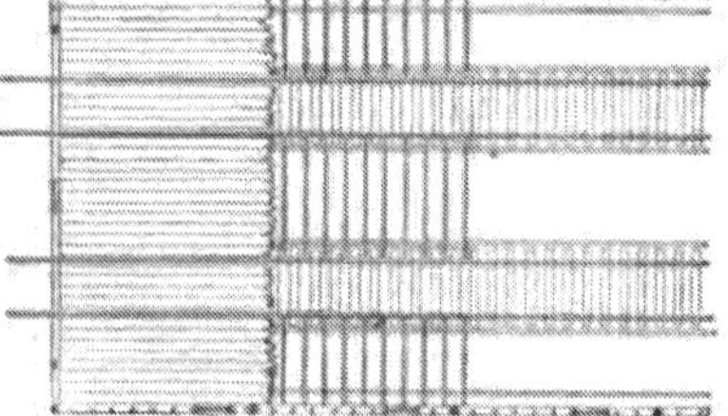

FIG. 136.—GROUND-PLAN.

The principal timbers used are as follows: sills, 10 in. × 10 in.; posts, 10 in. × 10 in.; studs, 2 in. × 4 in., spaced 24 in.; plates, 6 in. × 10 in.; rafters, 4 in. × 10 in., spaced 24 in.; tie-beams, 6 in. × 10 in.; ridge-purlins, two pieces, each 4 in. × 6 in.; purlin-braces and purlin-posts, 4 in. × 8 in.; roof-boards, 1 in., covered with shingles; floor, 2 in. plank; floor-joists, 2 in. × 12 in., spaced 24 in., and bedded on 6 in. × 6 in. mud-sills; outside of frame sheathed with weather-boarding; doors, 1¼ in. × 10 in frames, covered with ⅞ in. tongued and grooved boards.

Car-cleaning Platform at Jersey City, N. J., Central Railroad of New Jersey.—The car-cleaning platform of the Central Railroad of New Jersey, at Jersey City, N. J., shown in Fig. 137, is built between the tracks of the car-cleaning yard and consists of an open platform, 11 ft. 6 in. wide and 8 in. above the top of the rails, with a raised rack at the centre for piling and cleaning the car furniture and fixtures. The rack is 42 in. wide and 21 in. above the platform. It is slatted on top, so as to allow dust and dirt to drop to the ground. The tracks at this point are spaced 20 ft. centres. The dimensions of the lumber are as follows: blocking, 6 in. × 6 in.; floor-joists, 3 in. × 6 in.; flooring, 2 in.; posts, 3 in. × 3 in.; plates, 3 in. × 3 in.; slats, 1 in. × 3 in.; X-braces, 1 in. × 3 in.

FIG. 137.—CROSS-SECTION.

Car-cleaning Platform Shed at Jersey City, N. J., Pennsylvania Railroad.—The car-cleaning platform shed of the Pennsylvania Railroad, shown in Figs. 138 to 140, was built in the latter part of the year 1890 for the use of the Pullman Car Company at the special cleaning and storage yard for that branch of the service at Jersey City, N. J. There are several lines of these platform sheds, located between tracks spaced 24 ft. centres. The important feature of the design is the prominence given to the arrangements for allowing the linen and bedding to be properly aired under cover alongside the cars. The illustrations show racks provided for this purpose in every other opening of the shed, and there is a longitudinal hanger-beam under the louvred ventilator on which blankets, rugs, carpets, etc., can be hung.

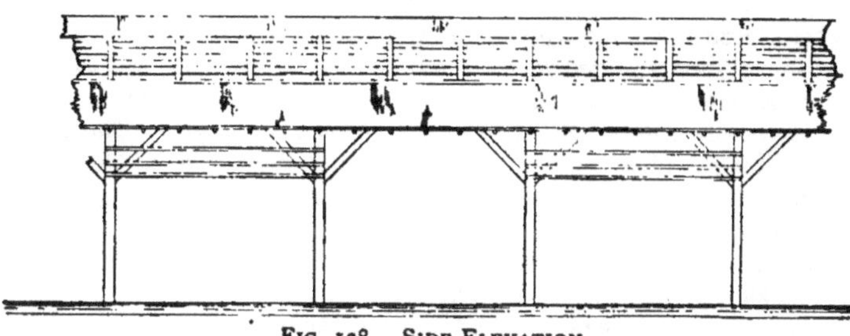

FIG. 138.—SIDE ELEVATION.

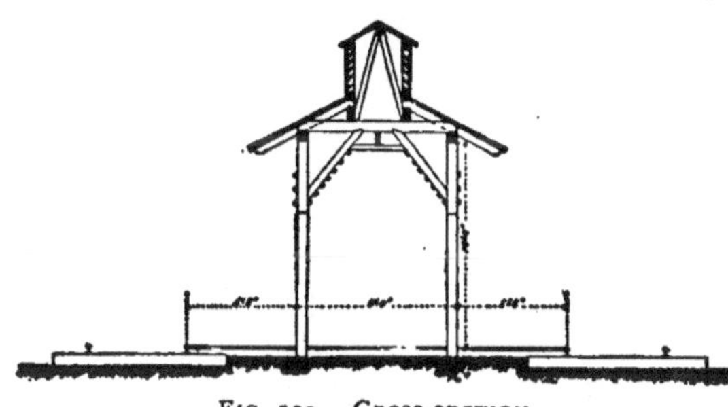

FIG. 139.—CROSS-SECTION.

The principal sizes of lumber used are as follows: posts, 6 in. × 6 in.; plates, 4 in. × 6 in.; ties, 4 in. × 6 in.; knee-braces, 4 in. × 6 in.; jack-rafters, 2 in. × 4 in.; roof, 1-in. boards covered with galvanized corrugated iron; longitudinal hanger, 2 in. × 8 in.; brace under same, 2 in. × 3 in.; slats of rack, 2 in. × 3 in. The louvre is built of posts, 3 in. × 3 in.; braces, 2 in. × 3 in.; ridge-plate, 3 in. × 4 in.; plates, 3 in. × 4 in.; louvre slats, ½ in.; and frame, 1 in.

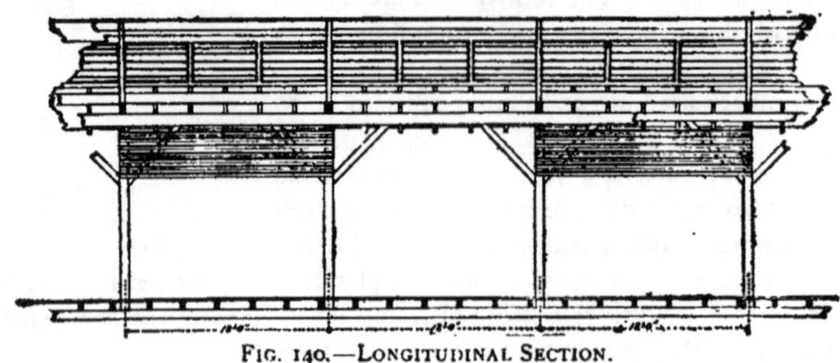

FIG. 140.—LONGITUDINAL SECTION.

Passenger-car Yard at Chicago, Ill., Pennsylvania Railroad.—The following description of the passenger-car yard of the Pennsylvania Railroad, at Chicago, Ill., copied from the issue of the *Railroad Gazette* of September 12, 1890, will prove interesting in connection with the subject of car-sheds, as showing to what extent on large railroad systems the equipment and facilities for cleaning passenger-cars are carried:

A neat brick building has been erected at one end of the yard, in the lower story of which storage-batteries are cleaned and repaired, and various stores are kept. Above these rooms are offices; the tracks are spaced an unusual distance apart. The tracks are all laid with very heavy rails, and the whole yard is floored with wood, even between the rails of each track. Just outside of each rail the flooring is composed of two heavy planks 1 foot wide. Beyond these and in between the rails the flooring is composed of narrow strips about 4 in. wide, spaced about ¼ or ⅜ in. apart. This floor is not laid in contact with the earth or ballast, but is a few inches above it. The planks are all laid parallel with the track. The whole yard is lighted by arc-lights placed upon high poles. It is piped with water, steam, and compressed air; the steam and compressed-air pipes are placed in the same boxing, which is located but a short distance below the floor. The water-pipes are located at a depth of about 3 ft. 6 in. Connections to the cars can be made between each pair of tracks, and at intervals equal to the average car length. The steam pipe has a branch which connects with the upright pipe from the water-main, and by regulating the water- and steam-valves any required temperature of water may be obtained for washing the cars. The lavatory tanks can be filled from the same water-pipe, the steam being shut off.

The water used is obtained from the city mains. The steam is taken from a plant which has been erected for that purpose, and for running the electric lights and furnishing compressed air. The building in which this apparatus is located is a new one, and has been erected near the roundhouse. In one end of this building there is a large stationary boiler of the locomotive type, with a Belpaire firebox, and in the same room there is an air-compressor, which maintains the required pressure of air on the pipes throughout the yard. The steam used in the yards is taken directly from the dome of this boiler. In an adjoining room there is an 80-H.P. Ball engine, and this is at present connected to a 30-light dynamo. At present 28 arc-lights are run.

CHAPTER IX.

ASHPITS.

Ashpits or clinker-pits are required along the main line of a railroad and at terminal and division yards, shop and roundhouse systems, to allow ashes and clinkers collecting in the fireboxes of engines to be dumped, and also, although to a more limited extent, to facilitate the examination and oiling of the engine machinery from below at points where stops are made. It is customary to prohibit the dumping of ashes on the track along the line of the road, and the cleaning of the fireboxes at special ashpits is made compulsory. The general design of ashpits is very similar to that of an engine-house pit, excepting that the paving and side walls must be protected in some manner from the deteriorating influence of hot ashes, and proper provision should be made for the economical and quick disposal of the ashes as they accumulate.

The location of ashpits varies according to whether they are in the main track, or on principal sidings along the line, or at division yards, shop or roundhouse systems. When placed in a main track the pits are usually short and located near stations, water tanks, or coaling platforms, in such a manner that the ashes can be quickly dumped while the engine stops for other purposes, and thus avoid extra delays. At large coaling systems for coaling engines preparatory to starting out on the road, at water stations, or at yard or shop systems, ashpits are placed so as to be readily accessible at all times from some open track. These pits are made much longer than those placed in main tracks, in order to enable a number of engines to use the pit at the same time. Where an ashpit is located in a main track it is absolutely essential to have a siding alongside for use as an ash-car track, to allow ashes to be loaded on cars without causing detentions to main-line trains.

The length of an ashpit varies according to its location, as outlined above, and according to the relative objections that may exist to requiring engines to wait their turn to use the ash-pit. The quality of coal has also an important bearing on the question, as inferior grades of coal produce a much larger percentage of ash and clinkers, and hence larger pits are required. Where a large number of engines are liable to require the use of an ashpit at the same time, as, for instance, at the close of a day's business, or preparatory to starting out a number of trains in close succession, due provision should be made to give quick dispatch to the engines.

The width of the pit is governed by the gauge of the track, the style of the coping on the side walls, and the method of fastening the rails to the coping. As a rule, however, the width of the pit is from 4 ft. to 4 ft. 3 in. in the clear, being narrower on main tracks than on side tracks, so as to give more stability to the side walls where there is fast running. The extra width of the pit is valuable, not only to gain storage room, but also to facilitate working under the engine in oiling and making light repairs.

The depths of pits vary considerably, but we can distinguish between two systems in use, namely, shallow pits and deep pits. Shallow pits are made from 14 to 16 in. deep below the top of rail, while deep pits are from 3 ft. to 4 ft. deep below the top of rail. Shallow pits should only be used where sufficient help is always on hand to remove the ashes promptly. If this is not the case, the length must be increased. Shallow pits are preferable in main tracks. Deep pits afford better storage and facilitate working under the engine. There are other questions dependent on local circumstances that may influence the depth of an ashpit.

It is desirable to have a water connection near the ashpit to allow the ashes to be cooled with water, so as to reduce their deteriorating effect on the pit and to allow the pit to be cleaned out sooner. While in one sense it is detrimental to play large streams of water on the masonry and paving in the pit, it is probably better to kill the fire promptly than to allow the heat to thoroughly penetrate the masonry.

The ends of the pits are generally built square. Steps or inclines can be introduced, where pits are deep, to facilitate getting into them or wheeling material out endways. This feature has, however, never been considered of sufficient importance in this country to warrant its adoption.

An ashpit located on a special track should be connected at both ends with open tracks, so that engines can leave the pit without interfering with other engines back of them. Where feasible, there should be a special depressed ash-car track alongside of an ashpit, so as to bring the car floor nearly on a level with the ashpit track. This siding should be close enough to the pit to allow ashes to be cast from the pit onto the car; but, on the other hand, there should be as much of a berm as possible left between the ash-car siding and the pit to serve for depositing ashes in case ash-cars are temporarily not available.

Further general distinguishing features of ashpits can be found in the construction of the side walls, which are either closed or open. Ashpits with closed sides have the disadvantage that they can be cleaned only when the track is clear, while pits with open sides can obviously be cleaned at all times, the ashes being either cast or drawn out between the iron rail-chairs, which is quite an essential feature where an ashpit is located on a much-travelled track.

In designing an ashpit the distinctive features to be considered are foundations, side walls, coping of side walls, rail-fastenings, paving, drainage, and the protection of the side walls and paving from the heat.

In building the foundations the usual rules for that class of work are followed, especial care being paid to give good foundations, particularly where rail-chairs are used, as the heavy concentrated loads on the chairs and the vibratory effects of rapidly passing trains, in addition to the deteriorating action of the heat and water, will soon destroy inferior work. The materials in general use for foundations are concrete, stone rubble work, or stone paving grouted with cement.

The side walls are usually built of stone or hard brick, from 18 in. to 24 in. thick, laid in cement mortar. It is desirable not to have too thin a wall, and all the materials should be of the best make possible, for similar reasons to those just recited for foundation work.

The coping of the side walls is made of large stones, timber stringers, or iron plates. Where coping-stones extend over the full width of the wall, it is not necessary to anchor them to the side walls below them; but where the stones are small they should be anchored to the wall and tied together with iron clamps. Timber coping should be fastened to the wall under it about every 5 or 6 ft. with iron anchor-bolts. Where wrought- or cast-iron coping-plates are used, special coping-stones are not required. The coping should always be properly secured in place, so as to prevent the rails spreading. In some designs transverse walls are provided at intervals to tie the side walls together, or iron tie-rods and braces are used in place of transverse walls.

The rail-fastenings vary according to the kind of coping used on the side walls. On timber coping the rails are either fastened in the usual manner with track-spikes with reversed heads (bridge-spikes), or with screw-spikes, or the rail is riveted to a wrought-iron plate, which plate is fastened to the timber coping about every 5 ft. with bolts or dowels, as shown in Figs. 144 and 145. Where a cast- or wrought-iron plate is used as coping, covering the top wall entirely, the rail is fastened to it by means of screw-bolts and small clips. Where stone coping is used the rails can be fastened by ordinary track-spikes driven into wooden dowels, about 2 in. in diameter, bedded in holes drilled in the stone. Another form of connection to stone coping is by rag-bolts or split-bolts with keys, set with cement, lead, or sulphur in holes drilled in the coping, the rail flange being caught by an appropriate clip, as shown in Fig. 141. Another method, shown in Fig. 142, is to use regular bed-plates or clip-plates under the rail, spaced at intervals of 3 to 4 ft., and properly fastened to the stone coping with rag-bolts or split-bolts, as above described. Where iron rail-chairs are used as rail supports and fasteners, they are either small cast-iron chairs, about 8 in. high, bedded in the side walls and spaced about 4 ft. apart, as shown in Figs. 153 and 154, or large cast-iron chairs spaced about 3 to 4 ft. apart, the side walls being either walled up between the chairs, as shown in Figs. 148 and 149, or left open, as shown in Figs. 150 to 152.

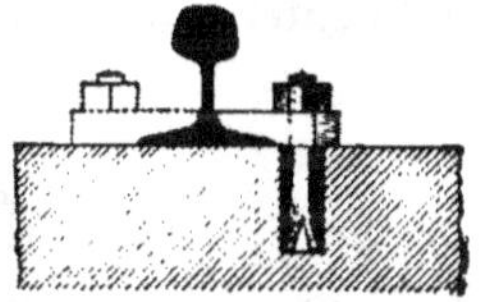

FIG. 141.—CROSS-SECTION OF RAIL-FASTENING.

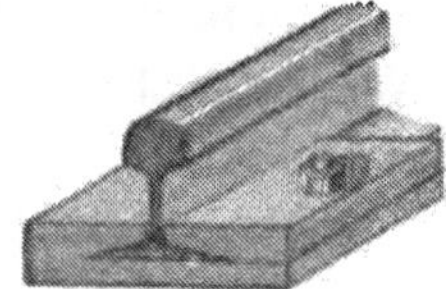

FIG. 142.—PERSPECTIVE OF RAIL-FASTENING.

The paving usually consists of brick or stone, although concrete is sometimes employed. The material under the paving should be carefully tamped and consolidated, and a sublayer of concrete under the brick or stone paving is to be recommended. Firebrick pavement resists the heat better than common hard brick, but it is soon worn out by the shovelling and from men working on it. Some roads, therefore, prefer to use common hard brick, which is easily and cheaply replaced when necessary. Stone flagging, unless well bedded, is easily broken, and, therefore, not desirable. Ordinary rough stone paving, such as is generally used under box culverts on railroads, is too rough for shovelling, if the bottom of pit is to be kept clean. City paving-blocks are generally too expensive, and do not present a much better surface to shovel on than ordinary paving-stones. A concrete bottom will soon disintegrate on the surface, and, once started, will grow rapidly worse. A pavement of common hard brick, set on edge, and laid on a good foundation or in a bed of concrete, will prove most desirable in the long-run.

To secure proper drainage of the pit, the paving is dished transversely and pitched longitudinally, the grade being arranged, according to the length of the pit, so as to drain toward one end of the pit, or from each end toward the centre, or from the centre toward the ends, or toward several points. The transverse dishing of the paving is usually in the form of a general depression, about 2 in. deep, from the sides toward the centre of the pit. Another method is to make the bottom straight transversely with a pitch toward one of the side walls, forming a gutter along the side wall; or the paving is built highest at the centre of the pit and pitches down toward each side wall, forming a gutter along each side wall. The dishing of the paving toward the side walls has the advantage of keeping the centre of the pit dry, but it has the objectionable feature of throwing the water against the side walls. The system of making the gutter at the centre of the pit is to be recommended, provided the dishing and curvature are not made so heavy as to impede shovelling. The longitudinal gradient of the paving must be sufficient to secure proper drainage lengthwise of the pit, and should be not less than 1 ft. in 100 ft. for brick pavement and more for rough stone paving. Large and well-designed sink-holes or catch-basins should be built either inside or outside of the pit, preferably the latter, as they can then be larger, and covered up in such a way as to be readily opened and cleaned out. Iron gratings at all drain-holes are essential so as to prevent, so far as possible, dirt and ashes carried along by the water from clogging up the drains. The drain leading from the catch-basin away from the pit should be large, especially where a good fall is not obtainable. It can either be an open ditch, a box culvert, a brick sewer, or a pipe drain. The cost of an iron pipe, 6 to 10 in. diameter, is from 75 cents to $1.25 per foot run; vitrified pipe will only cost about one half as much as iron pipe; and a stone box-drain, large enough to allow a man to enter it for cleaning it out, will cost from $2 to $2.50 per foot run. Where the length of the drain is short and the fall limited, a box-drain will prove the most advantageous.

The protection of the side walls from the deteriorating action of the heat is usually obtained by a facing of firebrick, or of cast-iron or wrought-iron plates. Where an iron facing is employed, an air-space is left between the iron and the face of the side wall, which is a very important element of the design. A cast-iron facing of the proper thickness will outlast any other material, but it is liable to crack under the sudden changes of temperature, in addition to the shock from the jarring of passing engines. Wrought-iron wears or rusts more quickly than cast-iron, especially when exposed to the combined attacks of heat and water. A firebrick facing, if well laid in fire-clay and built so as not to receive the weight and jars of the moving load to an appreciable degree, will give good service. Firebricks are easily damaged, however, by contact with shovels and other tools, and frequent repairs and the subsequent renewal of the facing would be eventually necessary. Where firebrick are not available or too costly, a facing of common hard brick will prove a cheap and efficient substitute for the firebrick, if built so as to allow renewals without tearing down the entire side wall. Ordinary stone or brick walls are doomed to destruction in a comparatively short time. If built, however, of first-class masonry, composed of large through stones, well jointed and bedded, and of a good heat-resisting quality, excellent results can be expected.

Thus far reference has only been made to stone or brick ashpits, or pits with large cast-iron chairs supporting the rails. All iron pits do not seem to have found favor in this country, although, under certain conditions, they have advantages over others that should not be disregarded. This is particularly the case with the general style of a proposed wrought-iron pit, shown in Fig. 143, which is practically a shallow wrought-iron pan or trough hung between timber track-stringers and resting at the centre on ordinary cross-ties under the stringers. If provided with iron guard-rails and safety points, or some rerailing device at each end of the pit, this arrangement can be considered as the very best for use in a main track at stations, water tanks, or coaling platforms, where trains stop a few minutes and it is desirable to dump a limited amount of ashes. Owing to the small weight of such a pit and the practicability of dividing it into short sections which are easily handled, it is especially adapted for use on temporary work in the construction of a road, or until the permanent location of the ashpit in connection with the development of a yard or shop system is determined. Such pits are also advantageous where the foundation is very soft or very deep, requiring expensive piling or other methods for supporting a heavy brick or stone wall. The iron trough rests on the usual cross-ties placed under a special set of track-stringers, requiring, therefore, no extra foundation work. In case of a settlement in the track, the pit can follow without serious damage.

FIG. 143.—CROSS-SECTION.

A step in the direction toward iron ashpits has been made in the cinder-loading plant of the Cincinnati, Washington & Baltimore Railroad, where the ashes and cinders are caught in iron drop-bottom buckets set into an ordinary stone or brick ashpit. When the track is clear, the buckets are hoisted out of the pit by means of a derrick, swung sideways, and emptied on ash-cars.

As a final method of comparing the different styles of ashpits, an effort has been made toward estimating the comparative cost of the different designs per foot run of pit, assuming the foundation depth to be about 5 ft. below the top of rail, with the following results: Ordinary brick or stone wall, with stone coping and rails fastened with spikes in wooden dowels, \$5; same, with rails fastened with rag-bolts, \$5.25; same, with rails fastened with iron bearing plates, \$5.50; ordinary brick or stone wall, with small cast-iron chairs built into the walls or set on top of wall, \$6; ordinary brick or stone wall with timber coping and rail fastened to wrought-iron plate over the timber, \$6.25; ordinary brick or stone wall with cast-iron or wrought-iron covering over top of wall, \$6.75; ordinary brick or stone wall with large cast-iron rail-chairs, filled in between the chairs with stone or brick work, \$9.25; ordinary brick or stone wall with large cast-iron rail chairs and cast-iron ties across the bottom of pit connecting the rail-chairs, the side walls being left open between the rail-chairs, \$10.75; a shallow, all wrought-iron pit, \$6 to \$8; a deep, all wrought-iron pit, \$9 to \$11. For a fireproof protection of the side walls, add about \$1 to the above prices. If the bottom of the pit is made of firebrick, in place of ordinary paving, add \$1 to the above prices.

As a rule, the cost of ashpits with unprotected sides and bottoms can be placed at about \$5 to \$9 per lineal foot run of pit. If the sides or bottom are properly protected by firebrick or iron in some shape or other, the total cost can be estimated at from \$7 to \$11 per lineal foot run of pit. If the foundations are not unusually expensive, the cost of ashpits, as actually used on American railroads, can be placed at from \$5 to \$12 per lineal foot run of pit.

Below will be found descriptions and illustrations of a number of ashpits and details of same actually in use.

Standard Ashpit, Atchison, Topeka & Santa Fe Railroad.—The standard design for ashpits of the Atchison, Topeka & Santa Fe Railroad, illustrated in Figs. 144 and 145, prepared from data furnished by Mr. J. M. Meade, Assistant Engineer, A., T. & S. F. R. R., shows a deep ashpit with side walls of common brick, protected on the face with firebrick, and coped with stone faced with firebrick. The rails are riveted to a wrought-iron plate resting in part on the stone coping and projecting over the firebrick into the pit 1 in. The standard size of the pit is 30 ft. long in the clear under ordinary circumstances, 4 ft. 2½ in. wide in the clear between side walls, 4 ft. ½ in. wide in the clear at the top between the projecting edges of the wrought-iron plates under the rails, and about 3 ft. 9 in. deep below the top of rail. The foundation of the side walls and the larger portion of the bottom of the pit consist of ordinary stone paving grouted with cement. The side walls are 18 in. thick, built of common brick, coped with stone, and faced all the way up with firebrick. In the bottom of the pit there are three rows of firebrick set on edge along each side wall and end wall. The iron foot-plate riveted to the rail is ½ in. × 12 in., and is anchored to the stone coping with 1-in. anchor-bolts every 5 ft. The rivets are spaced 18 in. centres. The firebrick facing is held to the stone coping by $\frac{3}{16}$-in. iron bolts set in the joints. The floor of the pit is straight transversely, pitching towards one side wall, thus forming a gutter along the latter. The drainage longitudinally is carried from the centre of the pit towards the ends, where drain-holes connecting with proper drains are provided.

FIG. 144.—CROSS-SECTION.

FIG. 145.—CROSS-SECTION OF RAIL-FASTENING.

The approximate cost of this style of pit will range, exclusive of difficult foundations, from about $7 to $8.50 per lineal foot. The protection of the side walls with firebrick is commendable, but the wrought-iron plate under the rail is not stiff enough to prevent the transmission of a considerable part of the weight of the moving load to the firebrick facing. The straight bottom and the drain along one side wall is advantageous for shovelling and keeping the pit dry, but will let considerable moisture into the side wall.

Ashpit at Heron, Mont., Northern Pacific Railroad.—The ashpit at Heron, Mont., on the Northern Pacific Railroad, shown in Figs. 146 and 147, is a deep pit, 84 ft. long in the clear. The width between the side walls is 4 ft. in the clear, the depth about 3 ft. 6 in. from top of rail. The side-wall foundations are of concrete, 2 ft. wide and about 1 ft. thick. The side walls are built of common brick, 17 in. thick. The coping timbers or stringers under the rails are 8-in. × 12-in. white pine, anchored to the wall every 6 ft. with ¾-inch bolts, reaching about 3 ft. into the brickwork. The rails are fastened to the timber stringers in the usual manner with ordinary track-spikes having reversed heads. The sides of the pit are protected by cast-iron plates, ½ in. thick, 18 in. wide, and about 3 ft. 4 in. long, which are hung on the timber stringer by a 3-in. top flange and fastened to same with ½-in. spikes. The bottom of these plates is set into the paving of the pit in such a way as to leave a 1-in. air-space between the back of the casting and the face of the side wall. The bottom of the pit is paved with common hard brick, set on edge and bedded in an 8-in. layer of concrete. The paving is dished transversely so as to form a gutter, 2 in. deep, at the centre of the pit. The longitudinal drainage is accomplished by giving the bottom of the pit a gradient from each end towards the centre of the pit, where a drain-hole through one of the side walls empties into a catch-basin, which is covered and is readily accessible for cleaning.

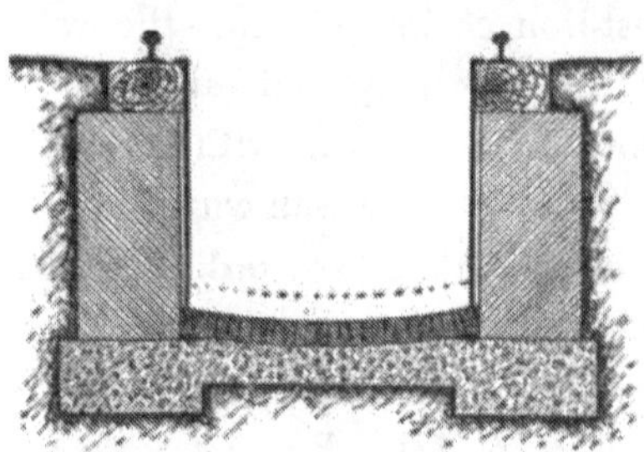

FIG. 146.—CROSS-SECTION.

FIG. 147.—PERSPECTIVE OF SIDE PLATES.

The cost of this style of ashpit will vary from $8.75 to $9.75 per lineal foot. The drainage of this pit and the cast-iron plate protection of the side walls are good features, but the unprotected timber stringers under the rails are liable to require frequent renewals. If a coping of large, well-jointed stones with a proper rail-fastening were substituted for the timber stringers, this design could be well recommended for deep pits. In sections of the country where stone is cheap, the brick side walls could be replaced by stone ones, built slightly wider, in which case this design, with the suggested modifications, would be worthy of consideration as a good deep pit standard for permanent work.

Ashpit at Packerton, Pa., Lehigh Valley Railroad.—The ashpit of the Lehigh Valley Railroad, built in connection with the yard and roundhouse system at Packerton, Pa., shown in Figs. 148 and 149,

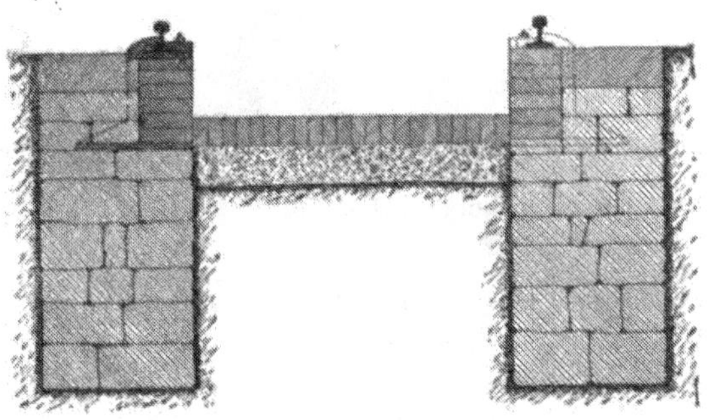

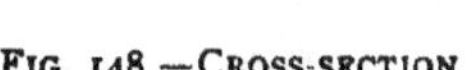

FIG. 148.—CROSS-SECTION.

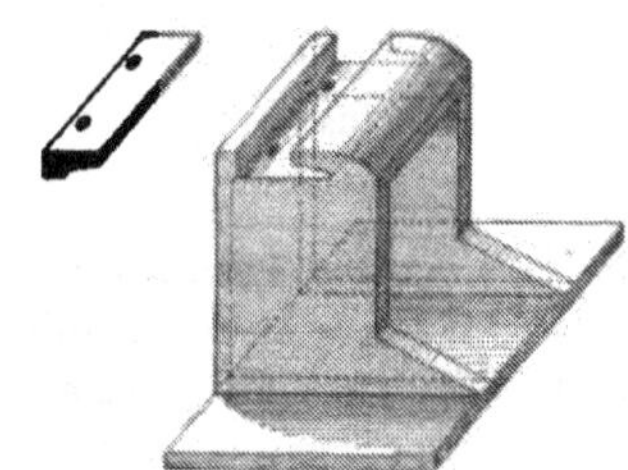

FIG. 149.—PERSPECTIVE OF RAIL-CHAIR.

designed by Mr. J. I. Kinsey, Master Mechanic, L. V. R. R., is a shallow pit with stone side walls, coped with large stone and protected along the inner face with firebrick. The rails are supported on large cast-iron rail-chairs, well bedded, and reaching down into the side walls below the bottom of the pit. The length of the pit is 240 ft., the width 4 ft. 1½ in. in the clear between the side walls, and the depth 1 ft. 2½ in. below top of rail. The side walls and their foundations are ordinary rubble masonry. The walls are 2 ft. thick; the coping-stones are 16 in. wide. The firebrick facing is 8 in. thick, and extends from the bottom of the pit to within 1 in. of the base of the rail. The rail-chairs are spaced 5 ft. centres along each rail. The base-plates of these chairs are 24 in. × 18 in., and are set 19 in. below the top of rail. The space between the two upright ribs of each rail-chair is filled with firebrick on the face and backed with ordinary rubble masonry, so that the only iron along the face of the pit directly exposed to heat is the outside edge of the ribs mentioned. The rail is held in the chair by a clip and screw-bolts, as shown. The paving consists of firebrick set on edge and bedded on a light layer of concrete. The bottom is concave transversely, the centre being about 2 in. lower than the sides. The ashpit track has a gradient of about 30 ft. to the mile, and the rail chairs had to be set accordingly. The drainage of the pit follows the down-grade of the track, but the fall is made slightly steeper. At the low end of the pit the water passes through a drain-hole in one of the side walls into a large, well-designed catch-basin, from which a stone box-drain leads to the low ground in the neighborhood.

The cost of this style of ashpit is from $9.75 to $11.25 per lineal foot. Though costly, this design possesses a number of good features for a shallow pit where permanency and a solid and lasting bedding for the rails is desired. Owing to the comparatively wide spacing of the chairs under each rail, it is essential that the masonry be well built under the chairs. Practical experience in this instance proves that the firebrick facing of the sides of the pit stands fairly well, probably owing to its thickness, and also to the fact that it carries none of the weight of the moving load. The firebrick paving was not a success, however, as it gave out very soon, owing to walking and working on top of it, so that it would be more economical to have used common hard brick. With certain modifications, therefore, this style of ashpit embodies the general features to be observed in a standard shallow ashpit.

Ashpit at Aurora, Ill., Chicago, Burlington & Quincy Railroad.—The style of ashpit in use at Aurora, Ill., and at other points on the Chicago, Burlington & Quincy Railroad, shown in Figs. 150 to 152, designed by Mr. William Forsyth, Mechanical Engineer, C., B. & Q. R. R., is a shallow pit without side walls above the bottom of the pit, the rails resting on large cast-iron rail-chairs, the space under the rails between the chairs being left open. At large roundhouse and shop systems the length of the pit is made 200 ft., and at some points on the line two or three pits of that length are required, where there are a large number of engines to be provided for, which burn a low grade of coal producing a large percentage of ash and clinkers. The pit is about 4 ft. 3 in. wide at the top of the rail-chair and about 3 ft. 6 in. wide at the bottom; the depth is 16½ in. below the top of rail. The foundations and side walls up to about 7 in. below the floor level of the pit are of ordinary stonework, over which there is concrete. Each side wall is coped with two longitudinal oak stringers, each 6 in. × 10 in. The iron rail-chairs are set on these timbers, the top of the bed-plate of the chairs being flush with the floor level of the pit. The chairs being spaced 3 ft. centres and the base being 2 ft. long, 1 ft. of the timber stringers between the chairs has to be protected by wrought-iron plates. The greatest peculiarity of this design is the use of the large cast-iron rail-chairs, set in pairs opposite each other, the bed-plates being connected by a channel-shaped tie across the floor of the pit, the whole being cast in one piece. The top of this tie is flush with the top of the bed-plates, and hence even with the floor level of the pit. The rails are held in the chairs by clips and screw-bolts, as shown. The pit being open on both sides and the floor level, the drainage takes place sideways, provided the ground slopes away from the pit, or proper ditches or drains are constructed outside of the pit.

FIG. 150.—CROSS-SECTION.

FIG. 151.—ELEVATION.

FIG. 152.—PERSPECTIVE OF RAIL-CHAIR.

The cost of this style of ashpit, or clinker-pit, as it is called on the C., B. & Q., is from $10 to $11 per lineal foot, exclusive of unusual foundations. Mr. Wm. Forsyth states that this style of pit is giving very good satisfaction on tracks where there are no fast trains run. Without a doubt this design offers great advantages in not having side walls exposed to the heat, in having all iron-work subjected to the action of the heat visible and open for inspection, and especially in being able to clean the pit from the sides even when engines are occupying the track.

Ashpit, Kansas City, St. Joseph & Council Bluffs Railroad.—From information kindly furnished by Mr. F. A. Chase, M. M., the Kansas City, St. Joseph & Council Bluffs Railroad uses a similar style of ashpit to that just described of the Chicago, Burlington & Quincy Railroad at Aurora, Ill. The principal difference consists in the side walls or foundations of the rail-chairs, which are built of brick throughout up to the level of the bottom of the pit, so that no timber stringers are required.

Rail-chair, Savannah, Florida & Western Railroad.—Figs. 153 and 154 show a form of rail-chair used in engine-house pits and ashpits on the Savannah, Florida & Western Railroad, prepared from data kindly furnished by Mr. W. B. W. Howe, Jr., Chief Engineer. This chair is about 8 in. high, and is built into the brick or stone side walls at intervals of about 4 ft. The base is about 8 in. × 12 in., and the thickness of the ribs about ¾ in. The rail is fastened to the chairs with screw-bolts. The weight of one chair is about 40 lbs. This design is presented as illustrating a method in actual use for bedding rails on top of side walls of pits, but it does not offer any distinctively commendable features.

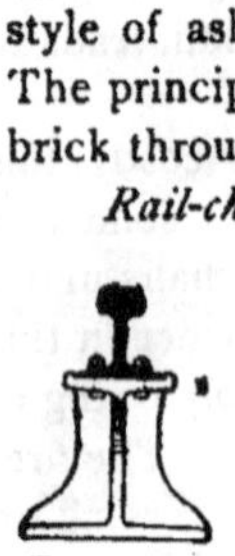

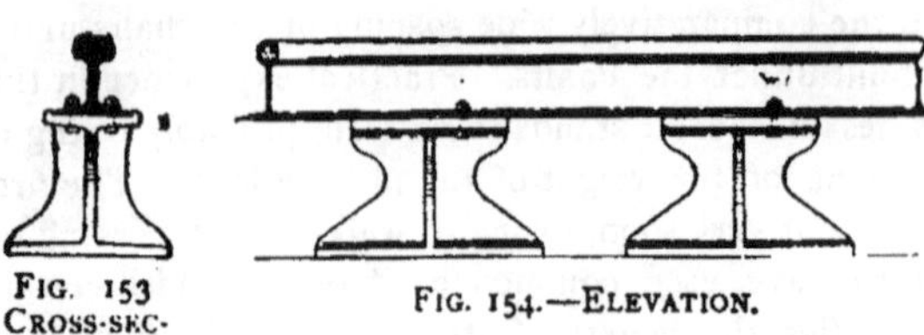

FIG. 153 CROSS-SECTION.

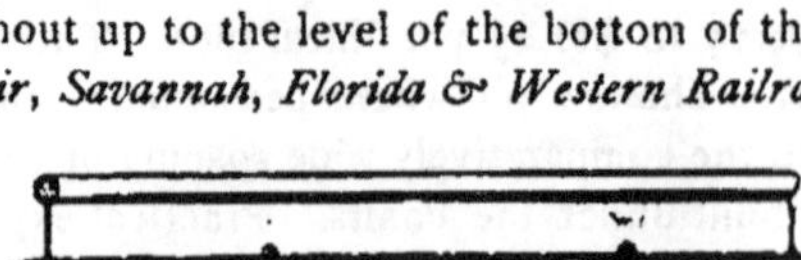

FIG. 154.—ELEVATION.

Ashpit, Lehigh & Susquehanna Railroad.—In Figs. 155 and 156 is shown a style of ashpit in use on the Lehigh & Susquehanna Railroad, near Walnutport, Pa., having ordinary rubble masonry walls covered with cast-iron channel-shaped coping-plates, to which the rails are fastened with screw-bolts and appropriate clips. The length of this pit is about 30 ft., with a cross wall connecting the side walls at the centre of the pit to prevent the side walls from bulging, as the pit is built in the main track. The cost of this style of pit is about $6 per lineal foot.

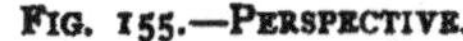

FIG. 155.—PERSPECTIVE.

FIG. 156.—CROSS-SECTION OF RAIL-FASTENING.

Ashpit Cinder-loading Plant, Cincinnati, Washington & Baltimore Railroad.—In connection with ashpits, a noteworthy labor-saving device for handling ashes at ashpits has been designed and built at Chillicothe, O., for the Cincinnati, Washington & Baltimore Railroad, by Mr. Edward Evans, Master Mechanic. According to the *Railroad Gazette* of June 6, 1890, the crane is located between the ashpit track and another track where a gondola car is kept for receiving ashes, which are raked out of the ashpans of engines directly into a sheet-iron box, about 8 ft. long, and in width the same as the distance between the walls of the pit. This box, when full, is lifted by the crane, and after being swung round so as to be over the gondola, its hinged bottom is tripped and the ashes drop into the car. The lifting chain of the crane passes down the centre of the mast and round a sheave at its foot, and can be either operated by a winch or attached directly to an engine. The saving in shovelling is obvious, and when a track can be reserved for cars to receive the ashes, the utility of the design is assured. For illustrations and further data see the issue of the *Railroad Gazette* above mentioned, and the issue of *Engineering News* of August 30, 1890.

Ash-conveyor, at Port Richmond, Philadelphia, Pa., Philadelphia & Reading Railroad.—Connected with the coaling station of the Philadelphia & Reading Railroad at Port Richmond, Philadelphia, Pa., there is an inclined ash-conveyor built on the trough-conveyor system, which passes below the tracks to sunken ashpits. The ashes are dumped from the engines into the sunken pits under the track and thence conveyed by conveyors up the incline to a large elevated, hopper-shaped steel pocket at the head of the incline, whence they are loaded on cars to be hauled away and disposed of along the road in one way or another. This coaling station with ash-conveyor is illustrated and described in the issue of the *Railroad Gazette* of May 13, 1892.

CHAPTER X.

ICE-HOUSES.

Railroads have to supply ice for drinking purposes at depots, offices, shops, and in passenger-cars, and for preserving perishable freight while it is in transit in refrigerator cars or stored in freight-houses. The consumption of ice on railroads has reached such proportions that it has been found advantageous to build special ice houses, so as to allow the railroad company to have control of its ice supply, and to be independent of local ice companies. These houses are stocked by the railroad company during the winter season, either from convenient sources under their own control, and with their own men, or the work is let out by contract. Ice-houses should be so located as to admit of a track being run alongside of them, in order to reduce the cost of handling the ice to a minimum. Two systems have been adopted by railroads for obtaining their ice supply. One is to locate large storage-houses at lakes, ponds, or rivers, in other words, adjacent to the sources of the supply, and to ship ice daily or at intervals from these large storage-houses to smaller houses along the line, from where it is dealt out in such quantities as required. In the other system, the ice, when harvested, is immediately loaded on cars and transferred, while the weather is cold, and hence with small wastage, to large storage-houses at important stations along the line, where considerable quantities of ice are used, as at junction or terminal stations, or where passenger-trains change engines and cars are iced, or at division yards where refrigerator-cars require icing before continuing on to their destination.

Ice-coolers of passenger-trains are usually iced at stations where engines are changed, the work being done by car-inspectors or station hands. For this purpose ice is generally carried in baskets from the ice-house to the station building before the arrival of trains. Where the ice-house is some distance from the station building, ice is brought in hampers or on trucks, once or several times a day, to a spare room or enclosure at the station building, and there washed, cut to size, and held ready for use. Refrigerator-cars are iced in the same way while *en route*, if necessary. Where feasible, however, they are run on to a special siding, as near the ice-house as possible, with a trestling or elevated platform alongside the siding at about the height of the top of the cars connecting with the ice-house to facilitate the handling of the ice from the house to the cars.

Relative to the quantity of ice used for various purposes, it is impossible to give data that will hold in all parts of the country. The following information can be taken as a fair average obtained from actual observation on one of the leading Eastern trunk-lines. There are, generally, one or two coolers in every passenger-car or Pullman coach, each cooler holding from 30 to 40 lbs. of ice. This amount will last about 16 hours in summer and about 24 hours in winter, although, if the cars are kept well heated in winter, the ice will melt about as fast as it does in summer. Thus, with the knowledge of the number of regular trains running on a road, the approximate amount of ice required for the passenger service can be ascertained. Provision should be made, however, for irregular and summer excursion trains, which latter require fully twice as much ice as regular trains. The quantity of ice needed for station and office use is determined by the number of coolers. Small stations, on the road referred to above, receive 30 lbs. of ice daily in summer, while large stations receive from 75 to 125 lbs. The amount of ice required at shops varies according to the number of men employed. Probably from 200 lbs. to 1000 lbs. daily during the summer months will answer, the latter amount being ample for the largest shop system. The data at hand relative to the ice capacity of refrigerator-cars varies considerably. According to the kind of car used and the service expected of it, one charge will take from 1000 to 4100 lbs., which charge will last from 2½ or 3 days to a week. Ice melts faster in cars that are in motion than when they are standing.

When estimating the probable quantity of ice to be stored, due allowance should be made for shrinkage while in store. The loss of ice by shrinkage in the brick ice-house of the Lehigh Valley Railroad at Mauch Chunk, Pa., is stated to be 10 per cent in one year, and slightly more in the frame ice-house of the same railroad at Phillipsburg, N. J. The shrinkage in a large house will be proportionately much less than in a small house, as the shrinkage is dependent on the exposed surface of the ice, which does not increase as fast as the cubical contents. Due regard should also be paid to the possibility of a short crop during one season, wherever the railroad company harvests its own ice supply.

The nominal capacity of an ice-house is generally taken to mean the capacity up to the eaves. By stocking the ice higher up under the roof, working from the gable ends or doors cut in the roof, the capacity can be increased 10 per cent. or even more. The capacity of an ice-house can be approximated by the following data. Sea-water weighs 64 lbs. per cubic ft., rain-water 62½ lbs., while pure solid ice averages 58.7 lbs. per cubic foot. Using the last figure, 34 cubic ft. of ice are equivalent to a ton of 2000 lbs. (the ton generally referred to in railroad work), or 38¼ cubic ft. of ice make a standard ton of 2240 lbs. A very usual assumption is, however, that ice weighs 60 lbs. per cubic ft., which gives 33⅓ cubic ft. to a short ton, and 37⅓ cubic ft. to a long ton. For practical purposes, in estimating the quantity of stored ice, it is correct to assume 36 cubic ft. per short ton or 40 cubic ft. per long ton, so as to make due allowance for the voids and irregular packing of the cakes. In comparing, however, the reported nominal capacities of different ice-houses with their actual cubical contents, the result shows 40 cubic ft. per short ton, and 45 cubic ft. per long ton. In some cases even larger variations are obtained, more particularly in very large ice-houses, where the lost space seems to be proportionately larger than in smaller houses.

The class of buildings used for ice-houses are either of a temporary nature or permanent and substantial structures, the size and kind of building being dependent on the importance of the location and the amount of ice to be stored. With very few exceptions, frame buildings are in general use, which allows cheap structures to be built, in addition to the advantage that wood is a very good non-conductor of heat. The essential features that should be embodied in an ice-house design to insure success are non-heat-conducting walls, the prevention of air penetrating the house from the sides and bottom, ample ventilation on top of the ice, good drainage at the bed, and proper appliances and arrangements for handling and stocking the ice economically.

To make the walls as non-conductive of heat as possible and to prevent the passage of air through them, an air-space, or a space filled with sawdust, shavings, ashes, or some non-heat-conducting material, is introduced in the walls. Layers of building-paper or tarred felting are also employed. A combination of several of these methods is usually the rule. Where an air-space is used provision must be made to keep the air pure by proper openings affording ventilation. Where the walls are filled in with sawdust or some similar material, it is very essential to prevent moisture, as far as possible, from penetrating the filling material, not only on account of the damaging effect of the filling in that condition on the life of the wood in contact with it, but also owing to the fact that the presence of water increases the heat-conducting qualities of the filling material. Suitable holes under the eaves of the building, connecting with the top of the spaces in the walls, should be introduced, so as to afford any moisture that may have penetrated the filling a chance to evaporate. A double roof is a very desirable construction, but, as a rule, the only protection against heat penetrating through the roof of the building consists of planking the roof rafters on top and bottom, creating an air space equal to the thickness of the rafters. The outside of the building should be painted some light color or whitewashed, as less heat of the sun will be thus absorbed. Doors and ventilator openings should be located preferably on the north side of the building, wherever feasible. Relative to the methods in use in American ice-houses for rendering the walls non-conductive of heat, it can be said, in a general way, that the width of the air-spaces or openings in the walls, to be filled with some insulating material, are too small to give the best results, and that, further, the insulation of the roof is usually very imperfect.

Good ventilation over the top of the ice is essential to prevent sweating of the ice. It must not, however, be created by a current of air, but simply be sufficient to keep the air sweet, as it is called in ice-house parlance, or, in other words, pure and dry. It is also advantageous to provide small board windows half-way down the sides, so that, when the level of the ice in the house gets below these windows, they can be opened during cold weather, or on cool nights, so as to purify the body of air at the lower level, the openings and ventilators in the roof not affording, as a rule, sufficient ventilation when the ice is well drawn down. The top of the ice is kept from direct contact with the air by a layer of sawdust, salt hay, or similar material. In the same way the sides of the ice pile are kept from direct contact with the walls of the building.

Proper drainage of the bed on which the ice rests is very important, and it must be done in such a way as not to allow currents of warm air from the outside of the house to penetrate the bed and thus come in contact with the bottom of the ice, and also to prevent the cold air in the house from escaping through the drain, thereby allowing the warm air at the top of the house to descend nearer to the bed. This can be accomplished by a properly constructed water seal in the drain-pipe or culvert, as shown in Figs. 157 and 158.

The floor in an ice-house should be higher than the surrounding ground, so as to keep surface water out of the bed, and also to decrease the possibility of the warmth of the earth affecting the ice. Unless the ground is composed of porous materials, as sand or gravel, it is necessary to use a heavy bed of broken stone, slag, cinders, or ashes, to afford better drainage.

FIG. 157.—CROSS-SECTION.

FIG. 158.—CROSS-SECTION.

In the coal regions coal dirt is used very extensively for this purpose, with good results. On top of the bed thus prepared it is customary to lay a loose floor of rough plank or mill slabs. It is preferable, however, to place this floor on mud-sills or scantlings in such a way as to leave an air-space below, which insures better drainage under the ice and assists to insulate the ice from the heat of the earth. A layer of sawdust, brush, or similar material is spread on top of this floor. It is a very common mistake in building ice-houses to simply level off the ground and lay down boards with a layer of sawdust on top to form the bed, the whole being surrounded by water-tight masonry walls or earth embankments. The result is that the bottom layers of ice are constantly in water, and hence melt much faster.

The top of the bedding material, whatever it be, should be dished from all sides toward the centre of the house or toward the centre of each compartment, if the house is divided into compartments, so as to give better drainage. An additional reason for this is, that, if the mass of ice should have a tendency to slide on its bed, the resultant pressure would more likely be toward the centre of the mass, and detrimental movements toward the sides of the building would be prevented. The side walls and partitions are frequently tied together by wrought-iron rods, so as to be better able to resist the pressure of the ice, in case it should move in a body and bring an outward pressure on the walls.

To facilitate the handling of the ice into and out of the house, doors should be arranged at different levels, or else one door provided leading into a shaft inside the building, the sides of the shaft being formed of loose boards, which can be adjusted to suit the change of level of the ice. A double set of doors are better than a single door, as in the first case an air-space is formed between the doors when closed. Large ice-houses are divided into compartments, so that the ice is only exposed in one compartment at a time when the doors have to be opened.

Small amounts of ice are handled by means of a tackle hung from a beam projecting out from the building over the doors. Where large amounts of ice are handled daily, or while stocking the house, it will be more economical to provide a small hoist, cage, elevator, or traveller, operated by steam or horse power, arranged to dump the blocks of ice automatically when the proper level is reached.

The erection of an artificial-ice plant has, as far as the author knows, never been undertaken by railroad companies. Having studied the question very carefully from the theoretical, practical, and industrial standpoints, the author is firmly convinced that the introduction of an artificial-ice plant on a railroad, especially in southern sections of the country, would not only result in a large saving to the railroad company, but if located at some large town along the route, would be the source of considerable outside revenue.

The following approximate sizes of ice-houses at different points, obtained from the best available information, will aid in forming a general idea of the usual dimensions employed:

Tyrone shops, Pennsylvania Railroad, 1200-ton capacity, 33 ft. × 93 ft.

Harrisburg shops, Pennsylvania Railroad, 1000-ton capacity, 25 ft. × 95 ft.

Cheyenne station, Northern Pacific Railroad, 700-ton capacity, 30 ft. × 50 ft.

Chicago, St. Paul & Kansas City Railroad, 500-ton standard, 28 ft. × 48 ft. × 18 ft. height of frame.

Phillipsburg, N. J., Lehigh Valley Railroad, 1600-ton capacity, 22 ft. × 125 ft. × 28 ft. height of frame.

Jersey City, N. J., Lehigh Valley Railroad, 2000-ton capacity, 30 ft. × 120 ft. × 24 ft. height of frame.

Sayre, Pa., Lehigh Valley Railroad, 1500-ton capacity, 32 ft. × 63 ft. × 32 ft. height of frame.

Nickerson, Kan., Atchison, Topeka & Santa Fe Railroad, 1500-ton capacity, 40 ft. × 120 ft. × 20 ft. height of frame.

Mauch Chunk, Pa., Lehigh Valley Railroad, 1500-ton capacity, 32 ft. × 86 ft. × 28 ft. height of brick side walls.

South Bethlehem, Pa., Lehigh Valley Railroad, 150-ton capacity, 18 ft. × 32 ft. × 12 ft. height of frame.

In regard to the cost of frame ice-houses it can be stated, in general, that, within certain limits, the larger the ice-house the cheaper it will prove per ton storage capacity. Thus, a 25-ton house will cost from $3 to $4 per ton storage capacity; a 50-ton house, from $2.25 to $3 per ton storage capacity; a 100- to 500-ton house from $1.75 to $2.25 per ton storage capacity; a 1000- to 2000-ton house, from $1.50 to $2 per ton storage capacity. Very large storage ice-houses at lakes or rivers, where the ice is harvested, can be built for about $1 per ton storage capacity, and even for less in sections of the country where lumber is cheap. Exclusive of very large storage-houses, the cost of frame ice-houses can be placed at from 4 to 7 cents per cubic foot, a good general average being 5 cents per cubic foot, or about $2 per ton storage capacity.

The following are descriptions of ice-houses in use on railroads in this country.

Design for a Fifty-ton Ice-house.—A very cheap ice-house of about 50 tons nominal capacity can be built as follows: size, 14 ft. square; height of frame from sill to eaves, 13 ft.; roof double-pitched and covered with two layers of 1-in. hemlock boards; sills, 4 in. × 6 in.; plates, 2 in. × 4 in., halved at corners; studs, 2 in. × 4 in., spaced 18 in., mortised into the sills and spiked to the plates. The inside and outside of the studding to be sheathed with hemlock boards, nailed horizontally, thus forming a 4-in. space, which is filled with sawdust. Two doors should be provided in one gable end, one above the other, both being made double by means of horizontal boards placed on the inside of the house as it is filled with ice, and removed as the ice is taken out. The roof projects over the side 1 ft., and the space between the roof-boards and the plate is left open to afford ventilation. A small ventilator or louvred lantern can be added on top of the roof if desired. The cost of such a building would be about $125.

Fifty-ton Ice-house, Jersey City Terminal, Lehigh Valley Railroad.—The small ice-house of the Lehigh Valley Railroad at its Jersey City terminal, used as a temporary storage-house, has a nominal capacity of 50 tons, although 60 tons can be packed into it. The house is 20 ft. × 14 ft. in size, and the height of the frame from the sill to the plate is 9 ft. 6 in. It has a double-pitched roof, boarded on the outside and beneath the rafters with 1-in. hemlock boards, and covered with tarred roofing-felt. The sills are 4 in. × 10 in.; studs, 2 in. × 6 in., spaced 16 in.; corner-studs, 6 in. × 6 in.; plates, 4 in. × 6 in.; rafters, 3 in. × 6 in., spaced 16 in.; nailers between rafters, 3 in. × 4 in.; outside and inside sheathing, 1-in. hemlock, the space between being filled with sawdust. There are two doors in one gable end of the house and a small louvred lantern on top. The cost is about $150.

One-hundred-and-fifty-ton Ice-house, at South Bethlehem, Pa., Lehigh Valley Railroad.—The ice-house of the Lehigh Valley Railroad at South Bethlehem, Pa., has a nominal capacity of 150 tons. It is 32 ft. × 18 ft. in size, and about 12 ft. high from ground to eaves. Its construction and timbers are similar to the fifty-ton ice-house of the Lehigh Valley Railroad at Jersey City, described above. Its cost can be placed at about $350.

Standard Five-hundred-ton Ice-house, Chicago, St. Paul & Kansas City Railroad.—The standard 500-ton ice-house of the Chicago, St. Paul & Kansas City Railroad, shown in Figs. 159 to 162, designed by Mr. H. Fernstrom, Chief Engineer, and Mr. C. A. Reed, Supervising Architect, C., St. P. & K. C. R. R., is a frame building, sheathed on the outside and inside with 1-in. boards, with a double-pitched roof covered with a double layer of 1-in. boards. The size of the house is 48 ft. × 28 ft., and the height from bottom of sill to top of plate 18 ft. At each gable end are three

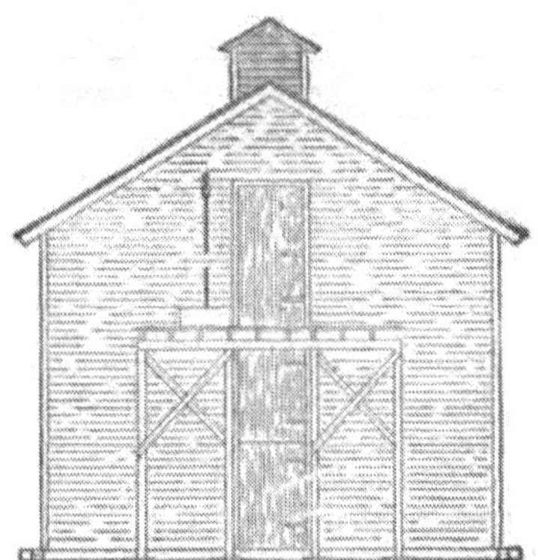

FIG. 159.—FRONT ELEVATION.

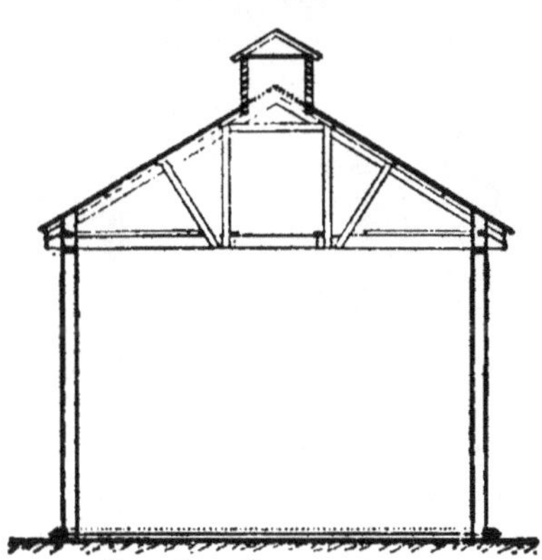

FIG. 160.—CROSS-SECTION.

doors above each other, and at the height of the top of a freight-car a platform or scaffolding with a swinging platform is arranged so as to be easily dropped on top of a car to facilitate the

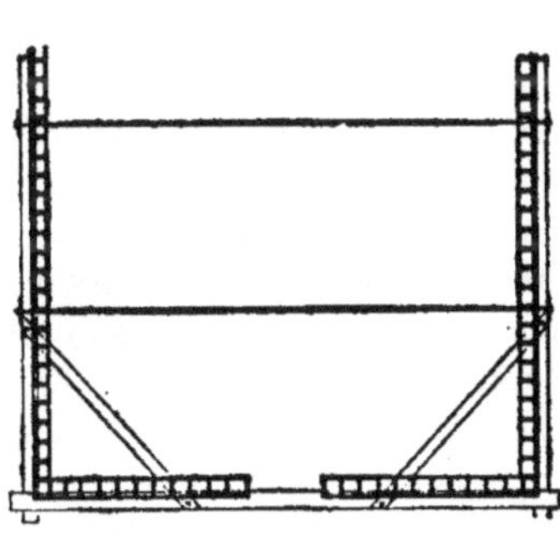

FIG. 161.—GROUND-PLAN.

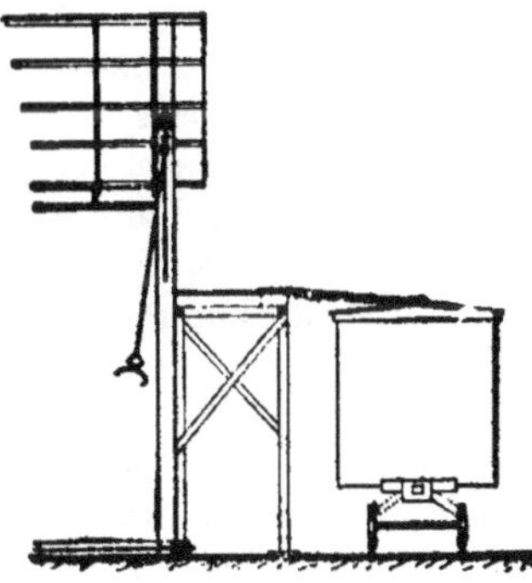

FIG. 162.—LONGITUDINAL SECTION.

handling of ice in icing refrigerator-cars. There is a small louvred lantern at the centre of the house, 5 ft. × 6 ft. in size. The sills are kept from spreading by four 1-in. iron rods placed across the house at the level of the floor.

The principal timbers used are as follows: sills, 8 in. × 10 in., laid flat; corner-posts, 8 in. × 8 in.; studs, 2 in. × 10 in., spaced 12 in., and notched over the inside of the sills to keep the foot of the studding from being crowded out by the pressure of the ice. The platform in front of the house is composed of 6-in. × 8-in. uprights, 6-in. × 6-in. caps, 2-in. × 8-in. joists, 2-in. floor-plank, and 2-in. × 6-in. X-bracing. The roof-trusses are spaced 3 ft. apart, and are formed of boards as follows: rafters, 2 in. × 8 in.; tie-beams, 2 in. × 10 in.; straps, 2 in. × 6 in.

The approximate cost of this house is about $1100 to $1200, and the capacity can be considered as nearer 600 than 500 tons, as stated above

Fifteen-hundred-ton Ice-house at Sayre, Pa., Lehigh Valley Railroad.—The 1500-ton ice-house of the Lehigh Valley Railroad at Sayre, Pa., designed by Mr. A. W. Stedman, Chief Engineer, L. V.

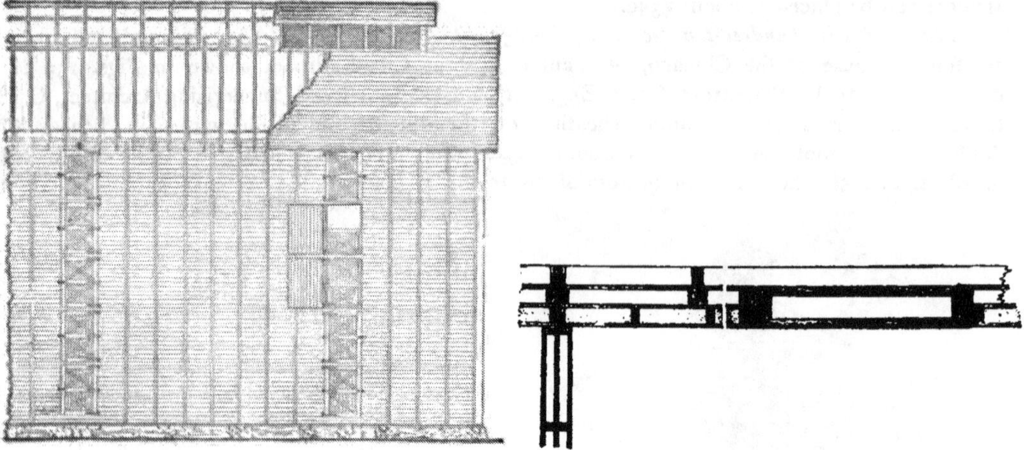

FIG. 163.—FRONT ELEVATION.

FIG. 164.—DETAIL PLAN OF WALLS.

R. R., assisted by Mr. F. E. Schall, shown in Figs. 163 and 164, is a well-designed frame ice-house, 63 ft. × 32 ft. 8 in., out to out, and 32 ft. high from bottom of sill to top of plate. The house is divided into two compartments, each 30 ft. × 30 ft. inside. The distinguishing feature of this design is the combined use of an air-space and a space filled with sawdust in the side walls, thus forming a double protection against the penetration of heat. A ventilator at the ridge of the roof, 8 ft. wide and 4 ft. high, extends nearly the entire length of the building, affording excellent ventilation. There are five double doors over each other on both outside walls of each compartment, and six such doors over each other in each gable end. These double doors, one outside and the other inside, are made to close tightly, leaving an air-space of 6 in. between them. The inner doors are made in two pieces, so-called Dutch or halved doors, to facilitate opening inwardly as the level of the ice is changed. The building rests on small masonry walls, and the floor consists of 1-in. rough hemlock boards laid open on a layer of coal dirt. A number of drain-holes, 6 in. square, are provided in the foundation-walls to allow drainage.

The principal timbers used are as follows: sills, 4 in. × 10 in., laid on top of the stone walls; inside studding, footing on the masonry on the inside of the sill, 2 in. × 4 in., spaced about 20 in.; inside corner-studs and door-studs, 3 in. × 4 in. The inside studding is planked on both sides with 1-in. rough hemlock boards, and the space of 4 in. thus formed between the boards is filled with sawdust. Outside of this inside studding, which is double sheathed, forming a space filled with sawdust, as explained, there are additional outside studs, 3-in. × 10-in. hemlock, planed on two sides, footed on the sill of the building. These outside studs are spaced 3 ft. 4 in. all around the outside of the building, excepting at the doors, where 4-in. × 9-in. special door-studs are set flush with the inside sheathing of the house. Hemlock nailing-strips, 4 in. × 1 in., are fastened on each side of the 3-in. × 10-in. outside studs, next to the outside sheathing of the inner sawdust space. These nailing-strips serve to support ⅞-in. tongued and grooved white-pine boards, planed on one side, which are fitted horizontally between the outside studs, thus forming a 4-in. air-space outside of the 4-in. sawdust space. The transverse partition at the centre of the house between the two compartments is formed of 2-in. × 6-in. studs, sheathed on both sides with 1-in. rough hemlock boards, the 6-in. space thus formed being filled with sawdust. Several doors are cut in this partition to afford connection between the two compartments. The plates of the side walls are 4-in. × 10-in. hemlock; rafters, 3 in. × 8 in., spaced 24 in.; tie-beams or ceiling-joists, 3 in. × 10 in., spaced 4 ft., and sheathed on top with 1-in. rough hemlock boards. The roof is covered with 1-in. tongued and grooved hemlock boards, not over 8 in. wide. The ventilator is formed of 4-in. × 4-in. sills, 3-in. × 4-in. plates; 3-in. × 4-in. rafters, spaced 39 in.; and 3-in. × 4-in. studs, spaced 39 in. The single outside doors are 5 ft. 8 in. high × 4 ft. 4 in. wide. The frames of the outside doors are made of 6 in. × 1½ in. stuff, and those of the inside doors are 4 in. × 1½ in. All the doors are X-braced with 3 in. × 1½ in. stuff, and covered with 1-in. boards. The spaces between the roof-boards and the plates are left open for ventilation. The building is tied together at the centre by two 1¼-in. iron rods.

The cost of this building can be placed at about $2500 to $3000, varying according to the locality and the depth of the foundations.

Two thousand-ton Ice-house at Jersey City, N. J., Lehigh Valley Railroad.—The two-thousand-ton ice-house of the Lehigh Valley Railroad, at Jersey City, N. J., shown in Figs. 165 to 168, designed by

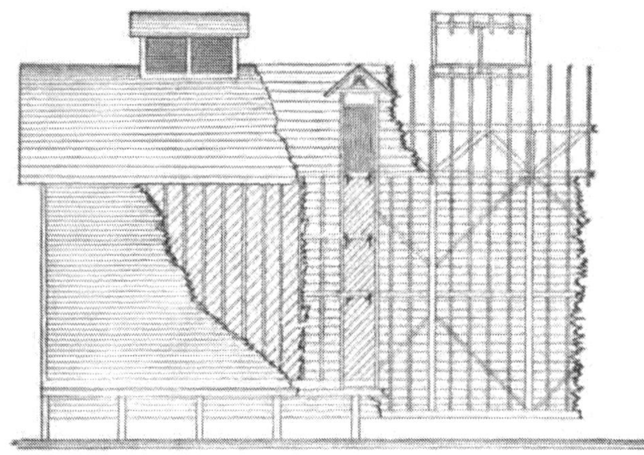

FIG. 165.—FRONT ELEVATION.

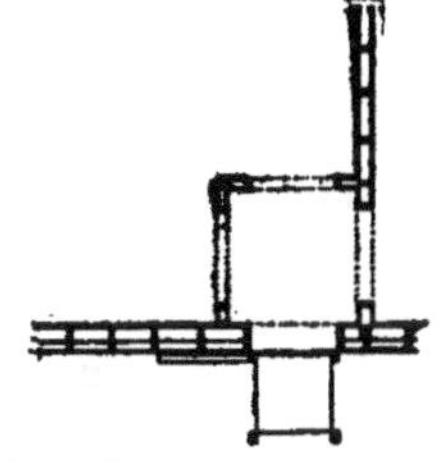

FIG. 166.—GROUND-PLAN AT SHAFT.

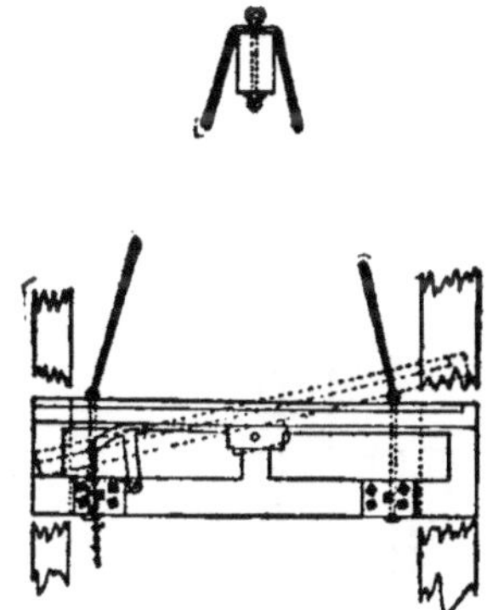

FIG. 167.—ELEVATION OF HOISTING-CAGE.

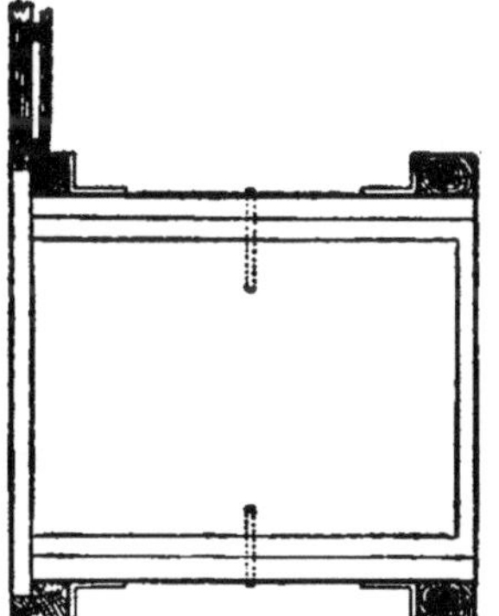

FIG. 168.—PLAN OF HOISTING-CAGE.

Mr. C. Rosenberg, Master Carpenter, Lehigh Valley Railroad, is a frame structure, 30 ft. 8 in. wide × 120 ft. 8 in. long, outside dimensions, and 24 ft. high from ground to eaves. It is divided into four compartments, each 30 ft. × 30 ft. There is a loading platform, 6 ft. wide on one side of the house along a track, the floor of the platform being level with the car-floor. Two hoists on this platform connect with shafts inside the building, each hoist supplying two of the four compartments in the house.

The side walls in this building have an 8-in. space filled with sawdust, and outside of that a 3-in. air-space. The studding is formed of 8-in. stuff, ceiled on the inside with 1-in. rough boards laid horizontally, and sheathed on the outside with 1-in. rough boards laid diagonally, thereby forming the 8-in. space filled with sawdust. The 3-in. air-space is obtained by nailing 3 in. × 4 in. pieces to the outside sheathing of the 8-in. studding, and then closing in the entire building with bevelled weather-boarding. The roof is ceiled underneath the rafters with 1-in. rough boards and covered with tarred roofing-felt on 1-in. boards. There is a 4-ft. × 10-ft. louvred ventilator in the roof over each compartment.

There are three sliding-doors in the side of the building and one door in the roof at each shaft or hoist. The sliding-doors are arranged so as to fit the openings tightly by means of suitable attachments and locking devices. The doors in the roof open inwardly. The sides of the shaft inside the building are made of loose boards working in slots, so that the top of the shaft can be kept at any desired height, or the shaft removed with the exception of the upright corner-pieces.

The foundations of the house are stone walls, with proper openings to allow for drainage. The floor in each compartment is dished from the corners to the centre, and is made of a layer of about 2 ft. of ashes on top of broken stone. Blind drains were built underneath the broken stone to give better drainage.

The principal timbers used are as follows: sills, 6 in. × 8 in.; principal studs, 8 in. × 8 in.; intermediate studs, 3 in. × 8 in., spaced 24 in.; outside studding to form air-space, 3 in. × 4 in.; plates, 6 in. × 8 in.; rafters, 3 in. × 6 in., spaced 24 in.

The cage of the hoist is provided with an arrangement for discharging the ice-blocks automatically into the house at any desired height. The cage consists of a frame supporting a platform pivoted at its centre. The side of the platform next to the house is held up by a cam underneath it, which cam is attached to the frame. This cam is connected by a chain or rope to a ring at the foot of the hoist, which allows the length of the rope to be readily adjusted. When the cage has been hoisted to the desired height, the rope becomes taut and draws the cam from beneath the platform, allowing the side of the platform next to the building to drop and shooting the block of ice into the house, where men are ready to receive it. While filling the house this hoist is operated by a small portable steam-engine or by horse-power. For drawing the daily supply from the house, a smaller platform worked by a hand windlass is used.

This building has given very good satisfaction. Its cost can be placed at about $3000 to $3500.

Fifteen-hundred-ton Ice-house at Nickerson, Kan., Atchison, Topeka & Santa Fe Railroad.—The ice-house of the Atchison, Topeka & Santa Fe Railroad at Nickerson, Kan., shown in Figs. 169 to 171,

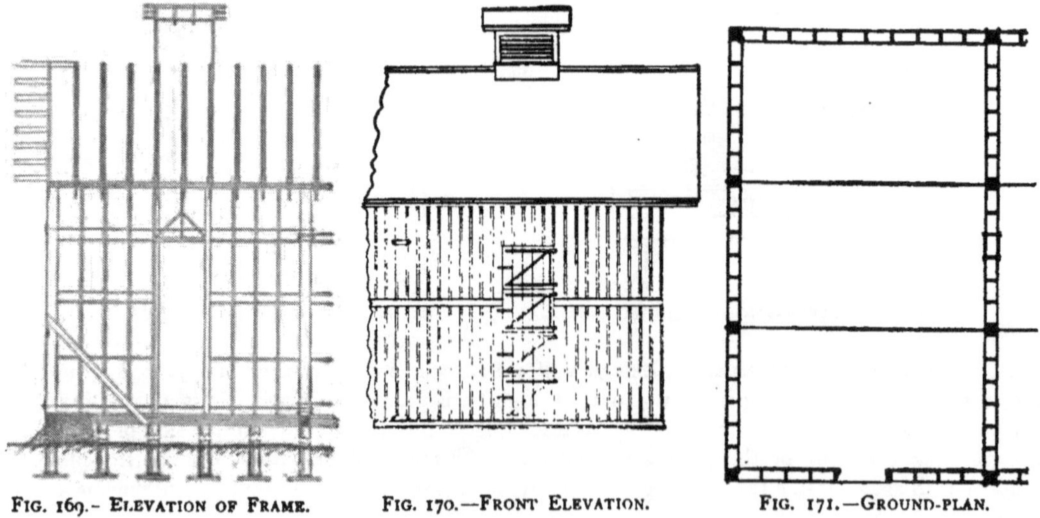

FIG. 169.- ELEVATION OF FRAME. FIG. 170.—FRONT ELEVATION. FIG. 171.—GROUND-PLAN.

with a nominal capacity of 1500 tons, but able to hold 1800 tons, is a frame structure divided into five compartments. The outside dimensions of the house are 120 ft. × 40 ft., and the height of the frame from the top of sill to bottom of plate is 20 ft. The side walls and transverse partitions are 14 in. thick. The inside dimensions of the compartments are 22 ft. 10 in. × 37 ft. 8 in. There are three louvred lanterns, each 5 ft. 6 in. × 4 ft. 6 in., on the roof, and four doors over each other for each compartment on one side of the house. The foundations are formed of posts, set on plank in the ground about every 5 ft., under the side walls and under the partitions. The sills are made of six pieces, each 2 in. × 12 in.; the plates are in three pieces, each 2 in. × 12 in. The corner-studs and intermediate studs in the gable ends and partitions are 12 in. × 12 in., and the door-studs are 6 in. × 12 in.; all other studs are 2 in. × 12 in., spaced about 27 in., and the corner-braces 2 in. × 6 in. The roof is double-pitched, with rafters spaced about 30 in.; rafters, 2 in. × 8 in.; tie-beams in two pieces, each 2 in. × 6 in. The building is kept from spreading longitudinally by four 1¼-in. rods in each compartment, and at each transverse partition by four 1-in. rods. Doors are each 3 ft. 10 in. high × 4 ft. 4 in. wide. Outside walls are ceiled on the inside with 1-in. rough boards, nailed horizontally, and sheathed on the outside with 1-in. upright boards and battens. The cross partitions are planked on each side with 1-in. rough boards. The ground inside the house is covered with a layer of broken stone to facilitate drainage. The cost of this ice-house can be placed approximately at $3500, dependent on local conditions and the depth of the foundations.

Fifteen-hundred-ton Brick Ice-house at Mauch Chunk, Pa., Lehigh Valley Railroad.—The brick ice-house of the Lehigh Valley Railroad at Mauch Chunk, Pa., shown in Figs. 172 and 173, has a nominal capacity of 1500 tons, but it can hold 1700 tons. The house was built of brick, partly to

FIG. 172.—PERSPECTIVE.

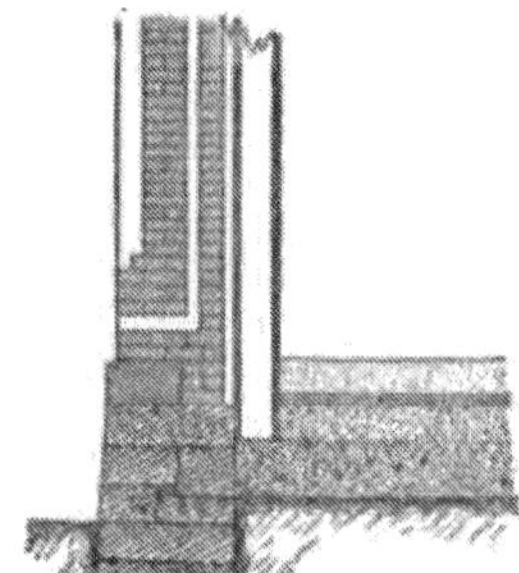

FIG. 173.—DETAIL SECTION OF WALL AND FLOOR.

lessen the danger from fire and partly on account of its proximity to the station building, there being a heavy passenger and excursion travel at this station. The building is 86 ft. long × 32 ft. wide, outside measurements, and 28 ft. high from the floor to the bottom of the tie-beam. The walls are built with a 2½-in. air-space in their interior. The brick wall outside of this air-space is 9 in. thick in the panels and 13 in. thick at the pilasters; the brickwork inside of the air-space is 4½ in. thick. The brick walls rest on stone rubble-masonry foundations. Inside the brick walls there is a timber frame, consisting of 3-in. × 6-in. studs, spaced 24 in., and sheathed on both sides with 1-in. rough boards, which thus form a 6-in. space that is filled with sawdust. The outside sheathing of this timber frame is kept 2 in. away from the inside of the brick wall, giving thus an additional air-space. The protection thus secured by the 2½-in. air-space in the brick wall proper, the 2-in. air-space between the brick wall and the timber lining, and the 6-in. sawdust space, has proved very effective. The bond between the two parts of the brick wall on each side of the air-space in the wall is maintained by iron plates laid between the bricks and extending across the air-space, the plates being spaced 24 in. apart. The air-space in the wall has openings near the foot of the wall and near the eaves, so as to keep the air fresh. The house is divided into two compartments by a partition at its centre. The floor is formed of an 8-in. to 10-in. layer of broken stones, on top of which there is a 6-in. course of coal dirt, covered by 2-in. rough boards laid open. On top of the boards a 6-in. layer of sawdust is spread before the ice is put into the house. Suitable drain-holes are provided in the foundation walls to allow proper drainage of the bed. There are two ventilators in the roof, three doors in each gable end of the house, and twelve doors on the side toward the tracks, the building being set with its back against the mountain. The roof is covered with slate on boards. The loss from shrinkage of the ice in this house is stated to be from 10 to 11 per cent during one year.

Sixteen-hundred-ton Ice-house, Phillipsburg, N. J., Lehigh Valley Railroad.—The ice-house of the Lehigh Valley Railroad at Phillipsburg, N. J., has a nominal capacity of 1600 tons, and is a frame building similar to the large ice-house of the same railroad built at Jersey City, described above, excepting that there is only a sawdust space, but no air-space, in the side walls. The size of the house is 125 ft. × 22 ft. outside dimensions, and 28 ft. high from ground level to the plate. The arrangements for proper ventilation of the side walls and the space above the ice in this house are good, and it has been found that, by exercising proper discretion in ventilating the house and keeping the air fresh, the so-called sweating of the ice is prevented to a large extent. When this house was first built, the 8-in. space in the side walls between the outside and inside sheathing was left as an air-space and no sawdust filling employed, the result being a shrinkage of ice in one year of from 25 to 30 per cent. After this space was filled with sawdust the loss was reduced at least 10 per cent.

CHAPTER XI.

SAND-HOUSES.

SAND-HOUSES are required on railroads to store sand for use on engines to increase the friction of the driving-wheels on the rails on heavy grades, or when the rails are in a slippery condition. The sand must be dry in order to run freely through the pipes leading from the sand-box of the engine to where the sand is spouted on the rails in front of the driving-wheels. Sand, freshly dug, is always more or less moist, and it absorbs moisture from the air very easily, even when properly stored under cover, so that artificial drying becomes a necessity. Sand-houses, therefore, have three distinct functions, namely, the storage of wet sand, the drying of the same, and the storage of the dry sand.

Sand-houses are usually provided at all points on a railroad where engines are changed, or in connection with engine-houses and coaling stations; in other words, wherever engines are supplied with coal, water, oil, sand, etc., before starting on a run. For this reason sand-houses will generally be found located along a track leading to or from an engine-house, yard system, coaling or water station. Even where the amount of sand to be used is very small, it will be found more advantageous to dry it at the place where it is to be supplied to engines, than to attempt to ship dry sand from a large, central sand-house at some distant point, because, if the weather be damp, the sand will collect moisture again during transit or while in store. It requires very little attention and labor to dry sand at intervals in small amounts with the ordinary cast-iron sand-drying stoves, and they do not, therefore, call for the regular employment of special help for that purpose.

The main consideration to be kept in view in designing a sand-house is economy in handling the material and in the amount of fuel required in the drying process. In the operation of a sand-house the several steps consist of storing the wet sand, keeping it as free from moisture as possible while in store, the drying process proper, the stocking of the dry sand, and, finally, the delivery of the dry sand to engines.

In storing sand it is best to put it under cover, but the structure should be arranged to admit plenty of light and air on pleasant days, the free circulation of dry air over the pile being very desirable. This is usually accomplished to a certain degree by leaving the sides of the shed open at the top, but the more effective construction is to introduce louvres or movable slat sash or shutters, which allow the house to be closed during very damp weather. Where the size of the house will warrant it, or steam is convenient, it will be found very advantageous to place a few steam-coils around the sides of the store-shed above the sand-pile, or to hang them from the roof, so as to slightly heat the air that circulates over the pile, and thus prevent moisture, especially in damp weather, from entering the sand.

Wet or green sand, as it is termed, is usually brought to the house in cars and cast into the storage-shed through openings in the sides of the building, or it is wheeled off the cars into the house. Where provision can be made for an elevated track, the car is either run into the house or over the top of the house, the sand being dumped from hopper-cars or cast off sideways. A very good location for a sand-house is under the tail-track of a coal-trestle, where this is feasible. Too much importance, however, should not be placed on an elevated delivery track, as the sand must be shovelled anyhow, except when delivered in hopper-cars. In other words, it would not pay to construct a special incline and trestle approach to facilitate unloading sand into store from an elevated track, unless the quantity to be handled is very large.

The drying process is conducted in several ways, the one most used being by means of so-called sand-drying stoves, of which there are a number of styles, the general features consisting of an ordinary cast-iron stove, with shallow pans near the top, or surrounded with a conical retort or drum around the body of the stove. The sand is packed in the pans or retorts, and a slow fire maintained until the sand is dry, when it is drawn off or scraped out through appropriate openings. Another form of a sand-drier is a revolving sheet-iron cylinder set at an angle in a furnace. A fire is kept up in the furnace while the cylinder is slowly revolved, the sand being fed into the upper end of the cylinder and passing out through a screen at the lower end. Another method is to put the wet sand in a trough with a system of steam-pipes forming a grating through which the sand, as it dries, gradually descends to the bottom of the trough, which is open, allowing the dry sand to drop on the floor. It is claimed that this system is very efficient and economical, where copper steam-pipes are used. In some sand-houses fires are maintained in brick or stone flues under the sand-pile. When the sand is thoroughly heated the fires are stopped until a fresh lot of wet sand is received.

After drying, the sand is generally screened and then shovelled into bins on the ground-floor of the building or on a level with the footboard of engines. Another system is to elevate the dry sand by an endless bucket belt, an appropriate hoisting apparatus, a cold blast, or an elevator system of some kind, to storage-bins overhead, whence it can be spouted down to the sand-boxes of engines or drawn into buckets by the enginemen. The Erie Railroad has on its Delaware division a sand-house, in which dry sand is elevated by a cold blast to a storage-bin, from where it is discharged directly into the sand-boxes of engines. In some sand-houses a large number of buckets are kept filled with dry sand on a platform adjacent to the track and on a level with the footboard of engines, so that the enginemen can pick up as many buckets of sand as they require and empty them into the sand-box without the delay incident to drawing the sand or filling the buckets. Another system in use is to have large buckets with drop bottoms standing filled with sand alongside the track; when an engine stops for sand, the buckets are picked up and swung around over the sand-box by means of a derrick arm or gallows frame, and then discharged upon releasing the catch. This method deserves mention for its simplicity, and it will give about as quick dispatch in supplying sand to engines as a more elaborate elevator and overhead storage-bin system.

In designing a sand-house, due regard must be paid to the quantity of sand to pass daily through the house. Where the usual help around a yard or engine-house system is to be relied on for its operation, it is essential to provide systems that involve a minimum amount of constant attention and labor. However, the introduction of labor-saving contrivances should not be carried to extremes, as illustrated in a sand-house of one of the leading Eastern trunk lines, where an elaborate trough-and-bucket system with belt conveyor is employed to take the wet sand to the drying troughs—a distance of about 10 ft., another bucket elevator being used to lift the dry sand to a platform 8 ft. higher than the floor of the drying-room, a 10-horse-power engine completing the plant. While this device might appear perfect at first glance, yet in actual operation it is a failure, requiring the constant attention of an engineer, and the output being entirely controlled by the speed with which a man can feed sand to the foot of the trough conveyor, which carries the sand a little farther.

The size and style of a sand-house to be adopted at any particular point depend upon the importance of the location, the grades that the engines have to pass, the number of engines to be supplied daily; also, whether the engine crew can be relied on to draw sand, or whether it is important to enable engines to take sand quickly without any assistance from the engine crew. As indicative, however, of the sizes in general use, the approximate dimensions of the following sand-houses can be mentioned: Richmond & Alleghany Railroad, at Richmond, Va., 16 ft. 6 in. × 14 ft. 6 in.; Atchison, Topeka & Santa Fe Railroad, 16 ft. × 28 ft.; Lehigh Valley Railroad, at Perth Amboy, N. J., 54 ft. × 20 ft.; design for Philadelphia & Reading Railroad, 16 ft. × 16 ft.; Chicago, Burlington & Quincy Railroad, at Burlington, Ill., storehouse, 50ft. × 29 ft., and sand-drying tower, 19 ft. × 19 ft.; Pittsburgh, Cincinnati & St. Louis Railroad, at Columbus, O., 91 ft. × 43 ft.; design for Lehigh Valley Railroad, 68 ft. × 18 ft.; Pennsylvania Railroad, at Connemaugh, Pa., 60 ft. × average width 27 ft.; Pennsylvania Railroad, at Pittsburgh, Pa., 16 ft. × 36 ft.; Pennsylvania Railroad, at Jersey City, N. J., 21 ft. × 29 ft.; Pennsylvania Railroad, at Tyrone, Pa., 20 ft. 6 in. × 12 ft.; Pennsylvania Railroad, at Huntingdon, N. J., 20 ft. 6 in. × 12 ft.; Pennsylvania Railroad, at Blairsville, Pa., 26 ft. × 15 ft. 6 in.; Pennsylvania Railroad, at Mifflin, Pa., 20 ft. × 15 ft.; Lehigh Valley Railroad, at Weatherly, Pa., 30 ft. × 20 ft.; Pennsylvania Railroad, at Washington, D. C., 30 ft. × 20 ft.

The ordinary cast-iron sand-drying stove is to be recommended, especially where only a small amount of sand is required daily, and where it is desirable that the usual help in the vicinity should also look after the sand-house. If steam can be introduced in the house, then a steam-pipe sand-drying trough with copper pipes will prove advantageous, especially where large amounts of sand have to be handled. In addition, the trough system diminishes the possible loss from fire.

Another economical method, referred to above, is that employed on the Lehigh Valley Railroad, at Weatherly, Pa., and on the Philadelphia & Reading Railroad, at Cressona, Pa., where a fire is kept up in the flues under the sand-pile for several days at a time. This method entails little labor, but, owing to the large quantities to be heated at a time, the sand dries very unevenly, besides being likely to collect moisture before being used. This last defect can be obviated by introducing steam-coils at the top of the sand-pile, as referred to above.

The lifting of the dry sand by elevators, hoists, or cold blast into an elevated bin, from where it can be shot down into the sand-box, or drawn by the enginemen from a spout into buckets, is quite a feature where large quantities of sand are to be handled daily, and one or more men are employed steadily for the sand service, and it is an object to enable engines to take sand quickly. Similar results, however, without elaborate appliances and such a costly building, can be practically obtained by keeping a number of buckets filled with sand on a platform adjacent to the track at a convenient elevation, or by the use of a swinging derrick-arm and a bucket with drop-bottom.

The patentees of a cylindrical drying-machine published in the *Railroad Gazette* of May 4, 1888, the following data for drying sand with a cast-iron sand-drying stove, as compared with the work of their patented machine:

	Railroad stove-drier.	Patented cylindrical apparatus.
Pounds wet sand dried and screened per hour	675	16,000
Pounds common soft coal consumed per hour	24	180
Pounds water dried out per lb. coal burned	1	$8\frac{1}{3}$
Average percentage of water in the two different sands	.035	.093
Men's labor required	1	3

Expense of drying one ton of sand:

Cost of labor at 15 cents per hour	44 cts.	$5\frac{1}{2}$ cts.
Cost of coal at $12\frac{1}{2}$ cents per bushel	$11\frac{1}{10}$ "	$3\frac{1}{3}$ "
Cost of steam motive power	....	3 "
Cost of interest, repairs, and depreciation	2 "	2 "
Total	$57\frac{1}{10}$ cts.	14 cts.

The following descriptions of sand-houses are introduced as forming an interesting addition to above general remarks on the subject.

Sand-house at Richmond, Va., Richmond & Alleghany Railroad.—The sand-house of the Richmond & Alleghany Railroad, shown in Figs. 174 and 175, is a good type of a cheap sand-house, where a

FIG. 174.—CROSS SECTION.

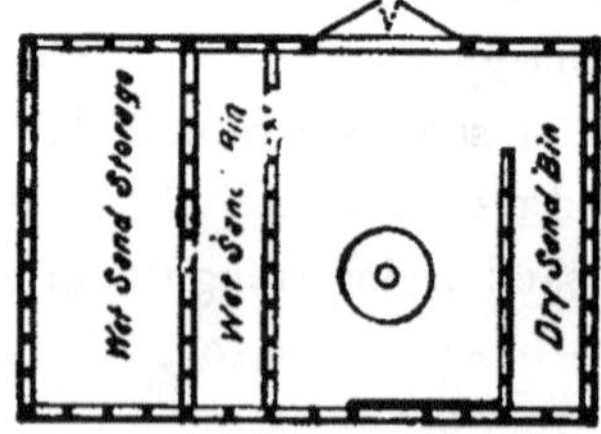

FIG. 175.—GROUND-PLAN.

limited amount of sand is used. The house is a low frame structure, 16 ft. 6 in. × 14 ft. 6 in., with an open bin, 6 ft. 6 in. × 14 ft. 6 in., adjoining one end of the building for the wet sand. In operating this house the wet sand is delivered from cars into the open bin, and from thence it is shovelled, as required, through an opening in the side of the building into an interior storage-bin for wet sand. A cast-iron sand-drying stove is located in the middle of the house, which is filled from the wet-sand bin. As the sand dries, it drops to the floor through openings in the sides of the stove, from where it is thrown on a screen placed over the dry-sand bin at the other end of the building. The enginemen are required to enter the house and fill their buckets with sand directly from the dry-sand bin.

The frame is 10 ft. high on the front of the building and 9 ft. on the rear. The principal sizes are as follows: sills, 4 in. × 6 in.; plates, 4 in. × 4 in.; corner and door studs, 4 in. × 4 in.; intermediate studding, 3 in. × 4 in., spaced about 18 in.; nailers, 3 in. × 4 in.; rafters, 2 in. × 6 in.;

posts for bin partitions, 3 in. × 4 in.; rails for bin partitions, 4 in. × 6 in.; floor in bins, 2 in.; outside sheathing, ⅞-in. vertical boards with battens; roof-sheathing, ⅞-in. boards, covered with tin.

While, as stated above, this is a representative design for a cheap sand-house, it could be improved by roofing over the outer wet-sand bin, and the second handling of the wet sand from the outside bin to the interior one should be avoided.

Sand-house, Atchison, Topeka & Santa Fe Railroad.—The sand-house in use on the Atchison, Topeka & Santa Fe Railroad, shown in Figs. 176 to 178, prepared from data furnished by Mr. J. M. Meade, Assistant Engineer, A., T. & S. F. R. R., is built on a similar plan to the foregoing one, excepting that it is on a larger scale and is arranged for two sand-drying stoves. The building is a one-story frame structure, 16 ft. × 28 ft. and 9 ft. high from sill to plate, with a double-pitched roof. The wet sand is shovelled from cars through an opening in the side of the house into the wet-sand bin, which is 6 ft. wide and 16 ft. long. From this bin the sand is fed to the sand-drying stoves as fast as required, and when dry the sand is thrown over a sand-screen, from where it is put into the dry-sand bin facing the track travelled by the engines. The floor of the dry-sand bin is inclined so as to form a hopper, the sand being drawn on the outside of the building through a funnel-shaped appliance with a stop-gate. A bin to keep the supply of coal required for the stoves is located in one corner of the house. The arrangement of the screen for screening the sand is noteworthy. Its upper end is hinged to the side of the building on a level with the sill of a small window, and its lower end is provided with a recess or pocket to catch stones and rubbish that do not pass through the screen. By means of a rope running over a pulley in the roof of the building and attached to the lower end of the screen, the latter is raised and the accumulated rubbish in the pocket discharged through the window without extra handling.

FIG. 176.—FRONT ELEVATION.

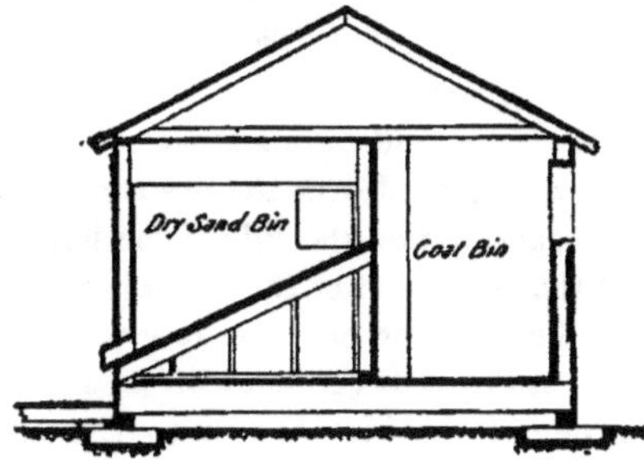

FIG. 177.—CROSS-SECTION.

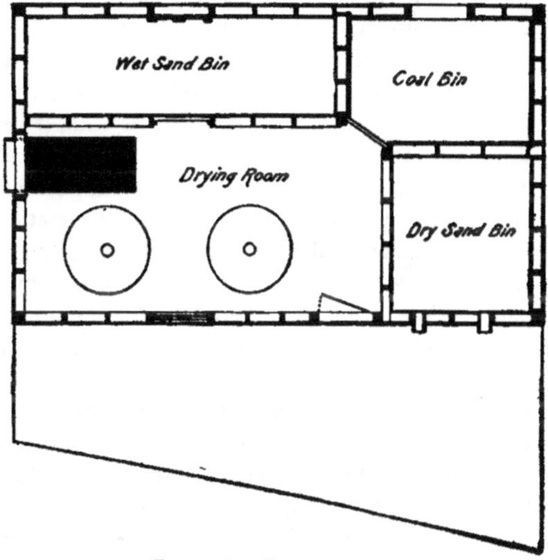

FIG. 178.—GROUND-PLAN.

The principal sizes used are as follows: sills, 6 in. × 6 in.; studs, 2 in. × 6 in., spaced 24 in.; plates, 2 in. × 6 in.; floor-joists, 2 in. × 12 in., spaced 16 in.; floor, 2-in. plank; rafters, 2 in. × 4 in., spaced 28 in.; lining of wet-sand bin, 1-in. boards; lining of dry-sand bin, 1-in. boards and No. 11 tank-iron; lining of coal-bin, 2-in. plank.

The interior arrangement of this building is very well planned, with the exception of the location of the sand-screen, which should be nearer the dry-sand bin, so as to avoid cross movements and extra handling of the sand in its passage from the wet to the dry-sand bin, unless the wet sand is screened before being put in the driers, in which case the location of the screen is all right.

Sand-house at Perth Amboy, N. J., Lehigh Valley Railroad.—The sand-house of the Lehigh Valley Railroad at Perth Amboy, N. J., shown in Fig. 179 is a one-story frame structure, 54 ft. × 20 ft., built under the tail track of the engine coaling trestle at that point. The house is divided into three compartments—one for the storage of wet sand, the middle one for the cast-iron sand-drying stoves, of which there are four, and an end compartment for the storage of the dry sand. The sand is dropped from hopper-cars, or shovelled off sideways from flat cars, through hatches in the roof into the wet-sand bin. The sand is then shovelled or wheeled through an opening in the partition wall to the sand-drying stoves. The dried sand drops on the floor around the stoves and is thrown on a screen placed over the dry-sand bin. A small door and platform are provided at the end of the dry-sand bin on the side of the house next to the track. The enginemen step off from the footboard of the engine, enter the house, and take sand directly from the bin, or, in busy times, buckets of sand are kept on the platform to give quicker dispatch to the engines.

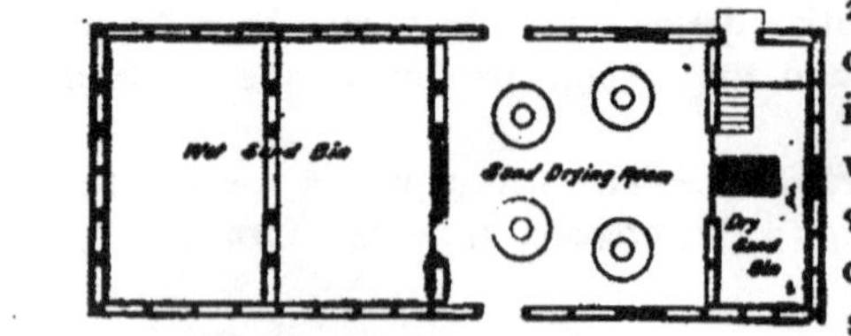

FIG. 179.—GROUND-PLAN.

As regards economy of labor, compactness of design, and cheapness of construction, this house is one of the best known to the author. It would be an improvement to have the same arrangement of the screen over the dry-sand bin as used in the sand-house of the Atchison, Topeka & Santa Fe Railroad, described above, so as to discharge the refuse and gravel outside of the house instead of on the floor of the sand-drying room in front of the dry-sand bin.

Sand-house Design, Philadelphia & Reading Railroad.—A sand-house design made for the Philadelphia & Reading Railroad, shown in Fig. 180, represents a frame building, 16 ft. × 16 ft. and about 18 ft. high. In the centre of the building there is an iron sand-drying stove with a large drum on top reaching up into a wet-sand bin located overhead. An ordinary stove-pipe or funnel is connected with the drum and projects up through the roof, it being the intention to utilize the heat of the gases ascending from the stove to effect a preliminary warming or drying of the sand, before it drops automatically into the large shallow drying-pan encircling the stove, as fast as the dry sand is drawn from the pan. While in this plan there is no labor connected with the placing of the wet sand in the drying-pan, there is extra labor connected with placing the sand in the elevated bin, unless dumped from an elevated track. To allow the entire contents of the bin to run automatically into the drum, the floor of the bin should be hopper-shaped. This design is interesting, however, as marking a step in the development of sand-houses, but it is costly, and not to be specially recommended.

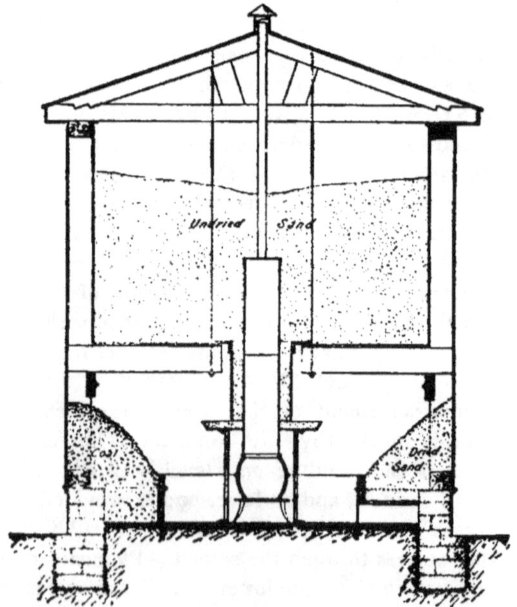

FIG. 180.—CROSS-SECTION.

Sand-house at Burlington, Ill., Chicago, Burlington & Quincy Railroad.—The sand-house of the Chicago, Burlington & Quincy Railroad, illustrated and described in the *Railroad Gazette* of July 22, 1887, is a brick structure of considerable proportions, divided into a wet-sand store, 50 ft. long by an average width of 29 ft., and a dry-sand tower, 19 ft × 19 ft. The height of the sand-store is about 24 ft. to the eaves, and that of the tower about. 33 ft. In operating the house, the wet sand is run into the wet-sand store in cars on a trestle track, and dumped from hopper-cars or shovelled off into store. The wet sand is wheeled, as required, from the store to driers of the steam-pipe trough pattern situated on the floor of the dry-sand tower. The dried sand drops from the troughs into a hopper leading to the foot of a bucket elevator operated by hand, which conveys the sand into a hopper-shaped dry-sand bin occupying the top of the tower. From this elevated storage-bin the sand is drawn through spouts directly into the sand-box of the engine, similarly to the manner that water is drawn from a water-tank through a goose-neck, or grain is spouted from a grain-elevator into boats or cars. The walls of the building are tied together by rods. The store-room is designed so as to be able to give good ventilation over the sand-pile. The trapezoidal shape of the store-house is due to local circumstances, the building being located between two converging tracks leading to an engine-house. The dry-sand bin in the tower is arranged so as to deliver sand to engines on either track. For some reason, the steam-pipe trough-driers originally intended to be used were replaced by cast-iron sand-drying stoves when the building was put into operation, the other arrangements of the building remaining the same. The valve at the end of the sand-delivery spout is an ingenious arrangement, consisting of a copper bucket hung on a pivot bar strapped to the pipe by a wrought-iron band. When the bucket hangs freely from the pivot, the sand runs from the pipe until it fills the bucket sufficiently to clog the mouth of the pipe, thus stopping the flow. To open the valve, it is simply necessary to swing the bucket upwards, and to hold it in that position so long as it is desired to draw sand; on being released the bucket drops and shuts off the flow. The track inside the house is a continuation of the tail track of a coal-chute trestle at that point.

Where large quantities of sand have to be handled, and the quick dispatch of engines is important, the general system embodied in this plant can be recommended, although the building need not be made as substantial as in the case described.

Sand-house at Columbus, O., Pittsburgh, Cincinnati & St. Louis Railway.—The sand-house of the Pittsburgh, Cincinnati & St. Louis Railway, plans for which were published in the *Railroad Gazette* of April 22, 1887, is divided into an open frame shed, 60 ft. × 43 ft., for the storage of the wet sand, and a brick dry-sand house, 31 ft. × 43 ft. The shed is 15 ft. high from sill to plate, and the brick building is 21 ft. high from ground to the eaves. The system of operation is to shovel the wet sand into the store-house through the sides of the shed, whence it is wheeled through a door in the back wall of the brick dry-sand house to the driers, which are located on the floor of the brick house, and consist of wrought-iron troughs, traversed by several rows of steam-pipes, about 2½ in. apart. The wet sand is thrown into the trough, and is held by the pipes while it is wet. As it dries, it gradually descends between the pipes till it drops to the floor. It is then screened and shovelled into the dry-sand bin, located on the ground-floor of the house, whence enginemen take the sand as they require it.

The sides of the shed are sheathed for 6 ft. from the ground. Above this movable shutters are provided, so that the sides of the shed can be closed or thrown open according to the state of the weather. The floor of this shed is paved with brick, set loosely on edge, tile-drains underneath the paving providing ample drainage. The principal timbers used are as follows: sills, 8 in. × 8 in.; plates, 8 in. × 8 in.; posts, 8 in. × 8 in.; knee-braces, 6 in. × 6 in.; corbels, 6 in. × 8 in.; inside sheathing, 2 in.; outside braces at foot of posts, 6 in. × 6 in.; roof-trusses, spaced about 9 ft. 6 in. apart; tie-beams, 8 in. × 8 in.; principal rafters, 6 in. × 8 in.; braces, 4 in. × 6 in.; purlins, 6 in. × 8 in.; common rafters, 2 in. × 4 in. The brick dry-sand house has 13-in. walls, with 17-in. pilasters; the floor is built of cement, and the roof-trusses are the same as those in the store-house.

The wet-sand house is stated to be of sufficient capacity to hold a supply for the four winter months, the average consumption in those months being about 17 car-loads per month.

Sand-house Design for Lehigh Valley Railroad—A sand-house designed for the Lehigh Valley Railroad, shown in Figs. 181 and 182, represents a good combination of the principal requirements of a large sand-house, utilizing some of the distinctive elements of the sand-houses at Burlington, Ill., and at Columbus, O. The building is divided into a storage-house, 50 ft. × 16 ft., and a dry-sand house, 16 ft. × 18 ft. The entire building can be a frame structure, or the store-house can be a frame shed with a more substantially constructed dry-sand house. The method of operating the house is to shovel the sand from cars through the sides of the storage-shed into store. The sand is then wheeled, as required, to the sand-driers on the lower floor of the dry-sand tower. After drying and screening, the sand is thrown into a hopper and hoisted by a bucket elevator, operated by hand, to a dry-storage bin in the upper part of the tower. This bin is hopper-shaped, and allows sand to be spouted directly to the sand-box of an engine on either side of the tower. Small bins for the storage of coal used for the drying process are located between the sand-store and the tower. This style of sand-house is especially economical where large amounts of sand have to be handled. Where it is feasible, the location of the house at the end of the tail track of a coal trestle is desirable to decrease the labor of storing the wet sand.

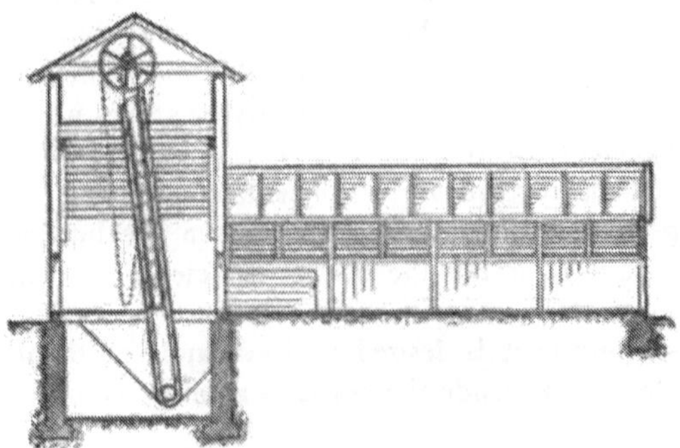

FIG. 181.—LONGITUDINAL SECTION.

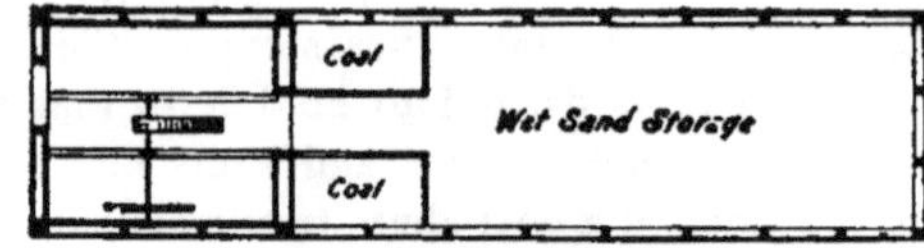

FIG. 182.—GROUND-PLAN.

Sand-house at Cressona, Pa., Philadelphia & Reading Railroad.—The sand-house of the Philadelphia & Reading Railroad, at Cressona, Pa., shown in a general way in Figs. 183 and 184, represents a method of drying sand by means of arched brick flues under the sand-pile, with fires at one end and connected at the other with a stack. The wet sand is dumped on the flues from overhead trestling, and the fires then started and maintained until the sand-pile has been thoroughly heated throughout. The flues are about 3 ft. wide and 40 ft. long. Alongside of each flue is a similarly built archway under the sand-pile, by means of which sand is drawn into wheelbarrows through openings in the arch, thus allowing the bulk of the sand in the pile to be drawn out without shovelling. The sand-pile is protected from the weather by a shed built over it.

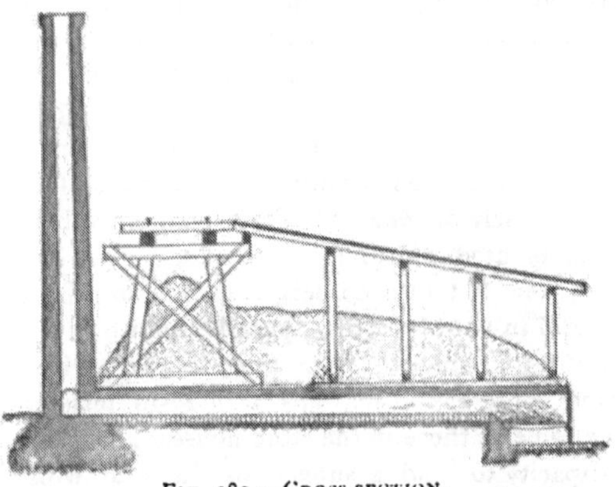

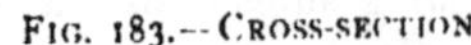

FIG. 183.—CROSS-SECTION.

FIG. 184.—FRONT ELEVATION.

Sand-drier at Connemaugh, Pa, Pennsylvania Railroad.—The sand-drier of the Pennsylvania Railroad, in use at Connemaugh, Pa., published in *Engineering*, June 29, 1877, and in the book "The Pennsylvania Railroad," by James Dredge, follows a system of drying sand with a wrought-iron cylinder, 2 ft. in diameter and 10 ft. 9½ in. long, inclosed in brickwork. The cylinder is covered with No. 9 sheet-iron for a length of 8 ft. 8½ in., and the remainder with wire netting of three meshes to the inch. This cylinder is mounted on a 2-in. square shaft and set at an angle over a furnace. At the upper end the shaft revolves in an ordinary bearing, and at the lower end in a bearing consisting of two cast-iron anti-friction rollers carried on a wrought-iron bracket, the shaft resting on a steel set-screw. The sand is fed into the upper end of the slowly revolving cylinder and, in descending, is exposed to the heat of the hot gases from the furnace. The sand is dry by the time it reaches the open wirework portion of the cylinder, and drops through the network to an inclined delivery chute.

Sand-house at Weatherly, Pa., Lehigh Valley Railroad.—The sand-house of the Lehigh Valley Railroad at Weatherly, Pa., is a very simple and substantial structure, in which the sand is dried in bulk by means of flues built under the floor of the house. The building is of stone, 20 ft. × 30 ft. out to out, and about 10 ft. high from ground to eaves. It is located at the end of the tail track of a coal-chute trestle, and the sand is dumped into store through hatches in the roof. Four transverse flues are built under the floor connecting with a large longitudinal flue, which opens into a chimney at each gable end of the house. The house is filled about once a month, and the fires maintained for about a week, sufficing to heat the entire contents. About three tons of refuse coal from the coal-dump is used per month. The storage capacity of the house is about 70 tons of sand. In the winter months about 35 tons are used monthly, which amount keeps 15 heavy grade engines supplied with sand.

This system is simple, very economical, and liable to run for years without repairs. It is claimed, however, that the sand is not dried uniformly throughout the pile, and that the sand nearest the flues is scorched and rendered lifeless. But the fact that this house has been operated successfully for years at the foot of a heavy grade on a much-travelled road would seem to justify the conclusion that the system of drying sand by flues underneath the sand pile is not to be considered an absolute failure. If the depth of the sand pile were reduced and the flues carried up through the pile, so as to distribute the heat more uniformly, better results could be expected.

Design for Sand-house, Lehigh Valley Railroad.—A design for a sand-house on the Lehigh Valley Railroad contemplated utilizing the general features embodied in the Weatherly sand-house of the same road, as described above, with the improvement of decreasing the depth of the sand overlying the flues during the heating process, so as to be able to reduce the degree of heat required and secure greater uniformity in drying. The sand after being dried in small batches on top of the flues is removed to a dry-sand storage bin on the ground-floor or elevated, as desired. The building has three compartments, one for wet sand, the middle one for the drying process, and the third one for the dry-sand storage bin. A small boiler connected with a steam-pipe coil system is provided to dry the air in the dry-sand store on damp days, and also to effect a preliminary drying of the wet sand. Two flues are located under the floor of the drying-room, fired at one end from the outside of the building, and connected with a stack.

Sand-house, at Washington, D. C., Pennsylvania Railroad.—The sand-house of the Pennsylvania Railroad at Washington, D. C., shown in Figs. 185 to 188, is a brick building, with wooden roof-trusses, and roofed with galvanized corrugated iron. The sand-house is combined with an oil-storage house in one building, the entire building being 20 ft. × 65 ft.; the part devoted to the sand-supply business is 30 ft. × 20 ft., to the oil-storage business 25 ft. × 20 ft., while the balance of the space is used for an office. There is a wet-sand storage room, 13 ft. 6 in. × 18 ft., and a sand-drying room, 14 ft. × 18 ft. The wet sand is shovelled from cars into the wet-sand store through openings on one side of the room. The walls of this room are tied together by iron rods, $\frac{3}{4}$ in. in diameter. A door leads from the wet-sand room to the sand-drying room. In the latter room there is, directly opposite the door from the wet-sand room, a sand-drying stove of the Pennsylvania Railroad standard. On the other side of the sand-drying room there is a hopper-shaped dry-sand bin with a screen over it for screening the sand as it is transferred from the sand-stove to the bin. The refuse and screenings drop to the floor between the bin and the stove, and have to be collected and wheeled out of the house. Enginemen enter the room by the door on the track side of the house, and draw the sand from a trap-door at the lower end of the dry-sand bin.

The foundations of the building are stone walls, 18 in. thick. The side walls are brick, 12 in. thick. The roof-trusses consist of 4-in. × 6-in. tie-beams; 4-in. × 6-in. principal rafters; 3-in. × 4-in. struts; $\frac{3}{4}$-in. diameter king-rod; and 3-in. × 5-in. purlins. The door between the sand-store and the drying-room is 3 ft. × 7 ft. 6 in. The outside entrance door is 3 ft. 6 in. × 7 ft. 6 in., with transom overhead. The windows are 3 ft. 5 in. × 6 ft. 2 in. The delivery openings for the sand in the side of the building are 3 ft. 6 in. × 6 ft. The dry-sand bin is 10 ft. × 7 ft. The screen is 4 ft. × 8 ft. There is a louvred ventilator at the peak of the roof for ventilation.

The balance of the building is used as an oil-storage house; it is described in the chapter on oil-storage houses, and illustrated in Figs. 201 to 204.

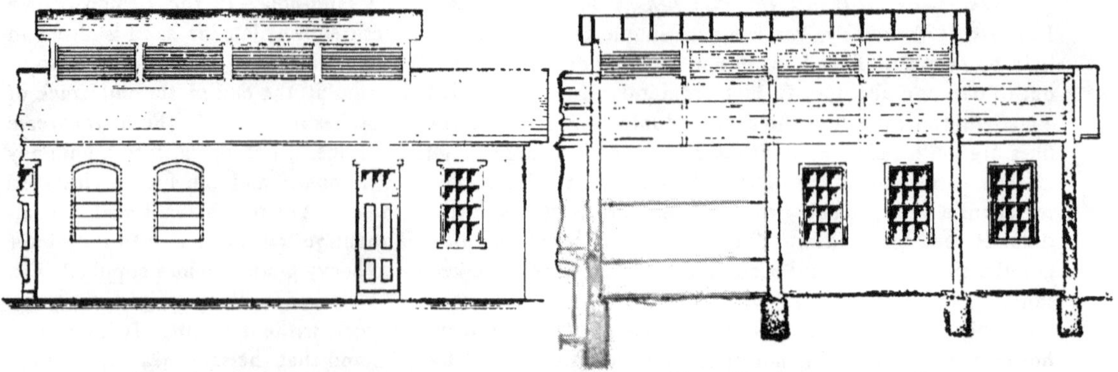

FIG. 185.—FRONT ELEVATION.

FIG. 186.—LONGITUDINAL SECTION.

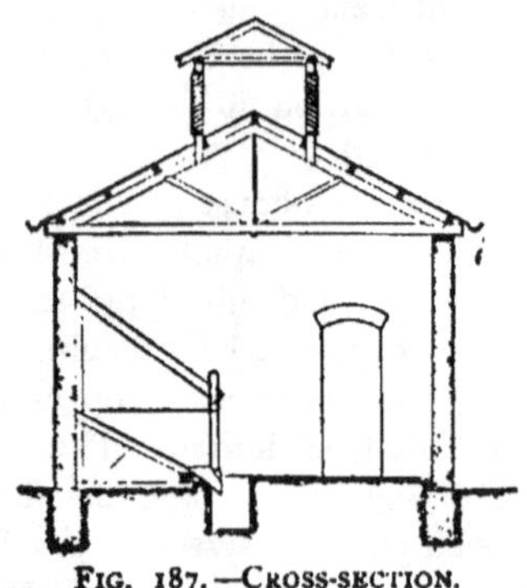

FIG. 187.—CROSS-SECTION.

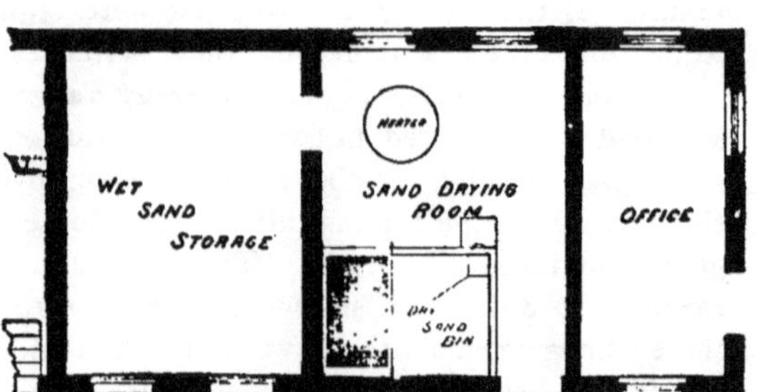

FIG. 188.—GROUND-PLAN.

CHAPTER XII.

OIL-STORAGE HOUSES.

OIL-STORAGE houses are required on railroads to store the oils employed to lubricate engines, cars, and shop machinery, or used in engine headlights, signal-lamps, switch-lamps, etc., or for lighting cars, station-buildings, and station-grounds. Oil-storage houses serve for the storage of the oils as received ready for use from oil works or dealers. The process of mixing the crude oils, where done by the railroad company, is conducted in so-called oil-mixing houses, which will be discussed separately. Storage-houses can be subdivided into general store-houses and supply-houses. In store-houses the oil is shipped from stock to different points along the line in barrels, iron drums, or large cans. In supply-houses provision is made for dealing out the current supply in small quantities, the oils being drawn either by a special attendant or directly by the enginemen, trainmen, shopmen, or roadmen, as required. While the above classification and division of oil-houses are correct, and, as a rule, clearly defined in practice, there are a large number of cases where the distinctive features of several of them are merged and contained in the same building.

Any structure or shed alongside a track offering space for the storage of barrels under cover will answer for a general store-house. A platform or skids for facilitating the handling of barrels to and from cars should be provided, and good ventilation is essential. It is also desirable to make proper provision (by suitable trestling or troughs inside the house), to allow oils to be transferred from damaged barrels to good ones, or to be drawn into iron drums or large cans for shipment over the road. The location of the structure and the question as to how far it should be made fire-proof, are entirely dependent on local circumstances and individual views in each case.

Oil-storage houses to be used as supply-houses for the current supply required in the vicinity call for a number of special features in their construction and operation, which, collectively, tend to make a good design. The oils are usually received in barrels, casks, or iron drums, which are either placed on a raised shelf or trestling, tapped and the oil drawn as required, or the contents are emptied at once into large iron tanks, from which the current supply is taken. The latter method is preferable where large amounts of oil are used.

In the first case the interior arrangements of the building are very simple, consisting of a raised shelf, bench-wall, or trestling for holding the barrels above the floor, with drip-boxes or drains underneath to catch any drippings from the faucets.

In case the oil is emptied into large tanks, suitable arrangements should be made for lifting the barrels on top of the tanks. The tanks should be set some distance above the level of the floor to allow oil to be drawn from them. It is, therefore, customary to put the tanks in a basement, the floor of which is sunk below the general yard level, with an upper story above it, from which the oils are dumped through holes in the floor into the tanks below. The barrels are either hoisted to the upper floor by suitable appliances, or rolled up an incline. This second floor is very useful to keep barrelled oil in excess of the tankage capacity of the house, and is also employed to store waste, tallow, and other similar supplies. Where a second floor is not desired, the barrels are hauled up skids with ropes on to runways of old iron rails on top of the tanks, and the oil discharged. When the amount of oil used is small, and shipments are made into store only at long intervals, the erection of a two-story building is not advisable, unless the additional storage space is desired.

Some oils, especially those required for lighting purposes and lubricating car-journals, where used in large amounts, are usually received in tank-cars, in which case large storage-tanks are placed in a cellar below or to one side of the building. The oil can thus be discharged from the tank-cars into the storage-tanks by gravity through a pipe with proper goose-neck, hose, and valve connections. It is then usually pumped, as required, into a smaller set of tanks, called supply-tanks, appropriately located in the main building with the tanks for barrelled oil. The tank cars could be run up an incline and the oil discharged directly into the regular supply-tanks; but the former method has the advantage of keeping the bulk of the stock in a separate, closed compartment, and does not require unusually large supply tanks inside the main building.

The location of an oil-storage house for dealing out the current supply of oil should be preferably alongside a track leading to or from an engine-house, coaling or water system, or facing any track that engines usually take when coming in from or preparing to start out on a run, so that they need not go out of their way to get their supply of oil. As a rule, the question of supplying oil promptly to engines will control the location, although in certain cases the wants of the car service or shop department will have preference.

Where the circumstances warrant, it is desirable to have a special attendant to look after the house and deal out the supplies, thus obviating many objectionable features, which would be brought into prominence in case any one of the company's employés could enter and draw oil at will. Where a special attendant is employed, the men pass their cans over a railing or through a small window, and the oil, waste, tallow, and other supplies they may require is handed to them. It is customary for the day man to draw the night supply into separate cans and set them in a small inclosure or on a shelf outside of the main building or immediately inside the entrance, unless the business is heavy enough to warrant a special night attendant.

In large yards or shop systems, small branch oil-shanties are established at different points for the convenience of car-inspectors and shop-hands, the supply being sent from the main oil-house in large cans or drums. These buildings are usually small frame structures, sheathed and roofed with corrugated iron. The interior is fitted up with shelves or trestles for the oil-cans, bins for holding waste, and racks, pigeon-holes, and shelves for miscellaneous supplies and car inspectors' tools.

In cold weather the oils in a supply-house must be heated, to render them sufficiently fluid to run properly in discharging from barrels into the supply-tanks, or in drawing oils. Where the stock carried in the house is very small, a stove is used, either in the same space, or in an adjoining room, the partition wall being either perforated or else cut away back of the stove, and the opening closed with wire netting or iron bars. Where the stock is large, and the danger and loss to neighboring structures in case of a fire would be considerable, steam-heat should be introduced, the steam being supplied from a special boiler, located in an annex to the building, or in a separate building, or supplied from stationary boilers in use in the vicinity. Where the oil is dumped from a second floor, it is customary to have steam-coils on that side of the room along which the barrels are placed before being emptied, while barrels not to be used immediately are kept on the cool side of the room. Steam-coils arranged along the walls back of the supply-tanks serve to heat the contents of the latter. As different oils require varying degrees of heat, it is best to put steam-coils mainly back of the tanks with the heavy oils, the general temperature of the room or a smaller number of coils sufficing to keep the lighter oils at the proper temperature.

The following general remarks apply to all classes of oil-houses. It is essential to keep the main stock, so far as possible, isolated from the room where the men enter to draw supplies. The most scrupulous cleanliness is requisite to reduce the danger from fire, and the fire service provisions should be the best obtainable. No open lights should be allowed in the building; the lighting should be done by electricity, if feasible, or by lamps with reflectors, arranged in recesses in the outside wall, the recess being closed on the inside of the house with a fixed glass panel and on the outside with a small door. A fireproof construction of the building is desirable at all important locations.

The following descriptions of oil-storage houses in actual use will be of value in connection with the above general remarks on the subject.

Frame Oil and Waste Storage Shed at Perth Amboy, N. J., Lehigh Valley Railroad.—In connection with a large oil-mixing plant at Perth Amboy, N. J., the Lehigh Valley Railroad has a frame oil and waste storage shed, shown in Fig. 189, which can serve as an illustration of a cheap storage shed.

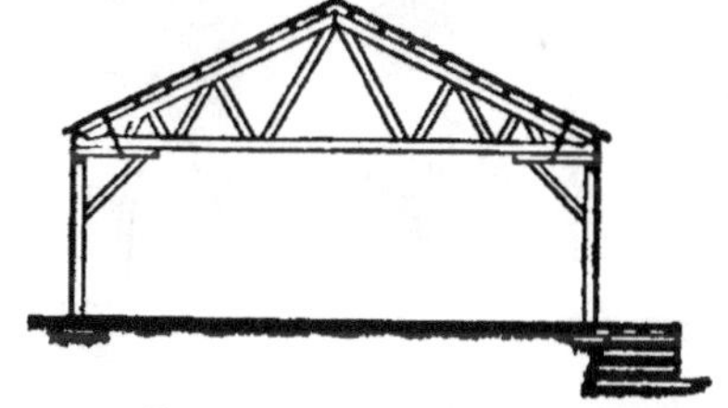

FIG. 189.—CROSS-SECTION.

The building is a one-story frame structure, 100 ft. × 38 ft., divided into two rooms, the one for storage of oils in barrels, and the other for storage of waste in bales. A loading platform runs along a track on one side of the house. The floor consists of 2-in. plank on mud-sills. The building is sheathed and roofed with corrugated galvanized iron. The roof-trusses are spaced 10 ft. centres. The height from floor to truss is 12 ft. in clear.

The principal timbers used are as follows: sills, 6 in. × 8 in., on blocking; posts, 6 in. × 8 in.; plates, 6 in. × 8 in.; tie-beams, two pieces, 3 in. × 10 in.; principal rafters, two pieces, 3 in. × 10 in.; truss-braces, 2 in. × 10 in. and 2 in. × 8 in.; purlins, 3 in. × 6 in.; roof-sheathing, 1-in. rough boards; corbels, 6 in. × 8 in.; knee-braces, 6 in. × 6 in.; studding, 2 in. × 4 in.

Brick Oil-house at Perth Amboy, N. J., Lehigh Valley Railroad.—The brick oil-house of the Lehigh Valley Railroad at Perth Amboy, N. J., shown in Figs. 190 and 191, is a small building with an arched brick roof covered with slate, forming a vault, as it were, in which oil is stored. The building is 20 ft. wide outside, 17 ft. 6 in. long, and 16 ft. 3 in. high from the ground to the eaves. The side walls and arch forming the roof are 21 in. thick. The building has two stories, the lower one being 9 ft. high, and the upper one 8 ft. 6 in. high at the soffit of the arch. The upper floor is carried by three 10-in. I-beams, supported at the centre by one 10-in. I-beam. The lower story has space for seven oil-tanks, each 4 ft. in diameter and 6 ft. high, set on brick benches. There is a cast-iron box in the upper floor over each tank with a screen and pipe leading to the tank underneath. Cast-iron drip-boxes are placed under the faucets in front of each tank to catch any drippings. Three small steam coils runs along the wall back of the tanks on one side of the house, which keep the temperature, as a rule, at about 60 degrees Fahr. The heavy oils, such as machine-oil and valve-oil, are

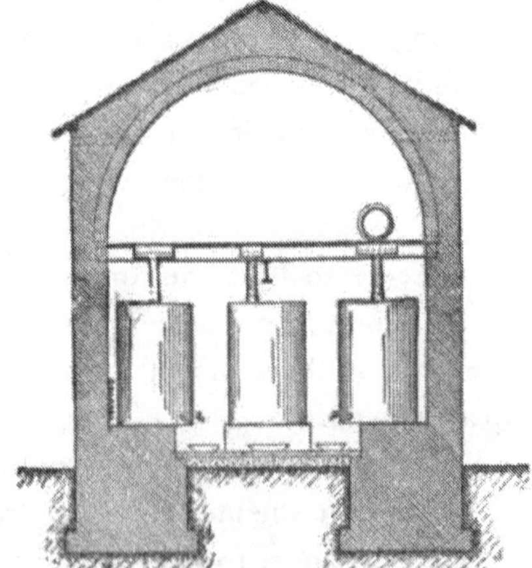

FIG. 190.—CROSS-SECTION.

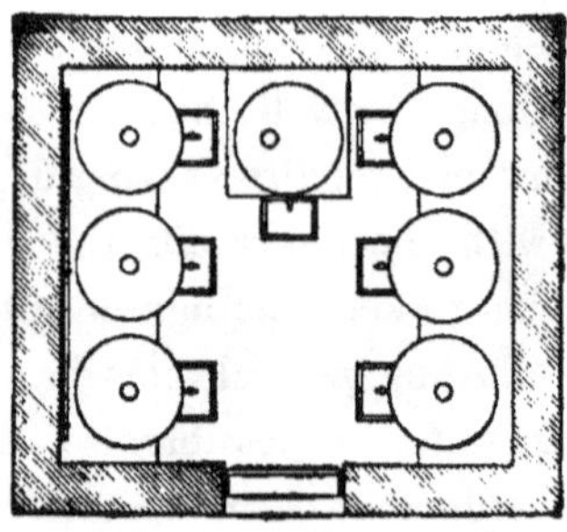

FIG. 191.—GROUND-PLAN.

placed in the tanks nearest the steam coils, while the lighter oils, as signal and headlight oil, are placed in the tanks on the opposite side of the house. The lower story is accessible through an iron door, so

FIG. 192.—FRONT ELEVATION.

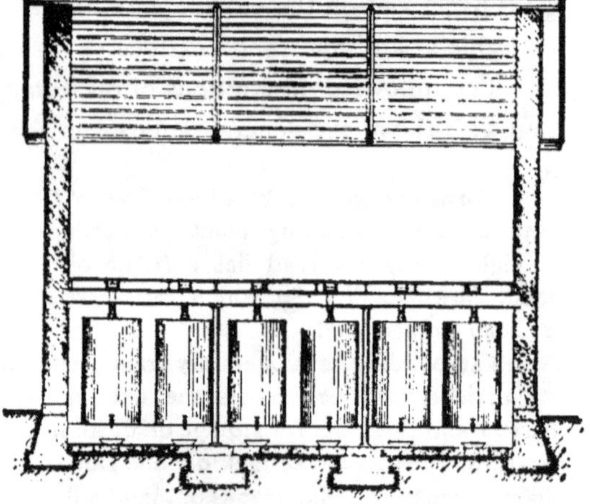

FIG 193.—LONGITUDINAL SECTION.

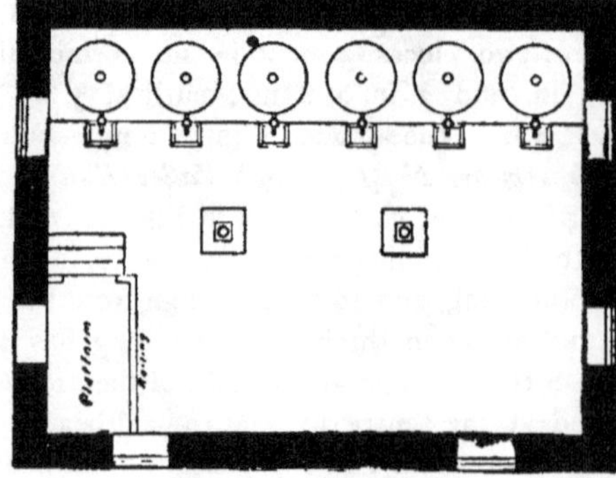

FIG. 194.—GROUND-PLAN.

as to allow oils to be drawn from the tanks into cans and buckets. The upper floor is reached by an inclined trestling on the outside of the house, up which barrels of oil arriving on cars are rolled, and the oil then dumped through the cast-iron boxes in the upper floor into the tanks below. A simple hoisting apparatus could be easily designed to hoist the barrels to the upper story, where the ground-space available does not allow an incline to be built. In the operation of this house the daily supply of oils is drawn by an attendant and placed on a small covered platform in front of the house, from where the enginemen take their supplies as needed.

The house should be a little longer for a large road, and a simple hoisting contrivance would prove cheaper than a special incline. This oil-storage house or vault can be considered a very good design in case a small amount of oil is to be stored in a permanent fire-proof structure.

Stone Oil and Waste House at Lehighton, Pa., Lehigh Valley Railroad.—The oil-house of the Lehigh Valley Railroad at Lehighton, Pa., shown in Figs. 192 to 194, designed by Mr. J. I. Kinsey, Master Mechanic, L. V. R. R., is a substantial two-story stone building with wooden roof covered with slate, 40 × 30 ft., and 21 ft. from the ground to the eaves. The walls are stone, 24 in. thick. The principal timbers are as follows: tie-beams, 6 in. × 12 in.; rafters, 6 in. × 8 in.; braces, 6 in. × 8 in.; tie-rods, 1 in. diameter; roof sheathed with 1½ in. boards. The basement floor is 3 ft. below the level of the track, and is flagged with stone. The second floor consists of cast-iron plates on 9-in. wrought-iron I-beams, the latter supported at the centre by a 12-in. wrought-iron I-beam, resting on two cast-iron columns. There are five windows in the first floor and six in the second one. Each window consists of twenty 8-in. × 12-in. lights. The window-sills and lintels are cast-iron. The enginemen enter the basement through a door facing the track, and receive their oil supply from an attendant, or draw it from the large storage tanks. A light trestle walk leads from a raised platform next to the track up an incline to a 6 ft. 6 in. double door in the upper story, facilitating the handling of materials from cars to the upper floor. Oil is shipped to the house in barrels ready for use. It is dumped from the upper story through openings in the cast-iron floor into the large iron storage tanks in the basement. The upper floor is also used for storing waste. A wooden chute for the delivery of waste leads from the upper story to the basement.

Brick Oil-house at West Philadelphia, Pa., Pennsylvania Railroad.—The oil-storage house at the West Philadelphia shops of the Pennsylvania Railroad, designed and built by Mr. Joseph M. Wilson, plans and descriptions of which were published in the "Journal of the Franklin Institute," volume 62, page 318, is a fireproof building with stone foundations and basement, brick upper story, and iron roof, 30 ft. × 24 ft. outside, with a boiler-house annex, 13 ft. × 13 ft. 6 in. The building is located at the rear of the roundhouse, and is intended for the storage of oil used in the shops. There is a platform in front of the building, 6 ft. × 14 ft., adjacent to a track, to facilitate the handling of material.

The main building is divided into a first floor and a basement, the latter having a door under the front platform wide enough to admit oil-barrels. The foundations and walls, up to the level of the first floor, are of stone finished off with a stone belt course, the front platform being of stone also. Above the first floor the walls are of brick, 9 in. thick, with pilasters 13 in. The basement floor is of brick laid in cement and having drainage into a sewer. On each side of a passage-way, 7 ft. wide, low platforms of brick are built on flat brick arches for the support of oil-tanks. The first floor is supported through the centre by two cast-iron columns sustaining wrought-iron I-beams, from which spring flat brick arches. The cast columns are of ½-in. metal, 3 in. external diameter at the top and 4 in. at the bottom, and rest upon firm stone foundations. The wrought-iron I-beams are 9 in. deep, weighing 89 pounds to the yard, and they are connected together, and also to 4-in. angle-irons on the end walls, at distances of 3 ft. apart in their lengths, by iron rods 1 in. in diameter, these rods taking and counteracting the thrust of the brick arches which spring from the I-beams and angle-irons. On top the arches are levelled off with concrete and paved with brick, thus forming the first floor.

Brick piers supporting stone slabs are built on the first floor for the support of oil-tanks, the top surface of stone being 2 ft. above the floor. The basement is lighted by openings in the crown of each arch of the ceiling filled with hammered glass 1 in. thick. The first floor has ample light from seven windows, the frames and sash of which are of cast-iron, and outside shutters of wrought-iron. The doors are of wrought-iron, with frames of cast-iron. The roof is a simple wrought-iron truss, the rafter being 3½ × 3½ in. T-iron, the ridge-pole of the same, and the purlins of 3 in. angle-iron. A covering of corrugated galvanized iron, with two large ventilators to carry off the disagreeable odors of the oil, completes the building.

To provide light at night and to prevent taking any fire into the oil-rooms, four small windows, one light each, 18 in. square, of heavy glass set permanently into an iron frame, are built into the wall between the main portion of the building and the boiler-room, and a gas-burner is placed before each window on the boiler-room side, so as to shine into the main building when lighted. Vertical pieces of 4-in. cast-iron pipe are built in the arches of the first floor over openings in each tank of the basement, to allow basement tanks to be easily filled from the oil-room above, and also to afford facilities for the introduction of pumps to transfer the oil from these tanks to tanks on the first floor.

The boiler-room is provided with a small vertical boiler, working at a low pressure (only the ordinary pressure in the service water-pipes) and having coils of steam-pipe in the basement and on first floor for warming in winter.

The basement tanks are rectangular in form, with an inclined bottom, being so made that any sediment may collect in front and be easily removed; when necessary, through an opening provided for the purpose. There are three of these tanks on one side and four on the other, the large tanks holding 1739 gals., one smaller one 1618 gals., and the remaining three 1130 gals. each. There are four large cylindrical tanks of 642 gals. each, and three smaller tanks of 361 gals. each. The total capacity of tanks is 13,867 gals., or 385½ bbls. The tanks are constructed of boiler-iron.

The building is so designed that a mixing apparatus, if desired, could be put on the first floor.

Brick Oil and Waste House, Mexican Central Railroad.—The brick oil and waste house of the Mexican Central Railroad, the design for which was furnished by Mr. F. W. Johnstone, Superintendent, Mexican Central Railroad, shown in Figs. 195 and 196, illustrates a novel departure from the customary methods in the United States of placing the oil-tanks in a closed building. In this case the oil-tanks are located under a small projecting roof outside of a brick building. Pipes lead from the foot of the tanks into the interior of the building, by means of which the oil is drawn as required.

The structure is a low brick building, 18 ft. 6 in. × 19 ft., and 18 ft. 3 in. high inside from floor to ceiling-joists. In the shed annex, which is 18 ft. 6 in. × 7 ft., there are seven oil-tanks, each 6 ft. 6 in. in diameter and 10 ft. high, with pipes leading into the main building, as mentioned above. Alongside the oil-shed annex, there is a raised platform, 5 ft. 9 in. wide, elevated 4 ft. above the top of the adjacent track. The oil is shipped to the house in barrels on cars. The barrels are unloaded on the platform and drawn up to the top of the tanks by means of skids and ropes. Two iron rails on top of the tanks form a runway, on which the barrels are rolled into position and allowed to drain into the proper tanks below. The waste is stored inside the house.

Mr. Johnstone states that this style of oil and waste house meets the requirements on the Mexican Central Railroad very satisfactorily, so that it would seem that for Southern climates the novel features introduced in this design would prove advantageous.

FIG. 195.—END ELEVATION.

FIG. 196.—CROSS-SECTION.

Oil-house at Denver, Col., Union Pacific Railway.—The oil-house of the Union Pacific Railway connected with the new shop system at Denver, Col., is 27 ft. × 38 ft. in size, with a basement and ground-floor. The ground-floor is on a level with the loading and unloading platform alongside of a track. There are six upright tanks for the storage of oil in the basement. Oil shipped in bulk in tank-cars is drawn from the cars into spouts and funnels at the face of the platform, and descends from there by gravity into the storage-tanks. Barrelled oil is emptied into the storage-tanks through openings in the main floor. The oil, as it is required, is pumped from the storage-tanks up to the supply-tanks on the ground-floor of the building.

Frame Oil-storage and Car-inspector's House at Perth Amboy, N. J., Lehigh Valley Railroad.—The oil-storage and car-inspector's house of the Lehigh Valley Railroad at Perth Amboy, N. J., shown in Figs. 197 and 198, serves as an example of a large number of similar structures on this road, varying in size according to local requirements. The one illustrated is 19 ft. 8 in. × 29 ft. 8 in., other sizes in use being 18 ft. × 12 ft. and 16 ft. × 24 ft.

These buildings are frame structures sheathed and roofed with galvanized corrugated iron, No. 20 gauge. The interior is usually divided by a partition into two rooms, one for the storage of oils in barrels or small iron tanks, the other for sundry supplies and tools in connection with car-inspecting.

The principal timbers used are as follows: sills, 6 in. × 10 in., upright; rafters, 2½ in. × 6 in., spaced 18 in.; floor-joists, 3 in. × 10 in., spanning 19 ft.; plate, 6 in. × 4 in., upright; side sheathing, 2-in. boards, nailed to plate and sill without any studding; floor, 2-in. plank. Height of frame from top of floor to top of plate, 11 ft.

FIG. 197.—END ELEVATION.

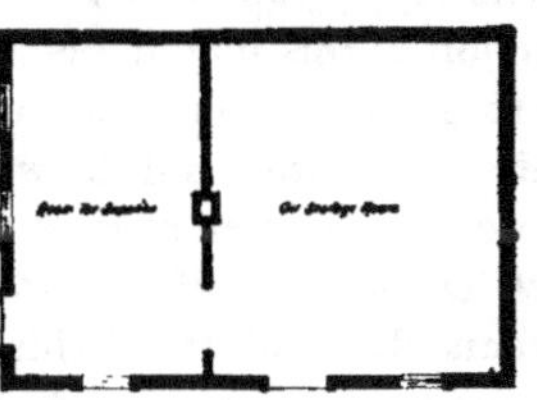

FIG. 198.—GROUND-PLAN.

Frame Oil-storage and Car-inspector's House at Packerton, Pa., Lehigh Valley Railroad.—The frame oil-storage and car-inspector's house of the Lehigh Valley Railroad at Packerton, Pa., shown in Figs. 199 and 200, is a one-story frame building with loft, 83 ft. × 20 ft., sheathed and roofed with galvanized corrugated iron, No. 20 gauge. The interior is divided into four rooms, namely, the oil-room proper, a room for storage of brasses and sundry car supplies, a room for bolts, chains, iron, etc., and a

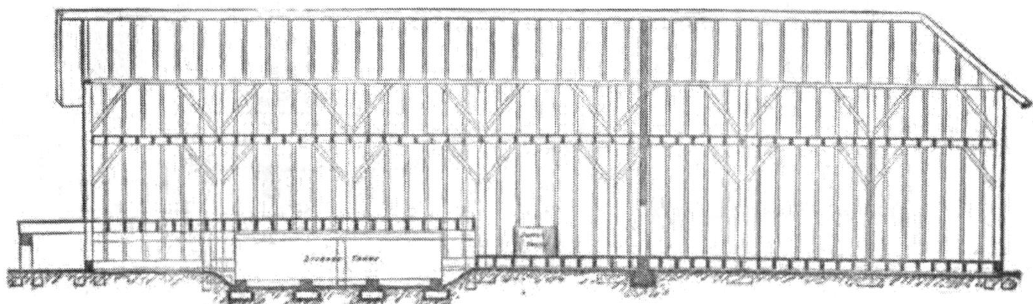

FIG. 199.—LONGITUDINAL SECTION.

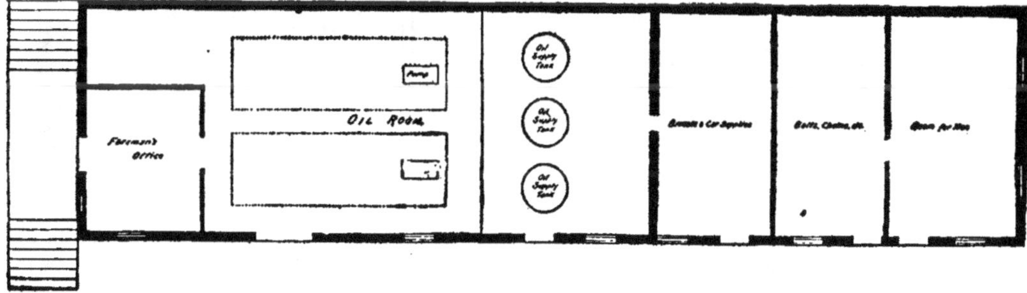

FIG. 200.—GROUND-PLAN.

room for the use of the men. The partition between the oil-room and the room for car supplies is of brick, and extends all the way to the roof, thus forming a fire-wall. All the other partitions are of wood. At one end of the oil-room the floor is raised to form a platform inside of the house level with the loading platform in front of the house, which is the same height above the track as a car floor. Oil arriving in bulk in tank-cars is discharged, through proper fixtures and piping, into two large iron storage-tanks in a basement or cellar underneath the platform in the oil-room. Oil arriving in barrels is dumped through openings in the floor into the storage-tanks below. On top of the platform are two rotary pumps, with which the oil can be transferred from the storage-tanks to three supply-tanks set in the lower part of the room. These supply-tanks or mixing-tubs are of iron, 30 in. high × 48 in. diameter, and are used to hold lubricating-oil for cars, and for mixing oil and waste for packing car-journals. Ranged around the walls are a number of pigeon-holes, each about 18 in. × 26 in., for the storage of oil and waste buckets, jacks, wrenches, tools, etc. All these tools and appliances are numbered, and each car-inspector or greaser has his own kit and place to keep it on the shelves. In one corner of the oil-room a 10-ft. × 12-ft. space is partitioned off for a foreman's office, on one side of which is the reporting window for men to report when going to or leaving the work. The supply-rooms and room for the men are suitably fitted with shelves, lockers, benches, etc. The loft of this building is used for the storage of waste in bales. There is an iron door in the fire-wall to allow communication between the two ends of the loft, and there is a small iron door down-stairs in the brick wall between the oil-room and the room for car supplies, to allow supplies to be passed out to the men as they come into the oil-room to get their tools or fill their buckets.

Brick Oil-house at Washington, D. C., Pennsylvania Railroad.—The oil-storage house of the Pennsylvania Railroad at Washington, D. C., shown in Figs. 201 to 204, is a brick building, with wooden roof-trusses, and roofed with galvanized corrugated iron. The oil-house is combined with a sand-house in one building, the entire building being 20 ft. × 65 ft.; the part devoted to the oil-

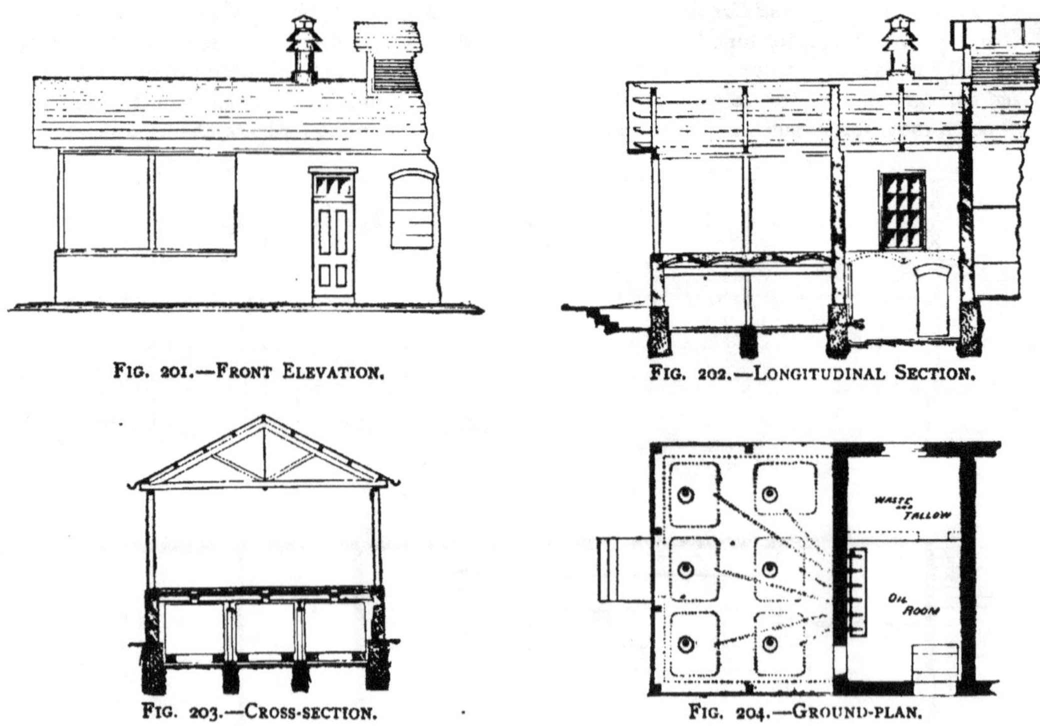

FIG. 201.—FRONT ELEVATION.

FIG. 202.—LONGITUDINAL SECTION.

FIG. 203.—CROSS-SECTION.

FIG. 204.—GROUND-PLAN.

storage business is 25 ft. × 20 ft., to the sand business 30 ft. × 20 ft., while the balance of the space is used for an office. There is an oil-vault, 14 ft. × 18 ft., in a basement floor with six tanks in it, each tank being 5 ft. × 4 ft. × 4 ft. deep. The floor of this basement is 18 in. below the yard level.

Above this oil-vault is a dumping-room for discharging oil from barrels through traps in the floor into the tanks in the basement. The floor in this room is 4 ft. 3 in. above the yard level, or 5 ft. 9 in. above the basement floor. The oil-vault is entered through a 5-ft. door at the end of the house, with steps leading down to it on the outside of the building. The side of the dumping-room next to the oil-room is closed by a brick wall, and the end of the room is closed by galvanized corrugated iron on studding. The front and rear of the dumping-room are closed by sliding-doors, covered by galvanized sheet-iron, so that barrels can be received or delivered from or to cars or the yard. Next to the oil-vault there is an oil-room, 9 ft. 6 in. × 11 ft., for drawing the oil. The floor of this room is 13½ in. lower than the floor of the oil-vault. Pipes lead from the six tanks in the oil-vault to the oil-room, so arranged that the oil runs by gravity. The ends of these pipes are closed by faucets, and oil is drawn into cans or buckets, as required. There is a gauge-glass in the oil-room for each pipe, so that the height of the oil in each tank can be seen in the oil-room. The oil-vault and the oil room are connected by a small iron door. The oil-room is reached from a door on the front of the house with steps leading down to the floor of the room inside of the house. Back of the oil-room is a waste and tallow room, 6 ft. × 9 ft. 6 in. The oil-vault and tallow-room are vaulted over with flat brick arches carried by I-beams. The floors are made of cement.

The foundations of the building are stone walls, 18 in. thick. The side walls are brick, 12 in. thick. The roof-trusses consist of 4-in. × 6-in. tie-beams; 4-in. × 6-in. principal rafters; 3-in. × 4-in. struts; ¾-in. diameter king-rod; and 3-in. × 5-in. purlins. The entrance-door to the oil-vault is 5 ft. wide × 4 ft. 8 in. high. The door between the oil-vault and the oil-room and the door leading into the tallow-room from the oil-room are 2 ft. 5 in. wide × 5 ft. high. The window over the waste-room, which serves to light up the oil-room, is 3 ft. 5 in. × 6 ft. 2 in.

The balance of the building, that is used as a sand-house, is described in the chapter on sand-houses, and illustrated in Figs. 185 to 188.

Brick Oil-house at Jersey City, N. J., Pennsylvania Railroad.—The oil and waste storage-house of the Pennsylvania Railroad at Jersey City, N. J., shown in Figs. 205 to 209, is a brick building, 53 ft. × 20 ft., with wooden roof covered with slate. The interior is divided by brick partition-walls into a lamp-room, 10 ft. × 18 ft.; a waste-room, 10 ft. × 18 ft.; an oil-room for drawing the oil, 14 ft. 4 in. × 18 ft.; and an oil-platform or discharging-room, 15 ft. × 18 ft., with an oil-vault of the same size below it. The floor of the oil-vault is 18 in. below the yard level, and the floor of the oil-room is 13½ in. lower than the floor of the oil-vault. The floors of the waste and lamp rooms are at the yard level. The floor of the discharging-room over the oil-vault is 4 ft. 6 in. above the yard level. There are six tanks in the oil-vault, which are filled with oil from barrels through traps in the floor of the oil-discharging room. The oil-vault is entered through a wide door in the end of the building, with steps leading down to it on the outside of the building. A small iron door connects the oil-vault with the oil-room. Separate pipes lead from each tank in the oil-vault to the oil-room, where faucets, glass gauge-tubes, and drip-boxes are provided, the same as shown in Figs. 202 and 204 for the oil-house of the same railroad at Washington, D. C. The oil-room is entered by a door on the front of the house, with steps leading down inside of the house. The end of the oil-discharging room is closed by galvanized corrugated iron on studding, while the front and rear of the room are closed by sliding-doors, hung on different rails so as to slide past each other. Barrels are handled through these doors to or from cars or the yard.

The foundations of the building are stone walls 18 in. thick. The side walls are brick, 12 in. thick. The partition walls are brick, 8 in. thick. The roof-purlins are 3 in. × 8 in., covered with 1-in. boards and slates. The corner and door posts of the framed sides of the oil-discharging room are 6 in. × 6 in., and the studs 3 in. × 6 in. The oil-vault is vaulted with 4-in. flat brick arches resting on iron I-beams and cast-iron columns at the centre of the room. All the floors throughout the building are made of cement. The entrance door to the oil-vault is 5 ft. 6 in. wide × 4 ft. 6 in. high. The doors leading into the oil, waste, and lamp rooms are 3 ft. 6 in. × 7 ft. 9 in., with transom-lights overhead. The windows have two sash, each 6 lights 12 in. × 12 in. The window-sills on the outside of the building and the window aprons on the inside of the window are of cast-iron. The door and window lintels consist of three pieces of oak, each 4 in. × 8 in. Ventilation is secured over the oil, waste, and lamp rooms by round, No. 22 gauge, galvanized sheet-iron ventilators at the peak of the roof, one over each room.

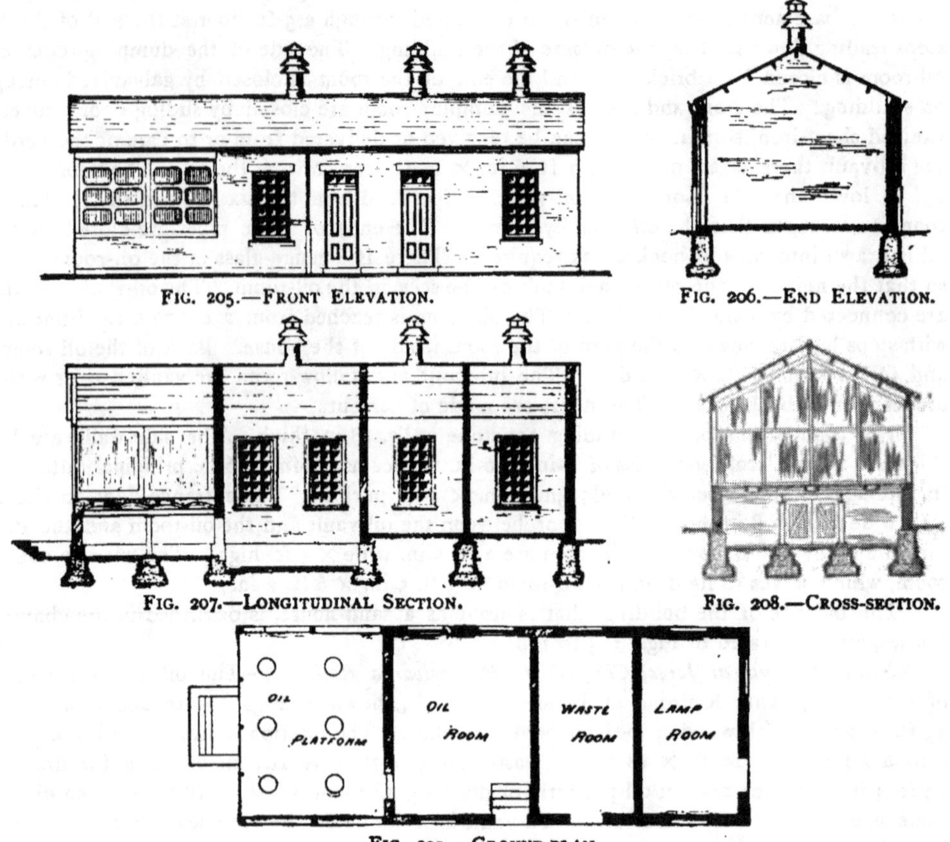

FIG. 205.—FRONT ELEVATION.

FIG. 206.—END ELEVATION.

FIG. 207.—LONGITUDINAL SECTION.

FIG. 208.—CROSS-SECTION.

FIG. 209.—GROUND-PLAN.

Brick Oil-storage House at Western Avenue, Chicago, Ill., Chicago, Burlington & Quincy Railroad. —The oil-storage house of the Chicago, Burlington & Quincy Railroad at Western Avenue, Chicago, Ill., shown in Figs. 210 to 213, prepared from data kindly furnished by Mr. Wm. Forsyth, Mechani-

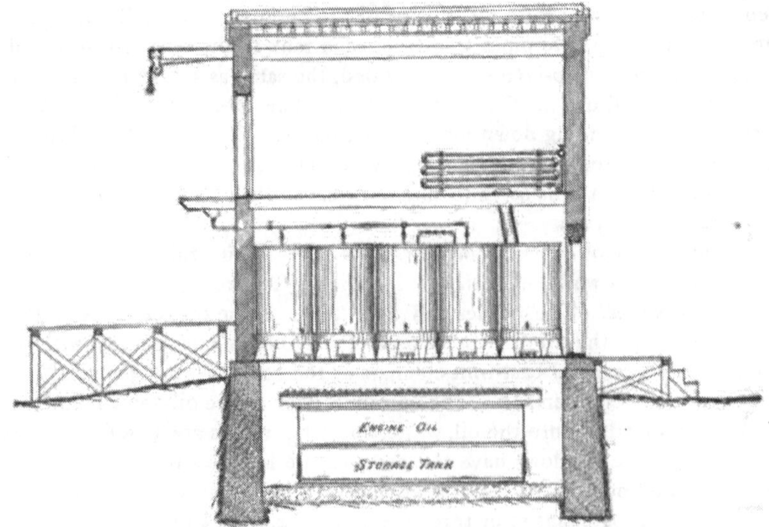

FIG. 210.—LONGITUDINAL SECTION.

cal Engineer, C., B. & Q. R. R., is a two-story brick structure, 20 ft. 8 in. × 19 ft. 4 in., with cellar. The structure is fireproof throughout. The foundations are stone walls. The floor-beams, roof-purlins, and rafters are iron T-beams, and the steps, railings, floor-plates, doors, door-frames,

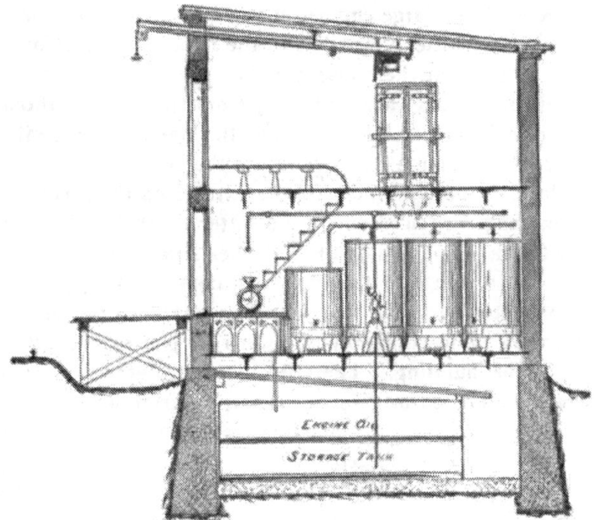

FIG. 211.—CROSS-SECTION.

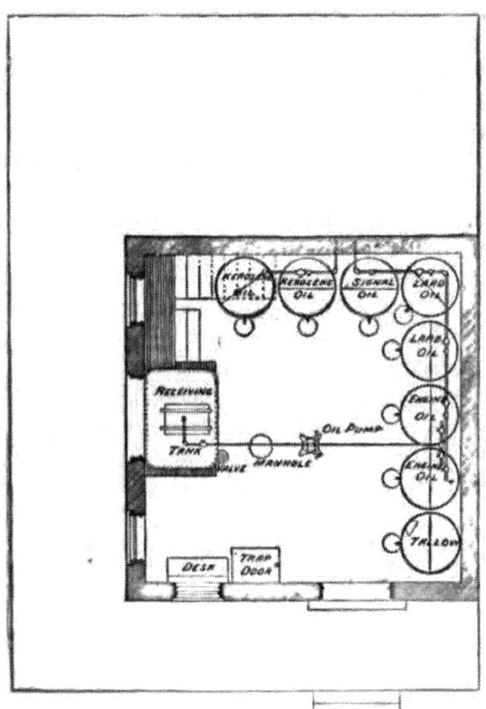

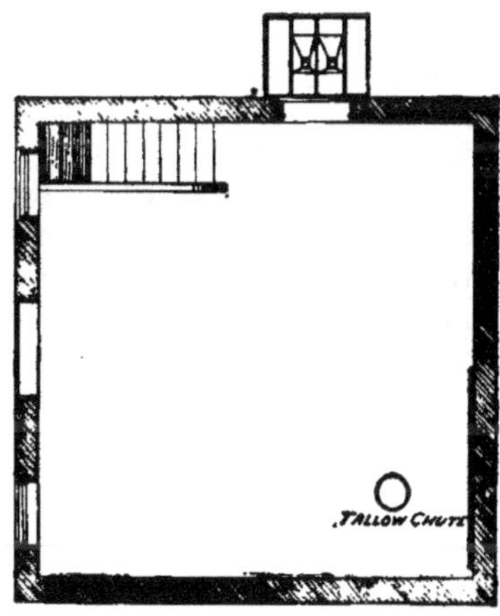

FIG. 212.—GROUND-PLAN.

FIG. 213.—SECOND-FLOOR PLAN.

window-frames, sills, lintels, and tank-stands are of iron. The roofing material is cement and gravel. The floor of the cellar is concrete. The platforms surrounding the building are of timber.

In the cellar there is a square iron tank for the storage of engine-oil, 13 ft. × 14 ft. × 4 ft. 4 in. deep, with a capacity of 9000 gallons. On the ground-floor there are eight supply-tanks, 3 ft. 2 in.

in diameter and 4 ft. 10 in. deep, each with a capacity of 270 gallons. The supply-tanks are used as follows: two for kerosene-oil, one for signal-oil, two for lard-oil, two for engine-oil, and one for tallow. There is at the entrance-door on this floor, situated inside of the house, a square sheet-iron receiving-tank, 5 ft. 3 in. × 4 ft. × 24 in. deep, covered with a grating of iron slats, and connected by a pipe, closed by a stem gauge-valve, with the large engine-oil storage-tank in the cellar. The top of the slats over this receiving-tank is level with the door-sill and the floor of the platform outside of the house, so that barrels of engine-oil received at the house can be rolled from the outside platform on to the receiving-tank, dumped, and then rolled back and away from the house without taking up floor-space inside the building. This receiving-tank serves to gauge the amount of the oil before it is discharged through the pipe mentioned into the large storage-tank in the cellar. The second floor is reached by iron steps from the lower floor. There are no tanks or fixtures on the second floor. There is a hole in the floor over the tallow-tank with a slide to the latter, so that tallow can be slid down to the tallow-tank from the upper floor. On one side of the upper floor is a large door leading to a projecting platform outside of the house with two troughs in it, connected by pipes with the supply-tanks. One of these troughs is connected with the two kerosene supply-tanks, the other trough connects with the signal-oil, lard-oil, and engine-oil supply-tanks. This platform is 4 ft. 4 in. wide, and projects 3 ft. 4 in. beyond the face of the building. There is a beam projecting out under the roof over this platform, with hoisting gearing attached to it for raising or lowering barrels. There is another door on another side of this room with overhead hoisting-tackle to enable barrels to be hoisted to the upper story and stored prior to being discharged.

The operation of the house is as follows: All oils are received at the house in barrels, ready for use. Engine-oil, which is used in very large quantities, is dumped from the barrels through the receiving-tank into the large storage-tank in the cellar. From here it is pumped by the hand-pump, situated at the centre of the first floor, to the two engine-oil supply-tanks, from which it is drawn, as required, into cans or buckets. In case engine-oil is to be shipped out of the house in barrels, the oil is pumped from the storage-tank in the cellar by the hand-pump through the pipe, shown in Figs. 211 and 212, ending 3 ft. 6 in. above the receiving-tank, which pipe has a short piece of hose attached to it for filling barrels placed on the grating over the receiving-tank. In case of an overflow or leakage the oil is caught in the receiving-tank and returned to the storage-tank in the cellar. The engine-oil supply-tanks can also be filled from the upper floor by means of the projecting trough platform, mentioned above. The kerosene-oil supply-tanks are filled from barrels dumped in the trough on the projecting platform of the upper floor. No other class of oil is run through this trough, as the kerosene-oil would be injured by any remnants of another oil being mixed with it. Signal-oil and lard-oil are dumped into the second trough on the projecting platform and run through the pipes, previously mentioned, to the corresponding supply-tanks. The tallow-tank is charged through the tallow-slide opening in the upper floor, as above explained.

The clear height of the cellar is 6 ft. 3½ in., of the first floor 9 ft., and of the second floor 7 ft. 6 in. at the lowest point. For heating purposes, there are on the first floor 110 lineal ft. of 1¼-in. piping, located back of the engine-oil and tallow tanks, the general heat of the room sufficing to heat the oils in the other tanks. On the second floor there are 55 lineal ft. of 1¼-in. piping located on the wall next to the tallow-slide.

CHAPTER XIII.

OIL-MIXING HOUSES.

OIL-MIXING houses on railroads serve for the process of mixing oils, where done by the railroad company, in place of buying the mixed oils used for illuminating, signaling, and lubricating purposes from special manufacturers of those articles. Oil-storage houses, discussed in the previous chapter, serve for the storage of oils as received ready for use from oil-mixing works or from dealers. In certain cases the distinctive features of oil-mixing houses and oil-storage houses are merged and provision made under one roof for both branches of the oil-supply service.

Oil-mixing houses have not been very extensively used on American railroads, although a few of the older roads have had small houses for mixing certain classes of oils in operation for a great many years. The Pennsylvania has maintained an oil-mixing plant at Altoona, Pa., for about twenty-five years, and has at present an oil-mixing house on each of its grand divisions. The Baltimore & Ohio operated a plant at their Mount Clare shops, Baltimore, Md., for nearly twenty years, until the latter part of the year 1889, when it was abandoned owing to the adoption of the policy of limiting the manufacturing required to be done by the railroad company. The New York, Lake Erie & Western operated an oil-mixing house at Susquehanna, Pa., for about three years, but abandoned it in March, 1888, owing to a change of policy similar to that of the Baltimore & Ohio. The Chicago, Burlington & Quincy has maintained an oil-mixing house at Aurora, Ill., for a number of years. The Lehigh Valley in 1887 built a very extensive oil-mixing plant at Perth Amboy, N. J., and is operating it with good results. The Chicago & Northwestern has an oil-mixing plant in operation in Chicago, Ill. The New York & New England maintains several oil-mixing houses along its route. The Chicago, Milwaukee & St. Paul has maintained a large plant at Milwaukee, Ill., since 1883, in addition to several smaller plants along its route.

The usual method employed by railroad companies is to buy ready-mixed oils from manufacturers, whose charges are based more or less on the reputation of their goods, and the prevailing idea that great skill and experience are required to manufacture mixed oils. The so-called mixing of oils is purely a mechanical affair, so far as the operation of a plant is concerned, while the saving to be accomplished by the erection of railroad works is very large. The first cost and operation of a plant are very small compared with the annual expense for the purchase of oils on a large railroad system. The proportions of the various ingredients to use to produce certain mixed oils are readily ascertained from general rules already established by the leading railroad companies, and experience will soon demonstrate what changes might be desirable to meet any special local conditions found to exist. The foreman for an oil-mixing plant need not be any more intelligent or skilful than the average railroad foreman in charge of a small shop or branch of a department. There is probably hardly a railroad in the country on which an oil-mixing plant could not be established, organized, and operated by men now in its employ, with one exception only, namely, the necessity of having the regular or occasional services of a chemist to analyze and report on the quality of crude stocks before being purchased, and to settle any doubtful questions that may arise involving chemical researches. As a matter of fact, in receiving crude stocks the foreman of an oil-mixing works can conduct the standard tests, which are very soon reduced to a mechanical following out of established rules. Doubtful cases and reports as to the relative value or properties of several brands offered for purchase are in reality the main points requiring the attention of a chemist, after the working routine of the plant has been well established. In the purchase of the various brands of mixed oils from manufacturers, a railroad company would anyhow require practically as much chemical expert work as if it were running an oil-plant of its own, in case it wished to feel certain of the quality of the mixed stocks purchased. The abandonment of the oil-mixing plants on the Baltimore & Ohio and on the New York, Lake Erie & Western cannot be considered as indicative of the failure of the methods used, as they were due to a change of policy or local conditions on the roads mentioned. The maintenance of special plants on the Pennsylvania, on the Chicago, Burlington & Quincy, on the Chicago and Northwestern, on the New York and New England, on the Chicago, Milwaukee & St. Paul, and on the Lehigh Valley, is sufficient evidence that on these large systems the plan has worked successfully. It is not only the saving in first cost of the oils that is material in the consideration of the economy of the subject, but the control of the uniformity and reliability of the oils shipped out for use along the road is a matter of prime importance.

Relative to the details of oil-mixing plants on railroads, the buildings used are either frame structures sheathed with galvanized corrugated iron, or brick buildings, the roofing material being either tin, galvanized corrugated iron, or slate. The storage of the main supply of barrelled crude and mixed oils in a separate storage-shed or building, away from the oil-mixing house proper, is advisable. The oil-mixing house proper is usually divided into a storage-room and a mixing-room. Where the mixing-tanks are located in a cellar or basement, the room above it is used to dump oils into the tanks below.

The mixing in the mixing-tanks is done by hand with paddles or dashboards, or by machinery with paddles attached to shafting operated by a steam-engine, or by blowing air into the oil at the bottom of the tanks with blowers operated by steam power, or by continuous pumping, drawing the oil from the bottom of the tank and returning it at the top.

Mixing by hand has been in use for a great many years on the Pennsylvania, the Baltimore & Ohio, the Chicago, Burlington & Quincy, and the New York, Lake Erie & Western; it consists virtually of stirring up and churning the oil by wooden paddles or dashboards worked by hand from the top of the mixing-tanks, and it is probably the best system to adopt for a small output, which would not warrant the introduction of steam-power and special appliances. The Pennsylvania has, to a large extent, introduced paddling by machinery in its oil-mixing houses, in addition to the older method of paddling by hand.

The method of continuous pumping is practiced by the Chicago, Milwaukee & St. Paul Railroad.

The method of agitating the ingredients in the mixing-tanks by blowing air into the mixture at the bottom of the tank has been adopted within recent years by some of the leading manufacturers of illuminating and lubricating oils in this country and abroad, and is the method practiced by the Lehigh Valley Railroad. Railroads purchasing mixed oils from dealers use brands manufactured by the blowing process to a large extent. Dr. Charles B. Dudley, Chemist, Pennsylvania Railroad, considers that the method of mixing oils by blowing air into them is not desirable, as it oxidizes the fatty oils and thereby leads to difficulty. Other chemists and manufacturers interested in the blowing process claim that the amount of oxidation which takes place is not sufficient to cause any deterioration in the lubricating or the general working qualities of the oils. It is also claimed that the mixture is more thoroughly agitated by blowing than by paddling, as in the latter process certain currents are created, and the different particles are not so finely subdivided as by the air forced through the oil in every direction from the bottom up, causing heavy particles sinking to the bottom to be thrown up toward the top of the tank.

The mixing-tanks are either cast-iron hemispherical-shaped kettles, or sheet-iron square or round tanks. Crude stock to be used for mixing is received in barrels, casks, or in tank-cars, and stored in storage-sheds or in storage-tanks until required in the mixing operations, when it is either discharged from the barrels or pumped from the storage-tanks into the mixing-tanks. After the oil has been mixed, it is either immediately drawn off into barrels, or pumped into supply-tanks, from which it is drawn as required for use in the vicinity or for shipments over the road. All pipes used for the transfer of oils should be at least 2 in. in diameter. In designing the piping and pumping system care should be taken, so far as possible, to prevent remnants of dark or light oils touching each other in the pipes or pumps, so as to avoid adulterations.

In designing a plant it must be borne in mind that it is essential to keep the main stock, if feasible, isolated from the oil-mixing house proper, and in the latter it is desirable to keep the mixing tanks in a separate compartment. The most scrupulous cleanliness is requisite to reduce the danger from fire. The fire-service provisions should be the best obtainable. The plant should be located as far as possible away from other important structures or yards, so that, in case of a fire, its spread would be limited or not attended with very serious losses. No open lights should be allowed in the building. The lighting should be by electricity or by lamps with reflectors, set in recesses in the outside wall, the recess being closed on the inside of the house by a fixed glass panel, and on the outside by a small door. A fire-proof construction of the building is desirable at all important locations or where the plant contained in the building is extensive. The heating of the building and of the oil in the tanks should be done by steam from a special boiler, located in an annex to the main building, or from some boiler in use in the vicinity.

The following descriptions of oil-mixing houses refer to oil-mixing plants that are or have been in actual use on railroads in this country, and will therefore prove of particular interest.

Oil-mixing House at Aurora, Ill., Chicago, Burlington & Quincy Railroad.—The mixing of oils on the Chicago, Burlington & Quincy Railroad is done at Aurora, Ill., the method in use being shown in Figs. 214 to 216, prepared from sketches and data furnished by Mr. Wm. Forsyth, Mechanical Engineer, C., B. & Q. R. R. The crude stock is received at the house in barrels, and dumped, as required, into a sheet-iron receiving-tank, 4 ft. × 6 ft. × 2 ft. deep, located in the house in front of a large double door leading from the platform into the house. The top of the receiving-tank is level with the door-sill and the floor of the platform, so that barrels can be rolled from the platform on to the receiving-tank, dumped, and then rolled back and away from the house, the space in the interior of the latter being limited. This receiving-tank serves to measure the ingredients, which form the mixtures for any particular oil. Underneath the house in a cellar there are two square sheet-iron mixing-tanks, each of 60 barrels capacity, with a manhole on top corresponding

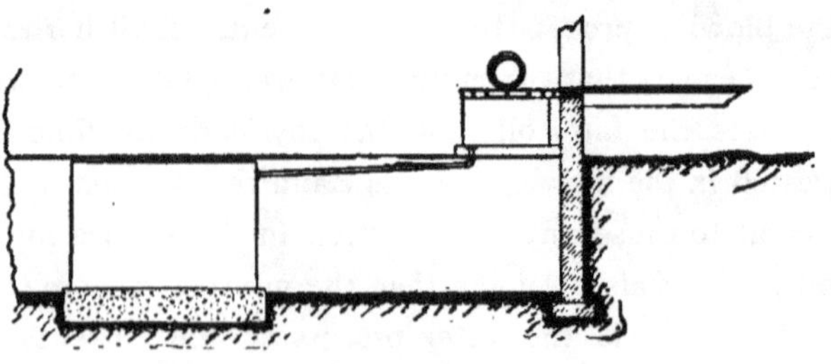

FIG. 214.—CROSS-SECTION.

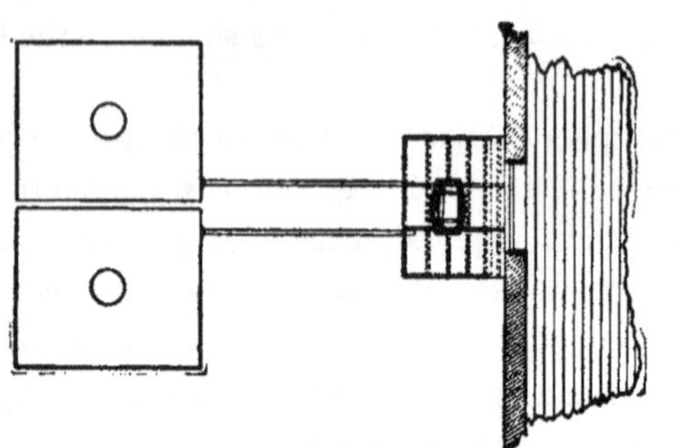

FIG. 215.—GROUND-PLAN.

FIG. 216.—PERSPECTIVE OF DASHBOARD.

with an opening in the floor of the mixing-room. These tanks are connected with the receiving-tank by pipes, as shown. The mixing of the oils is done by hand by means of a wooden mixing-dash (Fig. 216) inserted into the mixing-tanks through the manholes on the top, the oil being churned by the dash until thoroughly mixed. The dash consists of a 9-in. × 15-in. square board perforated with 26 holes, 1½ in. in diameter, with a wooden handle, 11 ft. long. The mixed oil is transferred by means of hand-pumps to storage-tanks or drawn into barrels for shipment over the road.

Oil-mixing House at Meadow Shops, Newark, N. J., Pennsylvania Railroad.—The oil-mixing house of the Pennsylvania Railroad located at Meadow Shops, Newark, N. J., shown in Figs. 217 and 218, is a one-story frame building, about 50 ft. × 175 ft., sheathed with galvanized corrugated iron, roofed with tin, and floored with plank. It is surrounded on three sides with wide platforms, which serve to store barrels and facilitate handling of supplies and materials to and from cars on tracks, one on each side of the house, the floor of the house and platforms being level with the car-floors. The oil-mixing plant is at one end of the building, and at the other end a small part of the floor-space is set apart for the storage of waste, while the balance of the house is used for the storage of oils in barrels. The mixing-tanks are in a small cellar, and immediately over them, raised above the floor of the house, are the storage-tanks for mixed oils, from which the mixed oil is drawn into barrels for shipment over the road. In addition to these tanks there are on one side of the house, as shown on the plan, a number of smaller receiving-tanks for mixed oils for local use at the shops and for the engine and car service in the vicinity, the oil being drawn into cans or buckets as required. All crude stocks arrive at the house in barrels, and, after mixing, the mixed oils are drawn into the same barrels for shipments out of the house. The account of stock and the quantity of the various ingredients used in making each batch of oil are tallied by actual weight, every barrel being weighed on a small portable scale. The different lots of crude stocks arriving at the house are kept separate, and the barrels of mixed oils from each batch are given distinguishing marks. There is a very simple and efficient set of books kept, so that at any time it can be ascertained exactly what lots of crude stocks were used in making the mixed oil contained in any particular barrel shipped out of the house.

The process of mixing the oil consists of agitating it inside the mixing-tanks by means of a system of paddles connected to a vertical shaft inside each tank revolved by the proper gearing and machinery. In order to create cross currents of the oil in the tank, the movement of the paddles is reversed from time to time, and fixed paddles are attached to the sides of the tank between the re-

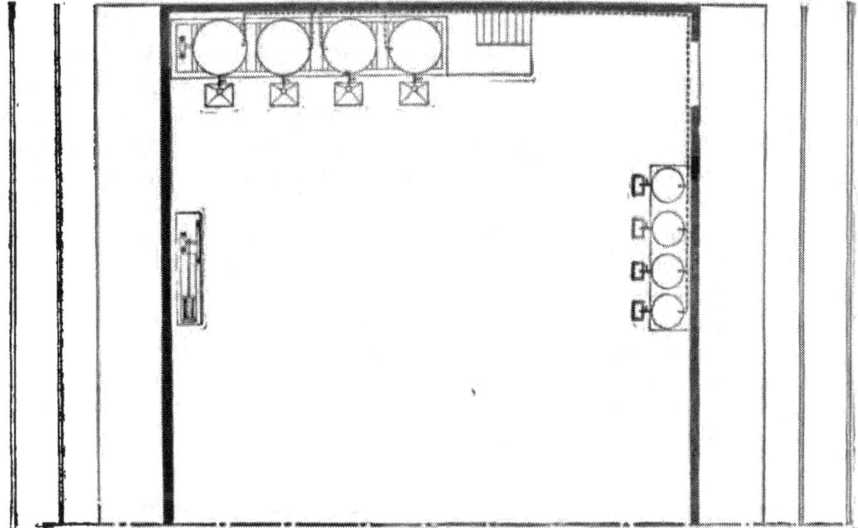

FIG. 217.—GROUND-PLAN.

volving paddles and pitched in an opposite direction. There are four circular sheet-iron mixing-tanks in the cellar, the crude stocks being dumped into them through a 16-in. × 20-in. opening in the floor over each one of them. These mixing-tanks are 4 ft. 6 in. in diameter by 7 ft. 8 in. high, and have a capacity of 16 barrels each. The paddles are 14 in. wide at the widest part and ¼ in. thick; the revolving ones are made of wrought-iron and the fixed ones of steel, their shape being similar to the blades of a screw-propeller. The paddles make about 15 revolutions per minute, and it takes about 3½ hours to mix a batch of oil. The speed is regulated by the quantity of oil in the tank, so as not to throw the oil out over the top. In front of each mixing-tank in the cellar there is an ordinary 2-in. plunger-pump, making four pumps in all, connected with one continuous pump-shaft, which pumps serve to transfer the mixed oil up to the storage-tanks or the receiving-tanks for local use.

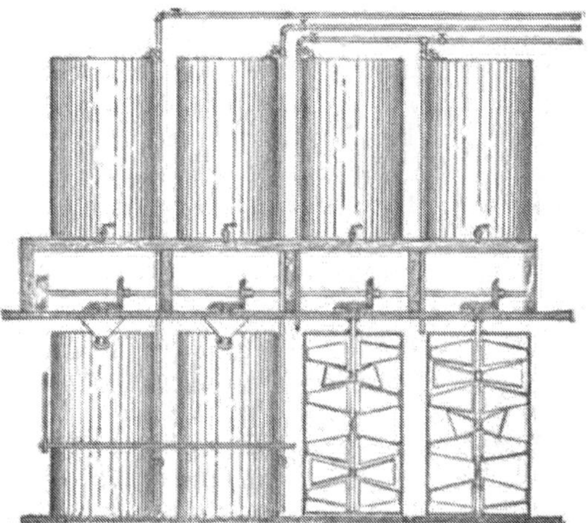

FIG. 218.—ELEVATION OF TANKS.

The power to drive the paddles and pumps is supplied by a small stationary engine, the counter-shaft of the mixing paddles being turned by a belt and the pump-shaft by a connecting-rod attached to the fly-wheel of the engine. The paddle shafts are thrown in and out of gear by means of clutches and levers situated above the floor just below the storage-tanks; but it is necessary to go down into the cellar to start or stop the pumps. The four mixing-tanks can be worked independently or all together, or mixing can be done in some of the tanks while pumping is going on from the others. There are four storage-tanks placed on a raised trestling immediately over the mixing-tanks, as previously explained. These storage-tanks are of the same size as the mixing-tanks. The receiving-tanks for local use are smaller. All pipes for transfer of oils are 2 in. in diameter. The oils in the tanks are kept liquid by a single coil of 1-in. steam-pipe in the bottom of each tank, the general temperature inside the building, especially in the small mixing-cellar, being kept quite high by steam-coils along the walls. Steam is supplied from the boiler connected with the shop system in the immediate vicinity. There is no provision made for lighting the building, as work is not allowed to be prosecuted after dark. The provisions for protection against fire consist of lines of hose connected with the water-system, kept uncoiled along the floor of the house at night ready for use, and fire-alarm boxes in the special circuit connected with the shop system.

This house has been in operation for about eight years, and supplies all the mixed oils and distributes all the cotton waste used on the New York Division of the road. There are about 700 barrels of oil mixed and distributed per month. The force employed consists of about three to five men, exclusive of the foreman, and they are kept busy for about nine hours a day the year round. The oils mixed are, as a rule, passenger-engine oil, engine-oil, navy sperm-oil, signal-oil, and heavy lubricating-oils. One of the mixing-tanks is used exclusively for engine-oils, another one for illuminating-oils, and the remaining two for heavy lubricants. Great care is taken to keep the dark and light oils separated in the pipes and mixing-tanks, so that the remnants of one batch will not injure the next batch of a different grade. In dumping the oils, the usual practice of boring vent-holes in the barrels is avoided by the use of a short piece of ½-in. pipe, bent in the shape of an elbow, which is inserted in the barrel through the bung-hole as the barrel is rolled over the dumping-trough, and serves to introduce the necessary air to allow the barrel to discharge quickly.

The general layout of this plant is good, and the operation very methodical and economical. The most serious objections are, that the tanks are located too close to the sides of the building, giving little opportunity for free inspection and repairs. The cellar or pit in which the mixing-tanks are located is very small and wet, and repairs are very difficult to make. Great care has to be exercised to prevent chips and other foreign matter from getting into the mixing-tanks, as the paddles break very easily and repairs are very difficult to make. The location of the storage-tanks immediately above the oil-mixing tanks cannot be considered as advantageous as locating the storage-tanks sideways from the mixing-tanks.

Oil-mixing House at Mt. Clare Shops, Baltimore, Md., Baltimore & Ohio Railroad.—The Baltimore & Ohio Railroad maintained an oil-mixing plant for nearly twenty years at Mt. Clare Shops, Baltimore, Md., but abandoned the operation of same in the latter part of the year 1889, owing to the adoption of the policy to do as little manufacturing by the company as possible. The following data on the subject has been kindly furnished by Mr. L. S. Randolph, Engineer of Tests, B. & O. R. R., who had charge of the house when in operation. The mixing-house was a one-story brick building, with iron roof and wooden floor, divided into two rooms, one for signal-oil and the other for cylinder-oil. The cylinder-oil room, about 60 ft. × 30 ft., was used to make cylinder-oil, and one end of it was also utilized for the storage of waste, where as many as 150 bales of waste could be stored at one time. The signal-oil room was slightly larger than the cylinder-oil room, and served to mix signal-oil in addition to providing storage space for a large quantity of crude stock and mixed oils. The only oils mixed were signal and cylinder-oils. The stock was delivered in barrels and stored inside, and also, at times, outside the building. The stirring was done by hand by means of paddles. There were two mixing-kettles for cylinder-oil, made of cast-iron, hemispherical in shape, holding each about 16 barrels, heated by steam-coils on the inside. The paddle used for cylinder-oil was spoon-shaped, and from 6 to 8 ft. long. The kettles were set high enough above the floor to allow the mixed oil to be drawn off into barrels placed below them. Barrelled crude stocks were hoisted up by block and tackle and swung on to skids over the kettles, from where they were discharged directly into the kettles. In the signal-oil room there was only one mixing-tank, sunk below the floor, made of wrought-iron, 10 ft. × 8 ft. × 4 ft. deep, with a capacity of about 60 barrels, although only 40 barrels were mixed at a time. The paddle used for signal-oil was a disk on the end of a rod, which was drawn up and down by a man who stood on the tank, working through a hole in the top of it. The mixed oil had to be pumped out of the signal-tank into barrels. The steam for heating the building and the oils in the mixing-tanks was supplied at first by a boiler placed in the building, but it was subsequently removed and steam obtained from a boiler in a neighboring mill. The interior of the building was lighted by oil lamps, when necessary. The mixed oils were drawn into the same barrels the crude stock had been delivered in, and shipped out on the road as called for.

The following mixtures were used for signal-oils: Winter oil, 8 parts 150 deg. fire-test, 8 parts 300 deg. fire-test, 15 parts lard and 10 parts rape-seed; summer oil, 8 parts 150 deg. fire-test, 8 parts 300 deg. fire-test, and 20 parts lard. Signal-oil was mixed at about 140 to 150 deg. Fahrenheit. When the temperature reached 140 or 145 deg. the steam was turned off and the oil was stirred for about five minutes. The stirring for that length of time was repeated five or ten times at intervals of from five to ten minutes.

The mixture for cylinder-oil was composed of 4 parts tallow and 12 parts stock. It was heated to from 200 to 300 deg. Fahrenheit, the heat being kept up for about five hours, with continual stirring during that time.

Oil-mixing House at Altoona, Pa., Pennsylvania Railroad.—The oil-mixing house of the Pennsylvania Railroad, at Altoona, Pa., shown in Figs. 219 to 222, has been in operation for about twenty-five

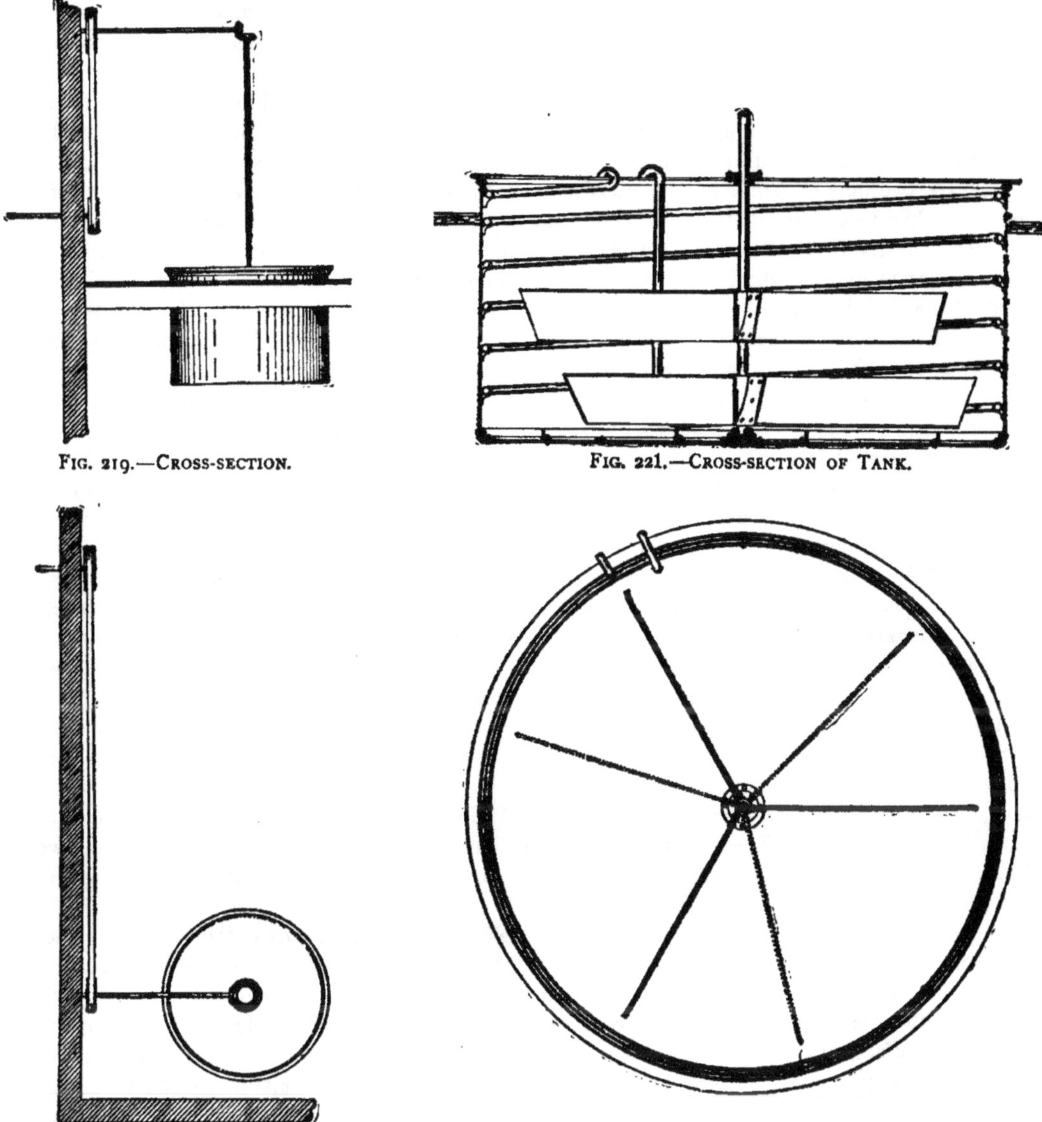

FIG. 219.—CROSS-SECTION.

FIG. 221.—CROSS-SECTION OF TANK.

FIG. 220.—GROUND-PLAN.

FIG. 222.—PLAN OF TANK.

years. It is a two-story fireproof structure with a cellar. The oils are mixed in tanks in the cellar. The main room on the ground-floor serves to store mixed oil in storage-tanks, from which it is drawn, as required, for local use or put into barrels for shipment over the road, and the second story is used for the storage of waste. In addition to the oil-mixing house there is an oil-storage house, located a short distance from the former, serving to store oils, tallow, etc., as received in barrels. There are dumping-troughs in one end of the storage-house connected by pipes with the mixing-tanks in the cellar of the oil-mixing house. The ingredients required to make a batch of oil are weighed and dumped into the troughs in the storage-shed, from where they run through pipes to the mixing-tanks. Mixing is done principally by hand, but agitating the oil in the mixing-tanks by means of paddles attached to shafts, driven by machinery, is also used, as shown in the illustrations, which represent more particularly the arrangement and details of the cylinder-oil mixer. There is a steam-pump on the main floor of the oil-mixing house for transferring oils from the mixing-tanks in the cellar to the storage-tanks overhead. The pump and shafting is driven by an engine and boiler placed outside the building, and steam from the boiler is employed to warm the building in winter and to heat the coils in the tanks. No lights are allowed in the oil-house, which is illuminated by gas burning outside the house and opposite windows provided for that purpose.

Relative to the cylinder-oil mixer, shown in the illustrations, the tank is 7 ft. 3 in. in diam. by 3 ft. 6 in. deep, covered on top, the top being set 6 in. above the floor. The thickness of the iron sheets is ¼ in., stiffened with angle-irons. The heating is done by a 1¼-in. spiral steam-coil, as shown. There are two tiers of paddles, each consisting of three arms, 8 in. high by ¼ in. thick by 3 ft. 4 in. long, attached to a 1¾-in. shaft, which makes about 15 to 20 revolutions per minute.

Mr. Charles B. Dudley, Chemist, Pennsylvania Railroad, has kindly furnished the following general data relative to oil-mixing houses on the Pennsylvania system: Each grand division on the P. R. R. has an oil-mixing house of its own. As a rule, the buildings used are of brick, roofed with slate and floored with cement or brick. They are sometimes one-story and sometimes two-story buildings, according to the location; in the latter case the upper story is used for the storage of waste. The oils are usually bought delivered in car-load lots in barrels, although at some places oil is received in tank-cars. If in barrels, they are unloaded and stored till required in a sort of open shed independent of the regular oil-mixing house or in an oil-storage house, which is usually built of brick with brick floor. The mixing is done in some houses by hand and in others with paddles and machinery. Mixing oil by blowing air is not considered good practice, as it oxidizes the fatty oils and leads to difficulty. The heating of the oils in the tanks is done by steam-coils, usually in the bottom of the tanks. The mixed oil is stored in large tanks situated on the main floor, and provided with gauge-glasses to indicate the amount in the tank, and is drawn from these tanks by faucets into cans and buckets for use in the vicinity, or it is also drawn into barrels and shipped to various points on the division. The power used at the oil-mixing houses for pumping and mixing is furnished by a small steam-engine, usually separated from the main building by a brick partition; and if it is not convenient to take steam from some adjacent boiler, a small upright boiler is put in the same building with the engine. The interior is best lighted by electricity, but if gas or oil must be used the jet is not allowed to burn in the open place where the storage of oil is; it is usually placed behind a window, or in a special compartment made for it. The main materials purchased are extra lard-oil, extra No. 1 lard-oil, paraffine-oil, 150 deg. fire-test burning-oil, 300 deg. fire-test burning-oil, well-oil, 500 deg. fire-test oil, and tallow. The oils usually mixed are signal-oil, engine-oil, passenger-car oil, cylinder-lubricant, and navy sperm-oil.

Oil-mixing House at Susquehanna, Pa., New York, Lake Erie & Western Railroad.—The operation of an oil-mixing plant at Susquehanna, Pa., on the New York, Lake Erie & Western Railroad, shown in Fig. 223, was abandoned in March, 1888, after having been in service successfully since June, 1885, the abandonment being due to a change in the policy adopted by the railroad company relative to manufacturing its own supplies. The following data have been kindly furnished by Mr. Walter D. Gregory, who formerly had charge of the plant as the chemist of the N. Y., L. E. & W. R. R. The building was one-story, brick, about 60 ft. × 35 ft., with a frame lean-to annex, about 60 ft. × 12 ft. The shed annex served to hold tank-cars and to heat them up sufficiently by means of steam-coils along the walls to enable the oil in the tank-cars to be discharged by gravity into two large receiving-tanks buried in the ground under the main building. These storage-tanks were built each of two old locomotive-tender tanks spliced and pieced out so as to form tanks of about 7500 gallons storage capacity. All petroleum stocks arrived in tank-cars; all animal oils and other materials arrived in barrels or casks. One end of the main building was used for the storage of barrels, and was arranged with a series of skids; the balance of the building had a wooden floor. At the other end of the building there were two mixing-tanks, set above the floor, so that the mixed oil could be drawn off into barrels placed under them. The charging of the mixing-tanks was accomplished by hoisting up barrelled stock by means of a small steam hoisting-engine and proper appliances, and swinging the barrels on to skids on top of the tanks, where the oil was discharged through strainers into the tanks. The oil in the receiving-tanks in the ground had to be pumped up into the mixing-tanks by means of a small steam-pump. One of the mixing-tanks was wrought-iron, hemispherical in shape, with a capacity of about 25 barrels; the other was of wrought-iron, cylindrical in shape, with a capacity of about five barrels. The house and mixing-tanks were heated by steam-coils. The mixing was done with paddles on shafts set into the mixing-tanks and operated by a small steam-engine. The lighting of the house was done by gas, without any special safety provisions. There was a steaming-trough inside the house on which barrels were steamed out. In addition to the skids in the building, there was a series of skids in the yard back of the house for the storage of empty barrels and barrelled stock. There was never much mixed oil to keep in store, as it was usually shipped out as fast as made.

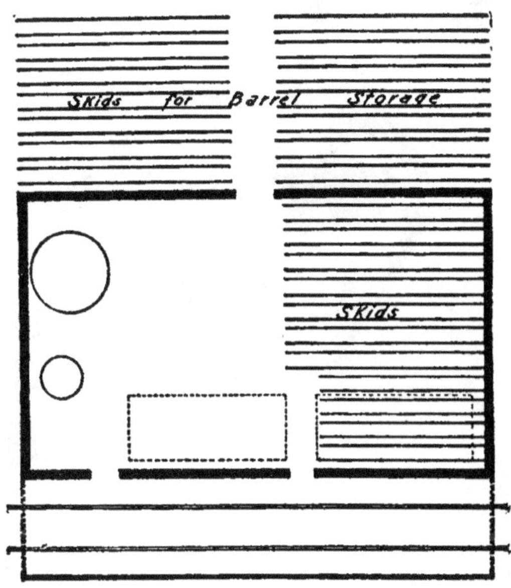

FIG. 223.—GROUND-PLAN.

Oil-mixing House at Milwaukee, Wis., Chicago, Milwaukee & St. Paul Railway.—The following information relative to the oil-mixing house of the Chicago, Milwaukee & St. Paul Railway at Milwaukee, Wis., has been compiled from data kindly furnished by Mr. George Gibbs, Mechanical Engineer, Chicago, Milwaukee & St. Paul Railway. This house forms the principal plant, although there are several smaller ones distributed over the road. The house is located near the general storehouse of the main shops of the road at Milwaukee, and consists of a one-story brick building, 48 ft. × 102 ft., roofed with corrugated iron. The interior is divided into two rooms, the front one, 48 ft. × 28 ft., for mixing oils and for the local supply; the rear one, 48 ft. × 74 ft., for storage of oil in barrels and of cotton and wool waste. The mixing-tanks, pumps, and tanks for storage and barrelling are located in the front or mixing-room. There are two large iron receiving-tanks, each of 18,000 gallons capacity, covered with iron roofs, sunk in brick-lined pits outside of the house. The crude stock arriving in tank-cars is stored in these underground receiving-tanks, and barrelled stock is stored partly in the house and partly on platforms surrounding the building. There are two upright wrought-iron mixing-tanks, each of 13 barrels capacity, set in pits in the mixing-room floor, the tops of the tanks being provided with strainers and covers. The oils are mixed by a steam-pump, which pumps the oil from the bottom of the mixing-tank and returns it at the top, which pumping operation is maintained until the ingredients are thoroughly mixed. The mixed oil is transferred by the same pump that does the mixing from the mixing-tanks to a series of storage-tanks for mixed oils located in the mixing-room, from which tanks the oil is drawn for use in the vicinity, or barrelled for shipments over the road. The oil is heated by steam-coils placed a little above the bottoms of the tanks. Steam for use in the house is drawn from the main shop boiler. The building is lighted by electricity.

The oils mixed at this house are signal-oil and bolt-cutting oil. The capacity of the two mixing-tanks is about 50 barrels per day. The entire road supply is handled at this house, amounting in the year 1888 to 18,097 barrels. The plant has been in operation since 1883.

Oil-mixing Houses of the New York & New England Railroad.—The New York & New England Railroad has maintained for several years small oil-mixing plants at South Boston, Boston, and Norwood, Mass., and at Hartford, Conn. The following information has been prepared from general data kindly furnished by Mr. A. Griggs, Superintendent of Motive Power, N. Y. & N. E. R.

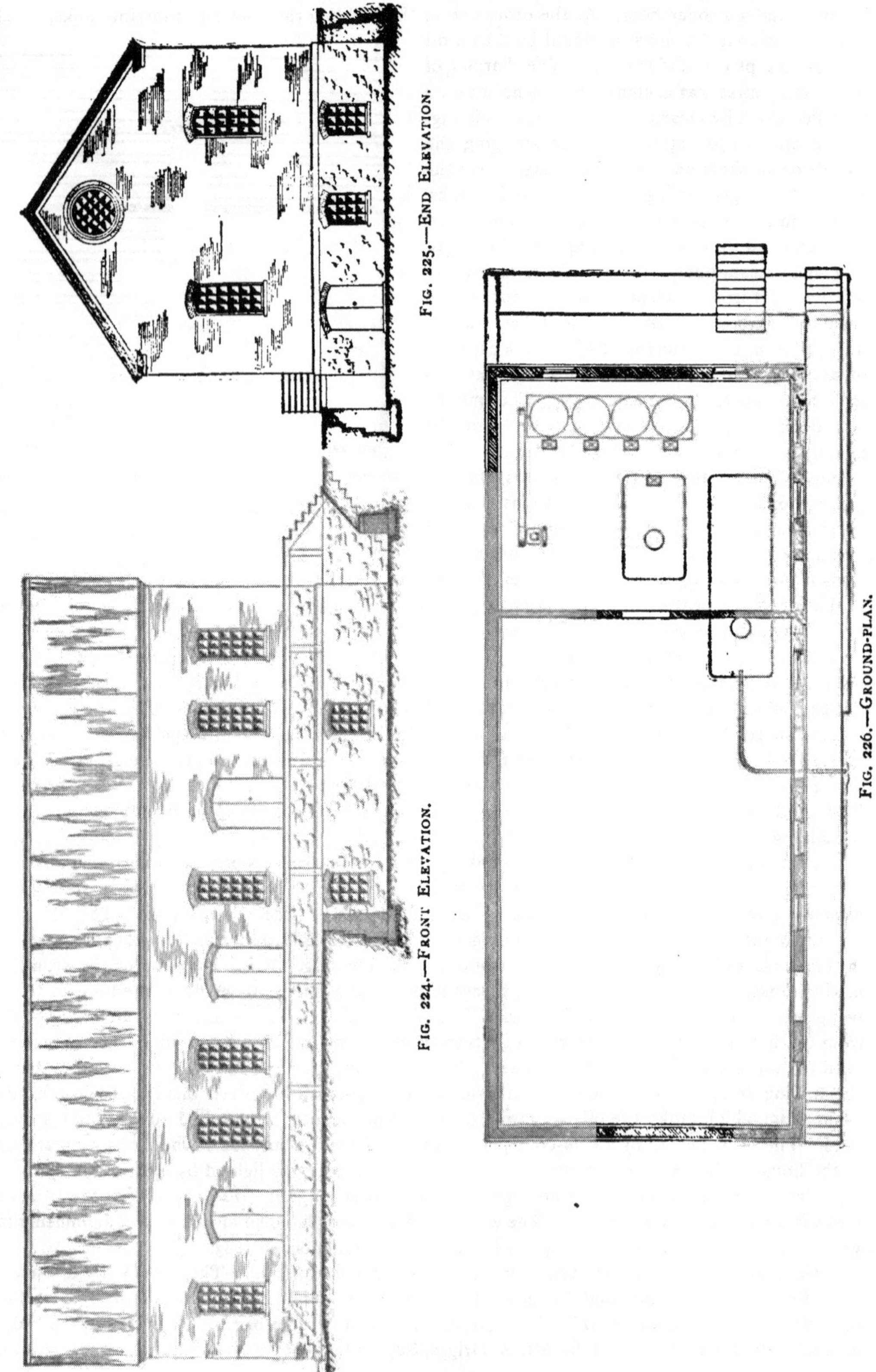

Fig. 225.—End Elevation.

Fig. 224.—Front Elevation.

Fig. 226.—Ground-plan.

R., and by Mr. P. H. Conradson, formerly chemist of the road. The buildings in use were not specially built for the service, and are in some cases only frame sheds. The floors are of wood or of sand. Some of the storage-tanks are in the building, and some of them are buried in the ground outside. Some of the mixing-tanks are made of old tender-tanks with paddles in the back ends worked by a belt from the shop engines. Some of the tanks are old water-tanks and some oil-tanks. All crude oils arrive in tank-cars, and are pumped into the storage-tanks by a steam-pump. The kettles used for boiling are open wrought-iron, such as are commonly used by roofers for melting tar, a wood fire being built under them in the usual way. The oil in the storage-tanks is kept warm in cold weather by means of steam-pipes. Power-pumps are used at most of the houses for handling and transferring the oils. The oils mixed are lubricating-oils for cars and engines, cylinder-oil for locomotives, lantern-oil, marine-engine and valve-oil for steamers. In the preparation of the car and engine-oils a so-called concentrated chemical solution is prepared only at the Norwood plant, which solution is distributed to the other houses, where it is mixed by agitation with a given amount of well-oil in the mixing-tanks. After this operation the mixed oil is pumped to storage-tanks, barrelled and shipped out on the road, as required. The plants have been in operation for several years.

Oil-mixing-house Design, Packerton, Pa., Lehigh Valley Railroad.—The design for an oil-mixing house of the Lehigh Valley Railroad, shown in Figs. 224 to 229, prepared by Mr. S. French Collins

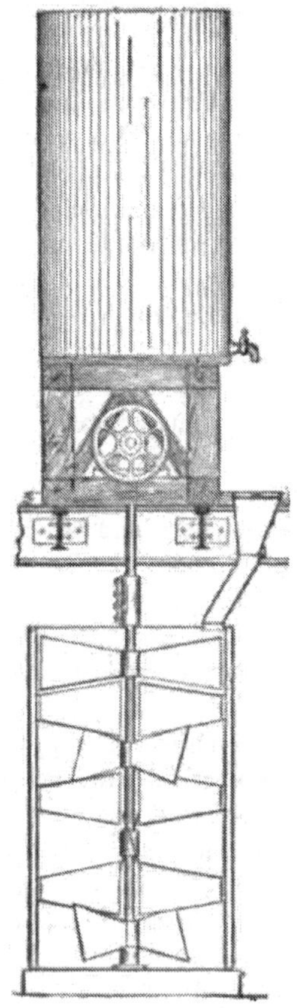

FIG. 227.—CROSS-SECTION OF TANKS.

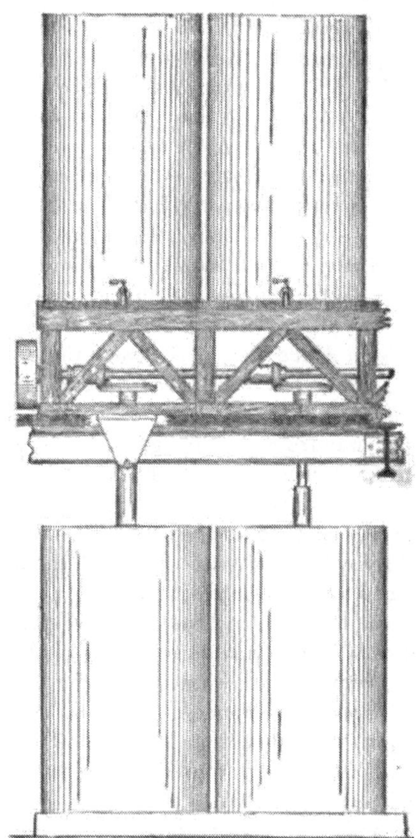

FIG. 228.—ELEVATION OF TANKS.

under the direction of Mr. John S. Lentz, Superintendent Car Department, L. V. R. R., was to have been carried out at Packerton, Pa., but was subsequently abandoned, principally owing to the limited space available. The plans show a one-story brick structure, 80 ft. × 33 ft., roofed with galvanized corrugated iron, divided into two rooms on the ground-floor, with a basement at one end of the building. The system to be used was similar to that employed at the Meadows Shops of the Pennsylvania Railroad, described above. The plans contemplated using four mixing-tanks in the basement, into which the oil to be mixed was to be dumped from the main floor overhead or pumped from the receiving-tank in the basement. The mixing was to be done by paddles attached to shafting, operated by machinery, as shown on the plans. The oils arriving in barrels were to be stored in the large room of the building, and oils arriving in tank-cars were to be stored in large receiving-tanks in the basement. Immediately over the mixing-tanks there were to be six storage-tanks, set on a

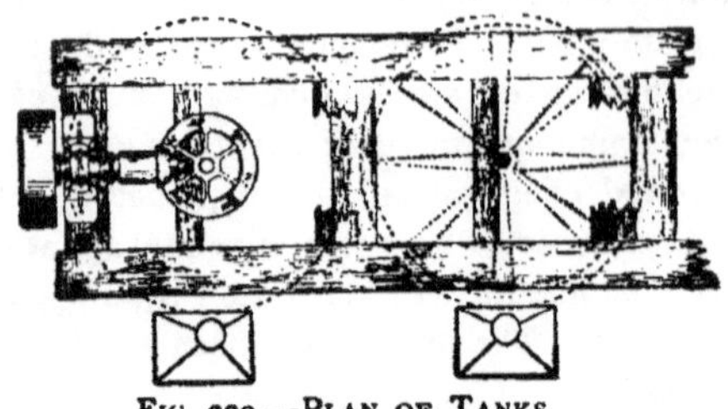

FIG. 229.—PLAN OF TANKS.

trestling raised 3 ft. above the main floor, which storage-tanks were to hold the mixed oils until drawn off for local use or put in barrels for shipment over the road.

Oil-mixing House at Perth Amboy, N. J., Lehigh Valley Railroad.—The oil-mixing house of the Lehigh Valley Railroad at Perth Amboy, N. J., designed and built by the author, shown in Figs. 230 to 235, is a very extensive and complete plant for mixing and storing oils, which has been operated very successfully for a number of years. The process employed is that of mixing the oils by blowing air into the mixing-tanks. An exhaustive description of this plant, including a complete set of illustrations, and a very thorough account of the operation of the works, and the methods employed for testing the oils, prepared by Mr. C. P. Coleman, Chemist, L. V. R. R., was published in the issues of the *Railroad Gazette* of April 10, 17, and 24, 1891. The following description and illustrations are taken from above publication:

The location of the oil-mixing works is at the coal and freight terminal of the Lehigh Valley Railroad at Perth Amboy, N. J., adjoining the creosoting works of the same company, the boilers at the creosoting works supplying steam to the oil-works. The general layout, as shown in Fig. 230, consists of the oil-mixing house proper, the tank-car discharging-house, and the storage-shed, located some distance away from the mixing-house. Two tracks run into the works, and ample yard space is provided for the storage of surplus stock, empty barrels, and sundry supplies.

The crude oils or stock not requiring to be mixed, when received at the works in barrels, are stored in the storage-shed until shipped off or needed in the oil-mixing house. Oil arriving in tank-cars is discharged by gravity from the tank-car discharging-house into the large storage-tanks in the basement annex to the oil-mixing house.

The oil-mixing house consists of a barrel-storage room, and a discharge and supply-room on an upper level, with a basement annex consisting of three rooms, respectively, the mixing-room, the storage-tank room for crude stock, and the engine-room. The main working-room (the discharge and supply-room), on the upper level, serves for dumping the barrel crude stock and tallow into the mixing-tanks in the basement. It is also utilized to store the mixed oils in supply-tanks located along one side of the room, from which the mixed oils are drawn into barrels for shipment over the road.

The storage-shed is a one-story frame structure, 100 ft. × 38 ft., divided into two rooms—the one for storage of oils in barrels, and the other for storage of waste in bales. A loading platform runs along a track on one side of the house, and barrel skids along the platform facilitate the transfer of barrels between the storage-shed and the oil-mixing house. The floor of the shed consists of plank on mud-sills. The building is sheathed and roofed with galvanized corrugated iron on a wooden frame. The roof-trusses are spaced 10 ft. centres. The height from floor to truss is 12 ft. in clear. This building is described more fully in the chapter on oil-storage houses, and illustrated in Fig. 189.

The tank-car discharging-house is a one-story frame shed, 20 ft. × 45 ft., sheathed and roofed with galvanized corrugated iron. This house serves in winter to heat heavy or congealed oils arriving in tank-cars till the oil gains the proper fluidity so as to be discharged into the storage-tanks in the adjoining basement. The cars are run into the house, the doors closed, and steam turned into steam-coils along the walls of the building. This building obviates the objectionable features of inserting a steam-pipe into the tank-cars, and discharging live steam into the congealed oil, and it offers a less cumbersome method than the system of placing horseshoe-shaped steam-coils over the tank-cars.

The oil-mixing house, shown in all the illustrations, consists of a one-story brick building, 38 ft. × 71 ft. 6 in., on stone foundations, with double-pitched iron roof covered with galvanized corrugated iron, divided by a brick partition-wall into the barrel-storage room, 35 ft. 6 in. × 38 ft. 6 in. in the clear, and the discharge and supply-room, 35 ft. 6 in. × 38 ft. 6 in. in the clear. The basement annex is a brick and stone structure, roofed with a flat roof, covered with a layer of cement, tar, and gravel, on 4-in. flat brick arches sprung between 6-in. I-beams, spaced 3 ft. centres, and spanning 11 ft., supported at their ends on the walls and on a 12-in. I-beam on 8-in. cast-iron columns. The basement has three rooms, respectively, the mixing-room, 12 ft. 6 in. × 32 ft. in the clear; the storage-tank room for crude stock, 22 ft. × 35 ft. in the clear; and the engine-room, 6 ft. × 24 ft. in the clear, The clear height of the upper rooms is 12 ft. 6 in.; the clear height of the basement varies from 8 ft. at the low end to 12 ft. at the high end. The engine-room is connected with the supply and discharge-room by stone steps, walled over with brick, and provided with iron doors at top and bottom. The upper floor is 12 ft. 6 in. higher than the floor in the basement, and 4 ft. above the track that runs along the 8-ft. loading platform on one side of the house. All the brick walls in the building are 13 in. thick, to afford greater stability and safety to the structure in case of fire. The iron roof-trusses over the main building, spanning 37 ft. between centres of walls, are spaced 10 ft. centres. They are pin-connected, and built of angle-iron principal rafters, star-iron struts, round-iron tie-rods and angle-iron purlins, spaced 5 ft. 6 in., and covered with No. 20 gauge galvanized corrugated iron fastened to the purlins with flat hoop-iron bands. The door and door-frames throughout the house are wrought-iron, and the door-sills are cast-iron. All window frames and sash, including the mullions, are cast-iron. All windows are provided with wrought-iron shutters. All sashes are fixed throughout the house, but there are two lights in each window hung in a cast-iron pivoting sash set in between the cast-iron mullions of the main sash. In addition to these openings in the sash, ventilators are provided, as shown on the plans. The sash in the mixing-room and storage-tank room are bolted into the window-frames in such a way as to be readily removed to allow tanks to be taken through the window openings in case of repairs or renewals being required. The floor of the loading platform and of the barrel-storage room is made of stone slabs, the floor of the discharge and supply-room of brick laid flat, and the floor in the basement of cement dished toward suitable sink-holes connecting with drain-pipes.

There are seven supply-tanks 4 ft. in diameter, by 7 ft. high, for the storage of mixed oils, placed on a raised platform on one side of the discharge and supply room. The platform is built of 6-in. I-beams on brick piers. The tanks are built of $\frac{1}{8}$-in. iron, and covered on top, and have faucets with copper-wire basket-strainers, glass gauge-tubes, and cast-iron drip-boxes on the floor under the faucets. Each tank holds 625 gallons.

On the side of the discharge and supply-room, next to the mixing-room, there are six cast-iron box troughs set in the floor, each connected by a 6-in. pipe, passing through the stone foundation-wall of the main building, with the top of the mixing-tanks in the basement. The sides of these troughs are raised a few inches above the floor, so as to form skids for the barrels to rest on when being dumped. The opening at the end of the trough leading into the 6-in. pipe is covered with wire netting, and kept closed, when not in use, by a heavy cast-iron hinged cover. Each trough is 12 in. wide by 5 ft. long, and from 6 in. to 10 in. deep.

In the mixing-room in the basement there are four mixing-tanks at present (space being left for two more, if ever required), set on a stone bench raised 1 ft. above the floor of the basement. Each mixing-tank is 4 ft. in diameter and 7 ft. high, built of $\frac{1}{4}$-in. iron, covered on top, and surrounded by a steam-jacket built of $\frac{3}{16}$-in. iron. The capacity of each mixing-tank is 625 gallons.

In the storage-tank room there are two cylindrical tanks, similar to tanks on tank-cars, each 5 ft. 6 in. in diameter, and 27 ft. long, with a capacity of 4680 gallons. The tanks are built of ¼-in. iron, and set on cast-iron saddles on the top of the floor.

In the engine-room there are a vertical engine, a rotary blower, and a steam-pump. The engine is of the New York Safety Steam Power Co.'s make, and is supplied with steam through a 2-in. pipe connected with the main steam-pipe from the boilers of the creosoting works adjacent to the oil-works, as explained above. It has a 7-in. × 9-in. cylinder, and a nominal capacity of 10 H.P. The engine drives the rotary blower by means of a 42-in. fly-wheel and belting. The rotary blower is of the Wilbraham Bros.' (size C) make, and serves not only to mix the oils in the mixing-tanks by blowing air into the tanks near the bottom of the tanks, thereby causing the contents of the tank to be thoroughly agitated, but it serves also as an oil-pump. The suction is 2 in. in diameter, arranged to work on the oil-pipes or to draw in air, and the discharge-pipe is 2 in. in diameter, connecting with the blow-pipes to the tanks or with the oil-pipes. In addition to the blower there is an ordinary steam-pump for transferring oils, supplied with steam through a 1-in. steam-pipe. This pump is of Guild & Garrison's make, and has a 6-in. × 7-in. steam-cylinder and a 3½-in. × 10-in. oil-cylinder, with a 2-in. suction and a 2-inch discharge-pipe.

The pipe system, shown in Figs. 233 and 234, consists of blow-pipes from the blower to the mixing-tanks in the basement and to the supply-tanks in the discharge and supply-room, in the first case to mix the oils and in the latter case to agitate the mixed oils slightly from time to time to prevent the ingredients separating to a more or less extent according to their specific gravities, if allowed to stand undisturbed for quite a time. The blow-pipe in each tank extends to within a few inches of the bottom of the tank, where it branches into four short horizontal perforated 1-in. pipes. The oil-pipe system consists of suction-pipes from the large storage-tanks in the basement to the pumps, and discharge-pipes from the latter to the mixing-tanks to allow crude stock from the storage-tanks to be transferred to the mixing-tanks. There are also suction-pipes from the mixing-tanks to the pumps to allow the mixed oils to be pumped up through delivery-pipes to the supply-tanks in the discharge and supply-room. There is also a delivery-pipe from the pumps to the storage-tanks, in case oil is to be transferred from the mixing-tanks or the supply-tanks to the storage-tanks. There is no special suction-pipe, however, provided in the supply-tanks, as the blow-pipe entering the same can be used as suction-pipe in connection with the rotary pump for transfer of oils from the supply-tanks to the different tanks in the basement, which operation is seldom required. There is also a suction-pipe extending to the tank-car discharging-house, so that oils can be pumped directly from the discharge-box alongside the cars through the pumps, in place of being discharged by gravity to the storage-tanks, which, under certain contingencies, might be found desirable. As previously explained, the blower can be used as a rotary pump to transfer oil, and the various suction and delivery pipes are connected in such a way with the blower and the regular oil-pump that either one or the other can be operated on any of the oil-pipes.

The system of delivery-pipes leading from the pumps to the mixing-tanks and to the supply-tanks, and the suction-pipes leading from the mixing-tanks to the pumps, is double, so as to enable the light-colored oils to be kept separate from the dark-colored oils, the one line being used exclusively for one class of oils and the other line for the other class. Except in cases of breakdowns, the rotary pump is used exclusively for light-colored oils and the regular oil-pump for dark or heavy oils, which, when slightly congealed, require considerable power to force them through the pipes. The pipes are all inclined as much as possible, so as to allow them to free themselves by gravity when pumping is stopped. At all low dead-ends drain-cocks are provided, and any oil left in the pipes after pumping is drained off into buckets before another grade of oil is pumped through the same pipe. In this manner the adulteration of one grade of oil by coming in contact in the pipes or pumps with remnants of another grade of oil is reduced to the least possible limit. The suction-pipe and the delivery-pipe between the storage-tanks in the basement and the pumps are single, as only dark oils pass through them. The blow-pipes are 1½ in. in diameter, and the oil-pipes are 2 in. in diameter.

The heating of the house and of the mixing-tanks is done by superheated steam, supplied from the superheater at the adjacent creosoting works. As shown in Fig. 235, there are steam-coils in the discharge and supply-room back of the supply-tanks, the number being larger back of the tanks for heavy oils than for light oils. There are also coils along the wall next to the dumping-troughs and on the partition next to the storage-room; as barrels prior to being dumped are brought in from the storage-room and placed along this partition the oil is thus rendered fluid enough to discharge easily. The temperature of the discharge and supply-room is generally kept at about 70 degrees Fahr. In the barrel-storage room the temperature is maintained at about 70 degrees Fahr. by means of coils hung

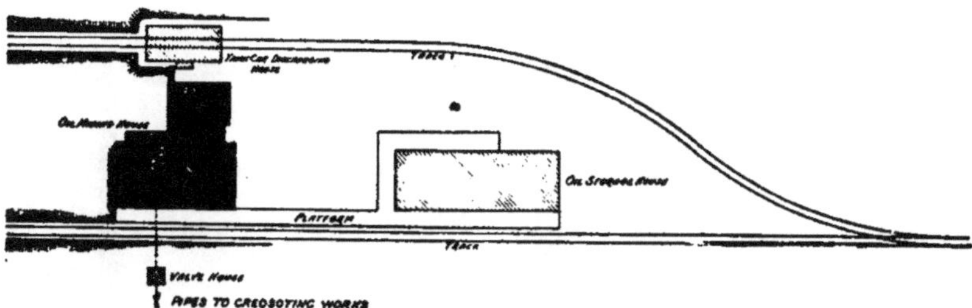

FIG. 230 GENERAL PLAN.

FIG. 231.—FRONT ELEVATION.

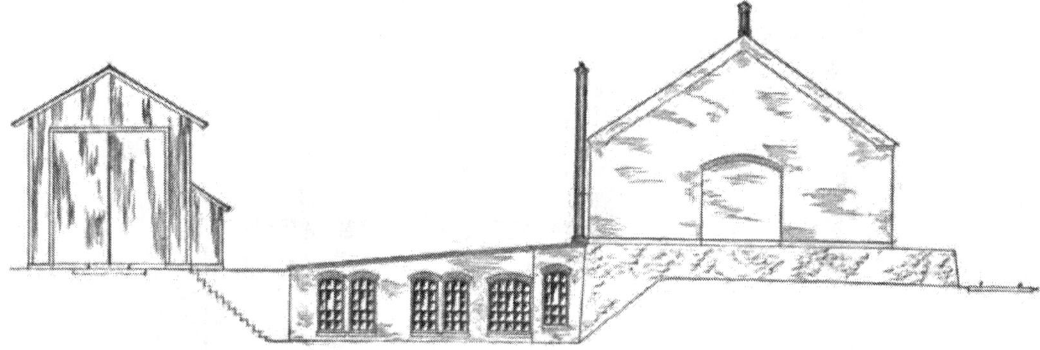

FIG. 232.—END ELEVATION.

from the trusses overhead, and by a set of coils along the partition next to the discharge and supply-room, the aim being to gradually heat the oils as they are transferred from the general stock in the storage-room till ready to discharge into the dumping-troughs. The general temperature of the oil-mixing room does not require to be over 70 degrees Fahr., but it is usually 110 degrees when working, due to the large amount of heat thrown off by the steam-jackets around the mixing-tanks. The tank-storage room in the basement is heated by a set of coils hung from the roof over the tanks, the temperature being kept at about 70 degrees Fahr. The pipes of the steam-coils are 1¼ in. in diameter.

The house is lighted throughout by incandescent lights supplied from the electric-light plant of the railroad company at the Perth Amboy terminal.

The provisions for protection against fire, as shown in Fig. 235, are particularly noteworthy in

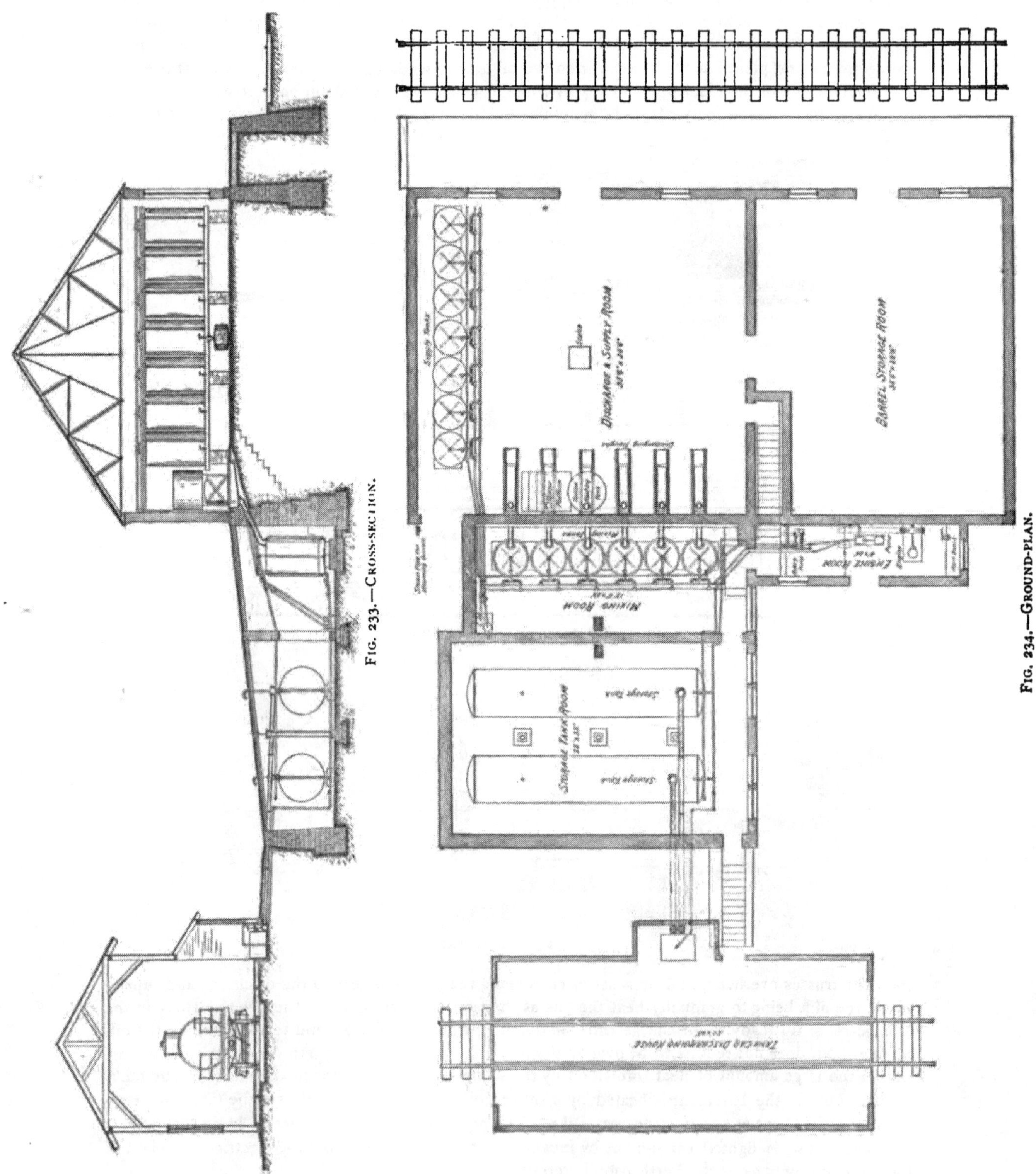

Fig. 233.—Cross-section.

Fig. 234.—Ground-plan.

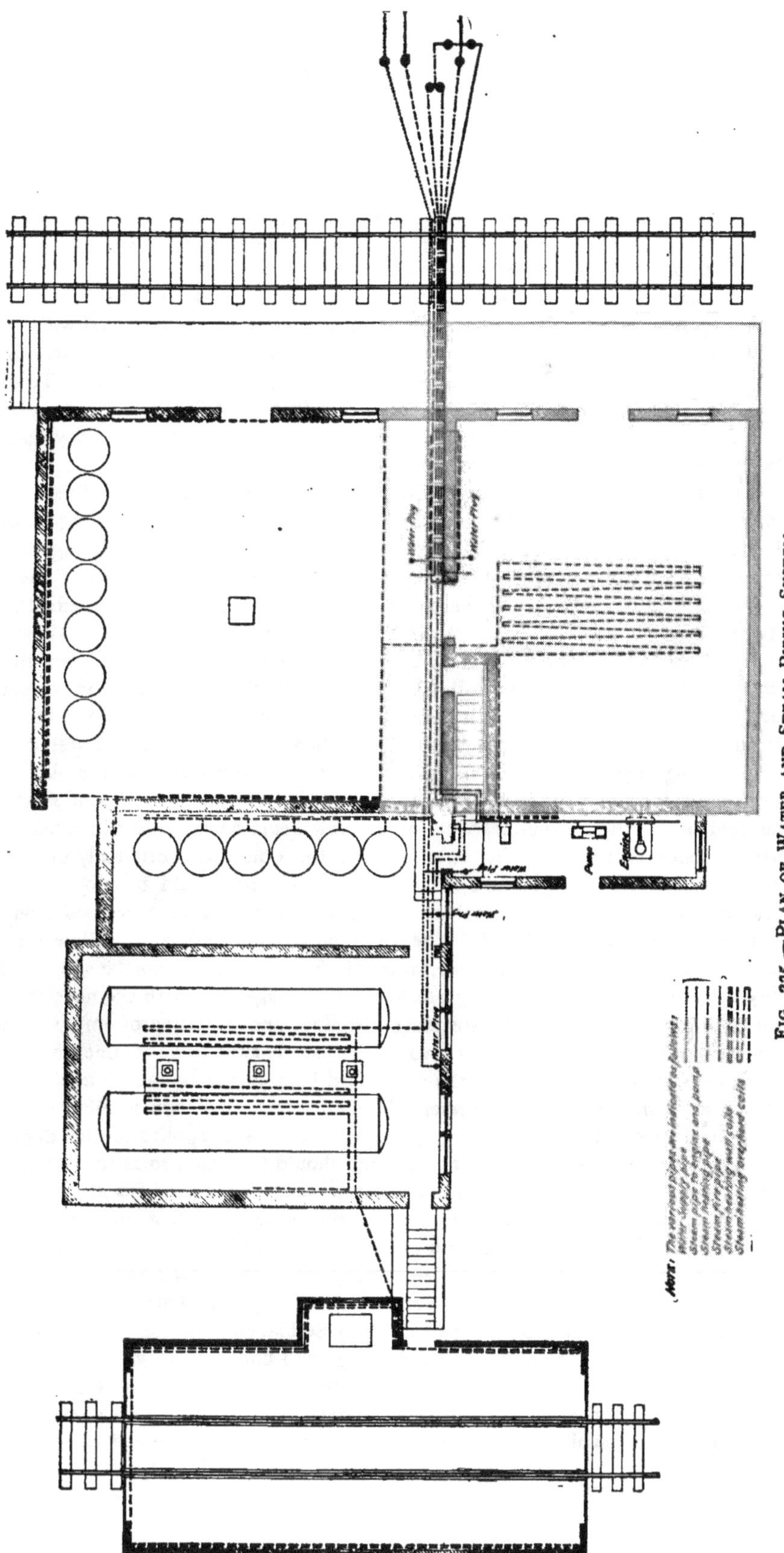

FIG. 235.—PLAN OF WATER AND STEAM PIPING SYSTEM.

this design, and have been carried out with great care and forethought. The idea of isolating the basement annex from the main body of the house and the distribution of the oil stock to different rooms and buildings, so as to limit the spread of fire, so far as possible, has been conscientiously carried out. In every room there is a 1½-in. water-pipe with about 25 ft. of hose attached ready for immediate service, the water being controlled by a valve on the wall next to the hose connection. In addition small portable chemical fire-extinguishers are placed on shelves in different parts of the building. In case a fire cannot be brought under control by the water-hose or the chemical apparatus, then the introduction of live steam into the room is employed to smother the fire: for this purpose there leads into each room a separate 1½-in. steam-pipe with an open end in the room, so that live steam can be turned into any of these rooms from the valve-house outside of the main building. To prevent the escape of the steam and to prevent the entrance of air, as also to retard the spread of a fire, all door-openings and passages have iron doors, the windows are provided with iron shutters, and all ventilators have dampers which can be closed from the outside of the house. In addition there are several hundred feet of 2½-in. fire-hose in the valve-house near the works. To prevent the large closed storage-tanks in the basement from exploding in case of fire, overflow or relief pipes are provided, which project above the shed roof over the tanks and serve to relieve any undue pressure that might be caused in the tanks by extreme heat.

After the works had been in operation for some time it was found that tallow could not be heated sufficiently, when dumped in the dumping-troughs, to run freely into the mixing-tanks, and that with steam-jackets around the mixing-tanks the tallow was not heated uniformly throughout the tank. The arrangement, shown in Figs. 233 and 234, was therefore introduced over one of the troughs leading to that one of the mixing-tanks in which tallow is used as one of the ingredients, consisting of a raised table on which the cask of tallow is rolled, the staves broken, and the tallow shovelled into a wrought-iron open tank alongside the table and immediately over the dumping-trough. This tank has steam-coils inside of it, and as the tallow melts it drains, through a pipe and wire strainer, into the dumping-trough, and reaches the oil-mixing tank in a fluid state. As the table and heating tank straddle dumping-troughs, the discharging of barrels beneath them is not interfered with.

The following suggestions are offered as desirable improvements in the plant, brought out by the experience gained in the operation of the works: It has been proved that steam-jackets do not heat the contents of the mixing-tanks uniformly, and steam-coils inside the tanks would be an improvement if kept steam-tight. The tanks in use in this house were originally ordered for the house designed for Packerton. The storage-tanks in the basement should be larger, so as to hold about 8000 galls., as the capacity of some tank-cars arriving at the works is over 6000 galls. The addition of one or two large storage-tanks would be an improvement, as it would allow a larger amount of crude oil to be kept in stock, and the operation of the works would not be so liable to interruptions caused by delay in the delivery of crude stock. A cooperage shed with the necessary appliances and steam-pipes or steam-chests for the steaming, cleaning, and repairing of empty barrels, would be a desirable addition in a new layout, as at present the barrels have to be steamed by a short steam-pipe connection, and the repairing done in the open yard back of the house. The difference in the floor levels of the main house and the basement should be increased so as to allow of heavier grades in the pipes to facilitate their drainage after pumping. This also applies to the discharge-pipes from the tank-car discharging-house. The engine-room should be larger, so as to give more room for the work-bench and better facilities for making light repairs. In a new design the disposition of the tallow-heating tank could be advantageously changed, so as to form a component part of the plan. With these modifications the buildings and plant can be considered as first-class.

Chemical Laboratory at South Bethlehem, Pa., Lehigh Valley Railroad.—In connection with the establishment of the oil-mixing house at Perth Amboy, N. J., the Lehigh Valley Railroad Company had a chemical laboratory erected in 1888 at South Bethlehem, Pa., for the use of the chemical department of the railroad. The building was designed and built by Mr. W. F. Pascoe, Superintendent Bridges and Buildings, L. V. R. R., from sketches furnished by Mr. C. P. Coleman, Chemist, L. V. R. R. This building, and especially the interior arrangements, combine a number of good features, worthy of adoption for similar structures, and it will not, hence, be out of place to devote space to

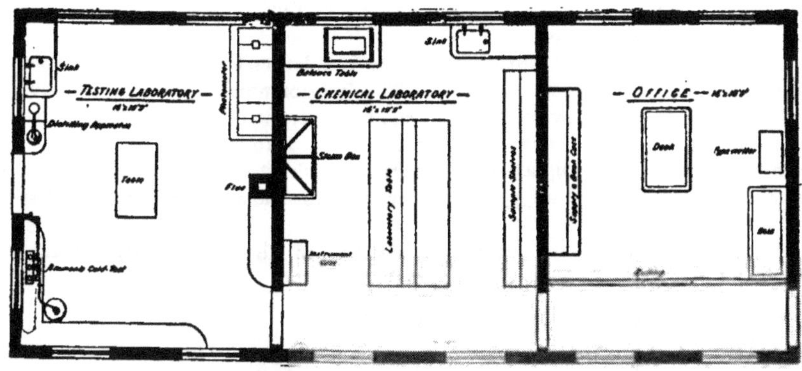

Fig. 236.—Ground-plan.

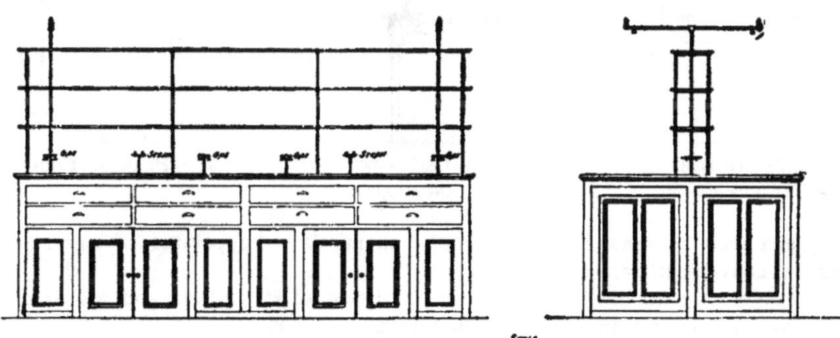

Fig. 237.—Front Elevation of Laboratory Table. Fig. 238.—End Elevation of Laboratory Table.

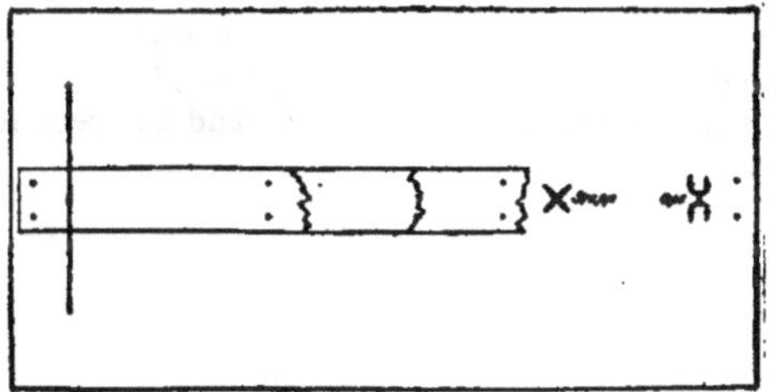

Fig. 239.—Plan of Laboratory Table.

Fig. 240.—Front Elevation of Steam-box.

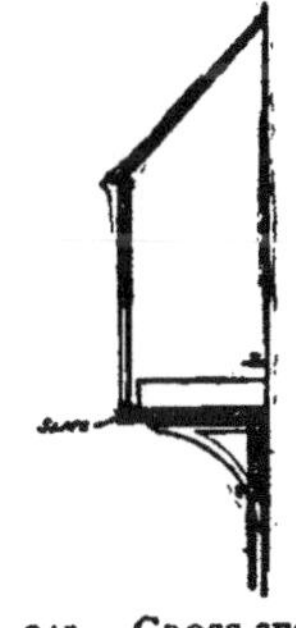

Fig. 241.—Cross-section of Steam-box.

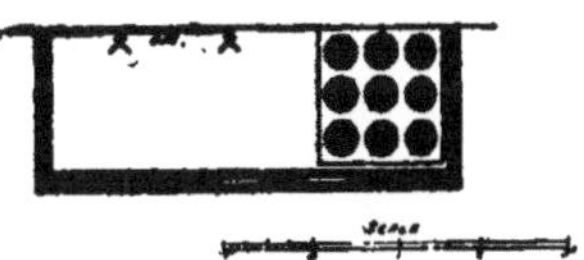

Fig. 242.—Plan of Steam box.

the following descriptions and accompanying illustrations, Figs. 236 to 245, copied from the issue of the *Railroad Gazette* of April 17, 1891:

The building is a frame structure, resting on a stone foundation, the exterior sides being sheathed with corrugated galvanized iron and roofed with slate. The interior finish is of Georgia pine throughout. It consists of three rooms, as shown by the ground-plan, Fig. 236, the office, 15 ft. × 19 ft. 9 in.; the chemical laboratory, 16 ft. × 19 ft. 9 in.; and the testing laboratory, 16 ft. × 19 ft. 9 in.

The chemical laboratory is equipped with laboratory table, steam-box or hood, balance-table, instrument-case, sink, sample shelves, and all apparatus necessary for chemical analyses. The special features of the room are:

1st. The laboratory table, a sketch of which is shown in Figs. 237 to 239, which is a table with a

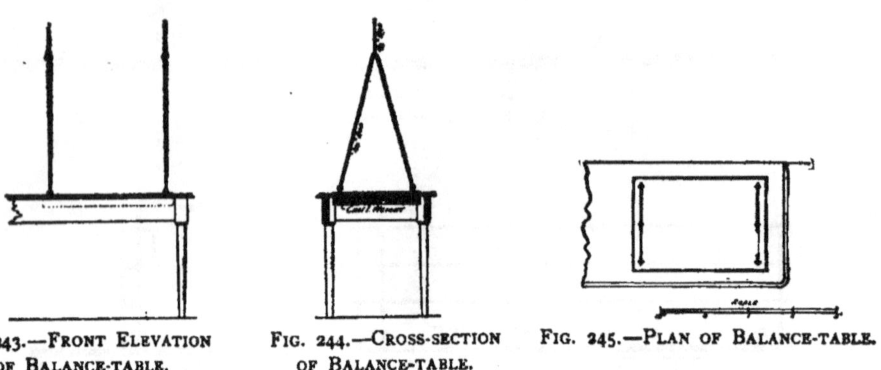

FIG. 243.—FRONT ELEVATION OF BALANCE-TABLE.

FIG. 244.—CROSS-SECTION OF BALANCE-TABLE.

FIG. 245.—PLAN OF BALANCE-TABLE.

soapstone top, and shelving, drawers, and closets for chemicals and apparatus, with gas, steam, water, and drain connections conveniently arranged on top.

2d. The steam-box or hood, Figs. 240 to 242, consisting of steam-bath and gas fixtures, and out of which a flue, shown in ground-plan, carries off the fumes.

3d. The balance-table, Figs. 243 to 245, consisting of a 1000-lb. casting, suspended by ¾-in. iron rods from a 9-in. × 6-in. iron-bound girder, the ends of which rest upon the base-beams of two of the roof-trusses. This arrangement does away with the vibrations of the balance-needle, which were caused, when the balance rested on an ordinary table, by locomotives passing over the tracks within 10 ft. of the building.

The testing laboratory is equipped with photometer, sink, distilling apparatus, ammonia and ice and salt cold-test boxes. It is also designed to admit of putting in a physical testing-machine, if it be so desired in the future. The building is heated throughout by steam, and has been found to meet every requirement of the work of the department.

CHAPTER XIV.

WATER STATIONS.

WATER stations are required on a railroad to supply water for locomotives, and are usually located from five to twenty miles apart, according to the importance and nature of the traffic on the road, ten miles being a fair average spacing. The water-supply for feeding stationary boilers, washing cars and floors, cleaning out boilers, cooling ashes, fire protection, and similar purposes, at shops, engine-houses, station buildings, etc., is very frequently connected with the water service for road engines at the same point. The provisions for the water-supply at each locality, therefore, depend to a large extent on the combination of requirements established for same. The choice and location of a system for supplying road engines is determined according to whether the tender is to be filled before the engine starts on its regular run, or whether its water-supply is to be replenished on the road, either while the train makes a stop at or between regular stations, or without stopping the train. The addition of the shop, engine-house, and station service to a water system for supplying road-engines will increase the quantity of water required and call for a greater pressure height. Where this additional supply is large the problems to be solved are analogous to those encountered in a water-works system, and hence this feature of the water-supply on a railroad will not be discussed in detail in this article.

It is essential to have double or independent water systems at all important points, so far as possible, so as not to cripple the road in case of temporary interruptions in one of the systems, caused by repairs, breakdowns, or extensions of the service. The water stations for the road supply should be so spaced along the line as to offer at all seasons of the year an absolutely reliable and ample supply for the heaviest possible traffic to be expected, and to allow for repairs or interruptions at one or several water stations at the same time. At important terminal or junction stations, shops or engine-houses, costly methods and long conduits have frequently to be employed to obtain the necessary water-supply. Water stations for the engine supply along the road, however, are generally located within a reasonable distance of the source of supply, wherever it is found, although the location at a regular station is preferable, where feasible, so as not to require engines to make special stops between stations.

The importance of the water service in the operation of a road arises not only from its necessity as a technical feature, but from the fact that it forms one of the permanent elements of the cost of operation. The United States census report of 1880 shows that the water-supply formed on an average 0.68 per cent of the total operating expenses of American railroads, the range on different roads being from 0.11 to 0.96 per cent, and the average cost per train-mile 0.6 cent. The cost of water service on the Pennsylvania Railroad system from

1879 to 1883 was reported as follows: Operating expenses, 0.602 cent per train-mile; maintenance, 0.368 cent per train-mile, or a total average expenditure of 0.97 cent per train-mile. On the Lake Shore & Michigan Southern Railroad the cost of water service from 1872 to 1881 is given as 0.6 cent per train-mile. The cost of water-supply, therefore, would seem to run from less than half a cent to a cent per train-mile, with a fair average of two-thirds of a cent.

The quantity of water required, the quality and the available sources are the essential features to be primarily considered in selecting and determining the water-supply at any point. These questions once settled, the consideration of the methods for collecting the water, conducting it to the place where it is to be used, storing it, and delivering it into the tender, is next in order.

The quantity of water required is dependent on the number of engines liable to take water per day, the duty required of them, their size and water consumption, the capacity of the tender tanks, the distance to the next nearest water station on the road, and any special duty in addition to supplying road-engines that the water service is to perform. The quantity thus ascertained should be increased at least 50 per cent to allow for fluctuations in the supply, rapidly repeated drafts on the supply at certain times during the day, waste of water in filling tenders, and loss by reason of the overflow in reservoirs. Mr. P. H. Dudley in 1882 ascertained that heavy and fast passenger-trains on the New York Central & Hudson River Railroad, working at 135 lbs. steam-pressure, evaporated 6.67 to 7.5 lbs. of water per pound of coal used, or about 40 gallons per mile on an average, the coal consumption having been from 40 to 50 lbs. per mile. A heavy freight engine burning 100 lbs. coal per mile would use about 80 gallons of water per mile. On stretches of a road with heavy grades the consumption is naturally larger, in addition to the allowance for pusher engines, where used. The capacity of tender-tanks varies considerably, ranging from 2200 to 4000 gallons, the usual size being about 2800 to 3000 gallons.

The quality of water used has a most important bearing on the repairs and the life of a boiler. Bad water induces priming, causes a deposit, or corrodes the iron rapidly. A chemical examination of the water to be used should always be made to determine its chemical composition and its percentage of incrusting matter, such as silica, oxide of iron and alumina, sulphates of lime and magnesia, and carbonates of lime and magnesia. On the Chicago, Burlington & Quincy Railroad it was found that in a tank of 2750 gallons there were 1.92 lbs. of incrusting matter in the best water used on the road, and 11.33 lbs. in the worst water in use. Theoretically, therefore, an engine, as above, consuming about 18 tanks of water per week, would in that time collect 34½ lbs. of incrustation under the best conditions and 204 lbs. under the worst conditions known on the road mentioned. While practically the actual deposit would not be so large, if the engine is kept properly cleaned out, and because considerable of the deposit is carried off mechanically, the figures, taken as they are from actual experience, serve to illustrate clearly the importance of the question. Muddy water should be avoided, or else settling basins or reservoirs introduced, in case the water constantly carries a large quantity of matter in suspension. Water from streams is generally better than water from wells or springs, but in rainy seasons it will carry considerably more sediment. Spring water that does not contain injurious alkalies or salts to a serious degree, and water collected in storage-ponds from the rainfall, if clear, are considered the best for use in boilers.

If the water available in the immediate neighborhood of a given point is found, on proper examination, to be too hard, chemically impure, or otherwise objectionable, it will, in all probability, prove advantageous to locate the proposed water station elsewhere, or even to adopt a costly pipe-line to bring good water from a more distant source. If no better source of supply is available, however, the water is frequently treated chemically with different mixtures, patented as a rule, reducing the tendency to foam and rendering the water less detrimental, or precipitating the incrusting matter before the water enters the boilers. The chemical treatment of the water prior to its entrance into the boiler is considered more desirable by the best authorities on the subject than to use so-called "boiler compounds" in the boiler.

The available sources to obtain water from are usually one or more of the following, namely, drawing from springs, from brooks or streams, from natural ponds or lakes, from artificial storage ponds or reservoirs, from dug wells or artesian wells, or from city water-works. Unless the source is unquestionably larger than the supply required, its volume should be carefully gauged or its watershed ascertained, and the minimum flow established with due regard to a probable reduction during protracted droughts. The permanency, steadiness, and capacity of a source, combined with its distance and relative elevation to the point on the road where the water is to be used, in addition to the quality of the water, would influence the choice as between several available sources.

Water is pumped from ponds, lakes, springs, wells, or streams below the level of the railroad by a suction-pipe, the end of which has a basket or hood, and is usually protected by a cribbing, grillage, or sheathing. In mountainous sections of the country, where a source is frequently found higher than the railroad, the water is collected in a settling box, basin, or reservoir, and thence allowed to run by gravity through a pipe to the railroad.

In taking water from its source to the place where it is to be used, and delivering it there at the proper height, the following methods are used, namely, transporting water along the railroad in specially constructed water-cars; or catching the water, where feasible, at sufficient height above the railroad to let it run by gravity through a pipe-line, or an open ditch and a pipe-line combined, to the railroad; or elevating it to the proper height by pumps worked by hand, steam, windmills, gas, hot-air, water or horse power. Relative to these several systems for conducting and elevating water it can be said that transporting by water-cars is used only for temporary service, or to help keep up the supply along the road during protracted droughts. The best method is, naturally, to draw the water by gravity from a basin or reservoir located in a gully or on some hill near the railroad. Pumps worked by hand or horse-power should only be resorted to as a temporary makeshift, or for a very small supply, or in connection with windmills to maintain the supply, when the water gets low, without any prospect of wind. Steam-pumps are either operated by a special boiler in connection with the pump, or steam is drawn in the vicinity of shops from the main shop boilers. Windmills give good service, where the storage capacity is comparatively large, the traffic small, and the prospects favorable for frequent winds. On the Pacific roads, artesian wells in connection with windmills are very frequent. The practicability and economy of introducing gas or hot-air engines, water-wheels, turbines, or connections with a city water service are dependent on special circumstances and conditions in each particular case. For a large water-supply a gravity system or pumping by steam or water power are the most approved methods.

For filling engine-tanks the water, after being conveyed and elevated by one of the foregoing methods, is stored in water-tanks located near the tracks and drawn from them, as required, by gravity, either through a goose-neck delivery-spout attached to the tank and projecting over the track, or through stand-pipes located along or between tracks either adjacent to or at some distance from the water-tanks. Other methods of supplying water to engine-tanks, without making use of storage-tanks or stand-pipes, are drawing the water up by a steam-injector located on the engine and worked with steam from the engine; or forcing the water up by an injector, steam-siphon, or pulsometer sunk in a well, pond, or stream alongside of the track and operated by steam from the engine or from a special boiler. Both of these methods are, however, not economical in the long-run owing to the large amount of steam required, and are only used as makeshifts in case of accidents or where a temporary supply is needed. They are used successfully, comparatively speaking, on construction work or new lines prior to the establishment of water stations. Finally, there is the system of filling the engine-tank without stopping the engine by means of a funnel-shaped pipe under the tender, which is lowered into a long, shallow water-trough between the rails, the speed with which the funnel is forced forward causing the water to rush up the pipe into the tank. This method is known as the Ramsbottom system, and is extensively and successfully used on the Pennsylvania Railroad for taking water on their fast express trains without stopping.

Relative to the location of water-tanks and stand-pipes in yards, they are usually placed along a track leading to or from the engine-house or coaling system, or located at the head of the yard, so that engines can take water along with their other supplies, such as coal, sand, oil, and waste, before starting on a run. It is customary at large layouts to either have several small water-tanks or else one large one, centrally located, with connections to the different stand-pipes. At stations on a single-track road the water-tank is located at one end of the station opposite to where the engine stands when trains in one direction make their regular stop, while at the other end of the station a stand-pipe, supplied from the water-tank, serves for the trains going in the opposite direction. Where a stand-pipe is omitted, the trains in one direction have to make a special stop for water before they pull up to the station building. At stations on double-track roads it is customary to combine a water-tank or stand-pipe along one track at one end of the station with a stand-pipe along the other track at the other end of the station; or the tracks are spread at one end of the station and a stand-pipe is placed between them, connecting with the water-tank, which in this case can be located off sideways somewhere, on probably less valuable ground. In locating water-tanks along a road the possible subsequent double-tracking or four-tracking of the road should be considered, and the tank located accordingly, which, however, in certain cases, would absolutely necessitate the use of stand-pipes. Where there are more than two tracks the spreading of the tracks and the placing of stand-pipes between the central tracks becomes necessary. The pipe connecting a water-tank with a stand-pipe should be not less than 6 in. in diameter, preferably 8 in., and even larger if the distance is considerable, so as to reduce the loss of head by friction and enable the water to reach the stand-pipe as fast as it can be drawn. Where the distance from the central or main tankage system to a stand-pipe is very great, as, for instance, an isolated stand-pipe at the far end of a station or yard layout, it will frequently prove more economical to locate a small auxiliary tank opposite the stand-pipe, with sufficient storage capacity to fill several engine-tanks, as the supply would be taken by gravity from the main tankage system through a much smaller pipe than if the engines were drawing directly from the pipe.

Wooden water-tanks are probably in universal use in this country, and they form a distinctive feature of American railroading as compared with European practice, where iron tanks are preferred. Wooden tanks are generally built circular in shape, and the staves and sundry parts are turned out to a large extent by machinery and kept in stock, so that repairs and renewals can be made very cheaply and quickly. In addition to these features, and the cheapness of the first cost, wooden tubs afford, when roofed over, in themselves a certain protection against cold, which could not be obtained in an iron tank construction without a special building or lining around it. With a view to making repairs, cleaning out sediments, and similar causes for interruption to the service, several smaller tubs are preferable to one very large one, although the first cost of a large tank is less than that of several smaller ones offering combined the same storage capacity.

Circular tanks are made of 14, 15, or 16 ft. staves, and the diameters most generally in use are 16, 18, 20, 22, 24, and 30 ft. According to the selected combination of height and depth, the capacities vary from about 20,000 gallons to 80,000 gallons. The floor of a tank is usually set about 12 to 15 feet above the track, unless a high-pressure service for other purposes is desired besides the delivery of water to engines. The foundations are usually wooden trestle-bents on mud-sills or on small stone foundation-walls. On some of the large roads in the country iron floor-beams resting on wrought- or cast-iron columns with substantial stone foundations have been extensively introduced.

The pipes in connection with a water-tank are the uptake or supply pipe, in warmer climates running up on the outside and discharging over the top of the tub, and in northern sections of the country entering through the floor with the proper protection against freezing; the discharge or delivery pipe, connecting with a goose-neck spout attachment at the face of the tank, or with a stand-pipe located at some distance from the tank; the overflow-pipe, either running down to the ground or back into the piping system, or consisting simply of a short trough or piece of pipe inserted at the top of the tub; and the waste-pipe, to draw off the water for inspections or repairs. Other fixtures in connection with a water-tank are automatic arrangements for the closing and opening of the valves in the supply and overflow pipes at the proper moment, the opening and closing of the delivery-pipe valve from the outside of the tank, either independently of the delivery-spout, or automatically in connection with the lowering and raising of the delivery-spout. An indicator or marker on a graduated staff is also universally in use to indicate the height of the water in the tank, and it is generally so arranged as to be readily seen from approaching trains. Where pumps supplying the tanks are located at some distance from the tanks, as for instance in the engine-room of a shop system, automatic indicators of various kinds are used to keep the help in the pump-room advised of the stage of the water in the tank, so as to enable them to regulate the pumping operations accordingly. Automatic signals are also used in certain cases; for instance, where a supply is intermittent or very irregular, to indicate to the operator in the nearest telegraph-office the condition of the supply, and from there it is telegraphed along the road, so that engineers of trains can be governed accordingly.

As mentioned above, the ordinary wooden tank, in connection with a tight roof over it, offers in itself a certain amount of protection against cold, owing to the low heat-conducting properties of wood, and the fact that the air above the tank is not in direct contact with the outside atmosphere and cannot be rapidly and steadily replaced by colder air from the outside, which would extract additional heat from the water, thereby gradually lowering its temperature and causing it eventually to freeze. In northern climates, where the cold is more intense, an additional safety against freezing is gained by the use of so-called frost-proof water-tanks, which merely consist of the usual wooden water-tank, with the addition of closed air-spaces above and below the tank. This is usually accomplished above the tank by sheathing beneath the rafters, or beneath or above the tie-beams of the roof, or both ways, thereby creating one or more enclosed air-spaces above the water-level. Below the tank the same result is accomplished by inserting an extra set of joists and closed planking below them, or by fitting boards tightly between the regular floor-beams under the tank. An additional precaution is to enclose the entire space under the tank, which space can be used as pump-room or for storing miscellaneous road supplies. Where the space below the tank is not enclosed, the pipes leading to the tank are protected from the cold by enclosing them in a box, which usually is filled with sawdust or straw. In very severe climates this box is made with several walls forming a number of spaces, some of which serve as air-spaces, while the others are filled with sawdust, straw, or some poor heat-conducting material. Enclosing the space below the water-tank, or the entire tank and the space below it, by a special building heated by a stove in winter, generally burning refuse coal from a coal-dump, is still used to quite an extent, although the adoption of the frost-proof water-tank is gradually superseding the older systems.

It is not feasible to discuss here in detail the question of stand-pipes, automatic valves, special water-tank appliances, pumps, steam, gas, and hot-air engines, injectors, pulsometers, steam-siphons, windmills, hand-pumps, artesian wells, hydraulic motors, etc., all of which form important elements of the subject. The principles governing these appliances are outside of the scope of this discussion, and, moreover, the best apparatus for any particular case is readily ascertained on making proper inquiries in the market, the competition between rival inventors and railroad-supply firms having caused the development and construction of machines and special appliances adapted for the water supply on railroads to reach a high degree of perfection combined with economy in operation.

Below will be found a series of descriptions and illustrations of water-tanks, for which probably every road has a standard, and which, in the main, form the most distinctive feature of the water supply on American railroads.

General Design of a Circular Water-tank.—In Fig. 246 is shown a design for a circular water-tank corresponding to the practice on a large number of railroads, more especially in the warmer sections of the country, where precautionary measures against the freezing of the water in winter are not essential. The supply-pipe can either enter the tub through the floor or be conducted over the top from the outside. The galvanized-iron delivery-spout is hinged to the delivery-pipe at the face of the tank and properly counterweighted. The delivery-pipe is closed with a lid-valve on the floor of the tank, which valve is opened by pulling on a rope on the outside of the tank, the weight of the water closing it as soon as the rope is released. The action of the valve and the movement of the spout are independent of each other.

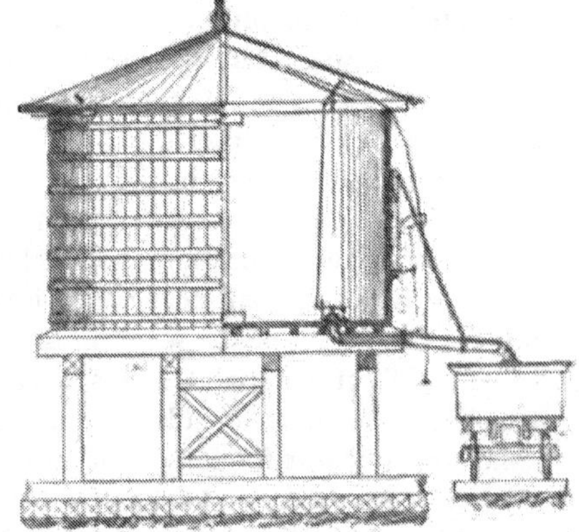

FIG. 246.—ELEVATION AND CROSS-SECTION.

Square Water-tank, Philadelphia & Reading Railroad.—The standard square water-tank of the Philadelphia & Reading Railroad, shown in Figs. 247 to 249, is a box-shaped wooden tank, 15 ft. wide in the clear, 29 ft. long in the clear, and 8 ft. deep, set on wooden floor-beams and brick piers. The floor of the tank is set 13 ft. above the top of rail. The floor-beams and supporting timbers under the tank are 12 in. × 12 in., spaced as shown. The tank is formed of plank fitted closely together, properly calked, and bound by yokes, standards, and iron tie-rods. The advantage claimed for this style of tank is that it is much cheaper to build than the usual circular tanks, and does not require as high a class of labor to put it together, and hence, under certain conditions, especially where lumber is cheap, has particular advantages over the circular tank, which is dependent on shop-work in order to be made economically.

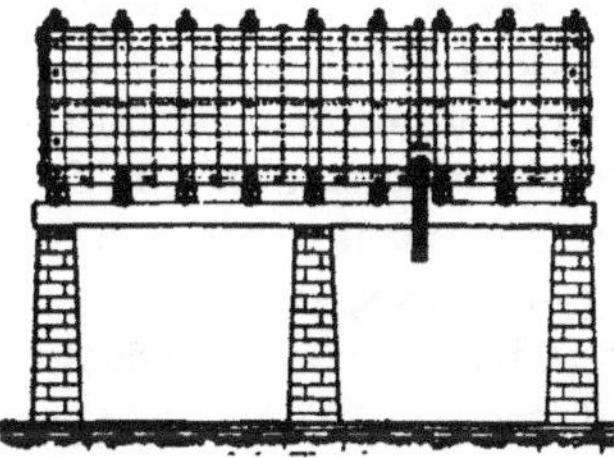

FIG. 247.—FRONT ELEVATION.

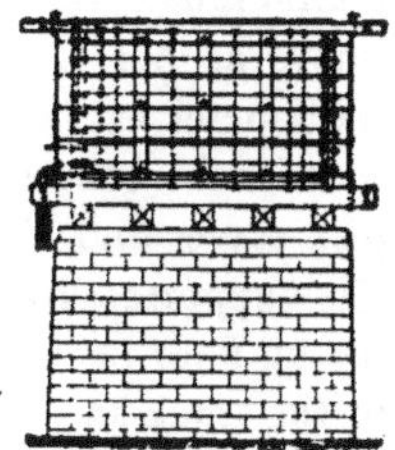

FIG. 248.—END ELEVATION.

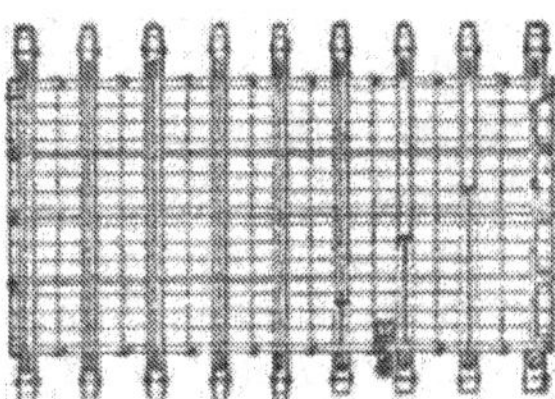

FIG. 249.—GROUND-PLAN.

Standard, 16 ft. × 24 ft., Circular Water-tank, Wabash, St. Louis & Pacific Railway.—The standard, 16 ft. × 24 ft., circular water-tank of the Wabash, St. Louis & Pacific Railway, designed by Mr. Charles Hansel, Resident Engineer, and Mr. J. E. Wallace, Superintendent, B. & B., is in its general features similar to the design shown in Fig. 246. The tub is 15 ft. 5 inches deep in the clear, 23 ft. 6 in. inside diameter at the top and 24 ft. inside diameter at the bottom, and has a capacity of 48,500 gallons.

The sides of the tub are formed of clear white-pine staves, 3 in. thick, surfaced on two sides, 16 ft. long and not exceeding 6 in. in width. The floor is made of the same kind of material as the sides. There are twelve wrought-iron hoops, each made in three sections, clamped and bolted as usual. Starting from the top downwards, there are, two hoops 3 in. × $\frac{3}{16}$ in., four hoops 4 in. × $\frac{3}{16}$ in., three hoops 5 in. × $\frac{3}{16}$ in., and three hoops 5 in. × $\frac{1}{4}$ in., varying in spacing from 22 in. centres at the top of the tub to 10 in. centres at the bottom of the tub.

The roof is circular, with a pitch of 7 in. in one foot, with sixteen rafters, 2 in. × 6 in., and five sets of nailers, 2 in. × 6 in., between the rafters. The roof is covered with $\frac{7}{8}$-in. narrow flooring, and has a man-hole, 18 in. × 26 in.

The floor of the tub is supported by a false floor of plank, 2 in. × 12 in., resting on 6-in. × 12-in. floor-joists, spaced 2 ft. centres, which in turn rest on five trestle-bents placed parallel with the track, and spaced 5 ft. centres. The caps and sills of the bents are 10 in. × 10 in.; the posts are 10 in. × 10 in., set about every 5 ft. in each bent, making twenty-one posts in all. The bents are braced from bent to bent on each side of posts with 6-in. × 8-in. X-braces, and the bents are prevented from spreading by 4-in. tie-rods, tying the outside bents together. The foundations of the trestle-bents are small masonry piers.

The supply-pipe is 4 in. in diameter and enters the tub through the floor, and is enclosed between the ground and the bottom of the tank by a 5-ft. box. The discharge-pipe is 7 in. in diameter and connected with an ordinary lid-valve on the bottom of the tub, which valve is kept closed by the weight of the water, but opened automatically from the outside as the spout is drawn down. As soon as the spout is released a counterweight draws the pipe up out of the way of the trains, and at the same time the valve closes the entrance into the discharge-pipe.

The top of the floor of the tank is set 12 ft. above the top of rail, and the centre of the tank is spaced 21 ft. from the centre of the track, using an 8-ft. 6-in. drop-pipe. The roof is painted with a mixture of mineral paint and boiled linseed-oil, and all finished work is painted with three coats of approved color. A ball-float is provided and connected with a gauge on the outside of the tank to indicate the height of the water in the tank.

The bill of material for this tank and trestle foundations is made up of the following items, namely: 10-in. × 10-in. sills; 10-in. × 10-in. posts; 10-in. × 10-in. caps; 6-in. × 12-in. joists; 2-in. × 12-in. rough boards for false floor; 2-in. × 12-in., clear, white-pine boards for tank floor; 3-in. × 6-in. × 16-ft. staves; 2-in. × 6 in. rafters; 2-in. × 6-in. ribbons; ⅞-in. narrow flooring for roof; mouldings and facia for cornice; braces, 6 in. × 8 in.; finial and finial brackets; 1-in. tie-rods for trestle-bents. Also the following material: washers, bolts, spikes, wrought-iron hoops, hoop-clamps, valve-rod lever, fulcrum, goose-neck, drop-pipe, Batavia valve, cut-off valve, float-ball for gauge, pulleys for drop-pipe, chain for drop-pipe, counterweights, gauge-weight, gauge-slide, rough 1-in. boards for box around supply-pipe, with door and fixtures complete for same.

Standard, 16 ft. × 24 ft., Circular Water-tank, Cincinnati Southern Railway.—The standard, 16 ft. × 24 ft., circular water-tank of the Cincinnati Southern Railway and associated roads, with a capacity of 50,000 gallons, is built in general as per the plan shown in Fig. 246. The tub is 15 ft. deep in the clear, and 22 ft. 3 in. inside diameter at the top and 23 ft. inside diameter at the bottom. The centre of the tank is set 21 ft. 5 in. from the centre of the track, using an 8-ft. 5-in. drop-pipe.

The sides of the tub are built of 3-in. staves and the floor of 2-in. plank. The tub is bound by twelve wrought-iron hoops. The floor is supported by 3-in. × 5½-in. joists, set 15 in. centres. The joists are supported in turn by 3-in. × 12-in. floor beams, spaced 16 in. centres. The floor-beams rest on four trestle-bents, placed parallel with the track and spaced 7 ft. centres. The outside trestle-bents have two posts, the inside bents have each four posts. The posts, caps, and sills of the bents are 12 in. × 12 in. The middle bents are braced by 4-in. × 6-in. X-bracing and tied together with 1-in. tie-rods. The roof is a regular circular roof with two thicknesses of 1-in. boards, with building-paper laid between them, resting on circular frames and covered with shingles.

The supply-pipe enters at the bottom of the tank, and is protected between the tank and the ground by a frost-proof box about 7 ft. square, sheathed on the inside and outside with 1-in. boards, leaving a 6-in. air-space. The discharge-pipe is 7 in. in diameter, and the entrance to it on the floor of the tub is closed with a lid-valve operated from the outside of the tank by a lever-arm and rope attached to it. The rope is drawn down by the engineman, and kept down as long as he wishes water to flow through the drop-pipe. The latter is counterweighted, and pulled down by hand prior to opening the valve. After the desired amount of water is taken the engineman lets go the rope attached to the valve-lever and then pushes the drop-pipe up to its original position. The foundations of the trestles are either stone piers or timber.

The specification for water-stations and water-tanks on the Cincinnati Southern Railway will be found embodied in the *General Specifications* for the construction of the Cincinnati Southern Railway, printed in the Appendix at the back of this book.

Standard, 14 ft. × 22 ft., Circular Water-tank, Pennsylvania Railroad.—The standard, 14 ft. × 22 ft., circular frost-proof water-tank of the Pennsylvania Railroad, shown in Figs. 250 to 258, with a capacity of 35,040 gallons, is 13 ft. deep in the clear, and 22 ft. inside diameter at the bottom and 20 ft. 10 in. inside diameter at the top. The sides are built of 3-in. staves, and the floor is built of 3-in. plank. The tub is bound by ten wrought-iron hoops, 4 in. × $\frac{5}{16}$ in. at the top of the tub and 5 in. × $\frac{5}{16}$ in. at the bottom, spaced 30 in. centres at the top and diminishing to a spacing of 8 in. centres at the bottom. The floor of the tub rests on 3-in. × 5-in. joists, spaced about 18 in. centres, resting on 5-in. × 12-in. floor-beams, spaced 18 in. centres, which in turn are supported by four trestle-bents placed parallel with the track and spaced 6 ft. 10 in. centres. Between the caps of the trestle-bents and the floor-beams there is a 1-in. floor, with a layer of building-paper inserted, which forms, together with the bottom of the tub, an air-space underneath the tank. The caps of the trestles are 12 in. × 16 in.,

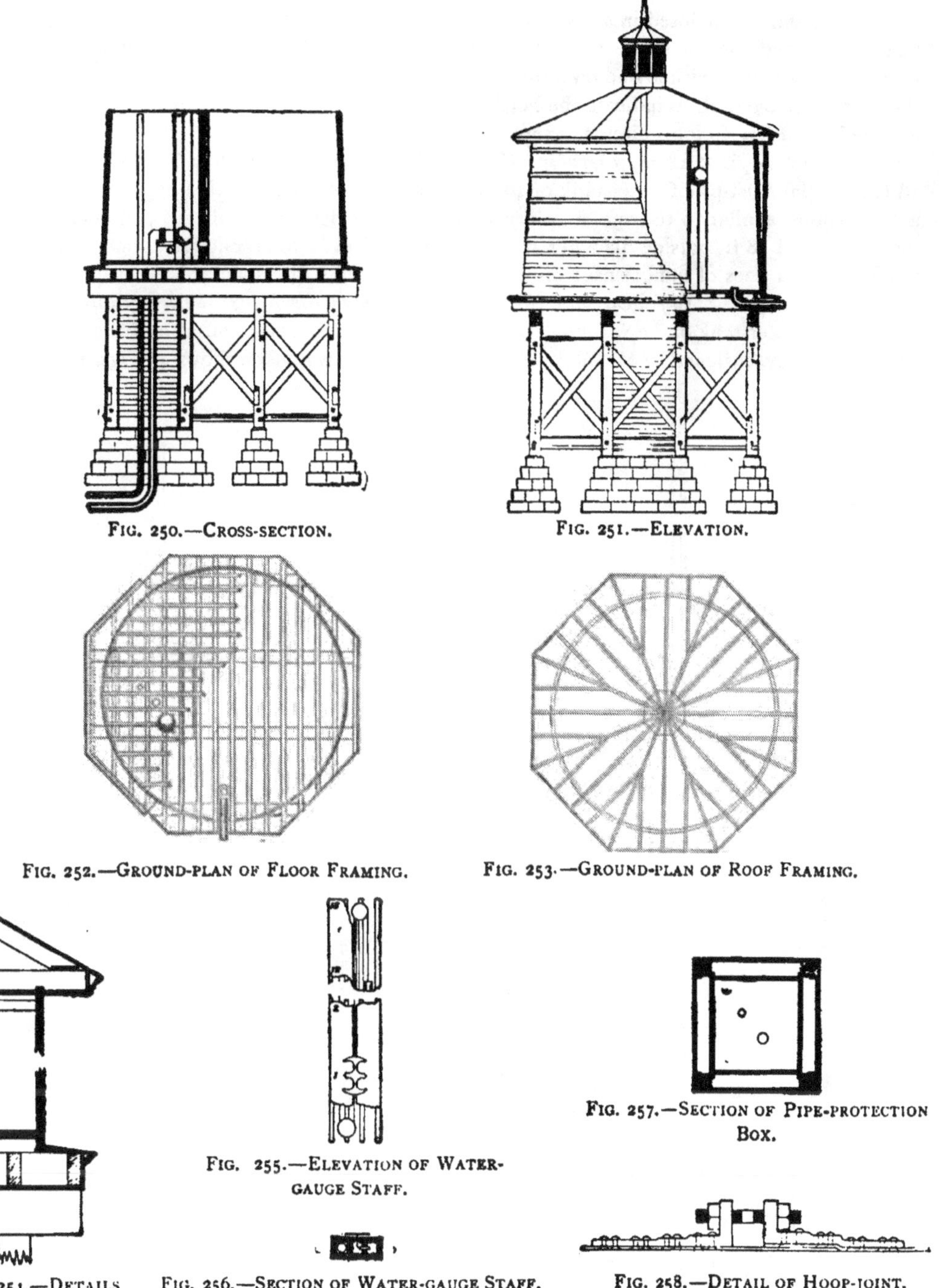

FIG. 250.—CROSS-SECTION.

FIG. 251.—ELEVATION.

FIG. 252.—GROUND-PLAN OF FLOOR FRAMING.

FIG. 253.—GROUND-PLAN OF ROOF FRAMING.

FIG. 254.—DETAILS OF TANK.

FIG. 255.—ELEVATION OF WATER-GAUGE STAFF.

FIG. 256.—SECTION OF WATER-GAUGE STAFF.

FIG. 257.—SECTION OF PIPE-PROTECTION BOX.

FIG. 258.—DETAIL OF HOOP-JOINT.

the posts are 12 in. × 12 in., the outside bents having each two posts, the inside bents each four, and the bents being prevented from spreading by 1-in. tie-rods, by 6-in. × 8-in. X-bracing, and by 4-in. × 6-in. horizontal struts near the ground level.

The roof is circular, with 3-in. × 6-in. rafters and 3-in. × 8-in. tie-beams, sheathed on top of the rafters and below the tie-beams with 1-in. boards. Building-paper is inserted above the sheathing under the tie-beams. Thus the tank has on the top and on the bottom a double sheathing, forming air-spaces, which prevent the water from freezing. The supply-pipes and overflow-pipes enter the tub through the bottom and are inclosed in an 8-ft. box between the bottom of the tank and the ground, which box is sheathed on the inside and outside with a layer of building-paper and 1-in. boards. The supply-pipe is closed with a Ludlow valve. An 18-in. copper ball-float is connected with a marker on the outside of the tank to indicate the height of the water. The height of the tank above the track is varied according to local circumstances.

Standard, 14 ft. × 18 ft., Circular Water-tank, Pennsylvania Railroad.—The standard, 14 ft. × 18 ft., circular frost-proof water-tank of the Pennsylvania Railroad, with a capacity of 23,628 gallons, is built almost similar to the one of a larger capacity just described. It is 13 ft. deep in the clear on the inside, and 18 ft. outside diameter at the bottom and 16 ft. 10 in. outside diameter at the top. All the details and sizes of lumber used are the same as for the larger standard.

Standard, 15 ft. × 16 ft., Circular Water-tank, Savannah, Florida & Western Railway.—The standard circular water-tank of the Savannah, Florida & Western Railway, and also of the Charleston & Savannah Railway, designed by Mr. W. B. W. Howe, Jr., Chief Engineer, shown in Figs. 259 and 260, is 15

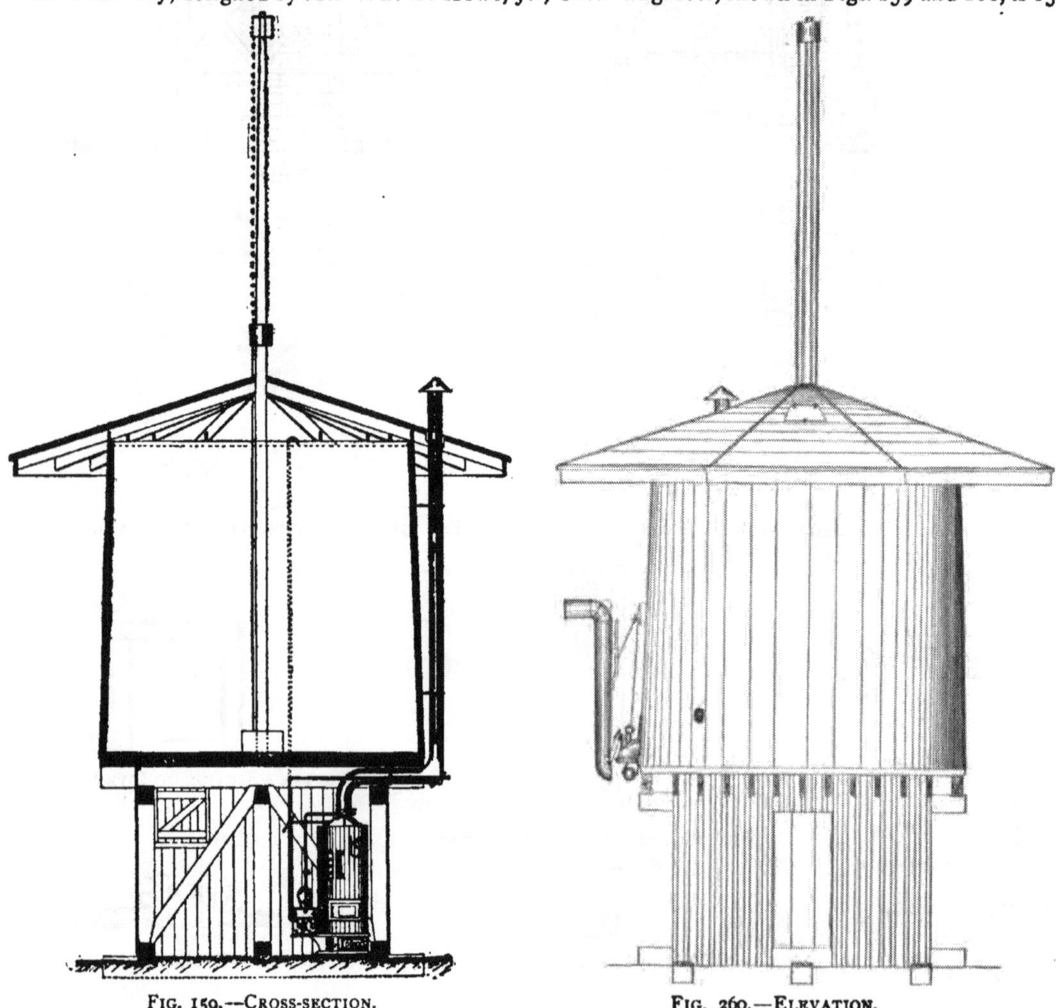

FIG. 159.—CROSS-SECTION. FIG. 260.—ELEVATION.

ft. deep in the clear, 16 ft. 1 in. outside diameter at the bottom, and 15 ft. outside diameter at the top. The bottom of the floor of the tank is set 8 ft. 6 in. above the top of rail, and the centre of the tank is set about 19 ft. from the centre of the track. The sides of the tub are made of 3-in. staves, and the bottom is made of 3-in. plank. The roof is octagonal, covered with 1-in. tongued and grooved boards on 2-in. × 6-in. rafters, and with 1½-in. × 9-in. facia boards. The roof has a man-hole, 16 in. × 20 in. in the clear.

The tub is supported on a solid 4-in. plank floor, 16 ft. × 16 ft., which rests on 3-in. × 12-in. floor-joists, spaced 15 in. centres. The floor-joists are supported by three trestle-bents, placed perpendicular to the track, and spaced 5 ft. 10 in. centres. Each trestle-bent has three posts, 10 in. × 10 in., and the sills and caps are 10 in. × 10 in. The bents are braced by 8-in. × 8-in. braces. The foundations of the bents are three 12-in. × 12-in. mud-sills.

The inlet-pipe enters the tank from the outside at the top. The outlet-pipe is tapped into the side of the tank just above the floor, and is closed automatically by a weight. As soon as the galvanized-iron delivery-spout is drawn down by the train hands and the back end of the spout strikes the socket of the discharge-pipe, the valve is opened, thus allowing the water to run freely. The method of tapping the discharge-pipe into the side of the tub above the floor will enable clearer water to be delivered, as mud and sediments collecting on the floor of the tank cannot be flushed into the pipe. The gauge for marking the height of water in the tub is a ring fitting around an upright pole, like a flagstaff, on top of the roof. The ring or circular disk moves up and down this pole according to the height of the galvanized-iron float inside the tank, thus allowing trainmen to see from quite a distance how much water is in the tank, without having to wait until they get up to and opposite the tank.

Standard, 16 ft. × 24 ft., Circular Water-tank, Chicago, St. Paul & Kansas City Railway.—The standard, 16 ft. × 24 ft., circular water-tank of the Chicago, St. Paul & Kansas City Railway, shown in Fig. 261, is 15 ft. 9 in. deep in the clear, 24 ft. outside diameter at the bottom, and 23 ft. 3 in. outside diameter at the top. The bottom of the floor is set 12 ft. 9 in. above the top of rail, and the centre of the tank is located 21 ft. 9 in. from the centre of the track.

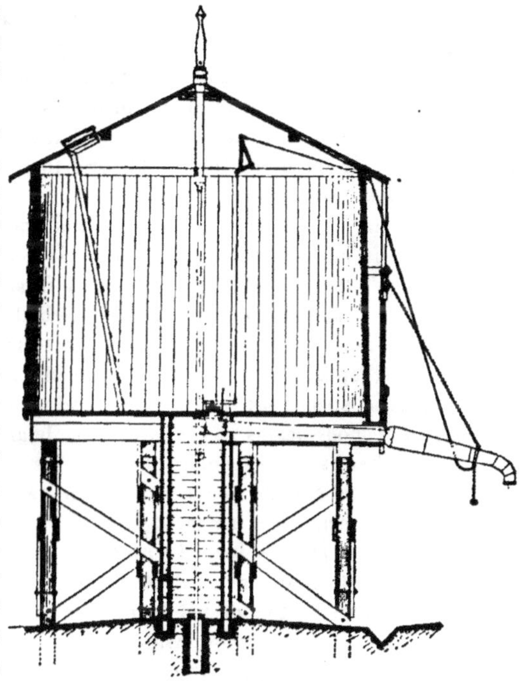

Fig. 261.—Cross-section.

The tub is built of 3-in. staves and 3-in. floor-planks. It is bound by 12 wrought-iron hoops, 3½ in. wide at the top and increasing to 6 in. in width at the bottom, spaced 24 in. centres at the top and running down to a spacing of 9-in. centres at the bottom. The roof is a regular circular roof made of two layers of 1-in. boards, resting on circular frames.

The tub rests on 3-in. by 6-in. floor-joists, spaced 15 in. centres, which rest on 3-in. by 12-in. floor-beams, spaced 15 in. centres. In the standard plan the floor-beams are supported by four pile trestle-bents placed parallel with the track and spaced 6 ft. 10 in. centres, with two piles in each outside bent and four piles in each inside bent. The caps of the bents are 12 in. × 12 in., the brace-plank in both directions 3 in. × 10 in., bolted to the piles. The inlet-pipe and the overflow-pipe enter the tank through the bottom and are enclosed from the ground up to the bottom of the tank in a 5-ft. double-sheathed box. The discharge-pipe leaves the tank at the floor near the centre of the tank and runs underneath the floor to the outside of the tank, where it discharges into a galvanized-iron goose-neck or delivery-spout. The discharge-pipe at the bottom of the tank near the centre of the floor is closed by an ordinary lid-valve operated by levers and a rope over pulleys from the outside of the tank. The delivery-spout is counterweighted, and has to be drawn down by the trainmen. As a rule, water-tanks on this road are supplied with water from wells, worked by windmills, placed as near the tank as possible.

Standard, 16 ft. × 24 ft., Circular Water-tank, Atchison, Topeka & Santa Fe Railroad.—The standard, 16 ft. × 24 ft., circular water-tank of the Atchison, Topeka & Santa Fe Railroad is 15 ft. 6 in. deep in the clear, 24 ft. outside diameter at the bottom, and 23 ft. 2½ in. outside diameter at the top, and corresponds in general to the design shown in Fig. 246. The top of the floor is 12 ft. 2 in. above the top of rail, the centre of the discharge-pipe at the back end of the goose-neck is set 10 ft. 8 in. above the top of rail. The centre of the tank is located 23 ft. 6 in. from the centre of the track.

The tub is built of 3-in. staves, 3-in. floor-planks, and is bound by fourteen wrought-iron hoops, 4 in. × $\frac{3}{16}$ in. in size, spaced 43 in. centres at the top and diminishing to 7 in. centres at the bottom of the tank. The roof is a regular circular roof, with 2-in. × 6-in. rafters, tie-beams and nailers, and covered by 1-in. boards and shingles.

The floor of the tub is supported by 4-in. × 6-in. floor-joists, spaced about 24 in. centres, and 5-in. × 12-in. floor-beams, spaced 24 in. centres. Between the floor-joists and the floor-beams there is a floor of 1-in. plank, forming an air-space in connection with the tank floor. The floor-beams are supported by five trestle-bents placed parallel to the track, and spaced 5 ft. 2 in. centres. The caps of the bents are 10 in. × 14 in., and the posts 10 in. × 10 in., resting on stone piers without any sills. There are twenty-one posts and piers, the inside nine of which are thoroughly braced together by 6-in. × 6-in. X-braces and 1-in. tie-rods.

The discharge-pipe leaves the tank near the centre of the floor, and is closed by a lid-valve worked from the outside of the house by appropriate levers, pulleys, and ropes. The discharge-pipe runs under the floor to the face of the tank, and connects there with a galvanized-iron 9-in. goose-neck or delivery-spout. The tank is provided with a float and marker similar to the other tanks described.

Standard, 16 ft. × 16 ft., Circular Water-tank, Northern Pacific Railroad.—The standard, 16 ft. × 16 ft., circular water-tank of the Northern Pacific Railroad, designed by Mr. C. B. Talbot, similar to the water-tank shown in Fig. 262, has a capacity of 21,000 gallons, and is 15 ft. 2 in. deep in the clear, 16 ft. inside diameter at the bottom, and 15 ft. 4 in. inside diameter at the top. The floor of the tank is set about 11 ft. 6 in. above the top of the rail. The top of the delivery-spout at the back end is set 10 ft. 7 in. above the top of rail, and the centre of the tank is located 17 ft. 9 in. from the centre of the track, using a 9-ft. 2-in. spout.

The tub is built of 3$\frac{3}{16}$-in. staves and floor-plank, and is bound with twelve wrought-iron hoops. The roof is circular, with 2-in. × 6-in. tie-beams and 2-in. × 4-in. rafters, covered with boards and shingles. The bottom of the tie-beams is sheathed with 1-in. plank, forming with the roof-sheathing an air-space on top of the tank, which, with the air-space at the bottom of the tank, as described below, renders the tank frost-proof. The floor of the tank rests on 2-in. × 6-in. floor-joists, spaced 8 in. centres, placed parallel with the track and resting on 3-in. × 12-in. floor-beams, spaced 15 in. centres, and placed perpendicular to the track. Between the floor-joists and floor-beams there are 1-in. boards, thus forming an air-space with the tank floor. The floor-beams are supported by four bents placed parallel with the track and spaced 4 ft. 8 in. centres. The outside bents have each two posts and the inside bents each four posts. The caps of the bents are 12 in. × 12 in., the posts 12 in. × 12 in., the sills 12 in. × 16 in. The bents are appropriately braced with struts and tied together with rods. The pipes entering the tank through the floor are inclosed between the ground and the floor of the tank in a pipe-chamber, a notable feature of the design being the care taken to protect this chamber from the cold. The chamber is 3 ft. 6 in. square inside, and is surrounded by four different walls of 1-in. plank, one outside of the other, forming thus from the outside in first a space of 18 in. filled with sawdust, then a 24-in. air-space, and lastly a 12-in. space filled with sawdust.

The discharge-pipe leaves the tank near the centre of the floor, and is closed by a lid-valve operated from the outside by appropriate fixtures; it runs under the floor between the floor-beams to the face of the tank, where it connects to a counterweighted goose-neck.

Standard, 16 ft. × 24 ft., Circular Water-tank, Northern Pacific Railroad.—The 16-ft. × 24-ft. circular water-tank of the Northern Pacific Railroad at Heron, Mt., designed by Mr. C. B. Talbot, similar to the water-tank shown in Fig. 262, has a capacity of 49,000 gallons, and in most of its details and general arrangements is almost identical with the 16-ft. × 16-ft. tank previously described. The outside staves and the floor are made of $3\frac{3}{16}$-in. plank, the floor-joists are 2 in. × 8 in., and the floor-beams are 4 in. × 14 in. The caps of the bents are 12 in. × 15 in. The distinctive feature of this design is the automatic arrangement for opening and closing the valve in the supply-pipe. This is done by means of a 14-in. cedar float on one end of a lever, the other end of which is connected by a

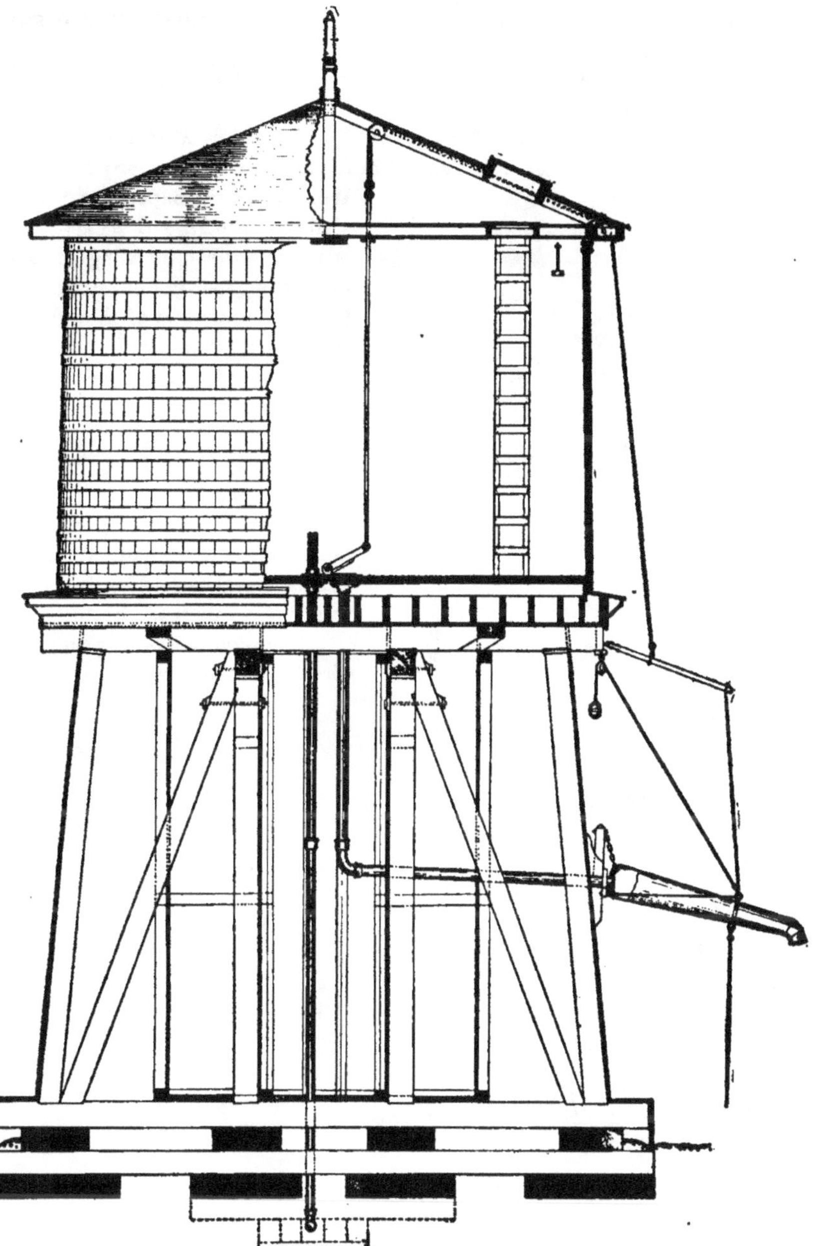

FIG. 262.—ELEVATION AND CROSS-SECTION.

pipe-rod with the valve-stem of a Chapman valve in the supply-pipe below the ground under the tank.

High Water-tank, Northern Pacific Railroad.—The high water-tank of the Northern Pacific Railroad, shown in Fig. 262, designed by Mr. C. B. Talbot, with a capacity of 49,000 gallons, is the usual standard, 16 ft. × 24 ft., circular water-tank of the same road, placed on a higher trestling than usual, in order to obtain a greater pressure at the outlet-pipe. The floor of the tank is set about 25 ft. above the top of rail, while the delivery-spout is kept at the usual elevation. The outlet valve on the floor of the tank is opened automatically when the delivery-spout is pulled down, and closes as soon as the spout is pushed upward.

Throughout this design the greatest care is taken to form air-spaces, and spaces filled in with sawdust, so as to protect the pipes under the tank, and also to keep the water in the tank from freezing. The outside of the trestling under the tank is sheathed with weather-boarding as an additional protection against severe weather.

Standard, 16 ft. × 20 ft., Circular Water-tank, Lehigh Valley Railroad.—The standard, 16 ft. × 20 ft., circular water-tank of the Lehigh Valley Railroad, shown in Figs. 263 and 264, designed by Mr. Wm. F. Pascoe, Superintendent of Bridges, Lehigh Valley Railroad, with a capacity of 34,292 gallons, is particularly interesting on account of the use of a wrought-iron and stone substructure for the tank. The tank is of the usual pattern, with 3-in. staves, 3-in. floor-plank, and 3-in. false floor, with 1-in. tongued and grooved boards nailed between the wrought-iron I-beam floor-joists under the false floor. The tub is bound by 14 wrought-iron hoops, $3\frac{1}{2}$ in. × $\frac{3}{16}$ in. The roof is octagonal, formed of 4-in. × 6-in. rafters, 3-in. × 4-in. nailers, and 4-in. × 7-in. tie-beams, held to the peak of the roof with a $\frac{7}{8}$-in. tie-rod. The tie-beams are sheathed on top and bottom, forming thus a 7-in. air-space on top of the tank.

The floor-joists rest on 6 wrought-iron plate-girder floor-beams, 18 in. high, spaced from 30 in. to 42 in. apart. The floor-beams are supported by 20-in. wrought-iron plate-girders on four sides of the hexagon formed by 6 wrought-iron columns, which transmit the load to a substantial stone foundation-wall. The floor-beams according to their length have a $\frac{7}{16}$-in., a $\frac{5}{16}$-in., or a $\frac{1}{4}$-in. web, and respectively 3-in. × 4-in. × $\frac{1}{2}$-in., 3-in. × 3-in. × $\frac{7}{16}$-in., or 3-in. × 3-in. × $\frac{1}{4}$-in. chord-angles; the stiffeners are in all cases $2\frac{1}{2}$-in. × 3-in. × $\frac{3}{8}$-in. angles. The 20-in. plate-girders connecting the columns have $\frac{7}{16}$-in. webs, 3-in. × 4-in. × $\frac{7}{16}$-in. chord-angles, 3-in. × $3\frac{1}{2}$-in. × $\frac{3}{8}$-in. stiffeners, and $\frac{7}{8}$-in. rivets. The columns are 9 ft. long, and each is composed of two 12-in. wrought-iron channels, with $2\frac{1}{4}$-in. × $\frac{1}{4}$-in. lattice-bars, 1-in. top and bottom plates, and $\frac{3}{4}$-in. rivets. The bed-plates are 22 in. square. The stone foundation-wall is 28 in. wide on top, with appropriate footings at its bed, and is built in the

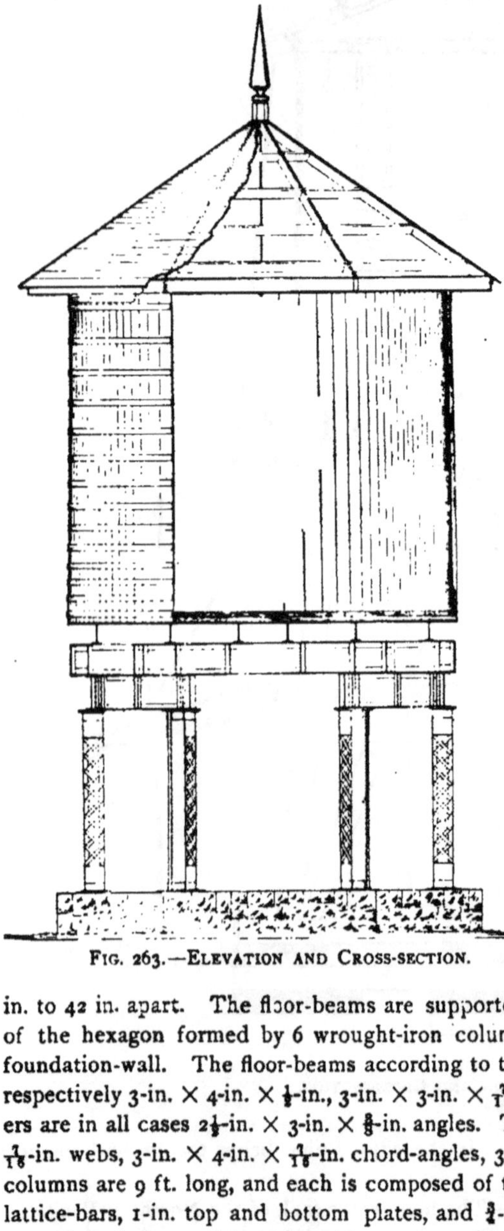

FIG. 263.—ELEVATION AND CROSS-SECTION.

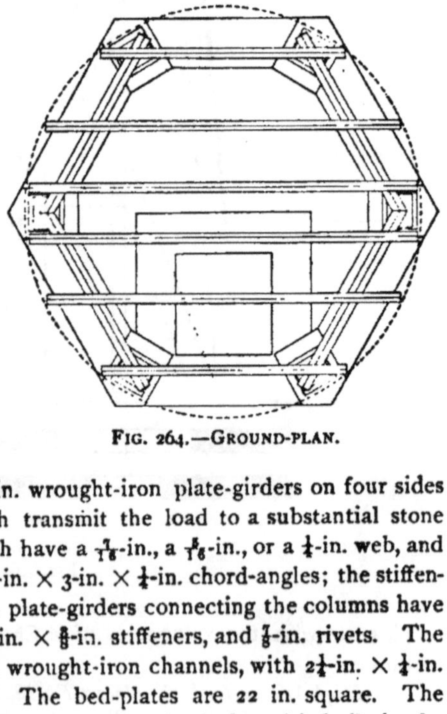

FIG. 264.—GROUND-PLAN.

shape of a hexagon, special large pedestal stones being set at the corners under the columns. On two sides of the hexagon 2-ft. openings are left in the foundation-wall, several feet below the surface, to admit the necessary pipes to the pipe-chamber in which the pipes ascend to the tank. This pipe-chamber is protected in the usual way by a frost-proof box. The floor of the tank is set about 14 ft. 9 in. above the top of rail.

Standard, 16 ft. × 30 ft., Circular Water-tank, Lehigh Valley Railroad.—The standard, 16 ft. × 30 ft., circular water-tank of the Lehigh Valley Railroad, shown in Figs. 265 and 266, designed by

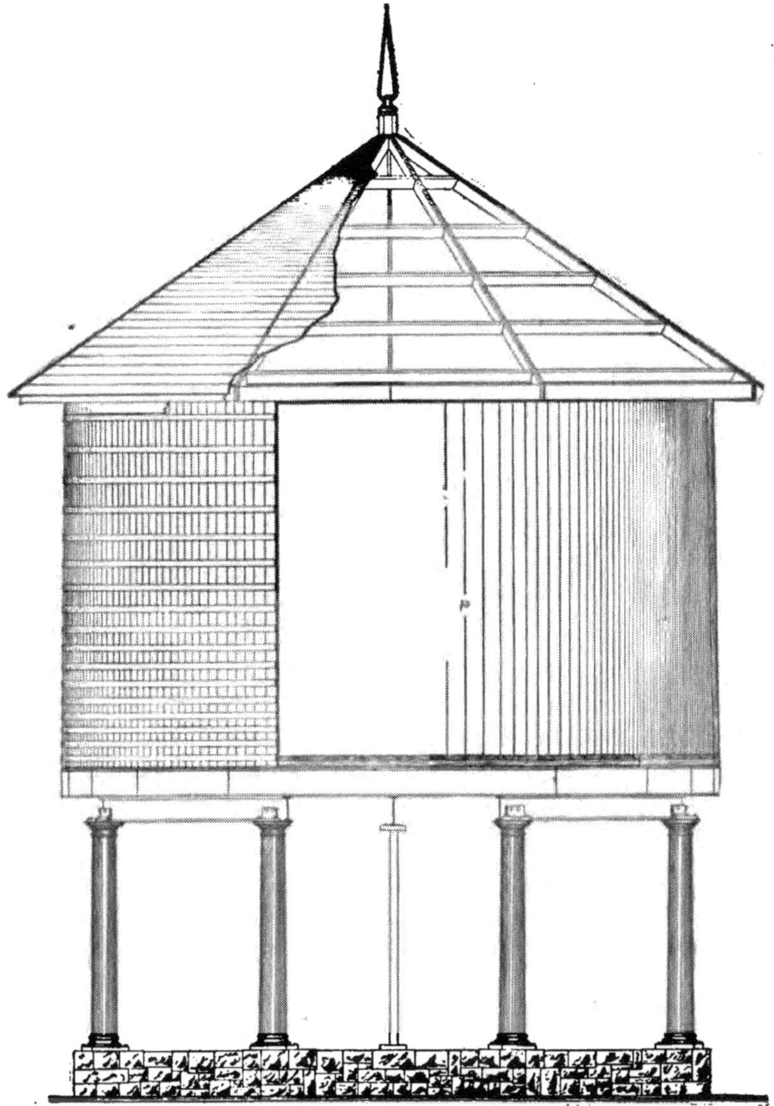

FIG. 265.—ELEVATION AND CROSS-SECTION.

Mr. Wm. F. Pascoe, Superintendent of Bridges, Lehigh Valley Railroad, with a capacity of 75,154 gallons, is noteworthy on account of its size and the permanent character of its substructure, namely, wrought-iron beams on cast-iron columns and stone foundation-walls. The construction of the tub and the dimensions of the materials used are exactly the same as for the 20-ft. standard of the same road, excepting that the tub is bound with 17 hoops in place of 14 as in the smaller standard. The tank rests on nine wrought-iron 15-in. rolled I-beams, 150 lbs. per yard, spaced from 37 in. to 44 in.

centres. These floor-beams are supported through the centre by a wrought-iron 15-in. rolled I-beam, 200 lbs. per yard, resting on four columns, each column consisting of a wrought-iron 9-in. rolled I-beam, 100 lbs. per yard. The floor-beams are supported at their ends by wrought-iron 12-in. rolled beams, 170 lbs. per yard, connecting on six sides the corners of an octagon formed by eight cast-iron ornamental columns, which transmit the load to the stone foundation. These cast-iron columns are 10 ft. high, 11¾ in. outside diameter at the top of the shaft and 14½ in. at the bottom, and have a

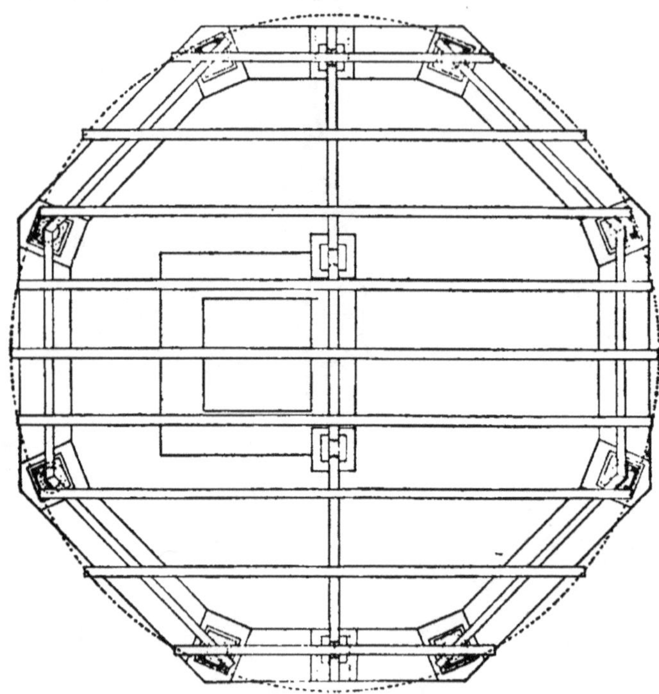

FIG. 266.—GROUND-PLAN.

base 20 in. square. The thickness of the metal in the columns is 1¼ in. The foundation-wall is 28 in. wide on top, with appropriate openings for the passage of pipes underneath the ground, which pipes ascend to the tank in a frost-proof pipe-chamber, for which a special foundation-wall is built, as shown on the plans. The floor of the tank is usually set about 15 ft. above the top of rail.

In general it can be said relative to the water-tanks on the Lehigh Valley Railroad that they are usually connected with stand-pipes located between the main tracks, or alongside of leaders, or at the head of yards, in which case attachments for the delivery of water directly out of the tank through goose-necks, etc., are not required. The supply-pipe and waste-pipe are 4 in. in diameter, and the delivery-pipe is 8 in. in diameter.

The following estimates of the cost of the standard 20-ft. and 30-ft. tanks on wrought-iron or cast-iron columns and on stone foundations have been kindly furnished by Mr. Pascoe, who states that the figures represent fair averages for usual conditions encountered:

Cost of a 20-ft. tank complete on wrought-iron columns.	
Masonry	$336 00
Wrought-iron (15,775 lbs.)	500 00
Tub	302 00
Pipes, valves, and laying	443 90
Erection	115 00
Total	$1,696 90

Cost of a 30-ft. tank complete on wrought-iron columns.	
Masonry	$402 00
Wrought-iron (28,936 lbs.)	927 00
Tub	461 00
Pipes, valves, and laying	486 30
Erection	189 00
Total	$2,465 30

Cost of a 20-ft. tank complete on cast-iron columns.		*Cost of a 30-ft. tank complete on cast-iron columns.*	
Masonry	$336 00	Masonry	$402 00
Cast-iron (14,568 lbs.)	291 36	Cast-iron (15,340 lbs.)	306 80
Wrought-iron (11,997 lbs.)	373 11	Wrought-iron (17,995 lbs.)	559 64
Tub	302 00	Tub	461 00
Pipes, valves, and laying	443 90	Pipes, valves, and laying	486 30
Erection	115 00	Erection	189 00
Total	$1,861 37	Total	$2,404 74

Standard, 16 ft. × 24 ft., Circular Water-tank, Union Pacific Railway.—The standard, 16 ft. × 24 ft., circular water-tank of the Union Pacific Railway, with a capacity of about 48,000 gallons, described and illustrated in the *Railroad Gazette*, issue of Sept. 5, 1890, is a wooden tank of the usual make, supported on eight ornamental cast-iron columns, bedded on stone piers. The tank is located between two tracks, and has spouts facing each track, affording thus extra facilities for the quick dispatch of engines taking water. The tank is covered with a ceiling of $\frac{7}{8}$-in. pine nailed to 2 in. × 6 in. joists, with one layer of building-paper above the ceiling. The roof is formed of $\frac{7}{8}$-in. pine laid over one layer of building-paper, with the joints covered with bevelled battens. The valves are of babbitt, and have rubber seats. All bolts passing through the tank are wound with oakum and white-lead to prevent leakage. The rafters in the roof are 2 in. × 6 in., and the staves are $2\frac{3}{4}$ in. thick and 6 in. wide, laid without dovetails. The hoops are $4\frac{1}{2}$ in. wide and $\frac{5}{32}$ in. thick, riveted to the buckles, which are drawn together by two bolts 1 in. diameter and $11\frac{1}{2}$ in. long.

Feed Water-trough, Pennsylvania Railroad.—The Pennsylvania Railroad has introduced with great success on its principal lines feed water-troughs in the track on what is known as the Ramsbottom system, enabling engines to take water while running, and thus save time which would otherwise be spent in stopping at water stations, which feature is especially valuable for fast through-trains. These tanks are generally about 1200 ft. long, and made of $\frac{3}{16}$-in. wrought-iron plates appropriately stiffened with angle-iron at the sides and half-round irons along the top. The width of the tank is 19 in. in the clear, and the depth 6 in. in the clear. The tank is placed in the middle of the track, and spiked loosely to the cross-ties, so as to allow for expansion and contraction of the material. The ends of the tanks are placed on appropriate inclines so as to prevent any loose rods hanging down from beneath cars ripping it up. Where the track is on a grade, the water is supplied at a number of points as fast as it flows off. To prevent the water from freezing in winter, live steam is turned into the tanks from a boiler placed in a shed near the road, the steam being led from the boiler through a 2-in. pipe parallel with the trough, from which main pipe branch pipes 1 in. in diameter are led off, at intervals of about 40 ft., discharging into the trough. These pipes are enclosed in appropriate wooden boxes, and properly protected from freezing in the usual way. Suitable valves are introduced at different points, and also protected with boxes. The water is taken from these troughs by a pipe or spout underneath the water-tank of the engine, which spout is lowered at the proper time into the water in the trough. The speed with which the spout is pushed through the water causes the water to rush up the pipe and fill the tank above.

For further data and illustrations, see the book "The Pennsylvania Railroad," by James Dredge.

CHAPTER XV.

COALING STATIONS FOR LOCOMOTIVES.

THE handling of coal on a railroad involves special appliances and structures, such as coal-runs and coal-tipples in the vicinity of coal-mines for delivering coal to cars for transit over the road, coal stocking and transfer systems, terminal coal-piers, coal-chutes or bins for supplying local coal dealers or large consumers, and coaling stations for locomotives. In this chapter the discussion will be confined to the methods in vogue for coaling locomotives, which investigation is rendered somewhat difficult owing to the large number of systems that have been adopted in practice to meet varying conditions and the individual views of railroad officers in charge of this branch of the service. The choice of a design will depend to a large extent on the topographical features of the locality, the ground space available, its shape and its value, the number of engines to be coaled in a given time, the kind of cars in which coal is to be delivered at the coaling station, the quality of the coal, whether hard or soft, and whether the coal will be supplied regularly all the year around, or only at certain seasons of the year; also, whether coal is to be delivered to engines on a side track with ample time allowance for coaling, or whether trains will stop to take coal on the main tracks, making a quick coal-delivery a prerequisite.

Ample provision for storage facilities is necessary wherever an irregular or intermittent supply is to be expected, caused either by possible labor troubles, temporary suspensions at the mines, or blockades on the road. On northern systems it is very desirable to store the bulk of the winter's supply before the full severity of the season sets in. In northern climates it will also prove economical to put a shed or roof over the pockets or storage-piles so as to prevent the coal from getting thoroughly drenched and freezing to a solid mass.

In designing a coaling system one of the main points to observe is to limit the number of handlings of the coal, so far as possible, thereby reducing the cost of operation and especially the breakage. Due regard should be paid to having some means for ascertaining and tallying the amount of coal delivered to engines, either by actual scale-weight or by measurement in bulk in buckets, dump-cars, or pockets, which latter method will prove practically just as accurate as scale-weights in the long-run.

The size of a coaling station will depend on the daily output to be expected and the storage capacity required, with proper allowance for a possible increase of business. The desirable storage capacity is determined after considering the points above mentioned pertinent thereto, while the daily output is a matter of simple calculation dependent on the number of engines to coal daily, multiplied by the coal-carrying capacity of their tenders, which hold usually from 2 to 7 tons, according to the size of the engines. Coaling stations will be usually found located on side tracks at all important stations, junction points, division yards, in fact at all points where engines are likely to be changed. Coaling stations have to be provided along the main track, wherever the engine run is longer than the coal-carrying capacity of the tender will allow, and the coal supply, therefore, has to be replenished *en route*. Engine runs for coal and freight trains are usually so regulated on large roads as to require the engines to coal only at the terminal points before starting on their runs, but passenger-engine runs are frequently much longer, and the engine has to coal *en route*, in which case rapidity of coaling is essential.

The methods in use for coaling locomotives consist of—

1. Shovelling directly into the tender from cars placed alongside the engine.
2. Handling by crane and buckets.
3. Platforms at about the height of the top of the coping on tenders.
4. Chutes at high elevation, either dumping sideways into the tenders or from an overhead bridge spanning the tracks.
5. Special systems, usually patented.

1. The method of *shovelling directly from cars into tenders*, requiring no special structures or appliances, is the most primitive method for supplying coal to locomotives, and is, naturally, only employed in connection with a very small output, or in case of necessity as a makeshift, or on new work until permanent arrangements are perfected. The total cost of handling is represented by the cost of one shovelling of the coal, or probably about 10 to 15 cents per ton, provided the coal is not frozen in the cars.

2. The method of handling coal by *crane and buckets* consists of loading iron buckets with coal from storage-piles or directly from cars, and swinging the buckets over the tender, as required, by means of a crane, the contents being dumped into the tender either by tipping the bucket or by opening trap-doors in the bottom of the bucket. The system can be subdivided according to whether a stationary crane with a swing-jib or a travelling-crane is used, the latter consisting either of a traversing crab on fixed end-trestles or of a so-called Goliath crane, in which the side supports of the overhead bridge travel on tracks laid on the ground. The bucket and crane system is more particularly employed where coal is delivered in flat cars and it cannot be dumped, but has to be shovelled out anyhow. The first cost of this system is small, as the storage of the coal is on the ground. It will take from five to ten minutes to coal a tender, the crane being worked by manual labor and the buckets having been previously filled.

Stationary cranes are in use on the Wisconsin Central Railroad, the Northern Pacific Railroad, the New York, Chicago & St. Louis Railway, the Des Moines & Fort Dodge Railway, and other roads. The cost of delivery is reported variously at from 7.5 to 15 cents per ton, including shovelling into the buckets, hoisting and discharging them.

A travelling-crane on fixed end-trestles is used by the Pittsburgh, Cincinnati & St. Louis Railroad at Columbus, O.; the average length of time for coaling an engine is stated to be six minutes, and the cost varies from 6.8 to 9.1 cents per ton, covering all expenses, including repairs and interest on first cost.

3. In the discussion of the system of using *platforms at about the height of the tender coping* it is necessary to distinguish between the methods for delivering the coal on to the platform and the methods of transferring it from the platform to locomotives.

The coal is delivered on to the platform either by horse and cart, or by shovelling from cars standing on the coaling track at the face of the platform, or from cars on a raised track near the rear of the platform and on a level with it. In the latter case the coal is either thrown toward the face of the platform for immediate use, or toward the rear into a surplus storage-pile, which system is frequently called the "compromise scheme" to allow for the numerous irregularities and fluctuations that take place in the coal supply. Coal is also delivered on to the platform by dumping from a raised trestling set on top of the platform, generally some distance back from the face of the platform, the height of the raised delivery track being usually from 8 to 9 ft. above the level of the platform. The platform level is usually placed from 10 ft. to 12 ft. above the top of rail of the coaling track along the face of the platform, so that the height of the elevated dumping track above the coaling track is from 18 to 21 ft. The height to climb with the loaded coal-cars in this system is much less than required for coal-chutes at a high elevation, and it is, therefore, frequently given the preference over the latter system.

The gradient usually adopted for the inclined approach trestling for the elevated dumping track is from 3.5 to 5 ft. rise per 100 ft. horizontal, which requires an incline of from 400 to 600 ft. in length. Where, owing to want of space, this length of incline is still too great, it is customary to increase the gradient on the incline to 8 ft. (in a few isolated cases even as high as 10 ft.) rise per 100 ft. horizontal, reducing the length of the incline to about 200 to 300 ft., allowing for vertical curves at each end. In operating a short incline on this heavy grade the locomotive does not run on to the incline, but a sufficient number of empty cars are placed between the locomotive and the loaded cars to allow the latter to be placed on the level part of the dumping trestling on top of the platform without the locomotive running up the incline. Vertical curves have to be inserted at each end of these heavy inclines so as not to break grade too suddenly, whereby the car-body might be thrown out of its bearings on the trucks.

Relative to the cost of delivering coal on to the platform it can be said, that the delivery by horse and cart from a storage-pile on the ground will cost about 7 to 15 cents per ton, in addition to the cost of unloading in the first instance into the storage-pile, but an expensive and extensive platform can be saved in this system, which feature may, at times, be in its favor. In shovelling on to the platform from cars on the coaling track the cost is not only equal to one shovelling with the disadvantage of having to throw the coal upwards, but, if it is desired to have a certain amount of storage or surplus coal supply on the platform, a second handling on top of the platform will be required to work the coal back from the face, so that the cost would be from 7 to 15 cents per ton. In shovelling from cars on a raised track near the rear of the platform and on a level with it, the cost of delivering on to the platform will be represented by one shovelling out of the cars under favorable conditions, or probably from 6 to 12 cents per ton. In dumping from a raised trestling the cost of unloading is merely nominal, if dump-cars are used and the coal is in a condition to run freely out of the cars. As the incline is not long and the trestling low, the fixed charge per ton to allow for the interest on the additional cost and maintenance of the elevated dumping trestle is small, especially so when the approach can be built on elevated ground, thereby reducing the extra cost of maintenance to a minimum.

Comparing, therefore, the different methods for delivering coal on to the platform, it can be stated that the method of dumping from a raised trestling is the most economical in the long-run, wherever the amount of coal to be handled is sufficient to warrant the erection of a regular coaling station, as the increased cost of construction and maintenance is insignificant compared with the much greater saving in the cost of the coal-delivery.

For a small or temporary supply, or where the space for a long incline is not available, shovelling from cars on the coaling track at the face of the platform, or on a track at or near the rear of the platform, is warranted.

The methods of delivering coal on to the platform having been discussed, the next question for consideration is the delivery of coal from the platform to locomotives, for which the following methods are actually in use in this country. The most primitive one is shovelling directly from the platform into the tender, which method is very slow, unless a large number of men are employed, in which case the cost runs up very heavily owing to unavoidable loss of time of the men between coaling. The next step is the use of small movable iron hand-carts or buckets on wheels, which are filled conveniently by the regular help stationed on the platform from the storage-pile on the rear of the platform and dumped directly into the tender of a locomotive as soon as it stops in front of the platform. The buckets usually hold from a half to one ton of coal. They are built either with a long projecting spout or chute at the front end, which serves as an apron in dumping into the tender, or there are a number of stationary aprons arranged along the face of the platform, which are lowered over the tender and serve to carry and guide the coal dumped from the buckets, in which case the buckets can be made smaller and less cumbersome. This, however, requires all coal to be brought to certain fixed points along the face of the platform, and locomotives have to stop accordingly; to obviate which objection, although not such a serious one, the device has been adopted of providing light iron hinged aprons sliding lengthwise on an iron axle or rod along the combing on the face of the platform, or else hung from staples or hooks in such a way as to be easily detached and transferred. The next method is a combination of the fixed-apron idea with a pocket or chute, consisting of a series of fixed tipping-boxes along the face of the platform, which are filled with coal by shovelling either directly from cars on a track back of the boxes or from a storage-pile on the rear of the platform. In the first instance there is only one handling of the coal, but there will be more or less extra shifting of the train to do, and detention to the switching engine to shift the cars opposite the boxes. In the case of drawing from the storage-pile the coal would have to be shovelled at least three times. The next method in use represents the attempt to improve on the foregoing method by drawing coal from the storage-pile in the rear without the extra handling just mentioned, and without increasing the time required for coaling an engine. It consists of having special dump-cars or tipping-boxes on trolleys, which run on tracks perpendicular to the face of the platform from the face to the rear of the platform. The cars are run back to the storage-pile, loaded there by shovelling from the pile, and then pushed forward to the face of the platform, and tipped. In some designs of trolley-cars the tipping is done automatically at the face of the platform by the impetus of the car, when pushed against special stops. The cars have either projecting ends which serve as aprons, or they discharge into fixed iron aprons attached to the combing of the face of the platform, or they run out from the face of the platform on a projecting track far enough to be able to discharge into the tender through trap-doors in the bottom of the car, which projecting track is hinged and counterweighted similarly to a one-arm lifting drawbridge. The objections to this method of only having transverse tracks on top of the platform, namely, that a special car has to be provided for each alley, and that each car can only be used for coal in its own alley, has caused the adoption of the method with transverse tracks, similar to the ones just described, connected however by a track running lengthwise or parallel with the face of the platform. Turntables are provided at the intersection of the longitudinal connecting track with the transverse tracks, or the longitudinal track is sunk into a pit below the level of the platform and serves for a transfer-table to work on. In some cases this transfer-table is utilized as a scale platform, and the coal in the trolley-car is weighed while on the table. The style of dump-cars and the methods of discharging at the face of the platform are the same as just described for the method with transverse tracks only.

Relative to the cost of delivering coal from the platform to locomotives with regard to the methods just discussed, it is difficult to give detailed figures, as the data, where obtainable, cover all the work connected with the coaling station. It can be said in general, however, that in shovelling directly to the tender the cost of delivery is not only the cost of one handling, but there is considerable lost time to allow for. The method of utilizing small hand-carts or buckets on wheels, while requiring from 5 to 15 minutes to coal an engine, will prove about as economical as any of the more elaborate methods described, which use fixed tipping-boxes or dump trolley-cars with a narrow-gauge track system, as the regular help stationed on the platform will be kept busy all the time, and the facility with which any part of the storage-pile can be reached and the coal taken to any part of the face of the platform is not to be underestimated. The apparent extra labor required to push a number of small hand-carts to the face of the platform, in place of one large trolley on rails, is not serious, and when the small buckets are ranged in line along the face of the platform, the attendants discharge them very easily and rapidly into a tender. In point of speed in coaling an engine the method with fixed tipping-boxes filled from a track behind the boxes is equivalent to the best elevated chute appliances, and it requires only one handling of the coal, but the extra cost of switching should be considered, besides surplus storage with this method being impracticable or very expensive. Relative to the methods with dumps on trolleys on narrow-gauge tracks, the speed of discharging is in most cases equal to the method with fixed tipping-boxes, but so far as the cost is concerned they are probably not materially better than the method with small movable hand-carts without tracks.

Comparing, therefore, the different methods for delivering coal to locomotives from a platform, it can be said that, where speed of coaling is an object, as for instance along a main track, the methods with fixed tipping-boxes or with tipping trolley-cars are the best, with the preference in favor of the latter method with transverse tracks connected by a longitudinal track, in case the coaling station is a large one and it is desired to offer considerable storage space. Where speed of coaling is not so essential, as for instance at a coaling station in connection with a yard or engine-house system, the small movable hand-carts will give a cheap and convenient service, and with less first cost for the plant. The use of aprons will admit of lighter hand-carts, in which case fixed revolving aprons at intervals along the face of the platform will answer as well as movable aprons. For temporary work or very small auxiliary coaling stations for use in case of necessity, or for coaling an engine on a small branch where the engine crew has plenty of spare time between runs, the method of shovelling from the platform to the tender is admissible.

Numerous combinations of the methods discussed above for delivering coal on to platforms and for delivering it from the platforms to locomotives exist in practice, the selection in each particular case being guided by the local conditions and requirements.

Relative to the total unit cost of storing and delivering coal to locomotives over platforms, it is dependent to a large extent on the daily output and the wages paid for labor. The Roadmasters' Association in 1885 adopted a report on "Handling Coal for Locomotives," in which it is stated that the replies received to a large number of letters of inquiry sent out indicated that the maximum price for handling coal over platforms of different constructions was 30 cents per ton, the minimum 11 cents per ton, with an average of 19.4 cents per ton. In the report on "Coal Delivery to Locomotive Tenders," adopted by the American Railway Master Mechanics' Association, in 1887, it is stated that on the Burlington & Lamoille Railway the cost of shovelling from a platform at level of footplate, delivering 30 tons per day, including measuring, but exclusive of delivery of the coal onto the platform, was 10 cents per ton; while on a Canadian road the cost of shovelling from car to platform and from platform to tender ran up as high as 34 cents per ton, where the output was small and the coal badly frozen. The same report states further, that on the Connecticut River Railway the cost of delivering 45 tons per day from a platform with trolley dump-cars was 14 cents per ton, and on the New York, Chicago & St. Louis Railroad, with the same system, the rate was eight cents per ton for 74 tons daily; on the Northern Central Railway the cost was only 4.6 cents per ton during the winter months for a daily output of 57½ tons, delivering the coal on to the platform from a dumping trestle and delivering to locomotives by tipping trolley-cars running on transverse tracks. From data collected by the author the cost on the Lehigh Valley Railroad of dumping coal from a dumping trestle on a platform and delivering it by means of small hand-carts to locomotives is about 5 to 10 cents per ton at the coaling station at Lehighton, Pa. The cost on the same railroad for shovelling coal from cars onto a platform at Jersey City, N. J., is about 7 to 9 cents per ton, and the total cost for shovelling from cars to the platform and then shovelling from the platform into the tender is about 13 to 15 cents.

4. *Chutes at high elevations* offer the advantage of coaling engines rapidly. They are either arranged to dump sideways into tenders on a coaling track running along the face of the chutes, or to dump from an overhead bridge spanning a number of tracks. The latter system has to be used where it is desired to coal engines on a number of parallel tracks, as for instance the main tracks and main sidings of a large road, while the former system is used where engines can coal from a track alongside the chutes.

This division between side chutes and overhead chutes having been pointed out, the next most important characteristic is the method adopted for elevating the coal to the proper height to be dumped into the chutes or pockets. One method is to convey the coal from cars or storage-piles on the ground by horse and cart up a proper ramp to the pockets. Another method, and the one most generally in use, is to have a long inclined approach on trestling or on high ground where the locality permits it. Where there is no space for a long inclined approach, a stationary engine with cable rope is employed, and the loaded cars are hauled up a steep incline or plane, as it is called. Another method is to fill small cars from a low dumping trestle and then to haul the small cars up an inclined plane to the proper elevation to allow them to be discharged into the high chutes. Another method is to store coal on the ground in bins or piles and fill small trolley-cars by hand from the storage-piles on the ground level, and then hoist the cars on a small platform elevator to the upper tier, where they are discharged into the chutes. A modification of this latter system, that is feasible and will probably be introduced in the near future, consists of increasing the size of the platform elevator and hoisting up the standard-gauge loaded cars in which the coal arrives, thus avoiding one handling of the coal, but of course with the objection of having to furnish a very powerful and heavy elevator. Another method, applicable where there is no space for a long incline or the other methods described are not desired, is to dump the coal into a pit underneath the track on the ground level, and then to convey it by a continuous bucket-belt elevator or a trough-conveyor to the upper tier, where it is distributed to the different bins by spouts, or by small tram-cars, or by the so-called automatic railroad system, or by a horizontal belt or trough-conveyor.

The claim that in the vertical bucket-belt elevator certain kinds of coal are badly ground to pieces and crushed in the pit at the foot of the elevator, is stated to be overcome by a form of loose swinging buckets (patented) in place of rigid buckets attached to the belt, and also by the improved patented trough-conveying system, in which the coal is dumped into a trough in a pit below the dumping track on the ground level. This trough has a continuous chain running through it, with vertical iron disks, called scrapers, attached to the chain at intervals. The chain is kept in motion by machinery, and each scraper pushes the contents of the trough in front of it gently forward without any grinding or crushing action. The trough as soon as it leaves the tracks rises gradually to the desired elevation, whence the coal is distributed to the pockets by spouts, or by a second longitudinal conveyor, or by tram-cars, as explained above for the bucket-elevator system. The patent trough-conveyor system has been used very successfully with the Dodge storage-pile system, reducing the timber structure connected with the coal-pockets to a minimum, and allowing a large storage capacity at a comparatively small first expense.

After the coal has been hoisted to the proper elevation for discharging into the chutes or pockets, the following variations in the designs in use can be noted: In most cases the coal is dumped from the elevated track on to a platform below it and level with the top of the pockets, thus giving considerable storage space under the track. In other designs there is no provision made for storage at this point, and the coal is dumped or shovelled directly into the pockets. Then there are designs where the coal is dumped into large hopper-shaped storage-bins, which are trapped off at the lower end, allowing coal to be discharged, as required, into regular chutes placed below the bins; this system requires extra height for the supply-tracks, but it avoids all shovelling of the coal. Wherever the coal is elevated in small trolley-cars it is usually discharged directly into the pockets. A peculiar combination of the high chute and low platform system is in use in a number of the older and in some more recent designs for coal-chutes, in which the coal is first discharged from a high track into pockets, which are trapped off at the lower end, so as to regulate the feed. Small trolley-cars, which run on tracks on a platform about 11 to 12 ft. above the coaling tracks, are placed under the pockets, filled, and discharged over the side of the platform, or run out on a projecting counterweighted platform, the same as described above in connection with the platform system. These cars serve also for the purpose of measuring or weighing the coal.

Where the coal is discharged into chutes under an overhead bridge, it is customary either to bring the coal up from the ground level in special trolley-cars which run out on the bridge and dump into the chutes, or a storage-pile is created on a high platform adjoining the overhead bridge, and the coal is transferred from the storage-pile to the chutes under the bridge in hand-carts, or in trolley-cars running on narrow-gauge tracks, or in buckets suspended from an overhead rail.

The height of the elevated dumping track above the ground level differs according to the variations in the design, as just outlined. In the case of dumping from an elevated track onto a platform, level with the top of the pockets or side chutes, the height of the dumping track is from 25 to 33 ft. above the ground. Where no provision is made for storage and the coal is to be dumped directly into the pockets, the height of the high track is not less than 22 ft. above the ground, and where the coal is to be shovelled off the cars sideways into the pockets, the height of the high track is from 12 to 15 ft. above the ground. Where the coal is dumped from an elevated track above a storage platform, which is level with an overhead bridge system, the height of the high track is from 28 to 32 ft. above the ground. In general, the top of the pockets for side chutes is from 18 to 23 ft. above the coaling track, and the floor of an overhead bridge is usually from 22 to 24 ft. above the tracks passing under it.

The height to which the coal has to be lifted having been determined, according to the system selected for the storage and delivery of the coal to locomotives, the next question to settle is the method to adopt for elevating the coal. With vertical platform elevators, bucket-belt elevators, and trough-conveyors, the yard space required for the coaling station is reduced to a minimum, and a slight additional lift, so as to provide better facilities or storage at the upper elevation, can be easily introduced into the system. Where inclined planes are used the gradient of the plane ranges from 18 to 22 ft. rise per 100 ft. horizontal. Inclined approaches with locomotive gradients, on trestling or on high ground, or on both, for reaching the high track of a coal-chute system are too long to be worked with a partial train of empties, as done on low-grade dumping trestles, and the momentum of a train acquired by taking a "run" is not sufficient to carry the train up. Hence the allowable gradient is limited to the safe grade for a locomotive to run on, and in practice the gradient on a high coal-chute inclined approach has been limited to 5 ft. rise per 100 ft. horizontal. Where possible, the gradient should not exceed 4 ft., especially in northern climates, where the rails are frequently in a very bad condition in winter. The following railroads have long coal-chute inclines with gradients as indicated, namely: Richmond & Alleghany Railroad (Chesapeake & Ohio), 3.75 ft.; Richmond & Danville Railroad, 3.6 ft.; Northern Central Railroad,

3.25 ft., Lehigh Valley Railroad, at Lehighton, Pa., 4 ft., and at Wilkesbarre, Pa., 5 ft.; Pennsylvania Railroad at East Tyrone, Pa., 5 ft.; New York, Lake Erie & Western Railroad, 4 ft.; Wabash, St. Louis & Pacific Railway, 3.75 ft.; Northern Pacific Railroad, 3.5 ft.; Atchison, Topeka & Santa Fe Railroad, 3.77 ft.

The detail design of the pockets or chutes varies according to whether the chutes dump sideways or lead down from an overhead bridge. The capacity of the pockets varies from 2 to 7 tons, the aim being usually to allow the entire coal supply required by an engine to be dumped in one operation into the tender. Where the coal is not weighed or measured in hoppers or buckets before being put into the pockets, it is customary to have a gauge marked off on the side of the pocket to indicate the capacity in tons at different levels. The pockets are closed by a hinged flap-door or a lifting-door, and there is a hinged counterweighted apron in front of the door. Some doors are opened and shut automatically by the movement of the aprons, while in other designs the doors are entirely independent of the aprons. The apron is sometimes provided with a screen for screening the coal. The so-called Clifton chutes have been designed with an inside division or intermediate flap, permitting the contents of a large pocket to be subdivided and a smaller amount of coal delivered to the tender than the full chute capacity, but this feature has not been found to be essential in actual practice.

The angle of slope of the chute floor and of the apron are very important features, and vary according to whether the coal to be discharged is soft or hard, in the former case the angle having to be greater. The following railroads have chutes with the angles of inclination from the horizontal as indicated, namely: Chicago, Rock Island & Pacific Railway, 34 deg. (Clifton chute); Baltimore & Ohio Railway, pocket 55 deg., apron 37 deg.; Michigan Central Railroad, 33 deg. (Kerr chute); Cincinnati, New Orleans & Texas Pacific Railway, 45 deg. (Kerr chute); Chicago, Milwaukee & St. Paul Railway, 30 deg. (Kerr chute), and a more recent design 38 deg.; Grand Trunk Railway, 36 deg.; New Orleans & North Eastern Railroad, pocket and apron, 45 deg.; Richmond & Alleghany Railroad, pocket 40 deg., apron 30 deg.; Northern Pacific Railroad, 45 deg.; Lehigh Valley Railroad at Wilkesbarre, Pa., 22½ deg.; Atchison, Topeka & Santa Fe Railroad (Clifton chute), 27½ deg.; Wabash, St. Louis & Pacific Railway, 48 deg.

Relative to the cost of coaling engines over a high-chute system the Roadmasters' Association report of 1885, on "Handling Coal for Locomotives," stated that where coal-chutes are used the maximum price per ton is 9 cents, the minimum 4.5 cents per ton, and the average 7.4 cents per ton, or an average of 12 cents per ton in favor of chutes as compared with the average cost of coaling over low-grade platforms; the time consumed in taking coal from high chutes is one minute and from other devices twelve minutes, a saving in time of eleven minutes for each engine coaled in favor of chutes; and where 3000 tons of coal are handled monthly an annual saving is realized of nearly $4500—over other devices. In the report on "Coal Delivery to Locomotive Tenders," adopted by the American Railway Master Mechanics' Association in 1887, it is stated that coal is delivered to locomotives over a high coal-chute system with long approach trestling and high dumping track on the Baltimore & Ohio Railroad, with a daily output of 115 tons, for $4\frac{8}{10}$ cents per ton; on the Michigan Central Railroad, with a similar system and a daily output of 175 tons, the cost is stated to be 7 cents per ton, which figure is increased to 8½ cents per ton, if allowance is made for interest, depreciation, renewals, and repairs at the rate of 20 per cent per annum of $4000, the first cost of the system of 40 chutes; on the Chicago & Eastern Illinois Railroad, with a daily delivery of 230 tons over a high coal-chute system, the average cost is stated to be 3.78 cents per ton, which figure is increased to 5 cents per ton, if allowance is made for interest, etc., at the rate of 20 per cent per annum on the first cost of $5031 for the plant; on the Chicago, New Orleans & Texas Pacific Railroad the cost of delivering coal over a high-chute system with drop-bottom cars, similar to the Baltimore & Ohio Railroad chutes, is stated to be 6 cents per ton in the slackest season with a daily output of only 18 tons, while in the busy season it is less, and the fixed unit to add to the above rate, if the chutes were worked to their greatest possible capacity of 320 tons per day, to allow for interest, etc., would be less than 1 cent per ton.

Comparing in a summary way the different methods used for high-chute systems, as just discussed, it can be said that the method of dumping from a high trestle with long inclined approach onto a platform level with the top of the pockets is the most economical method; it gives very little breakage of the coal, and offers considerable storage space, and the fixed charge per ton to add for the increased first cost of the structure, and the maintenance of same, is, in a large system, small as compared with the cost of handling coal by more expensive systems. Where the coal arrives in flat cars, and a large storage back of the pockets is not considered essential, the method of filling pockets from a track on the rear, by shovelling directly from car to the pockets, deserves the preference, as the structure is not so costly as in the regular high-chute system, and the length of the inclined approach for the dumping track is much less.

Where space for a long approach is not available, a vertical platform hoist or inclined plane for small trolley-cars, or an inclined plane for taking up the loaded road cars, is used to good advantage. The vertical lifting of the loaded road cars on a heavy platform hoist has never been tried to the author's knowledge, but it has been recommended by the American Railway Master Mechanics' Association, in the report previously referred to, as being worthy of a trial under certain conditions. For a small coaling station, with limited ground space, the use of a vertical bucket-belt elevator offers such decided advantages that it would be desirable to see this system used more frequently. At the coaling station for locomotives and for boilers for stationary engines in the yard of the National Docks Railway at Jersey City, N. J., a bucket-belt elevator has been operated at a less cost than would have been required for a high coal-chute system, if interest on the first cost and the maintenance of the structure are considered. The breakage of the coal, frequently claimed to be a serious defect of any bucket-belt elevator system, has not been found to be a detriment at this point. It should be stated, however, that at the coal-chute in question steam is constantly available from the boilers of the adjacent boiler-house, so that the small vertical engine for running the bucket-belt elevator is operated by ordinary labor. The use of the trough-conveyor system, with and without a storage-pile on the ground, has been introduced on a number of roads, and is deserving of more attention, as a most economical and practical system wherever ground is valuable, or the space for a long coal-chute approach is not available. The application of the elevator or of the trough-conveying system for lifting the coal from the ground to overhead bridges, for coaling engines on the main tracks of a road, is one of the most valuable and recent improvements adopted for supplying coal for locomotives, as it is very economical in operation, provided the daily output is sufficient to warrant the erection of some kind of a coaling station, and, in addition, the valuable land or limited space alongside the main tracks of a road will not be blocked by a long inclined trestle and coal-storage platform.

5. Under the heading of *Special Systems*, opportunity will be taken to review, briefly, a number of schemes, mostly patented, which offer individual characteristics, and cannot be brought readily under the classifications adopted above. Collin's Locomotive Hoist, which has been extensively adopted by the Pennsylvania Railroad, utilizes the tractive force of the locomotive to draw its own coal supply in road cars up to such a height that the coal can be delivered over a chute into its tender. The Dodge Coaling System consists of an inclined plane up which the loaded road car is hauled by a cable to the top of a coaling shed, where the coal is dumped and conveyed by horizontal belt-conveyors to whatever pocket it is desired to fill. Dockstader's System of a "side-dump coal-car and oscillating apron" is designed to deliver coal directly from the road car to tenders without the use of shovelling, at a minimum of expense and breakage, the car being run on a low trestling, along the coaling track, and then tipped sideways; the objection to this system lies in the fact that special cars have to be used to bring the coal from the mines, and that they will have to run back light in most cases. Mention has been previously made of the trough-conveying system, and of the bucket-elevator system with stationary or swinging buckets.

In case coal is delivered to a coaling station by water, in barges or canal-boats, the best method for transferring the coal to the coal-chutes or pockets consists of the tipping-bucket system, in which the buckets are loaded in the hold by shovelling, hoisted by horse or steam power, and tipped at the proper point by a suitable attachment, so as to discharge into a pocket or storage-pile. Where the coaling station is not located immediately alongside of the water front, the use of the Hunt Automatic Railway is clearly indicated. In this system the buckets are hoisted out of the hold of the vessel, and tipped at the proper height into a large hopper, from which tram-cars are filled which convey the coal to the pockets or storage-piles located some distance inland. The principal feature of this design is that the loaded car travels to the dumping point by gravity, while the empty car is brought back to the hopper by the impetus given to the empty car by a heavy counterweight attached to the car by a cable, the counterweight being brought into play as soon as the car has discharged its load. Where the coal supply by water is large enough to warrant it, a vertical bucket-elevator attached to a movable leg is used; the leg is lowered into the hold of the vessel, and the coal is elevated and transferred backward to the pockets or storage-piles.

Conclusions.—The five groups or systems, previously outlined, for supplying coal to locomotives having been considered in detail, the following remarks and conclusions, embracing the entire subject, will be of interest.

The Roadmasters' Association in the report adopted in 1885, quoted above, showed conclusively that the high coal-chute system was to be preferred in point of speed of coaling and of economy over all other known devices for coaling locomotives.

The American Railway Master Mechanics' Association in the report adopted in 1887, quoted above, offers the following conclusions on the question of the different methods for coaling locomotives:

"To summarize, it may be said that with regular coal supply from mine in drop-bottom cars, the cheapest and most rapid delivery is by using high central trestle, from which the coal is allowed to gravitate into dimensioned chutes, and from the chutes gravitates into tender.

"When sufficient land cannot readily be obtained for the long ramp (grade) this system requires, the economy in labor and slight injury to fuel is so marked under this system as to suggest the advisability of lifting the loaded mine cars, vertically (by some form of power elevator) up to the level of track on top of the high trestle.

"For a compromise system, where the daily fuel issues are sometimes taken from cars and sometimes from store heap, either the tipping pocket on truck or chute filled by horse and cart may be used, or, if the amount to be stored and lifted from heap be not large, an overhead girder crane will do. If a Goliath crane be used, the storage is practically limited only by the land obtainable.

"For leisurely delivering comparatively small amounts, the platform, or, better still, direct shovelling from car to tender, is as cheap as any manual-labor system known; and if it is desired to lessen the time actually occupied in delivering to tender, a hand crane and buckets on the platform will do so with but little outlay and but slight increase in cost over direct shovelling; in fact, if the use of buckets insures the men being steadily kept at work, the cost per ton may by use of crane be lessened."

The opinions and conclusions embodied in the reports of the Roadmasters' Association and of the American Railway Master Mechanics' Association, quoted above, can be considered as applicable to the conditions existing to day. There is, however, one additional feature to call attention to, namely, the lifting and transferring of coal by elevators or conveyors has, within recent years, been adopted under certain conditions with such good results by a number of railroads that any remarks on the subject under discussion would not be complete without calling attention to the valuable improvements in this class of coal-handling machinery, which have been brought prominently to the front since the reports of the associations mentioned above were adopted.

The following plans and descriptions of coaling stations for locomotives, as actually in use in this country, will prove interesting in connection with the above general remarks on the subject:

Derrick Coal-shed, Wisconsin Central Railroad.—The design for a coal-shed on the Wisconsin Central, shown in Figs. 267 and 268, is a coal-storage shed built on the stationary crane-and-bucket system for supplying locomotives. The shed is 20 ft. wide by any length desired, 150 ft. being the usual length. Coal is shovelled from cars into the shed through the side of the building, which is left open for that purpose from the eaves down to a point 7 ft. from the ground. A narrow-gauge track runs along one side of this shed, on which small tipping-bucket cars run. These buckets are filled by hand from the storage-pile in the shed, and are run to one end of the shed, where there is a raised platform and a swinging-jib crane, by which the buckets are hauled up and set on the platform. When an engine stops for coaling, the buckets are picked up by the crane, swung over the tender, and discharged.

The height of the shed is 12 ft. from sill to plate, and the bents are spaced 6 ft. apart. The principal timbers used are: posts, 6 in. × 8 in.; tie-beams, 8 in. × 8 in.; main sills, 8 in. × 10 in., running lengthwise of building, spaced 6 ft. apart, and resting on cedar posts spaced 6 ft. apart under

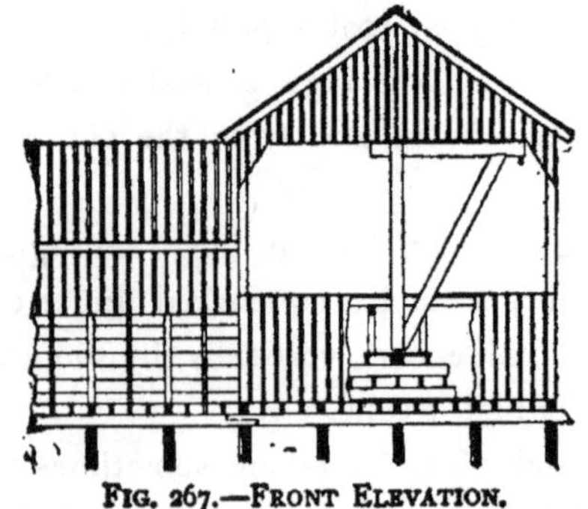

FIG. 267.—FRONT ELEVATION.

FIG. 268.—CROSS-SECTION.

each sill; floor-beams at bents, 6 in. × 10 in.; intermediate floor-beams, 3 in. × 10 in.; intermediate studs, 3 in. × 8 in.; plates, 3 pieces, 2 in. × 8 in.; rafters, 2 in. × 8 in., spaced 3 ft.; purlins, 2 in. × 8 in., laid flat; roof-boards, 1 in., with 1-in. × 3-in. battens; inside sheathing, 2-in. boards, for 7 ft. up from the ground; outside sheathing, 1-in. vertical boards, with battens.

Derrick Coal-house, Northern Pacific Railroad.—The Northern Pacific Railroad has a standard derrick coal-house, shown in Figs. 269 to 272, designed by Mr. C. B. Talbot, that is an excellent example of a first-class plan for the stationary crane-and-bucket system of coaling engines. The plan

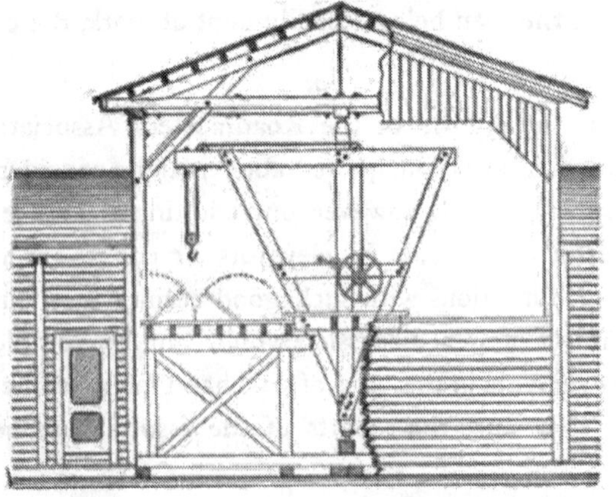

FIG. 269.—FRONT ELEVATION.

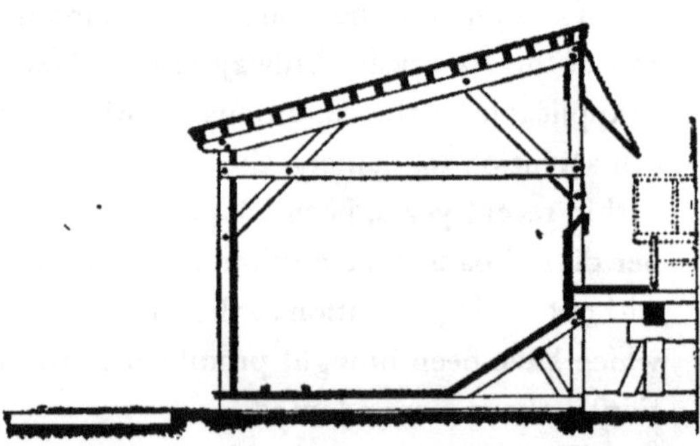

FIG. 270.—CROSS-SECTION.

consists of a low shed, 18 ft. wide and 250 ft. long, with a derrick-house, 18 ft. × 28 ft., at the centre. Along the face of the shed is the coaling track, on which engines stand opposite the derrick-house when receiving coal, while on the rear of the shed is an elevated coal-supply track, raised 6 ft. from the ground, to facilitate shovelling coal from cars into the house. This raised track has an inclined trestle approach on a grade of 3.5 ft. rise per 100 ft. There is a narrow-gauge track along one side of the shed on which tipping-bucket cars run. These are filled from the storage-pile, pushed to the derrick-house, raised there by the derrick through trap-doors to the upper floor, and placed around the derrick till needed, when they are swung out over the tenders and discharged.

The height of the shed is 10 ft. 9 in. in the clear from floor to tie-beam ; the principal timbers in the shed are sills, 8 in. × 10 in.; posts, 6 in. × 8 in., spaced 6 ft. apart; tie-beams, 2 pieces, 3 in. × 10 in.; rafters, 2 pieces, 3 in. × 12 in., spaced 6 ft. apart; purlins, 3 in. × 8 in., spaced 18 in., and spanning 6 ft.; roofing 3-ply roofing-paper, pitch and gravel, on two layers of 1-in. boards; inside sheathing of shed, 3-in. plank; floor-joists, 4 in. × 6 in., spaced 2 ft., and spanning 18 feet. The derrick-house is partially open towards the track, and the derrick is built and set, as shown on plans. The principal timbers in the derrick-house are sills, 8 in. × 10 in.; posts, 10 in. × 10 in.; tie-beams, 8 in. × 10 in.; rafters, 8 in. × 10 in.; purlins, 3 in. × 10 in.; roofing same as shed; outside sheathing, "V" Rustic.

This design allows of the use of either one shed only on one side of the supply track, or of sheds placed on both sides of same, with an additional coaling track on the rear.

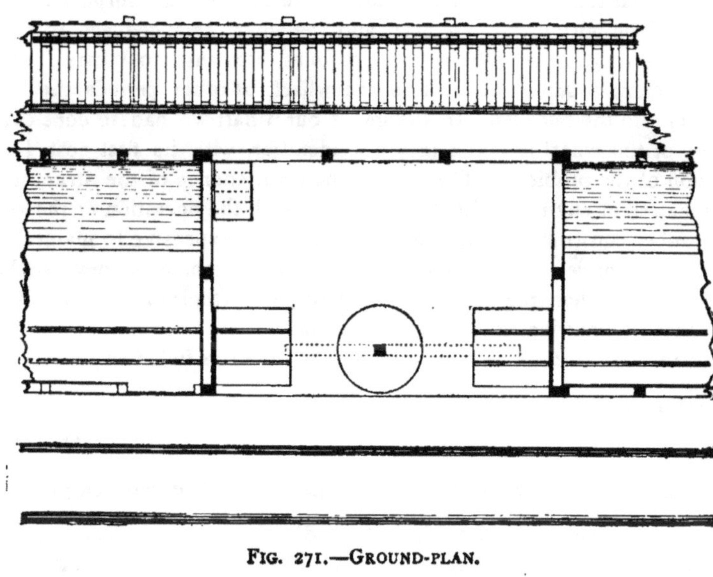

FIG. 271.—GROUND-PLAN.

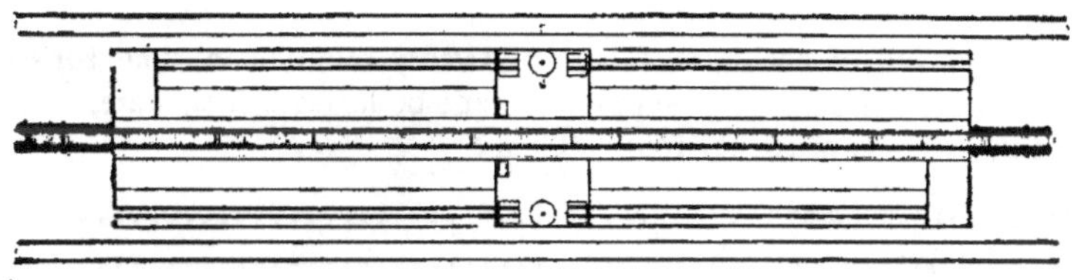

FIG. 272.—GENERAL-PLAN.

Stationary Crane-and-Bucket System, Des Moines & Fort Dodge Railway.—The Master Mechanics' Association's report, quoted above, states that on the Des Moines & Fort Dodge Railway two men handle 25 tons per day with one-half ton buckets and a stationary swing-jib crane, at a cost of 15 cents per ton. Each man, therefore, shovels into the buckets, and then lifts by crane and discharges into the tender 12½ tons per day, the daily wages being $1.87½.

Stationary Crane-and-Bucket System, New York, Chicago & St. Louis Railway.—The Master Mechanics' Association's report, quoted above, states that on the New York, Chicago & St. Louis Railway the results from two different coaling stations using the stationary crane-and-bucket system show the cost to be 7½ cents per ton, the rate of pay being 12½ cents per hour, and the rate of delivery 55 tons per day, one man shovelling and then lifting by crane 18 tons as a day's work.

Travelling Crane for Coaling-engines at Columbus, O., Pittsburg, Cincinnati & St. Louis Railway.—On the Pittsburg, Cincinnati & St. Louis Railway a travelling-crane or traversing crab-crane for coaling engines has been introduced at Columbus, O., by Mr. E. B. Wall, which was illustrated and described in the *Railroad Gazette* of April 1, 1887. It comprises a self-contained steam crab-crane, on a trolley having longitudinal movement over the whole length of an overhead travelling girder spanning three parallel coaling tracks, the girder having motion on rails carried on trestles 25 or 30 ft. high, one on each side of the coaling tracks. The coal shipped from the mine in ordinary cars is shovelled into 2½-ton iron buckets at ground level, and the crane lifts one of the filled buckets and moves it over the tender, when the latch securing the hinged bottom is released, and the contained fuel falls into the tender.

Relative to this system the Master Mechanics' Association's Report, mentioned above, quotes Mr. Wall as follows:

"I do not think that this form of coal wharf is the best for all purposes. Coal can be loaded more cheaply where drop-bottom cars are used and the wharf arranged accordingly. At Columbus, however, we receive our coal in straight-bottom gondolas, box and stock cars. At certain periods of the year we have to carry a supply of coal on the wharf; at other periods the coal can be loaded direct from the cars into the buckets. In designing our wharf we had to consider these conditions. When the capacity of this wharf is taken into consideration with its first cost, I consider it a very satisfactory solution of the problem. The cost of the maintenance of the structure is very light, and it can easily be renewed at any time without interfering with the operation of the wharf.

"The large timber constructions in general use are very expensive to maintain; they have to be renewed every six or seven years, and while with the drop-bottom cars they can be made to handle coal more cheaply per ton than the crane arrangement, nevertheless, when all items are taken into account, I think that the showing would be about even."

The capacity and cost of operation at Columbus is stated as follows:

Capacity of bucket, in pounds	5,000
Average weight delivered, per engine, in pounds	7,000

Probable maximum capacity with fifty buckets and trestle at present length:

Maximum number of buckets dumped per hour (tested)	20
Actual working hours (handling buckets)	21
Maximum number of buckets per month	12,600
Maximum number of tons per month	31,500

Allowing each bucket full of coal, also a loss of twenty minutes in time for each fifty buckets handled for the purpose of supplying crane boiler with fuel, water, etc., which equals about three hours in twenty-four. Then:

Present delivery in tons per month	9,120
Present delivery in buckets per month	5,142
Cost of plant	$7,700.00
Wages of (2) engineers per month, at eighteen cents per hour	129.60
Wages of (12) coal-heavers per month, at twelve cents per hour	518.40
Wages of (2) men dumping and signaling to craneman, per month, at twelve cents per hour. (These men are regular coal-heavers, and only do the work of signaling when the foreman is busy checking up the time or taking numbers of cars. One is employed at night and one in the day-time)	86.40
Foreman of wharf (1) per month, at thirteen cents per hour	46.80
Fuel, oil, waste, water, etc., per month	12.50
Repairs to apparatus, per month	5.00
Interest on investment, per month, at 6 per cent per annum	38.50
Total operating expenses, per month	$837.20
Cost of coaling, per ton, in cents	9.1
Cost of coaling, per engine, in cents	31.55
Not taking interest on plant into consideration, per ton, in cents	8.7
Probable cost per ton, at maximum capacity, in cents	6.8
Average length of time for coaling an engine	6 min.

The report mentioned states further: "It is possible that Mr. Wall's original plan might be improved by the use of a 'Gantry or Goliath Crane,' as used in Europe, described and illustrated in Mr. G. J. Appleby's paper on cranes, read before the American Society of Civil Engineers, October 17, 1883. (See Proceedings, p. 374.) This dispenses with the trestle, as the whole crane with its long vertical legs traverses on tracks at ground level. The first cost of the crane would be increased, and there would be an increase in the power required to move it, but the system and storage could at a few hours' notice be indefinitely extended at the slight cost of increasing the length of the tracks."

For additional data see the report of the Master Mechanics' Association mentioned, the issue of the *Railroad Gazette* of April 1, 1887, and the issue of *Engineering News* of September 24, 1887.

Coaling Platform at Jersey City, N. J., Lehigh Valley Railroad.—The coaling platform of the Lehigh Valley Railroad at Jersey City, N. J., shown in Fig. 273, will serve as an example of a small temporary and cheap coaling platform, the coal being delivered to the platform by shovelling from cars on the coaling track at the face of the platform, and delivery to tenders being made by shovelling directly from the platform into the tenders. The platform at Jersey City is 16 ft. wide and 90 ft. long, and will hold about 225 tons of coal. The floor is placed 6 ft. 3 in. above the coaling track, and the face is placed 6 ft. 6 in. in the clear from the centre of the coaling track. The cost of shovelling coal from the cars to the platform, with a daily output of about forty-five tons, is about seven to nine cents per ton, the rate paid for labor being twelve cents per hour. The coal is loaded into the tender by the engine crews between runs, and does not therefore appear as a separate charge, but costs presumably slightly less than unloading from cars, so that the total cost of unloading to platform and then loading tender will be from thirteen to fifteen cents per ton.

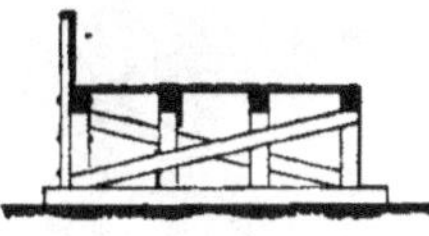

FIG. 273.—CROSS-SECTION.

The principal timbers used are as follows: bents perpendicular to coaling track are spaced 9 ft. centres; sills, 12 in. × 12 in.; posts, 12 in. × 12 in.; caps, parallel with track, 12 in. × 12 in.; floor-plank, 3 in.; brace-plank, 3 in. × 10 in.

Coaling Platform at Lehighton, Pa., Lehigh Valley Railroad.—The coaling platform of the Lehigh Valley Railroad at Lehighton, Pa., shown in Figs. 274 and 275, designed and built by the author, illustrates the system of delivering coal to engines from a platform by means of movable hand trucks or barrows over fixed revolving aprons along the face of the platform, the coal supply being dumped on the rear of the platform from a low dumping trestle. The approach to the dumping track is on an embankment on a gradient of 4 ft. rise in 100 ft. horizontal. The platform, 50 ft. wide by 275 ft. long, is located along a hillside, and is mainly in original ground. The face of the platform consists of a stone wall, varied in its dimensions according to the amount of new filling back of it. The wall is coped with stone coping, 34 in. wide by 12 in. thick, with an 8-in. × 14-in. oak combing-stick anchored to the masonry.

Along the face of the combing, at distances of about 60 ft., light timber gallows frames are erected with a chain drum operated by hand for raising and lowering aprons hinged to the timber combing. The floor of the platform consists of stone flagging. The centre of the dumping trestle is placed 30 ft. back from the face of the platform. The top of the floor of the platform is 11 ft. above the top of the rail of the coaling track; the top of the rail on the dumping trestle is 8 ft. above the floor of the platform. The face of the front wall at the height of the coaling track is placed 6 ft. 1 in. from the centre of the coaling track. The face of the wall has ½-in. batter. The face of the timber combing is 6 ft. from the centre of the coaling track.

The bents of the dumping trestle are spaced 12 ft. centres, and the principal timbers used are as follows: sills, 10 in. × 15 in.; posts, 12 in. × 12 in., 1 in 8 batter; caps, 10 in. × 15 in. × 12 ft.; track-stringers, one piece, 12 in. × 15 in., under each rail; 3-in. stay-plank on top of caps to hold stringers in place and prevent wear of caps in dumping coal; gang-plank on each side of trestle, 2 in. × 12 in. No ties are used, the rails being spiked to the stringers.

The force employed at this coaling station consists in general of five men during the day and three men at night. The rate of wages is twelve cents per hour. There are from one hundred to one hundred and twenty engines coaled every twenty-four hours, each engine taking from two to seven tons of coal. The barrows hold one ton, so that the number of barrows to dump is small. When rushed, seven tons of coal are dumped in six minutes, including lowering and raising the apron. According to the assumed daily output, the cost of delivery to tenders from the platform will be from two and one half to five cents per ton, to which must be added the cost of dumping from the trestle track into stock, and an extra allowance for interest on first cost and for the expense of maintenance, which latter item, however, is small, owing to the substantial character of the structure. On the basis of above data the cost would probably fluctuate from five to ten cents per ton.

FIG. 274.—FRONT ELEVATION.

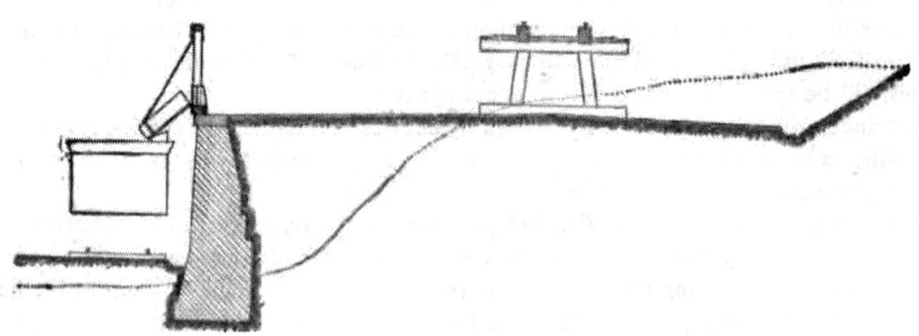

FIG. 275.—CROSS-SECTION.

Coaling Platform at South Easton, Pa., Lehigh Valley Railroad.—The coaling platform of the Lehigh Valley Railroad at South Easton, Pa., consists of a shedded platform with a dumping trestle on the rear. Owing to limited yard space the height of the dumping trestle is only 14 ft. 6 in. above the coaling track at the face of the platform. The approach trestle incline is only 198 ft. long, giving an 8 ft. in 100 ft. maximum gradient. The platform floor is placed about 8 ft. above the coaling track. The coal is discharged to tenders through hand-barrows with long projecting ends, as no aprons are used along the face of the platform. The incline is operated with a number of empties between the engine and the loaded cars.

Coaling Platform, Chicago & Grand Trunk Railway.—The coaling platform of the Chicago & Grand Trunk Railway, published in the Report of the Master Mechanics' Association, quoted above, republished in *Engineering News* of September 24, 1887, illustrates the system of locating fixed tipping dump-cars or pockets along the face of the platform, the coal being shovelled into the pockets from cars on a track immediately back of the pockets. This system gives as quick dispatch in coaling engines as a high-chute system. Where quick delivery is required and space for a long incline is not available, this style of coaling platform offers advantages. The cost of delivering coal to the pockets, however, especially if train service is considered, is quite an item, and storage of coal is not practicable.

Coaling Platform, St. Louis, Iron Mountain & Southern Railway.—The coaling-platform design of the St. Louis, Iron Mountain & Southern Railway, shown in Fig. 276, consists of a platform, 12 ft. 4 in. above the top of rail, with a supply-track at the centre of the platform, level with the floor. The coal is shovelled from the road cars on this supply-track, either to the rear of the platform into store, or toward the face of the platform for immediate use. There are narrow-gauge tracks running perpendicularly to the face of the platform, on which large wooden tipping coal-buggies run. The face of the buggy consists of an iron flap, which, when the buggy is tipped, serves as an apron. The tipping of the buggy is facilitated by having a gallows frame at the face of the platform, with the necessary chains, shafts, pulleys, etc. In the standard design the platform is 60 ft. wide, and 160 ft. long; the narrow-gauge tracks are spaced from 20 to 28 ft. apart, and the approach incline is 329 ft. long on a grade of 3.75 ft. in 100 ft. A light shed roof is built over the platform, so as to protect the coal from the weather.

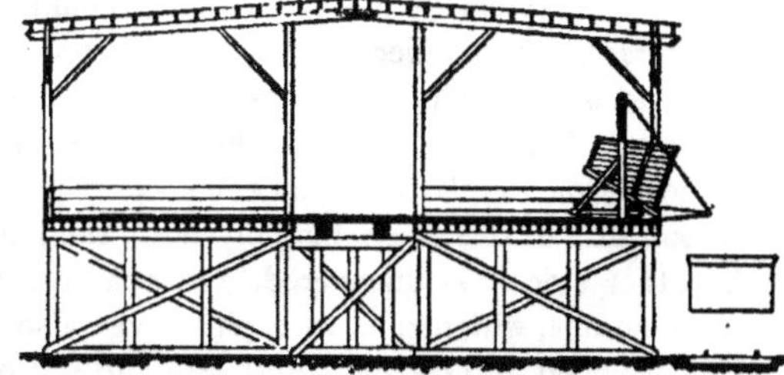

FIG. 276.—CROSS-SECTION.

In the coaling platform of the same road at De Soto, Mo., the platform is narrower, and it has no shed over it. There is no storage space provided on the rear of the platform. The coal-supply track runs immediately on the rear of the platform, and is sunk below the level of the platform, so that the floor of the car is about level with the floor of the platform. This design has the advantage that the approach incline is much shorter, but has the disadvantage that the storage capacity of the platform is limited.

Coaling Platform with Tipping Trolley Dump-car, Connecticut River Railroad.—The Connecticut River Railroad uses coaling platforms with tipping trolley dump-cars, plans for which were published in the Report of the Master Mechanics' Association, quoted above, the cars running on tracks perpendicular to the face of the platform. The coal is shovelled from the storage-pile on the rear of the platform into the dump-cars, which latter are then pushed to the face of the platform, tipped, and discharged. The cost is stated to be 14 cents per ton, with a daily delivery of 45 tons. The force employed is three laborers and one foreman, the former receiving 14½ cents, the latter 18¾ cents per hour. One man's shovelling and trolleying capacity is therefore about 11¼ tons per day.

Coaling Platform with Tipping Trolley Dump car, New York, Chicago & St. Louis Railroad.—On the New York, Chicago & St. Louis Railroad a similar system is in use to that described for the Connecticut River Railroad. The dumps hold 6 tons each, and dip to an angle of 45 degrees. The cost of delivery is 8 cents per ton, delivering 74 tons per day. The rate of pay is 12½ cents per hour. With four men employed each day, the capacity of each man is 18½ tons.

Coaling Platform with Tipping Trolley Dump-cars, Northern Central Railroad.—Plans showing the details of the tipping trolley dump-cars used by the Northern Central Railroad on coaling platforms were published in the Report of the Master Mechanics' Association, quoted above. The platform is located along the main track, 32 ft. wide and about 200 ft. long. The floor is placed 10 ft. above the top of the rail of the main-line track. Coal is delivered to the platform by dumping from a trestle on the rear of the platform, which dumping track is on an average about 9 ft. above the platform, with a light grade of 0.75 ft. in 100 ft. to facilitate the movement of cars by hand. The approach trestling is 447 ft. long, with a gradient of 3½ ft. in 100 ft. On the platform, spaced every 25 ft. (in every other trestle-bent), there are a series of narrow-gauge tracks running at right angles to the face and extending back the full depth of the platform. At a point 8½ ft. from the centre of the main track is a stop which serves the double purpose of first stopping the car at a given point, and, secondly, of releasing the hook on the back end of truck, the sudden impact of the truck dumping the coal into the tender. The inside dimensions of the dump-cars are 10 ft. 8 in. long × 5 ft. 10 in. wide × 1 ft. 10 in. high, holding 3 tons. One end of the truck is open. The car can be operated by one man. The system is preferred at coaling stations along the main track on account of the speed with which engines can draw their coal supply. The average cost per ton for the winter months is stated to have been 4.6 cents, employing two men and delivering 57½ tons every 24 hours. This gives an average of 23¾ tons coal handled per man.

Coaling Platform at Altoona, Pa., Pennsylvania Railroad.—Plans for the coaling platform of the Pennsylvania Railroad at Altoona, Pa., were published in the *Railroad Gazette* of September 15, 1882. The system in use consists of a coaling platform with tipping trolley dump-cars running on transverse tracks, connected by a longitudinal track with a transfer-table. The platform is about 90 ft. wide and placed 11 ft. above the coaling tracks, there being a coaling track along each face of the platform. Coal is delivered to the platform by shovelling from cars on a central supply-track near the centre of the platform, the track being placed at the same elevation as the floor of the platform. On one side of this central supply-track the platform is covered to serve for long storage, while on the other side it is uncovered, the coal on this side being intended for immediate use. The transfer-table, which runs in a pit, serves also as a weigh-scales. The trolley-cars are run on the table, weighed, transferred lengthwise and put off at any point desired along the face of the platform, where they remain till discharged.

Coaling Platform at West Philadelphia, Pa., Pennsylvania Railroad.—The coaling platform at West Philadelphia, Pa., on the Pennsylvania Railroad, plans for which were published in the *Railroad Gazette* of September 15, 1882, consists of a coaling platform with an elevated dumping track near the rear of the platform, coal being delivered to engines by tipping trolley dump-cars running on transverse tracks connected by a longitudinal track in a well with a transfer scale-table. The platform is about 50 ft. wide and the floor is placed 11 ft. above the coaling track. The location is along a side hill so that the floor of the platform is practically on original ground. The dumping-track is 9 ft. above the floor, and its centre is located about 40 ft. from the face of the platform. A 6-ft. well is located 10 ft. back from the face for the narrow-gauge transfer and scale table to run in.

Coaling Platform at East Tyrone, Pa., Pennsylvania Railroad.—The coaling platform of the Pennsylvania Railroad at East Tyrone, Pa., plans for which were published in the *Railroad Gazette* of September 15, 1882, is very similar to the coaling platform at West Philadelphia, on the line of the same road, excepting that at East Tyrone the entire structure is built on trestling, whereas at West Philadelphia the platform is cut into a side hill. The coaling platform is 46 ft. wide, and located 11 ft. above the coaling track along the face. The centre of the elevated dumping track is located 37 ft. from the face of the platform, and is 8 ft. above the floor of the platform. Nine feet from the face of the platform there is a well, 6 ft. in width, for the transfer-table to transfer the dump-cars up and down the platform. The trestle-bents are located 10 ft. centres, perpendicular to the coaling track, and rest on dry stone foundation-walls. The length of this platform is 200 ft., and the gradient on the incline leading up to the supply-track is 5 ft. in 100 ft.

Elevated Coal-shed, Northern Pacific Railroad.—The elevated coal-shed of the Northern Pacific Railroad, shown in Fig. 277, designed by Mr. C. B. Talbot, consists of a covered platform with a narrow-gauge track running lengthwise of the shed connecting by turn-tables with tracks running out over the coaling track on counterbalanced platforms or drawbridges, the coal being discharged into the tenders by small narrow-gauge tipping trolley dump-cars, which are loaded in the house from the storage-pile, turned on the turn-table, run out on the drawbridge, and tipped. The coal is put into the shed through openings in the side sheathing by shovelling from cars on an elevated track along the back of the shed. The platform in the shed is 14 ft. wide, and the floor is placed about 12 ft. 6 in. above the coaling track. The shed can be made any length desired; the standard plan shows it to be 240 ft. long, with a rated capacity of 500 tons. For this length of house there are two turn-tables and drawbridges for discharging to tenders. The elevated coal-supply track on the rear of the shed is placed 3 ft. 6 in. below the floor in the shed. The clear height of the shed above the floor is 8 ft. The centre of the coaling track is placed 6 ft. from the face of the building.

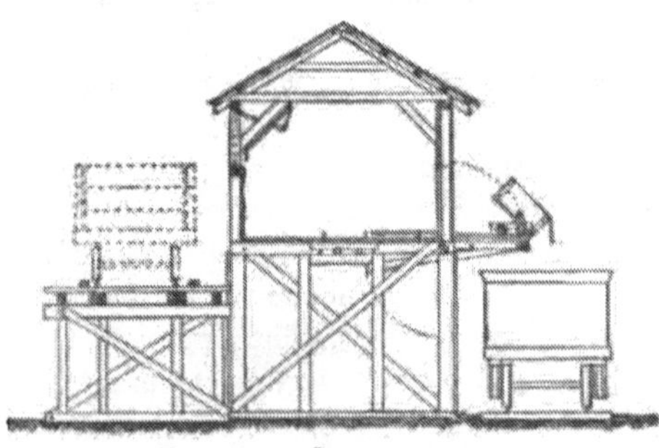

FIG. 277.—CROSS-SECTION.

Coal-chutes, Baltimore & Ohio Railroad.—The coal-chutes of the Baltimore & Ohio Railroad, plans for which were published in the *Railroad Gazette* of September 15, 1882, consist of a system of coal-pockets with an elevated dumping track. The trestling is about 42 ft. wide, there being a coaling track on each side, with pockets facing each track. The coal is delivered on an elevated supply-track at the middle of the trestle, about 33 ft. above the coaling tracks, whence the coal is dumped to a platform about 12 ft. lower, which is located at the elevation of the top of the pockets. The coal when dumped runs partly into the pockets, and the balance is shovelled in by hand as required. The pockets are closed at the lower end in the usual way with a trap-door and a counterweighted apron. The pockets are about 10 ft. wide, and contain three tons of coal when filled completely. The bottom of the pocket is set 12 ft. above the coaling track. The cost of delivering 115 tons per day over a high-chute system on the Baltimore & Ohio Railroad, similar to that described above, is stated to be $4\frac{3}{16}$ cents per ton.

Coal-chutes at Southport, N. Y., New York, Lake Erie & Western Railroad.—The coal-chutes of the New York, Lake Erie & Western Railroad at Southport, N. Y., plans for which were published in the issue of the *Railroad Gazette* of October 5, 1883, consist of an elevated dumping track from which the coal is dumped from the coal-cars to a lower storage platform. Along one side of this storage platform there is a row of pockets, triangular in shape, each of a capacity of two tons, the tops of which are on a level with the storage platform. The lower end of the pocket is closed by means of a trap-door and counterweighted apron in the usual manner. The trap-door is worked by means of a rod connected to its lower edge and running up to the level of the storage platform, so that the opening of the trap-door is independent of the lowering and raising of the apron. The cost of delivering 560 tons of coal to engines at these coal pockets, per month per each man employed there, is stated to be 7.85 cents per ton.

Coal-chutes, New Orleans & Northeastern Railroad.—The standard coal-chute of the New Orleans & Northeastern Railroad, part of the Cincinnati, New Orleans & Texas Pacific Railroad, lessee Cincinnati Southern Railroad, shown in Fig. 278, consists of a high trestle-track, from which coal is dumped

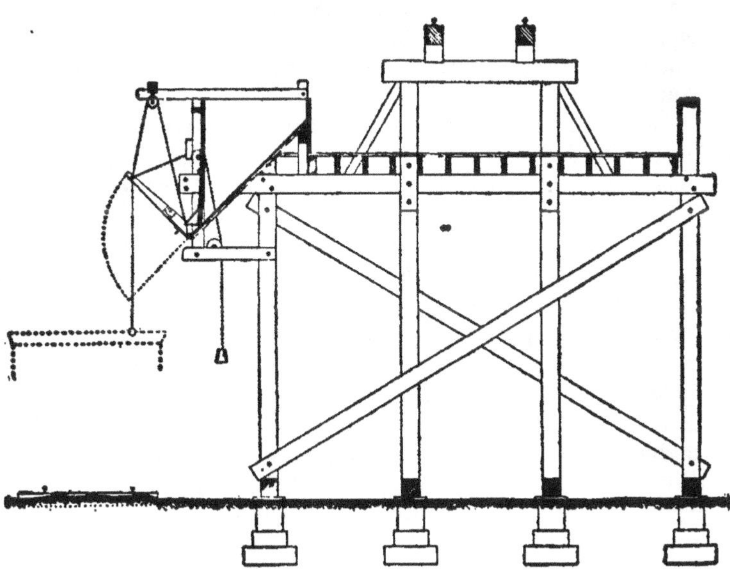

FIG. 278.—CROSS-SECTION.

on to a platform and then shovelled as required into a series of pockets along one side of the platform. The high track is 25 ft. 6 in. above the coaling track in front of the pockets, and 7 ft. 4 in. above the floor of the platform. The bottom of the pocket is set 11 ft. above the top of the rail of the coaling track. The width of the structure is 29 ft.

The dimensions of the principal materials used are as follows: the bents are spaced 10 ft. centres longitudinally; sills, running longitudinally, 12 in. × 12 in.; posts, 12 in. × 12 in.; caps, running transversely, 2 pieces, 6 in. × 12 in., clamping the posts; cap under track, 12 in. × 14 in. × 11 ft.; track-stringers, one piece, 12 in. × 12 in., under each rail; corbels, 12 in. × 12 in. × 3 ft.; floor-plank and side sheathing of platform and pockets, 2-in. oak; floor-joists, 3 in. × 12 in., spaced about 20 in. centres, bridged with 3-in. × 1¼-in. bridging; X-bracing, 3 in. × 8 in.

The bottom of the pocket is lined with $\frac{3}{16}$-in. sheet-iron. The apron is counterweighted, as shown, and the bottom of the pocket is closed by a flap-door, which is opened and closed automatically with the lowering and raising of the apron. The apron is 5 ft. long. The pocket and apron slope 45 degrees.

Coal-chutes at Scottsville, Va., Richmond & Alleghany Railroad.—The coal-chutes of the Richmond & Alleghany Railroad at Scottsville, Va., shown in Fig. 279, designed and built by the author,

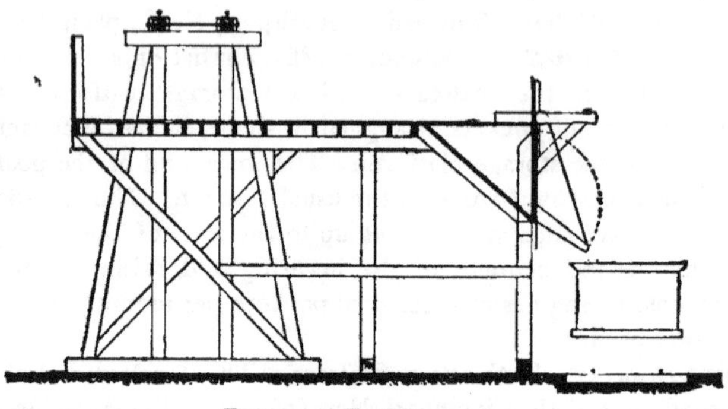

FIG. 279.—CROSS-SECTION.

consist of a timber trestle structure throughout, the coal being delivered onto a storage platform from a high dumping-trestle on the back of the platform and then shovelled as required into a series of pockets along the face of the platform, the top of the pockets being level with the floor of the platform. The chutes are located alongside of the main track of the railroad, as quick dispatch for coaling engines was desirable. The platform is 96 ft. long by 34 ft. 6 in. wide, and its floor is set 18 ft. above the top of rail on the main track. The face of the platform is placed 7 ft. from the centre of the main track. The end of the apron when lowered is 10 ft. 9 in. above the top of rail of the main track. The apron is 5 ft. 6 in. long, and reaches when lowered to within 2 ft. 3 in. of the centre of the track. The centre of the dumping track is placed 25 ft. from the face of the platform, and the top of rail on the trestle is 7 ft. 7 in. above the floor of the platform or 25 ft. 7 in. above the top of rail of the main track. The inclined approach is about 700 ft. long, with a maximum gradient of 3.75 ft. per 100 ft. There are three pockets along the face of the platform, each with a capacity of 3½ tons. The bottom of the pocket has a slope of 40 degrees, and the apron, when lowered, 30 degrees. The lower end of the pocket is closed by a flap-door locked by a pivoting-bar, so that the opening and closing of the door is independent of the movement of the apron, which is counterweighted in the usual way. In drawing coal the fireman pulls down the apron and then hits the bar lock of the door a light blow with a shovel or any handy implement, opening the door and allowing the coal to discharge. An engine can coal at these chutes in less than one minute.

New Coal-chutes at Waverly, N. Y., New York, Lake Erie & Western Railroad.—The coal-chutes of the New York, Lake Erie & Western Railroad at Waverly, N. Y., rebuilt in 1882, under the direction of Mr. O. Chanute, Chief Engineer, and Mr. W. Farnham, Roadmaster, plans for which were published in the *Railroad Gazette* of October 5, 1883, have a storage capacity for about 330 tons. The system consists of a high delivery track, from which the coal is dumped into a pocket or storage floor below. The coal is drawn, as required, through a measuring pocket into a chute, which is closed in the usual way by a counterweighted apron and flap-door. There are eleven pockets and chutes, making the storage platform 110 ft. long. The tail track is 60 ft. long. The approach incline is built with a gradient of 4 ft. per 100 ft., and high ground in the vicinity is utilized to reduce the length of trestling required. The track over the platform and tail trestle has a gradient of 0.8 ft. in

100 ft. to facilitate the movement of cars by hand. The cost of delivering 460 tons of coal to engines per month, per each man employed at these chutes, is stated to be 9.07 cents per ton.

Coal-chutes at Hornellsville, N. Y., New York, Lake Erie & Western Railroad.—The coal-chutes of the New York, Lake Erie & Western Railroad at Hornellsville, N. Y., built in 1881 and 1882, from a design and under the direction of Mr. J. W. Ferguson, Assistant Engineer, plans for which were published in the *Railroad Gazette* of October 5, 1883, consist of a system of coaling engines on both sides of a coaling trestle without any shovelling of the coal, requiring of all systems, thus far discussed, the least manual labor, as the coal passes from the supply-car to the tender entirely by gravity. The coal is dumped from two high tracks into hopper-shaped bins, which are trapped at the lower ends by measuring pockets. The coal, as required, is drawn through the measuring pocket into the chute below it, which chute is closed at the lower end in the usual way with a flap door and counterweighted apron. The supply-cars are taken up to the high tracks by a stationary engine and inclined plane with cable. The only objectionable feature in this system is the extra height that has to be given to the dumping tracks. Where, however, a stationary engine with plane is used, this is not a serious objection, as a few extra feet to climb after once placing cars on a plane does not cause a very noticeable expense. The system can therefore be recommended very highly under these conditions, and also where the approach can be located mainly on high ground. The cost of delivering 614 tons of coal to engines per month, per each man employed at the chutes, is stated to be 7.08 cents per ton.

Old Coal-chutes at Waverly, N. Y., New York, Lake Erie & Western Railroad.—The system of coaling engines on the New York, Lake Erie & Western Railroad at Waverly, N. Y., in use prior to the construction of the new pockets, was illustrated in the *Railroad Gazette* of October 5, 1883. It consists of two elevated tracks dumping onto a storage floor or pockets below them. The coal is drawn from the pockets through a measuring pocket into tipping trolley dump-cars with projecting end. The cars are run on a turn-table, which serves also as a scales, and transferred on a longitudinal track to whatever point along the face they are wanted, where they are again turned on a table, run out, tipped, and discharged. The cost of delivering 455 tons of coal to engines per month, per each man employed at the chutes, is stated to be 9.16 cents per ton.

Coal-chutes at Susquehanna, Pa., New York, Lake Erie & Western Railroad.—The coal-chutes of the New York, Lake Erie & Western Railroad at Susquehanna, Pa., plans for which were published in the *Railroad Gazette* of October 5, 1883, consist of three elevated tracks dumping into storage-bins and partly on a floor below them. The bins are hopper-shaped, and trapped at their lower ends with measuring pockets. The coal, as required, is drawn into narrow-gauge hopper-bottom trolley-cars of two tons capacity, which cars run on a system of tranverse tracks connected by turn-tables with a longitudinal track. To deliver coal, a counterbalanced, hinged platform is lowered over the tender and a car run out and dumped. The platform has chains attached to the outer end and to the timbers above, which prevent its dropping when loaded. It is raised and lowered by a hand-wheel and friction pulleys, around which the chains from the counterbalances are passed. The cost of delivering 675 tons of coal to engines per month, per each man employed at these coal-chutes, is stated to be 6.55 cents per ton.

Coal-chutes at Buffalo, N. Y., and at Connellsville, Pa.—The design for coal-chutes at Buffalo, N. Y., and at Connellsville, Pa., plans for which were published in the *Railroad Gazette* of September 15, 1882, consists of a coal-chute system with a high supply-track, from which the coal is dumped into triangular-shaped pockets, whence it is drawn into dump-cars on a lower platform. The trestle is 20 ft. wide and 24 ft. high. The dumping platform is 10 ft. above the rails and has a narrow-gauge track through the centre with appropriate turn-table arrangements to take the car from the central track to the face of the platform, whence the coal can be shot directly into the tender. There are no scales in this system, the coal being measured in bulk in the dump-cars.

Coal-bunkers, Northern Pacific Railroad.—The coal-bunkers of the Northern Pacific Railroad, designed by Mr. C. B. Talbot, shown in Fig. 280, are a combination of a number of the methods already discussed for storing and delivering coal to engines. The structure consists of a building, 34 ft. × 211 ft., with a delivery track at the peak of the building, 42 ft. above the ground. On one side of the building is the main track of the road and on the other side a yard track. The coaling of engines on the main track is done by hopper-bottom narrow-gauge trolley-cars, that run out on a counterbalanced platform or drawbridge and dump directly into the tenders. The coaling of engines

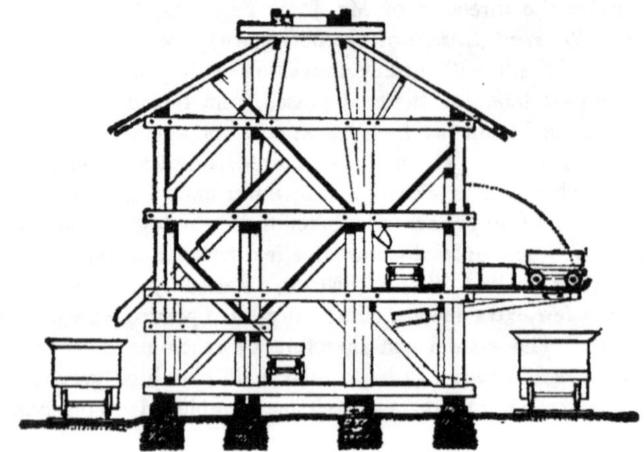

FIG. 280.—CROSS-SECTION.

on the other side of the house is done by an apron and flap-door leading out of a hopper-shaped bin. Storage-bins are provided, as shown, from which coal is drawn into the trolley-cars, and the cars then transferred to the upper tier again. The storage capacity of the building is 2000 tons.

Standard Coal-chute, Wabash, St. Louis & Pacific Railway.—The standard coal-chute of the Wabash, St. Louis & Pacific Railway, designed by Mr. Charles Hansel, Resident Engineer, shown in Fig. 281, consists of a system of elevated pockets with a supply-track on the rear, the coal being shovelled from the cars on the supply-track into the coal-pockets, the top of the pockets being 7 ft. above the supply-track. The centre of the supply-track is located 21 ft. from the centre of the main track, which is the coaling track, and the rail of the supply-track is 15 ft. above the main track. The face of the coaling pockets is located 4 ft. from the nearest rail, and the top of the pocket is 22 ft. 8 in. above the rail of the coaling track. The trestle-bents at the pockets are spaced 9 ft. 6 in. centres, while on the incline approach the bents are spaced 16 ft. ft. centres. The gradient on the incline leading to the elevated supply-track is 3.75 ft. in 100 ft. The lower end of the pocket is closed by a counter-balanced apron and a trap-door operated by a long lever arm, as shown in the plans. The standard coal-chute has about ten pockets, but any number can be used according to the varying conditions in different localities.

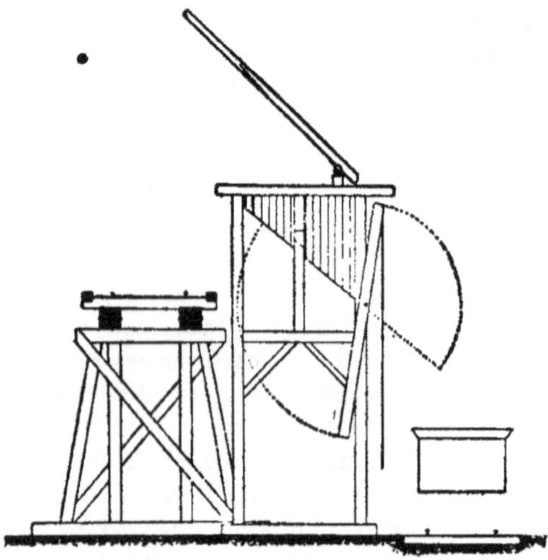

FIG. 281.—CROSS-SECTION.

The principal timbers in use on the supply-track trestling are: sills, 12 in. × 12 in.; vertical posts, 12 in. × 12 in.; batter-posts, 10 in. × 12 in.; caps, 12 in. × 12 in. × 12 ft. long; brace-plank, 3 in. × 10 in.; stringers, 2 pieces, 8 in. × 16 in., under each rail; ties, 6 in. × 8 in. × 10 ft. long; guard-rails, 6 in. × 8 in. The dimensions of the principal timbers used in the construction of the coaling pockets are as follows: sills, 12 in. × 12 in.; posts, 8 in. × 8 in.; caps, 8 in. × 8 in. × 12 ft. long; interties, 8 in. × 8 in.; intermediate-post, 8 in. × 8 in.; knee-braces, 4 in. × 6 in.

Coal-chutes at Black Diamond Mine, Wabash, St. Louis & Pacific Railway.—The coal-chute at the Black Diamond Mine, Wabash, St. Louis & Pacific Railway, designed by Mr. Charles Hansel, Resident Engineer, shown in Fig. 282, is arranged to allow mine cars from the Black Diamond Mine to discharge coal directly into a series of pockets or chutes along a coaling track. The details of the chutes are practically the same as described above for the standard coal-chute of the road. The delivery of coal to the pockets, however, is made from a platform at the height of the top of the pockets. on which the mine cars are turned, and run onto a tipple at the top of the pocket, by means of which the car is tipped and discharged into the pocket.

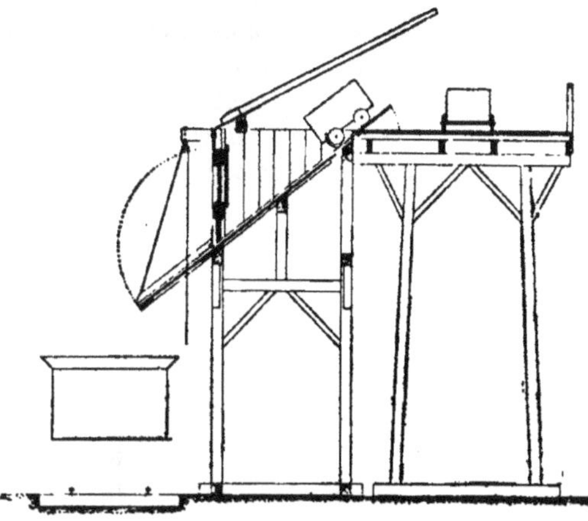

FIG. 282.—CROSS-SECTION.

Coal-chutes at Wilkesbarre, Pa., Lehigh Valley Railroad.—The coal-chutes of the Lehigh Valley Railroad at Wilkesbarre, Pa., designed by Mr. A. Mitchell, Division Superintendent, shown in Fig. 283, consist of a series of pockets, with a dumping track running directly over them, the entire structure being covered. The rail of the dumping track is placed 24 ft. above the rail on the coaling track, which runs along one side of the building. The approach incline, partly on trestle and partly on filling, is built on a gradient of 5 ft. per 100 ft. There are 15 pockets in the building all used for hard coal. The lower end of the pocket is placed 11 ft. 6 in. above the rail of the coaling track; and the slope of the bottom of the pocket is 5 in. in 12 in., or at an angle of about 22½ degrees. The pocket has a counterweighted apron, and is closed by a lifting-door. The shed over the pockets and dumping track has 15 ft. clear height above the rail and 18 ft. 8 in. clear width. Some of the pockets are used for fine coal, such as buckwheat and pea coal, and others for lump coal. The lump-coal pockets have screens in the bottom, screenings being collected, as shown in the sketch, in small coal-cars placed underneath the pockets. When full these cars are transferred to the upper track and the coal is dumped into the fine coal-pockets.

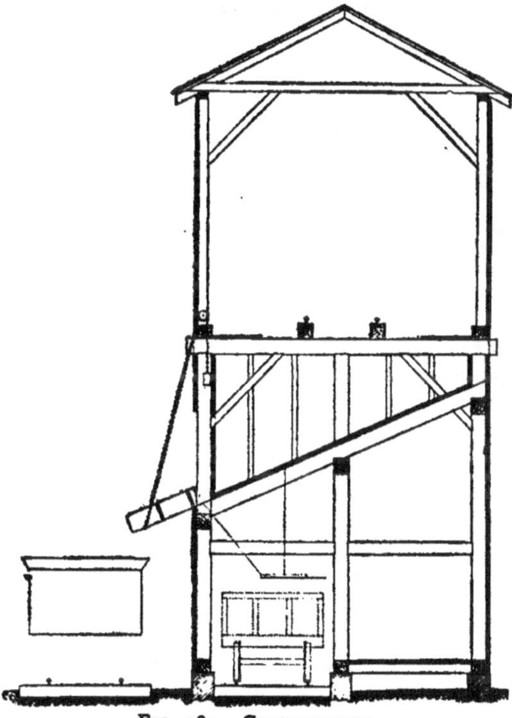

FIG. 283.—CROSS-SECTION.

The average amount of coal handled over these chutes daily is about 300 tons. The engine service is performed by the switching-engine employed at the shops in the immediate vicinity. The force regularly employed on the chutes consists of two day men and one night man, who dump the coal from the cars into the pockets and discharge the pockets, the rate of pay being 12½ cents per hour. The average cost, therefore, of dumping into store and discharging to engines will be about 1.5 cents per ton, exclusive of engine service, interest on first cost, and maintenance of the structure.

Coal-chute, Atchison, Topeka & Santa Fe Railroad.—The standard coal-chute of the Atchison, Topeka & Santa Fe Railroad, shown in Fig. 284, prepared from data kindly furnished by Mr. J. M. Meade, Assistant Engineer, A., T. & S. F. R. R., is built on what is known as the "Clifton" chute plan, which system has been very extensively adopted by a large number of railroads in the West, the same as the "Kerr" chute, which differs from the "Clifton" chute mainly in the details of the iron-work; but the general scheme or layout of the structure remains about the same, namely, an elevated covered supply-track, with covered bins or chutes on one or both sides of it, which bins are closed at the lower end with doors and provided with counterweighted aprons. The individual characteristics of the Kerr and Clifton chutes are the mechanical contrivances and fixtures for locking and working the door and the apron. In the Clifton chute the drawing down of the apron releases at the proper time certain catches or latches, and the pressure of the coal forces the door open and allows the coal

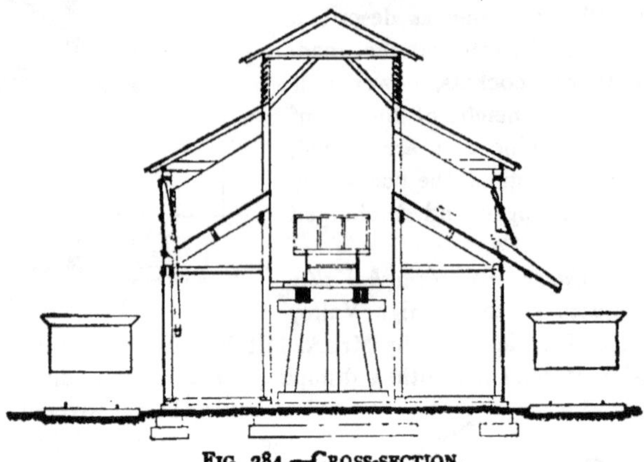

FIG. 284.—CROSS-SECTION.

to flow out. In pushing the apron back to place, the door and apron is locked again. The introduction of a second or inside door or flap in the Clifton chute allows the contents of the pocket to be subdivided, and only a part delivered at a time, if desired.

The design adopted for the Atchison, Topeka & Santa Fe Railroad places the rail on the supply-track 11 ft. 4 in. above the rail of the coaling track. The top of the pockets next to the supply-track is 8 ft. above the rail of the supply-track, so that coal, in being shovelled from cars into the bins, has to be lifted several feet. The width of the shed with pockets on both sides is 32 ft. The face is set 7 ft. 9 in. from the centre of the coaling track. The clear height of the shed over the supply-track is 18 ft. 6 in., and the clear width 11 ft. 6 in. The angle of slope of the bottom of the pocket and apron is about 27½ degrees. The gradient on the approach incline trestling is 3.77 ft. per 100 ft.

Collin's System for Coaling Locomotives, Pennsylvania Railroad.—Collin's system for coaling locomotives, plans for which were published in the *Railroad Gazette* of June 16, 1882, illustrates the method for coaling engines designed and patented by Mr. J. B. Collin, Mechanical Engineer, Pennsylvania Railroad, which method has been successfully introduced on the Pennsylvania Railroad at Lewiston, Pa.; Alleghany City, Pa.; Coalport, N. J.; Camden, N. J.; and at other points.

The report of the Master Mechanics' Association gives the following information relative to the operation of Collin's system for coaling locomotives at Elmira, N. Y.: "The rate of delivery is one truck-load of two tons in from 70 to 80 seconds, and four tenders have been loaded, with two trucks each, in 15 minutes and 25 seconds,—an average of 3 minutes 51 seconds each. This includes the time of attaching and detaching chain from the locomotive and clearing the track for another locomotive to enter. The cost, averaged over the first three months of 1887 (when the apparatus was not worked up to its capacity), is 7$\frac{8}{10}$ cts. per ton, delivering at the rate of 53.4 tons per day, and requiring three men per 24 hours, at 12 cts. per hour."

The main principle of this plan is that of using the power of the locomotive, which is to be supplied with coal, to raise the coal into a convenient position from which it can be dumped into the tender. This is done by means of an elevator or lift constructed alongside of the track, in front of which the locomotives stand when they are to be supplied with coal. This elevator has a suitable cage, which is raised by means of a rope or chain attached to the locomotive, the movement of the latter on the track drawing the cage up.

This system is hardly applicable, however, for coaling engines on the main line, as it is obviously impossible to allow an engine, while in service on the main line, to stop long enough to raise the coal to a sufficient elevation to allow it to be dumped into the tender. For coaling engines, however, before starting on a run, or before going into the engine-house to wait for their turn to start on the road again, this system would have its advantages under certain local conditions. For additional details see the issue of the *Railroad Gazette* above mentioned.

Overhead Coaling Station at Hackensack Meadows, Jersey City, N. J., Pennsylvania Railroad.—The coaling station of the Pennsylvania Railroad at the Hackensack Meadows, between Newark and Jersey City, N. J., built in 1887, plans for which were published in the *Railroad Gazette*, September 2, 1887, took the place of an old coaling station which had become inadequate for the business. In July, 1874, 3,700,067 lbs. of coal were delivered to engines, while in July, 1883, 11,813,000 lbs. were delivered, and during December, 1886, 17,491,000 lbs. were furnished, which statement conveys an idea of the amount of work to be done by a coaling station at this point, in addition to providing ample storage for coal. The system adopted consists of loading small narrow-gauge drop-bottom trolley-cars with coal on the ground level, hoisting them up by a platform elevator 22 ft. above the ground, and then running them out on an overhead bridge over the coaling tracks, and discharging directly into chutes leading down to the tenders when stopped underneath the bridge.

The structure is described as follows in the publication mentioned: The new station is located between the passenger and freight tracks. In the coal-yard are thirteen tracks having an average length of about 800 ft. These are connected with the east-bound freight track. The loading platform, connected with the coal-yard by tracks, consists of two low trestles and one high trestle. Midway between the two low trestles extends a depressed track, upon which runs a transfer car carrying the dump. Extending across the platform between each bent of the trestles are transfer tracks, upon which the dumps can be run under the trestles.

The loaded coal-car is brought to any point on either of the trestles. The dump is then brought opposite this point and rolled under the car, from which it receives its load. The dump is then run to one of the elevators, lifted to the upper platform, and taken over either the passenger or freight tracks. Coal-cars which are run upon the high trestle dump their loads upon the ground, the dumps being then loaded by hand. Upon the upper platform is standing-room for 70 dumps. Each dump is 8 ft. 6 in. long, weighs 2600 lbs., and will hold 7000 lbs. of coal.

From each turn-table on the upper platform extends a track, one leading over the passenger and the other over the freight tracks. Over the two passenger tracks are three chutes, the centre one of which is provided with two bottom doors in order that the coal from the dumps may be guided into a tender upon either track. Over the two freight tracks are two chutes located centrally between each pair of tracks, and furnished with double doors at the bottom. Each loaded dump is weighed upon scales placed on the upper platform, and the amount is handed down to the engineer.

The two Otis elevators are placed one at each side of the platform. The engines are double, with 10-in. × 10-in. cylinders. The face of the drum will hold 55 ft. of ¾-in. chain. The engines can be started from the ground or from the top of the trestle, and the hoists are automatically stopped both at top and bottom. The engines will lift a load of 20,000 lbs. The cage rises 26 ft.

According to the specifications, the piles are of Norway pine, spruce, or chestnut, 12 in. at the butt, and driven to hard bottom. The longitudinal caps are 12-in. × 12-in. yellow pine, secured by staggered ¾-in. wrought-iron spikes.

The transverse caps are also 12 in. × 12 in., and are mortised to receive the tenons of the trestle-posts. The main posts supporting the upper platform are 12 in. × 12 in. yellow pine, mortised and tenoned. The two posts adjacent to the transfer track are braced transversely and longitudinally by 3 in. × 12 in. strips bolted to the posts. The trestle is built with two straight and two battered posts, the latter having a spread of one quarter the height of the former. The trestle-caps are 10 in. × 12 in., and the stringers 12 in. × 14 in. The floor-beams of the upper platform are 3 in. × 12 in. yellow pine, spaced 24 in., and laid to break joints.

For additional data and details see the issue of the *Railroad Gazette* mentioned above.

Overhead Coaling Station at Gray's Ferry, Philadelphia, Wilmington & Baltimore Railroad.—The coaling station of the Philadelphia, Wilmington & Baltimore Railroad at Gray's Ferry, designed by

Mr. S. T. Fuller, Chief Engineer, plans for which were published in the *Railroad Gazette*, December 9, 1881 (the design being patented by S. T. Fuller and Charles A. Merriam), illustrates the system of having an overhead bridge thrown across the main tracks of the railroad, on which small narrow-gauge dump-cars containing the coal are run out and dumped through openings in the bottom of the bridge directly into the tender of the locomotives. In the coaling station as built at Gray's Ferry the coal is brought in cars up an incline to a coal-shed built sideways from the main tracks, the dumping track in the coal-shed being on trestling, so that the coal can be dumped from hopper-cars, if desired, to the floor at a lower elevation. The shed is 153 ft. long, the dumping track being in the centre of the shed, and on each side of it there are narrow-gauge tracks on the lower platform level, which tracks connect by means of turn-tables with the track running out on the bridge across the railroad. The iron narrow-gauge cars are filled with coal by hand, and then run out on the bridge as required. There are suitable openings in the floor of the bridge over each track, with aprons underneath, which latter can be raised and lowered by a lever as indicated on the plans. The operation of coaling the engines is very simple. When the tender comes to a stand-still underneath the bridge the apron or chute is lowered, the dump-car placed over the opening, and the drop-doors at the bottom of the dump-car opened, thus discharging the coal down the apron into the tender. It is claimed that the cost of handling the coal in this manner is one fourth of what it had been on the road prior to the introduction of this system by Mr. Fuller, independent of the saving in time, and that an engine can be coaled in from 1 to 2½ minutes without undue breakage or scattering of the coal, and with less dust than usual. Where it is impossible, owing to local conditions, to get the length or space required for an incline, a vertical platform lift, or a plane on a sharp incline with a wire rope to haul up the cars, can be used, but naturally with an increase in the cost of working the system.

For complete details, especially of the dump-cars, turn-table, apron, dumping trestle, and overhead bridge, see the issue of the *Railroad Gazette* mentioned above.

Overhead Coaling Station at Aurora, Ill., Chicago, Burlington & Quincy Railroad.—The overhead coaling station of the Chicago, Burlington & Quincy Railroad, plans for which were published in the *Railway Review* of June 15, 1889, consists of an overhead bridge spanning eight tracks, with chutes under the bridge between the tracks, arranged to deliver coal to the tracks on each side of each chute. The most novel feature of this coaling station is the method of taking the coal out on the bridge, which is done in buckets of three tons capacity, suspended from small buggies running on a system of overhead rails. A coaling shed is built parallel with the railroad, 31 ft. wide by about 200 ft. long, the floor of the shed and bridge being 21 ft. 3 in. above the main-line rails. On the back of the shed is the coal-supply track, at about the same elevation as the floor of the shed, the coal-cars being taken up to this elevation on an incline trestle approach. Parallel with the coal-supply track in the shed there are two lines of overhead rails on which the coal-buckets travel, connecting with similar tracks on the bridge. Coal is loaded into the buckets from the cars or from the stock on the platform in the shed; the buckets are then run out over the bridge and dumped into the chutes or pockets under the bridge. The pockets on the bridge are kept filled at all times, and as four pockets lead to every track, in addition to a number of loaded buckets being constantly kept on hand at the entrance of the bridge, it will be readily seen that the ability to coal a number of engines successively on any one track is good.

For further details, illustrations, and description, see the article in the *Railway Review*, mentioned above.

Coaling Station with Vertical Bucket-elevator at Jersey City, N. J., National Docks Railway.—The coaling station, designed by Mr. F. M. Slater, Chief Engineer, National Docks Railway, shown in Figs. 285 and 286, is intended for the joint purpose of coaling locomotives and furnishing coal to a boiler-house, but the illustrations herewith have been changed so as to show coal-chutes for locomotive-delivery throughout. The timber structure is 14 ft. 6 in. × 50 ft. × 34 ft. high, with storage-bins of a total capacity of about 200 tons in the upper part of the structure. The bins on one side of the centre of the building slope backwards for delivery of coal to the boiler-house on the rear of the coal-chutes, while the bins on the other side of the centre slope forward for coal-delivery to locomotives on a coaling track in front of the chutes. The bins are hopper-bottomed, and those for delivery to locomotives are closed at the lower end with gates and counterweighted aprons in the usual way.

The coaling track serves also as coal-supply track, the coal being dumped from cars on the coaling track into an underground pit under the track opposite the centre of the structure. This pit guides the coal to the foot of a vertical endless bucket-elevator with 39 ft. vertical lift, which hoists the coal up and discharges it at the head to the bins on both sides, a proper switch arrangement being provided at the head to feed the coal to any particular bin desired. The elevator is run by an 8-H. P. vertical engine. The buckets are 9 in. × 12 in. × 14 in., spaced 12 in. apart on the belt. The uptake capacity is stated to be 85 tons per hour. The machinery was furnished by the Link-belt Engineering Co., of Philadelphia, Pa. The cost of the machinery was about $1000; the timber structure cost about $1000 for the foundations, which had to be piled, and about $2000 for the superstructure.

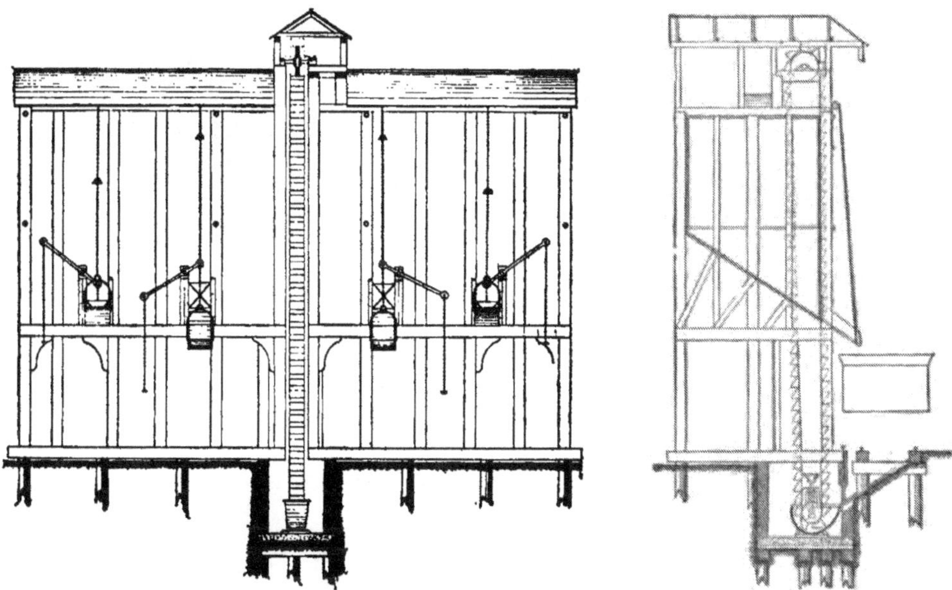

FIG. 285.—FRONT ELEVATION. FIG. 286.—CROSS-SECTION.

This system can be highly recommended for all localities where the ground-space available does not allow the usual methods for taking coal up to high chutes to be employed, or the daily output does not warrant the construction of a costly and large coal-chute system. Where steam can be drawn from a boiler in the vicinity of the coaling station, the same men that dump the coal can operate the elevator engine at any time without requiring an engineer or having to get up steam in a special boiler attached to the engine. Where the coaling track is also used for a running track and there is space behind the chutes, it will prove more advantageous to locate the coal-supply track with dumping-pit and elevator on the rear of the building. The cost of handling coal for a small coaling station on this system will prove less than over any of the platform systems, and will be as cheap as in a high-chute system, if the diminished first cost and maintenance in the elevator system is taken properly into account.

Coaling Station with Trough-conveyor Elevator at Oneonta, N. Y., Delaware & Hudson Canal Co.—The coaling station of the Delaware & Hudson Canal Co. at Oneonta, N. Y., used for coaling locomotives on the railroads controlled by the corporation mentioned, shown in Figs. 287 and 288, consists of a set of elevated pockets, the coal being carried up to the proper elevation for filling the chutes by an inclined trough-conveyor, designed and built by the Link-belt Engineering Co., of Philadelphia, Pa. The pockets are 60 ft. long × 20 ft. wide × 16 ft. deep, and are 36 ft. high from the ground-level to the top of the pocket, the storage capacity being 200 tons. The location is parallel to the main tracks, and four chutes with properly constructed aprons allow the coal to be delivered to tenders on the second track in front of the chutes, the track next to the chutes being used as a dumping track only. The incline for the trough-conveyor is only 80 ft. long, so that the entire structure and approach do not occupy more than 150 ft. in length. Coal is delivered to the foot of the elevator by dumping from cars on the nearest track into a pit below the track, as shown on the plans. In addition to the storage in the pockets, surplus storage on the ground is provided on the rear of the pocket, where a storage-pile on the Dodge Storage System is used, from which pile coal is fed to the foot of the incline when required. It is claimed that in this system the timber structure and ground-space occupied are reduced to a minimum, while the trough-conveyor does not damage the coal. The

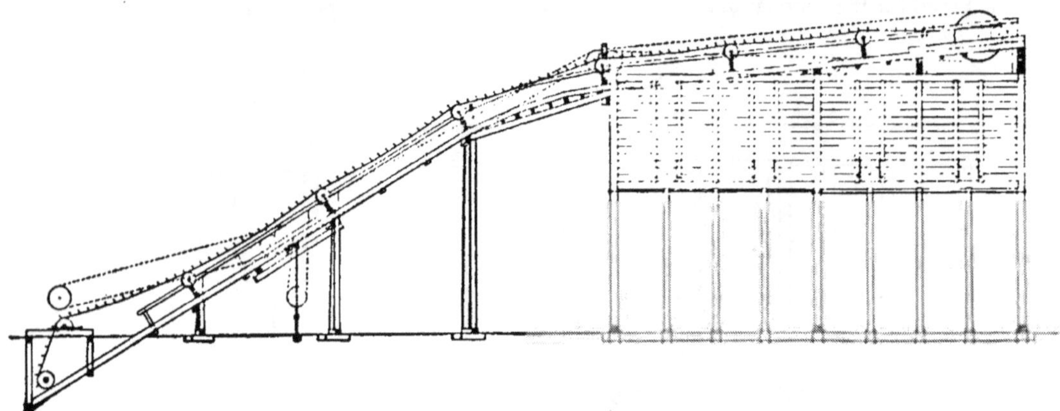

FIG. 287.—FRONT ELEVATION.

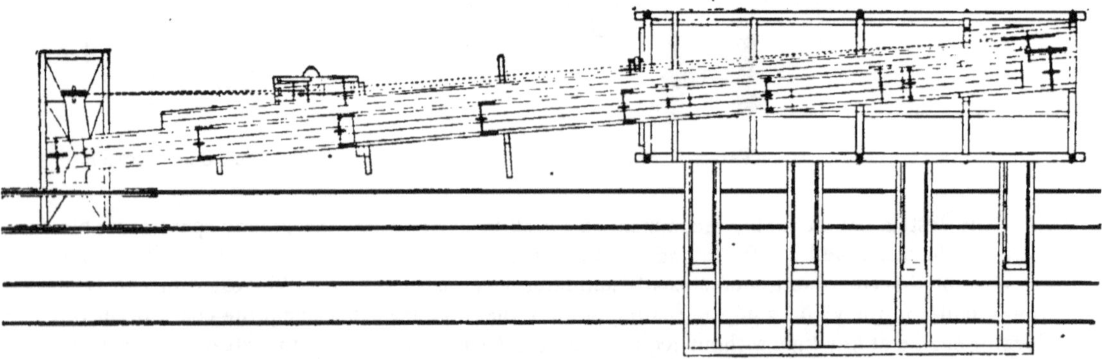

FIG. 288.—GROUND-PLAN.

cost of elevating the coal is only nominal, and a very large amount of coal can be carried in stock by the introduction of a Dodge storage-pile at the foot of the incline. The plant has been working successfully at Oneonta since 1889.

Proposed Overhead Coaling Station with Trough-conveyor Elevator at Hampton Junction, N. J., Central Railroad of New Jersey.—The overhead coaling station for two tracks, on the Central Railroad of New Jersey, proposed to be built at Hampton Junction, N. J., in connection with a large coal-storage plant on the Dodge storage-pile system, designed by the Link-belt Engineering Company, of Philadelphia, Pa., shown in Figs. 289 and 290, consists of a similar arrangement to that described above, situated at Oneonta, N. Y., excepting that the pockets are located over the main tracks and discharge through chutes vertically into the tenders underneath them. The pockets are 31 ft. long × 17 ft. wide, hopper-shaped, the bottom of the hopper being 24 ft. above the main tracks. The total storage capacity above the tracks is 75 tons.

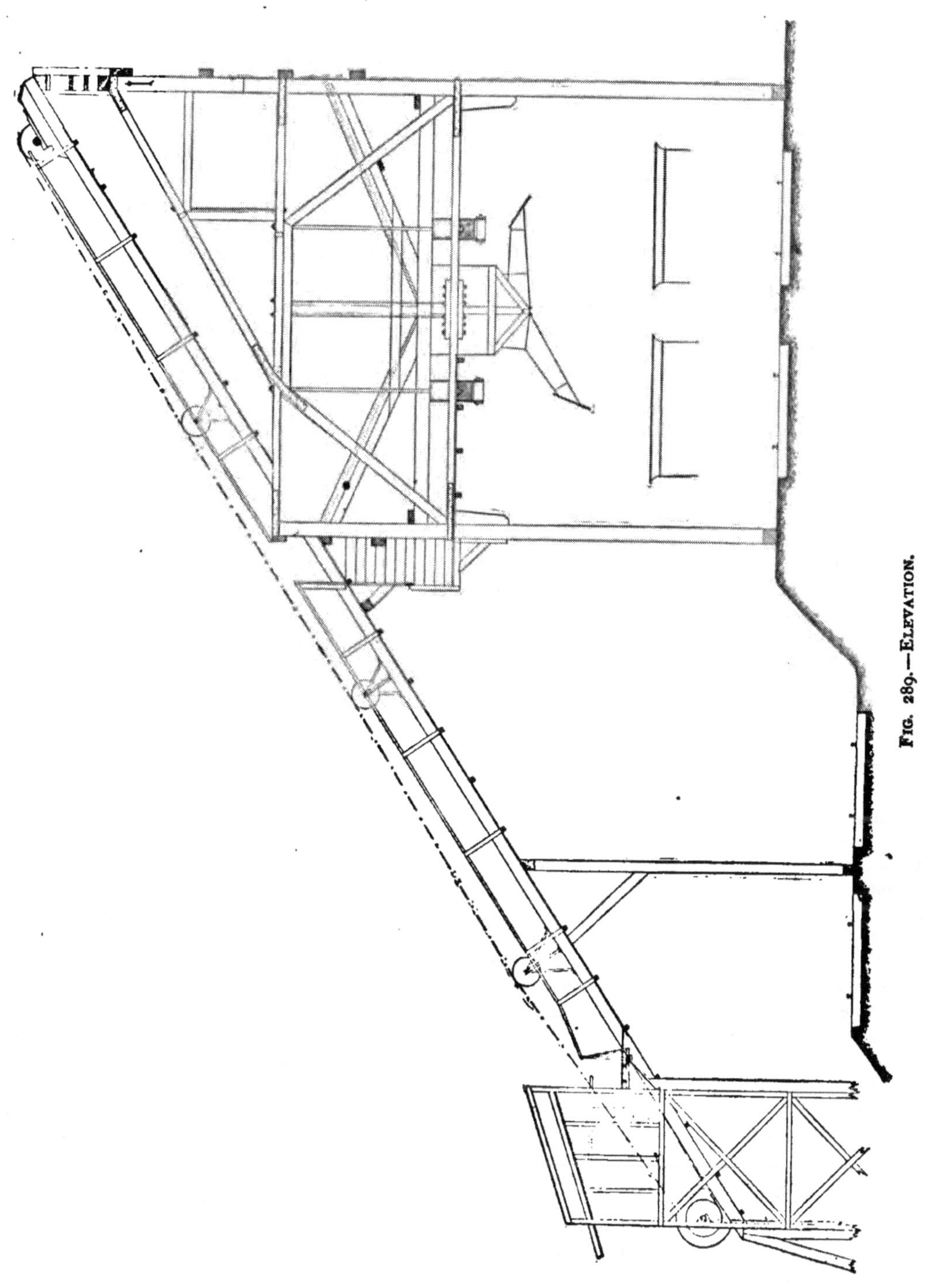

FIG. 289.—ELEVATION.

Susemihl Coal-chute at Jackson Junction, Mich., Michigan Central Railroad.—The form of chute illustrated in Figs. 291 to 294, copied from the issue of the *Railroad Gazette* of December 11, 1891, is particularly noteworthy for the peculiarity and originality of the devices for hanging and locking the apron and door. The following remarks on the subject are made in the publication mentioned:

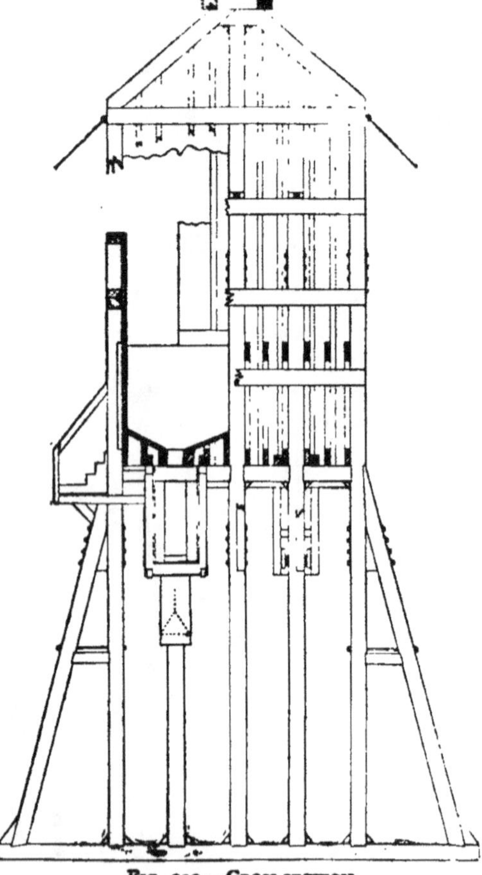

FIG. 290.—CROSS-SECTION.

The form of coal-chute pocket, designed by Mr. F. G. Susemihl, of the Michigan Central Railroad, in use at a number of points on western lines, has the chains and weights used in connection with the pocket so adjusted that the outward pull of the top of the apron due to its vertical thrust beyond the pivot is taken exactly for each position of the apron. This amount varies from nothing up to nearly the weight of the apron. The balance-block, in this case a 7-in. × 10-in. × 6-ft. oak timber, is suspended below the pocket from a point at the rear (*A*), about which it swings with the two ⅞-inch rods as radii, at either end. When the apron is down, the entire weight of this block is held by the other end of the apron chain, but as the apron rises, less and less of this weight is so sustained until the apron is closed, when nearly the whole of the weight of the block is carried from the point *A*. As will be readily understood, all necessity for latches is done away with, as the closed apron forms an absolute and reliable lock for the inner door. Two segmental castings are attached to the lower end of the inner door, and small angle-iron shoes are fitted over the lower end of the apron at each side. These shoes rub against the castings and thus keep the inner door closed until the apron is nearly down. The swinging radius of the corner of the shoe and the radius of the casting are the same, but the centre of the former is a trifle lower and forward of the latter, thus constantly relieving the pressure against the inner door as the apron is lowered. The casting is so made that it may be adjusted up or down somewhat by loosening the ⅞-in. bolt at the back. The friction here obtained between the angle-irons and castings is sufficient to prevent any gaining of momentum by the apron, and yet by the manner in which the weight is taken by the block from below it may be easily moved with but slight effort, and will remain at any inclination. The small sketches show clearly the relation of the apron and inner door to each other at the intermediate and two extreme points of movement.

The simplicity of construction, the absence of all latches and small parts, and the fact that there is so little to get out of order, would be sufficient to attract the attention of engineering and motive-power departments. The swinging of the apron from a point several inches inside its lower edge by means of hooked straps allows any coal dust or small pieces to drop through to the ground instead of clogging up the hinges. All the iron used in these chutes costs between five and five and a half dollars, the entire cost of building being considerably less per pocket than with many of the forms now used by different railroads. The older patterns used at coaling stations are not only difficult to operate, but frequently cause more or less serious accidents from their being only partially locked—a fault not uncommon with the latching devices.

Burnett-Clifton Coal-chute.—The style of coal-chute known as the Burnett & Clifton coal-chute, shown in Figs. 295 to 299, copied from the issue of the *Railroad Gazette* of December 18, 1891, is used by the Delaware & Hudson Canal and Railroad at Mohawk, N. Y., also by the Chicago, Rock Island & Pacific Railroad, the Chicago, Burlington & Quincy Railroad, the Union Pacific Railway, and many other prominent Western railroads. The chute combines the best features of the chutes patented by Messrs. Burnett & Clifton, who disposed of their interests to Messrs. Williams, White & Co., of Moline, Ill. The patents apply mainly to the irons and

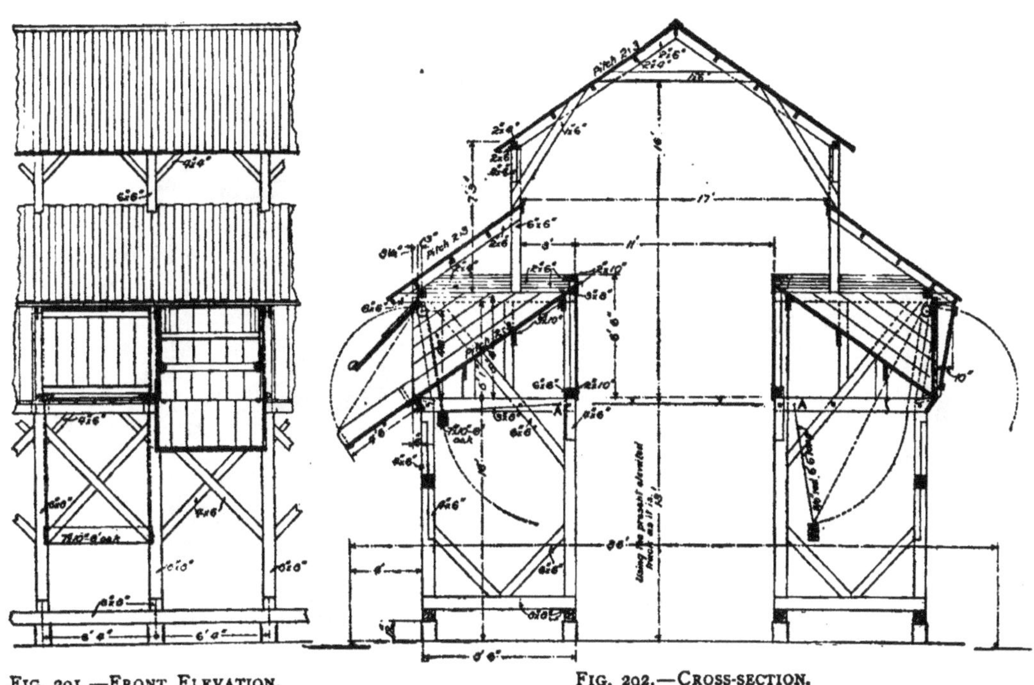

FIG. 291.—FRONT ELEVATION.

FIG. 292.—CROSS-SECTION.

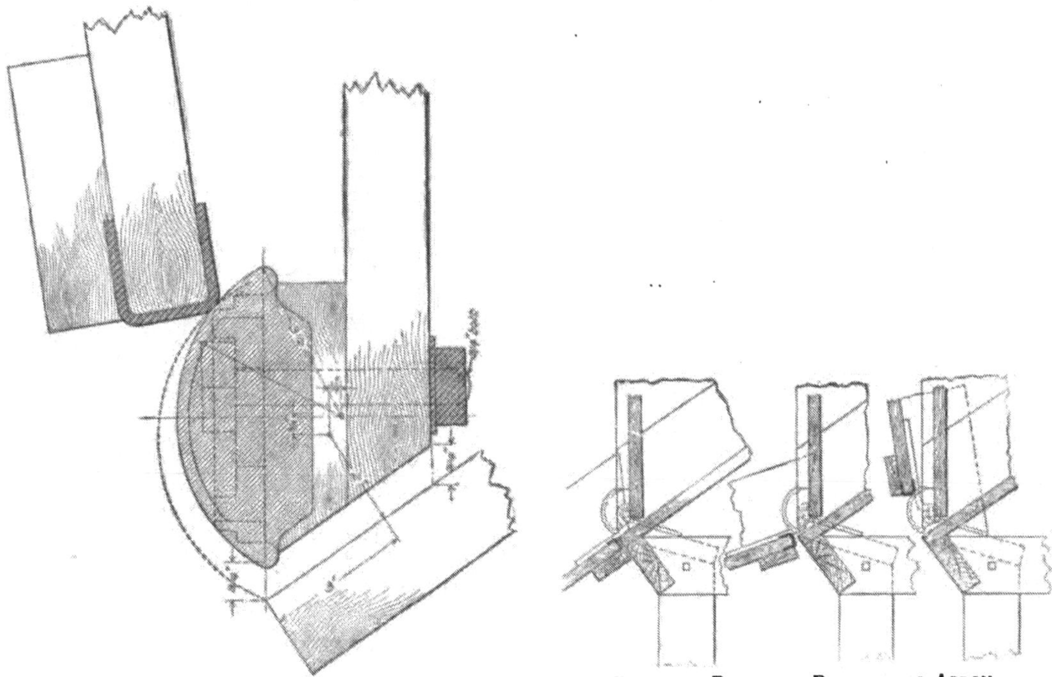

FIG. 293.—DETAIL OF LOCK.

FIG. 294.—DETAIL OF POSITIONS OF APRON.

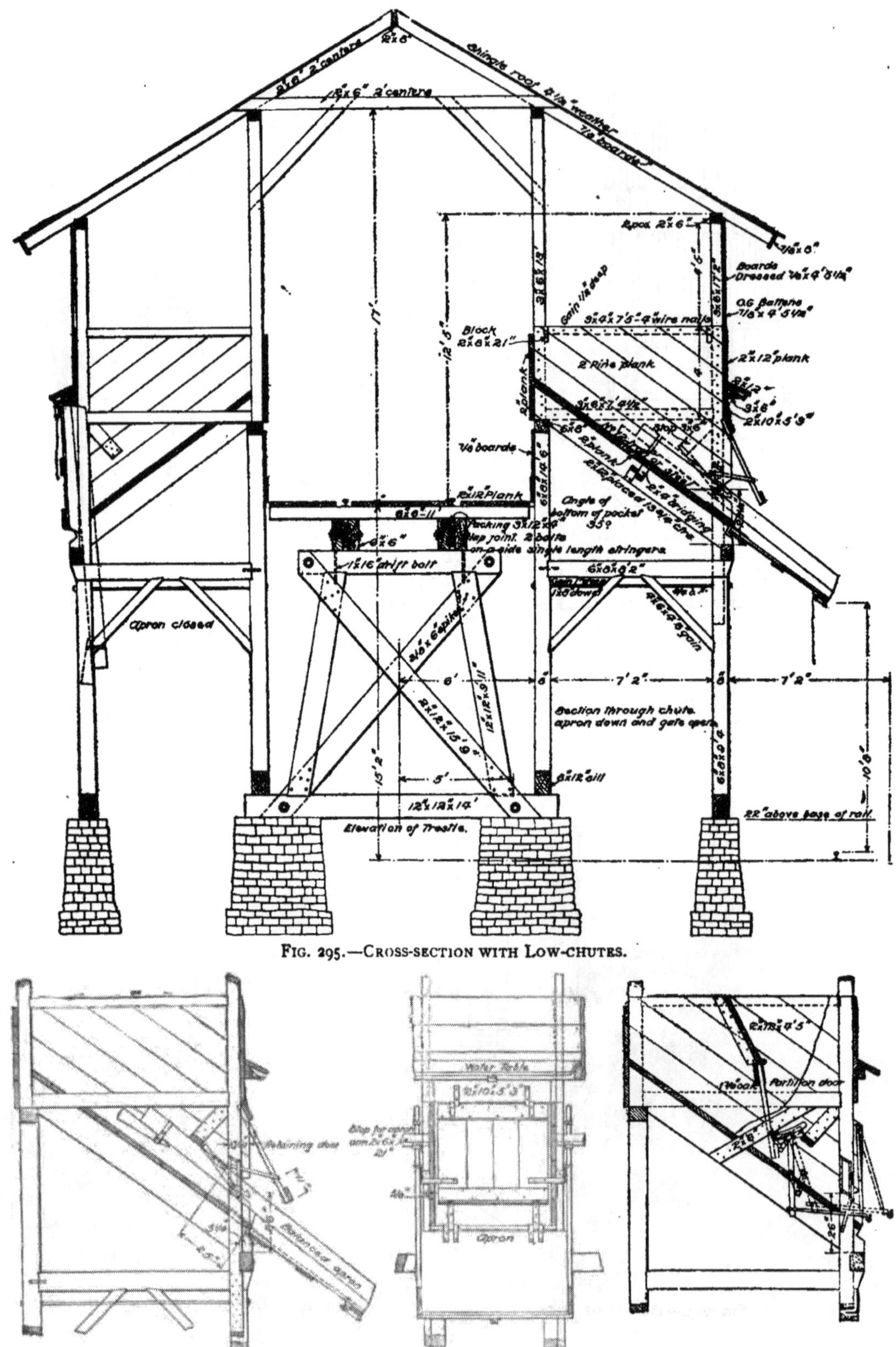

FIG. 295.—CROSS-SECTION WITH LOW-CHUTES.

FIG. 296.—CROSS-SECTION OF POCKET SHOWING LOCATION OF IRONS.

FIG. 297.—FRONT VIEW OF POCKET SHOWING APRON DOWN AND GATE OPEN.

FIG. 298.—CROSS-SECTION OF DOUBLE-POCKET.

details of the pockets proper, which style of pockets can be used either with the style of coal-chute shown in Fig. 295, delivering the coal by shovelling from cars, or with a regular high-chute dumping the coal from hopper-bottomed cars, as shown in Fig. 299.

The issue of the *Railroad Gazette* mentioned above contains the following remarks on the subject:

The change in this chute from the older methods in taking off the weight of the apron by a counterweight, whose vertical resultant shall vary the same as that of the weight of the apron, was a marked advance from the dead weights formerly used. The apron and arms are built of oak, and to the ends of the latter are fastened cast-iron blocks of about fifty pounds weight each, which may be moved forward or back to adjust the proper balance. In taking coal the fireman pulls a small latch at the top of the apron, which, when slipped, allows the easy lowering of the apron, because it is balanced. As the counterweighted arm rises it comes in contact with the tail of a pivoted latch, which releases the inner or retaining coal door. The sides of the apron are spread wider than this coal-door, and are formed by the forward end of the counterweight arm. To the lower part of the apron the hinges on which it and the arms are swung are fastened, there being a slight drop to the coal as it passes out of the pocket on to the apron.

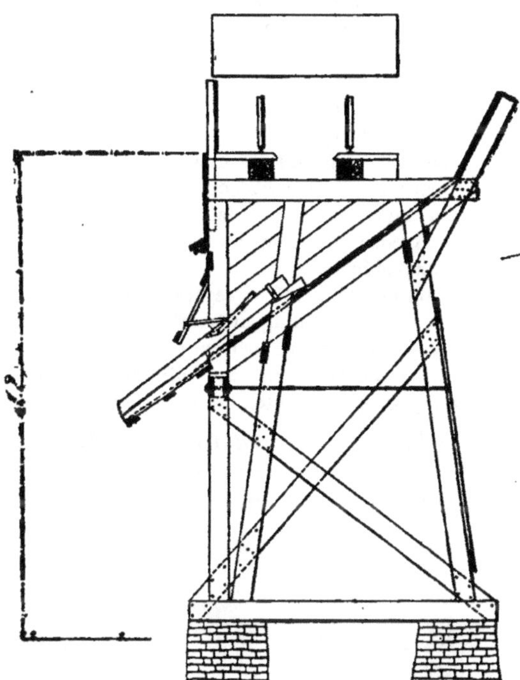

FIG. 299.—CROSS-SECTION WITH HIGH-CHUTES.

Back of the fulcrum line, about 2 ft. on each arm, is fastened a small ratchet plate, into which works a 1½-in. pawl, bent out 5 in. at the inner end, and held to a 2-in. flat strap by a split key, the strap being held to the door-frame with bolts. The retaining door-latch is offset 3 in., and, by means of a notch at the forward end, engages with the flat strap. A guide for this pawl is provided, which is made up of four pieces, pivoted together and fastened back by the short end pieces to the frame.

The sides of the apron are shod with 2-in. × 1-in. × ¼-in. channel iron, which is also used for stiffening between the sides and bottom, with several 24-in. strips bent at right angles at the middle.

This arrangement of catches (with the exception of the one at the top of the apron) is entirely automatic, and all the pieces have been made of such proportions as to especially provide for durability. This point requires special attention in the design of any structure of this character, as it is not desirable to be obliged to have any mechanism liable to break or get out of order at outlying coaling stations. There is not only the expense of taking down the parts and sending them to the shops for repairs, but the break may occasion the delay of trains either in getting coal or in the inability to close the pocket properly.

In Fig. 298 a special form of pocket is shown, for taking part or all of the coal, as is needed. The partition door is hung in the usual manner, and shuts against the iron-shod oak planking of the incline. The latching device is quite ingenious, and consists of long T-shaped arms pivoted a little below the centre, and tilted out of the perpendicular by a rod pulled from the front of the chute, thereby disengaging the small pin projecting from either side of the partition door. This pin slides in a guide slot, the arc of which is struck from the hinge centre. This form of pocket is only used occasionally, and then with but part of the pockets at a station. Their advantages over the single pocket are, however, becoming appreciated, and their use is increasing.

Fig. 299 shows the style of framing used where coal is unloaded into the pockets from bottom or side dumping cars. This form permits also the unloading from the ordinary car with shovels, and is well adapted to roads having large numbers of dump-cars, but which are liable to receive coal at times in foreign cars. The roof in this case is abandoned as unnecessary, in part at least.

Fig. 295 shows in a condensed form the pockets both open and closed, and the style of framing best adapted for use at division points with regular gondola-cars in the service.

With any form of locking device it is essential that there should be certainty of action at all times, and that both sides should work together. Otherwise the filling of the pocket would cause a bulging and straining of the hasps or catches, increasing the chances for failure of the fastenings at the next succeeding unloading. Or, should this defect be very marked, there might be an opportunity for the accidental unloading of the pocket on to the track below. With some of the designs of latches this is a source of continual annoyance, and when any of the parts become bent the trouble begins, so that the fewer the pieces and the straighter and simpler they are in outline, in so far is this evil avoided.

Another system is the raising of the centre track high above the pockets, so that the cars may be dumped in either direction and provided with runners between pockets to prevent overflow. This, however, allows considerable fall for the coal, and increases the quantity of dirt or slack. It also necessitates the building of the chute much stronger than otherwise, on account of the thrust against the front of the pocket, due to the momentum of a large body of coal falling this distance from the car above. The extra cost of a high trestle and the daily expense of raising the loaded cars this additional height would be factors against this form unless otherwise unavoidable.

As generally built the pockets are placed 6 ft. 6 in. centres, the inclined approach being on about a 1 to 16 grade, built up of bridge timbers, either on piling or trestlework with 16-ft. bents. This will, of course, be governed by the ground-space available and the position of adjoining buildings.

Wherever the work of erection is done by the railroad building department, the irons only, consisting of the latches, catches, weights, locking-bolts, stops, etc., are furnished by the manufacturers.

Coaling Station at East New York, Union Elevated Railroad, Brooklyn, N. Y.—The coaling station of the Union Elevated Railroad at East New York station, Brooklyn, N. Y., shown, in general, in Figs. 300 and 301, is an overhead coaling system for locomotives using the Hunt conveyor coaling

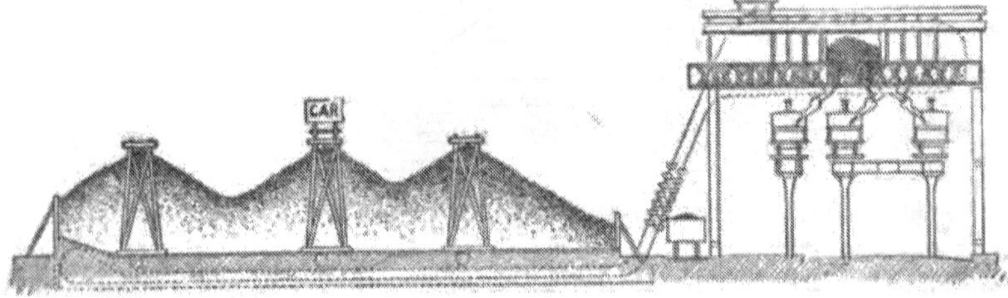

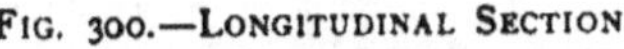

FIG. 300.—LONGITUDINAL SECTION.

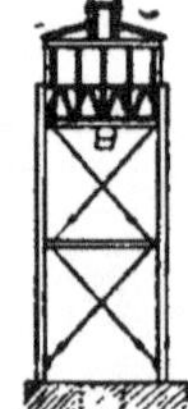

FIG. 301.—CROSS-SECTION.

system, controlled by C. W. Hunt Co., New York, N. Y. The coal is dumped from cars into a trough under the track at the ground-level, and conveyed thence by a Hunt conveyor with swinging buckets to the overhead bridge spanning the tracks, where the coal is dumped from the buckets at any point desired. There are pockets under the bridge properly trapped off and provided with aprons, so as to deliver into the tenders of engines below them. The pockets serve also as measuring pockets. In addition to the feature of putting coal up on the bridge, there is a storage-pile provided on the ground-level, to which coal can be delivered by the same conveyor. When required, coal is drawn from the storage-pile and taken by the same conveyor up to the bridge. The system is especially valuable where the land is limited, as efficient and cheap service can be combined with considerable storage on a very small ground-space and at a comparatively small first cost. The power is obtained from a small stationary engine of about 12 H. P. The uptake capacity is stated to be considerably over a ton per minute.

In Fig. 302 is illustrated the Hunt conveyor system as applied to a coal-stocking grounds.

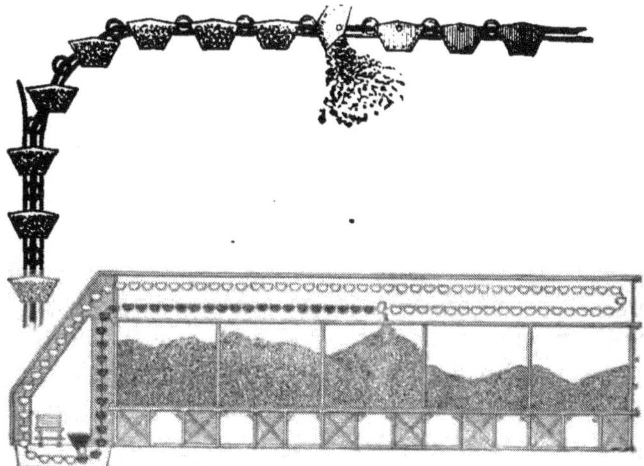

FIG. 302.—CROSS-SECTION OF HUNT CONVEYOR SYSTEM.

Coaling Station at Velasco, Tex.—The coaling station at Velasco, Tex., on the I. N. T. & C. T. N. R.R., shown in Figs. 303 and 304, shows the application of the Hunt coal-elevator and steam-shovel system controlled by C. W. Hunt Co., New York, N. Y., to a coaling station for locomotives, where the coal supply arrives at the coaling station in barges. There is a movable elevator-hoist on top of the pockets which takes the coal from the hold of the vessels with a steam-dredge (or in buckets filled by hand, if desired) and hoists it up to the proper elevation, where the bucket is tipped automatically and discharged through a hopper backwards into the coal-pockets proper. Where there is no space available at the water-front, the Hunt elevator in connection with a Hunt automatic railway for carrying the coal farther inland is a very good system to adopt, and can be highly recommended.

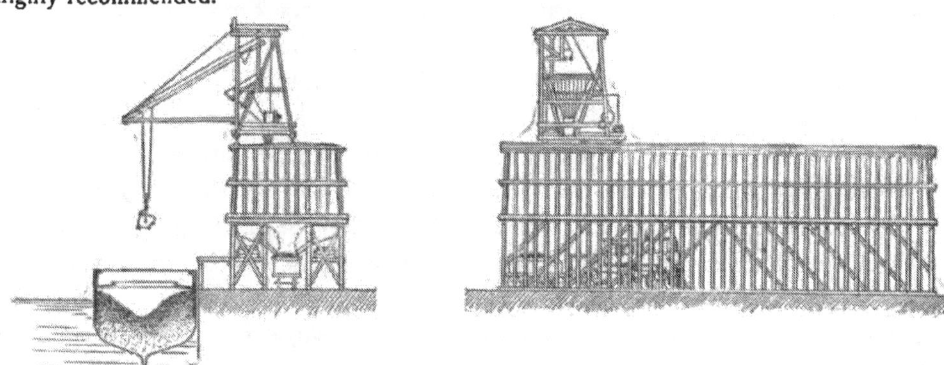

FIG. 303.—CROSS-SECTION. FIG. 304.—FRONT ELEVATION.

Coaling Station at Port Richmond, Philadelphia, Pa., Philadelphia & Reading Railroad.—The coaling station of the Philadelphia & Reading Railroad at Port Richmond, Philadelphia, Pa., illustrated and described in the issue of the *Railroad Gazette* of May 13, 1892, uses the trough-conveying system for transferring coal into a series of elevated pockets for delivery to locomotives. There is also connected with the coaling station an inclined ash-conveyor, which passes below the tracks and adjacent to sunken ashpits. This ash-conveyor takes the ashes coming from the engines out of the sunken pits up the incline to a large elevated steel pocket, whence the ashes are loaded on to cars.

CHAPTER XVI.

ENGINE-HOUSES.

ENGINE-HOUSES are used on railroads for housing engines when out of use, and for cleaning engines after runs, for making light repairs, washing out, etc. In some layouts, especially on small roads, or at points of minor importance on large systems, an engine-house has frequently a small shop for making more extensive repairs annexed to it, and sometimes a drop-pit is added to allow wheels and axles to be taken out.

Engine-houses along a railroad are generally located at terminal or division yards, at junction stations, and at all points where engines are changed or held in reserve. The site selected is usually in the neighborhood and in close connection with other structures for the train service and engine supplies, such as coal-chutes, water-tanks, oil-houses, sand-houses, ashpits, etc. These auxiliary structures for supplies, etc., are located in connection with the engine-house in such a way as to allow coal, water, sand, oil, waste, and other supplies to be taken on board the engine, either on its way in or out of the house, with due regard, however, to the fact that the drawing of such supplies or discharging of ashes must not be allowed to cause any serious detention to other engines passing in or out of the house. In other words, where the operation of taking certain of these supplies, or performing certain of these duties is accompanied by delays, then there should be a special open track leading to the engine-house. In all cases, engine-houses must be so located as to offer easy ingress and egress from the main tracks of a railroad, or be located close to an open track or a main leader.

The selection of the general style and size of an engine-house is dependent, more or less, on the section of the country that the building is located in, the available building materials in general use, and the number of engines that are to be housed simultaneously, with due allowance for possible future extensions. The topography of the site selected, the existence of other structures in the neighborhood, or a proposed layout for shop or yard purposes in the vicinity of the proposed site, may limit or define the shape of the ground-space available for the building and its track approaches, and influence the choice of the general design accordingly. Relative to how substantial and fire-proof a structure to erect, the importance of the house, in connection with the operation of the road, should be considered. If the building is to serve as an auxiliary house at some subordinate point, or intended to house one or more engines for a branch line at a junction point, the choice of a cheaper class of building is warranted, as, in case of fire or a rush of business, engines can be drawn from other points and allowed to stand on open tracks. If, however, an engine-house is to be located at an important terminal or division yard, where the traffic is constant and steady and large interests would suffer in case of a fire or a block, tying up a large number of engines at once, then the best policy to pursue is to build as first-class and substantial a structure as the financial condition of the road will permit.

While, therefore, a permanent and fire-proof construction is desirable, in fact, practically necessary, where a heavy traffic is to be considered and the location is permanent, it is a mistake to run up the construction account of a small road or of a new enterprise with expensive structures for housing engines. After operating a new road for some time it is frequently found desirable to make a change in the engine runs, to transfer a proposed shop system or yard to another point, or, through combinations with other roads, important junction points are created which were never thought of at the outset. The author knows of numerous cases where expensive roundhouses have been torn down or else used for other purposes than originally intended. Frame buildings, sheathed on the outside with weather-boarding and roofed with tarred felt or a gravel roof, are extensively used on the Northern Pacific Railroad. Other roads use frame structures, sheathed with corrugated iron and roofed with corrugated iron, tin, slate, or gravel roofing. Then there are buildings of a more substantial character, with brick or stone walls, iron fronts, and wooden, combination, or iron roof-trusses, covered with a slate or gravel roof.

Engine-house designs can be divided, according to the usual practice encountered in this country, into square houses and into polygonal houses or "roundhouses," as they are generally called. The former are in use mainly for smaller structures, the latter almost universally for larger houses. Large square houses are sometimes preferable, owing to the shape of the ground-space available for the house and track approaches, and also where an engine-house is to be used for considerable repair work in addition to housing engines. There are a large number of other possible forms of engine-houses, some of which have been used very extensively in other countries; but it can be stated that in this country, as a rule, under ordinary conditions, roundhouses have practically superseded all other designs for large engine-houses. Nevertheless, in the author's opinion, large, square houses have marked advantages under certain conditions, and merit, therefore, more attention in practice.

An engine-house for a limited number of engines consists, usually, of a square building, into which one, two, or more tracks enter at one gable end, the length of the building being in excess of the longest engine used, and the width being dependent on the number of tracks in the building. Sometimes the house is made long enough to accommodate two or more engines behind each other on the same track; it is not good practice to place more than two engines in the same stall, but even then there should be doors on the rear of the house, as well as on the front, as otherwise it would be difficult to get the rear engine out of the house if the front engine did not have steam up. The approach to these houses is, usually, by a track system leading off a leader, although sometimes, to economize space, the tracks run out of the building to a turn-table, which, however, is not good practice, unless a turn-table to turn engines would have to be built and maintained anyhow in the vicinity, in which case the turn-table could serve for both purposes. But, unless such is the case, a regular track approach is the best method to pursue with a small square house, provided there is sufficient ground-space available for that purpose.

For very large square engine-houses a transfer-table is used with good results, especially where the transfer-table is located some distance from the house, so as to give a space for engines to stand between the transfer-table and the face of the house, so that in case of fire the engines can be run out of the house quickly. The transfer-table system requires the least ground-space of all engine-house designs; but it has the same disadvantage compared with a track-approach system as a turn-table system has, namely, a breakdown of the transfer-table or of the turn-table, or a blockade on the open track leading immediately to or from the table, will cause a serious blockade of the entire business of the road, similar to the consequences of an accident on the main track. The track-approach system has the decided advantage of offering less opportunities for a general blockade, and it allows engines to be removed very quickly from the house in case of fire.

The usual style of an engine-house, known in this country as a roundhouse, consists of a house built in a circular form around a turn-table, with tracks leading from the turn-table radially into the house. The building can either be built as a full circle, known as a closed or full-circle roundhouse, or it can be a segment of a circle, known as an open or segmental roundhouse. The walls of the building are not actually built circular, but in the shape of a polygon, the circle being divided up into stalls or panels, the walls in each panel being built on the chords connecting the panel points. It is customary to provide two passage-ways into a closed roundhouse, through two of the stalls, so that in case of a block on one track the other track can be used. Two approach tracks to the turn-table are also frequently introduced in a segmental roundhouse, but in this case they do not usually run through the building, but in front of it, so that all stalls in the building are available to stand engines. The passage-ways to the turn-table through a closed roundhouse are walled on each side, so as to act as fire-walls and allow the house to be heated better in winter. In addition, in large engine-houses, special fire-walls are introduced, so as to divide the interior of the building into several parts, retarding thereby the spread of a fire throughout the building. Where the ground-space is available, it will be found more economical to place the building as far away from the turn-table as feasible, as a larger number of engines can be thereby accommodated under the same roof surface, while in case of fire the engines can be run out of the stalls in front of the tracks. The size of the house can generally be so selected, that the engines on every other stall can be run out of the house without interfering with each other, which feature offers the additional advantage, that surplus engines can stand temporarily between the house and the turn-table, when the house is full. Segmental polygonal houses have been built with track approach in place of a turn-table. This method offers all the advantages of a special track approach, but it is only feasible where the necessary ground-space is available, and as, usually, where a large engine-house has to be built a turn-table is required anyhow for the turning of engines, it seems more correct to always place a turn-table in combination with a roundhouse.

The advantages of a square house with special track approach are, that delays from breakdowns, blockades, or loss by fire are not so liable to occur; the house is cheaper and simpler to build, especially for a small house with only a few stalls; and the engine-house foreman will have a better oversight over the whole building than in a roundhouse,—which is quite important where there is considerable work and repairs to be done around the engines. But the disadvantage of a track approach is that it takes up considerable ground-space.

The advantages of a square house with a transfer-table are, that it takes up proportionately the least ground-space of any system; a cheaper and simpler house can be built; a better oversight had of the work going on in the building than in a roundhouse; and the extension of the building indefinitely is only limited by the land available. For a small house the construction of a transfer-table would not pay. The disadvantages are, however, that breakdowns are more liable to cause a blockade, and in case of fire the engines cannot be removed as expeditiously from the house as in a house with track approach, although by the use of a space between the house and the transfer-table, as above described, considerable can be done to eliminate this latter objection.

The advantages of a roundhouse with a turn-table are economy of ground-space, as compared with a large house with a track approach or a square house with tracks leading to a turn-table. A good light can be thrown on all engines, and the width of the stall is greatest at the outer wall, so that the best light and the most floor-surface around the engine exist at the head of the engine, as engines almost invariably run into a roundhouse head first. A roundhouse can also be built in sections at a time, without in any way harming the general design, as the wall at the end of each section, if built solidly, can remain as a fire-wall. The objections to a roundhouse are, that the building, as compared with a square house, is more costly and complicated, and a general oversight of the work going on in the house is not as easy as in a square house. A breakdown at the turn-table or on the main track leading to the house might cause a serious blockade, and in case of fire a roundhouse in combination with a turn-table, especially a closed roundhouse, even under the best conditions, is not much better than a fire-trap.

The following general remarks, relating more or less to all classes of engine-houses, are pertinent to the subject under discussion.

Practice in this country has developed beyond peradventure that the proper roofing material to use is slate or a tarred felt or gravel roof, as the sulphurous gases from the smoke of the engines destroy any other form of roofing material very speedily. If slate is used, a higher pitched and heavier roof has to be built, which causes greater expense, and the building being so high, it is more difficult to heat in winter. But a slate roof is more durable, particularly if a first-class grade of slate is used, fastened with copper nails, and laid on two or three layers of building-paper. A tarred felt, or tarred felt and gravel roof combined, especially the former, will allow of a very light roof construction ; but it is not very durable as against the weather, although it will withstand the gases penetrating to it from the interior of the house better than the usual metal roofing materials.

The ventilation of an engine-house is a very essential element. Large, properly designed ventilators at the peak of the roof are desirable, but in northern climates provision should be made for closing the ventilators when desired, so as to keep the heat in the house when required, while in southern sections of the country plain open-louvred ventilators are admissible. Smoke-stacks should be provided at the point over the stalls where the smoke-stacks of engines are when in the house. These stacks should have a movable lower bell-shaped piece, that can be lowered over the smoke-stack of the engine. The top of the stack should be arranged so as to exclude wind and weather. As sheet-iron smoke-stacks are eaten out very quickly, cast-iron is used to quite an extent, but it makes a very clumsy and heavy construction. Galvanized iron stacks have been introduced with considerable advantage, and terra-cotta flues have also been put on the market for this purpose.

The floor in an engine-house is made either of cinders, cement, stone, asphalt, or timber.

In all cases it is preferable to have the floor-level flush with the top of the rails of the house, so that trucking can be done through the house more conveniently. For small houses a cinder floor will answer, although it has the objection that trucking cannot be done readily through the house, and the cinder will get into the pits and help clog the drains. Where timber is cheap, a rough plank floor, two or three inches thick, laid on mud-sills, bedded in the cinder, will prove preferable. For a large engine-house, a stone slab, cement, or asphalt floor is preferable. The main objection to the asphalt flooring is, that heavy trucking and the use of hydraulic jacks, unless proper care is taken, will wear ruts and holes which are not very readily repaired. While a cement floor has similar objections, repairs can be made more easily and, what is of a further advantage, they can be made by the ordinary help connected with the engine-house. In sections of the country where stone slabs are cheap and easily obtainable, it will be found that they make an excellent floor, requiring very few repairs. Except on newly made ground, the use of plank floors on joists is not to be recommended, unless, possibly, in sections of the country where timber as a building material predominates. In all cases the floor should be properly dished, so as to allow drainage of the floor into the pits or into gutters. Cleanliness of an engine-house floor is an essential feature of good management, and flooring materials that will allow the floor to be frequently flushed with water, without detriment, should have the preference.

The drainage of an engine-house should be first-class, as all the elements which contribute to the rapid deterioration or the easy blocking of a sewer are present in the drain leading from an engine-house. The best method to drain the pits is to allow them to discharge at the lower end through a grating into a properly designed cesspool, which in turn overflows into a box-sewer, running around the house, between the ends of the pits and the wall of the building. The gradients of the drains should be ample, if possible, to allow water to run easily, and the box-sewer mentioned should be large enough to allow a man to enter and clean it out, by providing man-holes at proper places. If the closed sewer is not made large enough for a man to enter, then it should be an open box-drain, covered with timber or stone slabs in such a way as to be easily accessible without having to tear up the floor of the house in the vicinity of the sewer. For small engine-houses, of a few stalls only, and where the drain is short, pipes can be used, as they can be either flushed with water or else a swab introduced and run through. The roof water is usually drained through down-conductors inside the house into the pits or into the main sewer.

Engine-houses are heated by stoves or by steam-pipes. The former method is all right for small houses and for houses where a special steam plant for supplying steam for heating purposes only would not pay. Large round cast-iron stoves are usually employed for this purpose, set between two pits, the stove-pipe being generally led into the smoke-stack over one of the adjacent pits. For large houses, where feasible, steam heat is preferable, as it reduces the danger from fire and does not occupy floor-space. The main steam supply-pipe is usually carried through the house overhead, hung from the roof; but where an open box-drain exists, it will be found convenient to carry water and steam pipes on brackets in the upper part of the drain, as they are thus out of the way and yet readily accessible for inspection and repairs. As to the proper location of the steam-coils, considerable difference can be noted in practice. The placing of the steam-coils along the sides of the engine-pits has the advantage of allowing the heat to spread more uniformly throughout the house, and, in addition, it allows the heat to strike the bottom of the engine first, which is very desirable in winter, so as to thaw out the ice and snow adhering to the machinery when the engine is housed after a run. The only objections are that the steam-pipes narrow up the clear width of the engine-pits, which is objectionable in making engine repairs, and the closeness of the steam-pipes and the direct heat is objectionable for the wipers and repair men, who have to work in and around the pit. In other designs the steam-coils are placed along the walls, which method has the objection that the general heating of the house is more difficult and more heat is lost in that way, and if work-benches are placed along the walls it is very undesirable for the workmen to have to stand in such close proximity to the steam-coils. In other houses the steam-coils are hung from the roof, below the roof-trusses, the heat being thrown downwards and thus diffused throughout the house without causing any inconvenience to the workmen. This method, however, requires more steam to keep the temperature at the proper degree under the pits and at the floor-level, but where the roof is low and flat the loss is probably not very serious. In general it can be said that in northern sections of the country low flat roofs are preferable to high, double-pitched roofs, as the heating of the house in the former case is so much more readily effected. But, on the other hand, the roof construction would have to be heavier, and the roofing material would deteriorate more rapidly, owing to the greater accumulation of snow on the roof in winter.

Relative to light in an engine-house, large windows and transom-lights should be inserted wherever possible, as good light is a most essential requisite to insure cleanliness in the house, a thorough cleaning of the engines, and to facilitate inspections and repairs. When necessary, skylights should be introduced in the roof, but it is better to avoid them if possible. For a large square house the "saw-tooth" system of roof affords the best opportunity to light the interior of the building at all points by a diffused light from above, which is the best light that can be had in a workshop. The lighting at night is done, preferably, with electric lights where feasible, thereby reducing the danger from fire and the expense and trouble connected with having to maintain lamps throughout the building, in case work goes on extensively all night long in the house.

The engine-doors in an engine-house are always hung in pairs and should be well glazed, unless ample light is otherwise provided. They are either square-top or circle-top, the former being the cheapest. The selection between the two is generally dependent on the style of construction adopted to span the door-opening. The doors are very frequently made to swing outwardly, which allows the house to be made about five feet narrower; but this method has the objections that the wind is liable to catch the doors, and in northern climates the snow and ice collecting on the doors and on the ground will give considerable trouble. It is desirable, therefore, and the best practice, especially in northern sections of the country, to swing doors inwardly. One or more of the engine-doors in a house should be provided with a small wicket-door, so as to allow men to pass in and out of the house more easily.

Within recent years steel roller-shutter doors for engine-houses have been introduced on a number of railroads, among others in the roundhouse of the Housatonic Railroad at Bridgeport, Conn.; also in the roundhouse of the Chicago & Northwestern Railroad, at West Chicago, Ill.; and in the engine-house of the Lehigh Valley Railroad at Towanda, Pa.

The advantages are that the door is fire-proof and no floor-space has to be reserved inside the house to swing the doors open. The objections are that the cost is in excess of an ordinary wooden engine-door, although not very heavily in excess of the cost of a large, well-built and well-glazed circle-top door. The main objection, however, is that the lighting of the house has to be provided by transom-lights over the doors or skylights in the roof. If, however, the light in the house is otherwise well provided for, independently of the doors, and a first-class fire-proof structure is desired, then the use of steel roller-shutter doors can be highly recommended.

The questions involved in the construction of the engine-pits are similar to those discussed previously in the chapter on Ashpits, although the deteriorating effects do not exist to such an extent in engine-pits as in ashpits. The pits do not have to be lined with firebricks. Timber pits are only admissible in cheap engine-houses, or in sections of the country where timber is used almost universally for all building purposes. The choice between brick side walls or stone side walls will be dependent on the relative value of these two building materials. Stone walls, however, are generally made heavier than brick walls, and therefore require more material. Relative to the coping and the fastening of the rails to the coping, the remarks made in the chapter on Ashpits, referred to above, will practically apply to engine-pits.

An ample water supply is needed to clean the engines, wash the floors, flush out the pits and drains, and wash out the boilers. Engines have sometimes to take water by means of a small hose before leaving the house. Hydrants should be provided at intervals along the outside walls, or else sunk in pits under the floor at intervals between the stalls, the opening being covered with a suitable grating or door.

Relative to turn-tables, the size should be ample not only to accommodate the largest engine in use on the road, but to allow for the probable increase in the length of engines within the life of the turn-table or engine-house. Timber turn-tables are practically obsolete to-day, excepting for very small engines on lines with light traffic. Cast-iron turn-tables, while having some good features, are also seldom used to-day. Wrought-iron or steel plate-girder turn-tables are the best in use, provided they are not built to carry only the weight of an engine the same as for a bridge, but are proportioned with a great excess of strength to give ample stiffness, and also to allow for the probable increase in the weights of engines. The masonry connected with a turn-table, and especially the foundations, should be of the very best for the purpose, as a settlement of the centre pier or of the circular track would prove very detrimental to the easy working of the table. In northern climates a very good design is to keep the paving of the pit and the bench-wall for the circular rail some distance below the bottom of the table, so that the operation of the table does not have to be stopped for light snows, and it is only when a heavier snowfall takes place that the pit has to be cleaned out. Most of the remarks made above with reference to turn-tables will apply also to transfer-tables. Turn-tables are usually turned by hand, although for tables 60 ft. in diameter and over steam and electricity have been introduced. Transfer-tables are worked by steam, wire-cable, or electricity.

As referred to above, the walls of an engine-house can be either built as a frame structure, sheathed with weather-boarding or corrugated iron, or a more substantial structure with brick or stone walls can be adopted. In case of stone walls, it is best to make the wall heavier and omit all panelling and pilasters. In case of brick walls, ordinary panelling and pilasters can be used; but the elaborate cornice and frieze work, introduced so frequently on such buildings, should be reduced to the least possible amount consistent with the importance and the surroundings of the building. A plain cornice will generally be more effective, and prove in better harmony with the rest of the structure. In a fire-proof structure, cast-iron window sills and lintels are a good feature. Cast-iron window aprons, on the inside of the window, are very good to protect the inside ledge of the window opening; and, if built on a slope, will prevent the use of the window for depositing oil-cans, waste, tools, etc., which make an engine-house look untidy, and, to a certain extent, increase the danger of fires. The placing of a blind arch or lintel in the outer wall, opposite the end of an engine-pit, will prove serviceable in case an engine should be run off the pit and strike the wall, as there would be less chance of damage to the roof and cornice. Good patent rail-stops, provided at the end of the pit, will almost eliminate the chances of an engine striking the wall, so that making special provision for an accident of this kind is not particularly warranted.

The roof-trusses in engine-houses are either combination trusses of wood and iron, or all iron, or wooden girders on posts. The use of timber for roof-trusses is warranted for smaller houses, and where the fire-proof element of the design is not considered essential. With the exception of the greater danger in case of fire, a timber roof has the advantage over an iron roof in an engine-house, that it is not attacked so seriously by the sulphurous gases contained more or less in the atmosphere in the upper part of the house, so that a timber roof, kept well painted or whitewashed, will give, probably, in the long-run, about as efficient a service as an all-iron roof-truss. In regard to the fire-proof feature of the all-iron engine-house roof-truss, as usually made, it will prove, as a rule, in case of a fire, to be an illusion, the same as the bulk of so-called fire-proof constructions in buildings. The usual style of an iron truss for an engine-house is the triangular system, with deck-beam principal rafters and the bottom chord formed of tie-rods. The lateral bracing throughout the house consists of light rods, more serviceable for erection purposes and for lining up the trusses than for stiffness. The trusses are therefore dependent for lateral stiffness on the timber purlins and roof boards, so that when the latter are destroyed by fire the trusses will not have sufficient stability to stand alone. If iron roof-trusses are to be adopted, the author considers that more attention should be given to building stiff trusses, with more lateral stability and bracing and stiff bottom chords. Where a slate roof is to be used, the double-pitched high roof is preferable. The adoption, however, of a low, single-pitched roof is the very best construction in case a tarred felt or gravel roof is to be employed. For roofing over large square houses the "saw-tooth" system of roofs has decided advantages. In general, it can be said that the introduction of posts in the interior of an engine-house, if not placed too close to each other, is not such a detrimental feature as frequently assumed in designing an engine-house.

In order to facilitate the removal of engines from a house in case of fire, it is desirable to have, and the author has built, engine-houses with a down grade on the tracks in the house and extending across the space in front of the house for some distance.

While above remarks refer to roundhouses, as well as other classes of engine-houses, the following notes applying more particularly to roundhouses will prove interesting.

The choice of the size of a roundhouse is governed by the diameter of the turn-table selected, the width of the house required, and the arrangement of the tracks around the turn-table, so as to lead off properly from the turn-table, and give door-openings of ample clear width on the inner circle of the house. In some cases it is also desired to keep the inner front of the house sufficiently far away from the turn-table, to allow engines to stand outside of the house in front of the stalls, or at least in front of every other stall.

The tracks are arranged around the turn-table in three ways. First, so as to omit frogs entirely, the outside flanges of the nearest rails of neighboring tracks just touching each other at the face of the turn-table pit. The second method is to allow the same two rails, just referred to, to be joined together the same as in a frog; in other words, to place the point of the frog, if it can be so called, at the face of the turn-table pit, which method is, however, not desirable, as the point is soon battered down by the blows received when engines pass over it. The third method, and the one in most general use for houses with large diameters, is to arrange the tracks around the turn-table to suit whatever stall angle is selected, inserting frogs, and if necessary crotch-frogs, wherever required. In this case the only point to observe is to see that the dead ends of the rails around the turn-table coping can all be accommodated without interfering with each other, and that the frogs where inserted do not interfere with each other, and that the nearest frog point is far enough away from the turn-table pit to allow the frog to be introduced.

The angle of the stalls having been settled, the diameter of the inner circle of the house is dependent on the panel length required for the inner front of the house, which panel length is determined by the size of door-opening required in the clear, plus the width of the timber post, iron column, or brick pier desired to be placed between the doors. The width of the house is determined by the length of the largest engine in use, plus an allowance for the extra length of engines that may be adopted during the life of the house, plus an allowance to enable the doors to be swung inwardly, in case this construction method is adopted, plus whatever width is desired to be maintained for a passage-way along the outer walls of the roundhouse.

There is one other special feature in roundhouses that attention should be called to, especially where a slate roof is to be used, namely, the necessity of cutting the purlins on the outer slope of the roof convex, and the purlins on the inner slope of the roof concave, so as to follow the conical shape of the roof better, avoiding sharp angles at the truss lines, which would cause the roofing material to lie unevenly, in addition to not presenting as good an appearance. Where a tarred felt or gravel roof is used, the cutting of the purlins throughout is not so essential, the ends of the purlins, where they join at the truss line, being simply adzed down or shimmed up to make the break from one panel to the other less noticeable.

Summing up, therefore, it can be said in a general way, that for small engine-houses for the accommodation of a few engines only, a square house with track approach is the most preferable, but two engines should not stand in the same stall, unless there is an approach on the rear of the house. Where there are more than four stalls in width, the track approach will be long, and a turn-table can be inserted to advantage, especially at points where a turn-table is required anyhow to turn engines independent of the engine-house.

For large houses, with very limited ground-space available, the best method to use is a large square house with a transfer-table, the objection to handling the engines out of the house in case of fire being partly overcome by leaving sufficient space between the house and the transfer-table to stand engines. In northern climates, however, it is desirable to place the transfer-table under cover. Where ground-space is available for an extended track-approach, the plan of a large square house with roofs on the "saw-tooth" principle deserves more attention than hitherto granted to it in practice. This style of house with the track-approach at one end, or, better, if the stalls are built for two engines, with track-approaches at both ends, offers, in the author's opinion, one of the best systems of engine-houses known. The roof-construction is cheap; the side walls are low; the heating, ventilating, and lighting of the interior of the building are readily accomplished; the building can be easily enlarged at any time; engines can enter or leave the house at all times almost independently of each other; blockades on some of the tracks will seldom blockade the entire house; and engines can be taken out of the house very quickly in case of fire. The only objection is the ground-space required for the approaches, which objection can be eliminated to a certain extent by introducing transfer-tables.

As referred to above, roundhouses have been almost universally adopted for engine-houses in this country, partly, probably, from the inherent advantages they offer, and partly from the well-known fact that one road is very liable to copy the forms of construction that it finds apparently in general use on other roads in the vicinity. There is no doubt that the extensive adoption of any design is indicative of its having strong merits and points in its favor, but it does not absolutely decide the question of that particular design being the best under all circumstances. As a rule, roundhouses, especially closed or full-circle ones, can be considered as traps which will at times possibly cause a serious blockade to a large number of engines, and in case of a fire a large amount of valuable equipment will probably be destroyed and the road seriously crippled for want of motive power for months afterwards. However, much can be done to reduce the danger from fire by introducing provisions for an efficient, quick fire service to stop any fire before it gains headway, in addition to a thorough and substantial fire-proof construction of the pits, floors, walls, and roof of the building. Timber roof-purlins and the roof-sheathing, while not fire-proof, if kept whitewashed, will not endanger the building seriously, provided the roof-trusses or roof-girders and posts in the interior of the building are of iron. Attention has been called above to the necessity, however, of building heavier and stiffer all-iron roof-trusses than now generally practiced in this country.

The following descriptions and illustrations of engine-houses in actual use in this country will prove interesting in connection with above general remarks on the subject under discussion.

Engine-house at West Philadelphia Shops, Pennsylvania Railroad.—The engine-house of the Pennsylvania Railroad at the railroad shops in West Philadelphia, Pa., designed and built under the direction of Mr. Jos. M. Wilson, plans for which were published in the *Journal of the Franklin Institute*, Vol. LX., is a full-circle 44-stall brick roundhouse, with iron roof-trusses and slate roof. The outside diameter of the house is 300 ft., the inner diameter is 169 ft., and the diameter of the turn-table pit is 50 ft. The width of the house is, therefore, 65 ft. 6 in., and the space between the turn-table and the inner circle of the house is 59 ft. 6 in. The angle of the stalls is 8° 10′ 54″. The panel length on the inner circle is 12 ft. 0 39/64 in., and on the outer circle 21 ft. 4 13/16 in. The clear width of the interior of the building is 62 ft. 10 in., and the clear height from the top of rail to the tie-rod of roof-truss is 21 ft. 9 in. Two of the stalls are used for entrance tracks; all the others have engine-pits.

The foundations of the building are of stone, the outer walls being 2 ft. 6 in. thick, and all inner walls 2 ft. thick. The outer wall finishes off 4 in. below the ground, and is capped with a belting-course of cut stone, 9 in. × 15 in. All the doors on the inner and outer fronts have cut-stone sills, 12 in. × 17 in., the rails of the tracks being cut into these sills. The cast-iron blocks, at bases of columns of inside front, rest upon cut-stone blocks, 2 ft. square by 1 ft. thick. The outer wall above the belting-course is of brick, built in panels, with pilasters both inside and outside, and an ornamental outside cornice. The thickness of brick in panels is 13 in., and on pilasters 22 in. Two of the panels on the outside of the house are occupied by engine-entrance doors; the balance have windows, two in each panel, excepting in one panel, where there is a small entrance-door in place of one of the windows. A flush arch is built in the wall on the inside over every pair of windows, to provide against any injury to the cornice or roof in the event of accident to the wall below from locomotives. The engine-doors in the outside wall are in pairs, circle-top, and 3½ in. thick, panelled as shown, and hung on heavy cast-iron hinge-blocks, built into the brickwork, there being three wrought-iron hinges to each door. The doors leave a clear opening in width of 11 ft. 1½ in., and in height of 18 ft. at the centre of the circle. One door of each pair has a small wicket-door. The window-openings are square, 4 ft. 8¼ in. × 9 ft. 11 in., with cast-iron sills and lintels on the outside. They have box-frames, with two sash, each 12 lights 12 in. × 18 in., double-hung with cord, weights, and pulleys.

The inner front of the building is of cast-iron, 7/16 in. thick, excepting the columns, which are ⅝ in. thick. The doors are in pairs, circle-top, and 3 in. thick, panelled and glazed as shown, and leaving a clear opening in width of 11 ft. 1½ in., and in height of 18 ft. at the centre of the circle. Three of the 42 pairs of doors have small wicket-doors. Each door has three heavy wrought-iron hinges hung on lugs cast to the columns. All the doors open inward, and are provided with inside turning bars to fasten them when shut, and hooks to secure them in place when open.

The flooring consists of two layers of boards, the sub-flooring consisting of 1-in. white pine, worked to a thickness and laid close, and the upper layer being 2-in. white-pine flooring, worked, tongued and grooved. The floor-joists are 3-in. × 12-in. white oak, spaced 15 in. centres for half the house and 12 in. centres for the balance. They are cambered 1 in. at the outer wall, and proportionately less as they get shorter in approaching the inner front. The joists have one course of lattice-bridging, and are bedded on 3-in. × 12-in. white-oak wall-plates. The rails inside the house are laid upon 3-in. × 12-in. white-oak track-stringers, cut into the floor-joists, the top of stringer being laid flush with top of joists. A small gutter runs along each rail, draining into the pit.

The engine-pits in the stalls are 42 ft. 6 in. long by 3 ft. 11 in. wide in the clear, 2 ft. 9 in. deep at front, and 2 ft. 6 in. deep at back. The side walls are of stone, 2 ft. thick. The bottom is dished 1½ in. at the centre, and is paved with brick, laid on edge and grouted with cement. The pits drain at the lower end into a 12-in. circular brick sewer, that runs under the ends of all the pits, and discharges into the main sewer that leads from the house. The side walls of the pits extend all the way across the house so as to give a support for the floor-joists.

The roof-truss is constructed on the triangular system, of wrought-iron, having a span of 64 ft. 6 in. from centre to centre of bolt-holes in heel-blocks, an inclination of rafter of 22½ degrees from the horizontal, and a rise in tie-rod in centre of span of 6 in. above a horizontal line through the extremities. The diameters of the main tie-rods vary from 2 rods 1 in. in diam. to 2 rods 1¼ in. in diam. The counter-rods are 13/16 in. in diameter. The rafter is a 6-in. I-beam, weighing 40 lbs. per yard, and the struts and heel-blocks are of cast-iron. The heel-block on the inner front is firmly fixed to top of column; that on the outer front rests upon rollers on a cast-iron bed-plate, a wall-plate of white oak, 4 in. × 17 in. × 5 ft. long, being laid under the bed-plate on the brick wall. This arrangement allows of free expansion and contraction, owing to changes of temperature. The purlins are of white pine, 4 in. × 8 in. and 4 in. × 10 in., and are secured to the rafter by a wrought-iron angle-piece and clip, one arm of the angle-piece being bolted to the purlin, while the clip passes over the other arm and around the upper flange of the I-beam which forms the rafter. The purlins are cambered on the external circle, and made concave on the internal circle of the roof, so as to avoid hips and valleys, and allow the roof covering to be laid evenly. On the purlins is laid roof-sheeting of 1-in. worked white-pine boards. The sheeting is covered with the best quality slate from the Peach Bottom quarries of Pennsylvania. On the outside roof the slate run 11 in. and 10 in. × 20 in., laid to weather 8⅝ in., with the exception of nine courses from the ridge, which are 9 in. × 18 in., laid to weather 7½ in. On the inside roof the slate are 8 in. × 16 in., laid to weather 7 in. Gutters of double-cross roofing tin run around the eaves of inside and outside fronts, to receive the drainage from the roof. To protect this tin from the action of destroying agents in the atmosphere, it is well painted on the under side with two coats of red lead in oil before putting on, and afterwards on the upper side with one coat of the same, over which the finishing colors are laid. From the gutters a 4-in. eave-pipe runs down the outside wall on every alternate pilaster of the brickwork, discharging into a sewer which goes entirely around the building, and a 3-in. eave-pipe runs down the inside front on every alternate column, between the hinges at the back, discharging by a small box-drain into the pit sewer.

Ventilation is secured by 6-ft. octagonal wooden louvred ventilators placed in ridge of roof on every alternate stall, and there is a sheet-iron smoke-flue for every track placed directly over the position of the smoke-stack of the locomotive when in place. Water-plugs, with standard hose attachment, are placed in the floor at the centre of the house in alternate stalls, and are protected by cast-iron covers level with the top of floor. These plugs are supplied by a 4-in. cast-iron main pipe, passing under the floor of the building. Hydrants and wash-sinks are provided at necessary points. In every section, against the outside wall, is a work-bench and vise with the necessary tools for any slight work required on the locomotives. The building is warmed in winter by large cast-iron stoves, the pipes from which pass into the smoke-flues already described as provided in the roof for the locomotives. To retain the heat as much as possible within the building, the stalls of the entrance tracks are separated from the balance of the house by partitions extending from the floor to the roof, and in winter the roof ventilators are closed.

Between the house and the turn-table the rails of the track are laid on white-oak cross-ties, 6 in. × 8 in., bedded in 14 in. of stone ballast. The turn-table, 50 ft. in diameter, is a cast-iron centre-pivoted table, with anti-friction conical rollers. The outside circular track in the turn-table pit is laid upon white-oak cross-ties bedded on a stone foundation-wall. The spaces between the cross-ties under the circular rail are filled in with brick laid in cement, with a slight grade towards the pit so as to drain into it. The centre pivot is bedded on a stone foundation 6 ft. square, capped with a single stone, 5 ft. 6 in. square × 15 in. thick. The outside wall of the pit is of brick, 22 in. thick, bedded on a stone foundation and capped by a white-oak curb, 4 in. × 13 in., anchored to the brickwork with 1-in. anchor-bolts. The turn-table pit is paved with brick laid flat and grouted with cement, and drains into the main sewer of the house. The frogs are cast-iron, laid on oak ties bedded in stone ballast, the points of the frogs being about 7 ft. from the face of the turn-table pit.

For additional details and illustrations see the *Journal of the Franklin Institute*, Vol. LX., from which publication the above description is compiled.

Engine-house at 31st Street, West Philadelphia, Pa., Pennsylvania Railroad.—The engine-house of the Pennsylvania Railroad at 31st Street, south of Spring Garden Street, West Philadelphia, Pa., designed by Mr. Wm. H. Brown, Chief Engineer, Pennsylvania Railroad, and built in 1880, shown in Figs. 305 to 307, is one half of a 36-stall brick roundhouse, with combination roof-trusses and slate roof. The cross-section of this house is very similar to that shown in Fig. 308. There are eighteen stalls, all of which have engine-pits. The outside diameter of the house is 270 ft., the inner diameter is 138 ft., and the diameter of the turn-table pit is 60 ft. 6 in. The width of the house is, therefore, 66 ft., and the space between the turn-table and the inner circle of the house is 38 ft. 9 in. The angle of the stalls is 10 deg. The panel length on the inner circle is 12 ft. 0$\frac{9}{32}$ in., and on the outer circle 23 ft. 6⅝ in. The clear width of the interior of the building, measured on the centre-line of the stall, is 63 ft. 4 in., and the clear height from the top of rail to the tie-rod of roof-truss is 22 ft. 1 in.

The foundations of the building are of stone, the outer walls being 2 ft. 6 in. thick, and all inner walls 2 ft. thick. The outer wall finishes off 4 in. below the ground, and is capped with a belting-course of cut stone, 9 in. × 10 in. All the doors have cut-stone sills, the rails of the tracks being cut into the sills. The cast-iron columns of the inside front have cast-iron blocks at foot, 17½ in. × 17½ in. × 9 in., resting upon cut-stone blocks, 2 ft. square by 1 ft. thick, with a stone foundation, 4 ft. square. The outer wall above the foundation is of brick, built in panels, with pilasters both inside and outside, and an ornamental outside cornice. The thickness of brick in panels is 13 in., and on pilasters 22 in. There are two windows in each panel on the outside of the house, excepting at the back of the house, where the house butts against the retaining-wall of 31st Street. A flush arch is built in the wall on the inside over every pair of windows, to provide against any injury to the cornice and roof in the event of the wall below being damaged by locomotives running beyond their stall. The window-openings are square, 5 ft. 10½ in. × 11 ft., with cast-iron sills and lintels on the outside. The windows have two sash, each 24 lights 10 in. × 15 in. The cast-iron inner front of the building is 7/16 in., and the columns are ⅝ in. thick. The doors are in pairs, circle-top, and 3 in. thick, panelled and glazed as shown, and leaving a clear opening in width of 11 ft. 0½ in., and in height of 18 ft. at the centre of the circle. Three of the 18 pairs of doors have small wicket-doors. Each door has three heavy wrought-iron strap-hinges hung on lugs cast to the columns. All the doors open inward, and are provided with the proper fixtures for locking them, and also for holding them in place when swung open.

The engine-pits in the stalls are 42 ft. 6 in. long by 4 ft. wide in the clear, 2 ft. 9 in. deep at front, and 2 ft. 6 in. deep at back. The sidewalls are of stone, 2 ft. thick. The bottom is dished 2 in. in the middle, and is paved with brick laid on edge and grouted with cement. Each pit drains at the lower end through a 10-in. bell-trap into a 12-in. circular brick sewer that runs under the ends of all the pits and discharges into the main sewer leading from the house. The rails on the pits rest on 6-in. × 12-in. white-oak stringers, anchored every 4 ft. with a 1-in. anchor-bolt to the side-wall masonry. The top of the rail is flush with the floor-level in the house. The inner end of the pit is located 10 ft. 5 in. from the inside face of the door, and the rear end is placed 10 ft. 5 in. from the inside face of the outside wall. The track in the house outside of the pits is laid on oak ties bedded in ballast. The floor is made of cement, laid level with the top of the rails on the pits and slightly dished to insure better drainage.

The roof-trusses are built on the triangular system, of iron and wood, the span being 65 ft. 4 in. from centre to centre of end-pins, with a rise of 16 ft. 3 in. The cast-iron end-plate on the inner front is firmly fixed to the top of the column, while at the outer front it rests on a 4-in. × 14-in. white-oak wall-plate. The principal rafters are white pine, 8 in. × 11 in., and the struts are white pine, 4 in. × 8 in. and 3 in. × 8 in. The heel-blocks, king-blocks, strut-caps, and strut-shoes are of cast-iron, ⅝ in. thick. The main tie-rods vary from 2 rods ⅞ in. in diameter to 2 rods 1½ in. in diameter. The counter-rods are ⅞ in. in diameter. The purlins are of white pine, 4 in. × 8 in. on the inner circle, and 4 in. × 10 in. on the outer circle. The purlins are cambered or cut convex on the outer circle, the rise at the centre of the purlin being 3⅝ in. at the outer wall and 2⅞ in. near the ridge; and they are cut hollow or concave on the inner circle, the depression at the centre of the purlin being ⅞ in. at the inner wall and 1⅜ in. near the ridge. The purlins are sheathed with 1¼-in. hemlock boards, covered with slate laid on two layers of roofing felt. Gutters of tin are provided on the outer and inner fronts, from which a 4-in. galvanized corrugated-iron pipe-conductor carries the water down the outside wall on every alternate pilaster, discharging into an 8-in. clay-pipe drain that runs around the outside of the building, while a 3-in. conductor carries the water down the inside front at every alternate column, the pipe being located at the back of the column on the inside of the house and discharging through a 4-in. clay-pipe drain into the 12-in. circular brick sewer running under the ends of the engine-pits, as mentioned above.

Ventilation is secured by 6-ft. octagonal ornamental louvred ventilators placed in ridge of roof on every alternate stall. A sheet-iron smoke-flue is placed over every stall, the centre of the flue being 13 ft. from the inside face of the outer wall. The flue is 2 ft. in diameter, made of No. 14 gauge sheet-iron, and provided with a bell-shaped movable hood at the lower end, the bottom of the hood when raised being 14 ft. 11 in. above the top of the rail, and 13 ft. 7 in. when lowered. Water-plugs with 3-in. standard fire-hose connection, protected by cast-iron boxes and covers level with top of floor, are provided at the centre of the house in alternate stalls, supplied by a 6-in. cast-iron water-pipe. There is an 8-in. × 8-in. white-oak bumping-log with iron plate at centre fastened on the floor next to the inside of the outer brick wall opposite each pit, to take the blow from the cow-catcher of the engine in case it is run too far over the pit. The heating of the building is done by large cast-iron stoves, and the ventilators in the roof are closed when it is desired to retain the heat in the building.

Between the house and the turn-table the tracks are laid on oak ties in stone ballast. There are no frogs used around the turn-table, the outside flanges of the nearest rails of adjoining tracks just touching each other at the face of the pit obviating the necessity of using frogs. The turn-table pit is drained through a 10-in. pipe-drain into the main sewer from the house, which consists of a 12-in. clay pipe leading into a 3-ft. sewer on Spring Garden Street. The turn-table is 60 ft. in diameter, of wrought-iron, and worked by hand. The turn-table pit, side walls, foundations of circular track, and

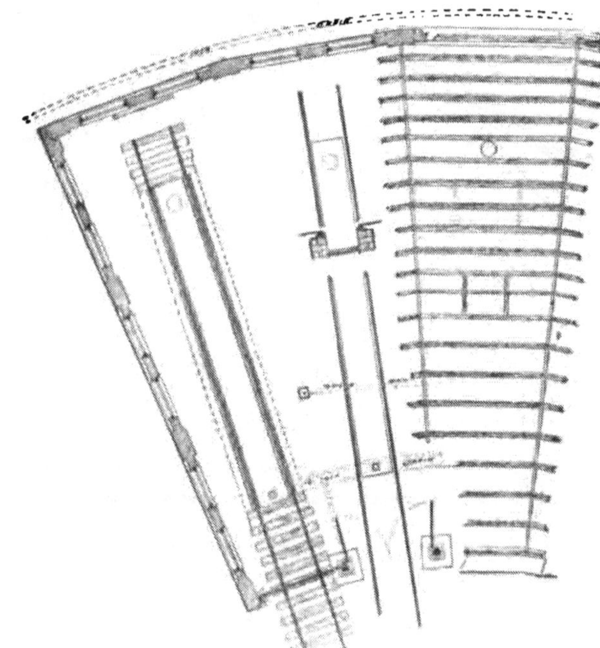

FIG. 305.—GROUND-PLAN.

FIG. 306.—ELEVATION OF ENGINE-DOOR.

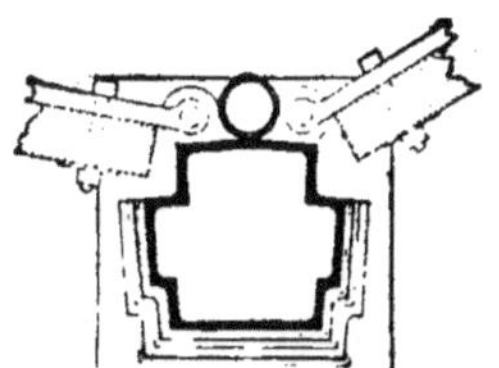

FIG. 307.—SECTION OF COLUMN.

paving are similar to the same class of work in the roundhouse at the West Philadelphia shops, described above.

The cost of the eighteen stalls, as per figures kindly furnished by Mr. Wm. H. Brown, was $21,750, exclusive of the retaining-wall to hold up the street at the back of the house, and exclusive

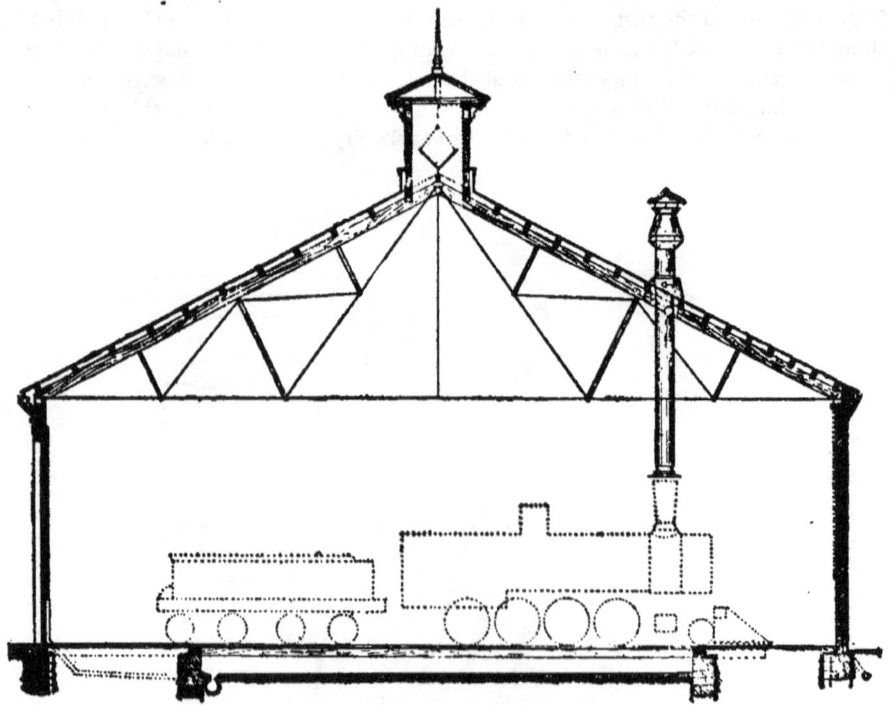

FIG. 308.—CROSS-SECTION.

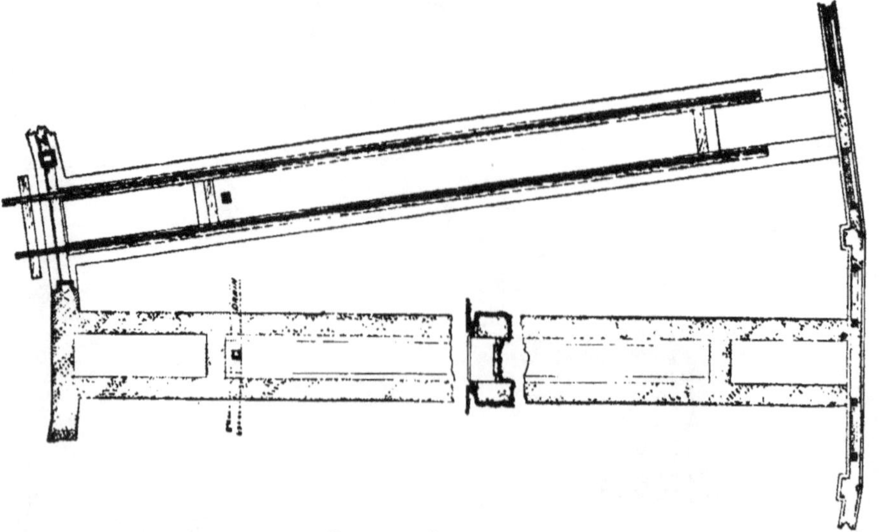

FIG. 309.—GROUND-PLAN.

of turn-table. The wrought-iron turn-table cost about $1500, so that the entire structure, exclusive of the special retaining-wall, cost $23,250, or, on an average, $1292 per stall.

Engine-house at Mt. Pleasant Junction, Jersey City, N. J., Pennsylvania Railroad.—The engine-house of the Pennsylvania Railroad at Mt. Pleasant Junction, Jersey City, N. J., shown in Figs. 308

to 314, built in 1890 under the direction of Mr. E. F. Brooks, Engineer Maintenance of Way, P. R. R., assisted by Mr. Martin L. Gardner, Assistant Engineer, is a full-circle 44-stall brick roundhouse

FIG. 310.—ELEVATION OF OUTSIDE WALL.

FIG. 311.—ELEVATION OF INTERIOR WALL AND ENGINE-DOORS.

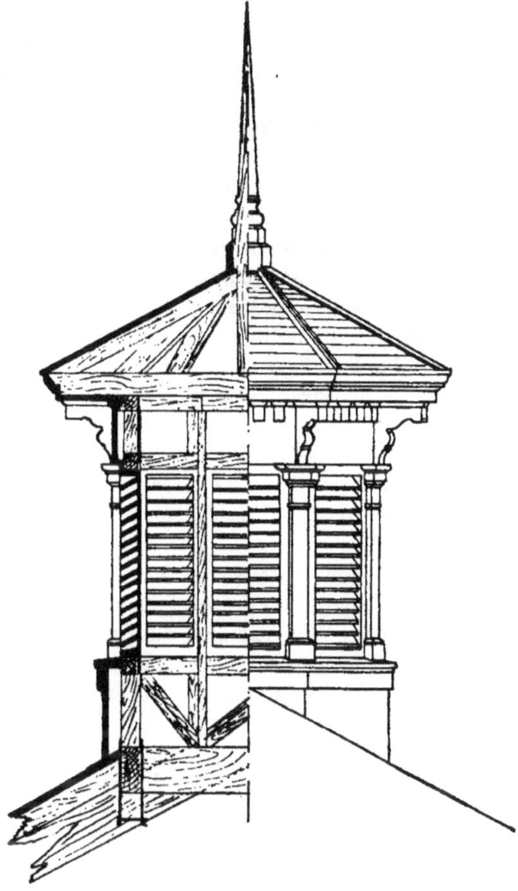

FIG. 313.—ELEVATION AND SECTION OF VENTILATOR.

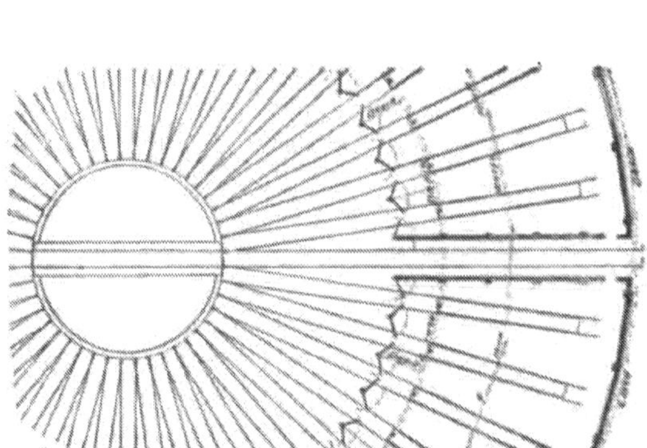

FIG. 312.—GENERAL PLAN.

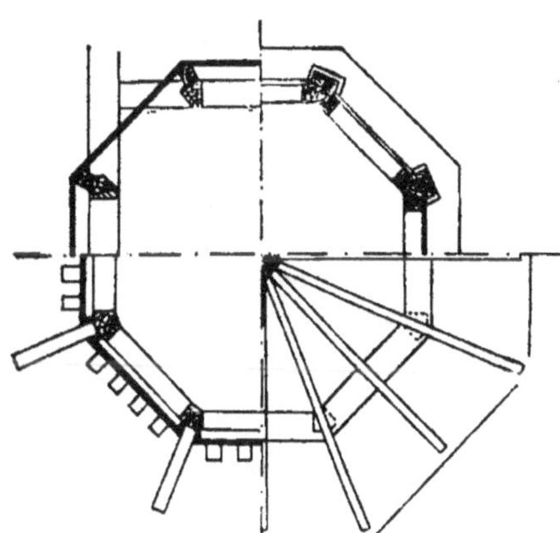

FIG. 314.—GROUND-PLAN OF VENTILATOR.

with combination roof-trusses and slate roof. The outside diameter of the house is 320 ft., the inner diameter is 168 ft. 6 in., and the diameter of the turn-table pit is 60 ft. The width of the house is, therefore, 75 ft. 9 in., and the space between the turn-table and the inner circle of the house is 54 ft.

3 in. The angle of the stalls is 8° 10′ 54″. The panel length on the inner circle is 12 ft. ½ in., and on the outer circle 22 ft. 9 15/16 in. The clear width of the interior of the building, measured on the centre-line of the stall, is about 74 ft., and the clear height from the top of rail to the tie-rod of roof-truss is 22 ft. Two of the stalls are used for entrance tracks, with brick fire-walls on each side of the track, the passage being 12 ft. wide in the clear; all the other stalls have engine-pits.

The foundations of the building are of stone, the outer walls being 1 ft. 7 in. wide at top in the panels, and 2 ft. 4 in. wide at top at the pilasters; all the inner walls, including the wall under the door-sills on the inner front, are 2 ft. thick. The outer wall finishes off 4½ in. below the ground surface, and is capped with a belting-course of cut stone, 4 in. × 14 in., set up edgeways. All the engine-doors have 8-in. × 12-in. white-oak sub-sills on 2-ft. stone foundation-walls; the rails are spiked to the sub-sills, and 4½-in. × 10-in. white-oak plank-sills are nailed to the sub-sill, so that the top of the sill is level with the top of the rails. The columns of the inside front rest on cut-stone base-blocks, 18 in. square by 12½ in. deep, the top of the base-block being level with the top of rail. The outer wall above the foundation masonry is of brick, built without panels on the outside, but with pilasters on the inside under the trusses, and with a plain but ample brick cornice on the outside. The brick wall is 12 in. thick between the pilasters, and 20½ in. thick at the pilasters. Two of the panels on the outside of the house are occupied by engine-entrance passages; the balance have windows, two in each panel. The window-openings are square, 4 ft. 8¾ in. × 13 ft. 2¾ in, with cast-iron sills and window aprons, and with three white-pine lintels, each 4 in. × 10 in. The windows have box-frames with two sash, each 24 lights, 12 in. × 12 in., double-hung. The entrance passages on the outside and inside fronts are walled over with semicircular brick arches—without any doors, however.

The inner front of the house has cast-iron columns between the doors. The columns are 12 in. × 9¼ in. in size, and consist of ⅝-in. metal. There are lugs cast on the back, to which the door-hinges are hung. The-engine doors are square-top doors, in pairs, with a clear height above top of rail of 18 ft. 1½ in., and a clear width of 11 ft. 3 in. The door-opening is spanned from column to column by a cast-iron, trough-shaped lintel, with a stop at the bottom for the doors to strike against. The lintel is 12 in. wide and 11 in. high, and is made of ⅝-in. iron. Four of the engine-doors have small wicket-doors.

The floor is of asphalt, level with the top of the rails. The engine-pits in the stalls are 45 ft. 8 in. long in the clear, by 3 ft. 11½ in. wide in the clear; 2 ft. 9 in. deep at front, and 2 ft. deep at back. The upper end of the pit is placed 13 ft. from the inside of the outer wall. The side walls are stone, 2 ft. thick. The bottom is laid with a slope from the centre of the pit down each way toward each side wall, along which gutters are formed, thus keeping the middle of the pit dry. The pits are paved with brick, set on edge and grouted with cement, and drain at the lower end through a 10-in. bell-trap with cesspool and cast-iron grate into a 12-in. circular brick sewer running under the ends of all the pits, and discharging into the main sewer leading from the house. The side walls of the pits extend all the way across the house so as to provide a support for the rails. The rails are spiked to 8-in. × 12-in. white-oak stringers, anchored with ¾-in. bolts every 4 ft. to the stone side walls.

The roof-trusses are built on the triangular system, of iron and wood, the span being 75 ft. 1 in. from centre to centre of end-pins, with a rise of 18 ft. 8 in. The cast-iron end-plate on the inner front is firmly fixed to the top of the column, while at the outer front it rests on a 4-in. × 14-in. × 2-ft. 6-in. white-oak wall-plate. The principal rafters are white pine, 9 in. × 12 in.; the struts are white pine, 4 in. × 9 in. and 3 in. × 9 in. The heel-blocks, king-posts, strut-caps, and strut-shoes are of cast-iron, ⅝ in. thick. The main tie-rods vary from 2 bars ⅞ in. square to 2 bars 1 in. × 2 in. The counter-rods are ⅞ in. square. The purlins are of white pine, 4 in. × 9 in. on the inner circle, and 4 in. × 10 in. on the outer circle. The purlins supporting the smoke-flues are 6 in. × 10 in., trussed by 2 rods ⅞ in. in diameter. The purlins supporting the ventilator at ridge are 6 in. × 12 in., trussed the same as just mentioned. The purlins are cambered or cut convex on the outer circle, the rise at the centre of the purlin being 2⅞ in. at the outer wall and 2¼ in. near the ridge, and they are cut hollow or concave on the inner circle, the depression at the centre of the purlin being ⅝ in. at the inner wall, and 1⅛ in. near the ridge. The purlins are sheathed with 1¼-in. hemlock, covered with slate laid on two layers of roofing-felt. Gutters of tin are provided on the outer and inner fronts. The gutter on the outside of the building is drained by a 3-in. × 4-in. galvanized sheet-iron down-conductor at every panel point into a 12-in. pipe-drain running around the outside of the building. The down-conductor is inserted in a 4-in. × 5-in. groove in the outside of the brick wall at the angle formed by adjoining panels. The gutter on the inside of the building is drained by a 3-in. circular galvanized-iron down-conductor on the inside of the house at every alternate column into a 4-in. pipe-drain that leads directly into the 12-in. circular brick drain at the engine-pits opposite the column. The down conductor is located on the back of the column on the inside of the house.

Ventilation is secured by 6-ft. octagonal ornamental louvred ventilators, placed in ridge of roof on every alternate stall. A sheet-iron smoke-flue is placed over every stall, the centre of the flue being 15 ft. from the inside face of the outer wall. The flue is about 20 in. in diameter, with a cast-iron stack of " None Such " patent at the top, and provided at the lower end with a bell-shaped movable hood, the bottom of the hood, when raised, being 15 ft. 2 in. above the top of rail and 14 ft. when lowered.

Water-plugs, with 3-in. standard fire-hose connection under the floor, protected by cast-iron boxes and covers level with top of floor, are provided at the centre of the house in alternate stalls, connected by a 6-in. water-pipe, and supplied by an 8-in. water-main. Four hydrants are located inside the house along the outside wall.

The heating of the building is done by steam, and the ventilators in the roof can be closed by flap-doors, as shown on the plans.

Between the house and the turn-table the rails are laid on oak ties in stone ballast. The frogs around the turn-table are rail frogs bedded on oak ties in ballast, the points of the frogs being 3 ft. $3\frac{7}{16}$ in. from the face of the turn-table pit. The turn-table pit is drained through a pipe-drain to the main sewer. The turn-table pit is 60.6 ft. in diameter in the clear. The turn-table is of wrought-iron, and is turned by steam-power.

A complete specification for this engine-house is given in the Appendix at the back of this book.

Engine-house at Roanoke, Va., Norfolk & Western Railroad.—The engine-house of the Norfolk & Western Railroad at Roanoke, Va., shown in Fig. 315, built in 1887 under the direction of Mr. S. B.

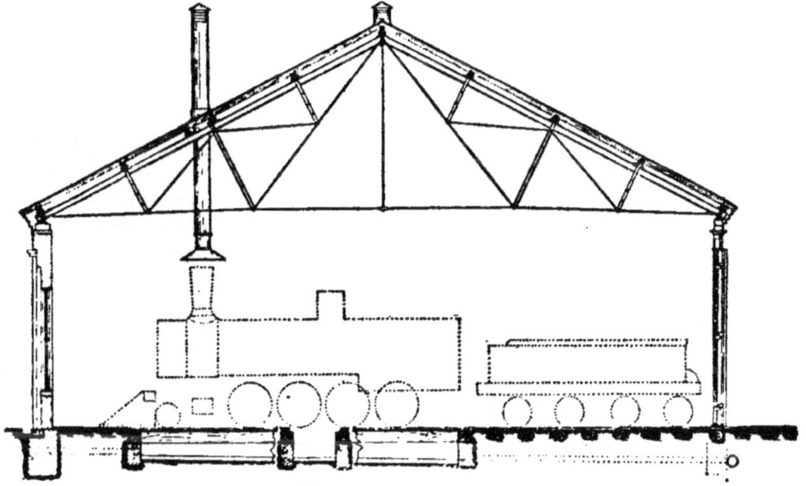

FIG. 315.—CROSS-SECTION.

Haupt, Superintendent, Motive Power, N. & W. R. R., is a segmental brick roundhouse with iron roof-trusses and slate roof. The outside diameter of the house is 314 ft. 3 in., the inner diameter is 186 ft. 3 in., and the diameter of the turn-table is 60 ft. The width of the house is, therefore, 64 ft., and the space between the turn-table and the inner circle of the house is 63 ft. $1\frac{1}{2}$ in. The panel length on the inner circle is 13 ft. 3⅜ in., and on the outer circle 22 ft. 4⅞ in. The clear width of the interior of the building, measured on the centre-line of the stall, is about 62 ft. 6 in., and the clear height from the top of rail to the tie-rod of roof-truss is about 18 ft.

The foundations of the walls are stone, finished at the ground-level with a 9-in. × 14-in. cut-stone belt-course. The door-sills are made of timber, and planks are spiked between the rails on top of the sub-sills, so that the top of the sill is level with the top of the rails and the floor in the house. The outer wall above the foundation masonry is of brick, with panels and pilasters on the outside, the thickness of the wall being 13 in. in the panels and 21 in. at the pilasters. There are two windows in each panel of the outside wall, each window having 24 lights, 12 in. × 16 in. The inner front of the house has cast-iron columns, 10½ in. × 12 in., between the doors. The engine-doors are square-top doors, in pairs, 16 ft. clear opening above top of rail, each door hung with heavy wrought-iron strap-hinges to lugs cast on the columns. The door-opening is spanned from column to column by a 12-in. channel-iron.

The floor consists of plank on mud-sills. The engine-pits are 30 ft. long in the clear by 4 ft. wide in the clear, 3 ft. deep at front and 2 ft. 6 in. deep at back. The upper end of the pit is placed 9 ft. from the inside of the outer wall. The side walls are brick, 21 in. thick. The pits are paved with brick set on edge in cement grout, and drain at the lower end through a 6 in. drain-pipe into a 12-in. circular drain that runs along the outside of the inner front of the building, which latter drain also takes the drainage from the roof-leaders along the inner front. The rails on the pits are spiked to 12-in. × 12-in. stringers, anchored to the side walls of the pits. The floor is laid flush with the top of the rails.

The roof-trusses are built on the triangular system, of iron, the span being 64 ft. from centre to centre, with a rise of 16 ft. The principal rafters are 8-in. deck-beams, 65 lbs. per yard; the main struts are two 4-in. channel-irons, 20 lbs. per yard; the intermediate struts are two 3-in. × ½-in. bars. All connections at joints are made of wrought-iron plates and shapes, pin-connected. The main tie-rods vary from two rods ⅞ in. in diameter to two rods 1⅜ in. in diameter. The counter-rods are ⅞ in. in diameter. The wooden purlins are spaced about 9 ft. apart, and support wooden rafters covered by boards.

Ventilation is secured at the peak by small 12-in. × 18-in. iron ventilators inserted over each panel. A sheet-iron smoke-flue is placed over the engine-pit in every stall, the centre of the flue being located 15 ft. from the centre of the outside wall. The flue is 18 in. in diameter, the upper fixed end being made of No. 12 gauge iron; the lower, movable, bell-shaped piece being of No. 10 gauge iron.

Engine-house at Lehighton, Pa., Lehigh Valley Railroad.—The engine-house of the Lehigh Valley Railroad at Lehighton, Pa., shown in Figs. 316 to 320, designed and built in 1883 under the direction of the author, is a 29-stall segment of a full-circle 56-stall stone roundhouse, with iron trusses and slate roof. The outside diameter of the house is 354 ft., the inner diameter is 206 ft., and the diameter of the turn-table pit is 60 ft. The width of the house is, therefore, 74 ft., and the space between the turn-table and the inner circle of the house is 73 ft. The angle of the stalls is 6° 40′. The panel length on the inner circle is 12 ft. and on the outer circle 20 ft. 7½ in., measured on the centre-line of the wall. The clear width of the interior of the building, measured on the centre-line of the stall, is 72 ft., and the clear height from the top of rail to the tie-rod of roof-truss is 21 ft. 2 in.

The foundations and walls of the building are throughout of stone. The foundations of the outer walls are 2 ft. 6 in. wide at top and 3 ft. 6 in. wide at bottom, finished off 4 in. below the top of rail and capped with a 12-in. × 25½-in. base stone. The wall above the base stone is 24 in. thick, perfectly plain, without any panelling, pilasters, or cornices, excepting on the gables. The foundations of the columns on the inner front are stone piers, 3 ft. square on top and 5 ft. square on bottom, finished off 12 in. below the top of rail, and capped with a 2-ft. square stone, 12 in. high, to which the bed-plate of the iron column is anchored. The engine-doors on the inner front have cast-iron hollow sills fitted in between the columns and the rails, the top of the sills being flush with the top of the rail. The iron sills rest on 2-ft. stone walls built in between the column piers. There are two windows in every panel of the outside wall. The window-openings are square, 4 ft. 6 in. × 11 ft., with cast-iron sills and sloping window aprons on the inside of the window. The window-opening is spanned by a cast-iron lintel on the outside of the wall and two white-oak, 6-in. × 14-in., lintels on the inside. The windows have box-frames with two sash, each twenty lights, 9 in. × 14 in., double-hung.

The inner front of the house is made of cast-iron. The engine-doors have semicircular tops, in pairs, each door hung with three heavy composition-metal hinges to lugs cast on the columns. The clear height of the door-opening at the centre of the arched top is 17 ft. 1½ in. above the top of the rail, and the clear width is 11 ft. 3 in. The door-opening is spanned by an ornamental cast-iron front, in two pieces, riveted together at centre of opening and riveted at the sides to flanges on the columns. The weight of the roof is carried across the opening by eave-purlins. A heavy galvanized-iron cornice and gutter, hung to the eave-purlin, finishes off the front. The engine-doors are 3 in. thick, panelled and glazed as shown. Three of the engine-doors have small wicket-doors.

The floor consists of 6-in. to 8-in. limestone flagging, set in sand and well grouted at joints. The floor is level with the base of the rails at the pits, and is slightly pitched between the pits, so as to afford better drainage. The engine-pits are 54 ft. long in the clear by 3 ft. 11 in. wide in the clear, 2 ft. deep below base of rail at front and 1 ft. 6 in. deep at back. The upper end of the pit is placed 9 ft. from the inside of the outer wall. The side walls of the pits are stone, 2 ft. thick. The pits are paved with stone paving, and dished from the side walls towards the centre of the pit. The drainage passes at the lower end of the pit through a cesspool with cast-iron grating into a 6-in. pipe leading into a stone box-sewer, 2 ft. × 3 ft., which serves as the main sewer of the house, taking the water from the down-conductors of the inner slope of the roof and the drainage from the turn-table pit. The side walls of the pits are coped with stone, the top being flush with the stone floor of the house. The side walls of the pits extend across the house, so as to provide a support for the rails between the pits and the outer walls of the building. The rails rest on the stone coping, and are held down and in place by rag-bolts and cast-iron rail-clips.

The roof-trusses are built of iron, on the triangular system, the span being 73 ft. 6 in. from centre to centre of end-pins, with a rise of 19 ft. The bed-plate on the inner front is firmly fixed to the top of the column, while at the outer front it rests on a white-oak wall-plate. The principal rafters are made of a 7-in. deck-beam, 65 lbs. per yard, 4-in. flange; the main struts are composed of 4 angles, 2 in. × 2 in. × ¼ in., and the intermediate struts are made similarly of 1¾-in. angles. All connections and joints are made of wrought-iron plates and shapes, riveted and pin-connected. The main tie-rods vary from 2 rods 1½ in. in diameter to 1 rod 1⅝ in. in diameter. The counter-rods are 1 in. in diameter. The purlins are white pine, 3 in. × 12 in. on the inner slope of the roof, 4 in. × 12 in. on the outer slope, and 6 in. × 12 in. at the ridge, at the eaves, and at the smoke-flue. The purlins are cut concave on the inner slope of the roof and convex on the outer slope. The roof-sheathing is 1-in. Michigan pine, tongued and grooved, and covered with slate laid on two layers of roofing-felt.

Ventilation is secured by 6-ft. octagonal ornamental louvred ventilators, placed in ridge of roof on every third stall. The smoke-flue for carrying off the gases and smoke from the smoke-stacks of the engines standing on the pits is quite a novel feature in this building, being the application on a larger scale of a system of overhead horizontal pipe-ventilators introduced by Mr. David Clarke, Master Mechanic, L. V. R. R., in an engine-house at Hazleton, Pa. A 33-in. horizontal iron pipe, connecting outside of the building with a brick stack, is hung from the roof-trusses over the pits, the centre of the pipe being 13 ft. from the inside face of the outer wall and 17 ft. 8 in. above the top of the rails. Over each pit this pipe has a vertical tube with a damper and a bell-shaped end to fit over the smoke-stack of the engine below it. The draught created in the brick stack outside of the house causes the gases and smoke in the smoke-stacks of the engines to be drawn into the ventilating tube, and thence out of the house. The system works very well in this house. The brick stack is 100 ft. high, and the smoke is drawn from engines 500 ft. distant from the stack.

Water-plugs are provided throughout the house at convenient points. The heating of the house is done by steam-coils hung from the roof-trusses overhead. This system is excellent, as far as producing a uniform heat throughout the lower part of the building, but it is accompanied with considerable waste of heat.

Between the house and the turn-table the rails are laid on oak ties in stone ballast. The frogs around the turn-table are steel rail-frogs bedded on stone walls connecting with the outside wall of the turn-table pit. The points of the frogs are 10 ft. 5⅜ in. from the face of the turn-table pit. The walls of the turn-table are of stone, 2 ft. 6 in. thick, coped with 12-in. × 30-in. coping, and with a 3-ft. offset or bench for the circular rail of the table. The centre pivot of the table rests on a 4-ft. square pedestal stone, 18 in. thick, with a stone pier-foundation under it, 7 ft. square at its bed. The pit is paved with brick, and drains into the main sewer of the building. The turn-table is of wrought-iron, and is turned by hand. The circular rail rests on cast-iron chairs, the base of the rail being 7 in. above the stone coping of the bench-wall under the chairs. This construction makes the pit deeper, but it allows the turn-table to be operated after a light snowfall, without waiting to have the snow shovelled out of the pit.

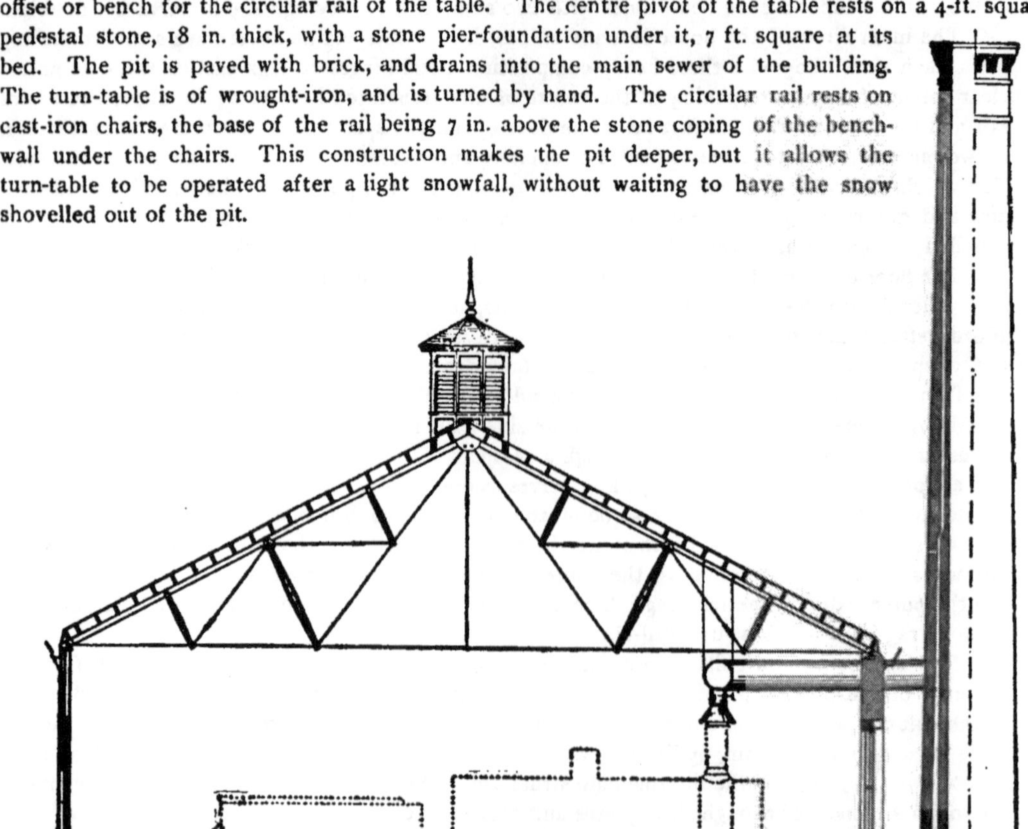

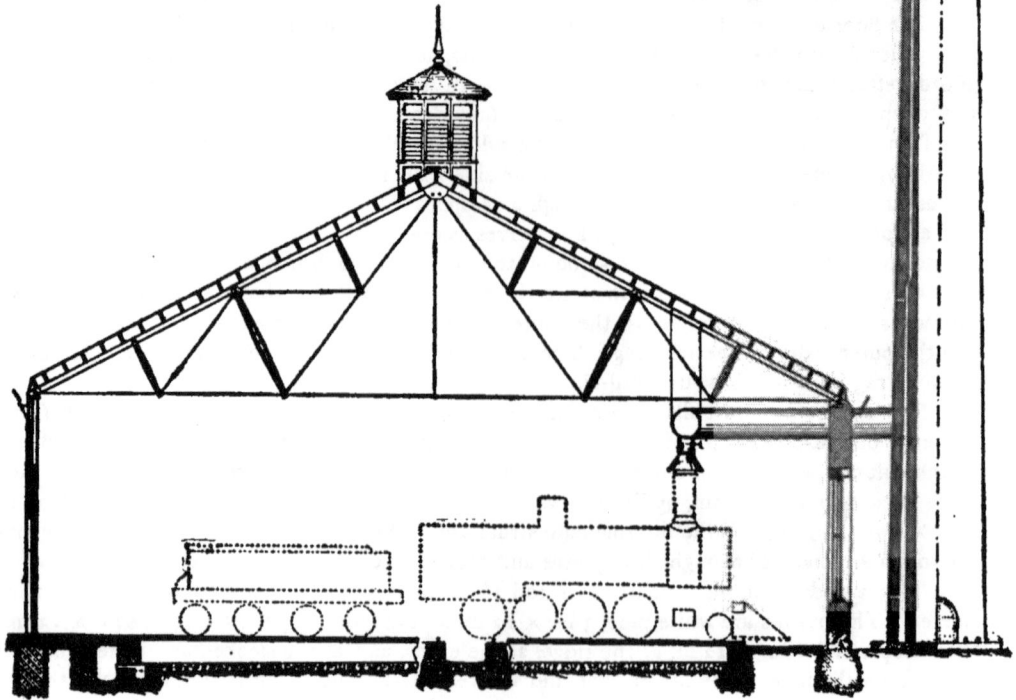

FIG. 316.—CROSS-SECTION.

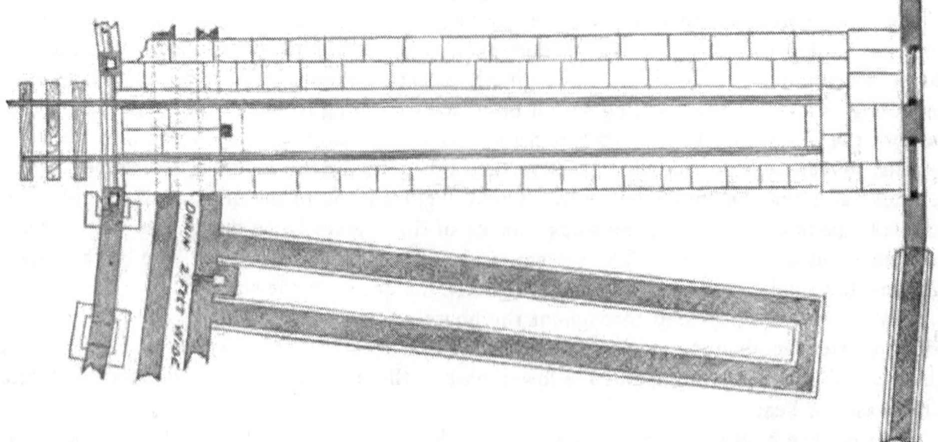

FIG. 317.—GROUND-PLAN.

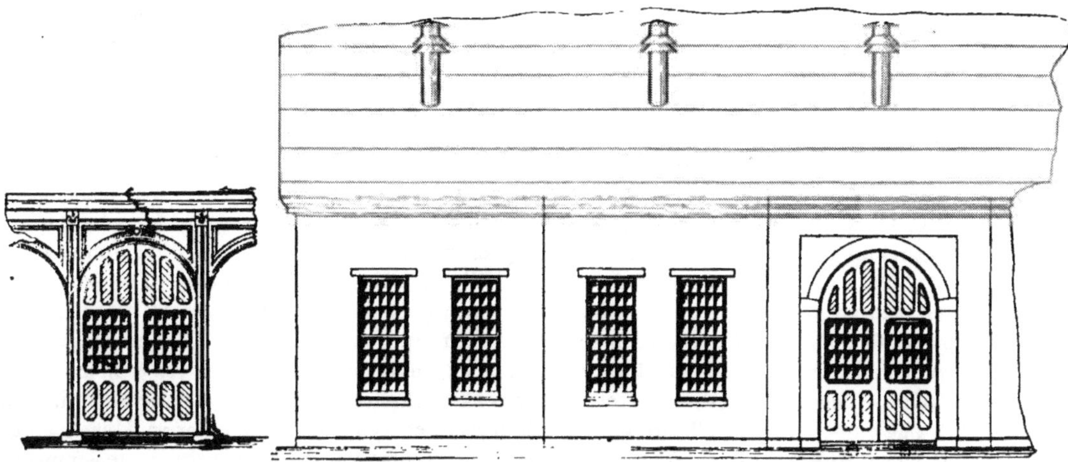

Fig. 318.—Elevation of Interior Wall and Engine-door.

Fig. 319.—Elevation of Outside Wall.

Fig. 320.—End Elevation.

Engine-house at Richmond, Va., Richmond & Alleghany Railroad.—The engine-house of the Richmond & Alleghany Railroad at Richmond, Va., plans for which were published in the *Railroad Gazette* of January 19, 1883, designed and built in 1880 under the direction of the author, is a 14-stall segment of a full-circle 56-stall brick roundhouse, with iron roof-trusses and a slate roof. There is a small machine-shop and blacksmith-shop attached to the roundhouse on the rear. The outside diameter of the house is 383 feet, the inner diameter is 252 ft., and the diameter of the turn-table pit is 51 ft. The width of the house is, therefore, 65 ft. 6 in., and the space between the turn-table and the inner circle of the house is 100 ft. 6 in. The panel length on the inner circle is 14 ft. 1 in., and on the outer circle 21 ft. 5½ in. The clear width of the interior of the building, measured on the centre-line of the stall, is 64 ft., and the clear height from the top of rail to the tie-rod of roof-truss is 22 ft. 6 in.

The choice of a roundhouse with 383 ft. diameter and 56 stalls to the full circle was caused by the necessity of having as many stalls as possible in one quadrant, the site being limited. The exact diameter was determined by the requirement that the track from each stall to the turn-table should allow a locomotive, a coach, or two flat cars to stand in front of the stall without blocking the tracks to the neighboring stalls. In this manner the standing capacity of the tracks was more than doubled, being especially advantageous for repair work. The tracks in the building have a downward grade towards the turn-table of ¼ ft. in 100 ft., and in front of stalls ½ ft. in 100 ft., to facilitate a speedy removal of cars and engines in case of fire.

The thickness of the outside wall is 2 bricks at top, and at pilasters 2½ bricks. The piers between the doors of the inner face are 3 bricks thick throughout. Engine-pits are 45 ft. long by 4 ft. 3 in. wide in clear, and 3 ft. and 2 ft. 6 in. deep; the upper end of pit is placed 12 ft. 6 in. from the inner face of the outer wall. The iron roof-trusses are built on the triangular system. The pine purlins supporting the slate roof are 2½ in. × 12 in. on the inner slope of roof and 3 in. × 12 in. on the outer slope, spaced about 28 in. The centre of smoke-flues is 17 ft. from the outer wall. The flues are telescopic, 20 in. in diameter, with double hood on top and expanding cone at bottom, 3 ft. 6 in. in diameter and 3 ft. high. The sheet-iron ventilators at the peak of the roof over each stall are 24 in. in diameter, with single hood on top. There are two windows in every panel of the outer wall, each window having 24 lights, 10 in. × 18 in. The engine-doors are circular-top doors, in pairs, batten-framed up to a height of about 7 ft., above which they are glazed. They are hung with strap-hinges to cast-iron wall-blocks built into the brick piers between the doors. The door-opening is 11 ft. 5 in. wide in the clear, and is spanned by a semicircular brick arch, 1½ brick high, the crown of the arch being 17 ft. in the clear above the top of the rail. The floor in the house is 2-in. plank on 10-in. joists. The rails

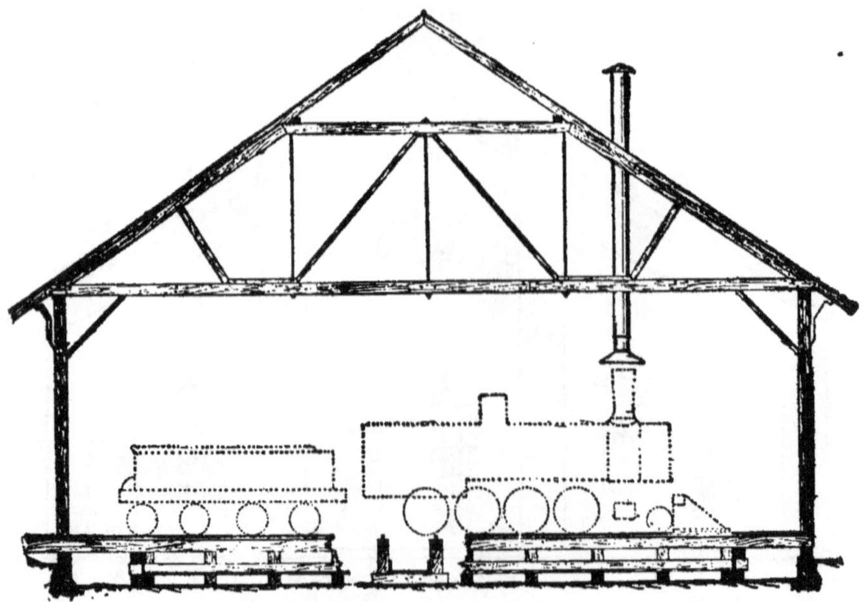

FIG. 321.—CROSS-SECTION.

on the pits are fastened to 12-in. × 12-in. oak wall-plates, the top of rail being level with the floor in the house. The walls of the pits and the foundations of the outside walls are of stone. The pits drain at their lower end through a cesspool, covered with a cast-iron grate, and a 6-in. drain-pipe into a stone box-culvert.

Engine-house, Northern Pacific Railroad.—The engine-house of the Northern Pacific Railroad, shown in Fig. 321, designed by Mr. C. B. Talbot, is a segment of a full-circle 51-stall frame roundhouse, with wooden roof-trusses. The outside diameter of the house is 351 ft. 6 in., the inner diameter is 211 ft. 6 in., and the diameter of the turn-table pit is 50 ft. The width of the house is, therefore, 70 ft., and the space between the turn-table and the inner circle of the house is 80 ft. 9 in. The panel length on the inner circle is 13 ft. ¾ in., and on the outer circle 21 ft. 6 in. The clear width of the interior of the building is 68 ft., and the clear height from the top of rail to the tie-beam of roof-truss is 21 ft. 8 in.

The foundations of the building are stone or brick piers, or blocking, according to circumstances. The wooden posts between the doors of the inner face and at the panel points of the outer wall are 10 in. × 10 in.; plates, 10 in. × 10 in.; studding of outside walls and gables, 2 in. × 5 in.; rafters, 3 in. × 8 in ; purlins, 6 in. × 12 in.; tie-beam of roof-trusses, 3 pieces, 4 in. × 12 in.; principal rafters, 10 in. × 12 in.; struts 6 in. × 12 in. and 4 in. × 12 in. The floor consists of 2-in. rough boards on 3-in. × 12-in. joists, spaced 20 in., which latter rest on 4-in. × 14-in. girders, spaced 6 ft., spanning the space between the pits. The pits are of timber, 4 ft. wide by 54 ft. long in the clear, and 3 ft. deep. The rise of the roof is one third of the span. The outside sheathing is $\frac{7}{8}$-in. dressed, "V" Rustic horizontal weather-boarding.

Engine-house Design, Philadelphia & Reading Railroad.—The engine-house shown in Fig. 322,

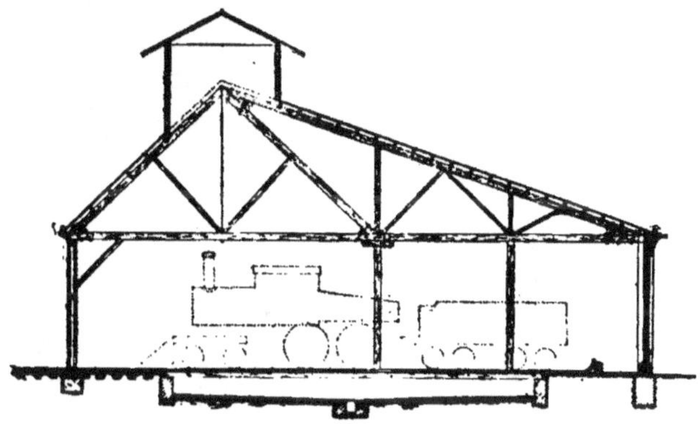

Fig. 322.—Cross-section.

designed for the Philadelphia & Reading Railroad, is a segment of a brick roundhouse with wooden roof-trusses wooden posts in the interior, and slate roof, the peak of the roof being placed excentric, so as to be located more immediately above the smoke-stack of the engines standing on the pits, giving thus a more direct ventilation through a continuous louvred lantern ventilator at the peak of, the roof. This house, built for 5 stalls, would cost $1400 per stall, exclusive of tracks, unusual foundations of walls, and track-pits; including the latter, the cost is $1600 per stall.

Engine-house at Grand Crossing, Wis., Chicago, Burlington & Northern Railroad.—The engine-house of the Chicago, Burlington & Northern Railroad at Grand Crossing, Wis., shown in Figs. 323

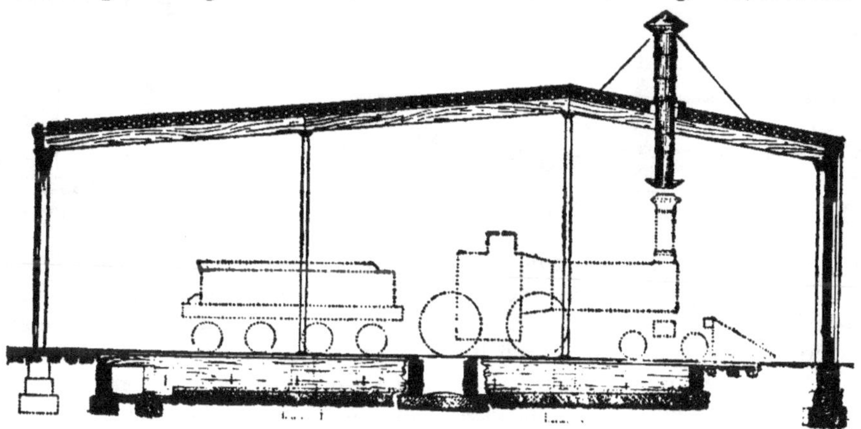

Fig. 323.—Cross-section.

to 328, plans for which were kindly furnished by Mr. H. S. Bryan, Master Mechanic, C., B. & N. R. R., is a full-circle 40-stall brick roundhouse, with a low flat girder roof, resting on cast-iron posts in the interior of the building, covered with a gravel roof. The outside diameter of the house is 304 ft., the inner diameter is 160 ft., and the diameter of the turn-table pit is 60 ft. The width of the house is, therefore, 72 ft., and the space between the turn-table and the inner circle of the house is 50 ft. The angle of the stalls is 9 degrees. The panel length on the inner circle is 12 ft. 6 in. The clear height from the top of rail to the roof girder at the outer walls is 18 ft. Two of the stalls are used as passage-ways, with brick fire-walls on each side.

The foundations of the walls are of stone. The outer wall is of brick, panelled on the outside, and with pilasters at the angles on the inside and outside of the wall, the thickness of the wall at the

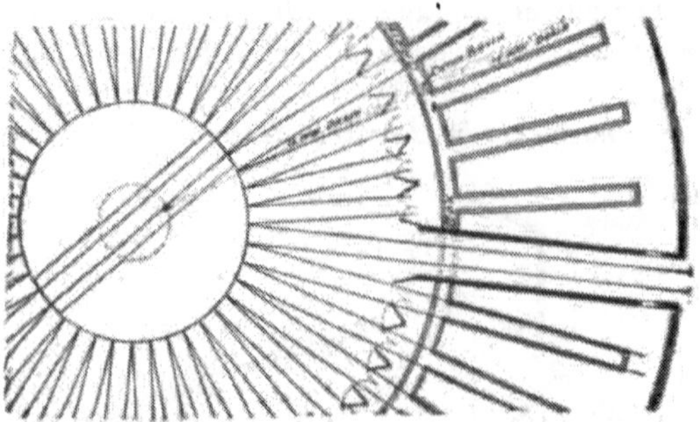

Fig. 324.—General Plan.

Fig. 325.—Elevation of Interior Wall and Engine-doors.

Fig. 326.—Elevation of Outside Wall.

Fig. 327.—Cross-section of Turn-table Pit.

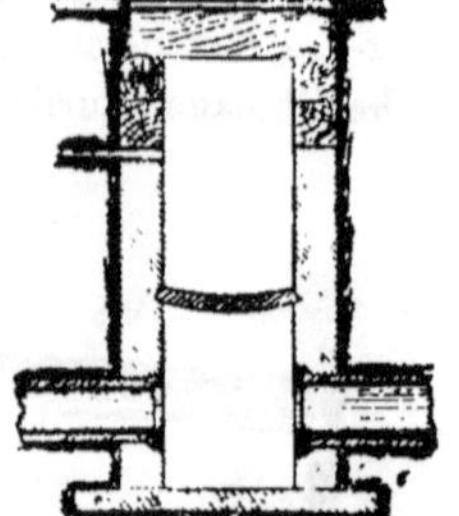

Fig. 328.—Cross-section of Drain.

pilaster being 2 ft. There is one triple window in each panel of the outer wall. The inner front consists of cast-iron posts between the doors, the door-opening being spanned by a semicircular 1½-brick arch springing from the top of the posts, and the balance of the space to the eaves filled out with brickwork. The crown of the arch is 16 ft. 4 in. above the top of rail. The doors are 3½ in. thick, panelled and glazed as shown. The cast-iron posts between the doors are 12 in. × 19 in. in section, of ½-in. metal, grooved to fit the doors, and with caps from which the brick arches spring.

The peak of the roof is placed, as shown in the plans, nearer the outer wall; the inner slope has a pitch of 1 in 12, the outer slope a pitch of 1 in 6. The roof-girders are supported inside the house by two 6-in. cast-iron columns, ¾-in. metal. The girders are two pieces, 6 in. × 16 in. The purlins are 2 in. × 10 in., spaced from 12 in. to 16 in. apart. The roof is covered with four-ply roofing-felt and gravel, on 1-in. boards. The engine-pits are 50 ft. long by 3 ft. 10 in. wide, and from 2 ft. 10 in. to 3 ft. 4 in. deep below the top of the rail. The pits are built with a foundation of stone flagging; the side walls are built up on this foundation for about 1 ft. in height with brick, and for the balance of the height with timber, the rail being spiked to the top timber. The bottom of the pit is paved with concrete, built convex, so as to form a drain along each side wall. The drainage of the pits is very thorough, through a cesspool and a brick and timber culvert.

Engine-house at Clinton, Ia., Burlington, Cedar Rapids & Northern Railway.—The engine-house of the Burlington, Cedar Rapids & Northern Railway at Clinton, Ia., shown in Figs. 329 and 330, designed by Mr. H. F. White, Chief Engineer, B., C. R. & N. Ry., is a 5-stall segment of a brick roundhouse, with iron posts on the inner circle, and timber posts in the interior supporting a low flat roof, covered with roofing-felt and gravel. The house is 70 ft. wide, outside measurement, and the panel length on the inner circle is 12 ft. 6¾ in. The foundations of the walls are of stone. The outside wall is brick, 13 in. thick, panelled on the outside and with pilasters at the corners, the wall being 17 in. thick at the

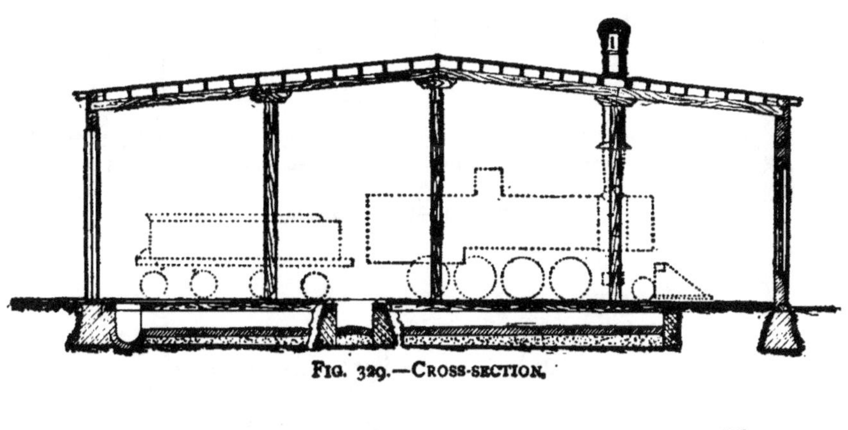

FIG. 329.—CROSS-SECTION.

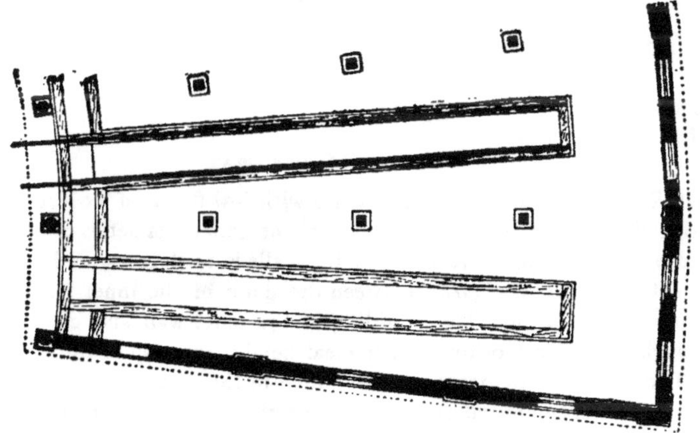

FIG. 330.—GROUND-PLAN.

pilasters. The posts between the engine-doors on the inner circle are of cast-iron, keystone-shaped, with the necessary grooves for the doors. The door-opening is spanned with an iron beam lintel. The opening is 16 ft. 6 in. high in the clear above top of rail. The wooden posts supporting the roof inside the building are 12 in. × 12 in. The girders of the roof are 10 in. × 12 in. on the inner slope and 12 in. × 12 in. on the outer slope of the roof. The purlins are 2 in. × 10 in. to 4 in. × 10 in., spaced from 24 in. to 30 in. apart. The pitch of the roof is 1 in 10. The pits are 52 ft. long by 3 ft. 8½ in. wide in the clear, and from 2 ft. to 2 ft. 6 in. deep below top of rail. The side walls are built of stone, capped with a timber stringer to which the rail is spiked. The bottom of the pits is made convex, and the drainage empties at the lower end into a stone box-drain. There is a small smoke-flue provided in the roof at the point where smoke-stacks of engines are when in the stall; otherwise there is no ventilation in the roof.

This house with 5 stalls cost in 1885, complete, $5200, or $1040 per stall. Mr. White states that he subsequently built a 10-stall house, with not such difficult foundations as the house at Clinton, complete for $8900, or $890 per stall.

Engine-house, Alabama Great Southern Railroad.—The engine-house of the Alabama Great Southern Railroad, shown in Figs. 331 and 332, plans for which were kindly furnished by Mr. G. B.

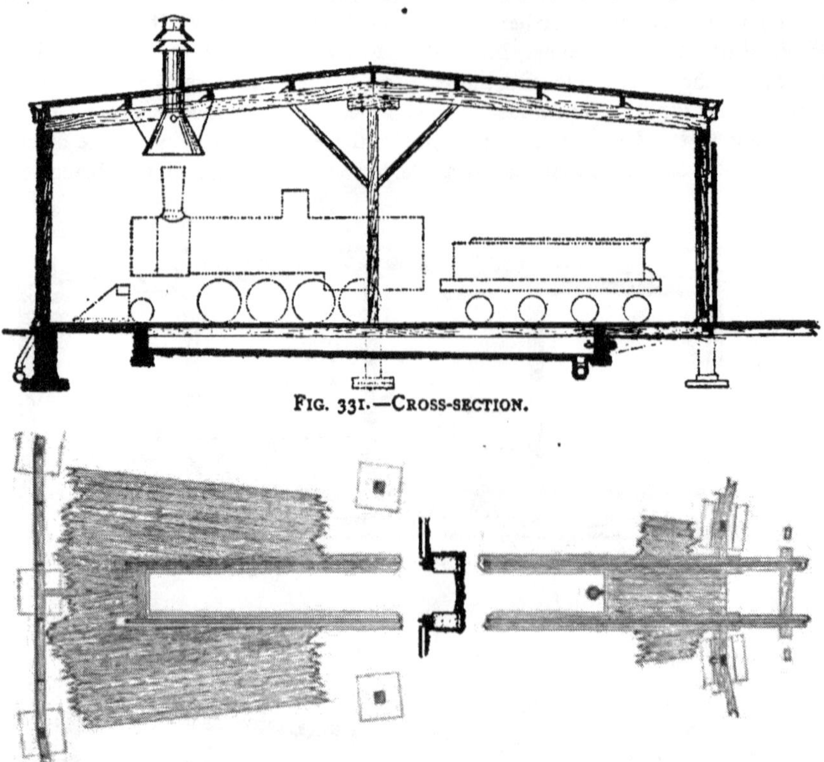

FIG. 331.—CROSS-SECTION.

FIG. 332.—GROUND-PLAN.

Nicholson, Chief Engineer, is a frame roundhouse with low flat roof covered with asphalt roofing-felt. The outside diameter of the house is 244 ft., the inner diameter is 114 ft. 8 in., so that the width of the house is 64 ft. 8 in. The angle of the stalls is 12 degrees, and the panel length on the inner circle is 12 ft. The wooden posts between the doors of the inner front and at the corners of the outer front are 8 in. × 12 in. The studding of the outer wall and gables is 3 in. × 8 in. The foundations throughout are on blocking. The clear height from top of rail to the roof girders at the walls is 18 ft. The doors on the front are 17 ft. high in the clear above the top of rail. The roof-girders are 10 in. × 12 in., supported at the centre of the building by a wooden 12-in. × 12-in. post. The purlins are 6 in. × 12 in., spaced about 8 ft. apart. The rafters are 2 in. × 4 in., covered with boards and 3-ply asphalt-roofing. The pitch of the roof is 1 in 10. The outside of the building is sheathed with 1-in. × 10-in. upright weather-boarding, and 1-in. × 3-in. bevelled battens. The engine-pits are 43 ft. long by 4 ft. 2 in. wide in the clear, and from 2 ft. to 2 ft. 6 in. deep below the base of rail. The side walls of the pits are brick, 13 in. thick, with oak wall-plates, 10 in. × 12 in., to which the rails are spiked. The pits are paved with brick on edge, dished towards the middle of the pit. The pits drain into a 10-in. vitrified-clay drain-pipe. The floor in the building consists of 2-in. oak plank on 4-in. × 6-in. mud-sills, spaced 3 ft. apart, and well bedded in cinder or ballast. The top of floor is level with the top of rails. A 2-ft. smoke-flue of No. 16 galvanized iron in each stall takes the smoke from the smoke-stacks of the engines.

Engine-house at Beardstown, Ill., Chicago, Burlington & Quincy Railroad.—The engine-house of the Chicago, Burlington & Quincy Railroad at Beardstown, Ill., shown in Figs. 333 to 337, plans for

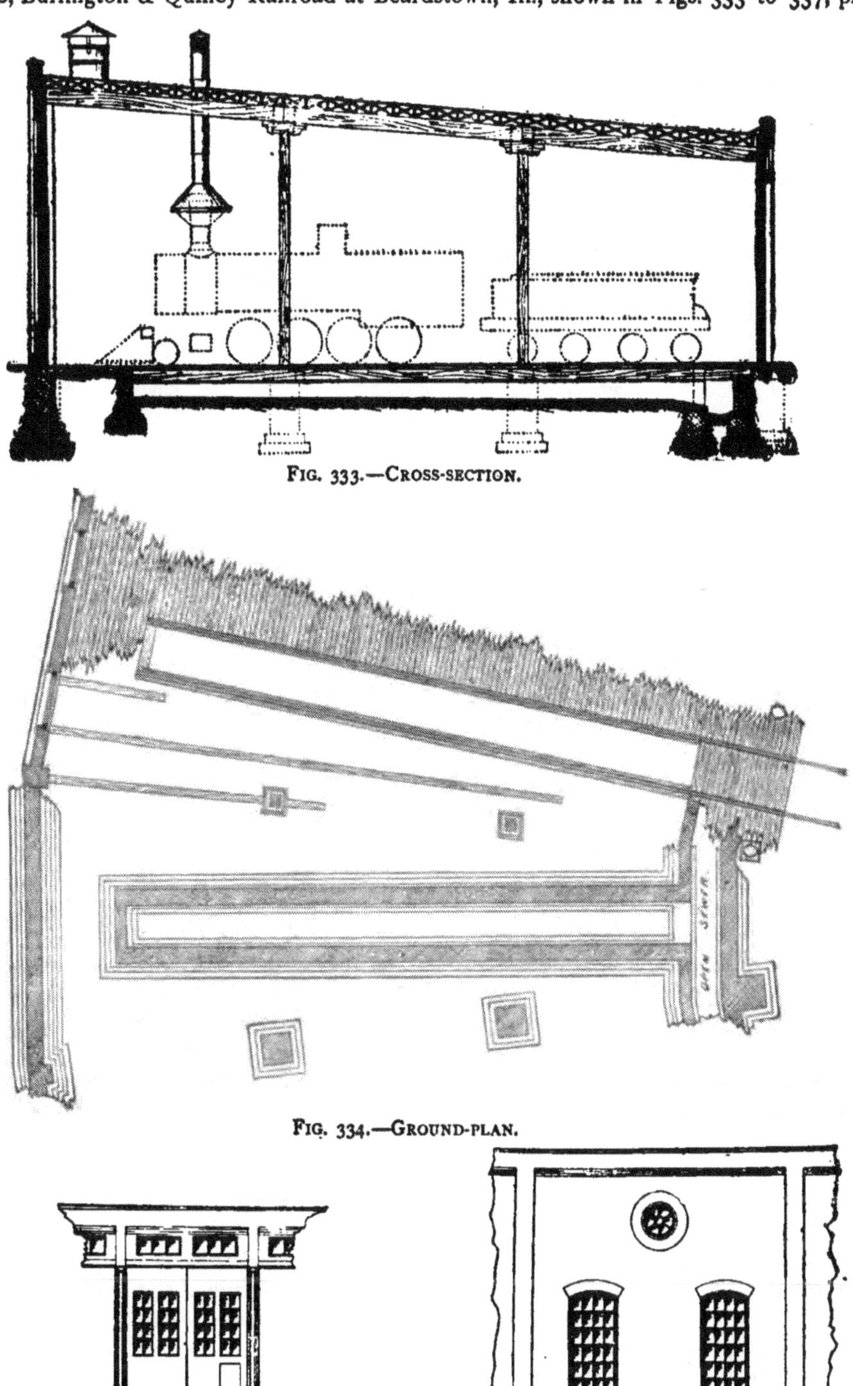

Fig. 333.—Cross-section.

Fig. 334.—Ground-plan.

Fig. 335.—Elevation of Interior Wall and Engine-doors. Fig. 336.—Elevation of Outside Wall.

which were kindly furnished by Mr. Wm. Forsyth, Mechanical Engineer, C., B. & Q. R. R., is an 18-stall segment of a 30-stall brick roundhouse, with a low flat girder roof resting on timber posts in the interior of the building, and covered with a tarred gravel roof. The outside diameter of the house is 256 ft., the inner diameter is 120 ft., and the diameter of the turn-table is 60 ft. The width of the house is, therefore, 68 ft., and the space between the turn-table and the inner circle of the house is 30 ft. The angle of the stalls is 12 degrees. The panel length on the inner circle is 12 ft. 6 in., and on the outer circle 26 ft. 7 in. The clear height from the top of the rail to the roof girder at the inner wall is 18 ft.

The foundations of the wall are of stone, 2 ft. thick, capped at the ground level with an 8-in. stone coping. The outer wall is of brick, 13 in. thick, panelled on the outside, and with pilasters at the angles on the inside and outside of the wall, the thickness of the wall at the pilasters being 26 in.

FIG. 337.—END ELEVATION.

There are two windows in each panel of the outside wall, each window having 24 lights, 12 in. × 18 in. The inner front consists of cast-iron columns between the doors, the door-opening being spanned by a cast-iron lintel. The door-opening is 11 ft. 5 in. wide in the clear and 16 ft. 3½ in. high in the clear. The doors are square-top, panelled and glazed, as shown, and swing inwardly.

The roof is a single-pitched roof on a slope of 1 in 12, the highest point being at the outer wall. The roof-girders are supported inside the house by two 10-in. × 10-in. timber posts, with cast-iron bed-plates resting on 12-in. stone pedestals, with a stone foundation 4 ft. 9 in. square. The girders are two pieces, respectively, 6 in. × 16 in., 7 in. × 16 in., and 8 in. × 16 in., for the three spans starting from the inner wall to the outside of the building. The purlins are 2 in. × 12 in., and 3 in. × 12 in., spaced to suit the span. The roof is covered with ⅞-in. boards and a tarred gravelled roofing-felt.

The engine-pits are 52 ft. 8 in. long by 3 ft. 10 in. wide in the clear, and from 2 ft. 8 in. to 3 ft. 2 in. deep below the top of the rail. The pits are built with a convex bottom, so as to throw the water toward each side wall. The top of the walls is covered with a 12-in. × 12-in. wall-plate to which the rail is spiked, the top of the rail being level with the floor of the house. The drainage of the pits is excellent, consisting of an opening at the lower end leading directly into a stone box-sewer 33 in. wide, with a concave concrete bottom and covered with the floor-timbers, making the sewer thus easily accessible for cleaning out and repairs. The flooring in the house consists of 2-in. plank laid on mud-sills.

The ventilation is effected at the high end of the roof next to the outer wall by a 3-ft. 4-in. round sheet-iron ventilator in the roof over each stall. There is also a smoke-stack with a movable bell-shaped lower piece hung in the roof, the centre of the stack being 14 ft. 4 in. from the inner face of the outer wall. The rain-water is carried down from the roof at every fourth column of the inner circle through a 4-in. round down-conductor to the box-drain inside of the house.

Engine-house at Waycross, Ga., Savannah, Florida & Western Railway.—The engine-house of the Savannah, Florida & Western Railway at Waycross, Ga., shown in Fig. 338, designed by Mr. W. B. W. Howe, Jr., Chief Engineer, S., F. & W. Ry., is a segment of a frame roundhouse with a low single-pitched flat roof covered with tarred roofing-felt. The outside diameter is about 276 ft., the inner diameter is about 138 ft, and the diameter of the turn-table is 54 ft. The width of the house is, therefore, 69 ft., and the space between the turn-table and the inner circle of the house is 42 ft. The clear height of the door-opening is 17 ft. above the top of rail.

The posts at the angles of the outer wall, also inside the house, and between the doors on the inner wall, are of wood, 8 in. × 8 in., with 6-in. × 8-in. plates. The posts rest on 12-in. stone pedestals, bedded on small stone piers. The roof-bents consist of 3-in. × 8 in. principal rafters, 2-in. × 6-in. tie-beams, and 2-in. × 8-in. braces, as shown. The purlins are 2 in. × 8 in., covered with 1-in. boards and tarred roofing-felt. The roof is single-pitched, with a slope of 1 in 7. The engine-pits are located centrally in each stall, and are 46 ft. long by 4 ft. 3 in. wide in the clear, and from 2 ft. to 2 ft. 4 in. deep. The design of the engine-pits, more especially the cast-iron chair for holding the rails on the side walls, has been previously described and illustrated in Figs. 153 and 154 in the chapter on Ashpits. The pits are built of brick, with 14-in. side walls, the rails being bolted to cast-iron chairs walled into the brick side walls at intervals of 4 ft. The bottom of the pit is built convex. The drainage from the pits is effected through a 4-in. terra-cotta drain-pipe leading into an open ditch

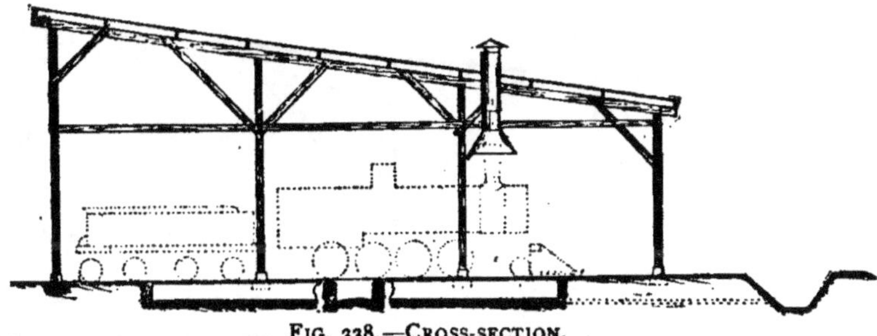

FIG. 338.—CROSS-SECTION.

around the outside of the building. The highest point of the roof is at the inner wall. Ventilation is effected by means of a smoke-stack in each stall hung in the roof over the pit, the stack having a movable lower bell-shaped piece to fit over the smoke-stack of engines. The outside of the building is sheathed with horizontal weather-boarding. There are two square windows in each panel of the outer wall, the windows being located next to the angles of the panel, the middle space of the panel opposite the end of the engine-pit being occupied on the inside of the wall by a series of closets.

Engine-house at Ashland, Wis., Wisconsin Central Railroad.—The engine-house of the Wisconsin Central Railroad at Ashland, Wis., shown in Figs. 339 and 340, is a 10-stall segment of a 32-stall full-circle roundhouse, with brick walls and a low flat single-pitched girder roof, covered with a tarred gravel roof. The outside diameter of the house is 262 ft., the inner diameter is 130 ft., the diameter of the turn-table is 54 ft. The width of the house is, therefore, 66 ft., and the space between the turn-table and the inner circle of the house is 38 ft. The angle of the stalls is 11° 15′. The panel length on the inner circle is 12 ft. 9 in., and on the outer circle 25 ft. 8 in. The clear height from the top of rail to the roof-girder at the outer wall is 16 ft. 6 in.

The foundations of the outer wall are stone, 2 ft. thick at top. The outer wall is of brick, 17 in. thick, panelled on the outside, and with pilasters at the angles on the inside and outside of the wall. There are two windows in each panel of the outside wall, each window having 40 lights, 10 in. × 12 in. The inner front consists of wooden posts between the doors, each post being made of one piece 12-in. × 12-in. oak in the front, with a 10-in. × 12-in. piece of pine back of it. These posts rest on stone piers. The sill of the engine-doors is a 12-in. × 14-in. stick of oak, the rail being spiked to it. The door-opening is 16 ft. high in the clear.

The roof is a single-pitched roof, on a slope of 1 in 12, the highest point being at the inner wall. The roof-girders are supported at the centre of the house by a 12-in. × 14-in. pine post, with 8-in. × 12-in. corbel at top, and 8-in. × 12-in. knee-braces. The girder consists of a 12-in. × 12-in. pine stick. The purlins are 2 in. × 12 in., spaced from 16 in. to 24 in. apart.

The engine-pits are located centrally in the stall, and are 51 ft. long by 4 ft. wide in the clear, and from 2 ft. 8 in. to 3 ft. deep below the base of rail. The side walls are of stone, 18 in. wide, coped with 10-in. × 12-in. pine wall-plates, to which the rails are spiked, the top of the rail being level with the top of the floor. The bottom of the pit is built concave, and paved with brick on edge.

The drainage is effected through a cast-iron plate at the lower end of the pit into a cesspool, the cesspools being connected between the pits by a 9-in. vitrified-pipe drain. The flooring in the house consists of 3-in. plank, laid on 4-in. × 6-in. mud-sills, spaced 24 in. apart. The ventilation of the house is effected by windows over the engine-doors at the inner front of the house, and through smoke-stacks of sheet-iron hung in the roof over each stall, the centre of the stack being placed 13 ft. from the inner surface of the outside wall. Although the house at Ashland has only ten stalls, there is a brick fire-wall in the house dividing it into two parts, so as to give greater safety in case of fire. This fire-wall is carried up some distance above the roof, and is only pierced by a small door.

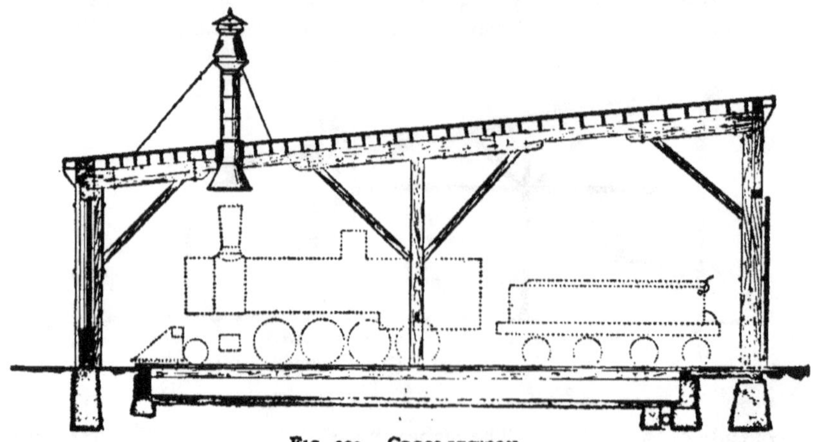

FIG. 339.—CROSS SECTION.

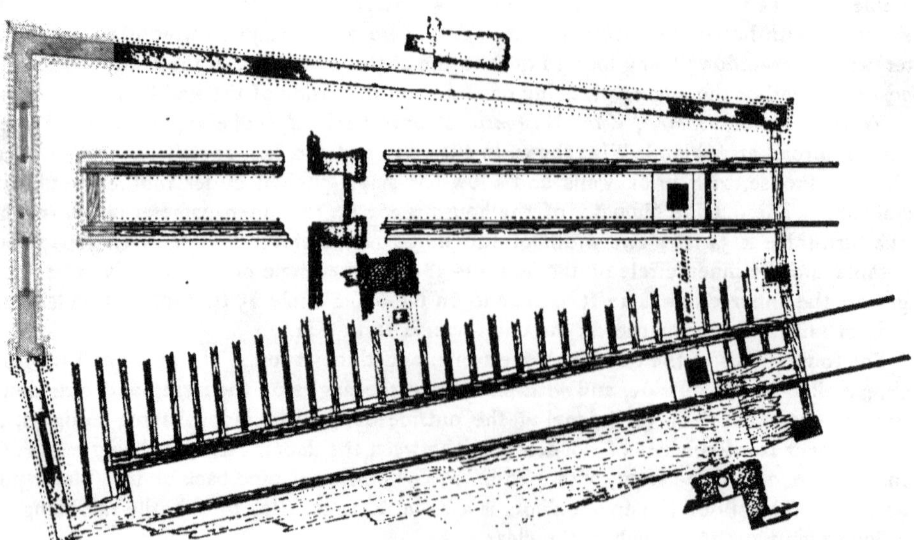

FIG. 340.—GROUND-PLAN.

Engine-house at Wilkesbarre, Pa., Lehigh Valley Railroad.—The engine-house of the Lehigh Valley Railroad, designed for Wilkesbarre, Pa., by Mr. A. W. Stedman, Chief Engineer, L. V. R. R., assisted by Mr. F. E. Schall, shown in Fig. 341, is a segment of a brick roundhouse, with a low flat girder roof, supported by iron columns in the interior of the building, and covered with a tarred gravel roof. The outside diameter of the house is 354 ft., inner diameter 206 ft., and the diameter of the turn-table is 60 ft. The width of the house is, therefore, 74 ft., and the space between the turn-table and the inner circle of the house is 73 ft. The panel length on the inner circle is 12 ft., and on the outer circle 20 ft. 7 in.

The outside wall is of brick, on a stone foundation. The wall is panelled on the outside with pilasters at the corners. Each panel of the outside wall has two large square windows with cast-iron sills and lintels. The inner front consists of Phœnix wrought-iron columns between the doors. The engine-doors are circle-top, hung in pairs. The door-opening is spanned by an ornamental cast-iron arch-plate and panel-plate above it, surmounted by a galvanized-iron cornice. The roof-bents consist of trussed I-beams, there being three spans, supported by the outer walls and by two cast-iron columns inside the house. These trussed beams carry purlins, which support the roof-boards and roofing material.

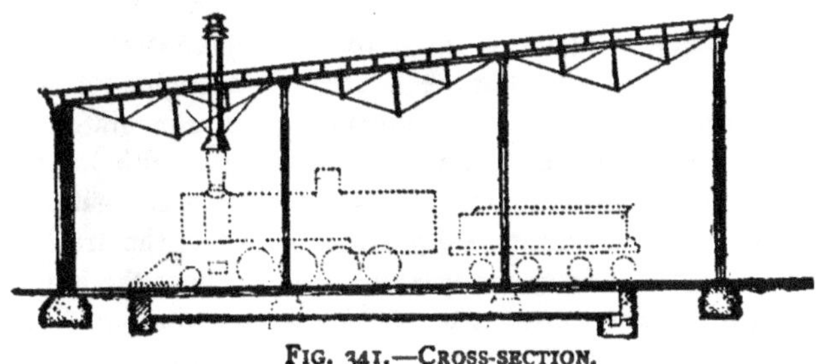

FIG. 341.—CROSS-SECTION.

Engine-house at Towanda, Pa., Lehigh Valley Railroad.—The engine-house of the Lehigh Valley Railroad at Towanda, Pa., designed by Mr. A. W. Stedman, Chief Engineer, L. V. R. R., assisted by Mr. F. E. Schall, shown in Figs. 342 and 343, illustrates a very unique method of

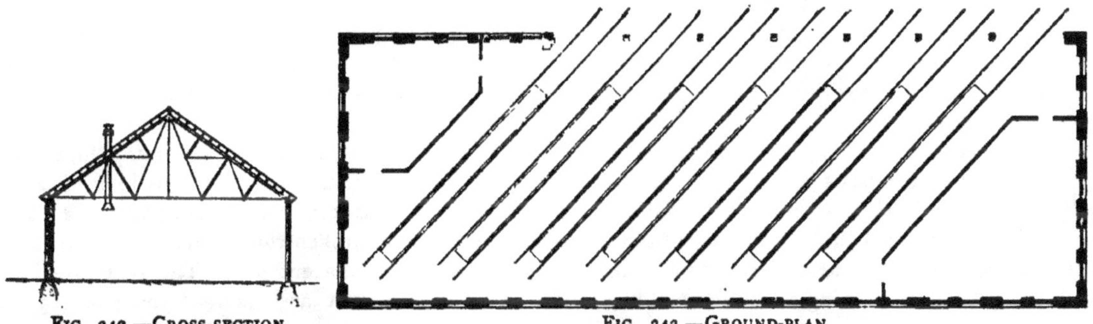

FIG. 342.—CROSS-SECTION. FIG. 343.—GROUND-PLAN.

utilizing a limited ground-space, adjacent and parallel to the main tracks of a railroad, for an engine-house. In the instance under discussion, the land available allowed of the construction of a square house, 63 ft. × 183 ft., with 7 tracks entering the building at an angle of 46 degrees with the face of the building. The tracks are spaced 13 ft. centre to centre on the square, or 18 ft. centre to centre on the skew, measured along the face of the building. The building is of brick, with an iron roof-truss, built on the triangular system, with purlins and roof-boards covered with slate. The columns between the doors, along the face, are cast-iron segmental columns, spaced 18 ft. apart. The engine-doors are steel roller-shutter doors. The opening is spanned by an iron lintel, surmounted by a heavy galvanized-iron cornice. The corners of the square building not occupied by the tracks are used for repairs and storage of supplies.

Square Brick Engine-house at Mauch Chunk, Pa., Lehigh Valley Railroad.—The brick car-shed of the Lehigh Valley Railroad at Mauch Chunk, Pa., described above in the chapter on Car-Sheds, and illustrated in Figs. 128 to 131, can serve as an example of a square brick engine-house for two engines. The building is 34 ft. 2 in. wide × 85 ft. long, of brick, with combination roof-trusses, roofed with slate. There are two tracks in the building, spaced 14 ft. 10 in. centres, which enter through two large circle-top engine-doors at one gable-end of the building.

Square Brick Engine-house at New Castle, Pa., New York, Lake Erie & Western Railroad.—The square brick engine-house of the New York, Lake Erie & Western Railroad at New Castle, Pa., is a brick structure, 53 ft. wide and 68 ft. long, with accommodations for three engines. There are three tracks running into the building, the central one of which has a track-pit under it. The foundations are of stone, and the walls of brick, 16 in. thick, panelled, the walls being 20 in. thick at the pilasters. The roof-trusses are spaced 14 ft. 5 in. centres, and are combination trusses with 8-in. × 12-in. white-pine principal rafters, cast-iron struts, and wrought-iron tie-rods. The purlins are 3 in. × 8 in., covered by 1-in. boards, and roofed with slate. The tracks are spaced 17 ft. centres, entering the house at one gable-end through three segmental-top engine-doors, hung in pairs. The clear opening of the doors is 12 ft. in width, and the tops of the openings are spanned by flat segmental brick arches. There are eight large windows on each side of the house and six on the rear gable, each window having 32 lights, 10 in. × 16 in. Smoke-stacks are hung in the roof to take the smoke from stacks of engines when in the house. The engine-pit is 45 ft. long, 4 ft. wide in the clear, and 2 ft. deep, draining at the lower end through an iron grate into a cesspool, from which an 8-in. drain-pipe leads. The pits are built of brick, and coped with longitudinal timbers, to which the rails are spiked. The floor of the house consists of plank on mud-sills, the top of the floor being level with the top of the rails. Hydrants are provided between the tracks. Small flues, built into the end wall, take off the smoke from stoves used in winter to heat the house.

Engine-house at East Mauch Chunk, Pa., Lehigh Valley Railroad.—The engine-house of the Lehigh Valley Railroad at East Mauch Chunk, Pa., designed and built under the direction of the author, assisted by Mr. F. E. Schall, shown in Figs. 344 to 348, is a large square brick engine-house, with a system of broken roofs supported on columns throughout the house. The house is 124 ft. wide × 132 ft. long, and has nine stalls running through it, each stall accommodating two engines, so that the capacity of the house is 18 engines. The stalls are spaced 13 ft. centres, and there are engine-doors at each stall at both ends of the house. There is a track approach at each end of the house, so that engines can pass in and out at either end of the building. The choice of this design was necessitated from the fact that the engine-house in question had to be built in a narrow mountain gulley. The track approach from one side of the house, if necessary, would have answered, but it was thought best to have approaches at both ends, so as to facilitate the movement of engines.

The foundations of the walls are of stone. The side walls are of brick, 17 in. thick, with pilasters. The posts between the doors are cast-iron segmental columns. The posts in the interior of the house are cast-iron round hollow columns, resting on cast-iron hollow bed-plates, the whole being so arranged that the drainage from the valleys between the broken roofs is taken down through the iron columns and pedestals to a drain-pipe leading into the adjacent pits. The roofs are built in 22-ft. spans, running across the building. The roofs at the front and back of the building are built on what is known as the "saw-tooth" principle, the long slope forming an angle of 30 degrees with the horizon, the front slope being set at an angle of 60 degrees with the horizon. Windows are inserted in the front slope, so that a large amount of light can penetrate the interior from above.

The interior roofs in the building under discussion were built as plain, symmetrical double-pitched roofs, but in the original design the intention was to have "saw-tooth" roofs throughout the building, with the windows facing the north, which is the best method of any known to the author to cover a large square building cheaply. This system offers the advantage of good ventilation and an excellent diffused light from above throughout the building, in addition to the feature that, the roof being low, the building is easily heated in winter. The objection to the fact that snow in winter lodges in the valleys between the roofs, and freezes solid in the gutters, is overcome in practice in this house, and in other places known to the author, by inserting a small steam-pipe along each valley. Where the house is heated by steam, as in the building at East Mauch Chunk, the small amount of steam required to thaw out the gutters, or keep the water from freezing, is inappreciable.

The pits are 114 ft. long by 3 ft. 11 in. wide in the clear, and from 2 ft. 4 in. to 3 ft. deep below the top of the rail. They are drained near the centre of the pit across the house, from pit to pit, by a 12-in. iron drain-pipe, connecting cesspools formed in the paving of each pit on the line of the pipe. The pits are built with stone side walls, coped with stone slabs, to which the rails are fastened with

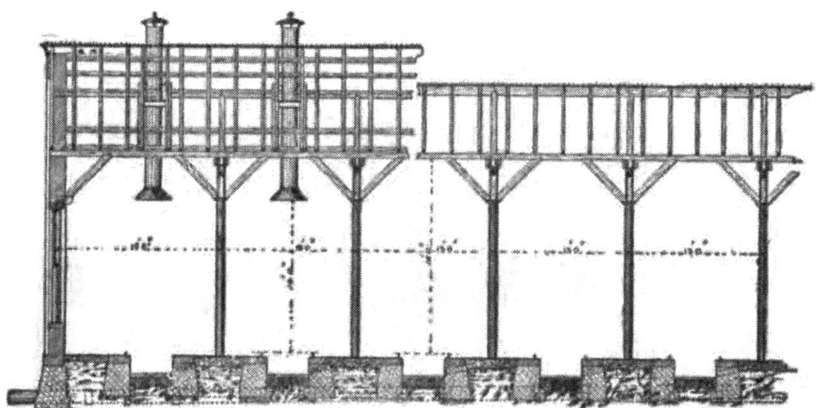

FIG. 344.—CROSS-SECTION.

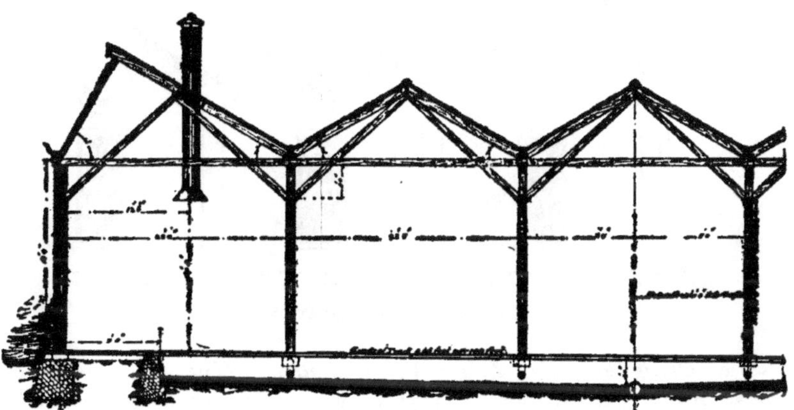

FIG. 345.—LONGITUDINAL SECTION.

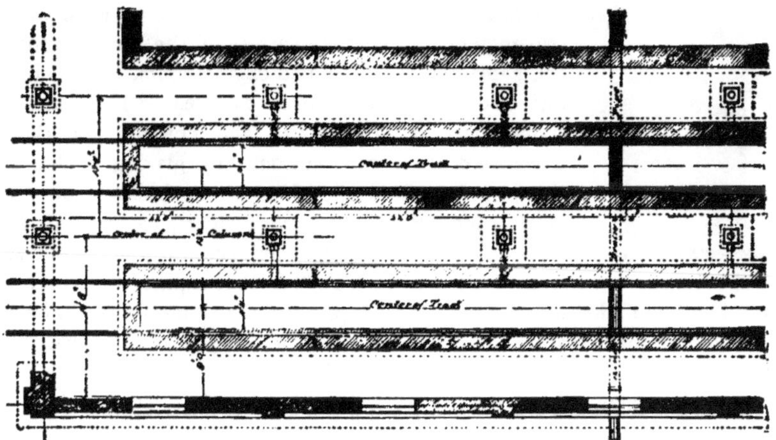

FIG. 346.—GROUND-PLAN.

clip rag-bolts. The floor is cement on gravel. The roof-trusses are very light, but braced both ways, so that the entire structure is very stable. Iron smoke-stacks are inserted at the proper points to suit the smoke-stacks of engines standing over the pits.

FIG. 347.—FRONT ELEVATION.

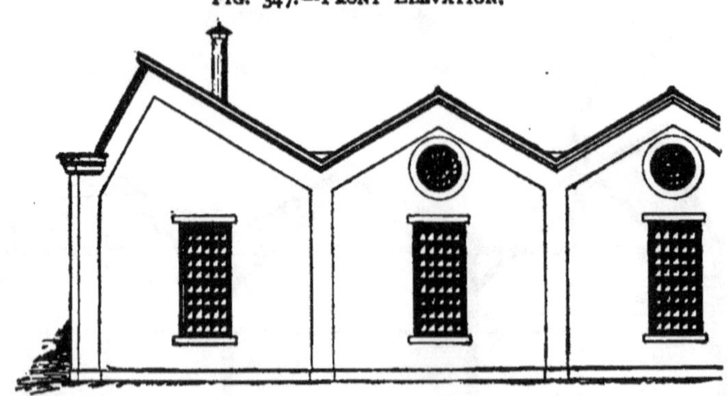

FIG. 348.—SIDE ELEVATION.

Engine-house at Orwigsburg, Pa., Lehigh Valley Railroad.—The engine-house of the Lehigh Valley Railroad at Orwigsburg, Pa., shown in Figs. 349 and 350, designed and built under the direction of Mr. Wm. F. Pascoe, Superintendent of Bridges, L. V. R. R., is a frame engine-house, 37 ft. × 140 ft., sheathed on the outside with corrugated iron, and roofed with slate. Two tracks enter the building, spaced 13 ft. centres, there being room on each track for two engines, so that the capacity of the house is four engines. At one gable-end there are two engine-doors, 11 ft. 6 in. wide × 16 ft. high above the top of rail in the clear. The doors are square-top frame doors hung in pairs, and covered on the outside with galvanized sheet-iron without any glazing. The rear gable has three windows, and the sides of the building have windows every 10 ft., each window having 32 lights, 10 in. × 12 in. There are three louvred ventilators provided, and four smoke-stacks are hung in the roof over each stall, so that engines can enter the house head first or back in. The foundation of the building and pits are 2-ft stone walls. The pits are 120 ft. long by 3 ft. 10 in. wide in the clear, and from 2 ft. to 2 ft. 6 in. deep below the base of the rail. The smoke-stacks are made of $\frac{3}{16}$-in. sheet-iron, 18 in. in diameter, with a 4-ft. bell at the base, the bottom of which is set 15 ft. 6 in. above the top of the rail. The height of frame is 17 ft. 6 in. from top of sill to top of plate. The bents are spaced in general 10 ft. centres throughout the house. The principal timbers are: sills, 8 in. × 10 in.; plates, 6 in. × 8 in.; posts, 6 in. × 6 in.; studs, 3 in. × 6 in.; principal rafters, 6 in. × 8 in.; tie-beams, 6 in. × 8 in.; truss-braces, 4 in. × 6 in.; purlins,

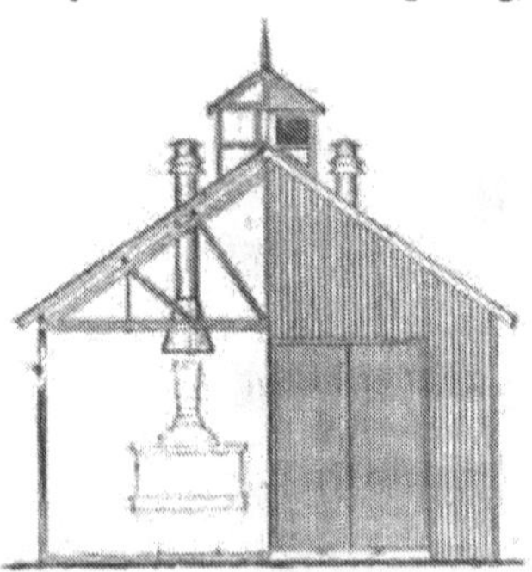

FIG. 349.—CROSS-SECTION AND END ELEVATION.

4 in. × 6 in.; rafters, 3 in. × 8 in., spaced 18 in. centres; roof-sheathing, 1-in. boards. Pitch of roof, $\frac{1}{4}$ rise. Rods of roof-trusses, $\frac{3}{4}$ in., 1 in., and $1\frac{1}{4}$ in. in diameter.

The cost of this house, including foundations, was $3629.38 for materials, and $2225.51 for labor, or a total cost of $5854.89, equivalent to $1463.72 per stall.

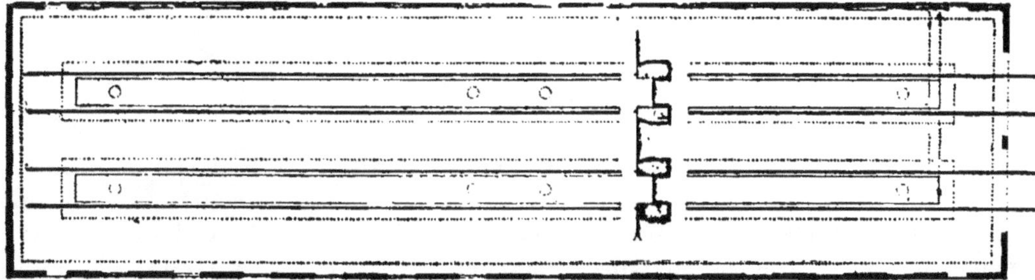

FIG. 350.—GROUND-PLAN.

Engine-house and Car-shop Rotunda at Mt. Clare, Baltimore, Md., Baltimore & Ohio Railroad.—The Baltimore & Ohio Railroad has at its principal repair-shops at Mt. Clare, Baltimore, Md., a rotunda, used at present as a car-repair shop, which design, however, can serve very well as an example of an engine-house rotunda. This style of engine-house is very common in Europe, but has not been adopted extensively in this country. The advantage of a rotunda design for an engine-house or car-shop is that the turn-table is covered, and there are no delays or trouble caused in winter from heavy snowfalls; in addition to which, especially for repair work, the superintendence and oversight of the work going on in the interior of the building is greatly facilitated.

Plans of this structure were published in the issue of the *Railroad Gazette* of August 22, 1884, in connection with the following description and remarks:

The external walls are built of hard brick, and the roof is slated. The space between the tracks is paved with Fall's Road stone, resting on a bed of salt-water sand rammed down tight. The building is divided into 22 stalls, and as it measures 235 ft. diameter inside, the longest passenger- or sleeping-cars can be easily accommodated. The whole building is completely roofed in, and is very well lit by the central lantern or clear-story, 100 ft. in diameter. The roof rises sharply from the outside walls to the base of the lantern, and is carried on lattice-girders, which, with the lantern, are supported by wrought-iron pillars, each composed of two 9-in. and two 12-in. channel-irons riveted together in the form of the letter H. Wrought-iron pillars can often be used very advantageously in lofty shops. They take up less floor-space than cast-iron columns, can be made considerably lighter, and are more easily transported and erected, and in certain cases these advantages render the wrought-iron columns the cheapest. The lantern is trussed, a precaution which is very generally thought unnecessary, the sloping sides being treated as struts, whose thrust is counteracted by a ring at the base of the cone.

The great height and size of this remarkably handsome structure are enhanced by the tasteful manner and light color in which the interior is painted. At first sight it might be thought an extravagantly large and costly structure to contain only 22 cars. But a little figuring will show that this is not the case. A rectangular building in three bays with a traverser down the centre aisle, and stalls right and left, enables each car to be moved without disturbing any other car, and in that respect gives similar advantages. A traverser, however, is not so easily moved as a turn-table, and would require a larger number of men to work it. The circular shed under notice gives a minimum clear space between cars of about 5 ft. 9 in. A comparison with a rectangular shed able to accommodate the same maximum length of car and giving a clear space of 6 ft. between cars shows that the rectangular shed requires the smaller roof to cover it, the area being 9 per cent less, while the four walls are 7 per cent longer than the circular wall of the turn-table shed, each, of course, having the same number of stalls. It would therefore appear that when it is a question of housing about 20 cars there is little difference in the cost, while the circular form gives more available space for benches, etc., as a turn-table occupies a smaller area than a traverser, and therefore less room is wasted. This difference is more considerable than might be supposed, and the circular form gives more working floor-space, in the proportion of about 13 to 8, when both sheds are full of cars and the space occupied by the turn-table in one case and the traverser-bed in the other is treated as unavailable.

CHAPTER XVII.

FREIGHT-HOUSES.

FREIGHT-HOUSES on railroads can be divided into terminal freight-houses and local freight-houses. The former are large separate buildings at important terminals of a railroad, while the latter are usually small structures at intermediate stations along the line of the road. Terminal freight-houses, when intended for the reception and delivery of local freight to and from a railroad, are located near some prominent thoroughfare, as close to the business portion of the town as feasible. If intended for receiving and shipping of freight by water, the freight-house is located on the water front, usually on a pier or bulkhead. At local freight-houses the freight is received from and delivered to wagons. At way-stations, where the passenger and freight trade are not very heavy, and especially where the freight traffic is more important than the passenger business, the use of combination depots is very generally adopted in this country, which class of buildings is discussed in a separate chapter under the heading of Combination Depots.

Relative to separate local freight-houses at way-stations, it can be said that the design almost universally adopted consists of a single-story frame structure, surrounded by high freight platforms on several or on all sides. If tracks are only on one side of the building, the station is termed a side-station, but if there are tracks on both sides of the freight-house, then it is called an island-station.

Where the business of a railroad is not very heavy, and car-load freight for a certain station is unusual, or else provided for by special car-load freight-delivery sidings, it is customary to locate the freight-house alongside the main track. If the road is a double-track road with light traffic, this arrangement is still feasible, as the small amount of freight passing to or from freight-trains on the far track can be skidded across the track nearest the freight-house, or a freight platform can be built on the opposite side of the main tracks from the freight-house, as shown in Fig. 351. At local stations considerable package freight is brought to the station shortly before train-time, and wagons are frequently waiting to take freight away as soon as unloaded from trains, so that very little freight would have to be transferred across the main tracks between the freight-house and the freight platform on the opposite side of the tracks. The introduction therefore of a special freight platform opposite the freight-house, as shown in Fig. 351, under the conditions mentioned, is a practical solution of the question of handling freight on a double-track road at a small way-station, where it is not desired to let the train cross from the far main track to the one next to the building, or the skidding of freight across the near main track to or from the train on the far main track is considered too dangerous.

Where the traffic on the railroad is heavy, a special siding has to be introduced, either in front of the freight-house between the building and the main track, as shown in Fig. 352, or at the rear of the building, as shown in Fig. 353. Topographical features, the land available, and especially the class and volume of business existing on the railroad and at the station in question, will usually govern and determine to a more or less extent what system of side tracks to adopt at a freight-house. In some cases the side track in the front or rear of the house has a dead-end, in other cases it is connected at both ends with the main track. In the former case, all trains have to back in or out of the siding, so that a dead-end siding should only be used, if possible, for cars left at the station, and not for loading or unloading freight to or from trains. In the second case, trains can run into the siding from either direction, and after discharging or receiving freight pass on. This siding should be, preferably, long enough to allow a freight-train standing on it to clear the main track, so that the siding can be used as a passing point for trains.

In regard to the relative advantages and disadvantages existing between the arrangement of tracks at a side-station, as shown in Fig. 352, and at an island-station, as shown in Fig. 353, the side-station has the advantage that less land is occupied; a much larger platform frontage is presented for wagon delivery; and teams and persons going to or from the freight-house do not, necessarily, have to cross tracks. The disadvantages of a side-station

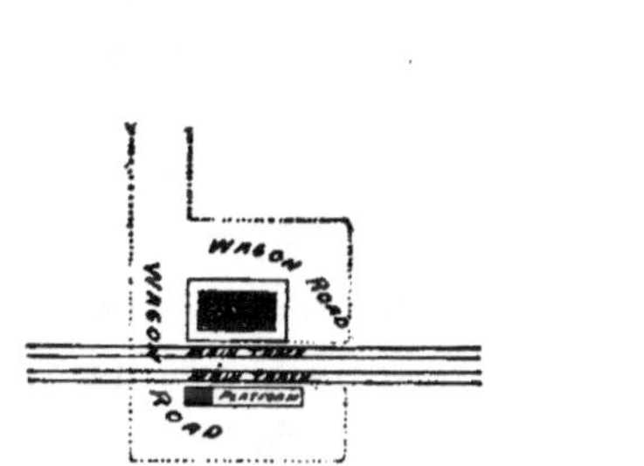

Fig. 351.—General Layout at Local Freight-station without Sidings.

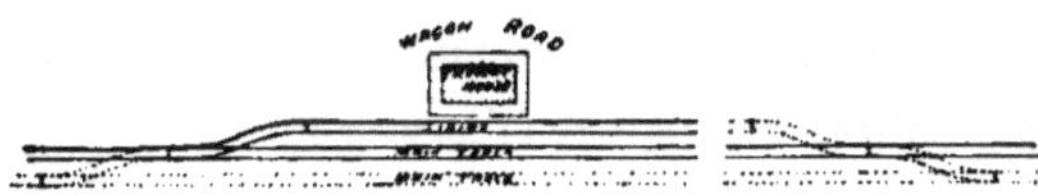

Fig. 352.—General Layout at Local Freight Side-station.

Fig. 353.—General Layout at Local Freight Island-station.

are, that package freight from or for freight-trains standing on the main track has to be skidded across the siding unless the train runs into the siding; and, if the siding is a through siding, then the cars standing at the freight-house have to be moved out of the way, while if the siding is a stub siding, then the train has to back in or out. The first objection mentioned, namely, the necessity of skidding freight across the side track, is frequently overcome in practice by stopping the car in the train on the main track opposite an empty or partially empty car standing on the siding and trucking freight between the main-track car and the platform through the car on the side track. The advantages of an island-station are, that the car-frontage of the platforms is increased; and the main-track trains can stop next to the platform without disturbing cars on the side track. The disadvantages of an island-station are, that more land is occupied; the wagon frontage of the platforms is reduced; all teams and persons going to or from the station have to cross tracks, unless the siding on the rear of the house is a stub siding, and the wagon-road can approach the station on the side of the dead-end of the siding; and the space at each end of the building between the main track and the siding is narrow, and therefore dangerous for teams, in case the horses are frightened by a passing engine, or otherwise.

A good combination of side tracks for a freight-house at a way-station on a single- or double-track road, where there is a heavy traffic on the main tracks and considerable package and car-load freight business to be done at the station, is shown in Fig. 354. If a special car-load delivery track is not desired, the upper end or the dead-end of the freight-house

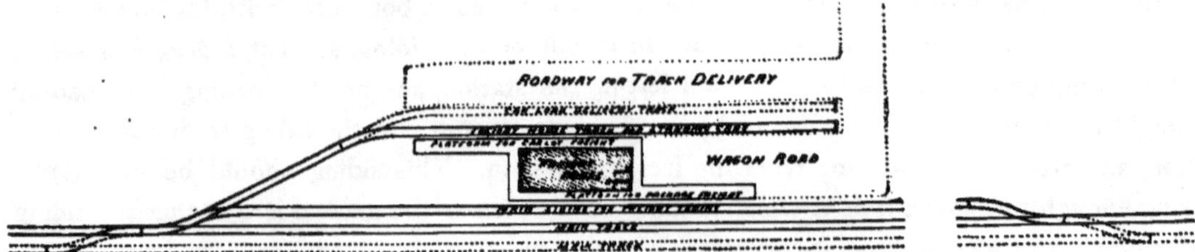

FIG. 354.—PROPOSED GENERAL LAYOUT FOR LOCAL FREIGHT-STATION.

track can be used for car-load freight. The extension of the rear platform along the freight-house track, as shown on the plan, is done to afford a larger car frontage on the platform, while the extension of the front platform gives a better frontage for freight trains and for wagon delivery, with the important additional advantage that package freight can be handled in most cases directly over the platform without passing through the house.

The characteristic distinctions between side-stations and island-stations for small local freight-stations having been discussed, the following remarks relative to the structures adopted in either case will be pertinent. It is generally customary to place the floor of the house at about a level with the floor of freight-cars, namely, about four feet above the top of rail. The platform is usually given a slope of from two to three inches down from the face of the building toward the face of the platform, so as to allow for drainage. The questions relating to the proper distance to place the face of the platform from the nearest track, so as to be safe and clear the widest car, and the correct height to set the face of the platform at, so as to be not only convenient for handling freight to and from cars, but also so as to allow the swinging-doors on certain classes of cars to open, will be discussed below in Chapter XVIII, on Platforms, Platform Sheds, and Shelters. It can be said, however, that the highplat form, placed about 3 ft. 8 in. to 4 ft. above the top of rail at the face of the platform, is the one most usually adopted for freight-houses, while the distance of the face of platform from the centre of the nearest track varies from 5 ft. 6 in. to 7 ft., the former distance, however, being only admissible for side tracks. The platform for receiving or delivering freight from or to freight trains need not be any longer than the building itself, as any part of the train can be stopped opposite the building; but the platform along the track for car-lot freight, where cars are left standing to be loaded or unloaded, should be longer, and it is generally extended away from the building, giving thus additional platform frontage, so that more cars can be reached from the platform without having an engine to shift the cars or necessitating moving the cars by hand. However, moving the cars by hand, assisted by pinch-bars, is not a serious objection, if the side track is placed on a slight down grade in the direction that the cars are to be moved. Car-load lots of freight are loaded, generally, from wagons directly into cars stationed on special sidings, and *vice versa*, unless each package has to be weighed, in which case the freight is passed over the scale in the house or over a small portable platform scale on the platform. The height of the platform above the wagon road should be less than the height of the platform above the rail. This is not so important in country settlements, as the class of wagons used are generally high; but in larger towns, and especially in cities, where there are a large number of low drays, it is desirable to have the platform for wagon delivery not more than 3 ft. above the street-level, preferably less. In cities, 2 ft. to 2 ft. 6 in. is a very customary height.

Relative to the class of building to adopt as a standard for small freight-houses at way-stations, it can be said that a substantial brick or stone building is not essential, as the increased cost of the large number of similar structures along a line compared with the value of the small amount of freight stored in one building, in case it is lost by fire, would hardly warrant the extra expense, unless a road is in a very flourishing condition or the contiguity of other buildings increases the danger from fire. Frame structures, therefore, sheathed on the outside with galvanized corrugated iron and roofed with tin or slate, or sheathed on the outside with weather-boarding or upright boards and battens and roofed with tin, slate, shingle, or roofing-felt, are warranted according to the importance of the building, the class of material in general use in each section of the country, and the financial status of the road. Freight-houses are generally left unceiled on the interior, excepting that protection boarding is usually run up on the sides for some distance above the floor to prevent freight piled in the interior of the building from damaging the outside sheathing. If the freight-house is located at a station where there is a separate passenger depot, and the freight business is run by an agent or clerk having his office in the passenger building or otherwise, it is not necessary to have a separate office in the freight-house. Where, however, the freight-house is run by a separate set of men, or it is inconvenient to get to the main office in the vicinity, then it is usual to partition off a small space at one end of the freight-house for an office. It is not customary to have windows in small freight-houses, as sufficient light can be obtained through the doors, which are practically always open when freight is being handled. In a large number of houses, however, transom-lights are provided over the doors, in which case the transom should have bars or a wire grating in front of it, so as to prevent entrance to the house by that means. The jambs of the doors should be protected for three or four feet above the floor by oak protection boards, or by cast-iron plates, or by angle-iron at the corners. Down-conductors for the rain-water are usually protected for four or five feet in height above the platform by wooden or cast-iron guard-boxes. Where the freight is heavy, it is customary to protect the upper edge of the face of the platform by an angle-iron, especially opposite the doors. It is also good to provide a wheel-stop at the level of the wagon-road in front of the platform, or else to fasten a wheel-guard on the front of the platform just below the top of the platform.

The questions affecting small local freight-houses having been discussed, the subject of the larger class of freight-houses at local or terminal stations will receive consideration. It can be said, in general, that for large freight-houses a substantial structure is very desirable, as the value of the freight stored in such a building is considerable, and the loss, in case of a fire, would be serious. Side-stations are usually adopted in preference to island-stations, as the business done through such a house and the rush of wagons at certain times of the day is so large, that it is necessary to provide as much frontage as possible on the street side of the building. In order to obtain, however, more track frontage, and also in order to be able to discharge freight without damage in bad weather, it is very customary to run one or more tracks into or through the building, in addition to one or more tracks along the face of the building on the track side of the house. It is essential in a large freight-house to make a clear distinction between incoming and outgoing freight. Incoming freight—that is, parcel freight arriving at the freight-house for distribution through the town—is unloaded promptly from the cars and stored in the house till taken away by the consignees. This class of freight, therefore, does not need much track-room for cars, as the freight can be unloaded at once and the empty cars promptly replaced by other loaded cars; but a large storage space will be required in the freight-house, as the freight will accumulate from day to day waiting for consignees to call. On the other hand, outgoing freight—that is, freight brought to the freight-house in wagons for shipment by rail—can be loaded at once into cars, if on hand, and removed promptly from the floor of the house. A much larger track-room is needed, however, for outgoing freight than for incoming freight. At some freight-houses cars are allowed to be loaded with freight for different points, the intention being to rehandle or reassort the freight at some distributing point or junction-station. At large freight-houses, however, a number of cars have to be placed along the house simultaneously, each car being destined for a special point, and the freight as it is received from wagons is distributed and loaded accordingly. In order to get more frontage on the track, platforms are frequently extended each way from the house. A platform annex to a freight-house, with a track on one side and a wagon-road on the other side of the platform, is frequently used for large lots of package-freight to be handled to or from cars or wagons without passing through the freight-house. The goods are tallied, and, if necessary, weighed by means of a small portable scale, as they pass over the platform. Car-lot freight is generally placed on separate side tracks along wagon-roads, known as track-delivery yards. Relative to the proper height of platforms, and the distance to set the face of platform back from the nearest track, the remarks made above with reference to small freight-houses apply equally well to large freight-houses, excepting that a large freight-house is never placed immediately along a main track. In order to increase the number of cars that can be reached from the building, it is very customary to run two tracks, or even more, along the face of the building, placing the doors of the cars standing opposite to each other in line, the cars on the nearest track serving to get to the cars on the far tracks. Tracks running into the building have the objections, that they require the roof-trusses to be placed higher than otherwise would be necessary, and the track pit cuts up the floor seriously, especially if two tracks run in the same pit. If the pit is only one track wide, it is very easy to skid freight across it, or to take freight through an empty car standing on the track. As mentioned above, it is very essential in large freight-houses to make a clear distinction between incoming and outgoing freight, and to design the house and the track system accordingly. The tracks for incoming freight should be opposite the main storage space of the building, which in turn should adjoin that portion of the street front allotted to wagons calling for freight. On the other hand, the wagon front intended for receiving freight from wagons should be as close as possible to the tracks for outgoing cars, with a certain amount of storage space provided between the street-doors and the tracks for temporary accumulations of freight. In a number of freight-houses the system prevails of shunting in loaded cars, which, after being unloaded, are reloaded with outgoing freight before being moved. Under certain conditions, and where the business is not very heavy, this system can be worked without serious delays; but in very large freight-houses the method of having separate tracks and portions of the house assigned for incoming and for outgoing business should be adopted, if feasible.

The following general remarks on certain characteristic details of freight-houses apply more particularly to the larger class of structures. The interior should be lighted by windows in the outer walls, or, better, by transom-lights over the doors, as the light from the windows is apt to be cut off by freight being piled up against the sides of the house. The light admitted through doors and transoms in a very large house is not sufficient for the varied amount of work, clerical and otherwise, that has to be done in the building, so that skylights or a clear-story are generally introduced. In large freight-houses one or more offices are usually provided at one end of the building, either on the ground-floor or in an upper story, or both combined. The freight-doors are usually sliding-doors, from 7 to 10 ft. wide and from 7 to 12 ft. high, either single or in pairs. The introduction of steel roller-shutter doors is very desirable, as it makes a fire-proof door, which occupies no floor-space when open, and can be shut at night without having to clear the floor space in case freight has accumulated around the door, as would be the case with swinging-doors. Wooden lifting-doors are used with similar advantages to steel roller-doors, where there is space above the door-opening for the door. Where this is limited, the author has in several cases used double lifting-doors to good advantage, the door opening being closed by two lifting-doors sliding in different grooves. Sliding-doors have the same advantages as lifting-doors and roller-shutter doors, so far as not taking up floor-space is concerned ; but in order to slide sideways the roof-construction has to be raised so as to allow the track and rollers to pass under the knee-braces of the trusses, or under the brackets supporting the projecting roof on the outside of the building. If sliding-doors are hung on the inside of the building, they have to be protected by guards or a partition, so that freight piled inside of the house will not damage or block the door. In northern climates it is preferable to hang sliding-doors on the inside of the building, although the rollers and overhead tracks can be protected to a certain extent from the weather by properly built hoods. A lifting swinging-door, hinged at the top of the door-opening and swinging upwards inwardly, has been very extensively used in connection with freight-houses and steamship piers, but it is a very undesirable device. The floor-space has to be cleared off for some distance from the door before it can be opened or closed; and if the hooks or ropes, which hold up the door when open, should get loose, the lives of men passing under the door would be in great danger. Ventilation is usually provided for through openings in the clear-story. In northern climates, however, the openings should be so arranged that they can be closed when desired. A platform is not necessary along the track side of the house, provided the freight-house doors are spaced, so as to correspond to the average spacing of car-doors in a train. For receiving freight from wagons a platform in front of the house will prove useful, where the street frontage is limited, as in case of a rush truckmen can place freight on the platform between the doors, and it is worked back into the house as fast as the freight-handlers can get to it. For delivering freight to wagons a platform is not needed, as far as the railroad company's interests are concerned, as each wagon as it is being loaded is backed up to the door. A platform, however, will frequently prove useful for truckmen to place part of the packages on while reloading or rearranging the freight on their wagons.

Relative to terminal freight-houses at the water-front for the delivery of freight to vessels and for receiving freight from vessels, it can be said that these structures are in nearly all cases built on piers projecting out into the water, usually with pile-foundations, although sometimes cribs with filling back of them are employed. Where there are several freight-piers at one terminal, a distinction is usually made between incoming and outgoing freight-piers and the piers are designed accordingly. Where the number of piers is limited, both classes of freight are handled over the same pier. The same conditions relative to the proportion of storage space required for incoming and outgoing freight exist in terminal-pier freight-houses as in large local freight-houses. Incoming freight—that is, freight for distribution by water craft around the harbor or for delivery to vessels or steamships—requires considerable storage space owing to delays waiting for the freight to be taken away. On the other hand, the unloading of the cars can be done very quickly. For certain classes of freight, for instance flour, the rules of the trade require railroad companies to hold the freight for a certain number of days before consignees are required to call for it, so as to allow for the proper inspection, classification, and distribution of samples before the consignee has to take the goods away. Incoming freight is also often consigned "to order," and railroad companies are obliged, in order to hold the trade, to store the freight in their terminal freight-house until the goods are placed on the market. Where the water-front is limited and very valuable, the use of two-story freight-sheds for the proper storage of incoming freight is daily becoming more prevalent. Flour and other freight, which will probably be left in store for some time, is transferred as soon as received to the upper floor by means of platform-elevators or barrel-hoists. In fact, the improvements in recent years in this class of machinery has been so marked, that it has practically removed the objectionable features of transferring freight to and from upper stories of a building. Methods for transferring freight lengthwise in a freight-house have not been thus far extensively used, but there is no doubt that in the future development of freight-house systems more attention will be paid to the mechanical movement or transferring of freight lengthwise of a freight-house.

Relative to the arrangement of tracks and the division of the floor-space in a freight-shed for incoming freight located on a pier with water-front on both sides, the best system is to have one or two tracks running the length of the pier in a track-pit at the middle of the house. There should be on each side of the track-pit at least five feet, preferably eight feet, left vacant as a passage-way. The space between the passage-way and the side of the building should be large enough to allow a car-load of freight to be piled in one row, which would require from 30 to 45 ft., according to the class of freight. Where the width of the pier will not allow this width for piling freight, then provision should be made for a width that would pile a car-load of freight in two rows. In other words, car-load lots have to, as a rule, be kept distinct and separated on the pier, and in order to use the floor-space to the best advantage it is desirable not to have broken rows. Platform scales are inserted in the floor of the pier at intervals at convenient points for passing the freight over them. Doors are located along the sides of the building at intervals corresponding to the average class of vessels to be expected. It is a mistake to introduce too many doors, as each door represents, practically, one passage-way useless for the storage of freight. On the other hand, if the doors are spaced too far apart the number of berths offered to vessels is diminished. The same remarks relative to doors, made above in connection with large local freight-houses, apply to doors in terminal-pier freight-houses, with the additional feature, however, that where there is an incline cut into the pier floor opposite the doorway the steel roller-shutter door deserves the preference over all others, as it can be easily made to run down below the pier floor to the foot of the incline. In connection with inclines at doorways on freight-piers, the advantages of movable gangway inclines cannot be overestimated. The upper end of the incline is hinged to the floor-timbers, or revolves on a rocker-beam, while the lower end is suspended by chains from an overhead gallows-frame, with the proper counterweights, shafting, wheels, etc., so as to readily raise or lower the bridge. The incline can thus be accommodated to any class of vessels lying at the pier, whether light or loaded, and at any stage of the tide. A light gang-plank from the end of the incline to the deck of the vessel completes the connection, and does away with the heavy and long gang-plank bridges which have to be used, at certain stages of the tide and with certain classes of vessels, when the incline is fixed. An additional advantage of the movable incline is, that a few turns of the wheel from time to time allows the bridge to follow any change in the height of the vessel due to the rise and fall of the tide or the loading of the vessel. The movable gangway incline has another very valuable advantage. It will frequently be found preferable to close some of the doors in the sides of the pier and utilize the space opposite them for storage. The movable gangway in this case has the advantage over the fixed incline, that it can be hoisted and held at the same level as the pier floor. As the chains and hoisting machinery are usually proportioned to hold only half the weight of the gangway bridge plus the heaviest load that is liable to be transferred over it, the author has introduced in a number of terminal-pier freight-houses, built under his supervision, toggle-irons or heavy bolts, which are run out under the ends of the incline by a lever worked from the floor of the pier. These toggle-irons are strong enough to allow the bridge to be loaded the same as any other part of the floor of the pier. For some classes of vessels and freight, doors and gangways are placed in pairs along the side of a pier, so that freight can be handled in and off a vessel at the same time, or the freight-handlers can pass through one door and back through the other, so as not to meet on the same gangway. Small doors in the upper story of a two-story freight-shed on a pier should be introduced to a limited extent. While freight would be seldom handled through them, they are useful in case of a breakdown of the elevators or steam-supply for running the machinery. In addition, these doors will give a better chance to ventilate the interior from time to time. In a single-story terminal-pier freight-house, windows in the sides of the building are generally omitted, as sufficient light and ventilation can be easily secured by skylights in the roof, or preferably by a clear-story. In double-story piers the upper floor is frequently extended across the track-pit, so as to utilize the entire floor-surface for storage, in which case side lights have to be introduced in the lower story in the sides of the building. These lights are usually made similar to transom-lights with fixed sash, and set high, so as not to be blocked by the freight piled along the sides of the building. In other double-story freight-piers, the upper floor is not extended across the track-pit, which reduces the storage space of the upper floor, but the advantages of this design are such that, in the author's opinion, it is the best plan to adopt. Ventilation and good light for the lower story is secured thereby in abundance; the clear height of the lower story can be reduced to what is actually needed for the storage of freight, independent of the height of the cars running in the track-pit; and a heavy and costly girder construction to carry the second floor over the track-pit is avoided. In this manner the total height of a two-story building can be made within a few feet the same as a single-story freight-shed.

In a number of cases, known to the author, terminal freight-houses on piers for incoming freight have been made very wide,—200 ft. and more in width,—with the intention of allowing two or three car-loads of freight to be piled in one row between the central passage-way and the outside of the shed. While the cost of construction in proportion to the storage space and water-front is decreased, such houses should only be used where the freight will remain for a long time in store and accumulate very heavily. The main objection to wide freight-piers is, that short-storage freight and freight that can pass from the cars almost immediately to vessels, if ready for it, have to be trucked a much longer distance than necessary. In such piers it would be more desirable, in place of a double-track well at the centre of the pier, to have two separate single-tracks wells, located nearer the sides of the building, so as to leave space between the track and the side of the building for the storage of car-load lots in one row. This would bring the track nearer the side of the building, and cause less trucking for short-storage or quick freight, while long-storage freight would be piled on the central portion of the floor between the two track-pits.

Freight-sheds on piers for incoming freight are usually made to cover the entire width of the pier, just leaving space enough on the outside for men to be able to pass lines back and forth and for placing mooring cleats and posts. Car-load lots of incoming freight, unless the freight has to be weighed separately, are generally not handled through the house, but from separate bulkhead tracks or tracks on open piers. In some cases it is desirable to place a track along the outside of an incoming-freight shed between the shed and the string-piece, so as to obtain the advantage that incoming car-lot freight can be handled and tallied by the same set of men as employed for package freight on the same pier, without the men having to leave the pier. Where business is heavy, however, an extra force of men can be easily maintained for car-load freight on open piers, and the water-front along the freight-shed will be reserved at all times for freight handled through the house. Where the business, however, in an incoming freight-house consists mainly of long-storage freight, and where at certain seasons the house may be fully stocked and yet very little freight movement be taking place, the railroad company will have a certain amount of water-front practically idle. Where water-front is scarce, a track along the outside of an incoming-freight shed, under these conditions, would prove advantageous in allowing the water-front to be used for other purposes than solely those connected with the house. Where such a track outside of the house is used, inclines at the doorways in the house are not required, as a gangway-plank thrown from the door to the string-piece across the track serves as an incline.

Terminal freight-houses along the water-front for outgoing freight—that is, for freight received from water-craft for shipment by rail—are one-story structures and generally built narrow, as the freight received is not kept any longer than possible in the house. The serious accumulation of freight in the house from one day to the other is only possible in case of the railroad company's inability to furnish the necessary cars, load them, and take them away as fast as the freight arrives. The same remarks as made above in connection with the doors of the lower story for incoming pier freight-houses will apply to the doors of outgoing pier freight-houses. The advantages of movable inclines remain the same. The lighting of the interior should be by skylight, or, preferably, by a clear-story. In the case of an outgoing freight-house on a pier with water-front on both sides, the best arrangement of tracks is to have one or two tracks running into the building in a track-pit at the centre of the house. Unless the house is very narrow, two tracks are desirable, so as to offer standing-room for a larger number of cars. There should be the usual passage-way left along the track. The width between the passage-way and the sides of the house cannot be specified in general, as it will depend upon the conditions under which outgoing freight arrives. A certain amount of storage space, however, should be given, as special lots of freight will have to be frequently stored temporarily on the floor, pending the arrival of a certain class of car intended for such special freight or for the special route the freight is to pass over. Some storage space is also needed for freight destined to stations for which a car is not put on the pier to be loaded for such a station until sufficient freight has accumulated to make a car-load lot. As this uncertainty or difference exists relative to whether storage space will be needed for outgoing freight, some outgoing-freight piers are designed with the track-pit located excentric to the centre of the house. Vessels with freight that will mainly pass immediately into cars are given berths on the side of the house where the track is nearest to the water-front, thus diminishing the trucking distance. Vessels arriving with a large amount of miscellaneous smaller lots of package freight, which has to be assorted, tallied, weighed, and partly stored on the floor of the house, are moored on the side of the building with the wider floor-space. It is very customary on outgoing freight-piers, such as last described, to have a track placed on the outside of the house, between the house and the string-piece, so that a large amount of outgoing freight that does not have to be weighed or distributed can be passed directly into the cars over the string-piece, and save the trucking through the house. Such a track, however, has the same advantages and disadvantages as mentioned above in connection with incoming-freight houses.

Where the number of piers at a terminal is limited, so that the separation of incoming and outgoing freight to different piers is not feasible, or where the relative proportion of each kind of freight to be handled is uncertain, which would be especially the case for a new enterprise or railroad, it is quite customary to build a freight-house that can be used by both classes of freight, which style of house could be appropriately called a compromise terminal-pier freight-house. The main feature in such a house is to place the tracks running into the house excentric from the centre of the house. The wider floor-space is allotted to incoming freight, and the side of the house with less floor-space is assigned to outgoing freight. In the case of one class of freight proving too large for its side of the house, it can be worked from the other side of the house, although to a certain disadvantage. If a track is added on such a pier outside of the house, between the house and the string-piece, the one structure will be adapted for incoming and for outgoing house freight, and also for car-load freight.

There will be the risk to run, however, that, like other finely elaborated schemes to accomplish a number of purposes at the same time, the conditions of the business will subsequently change, and be so entirely different from previous expectations that the system will not prove successful in actual working.

There is another class of terminal freight-houses along the water-front to which no reference has thus far been made, namely, freight-houses along the water-front of cities where the railroad terminal proper is situated across a river from the city, or in some other part of the harbor, so that there are no tracks in these houses. Incoming freight—that is, freight destined for distribution in the city—is brought to the pier either on lighters or in the original road-cars on board of car-floats, and then delivered to wagons. Outgoing freight—that is, freight from the city to be shipped out over the road—is delivered to the house in wagons, and then transferred to lighters or to cars on the car-floats for transfer to the railroad terminal proper. The advantage of using car-floats, in connection with transfer bridges for transferring cars from or to car-floats, is that the freight does not have to be rehandled in order to make the trip over the water. The adoption of car-floats, however, is only feasible where the business is extensive, as a large number of floats have to be kept on hand to handle the business, in addition to providing tugs, transfer bridges, etc. In these terminal city freight-houses the most customary arrangement is for the outgoing freight to be delivered into a bulkhead receiving-shed, whence it is trucked by hand to the car-floats. Incoming freight is usually unloaded and stored on the pier, which is arranged so as to allow teams to drive into the house the length of the pier and back up to the freight they are after. Where a bulkhead shed is not feasible, or where car-floats are not used, but the outgoing freight is loaded on lighters, the teams usually drive into the house and deliver the outgoing freight on the floor of the pier. As the space available for freight-houses along the water-front of a city is generally confined in one way or the other, the exact design to be adopted for such houses will be generally dependent upon a large number of local conditions. The necessity, however, for a strict division of incoming and outgoing freight, and for a proper proportioning of the relative floor-space required for the two classes of freight, is of the same importance in city freight-houses as for large terminal railroad freight-houses. In examining existing freight-houses along the water-front of a city, it will be found that incoming freight requires about three to five times as much floor-space as outgoing freight. For this reason, and on account of the great value of the ground along a water-front, two-story freight-sheds have been adopted, with good results. Long-storage freight is transferred at once to the upper story out of the way of quick freight. In this connection attention should be again directed to the advantages that modern hoisting machinery offers for transferring freight from different stories of a building, and to the advisability of adopting mechanical means for moving freight lengthwise of a freight-house. Mechanical appliances for moving freight from a second story down to a bulkhead shed for delivery to teams are worthy of serious consideration in localities where the ground-space is valuable and the street frontage limited.

The following remarks apply in general to all classes of freight-sheds located on piers. The structures are built of more or less permanent materials, and the method of construction deserves the preference that will allow of a downwards or sideways movement of the foundation to a limited extent without causing serious trouble, as however well and carefully a foundation in running water may be built, settlements or side movements from various reasons are liable to occur with time. Therefore, brick or stone structures are practically excluded. Freight sheds are generally built with a wooden frame, covered with sheathing or corrugated iron, with wooden or combination roof-trusses, and roofed with tin, roofing-felt, or a gravel roof. Slate roofs are excluded, as a rule, on account of the extra weight and the unstable character of the foundations. Where it is desired to have a more fire-proof structure, or to render repairs less frequent, which, if required constantly, would cause serious detentions to a heavy business, it is customary to build an all-iron shed. Relative to the roofing, a tin roof allows a very flat slope to be adopted, thereby cheapening the construction materially. Where piers are located, however, near salt water, it is claimed that a tarred felt and gravel roof will give better service than a tin roof, as the latter, unless kept well painted, deteriorates rapidly. A gravel roof, however, is heavier than a tin roof. Relative to the interior of the building, it can be said that costly designs of large-span roof-trusses, in order to avoid posts in the interior of the building, are not absolutely warranted, excepting where wagons drive into the pier, and even then posts can be distributed to a limited extent in such a way in the building as not to be a serious objection. In fact, under certain conditions and for certain classes of freight, which has to be collected, assorted, and distributed according to its destination point, it is actually convenient to have posts in the building, as the posts are labelled with the names of stations, and freight is piled around them accordingly.

There is another general feature with reference to all large pier freight-houses that should be mentioned, namely, the houses should not be so long that the length of train standing in the house becomes excessive. Either the work of the freight-handlers will be frequently interrupted to allow switching to be done, or else empty or loaded cars ready to leave will be held for hours till the entire train is ready to go out. Such delays are less noticeable where the trains are short. Freight-houses 2000 ft. long and more actually exist. Such freight-houses are in one sense magnificent structures, but they are failures as regards the practical working of them. Cars ready to leave the house in the early part of the day do not leave till late at night, or even the next morning, owing to the difficulties of sorting out a limited number of cars on such a long train. In addition, the lengthwise trucking of freight in such a house is liable to be something very serious. Therefore, short piers and short houses, with short slips, easy of ingress and egress, is the proper rule to adopt in designing the layout of a freight terminal at a water-front.

The proper floor load to allow for in designing a freight-house depends on the class of freight to be expected and other local conditions. The best method to pursue in any individual case is to ascertain how certain classes of package freight are usually piled in practice, and to design the strength of the floor for the heaviest load to be expected. Passage-ways are usually left between different rows of freight for inspection and to gain accessibility, which fact can be considered in establishing the unit-load to provide for; but it must be remembered, that an engineer in designing a structure may have certain rules in mind relative to piling freight that seem perfectly natural, and which may be impressed upon the freight department at the start, but which will be very soon forgotten in the run of years, especially where a change of men in charge takes place. The unit-load assumed, therefore, should be safe, and cover all ordinary contingencies. It is not necessary, however, to endeavor, unless specially asked to do so, to provide for such unusual features as storing pig-iron, steel ingots, lead or brass spigots, copper-ore in bags, etc., over the entire floor for the height that a man can pile it, as, when such freight is handled, the freight men in charge readily realize the character of the material they are handling, and will pile it in limited tiers, with ample floor-space between the rows.

Attention should be called, in a general way, to the fact that in Europe hydraulic machinery and mechanical-transfer methods are used in freight-houses to a much larger extent than in this country. Admitting that the conditions of the business encountered there vary considerably from those in this country, still the author stands not alone among engineers and railroad men in this country who have pointed out the desirability of more attention being paid to this feature of the freight-handling business.

The structures known as store-houses and bonded warehouses are connected with the subject of freight-houses, and can be considered as an extension on a large scale of freight-houses for long-storage freight. These structures, generally, consist of fire-proof brick or stone buildings, several stories high, built on land where the proper foundations can be obtained and the space is not as valuable as at the water-front, although sometimes they are built close to the water-front back of bulkheads. A full discussion of these structures does not come within the province of railroad structures, as they are usually built and controlled by other parties than railroad companies, although in individual cases railroad companies have built such structures to good advantage. A special kind of store-house is the so-called cold-storage warehouse, designed for the storage of perishable freight. In a number of cases railroad companies have erected and controlled such structures in connection with their freight terminals, and it can be said in general, that such a structure, if conducted properly, in a locality where the conditions warrant it, will always prove a source of revenue and be the means of drawing additional trade to the railroad company.

Connected with freight-houses and freight-handling systems, there are a large number of structures used on railroads for special classes of freight or materials, for which in each particular case a special study has to be made by the designing engineer, or else a specialist for that class of structures called in. Such structures are, for instance, grain-elevators; stock-yards; cattle-pens; stables; hay-sheds; and storage-houses for guano, phosphates, cement, cooperage stock, hides, flour, fire-clay, lime, etc. Each of these structures has its own peculiarities and distinctive features, and has to be designed in each case accordingly.

After above general remarks on the subject under discussion, the following descriptions and illustrations of freight-houses built in this country will prove important.

Freight-house for Way-stations, Boston, Hoosac Tunnel & Western Railway.—The freight-house design for way-stations on the Boston, Hoosac Tunnel & Western Railway, shown in Figs. 355 and 356, data for which were kindly furnished by Mr. Edwin A. Hill, consists of a frame building sheathed on the outside with vertical boards and roofed with slate. The building is 30 ft. × 20 ft., with platforms on the front and at each end, 8 ft. wide. The foundations of the building are stone piers, 2 ft. × 2 ft. 6 in. in size. The platform is supported by timber posts set in the ground.

The frame consists of 8-in. × 10-in. sills; 8-in. × 10-in. cross-sills and end-sills, framed into side-sills; 2½-in. × 12-in. floor-joists, spaced 18 in.; 6-in. × 8-in. posts, framed into sills and plates; 6-in. × 8-in. plates; 6-in. × 8-in. tie-beams at each post, framed into posts; 2-in. × 7-in. rafters, spaced 24 in. centres; 2-in. × 8-in. tie-piece, 4 ft. below ridge; 4-in. × 4-in. eave-braces, 3½-in. × 6-in. studding, and 2-in. × 6-in. nailers. The roof is covered with planed and matched 1-in. spruce boards, covered with slate laid on tarred felt building-paper. The outside of the building is sheathed with planed and matched 1-in pine or spruce boards, put on vertically, with bevelled or moulded battens, $\frac{7}{8}$ in. × 2 in. Flooring in the house and on the platforms is $2\frac{1}{2}$-in. spruce or pine boards. The corner-boards and casings are 1-in. × 5-in. pine; frieze, 1-in. × 12-in. pine; water-table, 2-in. × 5-in. pine; plank enclosing platforms, 2-in. hemlock or spruce. Transom light over freight doors is stationary, 8 ft. × 2 ft. 4 in. Doors in end of building, 2 in. × 2 ft. 10 in. × 7 ft. 6 in. Freight doors, one on front and one on rear of building, are 8 ft. wide by 7 ft. high, made of two thicknesses of planed and matched pine, $1\frac{1}{8}$ in. × 6 in., the inside layer vertical and the outside one diagonal, well nailed together with clinch-nails, and hung overhead with barn-door hangers. The gutter along the eaves is 6 in. deep, formed of galvanized iron, with 3-in. galvanized-iron down-conductors at each corner of the building, extending down underneath the platform, and enclosed for 5 ft. above the platform with 2-in. plank protection-boxes. There are no windows or partitions whatever in this freight-house. This design can serve as a very good example of a small, cheap freight-house for way-stations. A building of this kind costs about $750.

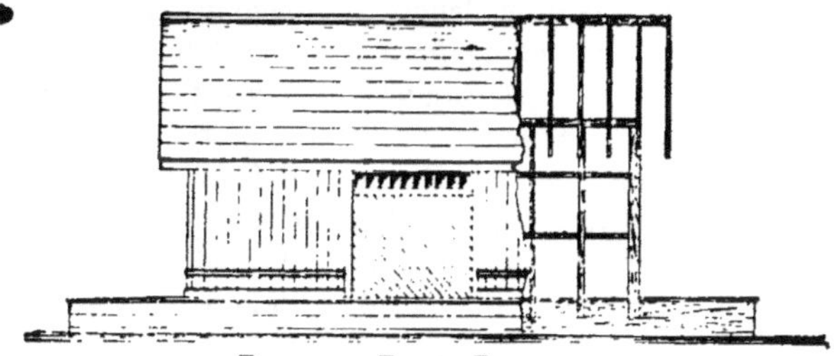

FIG. 355.—FRONT ELEVATION.

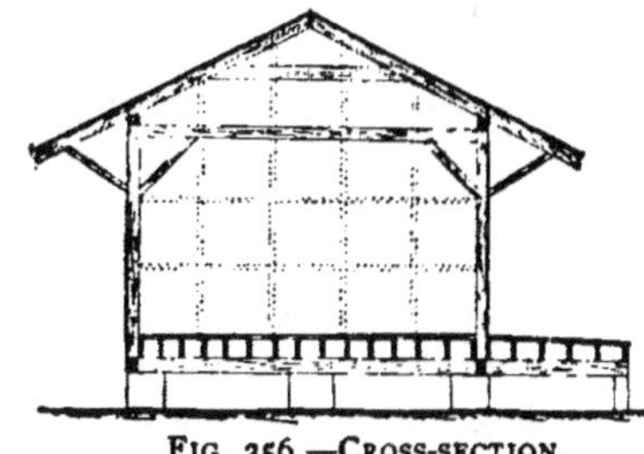

FIG. 356.—CROSS-SECTION.

Freight-houses at Brownwood, Tex., and at Gainesville, Tex., Gulf, Colorado & Santa Fe Railroad.—The standard freight-house of the Gulf, Colorado & Santa Fe Railroad, now part of the Atchison, Topeka & Santa Fe Railroad system, as built at Brownwood, Tex., and at Gainesville, Tex., designed by Mr. W. J. Sherman, Chief Engineer, G., C. & S. F. R. R., is a single-story frame structure, 22 ft. × 106 ft., surrounded by high platforms on all sides, sheathed on the outside with upright boards and battens, set on wooden blocks for foundations, and roofed with shingles on sheeting. The interior is divided into an office, 16 ft. × 22 ft., and a freight-room, 90 ft. × 22 ft. The office is ceiled on the interior, while the freight-room is left unceiled. The platforms on the front and the rear of the building and at the end next to the office are 8 ft. wide. There is at the other end of the building, as a continuation of the freight-room, a high open platform, 60 ft. long and 38 ft. wide. The design of the exterior of this building and the details and materials used are practically the same as in the freight end of the combination depot of the same railroad at Farmersville, Tex., described and illustrated below in the chapter on Combination Depots. This freight-house can be recommended on account of its cheapness and the simplicity of the design, and is especially adapted for pioneer roads, or where a cheap but efficient structure is desired.

Freight-house for Way-stations, Chesapeake & Ohio Railway.—The freight-house design of the Chesapeake & Ohio Railway, shown in Figs. 357 to 359, is a frame structure, 40 ft. × 25 ft., with

FIG. 357.—FRONT ELEVATION.

FIG. 358.—CROSS-SECTION.

a 7-ft. platform on all four sides. The interior is divided into a freight-room, 30 ft. × 25 ft., and an office, 10 ft. × 25 ft. The platform and the floor of the house are set about 4 ft. above the top of the rail. The foundations of the building are posts, bedded on blocks in the ground. The bents of the building are spaced 10 ft. apart. The posts are capped crosswise with 10-in. × 12-in. sticks, spaced 10 ft. apart. The building-sill is 12 in. × 12 in. The floor-joists are 3 in. × 12 in., spaced 18 in. centres, spanning 10 ft. The floor is 2½-in. plank. The studding is 2 in. × 6 in., spaced 16 in. centres; roof-rafters and tie-beams, 2 in. × 6 in.; plates, 6 in. × 6 in. The freight-room has a large sliding freight door at the front and rear of the building. The roof is a double-pitched roof, with hipped ornamental gables. The outside of the building is sheathed, partly with horizontal moulded weather-boarding, and partly with upright ornamental boarding. The interior of the freight-room is ceiled with 1-in. rough boards for 5 ft. from the floor up.

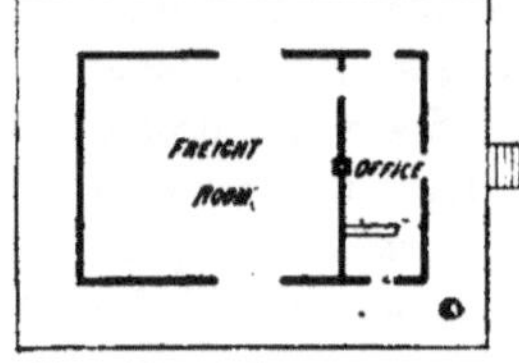

FIG. 359.—GROUND-PLAN.

Freight-house for Way-stations, Northern Pacific Railroad.—The freight-house design for way-stations on the Northern Pacific Railroad, shown in Fig. 360, is a frame structure 24 ft. wide and 80 ft. long, or any other length that may be desired. At one end 16 ft. is cut off for an office. The building is surrounded by 12-ft. platforms on all sides; the floor of the house is set 3 ft. 10½ in. above the top of rail. The platform facing the track is extended, 16 ft. wide, along the track each way from the building for any additional distance required by the business. The face of the platform is set 6 ft. from the centre of the track and 3 ft. 8 in. above the top of the rail. The building is sheathed on the outside with horizontal weather-boarding, and roofed with shingles.

FIG. 360.—PERSPECTIVE.

Freight-house for Way-stations, Northern Pacific Railroad.—The freight-house for way-stations of the Northern Pacific Railroad, shown in Figs. 361 and 362, is a frame structure 46 ft. × 100 ft. long, or any other length desired, surrounded by platforms on all sides. The platforms on the front and rear are 10 ft. wide, while at each end of the building the platform is widened, with an incline leading up to it. There is a track along the front and rear of the building, the nearest rail of each track being located 3 ft. 6 in. from the face of the platform. The platform is set 3 ft. 8 in. above

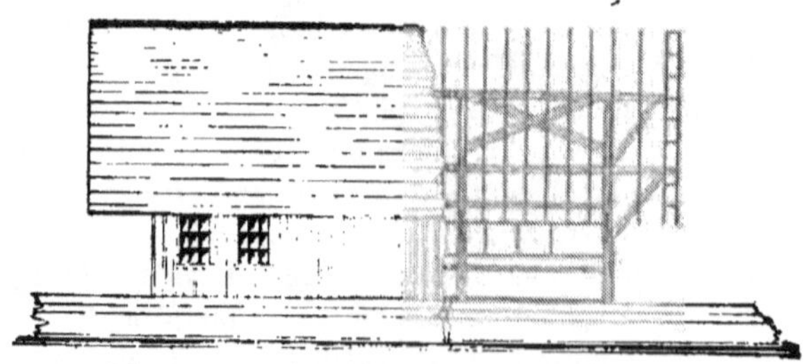
FIG. 361.—FRONT ELEVATION.

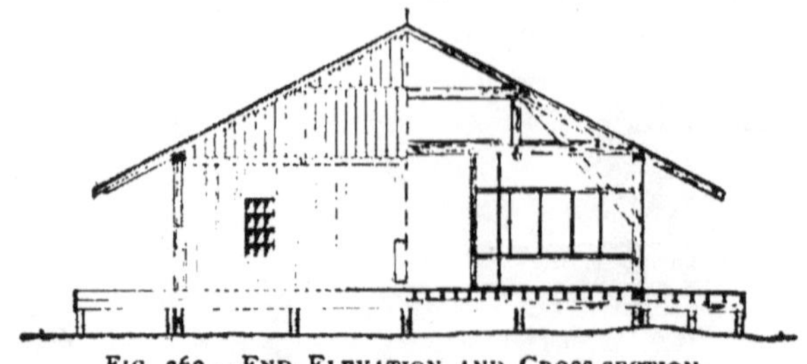
FIG. 362.—END ELEVATION AND CROSS-SECTION.

the top of the rail, and the floor of the house is 2½ in. higher. There is a small space, 14 ft. square, partitioned off at one end of the building, for an office. The outside of the building is sheathed with upright boards and battens, and the roof is covered with shingles. The freight-doors are 7 ft. wide, and are plain batten doors.

Standard Frame Freight-house for Way-stations, Pennsylvania Railroad.—The standard freight-house of the Pennsylvania Railroad, designed in 1886, shown in Figs. 363 to 365, plans for which were kindly furnished by Mr. Wm. H. Brown, Chief Engineer, Pennsylvania Railroad, is a

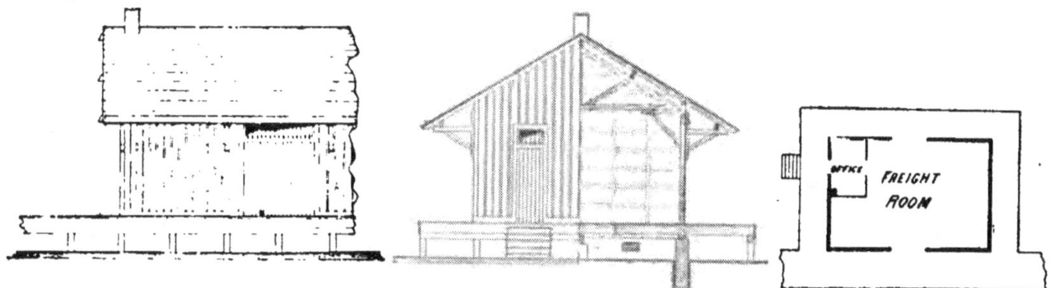

FIG. 363.—FRONT ELEVATION. FIG. 364.—END ELEVATION AND CROSS SECTION. FIG. 365.—GROUND-PLAN.

frame structure 24 ft. × 36 ft. 8 in., with a platform on all sides, the top of the platform and the floor of the house being set 3 ft. 10 in. above the top of the rail. The interior of the building has an 8-ft. × 12-ft. space partitioned off for an office. There is an 8-ft. × 8-ft. sliding-door at the front and at the rear of the building. The platforms of the sides and rear are 6 ft. wide, and on the front, facing the track, the platform is 8 ft. wide, extended for that width along the track for some distance each way from the house. The foundations of the house are stone walls, 18 in. thick, set on yellow-pine blocking below frost. The foundations of the platform consist of 8-in. × 8-in. yellow-pine posts, set on blocking in the ground. The frame of the building is of hemlock, the roof-bents being spaced 12 ft. apart. The corner-posts and posts under the bents are 6 in. × 8 in.; door-studs, 6 in. × 6 in.; intermediate studs, 4 in. × 6 in.; plates, 6 in. × 6 in.; sills, 6 in. × 10 in. Centre girder running through house under floor, 12-in. × 12-in. white pine, spanning 12 ft. Joists, 3-in. × 12 in. hemlock, spaced 16 in. centres, spanning 12 ft. Flooring, 2-in. yellow-pine rough plank. Roof-sheathing, 1-in. matched hemlock. Sheathing of outside of frame, 1-in. white-pine boards and battens. Roof-trusses, principal rafters, 6 in. × 6 in.; tie-beam, 6 in. × 6 in.; truss-braces, 4 in. × 6 in.; knee-braces, 4 in. × 6 in.; king-rod, ⅞ in. in diameter; purlins, 6 in. × 10 in.; ridge-pole, 4 in. × 10 in.; rafters, 3 in. × 5 in., spaced 24 in. centres. Platform roof projection, 6 ft., supported by brackets every 12 ft. The brackets, consisting of 6-in. × 6-in. horizontal piece, 4-in. × 6-in. vertical piece, and 4-in. × 6-in. knee-brace, bolted to frame with a 1-in. bolt, carry a 3-in. × 8-in. purlin. Roof-sheathing, 1-in. matched hemlock. The roof is covered with slate or tin on felt paper. The doors are made plain, battened on the back, hung on hinges for the office, and sliding on 6-in. cast-iron sheaves on ½-in. × 4-in. wrought-iron ways for the freight-house. Window in office, 3 ft. × 4 ft. 8 in. The transom-light over freight-house doors has a fixed sash of 1¼-in. white pine, with ½-in. round wrought-iron rods, spaced 6 in. apart in front of glass, as guards. The chimney-flue is hung in the roof, projecting 2 ft. above the peak of the building, and capped with a 2-in. flag-stone. The platform is reached by a pair of steps opposite the office, and by an incline at one end of the platform along the track. The face of the platform is sheathed with 2-in. × 15-in. yellow-pine plank all around the building, cast-iron grates being inserted, so as to afford ventilation under the house. The down-conductors are 2½-in. × 3½-in. galvanized iron. The office-door is 3 ft. × 8 ft., with transom overhead. The interior of the building is 12 ft. 4 in. high in the clear from the floor to the tie-beam. The interior of the office is lined and ceiled with 1-in. white or yellow pine worked boards. The woodwork on the outside of the building is painted with two coats of paint of standard tints, the interior of the office is finished in two coats of oil, and the inside of the freight-room has two coats of whitewash.

Standard Brick Freight-house for Way-stations, Pennsylvania Railroad.—The standard brick freight-house for way-stations of the Pennsylvania Railroad, designed in 1885, shown in Figs. 366 to 369, plans for which were kindly furnished by Mr. Wm. H. Brown, Chief Engineer, Pennsylvania

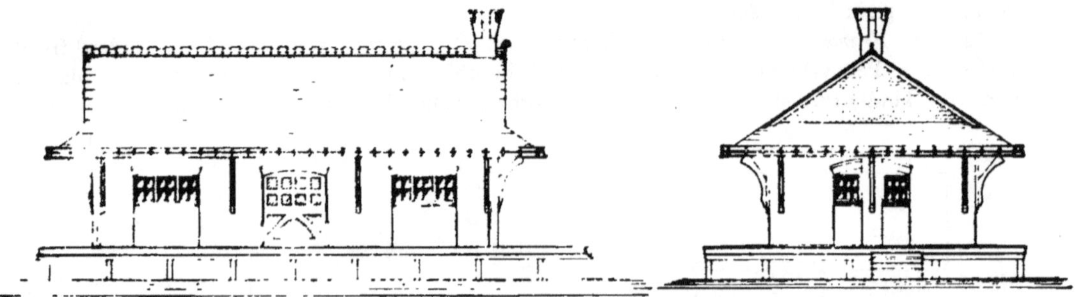

FIG. 366.—FRONT ELEVATION. FIG 367.—END ELEVATION.

Railroad, is a brick structure, 25 ft. × 50 ft., with slate roof. A platform surrounds the building on all sides, 6 ft. wide at each gable-end, 5 ft. on the rear, and 8 ft. wide on the front facing the

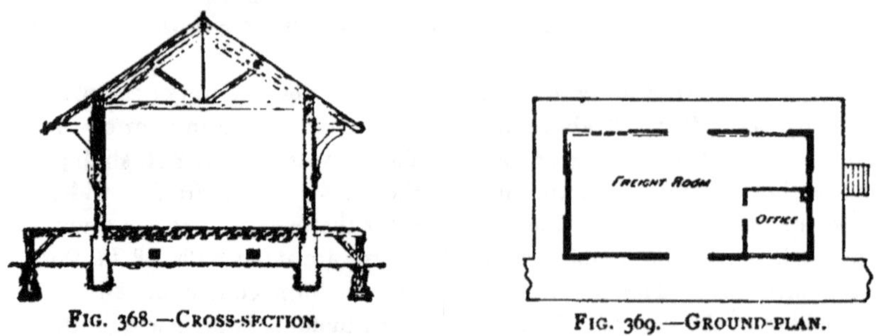

FIG. 368.—CROSS-SECTION. FIG. 369.—GROUND-PLAN.

track. The 8-ft. platform on the front is extended along the track each way from the building for some distance. The face of the platform along the track is 3 ft. 10 in. above the top of rail, and the floor in the house is set 2 in. higher. The interior of the building has in one corner an office, 12 ft. 4 in. square in the clear, partitioned off by a 4-in. glass partition. The remainder of the building serves as freight-room. The office is entered by a small door from the outside of the building. In the front and in the rear of the building there is an 8-ft. × 8-ft. sliding-door leading to the freight-room. The foundations of the building are 2-ft. stone walls around the outside, with two 16-in. cross walls. The foundations of the platforms are 8-in. × 8-in. posts set in the ground below frost, on yellow-pine blocking. The walls of the house are built of brick, 12 in. thick, with black joints. The doors and windows are set in panels in the wall, which panels are arched over with flat segmental arches. The roof-trusses are spaced about 16 ft. apart, and are built of hemlock timber, as follows: tie-beams, 6 in. × 6 in.; principal rafters, 6 in. × 6 in.; truss-braces, 5 in. × 6 in.; wall-plates, 3 in. × 8 in.; ridge-purlin, 5 in. × 8 in.; intermediate purlins, 5 in. × 8 in.; rafters, 3 in. × 5 in., spaced 2 ft. centres; roof-sheathing, 1-in. tongued and grooved hemlock sheathing, laid diagonally, and covered with roofing-felt and 8-in. × 16-in. or 9-in. × 18-in. Lehigh roof-slates. The rafters project over the platforms 6 ft. from the building, and are supported by a 3½-in. × 8-in. purlin, resting on ornamental brackets, spaced about 15 ft. apart. The pitch of the roof is ⅓. The gable-ends of the building above the platform roof are sheathed with ornamental shingles. The roof-cresting is of terra-cotta. The chimney is of brick, with ornamental top, covered with a 2-in. stone chimney-cap. The roof water is carried down at the corners of the building through 2¾-in. × 3⅛-in. galvanized-iron down-conductors, with cast-iron guard-boxes above the platform. The jambs of the freight-doors are protected by ¾-in. cast-iron guard-plates, 3 ft. from the floor up. The face of the platform next to the track is placed 3 ft. from the gauge-face of the nearest rail. The floor in the house consists of 2-in. narrow worked yellow-pine plank, on 4-in. × 12-in. white-pine or yellow-pine joists, spanning

15 ft., and bridged with three rows of 2-in. × 4-in. bridging. The foundation-walls, which are of rubble masonry in lime mortar, have at each gable-end two 12-in. × 18-in. openings for ventilation, which are closed by cast-iron grates. The platforms are floored with 2-in. narrow worked yellow-pine plank, laid on 3-in. × 8-in. hemlock joists, spaced 16 in. centres, spanning 8 ft., with 8-in. × 8-in. yellow-pine caps, resting on posts about 8 ft. apart. The height of the building in the interior is 13 ft. in the clear, and the height of the eaves of the platform roof above the platform is 10 ft. 3 in. The platform is reached opposite the office by a set of steps, and there are inclines at the ends of the platform along the track. In some sections a tin roof is adopted in place of a slate roof. The exposed woodwork of the exterior is painted with two coats of paint of standard tints; the interior of the office is finished in oil, and the freight-room is whitewashed with two coats.

Freight-house at New Hampton, Minn., Minnesota & Northwestern Railroad.—The freight-house of the Minnesota & Northwestern Railroad, at New Hampton, Minn., shown in Figs. 370 to 372, is a frame structure, sheathed on the outside with horizontal weather-boarding, and roofed with

FIG. 370.—FRONT ELEVATION.

shingles. The standard freight-house is 30 ft. wide by any length desired, the length at New Hampton being 120 ft. At one end of the building there is an office 15 ft. × 30 ft., divided off from the freight-room by a partition. A 6-ft. platform runs along the front of the house facing the track.

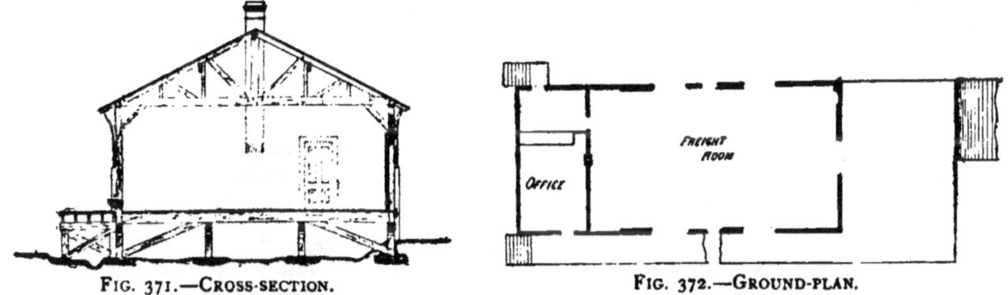

FIG. 371.—CROSS-SECTION. FIG. 372.—GROUND-PLAN.

At the end of the building away from the office, the platform is extended 36 ft. wide for a distance of 24 ft. An incline leads from the ground up to this platform extension, and at the office end of the building the platform is reached by steps. The doors of the freight-room are sliding-doors, 7 ft. × 7 ft., hung inside the house, with 20-in. stationary transoms. The foundations of the building are timber posts, set in the ground on blocking. There are four lines of 8-in. × 12-in. sills running lengthwise with the building. On top of these there are 2-in. × 12-in. joists, spaced 16 in. centres, spanning 10 ft. The floor is formed of 2-in. plank. The roof-bents are spaced 8 ft. 9 in. centres. Studding, 2 in. × 6 in., doubled at the bents; plates, 2 in. × 6 in. Height from floor to tie-beam, 8 ft. in clear. The roof-trusses have principal rafters, two pieces, 2 in. × 6 in.; tie-beam, 1 in. × 10 in.; plank-braces, from 2 in. × 4 in., to 2 in. × 10 in.; roof-boards, ⅞ in., covered with shingles; purlins, 4 in. × 8 in., hung under principal rafters of roof-bents; ridge-piece, 2 in. × 10 in.; intermediate rafters, 2 in. × 6 in. The 6-ft. platform is carried on 8-in. × 8-in. posts, with 8-in. × 8-in. caps, supporting five lines of 2-in. × 10-in. joists, spanning 8 ft. 9 in. The platform and floor of the house is set 4 ft. above the top of the rail, and the face of the platform is set back 6 ft. from the centre of the track. The wagon road on the rear of the building is 3 ft. below the floor of the house.

Freight-house at Gainesville, Fla., Savannah, Florida & Western Railway.—The freight-house of the Savannah, Florida & Western Railway at Gainesville, Fla., shown in Fig. 373, designed by Mr. W. B. W. Howe, Jr., Chief Engineer, S., F. & W. Ry., is a frame structure, 50 ft. wide by any length desired, with an 8-ft. platform on each side of the building. The outside of the building is sheathed with upright boards and battens. The foundations of the sides of the building are brick piers, while the intermediate floor-girders in the building and the outside floor-girders of the platform are supported by posts bedded in the ground. The building-sill is 8 in. × 12 in., and the floor-girders in the interior of the house and at the face of the platform are 6 in. × 12 in. The floor-joists are 3 in. × 12 in., spaced 24 in., spanning 12 ft. 6 in. The floor consists of 2-in. plank, the top being set 4 ft. above the top of the rail. The building is 12 ft. high in the clear from floor to tie-beam. The roof is carried by a set of posts at the centre of the building. The principal timbers are, posts, 6 in. × 8 in.; tie-beams, 2 pieces, 2 in. × 6 in ; ridge-purlin, 3 in. × 9 in.; plates, 6 in. × 6 in.; knee-braces, 2 pieces, 2 in. × 6 in.; rafters, 2 in. × 8 in., spaced 36 in. The freight-doors are 7 ft. wide by 9 ft. high, in pairs, built of 1-in. × 6-in. frame, covered with ⅞-in. narrow, tongued and grooved boards, laid diagonally. The platform slopes 2 in. from the house down towards the track.

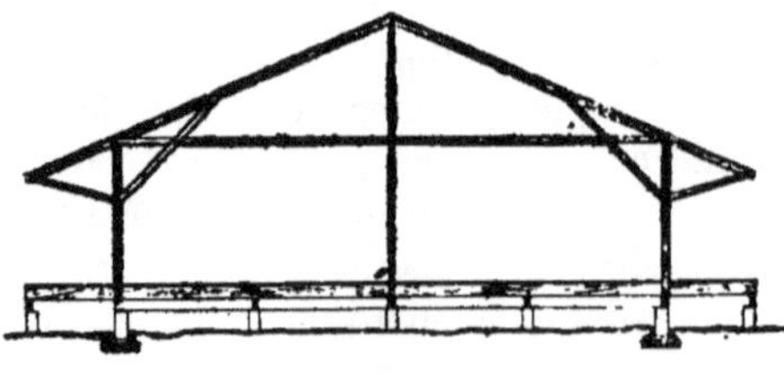

FIG. 373.—CROSS-SECTION

Terminal Freight-house at Jacksonville, Fla., Savannah, Florida & Western Railway.—The terminal freight-house of the Savannah, Florida & Western Railway at Jacksonville, Fla., shown in Figs. 374 and 375, designed by Mr. W. B. W. Howe, Jr., Chief Engineer, S., F. & W. Ry., is a one-story frame structure, 50 ft. × 294 ft., sheathed on the outside with upright boards and battens, and roofed with tin. There is a 6-ft. platform along the track, and a 6-ft. platform at one gable-end of the building. The building is divided by cross partitions into seven rooms, each 42 ft. × 50 ft. Sliding-doors, 9 ft. × 9 ft., are spaced 28 ft. centres along the front and the rear of the building. The interior is 13 ft. high in the clear from floor to tie-beams. The roof-projection over the platform is 6 ft. wide, supported by ornamental brackets. The foundations of the building are brick piers. The building-sills and intermediate floor-girders are 12 in. × 14 in., spanning 14 ft. The floor-joists are 4 in. × 12 in., spaced 24 in., and spanning 12 ft. 6 in. The floor is 2-in. rough planking. The joists on the platform are spaced 4 ft. centres, spanning 6 ft. The top of the platform is placed 3 ft. 10 in. above the top of the rail. The frame is built of 6-in. × 8-in. posts, 3-in. × 4-in. studs and nailers, and 4-in. × 8-in. plates. The roof-trusses are spaced 14 ft. centres, and are composed of 4-in. × 9-in. principal rafters; 4-in. × 9-in. tie-beams; 4-in. × 5-in. truss-braces; 2½-in. × 8-in. purlins, spaced 48 in.; truss-rods, ⅞ in. and 1 in. in diameter; roof-sheathing, 1-in. boards.

FIG. 374.—FRONT ELEVATION.

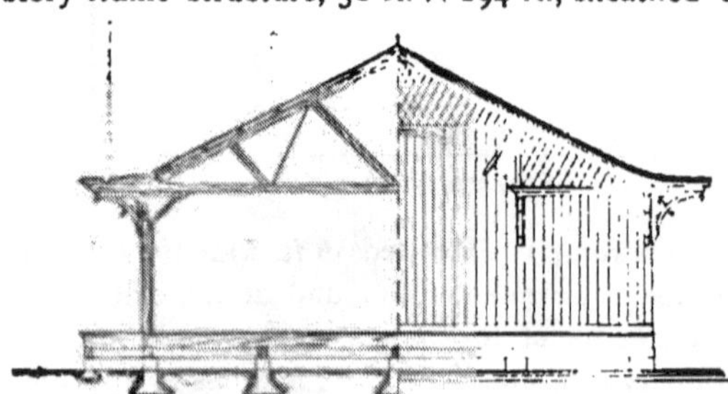

FIG. 375.—END ELEVATION AND CROSS-SECTION.

Terminal Freight-house at Grand Street, Jersey City, N. J., Lehigh Valley Railroad.—The terminal freight-house of the Lehigh Valley Railroad at Grand Street, Jersey City, N. J., shown in

Figs. 376 to 379, designed and built in 1890 under the direction of the author, assisted by Mr. Julius G. Hocke, Assistant Engineer, L. V. R. R., and by Mr. E. D. B. Brown, is a single-story, L-shaped frame structure, sheathed on the outside with galvanized corrugated iron, and roofed with tin. The location is at the junction of two important streets, Grand Street and Pacific Avenue, the tracks being parallel to Pacific Avenue, hence the necessity for the design as selected. In order to obtain more car frontage, covered platforms, 10 ft. wide, are run out from the freight-house along the tracks, as shown on the plans. The freight-house is 50 ft. wide, and 171 ft. long on the street frontage. The platform along the street is 6 ft. wide, and the freight-doors are 10 ft. wide and 14 ft. high, in pairs, sliding into recesses each side of the door-opening. Along the track the side of the house consists of sliding-doors hung alternately on two separate continuous rails, so that the house can be thrown open at any point. Attached to the freight-house is an office, 15 ft. × 23 ft., built as an annex to the main building. The end of the building away from the office is built so that the house can be extended along Pacific Avenue at any time without causing any serious changes. The floor in the house is set 3 ft. 8 in. above the top of the rails of the tracks, and the face of the platform is 2 ft. 9 in. above the wagon-road. The clear height in the house from the floor to the tie-beams of the trusses is 16 ft. 9 in.

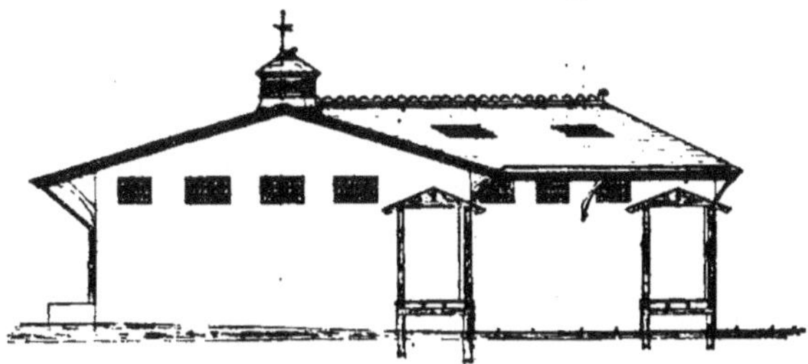

FIG. 376.—END ELEVATION.

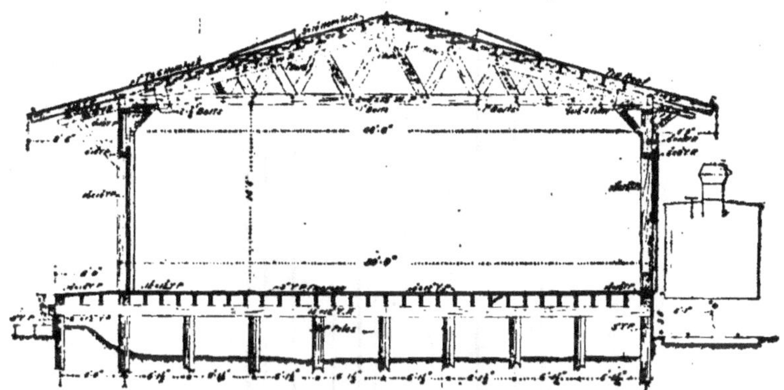

FIG. 377.—CROSS-SECTION.

The foundations of the building are yellow-pine piles, spaced about 6 ft. apart in each bent, the bents being spaced 10 ft. centres. The roof-trusses are spaced 20 ft. centres. The principal timbers used are yellow pine, 12-in. × 12-in. caps; 4-in. × 12-in. floor-joists; 12-in. × 12-in. building-sill; 3-in. floor-plank; 8-in. × 12-in. wheel-guard; 10-in. × 12-in. posts; 6-in. × 12-in. plates; 6-in. × 12-in. bolsters; 6-in. × 10-in. knee-braces; door-lintels 6 in. × 8 in.; extra upper door-lintel on track side of house for second set of sliding-doors, 6 in. × 14 in.; roof-brackets, 6 in. × 10 in.; false rafters on roof-projection, 3 in. × 8 in.; purlin on roof-projection, 6 in. × 8 in. The roof-trusses are built of white pine as follows: principal rafters, 2 pieces, 3 in. × 12 in.; tie-beams, 2 pieces, 3 in. × 12 in.; web-ties and struts, 2 in. × 10 in. The roof-purlins are 3-in. × 10-in. hemlock, covered by 1-in. tongued and grooved hemlock boards, roofed with tin on two layers of tarred roofing-felt. The outside of the building is covered with galvanized corrugated iron, the lower sheets being No. 20 gauge, the upper sheets No. 26 gauge. The interior is lighted by fixed sash in the sides of the building and skylights in the roof. The cornices, ridge-crestings, etc., are of galvanized iron.

Terminal Freight-house at Newark, N. J., Lehigh Valley Railroad.—The terminal freight-house of the Lehigh Valley Railroad at Frelinghuysen Avenue, Newark, N. J., shown in Figs. 380 to 382,

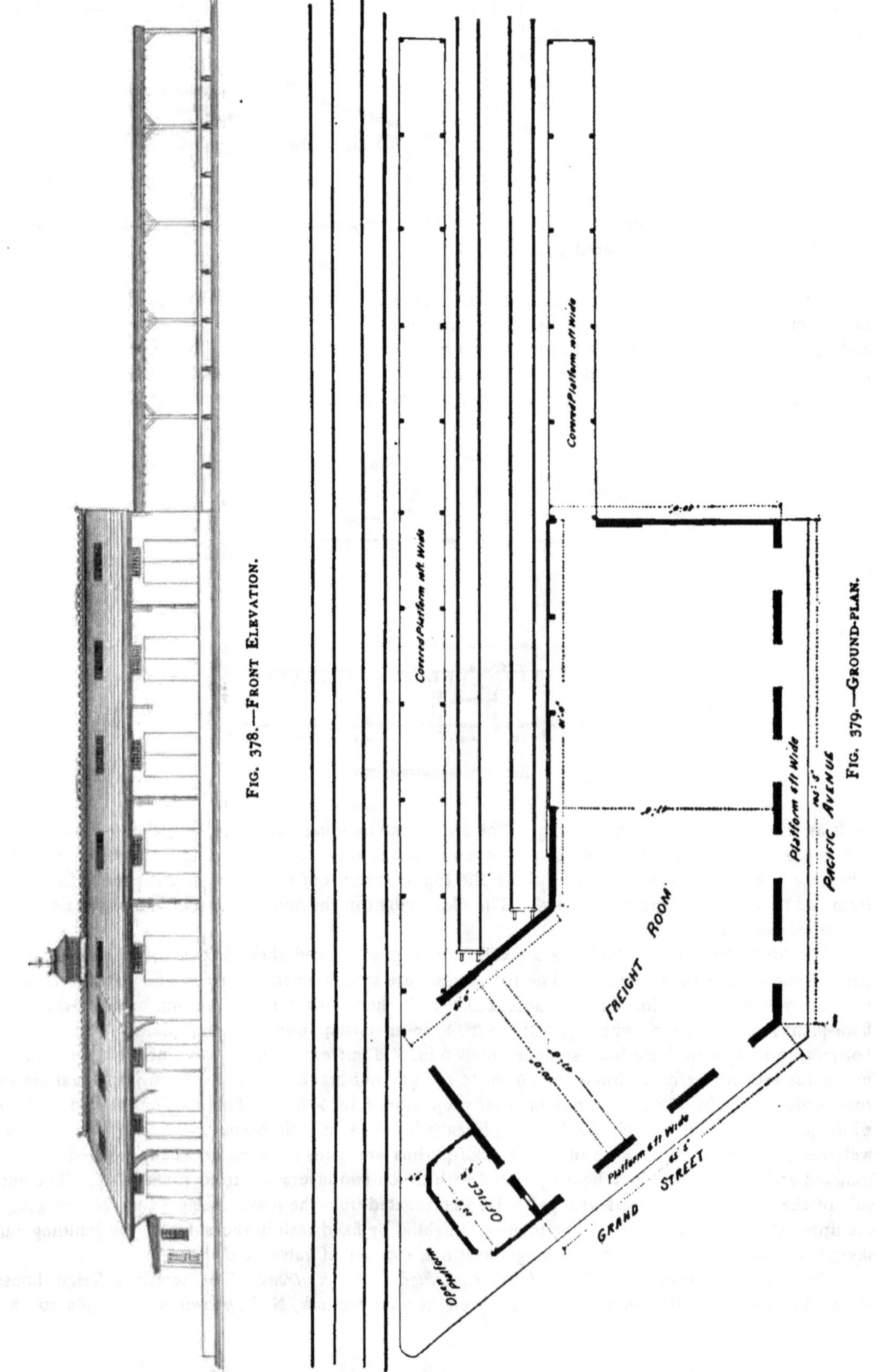

FIG. 378.—FRONT ELEVATION.

FIG. 379.—GROUND-PLAN.

designed and built in 1892 under the direction of the author, assisted by Mr. Phillip H. Dewitt and Mr. E. D. B. Brown, is a frame structure, 87 ft. × 145 ft., sheathed on the outside with galvanized

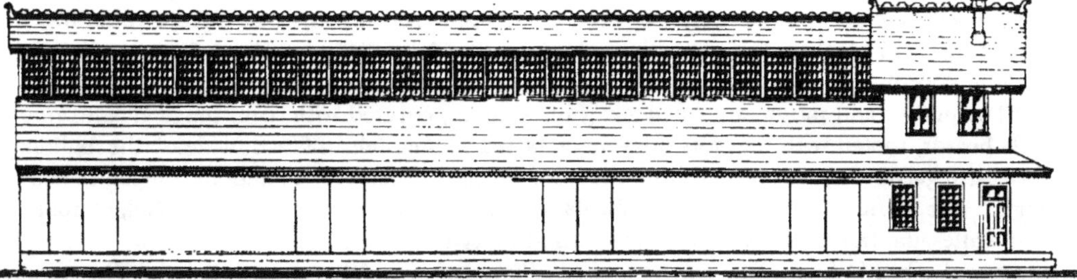

FIG. 380.—FRONT ELEVATION.

corrugated iron, and roofed with tin. Two tracks enter the building in one pit, spaced excentric, the floor-space on the narrow side being for outgoing freight, and the floor-space on the other side being

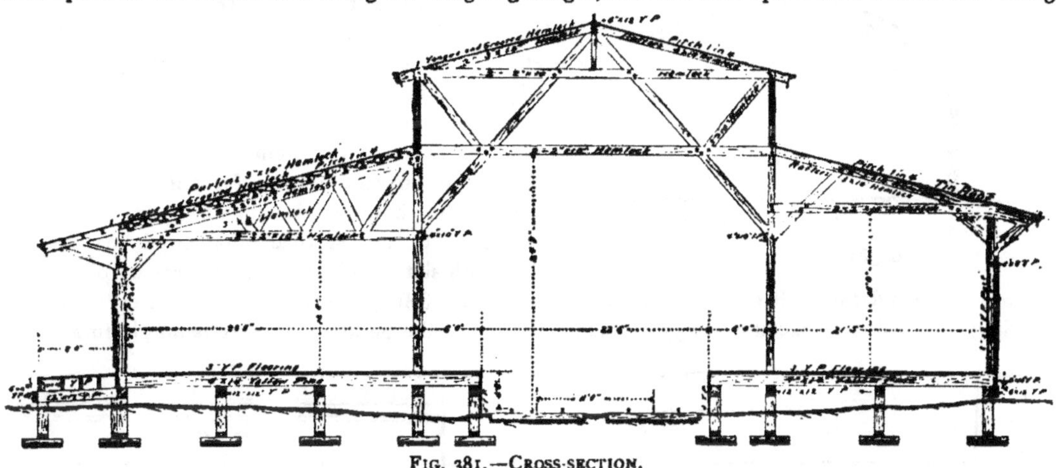

FIG. 381.—CROSS-SECTION.

for incoming freight. The site for this depot was limited to a lot with only 125 ft. front on Frelinghuysen Avenue. There is an 8-ft. platform along Alpine Street for incoming freight, and a 6-ft. platform along Frelinghuysen Avenue for incoming and outgoing freight. On the other side of the building there is no platform, the width of the property not allowing one; but this was not considered a serious detriment, as wagons bringing outgoing freight back up to the doors, and no trouble is experienced, if the freight is moved away from the doors as fast as deposited. The front of the building on Frelinghuysen Avenue is two-story, not only to add to the appearance of the structure, but so as to give an office for the local freight agent and his clerks, the office shown on the ground-plan being intended for the receiving and shipping clerks connected with business done on the floor of the house more particularly. The building is lighted and ventilated by a clear-story with glazed sash, every alternate sash being pivot-hung. The gable-end of the building away from the office is trussed over, so that the house can be extended at any time, if found desirable. Additional car frontage is obtained by covered platforms extending for some distance along the tracks outside of the house. The floor of the house is set 3 ft. 8 in. above the top of the rails of the tracks, and the face of the platform is placed 2 ft. 9 in. above the street. The freight-

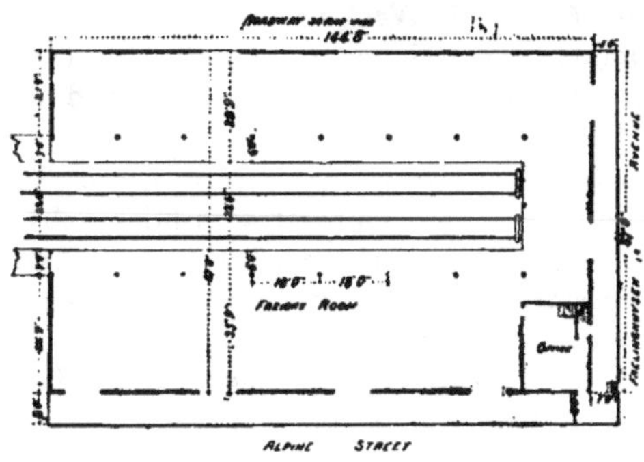

FIG. 382.—GROUND-PLAN.

doors are 10 ft. wide by 10 ft. high, hung in pairs, sliding each way from the door-opening. The roof-bents are spaced 18 ft. centres.

The foundations are creosoted posts set in the ground on creosoted blocking. The principal timbers are yellow pine, 12-in. × 12-in. caps; 4-in. × 14-in. floor-joists, spaced from 16 in. to 24 in. centres; 3-in. floor-planks; 6-in. × 12-in. wheel-guard; 8-in. × 8-in. posts; 6-in. × 8-in. plates; 6-in. × 8-in. door-lintels. The roof-trusses are built of hemlock, of the dimensions shown on the plans. The purlins and rafters are hemlock, 3 in. × 10 in., covered with 1-in. tongued and grooved hemlock boards, roofed with tin on two layers of tarred roofing-felt. The outside of the building is sheathed with galvanized corrugated iron, the lower sheets being No. 20 and the upper sheets No. 26 gauge. The cornices, ridge-crestings, finials, etc., are of galvanized iron. The freight-doors are made of white-pine frames, covered with galvanized sheet-iron No. 26 gauge.

Terminal Freight-house at Richmond, Va., Richmond & Alleghany Railroad.—The terminal freight-house of the Richmond & Alleghany Railroad, now the James River division of the Chesapeake & Ohio Railway, at Richmond, Va., shown in Figs. 383 and 384, designed and built in 1881 under the direction of the author, is a single-story frame structure, 40 ft. wide by 500 ft. long, one half of which length was enclosed and the balance built as an open shed. There were two tracks along the rear of the building, and one track ran into the open-shed portion of the house. The street delivery takes place along the front of the building. A two-story office building was located at the far end of the freight-house. The building is sheathed on the outside with horizontal and vertical ornamental boarding, and roofed with slate. The foundations are on piles, as the site is in the old James River Canal basin. There is an 8-ft. platform along the street front, with sliding freight-doors, spaced every 35 ft., along the side of the building. There is no platform on the rear of the building along the track, but the side of the closed portion of the house consists of doors throughout, so that any part of this side of the house can be opened, and the posts, supporting the roof-trusses every 11 ft. 8 in., are the only parts of the building that can interfere with loading or unloading cars. There are two continuous overhead roller-tracks for the door rollers to run on, and the doors in every alternate panel are hung on the same rail, so that any stretch of the house can be opened at will.

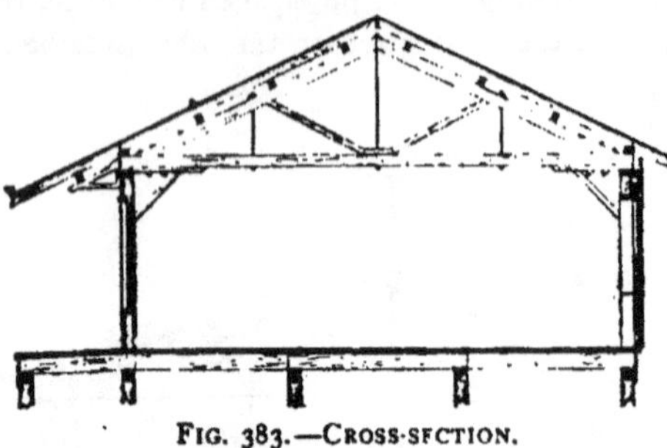

FIG. 383.—CROSS-SECTION.

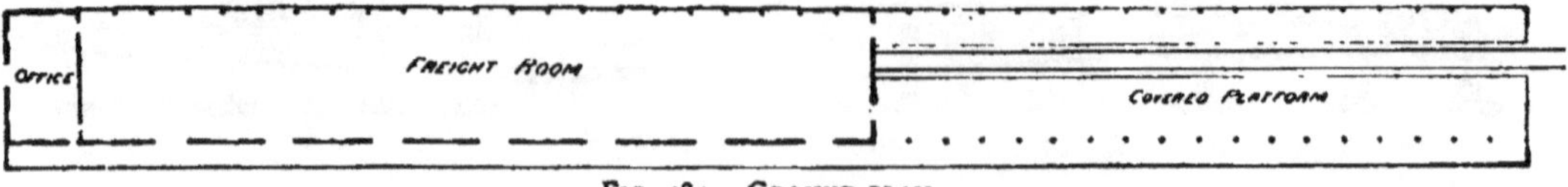

FIG. 384.—GROUND-PLAN.

Terminal Freight-house at St. Louis, Mo., St. Louis, Keokuk & Northwestern Railroad.—In the issue of the *Railroad Gazette* of Sept. 4, 1891, the following description is published of the new freight-house of the St. Louis, Keokuk & Northwestern Railroad at St. Louis, Mo., designed by Mr. G. S. Morison:

The south end of the building is to be so constructed as to give ample office quarters. These are to be 38 ft. × 141 ft., and five stories in height, with a severely plain front, with brick walls, and facing on the side street. On account of the incline along the front of the office, it is necessary to build heavy retaining-walls around three sides, as the basement is to be used for storage. The main floor is made up of 32-in. girders, 35 ft. 8 in. long, laid 9 ft. 6½ in. centres, and arched in with brick or hollow tiles. These girders are built up of ½-in. web, with 5-in. × 5-in. × ½-in. angles top and bottom, and will form a very stiff, solid floor. The lower basement floor is to be laid with concrete.

The main train-shed is 760 ft. long and 131 ft. wide, and spanned by an iron trussed roof, the main centre panels being mostly 60 ft. centres. The north truss has a latticed bottom chord to brace it against wind-pressure on that end of the building. These main trusses reach across the five tracks only, and rest on heavy composite Z columns bolted down to concrete foundations running down to rock bottom. These foundations are brought up to the platform level, and have bolts extending down into them 14 ft. The bolts are made U-shape, of 30-ft. rods, and sustain two pieces of rails of about 8 ft. in length on the lower part of the U. The rails are connected near their ends by short rods passing through holes drilled in the webs. It would seem that such a precaution as this against the disturbance of the holding bolts should be more than sufficient to guard against any possible pull from the upper end.

To the main posts at some 8 ft. below the eaves of the centre span is built a shed roof on either side, running down to a row of smaller posts built of Z-iron and plates, placed 20-ft. centres, and between which the doors are hung. Each 20-ft. panel contains a door (the full width of the panel) balanced on weights, which are suspended in the hollow of the Z-posts. Over the doors are large windows, so that when the door is down light may enter above, but on raising the door it shuts this off. Allowance is also made for light and air between the main and side roofs by having alternate frames set with slat ventilators and glass.

The five tracks extending the entire length of the shed are built on terraces, on an average slope of 1 in 20 to conform to the grade of the street at the north end, and are laid 11 ft. centres, it being the intention to load the three intermediate lines of cars through those on the tracks next the platforms. Beyond the north end of the shed the platforms extend for 87 ft. out, and have each an 11-ft. building at the inner end, and are also provided each with a 15-ton boom-crane having a 15-ft. swing. These will be used for transferring all heavy material, and will be of great assistance in the saving of time and labor on ordinary methods of loading. The need of such better facilities is being felt more and more by the carriers, and there is the additional advantage of locating the appliances at the general freight-house, in that frequently it may be better to unload part of the car by power, and at the same time it would not pay to switch that portion of the load to another part of the yard in order to reach the crane.

Inside the shed the platforms are furnished with Fairbanks scales of six tons capacity each, there being 22 in all, 18 on the west or receiving platform, and four on the east or delivery side. Both platforms throughout are built on the 1 to 20 slope, the receiving one being on the high side. When completed it will be possible to throw open the whole of the house with the exception of one 20-ft. panel on each side, so that every foot of floor-surface may be utilized to the best advantage. The end, across the tracks, is supplied with a large lattice-work gate nicely balanced by weights in pockets at the sides.

Terminal Freight-house at Cincinnati, O., Chesapeake & Ohio Railway.—The terminal freight-house of the Chesapeake & Ohio Railway at the corner of Third Street and John Street, Cincinnati, O., constructed during 1890, in connection with other terminal improvements at this point, is illustrated and described in the issue of the *Railway Review* of March 22, 1890. The approach to the freight-house is on an elevated trestling. The main floor of the house is used for receiving and delivering freight from Fourth Street, while a basement-floor is used for handling freight from the elevation of Third Street and John Street. The freight is transferred from the cars down to the basement, and from the basement up to the cars, by a large hydraulic elevator.

Single-story Terminal Freight-pier Shed at Jersey City, N. J., Lehigh Valley Railroad.—The single-story terminal freight-sheds of the Lehigh Valley Railroad, on Piers "B" and "C" of the freight terminus at Jersey City, N. J., described and illustrated in the issue of the *Railroad Gazette* of September 4, 1891, shown in Figs. 385 and 386, designed and built in 1889 under the direction of the author, assisted by Mr. Julius G. Hocke, Assistant Engineer, L. V. R. R., and by Mr. E. D. B. Brown, are frame buildings, 83 ft. wide, built on piers, 100 ft. wide and 600 ft. long. The sides of the building are sheathed with galvanized corrugated iron, and the roof is covered with tin. Owing to special local conditions governing the general layout of the terminus, the pier is built on an angle, so that the building has skew ends. There is one track running into the shed on each pier, and another track running outside the shed on the south side of each pier. This arrangement is a combination of an incoming and outgoing freight-pier; it gives a chance to ship or receive car-load freight directly over the string-piece, while package freight with a probable short storage is stored in the shed.

The entrance-doors to the engine-track in the pit are steel roller-shutter doors. Four movable freight inclines or gangways are provided on the north side of each pier, so that the inclines can be made to follow the tides or be adjusted to suit any boat, whether light or loaded. The south side of the shed

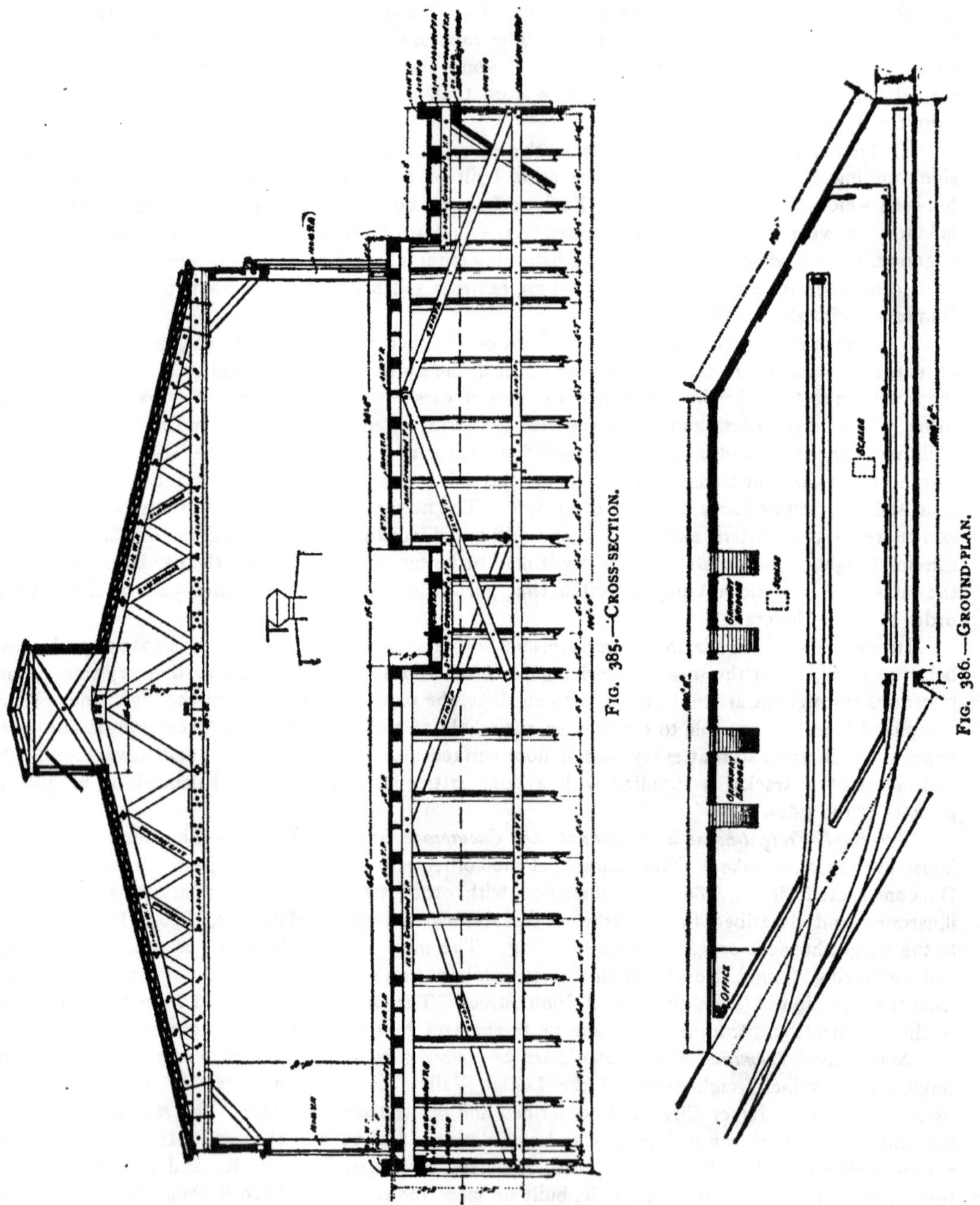

FIG. 385.—CROSS-SECTION.

FIG. 386.—GROUND-PLAN.

next to the string-piece track is built with a continuous system of sliding-doors, hung alternately on two different overhead rails, thus allowing any portion of the side of the house to be opened.

The top of the floor in the track-pits is placed 4 ft. above mean high-water, while the floor in the sheds is placed 4 ft. higher. The trusses in the sheds give 18 ft. 8 in. clearance above the floor under them. The pile-bents are spaced every 9 ft., while the upper or shed bents are spaced every 18 ft. The intermediate bents have 21 piles, the main bents 23 piles per bent.

The principal materials used in the substructure of the single-story covered piers are as follows: creosoted yellow-pine bearing and brace-piles, creosoted with 12 lbs. of dead oil of coal-tar per cubic foot; creosoted yellow-pine, 12-in. × 12-in. caps, 12-in. × 12-in. outside stringers, 12-in. × 12-in. building-sills, two 8-in. × 12-in. outside range-timbers, creosoted with 10 lbs. dead oil of coal-tar per cubic foot; untreated yellow-pine, 12-in. × 12-in. inside stringers and string-piece, 4-in. × 12-in. floor-joists, two 8-in. × 12-in. track-stringers under each rail, and 3-in. floor-plank; 6-in. × 12-in. oak fenders, 14 ft. long; 6-in. × 8-in. oak chocks between fenders, and oak cluster-piles at exposed corners. The superstructure or shed is built of Southern yellow pine, 10-in. × 10-in. posts, 8-in. × 12-in. plates; hemlock, 4-in. × 6-in. intermediate studs, 3-in. × 6-in. nailers; the outside sheathing is No. 20 galvanized corrugated iron; the inside of the shed is sheathed to a height of 6 ft. above the floor with 1-in. hemlock plank. The roof-trusses are built of white pine of the following sizes: tie-beams, 2 pieces, 4 in. × 14 in.; rafters, 2 pieces, 4 in. × 12 in.; studs and ties, 2-in. plank from 10 in. to 12 in. wide; and hemlock purlins, 3 in. × 10 in., properly bridged. The lantern is built of hemlock frame, with white-pine casings and sashes, the latter hung on centre pivots and operated with cords from below. The shed is roofed with 1-in. tongued and grooved hemlock boards, covered with tin laid on two layers of single-ply rosin-sized building-paper.

Single-story Terminal Freight-pier Shed at Jersey City, N. J., Pennsylvania Railroad.—The single-story terminal freight-shed of the Pennsylvania Railroad on York Street Pier, Jersey City, N. J., shown in Fig. 387, is a frame structure, 77 ft. 6 in. wide by 417 ft. long, the pier being 80 ft. wide. The shed is sheathed on the outside with galvanized corrugated iron, and roofed with tin. There is one track that runs into the building on one side of the pier. The doors along the sides of the house are swinging-doors, hinged at the top and swinging upwards when opened. This freight pier is used as a steamship pier for one of the transatlantic steamship routes, the track on the pier connecting with the Pennsylvania Railroad.

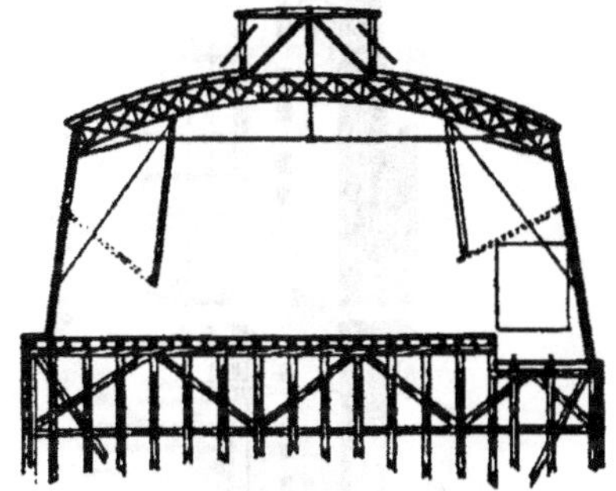

FIG. 387.—CROSS-SECTION.

Single-story Iron Terminal Freight-pier Shed at New York, N. Y., New York Central & Hudson River Railroad.—The terminal freight-shed of the New York Central & Hudson River Railroad on Pier No. 62, North River, at the foot of West Thirty-second Street, New York City, designed by Mr. Walter Katté, Chief Engineer, N. Y. C. & H. R. R. R., assisted by Mr. G. H. Thomson, Bridge Engineer, described and illustrated in the issue of the *Railroad Gazette* of March 1, 1889, is a single-story iron building, 94 ft. wide and 493 ft. long. There is a track running into the house at the centre of the pier. The pier substructure is 100 ft. wide. The roof is divided into three spans by means of two iron posts in each bent. The centre span, forming a clear-story, is 36 ft. high in the clear, and the side spans are 22 ft. high above the floor of the pier. There are seven large door-openings on each side of the pier for transferring freight to or from boats, there being a fixed inclined ramp at each door. The doors are closed by steel roller-shutter doors, the doors reaching down to the foot of the ramp, so that the house can be closed completely. The frame, roof-trusses and purlins are of iron throughout. The outside sheathing is galvanized corrugated iron, and the roof covering is gravel roofing on spruce boards.

Double-story Terminal Freight-pier Shed at Jersey City, N. J., Lehigh Valley Railroad.—The double-story terminal freight-sheds of the Lehigh Valley Railroad on Piers "G" and "H" of the freight terminus at Jersey City, N. J., described and illustrated in the issue of the *Railroad Gazette* of September 4, 1891, shown in Figs. 388 to 392, designed and built in 1891 under the direction of the author, assisted by Mr. Julius G. Hocke, Assistant Engineer, L. V. R. R., and by Mr. E. D. B. Brown, are frame buildings, 117 ft. 4 in. wide, built on piers, 120 ft. wide and 580 ft. long. The sides of the building are sheathed with galvanized corrugated iron, and the roof is covered with tin. Owing to special local conditions governing the general layout of the terminus, the pier is built on an angle, so

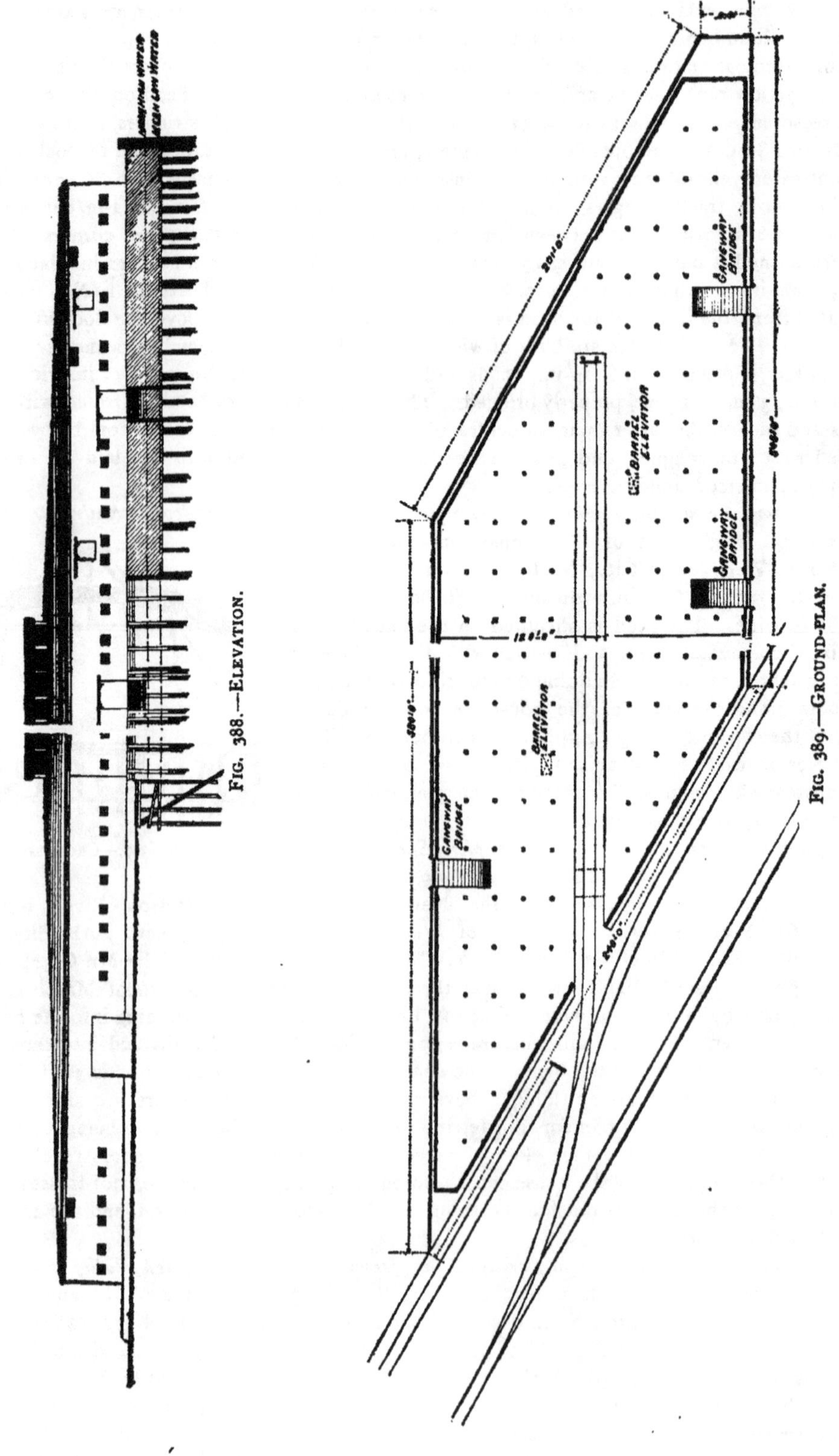

FIG. 388.—ELEVATION.

FIG. 389.—GROUND-PLAN.

that the building has skew ends. There is one track running into the shed on each pier at the centre of the shed. These piers are mainly intended for east-bound freight for which a certain amount of storage has to be provided. There are two stories, the lower one giving 10 ft. clearance between the bents, the upper one 8 ft. clearance at the bents, and more between them. The entrance-doors to the engine-track in the pit are steel roller-shutter doors. Four movable freight inclines or gangways are provided on each side of the pier, similar to those on the single-story covered piers, described above.

Freight is transferred to or from the upper story by means of six Ruddell barrel and freight elevators, shown in Fig. 392, operated by steam, arranged to carry barrels, bags, or package freight. These elevators are admirably arranged, so that freight can be hoisted to the upper floor and taken down from the upper floor to the lower story simultaneously, without stopping or reversing the

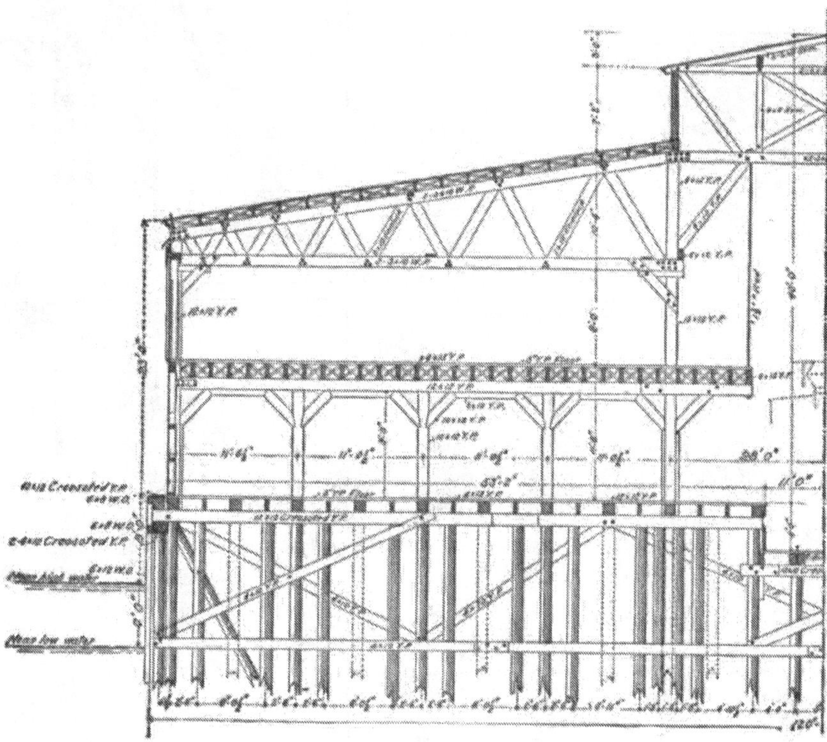

FIG. 390.—CROSS-SECTION.

engine. The machinery is equipped with safety appliances and automatic shut-off valves, so that one man can attend to all the engines on the pier, as in case of an accident the engine is stopped automatically.

By omitting the upper floor over the track-pit, the height of the building was reduced, while the ventilation and lighting of the lower floor were greatly facilitated, and a heavy and costly girder construction to carry the upper floor over the track-pit avoided—of course, however, with a certain loss of storage space. The top of the floor in the track-pits is 4 ft. above mean high-water, while the lower floor in the shed is placed 4 ft. higher. The pile-bents are spaced every 9 ft., while the upper shed-bents are spaced every 18 ft. The posts supporting the upper floor are spaced every 9 ft. lengthwise of the pier. The intermediate bents have 25 piles, the main or shed bents 37 piles per bent.

The principal materials used in the substructure of the double-story covered piers are the same as specified for the single-story covered piers, described above. The superstructure or shed is built of Southern yellow pine, 12-in. × 12-in. posts supporting upper floor and roof trusses; 12-in. × 12-in. floor-girders under upper floor; 4-in. × 15-in. floor-joists of upper floor, bridged between supports and spaced about 18in. centres; 3-in. upper floor-plank; and 6-in. × 12-in. plates; also hemlock, 4-in. × 6-in. intermediate studs, and 3-in. × 6-in. nailers. The outside sheathing of shed is No. 20 galvanized corrugated iron, and the inside is sheathed in both stories to a height of 7 ft. above the floor with 1-in. tongued and grooved hemlock. The roof-trusses, built as shown, consist of white pine, two pieces, 3-in. × 10-in., tie-beams; two pieces, 3-in. × 10-in., rafters; struts and ties, 2-in. hemlock, from 10 in. to 12 in. wide, and 3-in. × 10-in. hemlock purlins. The side-trusses are tied across the track-well with a 4-in. × 10-in. white-pine tie-beam, and the projecting parts of the upper floor next to the track-well

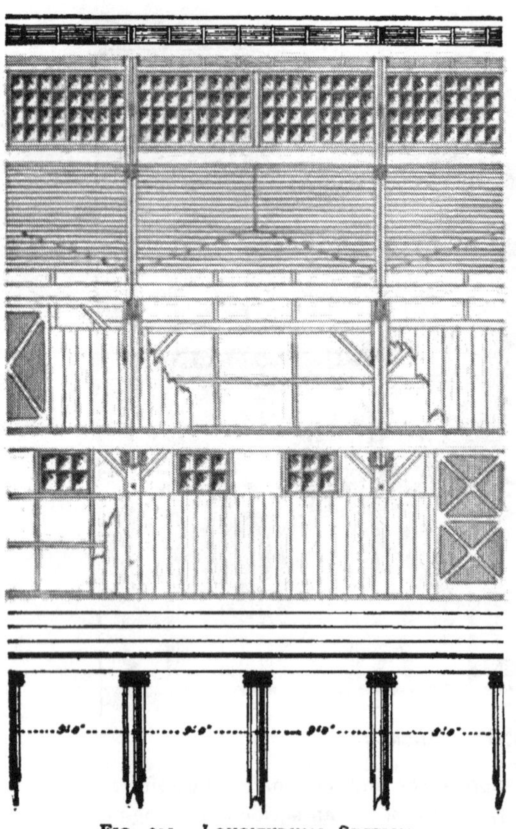

FIG. 391.—LONGITUDINAL SECTION.

FIG. 392.—RUDDELL BARREL AND FREIGHT ELEVATOR.

are suspended from the roof and supported by knee-braces, as shown. The lantern is built of hemlock frame, with white-pine casings and sashes, centre hung. The shed is roofed with 1-in. tongued and grooved hemlock boards, covered with tin, laid on two layers of single-ply rosin-sized building-paper.

Double-story Terminal Freight-pier Shed at Harsimus Cove, Jersey City, N. J., Pennsylvania Railroad.—The terminal freight-shed of the Pennsylvania Railroad on Pier No. 2, Harsimus Cove, Jersey City, N. J., shown in Fig. 393, is a double-story frame structure, 120 ft. wide × 460 ft. long, sheathed on the outside with galvanized corrugated iron, and roofed with tin. There are two tracks entering the house, near one side of the building, making a very good design for a combined ingoing and outgoing freight-shed. The clear height of the lower story is 15 ft.

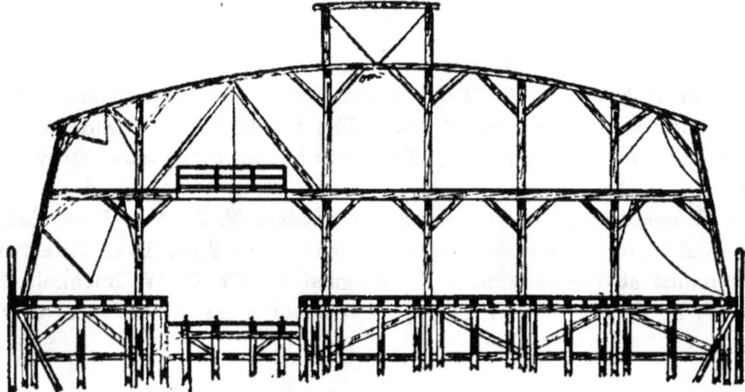

FIG. 393.—CROSS-SECTION.

Double-story Terminal Freight-pier Shed on Grand Street Pier, Jersey City, N. J., Pennsylvania Railroad.—The freight-sheds of the Pennsylvania Railroad on piers at Grand Street and at Sussex Street, Jersey City, N. J., shown in Fig. 394, are two-story frame structures, 125 ft. wide and about 500 ft. long, sheathed on the outside with galvanized corrugated iron, and roofed with tin. One track enters the building near the centre of the house. The lower story has 16 ft. clear height. These piers are used by transatlantic steamship lines, in connection with the Pennsylvania Railroad.

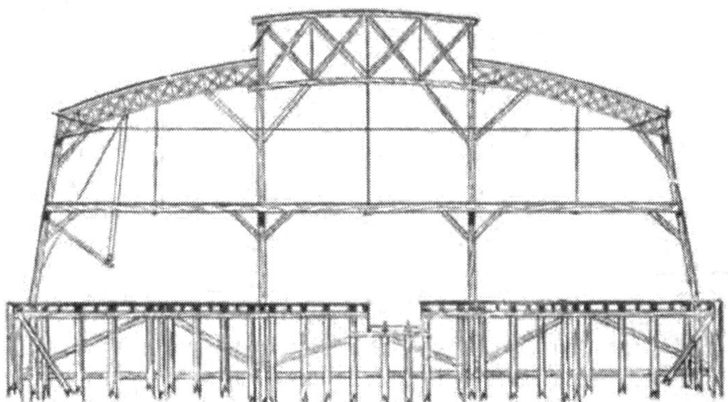

FIG. 394.—CROSS-SECTION.

Double-story Terminal Freight-pier Shed at Weehawken, N. J., West Shore Railroad.—The terminal freight-house of the West Shore Railroad, built on a pier at Weehawken, N. J., in 1883, described and illustrated in Mr. Gratz Mordecai's book on "Terminal Facilities of the Port of New York," is a double-story frame structure, sheathed on the outside with galvanized corrugated iron, and roofed with tin. The building is 200 ft. wide and about 2000 ft. long. The clear height of the lower story is 15 ft. 6 in., and of the upper story 11 ft. 6 in. at the outside of the building. There are two tracks entering the building at the centre of the house. The pier-bents are spaced 8 ft. apart, while the bents in the house are spaced 16 ft. apart. The doors on the first floor are 11 ft. wide × 10 ft. 6 in. high, with inclined fixed gangways, while the doors of the upper story are 7 ft. × 7 ft. The substructure, or pier proper, is built on piles, capped with two pieces, 6 in. × 12 in.; 12-in. × 12-in. stringers over piles, and 6-in. × 12-in. stringers between piles; track-stringers, 2 pieces, 7 in. × 12 in., under each rail; floor, 3-in. plank; posts, lower story, 12 in. × 14 in.; floor-girders, of second floor, 14 in. × 16 in.; knee-braces and straining-beams, 8 in. × 14 in.; floor-beams, upper floor, 12 in. × 16 in., and 8 in. × 16 in., spaced 24 in., spanning 17 ft. 6 in.; rafters, 8 in. × 10 in., and 5 in. × 12 in., spaced 24 in., spanning 17 ft. 6 in.

Double-story Terminal Freight-pier Shed on Pier B, at Weehawken, N. J., New York, Lake Erie & Western Railroad.—The terminal freight-shed of the New Yoik, Lake Erie & Western Railroad on pier B, Weehawken, N. J., described and illustrated in Mr. Gratz Mordecai's book on "Terminal Facilities of the Port of New York," is a double-story frame structure, sheathed on the outside with weather-boarding, and roofed with a gravel roof. The building is 70 ft. wide, and has a single track running into it at the centre of the house. The clear height of the lower story is 15 ft., and of the upper story 8 ft.

Double-story Terminal Freight-pier Shed at Weehawken, N. J., New York, Lake Erie & Western Railroad.—The double-story terminal freight-shed of the New York, Lake Erie & Western Railroad at its freight terminus at Weehawken, N. J., designed by Mr. C. W. Buchholz, Engineer B. & B., N. Y., L. E. & W. R. R., shown in Fig. 395, consists of a frame structure, 97 ft. wide by about

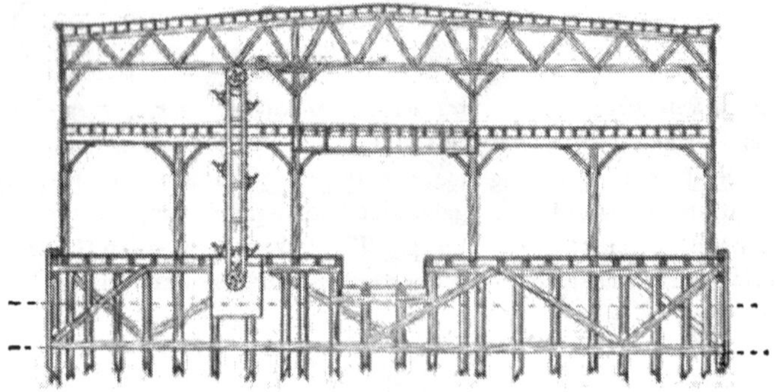

FIG. 395.—CROSS-SECTION.

750 ft. long, built on a pier in Hudson River. The outside of the building is sheathed with white-pine horizontal siding, with zinc casings around window and door openings. The roof is covered with a tarred felt gravel roof. There is one track in the house at the centre of the pier. The feature of this design is the use of iron beams and girders, to carry the floor of the second story, without a break, across the track on the lower floor. The necessary strength is obtained by a heavy wrought-iron plate-girder, which spans the track from post to post. The bents of the pier are spaced 10 ft. centres; the bents of the roof and the bents supporting the second floor are spaced 15 ft. centres. Freight is transferred to and from the upper floor by means of barrel-elevators.

Single-story Terminal City Freight-pier Shed, at Pier No. 21, North River, New York, N. Y., New York, Lake Erie & Western Railroad.—The terminal freight-shed of the New York, Lake Erie & Western Railroad for city freight on Pier No. 21, North River, New York City, described and illustrated in Mr. Gratz Mordecai's book on "Terminal Facilities of the Port of New York," is a single-story frame structure, 100 ft. wide, sheathed with galvanized corrugated iron, and covered with a gravel roof. The building is divided into two spans of 25 ft. each and a central clear-story span of 48 ft. The trusses are wooden lattice, of a style much in use on the Erie Railroad.

Single-story Terminal City Freight-pier Shed, on Pier No. 27, North River, New York, N. Y., Pennsylvania Railroad.—The terminal freight-shed of the Pennsylvania Railroad on pier No. 27, North River, New York City, for city freight, shown in Fig. 396, built in 1885, is a single-story frame structure, sheathed on the outside with galvanized corrugated iron, and roofed with tin. The roof-trusses are combination trusses. The building is 73 ft. wide by 533 ft. long, and gives 20 ft. clear height in the interior. The principal timbers used are posts, 12 in. × 12 in.; plates, 8 in. × 12 in.; principal rafters, 9 in. × 10 in.; purlins, 3 in. × 8 in.; rise of roof, $\frac{1}{6}$ of span.

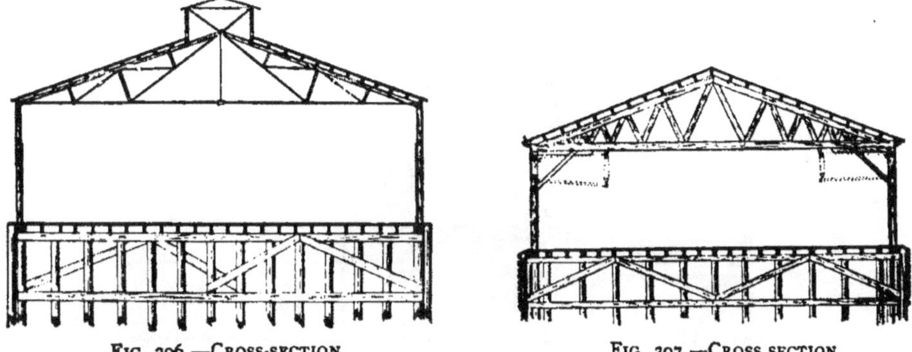

FIG. 396.—CROSS-SECTION. FIG. 397.—CROSS SECTION.

Single-story Terminal City Freight-pier Shed on Pier No. 1, North River, New York, N. Y., Pennsylvania Railroad.—The terminal freight-shed of the Pennsylvania Railroad on Pier No. 1, North River, New York, N. Y., built in 1883 for city freight, shown in Fig. 397, is a single-story frame structure, 63 ft. wide, sheathed on the outside with galvanized corrugated iron, and roofed with a gravel roof. The clear height in the interior is 16 ft. The rise of the roof is $\frac{1}{6}$ of the span. The doors are swinging-doors, 12 ft. high, hinged at the top and swinging inwards. The principal timbers used are, posts, 10 in. × 12 in.; plates, 8 in. × 12 in.; bottom chords of roof-trusses, 2 pieces, 3 in. × 12 in.; principal rafters, 2 pieces, 3 in. × 12 in.; web-members, 2 in. × 10 in.

Another similar frame freight-shed of the same railroad company at piers No. 4 and No. 5, North River, New York, N. Y., intended for delivery of city freight by teams entering the shed, has a span of 77 ft., and a clear height of 18 ft. 6 in. in the interior. The rise of the roof is $\frac{1}{8}$ of the span. The outside of the building is sheathed with galvanized corrugated iron. The roof is covered with gravel roofing. The principal timbers used are: posts, 12 in. × 12 in.; plates, 6 in. × 12 in.; corbels, 6 in. × 11 in.; knee-braces, 6 in. × 8 in.; bottom chords of roof-trusses, 2 pieces, $3\frac{1}{2}$ in. × 14 in.; principal rafters, 2 pieces, $3\frac{1}{2}$ in. × 12 in.; web-members, 2 in. × 13 in.; purlins, 3 in. × 7 in.

Single-story Terminal City Freight-pier Shed, at foot of Franklin Street, North River, New York, N. Y., West Shore Railroad.—In the issue of *Engineering News* of November 21, 1891, a description and plans are published of the new terminal of the West Shore Railroad at the foot of Franklin Street, on North River, New York City. An important element of the terminal is the freight-shed

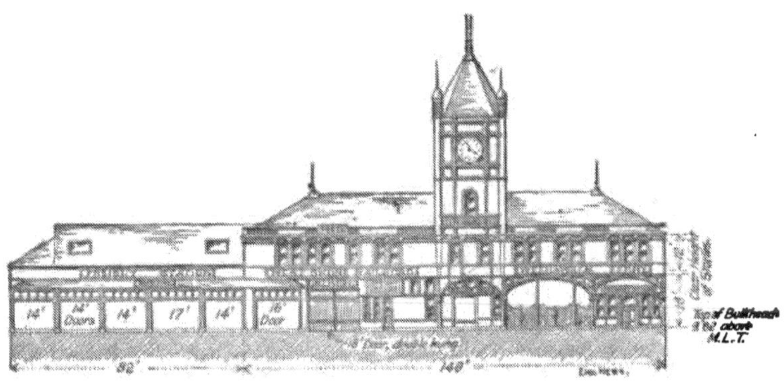

FIG. 398.—ELEVATION ON WEST STREET.

on the pier adjoining the ferry-house, which structure is designed for city freight going from teams to car-floats, and *vice versa*. The street elevation and the river elevation of the ferry and freight house are shown in Figs. 398 and 399, the cuts having been kindly furnished to the author by the *Engineering News*.

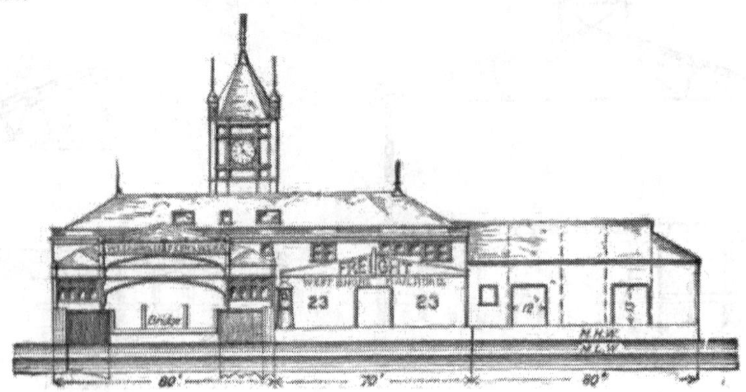

FIG. 399.—ELEVATION FROM RIVER.

Standard Guano Warehouse, Savannah, Florida & Western Railway.—The standard guano warehouse of the Savannah, Florida & Western Railway, designed by Mr. W. B. W. Howe, Jr., Chief Engineer, S., F. & W. Ry., shown in Fig. 400, represents a peculiar design for a special class of freight, namely, guano, which is handled to a large extent on the road mentioned. The house is 32 ft. wide by any length required. It is intended to store guano in bulk, the house being divided lengthwise into a number of bins so that different shippers can keep their stock in separate bins. The material arrives by railroad, and is thrown or wheeled out of the cars on to the platform along the face of the building next to the track. From here it is put into the stock-piles inside of the house. On the other side of the house is a wagon road, covered by a projecting roof, under which wagons stand when being loaded. The process of loading consists of throwing or wheeling the guano from the storage-pile in the house to a small platform along the rear of the house next to the projecting roof. From here it is thrown by hand into the wagons standing immediately below the roof projection.

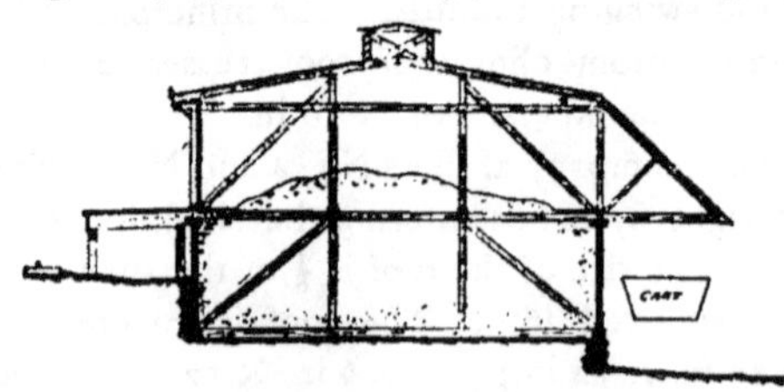

FIG. 400.—CROSS-SECTION.

CHAPTER XVIII.

PLATFORMS, PLATFORM-SHEDS, AND SHELTERS.

PLATFORMS have to be built along tracks at passenger and freight depots for the accommodation of passengers, and for facilitating the transfer of baggage and freight to and from cars. There are low and high platforms; the former are used more particularly for passengers, and the latter for the freight business. At passenger depots the platforms are always low, while at freight depots they are set invariably high. At combination depots the platforms are either low, high, or low and high combined. At freight stations a short, high platform with an incline or ramp at one end is frequently located at some convenient point in the freight-yard, to facilitate the handling of machinery or heavy building materials to or from cars without using cranes or travellers.

The height of passenger platforms and the distance of the face of the platform from the track are dependent on the location of the lowest step of the passenger-cars, and the clearance required near the level of the track for the rolling-stock in use on the railroad. The platform should be set close enough to the track, and at such a height, however, as to make it easy and safe for passengers to step on and off trains. Where there is a track between the platform proper and the track on which trains stop, the intervening track has to be planked over at about the level of the top of the rails. Where, however, the platform is alongside of the running track, it is customary to place the platform from 2 in. to 16 in. above the top of the rail, and to set the face accordingly from 4 ft. to 5 ft. 6 in. from the centre of the track. The length of a passenger platform is dependent on the average length of the regular trains stopping at the station. At stations of minor importance with a small passenger business the platform is only made the standard width near the depot, while the necessary total length of platform is secured by narrow footwalks from 4 to 6 ft. wide, extending each way along the track from the main platform. The width of a passenger platform is determined by the volume of business to be expected. It should be wide enough to accommodate passengers, and leave room for standing baggage and for the passage of baggage trucks without serious interference to passengers. In this connection attention should be called to the fact that ample and conveniently arranged platforms, especially where covered and provided with benches, will allow a smaller space to be allotted for waiting-rooms inside the passenger depot. In summer, when the travel is usually heaviest, the platforms will be occupied by passengers in preference to the waiting-rooms. These remarks apply also more particularly to passenger depots at suburban stations or pleasure resorts, where large crowds have to be handled only at fixed times of the day, or during certain seasons. Passenger platforms should be made never less than 12 ft. in width, and preferably more. Where there is a possibility that a single-track road might be double-tracked in the run of years, or a double-track road have a third or fourth track eventually added, it is a wise provision to locate all permanent structures along the road in such a manner as to admit of these improvements being subsequently carried out without causing extensive changes. With this feature in view, the width of a passenger platform in front of a depot building should be not less than 24 ft., so that in case an additional track is put through there will still be a reasonably wide platform left. In locating passenger depots along a railroad it is desirable to place them throughout on one side of the road, so far as possible, so that an extra track can be added at any time with comparative ease. This is particularly the case if the passenger depots have been placed back from the main track, as just outlined, and if freight depots, coaling trestles, water-tanks, yards, freight sidings, and similar structures, that have to be located close to the main track, are placed, where feasible, on the opposite side of the railroad from the passenger depots.

The height of freight platforms above the rail is dependent on the height of the floor in freight-cars and the height of the bottom of the swinging-doors, now extensively used on certain classes of freight-cars. The aim should be to have the platform about the same level as the car-floor, without interfering with the opening of the swinging-doors mentioned. Due allowance should also be made for the settlement of the car-body with time, owing to the wear of the springs and wheels, and a possible permanent set of the car-sills. An old rule for height of freight platforms was to set the top 4 ft. above the top of the rail. Since the introduction of swinging-doors, however, it is not safe to go over 3 ft. 10 in. The practice to-day is to adopt from 3 ft. 8 in. to 3 ft. 10 in., preferably the former figure.

Relative to the distance to place the face of a freight platform from the centre of the nearest track, it can be said, that the platform should be located as close to the track as possible, consistent with safety to passing trains, so that the open gap between the platform and the side of the car is reduced to a minimum. In track-pits in freight-houses this distance can be reduced to 5 ft. 3 in., although 5 ft. 6 in. is desirable. Freight-platforms along a siding are placed from 5 ft. 6 in. to 6 ft. from the centre of the track, while high platforms along a main track or a fast-running track should be invariably placed at least 6 ft. 6 in., preferably 7 ft., from the centre of the track. High platforms should either overhang their supports along the face of the platform, or else the space at the face of the platform between the floor and the ground should be left open, if possible, so that any person getting caught between the platform and a train can lie down between the track and the supports of the platform, or else crawl under the platform. The length of a freight platform is dependent on whether the platform faces a running track or a local side track. In the first instance the platform need not be much longer than the building, as cars in the train are moved successively, as desired, opposite the house. Where a freight platform serves to load or unload freight to or from cars left standing on a side track along the freight-house, the platform frontage should correspond to whatever number of cars it is desired to reach without having to do any shifting. Relative to the width of freight platforms, they vary from 6 ft. to 12 ft., while 8 ft. or 10 ft. is the general rule. A very customary standard, however, is to have the platform 12 ft. wide at the house, and to make the extensions along the track away from the house 8 ft. wide.

Combined high and low platforms are frequently used at combination depots. The most generally adopted design is to have low platforms in front of and in the vicinity of the waiting-rooms, while a high platform surrounds that end of the depot in which the freight-room is located. The passage from the low to the high platform near the centre of the front of the building is made by means of an incline, so that baggage or freight on trucks can be transferred conveniently from one to the other level. In other combination depots, especially where the package freight to or from passing freight-trains is light, while the passenger business is important, the high platform in front of the freight-room is made narrower than the low platform, so that there is a narrow, low platform between the high platform and the track. This design offers the advantage that passengers can pass, and baggage can be wheeled alongside the train on the low platform in front of the freight platform, while the small amount of package freight to or from passing freight-trains is lifted or skidded across the space between the car and the high platform.

The flooring material for a platform is dependent on the amount of traffic, the locality, and the exposure to the elements that can be expected. A good flooring should be durable, reasonably smooth for trucking, and not slippery. With the exception of platforms at terminal and large local stations, wood is universally adopted in this country for the construction of platforms. In most sections of the country lumber is the cheapest material that can be effectually employed for platforms, in addition to which the fact that the foundations of a timber structure are more easily and cheaply built and maintained, especially on new made ground, warrants the wholesale adoption of wooden platforms. For high freight platforms its cheapness over a more substantial and permanent class of materials is undoubted. A costly construction is also frequently not considered advisable, as subsequent changes and the introduction of additional facilities, especially on a new line, might cause existing platforms to be changed or modified. At terminal depots or large local depots the requirements are usually more closely defined, and a more permanent construction is desirable and indicated, especially as the necessity for making frequent repairs is more objectionable. The repair account of a railroad for the maintenance of wooden platforms is quite heavy, but, for the reasons given above, the use of such platforms, especially for high freight platforms, will have to be considered as good practice in the majority of cases.

Wooden platforms are cheap to build in the first instance, and repairs or alterations are easily made by the usual road force and with the class of materials kept in stock by the road department. Wood is more comfortable for passengers to stand on than other flooring materials. It is comparatively smooth for trucking purposes, and, unless grease and oils are handled carelessly, can be kept fairly clean. Wooden platforms should be left open underneath so as to afford ventilation around the timbers, and decrease the tendency to dry-rot. Where wooden platforms are to be bedded on mud-sills in the ground, it will prove advantageous to creosote the timber, or else to adopt a more durable foundation material. The flooring-planks are frequently laid with an open space between them to allow for the swelling of the timber when wet, and also offering better drainage. This is all right for freight platforms, where the planks are heavy, but on passenger-platforms the planks should be laid close so as to prevent small articles dropped by passengers from being lost through the crevices. A tight floor on passenger platforms is also desirable, so as to reduce upward draughts through the floor, which is objectionable for passengers. All timber floors are laid with a pitch towards the track to give better drainage, the grade being usually 1 in. in 5 ft. to 1 in. in 7 ft. for passenger platforms, and about 1 in. in 4 ft. for freight platforms. Freight platforms should be floored with 2½-in. to 3-in. oak planks, and passenger platforms with 2-in. oak or yellow-pine boards, the oak being preferable, if the platform is exposed to the weather.

Other classes of flooring materials, in addition to timber, are stone paving, stone flagging, asphalt, tiles, and "Granolithic" paving. Stone forms a very durable and good floor, but it requires a solid foundation, which cannot always be obtained without considerable expense. Paving-stones cost considerable when dressed and laid so as to make a smooth enough surface for trucks to run on easily. Stone flagging, in localities where it can be obtained readily, forms a first-class and comparatively cheap floor, provided the flagstones are large and well bedded. Asphalt forms a very smooth floor, but it is easily worn by truck-wheels, and in summer, if exposed to the sun, becomes very hot and uncomfortable for passengers. Tiles work loose easily, and hence a tile floor will seldom be found perfect. Granolithic paving is used very extensively for passenger platforms at important stations. It consists of a very fine grade of granite concrete with Portland-cement top-dressing, that presents a very hard, smooth, and durable surface.

Relative to the cost of different classes of flooring materials, it can be said, that, so far as first cost is concerned, a timber floor is the cheapest, and especially so for a high freight platform. Stone flagging is in some sections of the country nearly as cheap as timber flooring, particularly if the foundation is good, and does not require expensive preparation. The cheaper grades of asphalt flooring are about as costly as stone flagging, while the better grades and heavier-built floors of asphalt cost considerably more. Paving-stones, if dressed smoothly and laid properly, cost more than flagging and asphalt. Granolithic paving is usually the most costly, but it is one of the best known pavements for platforms at important stations. While prices vary in different localities, the comparative cost of different classes of flooring materials per square foot, according to the design adopted, can be placed as follows: timber, 10 to 20 cents; stone flagging, 15 to 25 cents; asphalt, 15 to 30 cents; stone paving, 25 to 40 cents.

Platforms are generally covered to a more or less extent by shed roofs. Immediately along the side of the depot building the platform covering consists of the roof overhang, but away from the building, or where the platform is wide, the roof is usually supported by a wooden or iron-column shed construction. The usual construction is to have two posts in each bent, unless the space to cover is very wide, and in that case a special girder is thrown from post to post in preference to introducing more columns. The post nearest the track should never be set closer than 6 ft. to the side of the car-body. It is customary in a number of designs to arrange the platform roof with a very large overhang over the rear of the platform, so as to protect passengers while passing to or from vehicles in stormy weather. One-legged sheds, that is, platform roofs supported on one post at each bent, as shown, for instance, in Fig. 413, can be used to good advantage in a great many cases, producing in addition a unique and pleasing effect. Platform-sheds are built of iron or wood, or a combination of both. The roofing is usually tin, shingles, or tarred felt. The design of the platform-sheds connected with a depot offers one of the best opportunities to produce a picturesque and handsome appearance of an otherwise square and bleak-looking building, and it merits, therefore, careful consideration, and relatively as much study as any other detail of the depot structures.

While on this subject it can be said that overhead passenger foot-bridges connecting opposite sides of a railroad can be designed with very little extra trouble and expense, so as to produce a most pleasing and harmonious effect with the rest of the depot structures, and add materially to the attractiveness of the station.

In connection with platform-sheds the subject of shelters should be considered, as these structures are simply short covered sections of a platform, so as to protect passengers from the weather while waiting for trains. Shelters are also used on double-track railroads with a heavy passenger travel to afford shelter for passengers waiting for trains or alighting from trains on the opposite side of the main tracks from the passenger depot, so as to avoid the dangerous features of passengers having to cross one main track in going to or leaving a train on the other main track. A fence is frequently built at such stations between the main tracks, and passengers cross to the shelter from the main depot platform on an overhead bridge, or through a tunnel or subway, or through gates in the fence opened by the station guards at the proper time. These precautionary measures for avoiding accidents in handling large crowds at suburban, city, or excursion stations on double-track railroads are absolutely necessary.

Shelters are also used at small flag-stations, where the business does not warrant a depot or an agent. The shelter affords protection to passengers from the weather or the heat of the sun while waiting for trains.

After above general remarks, the following descriptions of platforms, platform-sheds, and shelters, in actual use on railroads in this country, will serve to illustrate the subject further.

Platforms for passengers and for freight, of the dimensions and designs as described below, are in use on the following railroads:

Low Platform, Pottsville Branch, Lehigh Valley Railroad.—At the flag-stations of the Pottsville branch of the Lehigh Valley Railroad the platforms are 8 ft. wide in front of the building, and set 11 in. above the top of rail and 4 ft. 6 in. from the centre of the track.

Low Platform, Northern Pacific Railroad.—The low platform in front of combination depots and of flag-depot with dwelling, of the Northern Pacific Railroad, is 12 ft. wide, and is set 16 in. above the top of rail and 6 ft. from the centre of the track. The rise in the width of the platform is 2½ in. There are two steps leading from the platform down to the level of the track.

Low Platform at Flag-depot with Dwelling, Pennsylvania Railroad.—The low platform in front of the two-story frame flag-depot, with dwelling attached, of the Pennsylvania Railroad, is 12 ft. wide, extended 8 ft. wide each way from the building, and is set 8 in. above the top of rail and 4 ft. 6 in. from the centre of the track.

Low Platform at Flag-depot, Philadelphia & Reading Railroad.—The low platform in front of the flag-depot at Tabor, Pa., on the North Pennsylvania branch of the Philadelphia & Reading. Railroad, is 10 ft. wide, and set 9 in. above the top of rail and 5 ft. 6 in. from the centre of the track.

Low Platform, Minnesota & Northwestern Railroad.—The low platform used at local passenger depots and combination depots on the Minnesota & Northwestern Railroad is 14 ft. wide, and set 12 in. above the top of rail and 5 ft. from the centre of the track, with a rise of 2 in. in the width of the platform.

Low Platform at Combination Depots, Wabash, St. Louis & Pacific Railway.—The low platform in front of combination depots of the Wabash, St. Louis & Pacific Railway is set 4 in. above the top of rail, and 4 ft. from the centre of the track, with a rise of ¼ in. per foot.

Low Platform at Combination Depots, Union Pacific Railway.—The low platform at combination depots, with living-rooms attached, of the Union Pacific Railway, adopted in 1886, is set 14 in. above the top of rail and 5 ft. 3 in. from the centre of the track, with a rise of $\frac{3}{16}$ in. per ft.

Low Platform at Combination Depots, Burlington, Cedar Rapids & Northern Railway.—The low platform in front of the combination depots of the Burlington, Cedar Rapids & Northern Railway is 12 ft. wide, and is set 16 in. above the top of rail and 5 ft. 6 in. from the centre of the track, with a rise of 2 in. in 12 ft.

Low Platform at Local Passenger Depots and Combination Depots, Pennsylvania Lines West of Pittsburg, Southwest System.—The low platform in use on the Pennsylvania lines west of Pittsburg, Southwest System, is 16 ft. wide in front of the depot building, reaching within 4 ft. 6 in. of the centre of the track, and set 8 in. above the top of the rail.

High Platform at Local Freight-house, Northern Pacific Railroad.—The high platform in front of the local freight-depots of the Northern Pacific Railroad is 10 ft. wide, and set 3 ft. 8 in. above the top of the rail and 5 ft. 10¼ in. from the centre of the track, with a 2½-in. rise in 10 ft.

High Platform at Local Freight-house, Minnesota & Northwestern Railroad.—The high platform in front of local freight-houses of the Minnesota & Northwestern Railroad is 6 ft. wide, and set 4 ft. above the top of rail and 6 ft. from the centre of the track.

High Platform at Freight-house at Gainesville, Fla., Savannah, Florida & Western Railway.—The high platform of the freight-house at Gainesville, Fla., on the Savannah, Florida & Western Railway, is 8 ft. wide, and is set 3 ft. 10 in. above the top of rail.

High Platform Terminal Freight-house, at Jersey City, N. J., Lehigh Valley Railroad.—The high platform in terminal freight-houses on piers at Jersey City, N. J., of the Lehigh Valley Railroad, are set 3 ft. 8 in. above the top of rail, and 5 ft. 6 in. from the centre of the track.

High Platform Terminal Freight-house at Weehawken, N. J., New York, Lake Erie & Western Railroad.—The high platform in the terminal freight-house on pier B, at Weehawken, N. J., of the New York, Lake Erie & Western Railroad, is set 3 ft. 8 in. above the top of rail and 6 ft. from the centre of the track.

High Platform at Combination Depot, at Hilliard, Ga., Savannah, Florida & Western Railway.—The high platform in front of the freight depot of the Savannah, Florida & Western Railway, at Hilliard, Ga., is 10 ft. wide, and set 4 ft. above the top of rail, and 6 ft. 6 in. from the centre of the track.

High Platform at Local Freight Depots, Pennsylvania Railroad.—The high platform in front of small local freight depots of the Pennsylvania Railroad, facing the track, is 8 ft. wide, and is set 3 ft. 10 in. above the top of rail and 5 ft. 6 in. from the centre of the track, the rise in the width of the platform being 2 in.

High Platform at Combination Depots, Cincinnati Southern Railway.—The platform in front of combination depots of the Cincinnati Southern Railway is generally 12 ft. wide, and is set 3 ft. 8 in. above the top of rail and 6 ft. from the centre of the track.

Combined High and Low Platform at Combination Depots, Kansas City & Emporia Railroad.—The combination depot of the Kansas City & Emporia Railroad has a high and low platform. The low platform is set 12 in. above the top of rail and 5 ft. 1¼ in. from the centre of the track. The high platform is set 3 ft. 8 in. above the top of rail, and 5 ft. 7¼ in. from the centre of the track.

Standard Platforms, New York, Pennsylvania & Ohio Railroad.—The standard passenger or low platform adopted by the New York, Pennsylvania & Ohio Railroad, plans for which were described and illustrated in the issue of the *Railroad Gazette* of July 17, 1885, consists of a timber platform on stone or brick piers, the piers being generally spaced 12 ft. apart lengthwise of the platform. The platform starts 24 in. from the rail, or 4 ft. 6 in. from the centre of the track. The face is set 10 in. above the top of rail, and from there the platform rises, away from the track, at the rate of 1 in. in 9 ft. The floor consists of 2-in. plank laid crosswise of the platform, and supported by 3-in. × 8-in. floor-joists, spaced 16 in. centres, spanning 12 ft. generally. The joists are supported by caps, 6 in. × 10 in., resting on piers spaced about 8 ft. centres. The standard low platform in front of a passenger depot is shown to be 18 ft. wide.

The standard freight and passenger platform combined,—in other words, a low and high platform combined,—described and illustrated in the same issue of the *Railroad Gazette* mentioned above, has a high platform 6 ft. wide and 4 ft. 3 in. above the top of the rail in front of the house, while a low platform is inserted between the high platform and the track. The low platform is 6 ft. wide, the face of it starts 4 ft. 6 in. from the centre of the track, and it is 10 in. above the top of rail. The low platform is formed of 2-in. plank, on 3-in. × 8-in. joists, resting on 6-in. × 10-in. caps. The high platform is formed of 2-in. plank, on 3-in. × 12-in. joists, spaced 16-in. centres, supported on 6-in. × 10-in. caps.

Passenger Platform, Northern Pacific Railroad.—The platform design for passenger platforms, adopted by the Northern Pacific Railroad in 1884, shows a 12-ft. platform 16 in. above the top of rail, with two steps leading down in front of it, to the level of the track. The face of the platform is set 3 ft. 6 in. from the gauge face of the nearest rail, or 5 ft. 10¼ in. from the centre of the track. The platform rises at the rate of 2½ in. in the width of 12 ft. The floor consists of 2-in. rough plank, laid crosswise of the platform, on 3-in. × 10-in. joists, spaced 24-in. centres, and spanning 8 ft. The support of the joists are bents, spaced every 8 ft. lengthwise of the platform, consisting of 8-in. × 8-in. caps, each cap supported by three 8-in. × 8-in. cedar posts, set in the ground on cedar blocking.

Standard Platforms, West Shore Railroad.—In Fig. 401 are shown the standard high and low platforms adopted for the West Shore Railroad in 1888 by Mr. Walter Katté, Chief Engineer, designed by Mr. J. D. Fouquet, Engineer and Architect, N. Y. C. & H. R. R. R. and West Shore R. R. Two causes led to the revision of the standards previously in use, namely, refrigerator-cars had been introduced with swinging-doors, and allowance had to be made for the settlement of the car-body with time, owing to the wear and deflection of the springs, so that the doors, when opened, would clear high platforms. On the other hand, a snow-plough was introduced on the road, 10 ft. 1 in. wide, at a point 4⅜ in. above the top of the rail. The standard low or passenger platform starts 5 ft. 3 in. from the centre of the track, and is, at this point, 1½ in. above the top of rail. The pitch of the platform is ascending away from the track at the rate of 1 in. in 3 ft. The standard high or freight platform starts 5 ft. 6 in. from the centre of the track, and is, at this point, 3 ft. 10½ in. above the top of rail. The platform ascends away from the track at the rate of 1 in. in 4 ft.

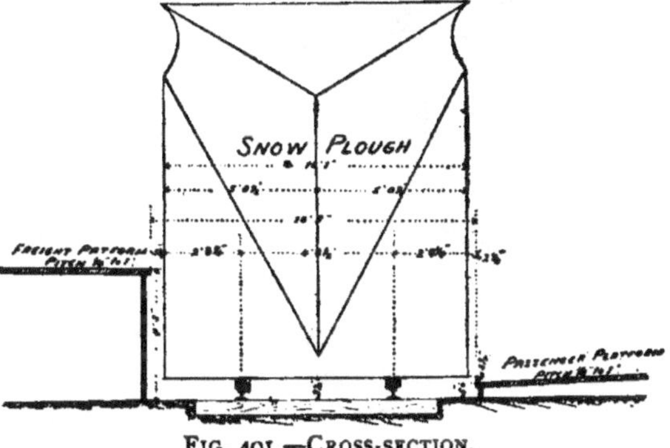

FIG. 401.—CROSS-SECTION.

Platform-shed and Shelter for Passenger Stations, Pennsylvania Railroad.—The passenger platform-shed, adopted by the Pennsylvania Railroad very generally, shown in Fig. 402, consists of trestle-bents, spaced about 18 ft. apart, supporting an unsymmetrical, double-pitched roof. Each bent has two ornamental posts, spaced 8 ft. apart, and the roof projects on the track side 6 ft. 9 in. beyond the nearest post. The eaves of the roof are 9 ft. above the platform, and the ridge is 14 ft. above the platform. The principal timbers used are 5-in. × 5-in. ornamental posts; 5-in. × 5-in caps; 5-in. × 9-in. purlins; 2-in. × 6-in. rafters, spaced 2 ft. centres; 1-in. roof-boards covered with tin.

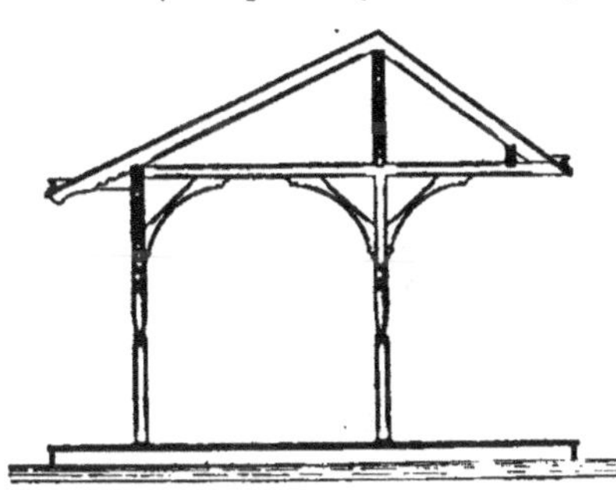
FIG. 402.—CROSS-SECTION.

This design of roof is also used very extensively by the Pennsylvania Railroad for shelters, in which case three sides of the space occupied by the roof are enclosed with studding sheathed on the outside with boards. The front towards the track is left open. According to the local requirements, these shelters in some cases have windows, and are also frequently ceiled on the inside with tongued and grooved boards, and finished and painted very neatly.

Platform-shed, Philadelphia & Reading Railroad.—The passenger platform-shed of the Philadelphia & Reading Railroad, shown in Figs. 403 and 404, consists of bents spaced 10 ft. apart

FIG. 403.—END ELEVATION.

FIG. 404.—FRONT ELEVATION.

lengthwise of the platform, each bent having two posts, spaced 8 ft. centres, as shown. The shed is roofed with tin. The finials, ridge-cresting, and board knee-braces, together with the ornamental finish of the posts, causes the structure to present a very striking and handsome appearance.

Platform-shed for Passenger Depot, Allentown, Pa., Lehigh Valley Railroad.—In Figs. 405 and

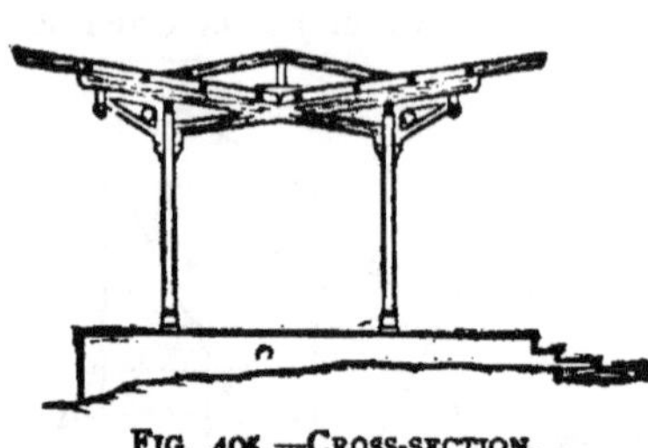

FIG. 405.—CROSS-SECTION.

FIG. 406.—END ELEVATION.

406 is shown a style of passenger platform-shed, designed by the author for a passenger depot of the Lehigh Valley Railroad at Allentown, Pa. The platform is 20 ft. wide, the posts are spaced 9 ft. 6 in. centres, the nearest post to the track being spaced 6 ft. 6 in. from the face of the platform.

Platform-sheds at Atlantic City, N. J., Philadelphia & Reading Railroad.—In Fig. 407 is shown a section of the platform-sheds in use at the terminal depot of the Philadelphia & Reading Railroad at Atlantic City, N. J. The symmetrical roof is used for platforms between tracks, while the unsym-

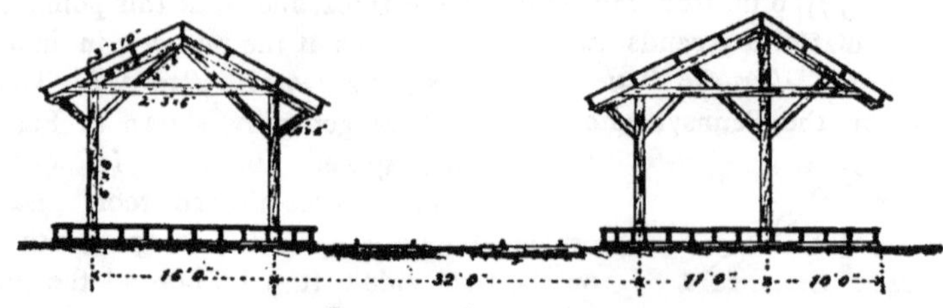

FIG. 407.—CROSS-SECTION.

metrical roof is used where there is a track on one side of the platform and a road on the other side. The illustration is copied from the *Railway Review* of May 10, 1890, in which issue the depot is fully illustrated and described.

Platform-shed at Passenger Depot, Rye, N. Y., New York, New Haven & Hartford Railroad.—The covered platform-shed of the New York, New Haven & Hartford Railroad at Rye, N. Y., shown in Figs. 408 to 412, published by permission of *The Engineering Record*, illustrated and described in the issue of *The Engineering Record* of November 23, 1889, is a two-legged platform-shed, with bents spaced 20 ft. centres. The posts in each bent are spaced 10 ft. centres. The roof projection in the rear of the building is 10 ft. beyond the post, so as to allow carriages to stand alongside the platform under cover. The foundations of the posts are stone blocks, 2 ft. square at the base, 18 in. square at the top, and 3 ft. deep, bedded on a suitable foundation. The principal timbers used are, posts, 6½

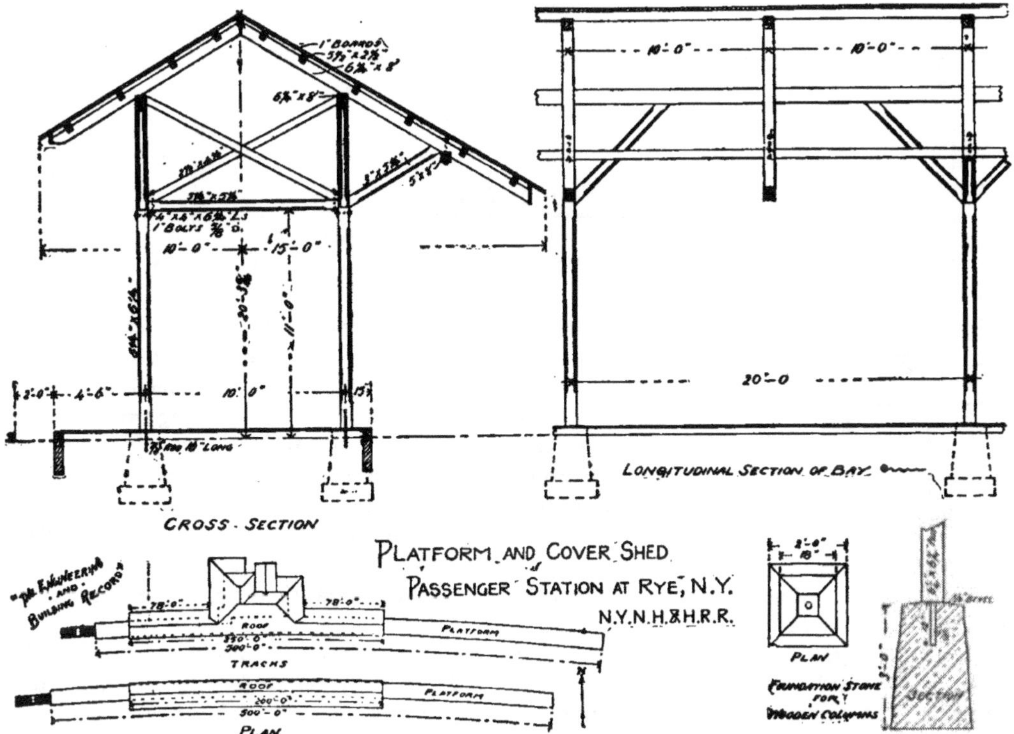

FIGS. 408 to 412.—CROSS-SECTION, LONGITUDINAL SECTION, AND GENERAL PLAN OF SHED, AND PLAN AND CROSS-SECTION OF COLUMN PEDESTAL.
(By permission of *The Engineering Record.*)

in. × 6½ in.; plates, 6½ in. × 8 in.; principal rafters, 6½ in. × 8 in.; purlins, 5½ in. × 2½ in.; roof-boards, 1 in. The length of covered platform on each side of the tracks is 250 ft.; the total length of platform is 500 ft. on each side of the tracks.

Platform-sheds, Union Depot, Kansas City, Mo.—In Fig. 413 is shown a section across the tracks at the Union Passenger Depot at Kansas City, Mo., copied from the issue of the *Railroad Gazette* of June 21, 1878. The peculiarity of this design consists of the use of one-legged iron platform-sheds over the platforms between the various groups of tracks and running parallel with the main depot building, thus avoiding the construction of a large and costly train-shed. The platform-

FIG. 413.—CROSS-SECTION.

sheds between the different tracks are connected at several points, across the tracks, by large specially designed roofs, which span the tracks from platform to platform. In this way, passengers can go to or from trains practically under cover by using the covered cross-passages to or from the platform-sheds proper.

Shelter for Horses and Carriages at Germantown Junction, Pa., Pennsylvania Railroad.—The

Fig. 414.—Front Elevation.

Fig. 415.—End Elevation.

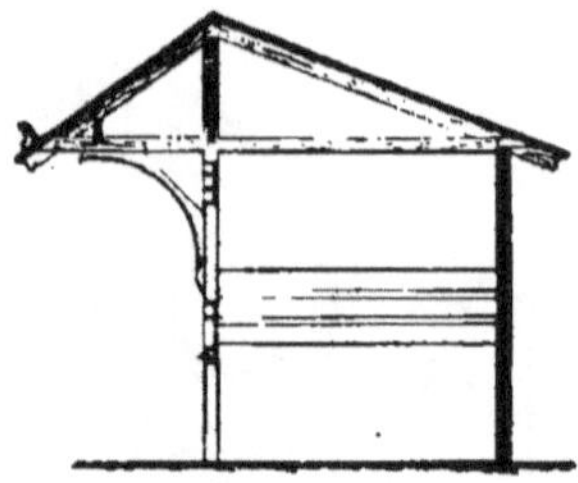
Fig. 416.—Cross-section.

design for a shelter for horses and carriages at Germantown Junction, Pa., on the Pennsylvania Railroad, designed by Mr. Wm. H. Brown, Chief Engineer, P. R. R., shown in Figs. 414 to 417, is a frame structure with unsymmetrical, double-pitched roof, supported by bents, spaced 10 ft. centres, each bent having two posts, spaced 10 ft. centres. The shelter is enclosed on three sides, being 10 ft. deep and 40 ft. long. The principal timbers used are, 6-in. × 6-in. ornamental posts; 6-in. × 6-in. caps; 2½-in. ornamental board knee-braces; 6-in. × 8-in. purlins; 3-in. × 8-in. purlin on the projection; 2-in. × 6-in. rafters, spaced 24 in. centres; 1-in. roof-boards, covered with a tin roof.

Fig. 417.—Ground Plan.

This style of roof and structure can be used, with slight modifications, for shelters for passengers and also for platform-sheds.

Shelter, Norfolk & Western Railroad.—The standard shelter of the Norfolk & Western Railroad, shown in Figs. 418 to 420, is 25 ft. long by 10 ft. wide, enclosed on three sides and open towards the track. A bench runs around the interior. There are two windows in each gable-end of the house.

Fig. 418.—Front Elevation.

Fig. 419.—End Elevation.

The outside of the building is sheathed with weather-boarding, and roofed with shingles. The principal materials used are, 6-in. × 6-in. posts; 2-in. × 4-in. studs; 2-in. × 4-in. purlins; 2-in. × 4-in. gable frame; 2-in. × 6-in. struts; 2-in. × 7-in. rafters; 2-in. flooring; 1-in. siding and roof-boards; 1-in. seats; 2-in. × 2-in. seat-legs; 2-in. × 7-in. ridge-pole; 2-in. × 8-in. floor-beams; 4-in. × 6-in. sills; ¼-in. × 6-in. casings; 1¼-in. wash-boards; 2-in. × 12-in. cresting; 2-in. curved brackets. The cost of the house erected complete is stated to be about $300.

Fig. 420.—Ground-plan.

Shelter, Philadelphia, Wilmington & Baltimore Railroad.—The design of an ornamental frame shelter with tin roof of the Philadelphia, Wilmington & Baltimore Railroad is illustrated in the issue of the *Railroad Gazette* of Feb. 20, 1875.

Shelter and Overhead Foot-bridge at Bedford Park, N. Y., New York Central & Hudson River Railroad.—The shelter and overhead foot-bridge of the New York Central & Hudson River Railroad at Bedford Park, N. Y., illustrated in Fig. 421, taken from the issue of the *Railroad and Engineering*

FIG. 421.—PERSPECTIVE.

Journal, Vol. LXVI., No. 2, the original plate having been kindly furnished to the author by the editor of the *Railroad and Engineering Journal*. The description in the publication mentioned is as follows:

Bedford Park is one of the prettiest of the recent suburban settlements around New York; it is on the west side of the Harlem Railroad, just above the old village of Fordham, while on the east side of the road is the new Bronx River Park, owned by the City of New York. The station is on the west side of the railroad, which has at that point four tracks, the two outer ones being used by the local trains, which stop at the station, and the two inner ones by express trains. The north-bound platform being on the east side of the tracks, a bridge was necessary to enable passengers to cross in safety, and one has been built which harmonizes well with the station and its surroundings.

The bridge is a single span of 60 ft.; the two plate-girders are supported on two columns at each end. The girders, which are spaced 8 ft. 6 in. apart between centres, form the railings, and the floor is carried on the lower flanges. The stairways on either side are supported by cast-iron columns. The bridge itself and the stairways are covered by a roof of ornamental design, carried on light iron columns.

This station, it will be noticed, is fenced in, and fences are placed to prevent persons from crossing the tracks on a level. This is the general practice followed on the Harlem line at the suburban stations.

CHAPTER XIX.

COMBINATION DEPOTS.

COMBINATION DEPOTS are used on railroads at local stations of minor importance, where the amount of freight or the volume of the passenger business does not warrant the construction of a separate freight-house or a separate passenger depot. In other words, a combination depot is a combination of the freight and passenger business under one roof. For the freight business a freight-room is required, with platform space along a wagon-road for transferring freight to and from wagons; and also the necessary platforms and facilities for handling freight to and from cars in freight trains or cars standing at the depot. A separate freight-office is not needed, because at stations where combination depots are used the entire business at the station is generally in charge of one man, with one or more assistants at important points, and the necessary clerical work, therefore, is done in one office, which serves as freight-office, ticket-office, and telegraph-office. This office should always have a projection on the track side, in the nature of a bay-window, so that the track is visible in both directions from inside the office. The passenger business is served by the introduction of waiting-rooms, either one general waiting-room or separate waiting-rooms for ladies and gentlemen. Where the passenger business warrants it, toilet-rooms are added. Separate baggage-rooms are also provided, where the passenger business is heavy, or a small space in one corner of the freight-room is picketed or partitioned off, so that baggage left at the station can be locked up, as the freight-doors of the freight-room are usually left open during the day-time. In a few individual cases, although very seldom, a separate room for express and a mail-room are added. A very frequent addition to a combination depot, however, is the provision for bedrooms and living-rooms for the agent and other help around the depot, or for the agent's family. This is very customary in the Western and Southern sections of the country, where it is not always feasible to get dwelling quarters in the neighborhood. Where local conditions require it, offices are sometimes added to such a depot for the use of a train-master, or a despatcher, or some other official of the railroad, whose office is located at the station in question. It will thus be seen that a large number of variations exist in combination-depot designs, according to the necessity of providing for and the relative importance given to the freight service, passenger business, baggage, express, telegraph, etc., and whether and how much room for dwelling purposes has to be reserved. There are combination depots, which are simply dwellings with a freight-room attached, and the clerical work is done in the living-room of the dwelling-house, while the platforms, the freight-room, and the agent's living-room are used indiscriminately for waiting and lounging rooms. On the other hand, there are combination depots where the provisions for dwelling purposes consist simply of a small bunk-room, for the use of a watchman or night-operator.

The requirements to be observed in dividing up the interior space of a combination depot are not many. Those for the freight business have been partly discussed in connection with local freight-houses, and those for the passenger business are similar to the questions discussed below in connection with local passenger depots. The location of the office should be facing the main track of the railroad. The ticket-window opening from the office to a general waiting-room should be so located in the office as to allow the necessary ticket-shelves, cases, etc., to be put along the wall without interfering with the operator's table or other work to be done in the office. Where there are separate waiting-rooms for gentlemen and ladies, tickets are either sold from a window leading on to a passage-way or lobby between the two waiting-rooms, or there are separate windows provided for each waiting-room. In the latter case, if possible, the windows should be located in such a way that the ticket-case is convenient to both windows, and that the ticket-seller does not have to move much in order to sell tickets from one or the other window. Where the freight business is large, and especially in northern climates, it is well to have a door between the office and the freight-room for the convenience of the agent in passing back and forth. At small stations, however, where the business is not very heavy, such a door only cuts up wall-space unnecessarily. Where feasible, it is desirable not to have the entrance to the office through the waiting-room, as trainmen, freight-handlers, and railroaders, desiring to speak to the agent or the office help, will have to pass through the waiting-room. Passengers will also be more liable to enter the office, crowding it and interfering with the work of the agent or his help. In small depots, however, such as mainly under discussion, these finer features of a depot design cannot be so readily observed, and are also less important.

One of the most important questions in connection with a combination depot is its location in relation to the tracks on one or both sides of the building, and also the extent, length, width, and height of the platforms. It has been previously stated in the chapter on Freight-houses that, where feasible, it is desirable to have the main track pass along the front of the building, and to put a side track for cars left at the station on the rear of the building. In combination depots, however, especially where more importance is attached to the passenger business, it is undesirable to have a side track on the rear of the building, as passengers have to cross it to get to the depot, and it makes it difficult and dangerous to drive up to the depot with carriages. For combination depots with considerable passenger business, therefore, the best construction will prove to be a side track, located between the front of the building and the main track. Passengers will have to step across the side track to get to the passenger-trains on the main track, while freight can be skidded from the freight platform across the side track to freight-trains. Cars left at the station for loading or unloading are placed on the side track in front of the freight-room and along the freight platform at the end of the depot away from that part of the building devoted to the passenger business. As a rule, however, special cars are not left at a station, unless it is for what is known as car-load freight, in which case the side track between the main track and the building can be omitted, as all freight passing through the house consists of package freight, which is handled directly to or from freight-trains. Provision for the accommodation of the car-load freight is made by having a special siding near the depot along a wagon-road. Therefore, unless standing cars will be loaded to a large extent from the house, the best plan to adopt is to let the main track or a main siding run along the face of the building.

Relative to the height of platforms, there are combination depots with low platforms throughout, others with high platforms throughout, and also others with a combination of low and high platforms. Where the passenger business predominates, low platforms throughout are warranted. Where the freight business is more important and the amount or class of passenger business does not have to be particularly considered, high platforms throughout will not prove detrimental, but on the contrary will be advantageous for the principal business, and also cheapen the construction. But where the freight and passenger interests are both important, high and low platforms should be adopted. In this case a high platform should be placed on both sides of the freight-room, and also across the end of the house where the freight-room is located, in case the house is a large one. This high platform should also be extended along the track for some distance, so as to reach more cars. At the other end of the house, where the passenger waiting-rooms are located, the platforms should be made low, and, where the business warrants it, this low platform should be extended for some distance along the main track. The high platform and low platform are connected at the front of the house by an incline. In some designs, an attempt is made to use one platform height around the building for both purposes, by placing the platform half-way between a low and a high platform; but this does not represent the best practice. Where two different heights are used, it is customary for passenger trains to stop, as far as possible, opposite the low portion, and freight trains are stopped so that the particular car from or to which freight is to be transferred is opposite the freight-room and the high platform. There is one objection usually made to the introduction of a high platform along a running track, even where it is only used in front of the freight-room, namely, that passengers might stand in front of the depot between the track and the high platform and get caught by a train. In a number of designs, therefore, a low platform is inserted between the high platform and the nearest track; in other words, the face of the high platform is kept 7 to 10 ft. away from the centre of the track, so that there is a low platform, 2 to 5 ft. wide, between the car-body and the high platform.

In Fig. 422 is shown a proposed layout for tracks and platforms at a combination depot, in which it is desired to have a low platform for the passenger business and a high platform

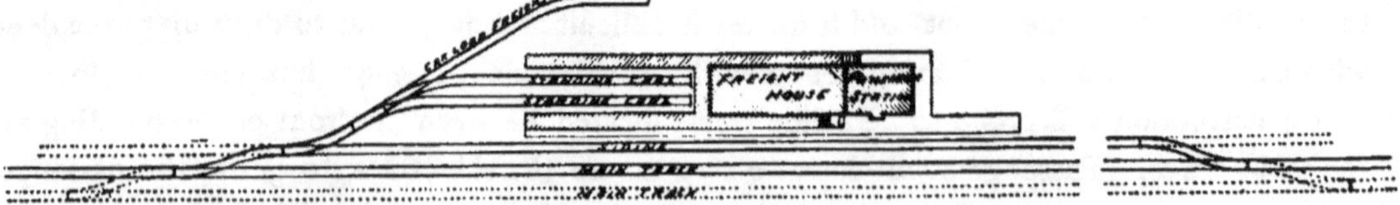

FIG. 422.—PROPOSED GENERAL LAYOUT FOR A COMBINATION DEPOT.

for the freight business, and to provide platform frontage for cars left at the depot to be loaded or unloaded with freight passing through the house, as also a track for car-load freight. The siding in front of the depot is intended for freight trains to pull into for receiving or delivering package freight to the house, and it will also serve as a passing siding for trains. The rear of the depot and the end opposite the passenger rooms are accessible for teams and carriages, without crossing any tracks or getting pocketed between tracks. The high platform is set 8 ft. back from the centre of the siding, which allows a passage-way for passengers and baggage between the siding and the high platform, while the space to be skidded across to get package freight to or from a freight-train on the siding is less than four feet, which does not require heavy skids.

Relative to the class of structure and materials to be adopted in each particular case, the same general rules and views will hold good as discussed in connection with small local freight-houses and local passenger depots. The same can also be said in connection with the design of the doors, windows, and other minor details of a combination depot.

The following descriptions and illustrations of combination depots in actual use on railroads in this country will serve to present more particularly the rules and methods generally observed in the construction of such structures.

Combination Depots, Minnesota & Northwestern Railroad.—The standard combination depots of the Minnesota & Northwestern Railroad and of the Chicago, St. Paul & Kansas City Railway, designed in 1887 under the direction of Mr. H. Fernstrom, Chief Engineer, by Mr. C. A. Reed, Supervising Architect, M. & N. W. R. R., consist of a series of alternate designs suitable for various localities and conditions. All the structures are one-story frame buildings, sheathed on the outside with upright boards or weather-boarding, and roofed with shingles. Low platforms surround the building on all sides, the top of the platform being 12 in. above the top of rail. The platform along the face of the house next to the track reaches within 5 ft. of the centre of the track.

Class "B" is 16 ft. × 40 ft., divided into a freight-room, 21 ft. × 15 ft.; a waiting-room, 17 ft. × 15 ft.; and a ticket-office, 6 ft. × 9 ft., with a square, 3-ft. × 6-ft., bay-window extension. This design, as shown in Figs. 423 and 424, is finished off verycheaply. There are platforms on all sides

Fig. 423.—Front Elevation, Class "B."

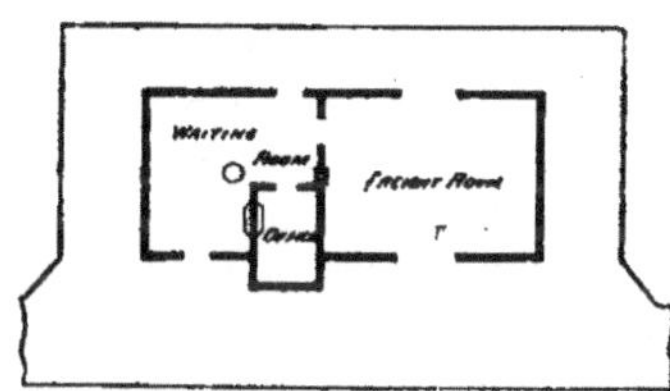

Fig. 424.—Ground-plan, Class "B."

of the building; the front platform is 14 ft. wide, the rear platform 6 ft. wide, and the end platforms 8 ft. wide. The front platform is extended, 8 ft. wide, each way from the building, so as to give a total length of 250 ft. of platform facing the track. The principal timbers for the platform construction are, sills on blocking, 6 in. × 8 in.; floor-joists, 2 in. × 10 in., spanning 8 ft.; flooring, 2 in. The principal materials for the frame are, sills, 6 in. × 8 in.; plates, two pieces, 2 in. × 4 in.; studs, 2 in. × 4 in.; ceiling-joists, 2 in. × 4 in.; rafters, 2 in. × 4 in.; truss-braces, 1 in. × 6 in.; floor-beams, 2 in. × 10 in., spanning 16 ft. The foundations are of blocking. Sliding freight-doors, 6 ft. × 7 ft.

Class "D" is a 20-ft. × 44-ft. structure, with a freight-room, 19 ft. × 24 ft.; a waiting-room, 18 ft. × 19 ft.; an office, 11 ft. × 6 ft., with a 3-ft. × 11-ft., square bay-window projection. The exterior of the building is finished off more handsomely than in class "B;" but the general arrangement, the width of the platforms, and the framing of the sides and roof remain about the same, excepting that the frame is a 6-in. frame in place of a 4-in. frame, and the ceiling-joists and rafters are 2 in. × 6 in., in place of 2 in. × 4 in.

Class "E" is a 22-ft. × 55-ft. structure, as shown in Figs. 425 to 428, and is in general similar to class "D." The interior is divided into a freight-room, 21 ft. × 28 ft.; a waiting-room, 21 ft. × 18 ft.; and an office, 21 ft. × 10 ft., with a 3-ft. 6-in. × 10-ft., square bay-window extension. The platforms remain the same, and the frame and roof consist of 6-in. scantlings, as described for class "D."

Class "G" is a 22-ft. × 70-ft. structure, practically the same as class "E," excepting the extra length, which is mainly utilized for a baggage-room inserted between the freight-room and the office.

Class "H" is a 22-ft. × 70-ft. building, exactly the same as class "E," excepting that the freight-room is lengthened out.

FIG. 425.—FRONT ELEVATION, CLASS "E."

FIG. 426.—END ELEVATION, CLASS "E."

Class "I" is 22 ft. × 90 ft., the same as class "E" in its general features, excepting the interior, which is divided so as to give a freight-room, 42 ft. × 21 ft.; a trainmen's and bulletin-room, 9 ft. × 21

FIG. 427.—CROSS-SECTION, CLASS "E."

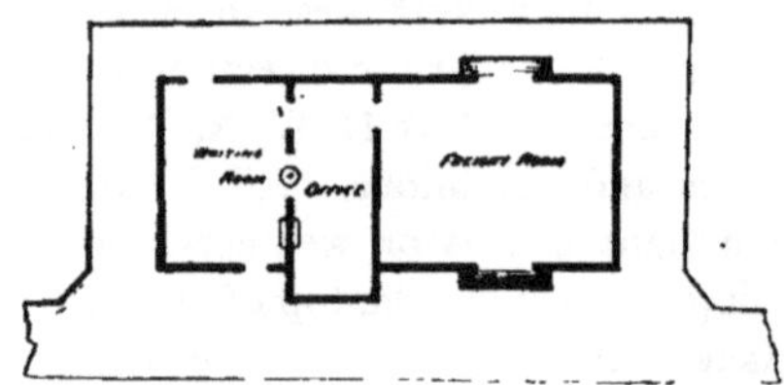

FIG. 428.—GROUND-PLAN, CLASS "E."

ft.; a general waiting-room, 20 ft. × 21 ft.; a ticket-office, 19 ft. × 7 ft.; and a trainmaster's and despatcher's office, 19 ft. × 16 ft.

Class "J" is 22 ft. × 90 ft., and similar to class "E," excepting that the interior is divided into a freight-room, 21 ft. × 38 ft.; a baggage-room, 21 ft. × 8 ft.; a gentlemen's waiting-room, 21 ft. × 15 ft.; a ladies' waiting-room, 21 ft. × 13 ft.; and a ticket-office, 11 ft. × 16 ft.

The materials for buildings of this kind, which have to be provided and allowed for in a bill of material, consist of brick, lime, sand, stoves, stove-pipes, elbows, cast-iron pan under stove, seats, shelves, paint, oil, varnish, drier, putty, shellac, turpentine, benzine, rough boards and scantlings, sized boards and scantlings, flooring, siding, ceiling, shingles, ornamental shingles, door-knobs, butt-hinges, sash-fasteners, spring sash-bolts, window-weights, sash-cord, barn-door hangers with rails, hinged hasps, padlocks, pin with chain and staple and wrought-iron door-handles for freight-doors, sash-locks, cupboard locks and hinges, stove-pipe thimbles and covers, tin for flashing and guttering, galvanized-iron down-conductors with elbows, zinc stove-screens, angle-iron protection for freight-door jambs, building-paper, nails, spikes, bolts, washers, outside doors, transoms, inside doors, freight-doors, door-frames, ticket-window, ticket-window shelves, operator's table, railings, windows, sash and frames, brackets for projecting roof, end brackets, finials, ridge-cresting, gutter-boards, cornices, mouldings, base-boards, wainscoting, oak door-sills, etc.

Combination Depot, Pine Creek & Buffalo Railway.—The combination depot of the Pine Creek & Buffalo Railway, shown in Figs. 429 and 430, designed by Mr. Theodore E. Hocke, consists of a single-story frame structure, 21 ft. wide × 57 ft. long, divided into a freight-room, 40 ft. × 20 ft.;

FIG. 429. FRONT ELEVATION.

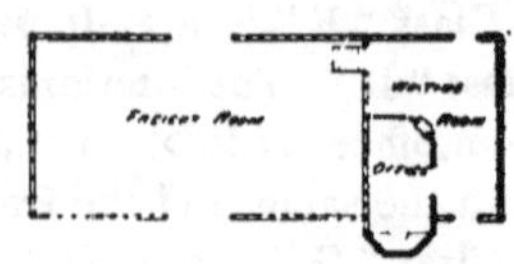

FIG. 430.—GROUND-PLAN.

a ticket-office, 12 ft. × 7 ft. 6 in.; and the balance for a general waiting-room. The waiting-room and ticket-office, including the platform surrounding that end of the building, is on a low level, while the freight-room is surrounded on all three sides with a high platform, connected with the low platform by inclines.

FIG. 431.—FRONT ELEVATION.

FIG. 432.—END ELEVATION.

Combination Depot at Cherry Ford, Pa., Lehigh Valley Railroad.—The combination depot of the Lehigh Valley Railroad at Cherry Ford, Pa., shown in Figs. 431 to 433, is a single-story frame structure, 15 ft. × 45 ft., sheathed on the outside with weather-boarding, and roofed with slate. It is divided into a freight-room, 17 ft. × 14 ft.; a general waiting-room, 17 ft. × 14 ft.; and an office, 8 ft. × 14 ft., with a 3-ft. × 8-ft., square bay-window projection.

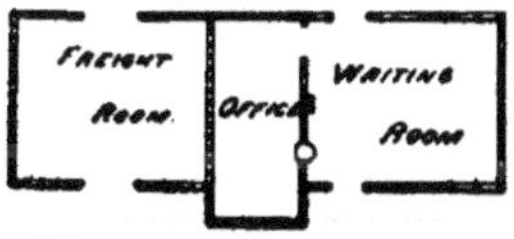

FIG. 433.—GROUND-PLAN.

Combination Depot, Class "A," Richmond & Alleghany Railroad.—The combination depot of the Richmond & Alleghany Railroad, known as class "A," shown in Figs. 434 to 436, is an island-

FIG. 434.—FRONT ELEVATION.

FIG. 435.—END ELEVATION.

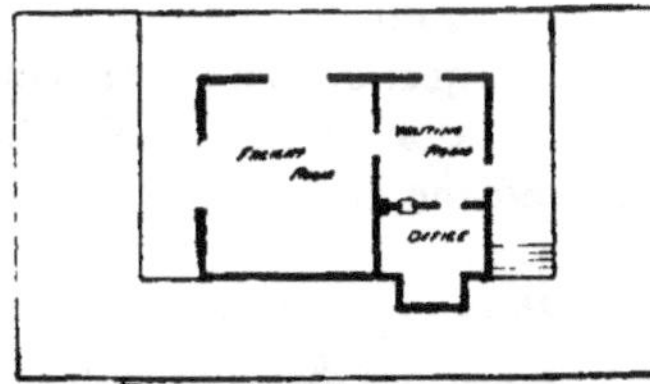

FIG. 436.—GROUND-PLAN.

depot, and consists of a single-story frame building, with a high platform at the ends of the building and on the rear along the side track, and a low platform on the face of the building next to the main track. The building is 25 ft. × 28 ft., and is divided into a freight-room, 22 ft. × 24 ft.; a waiting-room, 14 ft. × 15 ft. 6 in.; and a ticket-office, 8 ft. × 14 ft., with a square bay-window projection, 8 ft. × 4 ft.

Combination Depot, Class "B," Richmond & Alleghany Railroad.—The combination depot of the Richmond & Alleghany Railroad, known as class "B," shown in Figs. 437 and 438, is an island-depot, similar to class "A," and consists of a single-story frame

FIG. 437.—FRONT ELEVATION.

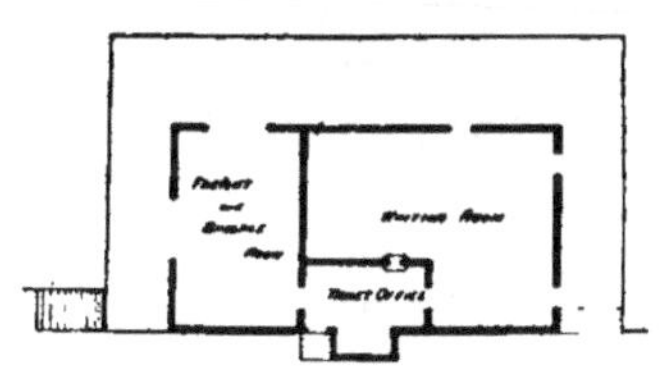

FIG. 438.—GROUND-PLAN.

structure, 25 ft. × 50 ft., divided into a freight and baggage room, 24 ft. × 16 ft.; a ticket-office, 8 ft. × 16 ft., with a square bay-window projection; and a general waiting-room. This class of depot is for use at an island-station, where there is a side track on the rear of the building, in addition to the main track along the face of the building. The platform at the face of the building next to the main track is a low platform, 8 ft. wide. The platform at the back of the building along the side track and at each end of the building is a high platform, 8 ft. wide.

Combination Depots, Pennsylvania Lines West of Pittsburg.—The combination depots of the Pennsylvania lines west of Pittsburg, Southwest System, designed by Mr. M. J. Becker, Chief Engineer, consist of three classes, respectively "A," "B," and "D," and are frame single-story structures, surrounded by low platforms on all sides, sheathed on the outside with vertical ornamental battened boarding and horizontal boarding, in panels, and roofed with slate. The walls of the offices and waiting-rooms are plastered. The foundations are stone piers. The platforms along the face of the building are generally 16 ft. wide, reaching within 4 ft. 6 in. of the centre of the track, and set 8 in. above the top of the rail.

The specifications for the depots class "A" and "B" are given in full in the Appendix at the back of this book, and the design for class "A" is illustrated in Figs. 439 and 440, the design for

FIG. 439.—FRONT ELEVATION.

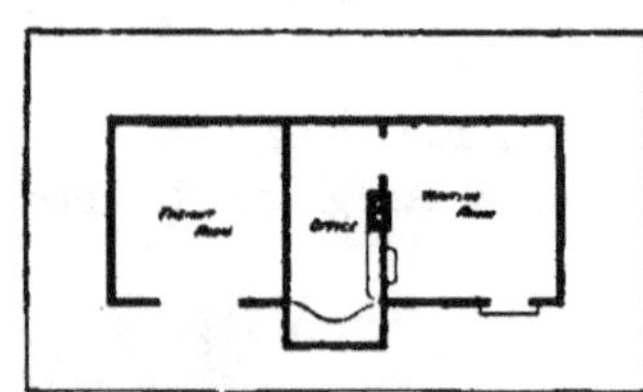

FIG. 440.—GROUND-PLAN.

class "B" being practically the same excepting in point of size, while class "D" is quite similar also. For detail data, see specifications.

The building in class "A" is 40 ft. × 16 ft., divided into a waiting-room, 15 ft. × 15 ft.; a ticket and telegraph office, 8 ft. × 19 ft., including a square bay-window projection on the track side; and a freight-room, 15 ft. × 15 ft.

The building in class "B" is 46 ft. × 18 ft., divided into a waiting-room, 17 ft. × 18 ft.; a ticket and telegraph office, 8 ft. × 20 ft. 6 in.; and a freight-room, 17 ft. × 18 ft.

The building in class "D" is 49 ft. × 17 ft., divided into a waiting-room, 20 ft. × 16 ft.; a ticket and telegraph office, 7 ft. × 19 ft. 6 in., including a square bay-window projection; and a freight-room, 20 ft. × 16 ft. The rear of the office in this plan is partitioned off as a ticket-office, while the front serves for a telegraph-office. There is a door between the office and the freight-room. The freight-room and waiting-room have also doors on the rear of the depot.

Combination Depot with Dwelling-rooms, Pennsylvania Lines West of Pittsburg, Southwest System.—The combination depot of the Pennsylvania lines west of Pittsburg, Southwest System, designed by Mr. M. J. Becker, Chief Engineer, known as class "E" of the standard depot plans, is a frame two-story building, 38 ft. × 17 ft., with a single-story annex, 25 ft. 6 in. × 14 ft. 6 in., for a living-room and a kitchen. The exterior of the building is treated similarly to the standard combination depots of the same railroad, described above and shown in Figs. 439 and 440, and the specifications are practically the same as for the combination depots and local passenger depots of the same railroad, the specifications for which are given in full in the Appendix at the back of this book. The outside of the building is sheathed with vertical ornamental battened boarding and horizontal boarding, in panels, and roofed with slate. The rooms are all plastered in the interior, excepting the freight-room. The ground-floor is divided into a waiting-room, 14 ft. × 16 ft.; an office, with a passage leading to the kitchen, and a stairway leading to the upper floor at the rear of the office; a freight-room, 14 ft. × 16 ft.; a living-room, 12 ft. × 14 ft.; and a kitchen, 12 ft. × 14 ft. The upper floor has two bedrooms, each 14 ft. × 16 ft.

Combination Depot, Chesapeake & Ohio Railway.—The combination depot of the Chesapeake & Ohio Railway, known as design No. 4, prepared in 1882, is a single-story frame structure, 16 ft. × 40 ft., sheathed on the outside with horizontal weather-boarding and with upright boards and battens, in panels, and roofed with tin or shingles. The interior is divided into a waiting-room, an office, and a freight-room. This design is practically the same as the standard combination depot, class "A," of the Pennsylvania lines west of Pittsburg, described above and illustrated in Figs. 439 and 440.

Combination Depot, Ohio Valley Railway.—The combination depot of the Ohio Valley Railway at Sturgis, Ky., designed by Mr. C. C. Genung, Chief Engineer, Ohio Valley Railway, is a single-story frame structure, 55 ft. × 20 ft., roofed with shingles, very similar in the general arrangement of the ground-plan to the combination depot of the Pine Creek & Buffalo Railway, illustrated and described above, with the exception, however, that the passsage from the high freight platform, in front of the freight-room, to the low passenger platform around the passenger end of the building, is made by steps and not by an incline. The interior is divided into a general waiting-room, 19 ft. × 15 ft.; a freight-room, 19 ft. × 28 ft.; and an office, 19 ft. × 10 ft., between them. The low passenger platform is 12 ft. wide and 120 ft. long in front of the building; the high freight platform is 8 ft. wide, and extends along the front and the end of the freight-room. The design of the exterior is similar to the standard local passenger depot of the same railroad illustrated in Fig. 520, the most striking feature of which is the upward curve of the roof at the eaves, the radius of the curve being about 10 ft. This feature, in connection with the knee-braces under the roof projection, which are cut to a bold semicircular pattern, causes the structure to appear very neat, without increasing the cost materially. The outside of the building is sheathed with vertical, horizontal, and diagonal plain and ornamental boarding, in panels. The inside finish is of wood. The vertical siding is painted a turkey vermilion, the horizontal and diagonal siding a very light drab, and the frames, belt-courses, etc., a very dark red, approaching a brown color. Mr. Genung states that this building cost about eleven hundred dollars, exclusive of platforms.

Combination Depot, Cincinnati Southern Railway.—The Cincinnati Southern Railway, now part of the Cincinnati, New Orleans & Texas Pacific Railway, had four classes of designs for combination depots, known as classes "A," "B," "C," and "D." All the designs are single-story frame structures, sheathed on the outside with boards, and roofed with tin. Design "A," shown in Figs. 441 to 444, is 58 ft. × 20 ft., divided into a freight-room, 22 ft. × 19 ft.; an office, 11 ft. × 19 ft.; and a general waiting-room, 22 ft. × 19 ft. At each gable-end of the building the roof is extended for 12 ft., forming an open shed extension to the building at each end. The outer end of the shed extension is supported by two posts. The building is surrounded on all sides by platforms. The front platform is 16 ft. wide, and is set 15 in. above the top of rail. The rear platform is 8 ft. wide, and set at the same height. The freight-doors are sliding-doors, 7 ft. 4 in. × 7 ft. 4 in.

FIG. 441.—FRONT ELEVATION.

FIG. 442.—END ELEVATION.

Plan "B" shows the same size building and division of the interior and general finish as plan "A." The shed-roof extension in plan "B," however, is only built at one end of the building, next to the waiting-room. Plan "B" differs from plan "A" in respect to the platforms. Plan "A" has low platforms on all sides of the house; plan "B" has a high platform, 12 ft. wide, on the front of the house, next to the track, a high platform, 8 ft. wide, on the rear of the house, next to the wagon-road, and a 12-ft. platform, on the same level as the other platforms, at the waiting-room end of the house under the shed-roof extension. The face of the front platform is set 6 ft. from the centre of the track, and 4 ft. above the top of the tie. The level of the wagon-road at the rear of the house is about three feet below the platform.

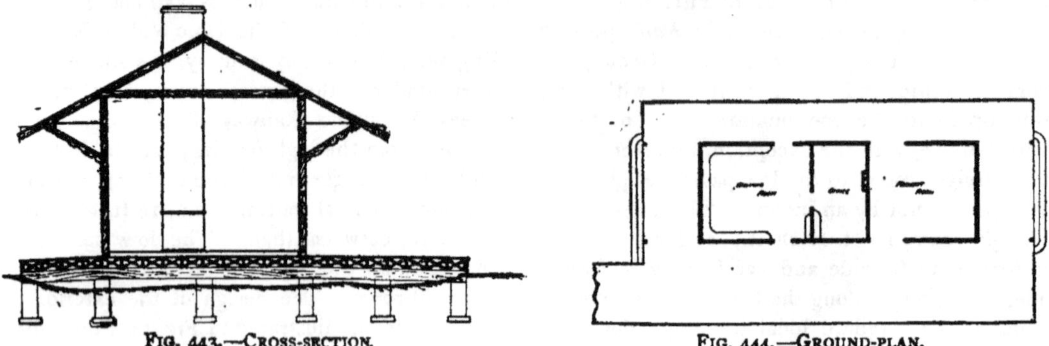

FIG. 443.—CROSS-SECTION. FIG. 444.—GROUND-PLAN.

Plan C is similar to plan D, excepting that the building is only 35 ft. long, and is divided into a freight-room, 23 ft. × 19 ft.; an office, 11 ft. × 8 ft.; and a waiting-room, 11 ft. × 10 ft.

Plan D is a very plain structure, without any attempt at ornamentation, 20 ft. × 46 ft., divided into a freight-room, a waiting-room, and an office. There is no shed-roof extension of the building, like in the other designs. There are high platforms on three sides of the building; the front platform is 12 ft. wide, while the end platform and rear platform are 8 ft. wide.

Combination Depot, Burlington, Cedar Rapids & Northern Railway.—The combination depot of the Burlington, Cedar Rapids & Northern Railway, shown in Figs. 445 to 447, consists of a single-story frame structure, 48 ft. × 18 ft., sheathed on the outside with horizontal weather-boarding. The interior is divided into a freight-room, 17 ft. × 20 ft.; a waiting-room, 17 ft. × 16 ft.; an office, 10 ft. × 17 ft., with a square bay-window projection, 3 ft. × 8 ft. The building is surrounded by a low platform on all sides, the platforms at the gable-ends and along the face of the building next to the track being 12 ft. wide, while the platform at the rear of the building is only 8 ft. wide. The face of the platform is set 5 ft. 6 in. from the centre of the track, and the top is placed 16 in. above the top of the rail. The foundations of the building are stone walls and piers. The freight-doors are 7 ft. wide by 8 ft. high, with large transom-lights. The roof projection on the front and rear of the building is 4 ft. 6 in. The principal timbers used are, sills, 6 in. × 8 in.; floor-joists, 2 in. × 12 in., spanning 9 ft.; corner and door studs, 4 in. × 4 in.; intermediate studs, 2 in. × 4 in.; plates, two pieces, 2 in. × 4 in.; ceiling-joists, 2 in. × 6 in.; rafters, 2 in. × 4 in; tie-beams, 1 in. × 6 in.; roof-boards, 1 in.; rise of roof, $\frac{1}{4}$ of span; platform-caps, 8 in. × 10 in.; platform-joists, 2 in. × 10 in., spaced 16 in. centres, spanning 9 ft.; freight-room and platform floor, 3-in. plank; floor in waiting-room and office, 1-in. dressed boards, laid on a rough plank under layer.

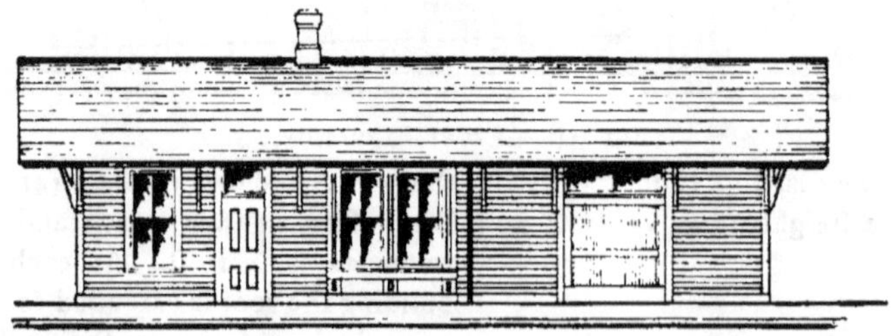

FIG. 445.—FRONT ELEVATION.

The data for above were kindly furnished by Mr. H. F. White, Chief Engineer, B., C. R. & N. Ry., who also states, that a depot as described above, with stone foundations, costs about $1000.

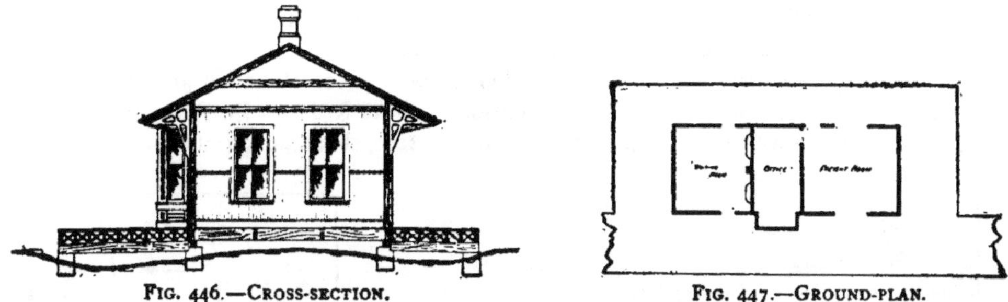

FIG. 446.—CROSS-SECTION. FIG. 447.—GROUND-PLAN.

Combination Depot, Wabash, St. Louis & Pacific Railway.—The combination depot of the Wabash, St. Louis & Pacific Railway, designed by Mr. Charles Hansel, Resident Engineer, shown in Figs. 448 to 451, consists of a single-story frame structure, 20 ft. × 50 ft., sheathed on the outside

FIG. 448.—FRONT ELEVATION.

FIG. 449.—END ELEVATION.

with upright boards and battens and diagonal sheathing, in panels, and roofed with shingles. The interior is divided into a waiting-room, 18 ft. × 17 ft.; a freight-room, 18 ft. × 23 ft.; and an office, 18 ft. × 8 ft., with a hexagonal bay-window projection, 3 ft. × 8 ft. The freight-doors are sliding-doors,

FIG. 450.—CROSS-SECTION.

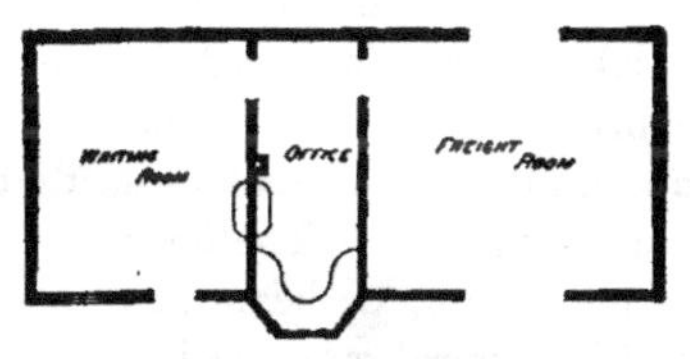

FIG. 451.—GROUND-PLAN.

7 ft. × 7 ft., with transom-lights overhead. The walls and ceilings of waiting-room and office, also the under side of the roof projection, is ceiled. The walls in the freight-room are boarded up to a height of 7 ft. with rough boards. The outside sheathing consists of half-dressed sheathing planks, covered with 3-in. O. G. battens. The shingles, before being laid, are dipped in a mixture of mineral paint and boiled linseed-oil. The platform at the face of the building, next to the track, is a low platform, 4 in. above the top of rail, and the face of the platform is set 4 ft. from the centre of the track. The height of the interior is 11 ft. 6 in. in the clear. The principal timbers used are, sills, 6 in. × 8 in.; floor-joists, 2 in. × 10 in., spaced 16 in.; plates, 2 in. × 6 in.; studs, 2 in. × 6 in.; ribbons, 2 in. × 4 in.; ceiling-joists, 2 in. × 8 in., spaced 16 in.; rafters, 2 in. × 6 in., spaced 20 in.; collar-beams, 1 in. × 6 in.; floor in waiting-room and office, 1-in. yellow-pine flooring; floor in freight-room, 2-in. rough plank; ceiling, ⅞-in. boards; outside sheathing and roof-boards, 1 in. The balance of the material required consists of shingles, battens, transom-lights, window-sash, outside doors,

inside doors, sliding freight-doors, nails, spikes, bolts, brick, lime, sand, base-boards, cap-boards, mouldings, brackets, ridge-piece, gutter-boards, down-conductors, window-frames, door-frames, sash-weights, door-hangings, locks, sash-fasteners, barn-door rollers and track, sash-cord, spring latch, ticket-window, and agent's table. The platform is set on posts planted in the ground, with 6-in. × 8-in. caps; 2-in. × 10-in. joists, spaced 20 in.; and 2-in. floor-plank.

Combination Depot, Kansas City & Emporia Railroad.—The combination depot of the Kansas City & Emporia Railroad, connected with the Atchison, Topeka & Santa Fe Railroad system, shown in Figs. 452 and 453, consists of a single-story frame structure, sheathed on the outside with board-

FIG. 452.—FRONT ELEVATION. FIG. 453.—GROUND-PLAN.

ing. The size of the building is 24 ft. × 42 ft., and the interior is divided into a freight-room, 13 ft. × 23 ft.; a waiting-room, 11 ft. × 18 ft.; an office, 11 ft. × 18 ft.; and a baggage-room, 9 ft. × 18 ft. The waiting-room, office, and baggage-room have low platforms in front of them, while the freight-room has a high platform around it. Connection is made between the low and high platforms by inclines, where they join each other.

Combination Depot at Hilliard, Ga., Savannah, Florida & Western Railway.—The combination depot of the Savannah, Florida & Western Railway at Hilliard, Ga., designed by Mr. W. B. W. Howe, Jr., shown in Fig. 454, is a single-story frame structure, 30 ft. × 32 ft., sheathed with upright boards and battens, and roofed with tin. The interior is divided into a warehouse, 15 ft. × 30 ft.; a waiting-room, 14 ft. × 14 ft.; and an office, 14 ft. × 14 ft., with an octagonal bay-window projection, 5 ft. × 10 ft. The building is surrounded on three sides by high platforms, 8 ft. to 10 ft. wide. The face of the platform next to the track is 6 ft. 6 in. from the centre of the track, and the top of the platform is 4 ft. above the top of rail. The roof projection on the front and rear of the building is 10 ft. Between the waiting-room and office there is a large brick chimney for wood fires in each room. The foundations of the building are brick piers. The sills under the building are 10 in. × 14 in., and under the ends of the platform and under the floor-beams inside the house they are 6 in. × 14 in. The floor-beams are 3 in. × 12 in., spanning 12 ft. The floor is 3-in. plank. The principal timbers of the frame and roof are, posts, 6 in. × 8 in.; tie-beams, two pieces, $1\frac{1}{2}$ in. × 6 in.; principal rafters, 3 in. × 8 in.; truss-braces, 6 in. × 6 in.; knee-braces, $1\frac{1}{2}$ in. × 6 in.; purlins, 3 in. × 8 in.; truss-rod, $\frac{3}{4}$ in. in diameter. The rise of the roof is $\frac{1}{4}$ of the span. The freight-doors are 5 ft. wide × 8 ft. high, hung in pairs and swinging inward.

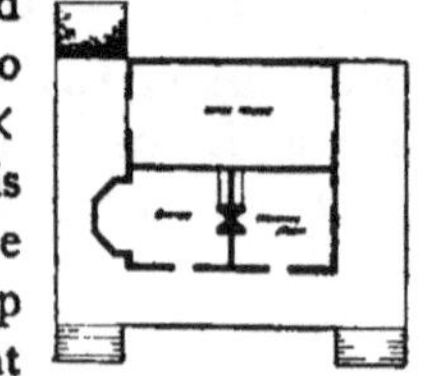

FIG. 454.—GROUND-PLAN.

Combination Depot, Philadelphia & Reading Railroad.—The combination depot of the Philadelphia & Reading Railroad, shown in Fig. 455, consists of a single-story structure, 80 ft. × 30 ft. One end is divided off for a freight-room, 31 ft. × 40 ft., and is surrounded by an 8-ft. platform on three sides, the top of the platform being 2 ft. 8 in. above the top of the rail, and the face of the platform being 5 ft. 6 in. from the centre of the track along the face of the house. The remainder of the house has an office, 18 ft. × 19 ft.; a gentlemen's waiting-room, 18 ft. × 15 ft.; a ladies' waiting-room, 18 ft. × 15 ft.; a baggage-room, 11 ft. × 6 ft.; and ladies' and gentlemen's toilet-rooms, each 6 ft. × 11 ft. in size. This part of the building is on a lower level than the freight-room, and has a low 8-ft. platform next

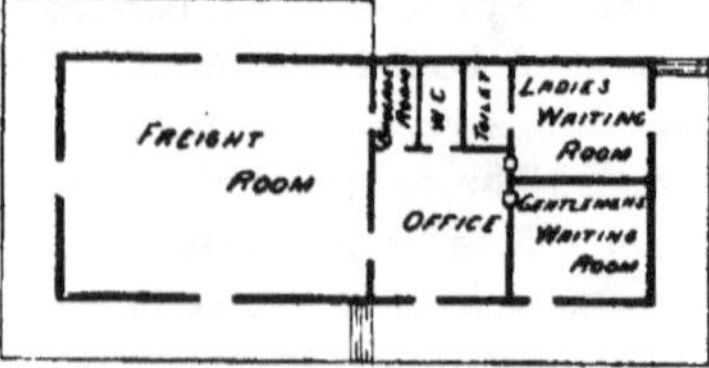

FIG. 455.—GROUND-PLAN.

to the track, and along the gable-end of the building. This low platform is 9 in. above the top of the rail, and connects with the high platform by steps or an incline.

Combination Depot and Office Building at Williamsburg, Va., Chesapeake & Ohio Railway.—The combination depot and office building of the Chesapeake & Ohio Railway at Williamsburg, Va., is a two-story frame structure, with a single-story freight-house annex, as shown in Figs. 456 and 457.

FIG. 456.—FRONT ELEVATION.

The outside of the building is sheathed with horizontal and upright boards and ornamental shingles, producing a pleasing effect. The two-story part of the building is 41 ft. × 21 ft. and the single-story freight-house is 26 ft. × 61 ft. The ground-floor has a freight-room; a gentlemen's waiting-room;

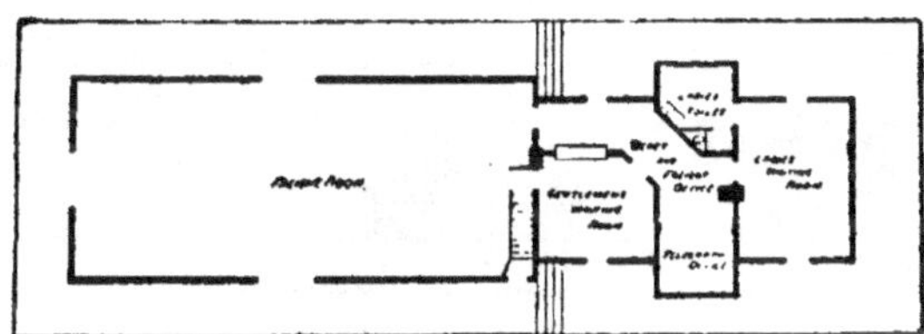

FIG. 457.—GROUND-PLAN.

a ladies' waiting-room with a ladies' toilet-room attached; also a large room for use as telegraph-office, ticket and freight office. A pair of stairs lead to the upper floor, where there are three rooms used as offices for the train-despatcher of the division, and other officials.

Combination Depot with Dwelling-rooms, Northern Pacific Railroad.—The combination depot of

FIG. 458.—FRONT ELEVATION.

the Northern Pacific Railroad, with dwelling attached, designed by Mr. C. B. Talbot in 1884, shown in Figs. 458 and 459, is a single-story frame structure, with the exception of one end where there is an attic room under the roof. The building is 22 ft. × 56 ft., and consists of one large freight-room, 22 ft. × 40 ft., which serves as freight-room, baggage-room, and waiting-room. Next to the freight-room there is a living-room and a bedroom, in addition to which there is, as previously mentioned, a bedroom upstairs, reached by a flight of steps. There is a platform 13 ft. wide in front of the house, along the track. This platform is set 16 inches above the top of rail, and 5 ft. 10 in. from the centre of the track. In front of the freight-house there is a 10-ft. wide, high freight platform, connected with the low platform by an incline. The face of the freight platform is 8 ft. 10 in. from the centre of the track, so that there is a narrow low platform for passengers between the high freight platform and the track.

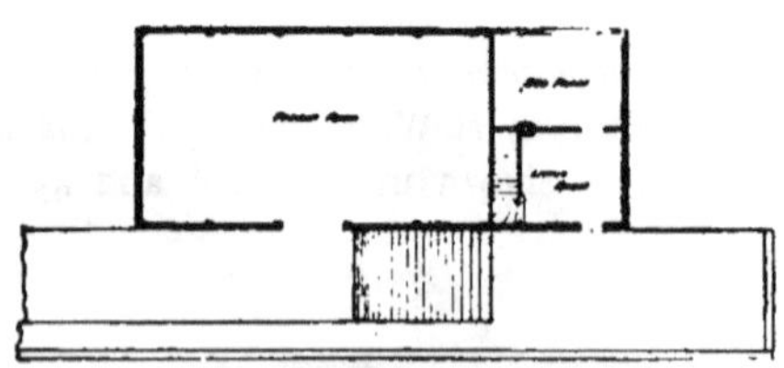

FIG. 459.—GROUND-PLAN.

Combination Depot with Dwelling, at Cœur d'Alene, Wash., Spokane & Idaho Railroad.—The combination depot of the Spokane & Idaho Railroad at Cœur d'Alene, Wash., connected with the Northern Pacific Railroad System, consists of a single-story frame structure, sheathed on the outside with upright boarding, 78 ft. long by about 20 ft. wide. There is a low platform along the face of the building next to the main track. The interior is divided into a freight-room, 30 ft. × 18 ft.; a general waiting-room, 17 ft. × 18 ft.; an office, 12 ft. × 12 ft.; a living-room, 18 ft. × 12 ft.; a bedroom, 10 ft. × 11 ft.; a bedroom, 8 ft. × 10 ft.; and a kitchen, 9 ft. × 13 ft.

Standard Combination Depots, Savannah, Florida & Western Railway.—The standard combination depot designs of the Savannah, Florida & Western Railway, kindly furnished by Mr. W. B. W. Howe, Jr., Chief Engineer, S., F. & W. Ry., provide for three classes, to suit varying conditions. Class No. 1 consists of a building 31 ft. wide × 60 ft. long; class No. 2 has the same width, but is 90 ft. long, while class No. 3 is 120 ft. long. In all cases the building has at one end a 30-ft. open shed extension. In Figs. 460 to 464 the design for class No. 1 is shown, and, as above explained, the other classes simply differ in the length of the freight-room.

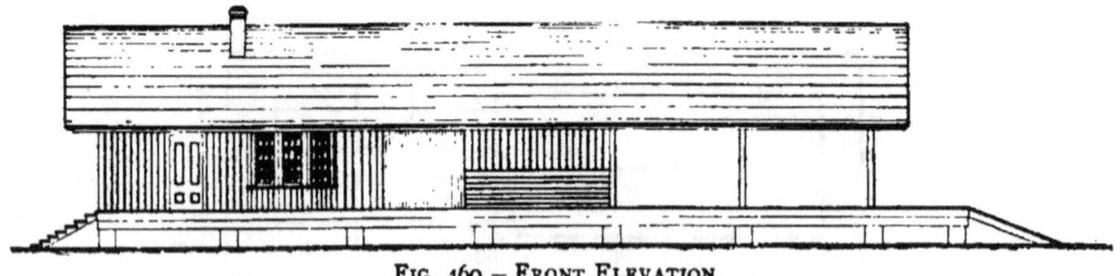

FIG. 460.—FRONT ELEVATION.

The building is a single-story frame structure, 31 ft. wide and of the length specified, according to which class of freight-house is to be employed. At one end of the building there is a waiting-room, a bedroom, and an office, each about 15 ft. square. The office has a large bay-window extension on the side towards the track. The rest of the building is occupied for the storage of freight. At the end of the building, away from the rooms above mentioned, there is a 30 ft. open shed extension. The platforms surrounding the house and shed on three sides, as shown on the plan, are 10 ft. wide, and are reached at one end by steps and at the other end by an incline. These platforms are set 4 ft.

FIG. 461.—END ELEVATION OF BUILDING.

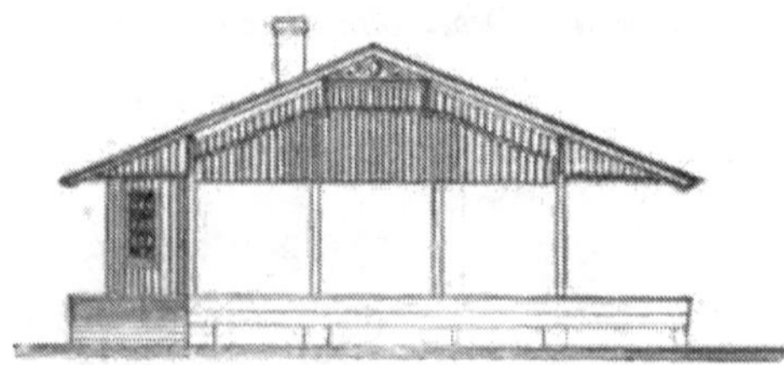

FIG. 462.—END ELEVATION OF SHED EXTENSION.

above the top of rail, and the face of the platform along the track is placed 6 ft. 6 in. from the centre of the track. The foundations of the building are brick piers, 13 in. × 27 in. on top. These piers

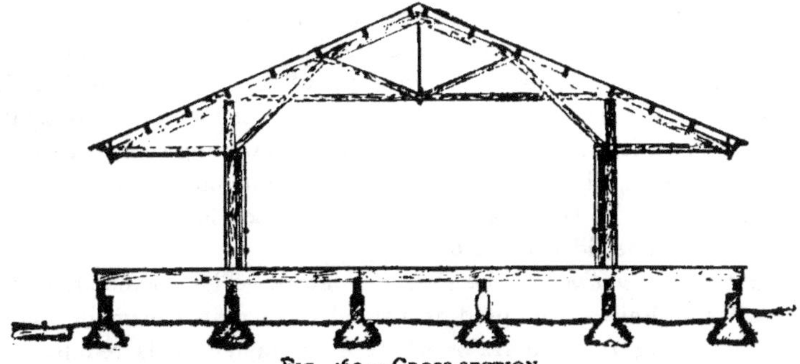

FIG. 463.—CROSS-SECTION.

support 10-in. × 14-in. sills under the walls, and 6-in. × 14-in. sills through the interior of the building and under the outside of the platform. These sills span 7 ft. 6 in. from pier to pier centres. The joists are 3 in. × 12 in., spaced 24 in. inside the house, spanning 10 ft. The joists are spaced 4 ft. apart on the platform. The floor consists of 2-in. plank. The frame is built of 6-in. × 8-in. posts, 3-in. × 6-in. studs, 4-in. × 6-in. plates, the height of frame being 13 ft. from floor to top of plate. The roof-trusses are spaced 15 ft. apart, and consist of 3-in. × 8-in. principal rafters; tie-beams, two pieces, $1\frac{1}{2}$ in. × 6 in.; truss-braces, 6 in. × 6 in.; knee-braces, $1\frac{1}{2}$ in. × 6 in.; king-rod, $\frac{3}{4}$ in. in diameter; purlins, 3 in. × 8 in.; roof-boards, 1 in. The rafters are extended over the platforms so as to form platform roofs projecting 10 ft. from the face of the building. The outside sheathing consists of upright boards and battens. The freight-doors are sliding-doors, 9 ft. square made of 2-in. × 6-in. frame, with 2-in. × 4-in. bracing, the frame being covered on the outside with 1-in. narrow tongued and grooved boards. Windows are inserted at the proper places, as shown on the plan. The construction of the open shed extension is similar to the building, excepting that the sides are left open. There is a large brick chimney with hearths in the office and in the waiting-room suitable for open wood fires.

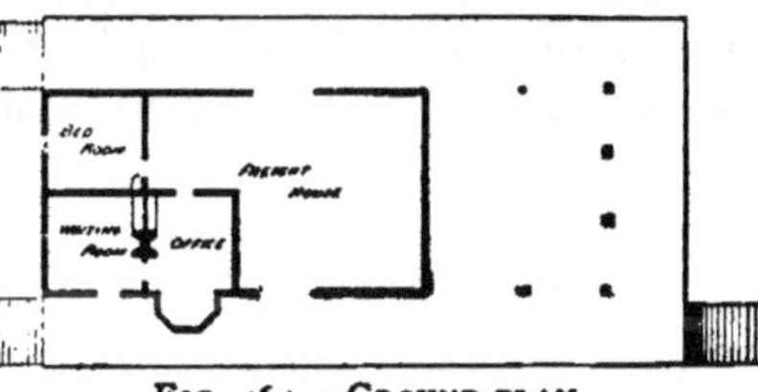

FIG. 464.—GROUND-PLAN.

Combination Depot, Class No. 1, Northern Pacific Railroad.—The combination depot of the

FIG. 465.—PERSPECTIVE.

Northern Pacific Railroad, shown in Figs. 465 and 466, known as Class No. 1, is a single-story frame structure, 24 ft. × 83 ft. The interior is divided into a freight-room, 24 ft. × 39 ft.; a general waiting-room, 15 ft. × 23 ft.; an office, 10 ft. × 15 ft.; a baggage and express room, 10 ft. × 15 ft.; a bedroom, 10 ft. × 10 ft., and a living-room, 12 ft. × 15 ft. Along the face of the building next to the main track is a 12-ft. low platform. Along the rear of the building, next to a side track, there is a high platform, 12 ft. wide. The high platform at the rear and the low platform at the front of the building are connected by inclines at each end of the building.

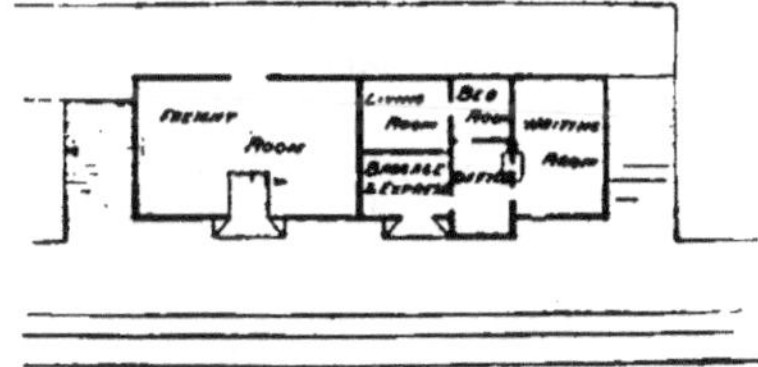

FIG. 466.—GROUND-PLAN.

Combination Depot, Class No. 2, Northern Pacific Railroad.—The combination depot of the Northern Pacific Railroad, known as class No. 2, is similar to the structure just described, excepting in size and the arrangement of the interior. The building is 24 ft. × 59 ft., and is divided into a freight-room, 23 ft. × 31 ft.; a general waiting-room, 23 ft. × 15 ft.; a bedroom, 10 ft. × 10 ft., and an office, 10 ft. × 12 ft., with a 3-ft. × 10-ft., square bay-window projection.

Combination Depot with Dwelling, Chesapeake & Ohio Railway.—The combination depot with dwelling of the Chesapeake & Ohio Railway, known as plan "A", designed by Mr. H. Jacob in 1883, consists of a two-story frame structure, sheathed on the outside with horizontal and upright boards, in panels, and roofed with tin. The ground-floor has a waiting-room, 14 ft. × 16 ft.; an office, 8 ft. × 10 ft., with a 3-ft. × 8-ft., bay-window extension; a freight-room, 14 ft. × 16 ft.; a living-room, 12 ft. × 14 ft.; and a kitchen, 12 ft. × 14 ft. The upper floor has two bedrooms, 14 ft. × 16 ft. There are low platforms on three sides of the building.

Combination Depot with Dwelling, Union Pacific Railway.—The combination depot with living-rooms of the Union Pacific Railway, adopted as a standard in 1886, shown in Figs. 467 to 470, is a single-story frame structure, 24 ft. × 60 ft., or whatever extra length is required to accommodate additional freight. The outside of the building is sheathed with siding and with upright boards and battens, panelled. The building is used as an island-depot, with a main track on the front and a side track on the rear. There are platforms on all four sides of the house, the height being 14 in. above

FIG. 467.—FRONT ELEVATION.

FIG. 468.—END ELEVATION.

the top of the rail, and the face of the platform next to the track approaches within 5 ft. 3 in. of the centre of the track. The passenger platform at the front of the house and the freight platform at one end of the house are 16 ft. wide, the freight platform at the back of the house is 10 ft. wide, and the platform at the end of the house away from the freight-room is 12 ft. wide. The interior is divided into a freight-room, 21 ft. × 23 ft., with a small space partitioned off for baggage; an office,

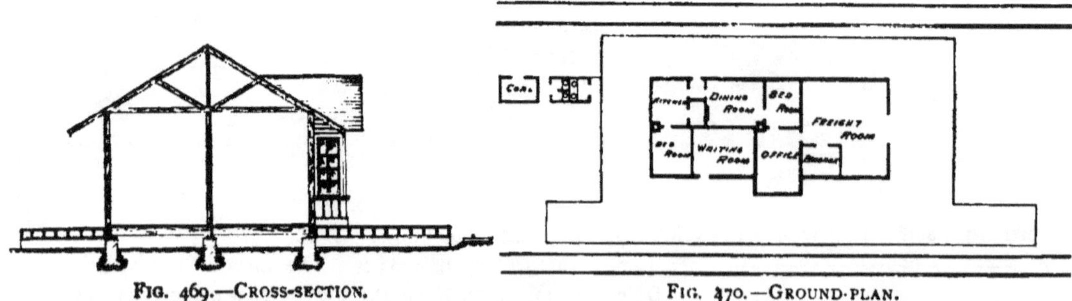

FIG. 469.—CROSS-SECTION.

FIG. 470.—GROUND-PLAN.

11 ft. × 12 ft., with a 4-ft. × 11-ft., square bay-window extension; a waiting-room, 15 ft. × 12 ft.; two bedrooms; a dining-room; a kitchen; and a pantry. There are two small detached buildings, one for the storage of coal and supplies, and the other for water-closets.

Combination Depot at Grovetown, Ga., Georgia Railroad.—The combination depot of the Georgia Railroad at Grovetown, Ga., designed by Mr. Bradford L. Gilbert, architect, New York City, described and illustrated in the issue of the *Railroad Gazette* of September 25, 1891, and in *The Engineering Magazine*, December, 1891, shown in Fig. 471, taken from the latter publication, is a very picturesque depot building, designed to meet the requirements of Southern railroad traffic at certain localities. The following remarks on this subject are made in the issue of the *Railroad Gazette* mentioned:

For a town of several thousand people, and somewhat of a suburban station as well, the requirements in the South are for a building with accommodation for first-class passengers (white) and second-class passengers (negroes), both under the general supervision of the station-agent, who is telegraph-operator and ticket-agent as well. It is also necessary to provide a freight-room and large platform for handling cotton

FIG. 471.—PERSPECTIVE.

and merchandise. The Grovetown station combines all these special features in a simple, picturesque, and quaint building—one which helps the town, and that advertises and builds up the railroad as well. The windmill (forming so picturesque a feature of the building) was designed with special reference to the necessary water supply in connection with the toilet accommodations, etc., of the building, as a practical and simple solution of this problem.

The building is 77 ft. × 24 ft., with waiting-rooms for white and colored passengers, baggage-room, toilet-rooms, office, and a large freight-room and freight platform for cotton. The street end of the building is occupied by the first-class passenger waiting-room, 24 ft. × 24 ft. in size, with a large alcove in the turret for ladies, and also ample toilet accommodations. The ticket and telegraph office is on the track side, 9 ft. × 15 ft., and, by means of a projecting bay-window, commands a view up and down the tracks. The second-class waiting-room, 14 ft. × 24 ft., and toilet accommodations, are located adjoining, with ticket-windows opening into each waiting-room. Beyond this the space is occupied by the freight building, 32 ft. × 24 ft., and platform, 10 ft. on the sides and 20 ft. on the end also, for whatever baggage and express business it may be necessary to handle. The platform extends around the building 10 ft. in width, covered by the projecting awning, and the *porte cochère* is provided for the convenience of those who drive to the station.

The material used at Grovetown for the exterior of the building has been cypress shingles (stained with creosote) on the sides, which, with metallic shingles on the roofs, form a durable and serviceable covering at minimum cost. The cost of the building is stated to be about $5000.

Combination Depot at Providence, Pa., New York, Ontario & Western Railroad.—The combination depot of the New York, Ontario & Western Railroad at Providence, Pa., shown in Fig. 472,

FIG. 472.—PERSPECTIVE.

copied from *The Engineering Magazine*, December, 1891, is a single-story frame structure, 24 ft. × 64 ft., divided into a waiting-room, office, and freight-room.

Combination Depot at Farmersville, Tex., Gulf, Colorado & Santa Fe Railroad.—The combination depot of the Gulf, Colorado & Santa Fe Railroad, now part of the Atchison, Topeka & Santa Fe Railroad System, shown in Figs. 473 to 475, designed by Mr. W. J. Sherman, Chief Engineer, G., C. & S. F. R. R., is a single-story frame structure, 20 ft. × 152 ft., surrounded by platforms on all sides. One end of the building is used for the passenger service and has low platforms surrounding it, while the other end is used for a freight-room with high platforms adjoining it. The ground-plan is divided into an office, 10 ft. × 16 ft., with a 3-ft. bay-window projection on the track side; a gentlemen's waiting-room, 14 ft. × 20 ft., and a ladies' waiting-room, 14 ft. × 20 ft., connected by a 4-ft. passage-way at the back of the office, tickets being sold to passengers in either room from ticket-windows at the rear angles of the office; an express-office, 14 ft. × 20 ft.; and a freight-room, 20 ft. × 100 ft., with a small space, 6 ft. × 10 ft., partitioned off as a baggage-room. There is an 8-ft. water-tub, 9 ft

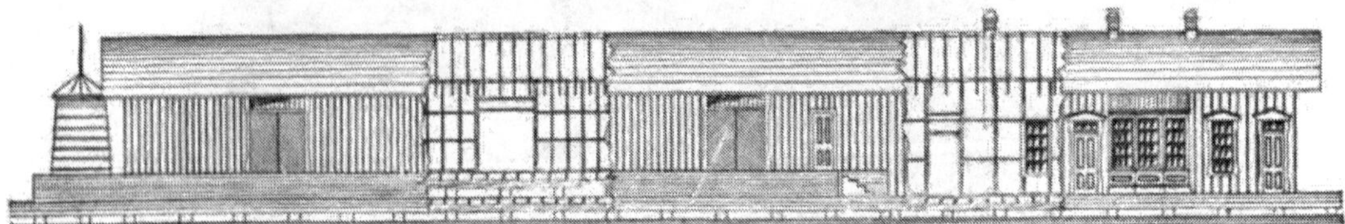

FIG. 473.—FRONT ELEVATION.

high, provided at the end of the freight-house to collect the rain-water from the roof, which is an essential feature in this section of the country. The top of the low platform is placed 6 in. above the top of the rail, and the face of the platform is set 4 ft. 6 in. from the centre of the track. The freight platform is set 3 ft. 6 in. above the top of the rail, and is 7 ft. wide on the front and the rear of the building and 12 ft. wide at the end of the freight-room. The high platform is connected with the low platform at the front and the rear of the building by steps. The face of the freight platform on the front of the building is set 11 ft. 6 in. from the centre of the track. The height of frame in the freight-room is 11 ft. from floor to plate, and the height of frame in the passenger rooms is 14 ft. The low platform around the passenger part of the building is 7 ft. wide on the rear and the end of the building, 14 ft. wide in front of the passenger part of the building, and 7 ft. wide in front of the high freight platform along the freight-room, and it is extended, 9 ft. in width, along the track each way from the building, so as to make a total low-platform track-frontage of 250 ft.

FIG. 474.—END ELEVATION AND CROSS-SECTION.

This building is especially to be recommended for the very good ground-plan layout and for the cheapness and simplicity of the design. It is built throughout of wood on timber foundations, with a 4-in. frame, sheathed on the outside with upright boards and battens, ceiled in the interior of the offices and passenger rooms with 1-in. tongued and grooved boards, and roofed with shingles on sheeting. The principal materials

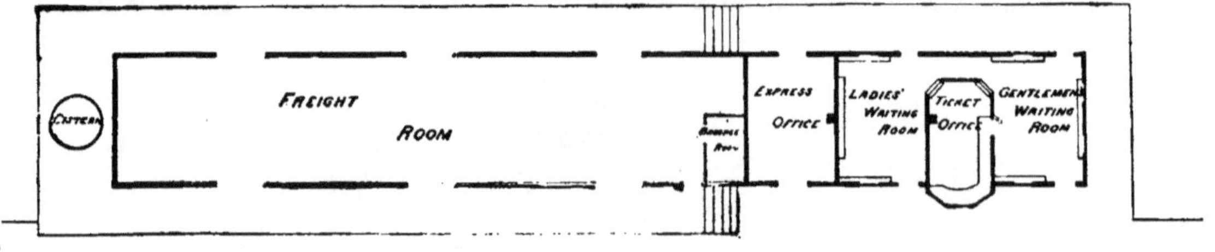

FIG. 475.—GROUND-PLAN.

used are foundation blocks of round timber, 12 in. to 15 in. in diameter; sills, 3 in. × 12 in., notched onto the blocks; joists, 2 in. × 10 in. in the waiting-rooms, offices, and passenger platforms, and 3 in. × 10 in. in the freight-rooms and freight platforms; plates, 4 in. × 4 in.; corner, door, and window studs, 4 in. × 4 in.; intermediate studs, 2 in. × 4 in.; nailers, 2 in. × 4 in.; rafters, 2 in. × 4 in., spaced 24 in. centres; ceiling-joists, 2 in. × 8 in.; ridge-piece, 1 in. × 6 in.; ties for ceiling-joists, 1 in. × 6 in.; roof-brackets, 2 in. × 4 in.; outside sheathing, 1 in. × 12 in., with O. G. battens; interior ceiling, 1-in. tongued and grooved boards; roof-sheeting, 1 in. × 4 in. The passenger doors are 7 ft. 6 in. × 3 ft.; the express-office doors are 7 ft. 6 in. × 4 ft. 6 in., hung in pairs; the office-doors are 7 ft. × 2 ft. 6 in.; and the freight-doors are 7 ft. wide × 7 ft. 6 in. high, hung in pairs, sliding sideways each way from the opening. All the outside doors have transom-lights overhead. There are three 16-in. brick flues hung in the roof for stoves in the waiting-rooms and offices.

Combination Depots, Port Huron & Northwestern Railway.—The depots along the line of the Port Huron & Northwestern Railway are cheap, single-story, wooden structures of the combination style. Mr. A. L. Reed, Chief Engineer, states that for settlements of a few hundred inhabitants the standard building in use is 16 ft. wide by 40 ft. to 50 ft. long, costing complete, including platforms, about $600. For towns of about one thousand or more inhabitants the standard building usually adopted is 20 ft. wide and 70 ft. or more in length, costing about $1000.

Standard Combination Depot, Macon & Birmingham Railroad.—The standard combination depot of the Macon & Birmingham Railroad is fully illustrated in the issue of *Engineering News* of May 26, 1892.

CHAPTER XX.

FLAG-DEPOTS.

FLAG-STATIONS on railroads are stations of minor importance at which only a limited number of trains stop,—usually on flag; hence the name. In reality flag-depots are small passenger depots at unimportant local stations, and they are frequently called second, third, or fourth-class passenger depots, according to the classification adopted by the railroad company. It follows, therefore, that the division between flag-depots and local passenger depots is difficult to maintain in discussing the subject, as in practice the passage from one class of buildings to the other is not clearly defined.

The business at flag-stations is necessarily limited. Where there is a freight business as well as a passenger trade, a small combination depot is usually erected. In other cases, a separate passenger building is constructed in addition to a small, separate freight-house. In the great majority of cases, however, flag-stations have only a depot building with accommodations for the passenger business, as the small amount of freight at such a station, if any, is handled on the platforms, or else separate tracks and facilities are provided for it.

The simplest form of flag-depot consists of an open or a covered platform. The next step is the adoption of shelters, described in a previous chapter, which are a special form of platform roofs usually enclosed on three sides and open towards the track. In other cases, especially in northern climates, an open shelter is too exposed, and a frame building with one small room is erected, the house being placed in charge of the track foreman employed in the vicinity, who keeps the place clean and sees that the door is unlocked during the day or at train time. The structures thus far described are used at stations where there is no agent, and it is simply desired to provide a place for the passengers to congregate and be protected, to a more or less extent, from the heat of the sun or during stormy weather pending the arrival of trains. As soon as a station gains in importance sufficiently to warrant a station-agent, flag-depots are used with an office in addition to waiting-rooms. According to the local requirements, there is either one general waiting-room or else there are separate waiting-rooms for ladies and gentlemen. Small baggage-rooms to store baggage in, and sometimes a special room for express matter, have to be added. In other cases a separate telegraph-office, a signal-tower, or toilet-rooms are found to be desirable. A very usual feature of a flag-depot, especially in sparsely settled sections of the country or where a station is located some distance from the settlement proper, is to connect some living-rooms or a complete dwelling-house with the depot building for the depot-help or the agent and his family to live in. There are designs where the building takes the character of a dwelling, with only one or two rooms on the ground-floor reserved for an office and waiting-rooms. In other cases, the main part of the building is devoted to the passenger service, and there are simply one or several rooms for dwelling purposes added, either in an annex or in an upper story. The local conditions and requirements will govern the selection of the design in each particular case.

The location of a flag-depot should be alongside of the passenger tracks. There should be a low platform in front of the building, extended along the track for whatever length it is thought desirable. Relative to the division of the interior, the structure will usually be so limited that general rules would not be of much use. However, it can be said, that, where a separate office is to be maintained, it is desirable to have a bay-window extension on the track side, excepting in the simplest and smallest class of flag-depots. The waiting-room should adjoin the ticket-office, and, where there are separate waiting-rooms for gentlemen and ladies, it is desirable, although not essential, that there should be a separate ticket-window for each room. The movement of baggage at the class of depots under discussion is so small, and as it is handled almost exclusively on the platforms, the location of the baggage-room, where one is introduced, is not a matter of great importance. Where feasible, however, it is desirable to have the baggage-room facing the track, or at one end of the building, at the most convenient location to allow baggage to be handled to and from trains and to and from teams. Where a dwelling is attached to the depot, it is desirable to have a private entrance to the dwelling independent of the waiting-rooms.

Relative to the style of structure to use for a flag-depot, the existing requirements and the importance of the locality will govern. Flag-depots in cities or at important suburban settlements are frequently built very substantially and artistically, while similar buildings in thinly populated districts on a pioneer railroad need not be anything more than the cheapest frame structure suitable for the purpose. The question of loss in case of fire is not serious, and would not warrant alone the construction of a more costly and fire-proof structure, as the value of the structure and the baggage, that might be stored in the building at the time of the fire, would be presumably small. An examination of the illustrations and descriptions for flag-depots given further below will show the great variety and difference existing in this country in the structures adopted for the accommodation of the passenger business at flag-stations. On Northern and Western roads the plainest class of frame structures without any attempt at ornamentation are utilized; while on Southern roads and on the more important Northern and Western roads, frame structures with more or less attempt at ornamentation and artistic finish, especially in the line of cottage architecture, are in vogue. In the more thickly settled sections of the East and in and around the large cities of the country, flag-depots are invariably finished off as handsomely as other depots on the line, and in some cases in the most substantial and best manner possible, as, for instance, the standard brick flag-depot of the Pennsylvania Railroad, illustrated below.

Relative to the materials in use, it follows from above remarks that no general rule can be established. In the majority of cases, however, frame structures are used, sheathed on the outside with plain boards or ornamental siding and shingles, and roofed with shingles, tin, or slate. Stone buildings exist in isolated instances. For a substantial building, however, a brick structure, with stone trimmings, slate roof, and ornamental gable-ends, cornices, ridge-cresting and finials, is used very extensively.

It can be said, in general, that all rules established for designing local passenger depots will apply to flag-depots, excepting that in the latter the rules need not necessarily be followed where the size of the building and the simplicity of the structure renders it difficult or impossible to do so.

After these general remarks on the subject, the following descriptions and illustrations of depot buildings in use in this country at flag-stations or minor stations of railroads will prove interesting.

Frame Flag-depot at St. Paul, Minn., Minnesota & Northwestern Railroad.—The flag-depot of the Minnesota & Northwestern Railroad, used on the Motor Line in the suburbs of St. Paul, Minn., designed by Mr. C. A. Reed, Supervising Architect, M. & N. W. R. R., shown in Figs. 476 to 479, consists of a single-story frame structure, 12 ft. × 20 ft., sheathed on the outside with

FIG. 476.—FRONT ELEVATION.

FIG. 477.—END ELEVATION.

horizontal and diagonal siding and ornamental shingles, in panels. The interior is divided into a ticket-office, 11 ft. × 6 ft.; and a waiting-room, 11 ft. × 12 ft. 6 in. The clear height of the room is

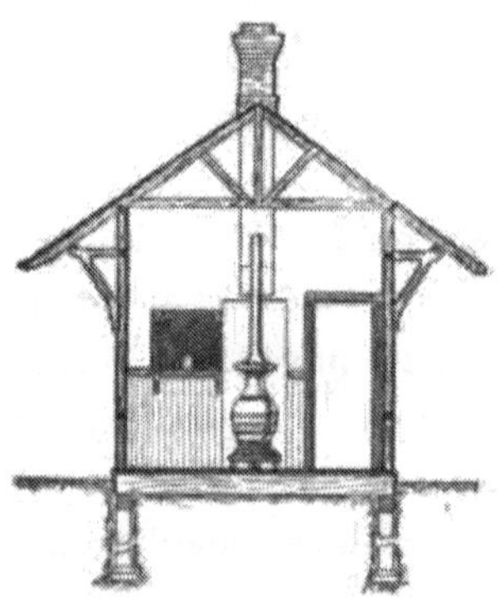

FIG. 478.—CROSS-SECTION.

FIG. 479.—GROUND-PLAN.

11 ft. There is a stove set in the partition between the ticket-office and the waiting-room, so as to heat both rooms. The doors are 2 ft. 6 in. × 7 ft. The windows have 8 lights, each 12 in. × 18 in. The foundations are posts set on blocking in the ground. The principal timbers are sills, 8 in. × 8 in.; floor-joists, 2 in. × 10 in.; and 2-in. × 4-in. studs, plates, nailers, rafters, and ceiling-joists.

Frame Flag-depot, Pottsville Branch, Lehigh Valley Railroad.—The flag-depot in use on the Pottsville Branch of the Lehigh Valley Railroad, shown in Figs. 480 to 482, designed by Mr. F. E.

Schall, and built under the direction of Mr. Wm. F. Pascoe, Superintendent of Bridges and Buildings, L. V. R. R., consists of a single-story frame structure, 21 ft. × 13 ft., sheathed on the outside with

FIG. 480.—FRONT ELEVATION.

FIG. 481.—END ELEVATION.

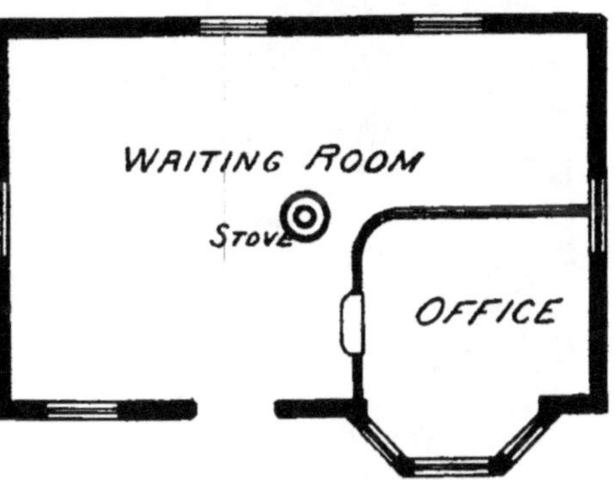

FIG. 482.—GROUND-PLAN.

matched diagonal sheathing and upright ornamental boarding, and roofed with slate. The interior consists of one large room, in one corner of which a space, 6 ft. × 8 ft., with a hexagonal bay-window extension, 2 ft. × 6 ft., is partitioned off by a railing for an office. The entrance door to the office in the railing has a shelf for the use of agents in selling tickets, etc. The roof is finished off very handsomely with galvanized iron ridge-cresting, finials, and smoke-flues. There is a semaphore signal projecting above the roof in front of the bay-window, as the stations are used as block-signal stations. The foundations of the building are brick or stone piers. There is a low platform extending around the building on all sides, 8 ft. wide on the face, and 5 ft. 6 in. wide on the rear and sides. The top of the platform is set 11 in. above the top of rail, and 4 ft. 6 in. from the centre of the track. The platform has a rise of 3 in. The principal timbers used are, sills, 4 in. × 6 in.; floor-joists, 3 in. × 10 in.; corner-posts, 4 in. × 6 in.; studding, 3 in. × 4 in.; plates and nailers, 3 in. × 4 in.; ceiling-joists, 3 in. × 8 in.; rafters, 2 in. × 6 in. The interior of the room is ceiled with yellow-pine narrow tongued and grooved boards, and wainscoted for 4 ft. in height from the floor. The clear height of the interior is 13 ft. 6 in. The door is 2 ft. 10 in. × 7 ft. The windows have 8 lights, each 12 in. × 18 in.

Frame Flag-depot at Wayne Station, Pa., Pennsylvania Railroad.—The flag-depot on the Germantown & Chestnut Hill Branch of the Pennsylvania Railroad, at Wayne Station, Pa., shown in perspective in Fig. 483, is a single-story frame structure, with an ornamental frame exterior, and roofed with slate. The foundations are stone walls. The panelling of the exterior, the cornices, roof-brackets, and gable-ends are finished in a very handsome and artistic manner, so that this design can serve to illustrate how effective and ornamental a structure can be erected in wood.

Frame Flag-depot, Ohio Valley Railway.—The standard design for a flag-depot of the Ohio Valley Railway is a plain, one-story frame building, 26 ft. × 16 ft., roofed with shingles, and divided by a central partition into a general waiting-room, 13 ft. × 15 ft.; and a baggage-room, 12 ft. × 15 ft. There is a 9-in. × 9-in. flue at the centre of the building. The design of the exterior is similar to the standard local passenger depot of the same railroad, illustrated in Fig. 520, the most striking feature of which is the curved roof at the eaves, and the knee-braces under the roof projection are cut to a bold, semicircular pattern. The outside of the building is sheathed with vertical, horizontal, and diagonal, plain and ornamental boarding, in panels. The inside finish is of wood. The vertical siding is painted a Turkey vermilion, the horizontal and diagonal siding a very light drab, and the frames, belt-courses, etc., a very dark red, approaching a brown color. Mr. C. C. Genung, Chief Engineer, Ohio Valley Railway, who designed the plans for these depots, states that a very neat, small flag-station building, about 12 ft. × 15 ft., can be put up complete for $100, exclusive of platforms.

FIG. 483.—PERSPECTIVE.

Frame Flag-depot at Tabor, Pa., Philadelphia & Reading Railroad.—The flag-depot at Tabor, Pa., on the North Pennsylvania branch of the Philadelphia & Reading Railroad, shown in Figs. 484 to 487, designed by Mr. Frank Furness, architect, is a single-story frame structure, 25 ft. 4 in. × 16

FIG. 484.—FRONT ELEVATION.

FIG. 485.—END ELEVATION.

ft. 4 in., with shed-platform roof extension at each end of the building. The outside of the building is sheathed with horizontal and vertical matched siding and ornamental shingles, in panels, and

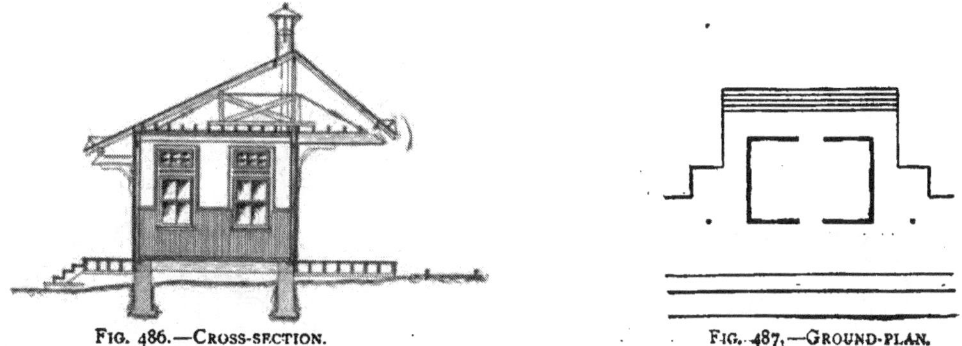

FIG. 486.—CROSS-SECTION. FIG. 487.—GROUND-PLAN.

roofed with slate. The projecting roofs with supporting brackets are finished in a handsome style. The cornices, ridge-cresting, finials, and smoke-flue are of galvanized iron. The entire design is finished off very artistically, and presents a very handsome appearance. The shed-platform roof extensions are supported by one post at each end of the building, as shown on the plan. The interior of the building consists of one general waiting-room, 15 ft. × 24 ft., with a clear height of 12 ft. 4 in. The interior is finished in wood, and wainscoted 5 ft. high from the floor. There are platforms on all sides of the building, 10 ft. wide on the face, and 5 ft. wide on the rear and sides. The platform is set 9 in. above the top of rail, and 5 ft. 6 in. from the centre of the track. The doors are 5 ft. × 8 ft., hung in pairs, panelled and glazed, as shown on the plans, with transom overhead. The windows are 3 ft. 6 in. wide, with transom-lights overhead. The foundations are stone walls.

Stone Flag-depot at Forest Hill, N. J., New York & Greenwood Lake Railroad.—The flag-depot of the New York & Greenwood Lake Railroad at Forest Hill, N. J., consists of a small stone single-story structure, roofed with slate, as shown in Fig. 488. The walls are rough stone, with

FIG. 488.—PERSPECTIVE.

dressed stone for corners, string-courses, cornices, and finish of windows and doors. This design is of the general style used very extensively for small depot buildings in England and on the Continent.

Frame Flag-depot, West Shore Railroad.—The flag-depots known as class "A," adopted for the West Shore Railroad, designed by Messrs. Wilson Bros. & Co., of Philadelphia, Pa., described and illustrated in the issue of the *Railroad Gazette* of April 23, 1886, and also in the issue of *Engineering News* of March 31, 1888, are single-story frame structures with a two-story tower. The building is 40 ft. ×17 ft., and it is divided into a ticket-office, 9 ft. × 20 ft., including a square, 3 ft. × 9 ft., bay-window projection; a general waiting-room, 16 ft. ×19 ft.; a baggage-room, 9 ft. × 5 ft.; a ladies' room, 9 ft. ×7 ft., with toilet-room attached; and a gentlemen's toilet-room. The upper part of the tower over the ticket-office is used as a signal-tower. The feature of this design is that in the finish of the exterior there are four different standards adopted, all of which correspond to the same ground-plan and frame, but vary in minor details connected with the tower, chimney, balcony, window-glazing, and form of roof. Thus, while uniformity in the ground-plan and the frame of all the depots of the same class is assured, there are sufficient changes in minor details of the exterior to cause each building to have certain individual characteristics.

Frame Flag-depot, Pennsylvania Railroad.—The flag-depot of the Pennsylvania Railroad, shown in Figs. 489 to 491, is a single-story frame structure, 53 ft. × 21 ft., sheathed on the outside with

FIG. 489.—FRONT ELEVATION.

FIG. 490.—END ELEVATION.

German siding and ornamental shingles, in panels, and roofed with slate. The interior is divided into a gentlemen's waiting-room; a ladies' waiting-room; and a ticket-office with an octagonal bay-window projection. The building is surrounded by low platforms on all sides. The top of the platform is 8 in. above the top of rail and reaches within 4 ft. 6 in. of the centre of the track along the face of the building. The platforms at the rear and at the ends of the building are 9 ft. wide, while the platform along the front of the building is 12 ft. wide, extended each way from the building along the track, the extensions being 8 ft. wide. The clear height of the rooms is 13 ft. The foundations are stone walls, 18 in. thick. The frame consists of 3-in. × 4-in. studding, covered on the outside with 1-in. rough hemlock sheathing and 1-in. German siding. The walls of the rooms are plastered. The roof consists of 2-in. × 8-in. rafters; 2-in. × 10-in. ceiling-joists; 2-in. × 6-in. collars; 3-in. × 8-in. ridge-poles; and 1-in. rough sheathing.

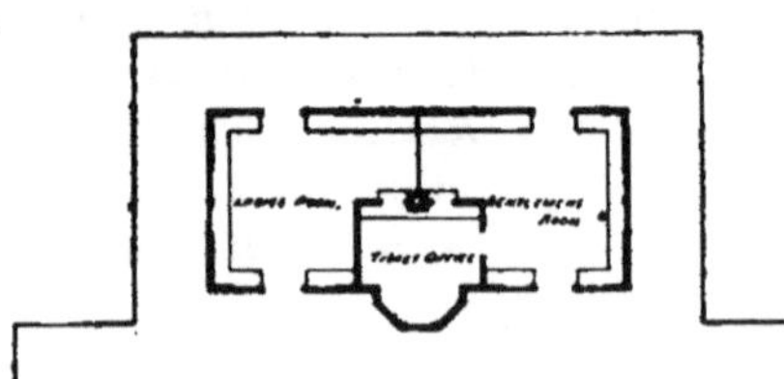

FIG. 491.—GROUND-PLAN.

Frame Flag-depot with Dwelling, Pennsylvania Railroad.—The frame flag-depot, with dwelling attached, of the Pennsylvania Railroad, shown in Figs. 492 to 495, consists of a two-story frame structure, 46 ft. × 30 ft. The building is sheathed on the outside with narrow white-pine

FIG. 492.—FRONT ELEVATION.

FIG. 493.—END ELEVATION.

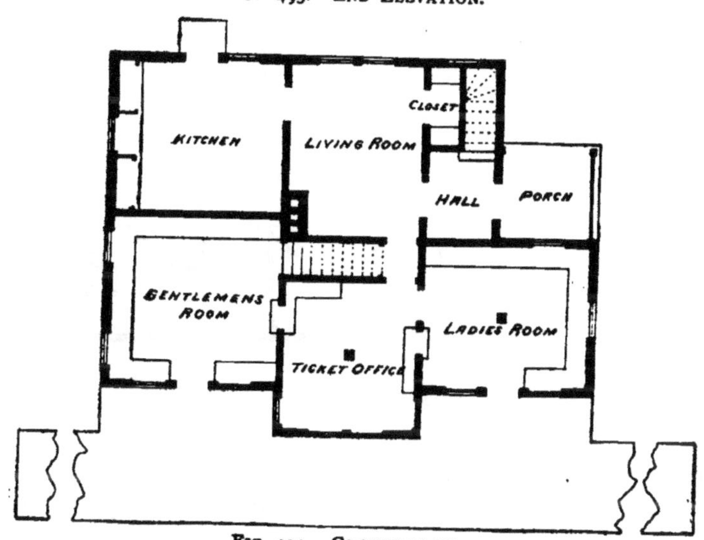

FIG. 494.—GROUND-PLAN.

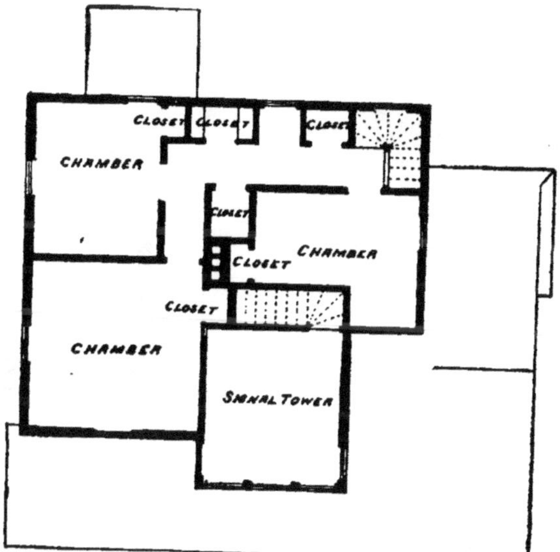

FIG. 495.—SECOND-FLOOR PLAN.

tongued and grooved boards, and ornamental shingles, in panels, and roofed with slate. There is a low 12-ft. platform in front along the track, extended 8 ft. wide each way from the building. The platform is 8 in. above the top of the rail, and 4 ft. 6 in. from the centre of the track. The total length of platform facing the track is 100 ft. There is a cellar under the living-room, 7 ft. 6 in. in height. The clear height of the first story is 10 ft., and the clear height of the second story is 8 ft. 8 in. The first floor is divided into an office, 12 ft. × 9 ft., with a 4-ft. × 12-ft., square bay-window extension; a gentlemen's waiting-room, 15 ft. × 14 ft. 6 in.; a ladies' waiting-room, 17 ft. × 12 ft. 4 in.; a kitchen, 13 ft. × 15 ft.; a living-room, 12 ft. × 15 ft.; a hall; and a porch. The second floor has three bedrooms and a signal-tower office, 12 ft. × 13 ft. The bay-window extension of the office on the first floor is carried up through the second floor, thus affording a very good place for a signal-station. A signal-lamp is placed in front of the building, as shown on the plans.

Brick Flag-depot with Dwelling, Pennsylvania Railroad.—The brick flag-depot, with dwelling attached, of the Pennsylvania Railroad, shown in Figs. 496 to 501, designed and adopted in 1884

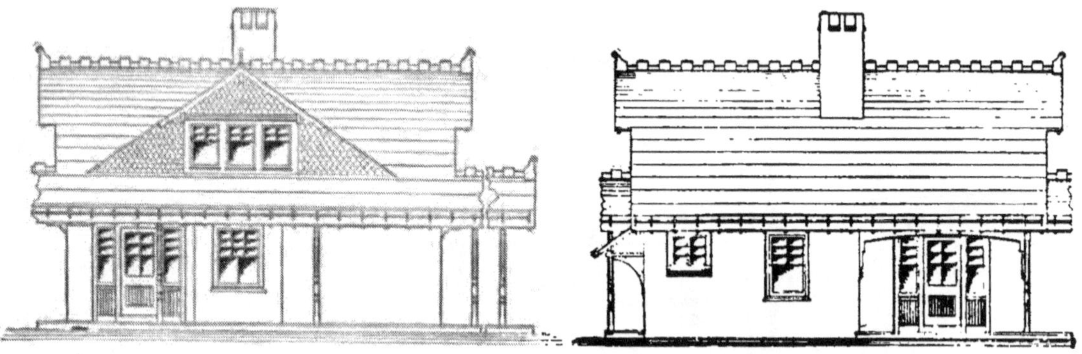

Fig. 496.—Front Elevation.

Fig. 497.—Rear Elevation.

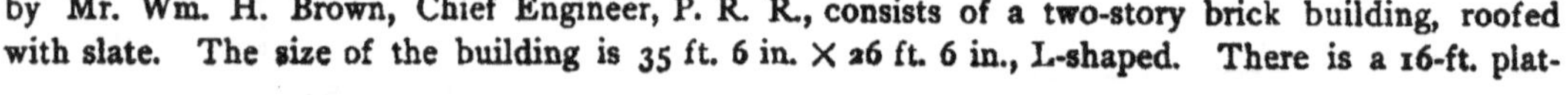

by Mr. Wm. H. Brown, Chief Engineer, P. R. R., consists of a two-story brick building, roofed with slate. The size of the building is 35 ft. 6 in. × 26 ft. 6 in., L-shaped. There is a 16-ft. plat-

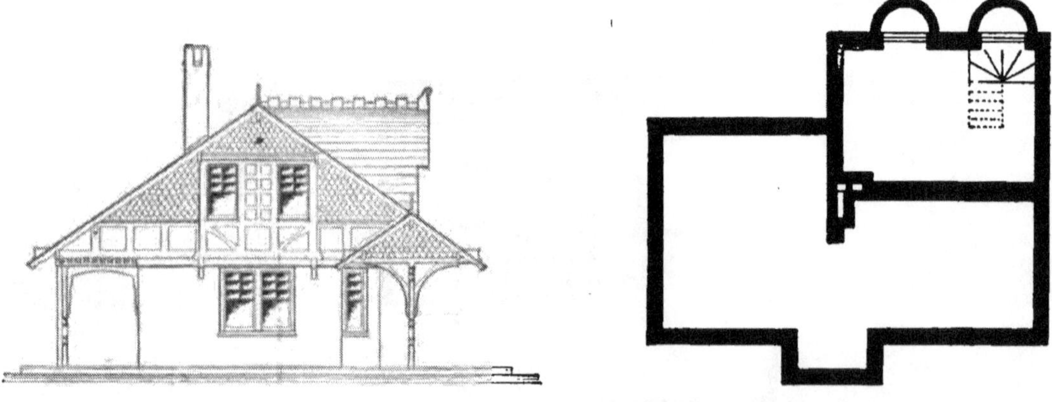

Fig. 498.—End Elevation.

Fig. 499.—Cellar-plan.

form on the front of the building, 81 ft. in length along the track, which platform is roofed with a single-post, ornamental platform roof. The platform is a low platform, and reaches within 4 ft. 6 in.

of the centre of the track. The platform on the side of the building is 5 ft. wide. There is a cellar

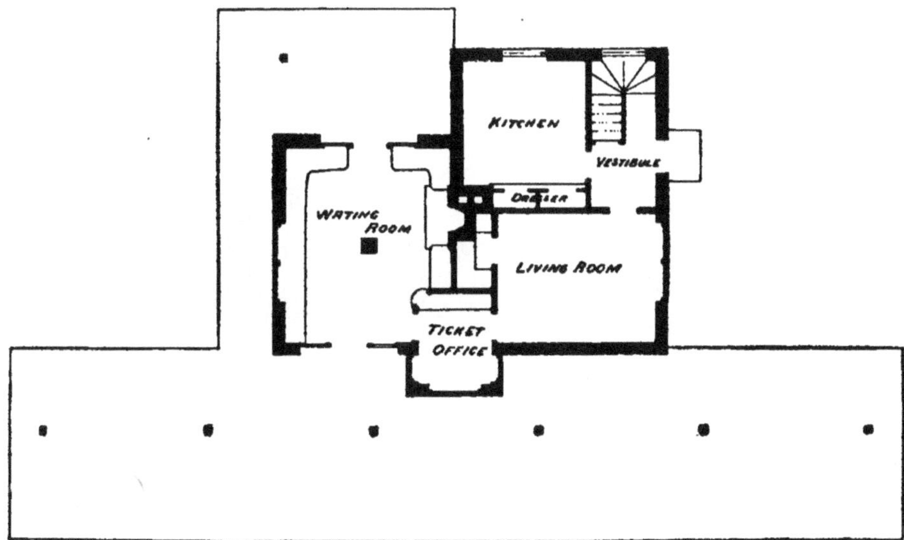

FIG. 500.—GROUND-PLAN.

built under one end of the building, with a furnace. The first floor is divided into a ticket-office, 6 ft. 7 in. × 8 ft., including a 2-ft. 6-in., square bay-window projection; a general waiting-room, 17 ft. × 15 ft.; a living-room, 14 ft. 5 in. × 11 ft. 6 in.; a kitchen, 11 ft. × 10 ft. 9 in.; and a vestibule. The second story has four bedrooms. The foundations are stone walls, 16 in. thick. The brick walls of the lower story are 12 in. thick, with wooden ornamental panels inserted at the doors. The windows have dressed flagstone sills. The slate roof is finished off with galvanized-iron cornices, ridge-cresting, and finials. The gable-ends of the upper story are sheathed with matched siding and ornamental shingles, in panels. The smoke-flue is of brick, with stone cap. The roof projections over the platform and the single-post platform roof are finished in a very ornamental and artistic manner.

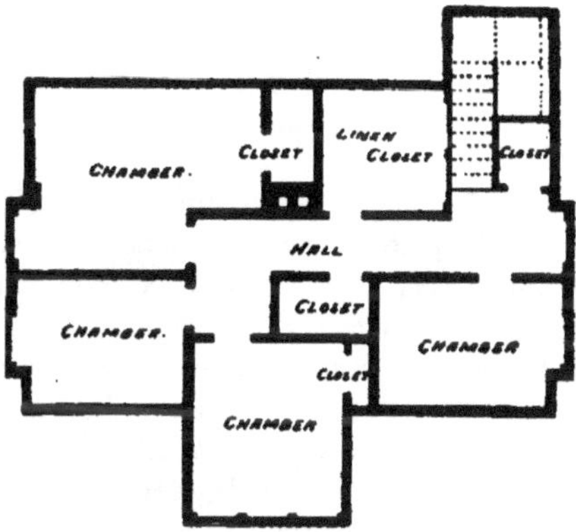

FIG. 501.—SECOND-FLOOR PLAN.

Frame Flag-depot with Dwelling at Principio, Md., Philadelphia, Wilmington & Baltimore Railroad.—The flag-depot, with dwelling attached, of the Philadelphia, Wilmington & Baltimore Railroad at Principio, Md., designed by Mr. S. T. Fuller, Chief Engineer, P., W. & B. R. R., described and illustrated in the issue of the *Railroad Gazette* of May 17, 1878, consists of a two-story frame structure with French mansard roof, and a single-story annex for a kitchen. The size of the building is 21 ft. × 36 ft. The first floor has a waiting-room, a living-room, a ticket-office, a kitchen, and two verandas. The upper floor has two bedrooms. The foundations are stone walls. The outside of the building is sheathed with horizontal and vertical matched siding, in panels, with a heavy ornamental wooden cornice. The roof is covered with slate.

Frame Flag-depot, with Dwelling, Northern Pacific Railroad.—The design for a flag-depot, with dwelling attached, of the Northern Pacific Railroad, shown in Figs. 502 to 504, designed by Mr. C. B. Talbot, consists of a single-story frame structure, 18 ft. × 46 ft., sheathed on the outside with upright boards and battens, and roofed with shingles. The finish of the exterior is plain and cheap. The height of the rooms is 10 ft. in the clear. The interior is divided into a waiting-room, 12 ft. × 18 ft.; an office, 8 ft. × 11 ft.; a baggage-room, 7 ft. × 8 ft.; two bedrooms, each 9 ft. × 12 ft.; a living-room, 12 ft. × 14 ft.; and a kitchen, 9 ft. × 12 ft. The building has a 12-ft. low platform along the front facing the track, a 12-ft. platform at the end of the building next to the waiting-room, and a 6-ft. platform on the rear. The platform is set 16 in. above the top of the rail, and 6 ft. from the centre of the track, with two steps leading down to the track. The platforms have

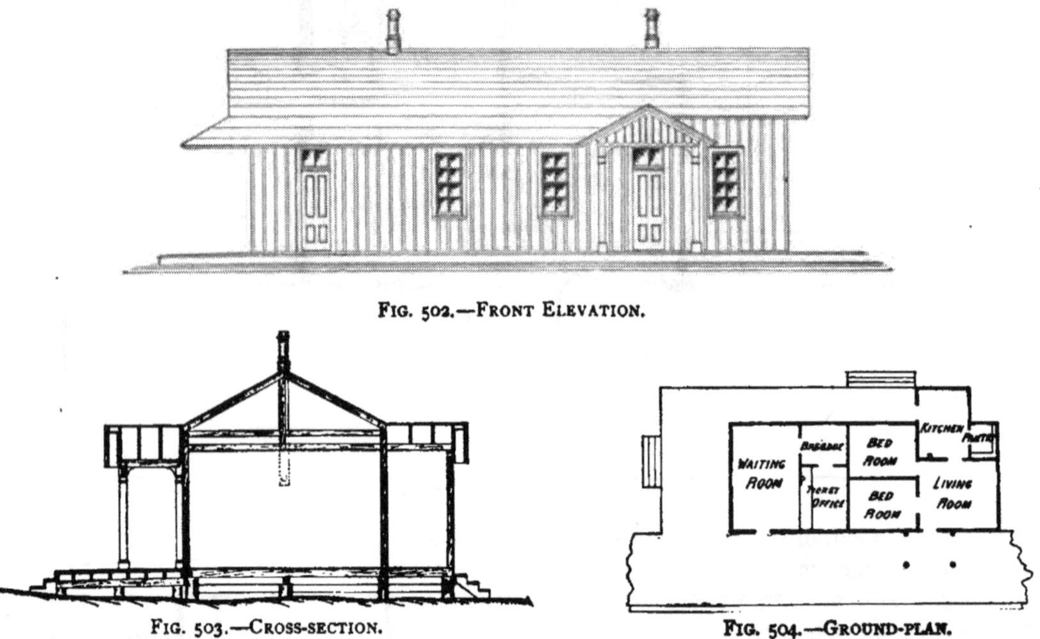

FIG. 502.—FRONT ELEVATION.

FIG. 503.—CROSS-SECTION.

FIG. 504.—GROUND-PLAN.

a rise of 2½ in. The building is built without a frame, consisting of two layers of boards nailed to the sills and plates. The foundations consist of posts set in the ground on blocking. The principal timbers used consist of 6-in. × 10-in. sills; 2-in. × 10-in. floor-joists, spaced 6 in. centres, spanning 9 ft.; ceiling-joists, 2 in. × 6 in., spaced 24 in. centres; plates, 2 in. × 6 in., upright; rafters, 2 in. × 6 in., spaced 24 in. centres. There are two 6-in. terra-cotta flues in the building. The doors are 2 ft. 8 in. × 6 ft. 8 in. × 1½ in. The windows have 8 lights, each 14 in. × 18 in.

Frame Flag-depot with Dwelling at Magnolia, Del., Philadelphia, Wilmington & Baltimore Railroad.—The frame flag-depot, with dwelling attached, at Magnolia, Del., on the Philadelphia, Wilmington & Baltimore Railroad, part of the Pennsylvania Railroad System, shown in Figs. 505 to 507, consists of a two-story frame structure, 45 ft. × 30 ft., very similar in exterior design to the frame flag-station building of the Pennsylvania Railroad, illustrated in Figs. 492 to 495. The out-

FIG. 505.—FRONT ELEVATION.

side is sheathed with narrow white-pine tongued and grooved boards and ornamental shingles, in panels, and roofed with slate. The building has a low, 12-ft. wide platform in front along the track, extended 8 ft. wide each way from the building. There is a cellar under the living-room, 7 ft. 6 in.

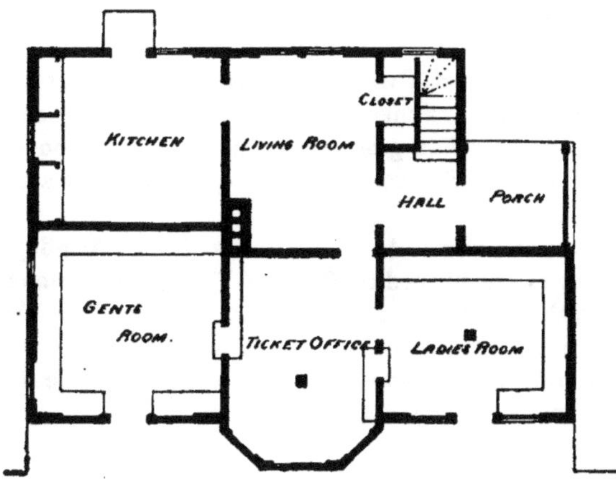

FIG. 506.—GROUND-PLAN.

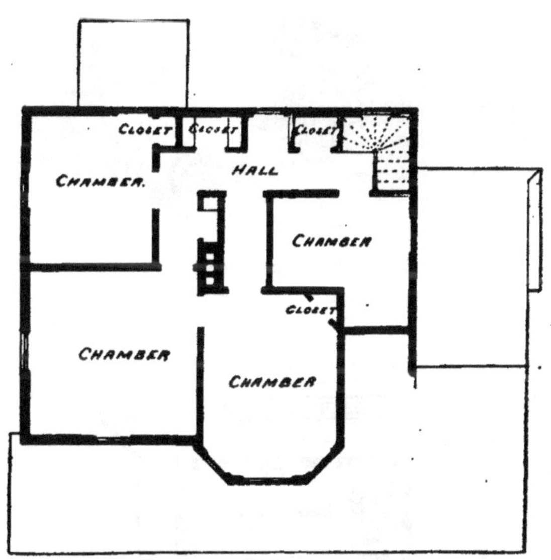

FIG. 507.—SECOND-FLOOR PLAN.

high. The clear height of the first story is 10 ft. and the clear height of the second story is 8 ft. 8 in. The first floor is divided into an office, 12 ft. × 12 ft., with a hexagonal, 3-ft. 6-in. × 12-ft., bay-window extension; a gentlemen's waiting-room, 15 ft. × 14 ft. 6 in.; a ladies' waiting-room, 17 ft. × 12 ft. 4 in.; a living-room, 12 ft. × 15 ft.; a kitchen, 13 ft. × 15 ft.; a hall; and a porch. The second floor has four bedrooms.

Flag-depots, Chicago & Northwestern Railroad.—In the issue of the *Inland Architect and News Record*, Vol. 10, No. 6, a number of flag-station depot buildings are illustrated, which were designed by Cobb & Frost, architects, Chicago, Ill., for the Chicago & Northwestern Railroad. The depots illustrated are at West Fifty-second Street, Chicago; Wayne Station; East Elgin Station; Hayes Station; and Waukesha Station.

Flag-depot at Van Buren Street, Chicago, Ill., Illinois Central Railroad.—The old flag-depot of the Illinois Central Railroad at Van Buren Street, Chicago, Ill., consists of an octagonal, two-story pavilion with French mansard roof, as illustrated in the issue of the *Railway Review* of June 28, 1879. A porch roof surrounds the octagon on all sides. The building is neatly finished, and presents a very ornamental appearance, but it is out of the run of the usual class of railroad buildings.

Flag-depot with Dwelling at Norwood Park, N. Y.—In the issue of *Building* of Sept. 1883, a design for a flag-depot at Norwood Park, N. Y., with dwelling attached, is illustrated, as designed by Mr. J. F. Lyman, architect, Yonkers, N. Y. The structure consists of a two-story frame building, finished very artistically. The ground-floor has a waiting-room, 23 ft. 6 in. × 48 ft. 6 in.; a ticket-office, and a small ladies' toilet-room. The upper story has a living-room, a kitchen, and two bedrooms.

Flag-depot Design with Dwelling.—A design for a $2500 flag-depot, prepared by Messrs. Leicht & Anderson, architects, is published in *Railroad Topics.* The materials are, first story, rock-faced stone; second story, shingle, and a slate roof. The ground-plan has a general waiting-room, a baggage-room, a ticket-office, toilet-rooms, and a *porte cochère.*

Flag-depot at Chestnut Hill, Mass., Boston & Albany Railroad.—The flag-depot at Chestnut Hill, Mass., on the Brooklyne branch of the Boston & Albany Railroad, shown in Figs. 508 and 509,

FIG. 508.—PERSPECTIVE.

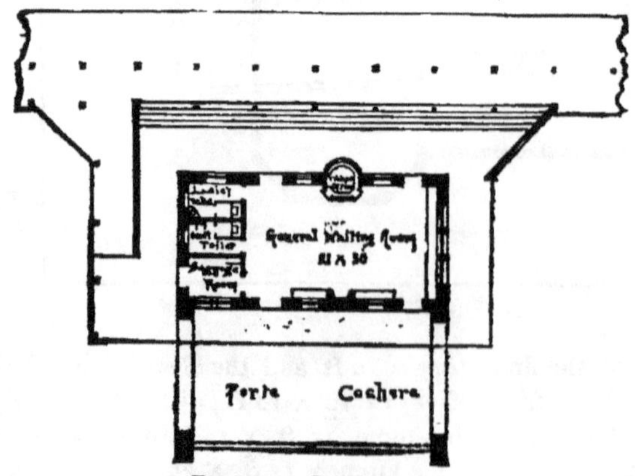

FIG. 509.—GROUND-PLAN.

designed by the late Mr. H. H. Richardson, architect, Brooklyne, Mass., plans for which were published in the *Railroad Gazette* of Nov. 5, 1886; in the *Sanitary Engineer*, Vol. 14; and in the *American Architect and Building News* of Feb. 26, 1887, is a small, single-story, granite building, with brownstone trimmings, and roof of red tiles. The principal and most striking feature of the design is a large *porte cochere* on the rear of the building, the full length of same, the drive-way being spanned by heavy granite arches in line with the ends of the building. The interior is divided into a general waiting-room, 21 ft. × 36 ft.; a small baggage-room; a gentlemen's toilet-room; a ladies' waiting-room; and a very small ticket-office. From an architectural and artistic standpoint this design is most effective and praiseworthy, but viewed from a railroad-engineer's standpoint there are serious defects in the ground-plan. It is very unusual and objectionable to have a gentlemen's toilet-room opening from a general waiting-room; an entrance from the outside of the building would have been preferable. The baggage-room is very small, although probably sufficient for the storage of the small amount of baggage remaining at the depot. The ticket-office is hardly large enough to warrant being called an office, so that two windows to sell tickets from, both leading into the same waiting-room, certainly seem unnecessary.

Flag-depot at Woodland, Mass., Boston & Albany Railroad.—The flag-depot of the Boston & Albany Railroad at Woodland, Mass., designed by the late Mr. H. H. Richardson, architect, Brooklyne, Mass., plans for which were published in the *American Architect and Building News* of February 26, 1887, consists of a single-story stone structure, 36 ft. × 16 ft., with heavy, sloping roofs. The façade towards the railroad is designed entirely from an architectural standpoint. There are stone seats under the sloping roof, alongside of the bay-window extension to the main building, which serves as ticket-office. The interior is divided into a general waiting-room; a baggage-room; a ladies' toilet-room; a gentlemen's toilet-room; and a ticket-office. The arrangement of the ground-plan has a large number of very objectionable features.

Flag-depot at Waban, Mass., Boston & Albany Railroad.—The flag-depot of the Boston & Albany Railroad at Waban, Mass., designed by the late Mr. H. H. Richardson, architect, Brooklyne, Mass., plans for which were published in the *American Architect and Building News* of Feb. 26, 1887, is a small, single-story stone structure, with tile roof. The size of the building is 38 ft. × 21 ft., divided into a general waiting-room; a baggage-room; a gentlemen's toilet-room; a ladies' toilet-room; and a small ticket-office located in a round bay-window projection at one corner of the general waiting-room. The arrangement of the interior ground-plan has several objectionable features.

Flag-depot at Wellesley Hills, Mass., Boston & Albany Railroad.—The flag-depot of the Boston & Albany Railroad at Wellesley Hills, Mass., designed by the late Mr. H. H. Richardson, architect, Brooklyne, Mass., plans for which were published in the *American Architect and Building News* of February 26, 1887, is a single-story stone structure, 21 ft. × 40 ft., with round bay-windows at the corners of the front of the building, and with large, sloping roof. The interior is cut up considerably so as to give a general waiting-room; a ticket-office; a baggage-room; a ladies' waiting-room. with toilet-room attached; and a smoking-room, with toilet-room attached.

CHAPTER XXI.

LOCAL PASSENGER DEPOTS.

PASSENGER depots solely for the accommodation of the passenger business of a railroad are used at all local stations of railroads where the passenger business is of sufficient importance to warrant a separate building, or where the freight business is handled in a separate building. The size, design, and class of structure used in each case will vary materially, according to the local conditions and the importance of the station. As indicated above in the remarks on flag-depots, it can be said that flag-depots are simply small local passenger depots, the distinction between the two being very hard to maintain, as the change from one group to the other in practice is frequently imperceptible, and not clearly defined. Railroads adopting standard sets of depot plans usually divide the designs into classes, flag-depots being the smallest and cheapest class of structures. The requirements for and the division of the interior of local passenger depots vary considerably, starting with a small building containing waiting-rooms, a ticket-office and a baggage-room, and ending with large two-story structures with capacious waiting-rooms, toilet-rooms, smoking-room, dining-room and appurtenances, baggage-room, express-room, mail-room, telegraph-office, parcel-room, news-stand, supply-rooms, rooms for conductors and trainmen, and offices. Structures of the latter class approach in character terminal side-stations, the distinction between the two, however, consisting in the feature, that in a terminal side-station the tracks, or a number of them at least, terminate at the station, while in a large first-class local passenger depot the tracks pass by the building. At terminal stations on pioneer railroads and in small towns the terminal passenger depot is built practically the same as a large local passenger depot. It will, therefore, be readily seen, that in the discussion of local passenger depots the remarks are necessarily general, and no special rules can be established, as the range of buildings embraced under the term of local passenger depots is very extensive.

The general style and size of a depot building will depend to a large extent on the proposed location with reference to the topographical features of the site, the amount of land available, the facilities required, and the importance of the locality. The size and ground-plan layout should correspond to the actual requirements of the business to be expected in the near future, considering also the possible growth of the town or settlement, so that subsequent enlargements of the structure can either be carried out easily or else the building made large enough at the start to exclude the possibility of having to make alterations for a great many years. The style of the building should correspond to the surroundings, with due regard, however, to the practical uses to which the structure is to be devoted. The class of building materials and the general finish of the building will depend on the amount of the appropriation set aside for the structure, and the materials found to be in general use and easily obtainable in each particular section of the country.

Local passenger stations on railroads with more than one main track can either be side-stations, island-stations, or overhead-stations. A special class of side-stations are so-called twin-stations and stations with covered platforms or shelters on the opposite side of the railroad from the depot building. Junction-stations occur at the crossing-point of two railroads, in which case the depot building is located in the angle between the two roads. Twin-stations, in other words two separate depot buildings, are used at junction points of railroads, where each road desires its own depot. They are also used, one on each side of the railroad, where the local passenger business is so heavy and there are so many trains running that it would prove a source of great inconvenience or danger to make passengers cross the tracks from one side of the station to the other. Of course two buildings require practically double help throughout, but there are conditions and localities which call for this class of station. Overhead-stations are very customary for railroads entering cities, where the road-bed is in a deep cut and the right of way obtainable is limited or the value of land very high. They not only afford a means of maintaining depots on the railroad company's original right of way, but offer the advantages of an island and a side-station combined. One set of offices, waiting-rooms, etc., serve for passengers going in either direction, while the respective platforms can be reached from the depot building without crossing tracks at grade. Island-stations, that is, stations with the depot building set between the tracks, which are spread for this purpose, have been used to quite an extent in this country. In case there are four tracks, and the inner two are used for way-trains, while the outer two are used for express trains, the adoption of island-stations offers some great advantages. But to make this method practical, all stations on the railroad should be island-stations, which it is not always feasible to accomplish, especially in running through towns or cities where the right of way is limited, or owing to the proximity of bridges it is impossible to spread the tracks to accommodate the island-depot. In addition, the use of the outer tracks for fast trains cannot be considered the best practice, if the requirements of the local freight business and the necessity for having sidings into factories and yards along the route are considered. Some four-track railroads run the fast trains on the two tracks on one side of the roadbed and the local trains on the other two tracks, so that depots located alongside the latter serve the local passenger business very well. But at stations where fast and local trains stop, this division of the tracks loses some of the prominent advantages claimed for it. At such stations the transferring of trains from one track to another by a system of cross-overs and leaders at each end of the station, well guarded by interlocking block-signals, offers a solution of the problem that has been quite frequently adopted. It can be said, however, in general, that, excepting where another style of station is required or distinctly indicated by the local conditions, side-stations represent the most general practice adopted in this country for local passenger stations on single, double, or four-track railroads.

Local passenger depots at side-stations have the objections that, where the railroad is a double-track or a four-track road, passengers are obliged to cross tracks at grade to get to trains on the far tracks. Where the business of the road is very heavy and the crowds to be expected at the depot at certain times are large, it is customary to place an open or covered platform or a shelter on the opposite side of the railroad from the depot building, thereby obviating some of the objectionable features of side-stations. At important points this platform or shelter is connected with the main depot building by a tunnel or subway beneath the tracks, or by an overhead foot-bridge over the tracks. The travelling public seems to have an aversion for subterranean passages, yet the vertical descent and ascent is fully ten feet less than the height the passenger has to overcome in passing from one side of a station to the other across an overhead foot-bridge. Where a subway can be properly drained and kept well ventilated and lighted, it should be preferred to an overhead foot-bridge, which, in addition, blocks the view along the road to a certain extent. Subways or foot-bridges are frequently provided by railroad companies, so as to have a strong legal point in defending any suits for damages resulting from accidents to travellers while crossing the tracks to get from one side to the other side of the station. It is, however, customary, where a subway or a foot-bridge is provided, to actually prevent travellers crowding across the tracks, even if it is at their own risk, by putting a fence between the main tracks or fences between each main track and the outside track next to it, in which latter case the outside tracks are used for local trains and the inner tracks for fast trains that do not stop at the station. Where the outside tracks on a four-track railroad are used for freight-trains only, and the inner tracks for all passenger trains, it is generally impossible to turn the outside tracks away from the main tracks, so that passengers are forced to cross a freight track to get to the passenger track. This is an objection which generally cannot be remedied, and has to remain, calling for increased vigilance and care on the part of trainmen and the station help.

The platforms at passenger depots are always low platforms, from 2 in. to 16 in. above the top of rail. According to the design adopted, they surround the building on all sides or only on certain sides. The platform along the track is usually extended each way from the building for some distance, so as to give a longer platform frontage for trains. The width of platforms varies in different designs according to the platform space required to handle the travel. Platforms should be never less than 12 ft. wide, and preferably not less than 24 ft. The conditions governing the selection of the height, length, and width of platforms at passenger depots, as also the proper materials to use, according to the circumstances presented in each particular case, are discussed at length in the chapter on Platforms, Platform-sheds, and Shelters. It should be mentioned, however, that platform roof projections along a carriage-road on the back of a platform, or a well-designed *porte cochère*, are a source of great convenience to travellers arriving or leaving in carriages during stormy weather.

As stated above, the division of the interior of a local passenger depot varies greatly, according to the requirements in each case. For the larger class of local depots the rules established below as a general basis for terminal side depots will apply, excepting that considerable liberty could be taken in following such general rules. The following general remarks will apply more particularly to the average-size local passenger depot.

The ticket-office, if used also as a telegraph-office, should be situated at the front of the building, facing the track, with a bay-window projection, so that the movement of trains on the track can be readily seen from the interior of the office. There should be, if feasible, separate ticket-windows for each waiting-room, and the windows should be far enough apart to allow space for a ticket case and shelf between them, without requiring the ticket-seller to move far in passing from window to window. Good light should be provided at day and night on both sides of the ticket-window. Selling tickets to a lobby or a large general waiting-room has some good and some objectionable features. If tickets are sold to a lobby or a general waiting-room, a large number of passengers after purchasing their tickets will pass immediately to the trains or platforms, and thus tend to make the special waiting-rooms more private. On the other hand, unless special windows are provided for ladies, the latter will be seriously inconvenienced when large crowds are at the depot. If the ticket-office is not used as a telegraph-office, it need not be located on the track side of the house ; but it is more advantageous to locate it thus in all cases, if possible, as the ticket-seller can keep better advised of the movement of trains. Finally, attention should be called to the desirability of making the offices large enough to be comfortable and convenient for the employés, and also to allow for the accommodation of extra help, if the business at the station should increase and require it.

Relative to waiting-rooms, it can be said, that separate waiting-rooms for gentlemen and for ladies are most desirable. But where there is only one general waiting-room, it is very important to provide, if possible, at least a small ladies' parlor with toilet-room attached. Where there is a special ladies' waiting-room, the parlor or dressing-room can be dispensed with, and the toilet-room open immediately from the ladies' waiting-room. It is very bad practice, however, to allow the door to the ladies' toilet-room to lead directly from a general waiting-room. Where the ladies' waiting-room is not completely closed off from the gentlemen's waiting-room or from the general waiting-room or corridor, it is desirable, where feasible, to place the door from the ladies' waiting-room to the toilet-room on a side of the room hidden from view from the corridor or the other waiting-room. If this is not feasible, it is customary to put up a screen or light partition, so as to partially mask the entrance to the toilet-room. The toilet-room for gentlemen should never have a direct entrance from the general waiting-room. There is no objection, however, to having the toilet-room for gentlemen lead from a smoking-room or from a separate waiting-room for gentlemen. But the best plan to pursue, when the toilet-room cannot be placed in the main building as an extension to a smoking-room or a gentlemen's waiting-room, is to place it in a separate building or else in the main building with an outside entrance from the rear or end of the building. In fact, the general rule should prevail, that the toilet-room for gentlemen should be accessible from the outside of the building. Attention should also be called to the advantages to be derived from introducing a generously proportioned and comfortably fitted-up smoking-room. It will not only accommodate smokers, but it will draw off from the waiting-rooms quite an undesirable element, as emigrants, laborers, hackmen, and loungers around the depot.

Relative to the location of the doors in the waiting-rooms, they should be so disposed that the passengers entering from the rear of the building can pass to the ticket-window and then out to the train on as direct a route as possible. Where large crowds are expected at times, and the doors leading to the train side of the house are kept closed till trains arrive or are ready to start, it is desirable to have the doors open with the crowd and not against it. At such depots, a large lobby or a general waiting-room is a good feature, as it allows large crowds and parties to pass directly to the train without tramping through or blocking the special waiting-rooms.

In connection with the handling of crowds going to trains, a word should be said about providing exits for the crowds from arriving trains. At small depots, passengers pass along the platform and around the building to the street. At large depots, where the building has considerable front along the track, special passage-ways are frequently provided near the centre of the main building to allow passengers to pass quickly from the arriving platform to the street at the rear of the building. The advantage gained is that arriving crowds leave the platform sooner, and do not conflict with the throng of people passing from the waiting-rooms to the train. The passage of arriving passengers through a general waiting-room, lobby, or corridor, which is used for outgoing passengers to pass through in going to trains, is very bad practice, as the outgoing passengers will be interfered with and delayed in buying their tickets, checking their baggage, etc. A separate passage-way is therefore more desirable, in case the incoming travel and the length of the building demand a short cut to the street. Excepting in very long depot buildings, the advantages of separate exits through the building for incoming passengers should not be overestimated, especially if the convenient and practical layout of the ground-plan with reference to outgoing passengers is thereby seriously disturbed. In this connection, the design of depots with a main building and an auxiliary building at one end or at both ends, separated from the main building, but connected with it by covered platforms, as shown in Figs. 564 to 566, is very customary. This style of design offers many advantages, one of the most important of which is the speedy manner in which arriving passengers can leave the depot without interfering with departing passengers.

The baggage-room at small local passenger depots, excepting in some cases at junction points where passengers change trains, need not be very large, as the baggage business is handled mainly on the platform next to the baggage-room, and the baggage-room proper serves more particularly as the baggage-master's office and for the storing of baggage over night. The same remarks hold good at large local passenger depots, especially for the incoming baggage; but the outgoing baggage is more liable to pass through the baggage-room, as it is received on the street side from wagons and passes through the baggage-room to the trains. The location of the baggage-room should be such that baggage can be easily received from the street side and also delivered to the street side of the depot. There should be considerable platform space available for the storing of baggage under cover, and the baggage-room should be located in such a way that passengers passing along the platforms are not blocked by the baggage and baggage-trucks, that will necessarily accumulate at times on the platform around the baggage-room. At the same time, however, it is desirable to locate it so that passengers can reach the baggage-room in passing to and from trains, without seriously going out of their way. Where there is a general waiting-room or a large lobby provided, it is good practice, if feasible, to have an opening or window leading from the general waiting-room or lobby into the baggage-room, so that passengers can leave hand baggage, arrange about checking baggage, make inquiries, etc., on their way to trains after purchasing their tickets without having to go outside of the building around to the entrance to the baggage-room. In small depots, as outlined above, this feature is not essential, as the checking of baggage is usually done on the platform in front of the baggage room; and, in any event, the distance the passengers would have to go from the waiting-room to the baggage-room is insignificant. Where the help at the depot is limited, and the agent or ticket-seller has to attend to the checking of baggage, the location of the baggage-room near the office is necessary. Where the volume of business warrants maintaining a separate baggage-master, the location of the baggage-room in an auxiliary building has advantages. The platforms around the main building can be kept clear of baggage, and the express-wagons and baggage-wagons will line up on the street near the baggage-room away from the passenger building proper, leaving the rear of the main building free for foot-passengers and carriages. The remarks in reference to the baggage business apply also to express-offices, to a more or less extent.

At dining-stations, according to the local requirements, small lunch-counters or large extensive dining-rooms, with all the necessary appurtenances, are provided. Where the building is two-story, the location of the kitchen and serving-rooms, etc., on the second floor is a good feature. Relative to the location of the dining-rooms, it will depend to a certain extent on whether provision is to be mainly made for through passengers, simply stopping at the depot for their meals, or whether the dining-rooms are for the accommodation of incoming and outgoing local passengers. In the first case, the main feature is to provide easy ingress and egress to and from the dining-room on the train side of the depot, without disturbing passengers in the waiting-rooms or passengers passing to trains. In the other case mentioned, the dining-rooms and refreshment-counters are part of the general layout in connection with the waiting-rooms and other facilities for the accommodation of incoming and outgoing local passengers, and the design should be made accordingly.

At small depots one office suffices for telegraph-office, ticket-office, and station-agent's office. At larger depots separate offices for the station-agent, telegraph-operator, train-despatcher, and other officials have to be provided. Also, supply-rooms for stores, fuel, lamps, oil, etc. Where two-story buildings are used, the upper floor is generally utilized for offices for the telegraph department, train-despatcher, clerks, and others connected with the road; also for trainmen's room, conductors' room, etc., where space for such purposes is desired. The style of depot with a main building and two auxiliary buildings or pavilions, situated some distance from each end of the main building, as shown in Figs. 564 to 566, offers advantages where space has to be provided for the various purposes just mentioned. The main building is usually devoted to the regulation accommodations for passengers, one auxiliary building is used for the baggage and express business, store-rooms, and gentlemen's toilet-room, while the other auxiliary building is used for offices for officials and rooms for men connected with the road.

Living-rooms for some of the help employed at depots are frequently provided. In some cases, regular dwelling-houses are attached to the depot building or dwelling-rooms provided for in an upper story.

The general remarks made above about waiting-rooms, toilet-rooms, baggage-rooms, and offices will hold good for junction stations, with the additional feature that in depots at junction points baggage-rooms and ticket-offices have to frequently be provided in duplicate, one for each railroad.

The heating, ventilating, plumbing, and lighting of a depot should be the very best obtainable, consistent with the general style of structure adopted. Large fire-places of quaint and artistic design in the waiting-rooms add not only to the general artistic effect and finish of the interior, but afford a good chance to warm the rooms and brighten them up in damp weather. They also give an opportunity to secure good ventilation. Where the size of the building warrants it, the heating of the building by steam or by a furnace located in a cellar under the building will prove the best method to adopt. Water-closets supplied with running water and waste drains should naturally be adopted, where feasible. Where water is not at hand, the next best possible system applicable to the case should be employed.

In the chapter on Platforms, Platform-sheds, and Shelters reference was made to the value of having ample and conveniently located covered platforms around a depot building, so that crowds could be accommodated on the platforms to a large extent, thereby allowing the waiting-rooms to be made proportionately much smaller. In addition it can be said, that, if convenient benches are provided on the platforms, a large number of travellers, and especially depot loungers, will congregate on the platforms in place of in the waiting-rooms. A drinking-fountain with running water located on the platform or near the depot will prove a great boon to passengers.

Relative to the style of structure to be adopted for a local passenger depot, it is very difficult to make any general recommendations. The importance of the station, the surroundings, the desires of the railroad management, and sometimes the wishes of the community, the prevailing class of architecture and building materials in each particular section of the country, will all influence the final choice. In a general way, however, it can be said that frame buildings are not as objectionable for small passenger depots as for freight-houses and other railroad structures, because in case of a fire the loss is practically limited to the value of the building, and the business of the road will not be blocked, although individuals will be personally seriously inconvenienced. In cities and at important stations a more substantial building is desirable, and it is usually required by existing building laws.

Relative to the design for the exterior of depots, much stress has been laid within recent years on providing artistic and picturesque structures for local passenger depots, especially at surburban points where the travel consists largely of wealthy patrons of the road. The artistic depot designs prepared by the late Mr. H. H. Richardson, the well known architect, of Boston, Mass., and a gradually increasing demand for artistic structures at passenger stations have given an impetus to the designing of more artistic buildings, with the result that architects of established reputation have been called on by railroad managers for designs. The architectural effect should be obtained by bold and original but graceful treatment, based on constructional outlines suitable to the materials used and adapted to the surroundings. In order, however, to produce quaint and artistic features in the exterior of a railroad structure, the practical requirements for the ground-plan layout should not be sacrificed. At smaller suburban depots defects of the ground-plan, caused by a desire to produce an architecturally picturesque building, are not so serious a matter. In large depots, however, any defects of the ground-plan layout are far more serious, and will entail for years constant trouble and extra expense. As above stated, picturesqueness of design in a small suburban depot is an important consideration; but in large depots the style of architecture adopted should be more indicative of the purposes to which the building is devoted. In other words, following the architectural maxim, that the style of the building should correspond to the use it is put to, it can hardly be considered good practice to design a large depot on the same outlines as a church or an old-fashioned country tavern, especially when very serious defects of the ground-plan layout are created by giving too much attention to the architectural effect of the building.

Where standard designs or "class-depots" are adopted, stress should be laid on having the designs modified in minor details, so as to avoid a monotonous sameness of similar structures along the road. This can be easily accomplished by making modifications in the details of the exterior finish, gables, dormer-windows, ridge-cresting, finials, roof-brackets, chimneys, etc., without in reality changing the ground-plan or the frame or the walls of the building.

The employment of a landscape architect in connection with the artistic design of rural stations has in a great many cases produced most picturesque and artistic depot surroundings. The planting of the ground around depot buildings and the maintenance of flower-beds and shrubberies at stations, together with the use of neat railings, gravelled walks and roads, have been introduced with good results by a large number of railroads in this country. The extent to which this can be carried is well shown in Fig. 585, representing the Ardmore Station of the Pennsylvania Railroad; as also in Figs. 594 to 596, illustrating the Auburndale Station of the Boston & Albany Railroad, where the drive-ways, in connection with the *porte cochère*, the foot-walks, and the masking of the fence lines by shrubbery, are admirably laid out.

After above general remarks on the subject, the following descriptions and illustrations, as also references to published descriptions and illustrations of local passenger depots in use, or designed for use, on railroads in this country, will prove interesting.

Single-story Passenger Depot, Chesapeake & Ohio Railway.—The passenger depot of the Chesapeake & Ohio Railway, known as design "B," April, 1883, is a single-story frame structure, 21 ft. × 50 ft., with extensions at each end, 13 ft. 6 in. × 11 ft. 6 in. The building is sheathed on the outside with vertical and horizontal boarding in panels, and roofed with tin. The interior is divided into a telegraph and ticket office, 8 ft. wide, running through the centre of the building, with a gentlemen's waiting-room, 20 ft. × 20 ft., on one side of it, and a ladies' waiting-room, 20 ft. × 20 ft., on the other side. In one annex, adjoining the ladies' waiting-room, there is a ladies' toilet-room, with entrance from the ladies' waiting-room; and a gentlemen's toilet-room, with separate entrance from the rear of

FIG. 510.—END ELEVATION.

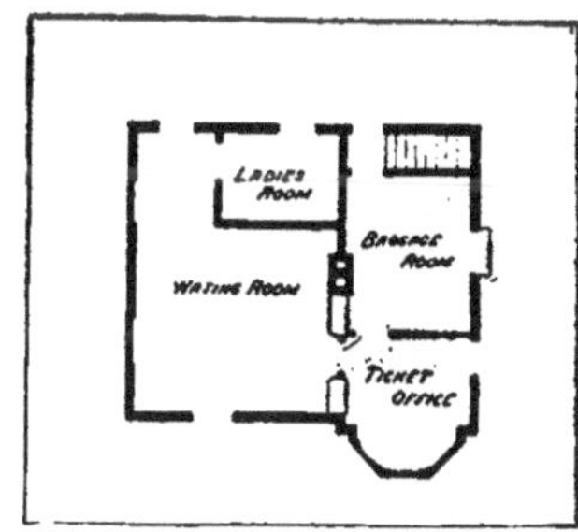

FIG. 511.—GROUND-PLAN.

the building. The annex at the other end of the building is used for a baggage-room. This design offers a very good ground-plan layout and a cheap structure, which is well adapted and sufficiently effective for country stations. The design is practically the same as the standard passenger depot, class "C," of the Pennsylvania lines west of Pittsburg, Southwest System, described below and illustrated in Figs. 512 to 514.

Two-story Passenger Depot, Chesapeake & Ohio Railway.—The passenger depot of the Chesapeake & Ohio Railway, known as design No. 2, 1881, shown in Figs. 510 and 511, is a two-story frame structure, sheathed with horizontal, vertical, and ornamental boarding, in panels, and roofed with tin. The building is 20 ft. × 25 ft., and has on the ground-floor a general waiting-room; a ladies' room; a baggage-room; and a ticket-office. On the upper floor there is a telegraph-office, and two rooms suitable for living-rooms or offices.

Standard Passenger Depot, Class "C," Pennsylvania Lines West of Pittsburg, Southwest System.—The standard passenger depot of the Pennsylvania lines west of Pittsburg, Southwest System, known as class "C," designed by Mr. M. J. Becker, Chief Engineer, shown in Figs. 512 to 514, is a

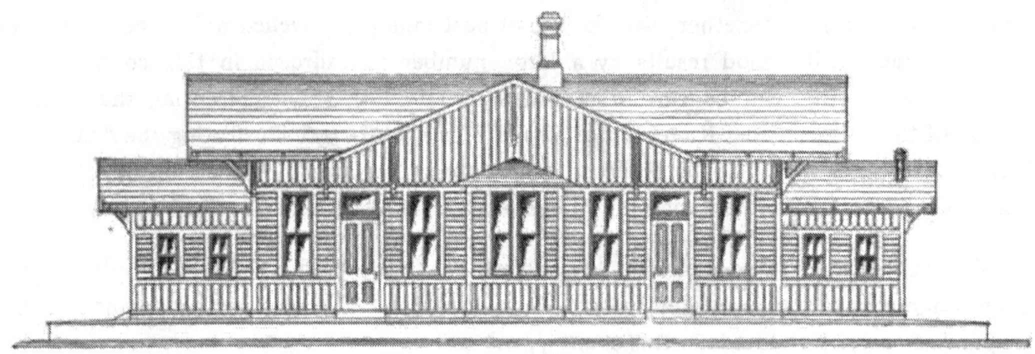

FIG. 512.—FRONT ELEVATION.

single-story frame structure, 21 ft. × 50 ft., with extensions at each end, 11 ft. 6 in. × 14 ft., sheathed on the outside with vertical ornamental battened boarding and horizontal weather-boarding, in panels,

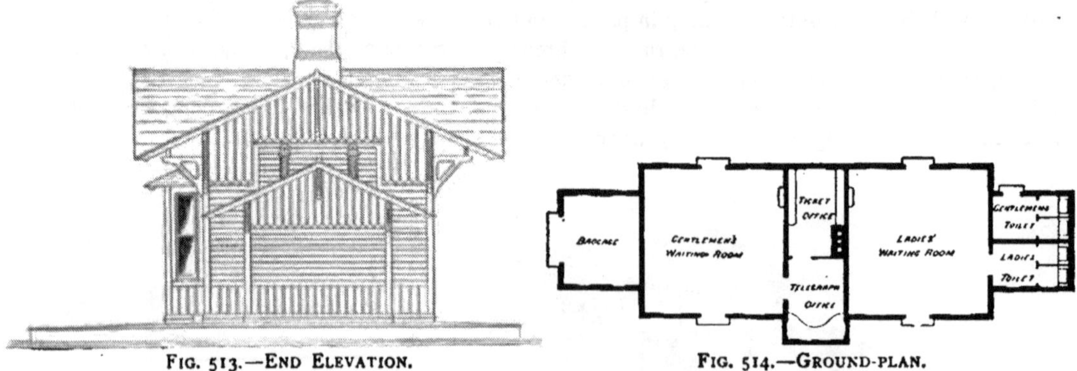

FIG. 513.—END ELEVATION.

FIG. 514.—GROUND-PLAN.

and roofed with slate. The interior is divided into a telegraph-office, 8 ft. × 11 ft. 5 in., with a square bay-window projection on the track side; a ticket-office at the rear of the telegraph-office, 8 ft. × 12 ft., partitioned off from the former; a gentlemen's waiting-room, 20 ft. × 20 ft.; a ladies' waiting-room, 20 ft. × 20 ft., with a toilet-room, 6 ft. 3 in. × 11 ft., attached; a baggage-room, 11 ft. × 13 ft.; and a gentlemen's toilet-room, 6 ft. 3 in. × 11 ft., with entrance from the rear of the building. The foundations are stone piers. The interior walls are all plastered, excepting in the baggage-room. The specifications for this building are practically the same as for the standard passenger depot, class "F," of the same railroad, the specifications for which are given in full in the Appendix at the back of this book. The ground-plan of this depot is first-class for the purpose, and the entire design can be highly recommended. The platform in front of the building is 16 ft. wide, set 8 in. above the top of the rail, and 8 ft. wide at the rear and ends of the building.

Standard Passenger Depot, Class "F," Pennsylvania Lines West of Pittsburg, Southwest System.—The standard passenger depot of the Pennsylvania lines west of Pittsburg, Southwest System, known as class "F," designed by Mr. M. J. Becker, Chief Engineer, shown in Figs. 515 to 517, is a single-

FIG. 515.—FRONT ELEVATION.

story frame structure, 70 ft. × 21 ft., sheathed on the outside with vertical ornamental and battened boarding and horizontal weather-boarding, in panels, with considerable scroll-work at the gables and galvanized-iron ridge-combings and gutter-cresting, the roof being covered with slate. The interior is divided into an office, 7 ft. × 10 ft.; a gentlemen's waiting-room, 20 ft. × 25 ft. 6 in.; a ladies' waiting-room, 20 ft. × 20 ft., with a ladies' dressing-room, 7 ft. × 10 ft., attached, from which a ladies' toilet-room, 6 ft. × 10 ft., leads; a gentlemen's toilet-room, 6 ft. × 10 ft., with entrance from the rear of the building; and a baggage-room, 12 ft. × 20 ft. All the walls are plastered and wainscoted, excepting in the baggage-rooms. The foundations are stone piers. The platform in front of

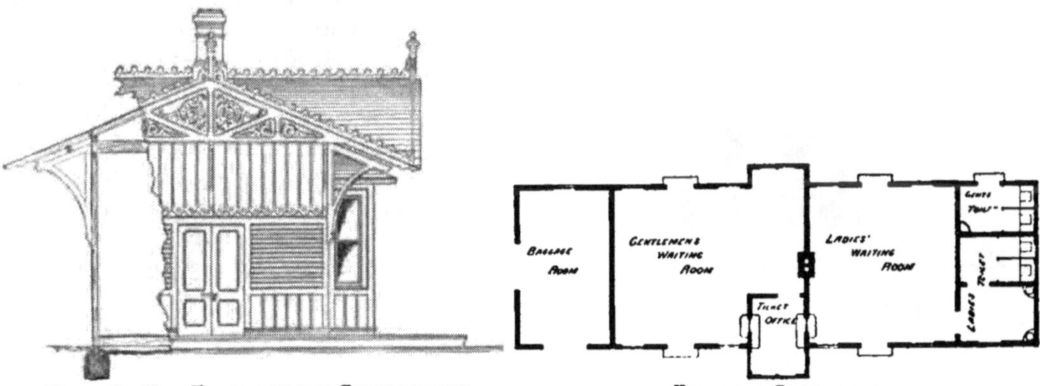

FIG. 516.—END ELEVATION AND CROSS-SECTION. FIG. 517.—GROUND-PLAN.

the building is 16 ft. wide, and it is 8 ft. wide at the rear and ends of the building. It is set 8 in. above the top of the rail. The specifications for this building are given in full in the Appendix at the back of this book. The ground-plan of this depot is first-class for the purpose, and the exterior design very ornamental, so that the entire structure can be well recommended.

Passenger Depot, Northern Pacific Railroad.—The passenger depot of the Northern Pacific Railroad, shown in Figs. 518 and 519, is a single-story frame structure, 24 ft. × 80 ft., sheathed on the outside with upright and horizontal boarding, in panels, and roofed with shingles. The building is surrounded by low platforms on all sides, 12 ft. wide at the rear and at the ends of the building, and

16 ft. wide along the front of the building, extended [illegible] ft. in width each way from the building along the track. The interior is divided into a ticket and baggage-office, [illegible] ft. × [illegible] ft., with a square bay-window projec-

Fig. 518.—Perspective.

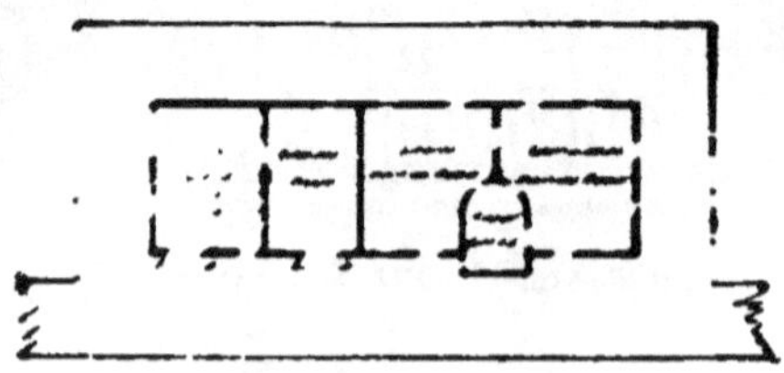

Fig. 519.—Ground-plan.

tion; a gentlemen's waiting-room, 22 ft. × 22 ft.; a ladies' waiting-room, 21 ft. × 22 ft.; a baggage-room, 15 ft. × 22 ft.; and an express-room, 18 ft. × 22 ft.

Passenger Depot, Ohio Valley Railway.—The standard design for a local passenger depot of the Ohio Valley Railway, shown in Fig. 520, designed by Mr. C. C. Genung, Chief Engineer, Ohio Valley Railway, consists of a single-story frame structure, 52 ft. × 18 ft., roofed with shingles. The interior is divided into a gentlemen's waiting-room, 17 ft. × 17 ft.; a ladies' waiting-room, 17 ft. × 17 ft.; a ticket and telegraph office, 20 ft. × 9 ft., including the front bay-window projection; and a baggage-room, 17 ft. × 9 ft. There is a low platform, 15 ft. wide, in front of the building. The most striking feature of this design is the upward curve of the roof at the eaves, the radius of the curve being 10 ft. This feature, in connection with the knee-braces under the roof projection, which are cut to a bold semicircular pattern, and the exterior panelling, causes the structure to appear very neat. The outside of the building is sheathed with vertical, horizontal, and diagonal, plain and ornamental boarding, in panels. The inside finish is of wood. The vertical siding is painted a Turkey vermilion, the horizontal and diagonal siding a very light drab, and the frames, belt-courses, etc., a very dark red, approaching a brown color. Mr. Genung states that buildings of this class cost about $1100, exclusive of platforms.

Fig. 520.—End Elevation.

A similar depot building at DeKoven, Ky., on the same railroad, cost about $1800. It is built on the same ground plan as the standard passenger depot described above, but there is a second story added, with a small tower over the telegraph-office, and the roof is covered with tin in place of shingles.

Single-story Passenger Depot, Richmond & Alleghany Railroad.—The single-story passenger depot of the Richmond & Alleghany Railroad, shown in Figs. 521 and 522, consists of a frame structure, sheathed on the outside with horizontal and vertical boarding, in panels, and roofed with slate. The building is 55 ft. 8 in. × 19 ft. 6 in., and is divided into a ticket-office; a gentlemen's waiting-room; a ladies' waiting-room; and a baggage-room.

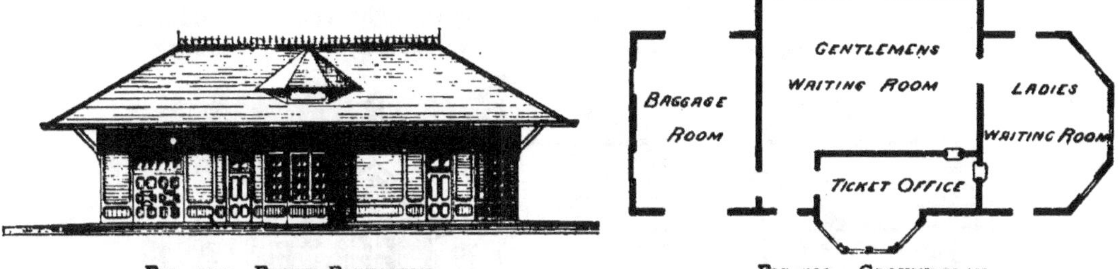

FIG. 521.—FRONT ELEVATION. FIG. 522.—GROUND-PLAN.

Two-story Passenger Depot, Richmond & Alleghany Railroad.—The two-story passenger depot of the Richmond & Alleghany Railroad, shown in Figs. 523 to 525, consists of a frame structure,

FIG. 523.—FRONT ELEVATION.

FIG. 524.—END ELEVATION.

sheathed on the outside with horizontal and vertical, ornamental boarding, in panels, and roofed with slate. The building is 57 ft. long × 21 ft. 6 in. wide at the narrowest part. The first floor has a ticket-office, 10 ft. × 13 ft.; a gentlemen's waiting-room, 16 ft. × 20 ft.; a ladies' waiting-room, 13 ft. × 19 ft.; a baggage-room, 16 ft. × 20 ft.; and a stairway leading to the upper floor, which is used as a train-despatcher's and telegraph office. While the design of the exterior of the building is neat, the ground-plan layout is defective in a number of points.

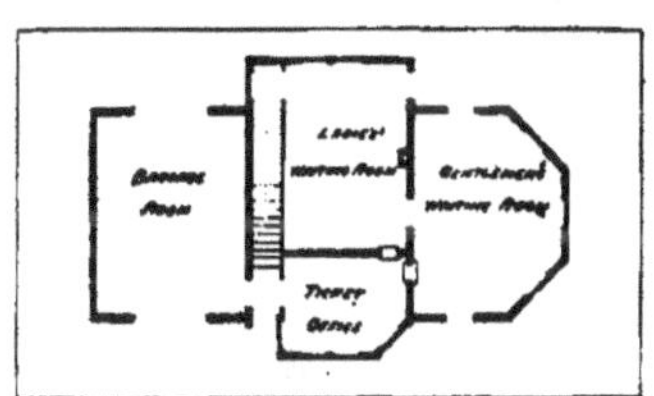

FIG. 525.—GROUND-PLAN.

Passenger Depot, Class "F," Minnesota & Northwestern Railroad.—The standard plan for a passenger depot, class "F," of the Minnesota & Northwestern Railroad and of the Chicago, St. Paul & Kansas City Railway, designed by Mr. C. A. Reed, Architect, St. Paul, Minn., under the direction of Mr. H. Fernstrom, Chief Engineer, M. & N. W. R. R., is a single-story frame structure. 22 ft. × 60 ft., roofed with shingles, built and finished in about the same manner as the combination depots of this railroad, previously described and illustrated in the chapter on Combination Depots. The building is divided, as shown in Fig. 526, into a ticket-office, 11 ft. × 16 ft., with a square bay-window projection; a gentlemen's waiting-room, 16 ft. × 21 ft.; a ladies' waiting-room, 15 ft. 6 in. × 21 ft.; and a baggage-room, 14 ft. × 21 ft.

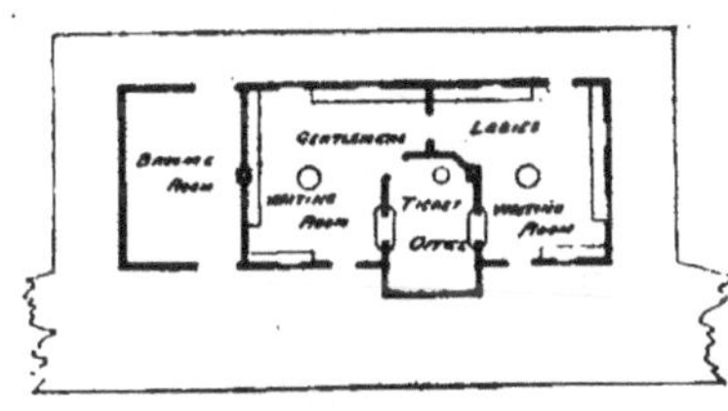

FIG. 526.—GROUND-PLAN.

Passenger Depot at Spokane Falls, Wash., Northern Pacific Railroad.—The passenger depot of the Northern Pacific Railroad at Spokane Falls, Wash., shown in Figs. 527 and 528, designed by Mr. C. B. Talbot, in 1886, consists of a single-story frame structure, sheathed on the outside with upright and horizontal, ornamental boarding, and roofed with shingles. The structure is divided into two separate buildings, connected by a covered passage-way, 19 ft. wide, both buildings and the passage-way being under one continuous roof. The building intended for the passengers more particularly has a ticket-office, 11 ft. × 16 ft.; a gentlemen's waiting-room, 31 ft. × 26 ft.; a ladies' waiting-room, 18 ft. × 24 ft.; and toilet-rooms for gentlemen and ladies connecting with the respective waiting-rooms. The other building contains a telegraph-office, 16 ft. × 18 ft.; an express, freight, and baggage room, 24 ft.

FIG. 527.—FRONT ELEVATION.

× 26 ft.; a battery-room; a fuel-room; a lamp and oil room; and a train-order room. The rooms are 11 ft. high in the clear. The interior is finished in wood. The foundations are stone walls. The principal timbers are, sills and floor-girders, 8 in. × 10 in.; floor-joists, 3 in. × 10 in., spaced 20 in.

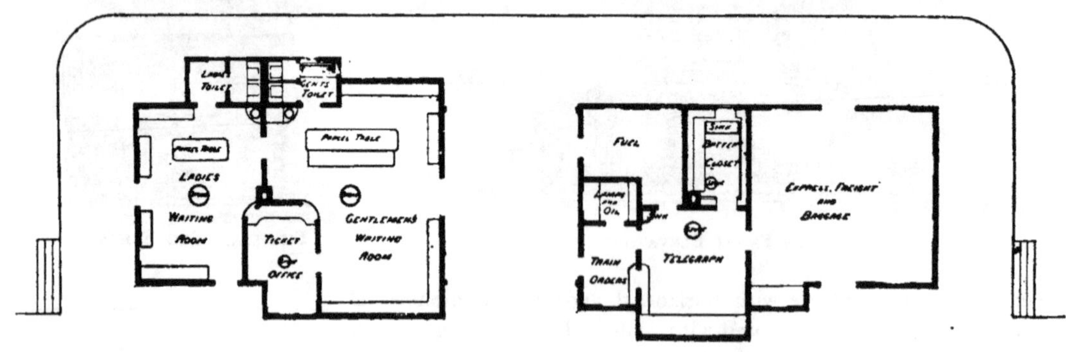

FIG. 528.—GROUND-PLAN.

centres; floor, double, with building-paper between; frame, 3-in. × 6-in. studs; plates, 3 in. × 6 in., double; rafters, 3 in. × 6 in., spaced 24 in. centres; ceiling-joists, 3 in. × 6 in.; struts and ties, $1\frac{1}{2}$ in. × 6 in.; 1-in. roof-boards.

Passenger Depot, Boston, Hoosac Tunnel & Western Railway.—The design for a second-class

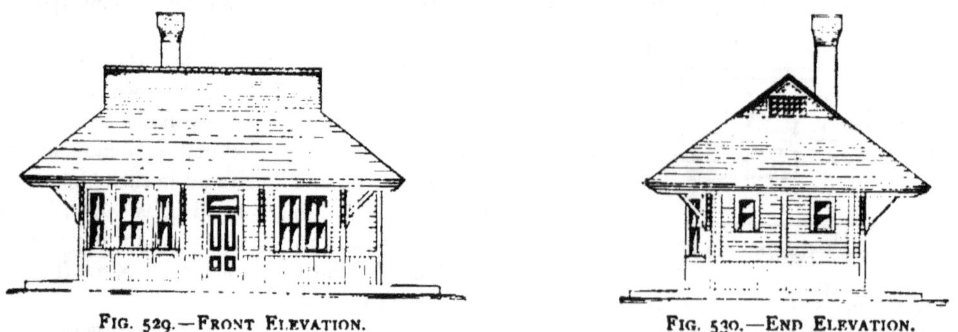

FIG. 529.—FRONT ELEVATION.　　FIG. 530.—END ELEVATION.

passenger depot of the Boston, Hoosac Tunnel & Western Railway, shown in Figs. 529 to 531, kindly furnished by Mr. Edwin A. Hill, is a single-story frame structure, 29 ft. 6 in. × 19 ft., surrounded by platforms on all sides, sheathed on the outside with upright and horizontal boarding, in panels, and roofed with slate. The platform on the face along the track is 8 ft. wide, and on the sides and rear 6 ft. wide. The floor of the house is set 15 in. and the platform 6 in. above the top of rail. The face of the platform is 5 ft. from the centre of the track. The interior of the building is divided into a ticket-office and baggage-room, 10 ft. × 19 ft., including a hexagonal bay-window projection; a general waiting-room, 16 ft. × 18 ft.; a ladies' toilet-room; and a gentlemen's toilet-room. The foundations of the building are stone piers, and the foundations of the platform are chestnut posts set in the ground. The chimney is of brick, 16 in. × 20 in. inside. The privy vault is 6 ft. deep, built of stone, and topped off with brick. The timber-work of the frame is spruce, the principal sizes being sills, 7 in. × 7 in.; girders, 6 in. × 8 in.; first-floor joists, 2 in. × 12 in. in waiting-room, and 2 in. × 10 in. otherwise, spaced 18 in. centres; platform front sills, 4 in. × 8 in.; platform cross-caps, 6 in. × 8 in.; platform-joists, 2 in. × 8 in., spaced 20 in.; posts, 4 in. × 8 in.; studs, 2 in. × 4 in., spaced 16 in.; window and door studs, 2 in. × 4 in., doubled; plates, 4 in. × 6 in.; rafters, 2 in. × 8 in., 25 in. centres; ceiling-joists, 2 in. × 8 in., 25 in. centres, and hung in centre from ridge; hips, 2 in. × 8 in.; outside sheathing, planed, matched, 1-in. spruce boards, laid close diagonally, and covered with heavy building-paper. The outside sheathing is planed and matched, narrow, ⅞-in. white-pine boarding, beaded on one edge. Corner boards, belt-courses, frieze, casings, etc., are 1-in. white pine. The roof is covered with 1-in. planed and matched spruce boards, laid close. The slate is laid on tarred felt, and nailed with galvanized nails. Flashings, gutters, and down-conductors are made of galvanized iron. The interior of the building is ceiled with planed and matched, seasoned, narrow, ½-in. white pine, beaded on one edge. The partitions are built of 2-in. × 4-in. spruce scantlings, 24-in. centres. The floor in the building consists of 1-in. hemlock, covered with two layers of heavy felt paper, and with planed and matched, narrow, seasoned, 1-in. Georgia yellow-pine flooring. Platforms are covered with 2-in. spruce plank, dressed on upper surface, and laid close. Sash, 1½ in. thick. Doors, white pine, 2 in. thick for outside and 1 in. thick for interior doors.

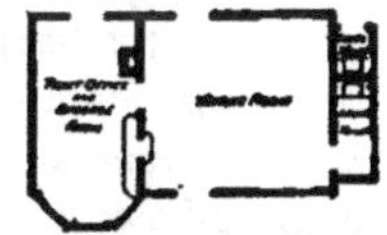
FIG. 531.—GROUND-PLAN.

A depot building of the kind described costs about $1100.

Local Passenger Depot, Louisville & Nashville Railroad.—A number of passenger depots at local points on the Louisville & Nashville Railroad are built on the ground-plan layout, as shown in Fig. 532. The platform is 10 in. above the top of rail, and reaches within 5 ft. 5 in. of the centre of the track. The interior is divided into a ladies' waiting-room, 18 ft. × 16 ft., with a small toilet-room partitioned off in it; a gentlemen's waiting-room, 16 ft. × 16 ft.; a baggage-room, 8 ft. × 16 ft.; a ticket and telegraph office, 15 ft. × 15 ft.; and a waiting-room for colored people, 15 ft. × 15 ft.

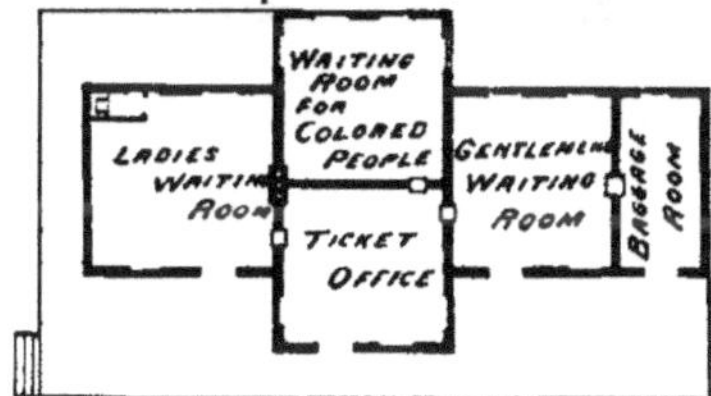

FIG. 532.—GROUND-PLAN.

Passenger Depot at Columbia, Ky., Louisville & Nashville Railroad.—The passenger depot of the Louisville & Nashville Railroad at Columbia, Ky., shown in Figs. 533 to 535, is a single-story frame

FIG. 533.—FRONT ELEVATION.

FIG. 534.—END ELEVATION.

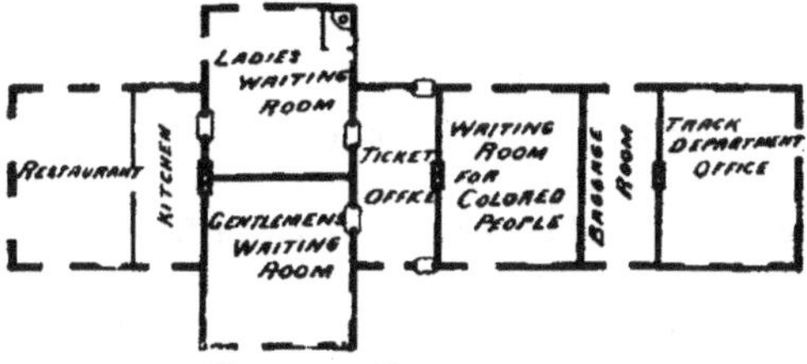

FIG. 535.—GROUND-PLAN.

structure, 20 ft. wide by about 90 ft. long. The interior is divided into a gentlemen's waiting-room; a ladies' waiting-room; a restaurant; a kitchen; a ticket and telegraph office; a waiting-room for colored people; a baggage-room; and an office for the track department.

Suburban Passenger Depot, New York Central & Hudson River Railroad.—In the issue of *Engineering News* of Aug. 25, 1888, a design for a passenger depot at a suburban station is illustrated, as designed by Mr. J. D. Fouquet, Engineer and Architect, New York Central & Hudson River Railroad, the ground-plan of which is shown in Fig. 536. The building is a stone and brick structure, one-story, with high roofs and ornamental towers. The ground-plan layout is especially commendable, as being first-class for the purpose. There is a gentlemen's waiting-room, 19 ft. × 22 ft., and a ladies' waiting-room, 19 ft. × 22 ft., which are entered independently of each other from a vestibule in the rear of the building. The ticket-office is 8 ft. 6 in. × 12 ft., with a round-tower projection in front of the building. There are special ticket-windows for each waiting-room, with sufficient space between them for the ticket case and shelf. A door leads from the gentlemen's waiting-room to the baggage-room, so that inquiries for baggage can be made and parcels checked from the waiting-room. The baggage-room is 8 ft. × 16 ft. Attached to the ladies' waiting-room is a ladies' toilet-room, 8 ft. × 8 ft., with the entrance door properly screened. A gentlemen's toilet-room, 8 ft. × 8 ft., is provided with an entrance from the rear of the building. As above stated, the ground-plan layout and the arrangement of doors and windows in this design can be considered as particularly well adapted for the purpose.

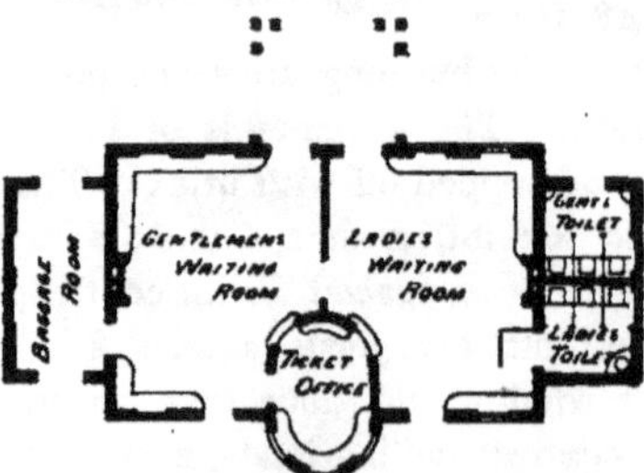

FIG. 536.—GROUND-PLAN.

Passenger Depot at Tamaqua, Pa., Central Railroad of New Jersey.—The passenger depot of the Central Railroad of New Jersey at Tamaqua, Pa., on the Lehigh & Susquehanna Division of the road is a very neat and good design for a local passenger depot at stations where trains stop to allow passengers to take meals. The building is a single-story brick structure, with brown-stone trimmings and tin roof, excepting the central vestibule portion, which is two-story. The building is built T-shaped, as shown in Fig. 537. At the centre of the building, facing the track, there is a central hall or

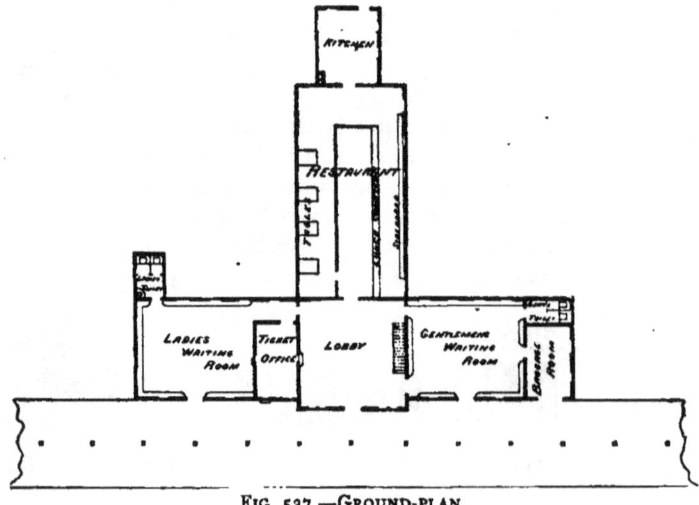

FIG. 537.—GROUND-PLAN.

lobby, 26 ft. × 26 ft. On one side of this hall is a gentlemen's waiting-room, 30 ft. × 24 ft., with a toilet-room attached, and a baggage-room. Ont he other side of the vestibule there is a ticket-office, and a passage-way leading to a ladies' waiting-room, 24 ft. × 30 ft., with a ladies' toilet room attached. At the rear of the vestibule there are large doors leading to the dining-room, 50 ft. × 26 ft., and at the end of the dining-room there is a kitchen, 18 ft. × 26 ft.

Junction Passenger Depots, Indianapolis, Decatur & Springfield Railway.—The passenger depot at the junction of the Indianapolis, Decatur & Springfield Railway and the E., T. H. & C. R. R., shown in Fig. 538, kindly furnished by Mr. Edwin A. Hill, Chief Engineer, is a frame building, built

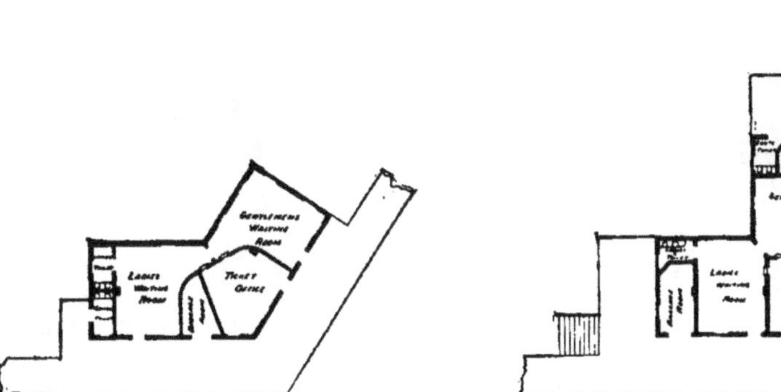

FIG. 538.—GROUND-PLAN AT SKEW CROSSING. FIG. 539.—GROUND-PLAN AT SQUARE CROSSING.

in the obtuse angle formed by the two railways. The building is 20 ft. wide, with 30 ft. front on one road and 35 ft. front on the other road. The interior has one ticket and telegraph office; one baggage-room; a gentlemen's waiting-room; a ladies' waiting-room, with toilet-room attached; and a gentlemen's toilet-room, with entrance from the outside of the building. The platform in front of the building is 12 ft. wide, extended 8 ft. in width for a distance of 200 ft. along each track. The building is finished neatly, and cost, exclusive of platforms, $1200. The platforms cost $616, making a total cost of $1716.

The standard plan for a junction-station passenger depot of the Indianapolis, Decatur & Springfield Railway, at a junction station where two railroads cross each other at right angles, is shown in Fig. 539, kindly furnished by Mr. Edwin A. Hill. The building is L-shaped, 20 ft. wide, with 40 ft. front on each railroad. In the angle, at the centre of the building, there is an office, 16 ft. × 17 ft., adjoining which, on one side, is a gentlemen's waiting-room, 16 ft. × 20 ft., and on the other side a ladies' waiting-room, 15 ft. × 20 ft., with toilet-room attached. At each end of the building there is a small baggage-room, so that each railroad has its separate baggage-room. There is a gentlemen's toilet-room at one end of the building, with a separate entrance from the exterior. The platform in front of the building is 12 ft. wide, extended 8 ft. in width for a distance of 200 ft. along each railroad.

Junction Depot at Humboldt, Tenn., Louisville & Nashville Railroad.—The depot building at the junction of the Louisville & Nashville Railroad and of the Mobile & Ohio Railroad at Humboldt, Tenn., shown in Fig. 540, is an L-shaped, single-story frame structure, with slate roof. The low platform is 30 ft. wide in front of the depot along each railroad. There is an agent's office at the angle of the building, 16 ft. 6 in. × 22 ft., which is brought out from the rest of the building and treated as a tower, giving quite a prominence to the front of the depot. The ladies' waiting-room, 22 ft. × 26 ft., and the general waiting-room, 22 ft. × 30 ft., adjoin the office. The waiting-rooms are connected by closed passage-ways with separate toilet-rooms in a small building back of the depot. At one end of the depot there is a baggage-room, 18 ft. × 28 ft., and at the other end an express-room, 20 ft. × 35 ft. The outside of the building is sheathed with upright and horizontal ornamental boarding, in panels, and is finished very neatly.

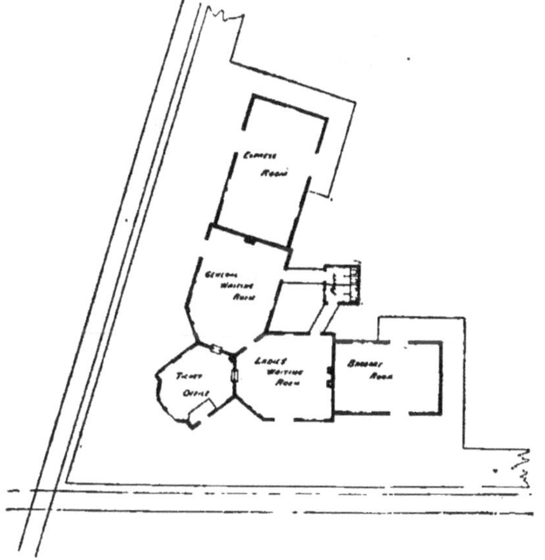

FIG. 540.—GROUND-PLAN.

FIG. 541.—FRONT ELEVATION.

FIG. 542.—END ELEVATION.

Passenger Depot at Picton, N. J., Lehigh Valley Railroad.—The passenger depot of the Lehigh Valley Railroad at Picton, N. J., shown in Figs. 541 to 543, designed by Mr. C. Rosenberg, Master Carpenter, L. V. R. R., is a two-story frame structure. The upper floor is used as a dwelling. The outside of the building is sheathed with horizontal, vertical, and diagonal, plain and ornamental siding, and the roof is covered with slate. Stained glass is used in the transoms on the lower floor and in the top sash of the upper floor, which, combined with an artistic selection of colors for painting the exterior, causes the building to present a very warm and bright appearance, without incurring heavy additional extra expenses to obtain an elaborate architectural effect. The ground-floor has a gentlemen's waiting-room, 14 ft. × 19 ft.; a ladies' waiting-room, 14 ft. × 19 ft.; a ticket and telegraph office, 9 ft. × 11 ft., including a 4-ft. bay-window projection; a baggage-room, 10 ft. 6 in. × 11 ft.; a gentlemen's toilet-room, 9 ft. × 7 ft. 6 in., leading from the gentlemen's waiting-room; a ladies' toilet-room, 10 ft. 6 in. × 7 ft. 6 in., leading from the ladies' waiting-room; and a stairway leading to the upper floor. The upper floor has a living-room; a kitchen; three bedrooms; a bath-room; and a toilet-room. There is a cellar under the building, with a cistern, coal-bin, heater, etc.

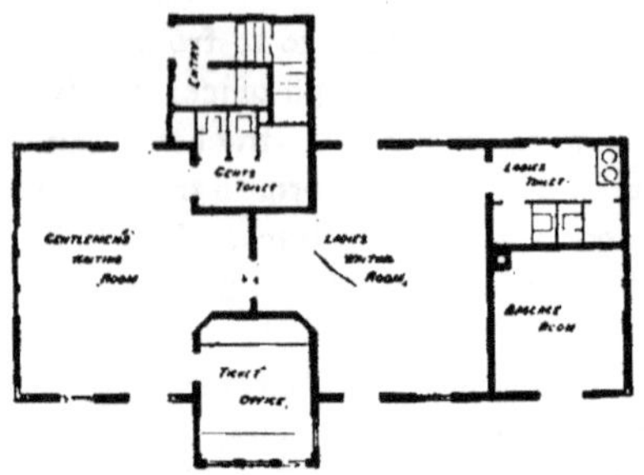
FIG. 543.—GROUND-PLAN.

Passenger Depot at Pottsville, Pa., Pennsylvania Railroad.—The passenger depot of the Pennsylvania Railroad at Pottsville, Pa., on the Pottsville & Schuylkill Valley Branch, designed under the direction of Mr. Wm. H. Brown, Chief Engineer, P. R. R., shown in Figs. 544 to 547, is a very well-designed structure, both as to architectural effect and the ground-plan layout. The building is built of brick, with slate roof, and ornamental, galvanized-iron ridge-crestings, finials, and tower. The building is 25 ft. × 100 ft. 6 in., part of which is two stories high. The ground-plan layout and the general style of the building, as mentioned above, is very good and well adapted for the purpose, and can be highly recommended as a standard worthy of adoption. There is a gentlemen's waiting-room, 21 ft. 8 in. × 34 ft. 6 in., and a ladies' waiting-room, 21 ft. 8 in. × 20 ft. 9 in., connected by a 7-ft. passage-way, closed by swinging-doors. On one side of the passage-way, facing the track, is a 12-ft. × 11-ft. 3-in. ticket and telegraph office, with ticket-windows opening into each waiting-room, and a ticket-shelf between the windows. On the other side of the passage-way there is a news-stand. In each waiting-room there is a large ornamental open fire-place. Connected with the ladies' waiting-room there is a ladies' toilet-room, 9 ft. × 16 ft.; and adjoining the ladies' toilet-room there is a gentlemen's toilet-room, with a separate entrance from the rear of the building. Beyond the toilet-rooms, and at the end of the building, is a baggage-room, 22 ft. 10 in. × 12 ft. The building is surrounded by covered platforms, and a two-post covered platform roof, 17 ft. 6 in. wide, is extended for some distance along the track each way from the building. There is a cellar underneath the building, in which the heaters are located. The upper floor is used for offices. The complete specification

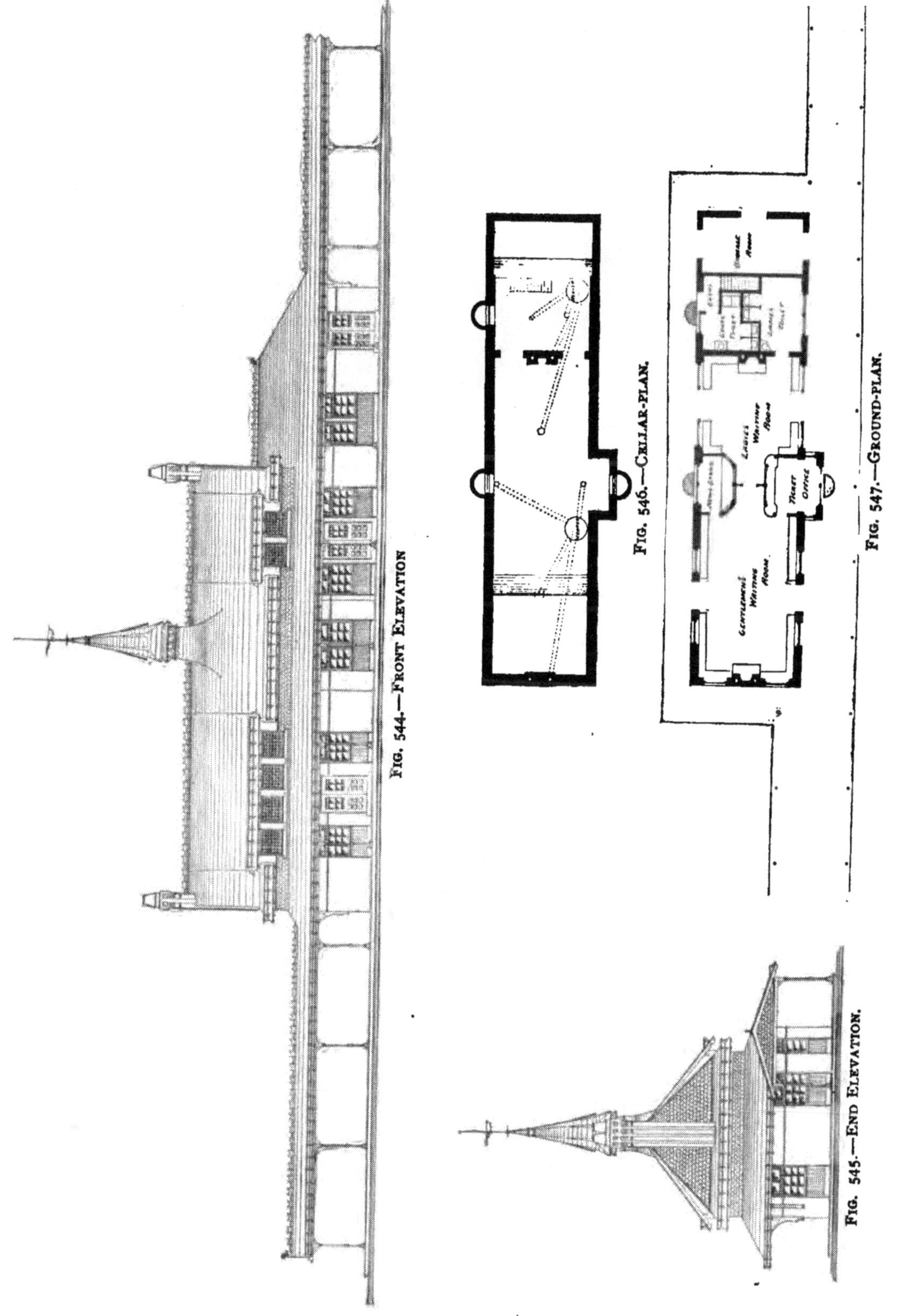

Fig. 544.—Front Elevaton

Fig. 545.—End Elevation.

Fig. 546.—Cellar-Plan.

Fig. 547.—Ground-Plan.

for this depot, kindly furnished to the author by Mr. Wm. H. Brown, Chief Engineer, Pennsylvania Railroad, is given in the Appendix at the back of this book.

Passenger Depot at Laury's, Pa., Lehigh Valley Railroad.—The passenger depot of the Lehigh Valley Railroad at Laury's, Pa., shown in Figs. 548 to 550, designed and built under the direction

FIG. 548.—FRONT ELEVATION.

of the author, is a single-story brick building, roofed with slate. The ground available for the depot building was limited to such an extent that an L-shaped ground-plan had to be adopted. The building is 34 ft. long and 25 ft. deep. It is divided into a gentlemen's waiting-room, 14 ft. × 11 ft. 6 in.; a ladies' waiting-room, 14 ft. × 11 ft. 6 in., with toilet-room attached; an agent's office, 9 ft. × 17 ft., with a square bay-window projection; a baggage-room, 8 ft. 6 in. × 14 ft.; and a gentlemen's toilet-room, with entrance from the rear of the building. The foundations are stone walls, 18

FIG. 549.—END ELEVATION.

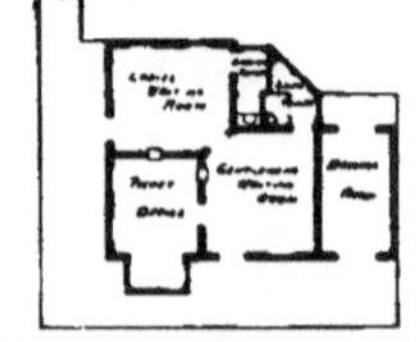

FIG. 550.—GROUND-PLAN.

in. thick. The brick walls are 9 in. thick. The framing of the roof consists of 2-in. × 6-in. rafters; 2-in. × 8-in. ceiling-joists; 1½-in. × 6-in. collar-beams; 1-in. rough sheathing.

Passenger Depot at Allen Lane, Pa., Philadelphia, Germantown & Chestnut Hill Railroad.—The passenger depot of the Pennsylvania Railroad at Allen Lane, Pa., on the Philadelphia, Germantown & Chestnut Hill Railroad, a branch of the Pennsylvania Railroad, designed under the direction of Mr. Wm. H. Brown, Chief Engineer, P. R. R., shown in Figs. 551 to 553, is a brick building with stone trimmings, timber panels, and a slate roof with terra-cotta crestings and finials, etc., located on top of the slope of a railroad cut, so that steps are provided to reach the level of the railroad, and a covered platform is built along the track, all as shown on plans. The building has a general waiting-room, 18 ft. × 25 ft.; a ticket-office, 9 ft. × 11 ft.; a ladies' toilet-room, with entrance from the general waiting-room; a gentlemen's toilet-room, with entrance from the rear of the building; and a baggage-room, 7 ft. × 10 ft. The covered steps leading down to the level of the railroad are 12 ft. wide.

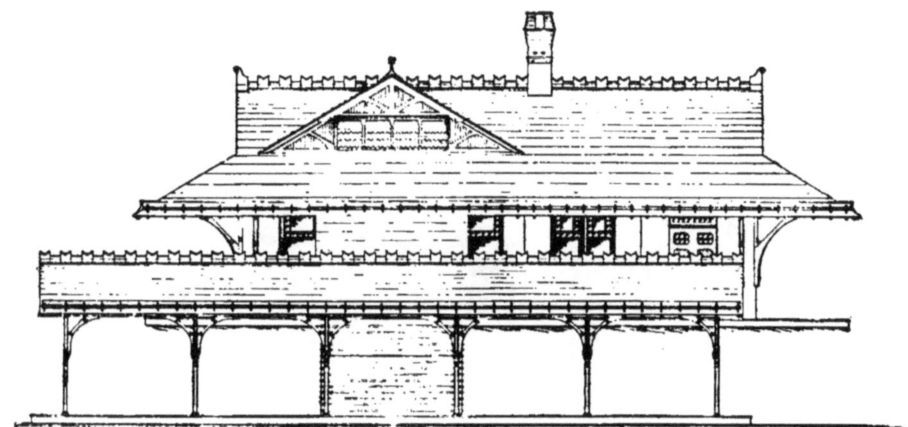

FIG. 551.—FRONT ELEVATION.

FIG. 552.—CROSS-SECTION AND END ELEVATION.

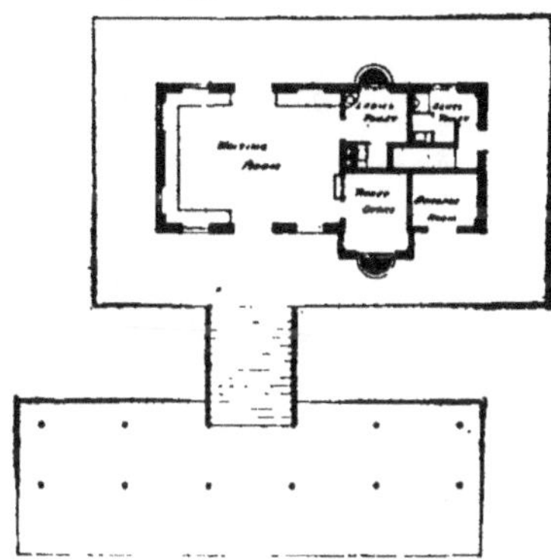

FIG. 553.—GROUND-PLAN.

Passenger Depot at South Park, Minn., Minnesota & Northwestern Railroad.—The passenger depot of the Minnesota & Northwestern Railroad at South Park, Minn., designed by Mr. C. A. Reed,

Supervising Architect, M. & N. W. R. R., shown in Figs. 554 to 557, represents a class of structures used by the Minnesota & Northwestern Railroad at suburban points. The building is of brick, 20 ft. × 38 ft., divided into a gentlemen's waiting-room; a ladies' waiting-room; and a ticket and telegraph office. There is a covered platform shed extension to the building, 20 ft. 6 in. long, at each end of the building.

FIG. 554.—FRONT ELEVATION.

FIG. 555.—END ELEVATION.

FIG. 556.—CROSS-SECTION.

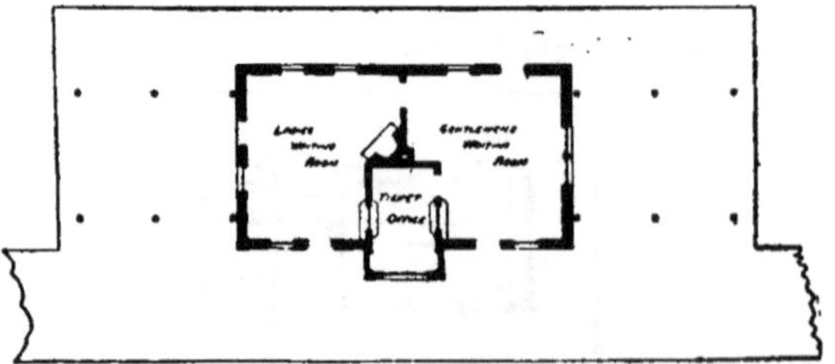

FIG. 557.—GROUND-PLAN.

Passenger Depot at Somerville, N. J., Central Railroad of New Jersey.—The passenger depot of the Central Railroad of New Jersey at Somerville, N. J., shown in Figs. 558 to 560, designed by Mr. Frank V. Bodine, Architect, Asbury Park, N. J., and built under the direction of Mr. Wm. H. Peddle, Superintendent, C. R. R. of N. J., is a stone building, with slate roof, the main portion of the building being only one story high. The ground-plan shows a general waiting-room, 21 ft. × 32 ft.; a ladies' waiting-room, 15 ft. × 16 ft., with toilet-room attached; a smoking-room, 12 ft. × 15 ft., with gentlemen's toilet-room attached; a baggage-room, 12 ft. × 17 ft.; and a ticket and telegraph office. The rooms on the upper floor are utilized for offices. The stone used in the building is light-

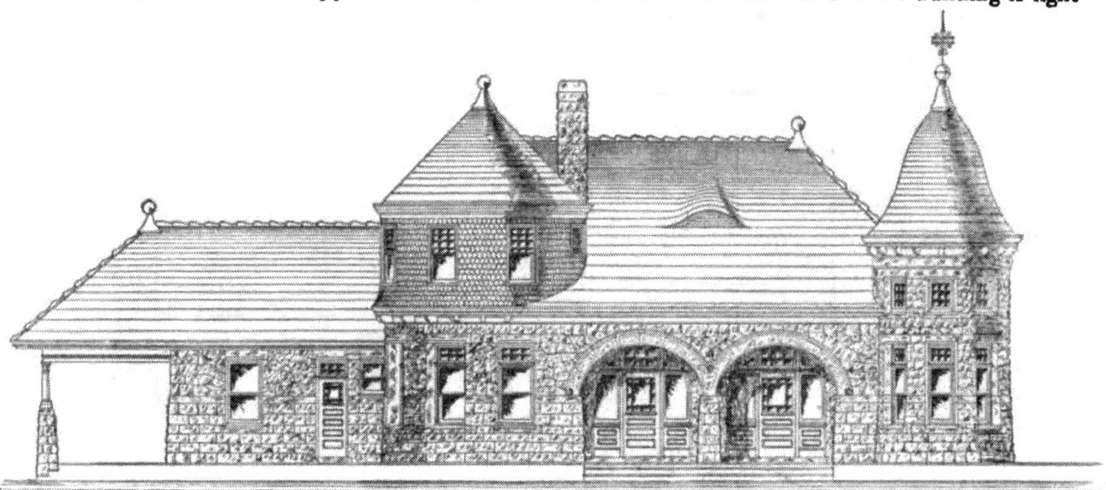

FIG. 558.—FRONT ELEVATION.

FIG. 559.—END ELEVATION.

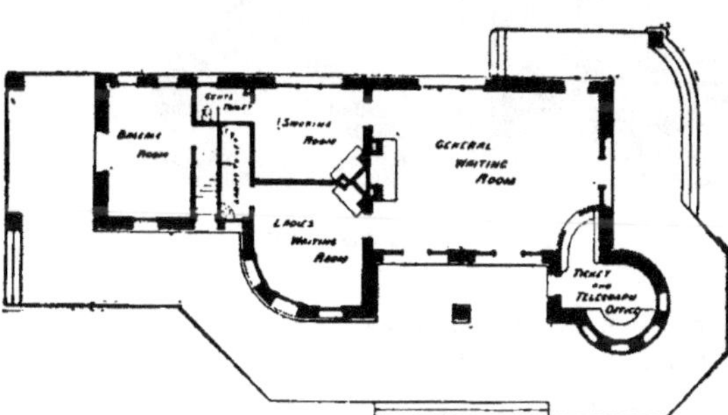

FIG. 560.—GROUND-PLAN.

colored Jersey sandstone. The interior is finished in wood. The building is lighted by electricity and heated by steam. There is a *porte cochère* at one corner of the building.

Passenger Depot at Wilkesbarre, Pa., Lehigh Valley Railroad.—The passenger depot of the Lehigh Valley Railroad at Wilkesbarre, Pa., shown in Figs. 561 to 563, is a handsome and well-designed two-story stone and brick building, with slate roof, 226 ft. long and from 34 to 60 ft. wide. At the

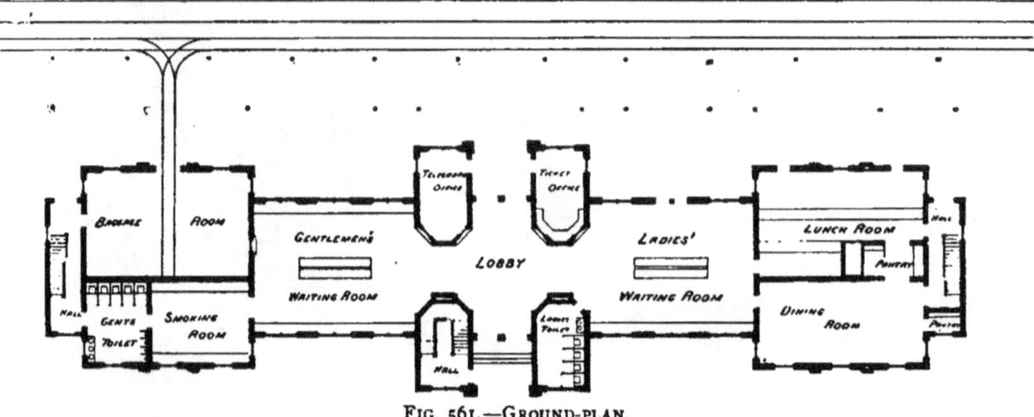

FIG. 561.—GROUND-PLAN.

FIG. 562.—PERSPECTIVE.

centre of the building there is a wide passage-way from the street to the train side of the depot, closed by vestibule doors. On one side of this passage-way is a gentlemen's waiting-room, 32 ft. × 40 ft., connecting with a smoking-room, and a gentlemen's toilet-room at the rear end of the smoking-room. There is also a baggage-room at this end of the building. On the other side of the passage mentioned is the ladies' waiting-room, 32 ft. × 40 ft. Beyond the ladies' waiting-room there is a lunch-room, a dining-room, and a pantry, with stairs leading to the kitchen on the upper floor. The four corners, formed by the passage-way through the centre of the building and the cross passage-way connecting the gentlemen's waiting-room with the ladies' waiting room, are utilized respectively for a ticket-office, with a ticket-window leading to the ladies' waiting-room, and a ticket-window

FIG. 563.—INTERIOR VIEW OF WAITING-ROOM.

opening on the general passage-way; a telegraph office; a ladies' toilet-room, opening from the ladies' waiting-room; and the stairs leading to the upper floor, where the division offices are located. The interior of the building is finished very artistically and handsomely. The depot was built under the general supervision of Mr. Alexander Mitchell, Division Superintendent, L. V. R. R.

Passenger Depot at Kalamazoo, Mich., Michigan Central Railroad.—The passenger depot of the Michigan Central Railroad at Kalamazoo, Mich., shown in Figs. 564 and 565, designed by Mr. Cyrus L. W. Eidlitz, Architect, New York City, illustrated and described in the issue of the *Railroad Gazette* of Aug. 5, 1887, and in the issue of the *Railway Review* of November 12, 1887, is a brick building with brown-stone trimmings, red-tile roof, and terra-cotta ridge-rolls and cresting. The general layout and design are excellent, and can be highly recommended. There is a central or main building, 73 ft. × 40 ft., with a gentlemen's waiting-room and a ladies' waiting-room, divided by a passage-way, on one side of which there is a ticket-office, and on the other side of which there is a ladies' toilet-room, with entrance from the ladies' waiting-room, and a stairway leading to a small conductor's room overhead. There are two small detached buildings about 60 ft. distant from the main building, connected with the latter by covered platforms. One of these buildings has a gentlemen's toilet-room, 13 ft. 8 in. × 19 ft., and a telegraph-office and battery-room, 19 ft. × 22 ft. 10 in. The other building has a baggage-room, 22 ft. 10 in. × 19 ft., and a telegraph-office, 13 ft. 8 in. × 19 ft. There is a *porte cochère* on the rear of the building. The finish of the interior of the waiting-

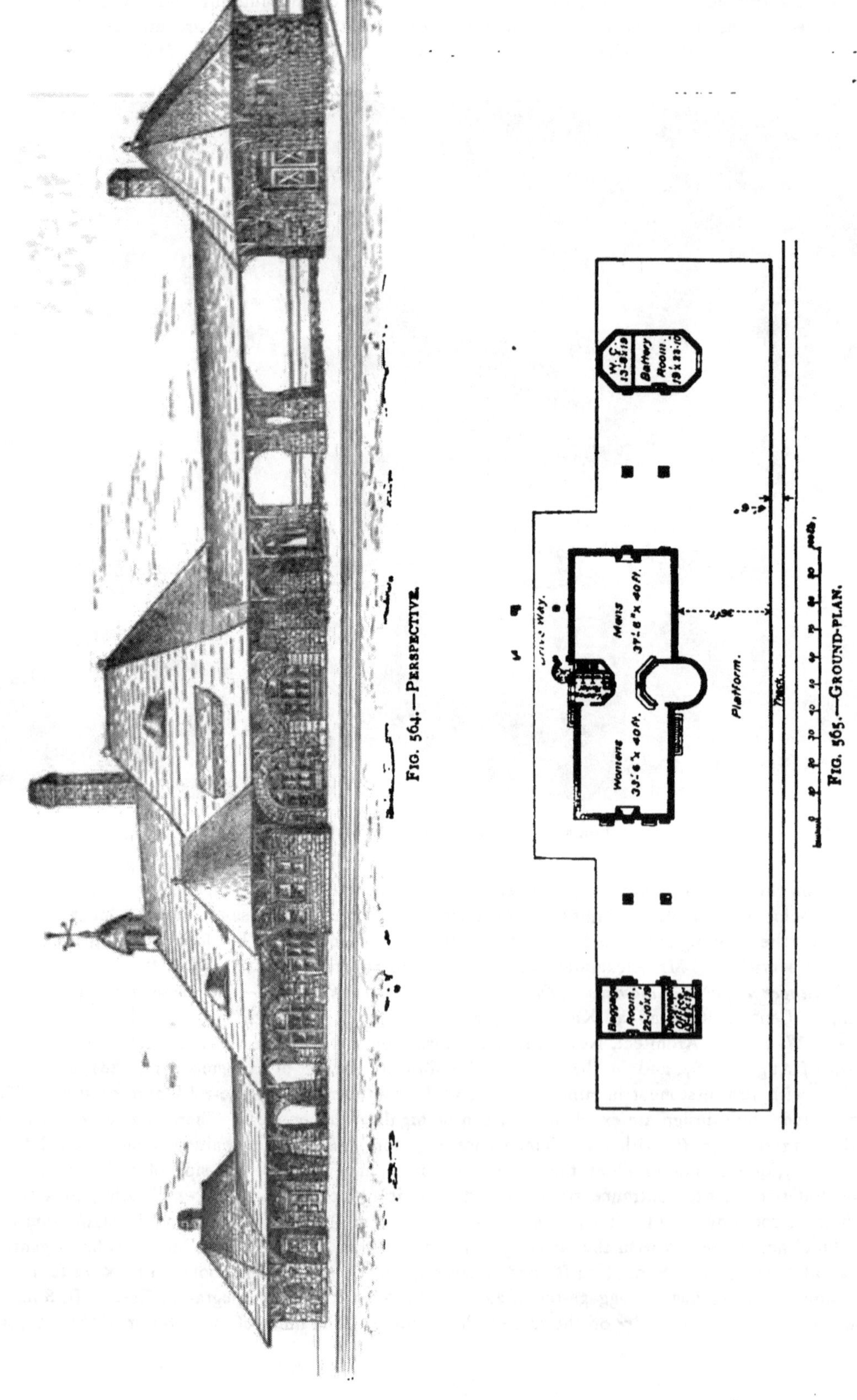

FIG. 564.—PERSPECTIVE.

FIG. 565.—GROUND-PLAN.

room is in quartered red-oak, with deep panelled and timbered ceiling. The walls are elaborately wainscoted in panels, 4 ft. 6 in. high, and plastered and fresco-painted to the ceiling. The two large fire-places in the waiting-rooms are of pressed and moulded brick and stone, with tile hearth and jambs. All upper sash is glazed with stained glass, and all clear glass is French plate.

Passenger Depot at Ann Arbor, Mich., Michigan Central Railroad.—The passenger depot of the Michigan Central Railroad at Ann Arbor, Mich., described and illustrated in the issue of the *Railroad*

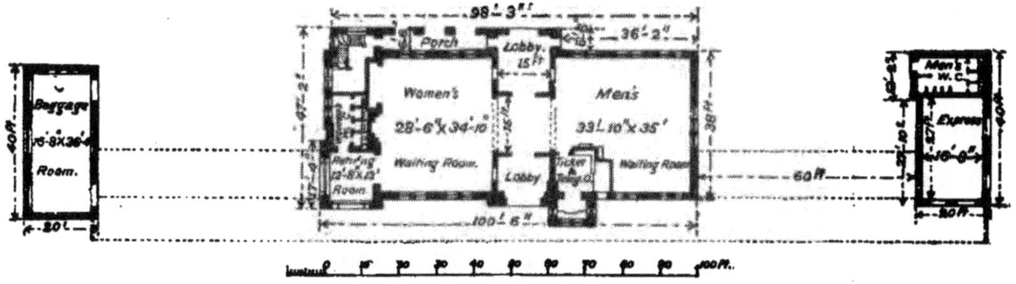

FIG. 566.—GROUND-PLAN.

Gazette of April 1, 1887, in the issue of the *Engineering News* of September 10, 1887, and in the issue of the *Railway Review* of November 12, 1887, designed by Mr. F. H. Speir, architect, Detroit, Mich., shown in Fig. 566, is a handsome stone building, with slate and red-tile roofs. The main building is two-story, 38 ft. × 100 ft., and has on the ground-floor a gentlemen's waiting-room, 23 ft. 10 in. × 35 ft.; a ladies' waiting-room, 28 ft. 6 in. × 34 ft. 10 in., with toilet-room attached; a ticket and telegraph office; a lobby or passage-way through the building; and a stairway leading to the upper floor. While the lobby in this design may add to the architectural effect of the building, and serves as a passage-way to and from trains, the introduction of this feature in the ground-plan is objectionable. It cuts off the possibility of having the ticket-office adjoin the ladies' waiting-room, so that ladies have to enter the gentlemen's waiting-room or stop in the lobby or passage-way to buy tickets, and if this lobby is used as a passage-way to and from trains it will prove very disagreeable for passengers in the waiting-rooms, especially in winter. In addition to the main building there are two separate buildings, each 20 ft. × 40 ft., located 60 ft. distant from each end of the main building, and connected with it by covered platform roofs. One of these buildings is used for a baggage-room and the other is used for an express-office and a gentlemen's toilet-room. This structure is built entirely of dressed boulders of various colors. The main roof is of slate, the roof of the large tower is red tile, and that of the small tower is of copper. The interior finish is of red oak throughout, and the ticket-office is quartered red-oak. The floors are of maple, and the vestibule is laid with French tiles; the clear-story windows are of stained glass. The building is heated by hot-water heaters.

Passenger Depot at Bay City, Mich., Michigan Central Railroad.—The passenger depot of the Michigan Central Railroad at Bay City, Mich., is a handsome stone building, two to three stories high; with large square clock-tower, designed by Mr. F. H. Speir, Architect, Detroit, Mich., illustrations of which were published in the issue of the *Railroad Gazette* of Dec. 26, 1890. The depot is divided into two buildings, the main building being 166 ft. and the small building 62 ft. long. The two buildings are connected by a covered passage, 58 ft. long. The ground-floor of the main building has a gentlemen's waiting-room; a ladies' waiting-room, with toilet-room attached; a ticket-office; lobbies; a *porte cochère;* a dining-room; a kitchen; a serving-room; a refrigerator-room; and pantries. The smaller building has a boiler-room; a baggage-room; an express-room; and a gentlemen's toilet-room. The structure is described as follows, in the publication mentioned.

The material of the main walls is of one kind throughout, a reddish-brown stone, rock-faced, and laid in broken courses, as shown. The roof is covered throughout with red tile.

The inside finish is mostly birch, except in the men's waiting-room, where it is red oak. The birch finish costs about the same as red oak, and gives a more pleasing effect. The ladies' room is provided with the usual retiring-rooms and a fireplace that burns wood. The buildings are heated throughout by a hot-water heater. The small building attached to the large one by a shed roof is used for the gentlemen's toilet-room, baggage-room, express-room, and boiler-room. At the extreme south end of the main building is a dining-room, attached to which are the necessary kitchens, carving-room, cold-storage-room, store-rooms, etc., with four sleeping apartments in the second story for the help.

The second story of the main building, together with a few rooms in the third story, is used for offices for the division superintendent and his assistants, the assistant general freight agent and his clerical force, the resident engineer, roadmaster, conductors and car-accountant.

Passenger Depot at Battle Creek, Mich., Michigan Central Railroad.—The passenger depot of the Michigan Central Railroad at Battle Creek, Mich., shown in Figs. 567 and 568, designed by

FIG. 567.—PERSPECTIVE.

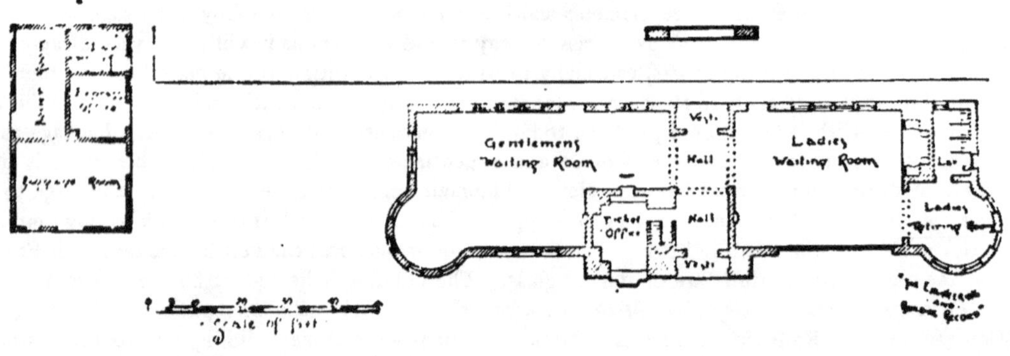

FIG. 568.—GROUND-PLAN. (By permission of *The Engineering Record.*)

Messrs. Rogers & McFarlane, Architects, Detroit, Mich., described and illustrated in the issue of the *Engineering News* of Sept. 10, 1887; in the issue of the *Railway Review* of Nov. 12, 1887; *The Engineering Magazine*, December, 1891; and in *The Engineering Record*, Vol. 20, is a brick building, with red-stone trimmings and red-tiled roof. The main building is about 36 ft. × 125 ft., and is divided into a gentlemen's waiting-room; a ticket-office; a ladies' waiting-room, with toilet-room attached; and a vestibule or hall, running through the centre of the building. This hall or passage-way has the same serious objections mentioned in connection with the Ann Arbor depot of the same road. There is a *porte cochère* at the rear of the main building. Located some distance from one end of the main building, and connected with it by a covered passage-way, there is a separate building, containing a baggage-room; an express-office; a gentlemen's toilet-room; and a boiler-room. The main building has a square clock-tower, 72 ft. high. The structure is built of Lake Superior red stone,

Detroit red bricks, and with an Akron red-tile roof. The interior finish is quartered white-oak, antique finished, with panelled wainscoting, and a large old-fashioned fire-place at one end of the ladies' waiting-room. The building is heated by hot-water heaters. The ceiling in the waiting-rooms is 16 ft. 4 in. high.

The complete specification for this depot is given in the Appendix at the back of this book.

FIG. 569.—PERSPECTIVE.

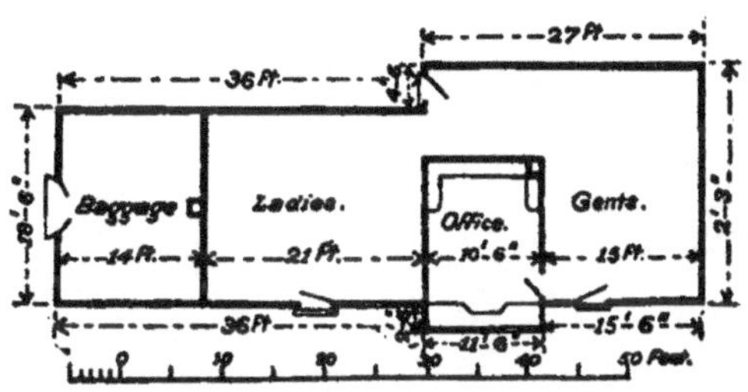

FIG. 570.—GROUND-PLAN.

Passenger Depot at Dexter, Mich., Michigan Central Railroad.—The passenger depot of the Michigan Central Railroad at Dexter, Mich., shown in Figs. 569 and 570, described and illustrated in the issue of the *Railroad Gazette* of April 1, 1887, and in the issue of the *Engineering News* of Sept. 10, 1887, designed by Mr. F. H. Speir, Architect, Detroit, Mich., is a single-story frame structure, 63 ft. × 20 ft., divided into a gentlemen's waiting-room; a ladies' waiting-room; a telegraph and ticket office; and a baggage-room.

Passenger Depot at Rye, N. Y., New York, New Haven & Hartford Railroad.—The passenger depot of the New York, New Haven & Hartford Railroad, at Rye, N. Y., designed by Mr. W. S. Babcock, Architect, New Haven, Conn., illustrated and described in the issue of *The Engineering Record* of Nov. 23, 1889, shown in Figs. 571 to 573, published by permission of *The Engineering Record*, is a single-story stone structure, with slate roof. The interior is divided into a general waiting-room, 30 ft. × 40 ft.; a ticket and telegraph office, 10 ft. × 13 ft., located in a square projection at one corner of the general waiting-room; a baggage and express room, 20 ft. × 30 ft.; and toilet-rooms for ladies and gentlemen. The building is surrounded on three sides by a covered platform shed, shown in Figs. 408 to 412, which is extended each way from the building, so as to make a total length of covered platform of 250 ft., the entire platform length being 500 ft. A similar platform and platform roof is built on the opposite side of the tracks from the depot building.

Junction-station Passenger Depot at Palmer, Mass., Boston & Albany Railroad and New London & Norwich Railroad.—The passenger depot at Palmer, Mass., a junction station of the Boston & Albany Railroad and of the New London & Norwich Railroad, illustrated in the issue of the *Ameri-*

can Architect and Building News of Feb. 26, 1887, designed by the late Mr. H. H. Richardson, Architect, consists of a stone building, located in the acute angle formed by the two railroads, the shape of the building being trapezoidal. The building has a general waiting-room; a dining-room with kitchen

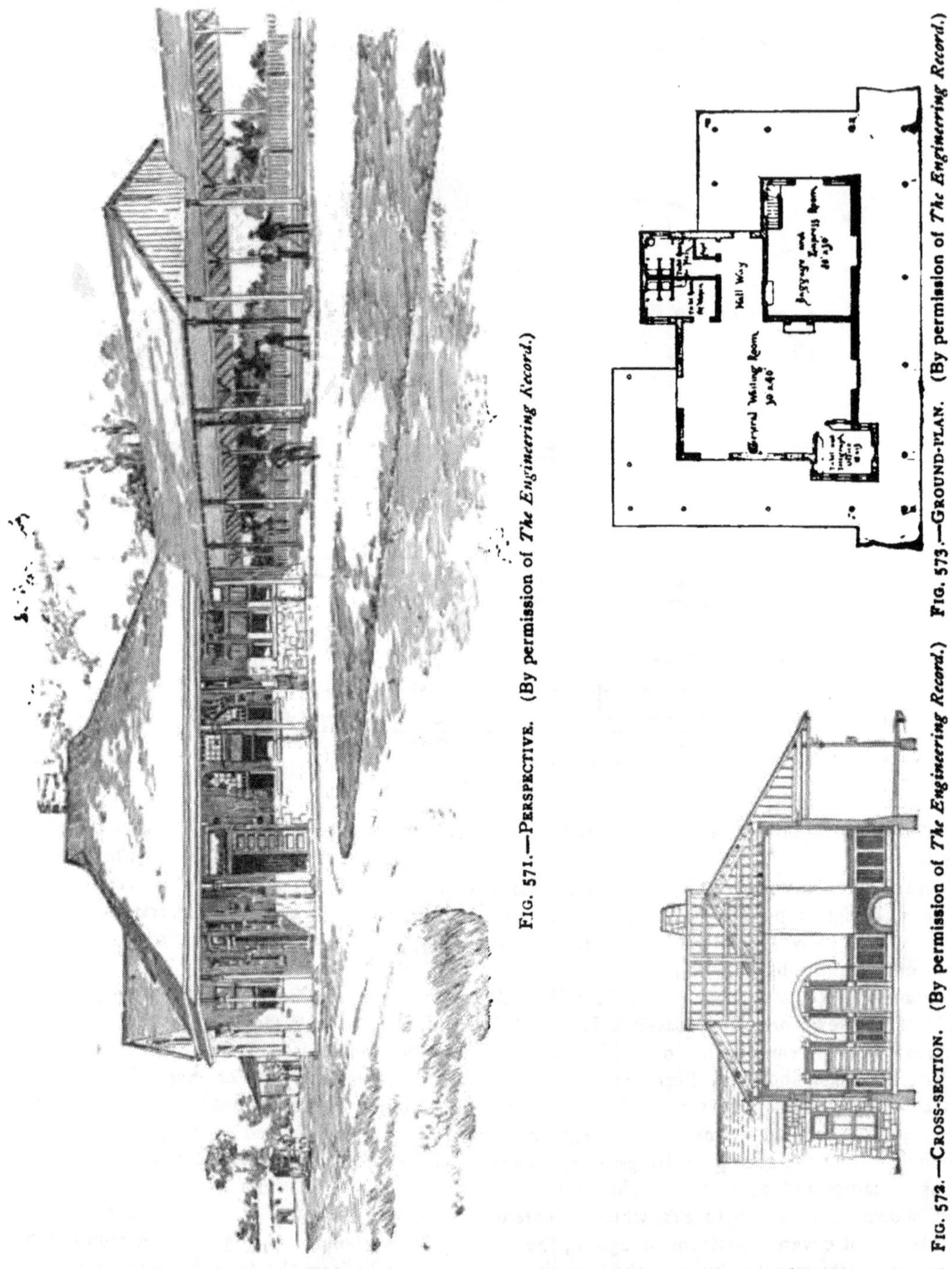

FIG. 571.—PERSPECTIVE. (By permission of *The Engineering Record.*)

FIG. 572.—CROSS-SECTION. (By permission of *The Engineering Record.*)

FIG. 573.—GROUND-PLAN. (By permission of *The Engineering Record.*)

and pantry; a ladies' toilet-room; a telegraph-office; one ticket-office for both railroads; a smoking-room, with gentlemen's toilet-room attached; an agent's room for the Boston & Albany Railroad; an agent's room for the New London & Norwich Railroad; and a baggage-room for the New London & Norwich Railroad. The baggage-room for the Boston & Albany Railroad is in a separate building.

Passenger Depot at Newcastle, Pa., Pittsburg & Lake Erie Railroad and Buffalo, New York & Philadelphia Railway.—The passenger depot at Newcastle, Pa., used jointly by the Pittsburg & Lake Erie Railroad and the Buffalo, New York & Philadelphia Railway, is illustrated and described in the issue of the *Railway Review* of Dec. 1, 1883. The description in the publication mentioned is as follows:

The building has a front of 60 ft. on Pittsburg Street, running back 26 ft. with a 12-ft. porch extending on each side and continuing around to the rear, connecting with a two story baggage-room, 12 ft. × 26 ft. The front and sides are laid with Rochester pressed brick, in black mortar, in a neat and artistic manner. The window-trimmings, string-courses, corner quoins, tablet-block, and such cut-stone work as called for by drawings, are all taken from Massillon white sandstone, and all work rubbed to a smooth surface. The rear of building, including the baggage-room, is laid with extra-select common brick, in same style of workmanship as the pressed-brick work. The roof of the entire structure is slate, and that of the lower part is cut to pattern with variegated pattern slate intermixed. The cornice is of wood, with brick panel frieze-work and brick dental foot-mouldings. The roof of the main building, including the baggage-room and bay-window roofs, is surmounted with a handsome iron cresting. The porch ceilings are panelled and moulded. The columns have rich carved capitals. The roof is covered with standing seam IX tin. The entire window and door frames throughout the building are made of cherry. All sash throughout are of walnut, and are hung with sash chain over polished brass axle-pulleys. On entering the building from Pittsburg Street there is a corridor of 240 square ft., the floor of which is laid with ornamental tile of a neat and artistic pattern. Passing to either side of same, we find the waiting-rooms, one gentlemen's and one ladies', all finished up in a rich manner. The wainscoting for these rooms and rooms of the entire first story, together with stair halls, is taken from Georgia yellow pine of select growth, and surmounted with walnut cap-mouldings and walnut base-work. The floors are also laid with same quality yellow pine. The inside finish of these rooms and throughout first story, including doors, shutters, and such like, is all walnut work, finished in cabinet style of workmanship. The ceilings have bold stucco cornice-work and rich centre-pieces, all stucco.

Each waiting-room is provided with toilet-rooms, fitted up with all the modern conveniences, together with stationary wash-stands, etc. The seating of these waiting-rooms is finished in walnut and ash work, extending along the walls and mitred together at each angle. The work was made to special design. The ticket-offices are in front, facing the corridor, and are partitioned off from each other with a strong and ornamental crimped-wire partition with artistic rosettes. The hardware used in first story of the building is genuine bronze. The stairs leading from the corridor lands one in the hallway in second story, from which access is easily gained to the different office-rooms occupied by each road. These offices are all finished up in a super-workmanlike manner, having inside shutters and such conveniences as are demanded in offices planned for railroad work. Stationary wash-stands are supplied. The superintendent of the River Division of the Buffalo, New York & Philadelphia Railroad Company occupies the entire suite of rooms in second story of one half of the building. The other side is exclusively taken up by the Pittsburg & Lake Erie Railroad Company for varying office-work.

The mansard or third story is reached by stairways from second floor, and the rooms here are devoted to the engineering department. The room in the tower is used as a general store-room for stationery, etc. The cellar under the entire building is 8 ft. high; the first story is 13 ft. 6 in.; second story, 12 ft. 6 in.; and mansard, or third story, 12 ft. high. All the exposed face of the cellar walls above the grade-line is finished with rock-face range-work, in regular courses, taken from Baden stone. The stone steps leading to the front entrance and the porches, together with sill and belt-course, are of the same material. The plans for the building were prepared by Mr. Joseph Angler, Architect, Alleghany City, Pa.

Passenger Depot at Fort Payne, Ala., Alabama Great Southern Railroad.—The passenger depot of the Alabama Great Southern Railroad at Fort Payne, Ala., designed by Mr. G. B. Nicholson, Chief Engineer, A. G. S. R. R., illustrated in the issue of *Engineering News* of September 12, 1891, from which publication Figs. 574 to 576 are taken by permission, is a handsome and substantially built brick and stone structure with slate roof. The building is in the main single-story, and is 89 ft. × 23 ft. in ground-plan. It is divided into a ladies' waiting-room, 21 ft. × 24 ft. 6 in., with toilet-room attached; a ticket-office, 10 ft. 6 in. × 15 ft., including a 3-ft. bay-window projection on the track side; a gentlemen's waiting-room, 21 ft. × 24 ft. 6 in., with toilet-room attached; a store-room, 5 ft. × 5 ft., back of the office; a stairway leading to the upper floor; and a baggage and express room, 32 ft. × 21 ft. There is a handsomely built veranda, 7 ft. wide, on the rear of the building facing the street, with a *porte cochère*. At the corner of the building next to the track there is a round

FIG. 574.—FRONT ELEVATION.

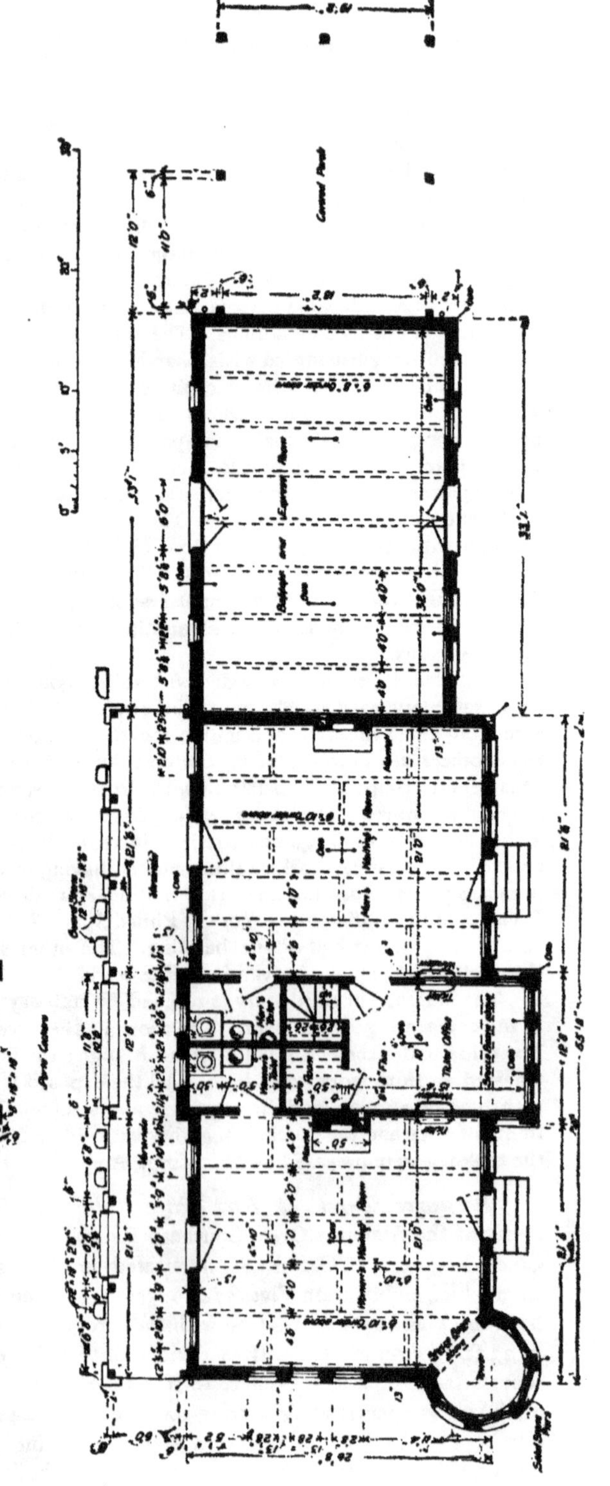

FIG. 575.—GROUND-PLAN.

tower, which forms in the interior a handsome alcove connected with the ladies' waiting-room. There is a covered porch extension of the building at the end of the building next to the baggage-room.

A full copy of the specifications for this depot, kindly furnished by Mr. G. B. Nicholson, will be found in the Appendix at the back of this book.

FIG. 576.—END ELEVATION.

Passenger Depot at Bowenville Station, Fall River, Mass., Old Colony Railroad.—The passenger depot of the Old Colony Railroad at the Bowenville Station, Fall River, Mass., shown in Figs. 577 to 579, is a large and artistically designed depot, plans for which were prepared by Mr. Bradford L. Gilbert, Architect, New York, N. Y., and published in the issue of the *Railroad Gazette* of Feb. 27, 1891. A perspective view of this depot is also published in *The Engineering Magazine* for Dec. 1891. The ground-plan has a *porte cochère* leading to a rotunda, 19 ft. × 22 ft., with a ticket-office, 8 ft. × 13 ft., and a telegraph-office, 9 ft. × 22 ft., and an agent's room, 14 ft. × 22 ft., leading from it. On one side of this rotunda is a gentlemen's waiting-room, 37 ft. × 40 ft., with a smoking-room, 16 ft. × 22 ft., and a gentlemen's toilet-room, 15 ft. × 16 ft., leading from the smoking-room. Beyond these rooms there is a lamp-room, 6 ft. × 18 ft., and two rooms for trainmen, each 18 ft. × 21 ft. On the other side of the rotunda, mentioned above, there is a ladies' waiting-room, 37 ft. × 40 ft., with a ladies' dressing-room, 10 ft. × 21 ft., leading from it, and a ladies' toilet-room, 10 ft. × 16 ft. Beyond these rooms there is a baggage-room, 27 ft. × 37 ft.; and a mail-room, 7 ft. × 9 ft.

The depot is described as follows in the issue of the *Railroad Gazette* mentioned above.

The station is located in the centre of a large square, under the main hill, and in order to break the monotony of the length and the low effect, the sky-line has been broken by carrying up the ticket loggia as a square turret or tower on the street side, the light from the windows overhead being utilized for the ticket loggia. On either side of this ticket loggia is shown on a blank wall-space a map of the Old Colony Railroad and connections.

Waiting-rooms are provided for men and women, with arched ceilings about 20 ft. in height at the centre. The woodwork of these rooms, including the flooring, and panelled wainscoting 9 ft. high, and columns in the openings, is entirely of oak. No plaster is used anywhere in the building. Two special features have been provided in the general plan—the smoking-room, and in the ladies' waiting-room several alcoves, with open fire-places, for the accommodation of private parties. There is also an open fire-place in the men's waiting-room. The general effect of the exterior is one of massiveness and solidity, and is produced entirely by constructional outlines, no fancy detail or ornamental work being provided anywhere.

The main superstructure is of rock-faced, dark pink, Milford (Mass.) granite, with trimmings, string-

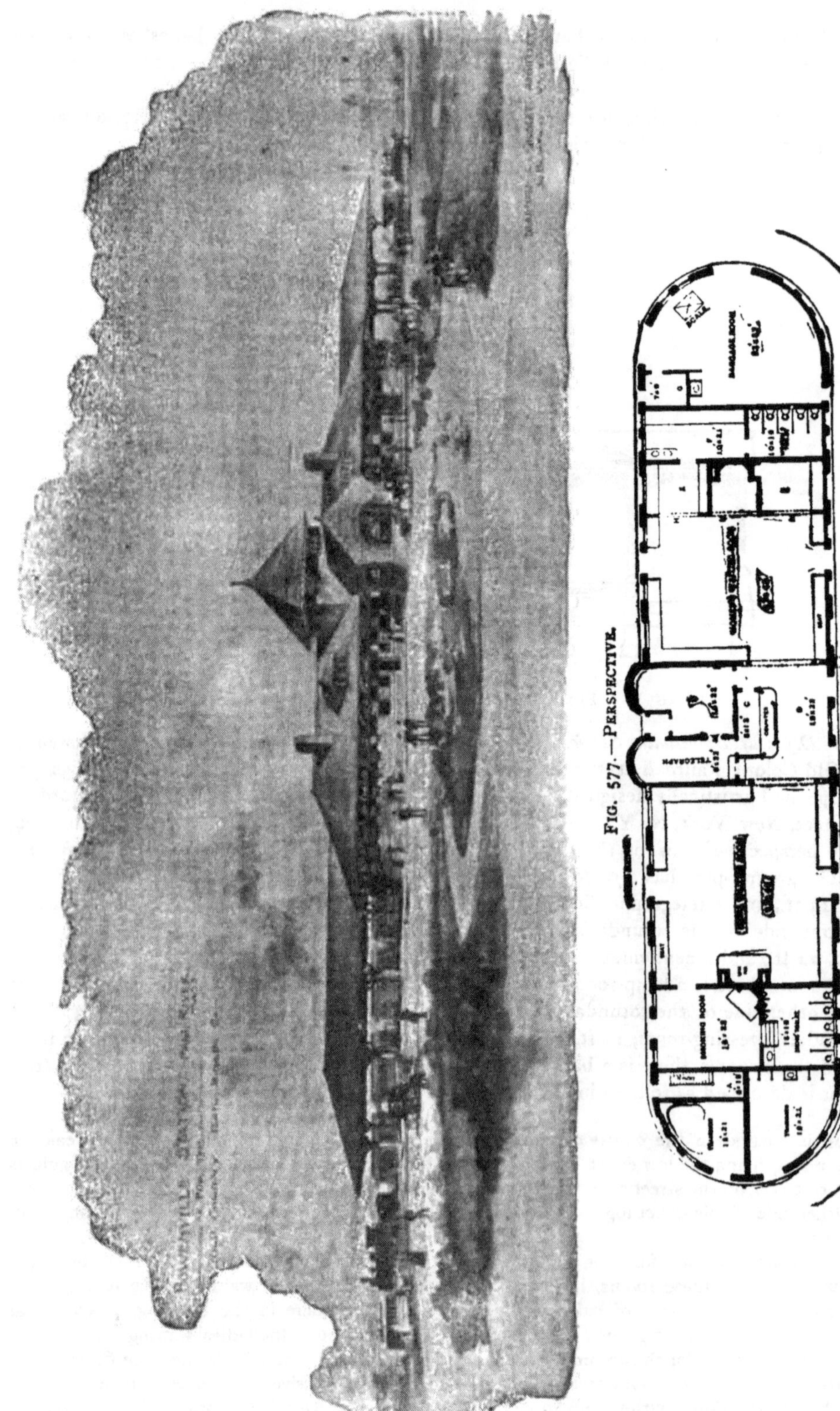

FIG. 577.—PERSPECTIVE.

FIG. 578.—GROUND-PLAN.

A, Lamp-room; *B*, Agent's Room; *C*, Ticket-office; *D*, Rotunda; *E E*, Alcove; *F*, Women's Retiring-room; *G*, Mail-room; *H H H*, Arches; *J*, Drinking-fountain for Horses.

courses and voussoirs of Longmeadow red sandstone. The platforms, together with the floor of the smoking-room, baggage-room, trainmen's and hackmen's room, will be of concrete pavement, and the interior walls of all these rooms will be finished in pressed brick (with wooden ceilings), while both toilet-rooms will be finished in marble on the floor and 6 ft. in height around the walls.

The roof of the building will be of slate, with a tile-cresting and finials as shown. The entire exterior woodwork will be of yellow pine, finished in natural color. The platforms are protected by awnings, and space is provided at the south end of the building for a hack-stand, while at the north end a covered space is provided for baggage and express wagons.

The building was estimated to cost less than $40,000.

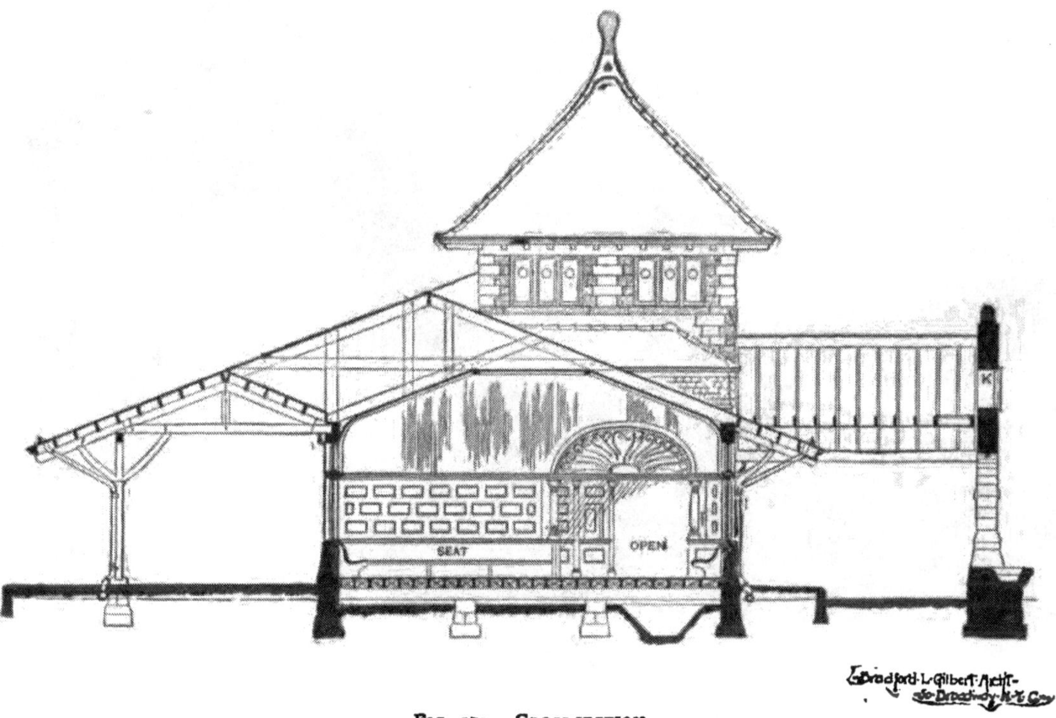

FIG. 579.—CROSS-SECTION.

Passenger Depot at St. Paul Park Station, Chicago, Burlington & Northern Railroad.—The passenger depot of the Chicago, Burlington & Northern Railroad at St. Paul Park Station, illustrated in the issue of the *Railway Review* of Nov. 12, 1887, is a neatly designed one-story brick building, with a two-story tower facing the track, and platform-shed extensions at each end of the building.

Passenger Depot at Mott Haven Station, 138th Street, New York City, New York Central & Hudson River Railroad.—The passenger depot of the New York Central & Hudson River Railroad at Mott Haven Station, 138th Street, New York City, designed by Messrs. Robertson and Manning, Architects, illustrated in the issues of the *Railway Review* of July 16, 1887, and of March 1, 1890, copied from *Architecture and Building*, is a two-story brick structure, with red-tile roof. The design is very picturesque, and while the structure is large, it is broken up by gables, arches, a clock-tower, and artistically designed platform roofs, loggia, and carriage entrance, so that the general appearance is perfect. The exterior is of brick and terra-cotta. An ornamental foot-bridge for passengers is thrown over the track, so as to enabie passengers to reach the opposite side of the tracks from the depot without crossing the tracks. From 138th Street there are four separate entrances to the depot; namely, for passengers, through a loggia; for carriages, through a large and imposing archway; for the street-cars, a special entrance; and another one for baggage-wagons. Inside the main entrance of the building, there is a large vestibule, from which doors lead to the general waiting-room, to the ticket and telegraph offices, and to the baggage-room, so that passengers can check their baggage from the vestibule after purchasing tickets. The waiting-room is 88 ft. × 26 ft., two stories high, with open timbered roof. Next to the waiting-room there is a large restaurant. On the second floor there are the general offices; a restaurant; a kitchen; a ladies' waiting-room; and toilet-rooms.

Passenger Depot at Melrose, New York City, New York Central & Hudson River Railroad.—The passenger depot of the New York Central & Hudson River Railroad at Melrose Station, 162d Street, New York City, shown in Figs. 580 to 581, designed under the direction of Mr. Walter

FIG. 580.—PERSPECTIVE.

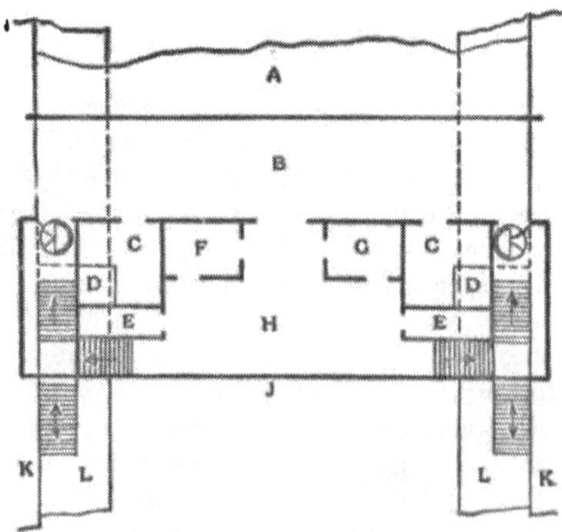

FIG. 581.—GROUND-PLAN.

A, Roadway of Bridge; *B*, Sidewalk of Bridge; *C C*, Baggage-raoms; *D D*, Baggage Elevators; *E E*, Closets; *F*, Ticket-office; *G*, Telegraph-office; *H*, Waiting-room; *L L*, Train-platforms. Windows not shown. Turnstiles at the exits prevent ingress except through the waiting-room.

Katté, Chief Engineer, described and illustrated in the issue of the *Railway Review* of Feb. 8, 1890; in the issues of *Engineering News* of Feb. 8 and 15, 1890; and also in the issue of the *Railroad*

Gazette of July 3, 1891, is a first-class example of a design of a passenger depot located on a bridge thrown over the main tracks of a railroad, where ground for a depot building outside of the space occupied by the tracks is not obtainable. In the issue of the *Railway Review* referred to above, a full set of plans are published for this building. The span of the bridge which supports the building, is 68 ft. 6 in. in the clear, which gives space for four tracks and a 10-ft. platform on each side. The building is about 26 ft. wide, with a 13-ft. sidewalk on one side. Passengers going to the depot cross the 13-ft. sidewalk along the building on the bridge to the centre of the span, where they enter through a commodious vestibule to the general waiting-room. On one side of the vestibule is a ticket-office, on the other side is a telegraph-office and an extra ticket-office. On one side of the general waiting-room there is a ladies' toilet-room; on the other side there is a gentlemen's toilet-room. There is a baggage-room, with lift, at each end of the building, one for outgoing, and the other for incoming baggage. At each end of the building a flight of stairs lead to the platform below, arranged so that passengers can get to or from the street without necessarily passing through the waiting-rooms. The express-trains use the two middle tracks, while way-trains use the outside tracks. There are fences on each side between the middle tracks and the outside tracks.

In the issue of the *Railroad Gazette* mentioned the following remarks are made in connection with the "Harlem Depression" work of the New York Central & Hudson River Railroad, necessitating overhead station buildings at Morrisania, Central Morrisania, Tremont, and Fordham, similar to the overhead station at Melrose.

These overhead depots are all built adjacent to one of the sidewalks of an overhead street bridge, and access to the station is from this sidewalk, the outer sidewalk girder being moved out to the rear of the station building so as to put the station practically on a very wide sidewalk. The station is 73 ft. wide across tracks, and 26 ft. longitudinally with tracks. The distance from the floor of station to the train platform is 17 ft., and there is 16 ft. clearance above top of rail. A central entrance from the sidewalk through a short vestibule, flanked on either side by small ticket and telegraph offices, admits the passenger into a waiting-room about 18 ft. × 32 ft., with closets off each end of the room. A door and stairway at each corner of the waiting-room leads to the train platform below. The stairways are 4 ft. 6 in. wide in the clear. Near each corner of the building adjacent to the sidewalk, and with a door from the sidewalk, is a baggage-room 11 ft. × 12 ft. At each corner of the building at the sidewalk is an exit turnstile and a passageway for passengers from trains.

From each baggage-room an elevator about 5 ft. square, and inclined about 5 ft. from the perpendicular in 16 ft. height, descends to the train platform below. For proper work, with very heavy travel, one man would be required up-stairs to receive, check, and lower baggage, and another below to take it from the elevator and handle it to train. These, with a ticket-agent and a gatekeeper in the waiting-room, would make four men required at each station. At present but two are employed—the ticket-agent and a baggageman.

The framework of the station is of iron; the interior is of oak, finished in hard oil. The exterior is covered with iron, arranged in moulded panels, with iron mouldings, cornices, and brackets, and with ornamental shingled roof, with crestings, tower, and gables. These stations cost from $22,000 to $24,000 each, and the artificial stone platform alongside the tracks about $1500 additional.

The retaining-walls are recessed to accommodate the track platforms of the stations. The necessities of the streets adjacent and parallel to the track made these platforms and the stairways narrower than was desired, but the frequency and shortness of the local trains and the fact that the stations are so near each other will doubtless obviate trouble from this lack of width.

Passenger Depot at Ottumwa, Ia., Chicago, Burlington & Quincy Railroad.—The passenger depot of the Chicago, Burlington & Quincy Railroad at Ottumwa, Ia., designed by Messrs. Burnham & Root, architects, Chicago, Ill., illustrated and described in the issue of the *Railway Review* of November 19, 1887, is a handsome two-story brick building, 196 ft. × 36 ft., with slate roof. The brick is of a dark color, and stone trimmings are used. The interior is divided, commencing at one end of the building, in an express-room, a baggage-room, a hallway, a gentlemen's waiting-room, with lunch-counter at one corner, a ticket-office, a ladies' waiting-room, toilet-rooms for ladies and gentlemen opening from the respective waiting-rooms, a lunch-counter at one end of the ladies' waiting-room, a dining-room, a kitchen, a bakery, and a laundry. The second floor is used for offices, supply-rooms, and living-rooms.

Passenger Depots, New York & Northern Railway.—The passenger depots of the New York & Northern Railway at Bryn Mawr Park Station, and at Yonkers, N. Y., are illustrated in the issue of the *Railway News* of October, 1890.

Fig 582.—Street Elevation.

Fig. 583.—Perspective.

Fig. 584.—Fire-place in Waiting-room.

In Fig. 582 is shown the street elevation of the depot at Yonkers, N. Y., which is a handsome three-story brick and iron building, facing Getty Square, with 100 ft. frontage. The passenger entrance is at the north end on the first floor, which also includes space for a restaurant and baggage-rooms. A marble staircase leads to the waiting-rooms and ticket-office on the second floor, in the rear of which are the exits to the trains.

Figs. 583 and 584 show the depot at Bryn Mawr Park, which is a small, picturesque, single-story stone building.

The illustrations are made from plates kindly furnished to the author by Mr. L. M. Allen, General Passenger Agent, N. Y. & N. Ry.

Passenger Depot at South Park, Ill., Illinois Central Railroad.—The passenger depot of the Illinois Central Railroad at South Park, Chicago, Ill., described and illustrated in the issue of the *Railway Review* of April 16, 1881, is a large and handsome two-story brick and stone structure, with slate roof, divided into three separate buildings, connected by covered sheds and platform roofs. The main portion, or central building, is 41 ft. × 90 ft., with an 84-ft. high main tower. The pavilions at each end are 10 ft. × 23 ft. The sheds connecting the main building with the pavilions at each end are each 26 ft. wide and 73 ft. long. The main building is divided on the ground-floor into waiting-rooms, ladies' toilet-room, offices, and restaurant. The pavilion at one end is used for a baggage-room; the pavilion at the other end is used for a gentlemen's toilet-room and store-room. The upper floors are used for offices, supplies, and rooms connected with the restaurant.

Passenger Depot at Charlotte, N. C., Richmond & Danville Railroad.—The passenger depot of the Richmond & Danville Railroad at Charlotte, N. C., designed by W. L. Poindexter & Co., architects, Washington, D. C., illustrated in the issue of the *Inland Architect and News Record*, No. 8, Vol. 14, and in the *Railway Review* of January 25, 1890, is a two-story brick structure, with a single-story extension. The building is surrounded by platforms on all sides. The railroad passes on one side of the building. The structure is large and finished very handsomely, and is built more on the character of a terminal depot. The ground-plan has a ladies' waiting-room, with toilet-room attached, a gentlemen's waiting-room, a ticket-office, a station-agent's office, a large restaurant, a gentlemen's toilet-room, a baggage-room, an express-room, a store-room, and stairs leading to the upper floor. The upper floor is used partly for offices, and partly for the kitchen and other rooms connected with the restaurant.

Passenger Depot at Kensington Avenue, Buffalo, N. Y., New York, Lake Erie & Western Railroad.—The passenger depot of the New York, Lake Erie & Western Railroad at Kensington Avenue, Buffalo, N. Y., illustrated in the issue of the *Railway Review* of June 4, 1887, is a single-story frame structure, with slate roof, costing about $3500. The interior is divided into waiting-rooms, offices, toilet-rooms, and baggage-room.

Passenger Depot at Atlanta, Ga., East Tennessee, Virginia & Georgia Railroad.—The passenger depot of the East Tennessee, Virginia & Georgia Railroad at Atlanta, Ga., designed by Mr. C. H. Waring, engineer and architect, Middlesborough, Ky., illustrated in the issue of the *Railway Review* of July 19, 1884, is a single-story frame structure, about 20 ft. × 120 ft., sheathed on the outside with horizontal, vertical, and diagonal boarding, in panels. The ground-plan is divided into a restaurant, 14 ft. × 25 ft.; a kitchen, 18 ft. × 17 ft.; a colored waiting-room, 20 ft. × 17 ft.; a ticket-office, 12 ft. × 14 ft.; a telegraph-office, 12 ft. × 14 ft.; a gentlemen's waiting-room, 22 ft. × 17 ft.; a ladies' waiting-room, 16 ft. × 17 ft., with toilet-room attached; an express-room, 11 ft. × 12 ft.; and a baggage-room, 14 ft. × 12 ft. At the centre of the building, over the ticket-office and telegraph-office, there are two small bedrooms provided on the second floor. The interior of the building is finished in selected Georgia pine, shellacked and varnished. The exterior is painted in two shades of green, with all the chamfered edges in terra-cotta.

Passenger Depot at Ardmore, Pa., Pennsylvania Railroad.—The passenger depot at Ardmore, Pa., of the Pennsylvania Railroad, shown in Fig. 585, designed by Messrs. Joseph M. Wilson and F. G. Thorn, of the firm of Wilson Bros. & Co., architects, Philadelphia, Pa., illustrated and described in the issue of the *Railroad Gazette* of March 30, 1877, and in the *Engineering Magazine*, December, 1891, is a very handsomely designed two-story stone structure, with slate roof. The walls are built of gneiss stone, with rock face, laid irregularly, with Ohio sandstone sills and lintels. The ground surface drops very heavily at one end and in the rear of the building down from the railroad, so that a light basement-story is obtained, which is utilized as a dwelling for the agent, consisting of a parlor, a bedroom, a dining-room, a kitchen, and a cellar. The ground-floor, on the level with the railroad, has a general waiting-room, 20 ft. × 35 ft.; a ladies' private room, 14 ft. × 18 ft., with toilet-room attached; a gentlemen's smoking-room, 11 ft. × 12 ft., with a toilet-room, accessible from the rear of the

FIG. 585.—PERSPECTIVE.

building; a baggage-room, 8 ft. × 12 ft.; a telegraph-office, in connection with the signai-tower; a ticket-office, 9 ft. × 18 ft.; and a small bedroom. The second floor has three bedrooms and a signal-tower. The illustration is from a plate kindly furnished by the railroad company.

Design for Passenger Depot, Pennsylvania Railroad.—The design for a suburban passenger depot on the line of the Pennsylvania Railroad, prepared by Messrs. Wilson Bros., civil engineers and architects, Philadelphia, Pa., described and illustrated, with a finely executed colored plate inset, in the issue of the *Railroad Gazette* of September 22, 1882, is a two-story brick structure, with red-tile roof. The ground-floor has a general waiting-room, 30 ft. × 40 ft., with a small ladies' waiting-room and ladies' toilet-room attached. Also, a telegraph and ticket office, a baggage-room, and a gentlemen's toilet-room, the latter with entrance from the rear of the building. The upper floor has a living-room, three bedrooms, and a store-room.

Passenger Depot at Thirty-ninth Street, Chicago, Ill., Illinois Central Railroad.—The passenger depot of the Illinois Central Railroad at Thirty-ninth Street, Chicago, Ill., illustrated in the issue of the *Railway Review* of January 8, 1887, is a two-story stone and brick structure, with slate roof. The exterior is finished very artistically and attractively. The interior is divided into gentlemen's and ladies' waiting-rooms, offices, toilet-rooms, baggage-room, etc.

Passenger Depot at Kewanee, Ill.—The passenger depot at Kewanee, Ill., designed by Messrs. Burnham & Root, architects, Chicago, Ill., illustrated in the issue of the *Inland Architect and News Record*, No. 4, Vol. 9, is a single-story structure with wide sloping roofs, surrounded by a low platform on all sides. The interior is divided into a gentlemen's waiting-room; a ladies' waiting-room; a ticket and telegraph office; a baggage-room; and toilet-rooms.

Passenger Depot at Newark, Del., Philadelphia, Wilmington & Baltimore Railroad.—The passenger depot of the Philadelphia, Wilmington & Baltimore Railroad, designed by Mr. S. C. Fuller, Chief Engineer, illustrated in the issue of the *Railroad Gazette* of April 26, 1878, is a handsome two-story brick structure, with slate roof. The size of the building is 21 ft. × 56 ft. The ground-floor has a gentlemen's waiting-room; a ladies' waiting-room; a ticket and telegraph office; a baggage-room; a kitchen; and a stairway leading to the upper floor. The upper floor has a sitting-room and three bedrooms.

Passenger Depot at Twenty-second Street, Chicago, Ill., Illinois Central Railroad.—The passenger depot of the Illinois Central Railroad at Twenty-second Street, Chicago, Ill., illustrated in the issue of the *Railway Review* of March 6, 1880, is a two-story ornamental brick structure, with slate roof and handsome square tower. The building is 25 ft. × 80 ft., and is divided into a gentlemen's waiting-room, 32 ft. × 23 ft., and a ladies' waiting-room, 20 ft. × 23 ft. The waiting-rooms are connected by a passage-way, on one side of which is a ticket and telegraph office with an octagonal bay-window projection, and on the rear of which are toilet-rooms for ladies and gentlemen, opening from the respective waiting-rooms. At one end of the building is the baggage-room, 12 ft. × 23 ft.; also the stairway leading to the second floor of the building.

Passenger Depot at Rockford, Ill., Chicago, Madison & Northern Railway.—The passenger depot of the Chicago, Madison & Northern Railway at Rockford, Ill., designed by Mr. Henry Schlacks, architect, plans for which were published in the *Railway Review* of June 2, 1888, and in the *Inland Architect and News Record*, No. 6, Vol. 11, is a stone and brick structure, with a covered platform on the track side, and a large, square, ornamental tower at the centre of the building. The interior is divided into waiting-rooms, toilet-rooms, offices, baggage-rooms, etc.

Passenger Depot, Utica, N. Y., Delaware & Hudson Canal Company.—The passenger depot at Utica, N. Y., of the Utica, Clinton & Binghamton Railroad, leased by the Delaware & Hudson Canal Company, is described as follows in the issue of the *Railroad Gazette* of February 6, 1885.

The building is in the Queen Anne style of architecture. It is of ordinary brick, laid in red mortar, and has brown-stone trimmings. In height it is two stories and attic. The principal waiting-room has two large entrances from Genesee Street. The room is a large one, and well lighted. In one end the ticket-office is partitioned off. Under the stairway leading to the second story is a news and book stand. Just beyond the ticket-office is a passage-way and a wide door leading to the depot-yard. Just beyond this passage-way is the ladies' waiting-room, adjoining which is a toilet-room and water-closet. Still further in the rear is the baggage-room, which has wide entrances from Water and Division Streets, and a wide baggage window in the rear, where baggage can be unloaded direct into the room. On the Division Street side is an ample shed, under which baggage and passengers will have protection from the weather. There is also a shed along the railroad front for the benefit of passengers. These sheds are ornamental in design and coloring. The floors are of Georgia pine, and the interior is well lighted. The side walls and ceiling are ceiled with 2-inch spruce, finished in the wood. The outer doors are of handsomely grained quartered oak, and the door and window trimmings and gas-fixtures are of brass. Over each inside door is a large transom, supplied with a transom-lifter. The seats in the waiting-room are of perforated woodwork, and comfortable and cleanly. The interior work is neat, attractive, and cheerful, the abundance of light and the bright appearance of the woodwork adding much to the effect.

On the second floor, the room facing Genesee Street is the superintendent's office, at the side of which is a private office. Next in rear, and communicating with the superintendent's office by a small window, is the conductors' room, supplied with large ash desks, and five closets for uniforms. Again in rear of this, and connected by a similar window, is the office of the train-despatcher. In this office, as also in the superintendent's office and the ticket-office on the first floor, there is a bay projection commanding an extensive view. The rooms on the second floor have a wainscoting of pine instead of the ceiling on the first floor. Suitable sinks, storage-rooms, etc., are provided for, and in all respects the building is very convenient. The rooms are high between floors, the first story being 16 ft. and the second 15 ft. high.

Passenger Depot at Manitou, Col.—The passenger depot at Manitou, Col., designed by Mr. Clinton J. Warren, architect, Chicago, Ill, illustrated in the *Inland Architect and News Record*, No. 6, Vol. 9, is an artistic, single-story stone structure with heavy sloping roof. The masonry is irregular rubble work, with cut-stone corners and arches. The interior has a waiting-room; baggage-room; toilet-room; and an office, located in a round-tower projection, at one corner of the building. The platform at the front and end of the building is covered, and a handsome *porte cochère* is built at the rear of the building.

Passenger Depot at Seymour, Ind., Ohio & Mississippi Railway.—The passenger depot of the Ohio & Mississippi Railway at Seymour, Ind., illustrated and described in the issue of the *Railway Review* of November 2, 1889, can be considered as representative of the class of depot buildings in use on the Ohio & Mississippi Railway. The same character of building and ground-plan arrangement of the interior is carried out, as far as possible, in general, for all similar structures along the railroad, with the necessary alterations to suit local requirements. The depot at Seymour is a two-story frame structure, sheathed on the outside with upright boarding and shingles, in panels. The size of the building is 24 ft. × 52 ft., with an 8-ft. × 30-ft. annex in the rear. The first floor is divided into a gentlemen's waiting-room, 23 ft. × 18 ft.; a ladies' waiting-room, 23 ft. × 18 ft.; an office, 17 ft. × 13 ft., with a circular bay-window projection; a battery-room, 6 ft. × 13 ft.; a ladies' toilet-room, 8 ft. × 8 ft., opening from the ladies' waiting-room; and the stairway leading to the second floor. The second floor has a trainmaster's office; a telegraph-office; a train-despatcher's office; a store-room; and a vestibule for trainmen. The gentlemen's toilet-room is located in a separate building, in the rear of the main building. The baggage-room is also located in a separate building, 50 ft. distant from one end of the main building.

Passenger Depot at Bates City, Mo.—The passenger depot at Bates City, Mo., illustrated in the issue of the *Railway Review* of May 24, 1879, is a two-story frame structure, with slate roof. The outside is sheathed with upright and ornamental boarding, in panels. The interior has a waiting-room, ticket-office, baggage-room, and toilet-room.

Passenger Depot at Glen Ridge, N. J., Delaware, Lackawanna & Western Railroad.—The passenger depot of the Delaware, Lackawanna & Western Railroad at Glen Ridge, N. J., illustrated and described in the issue of the *Railroad Gazette* of April 29, 1887, shown in Figs. 586 to 588, is a two-story stone structure, with slate roof. The railroad at this point passes through a sandstone cut, 18 ft. deep, so that the wagon-road is on a level with the upper story of the building. In addition to its use for a railroad depot, the building had to be designed to accommodate a post-office and an express-office. The walls are built of blue-black trap-rock rubble masonry, with red-brick corners and belt-courses. The wide porch roof at the front of the building, on a level with the wagon-road, is extended at one end so as to form a *porte cochère*.

Passenger Depot at Independence, Mo., Chicago & Alton Railroad.—The passenger depot of the Chicago & Alton Railroad at Independence, Mo., illustrated in the issue of the *Railway Review* of May 3, 1879, is a two-story frame structure with slate roof, sheathed on the outside with horizontal, vertical, and diagonal boarding, and ornamental shingles, in panels. The ground-plan shows a waiting-room, ticket-office, baggage-room, and toilet-rooms.

Passenger Depot at Oak Grove, Mo.—The passenger depot at Oak Grove, Mo., is illustrated in the issue of the *Railway Review* of May 17, 1879. It is a two-story frame structure, with slate roof. The ground-plan shows a waiting-room, ticket-office, baggage-room, and toilet-room.

Passenger Depot at Rahway, N. J., Pennsylvania Railroad.—The passenger depot of the Pennsylvania Railroad at Rahway, N. J., designed by Mr. Joseph M. Wilson, described and illustrated in the issue of the *Railroad Gazette* of July 5, 1878, is a two-story brick structure, with slate roof. The ground-plan has a gentlemen's waiting-room, 22 ft. × 40 ft., and a ladies' waiting-room, 22 ft. × 24 ft. The waiting-rooms are connected by a passage-way, on one side of which is a telegraph and ticket office, 16 ft. × 16 ft., with a square bay-window projection, and on the other side of which, on the rear of the building, located in a square projection of the main building, are toilet-rooms for ladies and gentlemen, opening from the respective waiting-rooms. There is also a stairway leading to the upper story, and at one end of the building a baggage-room, 11 ft. 6 in. × 22 ft. The face walls are built of French bricks, with pencilled black joints, relieved with black bricks. The belt-courses, window-sills, chimney-caps, and arch-stones of the windows and doors are of Ohio sandstone.

Union Passenger Depot, Canton, Ohio.—The Union Railroad Depot at Canton, Ohio, designed by Mr. W. Whitney Lewis, architect, Boston, Mass., illustrated in the issue of the *American Architect and Building News,* August 7, 1880, is a two-story brick building, with square ornamental clock-tower, and slate roof. The tracks pass on one side of the building. The building is about 40 ft.

FIG. 587.—FIRST STORY PLAN. FIG. 586.—PERSPECTIVE. FIG. 588.—CELLAR-PLAN.

wide × 190 ft. long, and the ground-floor was designed so as to give a gentlemen's waiting-room, 30 ft. × 37 ft. 6 in., and a ladies' waiting-room, 30 ft. × 37 ft. 6 in. The waiting-rooms are connected by a passage-way, on one side of which there is a small telegraph and ticket office, with hexagonal bay-window projection, and on the other side of which is a ladies' toilet-room. In addition, there is a gentlemen's toilet-room with entrance from the gentlemen's waiting-room; a baggage-room; a dining-room; a kitchen; a serving-room; and stairs leading to the upper floor. In the depot, as actually built, the dining-room and kitchen were omitted, and a small freight-room substituted.

Passenger Depots, West Shore Railroad.—The standard passenger depots designed for the West Shore Railroad, under the direction of Mr. Walter Katté, Chief Engineer, as illustrated and described in the issue of the *Railroad Gazette* of May 7, 1886, known, respectively, as class "A, B, C, and D:—agent," are two-story frame structures, built in general to the same ground-plan, but varying sufficiently in the minor details of each plan, principally in the roofs, so as to give each structure an individual and local character without essentially changing the main details of this class of structures. The standard ground-plans are also published in the issue of *Engineering News* of March 31, 1888.

Class "A" presents on the first floor, a ticket and telegraph office, 12 ft. × 12 ft., with a square bay-window projection; a gentlemen's waiting-room, 15 ft. × 16 ft.; a ladies' waiting-room, 15 ft. × 16 ft.; a baggage-room, 10 ft. × 15 ft.; a ladies' toilet-room, opening from the ladies' waiting-room; a gentlemen's toilet-room, with entrance from the outside on the rear of the building; and the staircase leading to the upper floor. The second floor has a living-room, 15 ft. × 16 ft.; a bedroom, 15 ft. × 16 ft.; and two smaller rooms.

Class "B" shows in the ground-plan, a gentlemen's waiting-room, 17 ft. × 23 ft., and a ladies' waiting-room, 17 ft. × 23 ft., connected by a passage-way, on one side of which is a telegraph-office, 11 ft. × 12 ft., with a square bay-window projection, and on the other side of which, on the rear of the building, is a ticket-office, 11 ft. × 12 ft., with a square bay-window projection. There is also a baggage-room; a ladies' toilet-room, opening from the ladies' waiting-room; and a gentlemen's toilet-room, with entrance from the rear of the building.

Class "C" is similar to class "B," excepting in the size of the rooms. The gentlemen's wait-room is 24 ft. × 23 ft.; the ladies' waiting-room 24 ft. × 23 ft.; and the baggage-room 12 ft. × 23 ft.

Class "D" is similar to class "C," excepting in the size of the waiting-rooms, which are each 32 ft. × 23 ft.

Passenger Depot at Terrace Park Station, Buffalo, N. Y., New York Central & Hudson River Railroad.—The passenger depot of the New York Central & Hudson River Railroad at Terrace Park Station, Buffalo, N. Y., designed by Messrs. R. H. Robertson and A. J. Manning, architects, New York City, plans for which were published in the *Railway Review* of March 19, 1887, and in the *Railroad and Engineering Journal* of May, 1887, is a very handsome and large structure, with stone base, pressed-brick walls, terra-cotta trimmings, and tile roof. A bridge or covered passage-way is thrown over the main tracks in front of the building, connecting with the shelter and platform on the side of the tracks away from the main building. The interior is divided into a large, square vestibule, with an elaborate entrance from the street, which is on a lower level than the railroad. Leading from this vestibule there is a passage-way and stairway, to get to the platform on the level of the track. A ticket-office, a parcel-room, and a baggage-room adjoin the vestibule on one side, while on the other side there is a general waiting-room, with a ladies' private room and toilet-room connecting with the general waiting-room. A gentlemen's toilet-room at the same end of the building is entered from the outside of the building.

Passenger Depot at East Douglas, Mass., New York & New England Railroad.—The passenger depot of the New York & New England Railroad at East Douglas, Mass., plans for which were published in the *Railroad Gazette* of April 8, 1881, is a single-story frame structure, sheathed on the outside with vertical and horizontal boards, and ornamental shingles, in panels, and roofed with slate. There is a small *porte cochère* on the rear of the building. The interior is divided into a gentlemen's waiting-room, 17 ft. × 19 ft.; a ladies' waiting-room, 17 ft. × 19 ft.; a ticket-office, 9 ft. × 9 ft.; a baggage-room; a ladies' toilet-room, with entrance from the ladies' waiting-room; and a gentlemen's toilet-room, with an entrance from the outside of the building.

Passenger Depot at Niagara Falls, N. Y., New York, Lake Erie & Western Railroad.—In the issue of the *Railway Review* of August 27, 1887, the plans were published for a proposed passenger depot at Niagara Falls, N. Y., for the New York, Lake Erie & Western Railroad.

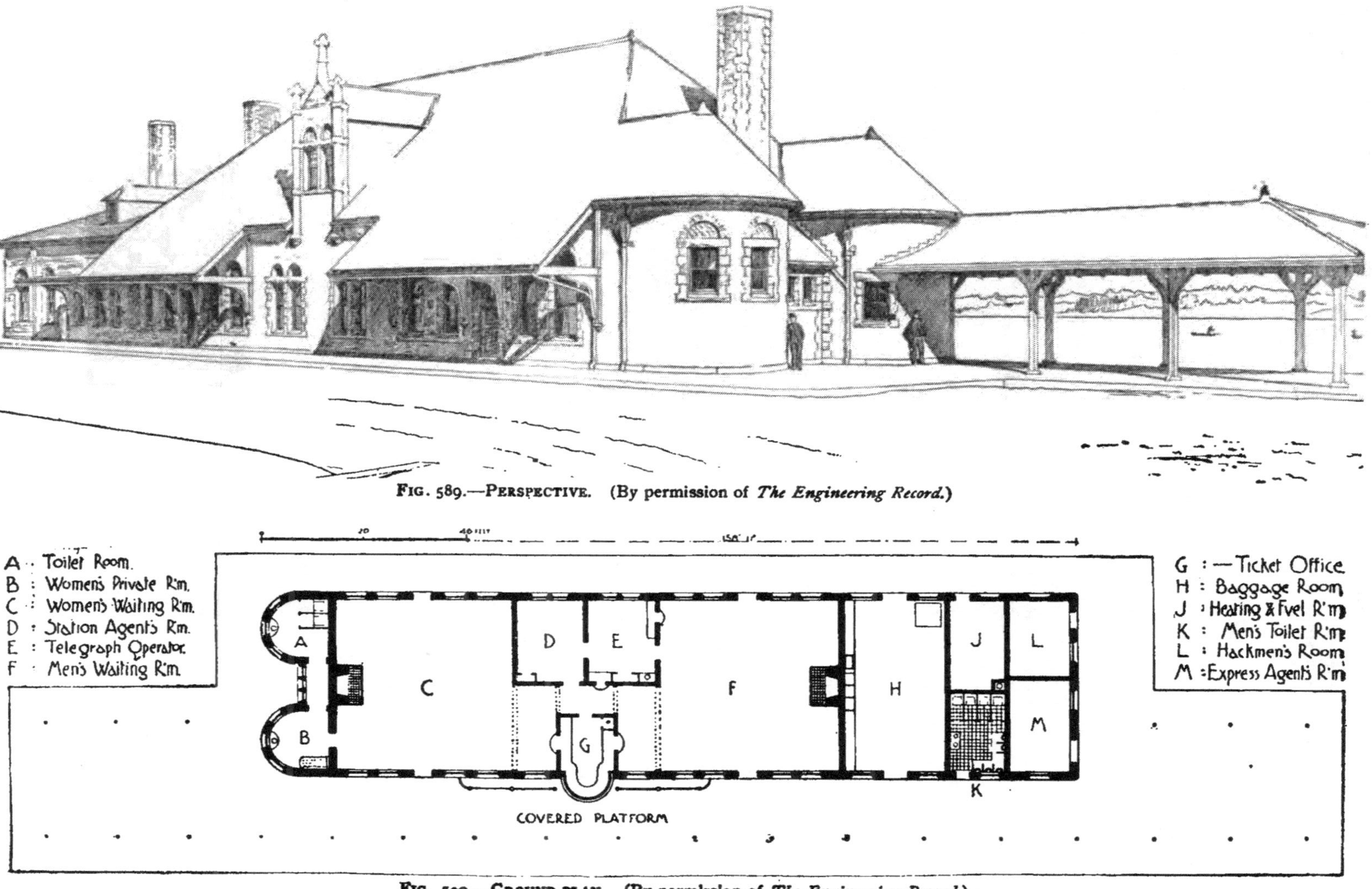

FIG. 589.—PERSPECTIVE. (By permission of *The Engineering Record*.)

FIG. 590.—GROUND-PLAN. (By permission of *The Engineering Record*.)

Passenger Depot at Walkerville, Ont.—The plans for a depot at Walkerville, Ont., designed by Messrs. Mason & Rice, architects, were published in the *Inland Architect and News Record*, No. 7, Vol. 14. The building is a stone structure, with heavy sloping roofs, and an elaborate and heavy square clock-tower. The interior is divided into waiting-rooms, offices, baggage-room, toilet-rooms, etc.

Passenger Depot at Dedham, Mass., Boston & Providence Railroad.—The passenger depot of the Boston & Providence Railroad at Dedham, Mass., designed by Messrs. Sturgis & Brigham, architects, Boston, Mass., plans for which were published in the *American Architect and Building News*, April 4, 1885, is a very elaborate and architecturally highly finished stone building, with sloping roof and clock-tower, built on an irregularly shaped ground-plan. The exterior of the structure has more the appearance of a chapel than a railroad depot. The interior is divided into a gentlemen's waiting-room, with toilet-room attached; a ladies' waiting-room, with toilet-room attached; a ticket-office; a baggage-room; and a telegraph-office. The interior finish is carefully studied, some of the details of which are illustrated in the publication mentioned.

Passenger Depot at New Bedford, Mass., Old Colony Railroad.—The passenger depot of the Old Colony Railroad at New Bedford, Mass., designed by Mr. Henry Paston Clarke, architect, Boston, Mass., plans for which were published in the *New England Magazine* of May, 1886, and also in the issue of *The Engineering Record* of April 6, 1889, shown in Figs. 589 and 590, published by permission of *The Engineering Record*, is an elaborate stone structure, with heavy sloping roofs. There is a covered platform along the face of the building next to the track, extending both ways along the track. The building is 160 ft. × 40 ft., and is divided into a gentlemen's waiting-room and a ladies' waiting-room, connecting by a passage-way, on one side of which is a ticket-office, and on the other side of which is a telegraph office and the station-agent's room. In each waiting-room there is a large open fire-place. At the end of the building, next to the ladies' waiting-room, there is a ladies' private room, with a toilet-room attached. At the other end of the building, next to the gentlemen's waiting-room (but without any door between them), there is a baggage-room. Next to the baggage-room is a gentlemen's toilet-room, with entrance from the platform; also a fuel-room; a hackmen's room; and an express-agent's room. The ground-plan of the building is very good.

Passenger Depot at North Easton, Mass., Old Colony Railroad.—The passenger depot of the Old Colony Railroad at North Easton, Mass., designed by the late Mr. H. H. Richardson, architect, Brooklyne, Mass., plans for which were published in the *American Architect and Building News* of Feb. 26, 1887, and in *The Engineering Magazine*, December, 1891, from which publication Fig. 591 is taken, consists of a single-story granite building, with brown-stone trimmings and tiled roof, 25 ft. × 90 ft., with a platform facing the track, and a heavy stone arched *porte cochère* on the rear of the building. The building is divided into a gentlemen's waiting-room and a ladies' waiting-room. A ticket-office is located between them on the side towards the track, and the waiting-rooms are connected back of

FIG. 591.—PERSPECTIVE.

the ticket-office by a lobby, which has an entrance door from the carriage-way under the *porte cochère.* At the end of the gentlemen's waiting-room there is a smoking-room; a gentlemen's toilet-room; and a door to the baggage-room. At the other end of the building a door leads from the ladies' waiting-room into a large ladies' parlor, with toilet-room attached. The ground-plan layout and the architectural artistic features of the building are first-class.

Passenger Depot at Holyoke, Mass., Connecticut River Railroad.—The passenger depot of the Connecticut River Railroad at Holyoke, Mass., shown in Figs. 592 and 593, designed by the late Mr. H.

FIG. 592.—PERSPECTIVE.

H. Richardson, architect, Brooklyne, Mass., plans for which were published in *The Engineering Record,* Vol. 14, and in the *American Architect and Building News* of Feb. 26, 1887, and in the *Railroad Gazette* of April 1, 1887, from which latter publication the cuts are taken, consists of a double-story granite building, with brown-stone trimmings and tiled roof, 40 ft. × 140 ft., surrounded by platforms on all sides. The first floor is divided into a general waiting-room, 36 ft. × 60 ft., with a ticket-office, partitioned off on one side, facing the track. At one end of the waiting-room there is a telegraph-office, and a lobby leads to a ladies' waiting-room, with toilet-room attached. The ladies' waiting-room has a separate entrance from the platform on the track side of the house. At the other end of the building there is a gentlemen's toilet-room, leading off from the general waiting-room; an emigrants' waiting-room, with toilet-rooms attached for men and for women; a baggage-room; and the stairway leading to the upper story.

FIG. 593.—GROUND-PLAN.

Passenger Depot at Auburndale, Mass., Boston & Albany Railroad.—The passenger depot at

FIG. 594.—PERSPECTIVE.

Auburndale, Mass., on the main line of the Boston & Albany Railroad, shown in Figs. 594 to 596, designed by the late Mr. H. H. Richardson, architect, Brooklyne, Mass., plans of which were published in the *Railroad Gazette* of Nov. 5, 1886, in *The Engineering Record*, Vol. 14, in the *American Architect and Building News* of Feb. 26, 1887, and also in the *Railway Review* of April 6, 1889, consists of a single-story granite building, with brown-stone trimmings and red-tile roofing. There is a covered platform along the face of the building and at the end of the building next to the

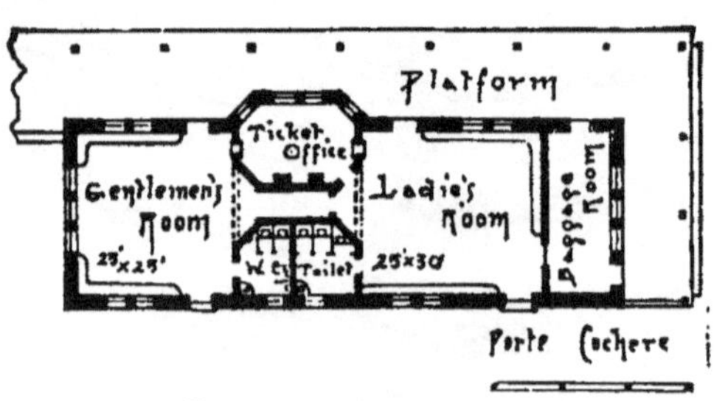

FIG. 595.—GROUND-PLAN.

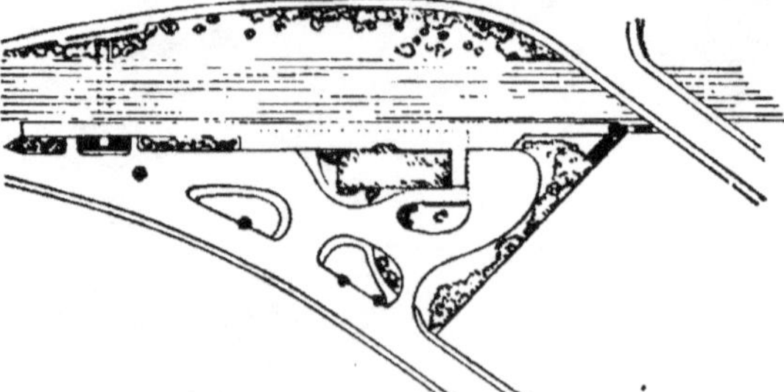

FIG. 596.—GENERAL PLAN OF STATION LAYOUT.

baggage-room, and an artistically designed *porte cochère* on the rear of the building. The interior is divided into a gentlemen's waiting-room, 25 ft. × 25 ft., and a ladies' waiting-room, 25 ft. × 30 ft., connected by a small passage-way, on one side of which is a ticket-office, and on the other side of which there are a ladies' toilet-room and a gentlemen's toilet-room. At one end of the building, adjoining the ladies' waiting-room, there is a baggage-room.

Passenger Depot at South Framingham, Mass., Boston & Albany Railroad.—The passenger depot at South Framingham, Boston & Albany Railroad, designed by the late Mr. H. H. Richardson, architect, Brooklyne, Mass., plans for which were published in the *American Architect and Building News* of Feb. 26, 1887, consists of a double-story structure, 120 ft. × 35 ft., with covered platforms surrounding it. The interior is divided into a general waiting-room, 33 ft. × 60 ft., on one side of which is a ticket-office, and on the other side of which is a large ornamental fire-place. Adjoining the general waiting-room, at one end of the building, there is a dining-room; a buffet; a smoking-room; a toilet-room for gentlemen; a serving-room for the dining-room; and a stairway leading to the kitchen on the second floor above the dining-room. At the other end beyond the general waiting-room the building is divided into a small ladies' waiting-room, with a toilet-room attached; a telegraph office; a package-room; the station-agent's office; and the stairway leading to offices on the second floor. The arrangement of the ground-plan in this building can be considered as first-class for the purposes to be accomplished.

Passenger Depot at Brighton, Mass., Boston & Albany Railroad.—The passenger depot at Brighton, Mass., of the Boston & Albany Railroad, designed by the late Mr. H. H. Richardson, architect, Brooklyne, Mass., plans for which were published in the *American Architect and Building News* of Feb. 26, 1887, consists of a single-story stone structure, 80 ft. × 30 ft., with long sloping roof, covering steps in front of the building, leading down to the level of the railroad. The interior is divided into a gentlemen's waiting-room and a ladies' waiting-room, connected by a passage-way, on one side of which is a ticket-office, and on the other side of which there are a ladies' toilet-room and a gentlemen's toilet-room. At the end of the building, next to the gentlemen's waiting-room, there are a small baggage-room and a telegraph office. The location of the telegraph office at the rear of the building, unless called for by some local requirement, is objectionable.

Passenger Depots, Chicago & Northwestern Railway.—Passenger depots designed by Messrs. Cobb & Frost, architects, Chicago, Ill., for the Chicago & Northwestern Railway at Oshkosh, Wheaton, and Kenosha, are described and illustrated in the issue No. 6, Vol. 10, of the *Inland Architect and News Record*, and also in the issue of January 20, 1888, of *The Railway Age.*

The depot at Oshkosh is a two-story structure, 78 ft. × 23 ft., divided on the ground-floor into a ladies' waiting-room and a gentlemen's waiting-room, connected by a broad passage-way, on one side of which is a ticket-office, and on the other side of which is the ladies' toilet-room, and the stairway leading from the outside of the building to the upper floor. Thirty feet from one end of the main building there is a baggage-room, 20 ft. × 23 ft., and 30 ft. from the other end of the main building there is a similar size building, which is used for fuel and supplies, and for a gentlemen's toilet-room. The space between the main building and the end building is covered by a wide shed roof, supported by columns and trusses. The building has stone foundations, with rock-face stone ashlar walls up to window-sills. Above the window-sills faced brick are used. The main building and tower is roofed with slate, the platform sheds with tin. The waiting-room ceilings are finished up into the roof, giving an opportunity for furnishing direct light from above the shed roof. The interior finish is in oak, with maple floors and high wainscoting. The cost of the building is stated to have been $13,000.

The depot at Wheaton has two waiting-rooms; a ticket-office; a baggage-room; and toilet-rooms; all in one building, 70 ft. × 20 ft. The platform is covered for 200 ft. along the track. The building is built entirely of frame, with a painted shingle roof. The lower portion of exterior of building, below window-sills, vertical sheathing, and above this to ceiling of sheds is narrow siding. The interior is finished in pine, painted, with wainscoting. The walls above wainscoting and ceiling are sheathed with narrow beaded pine. The floors are hard wood. The cost is stated to be about $4000.

The depot at Kenosha is 81 ft. × 23 ft. in size, with a lavatory annex, 8 ft. × 13 ft. The main building has a gentlemen's waiting-room; a ladies' waiting-room; a ticket-office; a baggage-room; and toilet-rooms. The building has stone foundations with rock-faced stone ashlar from platform to window-sills; above this point to roof, faced brick. The covered shed over platform, supported by columns and trusses, is 200 ft. long. Projection of the shed on track side of building 14 ft., with extensions on each end 20 ft. wide. The roof extends down, and projects 8 ft. on the other three sides of the building, supported on brackets. The entire roof of building, including shed, is covered with purple slate, using copper for ridge, hip, and gutter mouldings. The building has no second story, but the waiting-rooms are finished about one third into roof. Interior of building is finished in oak, with a high wainscoting, plastered walls and ceilings, maple floors throughout. The lavatory building is partially disconnected from the main building by the use of double doors and ventilators, built into the wall connecting the two. This lavatory has three seats and three urinals with vault underneath, with a ventilator extending from the same up through the roof, with door in rear for cleaning the same. No plumbing in building. Heated by means of stoves. Cost complete about $8400.

Passenger Depots, Philadelphia, Germantown & Chestnut Hill Railroad.—The passenger depots of the Philadelphia, Germantown & Chestnut Hill Railroad at Queen's Lane, Chelton Avenue, Chestnut Hill, and Wissahickon, Pa., shown in Figs. 597 to 604, designed by Mr. W. Bleddyn Powell, archi-

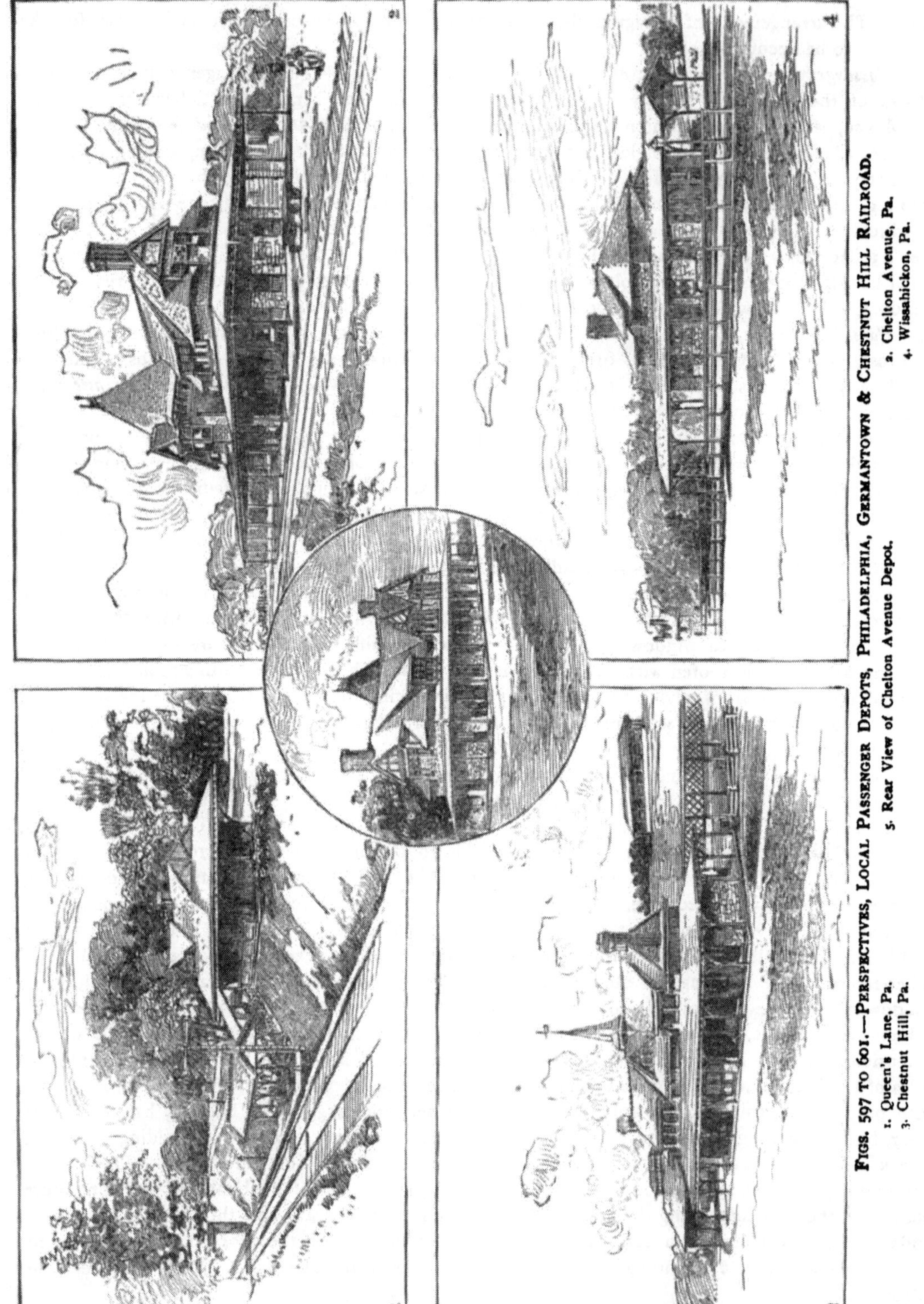

FIGS. 597 TO 601.—PERSPECTIVES, LOCAL PASSENGER DEPOTS, PHILADELPHIA, GERMANTOWN & CHESTNUT HILL RAILROAD.

1. Queen's Lane, Pa.
2. Chelton Avenue, Pa.
3. Chestnut Hill, Pa.
4. Wissahickon, Pa.
5. Rear View of Chelton Avenue Depot.

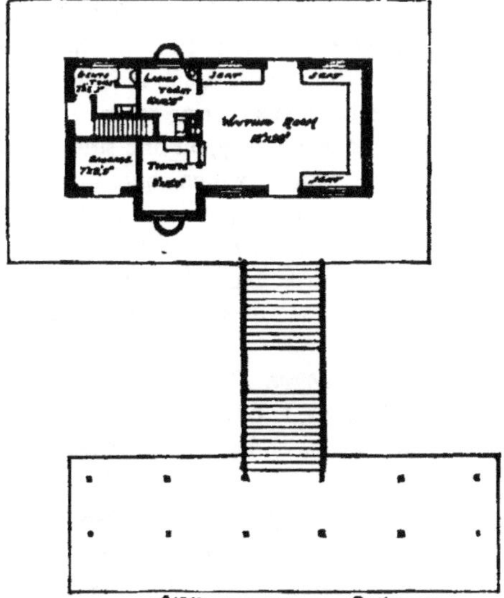

FIG. 602.—GROUND-PLAN, QUEEN'S LANE DEPOT.

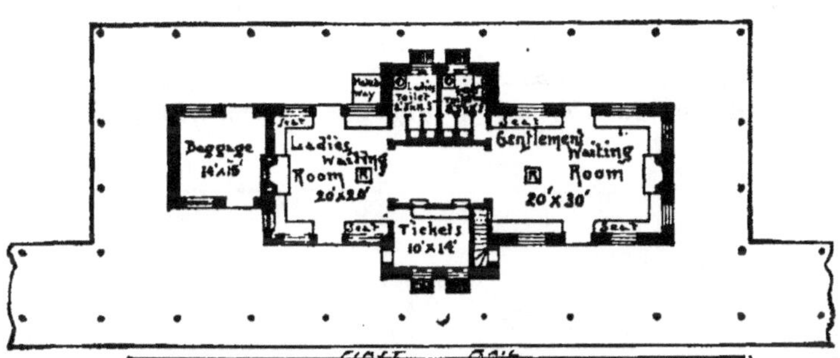

FIG. 603.—GROUND-PLAN, CHELTON AVENUE DEPOT.

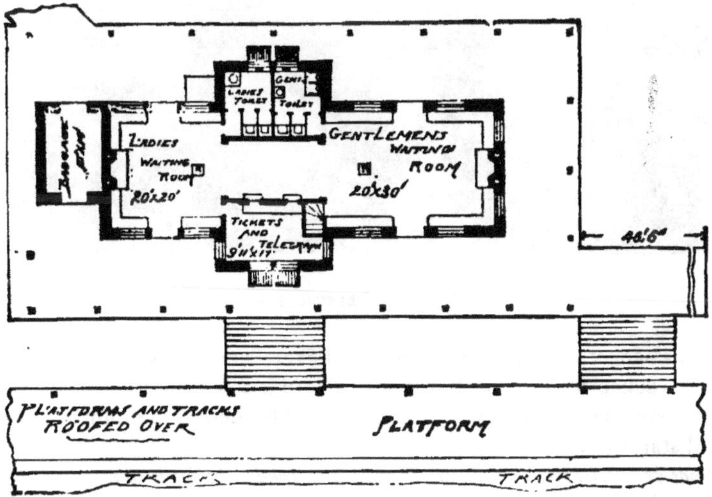

FIG. 604.—GROUND-PLAN. CHESTNUT HILL DEPOT.

tect, are described and illustrated in Vol. 14 of *The Engineering Record,* and in the *Railroad Gazette* of November 26, 1886, from which latter publication the cuts are taken. The depot building at Queen's Lane is of brick, the others are of stone, with some half-timber and shingle work in the upper stories. The Chestnut Hill depot has a gentlemen's waiting-room, 20 ft. × 30 ft., and a ladies' waiting-room, 20 ft. × 20 ft., connected by a broad passage-way, on one side of which there is a ticket and telegraph office, 10 ft. × 12 ft., and on the other side of which there are a ladies' and a gentlemen's toilet-room. At one end of the building there is a baggage-room, 10 ft. × 14 ft. The Chelton Avenue depot is similar, as far as the ground-plan is concerned, to the Chestnut Hill depot. The depot at Queen's Lane is smaller than the others, and has a general waiting-room, 18 ft. × 25 ft.; a ticket-office, 9 ft. × 11 ft.; a baggage-room, 7 ft. × 10 ft.; a ladies' toilet-room, 9 ft. × 10 ft.; and a gentlemen's toilet-room, 7 ft. × 10 ft.

Competition Designs for Local Passenger Depot, Toronto Architectural Sketch Club.—In the issue of the *Inland Architect and News Record,* Vol. 15, two plans for a passenger depot at a local station are illustrated, which secured the first and second prizes awarded in a competition arranged by the Toronto Architectural Sketch Club.

Competition Designs for Suburban Railway Depot, Chicago Architectural Sketch Club.—The *Railway Review* offered in 1889 three prizes to the members of the Chicago Architectural Sketch Club for the best plans of a suburban railway-station building, of which the cost of construction was to be $3000. The first prize was awarded to Mr. T. O. Fraenkel, of Chicago, Ill., and the plans were published in the issue of the *Railway Review* of April 13, 1889. The second prize was awarded to Mr. Henry Brown, of Chicago, Ill., whose plan was illustrated in the issue of the *Railway Review* of April 20, 1889. The third prize was taken by Mr. W. G. Williamson, of Chicago, Ill., whose design was published in the issue of the *Railway Review* of April 27, 1889.

Twin Passenger Depots at Desrover and Baker Parks, Minn., Chicago, Milwaukee & St. Paul Railroad.—In Fig. 605, copied from *The Engineering Magazine,* December, 1891, is presented a perspective of the "twin" passenger depots at Desrover and Baker Parks, between St. Paul and Minneapolis, on the Chicago, Milwaukee & St. Paul Railroad. There is a separate depot building, with waiting-rooms, ticket-offices, etc., on each side of the railroad. The depots are built on terraces reached by wide platforms and stairways.

FIG. 605.—PERSPECTIVE.

Passenger Depot at Sewickley, Pa., Pennsylvania Railroad.—In Fig. 606, copied from the *Engineering Magazine,* December, 1891, is shown a perspective of the passenger depot at Sewickley, Pa., on the Pennsylvania Railroad System. This illustration shows very clearly the method of using shelters with overhead foot-bridge and a fence between the main tracks at local suburban passenger stations

FIG. 606.—PERSPECTIVE.

on a double-track railroad with a heavy fast-train service. The depot building is about 27 ft. × 70 ft., divided into a general waiting-room; a ladies' private room; a baggage-room; a ticket-office; etc.

Passenger Depot at Acambaro, Mexico.—In Fig. 607, copied from *The Engineering Magazine*, December, 1891, is shown a perspective of the passenger depot at Acambaro, Mexico, designed by Mr. Bradford L. Gilbert, architect, New York, N. Y. The building is two-story, built of brick, about 100 ft. × 40 ft., with concrete platforms and tile roof. The first floor has the necessary offices and waiting-rooms with accommodations for first, second, and third class passengers, the European system of the division of the travelling public being in vogue. There is also a dining-room on the first floor. The second floor has hotel accommodations for passengers.

FIG. 607.—PERSPECTIVE.

Junction Passenger Depot at Reed City, Mich.—In Fig. 608, copied from *The Engineering Magazine*, December, 1891, is shown a perspective of the passenger depot at Reed City, Mich., designed by Mr. Bradford L. Gilbert, architect, New York, N. Y., used jointly by the Grand Rapids & Indiana and the Flint & Pere Marquette Railroads. The general waiting-room is in the shape of a large octagon, at one end of which is a lunch-room; on the track sides of the octagon the ticket-offices for the respective railroads are stationed; while on the other sides of the octagon doors lead to a ladies' waiting-room with toilet-room attached, and to a gentlemen's smoking-room with toilet-room attached. At each end of the building there is a baggage-room. The light for the rotunda is obtained from clere-story windows above the roof of both wings. The rotunda is 64 ft. square, with wings about 75 ft. in length.

FIG. 608.—PERSPECTIVE.

Passenger Depot at Grass Lake, Mich., Michigan Central Railroad.—In Fig. 609, copied from *The Engineering Magazine*, December, 1891, is shown a perspective of the passenger depot of the Michigan Central Railroad at Grass Lake, Mich. The building is about 63 ft. × 34 ft., divided into waiting-rooms, offices, baggage-room, toilet-rooms, etc. The material of the walls is field stone of various shades, with broken faces, laid up in rubble-work, the effect being very picturesque and unique.

FIG. 609.—PERSPECTIVE.

Passenger Depot at Laconia, N. H., Concord & Montreal Railroad.—The passenger depot of the Concord & Montreal Railroad at Laconia, N. H., designed by Mr. Bradford L. Gilbert, architect, New York, N. Y., shown in perspective in Fig. 610, copied from *The Engineering Magazine*, De-

FIG. 610.—PERSPECTIVE.

cember, 1891, is a picturesque, substantially built stone depot for the accommodation of a large passenger business. The most prominent feature of the design is the rotunda, 40 ft. square, with octagonal corners carried up above the roof, and with light from clere-story windows overhead. The interior of this depot is finished very handsomely. The floor of the rotunda is of marble, and a large chimney forms one of the features of the interior finish.

Passenger Depot at Galesburg, Ill., Atchison, Topeka & Santa Fe Railroad.—The passenger depot at Galesburg, Ill., on the Atchison, Topeka & Santa Fe Railroad, shown in Fig. 611, copied from

FIG. 611.—PERSPECTIVE.

The Engineering Magazine, December, 1891, is a handsome brick and stone building, 54 ft. × 168 ft. It is divided into offices, waiting-rooms, toilet-rooms, baggage and express room.

Passenger Depot at Mauch Chunk, Pa., Lehigh Valley Railroad.—The passenger depot of the Lehigh Valley Railroad at Mauch Chunk, Pa., shown in Fig. 612, copied from *The Engineering Magazine*, December, 1891, is a two-story brick building, with slate roof and an iron platform roof

FIG. 612.—PERSPECTIVE.

extending for several hundred feet along the track, as there is a very large excursion passenger business handled at this station. The most notable feature of the design is the fact that the depot and platforms are located alongside a heavy curve on the railroad, and the platforms and building follow the curvature of the tracks.

Passenger Depot at Wichita, Kan., Atchison, Topeka & Santa Fe Railroad.—The passenger depot of the Atchison, Topeka & Santa Fe Railroad at Wichita, Kan., shown in Fig. 613, copied from

FIG. 613.—PERSPECTIVE.

The Engineering Magazine, December, 1891, is a picturesque and handsome stone structure, 60 ft. × 156 ft., with an octagonal tower at one corner. The ground-floor has a large lunch-room in addition to the usual facilities and accommodations for the passenger service.

Passenger Depot at Evanston, Ill., Chicago, Milwaukee & St. Paul Railroad.—The passenger depot of the Chicago, Milwaukee & St. Paul Railroad at Evanston, Ill., shown in Fig. 614, copied from *The Engineering Magazine*, December, 1891, is a very substantially built stone two-story structure, 68 ft. × 21 ft., with metal shingles on the roof and sides of the dormers and tower, where projecting above the roof. The platform is roofed for some distance along the track.

FIG. 614.—PERSPECTIVE.

Passenger Depot at Highland, Mass., Old Colony Railroad.—The passenger depot of the Old Colony Railroad at Highland, Mass., shown in Fig. 615, copied from *The Engineering Magazine*, December, 1891, is a picturesque, single-story stone building with slate roof. The design is exceptionally bold and graceful, the prominent features being a large stone gable and chimney at one end of the building, and a *porte cochère* on the rear.

FIG. 615.—PERSPECTIVE.

Passenger Depot at Somerset, Ky., Cincinnati, New Orleans & Texas Pacific Railway.—The passenger depot of the Cincinnati, New Orleans & Texas Pacific Railway, at Somerset, Ky., shown in Fig. 616, designed by Mr. G. B. Nicholson, Chief Engineer, C., N. O. & T. P. Ry., is a two-story frame structure, 26 ft. × 180 ft. in ground-plan, surrounded by platforms on all sides, sheathed with horizontal weather-boarding on the outside, and roofed with flat iron-roofing on boards. The interior of the ground-floor, starting at one end of the building, is divided into a kitchen, 25 ft. × 25 ft.; a dining-room, 25 ft. × 44 ft.; a general waiting-room, 25 ft. × 30 ft., with lunch-counter, wash-room, and gentlemen's toilet-room; an office, 9 ft. × 13 ft., with a square bay-window projection on the track side, and ticket-windows leading into the gentlemen's waiting-room and into the ladies' waiting-room; a ladies' waiting-room, 25 ft. × 20 ft., with toilet-room attached; a stairway leading to the upper floor; a baggage-room, 25 ft. × 20 ft.; and an express-office, 25 ft. × 20 ft. The kitchen mentioned is built in the form of a single-story annex, so that the upper floor is only 153 ft. long, but

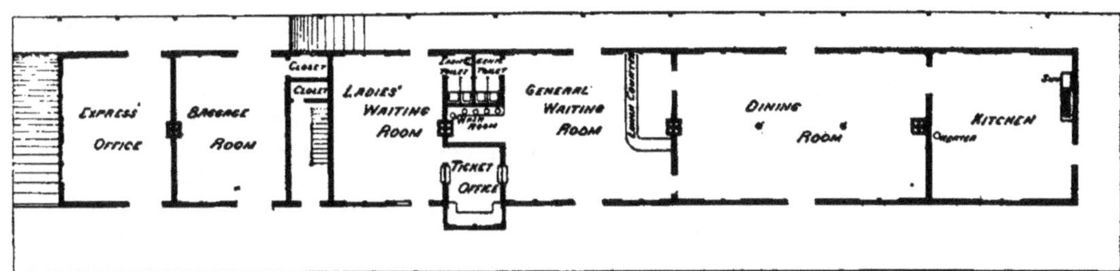

FIG. 616.—GROUND-PLAN.

the upper floor is built out on the rear over the porch or platform at the rear end of the building on the ground-floor, so that the width of the upper floor is 32 ft. There is a passage-way, 4 ft. wide, along the front of the upper floor, reached by the stairs previously mentioned from the ground-floor. The rooms on the upper floor, reached by the passage-way mentioned, are divided up as follows: superintendent's office, 31 ft. × 20 ft.; clerk's office, 26 ft. × 19 ft.; trainmen's waiting-room, 27 ft. × 26 ft.; despatcher's office, 25 ft. × 26 ft.; battery-room, 14 ft. × 11 ft.; storage-room for blanks and stationery, 14 ft. × 14 ft.; office of Superintendent of Bridges and Buildings, 22 ft. × 26 ft.; roadmaster's office, 22 ft. × 31 ft. The platforms around this building are all low platforms, with exception on the rear of the building back of the baggage and express rooms, where the platform is a high platform, connected with the low platforms by inclines. The high platform back of the baggage and express room is to facilitate the transferring of baggage and express matter to and from wagons. The low platform is set 16 in. above the base of rail, and the face of the platform is 5 ft. 6 in. from the centre of the track. The low platform is 6 ft. wide on the rear of the building, 8 ft. wide at the end of the building, and 12 ft. 6 in. wide along the face of the building.

Passenger Depot at Lexington, Ky., Cincinnati, New Orleans & Texas Pacific Railway.—The passenger depot of the Cincinnati, New Orleans & Texas Pacific Railway at Lexington, Ky., designed by Mr. G. B. Nicholson, Chief Engineer, C., N. O. & T. P. Ry., is a two-story frame structure with high attic, 28 ft. × 105 ft., sheathed on the outside with upright and horizontal ornamental boarding, in panels, and roofed with tin, similar in a great many of its features to the depot of the same railroad at Somerset, Ky., previously described and illustrated in Fig. 616, excepting that the exterior is more ornamental and the roof surface broken by gables and dormer-windows with ornamental stained-shingle panelling. The ground-floor is surrounded by low platforms, 16 in. high above the base of rail and set 6 ft. from the centre of the track. The platform along the front of the building is 24 ft. wide, and on the rear of the building and at one end of the building 8 ft. wide, while at the other end next to the general waiting-room it is 16 ft. wide. Connection is made at this point with a branch train, there being special platforms run out for this purpose along the extra tracks. The ground-floor has a general waiting-room, 40 ft. × 27 ft.; a ladies' waiting-room, 15 ft. × 19 ft., with toilet-room attached; an office, 9 ft. × 14 ft.; a stairway to the upper floor; a lunch-room, 14 ft. × 18 ft.; and a baggage-room, 30 ft. × 27 ft. The upper floor is arranged similarly to the upper floor of the depot at Somerset, Ky., previously described.

Passenger Depot at Science Hill, Ky., Cincinnati, New Orleans & Texas Pacific Railway.—The passenger depot of the Cincinnati, New Orleans & Texas Pacific Railway at Science Hill, Ky., designed by Mr. G. B. Nicholson, Chief Engineer, C., N. O. & T. P. Ry., is a small, handsome, and substantially built single-story frame structure, with high attic and gable front, sheathed on the outside with vertical and horizontal ornamental boarding, in panels, and roofed with tin. The building is 20 ft. × 40 ft., divided into a ticket-office, 10 ft. × 23 ft., including a bay-window projection on the track side; a gentlemen's waiting-room, 14 ft. × 19 ft.; and a ladies' waiting-room, 14 ft. × 19 ft. The rear of the office is picketed off so as to form a baggage-room, with a separate entrance from the rear of the building. The building is surrounded by low platforms, 12 ft. wide facing the track, and 8 ft. wide on the rear and at the ends of the building.

Passenger Depot at Eutaw, Ala., Alabama Great Southern Railroad.—The passenger depot of the Alabama Great Southern Railroad at Eutaw, Ala., designed by Mr. G. B. Nicholson, Chief Engineer, A. G. S. R. R., is a single-story frame structure, 20 ft. × 50 ft., with high attic and a two-story tower at one corner, sheathed on the outside with upright and horizontal ornamental boarding, in panels, and roofed with tin. The ground-floor is surrounded by low platforms, 12 ft. wide at the face of the building, and 6 ft. wide at the rear and ends. The interior is divided into a gentlemen's waiting-room, 15 ft. × 19 ft.; a ladies' waiting-room, 15 ft. × 19 ft.; a ticket-office, 9 ft. × 22 ft., including a bay-window projection on the track side; and a baggage-room, 10 ft. × 19 ft.

Passenger Depot at Brownwood, Tex., Gulf, Colorado & Santa Fe Railroad.—The passenger depot of the Gulf, Colorado & Santa Fe Railroad, now part of the Atchison, Topeka & Santa Fe Railroad System, designed by Mr. W. J. Sherman, Chief Engineer, G., C. & S. F. R. R., is a single-story frame structure, 18 ft. × 55 ft., surrounded by low platforms on all sides, sheathed on the outside with upright boards and battens, set on wooden blocks for foundations, and roofed with shingles on sheeting. The platforms are 8 ft. wide at the rear and ends of the building, and 14 ft. wide at the face of the building, extended along the track each way from the building, 9 ft. in width, so as to give a total platform track frontage of 150 ft. The interior is divided into an office, 9 ft. × 14 ft., with a bay-window projection on the track side; a gentlemen's waiting-room, 14 ft. × 18 ft., and a ladies' waiting-room, 14 ft. × 18 ft., connected by a 4-ft. passage-way at the back of the office, tickets being sold to passengers in either room from ticket-windows at the rear angles of the office; a baggage-room, 8 ft. × 18 ft.; and an express-office, 12 ft. × 18 ft. The ground-plan layout of this depot building, the design of the exterior, and the details and materials used are practically the same as in the passenger end of the combination depot of the same railroad at Farmersville, Tex., described above in the chapter on combination depots, and illustrated in Figs. 473 to 475. This depot can be recommended on account of having a very good ground-plan layout, and the cheapness and simplicity of the design renders it particularly adapted for pioneer railroads, or where a cheap but practical structure is desired.

Passenger Depot at Hopkinsville, Ky., Louisville & Nashville Railroad.—The passenger depot of the Louisville & Nashville Railroad at Hopkinsville, Ky., shown in Figs. 617 and 618, the data for

FIG. 617.—FRONT ELEVATION.

which were kindly furnished by Mr. R. Montford, Chief Engineer, L. & N. R. R., is a single-story frame building, roofed with slate. The main feature of the exterior is the tower at the corner of the ladies' waiting-room and the large circular bay-window projection of the agent's office at the centre of the building, which, combined with the cupola on the corner tower, the ridge-cresting and ornamental gable fronts, together with the general finish of the building, causes it to present a very handsome appearance. The ground-floor is divided into a ladies' waiting-room, 17 ft. × 20 ft., with an octagonal alcove inside the tower at the corner of the room; a ladies' toilet-room, 5 ft. × 8 ft. 6 in.; an agent's office, 14 ft. × 17 ft., with ticket-windows leading into the ladies' waiting-room, the general waiting-room, and the colored waiting-room; a colored waiting-room, 14 ft. × 14 ft.; a general

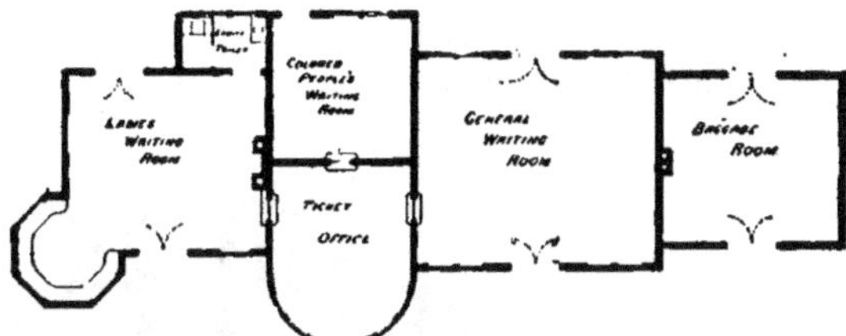

FIG. 618.—GROUND-PLAN.

waiting-room, 20 ft. × 24 ft.; and a baggage-room, 16 ft. × 18 ft. The exterior of the building is sheathed with horizontal and upright ornamental boarding, in panels, ornamental shingles and square panelling frieze-work and gable fronts. The doors leading into the ladies' waiting-room and the general waiting-room are double doors, 5 ft. × 7 ft. 6 in., with transom overhead. The lower sash of the windows have one large pane of glass, while the upper sash are surrounded with a border of small stained-glass lights.

Passenger Depot at Owensboro, Ky., Louisville & Nashville Railroad.—The passenger depot of the Louisville & Nashville Railroad at Owensboro, Ky., the data for which were kindly furnished by Mr. R. Montford, Chief Engineer, L. & N. R. R., is a single-story brick building with stone trimmings and roofed with slate, very similar, especially the ground-plan, to that of the depot at Hopkinsville, Ky., described above and shown in Figs. 617 and 618. The interior is divided into a ladies' waiting-room, 15 ft. × 18 ft., with a circular alcove at one corner in a tower projection with a prominent cupola; a ladies' toilet-room, 4 ft. × 7 ft. 6 in.; an agent's office, 12 ft. 9 in. × 13 ft. 6 in., with a prominent square bay-window projection on the track side and three ticket-windows; a colored waiting-room, 12 ft. 9 in. × 13 ft. 6 in.; a general waiting-room, 17 ft. × 18 ft.; and a baggage-room, 13 ft. × 16 ft.

Passenger Depot at Niles, Mich., Michigan Central Railroad.—The passenger depot of the Michigan Central Railroad at Niles, Mich., shown in Figs. 619 and 620, copied by permission from the issue of the *Railroad Gazette* of April 29, 1892, is described as follows in the publication mentioned:

FIG. 619.—PERSPECTIVE.

The building, which was erected under the supervision of Chief Engineer J. D. Hawks, and his assistant, C. W. Hotchkiss, is made of Ohio brown sandstone, and is 98 ft. × 40 ft., with a wing 40 ft. × 24 ft. The tower near the centre is 68 ft. high. The baggage-room, 22 ft. × 35 ft., is 55 ft. east of the main building, the intervening space being roofed over.

The plan shows the main floor, but the rooms immediately over the ticket-office are shown below the main plan, and the rooms above the kitchen (which are occupied by the family of the manager of the eating-house), are shown in a separate plan at the right of the kitchen. The other features of the floor-plan are self-explanatory.

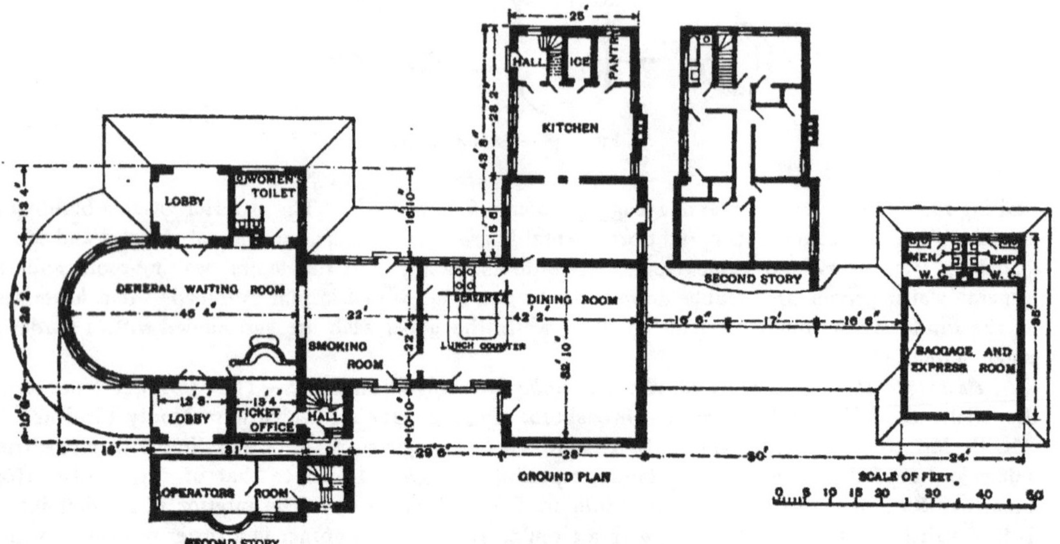

FIG. 620.—GROUND-PLAN AND SECOND STORY PLAN.

The interior of this building is exceedingly tasteful, the use of plate and stained glass and brass ornamentation having served to give a very pleasing effect in all parts of the building. The wainscoting and ceilings are quarter-sawed and carved oak, and the walls are decorated in light terra-cotta. The building is heated by hot water. The tower has an illuminated clock, with 5-ft. dial.

The grounds around this station are laid out on a well-designed plan, and there is an abundance of trees and shrubbery. There is a trout pond near the east end.

Passenger Depot at Port Huron, Mich., Port Huron & Northwestern Railway.—The passenger depot of the Port Huron & Northwestern Railway at Port Huron, Mich., which serves as a terminal depot and general office building for the railroad, is a two-story frame structure, 32 ft. × 150 ft., costing finished complete in hard wood, with steam heat, etc., about $15,000, according to data kindly furnished by Mr. A. L. Reed, Chief Engineer. The first floor has gentlemen's and ladies' waiting-rooms; toilet-rooms; ticket-office; vault; dining-room; lunch-counter; news-room; kitchen; boiler-room; baggage-room; train-despatcher's office; conductors' room; and customs-officers' room. The second floor has the general offices for the road.

Passenger Depot at Sheridan Park, Ill., Chicago, Milwaukee & St. Paul Railroad.—The passenger depot of the Chicago, Milwaukee & St. Paul Railroad at Sheridan Park, Ill., which is a picturesque, substantially built single-story structure, with prominent clock-tower, designed by Messrs. Holabird & Roche, architects, is illustrated in the *Inland Architect and News Record*, Vol. 19, No. 2.

Passenger Depot at Newark, N. J., Pennsylvania Railroad.—The new passenger depot of the Pennsylvania Railroad at Market Street, Newark, N. J., designed under the direction of Mr. Wm. H. Brown, Chief Engineer, Penn. R. R., described and illustrated in the issue of *Engineering News* of February 14, 1891, built in 1890 under the direction of Mr. E. F. Brooks, Engineer Maintenance of Way, P. R. R., to replace the old island-station building at this point, is a handsome side-depot, with an auxiliary building on the other side of the tracks, the two buildings being connected by a subway under the tracks. The buildings are built of dark-red brick, with brown stone trimmings, and the inside is finished in oak and light-colored woods. The arrangement of the ground-plan, and especially the successful design of the subway, so as to render this underground passage-way as unobjectionable to passengers as possible, are noteworthy features, and deserve attention.

FIG. 621.—PERSPECTIVE.

Passenger Depot at Windsor Park, Ill.—The passenger depot at Windsor Park, Ill., is shown in Fig. 621, prepared from a photograph. The building is a small two-story stone structure with a covered platform running along the railroad track.

CHAPTER XXII.

TERMINAL PASSENGER DEPOTS.

TERMINAL passenger depots are buildings erected for the accommodation of the passenger service at passenger terminals of a railroad. Frequently, several railroads entering the same town unite and use conjointly a so-called "Union Depot." It follows, therefore, that terminal passenger depots are located in large cities or towns, or at ferry terminals, or at important junction points of several railroads. As a rule, all the tracks of a railroad terminate at a terminal station, but very frequently certain tracks run past the depot, while others terminate at the depot. It will be readily recognized that the requirements and conditions will vary materially in each locality and at each point in question, so that it is practically impossible to establish any but the most general rules for guidance in planning such structures.

Relative to the general style and size to be adopted for a terminal depot building, the choice will depend to a large extent on the proposed location with reference to the topographical features of the site; the amount and shape of the land available; the location and elevation of the tracks in relation to neighboring streets; the location of the track approaches with reference to the terminal site selected; the facilities required; and the importance of the locality. A terminal depot involves such heavy expenditures, that it is a mistake to build it at the start on too small outlines. The size and ground-plan layout should correspond not only to the actual requirements of the business to be expected in the near future, but should be planned for the largest possible growth of the business, that can be plausibly expected for a long term of years, as subsequent alterations or enlargements of a previously adopted plan on a smaller scale are very difficult and expensive to make. The importance of planning for the future should be especially emphasized in acquiring terminal lands, as additional ground can be obtained prior to the construction of a terminal depot at much less rates than if the railroad company waits till the value of neighboring property is not only enhanced, but the necessity for acquiring the adjoining tracts becomes a vital railroad question of public importance. It is far preferable to build at first only part of a large layout, extending the buildings and adding extra facilities and more permanent arrangements as the business increases and the railroad company's exchequer allows it. Thus an extensive train-shed can be replaced temporarily by platform shed roofs, or the length of the shed reduced and covered platforms run out along the tracks beyond the shed, or the width of the shed reduced to one span, if the final plan contemplates several spans. The accommodations for baggage, express, mail, emigrants, etc., which are usually provided for in wings, detached buildings, or end pavilions, can be furnished of a more temporary nature or provided elsewhere temporarily. The import of these remarks is to emphasize the necessity in building a large railroad terminal of acquiring sufficient land at the start and making the general plans to cover the probable requirements for a great many years, even if all the ground is not occupied at once or the entire building erected immediately as planned. The class of building materials to use and the general finish of the building will depend on the amount of money available for the structure and the class of materials in general use or easily obtainable in each particular section of the country. It can be said, however, that, owing to the importance and cost of the structure, together with the serious difficulties and delays that would result to the entire passenger business of the road in case of a fire, it is desirable to have as fire-proof a structure as possible, equipped with the best fire-service provisions.

Relative to the style of architecture to be adopted for a terminal passenger depot, it will depend, more or less, on the importance of the station, the surroundings, the proximity and style of neighboring buildings, the size of the structure, the desires of the railroad management, the wishes of the public, the prevailing class of architecture and building materials in general use in the locality in question, and the individual views of the architect making the design. It follows, therefore, that no general style can be recommended for the exteriors of terminal passenger depots, nor would it be desirable to attempt to mould all such structures after the same pattern. Railroad managers in aiming to obtain the most artistic design for the exterior of a depot should rely on asking a number of architects for general plans or offering a prize competition based upon a general specification, in preference to establishing peremptory requirements for the exterior of the building, while the whole plan is still in an unsettled, chaotic state. In general, however, it can be said, that the character of the building should be expressed to a certain extent in its exterior, the structure should be built on broader and grander lines than local depots, presenting a bold and prominent front, relieved, however, by suitable disposition and divisions of the wall surface, the fenestration, roof lines, and other details, without detracting from the general features of the design as a whole. It will also prove better to follow, as a rule, well-established styles as precedents, applying the same principles modified to suit each individual case, in preference to attempting to produce something absolutely new and unique, which generally results in presenting for the edification of the inartistic public a kaleidoscopic conglomeration of architectural odds and ends from different climes and centuries. Attention should also be called to the absolute necessity of allowing in terminal passenger depots the requirements of the ground-plan to have actual precedence over the purely architectural features of the structure, as a defect of the ground-plan layout in a large depot is more serious than in smaller depots, causing not only constant annoyance and trouble, but entailing frequently for years afterwards continual outlays for increased expense in conducting the business or operating the various branches of the service at the terminal.

Terminal passenger stations can be divided into side-stations and head-stations. At side-stations the depot building is situated on one side of the tracks, at head-stations across the dead-end of the tracks. At some side-stations there are depot buildings on both sides of the tracks: either the main building is on one side and some auxiliary facilities for baggage, express, or waiting rooms on the other side, or there are main buildings on both sides, with a more or less double complement of accommodations for the passenger and baggage service, in which case the station is called a twin-station. Head-depots are frequently built with wings extending from the head-house along one side or both sides of the tracks, forming respectively an L or a U shaped building. In this way some of the features of side-depots are blended into a head-depot design.

In terminal passenger depots provision has to be made for a very large number of facilities and accommodations for the different branches of the service. Any one perusing the list given below will be impressed at once with the magnitude of the problem, when it is considered that all these interests, as far as required in any particular case, have to be provided for and placed not only in their proper position in the building as a whole, but also in suitable relation to each other. In some cases duplicate accommodations have to be provided, so as to cover the "in" and the "out" business in each branch; or, where several railroads use the same terminal depot, separate ticket-offices, waiting-rooms, or baggage-rooms are frequently demanded.

The facilities and accommodations at terminal passenger depots, that have to be provided to a greater or less extent according to the requirements in each particular case, and which are actually found in use in terminal passenger depots in this country, are as follows, grouped to the various branches of the service:

1. *Passenger Service.*—Waiting-rooms, consisting of, or a combination of, a general waiting-room, a gentleman's waiting-room, a ladies' waiting-room, a ladies' parlor, a reading-room, and a smoking-room.

Ticket-office, with ticket-windows leading to a vestibule, or to a general waiting-room, or to one or more of the waiting-rooms; ticket-agent's private office and vault.

Ticket-office for sleeping or palace car service.

Dressing-room, toilet-room, and lavatory for ladies.

Toilet-room, barber-shop, and boot-black stand for gentlemen.

Public telegraph, telephone, messenger service, U. S. mail-box, and express-office.

Parcel, hand-baggage, or coat room.

Bureau of information and time-table stand.

Newspaper and book stand.

Cigar, fruit, candy, soda-water counter, and flower-stand.

Lunch-counter, oyster-counter, bar, coffee-stand, restaurant, general dining-room, ladies' dining-room, ladies' lunch-room or lunch-counter, dining-rooms for private parties, etc., with all the necessary appurtenances, such as kitchen, pantries, serving-room, store-rooms, refrigerator-room, cellar, dumb-waiters, elevator for supplies, and sleeping quarters for the manager or the help.

Reception-room for conferences or receiving prominent travellers.

Waiting-room for emigrants, with toilet-rooms for men and for women, lunch-counter, coffee-stand, emigrant-agent's office, etc.

Waiting-rooms for colored people, frequently with separate toilet-rooms and a special ticket-window from the ticket-office leading into the waiting-room or on to a platform.

Waiting-room or a suite of waiting-rooms, with all conveniences, etc., for travellers forced to remain at the depot for considerable time between trains.

Cab, carriage, and omnibus stand or court, with agent's office and room for hackmen.

Entrance vestibules, lobbies near the trains for outgoing crowds to congregate in, and departure platforms.

Arriving platforms and exits for incoming travel.

Projecting awnings, shed roofs, or a *porte cochère* for passengers arriving or departing in carriages or omnibuses.

Elevators for passengers, or at least for invalids, where the track is not on the same level with the street.

2. *Baggage, Express, and Mail Service.*—Baggage-rooms, consisting of, or a combination of, a general baggage-room, receiving-room for "out-baggage," delivery-room for "in-baggage," store-rooms for lay-over baggage, for transfer baggage, or for unclaimed baggage, truck-stand, together with an office or offices for the baggage-master, clerks, porters, and others connected with the baggage business; also the necessary platform frontage for the receiving and delivery of baggage from and to wagons.

Express-rooms, consisting of, or a combination of, a general express-room, receiving-room for outgoing and delivery-room for incoming express goods, local express-room, storage-rooms, together with an office or offices for the express agent, clerks, local express or train agents, and drivers; also stand for express-wagons, etc., and the necessary platform frontage for the receiving and delivery of express goods from and to express-wagons.

U. S. mail-room, consisting of either one room or separate rooms for "in" and "out" mail; also platform frontage and stand for mail-wagons.

Rooms for custom-house officers at frontier stations, with detention and private searching rooms.

Room for dead bodies.

Elevators for baggage and express, where the track is not on the same level with the street.

3. *Station Service.*—Station-master's, train-master's, telegraph, and clerks' offices.

Gatekeepers' offices and porters' room.

Conductors' report-room, trainmen's room, and sleeping quarters for trainmen.

Lunch-room, lavatories, and toilet-rooms for employés.

Office for superintendent of railroad mail service, and room with letter-boxes for railroad mail.

Office of superintendent of sleeping, palace, or dining car service, with report-rooms for conductors, porters, etc., sleeping-quarters for lay-over men, and storage-rooms for miscellaneous supplies.

Office of superintendent of news company and store-rooms for supplies.

Room for station police or road detective force.

Physician's office, with small hospital ward for emergencies.

Water-plugs and gas-cocks along the tracks for supplying cars.

Car-cleaners' room, with racks and shelves for the sundry supplies and appliances used for cleaning cars while in the depot between runs.

Car-inspectors' room, with store-room for oil and sundry small supplies; also small work-room for making light repairs to car-fixtures.

Storage-room for ice, coal, and other supplies, required to be put on the cars before starting on a run or while stopping at the depot.

Construction-room for storage of tools, appliances, and supplies used by trackmen, painters, mechanics, and others in making repairs around the station.

Storage spaces for fire-service apparatus, chemical engines, hose-carriages, etc.

4. *Depot Service.*—Janitor's and watchmen's quarters.

Engine-room, engineer's room, engineer's work-shop for light repairs of machinery or building, pump-room, dynamo-room, boiler-room, heaters.

Lamp and oil-room, store-room for sundry supplies, fuel store.

Necessary facilities and appliances for heating, ventilating, cooling, and lighting the building.

Sleeping quarters or dwellings for janitor or other regular help employed in the building.

5. *Hotel Accommodations.*—At some terminal passenger depots, especially in the West and Southwest, a regularly equipped hotel is connected with the depot, with office, hotel lobby, restaurant and appurtenances, parlors, reading-room, writing-room, bedrooms for guests and the hotel help, toilet-rooms, lavatories, billiard-rooms, etc.

6. *General Offices.*—The upper floors of a terminal passenger depot are usually utilized to a more or less extent for offices for officials and clerks connected with the railroad or railroads using the depot, the accommodations consisting of general offices for the different departments, private offices for the chiefs of departments, vaults for documents, store-rooms for stationery and sundry supplies, directors' room, conference-room, toilet-rooms, lavatories, messenger-rooms, elevators, private entrance and staircase independent of the entrances and exits for passengers, as also in certain cases dwellings or private rooms for certain officials or employés, and a lunch-room for the officials and clerks.

The distinguishing features between a side-station and a head-station have been alluded to above. Relative, however, to the characteristic details of each class of station, it is impossible to establish any general precedent or rules, as each depot has its own peculiarities and requires special analysis, owing to the great variety of special requirements in each case, and especially on account of the restrictions and individual features introduced and controlled by the size and topographical features of the site selected and the relative location and elevation of the tracks with reference to the terminal tract and the neighboring streets. Some of the most usually adopted characteristic details of each class of station, where not absolutely controlled by local conditions, and provided the streets and the railroad tracks are about on the same level, are in general as follows.

In a side-station the entrance-hall, lobby, or general waiting-room is placed at the centre of the building, usually opposite the middle of the train shed or platforms in front of the building. The special waiting-rooms with their necessary appurtenances are located on one side of this central hall and the dining-rooms, etc., on the other side, the kitchen and other rooms connected with the dining-service being placed in a basement or more generally on an upper floor. The baggage-rooms then follow, there being very frequently two of them, one at each end of the building. The other accommodations are worked into the ground-plan to the best advantage, either in the main building or in auxiliary buildings, wings, or pavilions at the end or ends of the main building. In some cases, however, as for instance in the terminal passenger side-depot of the Atlantic Coast Line at Richmond, Va., the depot building is located alongside one end of the train shed, which offers the great advantage of passengers being able to reach the different longitudinal platforms in the train shed by using the end crosswalk immediately opposite the depot and, hence, not having to cross any tracks to get to trains on the far tracks. As all trains, however, practically stop at a terminal depot, even where some of the tracks are through tracks, the objections to allowing passengers to cross tracks at grade to get to or from trains are not so serious, provided the station tracks are properly protected by signals, and there is a fence with gates and gate-keepers provided to keep the public from overrunning the tracks indiscriminately. At a great many side-stations efficient cross-over systems and leaders are put in the tracks and thoroughly protected by interlocking signals, enabling trains to be passed speedily and safely to the tracks nearest the depot building, so that in most cases passengers do not have to cross tracks at all. As mentioned above, at some side-stations, especially where there are through tracks, there is an additional or auxiliary building with waiting-rooms and baggage-room located on the opposite side of the tracks from the main building, in which case the two buildings are generally connected by an overhead bridge or a subterranean passage, the latter being preferable, if the passage can be kept well lighted, ventilated, and drained. In some cases, however, where the street level is above the railroad tracks, an overhead bridge is the natural means for a connection between the two buildings. The adoption of such an auxiliary second building is especially indicated where there is a heavy local or suburban travel in addition to a large through travel, in which case the second building may have to be given such proportions and be so thoroughly equipped as to create a twin-station.

The most important characteristic details of the layout of a head-station, as far as they can be specified in general, are, that the entrance-hall, lobby, or general waiting-room in a regular head-depot is placed at the middle of the head-house, while in an L-shaped building it is frequently placed at the corner, although the centre of the head-house is usually preferred. The waiting-rooms and other accommodations are distributed on each side of the central hall to the best advantage. The tracks running into the station are generally divided into "in" and "out" tracks, one side of the station being reserved and planned for incoming business and the other for outgoing business. The baggage-rooms, express-offices, and other facilities are, therefore, frequently provided in duplicate, one on each side of the station, corresponding to the incoming and outgoing travel. For these purposes wings or separate buildings are run out from the head-house along the tracks on one or both sides of the station, forming respectively an L or a U shaped building, the adoption of one or the other of which styles of head depots is dependent to a large extent on the street frontage that can be obtained around the depot.

As has been previously indicated, the selection of a side-station or of a head-station is generally a matter of necessity and not a matter of choice, as the local conditions will usually predominate and govern the style of building to be adopted independent of the relative merits of the two classes of structures. In some cases, however, the site selected and the local requirements may admit of the question being raised as to the relative advantages or disadvantages of one or the other system, which are briefly, in a general way, as follows.

The principal advantages of a side-station are, that the waiting-rooms are closer to the middle of the trains for departing passengers, and that incoming passengers can reach the street by a shorter route than in a regular head-station with street frontage only along the face of the head-house. Where only one street adjoins the terminal tract, a side-depot, if feasible, offers usually a longer street frontage than obtainable for a head-station. Where all or nearly all of the tracks at the station are through tracks, a side-station has to be adopted.

The principal disadvantages of a side-station are, that passengers are obliged to cross tracks at grade to get to or from trains, although, as explained above, this objection can be partly remedied by switching the trains, where feasible, on to the tracks nearest the depot building, and also by erecting a fence in front of the building, so as to keep passengers from crossing the tracks at will. Where there are many fast through-trains, however, in connection with a heavy local travel, the objections mentioned become more serious, although they are modified to some extent by the introduction of an auxiliary building opposite the main building, connected with each other by a subterranean passage or an overhead foot-bridge, or else by the use of a twin-station layout. Further it can be said, that the superintendence of the work at a large side-station with many tracks in front of it is rendered more difficult than in a head-station, and crowds are not handled as easily, and the different classes of travel kept as independent of each other in passing through the depot as can be done with a head-station, especially an L-shaped or a U-shaped head-station with ample street frontage. As the width of a terminal tract is usually more limited than the length, it will frequently be found necessary to crowd the tracks up very close to the depot building in a side-station design, so that there is not much platform space left between the tracks and the building. The result is, that the waiting-rooms in such a depot will be more crowded at all times than in a head-station, where there is usually sufficient ground available for a large and ample crosswalk along the head-house at the dead-ends of the tracks for large outgoing crowds to collect in. Another disadvantage of a side-station is, that it is dangerous and even impossible at times to dispatch or receive several trains at the same time, and trains cannot be left standing on the tracks between runs without blocking the passage of travellers to or from other trains to a more or less extent.

The principal advantages of a head-station are, that passengers can pass to or from trains without crossing any tracks, and that any number of in-bound or out-bound trains can be discharging or receiving passengers at the same time without interfering with each other, and without any danger to the passengers. The superintendence of the work at the station is also easier, and the disposition and division of the tracks for the different classes of "in" and "out" travel much more readily established, maintained, and indicated to the travelling public. Crowds are handled with comparative ease, and the different classes of travel are readily kept distinct in passing through the depot. Outgoing crowds congregate on the crosswalk between the head-house and the ends of tracks, whence they pass to whatever platform their train adjoins, while incoming trains are generally run on to the tracks on one side of the station and the passengers pass out on that side of the building without interfering with the outgoing travel. Another very important advantage of a head-station is the ease with which additional tracks can be utilized for either the "in" or the "out" travel, according to the business at the time, without disturbing the general system governing the operation of the station. In this manner an increase of travel at any particular time of the day, as for instance the suburban travel in the morning and in the evening, or an unusual rush owing to some excursion, holiday, races, convention, etc., can be readily accommodated on short notice, and without serious interference with the regular travel at the station. A further advantage exists in the fact that an in-bound train, after discharging its passengers, can start off as an out-bound train from the same platform, if desired, without switching the train to another part of the station, which is particularly of value for local or suburban trains with short runs, where the same train passes continually back and forth. The tracks at head-stations can be used for the storage of cars, and a further advantage is, that more time can be given passengers to embark or disembark, without thereby interfering with the travel passing to or from trains on other tracks.

The principal disadvantages of head-stations are, that passengers have a much longer distance to travel on foot, and baggage has to be wheeled a much greater distance, than in a side-station, in order to pass between the train and the street or a ferry in front of the head-house. Where there is a ferry in front of the head-house, in connection with the depot, this extra distance, that has to be travelled by passengers, will affect the schedules for the train and ferry service to the extent of from one to three minutes. Where the depot, however, fronts on streets on two or three sides, the introduction of an L-shaped or a U-shaped head-depot, with the proper division of the various accommodations in the ground-plan layout, will accomplish much towards eliminating the most serious objections to head-stations. Where a head-station adjoins only one street at the face of the head-house, the street frontage will be usually more limited than in a side-station design with frontage along the side-depot. Where all the tracks are through tracks it is naturally impracticable to use a head-depot, but where only a few tracks are through tracks, they are arranged to pass by one end of the head-house. In a few individual cases, where the track level is below the street level, the through tracks at the station pass underneath the head-house.

Summing up, therefore, it can be said that for a very large terminal passenger travel, with all or most of the tracks stopping at the depot, a head-station design offers probably the most advantages, and by introducing, where feasible, some of the features of a side-station in connection with a head-station, by the construction of an L-shaped or a U-shaped depot building, much can be done to eliminate the most serious objections to a regular head-station, especially where street frontage can be obtained on several sides of the station tract.

The classification and distinctive characteristics of side-stations and head-stations having been discussed, the following general remarks applicable to all classes of terminal passenger depots, as well as to local passenger depots in a more limited sense, will prove interesting.

The waiting-rooms should be of ample size, airy, well lighted, heated, and ventilated, and comfortably fitted up. The latter feature is most essential in the special waiting-rooms, as cheerful and pleasant surroundings, especially in a ladies' waiting-room and parlor, aid materially in establishing the reputation of a railroad company for looking after the comfort of its patrons. More attention should be paid to the interior fittings and furnishing of a passenger depot, in preference to spending large sums on elaborate external ornamentation, in case the appropriation for the depot is limited. A terminal depot should always have, in addition to a central hall, vestibule, or general waiting-room, at least a special ladies' waiting-room, and preferably also a gentlemen's waiting-room. This is important, as the largest proportion of the outgoing travel will pass directly through the depot on the way to trains without much delay, and it is very objectionable to subject passengers, who have to wait some time at the depot or lay over between trains, to the annoyance of a continual stream of people passing through the waiting-room. This feature is more noticeable when there is an unusual rush, such as in the morning or in the evening, or on holidays, excursion-days, etc. For these reasons a design with a large central hall as a general waiting-room, or a generously proportioned vestibule leading from the street to the departure platforms, with all the necessary ticket-windows, counters, stands, etc, so located as to render it unnecessary for passengers to enter the special waiting-rooms, can be considered as the best practice for terminal passenger depots with a large travel.

The principal parts of a terminal depot design, which afford the architect the best opportunities to produce a pleasing and imposing effect, are the exterior *ensemble* of the structure, the entrance vestibule, the central hall or general waiting-room, and the interior of the train shed. This central hall is one of the important features of the general plan of the depot, and it is, therefore, usually designed as a large, high, and handsomely decorated room or rotunda with elaborate and effective ornamentation and fixtures. Ample light is generally introduced by windows located high enough to be above the platform and porch roofs that usually adjoin the building. The architectural treatment of these windows, and of the entrance and exit doors, the construction of the ceiling either as an open roof or with elaborate panelling, the chandeliers, the introduction of a staircase leading to trains, where different levels exist, or to the upper stories, and a gallery running around the hall for access to the rooms in the upper story, where required, together with the proper division of the wall surfaces for wall-maps, train index, standard clock, etc., and the suitable design and distribution of the sundry ticket-windows, counters, stands, and entrances to adjacent rooms and offices around the hall, all afford ample opportunities for the designer of the building to display ingenuity, good taste, and artistic ability. In some designs a great point is made of introducing an elaborate old-fashioned fireplace in the central hall, but in the author's opinion this feature is out of place in a large general waiting hall or vestibule such as described, and it will prove much more efficient to reserve it for the special waiting-rooms, where the character of the ornamentation and design of the interior should be more suggestive of home comforts, and a fireplace, therefore, forms a very appropriate element of the design. Where benches are introduced in a general waiting-room, they should be placed in the same direction as the crowds take in passing through the hall, so as to afford as little obstruction as possible, unless ample passage-ways are left on each side of the benches. The introduction of a large central hall or vestibule in a depot design will not only afford relief to the passengers occupying the special waiting-rooms by not having a continual crowd of people passing through the room with the attendant draughts and lowering of the temperature of the room in winter owing to the constant opening of the entrance and exit doors, but a large and undesirable element, such as depot loungers, laborers, hackmen, hotel porters, etc., and in Southern sections the colored element, will be more liable to patronize the general waiting-room, rendering the special waiting-rooms more quiet and select.

It is not absolutely necessary, although desirable, if feasible, to have a special gentlemen's waiting-room where there is a large and well-equipped general waiting-room. But, in any event, there should be a convenient, pleasant, and comfortably fitted up smoking-room provided. At some passenger terminals, where passengers are forced to wait considerable time between trains, when changing from one route to another, a reading-room is provided for the public.

A ladies' waiting-room should never be omitted, but should be considered as an absolute requirement. It should be fitted up comfortably, although not necessarily luxuriously. There should be, if possible, a ticket-window leading into this waiting-room from the ticket-office, or else a special ticket-window for ladies provided in the general waiting-room or vestibule, located as conveniently as feasible to the ladies' waiting-room, or to the route that ladies' would take in passing from the street to the ladies' waiting-room. It is also desirable, where possible, to have a ladies' refreshment-counter or lunch-room connected with or adjoining the ladies' waiting-room. A number of rocking-chairs and sofas, in addition to the regular seats, will prove desirable. A fireplace will add to the general appearance of the room. A very good feature to introduce in a ladies' waiting-room is to partially screen off small alcoves, or else have small separate rooms for wedding or funeral parties.

A ladies' parlor is quite a feature in a large number of depot layouts. In small terminal depots it takes the place of a special ladies' waiting-room, while in large terminal depots it forms a more select and quiet waiting-room, in addition to the special ladies' waiting-room, where there is naturally more or less bustle and passing back and forth all the time, and where gentlemen accompanying ladies are usually admitted. Hence the desirability in more ways than one of having a ladies' parlor, which also affords an excellent opportunity for catering to and obtaining the good-will of a very influential class of the travelling community. The cost of making the room luxurious, cosy, and attractive is small compared with the advantage to be gained and the cost of the entire building. The floor should be carpeted, the chairs and lounges upholstered, and the room rendered as warm, cheerful, and pleasant-looking as possible. Rocking-chairs and separate arm-chairs should be added. A small but unique fireplace will assist to give the whole room a cheerful and homelike appearance, and will, when used, especially on chilly days, relieve the atmosphere of any dampness, and also afford good ventilation.

Some of the minor but still essential provisions for the comfort of passengers are rolling-chairs for the use of invalids in passing to or from trains; stretchers for the sick or injured; and passenger elevators, at least for invalids, where the train story is not on the same level with the street. Large wall-maps, time-table racks, train index, and similar fixtures, are all valuable to assist passengers in gaining information. Drinking-fountains, water-coolers, and tables for depositing hand-baggage, the latter more particularly in the special waiting-rooms, will be found to be desirable additions.

It is necessary in some cases to provide special waiting-rooms with a more or less extensive set of appurtenances for the accommodation of travellers forced to lay over at a depot for considerable time waiting for a connecting train. In the South it is also very customary to have special waiting-rooms for colored people, frequently with a separate set of toilet-rooms. Tickets are generally sold to them from a special window leading from the ticketoffice into the waiting-room, or, where this is not feasible, there is a special ticket-window leading out to a platform in front of the building. At other points the emigrant service is such that it is necessary to provide special waiting-rooms for this class of travel, together with toilet-rooms, agent's office, etc. In order to prevent the emigrants from being swindled, and also so as to be better able to confine them to one section of the depot, it is desirable for the railroad company to see that a coffee-stand and lunch-counter is furnished and run properly in connection with the emigrant quarters. Finally, special mention can be made of the fact that at several depots in this country there is a spacious reception-room provided, usually in an upper story, for the holding of railroad conferences or the reception of prominent travellers.

In connection with waiting-rooms, the disposition of the lavatories, toilet-rooms, etc., is most important. The facilities in this line furnished for gentlemen consist of a toilet-room, lavatory, boot-black stand, and in some cases a barber-shop. The similar accommodations for ladies consist of a dressing-room, lavatory, and toilet-room. In some cases these conveniences are merged into one room for each class. It is very bad practice to allow the toilet-room for gentlemen or for ladies to open directly from a central hall or general waiting-room. There is no objection to a toilet-room leading directly from a gentlemen's or a ladies' special waiting-room or from a ladies' parlor or a smoking-room. Where there is a ladies' parlor in connection with a special ladies' waiting-room, however, it will prove preferable not to make the ladies' parlor a thoroughfare to the toilet-room, provided a dressing and lavatory room can adjoin the special ladies' waiting-room and serve for the passage-way to the toilet-room proper. Relative to the gentlemen's lavatory and toilet-room, it will prove advantageous to have a second entrance to it from one of the platforms on the outside of the building, as thus a constant passage of men through the gentlemen's waiting-room or the smoking-room will be prevented to a large extent. The objection usually made to this is that cleanliness is very hard to maintain when the toilet-room is accessible from the outside of the building, but as a porter has to be kept anyhow to look after these rooms in a depot of any size, it should not be difficult to enforce regulations and exclude undesirable parties. Where a ladies' waiting-room is open to some extent on the side next to the hall or general waiting-room, it is desirable to place the door leading to the dressing or toilet room either on a side of the room where it cannot be readily seen from the corridor or general waiting-room, or else to mask the entrance by a screen, a light partition, or shrubbery.

Relative to the ticket office or offices, they should be so located as to enable tickets to be sold not only to the central hall or general waiting-room, but also, if possible, to the ladies' waiting-room, and, where feasible, also to the gentlemen's waiting-room. Where it is impossible to have a ticket-window leading into the ladies' waiting-room, then there should be special windows for ladies provided in the central hall. There are frequently several ticket-offices or at least several ticket-windows provided for the different roads, routes, or classes of travel, or for use when the travel is unusually large. The main point to observe in locating a ticket-office, however, is to place it adjacent to the route that travellers usually take in passing from the street to the trains, with due regard to the fact that they have to get their tickets before they can check their baggage, and that they should not be required to retrace their steps, if possible. It is not necessary that the ticket-office should be located on the train side of the depot, although a ticket-agent can thereby keep better posted as to the movements of trains; and by having a ticket-window leading out on the platform facing the trains, through travellers, arriving at the depot on a train and forced to buy another ticket in only a few minutes' time, can be better accommodated. This latter point is not considered very essential in this country, although where it can be introduced without harming the location of the ticket-office for other purposes, it is just as well to do so. Where one ticket-agent has to serve at several windows, the windows should not be placed too far apart, but ample space should be left for shelves and ticket-racks between them. Good light should be provided at day and at night on both sides of the ticket-windows. Guard-railings are necessary outside the ticket-windows to keep passengers from crowding from all directions up to the windows. Ample shelves or racks should be provided at and near the windows, so that passengers can deposit their hand-baggage, umbrellas, or bundles while purchasing tickets. Finally, attention should be called to the necessity of making a ticket-office at a terminal depot large enough to accommodate not only the agent and clerks, but also the large number of ticket-cases, time-table racks, and other furniture that form the necessary appurtenances of a ticket-office. A designer of a depot familiar with the requirements at terminal depots will endeavor to give the ticket agent a large, well-lighted, and well-ventilated space, and not expect the enormous business that is done in a ticket-office to be conducted in a small kiosk or booth framed into one corner of the central hall. It is better to provide too much space and too many ticket-windows, than to err in the other direction. The ticket-offices for the sleeping or palace car service are frequently kept separate from the regular ticket-offices, or at least a separate ticket-window is provided for selling sleeping or palace car tickets. This window should lead on to the central vestibule, hall, or general waiting-room.

In addition to waiting-rooms and ticket offices, provision has to be made to a greater or less extent for a number of features, such as a public telegraph-office; telephone and messenger service; U. S. mail-box; express-office; carriage-office; parcel, hand-baggage, or coat room; newspaper and book stand; cigar, fruit, candy, and soda-water counter; a flower-stand; and a bureau of information. Suitable accommodations for all of these facilities and features should be provided, as far as possible, along the route taken by passengers in passing from the street to trains, in other words, they should be distributed at appropriate places along the entrance vestibule, central hall, or general waiting-room. At the telegraph-office there should be ample facilities for writing messages, and shelves should be provided to allow passengers to deposit hand baggage and bundles while thus engaged. It is desirable to have the telegraph-office and the mail-box as near the train side of the general waiting-room as possible, so that through passengers with only a few minutes to spare can make use of them more readily. It is also desirable to have the bureau of information near the trains or opening on to the lobby or platform next to the trains, where outgoing crowds congregate.

Relative to the dining-rooms, restaurant, lunch-counters, etc., and the necessary appurtenances, it can be said that the extent and the general arrangement of the accommodations for these facilities will depend entirely on local conditions. At some stations the proximity of hotels, restaurants, and bar-rooms makes it unnecessary to give much attention to them, while at other stations the facilities and equipment for this branch of the service are very complete. This is especially the case where the station is used very extensively for a meal station for through-trains, or where there is a hotel connected with the depot. Where the station serves as a meal station, the principal feature to observe is to locate the dining and lunch rooms as near the trains as feasible, and to give quick and easy means of ingress and egress from and to trains without, if possible, passing through the waiting-rooms. Where the service, however, is mainly for the local travel, the accommodations form part of the general layout of the depot, and should be worked into the ground-plan to the best advantage. As mentioned above, it is a very good feature to introduce a ladies' lunch-counter or lunch-room adjacent to the ladies' waiting-room. Otherwise, however, as far as the local travel is concerned, there is no absolute necessity of any special location of the dining and lunching rooms, provided they are accessible from the vestibule or general waiting-room.

Relative to the entrance and exit doors of the central vestibule or general waiting-room, they should be so arranged that passengers can pass by them on the shortest route from the street to the trains. Where the doors leading from the waiting-room to the train side of the house are kept closed till trains are ready for passengers, it is desirable to have the doors open with the crowd and not against it. Where feasible, however, as previously indicated, it is better practice to provide a lobby or covered platform for outgoing crowds to congregate in between the depot building and the departure platforms, thereby relieving the waiting-rooms considerably at times of an unusual rush of travel. If benches are added, and a drinking-fountain with running water provided in this lobby, it will be found that a great many people will prefer to remain outside the building, and a very undesirable element, such as depot loungers, laborers, colored people, hackmen, runners, and others will be drawn away from the waiting-rooms. A fence with gates and gate-keepers serves to control the crowd and keep them from spreading indiscriminately over the station. In handling passengers at depots the great feature to observe is to keep crowds moving in different directions from meeting each other. Incoming passengers generally disembark on special arrival platforms located on one side of the station, and pass thence to the street on that side of the station or through special exits or passages through the depot building to the street. This is more easily accomplished in head-stations than in side-stations. At the latter, owing to the extreme frontage of the building on the tracks, it is necessary to provide special exits or corridors leading through the building to the street. These passages are very important in a large terminal depot, as they enable arriving passengers to leave the platforms sooner. The passage of arriving passengers through the waiting-rooms or vestibules, used for outgoing travel in passing to trains, should never be allowed. In designing the special exits for incoming passengers, however, care should be taken that the ground-plan layout of the entire building, especially with a view to the accommodation of the outgoing and through travel, is not seriously interfered with. Where the train story is on a different level from the street, stairs have to be provided. They should be wide and ample to accommodate the largest crowds, and have broad treads with easy risers, and the flight be suitably broken by landings.

For the accommodation of passengers arriving or departing in carriages, cabs, or omnibuses, it is desirable to have projecting awnings or a *porte cochère* at the entrance to the building for outgoing passengers, and projecting awnings or a regular shed roof or covered carriage court for carriages and omnibuses for the incoming travel. More space and frontage is required for the incoming travel than for the outbound passengers, as the latter alight from the carriages and omnibuses at once, while carriages and omnibuses for the incoming travel have to line up and wait considerable time. In this connection attention should be called to the desirability of enforcing strict rules excluding hackmen from the waiting-rooms. A small room provided for them adjacent to the carriage-stand would do much towards keeping them in the background until wanted. Where the street level is below the track level, a carriage court is frequently created on a level with the street below the train-shed or main building.

The baggage-rooms at large terminal passenger depots have to be designed and located with considerable care and forethought, as an injudicious choice of location or too small facilities will entail in after years continually increased expenses for the handling of baggage. A clear and distinct conception should be had of the methods to be employed in handling the baggage to and from wagons and trains, and the accommodations located accordingly. Where several railroads use the same depot building there are in some cases a number of baggage-rooms. In most instances, however, the division of the baggage service consists of separating the "in" and "out" baggage, and locating the respective baggage-rooms with reference to the street delivery and the location of the baggage-cars of inbound and outbound trains when standing in the station. In side-stations there is usually a baggage-room at each end of the depot building. In side-stations with an auxiliary building opposite the main building and in twin-stations there is a baggage-room on both sides of the tracks. In head-stations there are usually two baggage-rooms, one on the side of the station where the departure platforms are mainly situated, and one on the side of the arrival platforms. In regard to the facilities required for the two classes of baggage, it can be said that "out" baggage is received at the outbound baggage-room at all times from express-wagons and other vehicles, especially shortly prior to train time. There must be sufficient storage space provided to store baggage delivered thus until it is claimed and checked by passengers. It is then loaded on trucks and transferred to the train. Inbound baggage is mostly claimed on the platform or baggage-trucks, as soon as unloaded from the train, by owners, drivers, hotel porters, and especially express agents, who hold the checks of the passengers. The inbound express-room, therefore, should be located conveniently to the arrival platforms and to the place where the inbound baggage is trucked to, so that the delivery of baggage to the express company can be made quickly and at once, relieving the railroad company of the necessity of storing the baggage. The result is that the floor-space of the "in" baggage-room can be much smaller than the "out" baggage-room, especially if a store-room is provided for left-over or baggage unclaimed after a certain time. One of the principal points to observe is to endeavor to have the baggage-trucks in their passage to and from trains interfere as little as possible with passengers going to or from trains, and that the trucking distance for each class of baggage should be reduced to a minimum. The accumulation of baggage on the platforms adjacent to the baggage-rooms should not be allowed, if the passenger service is thereby interfered with. The location of the inbound baggage-room should be such, if feasible, that passengers on the way from the arrival platforms to the street or ferry, if there is one, can look after their baggage without making too circuitous a route. The location of the outbound baggage-room should be near the waiting-rooms. The street-delivery side should be near the main passenger entrance, if feasible, so that passengers arriving in carriages or omnibuses with their baggage with them can see it properly delivered at the baggage-room. It is further good practice, if feasible, to have an opening or a window or a corridor leading from the central vestibule, hall, or general waiting-room to the baggage-room, so that passengers after purchasing their tickets can go to the baggage-room and check their hand-baggage, as well as heavier baggage previously delivered, without going outside of the building. Where the train story is on a different level from the street the baggage-rooms are located on the street level and the baggage is transferred on baggage-trucks by means of hydraulic platform-hoists to and from the train story. The baggage-rooms are provided with platform scales for weighing baggage; also the necessary baggage-counters for receiving baggage. Additional wall-surface for the storage of the large number of checks, that have to be kept in a baggage-room at a large terminal depot, is frequently made available by having a light gallery running around the baggage-room, the upper parts of the walls being studded with baggage-check hooks. Offices for the baggage-master and clerks have to be provided; also storage space for baggage-trucks.

The general remarks relative to the baggage service hold good to a large extent respecting the express business, with exception that the express-rooms do not have to be absolutely near any of the waiting-rooms.

Relative to the accommodations to be furnished for the various branches of the station and depot service it can be said, that they should be worked into the general layout to the best advantage possible, taking all circumstances into account. Special rules cannot be given, as the individual requirements and local conditions in each case will govern the choice materially.

Where hotel accommodations have to be provided, attention should be paid to keeping the part of the building reserved for the passenger business as distinct as feasible from the hotel section. Where a hotel is connected with a terminal passenger depot, the dining and restaurant facilities of the hotel proper serve for passengers, although in some cases there are additional private dining-rooms for more permanent guests of the hotel.

In the designing of general offices in connection with a terminal passenger depot, the same rules and requirements will govern the layout as in any office building. The general offices should, however, be kept distinct from the part of the building used by passengers, which is generally not difficult to accomplish, as the upper stories of the building are used mainly for offices, while the accommodations for passengers are on the ground-floor. The entrance and stairs leading to the general offices should be entirely independent of any entrance, vestibule, or central hall used by passengers, if the design will allow it. A separate private stairway and exit should be provided from the general offices to the train-shed.

Relative to the floors and platforms in a terminal passenger depot, similar remarks will hold good as made above in the chapter on Platforms, etc. In the entrance lobbies, vestibules, central hall, or general waiting-room, where there is a large amount of travel passing continually, an asphalt, tiled, or flagged floor will prove the best. A tile floor of suitable colors and pattern will add to the general appearance of the rooms and produce a warmer effect. If stone plinths are used at the base of the side walls, in place of wooden wash-boards, the floor can be washed more freely and readily without damaging the woodwork. In the special waiting-rooms and dining-rooms a wooden floor will be more suitable, although tile floors are sometimes used. Baggage-rooms and express-rooms are usually floored with wood, asphalt, or stone flagging. Platforms have either wood, asphalt, stone flagging, or "granolithic concrete" for a floor. The relative advantages and disadvantages of different classes of flooring materials have been discussed fully in the chapter on Platforms, etc. It can be said, however, that for platforms under cover, as for instance the platforms in a train-shed or under shed roofs and projecting awnings, wood, on account of being protected from the weather, will prove fairly durable, while an asphalt floor will not be heated by the rays of the sun, and will therefore prove less objectionable to passengers and less liable to be damaged by trucks passing over it. A floor of "granolithic concrete" is being used very extensively for platforms in a great many of the large terminal depots of the country. It makes an excellent floor, but unless truck-wheels are rubber-tired it will be found to chip easily. Wagon-courts and driveways for wagons or carriages should be paved with Belgian blocks or asphalt, where the travel is heavy. In some cases macadam roads are used. In selecting the proper flooring material for platforms, due regard should be paid to the fact that repairs are not only costly to make, but are attended with considerable annoyance to passengers and disturbance of the working routine of the station service. The flooring material should be durable, not slippery, comfortable for passengers to walk and stand on, reasonably smooth for trucking, and easily cleaned. In regard to this latter feature, a floor that can be flushed with water without damage and that dries quickly afterwards, will prove most advantageous.

The heating, ventilating, lighting, and plumbing of a terminal passenger depot should be the very best obtainable, consistent with the class of building adopted and the available appropriation. The heating should be by furnaces or by steam. Fireplaces in the waiting-rooms and principal offices add not only to the finish of the interior, but afford a good chance to warm the rooms and brighten them up in damp, chilly weather, when the regular heating of the building is suspended, and also offer good ventilation. Relative to ventilation of the building, it should be first-class, as it is very objectionable to passengers to be obliged to remain in close and badly ventilated rooms. The waiting-rooms, dining and restaurant rooms should be high and airy apartments, especially the general waiting-room. Mechanical ventilation should be introduced, where required, more particularly in the smaller offices. The lighting of the building should be by gas or electricity. The plumbing should be of the best kind possible. Water-closets should have, preferably, water running all the time; urinals should be furnished thus, in any event. Slate, glazed tiles, or polished marble are the best materials to use around a water-closet or urinals. The floor in a toilet-room should be made of tiles, asphalt, slate, or stone flags.

Train-sheds are used in connection with a terminal passenger depot, to cover the tracks and platforms in front of the depot on which passengers take or leave trains. At very large terminals, situated in cities, train-sheds are a necessary requirement of the depot structure; but at minor terminals, especially where the appropriation for the building is limited, satisfactory results can be practically obtained by a series of platform-sheds. If the general layout at the start is made with a view to building eventually a train-shed, when the business warrants it or funds are at hand to do so, then the introduction of temporary platform-sheds is a very commendable solution of the question. The first cost of a train-shed can also be diminished by reducing its length or omitting additional spans, where the final plan contemplates several spans, and substituting, if required, light temporary platform-sheds. At the Union Depot at Kansas City, Mo., one-legged iron platform-sheds, shown in Fig. 413, are used on the longitudinal platforms between the tracks, while large arched arcades, 50 feet in width, shown in Fig. 626, cover crosswalks connecting the longitudinal platforms with the covered platform along the face of the depot. Excepting during very stormy weather, this system provides ample protection for passengers and baggage, and offers, in addition to cheapness of first cost, the great advantages of being light, airy, and not seriously affected by smoke, soot, and the deafening noise from trains and engines, which renders a great many train-sheds very objectionable. In fact, a system of platform roofs on the longitudinal platforms, connecting at head-stations directly with the lobby or covered crosswalk in front of the head-house, and at side-stations by means of covered transverse arcades with the platform in front of the depot building, can be considered as far superior to the attempt to build a small and especially a low train-shed, in which the light and ventilation is bad, the smoke and soot a constant annoyance, while the acoustic properties are such that the noise of escaping steam from cylinders or safety-valves, the ringing of the bell, the sounds accompanying the slipping of the drivers in starting a heavy train, combined with the general confusion and bustle, all intensified by the reverberations caused by a low roof and side galleries, render the structure a nuisance to the travelling public, as well as a serious drawback to the quick and efficient despatch of the station service, where dependent on verbal communications or signals by sound. To obtain the best acoustic results a good height of the structure is most valuable, as also the absence of side galleries or low lean-to roofs on the sides of the main shed span, which are liable to catch the sounds more readily and intensify them by repeated reverberations.

The general arrangement of a train-shed is practically the same whether at a head or side station. The tracks are usually grouped in pairs, with longitudinal platforms between each pair of tracks. The tracks are connected outside the shed by leaders and crossovers, so that the tracks can be used at will for "in" or "out" trains, or through-trains run through the shed on any track desired. Interlocking switches and signals are an absolute necessity at every terminal depot of any magnitude. In this connection mention should be made, that the efficiency of the interlocking system, as far as promptness is concerned, is dependent to a much larger extent than frequently understood on establishing facilities and means for quick communication and interchange of signals between the train-despatcher, gate-keepers, train-starter, and the operations in the signal-tower outside of the depot, so that telephones, speaking-tubes, gongs, electric bells, and similar appliances, with a proper code of signals, etc., form a most valuable and essential element to any interlocking system.

The longitudinal platforms between tracks should never be less than 12 ft. wide, so as to accommodate passengers and baggage-trucks. Where posts are set on the platform, and where large crowds have to be handled, much wider platforms are used, a width of 20 or 24 ft. being quite usual. Side platforms that have only one track frontage can be made narrower. Crosswalks and outside lobbies for outgoing passengers to congregate in are made from 30 to 60 ft. wide or even more, according to the ground-space available, and the probable number of passengers to handle at unusual rushes. It is best to proportion the crosswalks or lobbies generously at the start, as it will be difficult to obtain additional space later, while they afford a most desirable means of relief in handling large numbers of passengers and prevent the overcrowding of the waiting-rooms to a great extent.

Relative to the height and spacing of platforms, in regard to the rails, reference should be made to the chapter on Platforms, Platform-sheds, and Shelters. In connection with terminal stations, however, it can be said in general, that at a great many side-stations the entire floor of the train-shed is planked at the level of the top of the rails, so that passengers can pass and baggage be trucked indiscriminately across the platforms and tracks on the shortest route. In this case all the tracks are frequently located close together without any longitudinal spaces for platforms between them. Longitudinal platforms between tracks at head-stations and also at side-stations, where used, are generally set from 6 to 12 in. above the top of the rail, and approach the centre of the track within 4 ft. 6 in. to 5 ft.

In regard to the grouping of the tracks and longitudinal platforms the following general remarks can be made. As previously stated, in side-stations the tracks are either located close together and floored over throughout level with the top of the rails, or else they are grouped in pairs, with longitudinal platforms between the pairs and connected by crosswalks with the main platform in front of the side building. At head-stations with only two tracks running into the depot there can be either one, two, or three platforms. In the first case the platform is located between the tracks and used for passengers and baggage service,—which, for instance, is the system in use at the terminal head-station of the Boston & Providence Railroad at Stoughton, Mass.: in the second case there are two platforms, one on each side of the pair of tracks, one platform being used for inbound and the other for outbound business; in the third case mentioned, there is a third platform added between the tracks, which central platform is used for baggage exclusively, as for instance the case at the depot of the New York & New England Railroad at Boston, Mass. Where there are more than two tracks running into a head-station, the tracks are usually grouped in pairs, with platforms between the pairs. The spacing of the tracks and platforms in connection with the train-shed construction is frequently such that an odd track is located on the outside of the shed proper, generally, however, covered in part by the roof projection of the main shed. In the proposed design for the train-shed of the Illinois Central Railroad at Chicago, Ill., the roof projection of the main shed is 36 ft. wide, so as to cover two tracks and a platform. In a few cases three or more tracks are grouped together between the longitudinal platforms, in place of the more usually adopted grouping in pairs. The middle tracks serve in such a case for the storage of cars.

Relative to the general construction to be adopted for a train-shed, reference has been made above to the desirability of having a high shed, constructed on good acoustic principles, and well lighted and ventilated. This is especially essential where the sides of the train-shed are enclosed practically solid on three sides by buildings or walls,—as for instance at a head-station. Where the shed is more or less open on the sides and at both ends, as frequently the case at side-stations, the nuisance from smoke and excessive noises will be greatly reduced. Ventilation is usually secured by a clere-story with louvred ventilator or movable sash built in the roof. As the gases accumulating in a train-shed are particularly injurious to iron work, and the peak of the roof forms a pocket to catch and hold them, it is very essential to provide some means of ventilation at the peak itself independent of other openings of the sides of the clere-story. Good light is obtained in the interior of a train-shed by introducing a large number of windows in the sides of the shed, where closed; also by windows and sky-lights in the clere-story and roof. Too many skylights in the roof proper is objectionable, as it will make the shed very hot in summer. The ends of a train-shed are usually closed to within 20 to 25 ft. of the rails. It is best to place as many windows as possible in these ends, as they assist materially in lighting up the interior of the shed. These end partitions have to be very thoroughly braced so as to withstand the wind pressure from the outside. The general light effect inside the shed will be greatly improved by painting the interior in light colors. The lighting of the shed at night should be preferably by gas or electric lights.

Train-sheds are usually built with iron roof-trusses resting on stone or brick side walls or on iron columns, covered with boards on wooden rafters or purlins, and roofed with tin on tarred felt or building-paper. The exposure of so much iron-work to the deteriorating effects of the sulphurous gases collecting under the roof is very objectionable. Skylights are very hard to keep water-tight in consequence of the constant damage being done by these gases. It can, therefore, be said, that practically repairs are constantly required in a large train-shed, if painting is included; in fact it is very seldom that painting or repair work of some kind is not going on inside or outside of a train-shed. For this reason prominent railroad men have frequently expressed it as their opinion, that the general adoption of iron for train-sheds cannot be considered as such an excellent innovation, as a heavily timbered roof or a combination roof has some decided advantages over an all-iron roof. The roof-trusses in train-sheds are usually spaced from 20 to 40 ft. apart. The longitudinal and sway bracing is very important so as to resist the wind-pressure.

Relative to the roof construction of a train-shed it can be said, that the general effect of the interior and its structural efficiency depend largely on the appropriate and artistic design of the roof. The engineering and architectural features of large-span train-sheds are blended to such an extent, that the greatest care should be observed to bring the best talent and experience to bear in every direction in making the plans. The number of tracks and platforms to be spanned determine to a great extent the general design to be adopted for the roof. Where there are only about six tracks to cover,—in other words, a width of about 100 to 120 ft.,—a single span is usually adopted, supported at the ends on the side walls or else on columns, with roof projections on the outside. Where there are additional tracks to cover, it is customary to make two or more small spans adjacent to each other,—in other words, to build a series of symmetrical roofs parallel to each other. Or the width is divided into one large central span, flanked by two or more smaller side spans. The next step is the adoption of one large roof span, resting on the side walls, or else supported on piers or columns at the ends and provided with cantilevered roof projections outside of the main span. The construction in each case can consist of either flat straight roofs or else curvilinear roofs. The curved roofs have the decided advantage of presenting a more graceful appearance, and they can be treated in a more artistic manner. A roof design should, however, primarily impress itself on the observer by its simplicity and the perfect fitness of all its parts in a structural sense, giving at once the appearance of strength combined with utility. Where, in addition to these necessary elements, a graceful contour can be obtained, and details are worked up artistically, the design should certainly prove meritorious. For large spans, arched constructions are almost universally used in this country; and we can point with pride to the fact that the largest existing single-span train-sheds are in this country,—one at the depot of the Pennsylvania Railroad at Jersey City, N. J., the width being 256 ft. out to out of truss and 252 ft. 8 in. centre to centre of end-pins; while the other one is at the depot of the Philadelphia & Reading Railroad at Philadelphia, Pa., which is the largest existing single-span train-shed, namely, 262 ft. 3 in. out to out of truss, 253 ft. 8 in. clear span inside measurement, and 259 ft. 8 in. centre to centre of end-pins. In addition, the Pennsylvania Railroad proposes to build a train-shed in Philadelphia, Pa., with a clear span of 294 ft. The train-shed at St. Pancras Station, London, England, has a clear span of only 243 ft.

The following summary data as to the size of different passenger train-sheds in this country have been compiled from different sources:

1. *Side-stations.*—Union Depot, Worcester, Mass.: length 504 ft.; width 250 ft., in two spans; stone segmental arch, with a clear span of 120 ft. at each end of the train-shed.

Concord Railroad, Concord, N. H.: length 770 ft.; width 120 ft.; flat straight roof, in one span.

Atlantic Coast Line, Richmond, Va.: length 486 ft.; width 76 ft. centre to centre of columns, and 92 ft. including overhang; one-span, straight flat roof.

Union Depot, Canal Street, Chicago, Ill.: length 1100 ft.; width 100 ft.

Chicago & Northwestern Railroad, Milwaukee, Wis.: length 440 ft.; 4 tracks.

Milwaukee & St. Paul Railway, Milwaukee, Wis.: length 600 ft.; width 100 ft.

Union Depot, Indianapolis, Ind.; length 700 ft.; width 180 ft., in 2 spans.

Philadelphia, Wilmington & Baltimore Railroad (Pennsylvania Railroad), Charles Street, Baltimore, Md.: length 250 ft.; width 80 ft.; one-span, straight flat roof.

Pennsylvania Railroad, Harrisburg, Pa.: length 420 ft.; width 90 ft.; 4 tracks; one-span, straight flat roof.

New York, New Haven & Hartford Railroad, New Haven, Conn.: length 400 ft.; width 126 ft.; 2 spans, each 63 ft.; 8 tracks.

2. *Head-stations.*—Baltimore & Potomac Railroad (Pennsylvania Railroad), Washington, D. C.: length 510 ft.; width 130 ft.

Pennsylvania Railroad, Broad Street, Philadelphia, Pa.: length 450 ft.; width 170 ft., in two spans; eight tracks.

New York, Lake Erie & Western Railroad, Rochester, N. Y.: length 270 ft.; width 72 ft.

Louisville & Nashville Railroad, Louisville, Ky.: length 400 ft.; width 100 ft.; five tracks.

Union Depot, Cincinnati, O.: length 700 ft.; ten tracks.

Pittsburg, Cincinnati & St. Louis Railway, Cincinnati, O.: length 360 ft.; width 85 ft.; four tracks inside, two tracks outside.

Canadian Pacific Railway, Montreal, Can.: length 500 ft.

Wisconsin Central Railway, Chicago, Ill.: length 560 ft.; width 119 ft., with overhang 143 ft.; six tracks inside.

Chicago & Northwestern Railroad, Chicago, Ill.: length 400 ft.; width 125 ft.

Chicago & Western Indiana Railroad, Chicago, Ill.: length 600 ft.; ten tracks.

New York, Lake Erie & Western Railroad, Jersey City, N. J.: length 600 ft.; width 140 ft., consisting of one central span of 66 ft., and two side lean-to spans each of 37 ft.

Pennsylvania Railroad, Jersey City, N. J.: length 653 ft.; width 256 ft. out to out of truss and 252 ft. 8 in. centre to centre of pins; one clear-span arched roof; twelve tracks.

Grand Central Depot, Forty-second Street, New York, N. Y.: length 650 ft.; width 200 ft.; one clear-span arched roof.

Baltimore & Ohio Railroad, Pittsburg, Pa.: length 400 ft.; width 84 ft.

Central Railroad of New Jersey, Jersey City, N. J.: length 520 ft.; width 216 ft., consisting of one central span of 143 ft., and two side lean-to spans each of 36 ft. 6 in.; twelve tracks.

Illinois Central Railroad, New Orleans, La.: proposed train-shed, width 148 ft., divided into three arched spans and two cantilevered side roof projections.

Illinois Central Railroad, Chicago, Ill.: proposed train-shed, width 180 ft., one central arched span of 108 ft., with cantilevered side roof projections.

Union Depot, St. Paul, Minn.: length 640 ft.; width 165 ft.; clear-span truss roof, supported on columns with roof projections; total width covered 189 ft.

Philadelphia & Reading Railroad, Philadelphia, Pa.: length 559 ft.; width 266 ft. 6 in. over all, and 262 ft. 3 in. back to back of chords; one clear-span arched roof; span in clear at level of tracks 253 ft. 8 in. and centre to centre of end-pins 259 ft. 8 in.; height of ridge above tracks, 95 ft. 6 in. from top of rail to top of ridge skylight, and 88 ft. 3 5/16 in. centre to centre of pins vertically; thirteen tracks.

Proposed Union Depot, Buffalo, N. Y., design by Mr. C. W. Buchholz: arched roof, one clear span of 280 ft.

Proposed Terminal Passenger Depot, Chicago Elevated Railway, Chicago, Ill.: arched roof, one clear span of 289 ft.

Proposed Union Depot, St. Louis, Mo.: length 700 ft.; width 601 ft.; five spans—one span of 141 ft. 3½ in., two spans each of 139 ft. 2¼ in., and two spans each of 90 ft. 8 in.; thirty tracks.

Proposed Extension Terminal Passenger Depot, Pennsylvania Railroad, Philadelphia, Pa.: length 707 ft.; width 306 ft. 9⅝ in. over all; one clear-span arched roof; span in clear 294 ft.; height of ridge 140 ft.; height in clear 104 ft. 6 in.; sixteen tracks.

After above general remarks on the subject of terminal passenger depots and train-sheds, the following descriptions and illustrations, as also references to published descriptions and illustrations, of terminal passenger depots and train-sheds in use, or designed for use, on railroads in this country will prove interesting.

Union Passenger Depot, Hartford, Conn.—The Union Depot at Hartford, Conn., is a large terminal side-station, plans for which were published in the issue of the *Railway Review* of June 2, 1888, and it is described as follows in the publication mentioned:

The site for the depot is peculiar, the lot being long and narrow, and the tracks coming in on an elevation. The station is 480 ft. long. The trains of the New York, New Haven & Hartford and New York & New England roads come in upon an elevated structure, the tracks being about 12 ft. above the level of the floor of the waiting-room. They are approached by broad staircases 14 ft. wide, both inside the waiting-room and in the platform between the tracks. Five ways are provided, through which the passengers may reach the staircases to the platform between the tracks. These stairs are used to avoid crossing the tracks.

The main feature of the building is the great central waiting-room, two stories high, 175 ft. × 60 ft. in size. This waiting-room has three large, double entrances, opening directly into the street, and is also reached by a corridor 16 ft. broad leading from Asylum Street. This room is handsomely finished and has broad unenclosed stairways on its west side. Two ticket-offices, one for each railroad, are placed on each side of the main entrance.

The wing next Asylum Street, 40 ft. wide and 136 ft. long, contains in the first story a restaurant and lunch-room which adjoin the corridor leading to the general waiting-room. The men's toilet and the news room are also in this wing. The wing on the other side toward Church Street, 40 ft. wide and 161 ft. long, contains in the first story the rooms for the baggage and express, which are, respectively, 66 × 36 and 56 × 36. Ample exits on both sides are provided for easily handling the baggage and express matter. Women's retiring-room and toilet are placed in this wing, adjoining the general waiting-room.

In the second story, which is on a level with the railroad track, the central portion is occupied by the general waiting-room, which, as has been said, extends up through two stories. The stairs from the lower story lead to a large landing 14 ft. wide and 60 ft. long. From this landing three double entrances lead out on to the platform.

In the wing next Asylum Street there is another waiting-room, 36 ft. × 28 ft., for the accommodation of passengers who come in on one train and go out on another without having occasion to leave the station. Ample toilet-rooms for men and women are provided for this waiting-room, also a ticket and telegraph office. Adjoining the waiting-room is a lunch-room, and back of the lunch-room is the kitchen, with serving-room, pantries, etc. Dumb-waiters and stairs connect the kitchen with the restaurant and lunch-room in the lower story. A large reception-room 28 x 36 is placed on the opposite side of the waiting-room. This room is intended to be used as a meeting-room for the officers of the different roads, and as a place where any prominent visitor may be suitably received.

From a lobby opening with arches into the upper part of the general waiting-room a staircase leads to the story above the waiting-room, which is intended to be used for offices.

In the wing next Church Street are placed four offices for the use of the New York & New England Railroad Company, with separate staircase leading to the street and entrance on to the tracks. Beyond the office of the New York & New England road is a room for the accommodation of the trainmen, 12½ ft. x 36 ft. Beyond this room are the rooms for the baggage and express on the track level, each 26 x 36. These rooms connect by large hydraulic lifts with the large baggage-room and express-room below. The lifts are of sufficient size to accommodate a truck loaded with baggage. The baggage-master and express-agent have private offices in the rooms on the track level. Next to the express-room are the supply and lamp rooms. A room in the extreme end of the wing is to be used as a construction-room, 16 x 36, where sufficient implements are kept to make slight repairs when cars are injured.

There is an elevator adjoining the general waiting-room which is intended only for the use of invalids or for people so crippled as to be unable to walk up-stairs.

In the basement under the baggage and express room is placed the heating apparatus. From this cellar tunnels extend over all parts of the building in which the steam and water pipes are to be placed. Under the restaurant is a vegetable-cellar and a coal-cellar.

In front of both the wings on Union Place are projecting sheds with glass roofs under which carriages will drive up.

As to the material of the building, the exterior walls are a reddish granite with red-sandstone trimmings. The roof is covered with slate.

The interior woodwork will all be of quartered oak. The floor of the general waiting-room, corridors, restaurant, etc., will be of granolithic pavement. The walls and floors of the lavatories will all be of marble. The floors of the baggage and express offices will be of rock asphalt. All the wood wainscoting rests upon a stone plinth which rests on top of the floor, so that all the rooms can be easily washed without injuring any portion of the woodwork. Everything is made as durable as possible. Great care has been taken to provide ample ventilation for all parts of the building. The station was designed by Shepley, Rutan & Coolidge, Brookline, Mass.

Union Passenger Depot at Springfield, Mass.—The Union Depot at Springfield, Mass., plans of which were published in the *Railroad Gazette* of March 14, 1890, reproduced by permission in Figs. 622 and 623, is a large terminal side-station, with the peculiarity and distinguishing feature that there are two distinct depot buildings, practically of the same size, one on each side of the railroad; in other words, this plan presents one of the best-known examples of terminal twin depots in this country. The depot is described, in the publication mentioned, as follows:

There are two buildings, one on each side of the tracks. Each is 275 ft. long and from 54 to 70 ft. wide. There are four tracks between the buildings. Between the two middle tracks is a covered platform, 34 ft. wide and about 850 ft. long, which, with the station platforms, gives convenient access to trains on all the tracks.

The Connecticut River Railroad is to occupy the north or Liberty Street building, and the New York, New Haven & Hartford the south or Lyman Street building, while the Boston & Albany will occupy both buildings, the north building for west-bound and the south building for east-bound business. The latter building will also be used for passengers arriving or departing by the New York & New England Railroad, whose line enters this yard from the east. Besides the four main tracks just mentioned, there are spur tracks at the ends of the buildings for the Connecticut River, New York, New Haven & Hartford, and New York & New England local trains.

The buildings are constructed of red granite, from the quarries of Norcross Brothers at Milford, Mass., with trimmings of brown sandstone, the chief portions of which are richly carved. The walls of each station are built in regular courses of squared stones with a smooth quarry face. In the general waiting-room, which is the principal apartment of each building, these are carried up to a greater height than for the adjoining rooms, and effectually break the monotony which would otherwise exist in a building so long and narrow as this. The Lyman Street building especially has an imposing appearance, being surmounted by a large tower about 70 ft. square and 80 to 100 ft. high, the interior of which is open from the floor to the springing-line of the rafters. The station platforms on the side next the tracks are 24 ft. wide, and the roof is supported by yellow-pine posts about 25 ft. apart, with curved braces at the top. The ceiling of the platform roof is covered with light yellow pine sheathing, finished in the natural color of the wood. On what may be called the back side of each building, the roof projects about 7 ft., and is finished with the same general appearance as on the platforms.

The two main buildings are alike in the interior arrangement and outward appearance of many of the rooms, as well as in the details of construction; but there are important differences which will be noted later on. Beginning at the west end of each building, there is first a large baggage-room, supplied with all conveniences, including large platform-scales. Next is a waiting-room for women only, out of which opens a women's lavatory, supplied with all modern conveniences and the latest improvements in plumbing. These toilet-rooms do not occupy the whole width of the building, the remainder being taken up by a conductor's room in the north-side building, and the office of the station-agent in the south-side building. These are between the women's waiting-room and the baggage-room.

The ceiling of the women's waiting-room is supported by two timber trusses. The spaces between the rafters, as well as the walls, are ceiled with quartered oak. The same kind of finish is used in all the other rooms in both buildings, except the baggage and express rooms, the walls of which are of face brick, and the kitchen, where the walls and ceiling are of yellow pine of the same quality as for the ceilings of the platforms. There is no paint or plastering in either building. There are groups of windows on either side of the women's waiting-room, at the top of the room as well as at the usual height. These can be opened when necessary for ventilation. Doors open from this room to the platform.

Next to the women's waiting-room is the general waiting-room. That in the Liberty Street building is built with a pitch roof, the apex of which is about 50 ft. above the floor. This has the appearance of being supported by four large semicircular arches of timber, the springing-line of which is from the top of large brackets about 16 ft. from the floor. The thrust of these is sustained by ornamental iron rods which span the arch at the springing-line. Windows open at each side both at the usual level and in the top of the room. Between this room and the women's room just described, on one side of the open space in the centre, is found a parcel-room and on the other a telegraph-office, with very wide windows for receiving packages and messages.

In the centre of the general waiting-room, on the side next the track, is the ticket-office, and directly in front of it in the roof which covers the platform is a large skylight. This relieves the ticket-sellers from the oppressive darkness characteristic of this location in most large railroad stations. The general waiting-room of the Lyman Street building is 70 × 71 ft., and is surmounted by a square tower supported on brick piers, about 6 ft. square, incased in oak sheathing. Between these piers are large arched openings connecting with the women's room on the one side and the restaurant on the other. On the other sides of this room are a series of doors which lead to trains on one side and on the other to a *porte cochère* where carriages may be taken, and from which there are also flights of steps leading to Lyman Street. A broad driveway from the *porte cochère* runs east and west by an easy descent to Lyman Street. The general waiting-room is covered by a flat ceiling 50 ft. above the floor, which is set with deep panels of very rich design. These are 288 in number, and between them the beams are cased with handsome mouldings. Just below the ceiling is a row of narrow windows on the four sides of the room, which make it amply light. From the east side of the waiting-room arched openings afford communication with the restaurant. The fittings of this room are of cherry. Folding-seats are arranged around the counter, which is recurved to give a greater length, and there is a generous number of tables. From the restaurant folding-doors give access to the serving-room, furnished with steam-tables, and in the Liberty Street building stairs lead to large store-rooms in the basement, and to the kitchen above, where all the cooking for both restaurants is done. This kitchen is a model of its kind.

A dumb-waiter and elevator (which is operated by hydraulic power) connects the kitchen with the serving-room and with store-rooms in the basement. Beyond the restaurant in each building, but entirely cut off from all the other rooms, is the smoking-room, out of which opens the men's lavatory. All the toilet-rooms are wainscoted with Tennessee marble—6 ft. high around the whole room. Slabs of the same material are provided for the set wash-bowls. Washout closets are used throughout. At the extreme easterly end of each building is an express-office, which is finished like the baggage-room with face-brick walls and doors, which slide from the bottom, on the side next the tracks and also next the driveway. Outside the baggage-room at the westerly end of each building is a covered enclosure for the storage of trucks, ladders, and other articles. A subway with broad steps leading to all the platforms connects the two buildings beneath the tracks, and from either end of this a paved walk leads westward to Main Street. From the northerly side of the Liberty Street building a broad carriage-drive and sidewalk leads to Liberty Street, and there is also a flight of steps at the northeast corner of the yard for foot-passengers to descend to Liberty Street.

It was determined to heat these buildings by steam, partly by direct and partly by indirect radiation. A considerable plant was therefore necessary. The boilers are located in a building at the easterly end of the car-shops, about 1300 ft. (west) from the centre of the new station. Four Hennessey boilers of 75 horse-power each are set side by side in brickwork in the basement of the shop, and connected with an iron smoke-stack 4 ft. in diameter and 80 ft. high. The boilers are all connected with a steam-drum running the whole length and a little in front. Independent valves allow each boiler to be connected or disconnected from the steam-drum at pleasure, so that any one or more of the boilers can be used without the others, whenever desired at a moment's notice. From the steam-drum a 6-in. pipe runs underground to the cellar of the Liberty Street building. This is supported on iron rods in a brick chamber. There are manholes in this chamber, and slip joints in the pipe, every 200 ft. Between these the pipe is covered with a thick coating of abestos cement. Two smaller pipes in the same chamber return the water of condensation by

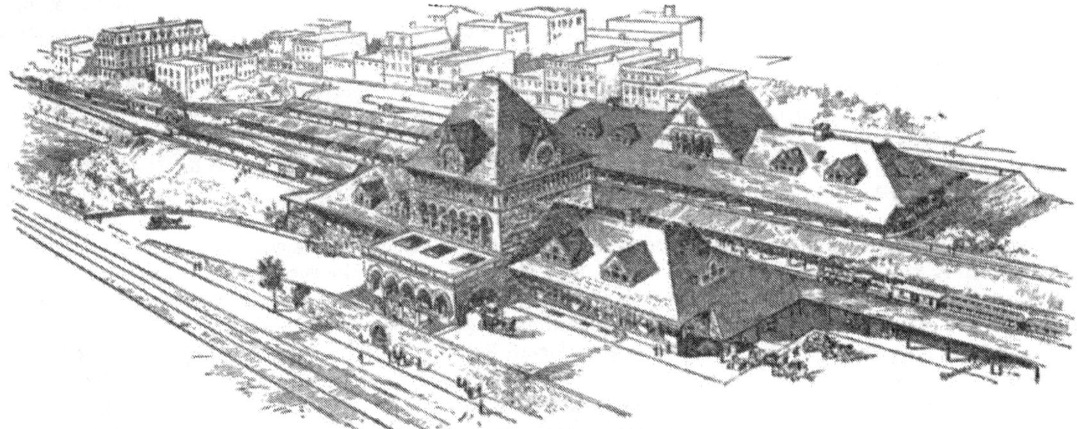

FIG. 622.—PERSPECTIVE.

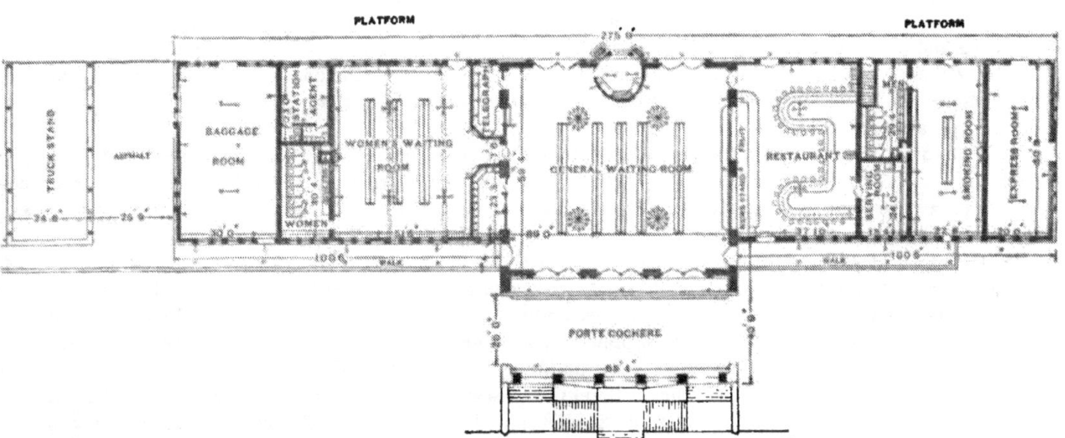

FIG. 623.—GROUND-PLAN OF MAIN FLOOR, LYMAN STREET BUILDING.

gravity to a hot-well, from which it is pumped to the boilers by two Worthington feed-pumps. The main valves, regulators, steam-traps, and pressure-gauges on each side of the main valve are located in the basement of the Liberty Street building, where the distribution begins. This can be regulated at will by means of valves, one for each branch. For indirect radiation there are also valves for each coil, which is located just below the floor of the room to be heated, and over which is a register. The coils are surrounded by a cold-air box leading from the outside of the building, with a slide to regulate the supply. A 6-in. branch from the main steam-pipe runs under the tracks to the basement of the Lyman Street building, where the steam is distributed in a similar manner. The main pipe, reduced to 4 in. in diameter, continues about one quarter of a mile farther east, where several connections furnish steam for heating the freight-offices and about twenty-five passenger-cars which stay over night at Springfield.

Only three boilers would have been needed to heat the buildings; the fourth was added to furnish steam for an electric-lighting plant. Preliminary estimates showed that these buildings could be more cheaply lighted by electricity than by gas, and that probably a considerable saving in the expense of lighting might be made if an additional boiler, and engines and dynamos for an insulated plant, were purchased. This was accordingly done.

Plans and specifications were prepared by the electrical engineer of the road. It was determined to use the Westinghouse compound engine, and, to provide as fully as possible against a breakdown which would extinguish the lights, it was decided to put in two engines, each of which should be of sufficient capacity to run the entire plant, and two dynamos, each capable of running *two thirds* of all the lights, or three dynamos, each capable of doing *one half* the entire lighting, as might be deemed best. Contractors were allowed to make their estimates on the basis of either of these plans. The arrangement of switches should be such that any of the lights could be run from either dynamo up to its full capacity, and the lighting could be transferred from one dynamo to another without extinction of the lights; that any dynamo could be started or stopped independently of the others, and finally the whole load could be transferred at any time from one engine to the other without delay or stopping either engine or any dynamo.

Several methods of doing this were proposed. In the one selected, the two engines are placed end to end in line with each other, with a shaft 4 in. in diameter and 17 ft. long between them, having a friction cut-off at each end, by which either engine may be attached or disconnected from the shaft at will. Either of the engines is of sufficient power to run the whole plant, and ordinarily only one is used; but should it be desirable at any time to change engines while running, the idle one is started, and when it has acquired its normal speed the friction coupling which unites it to the shaft is thrown in; the other one is thrown out directly after, and the engine, thus set free, is stopped at convenience. The governors were carefully set at the factory, and there is a difference of only about one revolution in the speed of the shaft, whether one or both engines are running. Two 500-light Edison dynamos are belted to this shaft with double rawhide belts, and run at a speed of 1200 revolutions per minute. (The main shaft runs 320, and the pulleys are 53 in. and 14 in., respectively.) A Brush dynamo for 16 lights is also run from the same shaft. Arc lights are used for lighting the driveways and approaches to the stations, and three roundhouses for locomotives.

Overhead wires lead from the dynamo-room to the basement of the Liberty Street building, where the distribution begins. The incandescent lamps vary from 16 C. P. to 50 C. P. The total number in use will be about 550, equivalent to about 700 of 16 C. P. Those in each room are turned on and off all at once, or in groups, by one or more switches, and those on the platforms in sections. Branches from the main wires go to the basement of the Lyman Street building, and to a set of mains for the lights in that building. The engines and dynamos are located on the floor of the shop, directly over the boilers. A 6-in. branch from the steam-drum conveys steam to the engines. The exhaust-pipe from the engines runs to a feed-water heater, and afterwards to the open air. Valves permit the heater to be shut off when desired, and the exhaust-steam then goes directly into the air.

The furnaces under the boilers are fitted to burn coal, should occasion require; but the fuel regularly used is oil. Along the front of the boilers run two pipes, one of which carries oil and the other compressed air. Three openings in the front of each boiler-setting admit a jet or nozzle, connected to both pipes. A valve in each pipe regulates the amount of air and oil. The oil is forced through a small orifice in a fine spray, and burns with a brilliant and very hot flame. To get up steam (starting with the boilers cold), a fire of wood is made under one boiler until the steam-pressure in that boiler has reached 20 lbs. The air-pump is then started and the oil turned on, the fires under the other boilers being lighted by a torch, or in any other convenient manner. The oil is supplied by a pump from two tanks of a capacity of 6000 gals. each, located underground some distance from the building. As the level of the oil is below that of the furnaces, the breaking of a pipe or valve can never flood the fires with oil, and cause a conflagration, as has happened several times in electric-light stations using oil for fuel where the supply from the tanks was kept up by gravity.

The oil and air pumps are automatic in their action, and maintain a constant pressure. The apparatus is easily managed, and works with practical perfection.

Only about 220 of the incandescent lamps are as yet in use, and for this number the consumption of oil is almost exactly 1 gal. per 16 C. P. lamp for 10½ hours (215 to 225 gals. per day), making 2¼ cents per lamp per day.

The construction of the new station was begun June 21, 1888, and the Liberty Street building was occupied July 7, 1889. The Lyman Street building will not be used until the completion of the bridge and the change in grade of the tracks. The electric lighting was put in service August 8, 1889.

The architects for the station and bridge are Shepley, Rutan & Coolidge, of Boston.

The plans and a full description of a depot at this same point, as proposed by the Boston & Albany Railroad in 1887, were published in the issue of the *Railway Review* of April 16, 1887. The final design described above, as adopted, shows two distinct buildings or twin depots, one on each side of the track. The proposal of 1887 was for a single main side-depot with a large train-shed spanning the tracks. While this proposed design was not adopted, it has a number of good features which might prove of value at points where local requirements call for the usual style of construction for a terminal side-station.

Union Passenger Depot at Worcester, Mass.—The Union Depot at Worcester, Mass., designed by Messrs. Ware & Van Brunt, architects, Boston, Mass., plans for which were published in the issue of the *Railroad Gazette* of December 18, 1875, is a large terminal station, combining some of the features of a side-station, but also of a head-station. It is one of the best-known structures of the kind in this country, owing to its original design and bold methods of construction, the entrance to the train-shed being spanned by a stone segmental arch with an opening of nearly 120 ft. in width. The building is described as follows, in the publication mentioned:

At the west end of the north section there is a projection built on a semicircle. It is generally called the round part, and is two stories high, with a nearly flat roof covered with tin. In the centre of the front is the main passenger entrance to the building. About 15 ft. from this entrance, and directly in front is a granite archway supported by double columns of granite. This is connected with the round part by a trussed roof, making three archways. The two at the sides are to be used as a driveway, thus enabling passengers to arrive and depart at all times without being exposed to the weather. On the outside of the round part a stationary awning has been built, which will cover a walk 10 ft. wide, which is to be built under it. At the northwest corner of the building is a stone tower, the cap-stone of which is 159½ feet from the ground. Above this rises a wooden extension covered with slate, 40 ft. in height, and surmounted with a rod and vane of 13 ft., making the total height 212½ ft. Near the top of the stone-work of the tower a large clock-room has been built.

The roofs of the two sections are each supported by eight heavy double trusses, one end resting on the walls of the building, the other on the girders running over the heavy iron pillars placed through the centre of the building. These two roofs are covered with slate, except a part of the two sides where they join in the centre of the building. Over this part of the roof there has been built a second roof which begins at the east and west ends of the building where it is about 3 ft. wide, and ascends with a gentle slope to the centre of the building, where it is about one third of the width of the building covered by the two roofs. This roof is made of concrete, and is built to catch the snow from the inner slopes of the two roofs, which would but for this slide down to the bottom of the pitch. The two roofs are surmounted with ventilators running the entire length of each. On the top of each is an ornamental iron railing, while over the top of each arch is a large vane. The roofs of the ventilators are covered with 7200 panes of glass, 12 x 34 in. in size, set in 360 sashes.

With the exception of a small corner in the west end of the north section of the building, and adjoining the round part, the entire area covered is to be used as a train-house for the five roads which are to concentrate there. In the centre and at the west end underground passage ways have been built. By descending into them the cars of any train can be taken without crossing the tracks. In the north section of the train-house the tracks are arranged in the following manner: First on the north side is the Boston, Barre & Gardner Railroad. Inside runs the Worcester & Nashua Railroad. These two roads enter the train-house through arches on the north side, and occupy the easterly end of the north section, the west end being used for the waiting rooms. The tracks of the other roads are in the south section of the train-house, and run through the house and under the arches at the east and west ends of this section. The first tracks on the outside are the Providence & Worcester Railroad, the next are for the Norwich & Worcester Railroad, and the inside for the Boston & Albany Railroad. The road-bed of each track is to be filled in with coal cinders, while between each an asphaltum pavement is being laid.

The waiting-rooms and business offices of the roads are located in the round part and a small portion of the west end of the north section of the building. The principal entrance to the business portion of the building is at the entrance on Washington Square and under the driveway. The large double doors open into a large, high passage-way of about 100 ft. in length. It runs through the business portion, and opens at the east end into the train-house near the Nashua tracks. That part of this passage-way which is in the round part is finished to the roof, the heavy wooden trusses which support the roof being exposed to view. Under each truss is an arch which springs from the ceilings of the rooms below. The sides of the west half of the second story are finished with windows similar to the rooms below, while the east half is left open, forming a large entry-way on each side, which is protected by a heavy rail and balustrade. At the east end of the east half is a bridge over the passage-way, connecting the two sides. The ceiling is finished in Norway hard pine, finished in oil and shellac.

That portion of this passage-way which is covered by the train-house roof is finished in the same way as the part just described, except that it is not carried up to the roof, but is built in the form of a semicircular archway. It is divided into ten sections. The arch springs from the ceiling of the rooms on the first floor, and is sheathed with hard pine, except near the top, where a space of about 12 ft. wide is covered with 20 sashes, each of which contains 12 panes of glass, 21 × 28 inches in size.

The finish of the passage-way, the two waiting-rooms, and the refreshment-room, as well as the style of architecture of the outside of the same in the train-house, is substantially alike. It is a wainscot base and Corinthian columns, with heavy capitals and cornice, the wood being brown ash finished in its natural colors. The walls in these rooms are delicately tinted. In the baggage-room the walls are sheathed in hard pine for about 7 ft. from the floor. This room has an entrance from the central passage-way from the train-house, and from the outside near the west archway.

The seats in the waiting-rooms present a unique appearance. They run almost entirely around the sides of the room, and are fastened to the walls and floor, while once in about ten or twelve feet there is a double seat projection from the side, which runs out into the room about ten feet. Rows of seats have also been placed in the centre of the room. The ends of these rows are designed to represent Corinthian columns, and remind one of the ends of the pews in some of the Episcopal churches or a cathedral. This style is quite common in English railway stations. The seats are similar to those in some of the modern horse-cars, and consist of alternate strips of black-walnut and ash. In the ladies' waiting-room there are 273 running feet of seating, while in the gentlemen's waiting-room there are 297 running feet.

Messrs. Ware & Van Brunt, of Boston, are the architects; Mr. E. S. Philbrick, the chief engineer.

Union Passenger Depot at Concord, N. H., Concord Railroad.—The Union Depot of the Concord Railroad at Concord, N. H., designed by Mr. B. L. Gilbert, architect, New York, N. Y., shown in Figs. 624 and 625, prepared from data kindly furnished by Mr. H. E. Chamberlin, Superintendent,

FIG. 624.—PERSPECTIVE OF DEPOT.

Concord Railroad, and Mr. J. M. Jones, Station-agent, plans for which were also published in the issue of the *American Architect and Building News* of April 4, 1885, is a large three-story terminal side-station, with high attic and basement. The main building is 218 ft. long × 62 ft. wide, built of brick, rock-faced granite, and terra-cotta. The train shed is 770 ft. long × 120 ft. wide. The ground-floor is used for passengers, while the upper floors are utilized for offices. The building is divided at the centre by a large open rotunda into two wings. This central rotunda is 62 ft. × 72 ft., and serves as a general waiting-room and passage-way. Adjoining this rotunda on one side there is a ticket-office, 18 ft. × 17 ft., and a ladies' parlor, 18 ft. × 39 ft., with toilet-room attached. Beyond these there is a smoking-room, 18 ft. × 23 ft., with entrance from the rear of the building, and with a gentlemen's toilet-room attached. Also, a baggage-room, 23 ft. × 57 ft.; a depot-master's room, 13 ft. × 17 ft.; and a baggage store-room, 14 ft. × 23 ft. On the other side of the rotunda there is a restaurant, 23 ft. × 31 ft.; a small mail-room; an office, 12 ft. × 23 ft.; a conductors' room, 15 ft. × 18 ft.; a tele-

FIG. 625.—PERSPECTIVE OF TRAIN-SHED.

graph-office, 19 ft. × 23 ft.; and an express-room, 22 ft. × 57 ft. The central rotunda is over 60 ft. high, open to the roof, showing the construction of the walls and open trusses. The finish of this room is exceedingly handsome, and of the most substantial character. The high wainscoting, panelled ceiling, ornamental beams and trusses, and bevelled chimney-piece are of solid oak. There is a large open fireplace upon the east side, faced with red sandstone. The floor is laid in squares of black and white marble. The walls are plastered in rough stucco, colored crimson and old gold. Stained glass has been introduced into the partitions and over the massive doors with pleasing effect. On either side of the west or street entrance are ornamental iron staircases leading to an open gallery which gives access to the offices on the second floor. Above this gallery, over the fireplace, is a large space on which is painted a railroad map of New Hampshire, with tablets on either side giving tables of distances from Concord. Upon the north and south sides of the gallery are massive iron arches, from which depend the electric lights by which the building is illuminated. All of the rooms on the ground-floor are handsomely furnished with oak woodwork, birch floors, and fireplaces. The woodwork of the offices in the upper stories is stained to imitate cherry. Nearly every room has a marble mantel and open grate. Radiators, set-bowls, speaking-tubes, electric bells, and all the modern conveniences are amply provided. Everything about the station is substantial and thoroughly built.

Union Passenger Depot at Portland, Me.—The Union Passenger Depot at Portland, Me., plans for which were published in the issue of the *Railway Review* of May 5, 1888, is a large, handsomely designed two-story terminal side-station. The building is constructed of granite, with a large square tower at one corner and with an iron train-shed along one side of the main building. The building is 304 ft. long and 48 ft. wide. There is, near the centre of the building, a large general waiting-room, 81 ft. × 46 ft., with a ticket-office at the centre of the room, on the track side. The entrance to this room from the street is by means of a broad platform, and also a *porte cochère*. On one side of this general waiting-room there is a door to a smoking-room, 38 ft. × 20 ft., with a gentlemen's toilet-room at the rear of the smoking-room. There is also a ladies' parlor opening from the general waiting-room, with a ladies' toilet-room attached. Beyond the smoking-room and the ladies' parlor at the end of the building there is a baggage-room 31 ft. × 46 ft. At the other end of the general waiting-room there is a small telegraph-office, and a passage-way to a dining-room, 66 ft. × 46 ft. Connecting with the dining-room there is a small private dining-room and a serving-room, with stairs leading to the upper floor, where the kitchen is located. Beyond the dining-room there is a second baggage-room, 26 ft. × 46 ft., and an express-office, 26 ft. × 46 ft. The architects of the building are Messrs. Bradlee, Winslow & Wetherell.

Proposed Union Passenger Depot at Providence, R. I.—In the issue of *Engineering News* of Aug. 2, 1890, the plans for a proposed Union Passenger Depot at Providence, R. I., as designed by Messrs. S. L. Minot and E. P. Dawley, engineers, are illustrated. The problem to be solved at this point was a particularly difficult one, the tracks being on a curve, and a street passing immediately under the proposed depot site, so that part of the building is supported on a bridge spanning the street. The depot is built alongside of the tracks, and follows their curvature.

Terminal Passenger Depot at Richmond, Va., Atlantic Coast Line.—The terminal depot at Richmond, Va., of the Atlantic Coast Line, designed by Mr. W. Bleddyn Powell, architect, plans for which were published in the issue of the *Railway Review* of April 30, 1887, is a large and handsomely designed terminal side-station. The improvements at this point, consisting of a new passenger depot, train-shed, freight depot, and necessary track changes, were commenced in 1885 and were completed in 1887. The passenger depot is described as follows, in the publication mentioned:

The style of architecture chosen for the passenger station is a free rendering of the Romanesque. The building covers a rectangle measuring 90 ft. on Seventh Street by 140 ft. on Canal Street equal to 12,600 sq. ft., and providing a total floor surface of 37,683 sq. ft. The accommodation for the public is located entirely on the ground-floor, and consists of a general waiting-room, 38 ft. × 76 ft. This room is located in the centre of the building, and serves as a general thoroughfare to and from all public rooms. Upon it opens the ladies' waiting-room, L-shaped, 33 ft. × 43 ft. This room is situated on the northeast corner, commanding views of Seventh and Canal Streets. On the opposite or northwest corner—a ticket-office 17 ft. × 33 ft. intervening—is located the dining room, 28 ft. × 33½ ft., communicating with the restaurant, 22 ft. × 32 ft. Adjoining the restaurant is the kitchen, 20 ft. × 22 ft., having its stair, pantry, etc., in an independent department, 10 ft. × 22 ft. Communicating with a store-room in the basement is a large lift capable of raising 2000 lbs. The toilet-rooms face on Canal Street, having direct communication with the waiting-rooms. The size of the ladies' toilet-room is 12½ ft. × 14½ ft.; that of the men's, 12 ft. × 13 ft. On either side of the entrance from Canal Street, 18 ft. in width and opening into the large waiting-room, are situated the offices for the Pullman Car Company and Western Union telegraph. The rear entrance, nearly the same width, affords access to a subordinate stair leading to the offices in second story, and opening from it is the smoking-room, 20 ft. × 28 ft., facing on the train-shed. For the convenience of management, the station-master's room (12½ ft. × 18 ft.), conductors' room (18 ft. × 20 ft.), and train-despatcher's (12½ ft. × 28 ft.), are located on the ground-floor, facing on the train-shed. The offices in the second and third stories are reached by a broad stairway approached from Canal Street, the entrance hall containing same measuring 12½ ft. × 26 ft. There is also a parcels and news room, 9 ft. × 25 ft., and a fire-proof vault, 8½ ft. × 9½ ft. The second story contains two stair halls, a directors' room, two fire-proof vaults, a toilet-room, and fourteen large offices, communication with which is had by a gallery extending around the general waiting-room. The third story contains stair hall, toilet-room, and seven offices. The fourth floor is one large room for storage. Many of the offices have open fireplaces, and the building throughout is heated by steam.

Externally, the building presents an unbroken wall-surface, relieved by bold fenestration and the introduction of a recessed bay over the office entrance. Further relief is obtained by the irregularity of roof lines and the emphasis given to the chimney-stacks. The building is divided into nearly equal blocks in plan, that next the train-shed being four stories in height, and that next to Seventh Street being two stories in height, and covered with a ponderous roof, 30 ft. to ridge from the eaves. The heights of stories are as follows: first floor, 18 ft.; second floor, 14 ft.; third floor, 10 ft.; and fourth floor, to ridge, 20 ft. The base, which runs entirely round the building, is of Richmond granite, 6 ft. 6 in. high, the stone is laid up in broken range, rock face. Above the base-line the facing and arches are laid up with Richmond pressed brick, laid in red mortar. A strong belt-course of specially-made bricks, with terra-cotta consoles and corner stops, indicates the height of stories, and the portion next Canal Street is crowned by a moulded brick and terra-cotta cornice.

A striking feature at the northwest corner is formed by the large panel of terra-cotta, 7½ ft. x 13½ ft., containing the coat of arms of Virginia, above which rises the chimney-stack from the fireplaces in the ladies' waiting-room, 8½ ft. wide by 22 ft. high, its base spreading out by means of curved wings to 15½ ft. high.

The gutters, down-spouts, and spout heads in connection with the building are made of cold-rolled copper, weighing one pound to the square foot. The roof is covered with dark slate on felt, having ridge tiles of red terra-cotta. External woodwork will be painted a dark bronzed green, to harmonize in color with the red brick.

Entering the vestibule on Canal Street and passing through the doorway in the heavy granite-framed screen, one stands in the lobby of the general waiting-room. This lobby is tiled from floor to ceiling with tile of a rich cream color, and the ceiling finished in worked chestnut. Passing under an arch 16 ft. wide and 14 ft. 3 in. high, formed of moulded and plain red pressed brick springing from massive blocks of Seneca sandstone, the general waiting-room opens up, 38 ft. wide, 76 ft. long, and 28 ft. 4 in. high. Red-brick arches similar to one just noticed occur at either end of the room, in the one case spanning the ticket-box, and in the other containing the screen leading to the entrance to the trains. Immediately in front of us a huge chimney-piece, in red brick and Seneca sandstone, raises its sloping roof lines nearly to the level of the under side of the gallery. The size of the mantel is worth recording: width, 14 ft.; height, 15½ ft.; width of niche, 8 ft. 4 in.; height, 4 ft. 4 in.; depth, 3 ft.; height of shelf above floor, 6 ft. 4 in.; the lintel over niche and forming the mantel-shelf is a single stone weighing 4½ tons.

The walls of the general waiting-room, together with those of the rear entrance, are tiled to the height of 10 ft., above which a broad chestnut moulding separates the buff brick in white cement running to the under side of the gallery floor. An ornamental belt of olive-tinted tiles 12½ in. wide runs around the room on a line with the springing-blocks under the arches. On a level with the chestnut cap-moulding are placed corbels of Seneca sandstone supporting the brackets carrying the gallery. The gallery edge is richly moulded, and the soffits of all ceilings filled in with selected panel lumber, and the angles suitably finished with grouped mouldings. An ornamental wrought-iron rail runs round the gallery, painted a rich bronze green. The walls above the gallery floor are plastered and colored to conform to the tints in the story below, and protected from injury by a chestnut wainscoting 5 ft. in height. The main ceiling is deeply coffered and the part next the walls panelled and moulded. The middle portion of this ceiling, consisting of a framework, 26 ft. x 24 ft., is raised 4 ft. above the part next the wall, from which curved brackets spring and assist in supporting the framework just mentioned. This frame is entirely filled with heavy glass; the light from the right light and four large windows (in rear wall opening on the depressed portion of the rear roof, and affording ventilation in midsummer) filters through pleasantly, illuminating the room below. The space between floor at third-story level and the bottom of the ceiling light is divided into panels, and the same filled with wrought-iron gratings of ornamental patterns.

The finish of the woodwork throughout the entire building is in imitation of antique oak, and it was intended by the use of chestnut (the grain being large) to depend mainly on it for the effect.

The ladies' waiting-room, restaurant, and dining-room are connected with the general waiting-room by openings, 8 ft. wide and 10 ft. in height, the lintel over the same being formed of heavy rolled beams and plates, painted in silver bronze and rivet-heads picked out in copper. The walls are wainscoted to the height of 6 ft. 4 in., the former room having a large pressed-brick mantelpiece, having panels of terra-cotta and buff brick, and a bevelled mirror let into the brickwork above the mantel-shelf. Panelled beams and hard-wood cornices, deeply moulded, make the finish for ceilings in these rooms. The main stairway is finished throughout in ash and chestnut, the railings of ornamental wrought-iron, similar in design to those of the gallery, but having no ash hand-rail.

The gas-fixtures in the several passenger-rooms are of wrought-iron, massive, and in design to conform to the architecture of the building.

The freight-house is of brick and is 90 ft. wide and 301 ft. 6 in. long, having at the north or Canal Street end an office two stories in height, with a total floor area of 2900.

The train-shed measures from centres of columns 76 ft., and together with the overhangings at sides, 8 ft. each, make a total width of 92 ft. by a total length of 486 ft. It is for the most part of wrought-iron.

In connection with the train-shed, and covered by an extension of the roof at the side toward Seventh Street, is the baggage-house.

The entire work on this building was designed and carried out from drawings and specifications prepared by Mr. W. B. Powell, architect for the Pennsylvania Railroad Company, under the general supervision of Mr. E. T. D. Myers, General Superintendent.

Union Passenger Depot, Birmingham, Ala.—The Union Passenger Depot at Birmingham, Ala, designed by Mr. H. Wolters, architect, Louisville, Ky., an illustration of which was published in the *Inland Architect and Builder*, Vol. 12, No. 1, is a large terminal side-station of stone and brick, with a long train-shed on one side of the main building.

Union Passenger Depot on Canal Street, Chicago, Ill.—The Union Passenger Depot on Canal Street, between Van Buren Street and Madison Street, in Chicago, Ill., is a large terminal side-station, two to three stories high, the street level being one story nigher than the track level. Plans and descriptions of this depot were published in the issue of the *Railroad Gazette* of May 13, 1881, and in the issue of the *Railway Reporter* of January 21, 1882. The description of the depot in the issue of the *Railroad Gazette* mentioned is as follows:

The grounds of the Pittsburg, Fort Wayne & Chicago Railway, operated by the Pennsylvania Company, front on the east side of Canal Street, between Madison and Van Buren Streets, a length of 1850 ft.; the south branch of the Chicago River, which is from 300 to 400 ft. from Canal Street, flows along the east line of the property. The depot grounds are crossed at the centre by Adams Street, the city traffic crossing the grounds and the river by a bridge, which is high enough above the rails to clear the locomotives and cars. The track-level is entirely below the streets, and but seven feet above the water surface of the river. Van Buren and Madison Streets both cross the tracks by viaducts, at the south and north ends of the ground respectively.

The fee of the property is in the Pittsburg, Fort Wayne & Chicago Railway Company, the Pennsylvania Company operating. The latter company entered into a contract with the four foreign roads for the joint use of the depot without in any way disturbing the title or leasehold.

The principal freight warehouse of the Pennsylvania Company is situated along the east side of the property parallel with and about 180 ft. distant from Canal Street, with a driveway along the river, approached by inclines from Madison and Van Buren Streets. This building is of brick, about 700 ft. long by 60 ft. wide.

The depot is to be used by the following railroad companies: The Pittsburg, Fort Wayne & Chicago, operated by the Pennsylvania Company; the Chicago, Burlington & Quincy Railroad; the Chicago & Alton Railroad; the Chicago, Milwaukee & St. Paul Railway; and the Pittsburg, Cincinnati & St. Louis Railway. The trains of the first three companies enter and leave the depot from the south, the other two from the north end.

The grounds occupied by the depot tracks were graded by excavating to two feet below the rail. New steel-rail tracks were laid on a solid foundation of broken limestone.

The train-house is 1100 ft. long, with open sides except at the buildings to which it is attached; the width is 100 ft.; 700 ft. lies north and 400 ft. south of Adams Street. The framework is supported by iron columns at intervals of 25 ft.; these columns rest on blocks of masonry, and are bolted to a heavy footing-stone. The entire shed is of iron and glass, except the wooden roof-sheathing and the small wooden rafters to which it is nailed. The roof is of the best charcoal tin manufactured. Platforms are laid at the level of the top of rail. Provision is made for drainage of roof and surface water, and for lighting the sheds at night. At one time it was thought that the electric light would be used, but gas has been introduced. Doubtless the electric light will ultimately be used; it is so suitable to the place that it was probably omitted only in the belief that great improvements in electric-lighting would be made shortly. The system of gas-lighting is as perfect as could be devised: three lines of lights extend the full length of sheds; these lines are divided at the centre so that any one or all of the six may be lighted and extinguished instantaneously by keys, at one convenient point. Small "tell-tale" burners, supplied by a small main, are kept constantly lighted; by turning on the gas to the main pipes the lamps are lighted. The tell-tales consume but little gas, and have proved efficient. Large "Dyott" lamps are used throughout the train-house.

The depot buildings are three in number, all fronting on Canal Street. The principal one—the passenger depot proper—is 200 ft. front by 58 ft. in depth. The other two front 150 ft. each on Canal Street, and are 25 ft. deep. All the buildings are three stories in height above the track level—two stories only above the street. They are all built of brick, with Warrensburg stone for trimmings. The foundations are of random coursed work, on squared-up footings of Joliet limestone. The faces of all walls are of Philadelphia pressed brick. This work has received many favorable criticisms on account of the exceptional uniformity of color and regularity of laying such a large number. Black mortar was used throughout the face-work. Over 425,000 pressed brick and 2,250,000 common Milwaukee and Chicago brick were used in the work. At each end of the main building granite stairways lead down to the track level; the walls along these stairways and the rear first-story walls are faced with enamelled brick in pleasing designs. This is to avoid the unsightly discoloration of pressed brick caused by persons rubbing or leaning against it. All exposed corners are protected by iron guards built into the walls.

The moderate depth which could be given to the building led to the supporting of the main rear wall on iron columns. The rear first-story wall is about 18 ft. nearer to the street than the main rear wall of the building; this gives a spacious porch, which is inclosed by an iron railing, with gates to train-house for passengers.

The roofs of all the buildings are covered with Peachbottom slate. The tinning of gutters, valleys, and flashings are of the best "IX" dipped charcoal plate. The same tin is used for the roof of the "porches" or verandas on Canal Street, which are iron framings extending from the curb to the walls the whole length of the three buildings, and crossing Adams Street by special construction in keeping with the other work. The cornice and open work patterns of iron forming a frieze below it combine to give a finish to this part of the work, while the porches themselves are of great utility, affording a complete protection to the sidewalk, so that passengers can enter the depot or train-house with comfort, and giving shelter to baggage, mails, etc., *in transitu*.

This veranda along Canal Street, in front of the buildings, is 580 ft. long and 16 ft. wide. Its importance as greatly adding to the facilities for handling passengers and baggage, cannot be overestimated. It is conceded by experts to largely increase the working efficiency of the depot.

The "main building" is the principal object of interest, and is well worthy a careful examination. Its general layout is unique in many respects, owing to the peculiar features previously mentioned.

The main entrance is at the centre by three pairs of swinging-doors admitting to a "vestibule" about 30 ft. by 40 ft. From the street-level one can pass by a flight of a dozen granite steps down to the track floor, or by seven steps on either side of this flight up to the waiting-room floor. There are four pairs of swinging-doors from the vestibule to the waiting-room. This vestibule is a striking feature: the frescoed ceiling is some 60 ft. from the floor; the walls are handsomely decorated, and the coat of arms of the States through which the railroads using the depot pass are artistically painted in the half-circle panels in the walls. A staircase opening off the principal waiting-room leads by one flight to the balcony, inside the main entrance over the doors, and by each of two flights from the balcony to the third-story hall. This stairway, entirely of wrought and cast iron, is in design and execution one of the finest in the country: its prominence in the vestibule made its appearance a matter of importance. Instead of being hustled into some obscure corner of the building, its bold introduction and successful treatment render it very effective. The vestibule and granite stairways are wainscoted with handsome marble-work; great care has been used here in the harmonious combination of color, as well as the selection of the most durable materials. The floor is also of marble. The handsome marble newels are surmounted by solid bronze "candelabra" newel lights. The following varieties of marble are among those used in the wainscot: Light and dark Knoxville, Glenn's Falls and Swanton black, Tennessee, Swanton dove, Lyonaise, Bongard, Lisbon, Formosa, Brocatelle, and other fine marbles, the most expensive being used in the panels. The floors of vestibule and waiting-rooms are of the best white Italian and Glenn's Falls black, one-fourth black, with black border. The large windows lighting the "rotunda," as this square vestibule has been named, are of handsomely designed stained glass, specially worked out with great skill in drawing and color.

Take it altogether, this rotunda is a success, and a fitting introduction to the rest of the building. The massive marble and granite work, the ornate staircase, the richness of coloring in the frescoing and stained glass, the beautifully cut plate-glass panels of the doors and the solid woodwork of the same form a *tout ensemble* pleasing to the eye, while the evident solidity of the work promises that it will need only an occasional renewing at the painter's hands to keep it bright and charming.

The main waiting-room, which, it will be remembered, is somewhat above the street level, is rectangular, about 54 by 120 ft. The vestibule cuts off about 28 ft. in depth by 38 ft. in width at the centre of the room. The ceiling is 25 ft. high, richly panelled and moulded. The walls and ceilings are frescoed. The wainscoting and other woodwork are of walnut and cherry carved and moulded in original and tasteful designs. The windows and glass door panellings are of plate-glass, the latter richly cut. The half-circle heads to the windows come above the level of the porch and train-house roofs where they join the main building; these half-circles are all glazed with cathedral and antique stained glass in special patterns, each room having a different treatment. The floor is of marble, laid in cement on concrete filled over corrugated-iron arches, supported in turn by iron beams. These iron arches form the ceiling of the story below, which, it will be remembered, is a trifle above the level of the tracks.

The dining-room is at the north end, on the same floor with waiting-rooms. The ladies' room is at the south end. These rooms are finished in the same style as the waiting-room, but the decoration of the ladies' room is worthy of a longer notice than can be given here. While nothing has been sacrificed in the way of substantial and durable work, the frescoing is remarkably delicate in design and coloring, and combines with the stained glass and other work to make this by far the most elegant waiting-room in the country; at the same time the necessary retiring-rooms have been provided with every comfort experience and care could suggest. In the waiting-rooms are perforated wall-seating and settees; the ladies' waiting-room has besides rocking chairs and other conveniences. A "ladies' lunch-room" adjoins this room for those who wish some light refreshment without going to the dining-room.

The ticket-office projects about 15 ft. into the general waiting-room, and has a window on the ladies' room; its face shows a combination of black-walnut, cherry, dark Knoxville marble shelf, and six windows on the waiting-room, two of these being at the cut-off corners. The design of all this work is entirely new and very striking. From the main waiting-room a stairway of granite steps leads down to the track level; it is easily approached from the ladies' room. The sides are panelled in fine marbles, while the well-hole is protected by unique and massive railing of solid brass, elaborately ornamented.

Retracing our steps to the vestibule and descending the main stair we find ourselves beneath the overhang of the main building on an asphaltum floor which completely surrounds the buildings and is enclosed by a stone curbing, on which stands the iron railing separating from the tracks and train-house. The rooms on this floor are: the engine-room (at the south end), one office, a wash-room and water-closet, a conductors' room, news-room, telegraph-office and depot-master's office, smoking and lunch rooms. All these except the engine-room have marble floors, and are handsomely finished in wood. The glass panels of the doors are finely cut. Neat but prominent lettering indicates the uses of the rooms. The engine-room contains two large boilers for the steam-heating apparatus and the pumps for the elevator system. The wash-room and water-closet connect by double doors; a barber-shop takes up part of the wash-room. The water-closets are arranged on an entirely new plan, with a view to perfect cleanliness and simplicity. The urinals are also simple, and we believe unique; they are of marble, and dispense with all plumbing except a pipe perforated with holes, into which small nipples are tapped and throw constant small streams against the slabs; the water is received into a marble trough cut out of the solid; thence by suitable simple devices it enters the sewer. The pipe is nickel-plated, as are the brass legs which raise the marble back and side slabs clear of the marble floor of the urinal, which is one step above the marble floor of room. A similar urinal is provided in a small room off the general waiting-room above.

A reference to the first part of this description shows that this floor is at so small an elevation above the ordinary water in the South Branch that a cellar, as ordinarily understood, was not to be thought of. Accordingly a "subway" of masonry was provided along the rear of this story for water, steam, and drain-pipes; all these are of iron, except the smaller water-pipes, which are of lead. The drain-pipes connect to a private sewer which leads to the river. The plumbing-work was designed to be as substantial as possible; marble slabs of wash-basins are of more than ordinary dimensions and thickness, and of the best marbles obtainable; basins, basin-cocks, trimmings, and traps are of the best; the water-closets are of one style throughout the buildings; about thirty in all were used, all well ventilated.

The gas-fixtures are very elegant and suitable; they were selected especially, and prepared in ample time. Nickel and gold finish is used in the main floor, brass in the story below, and bronzed goods in the third story and baggage buildings. The solid bronze newel lights in the rotunda have been spoken of before.

The seating of the waiting-rooms has been carefully studied out; perforated wooden side seating and settees have been adopted, made especially to fit their places. For cleanliness and general comfort this seating is preferred, No upholstered work has been admitted. A few chairs are in the ladies' apartments.

The hardware of the buildings may be mentioned here. It was selected with care, and is in every way far superior to the ordinary builders' goods so freely used. It is uniform in design; all locks are hand-made, with brass works; every lock has two brass keys, marked to show where they belong. Only bronze and brass are used for door and window trimmings; all is massive and substantial.

The third story of the main building is occupied by offices; the north end has been divided off as a kitchen, as convenient and perfect as could be desired, with ranges, ovens, and all appurtenances complete, including dumb-waiters to the dining-room, just below it, and the lunch-room on the track-level floor. There is also an elevator for heavy work, a stairway for the kitchen from the lowest floor, refrigerators of large size, vaults, store-rooms, pantries, and closets.

A lofty attic is reached by stairs from both ends of the third story. It is divided into three main rooms. The huge iron tank which holds the reserve supply for the elevators is supported on the vestibule walls, about 85 ft. above the tracks. The deck of the central roof is 100 ft. above the tracks. The roof is reached by ladders and trap-doors at three points. A flag-staff stands at the central point of the roof.

The baggage buildings require special mention. A description of one applies equally to the other, except as to the third stories. The size is already given. Baggage is received and delivered at the street level; from this story it is lowered or raised by hydraulic elevators, two to each building; the platforms are large enough to hold two of the large "special" trucks loaded to a maximum. The elevators have been tested to 8300 lbs. each, and further by running all the elevators at as close intervals as could be reached in practice. The "receiving" and "delivery" rooms of each building are supplied with every facility for the rapid handling of baggage and mails. At present two roads receive baggage at the southern building and deliver at the northern one, while the other two roads reverse the operation. In the lower story of the baggage buildings is ample room for storage; and water-closets, sinks, etc., are provided. The third story of the northern (called western) baggage building is used for offices, and is approached by an outside covered stairway of iron. The third story of the eastern baggage building is divided into "emigrant" rooms, with all conveniences.

The elevator system is worked under a water-pressure of some 36 lbs. to the inch, obtained by pumping water into a stand-pipe 10 in. in diameter, built in a flue in the wall and supplying the reserve tank before mentioned. Every possible arrangement is made in the way of reserve pumping power to reduce to the minimum the chances of accident to the apparatus. In a trial 46 trips were run by the elevators without using the pump. The return water flows into two cisterns sunk 16 ft. below the engine-room floor, and is thence pumped back to the stand-pipe and tank. The cisterns are two iron cylinders, connected after sunk, lined with brick in Portland cement.

All but some 400 ft. of the long front of the property on Canal Street is laid with a heavy flagstone sidewalk, with vaults underneath and wrought-iron railings at areas in front of buildings and all along the property, which lies from 10 to 15 ft. below the street.

Terminal Passenger Depot at Milwaukee, Wis., Chicago & Northwestern Railroad.—The plans for the terminal depot of the Chicago & Northwestern Railroad at Milwaukee, Wis., designed by Mr. Chas. S. Frost, architect, Chicago, Ill., were published in the issue No. 3, Vol. 13, of the *Inland Architect and News Record*, and in the issue of the *Railway Review* of March 16, 1889. The building is a three-story stone and brick building, with a large square clock-tower. The depot is an L-shaped side-station. The train-shed is 440 ft. long, and has four tracks running through it. The building has a general waiting-room; a ticket-office; a smoking-room, with a gentlemen's toilet-room attached; a baggage-room; a ladies' waiting-room, with toilet-room attached; a dining-room; and a lunch-room. The upper stories are used for hotel accommodations, in connection with the restaurant. The general waiting-room has an iron and tile floor with face-brick walls, and an open timbered oak ceiling. The ladies' waiting-room is furnished like a sitting-room. The exterior of the building is of stone from the ground up to the first-story window-sill, above which red face-brick and terra-cotta are used. The tower is 176 ft. high. The main roof is slate, and the roof of the tower is red Akron tile with copper trimmings. In the publication mentioned it is stated that the entire building, including train-shed, would cost $150,000.

Terminal Passenger Depot at Milwaukee, Wis., Chicago, Milwaukee & St. Paul Railway.—The passenger depot of the Chicago, Milwaukee & St. Paul Railway at Milwaukee, Wis., plans for which were published in the issue of the *Railway Review* of Dec. 25, 1886, and in the issue of the *Scientific American* (Architects and Builders' Edition) of March, 1887, is a large terminal side-station, described as follows in the publications mentioned:

The new passenger station of the Chicago, Milwaukee & St. Paul Railway at Milwaukee is situated between Third and Fourth Streets, one and one-half blocks from Grand Avenue, and fronts on a park on Everett Street. The ground-plan of the building shows a surface of 120 × 65 ft. There are three floors—the first 16 ft. in the clear and the other two 14 ft. each. In the centre of the façade rises a tower to the height of 160 ft., reminding one in its graceful lines of some Venetian campanile, and dominating the landscape in every direction. The style of the structure is modern Gothic. The foundations are solid and enduring, being constructed of stone, with granite facings above grade. The material used in the construction of the walls is Milwaukee brick, faced with pressed Philadelphia red brick. The trimmings are of red sandstone and terra-cotta in handsome patterns.

The main entrance of the building is formed of a triple arch, supported by columns of polished granite. It is reached by a flight of six easy steps. The swinging-doors of polished oak are a few feet inside the arch, being surmounted by stained-glass windows in beautiful designs. These admit the visitor into the large central hall which bisects the building. This is 30 × 65 ft. The floor is of tile, in a well-defined pattern, and soft, pleasing colors. The walls are of red brick up to the spring of the arch. From there on they are in a soft, creamy brick. The lower portion of the wall is marked with geometrical patterns in different-colored brick, while the creamy surface above is picked out here and there with a dash of dark color.

Around the rear of the hall runs a gallery, which serves to give the light and lightness needed to the whole. This gallery is surrounded by a railing in hammered dull brass.

On the right of the main entrance is the ladies' waiting-room, an apartment of handsome proportions, 30 x 84 ft., with tile floor, and finished in oak in natural color. To the rear of the apartment are well-appointed toilet-rooms. On the same side of the hall, and occupying the south side of the building, is the gentlemen's waiting-room, of the same size as the other room, less a slight abridgment in length. Between the two is a bijou ticket-office with three ticket-windows, one to the hall and one to each waiting-room. All these rooms, as well, in fact, as all the rooms down-stairs, with one exception, are finished in a similar manner to the ladies' room, and have tiled floors. The ceiling on this floor throughout is ribbed by heavy beams, whose possible heaviness is relieved by tinting in light color approaching a soft shade of Nile green. On the left of the entrance is the dining-room of the hotel connected with the depot, a room 40 x 52 ft., finished as the other rooms, but with a wood floor. The lunch room, on the same side, is 16 x 52 ft. in size, and is furnished with folding-stools for the benefit of its patrons. Between the two rooms is the telegraph-office and the parcel counter.

To the right and rear of the hall an alcove gives room for a handsome oak stairway that leads to the second floor. This, in the west end of the building, is occupied by the train-despatchers of the different divisions, and it is safe to say that never before did train-despatchers have more comfortable or beautiful quarters. The most of the offices look directly out on the park. The east end of the building is occupied, with the exception of one room, for hotel purposes. Descending to the first floor, in the extreme west end of the building, is found the baggage-room, an apartment 52 x 56 ft. in its floor dimensions. Immediately above it and reached by a water-elevator is a room of similar size for the purpose of storing baggage not called for immediately. In the east end of the building is the emigrant room, of size the same as the baggage-room, with heavily timbered ceiling and tiled floor. This room and the one above it, also intended for the same purpose, are well appointed for their special object. The building is lighted throughout by electricity and heated by steam, both being furnished by boilers and engine located in the east end of the basement.

Outside are large car-sheds, 600 ft. in length and 100 in width, supported by iron columns and girders, and roofed with corrugated iron. They cover five tracks, on which the highest skill of the road-masters' art has been displayed. There is placed in the tower, at a height that will make it easily seen from a good part of the city, a big clock, the dials of which will at night be illuminated by electricity. The clock is one of the finest as well as the largest in the country. It has four dials. Those on the north and south sides are 11 ft. in diameter, and those on the east and west are 9 ft. Each of these dials is composed of six sections of the finest ground glass, so joined together as to appear one solid piece. The pendulum of this mammoth clock is 14 ft. in length, and weighs 400 lbs. It is regulated for heat and cold. The cost complete is $500,000.

Union Passenger Depot at Stillwater, Minn.—The Union Depot at Stillwater, Minn., an illustration of which was published in the *Northwestern Railroader* of March 9, 1888, is a small terminal side-station, described as follows in the publication mentioned:

The building is an extremely effective structure of red Kasota sandstone, fire-brick, and terra-cotta, covering an area of 114 by 63 feet. A handsome vestibule leads to a wide corridor, with waiting-rooms for ladies and gentlemen on either hand, 40 by 24 ft. and 28 by 24 ft. in size, respectively. A toilet-room 16 by 20 ft. opens off the latter, and large toilet-room and barber-shop off the former. Behind the gentlemen's waiting-room are news-depot, lunch-room, etc. The baggage-room and express-room open on the platform in the rear, and are 40 by 18 ft. and 24 by 18 ft., respectively, in size.

The kitchen and dining-room, with private dining-rooms, telegraph-office, private offices, etc., are on the second floor; the main dining-room being 18 ft. by 26 in size, and opening through a handsome arch into a second apartment nearly as large.

The point of the main tower is 72 ft. from the ground, the roof of the whole building being metal-shingled, with copper finials and castings. Messrs. Bupling & Whitehouse, of 36 Clark Street, Chicago, are the architects.

Union Passenger Depot at Atchison, Kan.—The Union Passenger Depot at Atchison, Kan., an illustration of which was published in the issue of the *Railway Review* of Sept. 18, 1880, is a large terminal L-shaped side-station of stone and pressed brick. The building is two stories high, excepting at the junction of the "L," which has a high mansard story added. The main building is 234 ft. ×

46 ft., and the "L" is 96 ft. × 44 ft. At the end of the main building there is an open shed extension, about 120 ft. long.

Union Passenger Depot, Kansas City, Mo.—The Union Depot at Kansas City, Mo., plans for which were published in the issue of the *Railroad Gazette* of June 21, 1878, from which Figs. 413, 626, and 627 are reproduced, is a large terminal side-station, the most noteworthy feature about it being the replacing of the usual style train-shed by a system of longitudinal one-legged platform-roofs (shown in Fig. 413), connected by covered transverse platforms or arcades (shown in Fig. 626). The letters on the ground-plan, Fig. 627, indicate the use the different spaces are put to, as follows: *a.*—Ladies' Waiting-room; *b.*—Gentlemen's Waiting-room; *c.*—Ticket-office; *d.*—Baggage-room; *e.*—Restaurant; *f.*—Kitchen and Office; *g.*—Express-office.

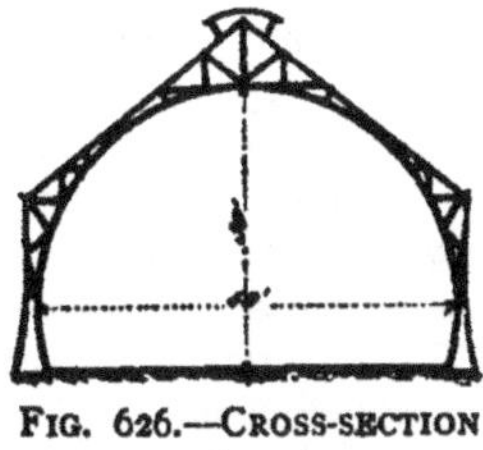

FIG. 626.—CROSS-SECTION OF ARCADE.

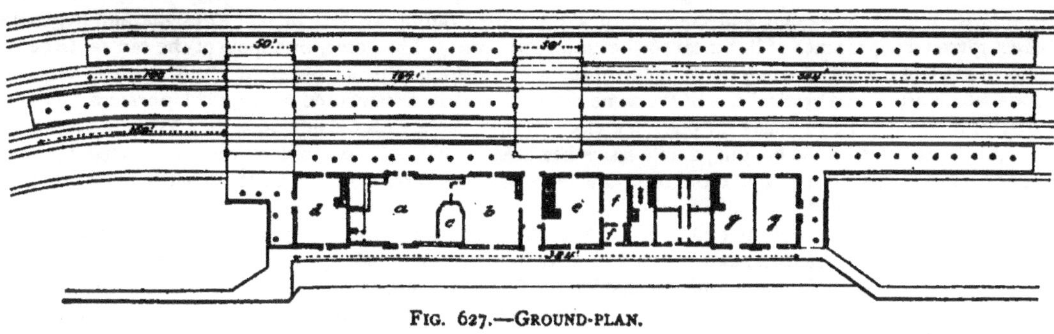

FIG. 627.—GROUND-PLAN.

The structure is described as follows in the issue of the *Railroad Gazette* mentioned above:

The general plan of the depot is that of a main building for waiting-rooms, hotel, offices, etc., with iron arcades or sheds for covering the tracks, instead of an immense and costly building to cover them with a single span. The main building fronts on Union Avenue, and has a covered platform in front and rear. The space in the rear of the building is traversed by six railroad tracks connecting with all the railroads entering the city. These tracks are arranged by placing two of them sufficiently far apart to allow trains to pass each other, then leaving a space twenty feet wide, then two more tracks. A "spur" track is also placed at each end of the building. The space between the tracks and also between the rails has been floored with plank three inches in thickness, thus forming a platform 1000 ft. in length, and when completed 90 ft. wide. In the spaces between the tracks iron sheds, 18 ft. high in the centre and 15 ft. in width, have been erected. They are supported on iron columns, placed in line at distances of 15 ft., and firmly bolted to stone foundations. The framework is of angle-iron, and the roof of corrugated sheet-iron. These longitudinal sheds are connected with each other and with the main building by two transverse "arcades," one at the centre of the main building, and the other at the end.

Of this general plan Mr. O. B. Gunn, the engineer and superintendent of construction of this work, writes:

"The arrangement of iron arcades or sheds we find very convenient and inexpensive compared with a heavy trussed shed over all the tracks, for the same width and length. These heavy covered depots into which the cars run are very smoky, very dirty, and very noisy, especially when steam escapes and engines run or stand in them. By the arrangement of light sheds we have more light and less noise, while the smoke passes away freely, and the cost is small comparatively. Our light sheds have single posts, which give much better room between the trains than with the usual double posts. The light arcades are parallel with the tracks and protect the passengers while reaching and entering the cars, while the heavy sheds cover all the tracks at right angles to the main building, opposite the main entrance and again at the baggage end of depot. The only objection to this arrangement is that in heavy storms passengers will be subject to a slight dripping from the cars when getting into and out of them.

"All the arrangements of tracks, sheds, and the rooms in the main building seem to give great satisfaction to every one connected with them and to all railroad men."

The following description of the building is copied from the Kansas City *Journal of Commerce:*

The building fronts toward the northwest and is 384 ft. long, with an average depth of 50 ft. It presents the general appearance of a main building two stories in height, connected by walls one story in height, with wings, also two stories high, the whole surmounted by mansard roofs with flat tops. The main building and wings are 75 ft. in height, and from the front centre of the main building a tower 20 ft. square is carried up continuous with the front wall to a height of 84 ft. and is surmounted by a cupola, the top of which is 125 ft. from the ground. The walls are of brick, laid in black mortar, 20 in. in thickness, and rest on solid masonry, 15 ft. deep, and laid in the best Fort Scott cement. Eight transverse walls, at various distances, are carried across the building from side to side, and upon these and a line of iron columns resting on stone foundations, and running lengthwise through the centre of the entire building, the upper floors are supported. The wall-trimmings are of cut stone, and the cornices, dormer-window fronts, etc., are of zinc, painted in imitation of stone. The mansard roofs are laid in colors, and are relieved by Gothic gables and French dormer-windows, which present the appearance of pilasters rising from the cornice of the building and supporting a four-sided roof covered with slate and surmounted by a cap of the same shape and cornice of the same style as those surmounting the mansard roof. The roof of the main building contains twelve of these dormer-windows and each of the wings eight. The "cresting" which crowns the dormer-windows, roof, and towers is of modern design, and consists of a light iron railing worked in fancy designs, and in general effect gives an appearance of lightness to the entire structure. The dome, or cupola of the central tower, is also of modern design, starting on a square base and finishing with an octagon. It is covered with tin, upon which are placed vertical ribs of the same material, and is ornamented with "clock dormers" on each side. Provision has been made for placing a clock in the cupola with outside dials four feet in diameter.

At the east end of the building ample space has been provided for the use of the 'bus company, and in front between the platform and the street is a macadamized carriage-drive, 20 ft. in width. The waiting-rooms for passengers are entered directly from the front platform, and there are also two open passages from the front to the rear of the building, one 8 ft. wide, and the other, which is the main entrance, is 16 ft. wide, floored with marble tiles, and opens in the rear under an arcade, 32 ft. in height at the centre, 50 ft. wide, and extending 78 ft. across the rear platform. The space under this arcade is intended as a passage-way to and from the trains, which will stand on either side. A similar arcade is to be erected across the rear platform at the east end.

The baggage department occupies the room at the east end of the building. This room is provided with three large sliding-doors, and 47 ft. square, and is fitted up with every possible convenience for the prompt transaction of the business of its department. A platform 6 ft. below the ceiling passes around two sides of the room, and on the walls above this platform are ranged hooks by the hundred, whereon to arrange in systematic order the 30,000 to 40,000 checks which are constantly kept on hand. Four check-stands on the floor will accommodate 1000 different forms of checks.

The clerk's desk is on an elevated platform reached by a stairway, and here a record will be kept of every piece of baggage received and forwarded.

Next to the baggage-room are the waiting-rooms for passengers. The ceiling of these rooms is 19 ft. from the floor. The floors and wainscoting are of alternate strips of oiled black-walnut and ash, 3 in. in width, the other woodwork being richly grained in imitation of oak. The seats are a framework of oiled black-walnut with bent ash seat and back. The ladies' room adjoins the baggage-room, and is 53 × 43 ft. in size, and is provided with tastefully fitted dressing-rooms. Brussels carpets cover the floors, and marble wash-stands, mirrors, and elegant seats adorn the rooms. The gentlemen's room is 40½ × 47 ft., and between these two rooms is placed the ticket-office, supplied with the latest improved ticket-cases and all other appliances necessary for the convenience of the ticket-agent and his assistants. Including the "local tickets," about 6000 different forms of tickets are issued from this office.

Crossing the main hall, which adjoins the waiting-rooms, the dining-room (47 ft. long and 40½ ft. wide) is reached, finished in the same manner as the waiting-rooms, and provided with the same style of furniture. The dining-room will seat 100 guests, and the tables will at all times be supplied with the best the market affords. No liquors will be sold on the premises. The telegraph-office is next, and is connected by a bewildering array of wires with all the telegraph lines entering the city. In one corner of this room a stone pedestal rises a few inches above the floor, resting on a foundation which is entirely disconnected from the building. This pedestal is occupied by the depot clock.

The general plans for the depot, iron sheds, and tracks were designed by Major O. B. Gunn, who has had general charge of the work as engineer and superintendent of construction, with Mr. Wm. E. Taylor as assistant. The work of grading, ballasting, track-laying, and building platforms was under the immediate supervision of Mr. G. M. Walker, assistant engineer. The general plans were elaborated in detail by the firm of Cross & Taylor, architects, Kansas City, Mo.

Union Passenger Depot at Leavenworth, Kan.—The Union Depot at Leavenworth, Kan., designed by Messrs. Henry Ives Cobb and Chas. S. Frost, architects, Chicago, Ill., a plan of which was published in the *Inland Architect and News Record*, Vol. 9, No. 10, is a terminal side-station of fair proportions, the greatest peculiarity being that the street on the rear of the building is level with the second story, while the tracks passing on the other side of the building are on a level with the ground-floor.

Union Passenger Depot at St. Joseph, Mo.—The Union Passenger Depot at St. Joseph, Mo., is a large, handsomely designed, and substantially built terminal side-station, a plan of which is published in the *Railway Review* of March 5, 1881. The description of the depot in the publication mentioned is as follows:

The style of the building is English domestic Gothic, and contemplates a building 400 feet in length and 50 feet in width, set back from Sixth Street 37 feet, so as to give room for carriage-way between present street line and front of building. The front on Sixth Street will present a central division of 120 feet front, and three stories in height, with a clock-tower in the centre rising to the height of 150 feet from grade. On each side of this central division there will be wings of two stories in height, and extending 90 feet in each direction to the end pavilions which are three stories in height. All exterior walls will be faced with pressed brick laid in black mortar, with elaborate trimmings of stone, black and moulded brick, and encaustic tile. All windows will have transoms over them filled with stained cathedral glass in varying designs, set in lead sash. This work will be of the best description of stained-glass work, and will give a most beautiful effect to the various rooms of the building.

The first floor of the building will be divided into three parts by open corridors or passage-ways 16 feet 6 inches wide; these corridors will be arched over, and faced with pressed brick, with trimmings to correspond with the exterior of the building. From these passage-ways the stairways to the second story of the building will start. The north division will contain the baggage-room, 50 × 50 feet; two express-offices, 22 × 50 feet; mailing-room and superintendent's room, each 15 × 25 feet. The central division between passage-ways will contain ladies' and gentlemen's waiting-rooms, each 50 × 50 feet; ladies' and gentlemen's wash-rooms, etc., each 18 × 25 feet; barber-shop and telegraph-office, each 18 × 25 feet; general ticket-office, lunch-counters, etc. The south division will contain the dining-room, 50 × 50 feet; hotel office, with wash-rooms, etc.; billiard-room; kitchen, with all necessary pantries, etc.; and hotel stairway to second story of building. The second story will contain the railroad offices, 18 in number, and 35 large sleeping-rooms, hotel parlor, bath-rooms, etc. The third story over north pavilion will contain janitor's apartments, the third story over central part 15 sleeping-rooms for hotel, and that over south pavilion the servants' rooms.

The finish throughout the building will be rich and massive, and of the style generally known as the "Eastlake." The trimmings for doors and windows will be of gold bronze of rich design. The building will be heated throughout by steam, and be supplied with hot and cold water.

Union Passenger Depot at Pueblo, Col.—The Union Depot at Pueblo, Col., designed by Messrs. Sprague & Newell, architects, Chicago, Ill., a plan of which was published in the *Inland Architect and News Record*, Vol. 13, No. 7, is a large three-story stone and brick terminal side-station, with square clock-tower.

Union Passenger Depot at Denver, Col.—The Union Depot at Denver, Col., plans for which were published in the issue of the *Railway Review* of June 18, 1881, is a large terminal side-station, described as follows in the publication mentioned:

The depot grounds comprise twelve acres adjoining Wynkoop Street and extending from Sixteenth to Eighteenth Streets. The building is 503 feet long, 65 feet wide, and two stories high, with a dome or tower 180 feet high, which is to be supplied with five electric lights. The central building and both wings of the structure are ornamented with a handsome French roof, cut-stone dormer-windows, and gable-ends. The trimmings around the openings and at the corners are of white Manitou sandstone. All the doorways and entrances have richly carved caps. The main entrance has two columns of Scotch granite, surrounded with carved Gothic caps. The style followed by the architect throughout is Gothic. The ground-floor is for baggage-room, ticket-offices, express, dining-hall, lunch-counters, telegraph-office, sample-room (bar), barber-shop, closets, etc. The kitchen and closets are marble tiled floor. The second story is used entirely for the offices of the Denver & Rio Grande and Union Pacific Railways. The offices are elegantly furnished, many of them being finished with black-walnut and French walnut. They are models of elegance and comfort.

The building is of lava stone, rough-hewed, trimmed with white and red sandstone. Slate roof. The entire building is heated by steam and lighted by gas. The main platform is 530 x 30, and the Wynkoop Street platform is 13½ x 500 feet. Six sets of tracks are laid and planked between rails, forming a platform 880 x 140 feet.

Union Passenger Depot at Indianapolis, Ind.—The Union Depot at Indianapolis, Ind., shown in Fig. 628, is a large three-story building about 150 ft. square, of stone, brick, and iron. The train-sheds are 700 ft. long and about 180 ft. wide. An illustration of this depot is published in the issue of the *Railway Review* of December 11, 1886, and in the article accompanying the illustration it is

FIG. 628.—PERSPECTIVE.

stated that the depot building would cost about $300,000, and the train-sheds $275,000, in addition to about $250,000 which the various companies who would use the depot expected to pay for improvements connected with the new terminal.

Union Passenger Depot at Ogden, Utah.—The Union Passenger Depot at Ogden, Utah, designed by Messrs. Van Brunt & Howe, architects, Boston and Kansas City, plans for which were published in the issue of the *American Architect and Building News* of November 6, 1886, consists of a large three-story building with clock-tower, located on one side of the tracks. The ground-floor is divided into two parts by a wide passage-way, at the centre of the building, serving as a quick exit for passengers arriving on trains. The section of the ground-plan on one side of the passage-way, shows a gentlemen's waiting-room, with toilet-room attached ; a ladies' waiting-room, with toilet-room attached; a ticket-office and telegraph-office; a news-counter; a baggage-room; and an emigrants' room, with toilet-rooms attached. The other section of the ground-plan shows a large hotel-hall, with the offices and other accommodations usually connected with a hotel-lobby; a dining-room; a kitchen; and an express-office. The upper floors are used for offices and hotel purposes.

Union Passenger Depot, Cheyenne, Wyoming, Union Pacific, Denver Pacific, and Cheyenne & Northern Railroads.—The Union Depot at Cheyenne, Wyoming, of the Union Pacific, Denver Pacific, and Cheyenne & Northern Railroads, illustrated in the issue of the *Railway Review* of May 11, 1889, is a large terminal side-station, partly two-story and partly three-story, with a large square clock-tower. The ground-floor is divided by a large passage-way into two wings. One wing contains the waiting-rooms, ticket-office, baggage-room, etc.; the other wing has dining-rooms, offices, and hotel accommodations.

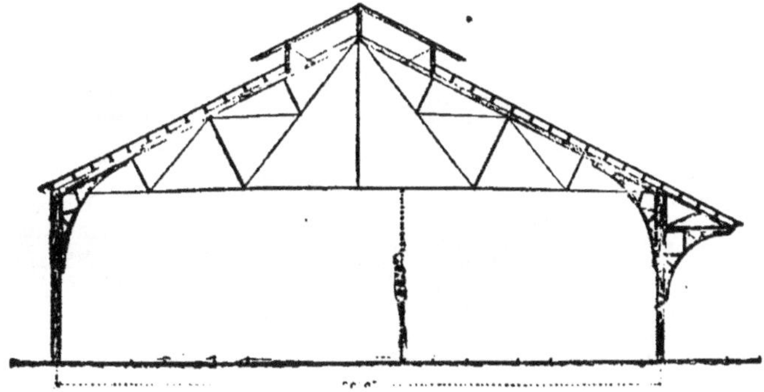

FIG. 629.—CROSS-SECTION OF TRAIN-SHED.

Terminal Passenger Depot at Harrisburg, Pa., Pennsylvania Railroad.—The new passenger depot of the Pennsylvania Railroad at Harrisburg, Pa., built in 1885 under the direction of Mr. Wm. H. Brown, Chief Engineer, Pennsylvania Railroad, is a large terminal side-station. In Fig. 629 a section of the train-shed is shown. The shed is 420 ft. in length and has a span of 90 ft. from column to column. The clear height from the rail to the tie-beam of the truss is 24 ft. The trusses are spaced 20 ft. centres. There are four tracks inside the shed. The elevation of the street is above the track-level. Passengers have to descend to get to the platform in front of the depot. There is an overhead foot-bridge across the tracks, so that the other platforms can be reached by stairs leading down from this overhead bridge.

Passenger Train-shed at New Haven, Conn., New York, New Haven & Hartford Railroad.—The train-shed of the New York, New Haven & Hartford Railroad at New Haven, Conn., shown in Fig. 630 is an all-iron structure, 400 ft. long and 126 ft. wide, consisting of two symmetrical flat roofs,

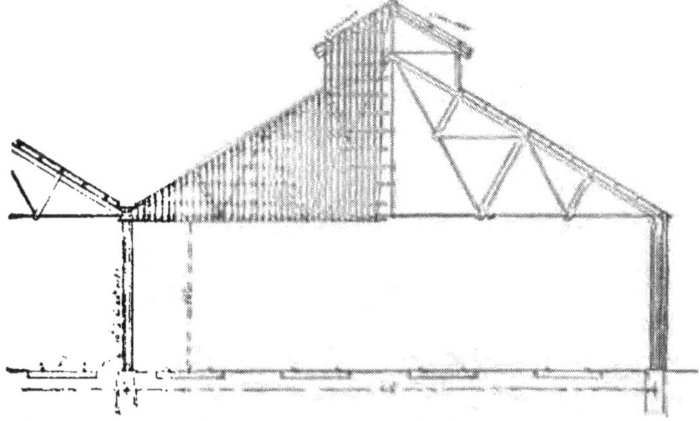

FIG. 630.—CROSS SECTION OF TRAIN-SHED.

each of 63 ft. span. There are four tracks in each span spaced 15 ft. centres. The train-shed is used at a terminal side-station, and the floor of the shed is floored flush with the rails. The posts and the principal rafters consist of channel-irons, the truss-struts of angle-irons, the tie-rods of round iron, and the purlins and studding of channel-irons. The shed is sheathed on the outside and roofed with No. 20 gauge galvanized corrugated iron.

Above data were kindly furnished by Mr. F. S. Curtis, Chief Engineer, N. Y., N. H. & H. R. R.

Terminal Passenger Depot at Charles Street, Baltimore, Md., Pennsylvania Railroad.—The terminal passenger depot of the Pennsylvania Railroad at Charles Street, Baltimore, Md., shown in Figs. 631 to 633, is a side-station with a substantially built depot building and train-shed. The tracks run

FIG. 631.—PERSPECTIVE OF DEPOT.

FIG. 632.—PERSPECTIVE OF TRAIN-SHED.

past this depot. The peculiarity of the design consists in the fact that the street-level is above the train-level. Passengers enter the depot at the street-level at one end of the depot and descend to the waiting-rooms, which are on the train-level. An inclined roadway leads down from the street to

FIG. 633.—PERSPECTIVE OF INTERIOR OF WAITING-ROOM.

the space around the depot, so that carriages and wagons can drive down to the train-level from the street. On the train-level there is a general waiting-room; a ladies' waiting-room; and on the sides of the entrance stairway from the street at the train-level there is a gentlemen's waiting-room and a restaurant. The train-shed connected with the depot is 80 ft. wide by about 250 ft. long. It is open on the sides, being supported on iron columns throughout.

Terminal Passenger Depot at Washington, D. C., Pennsylvania Railroad.—The passenger depot at Washington, D. C., of the Baltimore & Potomac Railroad, the terminus of the Pennsylvania Railroad System at Washington, D. C., shown in Fig. 634, kindly furnished to the author by the Passenger Department of the Pennsylvania Railroad, is a large terminal head-station, designed by Mr. Joseph M. Wilson, engineer and architect, Philadelphia, Pa. The building is illustrated and described in the issue of the *Railroad Gazette* of July 19, 1873; in the issue of *Engineering* of March 2, 1877; in the issue of the *Scientific American*, supplement, of May 12, 1877; and in the book "The Pennsylvania Railroad," by James Dredge. The depot is described in the publications mentioned as follows:

It is constructed of the best pressed bricks, with Ohio-stone dressings, the base course up to the level of the first-story windows, and the entrance steps, being of Richmond granite. It has a frontage on B Street of 137 ft., and on Sixth Street of 95 ft.; the main entrance being on Sixth Street, and the ladies' entrance on the former.

The accommodations on the first floor for passengers are ample and convenient, comprising a general waiting-room, 40×68, a ladies' room, 23×45, a gentlemen's room, 37×20, a restaurant and dining-room 45×55, with complete kitchen arrangements, a baggage-room, offices, etc., etc. The second and third floors

Fig. 634.—Perspective.

are devoted to offices for the company, janitor's rooms, etc. The whole building is finished in first-class style, and is heated by steam throughout.

At the rear of the main building, extending along Sixth Street, and covering a space of 130 ft. × 510 ft., is the roof under which the passenger-cars enter, and receive and discharge the passengers. It is spanned by a handsome wrought-iron arch, is well lighted and ventilated, and affords ample protection to passengers from the weather. The design for the southern entrance to the roof is exceedingly handsome.

The complete specification for the construction of this depot will be found on pages 124 to 139, in Mr. Lewis M. Haupt's book on "Engineering Specifications and Contracts," covering the general requirements, and the detailed specifications for stone-work, brick-work, iron-work, carpenter-work, plastering, plumbing, gas pipes and fitting, painting and glazing, hardware, tin-work, slating, heating, etc.

Passenger Depot at West Philadelphia, Pennsylvania Railroad.—The old terminal passenger depot of the Pennsylvania Railroad at West Philadelphia, Pa., used as an office-building and car-shed since the construction of the new Broad Street station in Philadelphia, is a large terminal head-station, plans for which were published in the issue of *Engineering*, March 9, 1877, and also in the book "The Pennsylvania Railroad," by James Dredge. This depot was designed and built under the supervision of Mr. Joseph M. Wilson, engineer and architect, Philadelphia, Pa., and it is described as follows in the publications mentioned:

The depot stands back from the main road, being reached by a carriage-drive that passes underneath a timber ornamental covered way in front of the façade. The building is a two-story structure, the upper floor being chiefly occupied by the company's offices. The façade is constructed of different-colored bricks arranged with a very good effect. Behind the station building are two covered sheds, about 900 ft. long, each of them covering three lines of rails. The sheds consist of columns spaced about 15 ft. apart, and carrying a curved timber truss with iron ties. This truss is extended on each side beyond the columns, and is supported by brackets as shown. The longitudinal girders between the columns are braced together with double ties converging into a single rod running across the span, and supported at two points in its length by a light suspension-rod. An adjusting screw-sleeve is placed in the middle of each tie-rod. The roof is covered with tinned sheets carried on purlins, and a lifted ventilating roof with louvres in the sides is placed in the centre. There are altogether twelve tracks in the station, six of which are under the shelter of the two sheds, and the remaining six are used for storage of cars, etc. There are ten platforms. The station comprises three independent structures—the station building proper, the departure baggage-room, and the arrival baggage-room. There is besides on the end platform a small office for receiving parcels. The space around the station building is covered in with a flat roof as far as the gable-end of the enclosed roofs over the tracks. The main building is about 180 ft. × 100 ft. The general waiting-room does not occupy a central position in the building, having on one side of it a general and a ladies' restaurant 40 ft. wide, and occupying together the whole depth of the building, while on the other side is a ladies' waiting-room, 40 ft. wide by about 100 ft. long, approached by a passage from the general waiting-room, and having on one side of it the ticket-office, and on the other lavatories, occupying a width of about 20 ft. On the second floor, which is reached by a winding stair, are situated on one side the kitchen and offices of the restaurant, and on the other the offices of the general agent, general baggage-agent, conductor and train-agent, telegraph-clerks, stores, etc. A second spiral stairway leads from these rooms to the ground level. This part of the building is covered by a flat roof. The general waiting-room rises unbroken up to the roof, the centre of which is about 65 ft. from the ground. A very spacious hall is thus obtained, measuring approximately 81 ft. × 100 ft.

Terminal Passenger Depot at Broad Street, Philadelphia, Pa., Pennsylvania Railroad.—The passenger depot of the Pennsylvania Railroad, at Broad Street, Philadelphia, Pa., designed by Messrs. Wilson Brothers & Co., architects and engineers, Philadelphia, Pa., shown in Figs. 635 to 641, is a large and handsomely constructed terminal head-station, with an elevated track approach. An illustration of this building, with a description of the improvements, was published in the issue of the *Railway Review* of Dec. 31, 1881. The illustration, Fig. 636, was prepared from data kindly furnished the author by Mr. Wm. H. Brown, Chief Engineer, P. R. R., under whose direction the depot was built, and Fig. 635 and Figs. 638 to 641 are published through the courtesy of the Passenger Department of the Pennsylvania Railroad, and of Messrs. Wilson Brothers & Co., who have described the depot as follows in their album of designs:

The building was opened to the public in January, 1882. The arrangement is peculiar, owing to the fact that the railroad tracks, after crossing the Schuylkill River, are carried on a brick arcade along the south side of Filbert Street, at a considerable elevation above the street, and enter the station at the level of the second floor. The first story thus becomes a kind of basement above ground, and is so treated architecturally.

FIG. 635.—PERSPECTIVE OF DEPOT.

The front on Broad Street measures 193 ft. 5 in., and the depth on Filbert Street is 122 ft. 10 in. On the right about 80 ft. of the frontage is occupied by ticket-offices, baggage-room (departing), 30 x 73, and a lobby, 40 x 80, for passengers in connection therewith, which lobby contains stairs and elevators to the waiting-rooms on second floor. On the left about 34 ft. is occupied by the exit staircase, behind which is the baggage-room (30 x 80) for arriving baggage. The central portion, about 80 ft., is left open from front

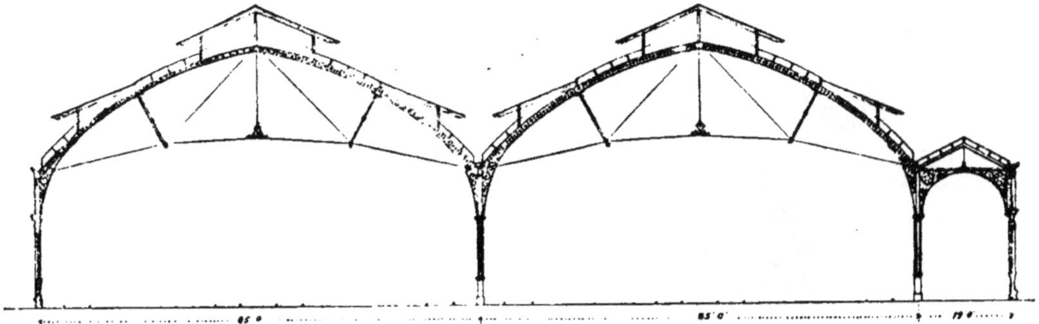

FIG. 636.—CROSS-SECTION OF TRAIN-SHED.

FIG. 637.—PERSPECTIVE OF TRAIN-SHED.

to rear, providing a convenient passage way for carriages, to which passengers have access from either street under cover.

In the second story the entire frontage on Broad Street is occupied by the ladies' waiting-room (29 x 80) with private room (13 x 28) and toilet attached, and the dining-room (29 x 74). The restaurant (40 x 50) opens from the dining-room, and is served by private stair and dumb-waiters from kitchen above. The general waiting-room (50 x 80) adjoins the ladies' waiting-room and the restaurant. It is approached by the entrance stair and elevators from first floor, and opens on the train lobby (30 x 190), extending the whole length of the building on rear (Fifteenth Street), and communicating with trains by gates. The exit stair descends directly from this lobby, and a baggage-lift is provided at each end, connecting with the baggage-

FIG. 638.—DETAIL OF EXTERIOR.

FIG. 639.—DETAIL OF PUSH-PLATES OF DOORS.

FIG. 640.—GENERAL VIEW.

rooms for arriving and departing baggage. The offices in the upper stories are approached from this lobby by a private stair and passage on the Filbert Street front, which also affords access to the toilet-rooms for gentlemen.

The train-house, which begins at the gates from the lobby, extends 450 ft. in length to Sixteenth Street, being carried across Fifteenth Street on girders. It contains eight passenger tracks and platforms.

Looking up Filbert Street from the Masonic Temple the view of the building is very pleasing, the color showing up richly against the white marble of the new City Hall, which sets well back, making a sort of plaza.

The style of the building is a modern adaptation of Gothic architecture. The eastern or principal front

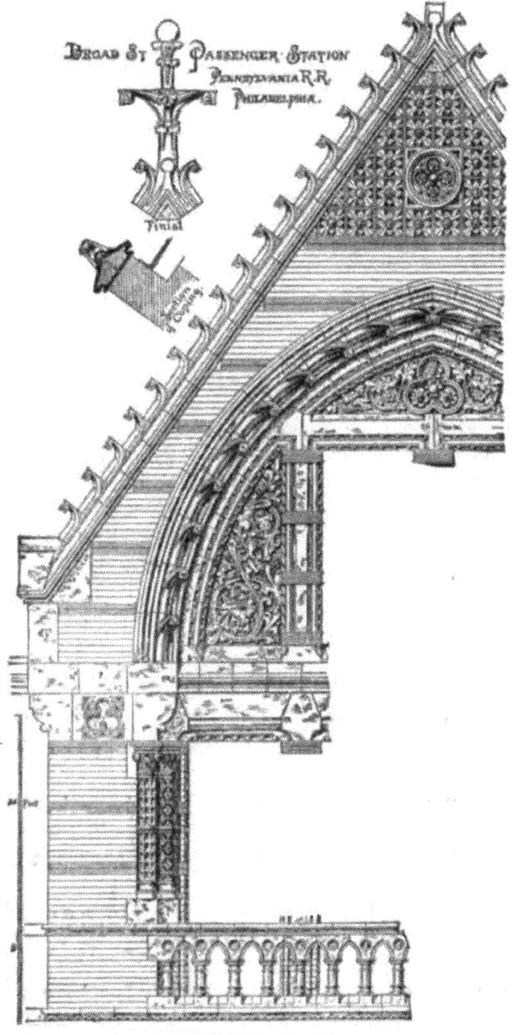

FIG. 641.—DETAIL OF EXTERIOR.

is divided into six unequal bays by piers and buttresses, flanked on the north by a clock-tower, and on the south by a gable, in which are the openings to the exit hall and stairs. The tower and two bays next to it include the ticket-offices, lobby, entrance stairs, etc., the other bays being open through on the street level, so that carriages may drive under.

The basement or first story is of granite, above which are three stories of red brick and terra-cotta. The second floor, as before mentioned, is at the level of the tracks, where all the principal apartments are located. The second-story is therefore the principal one, and is so treated architecturally, the height of the large rooms being divided at either end by entresols.

The piers are carried up from their granite bases in terra-cotta as far as the springing of the large windows of the second story, the jambs of which are decorated with slender terra-cotta columns, two to each side, with enriched shafts and caps, from which rise the great arches of elaborate terra-cotta work in three orders, as shown in detail in Fig. 638.

The transom-lights are kept rectangular, forming spandrels under the arches, which are of terra-cotta, richly decorated. Over the piers between these arches are circular panels, containing finely modelled heads typical of the races of humanity, indicating the cosmopolitan character of the institution and its widespread benefits. The upper stories, being occupied by officers of the company, are more plainly treated, and the openings are made smaller and more numerous to suit the necessary subdivisions. At the level of the fourth floor a balcony is got in the thickness of the wall, the face above being set back, and the line of the wall face below carried up by buttresses, through which openings are pierced, making the balcony continuous. Two of the bays of this front are carried up through the cornice and form gables, shown in Fig. 641, which contain windows lighting an attic story extending over the whole building, and serve to break the otherwise long lines of the cornice. The front on Filbert Street is treated in a similar manner, extending from the clock-tower to the bridge crossing Fifteenth Street, and connecting with train-house.

The granite-work is executed with extreme simplicity, the blocks being large, and the natural unworked surfaces being used wherever practicable. The mouldings and enrichments there used are bold and simple in character. The terra-cotta work, on the other hand, is very elaborate. The individual pieces are small, and plain surfaces are avoided as much as possible, to obviate the difficulties met with in manufacturing large pieces, and the bad effects of warping and shrinking. Delicacy and elaboration of detail naturally follow—qualities which characterize the ancient Italian work, and also the best modern English essays in this material. The red-brick work is relieved by bands of moulded brick of the same color at intervals, which serve to break agreeably the plain surfaces without destroying the solid effect.

The interior is thoroughly carried out in the same style as the exterior. In the lower story the walls of the lobby and stair halls are faced with enamelled brick in buff and white, with dado of chocolate and black, and frieze of white and blue in patterns. Caps and corbels, arches, skirtings, etc., are of blue marble. The ceiling is arched in brick between rolled-iron beams, supported on heavy wrought-iron girders, which in turn are upheld by powerful cast-iron columns, consisting of a square centre section, surrounded by a cluster of four shafts with caps and bases, from which spring ornamental cast-iron brackets, in the shape of a quarter circle, connecting with the under sides of the girders. The iron-work is all exposed to view, and decorated in colors. The floor of the driveway is laid with a pavement of asphalt, and the rest of this floor is artificial stone. The wood finish of this story is ash. The stairs to the waiting-rooms above are marble, with a handsome wrought-iron railing.

In the second or principal story the jambs and arches of the openings are marble, and the floors marble tile, except in the lobbies, etc., where artificial stone is used in colored patterns with good effect. In the lobbies and other exposed portions the walls are colored and enamelled bricks; elsewhere panelled wooden dados are used.

The ceilings of the ladies' waiting-room, dining-room, exit-stair hall, and lobby to train-house are hardwood, divided into panels by the girders supporting the floors above, and subordinate moulded ribs running between them.

In the ladies' waiting room, dining-room, and exit-stair hall the ceiling is supported by curved trusses springing from the walls at the same level as the springing of large windows, and resting on marble corbels built in the walls. These arched trusses are quite elaborate in design, and add much to the beauty of the apartments.

The waiting-rooms, dining-room, and ladies' private room have large open fireplaces, and the transoms of windows and doors and the ceiling over main waiting-room are glazed with cathedral glass in lead, plate-glass being used elsewhere.

The train-house is divided into two equal spans of eighty feet by a row of wrought-iron columns enclosed in ornamental open casings of cast-iron, which carry the roof-trusses. These trusses are wrought-iron, in the form of a double segment, meeting at the ridge in a low Gothic arch, with ornamental struts and tie-rods. The walls are red pressed bricks, divided into panels by moulded pilasters and arches, the pilaster caps being red terra-cotta, and the spandrels filled with buff moulded bricks, arranged in patterns. Along the base is a skirting of blue marble, and a moulded sill-course of the same stone extends the whole length below the windows, which have semicircular heads following the lines of arches between the pilasters.

Every provision has been made for the comfort and convenience of passengers, and every detail, down to the seats and the push-plates on doors, etc., has been carefully considered.

Passenger Depot at Atlantic City, N. J., Philadelphia & Reading Railroad.—The passenger depot of the Philadelphia & Reading Railroad at Atlantic City, N. J., is a terminal head-station, plans for which were published in the issue of the *Railway Review* of May 10, 1890, in connection with the following description :

There are six tracks terminating at this depot, arranged in pairs in such a manner that wide platforms are obtained for the approach of each train. These platforms are 450 ft. in length, and are covered. The waiting-rooms, baggage and express rooms, etc., are grouped together at the end of these tracks in a head-house. There are numerous entrances into the building from Atlantic Avenue and one from Arkansas Avenue. On the latter street there are a number of gateways communicating to the platforms, forming means of ready exit. The lobby is covered by a shed roof extending at right angles with the tracks. From this gable roofs extend parallel with the tracks, covering the platforms their entire length. There are numerous features of interest in the building, the style of architecture being novel. The waiting-rooms are nicely finished in oak, with mahogany furnishings and rich curtains. The station is one which has attracted a great deal of attention and favorable comment.

Passenger Depot at Boston, Mass., New York & New England Railroad.—The passenger depot of the New York & New England Railroad at Boston, Mass., is a terminal head-station, plans for which were published in the issue of the *Railroad Gazette* of Sept. 30, 1881. The train-shed has two tracks entering it, one for in-bound and the other for out-bound trains. There is a baggage platform between the two tracks, while wide passenger platforms are provided along the outside of each track. Baggage is thus handled entirely independently of the passenger platforms, and arriving passengers and departing passengers use separate platforms. The depot building has a general waiting-room, 40 ft. × 46 ft. 10 in.; a baggage-room, 33 ft. × 34 ft.; a kitchen, 19 ft. × 16 ft.; a dining-room, 30 ft. × 16 ft.; a depot-master's room, 23 ft. × 10 ft.; a refreshment-room, 30 ft. × 7 ft.; a telegraph office and package-room, 19 ft. × 7 ft.; a news stands; a ladies' waiting-room, 40 ft. × 23 ft.; a ticket-office, 19 ft. × 17 ft.; lavatories and toilet-rooms for gentlemen and ladies. The general waiting-room is entered through a vestibule from the street. On one side of the depot is a small *porte cochère*. The inside of the building is finished in wood. The offices and dining-rooms are heated by steam, and the waiting-rooms by stoves. The building is covered with galvanized iron on building-paper and boards, and roofed with slate.

Passenger Depot at Stoughton, Mass., Boston & Providence Railroad.—The passenger depot of the Boston & Providence Railroad at Stoughton, Mass., designed by Messrs. Sturgis & Brigham, architects, Boston, Mass., is a small but very substantially built head-station. The head-house is of stone, with slate roof and a large square clock-tower. The train-shed has two tracks running into it, with a platform between the tracks. The ground-plan shows a gentlemen's waiting-room; a ticket-office; a ladies' waiting-room, with toilet-room attached; a baggage-room; a telegraph office; a gentlemen's toilet-room; and a *porte cochère*. The ladies' room is located in the circular-shaped end of the building next to the street, which gives a very pleasing effect both for the exterior as well as the interior. Plans for the building were published in the *Stoughton Sentinel* of April 9, 1887, in which issue the structure is described as follows:

The proposed new depot is to be comprised of a head-house and a train-house. The head-house is to face on Wyman Street. The structure is to be of granite, and is to have a tower and a clock. The tower is to be 62 ft. in height, 15 ft. square on the base, 32 ft. to the ridge or coping, and 14 ft. to the roof of the depot. The extreme length of the main building is 88 ft., and the total width 35½ ft. In the rear the train-house will be of sufficient length to accommodate the entrance of a passenger train and the delivery of the passengers on the inside platform, from which they will proceed to Wyman Street in the main building. The building is to be of Stoughton granite, rough-hewn. The roof will be slated, and the outside wood-work will be of hard wood. On the inside the station will be framed to be at once beautiful and convenient.

The women's room will be on the west side of the building, and will be a beautiful twelve-sided room, 32 ft. square. The men's room will be 32×36 ft. square, large and convenient. The ticket-office will be between the two rooms on the south side facing Wyman street, and will be so arranged as to permit the sale of tickets in either room in a very handy manner. This room will be 10×14½ ft. The baggage-room will be in the east side of the building and will be 11 ft. square. The telegraph office will be 14×6½ ft. and convenient of access. Suitable and convenient toilet-rooms for men and women will be found.

The *porte cochère* or driveway entrance will be on the extreme east of the building, and will be 20 x 24 ft. The interior will be finished in hard wood in the most substantial and elegant manner, with hard-pine floors.

Passenger Depot at Boston, Mass, Boston & Providence Railroad.—The passenger depot of the Boston & Providence Railroad, built about the year 1874, and designed by Messrs. Peabody & Stearns, architects, Boston, Mass., is a very handsome head-station, a plan of which was published in the issue of the *Railroad Gazette* of June 19, 1875, in connection with the following description.

The building is situated on the triangular lot bounded by Park Square, Columbus Avenue and Providence Street, and is Gothic in design, and built of brick laid in black mortar, with Nova Scotia stone trimmings. The head-house is 200 ft. long and 150 ft. wide. The train-house is 600 ft. long, 128 ft. wide, and 65 ft. high. The main entrance to the building is on Columbus Avenue, through a vestibule 25 x 32 ft., paved with tiles, and the ceiling finished with hard pine. On the left of the main entrance, on Park Square, is a brick tower 150 ft. high, containing an illuminated clock with four faces, each 10 ft. in diameter. The vestibule leads into a general waiting-hall 170 ft. long, 44 ft. wide, and 80 ft. high, extending up above the rest of the building so as to admit light through clear-story windows. Additional light is also obtained through skylights in the roof. This hall, as well as the remainder of the first story, is paved with black, white, and red tiles, and is heated by means of three stacks of marble-topped steam radiators. Around this hall, and on a level with the second story, runs a gallery, connecting the corporation offices in the second story, supported by wooden columns and brackets; between these columns are pointed arches, finished in ash, and glazed with plate glass, dividing the hall from the waiting-rooms on the sides and at the end opposite the entrance from the train-house. The main hall is covered by a roof supported by hard-pine trusses, and sheathed with pine varnished and decorated. On the left of the hall is the smoking-room, 44 x 27 ft., gentlemen's waiting-room, 50 x 40, ticket-office, and ladies' room, 50 x 62. The parcel-room is between the waiting-rooms and behind the ticket-office. Connected with the ladies' waiting-room is a dressing-room, 15 x 24 ft., and water-closet.

On the right of the hall is the main staircase to the corporation offices in the second story (which are also connected with Park Square by means of a private vestibule), gentlemen's dressing-room, 15 ft. square, gentlemen's water-closet, 34 x 13 ft., telegraph office, news-stand, barber-shop, restaurant, 50 x 30 ft., private dining-room and serving-room. All of these rooms are 20 ft. high and finished in ash. The windows are glazed with plate glass and leaded glass above the springing of the arch. On the walls of the ladies' room are painted maps of the road and its connections. Next to the ladies' room is a corridor leading to the Columbus Avenue entrance and which connects with the outward baggage-room.

In front of the building, in the second story, is the superintendent's general office, superintendent's private office, and president's private office. On the left of the building is the president's and directors' room, treasurer's general and private office, ticket-agent's and conductors' room, and connected with these rooms are the necessary dressing-rooms. On the right of the building is a room for the storage of supplies, travellers' reading-room, billiard-room, 30 x 50 ft., spare office, kitchen and bakery, the latter being over the restaurant and accessible therefrom by a private staircase. In the third story, over the front office, are sleeping-rooms and bath-rooms for the president, superintendent, and treasurer. The entire building is finished in ash, the walls and ceiling painted and decorated with oil colors, and is heated by steam furnished by four large boilers in the basement. The train-house is entered from the main hall on the first story through three arched doorways. On the right of the entrance is the depot-master's room, and a staircase leading to the gallery of the head-house. On the left is the outward baggage-room, which connects with the Columbus Avenue carriage-entrance. About half-way down the length of the train-house, and outside the building, is a room for the storage of inward baggage and a waiting-room for hackmen. The roof, which covers five tracks, is supported by arched iron trusses, 24 ft. on centres and 125 ft. span. Light is furnished through large windows in the sides and glass in the roof. The trains enter through arches in the end of the train-house, the largest of which is 68 ft. span.

Proposed Union Passenger Depot at Buffalo, N. Y.—The plans for a proposed Union Passenger Depot at Buffalo, N. Y., were published in the issue of the *Railway Review* of Feb. 18, 1888. The design, prepared by Mr. C. W. Buchholz, Engineer of Bridges and Buildings, New York, Lake Erie & Western Railroad, shows a large and handsome terminal head-station, described as follows in the publication mentioned:

The efforts to solve the grade-crossing problem in Buffalo have resulted in a scheme which is so favorably received by the railroads and the public that it seems likely to be brought to a fulfilment. The proposition, as submitted to the sub-committee of the joint committee on grade-crossings, was illustrated by plans prepared by Mr. C. W. Buchholz, of the Erie Railroad. The total cost of the projected improvement is estimated at between $2,000,000 and $3,000,000.

It is proposed by the Buchholz plan to have the roads entering the city approach their terminus by a common route, the tracks of which shall cross the streets east of Louisiana Street above grade, but shall run under Louisiana, Chicago, and Michigan streets. The tracks are to run into a union depot which will front on Washington Street, at the corner of Exchange. West of the depot the tracks of the New York Central will cross Washington and Main streets below grade, coming to grade on the Terrace about opposite the foot of Franklin Street.

It is proposed to begin the depression of the tracks at Van Rensselaer Street and continue the descent until a level is struck two feet below the present grade at Louisiana Street. This level will be continued to Michigan Street, and thence carried into the train-house at such a grade that the platforms of the cars will be on a level with the landings.

The passenger depot provided for in Mr. Buchholz's plans is worthy of a description in detail. The Washington Street elevation presents an ornate brick and cut-stone building, with a frontage of 300 ft., seven stories high, covered by a Mansard roof with numerous dormer-windows, and overtopped by a massive clock-tower over 200 ft. high. A paved plaza 100 ft. wide separates the building from the street proper. Over the main entrances is a broad *porte cochère*, and to the right of this, about 75 ft. farther south, is a massive arch from which emerge the double tracks of the Central Belt Line and the Niagara Falls branch. The Exchange Street elevation drops to three stories after passing the tower, and continues for 300 ft. Beyond this stretches away the train-house for 500 ft. more. A heavy archway securely gated on this side furnishes an exit for all passengers leaving the depot. Some of the express and baggage rooms are on this side, and the other express and baggage rooms are in the corresponding building on the canal side of the station, which is separated from the canal by a driveway of ample proportions. The ground-plan of the passenger station shows a general waiting-room, 76 × 132; a smoking-room, 37 × 81; a spacious ladies' room, wide hallways extending up to the roof to afford light and ventilation, a grand staircase leading to the regions above from the hall on the right of the general waiting-room, four elevators, a spacious ticket-office, and a platform 50 × 280 between the waiting-room and the train-house.

On the second floor is a restaurant, while all the floors above are given up to offices of the railroad companies making use of the terminal facilities. The south wing contains baggage-rooms, express-rooms, a store-room, and a kitchen, with offices on the two floors above.

The north wing, on the Exchange Street side, contains baggage and express rooms only on the ground floor, with offices above. The plans for the train-house call for an arched structure 108 ft. high in the centre and 280 ft. wide, with 14 tracks and eight broad platforms between them.

The estimated cost of the passenger station complete is $700,000.

Passenger Depot at Rochester, N. Y., New York, Lake Erie & Western Railroad.—The passenger depot of the New York, Lake Erie & Western Railroad at Rochester, N. Y., is a terminal head-station, plans for which were published in the issue of the *Railway Review* of August 27, 1887; in the issue of the *Scientific American* (Architects and Builders' Edition) of November, 1886; and in the issue of the *Railroad Gazette* of March 20, 1885. The description of the building in the *Scientific American* is as follows:

The new depot is located on the south side of Court Street, near the river. The style of the architecture is based on the modern Renaissance, being treated in a free and unconventional manner suitable for this class of building. On the first story there is a general waiting-room, 38 ft. × 35 ft., with a gentlemen's toilet-room opening from it. Also a ladies' waiting-room opening from it, with a ladies' toilet-room attached. There is also a baggage-room, 39 ft. × 15 ft.; an agent's room, with ticket-office; a news-stand; and a telegraph-office. On the second story there are a superintendent's office, conductors' room, division freight agent's office, hall, lobby, and toilet-room. The main building is 76 ft. × 60 ft. A tower on the northeast corner rises to the height of 110 ft. above the pavement. Brick and stone have been used for the walls, with Medina stone laid up in regular courses of ashlar, with quarry faces and chiselled draught below the first-floor sills. Above this point the exterior courses of walls are laid up with pressed brick in black mortar. Window-sills, bracket corbels, key-stones, and first-story sill-course are of Ohio sandstone. Trimmings of terra-cotta and moulded brick are freely used in belt and string courses and in the arches. The roofs of main building and awnings are covered with slate and copper, and the roofs of wings with tin. The interior of the building will be finished in white ash and cherry, the floors of waiting-rooms and vestibules laid with black and white marble tiles, and the floors of the toilet-room with slate tiles. An open staircase in oak, ash, and cherry is located in the tower. Steam will be used to heat the building, and electricity for lighting. The tower clock has four 5-ft. glass dials, and will be lighted automatically by electricity. A train-shed 270 ft. long and 72 ft. wide, of ornamental design, in iron, is to be erected adjoining. The cost of passenger station and train-shed will be upward of $50,000. The work is being executed under the direction of C. W. Buchholz, engineer, from drawings and designs of George E. Archer, architect to the company.

Terminal Passenger Depot at Louisville, Ky., Louisville & Nashville Railroad.—The passenger depot of the Louisville & Nashville Railroad at Louisville, Ky., designed by Mr. H. Wolters, architect, Louisville, Ky., commenced during the summer of 1882 and completed in 1887, shown in Figs. 642 and 643,

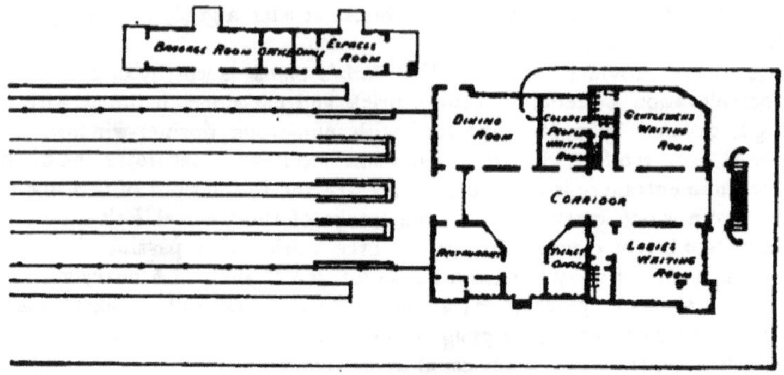

FIG. 642.—GROUND-PLAN.

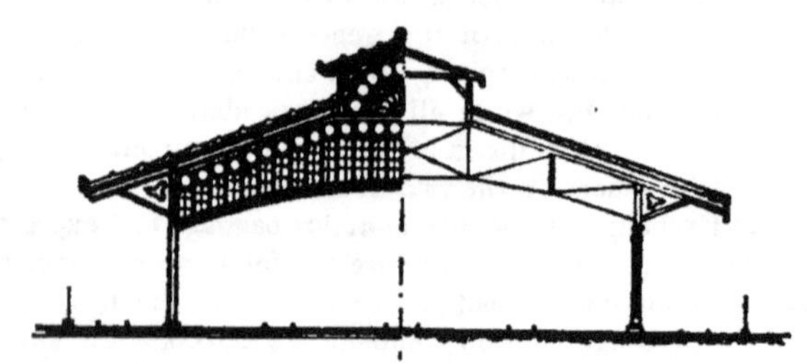

FIG. 643.—CROSS-SECTION AND END ELEVATION OF TRAIN-SHED.

from data kindly furnished to the author by Mr. R. Montford, Chief Engineer, L. & N. R. R., is a large terminal head-station, plans for which were published in the issue of the *American Architect and Building News* of May 20, 1882, and in the issue of the *Railway Review* of May 20, 1882. The description of the building in the latter publication is as follows:

The depot is located on the corner of Broadway and Tenth Streets. The front of the building will be 100 ft. wide and 130 ft. deep, and will have a basement and three stories. The first floor will have, besides a corridor 20 ft. wide, waiting-rooms for ladies, for gentlemen, and for colored people, together with a ticket-office, coffee-stand, and dining-room. On the second floor will be offices for the transportation and the engineering departments, and a large room for the Louisville & Nashville branch of the Young Men's Christian Association. The walls will be faced with pressed bricks, and the sills, lintels, and ornaments will be made of the white oolitic limestone from the quarries at Bedford, Ind., while the front stairway will be made of granite. All the inside finish will be of hard wood. The car-shed will be 100 ft. wide and 400 ft. long; it will be made entirely of wrought-iron, and will cover five tracks, three of which will be for the exclusive use of the Louisville & Nashville Railroad Company's trains, while the two on the west side will be made accessible to trains of the Chesapeake, Ohio & Southwestern, as well as of the Ohio & Mississippi, and of the Jeffersonville, Madison & Indianapolis, from the north side of the Ohio River. West of the shed there will be a detached brick building, 130 ft. long, for the baggage and express business.

Union Passenger Depot at Cincinnati, O.—The Union Passenger Depot at Cincinnati, O., designed by Mr. W. W. Boyington, architect, Chicago, Ill., is a large terminal head-station, a plan of which was published in the issue of the *Scientific American Supplement* of Nov. 12, 1881. The structure is described in the *Railway Review* as follows:

This structure is to be located upon the corner of Central Avenue and Third Street. The end front will be 233 ft. on Central Avenue. The side front will be 475 ft. on Third Street. On the corner of Central Avenue and Third Street will be an office-building 80 × 90 ft., six stories high. This is intended to accommodate local offices for the four or five different railroads that will occupy the station. In this building there will be a series of three large fire-proof vaults on each floor. A passenger elevator and all modern conveniences for office purposes will run to the roof. There will be a light-shaft in the centre, affording light to all parts of the building, and at the same time a thorough ventilation. The depot proper will be approached either from Central Avenue or Third Street. The main passenger waiting-room will be on a level with Third Street, 220 ft. long by 36 ft. wide in the clear, and three stories high, with ticket, Pullman, and telegraph offices included. There will be large and commodious parlors and living-rooms and lunch-counters on a level with this floor in the office-building.

The passenger building will recede 30 ft. back from the office-building on Third Street. This 30 ft. will be covered over to the sidewalk with an iron canopy for the convenience of passengers alighting from carriages. In addition to this covered roadway there will be a covered carriage and 'bus rotunda, 100 × 80 ft., opening from Central Avenue.

The platform or car-shed story will be 15 ft. down from Third Street, and will be reached by the rotunda before mentioned on Central Avenue, and by a large archway 30 ft. wide between the office building and main passenger-room, also by a large double flight of stairs through the centre of the main waiting-room. There will be a general ticket-office, waiting-rooms, lunch-counter, smoking-rooms, barber-shop, etc., on the platform floor.

The baggage-room and building, 36 × 175 ft., and two stories high, will be on Third Street, west oı the main waiting-room. This will be arranged so that the baggage-room floor will be on a level with the car floor, and the 30-ft. road so graded on the street front that baggage wagons can load directly from the baggage-room without elevators.

An incoming-baggage room will be provided on Central Avenue, approached by the rotunda before mentioned. It will be otherwise similar to the main baggage-room. The platforms will be about 700 ft. long under the viaduct of Smith Street.

The car-sheds cover ten tracks, with sufficient platforms to accommodate five roads with two tracks each.

The style of the building is to be Eastlake and modern Gothic, treated with Queen Anne features. This will be relieved by bold projections, giving a picturesque outline and a very attractive and impressive façade, quite dissimilar to any depot in this country. Its material will be stone in the first or platform story, and red pressed brick above, with light-colored stone trimmings and red terra-cotta ornaments interspersed to relieve the plain surfaces.

The building itself will cost about $400,000. The entire cost of ground, track, and buildings will be about $1,000,000.

The railroad immediately in charge of the enterprise is the Cincinnati, Indianapolis, St. Louis & Chicago Railway Company, with M. E. Ingalls, Esq., president, at the head of the enterprise. W. W. Boyington, Esq., of Chicago, is the architect of the building.

Terminal Passenger Depot at Cincinnati, O., Pittsburg, Cincinnati & St. Louis Railway.— The passenger depot of the Pittsburg, Cincinnati & St. Louis Railway at Cincinnati, O., designed by Mr. S. J. Hall, architect, under the direction of Mr. M. J. Becker, Chief Engineer, P., C. & St. L. Ry., is a large terminal head-station, plans for which were published in the issue of the *Railroad Gazette* of Oct. 27, 1882. The improvements made at this point, including the passenger depot, are described as follows, in the publication mentioned:

The new passenger station is located on the southeast corner of Pearl and Butler streets, extending with its main entrance front along Butler Street, 116 ft. 4 in., and 89 ft. 6 in. along Pearl Street.

Its foundations consist of blue limestone masonry, reaching to the base of the lower story windows, where they are capped with a bevelled water-table of white Dayton limestone. All outer walls are of pressed brick of Zanesville, O., manufacture, trimmed with Cincinnati freestone. The roof is partly of slate and partly of tin.

The ground-floor contains a main waiting-room in the central part of the building, open to the roof; on the left of the main entrance is a passage leading to the ladies' waiting-room, and connected with that room is a toilet-room and closets. The general ticket-office, the Pullman office, a package-room, and water-closets are all located upon the left of the general waiting-room, as is also an exterior hall and stairway leading to the offices in the upper story.

In the rear of the general waiting-room and directly opposite the main entrance are the doors leading to the train-shed. On the right of the general waiting-room are the dining-room and lunch-room, with kitchen between the two; also telegraph-office, depot-master's office, and conductors' room.

In the upper story of the building are the offices of the Superintendent of the Little Miami Division, the train-despatcher's office, conductors' rooms, and closets. All these rooms are located along the outer walls of the building, leaving the entire interior space open for light and ventilation for the main waiting-room below. A gallery connects the rooms of the upper story, and affords a view over the general waiting-room and lower story of the building.

The interior walls are frescoed in oil, and the woodwork is finished in black-walnut, all of modern designs and workmanship. The floors are tiled. The gas-fixtures are of polished bronze of tasteful designs.

The rear of the building is sheltered by a porch inclosed by an iron railing, with iron gates for access to the train-shed.

The train-shed is 360 ft. long and 85 ft. wide between columns, affording entrance for four tracks and sheltering two additional tracks under the projections of the roof. It is composed of wrought-iron columns anchored to stone foundations, roofed by wooden arched ribs and covered with tin. A substantial wall, surmounted by an iron fence, encloses the yard along Pearl Street. The widening of Butler Street and the space south of the passenger station afford ample room for approach of carriages and vehicles for the landing of passengers and baggage.

Near the southeast corner of the passenger station is a brick building, 85 ft. long and 24 ft. wide, for baggage, mail, and express rooms. The passenger yard is separated from the freight yard by a division wall extending from the ice-house eastwardly to a point east of Kilgour Street.

The elevation of Pearl Street at the corner of Butler Street is about 11 ft. above the level of Front Street, which difference made it necessary to establish the two yards on different planes in order to afford access to each from the adjacent streets. The tracks of the passenger yard are therefore ascending from the point of divergence east of the city water-works towards the passenger station, and the freight tracks are descending in the same direction, the division wall rising in height with the increasing difference in the elevation of the tracks.

Immediately south of the division wall is a spare track for delivery of bulk freight. Next to this is the track leading to the Newport and Cincinnati Bridge, upon a rising grade of 110 ft. per mile. Between this bridge track and Front Street are the freight tracks and freight stations. The new freight-house is 505 ft. long and 94 ft. wide; it is composed of iron columns supporting a combination roof covered with tin. Adjoining the new freight-house on the west are the offices of the local agent, cashier, and their clerks, in a two-story brick building facing on Front Street.

An old freight-house, east of Kilgour Street, has been retained for a local delivery station.

The former passenger station on the south side of Front Street has been converted into a freight station for use of the Louisville & Nashville Railroad.

The total cost of the improvements foots up as follows:

Passenger station,	$79,422 39
Passenger shed,	28,995 48
Baggage building,	5,660 71
Freight station,	53,090 32
Converting old passenger station into freight station,	2,646 78
Yard tracks,	44,319 76
Retaining-walls,	10,134 93
Grading,	7,688 77
Street-paving,	17,269 95
Total cost,	$249,229 09

Terminal Passenger Depot at Cincinnati, O., Chesapeake & Ohio Railroad.—The passenger depot of the Chesapeake & Ohio Railroad at Fourth Street, Cincinnati, O., which was in course of construction during the year 1890, in connection with other terminal improvements at this point, is a terminal head-station, the ground-plan of which, with a description, was published in the issue of the *Railway Review* of March 22, 1890.

Terminal Passenger Depot at Montreal, Can., Canadian Pacific Railway.—The new passenger depot of the Canadian Pacific Railway, at Montreal, Can., shown in Fig. 644, is a very large and handsome head-station, designed by Mr. Bruce Price, architect, New York, N. Y., plans of which were published in the *Engineering & Building Record*, and subsequently published in the issue of the *Railway Review* of Feb. 25, 1888. The building is described as follows, in the publications mentioned:

There are four full stories above the basement, besides a finished story in the roof. The basement is a full story at one end, and wholly under ground at the other, as the building stands on rising ground. The general dimensions of the building are 204 ft. front and 70 ft. deep. The train-shed in the rear of the building is 500 ft. long. The cost is stated to be about $250,000. The upper floors are used for the general offices of the company. The material used in the building is stone, Scotch rubble-face, with rock-face belt-courses. The interior finish is in Vancouver cedar. The general waiting-room on the first floor is arched over, with granite columns and arches finished in plaster. The floor-beams throughout the building are iron, with fire-proof finish.

This depot and the stone viaduct approach are described and illustrated in the issue of *Engineering News* of March 3, 1888.

Terminal Passenger Depot at Detroit, Mich., Michigan Central Railroad.—The passenger depot of the Michigan Central Railroad at Detroit, Mich., is a large and handsomely constructed head-station, designed by Mr. Cyrus L. W. Eidlitz, architect, New York, N. Y., plans for which were published in the issue of the *Railway Review* of Aug. 25, 1883, the description of the depot being as follows, in the publication mentioned:

The depot is located at the corner of Third and Woodbridge Streets. The main building will have a frontage of 182 ft. 6 in. on Third Street and 280 ft. on Woodbridge Street. From the line of Third Street to the front of the building there will be an open space of 27 ft. deep, intended for a grass plat, fountains, and flowers. The westerly 84 ft. on Woodbridge Street will be covered with a lower range of buildings, in which will be the boiler-rooms and express-offices, leaving an area of 182 x 196 ft. for the main building.

The principal entrance will be in the centre of the Third Street front, and will be one of the chief features of the structure. This central division will project 13 ft. from the line of the main wall, and the entrances will be five in number; three arched openings in the front and one on each side of the projection will give access to a large and lofty lobby 40 ft. wide and 45 deep. In this lobby there will be an ornamental wrought-iron staircase leading to the general offices of the company on the second floor. At the westerly end of the lobby, and directly opposite the main entrance, there willbe large double doors leading to the trains. The space above the doors and the transom will be filled with stained glass.

On the right-hand side of the lobby there will be large double doors leading to the gentlemen's waiting-room, which will occupy the space between the main entrance and the tower.

To the left of the lobby will be similar doors opening into a spacious dining-hall, which will be first-class in every respect.

Around the corner, in the Woodbridge Street front of the main building, there will be a ladies' entrance. This front is also projected beyond the line of the main wall sufficient to give space for a vestibule, from which will be the entrance to the ladies' waiting-room, a spacious apartment 43 x 30 ft., with its high ceiling panelled with hard wood, and with a hard-wood panelled wainscoting extending 6 ft. above the floor. To the right of the waiting-room there will be dressing-rooms, to the left the ticket-office, while at the southerly end there will be wide doors leading to the train platform.

The ticket-office will be in the base of the tower, occupying the angle between the two waiting-rooms with office windows opening to each.

The baggage-rooms will be next west of the ladies' waiting-room, with which they will be connected by an enclosed passage-way.

Large terra-cotta fireplaces of original design and extending from the floor to the ceiling will be conspicuous features in the ladies' waiting-room and the dining-hall. A novelty in the interior arrangement of the station will be the wide platform, 30 ft. in width, which will extend the whole length of the Third Street front. It will be surmounted with a roof of glass and be railed off from the tracks by an ornamental paling, in which will be gates which will be kept closed except when passengers are entering the cars or coming in from trains. Between the tracks there will be wide, sheltered verandas, beneath which passengers can step from the trains without exposure to the weather.

The second story will be devoted to the offices of the company, to which, besides the main staircase in

FIG. 644.—PERSPECTIVE.

the entrance lobby, there will be a private spiral staircase in the turret attached to the great tower at the angle of the building. The general and private offices of the president will be in the tower, above the ticket-office; and clustered around these will be the offices of the other officers of the road, such as the president's private secretary, the general attorney, auditor, superintendent, and chief engineer. Across the broad hall at the rear of the building and facing the tracks will be the offices of the general freight-agent, paymaster, fuel-agent, superintendent of the Canada Southern, division superintendent, and purchasing agent.

The main motive for the architectural treatment of the building is the leading up of all its parts, from both directions, to the main tower. This tower will be 157 ft. in height to the ridge, and will be a conspicuous and imposing object from every point of view. From this culminating point the masses of the building diminish in height towards the end, although this recession is prevented from becoming monotonous by the bold and emphatic perspective of the gable mass at the base of which will be the main entrances, and by the lesser projection that will relieve the Woodbridge Street front.

The materials to be used in the construction of the building are Philadelphia pressed brick, red terra-cotta, a reddish-brown sandstone from New Jersey, and blue and red slate,—the latter for the tower only. The stone will be used rock-face, and will form the footing-courses, steps, string-courses, and the first stage of the tower and turret. The terra-cotta will be used in the arches, string-courses, crestings, and ridges of the roofs.

Union Passenger Depot at Fort Street, Detroit, Mich.—The Union Passenger Depot at Fort Street Detroit, Mich., on which construction was started in 1890, is a large terminal head-station, designed by Messrs. Jas. Stewart & Co., architects, of St. Louis, Mo., plans for which were published in the *Railway Review* and also in the issue of *Engineering News* of Jan. 31, 1891, Fig. 645 being taken from the latter publication. The same issue of *Engineering News* contains the plans for a proposed design for the same depot, prepared by Mr. Bradford L. Gilbert, architect, New York City, N. Y. The description of the adopted design, in the publication mentioned, is as follows:

The site for the new station is at the corner of Fort and Third Streets, a few blocks north of the Michigan Central Station, and somewhat further removed from the river than that building. The heavy expense for foundations necessary in the made ground near the river was therefore avoided here. Fort Street is one of the principal residence streets of the city, and a large church with high spire on the corner opposite the site of the station made a building of considerable height necessary in order that it should not be dwarfed by the church. A train-shed was not called for, it being considered better to put all the money available into the main structure and place shed roofs over the platforms, leaving the train-shed to be built, perhaps, at some future day.

The adopted design has six tracks running into the depot. The estimated cost for the new depot is set at $225,000. The frontage on Third Street is 138 ft. and on Fort Street 125 ft. The tower is about 170 ft. The materials are to be red brick and stone.

Terminal Passenger Depot, Chicago, Ill., Wisconsin Central Railway.—The Central Station of the Wisconsin Central Railway, at the corner of Fifth Avenue and Harrison Street, Chicago, Ill., designed by Mr. S. S. Beman, architect, and built under the direction of Mr. W. S. Jones, Chief Engineer, W. C. Ry., plans for which were published in the *Inland Architect and News Record*, Vol. 13, No. 1, and in the issues of the *Railway Review* of February 23, 1889, and of December 20, 1890, is a large L-shaped terminal head-station. It is described as follows in the *Railway Review* of December 20, 1890:

On December 8, 1890, the Grand Central Station of Chicago was formally opened to the public. The construction of this building was begun in October, 1888, and in the time which has since elapsed there has arisen the finest depot building in Chicago, and one of the most magnificent in this portion of the country. Complete in all its appointments, grand in its proportions, and imposing in its architecture, it commands admiration, and reflects great credit upon those who conceived and carried out the enterprise to a successful completion. The Chicago & Northern Pacific R. R., the Wisconsin Central lines, and the Chicago, St. Paul & Kansas City R. R. are occupying the building jointly, and they may all greatly increase their passenger traffic without becoming cramped in their facilities. The station is very conveniently located, being almost in the centre of the city, and but a short distance from most of the other prominent railway stations of Chicago. The enterprise was undertaken by what was at that time known as the Chicago & Great Western Railway, a short double-track road by which the Wisconsin Central lines and the Chicago, St. Paul & Kansas City Railroad obtained an entrance into the city. Since that time the Wisconsin Central has been leased by the Northern Pacific Railroad, and the Chicago & Great Western is now known as the Chicago & Northern Pacific. The engineer in charge of the work from its conception was Mr. W. S. Jones, Chief Engineer of the Chicago & Northern Pacific Railroad. The architect was Mr. S. S. Beman, of Chicago, and the iron and steel work of the train-shed has been constructed by the Keystone Bridge Co., Pittsburg, Pa., of which C. L. Strobel, of Chicago, is chief engineer.

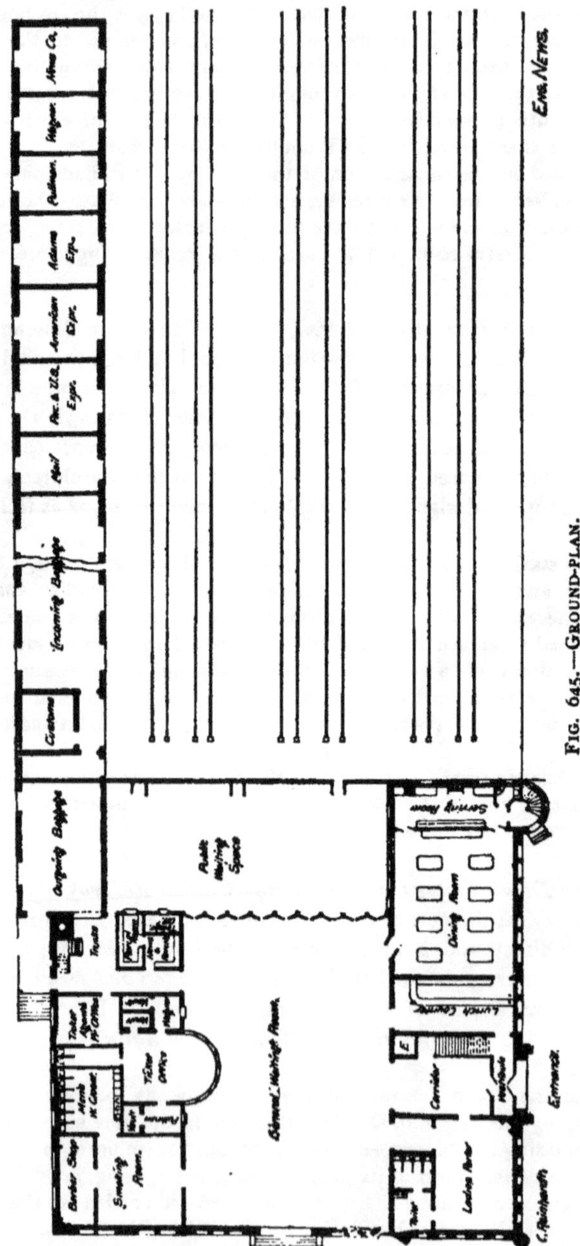

FIG. 645.—GROUND-PLAN.

The property on which this building stands extends south from Harrison Street to the railroad draw-bridge across the south branch of the Chicago River, some 300 feet below Taylor Street, and west from Fifth Avenue to the river, and comprises an area of over 15 acres. South and west of the river there is also a tract of land comprising about 8 acres on which railroad buildings, roundhouses, etc., are located, and still further south there is another piece of land 24 acres in extent which will be used for warehouses, freight-depots, etc. The building has a frontage on Harrison Street of 226 feet, and the entire building, including baggage-rooms, express-offices, etc., has a frontage of 837 feet on Fifth Avenue. The foundations of the buildings are very massive, and the superstructure is composed of brown pressed brick and Connecticut brown stone. The foundations are carried on piles, which are 30 feet long under all the lighter walls, while under the main walls and the tower they are 50 feet in length. The piles are capped with 12 × 12-in. oak timbers, and the space from a point 12 in. below the top of the piles to a level with the tops of the caps is rammed full of Portland cement concrete, and above this there is a course of 12-in. timber spaced about 4 in. apart and filled in with concrete. The whole is then covered with 18 inches of concrete on top of which the walls are built.

A portion of the building is seven and the remainder four stories in height. The tower is 212½ ft. high above the sidewalk. The lower story of the building is used for the station proper, and the upper stories for offices.

At the corner of the building four very heavy walls form a square about 80 ft. each way. This portion of the building extended up around the tower forms that part of the structure which is seven stories high. The remainder of this plan exterior to the square is carried up four stories only. The office portion of the building is in most respects very similar to modern buildings devoted to these purposes, and needs no special description. One peculiarity in the location of the vaults is perhaps worthy of notice. A number of them are located in the interior of the building, but every pilaster in the north and east walls of the building is made hollow and utilized for the location of a vault.

The ground-plan of the building is devoted to various station purposes, and the baggage-rooms are located in an annex which extends south from the depot along Fifth Avenue; the express-offices are located still further south under the approach to a viaduct, which will be again referred to. The general waiting-room is 207 ft. long and 71 ft. wide, and is most magnificent in its appointments. The floor is of marble tiling, and the walls are faced with Tennessee marble to a height of about 8¼ ft. from the floor. Above that the walls are perfectly plain, and the ceiling, though elegant in appearance, is also characterized by its simplicity of design and color. The columns are circular in section, and finished in light colors corresponding with the ceiling and walls. The whole effect in color is that of a yellowish tint, verging upon a cream color. The ceiling, which is 25 ft. high, is divided, by the columns and concealed girders resting upon them, into a number of squares, in the centre of each of which is placed a circle of incandescent lights. There are two entrances from Fifth Avenue and one from Harrison Street, in addition to those through the base of the tower. On the west side of the room is the large ticket-office, a portion of which is divided off for the use of palace-car ticket-agents. Along one side of the ticket-office, and encroaching somewhat on its floor area, a news-counter is located, and just north of it there is a commodious check-room. It is almost impossible to do justice to the fine appearance which this corner of the room presents.

At the south end of the waiting-room there is a passage-way leading out to a corridor extending east and west between the main building and the baggage-room. On the east of the passage-way there is a ladies' waiting-room, 28 × 38 ft., with a private-room and a toilet annex. On the other side of the passage-way the space is divided into a lunch-room, barber-shop, and gentlemen's toilets, all three of which rooms are approached from the platform of the train-shed, or may be entered from the general waiting-room The general finish of these rooms is in entire keeping with the remainder of the building. The baggage-room is very large, being 160 ft. long and 32 ft. wide. The baggage-room has eight doorways opening out on a platform which extends along the baggage tracks from which these cars are loaded and unloaded. The exact manner of handling the baggage will be explained in connection with the train-shed and the uses to which the tracks are put. The baggage-room has also six doorways upon its Fifth Avenue side by which baggage can be received or delivered.

There is a mezzanine floor located south of the general waiting-room, with a very elegant restaurant, 56 × 74 ft., which is reached by a marble staircase from the general waiting-room, and also by means of a hallway and staircase which lead to the corridors between the baggage and general waiting-room. Adjacent to the restaurant there is a kitchen, store-room, etc., and an elevator shaft by which supplies can be obtained from the basement under the baggage-room. The emigrants' waiting-room occupies all of the floor above the baggage-room, and is entirely detached from the remainder of the depot. The entrance and exit to this room are at the south end, where a flight of stairs leads down to a vestibule on the first floor, from which doorways lead to the street and also to an adjacent platform.

Just south of the train-shed Polk Street crosses the tracks, and it became necessary to construct a viaduct at this point in order to avoid a grade-crossing. The nature of the locality made it necessary that the approach to the viaduct should be made parallel to Fifth Avenue, and the entrance to it has been located just south of the baggage-room. Rising by an easy incline, it continues parallel with Fifth Avenue until Polk Street is reached, where it connects with the viaduct extending across the tracks. The approach is constructed entirely of masonry, filled with earth until a sufficient height is reached to enable the space enclosed by the walls to be utilized, and from that point the earth filling ceases and the masonry walls are pierced by windows and doors necessary for utilizing the interior as express-offices. The express storage-room is 27 × 144 ft., and at the north end of it there are two offices, each 18 × 13 ft. 6 in. Across the passage-way there are suitable toilet-accommodations provided. The express-room is situated, in relation to the street and railroad tracks, in much the same manner as the baggage-room.

Facing upon Harrison Street there is a very large carriage court, 117 ft. deep and 149 ft. wide, to which entrance is obtained by three large archways. It is separated from the train-shed by a partition which is composed largely of glass. The court is paved with lithogen. The platform surrounding it on three sides is one step higher than the court, and is six steps higher than the platform in the train-shed. The descent to the platform in the shed is made just inside of the partition between the shed and carriage court. Underneath this court are located the boilers, steam-engines, and other machinery necessary for the heating and lighting of the entire plant, the operation of its elevators, etc. Two large vertical boilers of the Hazleton type are located close to the west wall of the building, and extend up from the basement into the court, where they are entirely encased with brickwork. The stack is located between the boilers, and the gases pass into it at a point just above the boilers, thus making a very neat and compact arrangement, which not only has the advantage of saving much valuable floor-space, but makes it possible to employ one of the most economical types of boilers. Each boiler has two furnaces fitted with Roney automatic stokers. The dynamo-room contains two Sperry dynamos for arc-lighting, and five Edison machines for incandescent lamps, and these machines when used to their full capacity will furnish power for 60 arc-lights of 2000 candle-power each, and 5000 incandescent lights, of which about 500 will be 32 and the remainder 16 candle-power. The elevator machinery is of the type employing horizontal cylinders and rams located in the basement, and the water for their operation is furnished by Worthington compound duplex pumps.

The train-shed and system of tracks connected with this depot form a most interesting feature of these terminals, and are deserving of considerable attention. The roof of the train-shed is supported by 15 trusses, having a clear span of 119 ft. They are spaced 40 ft. apart from centre to centre, making the length of the shed 560 ft. between centres of end trusses. From out to out it is 562 ft. 6 in. The radius of the inner circle of the arch is 59 ft. 6 in., or one half of the clear span, thus making the arch a semi circle. The radius of the outer circle is 76 ft. 6 in. The truss is 3 ft. deep at the centre and 2 ft. 6 in. wide throughout. At the intersection of the outer circle with the vertical member projected up from the foundation, the truss is 9 ft. 10½ in. deep (measured radially), and at the base it is 3 ft. × 2 ft. 6 in. The lower chord is composed of two angle-irons 6 × 6 in., and the upper chord of two angles 4 × 6 in. The roof has an overhang of 11 ft. 9 in. on each side, making the total width of the train-shed 142 ft. 6 in. The monitor is 17 ft. 6 in. high and 14 ft. wide, and has a glass roof. There is also 24 ft. of glass on each side of the monitor for its whole length, and about two thirds of the roof of the overhang on each side is of glass. The courses of masonry in the piers which constituted the foundation of the trusses are inclined sufficiently to be at right angles to the line of thrust, and there is a heavy compression member extending diagonally from the base of the perpendicular member to the angle-irons which form the inner arc of the truss. This transfers the thrust to the foundation-stone, and the inner arc of the truss, though continued below its connection with the diagonal, has no direct bearing upon the foundation. The train-shed is open at the sides. That portion of the roof not covered with glass is covered with corrugated galvanized steel, and the south end truss is also covered on its outer face with the same material. The two feet of this truss are encased in a cast-iron base of suitable design, which enhances the architectural effect.

There is a certain amount of space between the arched roof of the train-shed and the main building which must be roofed over to protect the platforms. This roofing is supported upon light girders, and consists partly of corrugated steel and partly of glass. It has a slight dip toward the train-shed roof, so that the water is drained off at the junction between the two. One end of these light girders is supported on the train-shed roof, and the other is built into the wall of the main building. The tracks between the baggage-room and the train-shed proper are also covered in the same manner, but as the span is a great deal longer the roof-trusses are considerably heavier. A large portion of this roof is also of glass.

There are six tracks within the train-shed, and one extending along the east and west sides, just under the overhanging roof. Still further east there are three more tracks, two of which terminate in front of the baggage-room, and the third in front of the express-office. Taking the tracks in their order from Fifth Avenue west, the first is used wholly for loading and unloading express-cars at the office. The next two tracks are used for baggage, the first being for in-bound and the second for out-bound baggage. The in-bound baggage is taken from the cars directly on to a platform the same height as the floor. The out-bound baggage is carried over the same platform and around the inner ends of the tracks, where it is delivered on trucks which are operated on a lower platform between the second baggage-track and the one west of it. This next track, the fourth from the street, is intended for suburban traffic only. The remaining six tracks within the train-shed, and the one extending along the west side of it, are used for regular passenger traffic, both in and out bound. The track farthest west also extends north along the west side of the main building, so that coal can be taken in cars directly to the basement in which the boiler-furnaces are located, and ashes and other refuse can be taken therefrom.

The tracks in this train-shed are laid in a most substantial manner, and no expense has been spared to make them all that could be desired. When the ground was cleared preparatory to putting in the tracks and platforms the space occupied by the tracks was first filled to a depth of four inches with broken stone, which was rammed and solidly packed. The next course was four inches of screenings, which was rolled by a seven-ton roller. Above this were placed the Portland-cement walls for the support of the track, with concrete bases. The space between these walls was floored with eight inches of brick laid to form an inverted arch. The troughs were then filled as shown, on which was placed a four-inch course of broken stone, and the whole covered with four inches of concrete. The longitudinal wooden beams on which the rails are laid are 8 x 12 in. and secured by anchor-bolts about four feet apart. The surface between the tracks is dished for drainage purposes, and is also graded longitudinally with the train-shed, having slight summits 80 ft. apart, midway between which there are catch-basins covered with iron gratings and connecting with the sewer. The six tracks within the train-shed are grouped in pairs, and between each group there is a platform 19 ft. wide, composed of lithogen 6 in. thick, supported upon 12-in. walls of the same. The space between the rails of one track, instead of being filled with earth, is used as a conduit. This conduit will be used for pipes supplying steam the whole length of the train-shed, so that cars may be heated before the locomotive is attached. It will also contain air-pipes supplying the electro-pneumatic interlocking signals used in the yards below, and water-pipes by means of which an abundance of water for flushing the tracks and platforms can be obtained. It will also be utilized for electric wires which will lead from various parts of the shed to the train-despatcher's office, located above the depot-master's office at the head of the train-shed. When trains are ready to proceed a signal can thus be given by the conductor to the despatcher, who in turn will operate an enunciator in the signal-tower, calling attention of the operator at that point to the fact that a certain route is desired through the yards and out onto the main line.

Just south of the viaduct over Polk Street an interlocking tower is located, which contains a 24-lever electro-pneumatic signaling machine, furnished by the Union Switch and Signal Co. This machine controls all the switches and signals in its immediate vicinity. The two tracks (Nos. 1 and 2), from which all others branch out to the depot and to express and baggage tracks, are the in and out bound main lines. The three tracks (Nos. 4, 6, and 8) to the west of them are passenger sidings, as are also two tracks (Nos. 3 and 5) to the east of them. Next to the freight-house on Fifth Avenue south of Polk Street there are two freight-tracks (Nos. 9 and 11), and between them and the passenger sidings there is one neutral track (No. 7). The tracks all unite into two lines which pass over the drawbridge. On this bridge there is another interlocking tower, containing a 12-lever machine, which controls all switches and signals grouped at the southern end of the yard. The compressed air for operating all the machinery connected with both interlocking cabins is furnished by air-compressors in the basement of the station building. There are several features of interest in connection with the cabin on the drawbridge, one of the chief of which is the fact that the engine for swinging the bridge will hereafter be run by air. As compressed air was piped to the bridge anyway, it was deemed advisable to do away with the steam-boiler and its attending annoyances, and put in a second air-main to run the engine. A three-inch pipe is carried down the yard for this purpose, and a two-inch one for the operation of switches and signals. These extend to the bank of the river, and in company with two other three-inch pipes containing electric wires, pass down into the river-bed, across to the central pier, and thence up to the bridge and cabin. The construction of the central pier made it impossible to go up through the centre of it; consequently the pipes were carried up the outside, and elbow-joints are employed to make connections with the bridge, and permit the latter to be swung. The machine in this cabin also differs from others heretofore constructed, in that the valves of the machine, instead of being operated by air, are electrically controlled, and air does not come into service at any point between the switch and the lever-machine. Some distance south of the drawbridge a third tower is located, also containing a 12-lever machine, and the electro-pneumatic block system is employed as far as Ogden Avenue, a distance of 3.7 miles, in which distance there are ten blocks.

Terminal Passenger Depot at Chicago, Ill., Chicago & Northwestern Railway.—The passenger depot of the Chicago & Northwestern Railway at Chicago, Ill., shown in Fig. 646, designed by Mr. W. W. Boyington, architect, Chicago, Ill., is a large and handsome, substantially built head-station, plans for which were published in the issue of the *American Architect and Building News* of Feb. 19, 1881, and in the issue of the *Railroad Gazette* of June 3, 1881, and is described as follows in the latter publication:

This structure is intended for a general passenger depot and office building of the Chicago & Northwestern Railway in Chicago, at the corner of North Wells and East Kinzie streets. The material is red pressed brick and Lake Huron French gray sandstone, treated in the Queen Anne style.

There are two passenger waiting-rooms. One, which is termed the platform story, down from the principal streets half a story. The size of this room is 126 ft. x 56 ft. It contains a ticket-office and lunch-room, gentlemen's and ladies' departments, etc. This floor has also the baggage-rooms, 217 ft. x 25 ft., in a side building; also an express building, 150 ft. x 15 ft. This is but one story high.

The main and grand gentlemen's and ladies' waiting-room is upon a level with the main street entrance. It in itself is, without doubt, one of the most complete and commodious passenger rooms yet erected. It is 144 ft. x 60 ft. in the clear. It has been finished in hard wood, void of all gingerbread finery. The walls

FIG. 646.—PERSPECTIVE.

are painted in oil, the ceilings beautifully frescoed in keeping with the wood work, all of which is in the Eastlake or modern Gothic style. On this floor there are a commodious dining-room, kitchen, store-room and pantries, lavatories for ladies and gentlemen, a ladies' parlor (a little gem), the main ticket-offices, and the Pullman ticket-office. From this main floor there are two large flights of hard-wood stairs leading to the two stories of offices above, which are finished off in hard-wood, and now occupied by several departments of the road.

The main platforms and tracks are covered with an iron shed 125 ft. x 400 ft., containing nine tracks.

The total cost of the buildings and platforms is $250,000.

The Chicago & Northwestern has three separate lines out of Chicago, and originally each of these had its own Chicago station, and until this building was completed one important station was on the west side of the river. At the new structure, which is very near the business centre of the city (connected with it by a bridge and a tunnel), there will be room to concentrate the whole passenger business.

Union Passenger Depot at Van Buren Street, Chicago, Ill.—The Union Passenger Depot at Van Buren Street, Chicago, Ill., for the use of the Rock Island, the Lake Shore, and the N. Y., C. & St. L. Railways, is a very large and substantially built terminal head-station. The depot is 600 ft. long, and 172 ft. wide, with towers at the front about 200 ft. high. A cut of this depot was published in the *Railway Review* of Nov. 12, 1887.

Terminal Passenger Depot at Chicago, Ill., Chicago & Western Indiana Railroad.—The passenger depot of the Chicago & Western Indiana Railroad at Chicago, Ill., designed by and built under the supervision of Mr. Cyrus L. W. Eidlitz, architect, New York, N. Y., is a large and handsome head-station, plans for which were published in the issue of the *Railway Review* of July 12, 1884, in the issue of *Building* of September, 1885, and in the issue of *Harper's Weekly* of November 7, 1885. The description of the building in the issue of the *Railway Review* mentioned is as follows:

The depot will be in the shape of an L, and will have a frontage on Polk Street of 213 ft. On the right, Fourth Avenue, it will run back 200 ft., and on the opposite side, Third Avenue, the building proper and the one-story extension will have a depth of 446 ft. The materials to be used in the construction are Philadelphia pressed brick; red terra-cotta trimmings, from the Perth Amboy, N. J., works; a reddish-brown sandstone from New Jersey; and a blue and red slate, the latter for the roofs. The stone will be used rock-faced, and will form the footing-courses, steps, string-courses, and the first stage of the tower and turret. The terra-cotta will be used in the arches (which are quite numerous), string-courses, and ridges of the roof.

The building will be three stories high on the corners, and two and a half, including the dormer-windows, in the centre. A feature of the new depot is the three-story part on the corner of Polk Street and Third Avenue. Its dimensions are 48 × 65 ft., and its tall gable-roof and dormer-windows will have quite a picturesque effect. The ground-floor of this building will be a large open lobby, with three large arched entrances on each corner, which are protected by an iron veranda projecting over the sidewalk. Access from this lobby is obtained to the ticket-offices, the ladies' and general waiting-rooms, and lobby vestibule to train-shed. The ladies' waiting-room, 40 ft. square, and toilet-rooms, directly south of the Polk Street entrance, are to be fitted up elaborately. The floors will be of marquetry, and the ceilings and wainscoting will be finished in hard woods. The same attention will be paid to the general waiting-room, which occupies a space of 135 × 40 ft.

The remainder of the Polk Street front is a two-story and dormer-window building, broken a little to the right of the centre by a tall clock-tower, which will be 195 feet in height and directly facing Dearborn Street, and when that thoroughfare is opened for travel will be seen from the heart of the city. The tower will contain the main entrance, the vestibule of which will be ornamented with terra-cotta and glazed brick of variegated designs. The floor will be a handsome tile one, also of various colors. The interior decoration of the large lobby on the northeast corner will resemble the tower vestibule. The ground-floor, corner Polk Street and Fourth Avenue, 25 × 80 ft., will be devoted to a large dining-room, which will have a complete restaurant attachment. The window transoms of the first-story will be of stained glass, cathedral pattern.

The extension on the east side will be fitted up for outgoing baggage and express traffic. On the opposite side the incoming baggage will be taken care of.

Particular attention will be paid to the fitting up of the basement which is very large and roomy, having 12 ft. headway. It will be used for a variety of purposes, boiler and engine-room for steam-heating, elevating power, etc. That part directly under the dining-room will be used for a kitchen; that under the waiting-room for barber-shop, closets, etc.; and that under the main lobby will be fitted up tastefully for an emigrant waiting-room. This room will be wainscoted and plastered. Ventilation will be made as nearly perfect as possible, and light will be obtained by the means of the Hyatt lights. The second story is reached in two places. There will be two iron flights of staircases in the tower and one on Third Avenue, back of the ladies' waiting-room. The second and third stories will contain the offices, and they will be elegantly finished in hard woods, and will be used by the officers of the company and their assistants.

The train-shed will commence at the rear of the main building and between the two wings, and extend out beyond the wings,—in all a distance of 600 ft. The shed will contain 10 parallel tracks, and just outside there will be 14. The roof will be of glass and corrugated iron, and will be supported by iron trusses 20 ft. apart. The ornamentation at the south end of it will be quite striking, being made up of circular and square window-heads, ornamental posts, brackets, etc. Both the depot and yard are to be lighted by electricity. The following companies will enter the new depot: Chicago & Grand Trunk; Wabash, St. Louis & Pacific; Chicago & Atlantic; Louisville, New Albany & Chicago; and Chicago & Eastern Illinois. The estimated cost of the completed structure is $500,000.

Union Passenger Depot at St. Louis, Mo.—In the issue of the *Engineering News* of October 3, 1891, the first-prize design for a proposed Union Passenger Depot at St. Louis, Mo., is illustrated

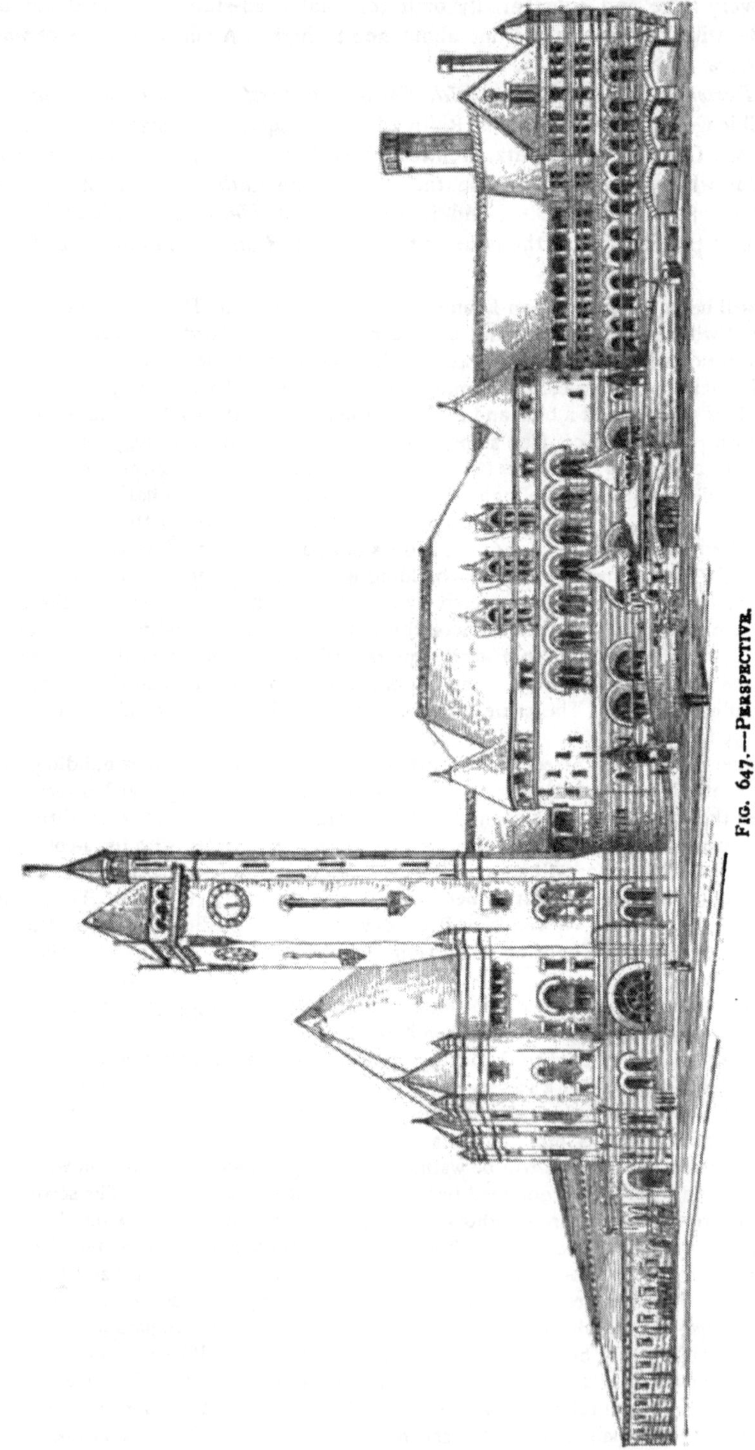

FIG. 647.—PERSPECTIVE.

and described, from which publication Fig. 650 is reproduced by permission. The accepted design was prepared by Messrs. Theodore C. Link and Edward A. Cameron, architects, St. Louis, Mo. It is also illustrated in the issue of the *Railroad Gazette* of July 24, 1891, reproduced by permission in Figs. 647 to 649, the description of the structure as published in the *Railroad Gazette* being as follows:

The Terminal Railroad Association, operating the St. Louis Union Depot and the Bridge and Terminal Railroad System, some months since acquired land at Twentieth and Market streets for a new station to take the place of the present insufficient quarters, and a number of architects presented plans in competition for the proposed new depot. The accepted design is a handsome stone and brick head-station, with a train-shed covering thirty tracks. This train-shed will be larger than any existing station in this country, being 606 ft. wide, including the baggage-room, etc., at the sides. It is 600 ft. long, exclusive of the 50-ft. transverse platform between the head-house and the ends of the tracks, but some of the tracks are 1000 ft. long.

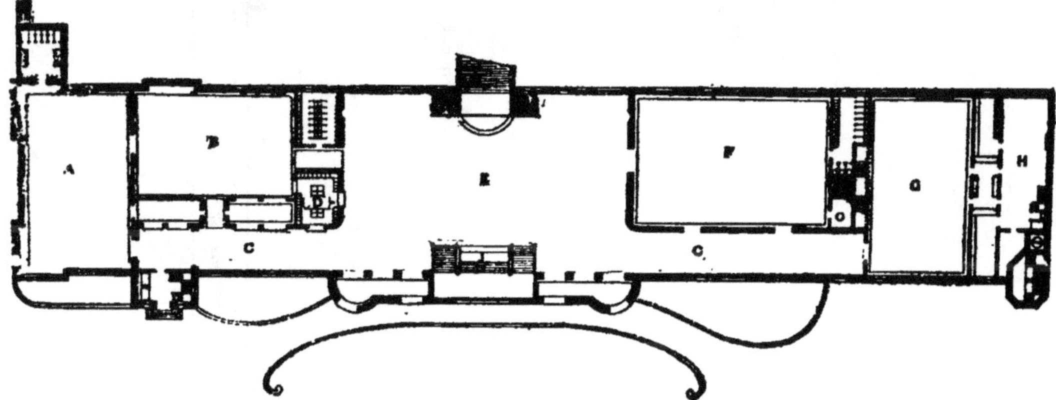

FIG. 648.—GROUND-PLAN OF MAIN FLOOR.
A, Smoking-room; *B*, Gentlemen; *C C*, Ambulatory; *D*, Package-room; *E*, Main Hall; *F*, Ladies; *G*, Dining-hall; *H*, Kitchen.

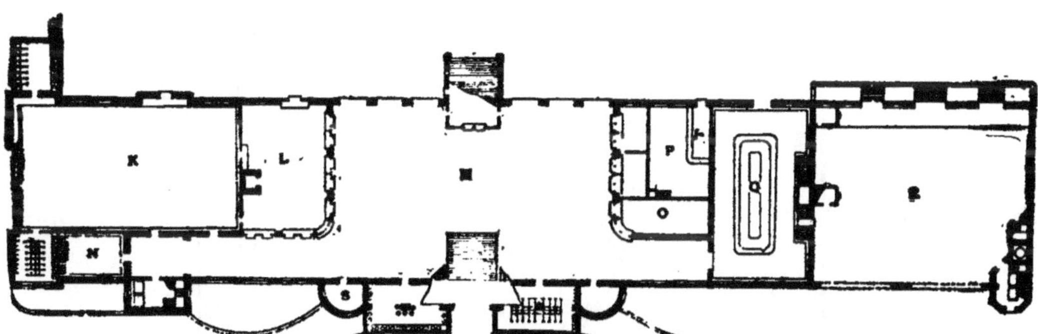

FIG. 649.—GROUND-PLAN OF BASEMENT.
K, Emigrant Waiting-room; *L*, Ticket-office; *M*, Concourse; *N*, Barber-shop; *O*, Mail-room · *P*, Telegraph; *Q*, Restaurant; *R*, Carriage Concourse; *T*, Conductors' Lobby.

It is not proposed to cover the whole with a single-span roof, there being four rows of pillars for intermediate supports.

The head-house is 456 ft. long by 80 ft. wide. The basement-floor is on a level with the tracks, and the "concourse" in the centre contains 10,530 sq. ft. The telegraph-office in this story has a mezzanine floor. The floor of the carriage concourse is on a level with the street and about 4 ft. higher than the track. On the main floor the general waiting-room aggregates 10,530 sq. ft.; the gentlemen's rooms 3300, and the ladies' rooms, including the retiring and matron's rooms, 5760; the dining-room 4500, and the smoking-room 2340 sq. ft. It will be observed that the main entrance is approached by an inclined walk from either direction, so that there are no steps to climb, and wide stairways on either side of the main entrance lead to the concourse in the basement. The *porte cochère* is located outside the inclined approaches. The train platforms are reached from the main waiting-hall directly by two stairways.

The general waiting-room has ample skylight and ceiling light. There are numerous exits for incoming passengers at the sides of the train-shed on the side streets. There are two entrances specially for the

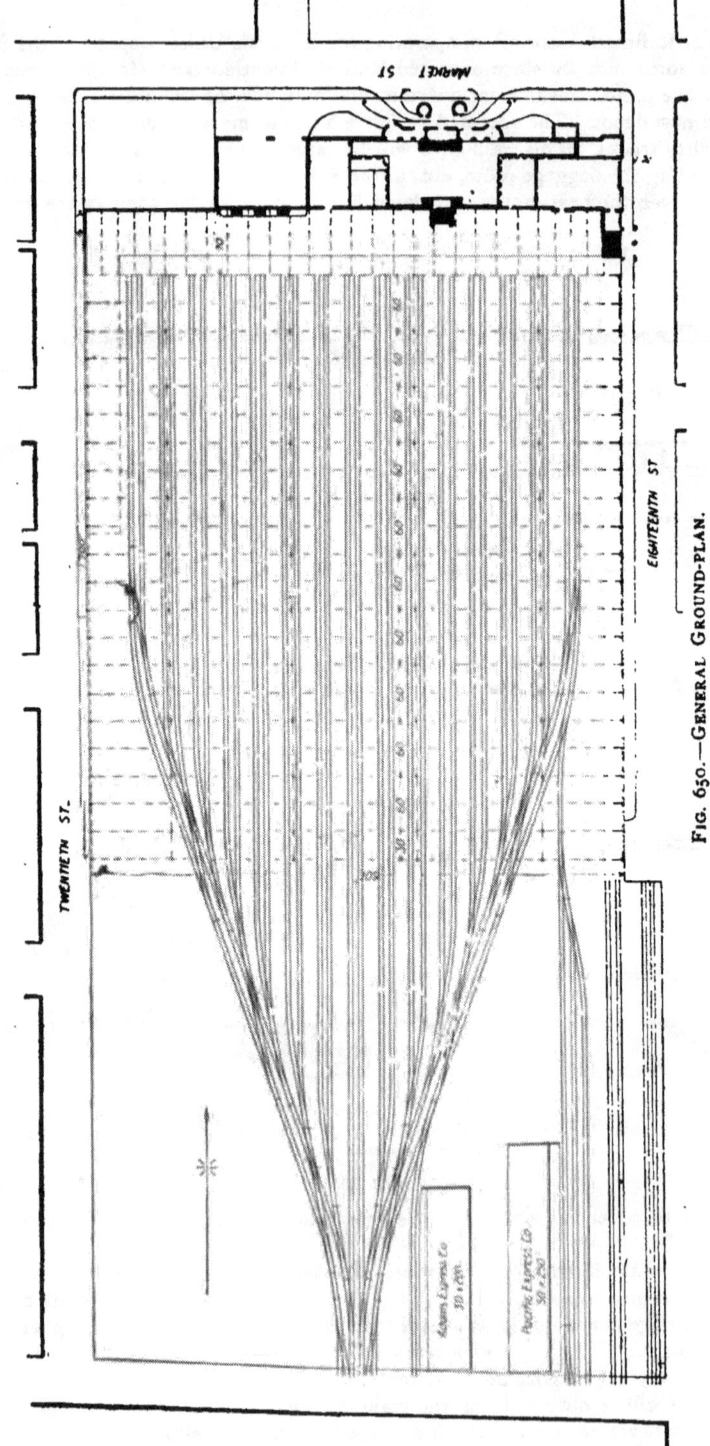

FIG. 650.—GENERAL GROUND-PLAN.

office floors in the upper part of the building, and each has two hydraulic elevators. The kitchen, connected with the restaurant, has a separate freight-elevator. The plans include a sub-basement 7 ft. 6 in. high, not without some daylight, to protect the basement-floor from dampness. The boiler-room is under the carriage concourse. Each of the two office floors has about 30 large rooms.

The architects have made elaborate plans for heating and ventilation, using power fans and heated flues. Steam radiators are provided in every room, and it is proposed that the air forced in by the fans shall be heated only to 70 degrees, so as not to produce an unpleasant draught at the discharge. Dust-screens and spray-washers will be provided to remove the dust from the air and to moisten it so as to do away with the unpleasant dryness of heated air. It is expected to so arrange the water-closets that the circulation of air will always be from the corridors to the closets and out through the exhaust flues. All the ventilating flues will discharge into the roof-space, and each will have a self-closing valve at the top.

The outer walls of the building are to be of Missouri gray granite, backed with brick up to the second-story sill, and brick with stone trimmings above; and the style is Romanesque. The tower will be about 200 ft. high. For the interior decoration of the two main floors materials will be employed which are of a permanent character and will not require painting. The walls of all rooms on the ground-floor are lined with enamelled brick or tiling about 5 ft. high, and above this buff Roman bricks. They will show exposed ceiling-beams and have marble floors. The walls of the main floor, however, are treated with a composition known as art marble. The public rooms in this story have Mosaic floors. The estimated cost of the entire improvement, including the train-sheds, is placed at $800,000.

The train-shed, designed by Mr. Geo. H. Pegram, consulting engineer, is very well described and fully illustrated in the issues of *Engineering News* of April 2, 21, and 28, 1892, from which publication the illustrations Figs. 651 to 653 are taken. The following description is taken from the same source :

The train-shed is 601 ft. wide from c. to c. of outer columns, covering thirty tracks, and 700 ft. long from wall of head-house to centre of end columns. Of this length 70 ft. will be an auxiliary shed, covering the wide transverse platform and connecting the head-house with the train-shed proper, the main part of the latter being, therefore, 630 ft. long. The height to centre pin of top chord of middle span at the head-house end will be 74 ft. and the height of end pins of bottom chords of side trusses 20 ft. The total width of 601 ft. is made up of a centre span of 141 ft. 3⅛ in., two flanking spans of 139 ft. 2¼ in. each, and two side spans of 90 ft. 8 in. each. The side columns are placed 30 ft. apart, c. to c., longitudinally, while the columns of the three interior rows are placed 60 ft. apart. The roof-trusses are 30 ft. apart, every alternate truss resting on the longitudinal girders carried by the columns.

The design of the train-shed was limited by these conditions: the height should not exceed a certain amount, in order to avoid overshadowing the head-house; the plan was to be accommodated to a previously adopted system of tracks; and the cost was not to exceed a given figure.

The natural tendency in designing a building of this great width and small height would be to make what would appear to be more or less a set of parallel buildings. The main aim, architecturally, was to preserve the unity of design and make its size more impressive, by avoiding as far as possible any idea of division which the necessary intermediate lines of supports would cause. The conspicuous part of the interior will, of course, be the roof-sheathing, which limits the vision, and this has been made in the form of a single arch. It is believed that the bottom chords, hanging like chains from the columns, will produce an effect of drapery, or at least an effect of continuity, over the columns something like the sag in a circus tent from the poles, which will tend to neutralize the rigid divisions by intermediate supports.

The central skylight is covered with glass its entire length, with louvre slats in the sides. The lateral skylights have glass and louvres in the sides to prevent a darkening effect of the building from the fall of snow, and also to give better ventilation, as the building fronts south, from which the prevailing wind blows. The building is made as good as possible in detail; no wood being used, except for sheathing, and all glass being of a heavy corrugated pattern, set in copper bars, the glass being all clear, except in the south end, where it will have an amber tint. The train-shed will be symmetrical, except that eight rafters over the baggage-room will be strengthened to carry the second floor thereof, and the longitudinal girders between the outer columns will be modified along the baggage-room. The tops of columns will be in horizontal planes. The tracks will be on a rising grade of 0.48 per cent into the station, to which grade the bases of the interior columns are to conform. The bases of the outer columns will be in horizontal planes in sets of four in each row, the sets conforming to the above grade, except the end columns, two in each row, which will be at grade.

The train-shed is practically at right angles to the main lines, which run east and west through the city, and it is approached by two double-track lines, one from each direction, which form a Y, the apex of which is close to the train-shed. From this point tracks will diverge to connect with the thirty tracks of the train-

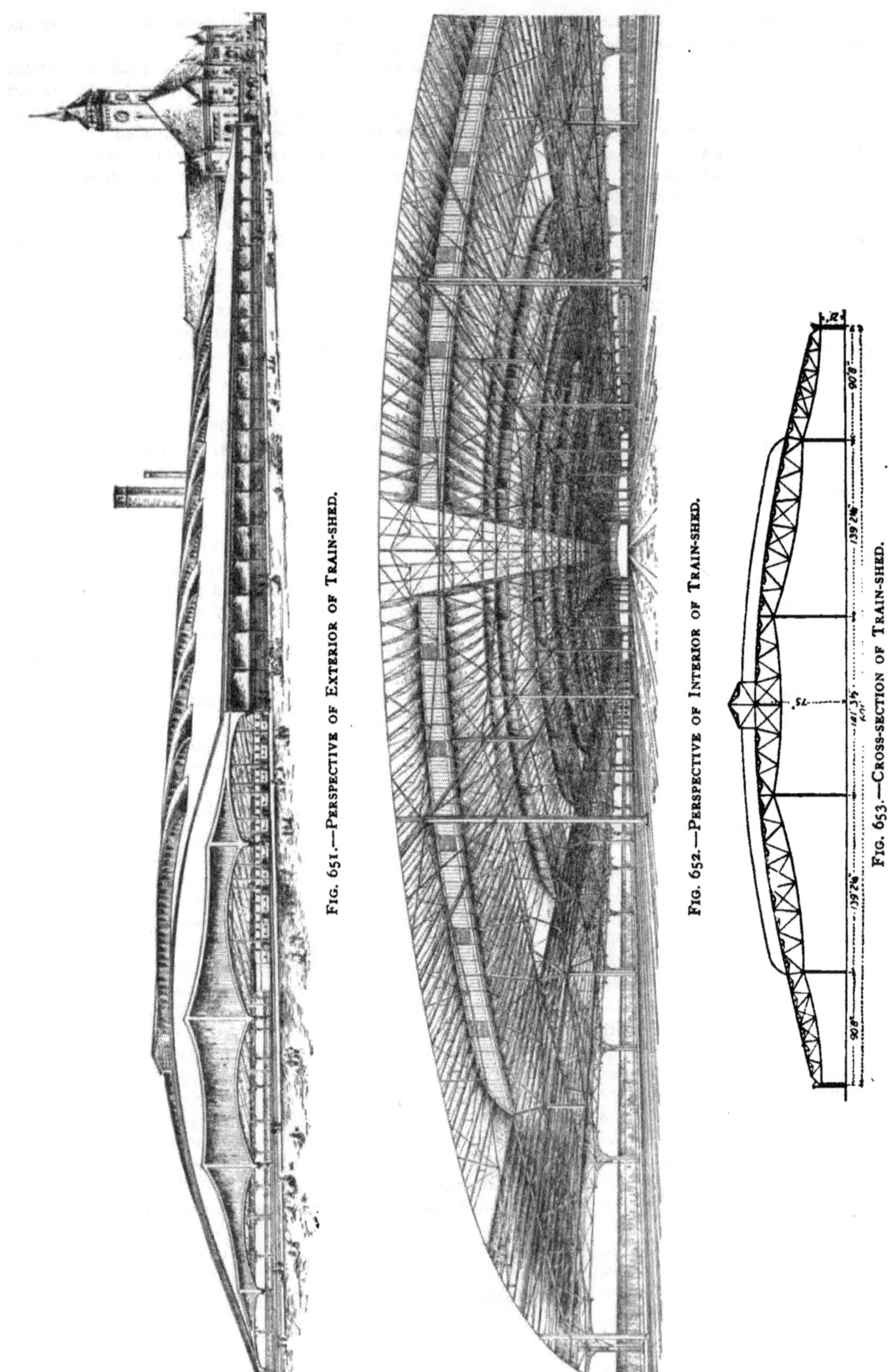

FIG. 651.—PERSPECTIVE OF EXTERIOR OF TRAIN-SHED.

FIG. 652.—PERSPECTIVE OF INTERIOR OF TRAIN-SHED.

FIG. 653.—CROSS-SECTION OF TRAIN-SHED.

shed, the arrangement being such that all these tracks are accessible from either branch of the Y and from the main tracks in either direction. The tracks are on a slight rising grade of 0.48 per cent into the train-shed, and are arranged in pairs, seven pairs on each side of the centre pair. The main transverse platform will be 50 ft. wide, with a platform 22 ft. 6 in. wide between each pair of tracks. The tracks of each pair will be spaced 12 ft. apart, with the exception of the second pair on each side of the centre pair and the second pair from each side, which will be 14 ft. apart.

The ground is of variable character, some parts being solid and other parts filled in, and there are a few artificial obstructions. The foundations consist of concrete piers resting upon solid ground or upon piling, and capped with stone, as shown by the accompanying drawings. The piers for the outside rows of columns have a base of 9 ft. × 11 ft. 6 in. with piles, or 9 ft. × 12 ft. without piles, and are reduced by offsets to a uniform size of 4 ft. × 6 ft. at the top. The piers for interior columns have a base of 7 ft. × 8 ft. to 8 ft. × 9 ft. on piles, or 8 ft. × 9 ft. to 9 ft. × 10 ft. without piles, and are reduced by offsets to a size of 4 ft. × 5 ft., 4 ft. × 6 ft., or 5 ft. × 6 ft. on top, according to location. The bottom of each excavation is to be rammed and drained, and the back filling well tamped in layers 6 in. thick. The piles are to be of white oak or red cypress, not less than 10 in. diameter at the small end, and with the bark removed. They will be driven to a ½-in. set from a 2500-lb. hammer falling 25 ft. The piles will be sawed off to a level plane, and the ground around and between them thoroughly tamped.

The piers will be built of Portland cement concrete mixed in proportions of one part of cement to three of sand and six of broken stone. The cement is to have a minimum strength of 400 lbs. per square inch when tested in briquettes which have been 24 hours in air and seven days in water. The sand is to be clean, coarse, sharp river sand. The stone is to be of approved quality, broken to pass through a 2½-in. ring, and screened, and if too dusty or dirty it is to be washed. The cement and sand will be thoroughly mixed dry and then mixed with water. The stone, having been previously wetted, is then to be added, and the mass worked until all the stones are well coated with mortar. The concrete is then to be immediately deposited and tamped in layers of about 6 in., within wooden forms which are not to be removed until after the concrete has set. Care must be taken to use the least amount of water necessary. The concrete for the outside columns will be deposited continuously until the pier is completed, but the concreting of the interior piers may be stoped at the level of an offset when required. Wooden frames will be used to hold the anchor-bolts in position during the construction of the pier. The cap-stones will be of granite or limestone, the former being used probably for the exterior and the latter for the interior piers. They are specified to be of best quality and of uniform grade and color. The top will be bush-hammered, with a 1-in. bevelled chisel draught around the edges, and the four sides will be hammer-dressed to a depth of 6 in. from the top, the lower part of the sides being rock-faced. The stones will be set in a bed of mortar composed of one part cement to two of sand, freshly mixed, the mortar joint to be not less than ⅜ in. nor more than ¾ in. thick. The spaces round the anchor-bolts will be filled in with Portland cement mortar, composed of one part cement to one of sand.

The anchor-bolts for the outer piers are 2 and 2½ in. diameter, with the upper 6 or 7 in. upset and threaded. They are about 8 ft. 6 in. to 10 ft. 6 in. long, 17½ to 24½ in. projecting above the cap-stones. The lower ends of each pair are connected by cast-iron washers. For the interior piers the anchor-bolts are 1½ in., 1⅝ in., and 2 in. diameter, 4 ft. to 5 ft. 6 in. long from washer to top of caps. The ends are not upset, and a separate round washer is used on the end of each bolt.

The train-shed itself is an interesting and important work, both from its design and its great size. The columns, trusses, and purlins will be generally of steel, and all other parts generally of iron. Steel is to be used except where iron is specified. The steel is to have an ultimate strength of 60,000 lbs. per sq. in., with 4000 lbs. allowance either way. It is to be reamed in tension-members, but need not be reamed in compression-members except to avoid the use of drift-pins. The specifications require the quality of materials and workmanship to be in accordance with the bridge-builder's specifications, as given in Carnegie, Phipps & Co.'s "Pocket Companion," edition of 1890. In the latest edition of this "Pocket Companion," however, the bridge-builder's specifications are replaced by Mr. Theodore Cooper's standard specifications. Where truss-rods are connected at the ends with rivets, the holes need not be bored, but must be of proper diameters to suit the rivets used. The specifications suggest that the manufacture of the bent truss-rods may be facilitated by using washers of various diameters on the post rivets, thereby compensating for inequalities in length. The bends in these rods must be exactly in the middle.

The lumber for sheathing will be all heart yellow pine, in widths of 6 in. It will be clear of sap and dry, tongued and grooved, and milled to a thickness of 1¾ in. The base-boards and sills of the skylights will be red cypress of the same description.

It is not decided whether iron or wooden mullions will be used for the vertical glass-work. The glass in lateral skylights and in the end designs will be $\frac{3}{16}$ in. thick, with a uniform width of 20 in., and will be in single lengths of about 8 ft. The central ventilator will be covered with glass for its entire length. The auxiliary shed between the main train-shed and the head-house will be covered with glass for a width of 23 ft. and a length of 600 ft. along the head-house. The glass will be ¼ in. thick, set in metal longitudinal-bars. The glass in the front and rear of the building will be $\frac{3}{16}$ in. thick, set in iron mullions. The end trusses will be covered with galvanized corrugated iron, and there will be a galvanized-iron cornice 3 ft. deep across both ends of the building and along the sides, except the 250 ft. along the baggage-room. There will also be a galvanized-iron frame about 1 ft. deep around the glass designs in the ends of the building, and covering the columns above the brackets. All galvanized iron will be of No. 22 gauge. Galvanized-iron posts and louvres, extending from the sills to the eaves, will be fitted in the central and lateral skylights. The roof-sheathing will be covered with a thick layer of roofing-felt, lapped and tacked, and then covered with I. C. tin. The seams are to be well soldered, using resin as a flux, the solder being thoroughly soaked into the seams. Standing seams are to be used on the portions of the sides of the main shed, extending from the gutters to a distance of 10 ft. above the ends of lateral skylights, and on the auxiliary shed, flat seams to be used on other portions of the roof. All roof-sheets are to be 28 × 20 in., showing 18⅛ × 26⅛ in. for a flat seam, and 18⅞ × 25¼ in. for standing seam when laid on the roof.

The tin and galvanized-iron work will receive two coats on both sides. The paint is to be red lead mixed with 1 ounce of lamp black per lb. and pure linseed-oil.

The quantities required are approximately as follows:

Iron-work, ...	5,115,740 lbs.
Z-iron sills and T-iron mullions in lateral skylights (if used),	172,180 "
T-iron mullions in end designs (if used), ...	44,968 "
Lumber, ...	896,000 ft. B. M.
Wooden mullions in lateral skylights (if used), ...	34,560 lin. ft.
Wooden mullions in end designs (if used), ...	12,850 " "
Glass in lateral skylights, ...	51,840 sq. ft.
Glass in end designs (both ends), ...	22,000 " "
Glass in roofs of central skylight and auxiliary shed, . . .	39,630 " "
Tin, ...	402,840 " "
48 cast-iron down-spouts, ...	12,000 lbs.
48 galvanized-iron down-spouts, ...	900 lin. ft.
Galvanized iron, including louvres, ...	17,920 sq. ft.
Galvanized corrugated iron, ...	19,170 " "
Galvanized-iron cornices, ...	2,260 ft.

The iron and steel work is to receive two coats of paint at the shops and one coat after erection.

The peculiarity of the arrangement of wind-bracing is, that it consists entirely of a system of diagonal bracing between the two sets of trusses next the front end and the columns which carry them. The ends of the train-shed will be covered by glass and corrugated iron down to the level of the tops of the columns, with a clear headway of openings of 20 ft. at the columns and 28 ft. at the middle, as shown by the elevations.

Second-prize Design for Union Passenger Depot at St. Louis, Mo.—In the issue of *Engineering News* of October 3, 1891, the second-prize design for a proposed union passenger depot at St. Louis, Mo., is illustrated, as shown in Fig. 654, the original plate having been kindly furnished to the author

Fig. 654.—Perspective.

by *Engineering News*. The design was prepared by Messrs. Grable & Weber, architects, St. Louis, Mo. For further data and ground-plan see *Engineering News.*

Terminal Passenger Depot at Jersey City, N. J., New York, Lake Erie & Western Railroad.—The passenger depot of the New York, Lake Erie & Western Railroad at Jersey City, N. J., shown in Figs. 655 to 657, is a large terminal head-station, in connection with a ferry to New York City. Plans for this depot were published in the issue of the *Railroad Gazette* of May 6, 1887; in the issue of the *American Contract Journal* of May 29, 1886; and in the issue of the *Railway Review* of August 27, 1887. The drawings and specifications were made by Mr. George E. Archer, architect, N. Y., L. E. & W. R. R., and the work was executed under the supervision of Mr. C. W. Buchholz, Engineer of Bridges and Buildings, and Mr. J. W. Ferguson, Assistant Engineer. The train-shed was built by the Phœnix Bridge Company, and the passenger house was erected by Messrs. Cofrode & Saylor, contractors, Philadelphia, Pa. The structure is described as follows in the issue of the *Railroad Gazette* mentioned:

The main building has a frontage of 127 ft. on Pavonia Avenue and a river front of 120 ft. exclusive of the 24-ft. awnings on their sides. The train-shed is 140 ft. by 600 ft. The tower at the southeast corner is to be about 115 ft. high, including the finial of 15 ft. The main structure will be about 60 ft. high. The disposition of waiting-room and other rooms on the ground-floor is shown on the plan. On the second floor are to be the offices of the operating department, and on the third floor offices for the car-record clerks.

The foundations of the head-house are of hard brick, laid in Portland cement, coped with North River sandstone. The brickwork rests on 525 piles, 55 ft. long. The site of the new building is full of old piles and cribs, which have, in their turn, supported different structures. These form, with the new piles driven among them, a very solid mass, preventing any outward sliding on the deep mud of the river. To avoid overloading, however, this part of the structure is almost wholly built of wood; the train-shed is of wrought-iron, sheathed with wood and galvanized iron.

The extension of the building is to be finished with "novelty" siding, shingles, panels, etc., painted in parti-color to accentuate the details. The finials are iron and copper, gilded. The tower-clock will have six-foot dials, lighted from within by electric light. The interior will be in hard wood, in natural colors. The floors of the vestibules and toilet-rooms will be of maple. The main waiting-room is 66 ft. by 100 ft., and 50 ft. high in the clear, and lighted by stained-glass windows in the clere-story. A gallery runs around three sides of the waiting-room at the level of the second story, and from this various offices open off.

There will be a ferry ticket-office at the southeastern corner of the building for the use of Jersey City passengers only. As at the Jersey City depot of the Pennsylvania, passengers from the trains will go on board their boats without passing through the ferry wickets. It is to be regretted that in neither of these fine depots has it been found practicable to pass the suburban traffic directly to the trains without going through the waiting-room.

The building is to be lighted throughout by electricity, and heated with steam by about 60 Bundy radiators.

The cost of passenger station, train-shed, and the iron shed to connect the station with the ferry-house will be over $200,000. The drawings and specifications were made by Mr. Geo. E. Archer, the company's architect, and the work is executed under the supervision of Mr. C. W. Buchholz, Engineer of Bridges and Buildings, and Mr. J. W. Ferguson, Assistant Engineer.

Old Passenger Depot at Jersey City, N. J., Pennsylvania Railroad.—The old passenger depot building of the Pennsylvania Railroad at Jersey City, N. J., partially destroyed by fire, and since replaced by a new structure and layout, owing to the elevation of tracks at this point, was a large terminal head-station, in connection with the ferry to New York City. Plans of the old structure were published in the issue of *Engineering* of March 2, 1877, and in the book "The Pennsylvania Railroad," by James Dredge. This structure is described as follows in the publications mentioned:

In designing the terminal station of the Pennsylvania Railroad at Jersey City considerable difficulty was encountered, as the same ferries had to be employed for the train passengers and for local traffic to and from Jersey City and New York. The local ferry traffic is accommodated with a separate building adjacent to the depot building proper, leading from the street, with a waiting-room 80 ft. × 48 ft., and the necessary ticket-offices. On each side of this building there is a drive from the street, leading to a 60-ft.-wide roadway, along the back of the ferry slips, from which access is obtained to the boats. The train-shed is roofed over in five spans, and has platforms 620 ft. in length, there being twelve tracks and six platforms. At the end of the station is a covered passage, 40 ft. wide, on to which the doors of the general waiting-room

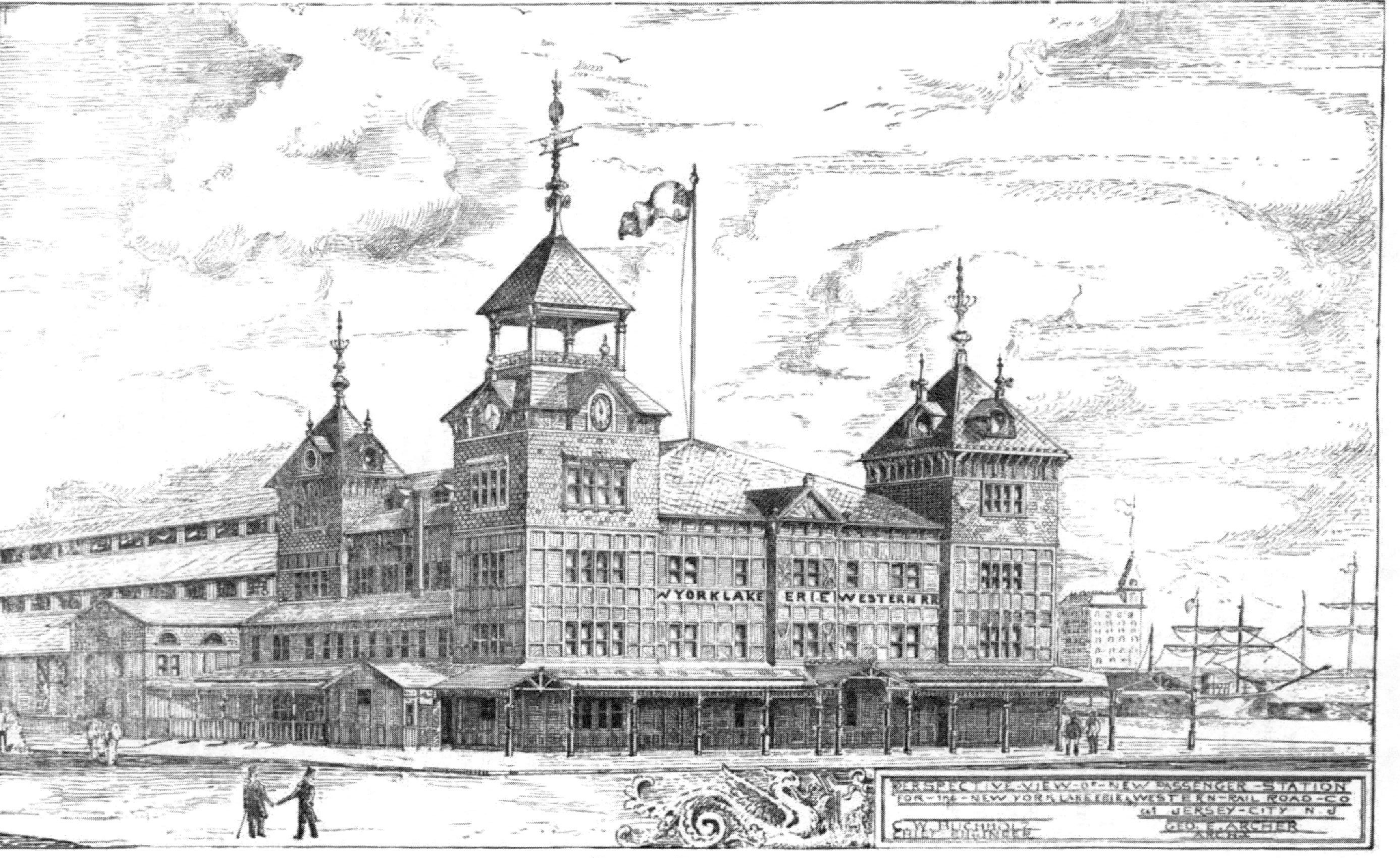

FIG. 655.—PERSPECTIVE.

open. At the south side of the station are placed the offices, stores, baggage-rooms, etc., which are built of brick, as also is the boundary-wall on the north side. With these exceptions, the station is entirely of timber. The station building comprises a general waiting-room, 80 ft. × 84 ft.; a restaurant; kitchen; offices;

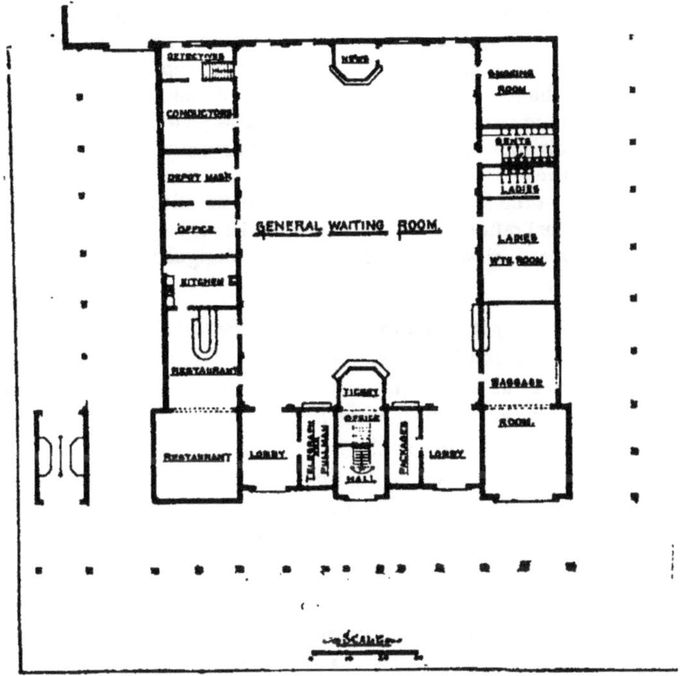

FIG. 656.—GROUND-PLAN.

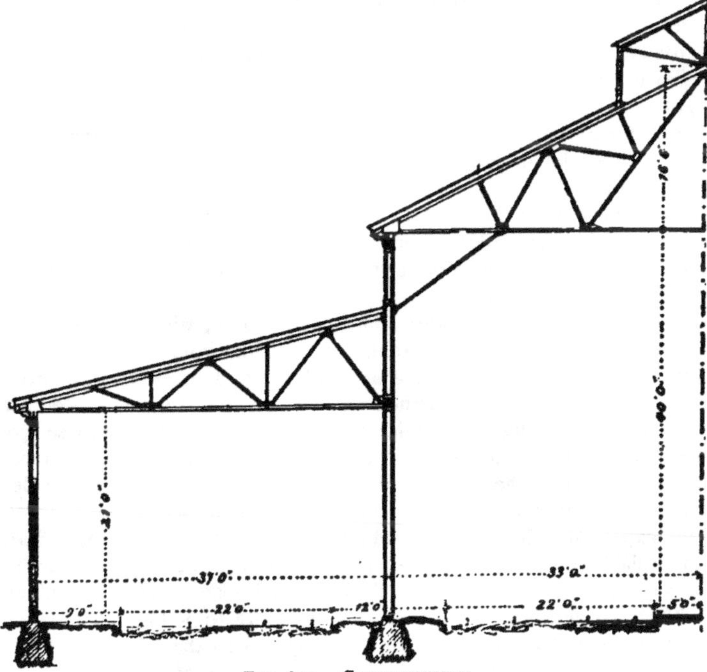

FIG. 657.—CROSS-SECTION.

ticket-office; ladies' waiting-room; etc. At one end of the room are exit doors, leading to steps, at the top of which is a bridge, forming a connection with the street. Train passengers for Jersey City reach the street by a second series of steps, while those going on to New York pass underneath the bridge and through the gate to the ferries. On the other hand, passengers from New York enter the general waiting-room of the station, but cannot return without purchasing ferry tickets. From the waiting-room they pass out to the platforms. Four of the tracks in the train-shed are used for arriving and four for departing trains; the other four being used for storing cars. The foundations for this work were difficult and costly, as the ground on which the station stands is very soft, and the whole area required piling. Indeed, the station building and all in front of it to the ferry slips is over the water. The whole of the piles underneath the building were cut off at low-water level and iron columns placed upon them to carry the floors and walls. The various structures are all built with solid timbers, instead of framing throughout, so as to leave no concealed spaces, the object being to reduce danger by fire as far as possible. The roof over the general waiting-room is arranged with only four main trusses, running diagonally from the corners of the room to the peak of the roof over the centre of the room. The view from below is not intercepted by any bracing, as the trusses are only tied together at the feet over the walls, and an excellent effect is thus obtained. Each truss is of iron, excepting the principal rafter, which is of timber. The roofs are covered with tin, and well lighted by skylights, with ⅛-in. roughened glass. The structure was designed by Mr. Joseph M. Wilson, engineer and architect, Philadelphia, Pa.

New Terminal Passenger Depot at Jersey City, N. J., Pennsylvania Railroad.—The new passenger depot of the Pennsylvania Railroad at Jersey City, N. J., built in 1891, to replace the old depot, owing to the elevation of tracks at this point, is a large terminal head-station, forming the New York terminus of the road, the transfer to New York being made by means of a ferry. Full plans and descriptions of this depot were published in the issue of the *Railroad Gazette* of October 2, 1891, and in the issues of the *Engineering News* of September 26, 1891, and of October 3, 1891. The illustrations, Figs. 658 to 668, are taken from the *Railroad Gazette*, with the exception of the general ground-plan, Fig. 666, which is copied from *Engineering News*. The following description of this terminal depot is taken from *Engineering News:*

For over four years the Pennsylvania Railroad Co. has been at work upon the improvement of its terminals at Jersey City, to enable it to handle with safety and despatch the vast and rapidly growing traffic which concentrates at this point, the eastern terminus of the Pennsylvania Railroad System, which now has a total extent of 7750 miles. One of the most important features of the Pennsylvania's improvements was the elevation of the passenger tracks across the city to do away with the grade-crossings. At the end of the embankment at Brunswick Street a four-track viaduct begins and extends to Henderson Street, a distance of 1000 yds. The designs for this viaduct were illustrated in the issue of *Engineering News* of June 25, 1887.

The viaduct ends at Henderson Street, and from here to the terminus, a distance of 2475 ft., the ground was filled to a height of 15 to 20 ft. above the original level, which necessitated the bringing in by train of about 350,000 cu. yds. of material from borrow-pits 10 to 20 miles distant. Warren Street and Washington Street are crossed by plate-girder deck-bridges. The total area filled in is over 11 acres, of which nearly 3½ acres are covered by the train-shed.

From a structural point of view the train-shed is the most important feature of the terminal, and it certainly is its most noticeable feature. Seen from the ferry-boats on the river, its colossal arched roof and great glass gable loom up in such proportions as to dwarf into insignificance every building in the vicinity with the exception of the lofty grain-elevators.

The main dimensions of the structure are: length, 652 ft. 6 in.; width, 256 ft.; clear height at centre, 86 ft.; height from top of rail to ridge of monitor roof, 110 ft. The whole weight of the structure is carried by twelve pairs of main roof-trusses, each with a span of 252 ft. 8 in. between centres of end-pins. The decision to cover the train-shed by a single arched roof of large span was made after a thorough comparison of the merits of this design and a design in which the roof was divided into three spans and two rows of columns were used through the centre of the building. The disadvantages connected with the use of columns in the interior of a train-shed are the danger of a fall of the roof in case derailment or a boiler explosion should wreck one or more columns; the obstruction presented by the columns; the fact that unless very high and expensive columns or braced piers are used the roof is low, affords less air-space, has less pitch, and is more liable to leakage. The connection of the central bay of the roof to the two side bays of the design with two rows of columns through the building is also somewhat troublesome to make secure against leakage. These considerations, together with the desire to build a monumental structure, in keeping with the circumstances and traditions of the company, led to the adoption of a design for an arched roof of a single span, greater, so far as we now recall, than the span of any roof-truss ever built. The only roof approaching it is the St. Pancras station of the Midland Ry. in London of 243 ft. span, which was built about twenty-five years ago. On an inset sheet is shown the strain-sheet of the main roof-trusses, with the details of the work which are of principal engineering interest.

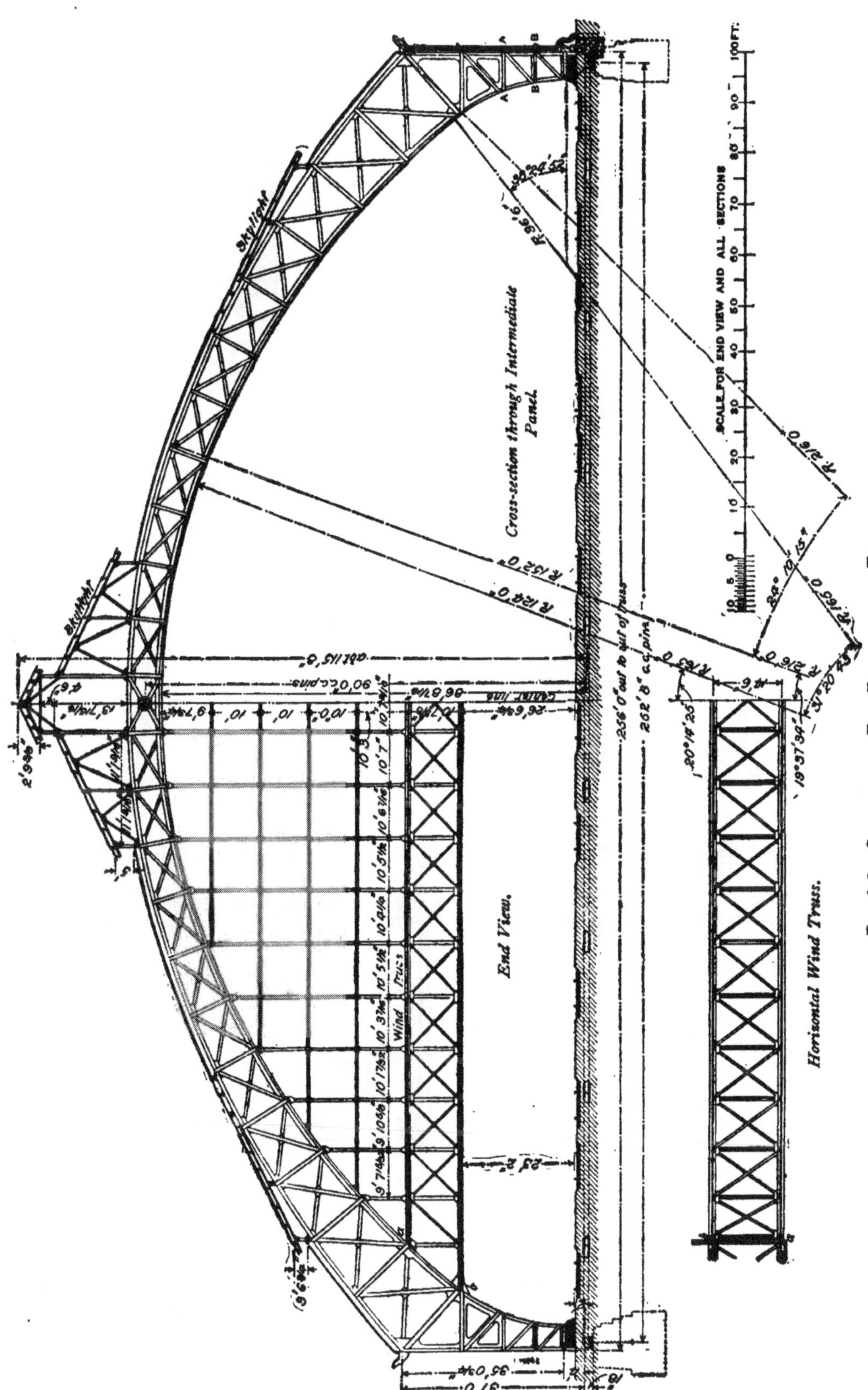

FIG. 658.—SECTION AND END ELEVATION OF TRAIN-SHED.

FIG. 659.—LONGITUDINAL SECTION OF TRAIN-SHED.

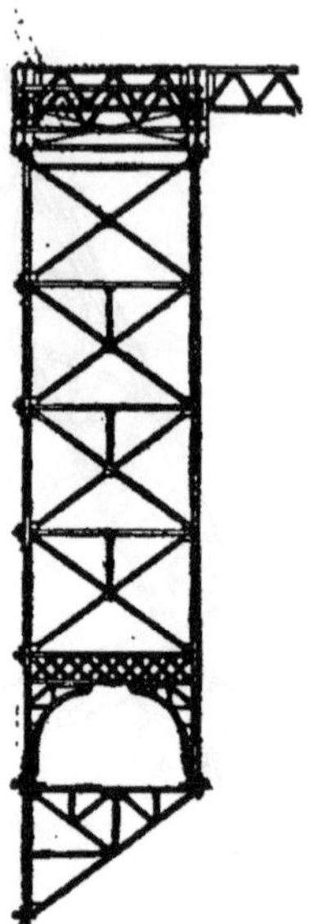

FIG. 660.—CROSS-SECTION OF WIND-BRACING AT END OF TRAIN-SHED.

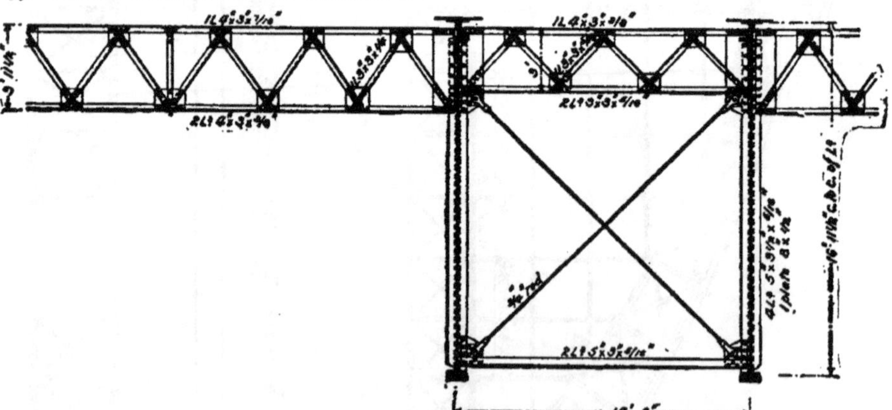

FIG. 661.—SECTION OF PAIR OF TRUSSES, SHOWING PURLINS.

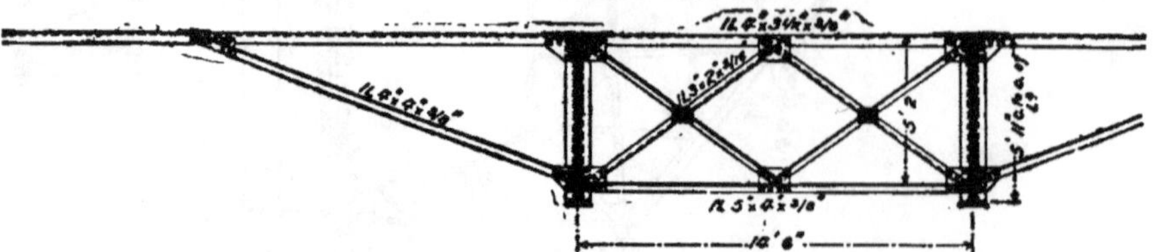

FIG. 662.—SECTION OF PAIR OF TRUSSES NEAR FOOT OF ARCH.

The main roof-trusses.—The whole weight of the structure above the foundation is carried by 24 main roof-trusses, of arch form, with riveted joints, and hinged at each foot and at the apex to permit movement with changes of temperature. The centre-pin is 5 in. in diameter and the pins at the foot are $5\frac{11}{16}$ in. The assumed loads, given on the strain-sheet, are a little over 30 lbs. per sq. ft. for dead load (consisting of the weight of the iron-work and the roof, the covering of the roof being assumed at 13 lbs. per sq. ft. of roof surface), 17 lbs. per sq. ft. for snow load, and 35 lbs. per sq. ft. of elevation for wind-pressure. In calculating maximum strains, the dead load is of course constant; the snow load is figured: first, all over; second, on twelve centre panels only; and third, on one side only; the wind is assumed to blow either toward the anchored side or toward the expansion side. The foundation-shoes of the north side rest on roller bearings, to permit motion with temperature changes. At first sight it would seem impossible for a compressive strain to be induced in the lower chord; but the strain-sheet shows that with the wind blowing against the expansion side, at the maximum assumed force, a compressive strain of 8000 lbs. may be produced in the lower chord. The lower chord is an I-beam weighing 100 lbs. per yd. It runs across the station, beneath the tracks, its top surface being 1 ft. below the base of the rail. To protect it from corrosion and from temperature changes, it is enclosed in a wooden box and the space around it inside the box is filled in solidly with pitch and gravel.

To permit motion at the apex when temperature changes occur, the members above and below the pin at the apex have the rivet-holes slotted at the junction, and are joined by bolts instead of rivets.

The fact that the two feet of each arched truss are joined at the bottom by a lower chord which sustains a tensile strain from the weight of the roof and iron work alone of 35 tons, is one which will not be suspected by one person in a thousand who examines the station. The lower chord is buried beneath the tracks and platforms; and a false cast-iron base is bolted to the foot of the truss at the base of the first panel above the pin. A hollow brick pier is built up under this base, enclosing the real foot of the truss from view. To the cursory observer, therefore, the arch seems to rest on the cast-iron base and brick pier. As a general rule, to make appearances deceitful is bad taste, architecturally; but in this case there is something to be said for this arrangement. The sides of the arched truss come down to the ground level so nearly vertical that the fact that a horizontal thrust exists there is not suspected. Even an engineer who did not stop to reason that the truss must be hinged at its apex to allow for temperature changes would be deceived. Certainly to have given the structure an appearance of strength which it did not possess, or to have brought the trusses down on their bases at an angle, so that they would have appeared to be in danger of spreading, would have been very bad taste. The arrangement adopted, however, while not exactly what it appears to be, does not seem an objectionable one.

At first sight the permissible loading of 14,000 lbs. per sq. in. for combined dead load and wind or combined dead load and snow, and 18,000 lbs. per sq. in. for combined dead load, wind, and snow, may seem excessive strains for wrought-iron; but it is to be remembered that neither of the assumed maximum loads of 14,000 lbs. for wind or for snow are likely to occur oftener than once in perhaps a score of years. The mathematical chances that these two maximum loads will both occur at the same time are therefore seen to be practically infinitesimal. Even the blizzard of March, 1888, which was probably as great a conjunction of snowfall with wind as has ever been recorded at New York, would by no means have subjected the structure to an excessive load; for the wind pressures probably did not exceed 13 to 20 lbs. per sq. ft. at most, and on the exposed flat surface of the roof the snow would have been swept off by the wind as fast as it fell. As for the strain of 14,000 lbs., due to dead load and wind, or dead load and snow combined, even this will probably come on the structure only at extremely rare intervals, and possibly never. To have a load of snow of even 10 lbs. per sq. ft. on such an elevated and exposed surface as this roof is uncommon in a New York winter, and either wind, sun, or rain will be apt to remove a heavy snowfall in a short time. As for wind pressures, the assumed load of 35 lbs. per sq. ft. is 5 lbs. greater than the wind pressure usually assumed in bridge specifications at the present time by the best engineers.

The train-shed tracks are on a grade of 0.4 per cent, falling toward the west, to facilitate the starting of heavy trains. The train-shed roof, however, is kept level by making each successive pair of trusses $2\frac{3}{4}$ in. higher than the pair to the east. To avoid, so far as possible, changes in the iron-work, the change is made by increasing the height of the first panel above the foot of the truss. Except for this and some slight changes in the trusses at the ends, on account of the wind-bracing of the gable-ends, the 24 main trusses are duplicates of each other.

The operation of erecting these trusses and the traveller used were described at length with illustrations in the issue of *Engineering News* of Dec. 27, 1890. In brief, we may say that the train-shed tracks were laid and surfaced, and on them were set freight-car trucks for carrying the traveller. This was a huge timber frame, with its top made to fit the lower curve of the roof-trusses. It was long enough to permit erecting one pair of trusses and the nearest truss of the next pair ahead upon it. After these were erected and braced, the traveller was moved ahead and three more trusses were placed in position. Of course the first step in the erection was to place the lower chord and the feet of the trusses in position. The material was delivered on the ground in sections small enough to be hoisted into place by a single hoisting-engine.

The 24 main trusses form the main members of the roof. The space between each pair is 14 ft. 6 in., and the space from each pair to the next pair is 43 ft. 6 in. This space is also divided into 14 ft. 6 in. panels by two light intermediate trusses, which with the main trusses form the rafters for the roof. The intermediate trusses are supported from the main trusses by purlins 3 ft. in depth, running horizontally the length of the building through each panel of the main trusses.

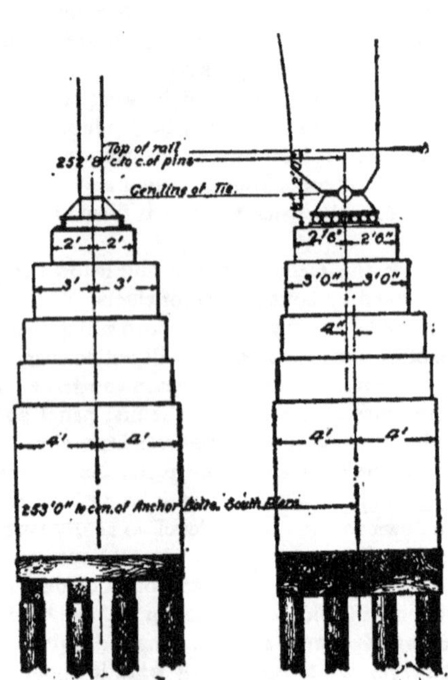

FIG. 663.—DETAILS OF MOVABLE END OF ARCH.

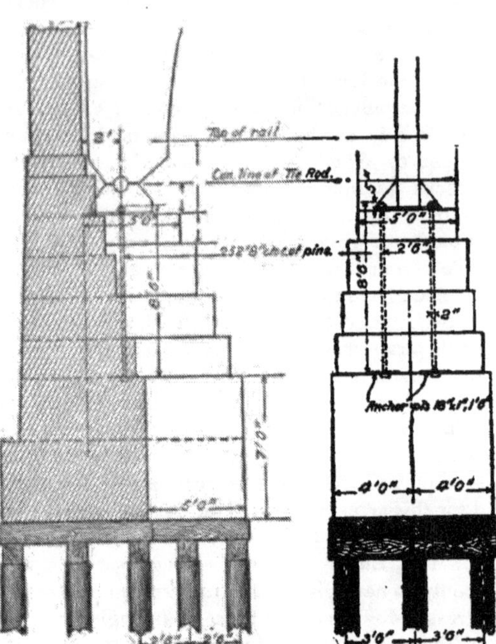

FIG. 664.—DETAILS OF FIXED END OF ARCH.

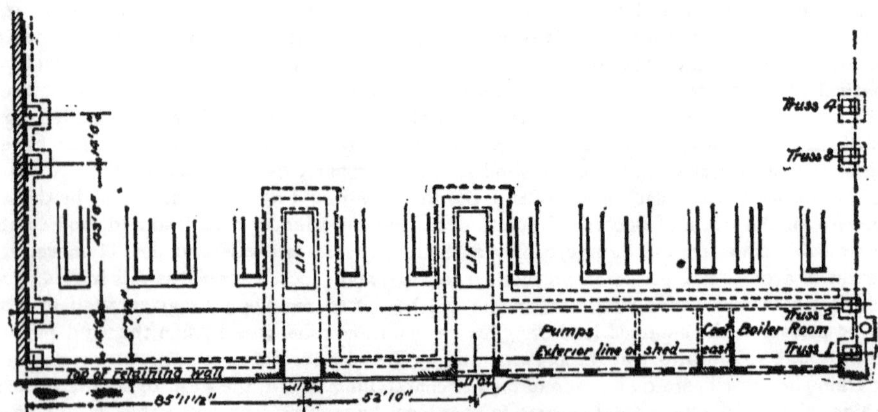

FIG. 665.—PLAN OF FOUNDATIONS.

The iron-work of the gables is especially interesting on account of the large surface there exposed to wind-pressure, about 12,000 sq. ft. The total pressure upon the gable-end at the maximum wind-pressure assumed of 35 lbs. per sq. ft. is upward of 200 tons. The gable is divided into panels about 10 feet square by light vertical trusses with horizontal bracing. The load from wind-pressure at the top of these vertical trusses is transmitted to the purlin trusses, which distribute it to the main trusses of the train-shed. The lower end of these vertical trusses is supported by a horizontal truss, 14 ft. 6 in. deep, running across the train-shed and carrying the strain from wind-pressure to the end main truss at the top of the first section.

In each panel of the gable is a galvanized-iron frame supporting 10 panes of hammered plate-glass, each ft. × 22 in. and ¼ in. thick. This glazing extends over the whole area of the gable inclosed by the inner

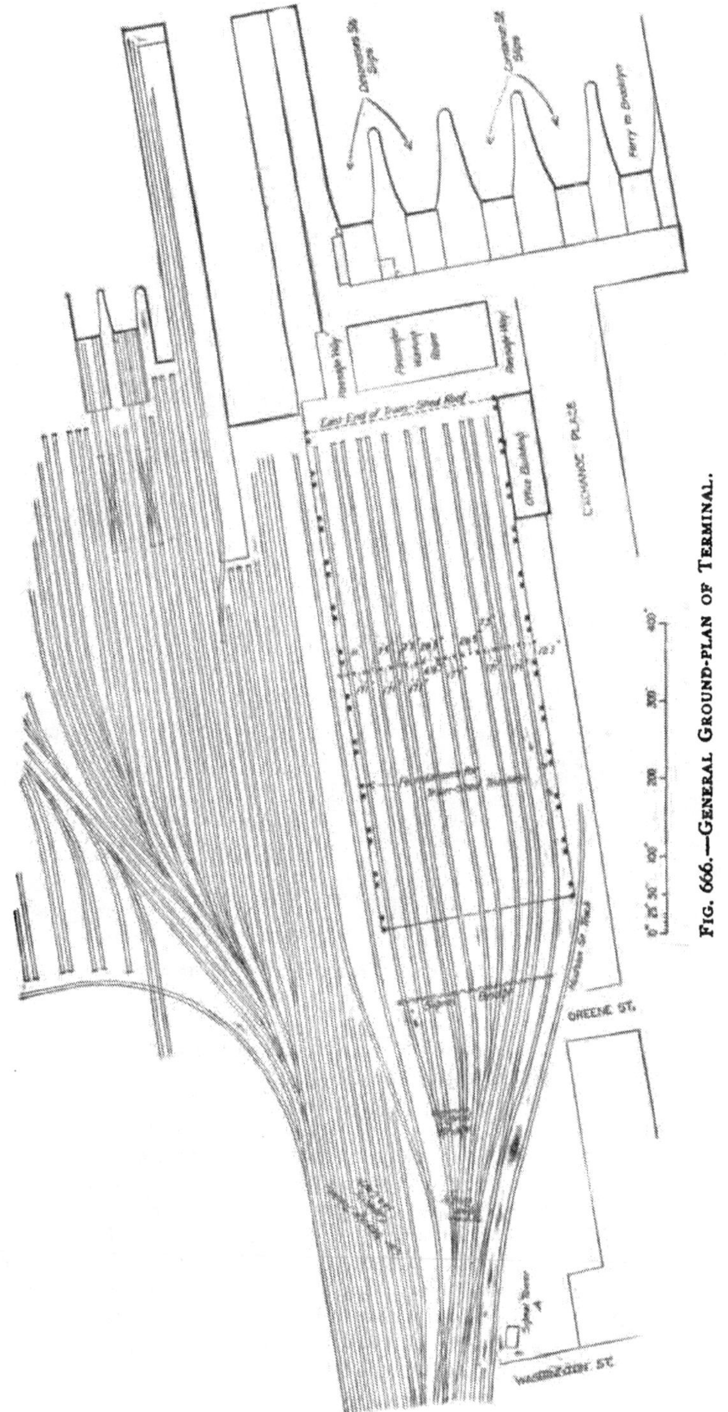

FIG. 666.—GENERAL GROUND-PLAN OF TERMINAL.

chord of the end main truss. The end truss itself is finished with a corrugated-iron covering, panelled to correspond to the panels of the truss, and with false verticals and diagonals on the outer side, giving the appearance of a truss from the exterior.

Besides over 6000 sq. ft. of glass in each gable, there is a row of windows in the north wall, running the whole length of the building, and a row in the south wall for a part of its length. These windows are hung on trunnions so that they can be swung open for ventilation whenever the weather permits. The main sources of light for the train-shed, however, are the skylights in the roof, of which there are four, one on each side of the roof half-way between the ridge and the eaves, and one on each side of the roof of the clere-story. One half the total area of the roof is of glass. There are four ventilators in the clear-story and two in the roof.

FIG. 667.—PERSPECTIVE OF TRAVELLER USED IN ERECTION OF TRAIN-SHED, SIDE VIEW.

The main and intermediate trusses running transversely and the purlin trusses running longitudinally divide the roof in panels 14 ft. 6 in. in length and a little less in width. These panels are filled with the framing for either the glass panes or for the corrugated-iron roofing, according to their position. The skylights are all glazed on the Helliwell system. The glass used is rough plate, ¼ in. thick. The elevation of the glass above the train-shed platform, from 50 to 100 ft., would make the breakage of a pane and its fall a rather dangerous thing for any one below. To guard against any accident of this sort, a copper netting of 1½-in. hexagonal mesh is stretched below the whole surface of the skylight.

The very large area of glass and the large air-space furnished by the high open roof makes the train-shed very light and free from smoke. As an example of the pains taken to make the interior of the train-shed as light as possible, the wall of the office building which extends for a distance of 160 ft. along the south side of the train-shed is faced with light-colored bricks. At night the train-shed is lit by arc-lights suspended about 20 ft. above the station platforms and furnished with current by a dynamo plant operated by the Railroad Co. The whole number of lamps in the train-shed is 64, or one to each 2600 sq. ft. of area lighted.

The whole train-shed is founded on piles, driven to a good bearing in the silt which underlies the whole water front of Jersey City. The north ends of the main trusses rest on separate piers of masonry 8 ft. 6 in. square at the base, each of which is supported by 16 piles in rows of four, each row capped by a 12 x 12 in.

timber and a tight timber platform laid on top of the caps. The south ends of the main trusses rest on counterforts projecting from the retaining-wall, which runs along the south side of the train-shed. The three rows of piles to the left are continuous along the whole length of the retaining-wall, and six additional piles are added for each counterfort.

The truss-shoes at the north end rest on a nest of 8 rollers $2\frac{11}{16}$ in. in diameter, and a little less than 2 ft. long. The south shoes are secured to the masonry by two $2\frac{1}{8}$-in. bolts.

The train-shed is built throughout of wrought-iron. The specifications for its quality and for the workmanship were the same as the standard specification of the Pennsylvania Railroad for the material and workmanship of wrought-iron bridges. All the iron-work of the building is painted three coats with red

FIG. 668.—PERSPECTIVE OF TRAVELLER USED IN ERECTION OF TRAIN-SHED, FRONT VIEW.

oxide-of-iron paint mixed with linseed-oil. The question of what is the best paint to preserve the iron roofs of train-sheds from the corrosive effect of the gases from the locomotive is an important one; but so far the Pennsylvania Railroad engineers have found nothing superior to iron oxide for this purpose.

Twelve tracks run the length of the train-shed, terminating 25 ft. from its east end. The total length of the train-shed is 652 ft. The total standing room for cars on the train-shed tracks, measuring from the clearance points, is 8571 ft. There are three double-track lines and six single tracks. The twelve tracks in the train-shed connect with five tracks in the yard. The arrangement of switches is such that any track in the train-shed can be connected to any one of the five yard tracks; hence any track can be used for either incoming or outgoing trains. This is of especial advantage in case of the blockade of any part of the yard by derailment or other accident, and is also a convenience in handling very heavy traffic.

The junction of the train-shed tracks with the yard tracks is made with a crossing using No. 8 movable-point frogs and slip-switches. The curves through these slip-switches are the sharpest in the yards, being 484 ft. radius. No other yard curves have less than 600 ft. radius. The switches and signals are all operated by the Westinghouse electro-pneumatic interlocking system, erected by the Union Switch & Signal Co. The signals are of the semaphore type, standard on the Pennsylvania, the signals for full-speed movements being mounted on posts, while dwarf signals are used for switching movements.

The compressed air for operating the switches and signals is supplied by compressors at the yards on the west side of Jersey City, and is carried through a 2-in. main. A reserve compressor, located at the terminus, can be started at a moment's notice, and is run for half an hour on three days in the week. An auxiliary reservoir is located at each switch and signal. The electricity for working the plant is supplied by storage-batteries, which are kept charged by a current from the Jersey City electric-lighting station.

A novel signaling arrangement has been introduced to notify engineers of incoming trains that a train is standing on the track they are to enter. On the signal bridge 400 ft. west of the train-shed are located the distant signals governing the train-shed tracks, while the home signals are located on a bridge 100 ft. in front. Each train-shed track is connected to form a track circuit, and when a train is on the track the distant signal is thrown automatically to the "caution" position, and remains there until the track is cleared. An engineer, therefore, who finds the distant signal at caution and the home signal at safety, knows that another train is standing in the train-shed on the track he is to enter, and that he must come in with his train under control.

Besides the train-shed tracks there is one track leading down on the south of the train-shed to a terminus at Hudson Street on the water front; and to the north of the train-shed is a yard of twelve tracks, for the storage of passenger-cars. To the north of this, on a track not filled above the old level, are the yards for handling Jersey City local freight and tracks for Adams Express cars.

The arrangement of tracks in the train-shed is in three double tracks and six single tracks, between which are the eight platforms. These are of varying widths, two having the very generous width of 22 ft. and the others being 12 ft. 2 in. wide. At present wooden platforms are in use; but after the fill on which the tracks are built is thoroughly settled and consolidated, these will be replaced by platforms of granolithic pavement. All the tracks will be ballasted with broken stone to discourage passengers as much as possible from walking across them. The arrangements for supplying water and compressed gas to the cars are unusually complete. On each track there is a gas-cock every 50 ft., with hose attached for filling cars, and there is a water-cock every 100 ft.

The general design of the new passenger station which is to replace the old one that had done service for so many years has been decided upon. It is located on the east end of the train-shed with its centre a little south of the centre-line of the train-shed. The old building had only one story; but the train-shed tracks being now at an elevation of about 15 ft. above the street level, the new structure will have two stories, of which the upper floor will be the one chiefly used by travellers, the lower story being only for Jersey City passengers, ferry waiting-rooms, storage, offices, etc.

The depot proper covers a space 188 ft. × 84 ft., and a covered passage-way about 41 ft. wide extends along the side toward the train-shed and across each end. The passage-ways across the ends of the waiting-room permit passengers to pass directly from the ferries to the trains or in the contrary direction without passing through the waiting-room.

Like the train-shed, the station is founded on piling; but there is a considerable depth of water here, so that the placing of masonry to carry the structure from below low-water mark to above high-water mark would be expensive. Moreover, the foundation secured by piling at this point is not especially stable, and as little weight and as much flexibility as possible in the structure to be supported are desirable ends to be attained. The piles, which are driven in clusters of four, are therefore cut off below low-water mark, and are capped with a timber platform which supports a cast-iron column 7 ft. 8 in. high. Tie-rods 1¼ in. square brace these columns. On top of these columns 20-in. wrought-iron girders run across the building, and on these the floor-timbers are laid. The floor of the second story and the roof are supported on iron columns.

The passages across the ends of the station are supported on piles cut off just below the level of the lower floor and braced with timbers. The roof-trusses over these passages are similar to those over the transverse platform. This latter truss is supported on one side by the lower chord of the truss which runs across the gable of the train-shed. This leaves an open space free from columns and 65 ft. in width across the whole end of the train-shed,—a very desirable feature for handling large crowds.

As the teredo sometimes works in these waters, all the piling and timber used in these foundations have been well creosoted with dead oil or coal-tar creosote.

The allowable working-stresses in the iron-work for the station are 14,000 lbs. per square inch for wrought-iron in tension; 13,000 lbs. per square inch for wrought-iron in compression, properly reduced; 10,000 lbs. per square inch for single shear on rivets; 20,000 lbs. per square inch for bearing value of rivets. Where strains include wind and snow, the above tensile and compressive stresses may be increased to 17,000 lbs. and 16,000 lbs., respectively.

As in all the other work connected with the improvement of these terminals, the time and expense of constructing the station are considerably increased by the necessity of providing temporary accommodations for the heavy traffic, which must be moved with the least possible hindrance no matter what changes are going on.

A new five-story office building, 50 ft. × 159 ft., adjoining the southeast end of the train-shed, serves for the general offices of the New York division of the railroad.

A system of bridges and passages will cross the ferry-house on a level with the second story and waiting-room, connecting with foot-bridges at each slip leading to the upper deck of the ferry-boats. These bridges, which are very light, being only for foot traffic, are suspended from a gallows frame, and are counterweighted so that they are easily adjusted by hand by the ferry attendants to suit the stage of the tide. The bridges leading to the lower decks, which are much heavier, being used for teams, are supported on pontoons, so that they adjust themselves to the rise and fall of the tide. Baggage is brought across the river on the lower decks in a baggage-van or on a truck, and is drawn through the ferry-house and onto the platform of a hydraulic elevator at the rear of the train-shed, which raises it quickly to the level of the train-shed platforms.

The credit for the general design of the train-shed is due to Mr. C. C. Schneider, M. Am. Soc. C. E. The structural details were worked out by the Pencoyd Bridge and Construction Co., who were the contractors for the work. The whole work was done under supervision of the engineering staff of the Pennsylvania Railroad; those to whom special responsibility in connection with the work was entrusted being Chief Engineer Wm. H. Brown, assisted by Mr. Wm. A. Pratt at the general offices of the company, and Mr. E. F. Brooks, Engineer of Maintenance of Way of the United Railroads of New Jersey Division, assisted by Mr. Martin L. Gardner.

For further data, details of iron-work, strain-sheet, method of erection, etc., see the publications mentioned above.

Passenger Train-shed at Pittsburg, Pa., Baltimore & Ohio Railroad.—The passenger train-shed of the Baltimore & Ohio Railroad at Pittsburg, Pa., was described and illustrated, in a paper read before the Engineers' Society of Western Pennsylvania, by Mr. J. E. Greiner, C.E., partly republished in the issue of *Engineering News* of February 23, 1889. This shed is 385 ft. long, and consists of a clear span of 84 ft. resting on columns with outside roof projections. The great peculiarity of this design is that the entire shed rests on a second set of columns below the train story, so that the design involved considerable ingenuity and nicety of calculations to provide for all the possible combinations of dead weight, live load, snow, wind, etc., and also give ample stiffness and stability. The specifications for the shed are reprinted partly in the publications mentioned. The methods and assumptions utilized in calculating the roof structure and its supports are given in full in the paper.

Ferry Passenger Terminus at Franklin Street, New York, N. Y., West Shore Railroad.—The plans for the ferry passenger terminus of the West Shore Railroad at foot of Franklin Street, New York, N. Y., designed and built under the supervision of Mr. Walter Katté, Chief Engineer, were illustrated and described in the issue of *Engineering News* of November 21, 1891. The ferry-house is partly shown in Figs. 398 and 399, and the description in the publication mentioned is as follows:

The facilities include a freight pier in addition to the passenger ferry. The slip for the passenger ferry-boat is on the north side of the freight pier, which is protected from injury by a row of fender-piles. The conveniences provided in the passenger station are about those usually arranged, with the addition of a ladies' waiting-room and a smoking-room. The West Street front of the building is ornamented by a clock-tower 22 × 20 ft., the face of the clock being about 60 ft. above the street surface and the spire rising to a height of about 100 ft. This feature is a most commendable one, especially on a road carrying a considerable number of commuters, a class of passengers whose habit of arriving at the ferry very close to the time of departure of the boat connecting with their train is well known.

Another noticeable feature of the terminal is the abundant light provided for the passage-ways to and from the ferry-slip by a large skylight in the roof, 63 × 22 ft. in size.

The buildings are heated by steam; and both gas and electric lights are provided, with arc-lights over the wagon driveways. The frames and roof-trusses are of iron, while the roof and sides are of galvanized sheet-iron. The roof is covered with asphalt and gravel.

Ferry Passenger Terminus at Boston, Mass., Boston, Revere Beach & Lynn Railroad.—The passenger depot of the Boston, Revere Beach & Lynn Railroad on Atlantic Avenue, Boston, Mass., is the Boston terminus of the ferry across the Charles River, connecting with the Boston, Revere Beach & Lynn Railroad. Plans and a very full description of this depot, designed by Mr. George Finneran, architect, were published in the issue of the *Railroad Gazette* of August 1, 1880.

Proposed Train-shed at New Orleans, La., Illinois Central Railroad.—In Fig. 669 is shown the half-section of a design for a proposed iron train-shed of the Illinois Central Railroad at New

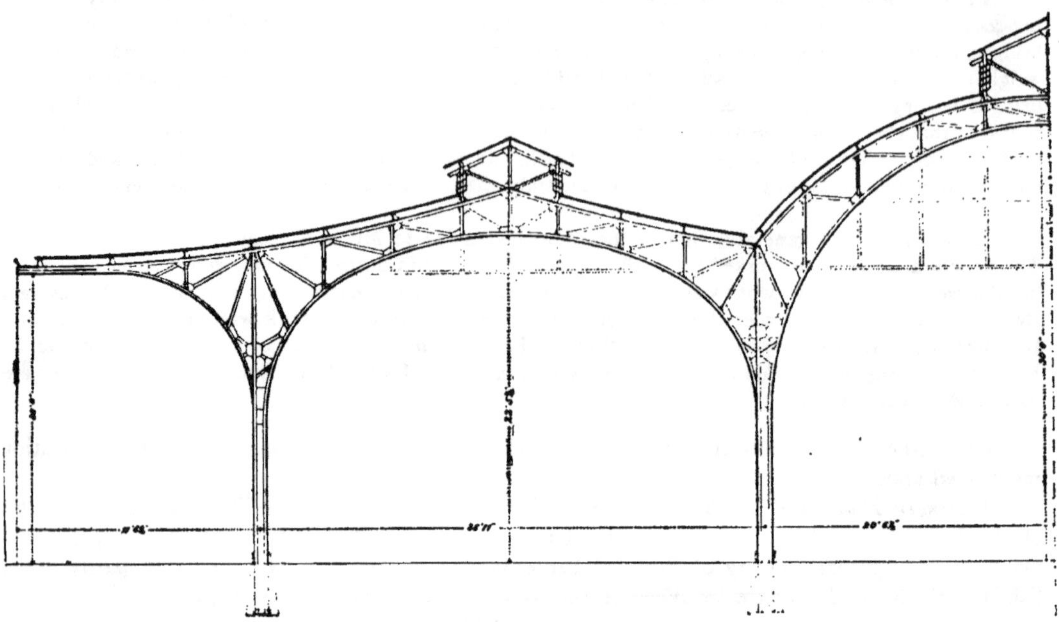

FIG. 669.—CROSS-SECTION OF TRAIN-SHED.

Orleans, La., data for which were kindly furnished by Mr. J. F. Wallace, Chief Engineer, Illinois Central Railroad. The design of this shed is novel and original. It consists of three arched spans, with two cantilever side roof projections. The entire width spanned is 148 ft. The central span is 41 ft. wide and 30 ft. high in the clear above the track at the centre of the span. The adjoining side spans are each 36 ft. wide and 22 ft. 6 in. high in the clear above the track at the centre of the span. The roof projections on each side extend 17 ft. 6 in. beyond the side column. The roof-trusses, purlins, columns, and longitudinal bracing are all of iron plates or shapes riveted together.

Proposed Terminal Passenger Depot at Chicago, Ill., Illinois Central Railroad.—In Fig. 670 is shown a section of the iron train-shed to be built at the proposed passenger depot at Chicago, Ill., of

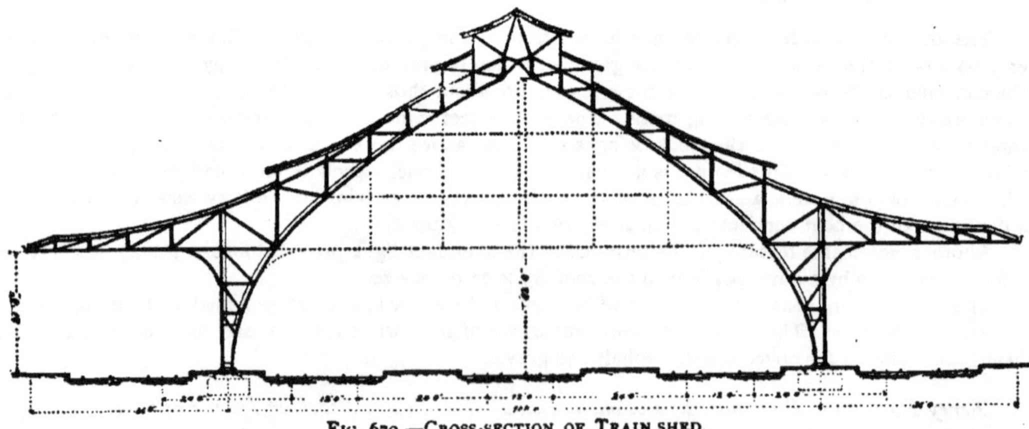

FIG 670.—CROSS-SECTION OF TRAIN SHED.

the Illinois Central Railroad, the data for which were kindly furnished by Mr. J. F. Wallace, Chief Engineer, Illinois Central Railroad. The shed is built with an arched central span, 108 ft. wide, and a cantilever roof projection, 36 ft. wide, on each side of the main span, so that the total width covered is 180 ft. The clearance is 21 ft. above the rail. There are 10 tracks covered, 6 under the main span and 4 under the roof projections. The tracks are grouped in pairs. The tracks in each pair are spaced 12 ft. centres. The platforms between the tracks are 14 ft. wide.

The proposed depot building is illustrated and described in the issue of *Engineering News* of April 28, 1892, from which publication Fig. 671 is taken. It is also very thoroughly described and illustrated in the issue of the *Railroad Gazette* of October 14, 1892.

The description of the depot in *Engineering News* is as follows:

FIG. 671.—PERSPECTIVE OF DEPOT.

The site is on the lake front at the south end of Lake Front Park, and near Twelfth Street and Park Row. It will be a terminal station for main-line trains, but suburban trains will run through as far as Randolph Street, where a new station for suburban traffic will be built eventually. The location and general arrangement of the main terminal station have been settled by Mr. J. F. Wallace, Chief Engineer, and Mr. Bradford L. Gilbert, of New York, is architect for the building. The illustration represents the up-town or north face of the building, showing the openings through which the suburban tracks pass to the train-shed. The building will be of fire-proof construction. The first three stories will be of dark granite on the main front, while the upper part and the other sides will be of buff mottled brick. The roof will be covered with dark glazed Spanish tiles. Adjoining the building will be the train-shed, 600 ft. long.

The first and mezzanine stories of the building will be devoted to waiting-rooms, ticket-offices, and other offices for the use of the public. Special provision has been made for the accommodation of suburban traffic, and ingress and egress can be had from the platforms and special waiting-room without the necessity of entering the main station building. Carriages will drive from Park Row into a large covered court.

The principal ticket-offices will be on the street level. Provision has been made for passengers to check their baggage, and by means of subways reach the train platforms without the necessity of going up-stairs into the waiting-rooms, which will be in the portion of the building extending over and above the tracks, and forming, in addition to the office building, a structure about 150 ft. square. Private waiting-rooms for ladies, a smoking-room, restaurant accommodation, and other conveniences have been provided for. The rotunda, or general waiting-room, will be 100 ft. by 150 ft., with a large, circular-domed roof. Wide stairways are provided from this room connecting with all passenger platforms, and to avoid the necessity of incoming passengers having to pass through the waiting-room, provision has been made by well-lighted subways carried under the tracks for entrance from Twelfth Street, Park Row, and the covered carriage court. The cost of the station, including main building and train-shed, is estimated at $900,000.

Terminal Depot at Oakland, Cal., Central Pacific Railroad.—The western terminal station of the Central Pacific Railroad is situated near Oakland, Cal, upon a pier of earthwork and rock running out into San Francisco Bay from its eastern shore, a distance of 1¼ miles, having a wharf and ferry-slip at its western extremity.

The building is constructed in three main divisions crosswise. The central part is 120 ft. wide and 60 ft. high, and accommodates overland trains, and the divisions on either side of this are 60 ft. wide and 40 ft. high, being exclusively for suburban trains running to and from Oakland, Alameda, and Berkeley, connecting with the San Francisco ferry-steamers.

At the west end of the main or central division are two commodious waiting-rooms for passengers. The upper or main waiting-room, 120 × 120 ft., connecting by side aprons with the saloon deck of ferry-steamers, and the lower waiting-room, connecting by end apron with the main deck of steamers, give quick and easy passage to and from the boats.

The building also contains a restaurant and various offices and apartments for railroad employés.

The structure, 1050 ft. total length, covers an area of over four acres, and is constructed mainly of wood and iron, the supports resting on concrete and pile foundations. The roof is covered with corrugated iron and glass. At night the building is illuminated with electric lights.

Union Depot at Omaha, Neb.—The proposed Union Passenger Depot at Omaha, Neb., is described and illustrated in the issue of *Engineering News* of August 17, 1889.

Proposed Terminal Passenger Depot at Chicago, Ill., Chicago Elevated Terminal Railway.—The proposed terminal passenger depot of the Chicago Elevated Terminal Railway at State and Twelfth streets, Chicago, Ill., designed by Mr. S. S. Beman, architect, Chicago, Ill., is shown in Figs. 672 and 673, taken by permission from the *Engineering News* of May 5, 1892, in which publication the depot is described as follows:

The main building will be eight stories high, and surmounted by a steep tiled roof, and will have a frontage of 350 ft. on State Street, the style of architecture being that of the English renaissance. About 80 ft. south of this main building will be a train-shed with a length of 1000 ft. on State Street. At the corner of the building will be a tower 60 ft. square and 420 ft. high to the top of the flag-staff. In the tower there will be a clock with dials on each side 19 ft. diameter, while at the top there will be a frieze about 16 ft. wide, emblematic of railway construction.

The exterior will be constructed of stone, very likely brown-stone, for the first and second stories, and above this the walls will be of terra-cotta. There will be two entrances to the main waiting-room from State Street and two through the tower, while the passengers for the suburban trains will reach the trains from the south end of the main building through the court between the latter and the train-shed. The fronts of the ground or first story of both the main building and train-shed will be leased for stores, with the exception of the space used for entrances. The main waiting-room will be 174 × 350 ft., and will be arched, with a skylight overhead, this being the size of the court by which the offices above will be lighted. Opening onto this room there will be a suburban waiting-room, 50 × 160 ft.; ladies' parlor, 50 × 80 ft.; and dining-rooms, barber-shop, news-stands, etc.

Off the main waiting-room there will be a loggia 18 ft. wide and about 130 ft. long, beneath which will be a carriage entrance to the elevators, and steps leading up to the grand waiting-room. This carriage court will be 150 × 50 ft. The upper part of the building, including the tower, will be used for offices, of which there will be 106 on each floor. In the train-shed will be 14 tracks, with a transfer-table by which trains can be immediately transferred from one track to another, so that they can arrive and depart without interruption. At the north end of the shed there will be eight elevators for receiving and lowering the baggage from

FIG. 672.—PERSPECTIVE.

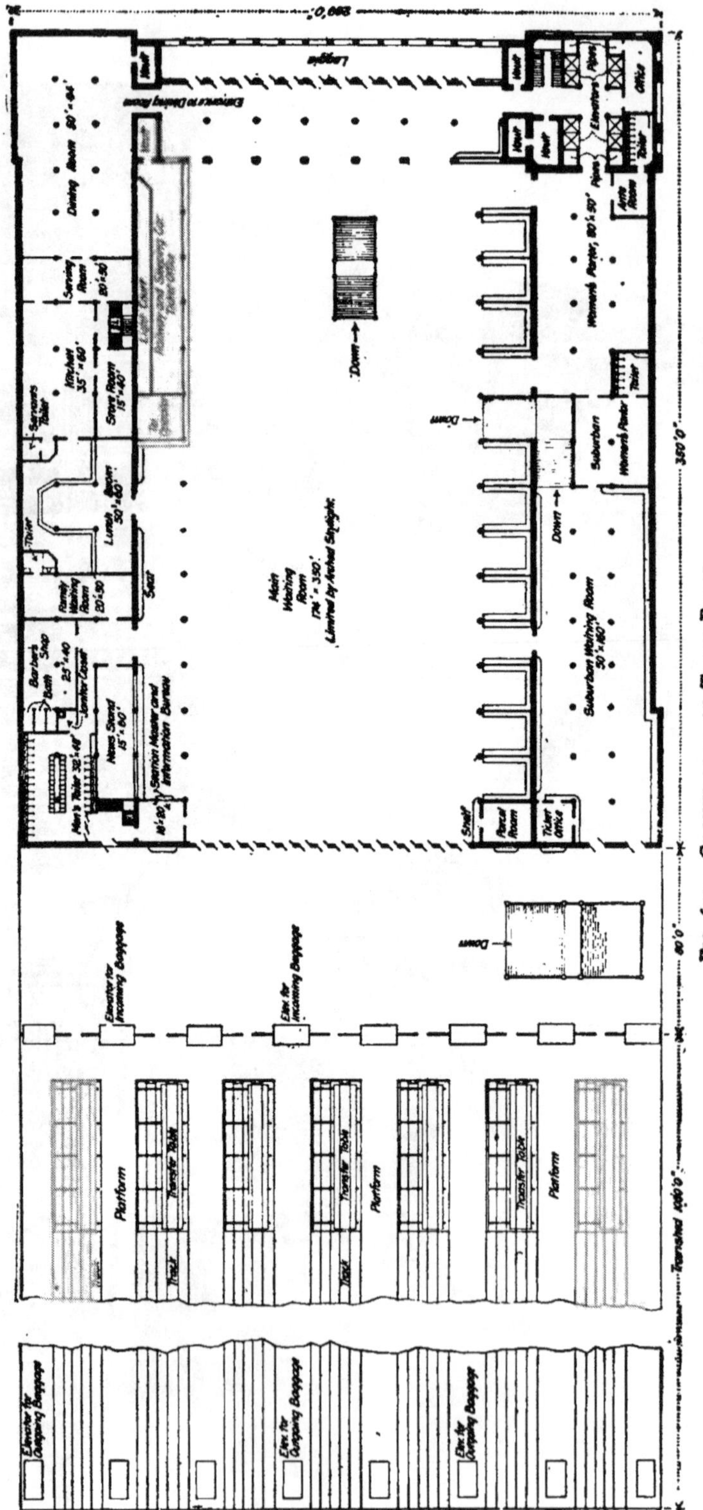

FIG. 673.—GROUND-PLAN OF TRAIN FLOOR.

incoming trains to the baggage-rooms beneath, while at the south end there will be the same number for handling outgoing baggage. The steel roof-trusses of the train-shed will have a clear span of 289 ft., and will be of elliptical form, rising to a height of 125 ft. They will be placed 40 ft. apart and arranged in pairs braced and riveted together. The platforms of the train-shed will be of Portland cement, and the tracks will be 12 in. below the platform level.

The entire structure will be of fire-proof construction, and equipped with all modern conveniences. The estimated cost is $3,500,000. It is intended to begin work as early as possible, and it is thought that two years will be required to complete it.

A large cut of this depot is published in the *Inland Architect and News Record*, Vol. XIX., No. 2.

Union Passenger Depot at St. Paul, Minn.—The Union Passenger Depot at St. Paul, Minn., designed by Mr. L. S. Buffington, architect, shown in Fig. 674, is a large terminal head-station, with six tracks terminating at the head-house, and three through tracks. Plans for this building were published in the issue of the *Railway Review* of October 30, 1880, and described as follows :

The depot building, now in process of construction and nearly completed, is located at the foot of Sibley Street, partly on the public levee and partly on the adjoining tier of lots. The width of this portion of the ground is 208 ft.; the length from Sibley Street to the east end of the station is 720 ft., and the approach is about half a mile long. The area of the entire depot ground is 9½ acres. For passenger business nine tracks enter the grounds, six of them being terminal and three forming continuous lines past the south side of the head-house. These latter connect with a tenth track that is continuous to the extreme south, and is intended for transfer business. This system of tracks is arranged in pairs. Between these pairs extend platforms, 475 ft. long by 88 ft. wide, connected at the depot end by a cross platform, 30 ft. wide and covered by an iron porch roof.

The depot building, constructed of St. Louis pressed brick and Ohio sandstone trimmings, has a 130 ft. front across the tracks, and is 150 ft. deep. It is divided longitudinally by a central hall 112 ft. long and 30 ft. wide. This hall is carried up through two stories, and is 40 ft. high. The effect thus produced is very striking, and is heightened by the artistic decorations. These latter consist of tasteful mosaics of Philadelphia enamelled and Racine pressed brick, with which the hall is lined. The colored enamelled brick are carried up some 10 ft., harmoniously combined in a graceful design, and thence the cream-colored brick are carried up to the ceiling. The result is a very pretty and withal light hall. At the second-story a series of arches is encountered. These arches form the upper hall. The dwarfing effect of projecting balconies, found in some similar structures, is here obviated by making the balconies flush, and taking the extra space from the upper series of rooms. Thus there is in the central hall a clean sweep of two stories. The interior of the cross hall is also tastefully decorated. The artistic effects of these halls are quite striking. The ladies' and gentlemen's rooms are each 46 ft. square, and there are commodious restaurants, lunch and baggage rooms, depot offices, employés' rooms, etc. Taken altogether, this is a model depot. The arrangement of tracks is admirable, and well calculated to facilitate a systematic handling of St. Paul's very rapidly increasing passenger traffic. The comfort and convenience of the public has been especially studied, and ventilation and heating have been closely looked after.

This building was destroyed by fire in 1884 and immediately rebuilt, the old walls being partly used and the interior arrangements being practically the same as previously built. The baggage-building on the north side of the grounds, built in 1883, is a two-story brick building. The lower floor is used for baggage and express and for the heat and power plant, while the upper floor is fitted up for emigrant waiting-rooms.

The longitudinal platforms between the tracks were covered by wooden platform shed roofs, supported on two posts about every 16 ft. These temporary wooden platform sheds, as also the iron porch roof over the transverse platform at the back of the head-house, were removed in 1889 and replaced by a handsome iron train-shed, as illustrated and described below.

Train-shed of Union Passenger Depot at St. Paul, Minn.—The train-shed of the Union Passenger Depot at St. Paul, Minn., designed by and built in 1889 and 1890 under the direction of Mr. Chas. F. Loweth, civil engineer, St. Paul, Minn., shown in Figs. 674 to 677, is described as follows by Mr. Loweth, who has kindly furnished some very valuable data as to the details of the work and the unit costs, which will prove of especial interest, and hence are reproduced here in full:

The shed is at rear of and adjoining the Union Depot building. The area covered is 640 ft. in length by about 189 ft. in width, and deducting the area in adjoining baggage building amounts to 115,128 sq. ft. The outer right-hand corner was cut off to conform to the property line. Shed covers nine tracks and five platforms, the lower track being a freight-transfer track.

The structure consists of a series of nineteen trusses, spaced generally 33 ft. 6 in. c. to c., and varied to suit openings in baggage building. These trusses are supported on posts generally 165 ft. 10 in. c. to c., with projecting brackets, making a clear span of about 164 ft. 6 in., and a total width of building of about 189 ft. out to out of roof.

Sides of structure between posts are open, except such bracing as required for stability, and consisting of a 7-ft. deep latticed purlin-strut at top, and a 4-ft. deep plate-girder curtain strut, the bottom of which is level with the top of car-windows, and which is ornamented by rosettes and open holes arranged in scrolls. The second and fourth trusses from east end at north side are carried by longitudinal trusses to adjoining posts in order to allow for side tracks.

FIG. 674.—SIDE ELEVATION OF HEAD-HOUSE AND TRAIN-SHED.

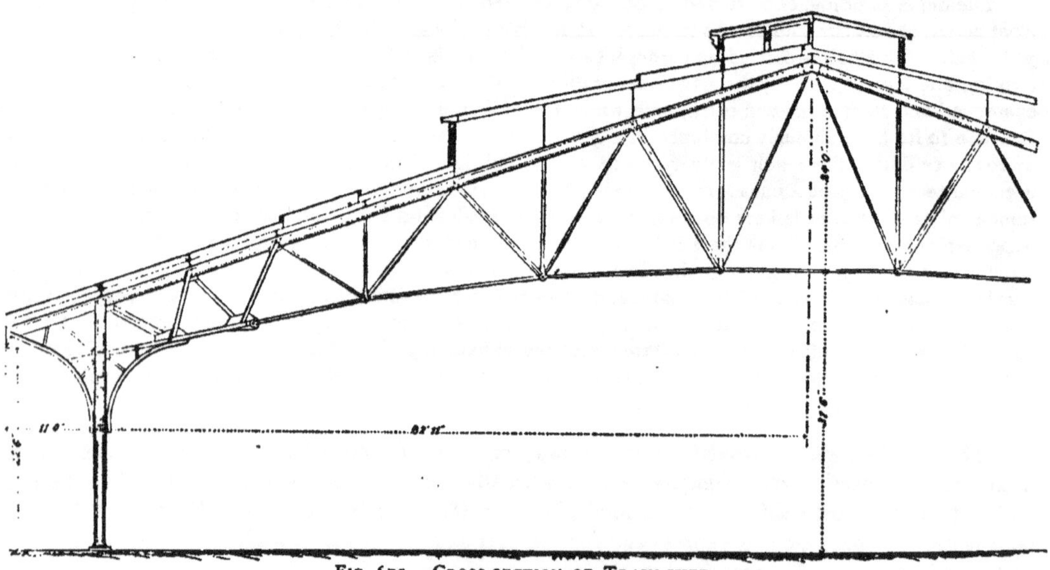

FIG. 675.—CROSS-SECTION OF TRAIN-SHED.

Foundations.—Foundations along south side and the two at N. E. corner are on piles. End piers have six piles and intermediate ones nine; largest foundation at N. E. corner of building has twelve piles. All piles were cut off at about 6 ft. 6 in. below ground and pit excavated 6 in. below top of piles; on piles was placed a bed of American natural-cement concrete 2 ft. thick and generally 6 ft. wide by 9 ft. long. On concrete was built a masonry pier of first-class ashlar masonry with granite cap-stones about 6 in. above top of rails.

Foundations along baggage building were carried down to level of bottom of building foundation, about 6 ft. 6 in. below tracks; foundation wall cut away for length of about 7 ft. 6 in., and a Portland-cement concrete foundation 7 ft. 6 in. by 15 ft. laid, the length being transverse to building. Eight 10 in. steel beams 14 ft. long were bedded in each concrete base; on this foundation masonry was built similar to other piers except that the cap-stones were Mankato stone and the space between building wall and new piers was filled with masonry.

All foundations are on made ground, consisting of 20 to 25 ft. of gravel filling on old slough and river bed, put in from nine to twelve years previously.

Quantities, prices, and total cost are as follows:

2265 ft. pine piling, at 30 c.,	$679 50
150.99 cu. yd. Milwaukee cement concrete, at $4.50,	679 45
88.20 " " Portland cement concrete, at $6.50,	573 30
144.06 " " Mankato stone masonry, at, $14,	2,016 84
5.62 " " " " pier caps at, $16,	91 00
10.4 " " granite pier caps, at $50.75,	527 80
Extra work, repairing sewer damaged in driving piles, etc.,	69 97
Steel beams for foundations, 25,704 lbs., at 3 c.,	771 12
Total,	$5,408 98

Cost of foundation per square foot of area covered, 4.7 cents.

Iron Work.—Trusses are 6 ft. deep at ends, 23 ft. deep at centre, with bottom chord curved and raised at centre 10 ft. above ends. Trusses are pin-connected except the two panels at ends, which were made of the

FIG. 676.—PERSPECTIVE OF EXTERIOR OF TRAIN-SHED.

riveted lattice form in order to admit of a stiffer connection to the supporting posts. All eye-bars, counters, top chords, pins and supporting posts are of steel. All else of wrought-iron. All rivet-holes in steel were reamed.

Structure was proportioned for a combined dead and live load of respectively 20 and 25 lbs. per square foot of roof surface, and also for the above dead load, and in addition a combined live snow-load of 20 lbs. per square foot and a horizontal wind-pressure of 50 lbs. per square foot, both acting on the same half of truss only.

Allowable unit stresses are generally on a basis of a factor of 4, which is a minimum and increased somewhat as the importance of the member. Minimum thickness of metal $\frac{5}{16}$ in. Purlins are riveted lattice girders spaced about 10 ft. 10 in. apart measured in plane of roof, and are generally 3 ft. deep. Purlins are prevented from sagging by 3 in. × 3 in. × $\frac{5}{16}$ in. angle-iron extending from centre of purlins to ridge purlins, or diagonally each way to the main trusses.

Lateral bracing occurs in every other space between trusses at top chord only, except in the two spaces at east end of shed, where heavy lateral bracing occurs at lower chord level to provide for wind-pressure on end gable.

The total weight of iron and steel in superstructure is 1,690,290 lbs., equivalent to 14.7 lbs. per square foot of area covered. Contract price was 4.25c. per pound erected and painted, amounting to $71,837.32, or 62.5c. per square foot of area covered.

Extras in iron-work contract amounted to $524.41 and included cost of 6160 lbs. eye-bars broken in

FIG. 677.—PERSPECTIVE OF INTERIOR OF TRAIN-SHED.

testing and 2033 lbs. iron-work injured by other contractor, extra painting, etc.; making total cost of iron-work $72,361.73.

Roof-covering.—Roof-covering is of 1½-in. matched and dressed pine sheathing laid on 3-in. × 8-in. pine jack-rafters spaced about 4 ft. 3 in. apart and bolted to purlins. Skylights arranged as shown on plans. Glass ⅜ in. thick in first 125 ft. next to Union Depot building, and balance ¼ in. thick, all best quality rolled ribbed glass, set in galvanized-iron frames, thoroughly painted. Skylights constitute 26.3% of roof surface. Ventilation of shed obtained by continuous wood louvres, one on each side of roof at about the centre, and by four large ventilators at ridge, each one panel long with wood louvres at sides; also by ten cast-iron "None such" smoke-jacks at ridge.

Roofing of tin (Gilbertson's "Old Method" or Taylor's "Old Style," extra heavy coated). All tin painted on under side at shop and laid with one layer of strawboard building-paper between it and the sheathing. Gutters made of No. 24 galvanized iron.

The entire cost of this roof-work, including enclosing ends of shed, gutters, leader-pipes, etc., was $34,825.54, or equal to 30¼c. per square foot of area covered.

The following are some of the quantities in the work and prices paid:

96,680 sq. ft. of tin roofing, at $9.00 per 100 ft., including flashings, painting under side, and paper layer.

32,060 sq. ft. of skylights, 7480 ft. being ⅜ in. glass, balance ¼ in. thick. Cost 53c. and 45c. per square foot respectively, set in place.

896 lineal ft. of 24-in. girth galvanized-iron gutter.
648 " " " galvanized-iron leader-pipes.
168 " " " cast-iron leader-pipes.
311 " " " 31 in. × 24 in. iron cornices.
3,460 sq. ft. corrugated-iron siding.
1,280 lineal ft. of 4 ft. 10 in. wood louvres.
264 " " " 3 " 5 " " "
83 " " " glazed light frame in east-end gable.
193,480 ft. B. M. in rafters and sheathing.

Above price did not include painting of wood and sheet-metal work, except such surfaces as would be inaccessible for painting after erection; separate contract for painting amounting to $3500, including one coat for all rafters and under side of roof sheathing, and two coats on all outside wood-work, tin-roofing, cornices, gutters, and corrugated and other sheet-iron work, but not including painting of any structural iron-work. Above price is equivalent to 3.4 c. per square foot of area covered.

Cost of structure should include, in addition to above items, one of $2251.77 for miscellaneous expenditures, such as supplies, extra help, electric lights, building permit, switching cars, etc., and including $709.42 for sewers along both sides of building.

Summary of Cost:

Foundations,	$5,408 98
Iron-work,	72,361 73
Roof-covering, etc.	34,825 54
Painting,	3,500 00
Miscellaneous,	2,251 77
Total	$118,348 02
Engineering and inspection, including inspection of iron-work at mill and shop,	4,848 07
Total cost,	$123,196 09

Total cost per square foot of area, $1.07.

The iron-work was furnished and erected by the Keystone Bridge Co.

Terminal Passenger Depot at Forty-second Street, New York, N. Y., New York Central & Hudson River Railroad.—In Fig. 678 is shown the ground-plan of the terminal depot of the New York Central & Hudson River Railroad at Forty-second Street, New York, N. Y., which is built as a U-shaped head-station. This station serves for several railroads, and hence there are a series of waiting and baggage rooms. The train-shed for departing trains has twelve tracks, while the shed for arriving trains has seven tracks. The train-sheds are 650 ft. long. The main shed is covered by a single-span arched iron roof construction of 200 ft. span.

Terminal Passenger Depot at Jersey City, N. J., Central Railroad of New Jersey.—The passenger depot of the Central Railroad of New Jersey at Jersey City, N. J., shown in Figs. 679 to 683, described and illustrated in the issue of *Engineering News* of October 6, 1888, from which publication Figs. 679 to 682 are copied, is a large, handsome, and substantially built terminal head-station, described as follows in the publication mentioned:

The building is of brick and iron, with stone trimmings in the front. The general dimensions are 215 ft. in width by 717 ft. in length, the train-shed being 512 ft. long. The accompanying plan and front and side elevations convey a clear idea of the arrangement of the ground-floor and of the appearance of the exterior.

The foundations of the walls and piers are of piles of an average length of 60 ft. Under the walls the piles are placed zigzag, from 5 to 6 ft. apart, in two rows 2 ft. centre to centre. On top of the piles are 12 × 12 caps, upon which are 3 × 6 cross-pieces on which rests the masonry. All the wood is below high-water mark. The pier foundations are clusters of from 7 to 9 piles capped with 12 × 12 and 3 × 6 timbers, and then a brick pier capped with a 3 × 4 bluestone. These support the iron columns carrying the main roof of the train-shed. The load on a single pile is limited to 9 tons.

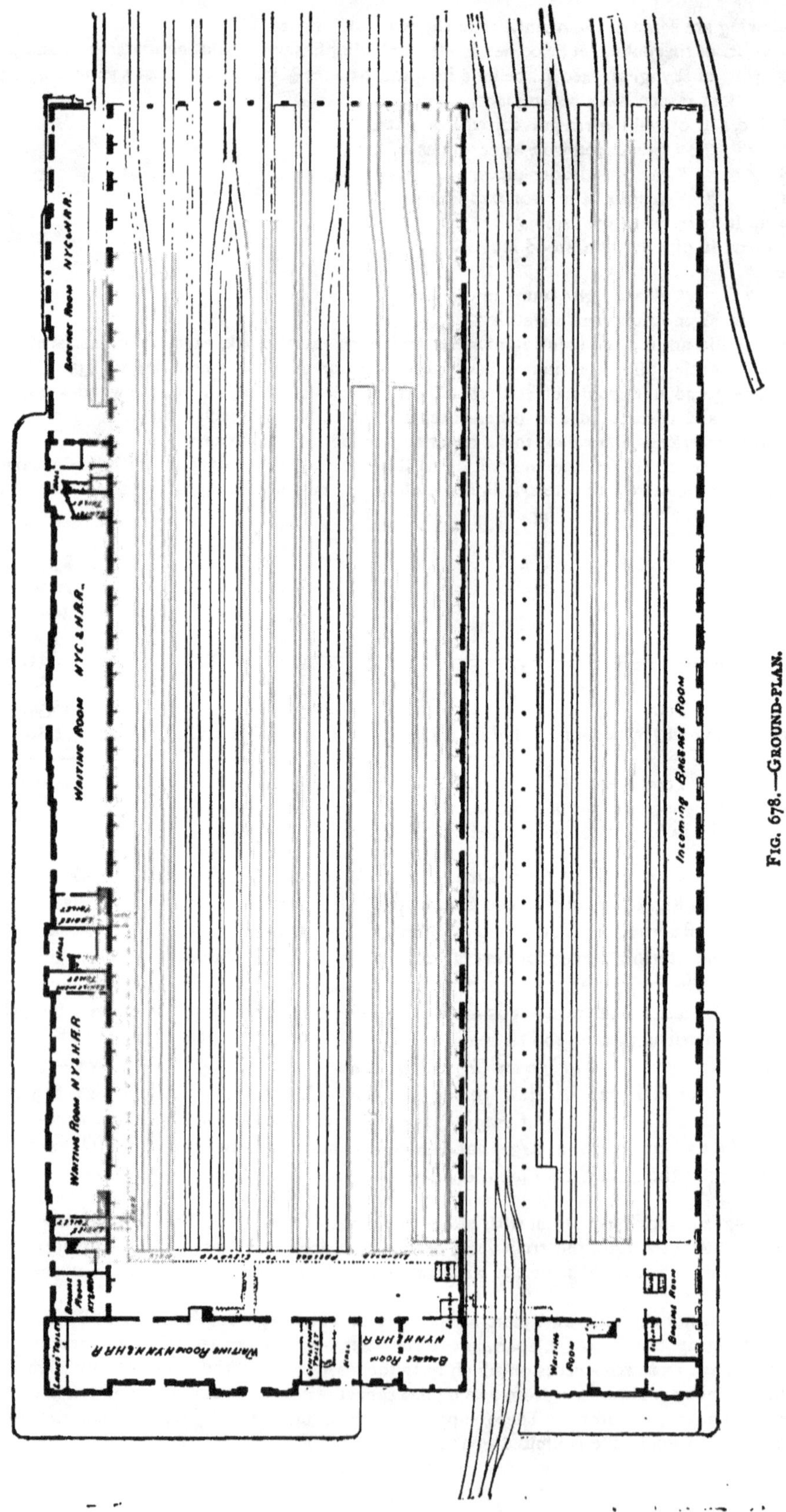

FIG. 678.—GROUND-PLAN.

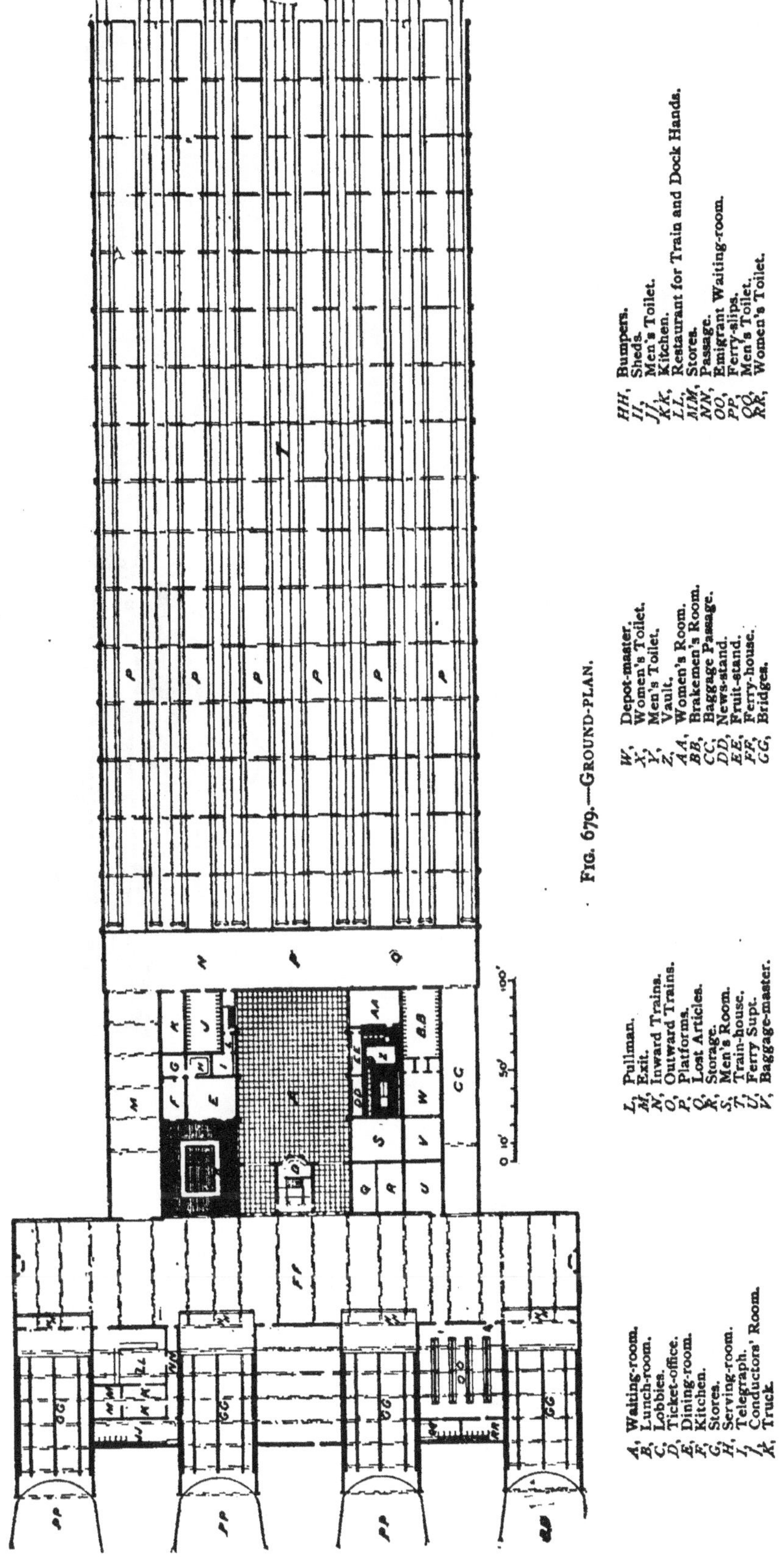

FIG. 679.—GROUND-PLAN.

A, Waiting-room.
B, Lunch-room.
C, Lobbies.
D, Ticket-office.
E, Dining-room.
F, Kitchen.
G, Stores.
H, Serving-room.
I, Telegraph.
J, Conductors' Room.
K, Truck.
L, Pullman.
M, Exit.
N, Inward Trains.
O, Outward Trains.
P, Platforms.
Q, Lost Articles.
R, Storage.
S, Men's Room.
T, Train-house.
U, Ferry Supt.
V, Baggage-master.
W, Depot-master.
X, Women's Toilet.
Y, Men's Toilet.
Z, Vault.
AA, Women's Room.
BB, Brakemen's Room.
CC, Baggage Passage.
DD, News-stand.
EE, Fruit-stand.
FF, Ferry-house.
GG, Bridges.
HH, Bumpers.
II, Sheds.
JJ, Men's Toilet.
KK, Kitchen.
LL, Restaurant for Train and Dock Hands.
MM, Stores.
NN, Passage.
OO, Emigrant Waiting-room.
PP, Ferry-slips.
QQ, Men's Toilet.
RR, Women's Toilet.

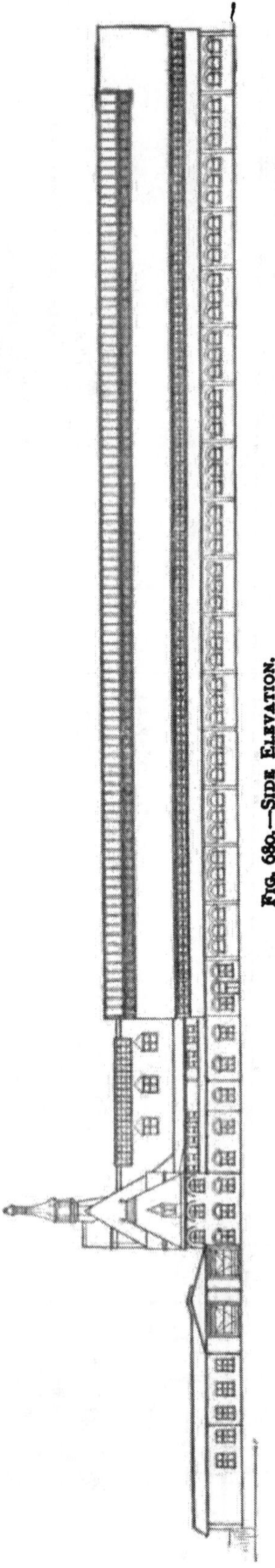

Fig. 680.—Side Elevation.

Fig. 681.—Front Elevation.

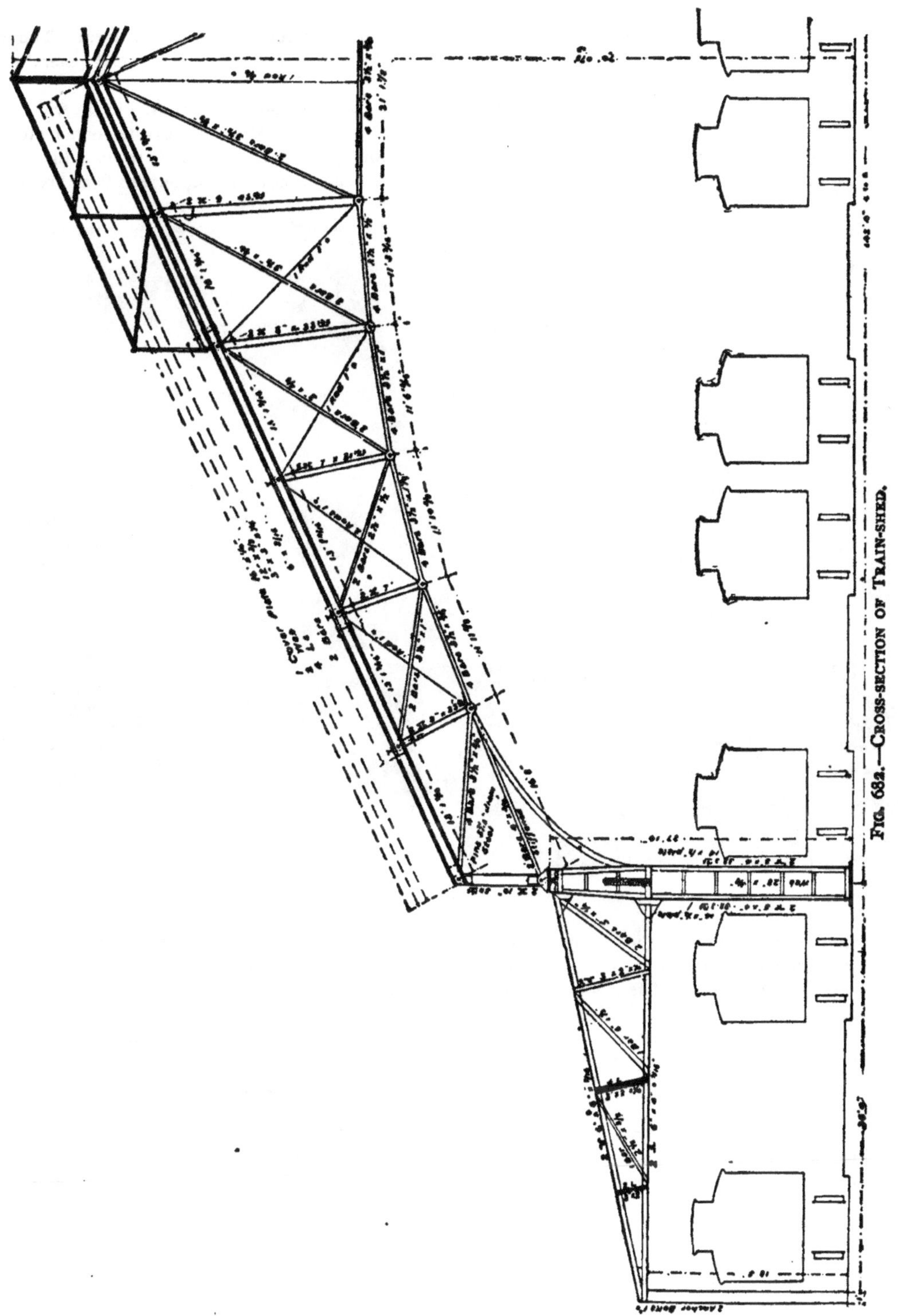

FIG. 682.—CROSS-SECTION OF TRAIN-SHED.

The truss of the train-shed roof is shown in the accompanying half-section. The trusses are spaced 32½ ft. The lean-to roofs are tin, the others slate. Extending the length of the train-shed is a monitor roof of glass. Fixed windows are placed above the lean-to roof.

The train-shed will accommodate 12 tracks, 6 for outgoing and 6 for incoming passengers. The tracks are arranged in pairs, separated by concrete walks, 13 ft. 10 in. wide. The tracks are spaced generally 12 ft. centres.

The waiting room in the centre of the head-house is 85 ft. 4 in. in length, and 66 ft. 8 in. in width. The ticket-office is located at the entrance, and at the sides are news-stands, restaurant, private rooms, etc. The walls are of English cream-colored glazed brick, and the flooring of bluestone. This room is lighted by 3 large dormers and a skylight extending the whole length. All the other rooms upon this floor are finished

FIG. 683. PERSPECTIVE OF EXTERIOR OF TRAIN-SHED.

in North Carolina hard pine, the ceilings being formed by the beams and flooring of the second story. The exit for incoming passengers, on the south side of the building, is 29 ft. wide, is paved with concrete and walled with English brick. The platform between the head-house and train-shed is 31½ ft. wide. The baggage passage is on the north side of the depot.

The vault measures 17 by 10½ ft. inside. The foundation consists of three rows of piling (longitudinal) carrying arches supporting the floor, which is on a level with the main floor. The centre wall is 12 in. thick, the outer ones 24 in. In the latter is a 4-in. air-space. The vault is entered from the second floor by means of a spiral stairway.

The upper stories of the head-house are to be used as offices.

Four new slips, arranged symmetrically with the building, and a new ferry-house, are being built.

The depot building was designed by Messrs. Peabody & Stearns, architects. The work throughout was built and carried out under the immediate supervision of Mr. Wm. H. Peddle, Engineer and Superintendent, C. R. R. of N. J.

Terminal Passenger Depot, Philadelphia, Pa., Philadelphia & Reading Terminal Railroad.—The passenger station of the Philadelphia & Reading Terminal Railroad Company at Twelfth and Market streets, Philadelphia, forms the Philadelphia terminus of the Philadelphia & Reading Railroad. It is a large and substantially built terminal head-station, designed by Messrs. Wilson Brothers & Co., civil engineers and architects, Philadelphia, Pa., as shown in Figs. 684 to 688, prepared from data kindly furnished by them. The head-house, which fronts on Market Street, has a frontage of 266 ft. 6 in. and a depth of 100 ft. It is eight stories high with a half-basement; the height from the pavement to the top of the balustrade being 153 ft. The train-shed is 266 ft. 6 in. in width and 559 ft. long, including the lobby 50 ft. wide in rear of head-house. The entire space covered reaches from Market Street to Arch Street, a distance of 659 ft. The trains enter the station by an elevated structure, so that the platforms in the train-shed are on a level with the second floor of the head-house. Filbert Street, which runs between Market Street and Arch Street, and parallel thereto, passes under the train-shed. The ground-floor from Market Street to Filbert Street is occupied by the railroad company for sundry purposes, explained below, while the space under the train-shed from Filbert Street to Arch Street is utilized for a public market-house.

This structure is especially noteworthy, as it is the most recent passenger terminal station of magnitude erected in this country, its construction having begun in the fall of 1891. It presents, therefore, so far as feasible under the circumstances, the best arrangements and the latest improvements applicable to railroad passenger-stations. It has the largest existing single-span train-shed roof, which fact alone entitles this structure to rank with the most prominent railroad terminal stations of this or any other country. The Philadelphia & Reading Railroad Company has succeeded in erecting one of the handsomest terminal passenger stations in the world, so that due credit should be given to the railroad company and to the designers for an achievement that every American can be justly proud of.

The exterior of the building, as represented in Fig. 684, shows a design in the Italian Renaissance, which is very artistic and effective. Since the design was made from which the illustration is taken, an additional story has been added to the head-house between the third and the seventh floors, which will improve the appearance. The basement and the first stories are built of pink granite, and the remainder of pink brick and white terra-cotta.

The several floors of the head-house are used as follows: The basement is fitted up for stores. The first floor serves as an entrance-lobby for passengers, with the necessary ticket-offices, baggage-rooms, carriage-court, and accommodations for a number of interests and departments connected with the railroad and station service. The second floor, which is on a level with the platforms in the train-shed, contains a large general waiting-room, a ladies' waiting-room, dining-room, restaurant, toilet-room for gentlemen and ladies, etc. The remainder of the building is used for general offices of the railroad company and of the operating service of the terminal.

The half-basement on each side of the main passenger entrance from Market Street is fitted up very handsomely, and contains six stores on the Market Street front and one on Twelfth Street. It is reached by a few steps leading down from the street.

The large passenger lobby on the first floor, 58 ft. × 80 ft., forming the main entrance, is reached, as shown in Fig. 685, by two steps leading up from the level of Market Street through an open arcade, 114 ft. front and 12 ft. in depth. On the left-hand side of the lobby there is the ticket-office, 37 ft. × 48 ft., with a fire-proof vault; also a branch office of the U. S. post-office, 31 ft. × 37 ft. In the rear wall of the lobby there is an entrance to a 20-ft. corridor leading from the lobby to the carriage-court, and also two openings to the outward-bound baggage-room, so that passengers after purchasing tickets can attend to checking their baggage before ascending to the train-floor of the building. On the right-hand side of the lobby there is a 10-ft. staircase leading to the train-floor; also two elevators for passengers, and a Pullman ticket-office.

On the Market Street front, beyond the arcade to the right, there is a large office, 43 ft. × 58 ft., with a fire-proof vault, for the Philadelphia & Reading Coal and Iron Company. In the rear of this office there is the store-room for railroad-tickets, 32 ft. × 37 ft.

To the left of the arcade, at the corner of Market Street and Twelfth Street, is the office for the treasury department of the Philadelphia & Reading Railroad Company. This office is 64 ft. × 73 ft. and has connected with it large burglar-proof and fire-proof vaults.

Between this office and the ticket-office is located the main exit stair leading to Market Street; and there is also a similar stair leading to Twelfth Street, as shown on the plan.

At the extreme right of the Market Street front, and also on the Twelfth Street front, there are

Fig. 684.—Perspective of Exterior.

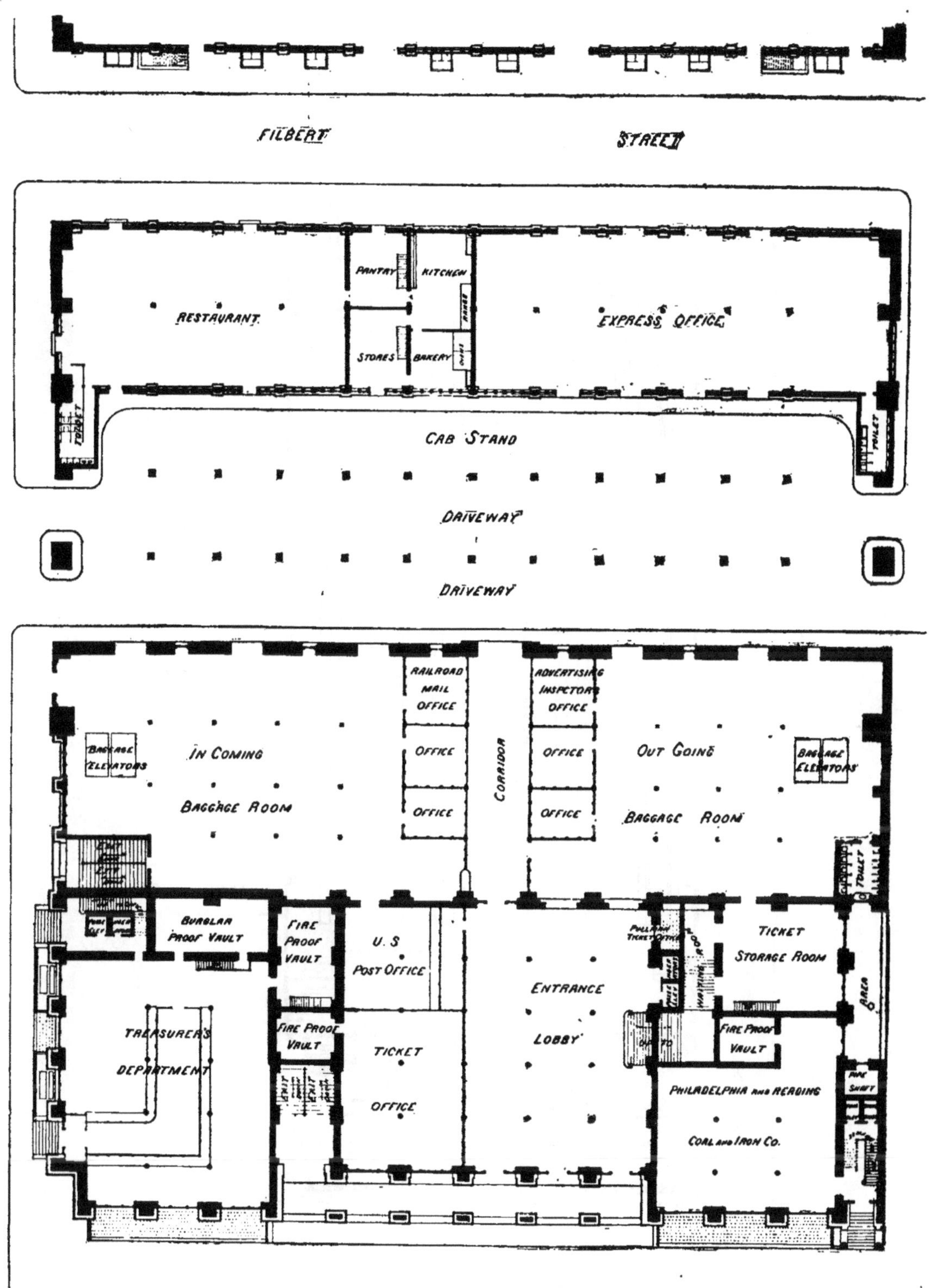
FILBERT
STREET
PANTRY
KITCHEN
RESTAURANT
STORES
BAKERY
EXPRESS OFFICE
TOILET
CAB STAND
TOILET
DRIVEWAY
DRIVEWAY
RAILROAD MAIL OFFICE
ADVERTISING INSPECTORS OFFICE
OFFICE
OFFICE
OFFICE
OFFICE
CORRIDOR
BAGGAGE ELEVATORS
IN COMING
BAGGAGE ROOM
OUT GOING
BAGGAGE ROOM
BAGGAGE ELEVATORS
TOILET
BURGLAR PROOF VAULT
FIRE PROOF VAULT
U. S POST OFFICE
ENTRANCE
LOBBY
TICKET STORAGE ROOM
AREA
TREASURER'S DEPARTMENT
FIRE PROOF VAULT
TICKET OFFICE
FIRE PROOF VAULT
PHILADELPHIA AND READING
COAL AND IRON CO.
EXIT
EXIT

FIG. 685.—GROUND-PLAN OF FIRST FLOOR.

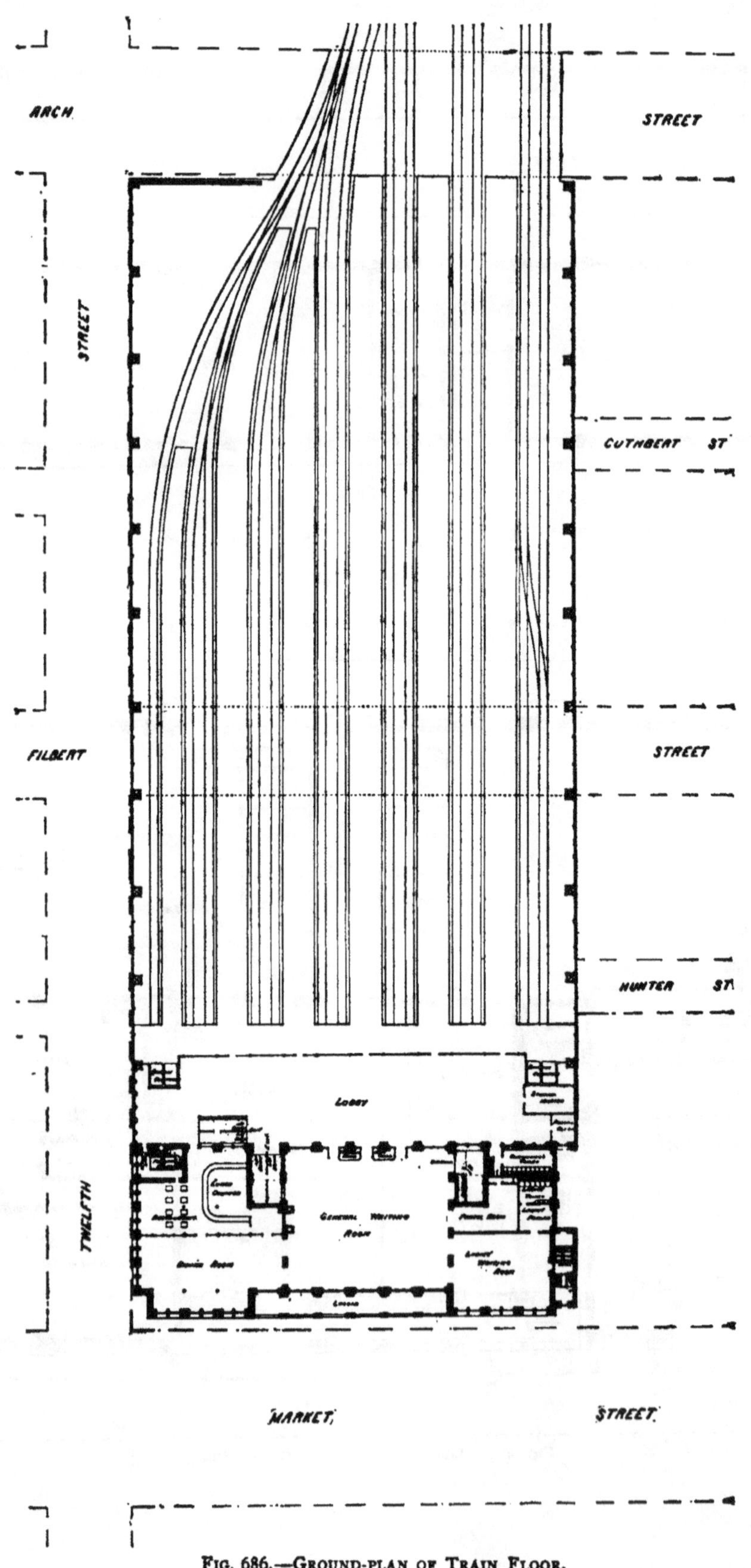

FIG. 686.—GROUND-PLAN OF TRAIN FLOOR.

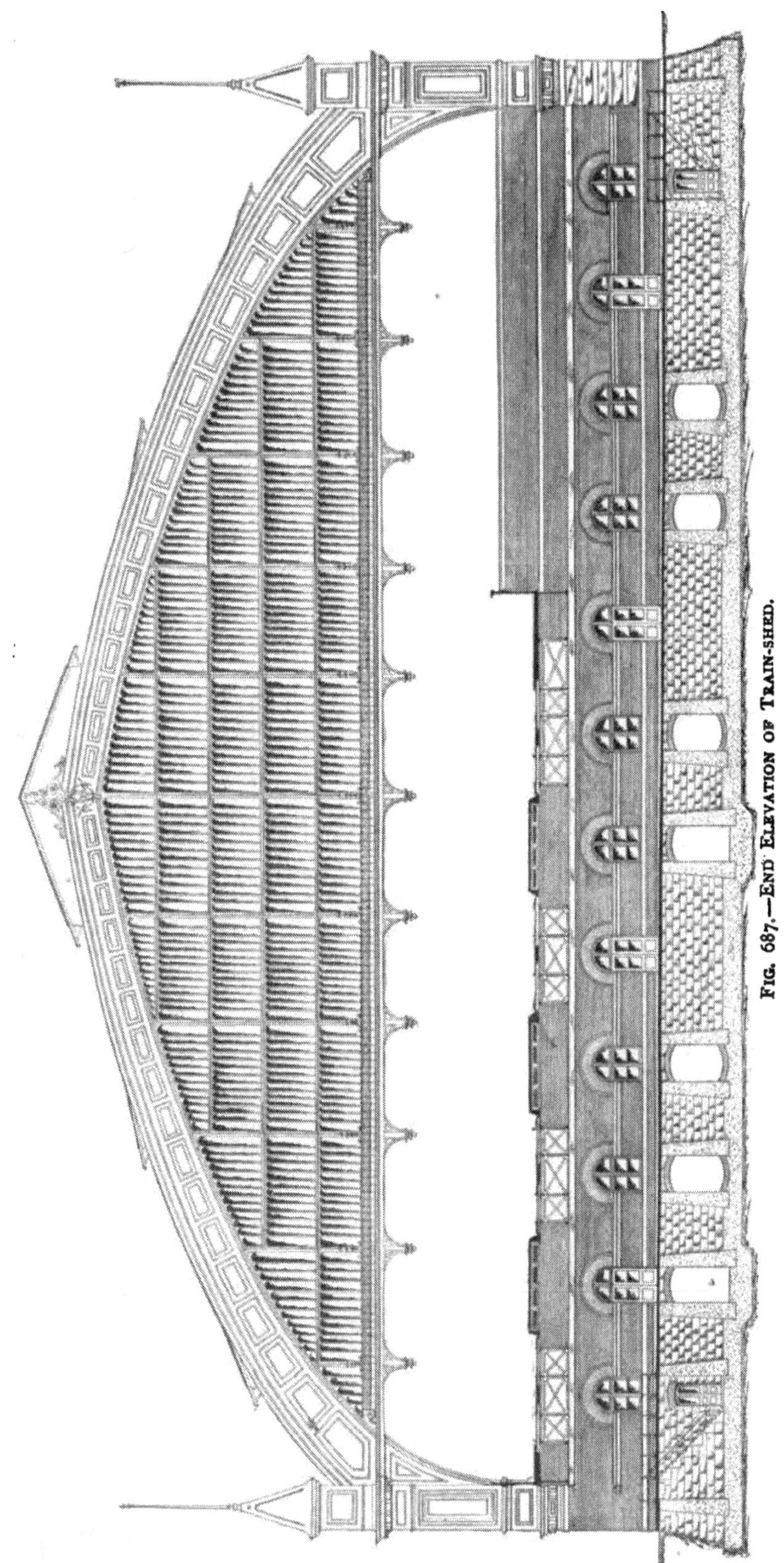

FIG. 687.—END ELEVATION OF TRAIN-SHED.

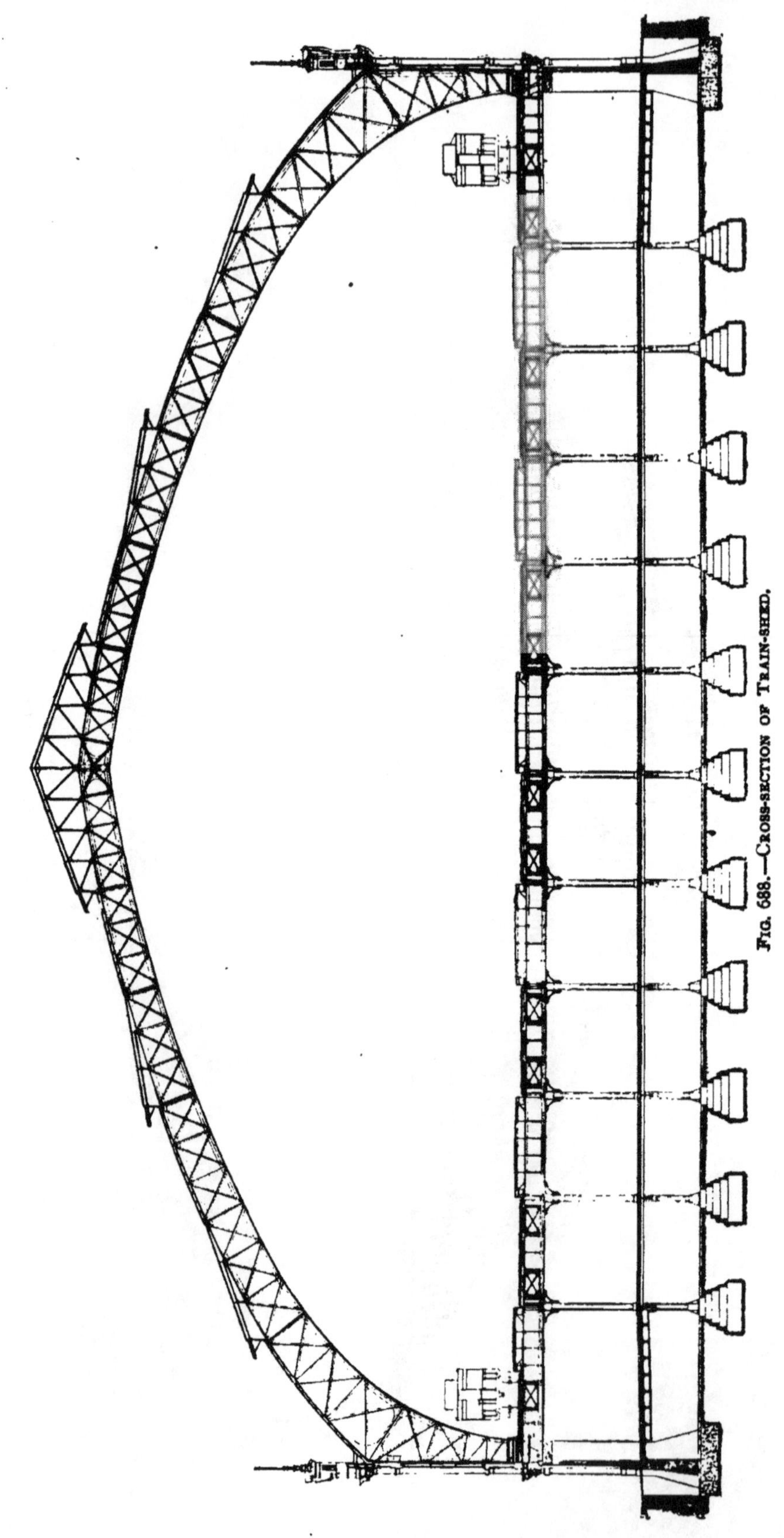

FIG. 688.—CROSS-SECTION OF TRAIN-SHED.

special entrances with staircases and elevators leading to the general offices of the railroad company on the upper floors.

The baggage-rooms are located between the head-house and the carriage-court in the rear, from which, as previously mentioned, there is a 20-ft. corridor leading to the entrance-lobby. This corridor is flanked by a number of small offices for various purposes, such as railroad mail and the advertising inspector.

The out-bound baggage-room is 72 ft. × 90 ft. Baggage is received from wagons standing in the carriage-court and hoisted to the train-floor level by means of two baggage-elevators at one end of the room. Passengers can check their baggage or make inquiries concerning same at the two openings from the lobby previously mentioned. At one corner of this baggage-room there is a water-closet for employés. At the corner next to the carriage-court there is a mail-chute, so that incoming mail-bags can be delivered from the upper or train-floor level to a platform on the lower level, whence they are loaded into the mail-wagons.

The in-bound baggage-room is 72 ft. × 105 ft. Baggage is transferred to it from the train-floor level by two baggage-elevators, located as show on the plans, and thence delivered to wagons standing in the carriage-court or on Twelfth Street. At the corner of this baggage-room, next to the corridor from the carriage court previously referred to, and near the entrance-lobby, there is an in-bound baggage-delivery window, where in-bound passengers passing to the carriage-court can obtain hand-baggage or make any necessary arrangements.

The carriage-court in the rear of the baggage-rooms is 74 ft. wide and runs through under the train-shed from Twelfth Street to Hunter Street, to which it forms a prolongation, as shown on the plans. The middle of the carriage-court is used as a driveway; the side next to the baggage-rooms serves for wagons to stand when delivering or receiving baggage, while the other side of the court is utilized as a cab-stand.

The space on the ground-level between this carriage-court and Filbert Street is used for a restaurant for employés and market people, and for an express-office. The restaurant, 47 ft. × 89 ft., fronting on Filbert Street, Twelfth Street, and the carriage-court, has connected with it a store-room, 18 ft. × 24 ft.; a kitchen, 19 ft. × 29 ft.; a pantry, 18 ft. × 23 ft.; a bakery, 17 ft. × 19 ft.; and water-closets for men and for women. The express-office, 47 ft. × 129 ft., is accessible from Filbert Street and from the carriage-court, and is provided with a toilet-room for employés.

The remainder of the ground-floor under the train-shed between Filbert Street and Arch Street is used as a public market-house, as before stated.

The ground-floor having been explained, it will now be in order to describe the second or main floor of the building, as shown in Fig. 686, which is on a level with the platforms in the train-shed. The outgoing passengers, after purchasing their railroad-tickets and checking their baggage, ascend from the entrance-lobby on the ground-floor by the entrance stairs or elevators, shown on the plans, to the general waiting-room, 78 ft. × 100 ft., which is a lofty and handsomely finished room. In front of this room, facing Market Street, is a loggia, 14 ft. × 120 ft., which adds materially to the beauty of the exterior design of the building, while it lends additional attractions to the general waiting-room, as it will prove in summer a welcome extension.

On the right of the general waiting-room is located the ladies' waiting-room, 39 ft. × 43 ft., with ladies' parlor, 15 ft. × 17 ft., and a ladies' toilet-room, 15 ft. × 17 ft., a parcel-room, and the stairs and elevators for passengers. On the left is the dining-room, 43 ft. × 84 ft., and the restaurant, 48 ft. × 64 ft., with lunch-counter. A telegraph-office, for the use of the public, and a news-stand are located on the side of the general waiting-room next to the train-shed.

There is a lobby 50 ft. wide between the head-house and the train-shed, extending across the station, in which outgoing crowds congregate while waiting for the gates to be opened, and from which incoming passengers have access to the main exit stairs to Twelfth Street and to Market Street. The lobby is enclosed on the train-side by an ornamental iron fence with gates opposite the longitudinal platforms in the train-shed. The elevators from the baggage-rooms on the ground-floor are located at the ends of this lobby, which also contains small offices for the station-master and the United States postal clerk. The second story of the head-house is 35 ft. high, and the main waiting-room occupies the whole of it; but on either side a half-story is obtained over the ladies' waiting-

FIG. 689.—PERSPECTIVE OF DEPOT.

room, dining-room, etc. A small service stair leads from the lobby to the portion of this half-story on the ladies' waiting-room side, where the station operating force is accommodated. The gentlemen's toilet-room, 15 ft. × 29 ft., also opens on the lobby at this end.

The remainder of the building is used for the general offices of the railroad company and its affiliated interests, and is fitted up for offices in the very best and most approved manner.

The train-shed extends from the lobby to Arch Street, a distance of 509 ft. The lobby, 50 ft. wide, is covered with a low-pitch roof and skylights, so as to afford better light to the offices in the rear of the head-house above the train-shed floor.

The roof of the train-shed is designed as shown in Fig. 688, the trusses being grouped in pairs spaced 50 ft. 2 in. centre to centre of pairs, the trusses in each pair being 5 ft. centres. The horizontal thrust at the foot of the arch is taken up by a system of eye-bar ties running across the train-shed under the floor alongside of the cross-girders supporting the tracks. The illustration Fig. 688 shows the space devoted to the market-house below the train-shed floor, and Fig. 687 shows the elevation of the Arch Street end of train-shed.

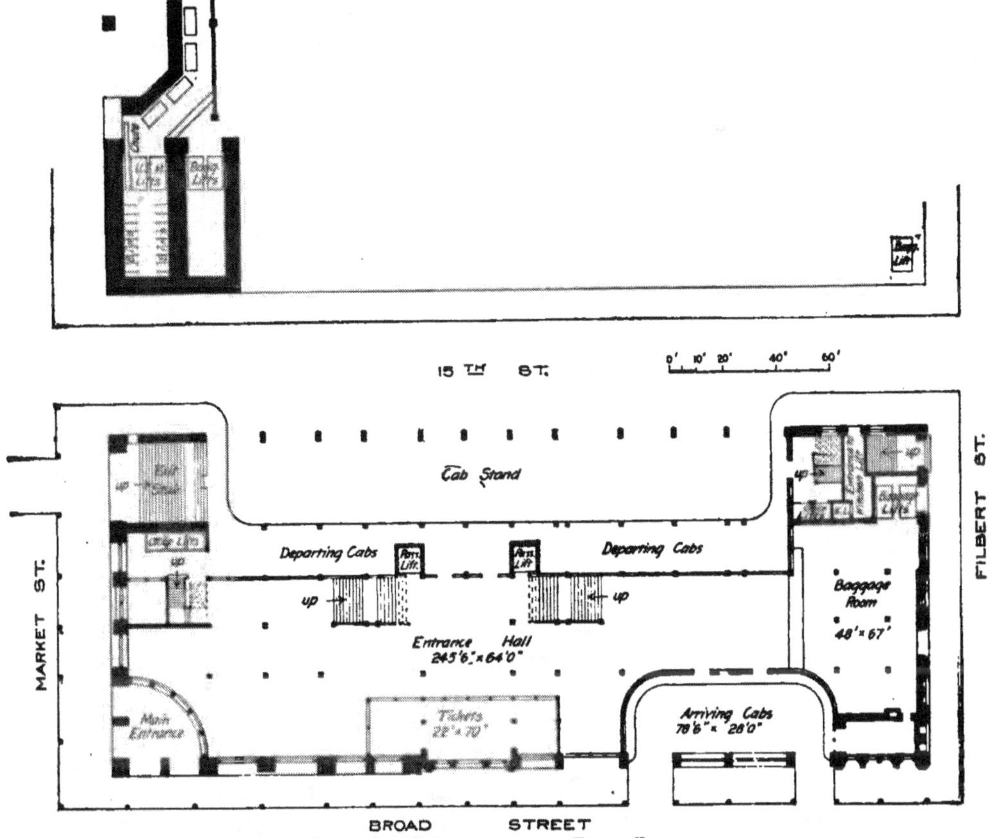

FIG. 690.—GROUND-PLAN OF FIRST FLOOR.

The following are the official data regarding the dimensions of this train-shed roof, which, as previously stated, is the largest existing single-span train-shed. Clear span at level of tracks, 253 ft. 8 in. Span, 266 ft. 6 in. over all and 262 ft. 3 in. back to back of chords. Span centre to centre of end-pins, 259 ft. 8 in. Height from top of rail to top of skylight ridge, 95 ft. 6 in. Vertical height centre to centre of pins, 88 ft. $3\frac{5}{16}$ in. Height in clear at centre of span from top of rail to underclearance line, 80 ft.

There are thirteen tracks in the train-shed, grouped in pairs with longitudinal platforms between them, the tracks in each pair being 12 ft. on centres and the platforms 19 ft. wide. The platforms are 8 in. above the top of the rails and 4 ft. 6 in. from the centre of the nearest track. The rails are laid on creosoted oak cross-ties bedded in asphalt concrete. The floor of the train-shed, forming the ceiling of the market-house, is constructed as shown in Fig. 688, and floor-lights are inserted in the longitudinal platforms between the tracks. The roof is covered with tin over wooden sheathing on wrought-iron purlins. The skylights are glazed with ⅜-in. rough plate glass set on sash-bars made of sheet copper with wrought-iron coves. The sides of the shed are of cast-iron, panelled and provided with windows, pivot-hung, so as to give ample light and ventilation.

Proposed Extension of Terminal Passenger Depot at Broad Street, Philadelphia, Pa., Pennsylvania Railroad.—In the issues of the *Railroad Gazette* of September 30 and October 21, 1892, and in the issues of the *Engineering News* of October 6 and October 13, 1892, the proposed extension of the terminal passenger depot of the Pennsylvania Railroad at Broad Street, Philadelphia, Pa., as shown in Figs. 689 to 691, copied by permission from the *Engineering News*, is described and illustrated. The old depot at this point, described above and illustrated in Figs. 635 to 641, built about 1882, having become inadequate to accommodate the increased passenger travel at this station, the railroad

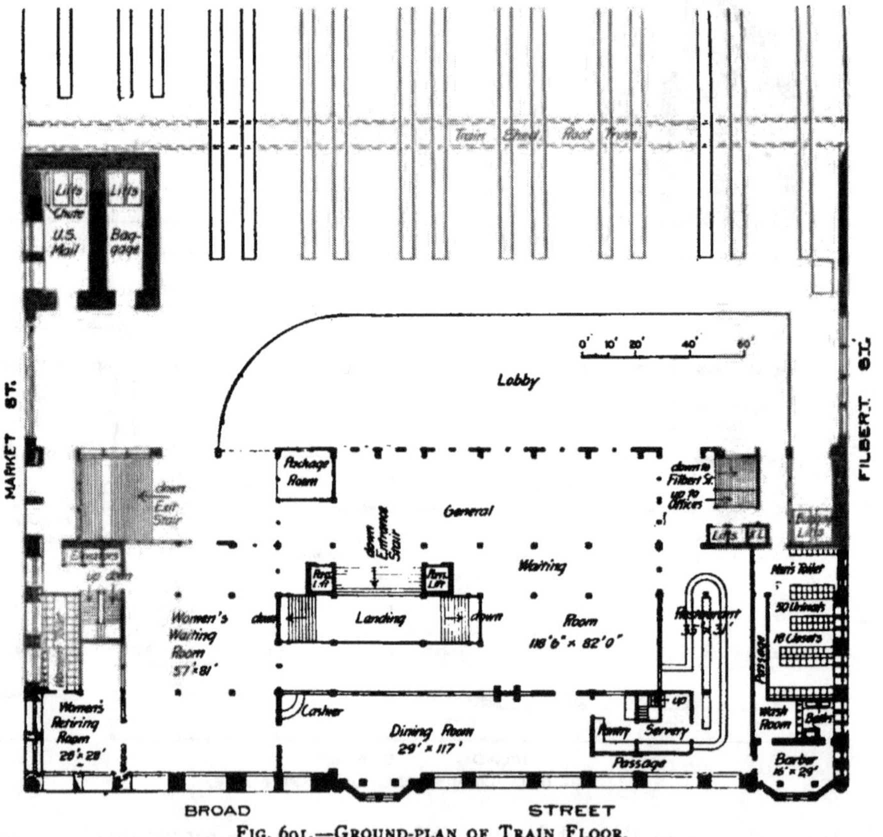

FIG. 691.—GROUND-PLAN OF TRAIN FLOOR.

company was forced in 1892 to acquire the remainder of the property facing on Broad Street between Market Street and Filbert Street, and to make arrangements for the construction of the new depot building and train-shed, as shown in Figs. 689 to 691. The old depot building at the corner of Broad Street and Filbert Street will remain, with extensive changes, however, in the interior. At the corner of Market Street and Broad Street a new building, 14 stories high, as shown in Fig. 689, is to be built with a train-shed extending across the rear of both the old and the new building, which train-shed will be 306 ft. 9⅝ in. wide and 707 ft. long, accommodating 16 tracks, which is double the number of tracks in the old layout. The train-shed will be 140 ft. high at the centre, the main arches having a clear span of 294 ft. and a clear height of 104 ft. 6 in. The layout of the ground-floor with the entrances from and exits to the street is shown in Fig. 690, and the arrangement of the second floor, which is on a level with the tracks in the train-shed, is shown in Fig. 691. The upper stories will be utilized for the general offices of the railroad company.

APPENDIX.

SPECIFICATIONS.

PENNSYLVANIA RAILROAD.

SPECIFICATIONS FOR LOCAL PASSENGER DEPOT AT POTTSVILLE, PA.*

EXCAVATIONS AND FOUNDATIONS.

Excavate for foundations to depth indicated on the drawings; the foundation masonry to be built to correspond with the dimensions and in the manner shown on the *drawing*.

Excavations for drain and other pipes, except for plumbing and gas-fitting, will be done by the mason.

The stone used for foundations must be submitted to and have the approval of the Engineer in charge before being permitted to be laid in the walls. No stone to have less bed than face, and the footing courses to be laid with extra large flat stone; all to be carefully bedded on their broadest faces, well bonded together, and laid in strong, sharp mortar, made of good lime and clean, sharp sand, or sharp screened gravel, as the Engineer may direct.

AREAS.—Build in substantial manner all walls for ways to outside cellar-doors, areas to cellar-windows, and such other walls as indicated on *plans, etc.*

DAMP COURSE.—On the top of cellar walls, and under joists, girders, plates, sills, etc., lay a course of slate thickness in cement, to prevent the rise of moisture.

CESSPOOL.—Locate where indicated, and excavate for cesspool to a depth of 12′ 0″ or such depth as the Engineer in charge shall direct; wall up with hard brick 8½″ deep, the finished diameter to be 5′ 6″. The bricks will be laid from bottom of well up to within 3′ 0″ of the top. Cover the cesspool with a flag-stone 7′ 0″ × 7′ 0″ × 6″, having manhole 2′ 0″ diameter, and cover of cast-iron.

STONE-WORK.

CUT STONE.—All the cut stone-work, of every description, to be of the dimensions, form, kinds, and finish as per *plans, elevations, etc.;* the same to be delivered in first-class conditions, free of all defects, properly lewised, drilled, dowelled, anchored, fitted and set, close-jointed, carefully pointed, and cleaned off at completion.

Spalled or patched stone-work will be condemned.

BOND STONE.—Bond stone must be built in all walls and piers, wherever required by the drawings the bonds to be made every *three feet in height* with *North River flagstone not less than five* inches thick, by the thickness of the walls or size of the piers in which they are intended to be used.

NOTE.—Iron clamps and dowels to be used wherever necessary for the stability of the work. *The stone-work of superstructure shall be of approved brown sandstone laid broken range, rock face, pitched; the door and window sills to be same material. Supply dressed flagstone covers for the chimneys 2½″ thick.*

---

* Mr. Wm. H. Brown, Chief Engineer, Pennsylvania Railroad, who has kindly furnished this specification for publication, states that for the smaller and standard buildings erected under his charge the quality of materials and the dimensions are clearly noted on the drawings, so that a separate specification is not required, the *General Specifications* for all classes of construction work, in connection with the drawings, being ample. For larger and more varied structures a separate specification is usually prepared, although sometimes an attempt is made to use a skeleton specification. The specifications for the Pottsville Depot are based on such a skeleton specification in use to a limited extent on the Pennsylvania Railroad. The parts in *italics* are filled in by hand in the original, while the balance is the printed text of the original skeleton specification.

This depot is described on pages 294 to 296 and illustrated in Figs. 544 to 547.

BRICKS AND BRICK-WORK.

All interior brick, and the backing of face brick, shall be good, sound, and well burnt, the walls to be built true and straight, and properly bonded with the requisite number of heading courses. All exterior brick-work will be laid up with first quality *Reading or Hamburg pressed brick. Start the brick-work from one course of No.* 13 *Peerless moulded brick.*

Akron Tiles.—Gables at end of Waiting-room, also the space between end piers of dormers, to be covered with round-end Akron tiles.

Keep the face of brick-work in gables 6" back from face of brick-work below.

CHIMNEYS.—The chimneys will be built of hard brick only, the facing brick to be *same as in wall.* All the flues to be well built, *pargeted throughout their entire length,* and started two feet below first floor-joist to insure proper connection with the furnace. *The tiling specified below will be selected by Architect.*

FIREPLACE.—*Build and face fireplaces in manner shown by detail drawings. Supply the required floors of soapstone* $1\frac{1}{2}''$ *thick (encaustic tile hearths 2' 0" wide), iron backs and jambs* ($16.00) *each, and the same fitted with patent chimney-throat.*

RELIEVING ARCHES.—Relieving arches must be turned over all openings that will admit of them.

BRICKNOGGING.—Bricknogging must be introduced between the ends of all joists resting on exterior and brick partition walls.

MORTAR.—*The* mortar to be used for pointing the *outside walls* shall be colored with *mineral red* in such proportions as to insure permanent color. Common mortar shall be compounded of sharp, clean sand and wood-burned lime, in approved proportions.

IRON-WORK.

IRON-WORK.—All truss-rods, bolts, and other wrought-iron work required in the various parts of the building to be furnished of first-quality double-rolled wrought-iron, and to be subject to the approval and directions of the Engineer in charge; it being understood by the parties to the contract that such bolts, rods, etc., are to be introduced at the discretion of the said Engineer in charge, wherever he may deem it to be necessary to insure the strength and permanency of the structure. All window and door frames to be secured with iron joggles, and iron clamps and dowels to be used wherever necessary. *Two* 12" 125-lb. *I-beams shall be employed to carry spire. (See plan for position.) Two 9" 70-lb. I-beams, combined with web separators at standard distances, shall be used as girder to carry brick-work, etc., over the Ticket-office. Cast-iron columns to be made from moulds dusted with "fine facings" to produce smooth castings. Chip off or file away any blisters or other imperfections of surface.*

WINDOW-GRATINGS.—Substantial wrought-iron gratings to be placed in the windows of cellar, set in the platform. *Two* of these to be hinged double for coal-chute, and to be secured by bolt and strong padlock.

Galvanized-iron wire screens, No. 8 wire gauge and one-inch-square mesh, to be placed in all windows of Ticket-office two inches (2") from shelf or sills, and extending upwards the whole height of openings.

CASTINGS.—All castings required in the execution of the work to be made from good, tough iron, true and sound, holding the full sizes according to the drawings, and to be free from cracks, flaws, bubbles, or defects of any kind whatever.

PAINTING.—All wrought-iron to be painted while hot with red oxide of iron, and cast-iron work to be painted with the same material after inspection by the Engineer.

LUMBER AND CARPENTER WORK.

LUMBER.—All the lumber throughout the building, except where particularly specified to the contrary, to be first-quality *hemlock* free from shakes, flaws, and unsound knots, thoroughly seasoned, dry, and in every way suitable for the various purposes for which it is intended.

JOISTS.—All joists to be of *spruce or hemlock.*

The rule for spacing the joists throughout the building shall be sixteen inches from centre to centre, with double joists under partitions. Each joist must be properly backed, and have a bearing of   inches at each end, on the walls and partitions. All joists *in the Waiting-rooms* to have *three* rows of cross-bracing, *elsewhere one row.*

Flues and other openings are to be framed around with double trimmers in all cases where there is more than one tail-joist. Particular attention must be paid to keeping all wood-work sufficiently far from the flues to insure absolute safety from fire.

PARTITIONS.—The wooden partitions throughout the building are to be made of good 3in. × 4in. hemlock or spruce scantling, spaced sixteen inches from centre to centre, securely attached to the floors and ceilings, and stiffened with two rows of horizontal bracing. In all cases the broad side of the timber is to be placed crosswise of the partitions, and double studs are to be placed on each side of all openings and at angles.

Partitions will have, where possible, long studs passing through floor-timbers, to stand on girders, and to have plates 3 in. × 5 in. on which to foot studs coming above, and to carry *upper* timbers.

Studs in partitions to be sized, jointed, and set to a true line. Partitions to be set perfectly plumb. No studs to stand on floor-joist, but to foot on plate below; in case no partition should be underneath, the studs must foot on a sill-piece 3 in. × 5 in., spiked to and extending across tops of floor-joist (avoiding openings), so as to render the whole work stiff. Truss over all openings.

Long braces, cut in barefoot and well spiked top and bottom, must be placed where necessary. Studs to cut on bracings.

WINDOWS.—All the window-frames *throughout the house are* to be made, as shown on details, of sound, well-seasoned *white pine* lumber, fitted with all the necessary pulley-stiles, boxes, pockets, parting strips, beads, etc., in accordance with the drawings, *to be stained in imitation of yellow pine in rooms with this finish.*

FINISH.—The finish around the windows *in Waiting and Ladies' Toilet Room* to be made as shown by details. Outside roof-finish, brackets, etc., to be of *yellow pine* lumber, and finished in accordance with elevations and details.

SASH.—The sash to be composed of first-quality *chestnut in W. R., elsewhere white pine*, made in accordance with the drawings. All to be double-hung on strong axle-pulleys, with the best patent cord, and finshown.

DOORS.—The outside doors to be *of fine-grained selected chestnut*, made the thickness and in the manner shown on details. The inner doors to be *of the same material, all to be* panelled and moulded as shown on ished as details.

The baggage-room doors to be of two thicknesses, made as shown on the elevations, but to be hung on *Philadelphia pattern sheaves (6" wheels) and wrought-iron ways.*

All the doors throughout the building to be made of the best *materials*, mortised one inch deep, dowelled and glued up in the best manner, hung on the most approved strong butt-hinges, and furnished with locks, bolts, etc., complete, as provided under the head of Hardware.

The water-closets to have short slat-doors, hung twelve inches above the floor. Thickness of water-closet doors one and one-quarter inches. *The finish in Gents' W. C. Room to be of selected yellow pine.*

TRANSOMS.—The doors *throughout the station are* to have square heads and transom lights, with movable sash hung on transom plates, secured by spring catches, let in flush, and operated by *Wollensak transom-rods.*

ROOFING.—The carpenter shall frame and construct, according to the drawings furnished, all roofs in the most thorough manner, provide and fix all bolts, rods, straps, and other iron-work necessary to fully carry out the work as designed.

Prepare and firmly fix all the carpentry necessary to form the eaves and eaves' gutters, cornices, brackets, consoles, barge-boards, etc.; grade the gutters in the metal lining—never in the wood-work—so as to throw the water to points indicated or specified for the location of the leaders.

The end gables (see Elevations) are to be *tiled* with *Akron round-end red tiles* in three thicknesses, and to show 5" to the weather, the ends to be cut in the manner shown.

SHEATHING.—The sheathing of the roof and frame to consist of best quality hemlock sheathing-boards, one inch thick, planed on one side, put on diagonally, with planed side out, and well nailed to the rafters. Exposed portions of eaves of main roof and roofs of porches to be best-quality *double-beaded* 1 in. × 3 in. *yellow pine tongued and grooved boards, surfaced one side.*

FELTING.—Cover the entire sheathing with brown felting-paper, the felting to extend down and under water-table, frieze-boards, corners, casings, etc., in order to insure a water-tight job.

WAINSCOTING.—All the walls of Waiting-rooms *and Ladies' Toilet* to be wainscoted and capped to a height of *six feet* (6'.0") with *selected chestnut* boards, tongued, grooved and beaded, and laid vertically with base and cap, as per drawings. Wainscot behind seats.

SEATS.—*Seats will be furnished by the Company.*

Baggage-room to be lined and ceiled with narrow tongued and grooved seven-eighth-inch yellow-pine boards, tongued, grooved, and beaded, planed smooth, secret-nailed, wedged tight, tight joints, and nail-holes closed with colored putty.

FLOORS.—All the floors, except otherwise noted, to be composed of first quality *maple* flooring-boards, one inch thick, in width not exceeding three inches. The whole to be free from sap, unsound knots and shakes, and to be tongued and grooved, well planed on top, and securely secret-nailed to the joists. All the floors in the building to be planed and left clean and perfect on the completion of the work. Outside platforms to be 2 in. × 4 in. yellow pine, laid.

All floors must be run up close to brick-work or framing; flooring-boards must run between all partition-studs, making close all spaces to prevent the circulation of vermin through the house.

STAIRWAY.—Build stairway as shown by the *floor-plan* and *details* for the same. The stair to be constructed in a substantial manner on 3" × 12" *yellow-pine* horses, to have ⅞ in. *yellow-pine* risers and 1¼ in. *yellow-pine* treads; house all steps into the wall-string.

The hand-rail must be closely bolted at all joints; posts, balusters, etc., to be secured to hand-rail in an accurate and substantial manner, and to conform in every respect to first-class finish. Finished work of stairs will not be set up until plastering is completed and dry.

HATCHWAY DOORS.—Hatchway doors, if any, will be constructed of yellow pine 2" thick, tongued, grooved, and having grooves filled with colored lead paint, and wedged up tight; to have strong strap-hinges secured to the leaves with rivets, and having bar or other fastening as directed.

TOILET-ROOMS.—All wood-work necessary for fitting up of plumbing to be done with best *chestnut* (*or y. p.*). Seats of water-closets to be ash, 1¼" thick. Partitions dividing water-closets from toilet-rooms to be made of inch-thick tongued and grooved *chestnut* (*or y. p.*) boards, 3" wide, double-faced and beaded. Partitions to be 7' 0" in height, and to have base and cap.

PORCHES.—Porches shall be constructed of *yellow pine* in the manner shown by details for the same.

Note.—The eaves and plates on cast-iron columns shall be painted three colors, as per example Park Station on the P. S. V. R. R. near Philadelphia, or the station at Douglassville on the line of the same road; the ends of the rafters and the sheathing to be left natural and coated with Crockett's No. 1 Preservative. The iron columns will be painted to harmonize with the above.

All the carpenter work that may be required to be done throughout the building must be executed according to these specifications, and the drawings hereinbefore referred to, and such additional drawings as may hereafter be made in exemplification of the same; and all carpentry not herein mentioned, and which may be necessary for the complete and proper execution of the work, to be faithfully done and furnished as if fully specified and at length set forth. Mill-stock mouldings will not be accepted as substitute for those indicated to be used on the several detail drawings.

PLASTERING.

The walls and ceilings of all rooms to be well plastered in three coats, the first two scratched and the last coat to be sand-finish floated, colored with *buff calsomine* (*two or more coats*) *after hardening.*

The materials used to be of the best quality, and the work to be executed in a good and workmanlike manner. Long slaughter hair will be required to be used for the first and second coats.

Whatever jobbing and repairing may be necessary to render the building perfect before its final acceptance by the Engineer is to be well and truly done without extra charge.

FURRING.—Diagonal furring strips, 1 × 3 inches *hemlock*, must be securely nailed every sixteen (16) inches between centres to the inside of *the Waiting Rooms. Brick walls* to receive *wire* lathing.

Prepare sufficient cradling to receive furring for cornices, panels, beams, and other work, as per working drawings of the same.

All circular corners on partitions or walls to be furred horizontally, and the lath nailed on diagonally.

SLATING.

Cover the roofs with best selected Peachbottom (*Bangor or Portland*) *roofing slates* 9 in. × 18 in., laid in *three* thicknesses, butt and tip lapping three (3) inches; secure to sheathing boards with best tinned flat-head nails, two nails to each slate, and leave the same free of all defects.

The slates at tips, valleys, eaves, and heading course to be so laid that their bond will be uniform with the rest; bed the same in slaters' putty. Slate the hips with slates set up on ⅞" strips, so as to avoid covering the same with metal. Bed hip slates and cresting slates, if not covered, in slaters' putty, to prevent leaks.

CRESTING.—*Cresting shall be of the Perth Amboy Terra Cotta Company's manufacture, of the shapes, size, and finish shown on the Elevations and Details.*

TINNING.

Furnish only the best charcoal IX tin of the following brands: "M. F.," "Old Style," "Talbot," "Melyn," or "S. T. P." brands.

TIN-WORK.—All flashings to be done with tin of the above brands, painted on under side with one coat and on upper side with two coats Venetian red. The exposed parts of tin-work to be laid flat, joints well locked and soldered where necessary; use three nails to the sheet, and solder over nail-heads. Tin all places that require to be water-tight, and go over the work, stopping all leaks, if any, after the workmen shall have left the building. Valleys to be made narrow and painted slate-color.

GUTTERS.—Gutters to be formed and lined as per drawings. Run the tin up under the slates at least four inches (measured vertically) above the overflow line; tack close and smooth over edges,

Fix where indicated galvanized-iron leaders *corrugated* 2½ in. × 2½ in., fitted with the necessary curves, bends, breaks, and other connections to convey the water from the roofs to grade. Secure conductors to walls with the proper fastenings, galvanized; lap joints and solder, and secure fine wire screens, muzzle patterns, over openings in gutters. The contractor will be required to run the water-pipes to *a point* 10' 0" *away from the Building; from thence the Contractor will be required to state the price per lineal foot, including excavation for additional drain pipe and laying the same for use, complete.*

PAINTING.

The painting to be performed with the best materials and labor, and every item requisite for a first-class job of work must be furnished.

PRIMING.—All wood-work, inside and out, required to be painted must be primed; all sap, knots, and other defects in lumber to be covered with a good coat of strong shellac before applying the priming coat; putty up nail-heads, etc., after priming, and go over the same before applying the final coat.

PAINTING.—The several portions of the structure to have three coats of pure white lead and linseed oil, tinted, as may hereafter be directed.

The rooms shall be designated from without by painting in black letters on the lock rail of the doors the words Gents' or Ladies' Waiting-room, if there are two; if one, simply Waiting-room, Baggage-room, Ticket-office, etc., etc.

HARD WOOD.—All *the interior work* to be filled with the *Crockett's* filler, properly applied, rubbed down and cleaned off when wet, and finished with three coats of *Crockett's No. 1. Preservative,* properly applied and rubbed down with *water* and powdered pumice, the last coat to be rubbed to a dull finish. *Apply Crockett's No. 1. Preservative to all outside yellow pine.*

GLAZING.

All the windows and transom lights throughout the building, together with all glazed panels of doors not otherwise specified, to be glazed with *double thick* glass, well bedded, bradded, and back-puttied in soft putty; left clean and perfect on completion of the work. The sash must receive two coats of paint or other finish (as previously specified) before the putting in of the glass. *Provide ground glass for sash in the Toilet-rooms (and heavy hammered plate glass in doors of the Baggage-room).*

Glass in upper sash of the lower windows, also the dormers, shall be white "fluted," arranged to produce a play of light. Glaze the sash of Ticket Office and the News Room with the same glass arranged vertically and horizontally as to the flutings.

HARDWARE.

All outside doors (not sliding) to be hung with 5 × 5-inch *imitation bronze* loose-pin acorn-butts, *three* to each leaf.

All other doors to be hung with 4 × 4-inch *bronze* loose-pin acorn-butts, *three* to each door or leaf of double doors.

Doors to *the Toilet-rooms and Cellar stair* to have spring hinges, and to swing *one* way. W. C. doors to have brass hinges.

All exterior doors to have six-inch patent front-door mortise lever lock, with *bronze* face and striking-plate. All other doors to have five-inch mortise locks, with *bronze* face and striking-plate.

The furniture to locks throughout to be *bronze.*

Ticket-office door will be supplied with *patent alarm bell-knob.*

All outside doors are to have bronze metal mortise flush-bolt at top and bottom of the leaf. Doors to *Water-closets* to be provided with brass bolts and knobs.

Padlock of the Yale Manufacturing Company's make must be placed on hatchway doors, *if any.*

All balanced sash to have Morris's patent brass sash fasts, or others equally as good.

Put heavy triple hooks of japanned cast-iron in water-closets and other places as may be directed.

All brass hardware to be put on with brass screws, and all *bronze* hardware to be put on with *bronze* screws.

Supply the necessary sash-lifts, transom-bolts, rods, pivots, plates, and other hardware that may be required to make a thorough and complete job.

Baggage-room doors to have cast-iron sliding-door lock of approved pattern, and six-inch cast-iron sheaves running on one-half-inch wrought-iron ways.

HEATING.

***Supply two portable c. i.* heaters in cellar warranted to warm all parts of the building to a uniform temperature of 70° with the outside temperature at 0°. Heaters to have anti-clinker grates and cast-iron firepots.**

All brick flues for warm air to have tin lining, those running up in the frame partitions to be double and parts around the same lined with asbestos paper.

Supply japanned registers to all rooms. Registers in floors to have soapstone or slate frames let in flush. Registers in partitions to be double-boxed with tin and space filled with plaster of Paris. Pedestal registers shall be placed where indicated on plans, and shall be of Tuttle's make or others equally as good, 16" x 21" on base, bronzed sides and marble top.

PENNSYLVANIA RAILROAD.

SPECIFICATIONS FOR ENGINE HOUSE AT MT. PLEASANT JUNCTION, JERSEY CITY, N. J.*

DESCRIPTION.—The building will be a polygon of 44 sides as shown on plan. The inner space over the turntable and around it will not be roofed. The outside wall and walls at sides of entrances shall be brick. Outside wall shall have windows in the sides as shown. The inside front shall be cast-iron and glazed doors. The roof-trusses will be a combination of wood and iron. The roof will be slate.

DIMENSIONS.—The radius to outside of brick pilasters will be 160 feet. The radius to face of cast-iron column in inside front will be 84 feet 3$\frac{5}{16}$ inches. The distance between the centres of the brick pilasters on the faces will be 22 feet 9$\frac{11}{16}$ inches. The distance between the centres of the faces of cast-iron columns will be 12 feet 9$\frac{1}{4}$ inches. The height from top of rail to centre of tie-rod of roof-truss will be 22 feet 1$\frac{1}{4}$ inches. The roof will be one quarter pitch.

CUT STONE.—The foundation walls are built, anchor-bolts are in pit walls.

A 4" x 14" North River flagstone base course to be run around the outside wall of the building.

Cut-stone blocks 18 inches square by 12$\frac{1}{4}$ inches high to be set on the piers of inside front for the cast-iron column bases to rest on; tops to be dressed.

Cut-stone sills for four small doors in entrance walls to be of the sizes shown.

BRICK-WORK.—The outside and entrance walls shall be built of good, sound, and well-burned bricks, laid true and straight and properly bonded together with heading courses. The mortar to be composed of the best quality of lime and clean, sharp gritted sand, properly mixed and thoroughly manipulated. The exterior shall be faced with the best quality of "Haverstraw" or "Hackensack" bricks of uniform color. The pointing mortar for outside to be the same color as bricks. The inside exposed face of the brick-work shall be laid with straight hard bricks. The entrance walls shall be carried up to the roof. The track-pits shall be paved crowning as per drawing with straight hard bricks, laid on edge and grouted with cement. The filling in and backing of the brick walls of the building shall be of sound hard bricks. All bricks shall be laid with flashed solid joints, leaving no interstices or empty spaces in the walls.

CAST-IRON.—All the castings required in the execution of the work shall be made from good tough iron, true and sound, and free from cracks, flaws, bubbles, or defects of any kind whatever.

The heel-blocks of roof-trusses, king-blocks, feet of struts and caps of main struts, the inside and outside sills of windows shall be cast-iron. All the cast-iron work shall have a coat of metallic brown and linseed oil before being sent to the work.

The inside front will be cast-iron; it will be furnished, fitted, and delivered on cars near the site of the building by the said party of the second part. The said party of the first part shall unload the front and erect it, and be responsible for any damage that may occur to it after it is delivered to them. The columns of cast front at entrance-walls shall be cramped to the brick-work.

WROUGHT-IRON.—The rods, pins, and bolts for roof-trusses, purlin-bolts, truss-rods for purlins supporting canopies and ventilators, hinges, hinge-bolts, and whatever other forged iron-work may be required in the various parts of the structure, or shown on the drawings, shall be furnished of the best quality of wrought-iron, made in the best manner and subject to the approval and directions of the Engineer in charge,

---

* This specification was kindly furnished for publication by Mr. Wm. H. Brown, Chief Engineer, Pennsylvania Railroad.

This engine-house is described on pages 180 to 183 and illustrated in Figs. 308 to 314.

it being understood by the parties to this contract that such bolts, rods, etc., are to be introduced at the discretion of the said Engineer in charge, wherever he may deem it to be necessary to assure the strength and permanency of the structure.

There will be no roof-trusses at sides of entrances.

All window-frames shall be secured with iron joggles.

All the wrought-iron work shall have one coat of boiled linseed-oil before delivery to the work.

All the wrought-iron work shall be according to the following specifications.

CARPENTRY WORK AND LUMBER.—All the lumber throughout the structure, except where particularly specified to the contrary, shall be first-quality yellow pine, free from shakes, flaws, and unsound knots, and in every way suitable for the various purposes for which it is intended.

ROOF.—The principal rafters, roof-struts, purlins, and ridges shall be sound yellow pine, free from large, objectionable or rotten knots, sap, or bark edges. The purlins and supports for canopies and ventilators shall be backed to a camber on the outer slope of the roof and curved concave on the inner slope to the dimensions given on the drawings, so as to avoid hips and valleys.

Entrances will be roofed over.

SHEATHING.—The roof-sheathing shall be first quality hemlock, 1¼ inches thick, surfaced to uniform thickness, grooved and tongued, no board over 8 inches wide, laid with rough side down and well nailed to the purlins.

WHITE OAK.—The stringers on track-walls, and at sides and ends of track-pits, the plates under heel-blocks of roof-trusses, and sills for large doors, shall be first-quality white oak, sound and free from all imperfections. The track-stringers shall be anchor-bolted to the walls as shown.

WINDOWS.—All the window-frames shall be made as shown, of well-seasoned white pine.

SASH.—All the sash shall be made of first-quality well-seasoned clear white pine, 1¾ inches thick, pinned and jointed with white lead, to be double-hung on strong 2½ inch-diameter turned pulleys with the best Italian braided sash-cord and round weights, and fastened with japanned stops.

DOORS.—The doors in cast-iron front shall be 3 inches thick, made in two thicknesses of the best quality of well-seasoned white pine, nortised, tenoned, wedged and pinned together in the best manner with white-lead joints. The upper portion shall be sash as shown; the under part outside shall be panelled, and the inside to be bead and flush. There shall be four pairs of forged hinges to each set of doors. The doors shall be fastened with stout bolts at top and bottom at one side and at shoulder high on other side, and kept open by hooks attached to dwarf post sunk in floor. In four of the doors there shall be wickets on one side, as shown, hung with strap-hinges and have stout thumb-latches.

The open space under each door at each side of the rails and between them shall be closed with white oak 4½ inches thick by 10 inches wide, spiked to the sill.

VENTILATORS.—Ventilators shall be built in roof over alternate tracks as shown, fitted with slat frames and finished as indicated. Valve-doors to be formed in lower part to regulate the ventilation, operated from below by cords as shown.

GALVANIZED SHEET-IRON.—The conductors shall be of No. 20 iron; those on the outside wall shall be 3×4 inches, galvanized, and be placed in each angular recess. Those at inside shall be 3 inches diameter, galvanized, and be secured to back of alternate cast columns. All the conductors shall have galvanized-wire guards at top, and shall extend down to within 3 feet 9 inches of level of top of rail; from thence the water will be conveyed away by cast pipe, etc., as specified under the head of Plumbing. Frieze and cornice on inner front over doors to be made of No. 22 galvanized sheet-iron.

The upper part of back of cast-iron front shall be enclosed with No. 20 galvanized iron riveted to the cast-iron back and nailed to the roof-sheathing.

The hanging gutters on outside and inside to be of No. 24 galvanized sheet-iron with riveted joints supported on hooks made of 1½ × ⅜ wrought-iron spaced 4 feet apart with uniform fall to conductors.

TIN-WORK.—The flashings around canopies and ventilators shall be made of the best quality IX charcoal tin leaded, "Talbot" or "Melyn" brand, brand and thickness stamped on each sheet, painted two coats on both sides with oxide of iron and linseed oil.

CANOPIES.—Over each stall there shall be a Roe cast-iron smoke-stack as shown. The lower portion shall raise and lower by means of lever, ropes, and pulleys as shown.

SLATE ROOFING.

FELT.—The main and ventilator roofs shall be covered with two layers of the best waterproof felt, containing not more than 20 square feet to the pound.

SLATE.—On this felt shall be laid the best sound hard Peachbottom roofing-slate, 10 inches wide by

18, 20, or 22 inches long, lapped three inches, well secured with two galvanized nails to each slate. All slates on each slope to be the same size.

LEAD.—The hips of ventilators and the ridges of the main roof shall be covered with strips of 4-pound sheet-lead, nine inches wide.

PAINTING.

PAINTING.—All exposed iron and wood work, inside and outside, the galvanized gutters and conductors, and other work usually painted shall have a priming and two coats of best white lead and linseed oil, outside tinted in standard party colors as may hereafter be directed. Sash to be primed before glass is put in. Inside work to be white. Galvanized iron to be primed with red lead. Five feet up on inside of brick wall shall be painted dark green.

KALSOMINING.—The inside of the brick walls above the dark green paint mentioned previously shall be kalsomined white two coats; the roof-timbers and roof-sheathing one coat.

GLAZING.—All the windows and doors shall be primed. They shall then be glazed with second-quality 12″ × 12″ American glass, single thick, well bradded, puttied, and be back-puttied where necessary and left clean and perfect on completion of the work.

CARE OF MATERIALS.—The said party of the first part will take care of and be responsible for the safety of the material furnished by the said party of the second part, including the cast-iron front and the canopies.

TRACK MATERIALS.—All the track material, including the rails, spikes, joints, etc., shall be furnished and laid by said party of the second part.

TIME.—It is understood that the said party of the first part will not be responsible for any delay that may be caused by the said party of the second part.

PLUMBING.

PLUGS.—In the alternate spaces between the tracks as shown there shall be a water-plug for round-house floor, with 3-inch standard hose coupling. They shall each have a cast-iron box around them and have a flush iron frame and lid, and be connected with the supply-pipe.

SUPPLY-PIPE.—The supply-pipe to floor plugs shall be 6 inches internal diameter. It shall be laid in position shown on plan. The top of it shall be not less than 3 feet 6 inches below top of rail. All pipes, branches, etc., shall be cast-iron, sound and true, and shall be coated with coal-pitch varnish.

HYDRANTS.—There shall be four $\frac{3}{4}$-inch iron hydrants, as shown on plan. They shall have screw nozzles. Supply-pipe shall be one inch, galvanized. Each hydrant shall have cast iron hydrant cesspool 18″ × 18″ × 6″ with bell-trap, and be connected to drain by terra-cotta pipe 4″ diameter.

RAIN-WATER LEADERS.—The spouts from roof at each angle of outside wall and at alternate iron columns inside shall discharge into cast-iron leaders four feet high above top of rail and one foot below it, as per detail drawing. To have lugs tap-bolted to columns and spiked to brick wall; from these the water will be conducted away by terra-cotta drainage-pipes 4″ diameter.

PIT DRAINAGE.—Each track-pit will drain through 12″ cess pools with bell-traps and grates into 12-inch terra-cotta drain, as shown.

DRAIN-PIPES.—The lines and sizes of pipes are given on drawing. Pipes to be vitrified, first quality, to be straight, sound, and well burned, free from all imperfections. Broken, cracked, crooked, bent, or misshapen pipes will not be received. Outside drain to be 3 feet clear from wall. Trenches to be excavated to levels given by Engineer. Pipes to have a uniform descent of six tenths of a foot per one hundred feet and discharge into present drain from turn-table pit. Bottom of drains are 3 feet below ground surface at heads. Joints to be filled with approved hydraulic cement, and pipes carefully cleaned out afterwards. Trenches must not be filled until lines of pipes are inspected and approved by Engineer.

CAST PIPES.—All cast-iron pipes to be coated; joints to be oakum and molten lead; the weight per length of pipe to be as follows:

6-inch pipe 12′ 3″ long to weigh 370 lbs.
8- " " 12′ 3$\frac{1}{2}$″ " " " 500 "

GAS-PIPING.

Under the centre of each roof-truss there shall be a two-light drop, and at inside of each of the entrance walls there shall be two one-light brackets. At each alternate pilaster inside there shall be a one-light bracket for vice-bench. Under cornice of inner front at two opposite sides there shall be one-light reflector to light turn-table. Fixtures not to be included.

TRANSPORTATION NOT FURNISHED.—The said party of the second part will not transport free any of the workmen or materials for this work, but all material must be shipped in the name of the party of the first part, and in no case shall it be shipped in care of or in the name of the railroad company or of any of its officers or employés, and said party of first part must pay the regular freight rates arranged for with the freight department, none of which will be refunded.

ALABAMA GREAT SOUTHERN RAILROAD COMPANY.

June 1st, 1890.

SPECIFICATIONS FOR PASSENGER DEPOT AT FORT PAYNE, ALABAMA,*

Located 51 Miles South of Chattanooga, and 93 Miles North of Birmingham.

WORK TO BE DONE.

1. WORK TO BE DONE.—The work to be done consists of the construction complete (exclusive of foundations, and grading of the grounds) of a one and one-half story building, with passenger shelter annex, to be used as a passenger depot. The building to be of stone, or of brick faced with pressed brick and having stone trimmings, as may be determined by the Engineer. The foundations have been built under another contract, and the Contractor must inform himself of the exact nature of the same.

2. LETTING OF CONTRACT.—The work is to be let as an entire contract, and parties bidding must thoroughly inform themselves of all that is required to be done to build the structure complete ready foı occupancy, on the basis of these specifications and the plans to which they refer.

GENERAL CONDITIONS.

3. BASIS OF CONTRACT.—The several drawings with all figured dimensions and written explanations thereon, with these specifications, are to be the basis of the contract, and of equal force.

OMISSIONS IN PLANS OR SPECIFICATIONS.—Whatever work may be specified and not drawn, or drawn and not specified, is to be executed as if described in both ways; and should any material or workmanship be wanted, which are not directly or indirectly denoted in these specifications or drawings, but is, nevertheless, necessary for the proper carrying out of the obvious intentions thereof, the Contractor is to understand the same to be implied, and to provide for it in his tender as fully as if it were particularly delineated or described.

4. INTERPRETATION OF DOUBTFUL POINTS.—Any doubts that may arise regarding the intent and purpose of the drawings or the specifications, or discrepancies between any parts of the drawings or specifications, shall be referred to the Engineer for decision.

5. MATERIAL AND LABOR.—The Contractor must furnish all material, labor, tools, machinery, and scaffolding required to fully execute the work as shown on plans or in these specifications, or reasonably implied in the drawings or specifications.

6. EXTRAS AND CHANGES.—No extras will be allowed unless they have been executed on the written order of the Engineer.

No departure from the drawings or specifications will be allowed unless on the written order of the Engineer.

7. QUALITY OF MATERIAL AND WORK.—All materials throughout must be the best of their several kinds, and the entire work executed and completed in the best, most substantial and workmanlike manner, according to the true intent and meaning of the plans and specifications; which are intended to include everything dependent upon, or necessary and requisite to the proper and entire finishing of the work with the materials best adapted to the purpose, even though every item of work or materials involved is not particularly mentioned; to the entire satisfaction, approval, and acceptance of the Engineer.

---

* This specification was kindly furnished for publication by Mr. G. B. Nicholson, Chief Engineer, Cincinnati, New Orleans & Texas Pacific Railway and Alabama Great Southern Railroad.

This depot is described in pages 307 to 309 and illustrated in Figs. 574 to 576.

8. Faulty Material or Work.—Should at any time improper, imperfect, or unsound material or faulty workmanship be observed, whether before or after the same has been built into the structure, the Contractor shall, upon notice from the Engineer, cause the same to be removed, and good and proper materials and workmanship substituted without delay: in default of which the Engineer may effect the same by such other means as may be deemed best; and shall charge the cost of such alterations to the Contractor, and the amount shall be deducted from the sum due and payable to the Contractor under this contract.

9. Prosecution of Work.—The Contractor shall prosecute the work at such times and with such force as the Engineer may direct; and if at any time he fails to do so the Railroad Company shall have the right to go in the open market and purchase material and employ men to execute the work, the cost of which shall be borne by the Contractor.

10. Alterations.—Should the Railroad Company, at any time during the progress of the work, require any alteration, deviation, additions or omissions of work or materials herein specified or shown on the drawings, it shall be at liberty to do so, and the same shall in no way vitiate or make void the contract, but the cost of the same will be added to or deducted from the amount to be paid under this contract, as the case may be, by a fair and reasonable valuation to be decided by the Engineer.

11. Risks.—The Contractor shall assume all risks from storms, fires, and casualties of every description until the final completion and acceptance of the work under the terms of this contract.

Precautions and Liabilities for Damages.—He must provide all necessary safeguards during the progress of the work, and shall protect and hold harmless the Railroad Company from any liability for damage or injury to persons or property in or about said work, resulting from any act which he may have done or omitted to have done, by accident, negligence, or otherwise.

12. Laws, Fees, and Protection of Work.—The Contractor shall comply with all laws and regulations of properly constituted authorities, in case there be any such affecting the work, and pay all proper fees for the same, if any there be. He must also protect his work from damage as the Engineer may direct and provide, and maintain all requisite guards, lights, temporary side-walks and fences.

13. Insurance.—The Contractor must take out a builder's insurance to cover the full value of the work as it progresses, and made payable to the Railroad Company as far as its interest may appear.

14. Care of Finished Work.—Particular care must be taken by the Contractor of all finished work as the building progresses, such as exterior projections, cut stone, stairs, wash-stands, etc., which must be covered up and thoroughly protected from injury or defacement during the erection and completion of the building

15. Foreman.—The Contractor must give the work his personal attention and keep a competent foreman constantly on the ground.

16. Rubbish.—The Contractor must remove from the premises all his rubbish and surplus material, and must clean the windows, and leave his work clean, uninjured, and in perfect condition ready for occupancy.

No shavings or wood which might cause damage from fire shall be allowed to remain over night in an exposed situation.

17. Transportation.—The Contractor will receive free transportation on the line of the Alabama Great Southern Railroad for men engaged on the work and for tools and materials used on the work.

18. Payments.—Payments will be made on the 20th day of each month for 90 per cent of the relative value of the work done to the last day of the preceding month. The retained 10 per cent will be paid on the final completion of the entire work.

19. Partial payments made as the work progresses will be payments on account, and shall in no wise be considered as an acceptance of any part of the work or material of the contract.

20. Engineer.—The word Engineer used in these specifications means the Chief Engineer of the Alabama Great Southern Railroad Company.

HYDRAULIC CEMENT.

21. Quality of Cement.—The cement used must be fresh, finely ground hydraulic cement, subject to the approval of the Engineer. It must stand 100 pounds tensile strain per square inch in a briquette of pure cement made seven days before testing.

22. Inspection of Cement.—If Louisville cement is used, it must have the inspection brand of Mead & Shaw. The expense of the inspection will be borne by the Railroad Company.

SAND.

23. All sand used in mortar must be clean, sharp, and well screened. If perfectly clean sand cannot be obtained in natural beds, it must be thoroughly washed to free it from impurities.

CONCRETE.

24. Should it be determined to use concrete in foundations, although not shown upon plan, it must be composed of 4 measures of clean gravel; or of stone broken to a size not exceeding 4 inches in any direction; 2 measures of clean, sharp sand and one measure of hydraulic cement; the cement and sand to be mixed dry before the incorporation of stone or gravel; to be made and thoroughly mixed just before using, and well rammed in place. It must contain just sufficient water to film the surface of the concrete when rammed, but not enough to make it quake. Concrete must be mixed on wooden mortar-beds.

CEMENT MORTAR.

25. The cement mortar must be made of the best freshly burned cement, as above described, mixed with sand, also as above described, in proportion of one of cement to two of sand, or such other proportions as may be required by the Engineer. The cement mortar shall be mixed only as required for use, and must be used as soon as mixed, as none left standing until set will be allowed in the work. It must be mixed on wooden mortar-beds.

LIME MORTAR.

26. Lime mortar is to be composed of 1 measure of cement, 1 measure of lime, and 4 measures of sand. It must be mixed on wooden mortar-beds. The cement and sand to be the same quality as specified above. The lime must be of the best quality—well slacked before using.

The cement and sand must be mixed dry, and the lime added just before using.

BRICKWORK.

27. THICKNESS AND KIND.—The partition wall between the baggage-room and the men's waiting-room is to be of brick, 13 inches thick.

The exterior walls, if built of brick, are to be 13 inches thick, and are to have the outer showing face of pressed brick.

The chimneys are to be of brick up to the roof.

28. QUALITY AND WORKMANSHIP.—All brick, except pressed brick facing of exterior walls, are to be of the best quality; hard burned and of uniform texture. No soft or salmon-colored brick will be allowed. All brick are to be wetted before laying, and *all joints to be completely filled with mortar*. The mortar must be lime mortar above described.

Where bricks come in contact with anchors, each brick shall be "brought home" to do all the work possible. In all brickwork the courses shall be kept level, the bonds shall be accurately preserved, the walls shall be laid to lines and be kept perfectly plumb and straight. The work is to be well bonded with headers every seventh course, and to have all joints struck. No joint to be over ½ inch thick.

29. ARCHES.—Relieving arches are to be turned over all openings in brick walls, and trimmer arches are to be built for fireplaces. Centres to be used for all arches.

30. FLUES.—All the flues to be well built, laid true to line, with struck joints inside and outside. Office flue to be started at the floor line, and a cast-iron-flue-door for cleaning out the flue to be put in at the floor level. Flues for grates to be started with a throat immediately above the arch of the fireplace. All flues to be lined with 1-inch fire-clay flue-lining. Flue-holes in office to have flue cylinder and cap built in. Partitions in flues to extend in every case to the top of the chimney.

31. PRESSED BRICK.—The pressed brick for the face of the exterior walls are to be the best No. 1 pressed brick, to be approved on sample by the Engineer before delivery at the work. They are to be laid with ⅛-inch sunk red cement-mortar joints in courses, and to be well tied to backing with blind headers.

32. CLEANING WALLS.—Showing faces of walls must be cleaned from all mortar stains at completion of work, with diluted muriatic acid, but all stones must be thoroughly wetted before applying same, and washed off at completion so as not to be damaged thereby.

33. OPENINGS.—Vertical recesses for the reception of pipes for plumbing, gas, water, heating, or ventilation, to be built in the walls where necessary or where indicated on plans, and not cut afterwards.

STONE-WORK.

34. KIND OF STONE FOR STONE BUILDING.—If the building be built with exterior walls of stone, the stone in the body of the building must be gray-colored sandstone, and the water-table, window-sills, door-sills, lintels, arches, copings, finials, belt-courses, carved work, and chimney-caps must be red-colored sandstone.

35. Stone Trimming for Brick Building.—If the building be built with the exterior walls of pressed brick, the trimming stone, mentioned in paragraph 34 as red sandstone, may be either gray or red sandstone, as shall be determined by the Engineer.

36. Quality of Stone.—All stone must be of a durable quality, that will not crack or disintegrate under weather; to be of uniform color of its particular kind, free from cracks or blemishes, and to be approved by the Engineer.

Rock-face Masonry.—Unless otherwise specified, all showing stone to be rock-face with square joints, and beds and ends pitched off to a line, so that all joints shall be truly horizontal or vertical. The showing face to show new split surfaces; no seam-face or quarry-surface stone will be allowed.

Blemishes.—No tool-marks, lewis-holes, or other marks or holes will be allowed in the showing surface of any stone.

Projection of Rock-face.—The rock-face is not to project more than 2 inches from the line of the wall at any point. The inner faces of the stones are not to have more than 1 inch projection beyond the face of the wall at any point. The entire stone-work is to be washed down and cleaned upon completion of the building.

37. Courses under Water-table.—There will be two 8-inch courses of stone on the exterior walls under the water-table. These stones to be laid in uniform courses, breaking joint; to be of full thickness of wall; to be laid on their natural or quarry beds; to have a 1-inch draft on all quoins; to have all joints completely filled with cement mortar and neatly pointed on both faces. These courses to be well bonded with the stone foundation of the cross-wall.

38. Exterior Stone Walls.—The exterior walls, if built of stone, are to be 18 inches thick. This masonry is to be broken-range, of superior quality, with no stone less than 6 inches thick, unless otherwise directed by the Engineer; to be well bonded and levelled; to be laid flush in soft cement mortar; to have horizontal beds and vertical joints on the face, with no face joint over ½-inch thick. All stones to be firmly bedded, and all spaces to be filled with mortar and spalls forced into the spaces so filled, but no spalls to be used in the beds.

All walls to be built straight, plumb, and level.

39. Beds.—All stones to be laid on their natural or quarry beds in full beds of cement mortar.

40. Headers.—At least one-fourth of the stones shall be through-stones acting as headers, evenly distributed through the work. No stone shall be used which does not bond into the wall at least 8 inches.

41. Quoins.—All the quoins are to have hammer-dressed beds and joints, and drafted corners.

42. Pointing.—All joints on all faces shall be neatly pointed with cement mortar. The joints on rock-face masonry must be cleaned out to a depth of one inch while the mortar is fresh.

Before applying the pointing, the joints shall be well cleaned by scraping and brushing out loose mortar, and then be moistened so as to neither give to nor take water from the pointing mortar.

Pointing mortar shall be one cement to one sand, mixed in small quantities as used, and pressed firmly into the joints, completely filling vacant spaces. It must be rubbed smooth on the outside flush with the edge of the stone.

43. Lines of Walls.—All walls shall be built to a line, both inside and outside faces.

44. Top of Stone Walls.—The upper courses of all walls shall be levelled off for the reception of the superstructure, and shall be provided with a through-stone at each corner, and also one through-stone at least every 5 feet. These through-stones shall be dressed on their top beds and accurately set to the level of the wall, as shown on the drawings.

Between these through-stones the walls must be carefully laid with the upper beds of the stones brought up flush with the top of the through-stones, so as to secure a perfectly level surface for the top of the wall.

45. Joints.—All joints and spaces must be completely filled with cement mortar.

46. Wetting.—All stone must be wetted before laying.

47. Cut Stone.—The cut-stone water-table, window-sills, door-sills, lintels, trimmings over arches, copings, finials, chimney-caps, etc., are to be furnished of the sizes marked on the plans, all to be cut and dressed to line with a disk-edged chisel. All projecting courses are to have a drip cut underneath. Particular care must be taken with this stone-work, as no poor workmanship or defective stone will be allowed in the work on any pretence. Chimney-caps must have flue-holes neatly cut out of solid piece. Iron clamps and dowels to be used wherever necessary for the stability of the work.

48. Carving.—All carving in stone is to be done from models approved by the Engineer.

49. Chimneys.—The chimneys above the roof will be built of stone, as shown on plans, whether the building be of stone or pressed brick.

50. Voussoirs.—All stone voussoirs are to be the full thickness of wall, and must have joints radial to the centre of the arch.

51. JAMBS.—The window and door jambs will be finished as specified for cut stone.

52. POINTING OF FLASHINGS.—The masons must point up under all galvanized iron, and for the flashings on roof, and other places where required.

53. WOOD-BLOCKS AND GROUNDS.—Blocks are to be built in walls for doors and windows, to secure joinery, and lookouts for cornices are to be built in.

Strips 1 inch × 4 inch are to be built in the horizontal joints every 2 feet, for attaching furring on outside walls to be plastered.

RECESSES, ANCHORING, ETC.—The mason is to make proper recesses in walls for plumbing and gas-fitting or other piping that may be required. He is to fix all iron anchors, clamps, etc., which are used in his work, cut all necessary raglets for flashings and point up around window-frames, and to call upon the carpenter when required to put up rough casing around window-frames, and cut-work where necessary to protect it from damage.

PLASTERING.

54. PARTS TO BE PLASTERED. LATHS.—All stud partitions and ceiling for ticket-office and the under side of stairs are to be plastered. Laths to be of the best quality of dried sawed pine or poplar laths, laid full ¼ inch apart, with the joints well broken every ninth course, with four nailings to each lath and two nails at each end.

55. LATHING.—Long vertical joints will not be allowed, nor lath put on vertically to finish up to angles or corners. All laths at angles and corners must be nailed on solid furring, and lath will not be allowed to run from one room to another behind the studding. The lather must call upon the carpenter to fur and straighten all walls, ceilings, etc., and block and spike all studs together solidly at angles.

In all cases lath below grounds to the floor, and behind all wainscoting.

56. Grounds will be required to be put around all openings against which to finish plastering and horizontal grounds for wainscoting. The plasterer must take care that all grounds are true and straight, and all angles and mitres true and sharp. All sharp angles to be protected by wooden guards screwed on with round-headed brass screws.

57. FURRING.—All outside walls are to be furred as shown on drawing No. 16, and all ceilings are to be cross-furred on the joists before lathing, with 1-inch × 2-inch strips. The plaster will be put directly on the brickwork of the brick partition-wall.

58. PLASTERING.—The store-room, stairs, and brick partition-wall are to have the best two-coat work. All other work throughout is to be plastered three good coats of the best lime, hair, and sand plaster, and the same is to have a fine washed sand finish (except store-room and stairs), and is to be stained such color as shall be approved by the Engineer.

59. STUCCO-WORK FOR WAITING-ROOMS.—All plastering is to run down to the floor. Plain stucco cornices, 16-inch girth as per detail, are to be run for men's and women's toilet-room, and ticket-office, and brackets are to be put up for same by plasterer.

60. STUCCO-WORK FOR TOWER.—Stucco beams and brackets are to be put up for tower-bay and other places where marked, as shown on drawings.

61. SCAFFOLDING AND COMPLETION OF PLASTERING.—The Contractor is to furnish all scaffolding required for his work, make good any injury his work may sustain from the carpenter or otherwise; and the whole is to be left sound and clean upon completion. Also, to remove from the premises all rubbish caused by him.

GALVANIZED-IRON, TIN, AND SLATE WORK.

62. RIDGE AND FINIALS.—All galvanized iron is to be No. 26. The ridge-mouldings, finials, and cornices are to be made in the best manner as per drawings, and to be well riveted and soldered at each joint.

63. DOWN-SPOUTS.—There will be three 4-inch and two 3-inch round galvanized-iron down-spouts; also, five branches from verandas and balcony in tower.

Down-spouts are to be extended from gutters, and to be connected to stoneware drain-pipes 1 foot above final grade-line; to have flared inlets, copper-wire basket-strainer in gutter, and to be well secured to walls by galvanized-iron hooks. One galvanized-iron box is to be put up to drain flat in balcony of tower.

64. TIN ROOF.—The balcony over tower is to be covered with N. & G. Taylor's (Philadelphia) extra-coated old style I. C. tin, 14-inch × 20-inch plates, laid with flat seams, with ½-inch lock well secured with cleats, and securely soldered.

65. FLASHINGS.—Flashings of the same tin are to be turned up at least 6 inches against all brick or stone work, and counter-flashed 2 inches into the joints. Joints to be pointed with cement mortar.

66. **Gutters, Hips, and Valleys.**—Gutters are to be lined with same tin run up at least 4 inches under slate. Hips and valleys are to be flashed and counter-flashed with the same tin, so as to be water-tight.

67. **Painting Tin.**—All tin is to be painted on the under side, before laying, with one good coat of metallic paint and pure linseed-oil, mixed in the proportion of seven pounds of dry paint to one gallon of oil.

Resin on Tin.—All resin is to be removed from the upper side of the tin before painting.

Tin Cover for Flue.—A moulded tin cover is to be provided for office flue-hole.

68. **Slate Roof.**—All remaining portions of roof are to be covered with the best quality of 10 × 20-inch Black Virginia slate, of a uniform color, and free from spots, and be well nailed with tinned nails, and to have not more than 8½ inches of each slate exposed to the weather.

69. The lower courses are to be of double thickness, laid on wooden tilting strips. The roof of tower is to be slated with 8 × 16-inch slate, of the best quality of the same material.

70. **Sheathing-paper.**—All sheathing is to have a layer of Sachett's No. 1 sheathing-paper before the slate or tin is put on.

71. **Copper-work.**—The Contractor is to state in his bid what the additional cost will be if the entire galvanized-iron work is make of 20-oz. cold-rolled copper, including the down-spouts, gutters, linings, and flashings.

72. **Guarantee of Roof.**—The Contractor will be required to give a written guarantee that the roof will be water-proof for one year from time of completion, and will be required to repair any leaks that may occur within that time on account of faulty work.

IRON-WORK.

73. **Anchors.**—¾-inch bolts, 2 feet 9 inches long, with ½ × 4 × 4-inch plate-washer on each end, will be put in wall, at least every 8 feet, for anchoring down wall-plate.

74. Ceiling-joists are to be anchored to walls at least every 8 feet, by means of ⅜ × 1½-inch anchors, 2½ feet long, turned up 4 inches in wall, and secured to rafters with two spikes, ½ × 6 inches.

Floor-joists are to be anchored to walls at least every 8 feet, with ⅜ × 1½-inch anchors, 5 feet long, turned up 4 inches in the wall, and secured to joists with three spikes, ½ × 6 inches.

The stone gables and dormer-windows are to be anchored to roof-rafters with ⅜ × 1½-inch anchors, 3 feet long, turned up 4 inches in wall, and secured to rafters with ½ × 4-inch spikes. Three anchors to each gable and dormer.

The wall-plate of tower is to be anchored to each stone pier with a ¾-inch × 2-feet 9-inch bolt, with ½ × 4 × 4-inch plate on each end.

Wicket.—A wrought-iron wicket for ticket-window, as per detail, is to be provided.

CARPENTER-WORK.

75. **Quality of Lumber and Framing.**—All lumber throughout the building must be the best of their several kinds; thoroughly seasoned, sawn true and square, free from large and unsound knots, shakes, wanes, dry-rot, or other imperfections impairing its strength or durability. Sap-wood to the extent of 10 per cent will be allowed, except where clear-heart is specified. All timbers used throughout must be prepared and framed to exact dimensions given, according to plans, sections, and details, as no shimming or blocking up will be allowed.

Work to be Done by Carpenter.—The carpenter must size and fur all frame partitions on both sides, and the under sides of ceiling or floor-beams, if required, where plastering is used, and leave everything straight and true for the lathers. All trimmers and headers, and rafters around scuttle, must be framed double, and be well spiked together. In no case allow less than 4 inches between chimney-breast and trimmers. Frame all trusses as per detail for the same. The carpenter must do all usual and necessary wood-work for and after the several craftsmen of the building. He must provide and set centres on which to turn arches, and no arches shall be turned without one, and he shall provide patterns for tower. He must make all patterns that may be required; provide all temporary means for conducting water from the building; provide all temporary doors and windows for locking up the building when needed, and furnish and put up meter-shelf for plumber when required.

Where walls have been plastered, no joiner-work, such as doors and architraves, window-finish, shutters, bases, etc., is to be put up until the same have become dry enough to receive the finish.

Clean the building and premises, at the completion of the work, of all rubbish caused by building operations, and leave the building perfectly clean.

Studding.—The general dimensions of all timber are given in figures on plans. All door-openings in studded partitions are to be double studded. Set studs generally 16 inches from centres.

TRUSSING AND BRIDGING.—Truss all door and window openings, and bridge vertical studding about every 4 feet in height, and set with sill and plate, 2 × 4 inches. All studs to be set with broad side crosswise of the partition.

76. FLOOR-BEAMS.—All floor-beams and girders for building and veranda, and all first-floor joists, are to be of clear-heart close-grained long-leaf yellow pine or red cypress.

77. JOISTS.—Joists are to be of sizes marked on drawings, and are to be spaced 16 inches on centres and to be braced with double 1 × 3-inch bridging, in rows not more than 5 feet apart, with 2 nails in each end. All joists are to be dressed on one edge to exact depth marked on drawings. All joists to be of close-grained long-leaf yellow-pine, of quality specified in paragraph 75.

78. ROOF-TIMBERS AND PLATES.—Rafters and wall-plates to be of sizes marked on drawings, spaced as shown, and rafters to be well spiked to wall-plates and ridges, and all wall-plates to be set in a full bed of mortar. All roof-timbers to be of close-grained long-leaf yellow-pine, of quality specified in paragraph 75.

79. SHEATHING.—Sheathing to be of 1-inch close-grained long-leaf yellow-pine, tongued and grooved and matched, not over 6 inches wide, and securely nailed to rafters. Gutters to be lined with the same material, and to have proper falls to down-spouts.

80. CEILING.—The ceiling of men's and women's waiting-rooms and verandas are to be ceiled with selected clear-heart close-grained long-leaf yellow-pine, tongued and grooved, and dressed and beaded on one side. To be not over 3 inches wide. The 6 × 10-inch ceiling-joists are to be of the same grade of the same material.

81. FLOORING.—The entire first floor and the second floor over ticket-office is to be floored with close-grained long-leaf yellow-pine, tongued and grooved and matched, of a uniform width of 3 inches, of quality specified in paragraph 75, and secret-nailed to each joist.

Veranda is to be floored with $1\frac{1}{8}$-inch close grained long-leaf yellow-pine, tongued and grooved and matched, and of a uniform width of 6 inches, with joints white-leaded, and secret-nailed to each joist.

82. STAIRS.—The veranda steps are to have 6-inch risers, 11-inch treads made of oak $1\frac{1}{8}$ inches thick, dressed, and with rounded nosing and return. Horses to be 2 × 12 inches, spaced 2 feet on centres. Steps blocked and framed in strongest manner.

Stairs from first to second floors are to have $1\frac{1}{4}$-inch tread, with rounded nosings; $\frac{7}{8}$-inch risers; 3 horses 2 × 12 inches, and to be enclosed with $\frac{7}{8}$ × 3-inch boards, tongued and grooved, and beaded and dressed on both sides, topped out in attic with moulded cap as shown on longitudinal section. All to be of close-grained long-leaf yellow-pine, of quality specified in paragraph 75.

83. TRAP-DOOR.—A trap-door 2 × 3 feet is to be framed in the roof, with ladder to same of dressed stuff, 2 × 4-inch uprights and 1 × 3-inch rungs, and located where the Engineer directs.

84. BLOCKS AND GROUNDS FOR MASON.—Blocks to secure joinery are to be furnished to the masons to build in wall. Strips 1 × 4 inches must be furnished the masons to build into the exterior walls. Carpenter is to put shelving in store-room, three shelves 15 inches wide all around room.

85. VERANDA FINISH.—Veranda is to be encased under floor with strong lattice-work between the posts.

The posts, spandrels, and trimmings of the verandas are to be of clear white pine carved from the solid piece, and finished in the most artistic manner.

86. DOORS.—All outside doors will be of quartered oak $2\frac{1}{4}$ inches thick, with stiles and rails with white-pine core as per plans. The frames to be of quartered oak. All other doors will be of solid quartered oak $1\frac{3}{4}$ inches thick, of same style as outside doors, except the doors to water-closets, which will be of solid quartered oak, $1\frac{3}{8}$ inches thick. All doors to be mortised, tenoned, glued, and wedged in the best manner, hung on butt-hinges, and furnished with locks, bolts, etc., complete, as provided under the head of Hardware. All doors to have quartered-oak thresholds, and to have oak stoppers with rubber buttons.

TRANSOMS.—Transoms to be provided over doors as shown on drawings. All transoms to be hung on pivots, and to be provided with Wollensack's patent transom-lift.

87. INTERIOR FINISH.—The waiting-rooms, ticket-office, and water-closets will be finished in clear quartered oak. All remaining portions of building will be finished in clear close-grained long-leaf yellow pine, but all window-stools are to be of clear quartered oak. The walls of waiting-rooms, ticket-office, and water-closets are to be wainscoted 3 feet 8 inches high, including cap with $\frac{7}{8}$ × 3-inch clear, beaded, tongued, and grooved quartered oak, with moulded cap and base.

88. WAINSCOT FOR BAGGAGE-ROOM.—Wainscoting for baggage room will be of clear close-grained long-leaf yellow pine, $\frac{7}{8}$ × 3 inch, tongued and grooved, dressed and beaded on one side, with moulded cap and bevelled base.

89. MOULDING-BOARDS AND BOXING.—All necessary moulding-boards are to be put up by the carpenter for the plumber, electrician, and gas-fitter. All pipes are to be boxed with lids screwed on with brass screws with round heads.

90. PICTURE-MOULDING.—A picture-moulding is to be put up in all rooms on the first floor, of same material as finish of room, as shown in details.

91. WINDOWS.—All the windows are to have full box frames, made as shown on drawings, of clear white pine, well seasoned and kiln-dried. To have 1¾-inch white-pine hanging stiles, and pulley-stiles of close-grained long-leaf yellow pine, to have all necessary boxes, pockets, pendulum, and parting strips, beads, etc. The inside beads are to be screwed to the frames with 1¼-inch No. 9 round-headed brass screws.

92. Beads are to match finish of rooms. All window-sash will be 1¾ inches thick, with check-rails and lugs at meeting-rails, and acorn-moulded stiles, rails, and muntins; to be double-hung with axle-pulleys, best braided sash-cord and round-eyed cast-iron weights, as provided under Hardware.

93. SETTING FRAME.—All window and door frames must be set, stay-lathed, and plumbed in the walls by the carpenter.

HARDWARE.

94. KIND OF HINGES.—All rooms on the first floor are to have plain polished bronze hardware.

Hinges to be loose-pin butt-hinges, with double steel bushings of proper size, and three to each door over 7½ feet high.

KNOBS AND ESCUTCHEONS.—Knobs for all doors, except water-closet doors, to be egg style, combined rose and escutcheon, 3 inches wide by 10 inches long.

LOCKS.—All outside and office doors to have Yale & Towne Standard No. 2000, catalogue of 1884, mortise spring-locks with duplicate keys, and swivel spindles. Double doors in baggage-room to have bronze flush-bolts on top and bottom of one leaf of door. All other doors, except water-closet doors, to have Yale & Towne Standard No. 1500, catalogue of 1884, mortise spring locks with duplicate keys. Water-closet doors to have ½-inch bronze barrel-bolts.

TRANSOM-LIFTS.—All swinging transoms to have bronze pivots and bronze Wollensack's patent transom-lifts.

95. WINDOW HARDWARE.—All windows to have two bronze sash-lifts on each lower sash, to have bronze burglar-proof sash-locks, and cast-iron weights of proper size. All window weights to be hung with best Silver Lake braided sash-cord; and to have 2-inch steel axle-pulleys with bronze face.

96. SCUTTLE-HOOKS.—Scuttle in roof to be provided with two wrought-iron hooks and staples.

COAT-HOOKS.—Provided bronze coat-hooks, one for each water-closet, two for office, and two for second-floor room.

PAINTING AND GLAZING.

97. CATHEDRAL GLASS.—The cathedral glass shall be of a design approved by the Engineer, to cost not more than one dollar per square foot, and to be securely leaded and wired to iron rods.

SAND-BLAST GLASS.—Glass in lower sash of office and water-closet windows to be double-strength American plate sand-blast glass.

PLAIN GLASS.—All other glass will be first quality double-strength-American plate-glass; to be free from flaws and imperfections of all kinds; to be set in putty, back puttied and well sprigged, and to be left sound and clean upon completion of building.

98. PAINTING WOODWORK.—All sashes are to be prime before glazing. All exterior dressed woodwork is to be painted one good coat of yellow ochre, and two good coats of white lead, pure linseed-oil, and driers, of such tints as the Engineer may direct.

99. PAINTING METAL-WORK.—All galvanized iron and tin to be painted two good coats of best metallic paint.

100. VARNISHING.—The ceilings of verandas and balcony in tower are to be varnished three good coats of the best copal varnish. All interior dressed woodwork throughout is to be well sand-papered, and then varnished with three good coats of the best copal varnish. The last coat to be of the best coach varnish.

101. CABINET-FINISH.—The waiting-rooms, ticket-office, and water-closets must be finished in oak, and all to have one good coat of Wheeler's Patent Filler, and three good coats of the best rubbed copal varnish, and to be well rubbed after each coat with pumice-stone and water, and to be finished with a cabinet finish.

Doors and frames for same are to be done in the same manner.

102. OILED-FINISH.—The treads, risers, and platforms of stairs and runners of all box-frames are to be oiled with two good coats of boiled linseed-oil.

PLUMBING.

103. FIXTURES.—Provide two water-closets, two wash-stands, and one urinal.

104. SUPPLY-PIPES OF LEAD.—Rising main to be ¾-inch lead pipe, weighing 4 pounds per lineal foot, and connected to water-main at such point as the Engineer may approve, laid at least 3 feet below final grade-line, and carried up so all supply-pipes will lead from it, and provided with a stop and drainage cock.

Supply-pipes to water-closet tanks and to urinal to be ½-inch lead pipe, weighing 2 pounds per lineal foot.

Supply-pipes to wash-stands to be ⅝-inch lead pipe, weighing 3 pounds per lineal foot.

105. WASTE AND VENTILATOR PIPES.—Water-closets to have 4-inch cast-iron double-strength wastes leading into a 4-inch cast-iron double-strength soil-pipe, carried 10 feet outside of the building, and ventilated through a 4-inch single-strength cast-iron pipe, carried 2 feet above the roof, with a globe ventilator on top. The ventilator-pipe to be provided with Y's for connecting air vent-pipes from each fixture. The soil-pipe is to have a trap, placed with an accessible clean-out, outside the foundation-walls, and provided with a fresh-air inlet 4 inches diameter on the house side of the trap, extending to the external air in such a location as not to be offensive. Rain-water leaders are to be provided with traps at the foot of the pipes.

Urinal and wash-stands are to waste through 1½-inch lead pipes, weighing 4 pounds per lineal foot, and provided with 1½-inch brass "Sanitas" traps, and vented beyond traps through a 1½-inch lead pipe into 4-inch cast-iron ventilating pipe. Overflow-pipes to wash-bowls and urinal will be 1¼-inch lead pipes, connected with 1½-inch waste above trap.

106. All showing pipes for wash-stand and urinal to be drawn-brass pipe of same size as lead pipe.

SUPPLY-PIPES OF BRASS.—Supply-pipes from cisterns to water-closets will be 1¼-inch drawn polished brass pipe, lacquered.

107. CAST-IRON PIPES.—All cast-iron pipes to be of best quality, with proper fittings, elbows, T's, and Y's; to be coated inside and outside with asphaltum; to be put up in the best and strongest manner with iron hooks and stays, and the joints calked with oakum and melted lead.

All connections with iron pipes to be made with Y branches.

108. LEAD PIPES.—All lead pipes to be put up in the best manner on boards set in place by the carpenter, and to be secured with brass bands and screws or hard-metal tacks. All joints in lead pipe throughout are to be wiped joints. All connections between lead and iron pipes and traps are to be made with cast-brass ferrules the same size as the lead pipes, with wiped joints, and calked with oakum and melted lead run into the iron pipes.

109. COVERING OF PIPES.—Where pipes come within walls or partitions they shall be covered with face-boards matching finish of room, fastened with brass round-headed screws.

110. TRAPS.—Each basin, urinal, and water-closet shall be furnished with a trap, which shall be placed as near as practicable to the fixture that it serves; traps shall be protected from siphonage or air-pressure by special air-pipes of a size not less than the trap; but air-pipes connected with water-closet traps shall not be less than 2-inch bore, and in every case of proper proportion for their purposes, as may be approved by the Engineer. They may be branched into the soil or waste pipe vent, not less than three feet above the inlet from the highest fixture. No trap-vent shall be used as a waste or soil pipe.

111. INSPECTION.—Pipes and other fixtures shall not be covered from view or concealed until the work has been examined by the Engineer, and he shall be notified by the plumber when the work is sufficiently advanced for inspection. Plumbing work shall not be used unless the same has first been tested in the presence of Engineer, and by him found satisfactory.

112. WATER-CLOSETS.—The water-closets will be flush-rim washout closets, of the style described as "Embossed Inodoro" in the J. & L. Mott catalogue G, 1888, plate 93 G, with copper-lined cabinet-finished quartered oak after-wash cistern No. 4½, design E; open seat, and cover of quartered oak with brass back, as shown on plate 874 G; with polished-brass 1¼-inch flush-pipe; polished-brass curved trap-vent calked into hub of Y of cast-iron vent-pipe. To be connected by a four-inch lead waste-pipe weighing 8 pounds per lineal foot, to the hub of Y of cast-iron soil-pipe; joint with bowl to be sealed with red lead.

To be set on a recessed slab of dark Tennessee marble 1¼ inches thick, 27 inches × 27 inches.

113. WASH-STANDS.—The wash-stands are to be of the style described and shown in J. & L. Mott catalogue G, 1888, plate 411 G. To have 17-inch × 14-inch white-porcelain bowls with silver-plated "Duplex" waste, dark Tennessee marble recessed slab 22 inches × 33 inches, marble back 14 inches high, and marble sides and front 5 inches deep, and polished-brass legs. One low-down silver-plated compression-cock to each basin.

114. URINAL.—The urinal is to be of white porcelain flat-back lipped urinal with nickel-plated brass fittings, with dark Tennessee marble back 30 inches × 4 feet high, and one marble side next to wash-stand 22

inches × 4 feet high, and 1¼-inch recessed slab of same marble 22 inches × 33 inches. To be supplied with silver-plated ½-inch compression flush-cock.

All marble secured in strongest manner with brass brackets and brass round-headed screws.

DRAINAGE.

115. STONEWARE DRAINS.—The drain-pipes outside the building shall be laid of the sizes and in the location shown on drawing No. 1. They shall be of the best salt-glazed vitrified stoneware drain-pipe laid to a true and uniform grade, with all joints completely closed with cement mortar and made smooth on the inside.

TRENCHES.—The trenches for drain-pipes are to be dug to a true grade, and hollows made to receive the bell-ends of the pipes, and the earth well tamped around the pipe, and the trenches filled and well tamped in 6-inch layers. Provide all necessary "Y," "U," and "T" joints,

116. GRADIENT OF DRAINS.—The drains shall have a fall of not less than ⅛ inch per foot.

117. MAN-HOLE.—The sewer-pipe is to be provided with a man-hole and a trap on house side of man hole at point shown on sheet No. 1.

The man-hole is to be 2 feet in diameter at top, and 3 feet diameter at bottom in the clear. Wall to have two rings of brick, with joints completely filled with cement mortar, and interior of wall plastered with cement mortar. The foundation of man-hole to be 12 inches of concrete laid on two courses of timber grillage, each 4 inches thick with 2-inch spaces between timbers, filled with cement mortar.

To be capped with a stone coping 8 inches thick, 3 feet 6 inches in diameter, of hard, durable sandstone, in one piece, with a hole 2 feet diameter cut in centre, and provided with a cast-iron grating cover, set flush in stone coping. Top of man-hole to be level with ground.

GAS-FITTING.

118. PIPING.—Where shown on the drawings, to be of the best wrought-iron piping, of the various sizes required. The mains to be run as direct as possible, and so graded that the water can run out at a convenient place near the meter. The following table will govern the sizes of pipes:

SIZES OF PIPES.—	Size of tubing.	Greatest length.	Number of burners.
	⅜ inch.	20 feet.	3
	½ "	25 "	6
	¾ "	40 "	20
	1 "	60 "	30
	1¼ "	110 "	60

DETAILS OF PIPING.—No rising pipe to be less than 2 feet in length, all properly graded. Secure all piping in place with iron hold-fasts, and secure the drops and other outlets with galvanized-iron straps and screws. All centre-lights, where shown, to be secured with galvanized-iron waste-nuts instead of screws, the pipes to be run to supply side-lights where indicated on plan. The side-wall pipes to project the proper distance for brackets, with rosettes, and pipe-ends for drop-lights to hang perfectly straight, true, and plumb. Put all pipe-joints together in red lead. Cap all pipe, and leave caps on and prove, and locate the meter, and provide all shut-offs and alcohol cocks. The gas-fitter will not be allowed to cut away any of the woodwork. This will be done by the carpenter.

MANTELS.

119. LOCATION.—Mantels and grates will be provided in the waiting-rooms.

WOMEN'S WAITING-ROOM.—In the women's waiting-room provide and set a mantel and top of quartered oak, of style numbered 240 in the Robert Mitchell Furniture Company of Cincinnati, catalogue No. 24, page 65; with antique cast brass frame, radiant setting, polished basket, jambs and screen, with ashpan; with facing of enamelled and embossed tile, slabbed of a rich olive tint; with hearth 5 ft. × 2 ft. of enamelled tile, and embossed border of same tint as facing; with fireplace lined with the best fire tile and brick. This mantel and trimmings will be furnished complete by the Mitchell Furniture Company for $150.00.

MEN'S WAITING-ROOM.—In the men's waiting-room provide and set a mantel of quartered oak, of style numbered 113 of the Meader Furniture Company of Cincinnati. To have antique cast-brass frame, radiant setting, polished basket, jambs and screen, with an ashpan; with facing of enamelled tile of rich orange tint, and 5 ft. × 2 ft. hearth of same tile; with fireplace lined with best fire tile and brick. The Meader Furniture Company will furnish this mantel and fittings complete for $85.00.

INSPECTION.

120. CONDEMNED MATERIALS.—All materials will be subject to rigid inspection, and any that have been condemned must be immediately removed from the site of the work.

121. GENERAL INSPECTION.—The work will be done under the supervision of an Inspector, whose duties will be to see that the requirements of these specifications are carried out; but his presence is in no way to be presumed to relieve in any degree the responsibility or obligation of the Contractor.

JUNE 1, 1890.

N. B.—Proposals must be made on this Form and sent in without detaching Specifications.

ALABAMA GREAT SOUTHERN RAILROAD COMPANY.

PROPOSAL FOR BUILDING A PASSENGER DEPOT AT FORT PAYNE, ALA.

The undersigned, having examined the specifications attached hereto and the plans for the work, do............hereby propose to the Alabama Great Southern Railroad Company to furnish all the necessary material and labor to build the passenger depot at Fort Payne, in accordance with the requirements of the said plans and specifications; and on the acceptance of this proposal do............hereby bind..................to enter into and execute a contract for the said work at the following

PRICES.

1. Building complete with exterior walls of hard-burned brick, and faced with pressed brick and stone trimmings, ... $..................
2. Building complete with exterior walls of stone, ... $..................
3. Additional price, if copper is substituted for galvanized iron (per paragraph 71), . . $..................

The undersigned further propose........to commence work within..............days from notice of award of contract, and to complete the same within............days thereafter.

Signed this..............day of..................1890.

(Name of firm)

....

References: By

....

Address:

....

PENNSYLVANIA LINES WEST OF PITTSBURG—SOUTHWEST SYSTEM.

SPECIFICATIONS FOR DEPOTS.—CLASSES A AND B.*

For the construction of a Joint Passenger and Freight Building at............on..........Division of the..........Rail..........Said building to be..............feet, outside measurement, and placed 17 feet 6 inches from the nearest rail of the main track of said railway, as per plan; to have one Waiting-room, one Freight-room, and a Ticket and Telegraph Office. For dimensions see plan. The final location of building site to be determined by the Superintendent of the..........Division of said railway.

FOUNDATION.

The building will rest upon stone piers, at least 18 inches square, to be set into the ground a sufficient depth to insure a good and firm foundation for the building. There will be 16 piers, placed as indicated on the plan.

CARPENTER-WORK.

All timber for the framework to be of good, sound, well-seasoned white pine, free from sap, rot, or large knots, and sawed to the full dimensions of the parts required.

---

* This specification was kindly furnished for publication by Mr. M. J. Becker, Chief Engineer, Pennsylvania Lines West of Pittsburg. This depot is described on page 252 and illustrated in Figs. 439 and 440.

Sills to be 8 × 8 inches, of sufficient length to reach from corner to corner, halved at the angles and spiked together.

Corner-posts to be 4 × 4 inches. Door and window posts 4 × 4 inches, properly framed together and pinned in connection with top plate for ceiling-joists to rest upon.

Studding, 2 × 4 inches, placed 16 inches centre to centre; to be of uniform height, squared at the ends and spiked to the sills and capping plates.

Floor-joists, 3 × 12 inches, in freight-room, spaced thirteen (13) inches centre to centre, and 2 × 12 inches, spaced 16 inches centre to centre, in the balance of building. Joists in freight-room to be boxed into sills and set 6 inches lower than rest of floor. All other joists to rest securely on and be spiked to sills, and all joists bridged twice in the width of building. Joists to be spiked to studding when their position will admit of its being done. Cap-plates, 4 × 4 inches, framed into corner and door posts. Ceiling-joists, 2 × 8 inches, spaced 16 inches from centre to centre, spiked to plate and have two rows of bridging, except in freight room, which will have no ceiling.

The roof is to be constructed as per plan, and is to project on each side and end, six (6) feet from the face of the building. The projections are to be supported by brackets of 4 × 6-inch pine, and be firmly bolted to building and made as per plan. All projecting timbers and eaves to be properly moulded and planed smooth, ready for the painter.

Roof to be covered with one-inch pine sheeting-boards.

SIDING.—The middle course to be of patent moulded ⅞-inch weather-boarding, ends shouldered to the trimmings and placed as per plan. The courses between the water-table and belt-course, and also the courses below the roof and the gable-ends, to be 1 × 12-inch battened boards, joints to be covered with two (2) inch moulded battens, as per plan.

There will be a belt-course under window-frames and a belt-course 1 × 6 inches, with a moulded cap on the upper side of middle course of weather-boarding, upon which the battens rest, as per plan.

A water-table 1⅛ × 10 inches with bevelled cap, will extend around the building.

Flooring of 1 × 4 inch yellow pine, tongued and grooved and blind-nailed in all rooms, except freight-room, which will be floored with two (2) inch white pine, gauged to uniform thickness, and laid close joints.

All rooms, except freight-room, to have a wainscot, 3½ feet high, of tongued, grooved, and beaded strips four (4) inches wide, of white pine, to be finished on top with a moulded projecting cap, with a ¼ round moulding at the base.

All rooms, except freight-room, to have all window and door frames finished with casings, 1 × 6 inches, with moulded edges.

All doors and windows on the outside to be trimmed with one-inch stuff, as per plan.

There will be six (6) windows, having four (4) lights each, and two (2) front bay-windows, of two (2) lights each, with clear double American glass. The sash to be 1⅛-inch well-seasoned white pine, with mouldings, and properly hung with weights and pulleys.

There will be one ticket-window, 20 × 24 inches, placed as per plan, and have upward sliding panel, with two (2) spring catches, also have shelves of 2-inch oak, supported by neat brackets, and be neatly trimmed around the opening.

In addition there will be a telegraph operating-table, properly constructed and placed, as per plan.

All outside doors will have fixed transoms, having three glass lights, 18 inches high, except freight-room door, which will have six (6) lights, each 18 inches high. There will be one (1) outside door 3⅛ × 8½ feet, made of 1¾-inch well-seasoned white pine, with moulded and raised panels, also one (1) inside door, 3 × 7½ feet. Freight-room will have one (1) double door, 7 feet 2 inches by 9 feet 4 inches, to be framed of 2-inch stuff, with panels of ⅞ × 4-inch beaded and matched boards, rabbeted in frame and well-fastened with screws.

Partitions will be made 2 × 4-inch studding. The walls of freight-room to be lined with one (1) inch rough boards to the height of ten (10) feet.

SLATING.

Roof-sheeting is to be covered first with a layer of tarred felting-paper, then slated with the best black Pennsylvania slate, 8 × 20 inches, with eight (8) inches exposed to the weather. All to be securely nailed with galvanized slating nails. Slate to be from the American Bangor Slate Company's quarry.

GUTTERS, ETC.

Gutters are to be lined with tin, and the tin to run up under slate eight (8) inches, be exposed eight (8) inches, and be four (4) inches high, pitched to carry the water to corners of building; all to be securely nailed to sheeting.

There will be conductor-pipes of three (3) inch galvanized iron No. 22 at each corner of building, to run down below the platform, and each to have a 12-inch elbow at bottom.

Chimney to be flashed with tin.

There will be galvanized-iron ridge-combings on roof, as per plan.

All tin-work to be best I X double-dipped, bright tin plate. Gutters and flashings to be painted 2 coats on back before being laid.

PLASTERING.

The ceiling and walls, except in freight-room, to be plastered with two (2) coats of good hair-lime plaster. The ceiling to be finished with one (1) coat of hard finish, and the walls with one (1) coat of rough-cast, of fine sand finish, tinted in distemper colors, to be selected by the Superintendent. Laths to be of best quality, and be nailed with No. 3 lath-nails at every joint and studding.

CHIMNEYS.

There will be one (1) chimney, as per plan, with two flues, 8 × 8 inches each, all to have 8-inch walls, with 4-inch division walls. Chimney to be carried above the apex of the roof and finished with stone cap 6 inches thick, composed of one piece, as per plan.

PAINTING.

All painting to be done with the best quality white-lead and pure linseed-oil paint, well mixed. Inside of building to have two (2) coats and outside three (3) coats, in two (2) colors, to be selected by the Superintendent. Gutters and down-pipes for roof-drainage to have two (2) coats of paint.

HARDWARE.

All outside doors, except freight-room, to be hung with 3 pairs of 4½-inch loose-pin butt-hinges; the inside doors to have 3½-inch loose-pin butt-hinges. All doors, except freight-room, to have heavy upright mortise knob-locks, equal to No. 305 of Norwalk Lock Company make. Window-sash to be hung with Silver Lake Company's solid braided window-sash cord, on 2-inch axle-pulleys, sash-weight to be sufficient to balance sash. Freight-room door to be hung on heavy iron hangers with six (6) inch wheels, running on horizontal iron guides and have iron fastenings on door for padlock.

GENERAL CLAUSES.

All materials are to be furnished and all work done which may be necessary to complete the building according to the plan, though the same may not be specially mentioned herein. All materials and work not otherwise specified are to be of the best qualities of their several kinds. All alterations and deviations from these specifications, and all additions to the same, must be fully stated in writing, and the price agreed upon or such extra work must be stated in an appendix to these specifications and signed by both parties, before payment will be made for the same. All materials needed in the construction of the building, and all laborers and mechanics actually employed in its construction, will be transported free of charge over the ...... Division of the Pittsburg, Cincinnati & St. Louis Railway.

PENNSYLVANIA LINES WEST OF PITTSBURG—SOUTHWEST SYSTEM.

SPECIFICATIONS FOR DEPOTS.—CLASS F.*

For the construction of a Passenger Depot at..... , on..... Division of the Pittsburg, Cincinnati & St. Louis Railway.

The main building to be 21 × 70 *feet, outside measurements, and placed* 17 *feet* 6 *inches from the nearest rail of the main track of said railway as per plan; to have two* (2) *Waiting-rooms and one Ticket and Tele-*

* This specification was kindly furnished for publication by Mr. M. J. Becker, Chief Engineer, Pennsylvania Lines West of Pittsburg.

This depot is described on page 287 and illustrated in Figs. 515 to 517.

graph Office, one Baggage-room, one Toilet-room, and two Water-closets. For dimensions, see plan. The final location of building site to be determined by the Superintendent of the...... Division of said railway.

FOUNDATIONS.

The building will rest on stone piers at least 18 inches square, to be set into the ground at a sufficient depth to insure a good and firm foundation for the building. There will be 37 piers, placed as indicated by plan.

CARPENTER-WORK.

All timber for the framework to be of good, sound, well-seasoned white pine, free from sap, rot, or large knots, and sawed to the full dimensions of the parts required.

Sills to be 8 x 8 inches, of sufficient length to reach from corner to corner, halved at the angles and spiked together.

Corner-posts to be 4 x 4 inches. Door and window posts to be 4 x 4 inches, properly framed together and pinned in connection with top plate for ceiling-joists to rest upon. Studding 2 x 4 inches, placed 16 inches centre to centre, to be of uniform height, squared at the ends, and spiked to the sills and capping plates.

Floor-joists 3 x 12 inches in baggage-room, spaced 13 inches centre to centre, and 2 x 12 inches, spaced 16 inches centre to centre, in the balance of building. All joists to rest securely on and be spiked to sills, and bridged twice in the width of building. Joists to be spiked to studding when their position will admit of its being done. Cap-plates 4 x 4 inches, framed into corner door-posts. Ceiling-joists to be 2 x 12 inches, all spaced 16 inches from centre to centre, spiked to top plate, and bridged twice in the width of the building.

The roof is to be constructed as per plan, and is to project on each side and end seven feet ten inches (7 ft. 10 in.) from the face of the building. The projections are to be supported by brackets of 4 x 6-inch pine, and be firmly bolted to building, and made as per plan. The gables to have framed ornaments made of 2 x 6-inch pine, and 1-inch backs to panels, scroll-sawed as per drawings. All projecting timbers and eaves to be properly moulded and planed smooth, ready for the painter.

Roof is to be covered with 1-inch pine sheeting-boards.

SIDING.—The middle course to be of patent moulded ⅞-inch weather-boarding, ends shouldered to the trimmings and placed as per plan. The courses between the water-table and belt-course, and also the courses below roof and gable-ends, to be of 1 x 12-inch battened boards. Joints to be covered with 2-inch moulded battens, as per plan. The upper course of battened boards to have their lower ends finished as per plan.

There will be a belt-course under window-frames and a belt-course 1 x 6 inches, with a moulded cap, on the upper side of the middle course of weather-boarding.

A water-table 1¼ x 10 inches with bevelled cap will extend around the building. Flooring 1 x 4-inch yellow pine, tongued and grooved, and blind-nailed in all rooms, except baggage room, which will be floored with 2-inch white pine, gauged to uniform thickness and laid close joints.

All rooms, except baggage-room, to have a wainscot 3½ feet high, of tongued, grooved, and beaded strips four (4) inches wide, of white pine, to be finished on top with a moulded projecting cap, with ¼-round moulding at the base.

All window and door frames to be finished with inside trimmings 1 x 6 inches, with moulded edges.

All doors and windows on the outside to be trimmed with 1-inch stuff, as per plan.

There will be ten (10) windows, having four (4) lights each, and eight (8) windows of two (2) lights each, with clear double American glass. The sash to be of 1½-inch well-seasoned white pine, with mouldings, and properly hung with weights and pulleys.

There will be two (2) ticket-windows 20 x 24 inches, placed as per plan, and have upward-sliding panel, with two (2) spring catches; also, have shelves of 2-inch oak, supported by neat brackets, and be neatly trimmed around the openings.

In addition there will be a telegraph operating-table, properly constructed and placed as per plan.

All outside doors will have fixed transom, having one light of glass 18 inches high, except baggage-room doors, one of which will have no transom, and one will have a six (6) light transom.

There will be four (4) outside doors, 3½ feet by 9 feet, and one (1) door 3 feet by 9 feet, made of 1¾-inch well-seasoned white pine, with tongued and grooved and beaded panels; also three (3) inside doors, 3 feet by 8 feet, and four (4) doors 2 feet 3 inches by 5 feet, for closets.

Baggage-room will have two (2) double doors 6 feet by 9 feet 6 inches, to be framed of 2-inch stuff, with panels of 4-inch beaded and matched boards, well fastened with screws.

Partitions will be made of 2×4-inch studding. The walls of baggage-room to be lined with one (1) inch rough boards to the height of ten (10) feet.

SLATING.

Roof-sheeting is to be covered first with a layer of tarred felting-paper, then slated with the best black Pennsylvania slate, 8×20 inches, with eight (8) inches exposed to the weather. All to be securely nailed with galvanized slating nails. Slates to be from the American Bangor Slate Co.'s quarry.

GUTTERS, ETC.

Gutters are to be lined with tin, and the tin to run up under slate eight (8) inches, be exposed eight (8) inches, and be four (4) inches high, pitched to carry the water to corners of building; all to be securely nailed to sheeting.

There will be conductor-pipes of three (3) inch, No. 22 galvanized iron at each angle between main and out building, to run down below the platform, and each to have a 12-inch elbow at bottom.

Valley gutters to be tin of 16-inch girth, 8 inches exposed to the weather.

There will be galvanized-iron ridge-combings and gutter-crestings on roof, as per plan.

PLASTERING.

The ceiling and walls, except in baggage-room, to be plastered with two (2) coats of good hair-lime plaster. The ceiling to be finished with one (1) coat of hard finish, and the walls with one (1) coat of rough cast of fine sand finish, tinted in distemper colors, to be selected by the Superintendent.

Laths to be of best quality, and be nailed with No. 3 lath-nails at every joist and studding.

CHIMNEYS.

There will be one (1) chimney, as per plan, with two (2) flues, 8×8 inches each. All to have 8-inch walls, with 4-inch division walls. Chimney to be carried above the apex of the roof and finished with stone cap, composed of one piece pierced for flues as per plan; also two (2) ventilator flues from the water-closets, of galvanized iron above roof, as shown on plan. Chimney to be flashed with tin.

PAINTING.

All painting to be done with best quality white lead and pure linseed-oil paint, well mixed. Inside of building to have two (2) coats and outside three (3) coats, in two (2) colors, to be selected by the Superintendent.

Gutters and down-pipes for roof-drainage to have two (2) coats of paint.

All tin-work to have two (2) coats of paint on the under-side before laying.

HARDWARE.

All outside doors, except baggage-room, to be hung with 3 pair of 4½-inch loose-pin butt-hinges; the inside door to have 3½-inch loose-pin butt-hinges.

All doors, except baggage-room, to have heavy upright mortise knob locks, equal to No. 305 of Norwalk Lock Company make.

Window-sash to be hung with Silver Lake Co.'s solid braided window-sash cord, on 2-inch axle-pulleys. Sash-weights to be sufficient to balance sash.

Baggage-room door to be hung on heavy sliding-door hangers with six (6) inch wheels and iron track rail at top, and provided with heavy flush-bolts, and strong hasp for padlock.

GENERAL CLAUSES.

All materials are to be furnished and all work done which may be necessary to complete the building according to the plan, though the same may not be specially mentioned herein. All material and work not otherwise specified are to be of the best qualities of their several kinds.

All alterations and deviations from these specifications and all additions to the same must be fully stated in writing, and the price agreed upon for such extra work must be stated in an appendix to these specifications, and signed by both parties before payment will be made for the same.

All materials needed in the construction of the building, and all laborers and mechanics actually employed in its construction, will be transported free of charge over............. Division of the Pittsburg, Cincinnati & St. Louis Railway.

CINCINNATI SOUTHERN RAILWAY.

June 1, 1878.

GENERAL SPECIFICATIONS FOR BUILDINGS, WATER STATIONS, CATTLE-GUARDS, ROAD-CROSSINGS, TURN-TABLES, FENCING, AND TELEGRAPH LINES.*

FOUNDATIONS OF BUILDINGS.

Foundations, unless they rest on solid rock, must be sunk at least three feet below the surface of the ground, and as much more as may be necessary to reach a solid bed.

The bottoms of foundation-pits must be dressed level, and the material excavated must be deposited at such a place as may be directed by the Engineer.

The foundations will be either of stone or wood.

STONE.—The walls or piers must be built in accordance with plans furnished, of large flat bedded stone of quality approved by the Engineer; laid flush with broken joints in good fresh-mixed cement mortar; composed of the best quality of cement, sharp sand, and clear water, mixed in such proportion as the Engineer may direct.

The first footing-course must be composed of selected stone, well rammed to position in a 2-inch bed of cement mortar. The masonry must be well bonded, built straight, plumb, and level; no spalls to be allowed in the beds. Spaces between bedding-stones to be filled with spalls laid flush in good cement mortar.

All faces exposed to view or above ground must be neatly pointed. All piers must be capped with a single stone roughly squared, and walls with selected stones reaching across the wall.

The spaces between the masonry and the sides of excavations must be filled with the material excavated well rammed in.

WOOD.—Foundations of wood will consist of white-oak blocks well charred, not less than 12 inches in diameter, resting on white-oak sills.

The sills must have a full and equal bearing on the bottom of the pit. The blocks must be straight stand vertically in line, sawed level at the top and bottom, and of the proper height. The pit must be filled with the material excavated well rammed in.

When solid rock or other solid foundation-bed is reached the sills will be dispensed with.

BRICKWORK.

All brickwork must be of the best quality of hard-burned brick, well shaped and laid wet in the best hydraulic cement or strong fresh lime mortar as may be required, mixed with clear water, the proportion of sand to cement being such as the Engineer may direct.

All beds and joints to be well filled with mortar, to be neatly pointed on the face of the wall, and not to exceed three eighths (⅜) of an inch in thickness. No bats, cracked or salmon brick will be allowed.

The walls to be well bonded, every seventh course to be of headers. All flues to be lined with terra-cotta pipe, provided with the necessary thimbles and capped in approved manner.

TIMBER AND FRAMING.

All timber must be of the best quality of the kind specified, sawed true and out of wind, full size, free of wind-shakes, large or loose knots, worm-holes, sap, or any defect impairing its strength or durability.

All framing must be done to a close fit, and in a thorough and workmanlike manner. No open joints or filling shims will be allowed.

---

* This specification was used in the construction of the Cincinnati Southern Railway, Mr. G. Bouscareu, Consulting and Principal Engineer, and R. G. Huston & Co., Contractors. The specification and the annexed copy of Messrs. R. G. Huston & Co.'s bid for the different classes of work covered by the specifications is copied from the report of the Consulting and Principal Engineer to the Board of Trustees, dated March 6, 1880.

The depots, Classes A, B, C, and D, mentioned in these *General Specifications* are described above on pages 253 to 254, and the Depot Class "A" is illustrated in Figs. 441 to 444. The Water Station is described on page 120. The Tool-house is described on pages 9 to 10, and illustrated in Figs. 25 to 27.

Floor-joists must be well stayed by rows of bridging, 1" x 3", not more than 6 feet apart, secured with two nails at each end.

Rafters to be notched on wall-plates and spiked to ridge-pieces and wall-plates. All bolts to be square-headed, and provided with washers under nut and head.

WEATHER-BOARDING.

To be of good second common pine or yellow poplar, without cracks or loose knots, thickness one inch, width not to exceed nine inches, securely nailed to studding with *close joints*, and battened with 1" x 3" strips, bevelled and dressed.

FLOOR.

Will be of two kinds: No. 1, used in passenger rooms, offices, etc., will be of 1" x 4½" first common yellow pine, well seasoned, dressed and matched, secret-nailed, and smoothed off after completion.

No. 2, used on platforms, freight-rooms, etc., will consist of 2" x 8" seasoned white oak, well spiked to joists or sills with close joints, and smoothed off after completion.

Header-joints of all flooring to be brought over joists.

CEILING AND WAINSCOTING.

To be of first common well-seasoned matched flooring 1" x 4½", of uniform width, header-joints on studding and joists, secret-nailed, beaded for walls and partitions, and smoothed off. Ceiled rooms must be provided with an eight-inch base-board and with a neat moulding at the junction of ceiling and walls.

ROOF.

The roofs will be covered with shingles, tin, or slate. The sheathing will be of second common dressed pine or yellow poplar, laid with close joints and securely nailed to rafters.

The shingles must be of the best quality of pine or yellow-poplar shaved shingles, 16 inches long, of uniform width and thickness, well nailed, and showing 4 inches to the weather.

The tin must be the best quality of I. C. leaded charcoal roofing-tin, sheets 14" x 20", with standing lock-joints 1½" high running with the slope of the roof, well secured and soldered to gutter and flashing-tin, and fastened occasionally to sheathing by soldering small strips at joints and nailing down.

The slate to be of the best quality of Virginia slate 10" x 20", laid 8" to the weather, carefully gauged and punched, each slate to be fastened with tin-composition nails, with heads countersunk in slate. The ridge of roof must be covered with No. 22 galvanized iron, rolled as per detail approved by the Engineer and well secured in place.

Flashings around chimneys and ventilators to be of the same quality of tin as that used on the roof, and secured in the best manner, to the satisfaction of the Engineer. All roofs must be water-tight.

Gutters must be lined with tin of the same quality as that used on the roof. the tin must reach beyond the first lap of shingles or slates. Connections of gutters to water-spouts must be well made, and perfectly water-tight.

Down-spouts must be of the number and size specified; they must be of No. 22 galvanized iron, each provided with flaring mouth and copper-wire strainer, joints well soldered and riveted. They must be firmly fastened to the building with No. 16 galvanized-iron holders, and boxed with one-inch plank where exposed to blows.

DRAINAGE.

The water from the down-spouts of buildings must be collected in box-drains and run out to the side ditch along the track.

PLASTERING.

The laths for plastering must be the best sawed-pine laths, well seasoned. They must be strongly nailed to the studding, and break joints every eight laths.

The plastering must be of three good coats, finishing hard white, and composed of fresh strong white lime, clean sharp sand, long strong hair, and clear water.

WINDOWS.

All box-framed windows to be hung on pulleys with best quality of cotton sash-cord, must be well balanced by cast-iron weights, and fitted with approved lock and strong brass hook-lifts. The lower half of common sash-windows must be made to slide easily, and fitted with approved spring-lock and brass hook-lift.

DOORS.

Large exterior doors will be $1\frac{3}{4}''$ in thickness, interior doors $1\frac{3}{8}''$. All doors must be of the best quality of seasoned pine, double panelled, hung on three hinges, fit closely, work easily, and fitted with approved mortised knob-lock for exterior doors, and rim knob-locks for the others. Hinges for outside doors to be $4'' \times 4''$, and for the others $3'' \times 3''$.

HARDWARE.

All hardware required for the full and complete finishing of all structures must be furnished and fitted, and be of quality and style approved on sample by the Engineer.

FINISH AND TRIMMINGS.

The outside trimmings of the buildings and the inside finish of passenger rooms, offices, and section houses will be plain, but neatly done, in such style as the Engineer may direct.

PAINTING AND GLAZING.

The exterior of all buildings, unless otherwise specified, will be painted with two coats of the best quality of Iron-clad paint mixed with boiled linseed-oil; the outside trimmings and the interior of passenger rooms and offices with two coats of white lead mixed with boiled linseed-oil, and be of such color as the Engineer may direct.

Tin roofs will be painted with two coats of Iron-clad paint. All the tin and iron about the roof and gutter to be painted in like manner.

Water-tanks, spouts, and turn-tables to be painted with two coats of Iron-clad paint. All water-pipes, smoke-funnels, and smoke-stacks to be painted inside and out with two coats of hot coal-tar thickened with lime.

GLAZING.—All glazing must be done in the best manner, bedded, sprigged, and back puttied. All window-sashes and transoms to be glazed with the best Pittsburg glass, free from color, bubbles, waves, and other defects.

GENERAL CLAUSE.

All materials must be of the best quality of the kind specified, and be subject to the inspection and acceptance of the Engineer.

The workmanship must be of the best character, and to the satisfaction of the Engineer.

If there should be any omissions in these specifications or plans furnished, the Contractor shall, nevertheless, supply without extra charge all the material and labor necessary for the completion of the buildings and other structures in the style contemplated by these specifications and plans.

The Contractor takes all risks of damage or destruction by fire, storm, or any cause whatsoever, and must maintain all finished structures in a complete state of repair until their final acceptance. No structure will be finally accepted until the completion of the entire work under contract.

STATION-HOUSES.

PLAN A.

Will be built in accordance with the general plan marked "A."

Platforms eighteen inches above grade. All inside walls and ceilings to be ceiled with white or yellow pine. Flues to be plastered. Ceilings of water-closet and baggage-room to be ten feet above the floor; each seat in the water-closet to be fitted with a hinged cover and be enclosed in a pine ceiling partition, six feet high, with a venetian door. Provide basins and traps with all improvements and pipe attachment for water supply. The gentlemen's closet to have enamelled urinal basins for two. The ladies' closet to have a wash-stand with enamelled basin with supply water-pipe and cock, and discharge pipe to the vault. Provide for ladies' and for gentlemen's closet a hinged transom-window of three lights, of the same size as transom over doors, at the same height and with the same finish.

The vault to be six feet in diameter in the clear, and twelve feet deep below surface, lined with brick and cement on side and bottom, and ventilated by a box-flue extending to the top of the roof.

Floor to be No. 1 for all rooms, and No. 2 for platforms. Steps in sufficient number must be provided to connect end of building with the surface of the ground, All windows to be box-framed.

Roof to be covered with shingles and drained by four 3½" down-spouts, one at each corner of the building.

Wooden benches in passenger rooms to be as shown on plan, of clear yellow pine or yellow poplar, with iron brackets between seats, of a pattern approved by the Engineer.

PLAN B.

Will be built in accordance with the general plan marked "B." Platform four feet above grade. The walls and ceiling of the passenger room and office to be ceiled and finished the same as for plan A. Windows in waiting-room and office to be box-framed. The brick flues to be plastered.

The roof to be covered with shingles and drained by four 3½" down-spouts, one at each corner of the building. Sufficient steps to be provided at each end of the building to connect the platforms with the surface of the ground.

Floors to be No. 1 for passenger-room and office, and No. 2 for freight-room and platforms.

Hangers of freight-doors to be of wrought-iron, and the track for the same to be also of wrought-iron firmly screwed to the frame of the building. Freight-doors must fit well, work easily, and be provided with approved bolt.

PLAN C.

Will be built in accordance with the general plan marked "C."

Platform four feet above grade.

Ceiling of office and waiting-room to be ten feet above the floor; ceiling and walls to be ceiled. Windows in waiting-room and office to be box-framed.

Opening for stove to be made in partition, properly consolidated by a frame and protected by a zinc lining.

Freight-room to be the same as in plan B.

Roof to be covered with shingles and drained by four 3" down-spouts, one at each corner of the building.

Floor to be No. 1 for waiting-room and office, and No. 2 for platform and freight-room.

PLAN D.

Will be built in accordance with the general plan marked "D."

Platform to be four feet above grade.

The entire building to be ceiled inside, the weather-boarding omitted, and all showing parts of the frame to be dressed and chamfered where required.

The partitions to be carried up to the roof, which will be sheathed with ceiling stuff throughout, covered with tin, and drained with four 3" down-spouts, one at each corner of the building.

The brick flues to be plastered; office and waiting-room to be finished the same as in plan A. All windows in office and waiting-rooms to be box-framed.

Floor to be No. 1 for waiting-room and office, and No. 2 for freight-room and platforms.

Sign-boards must be placed on each end of every station-house of all plans, and painted with three coats of white lead, with the name of the station and the number of miles in black.

PLATFORMS.

Platforms will be built in accordance with plan furnished, generally twelve or six feet in width. The twelve-feet platform being built at the end of station-houses on foundations similar to that of the building itself, the six-feet-platform between the main track and siding, on sub-sills. The floor of all platforms to be No. 2.

CATTLE-PENS.

Cattle-pens will be built as may be laid out and in accordance with the general plan furnished. The posts must be of white oak, black locust, or cedar, nine feet long, 8″ × 8″. They must square not less than six inches if round. They must set three feet in the ground, and if of white oak must be charred to one foot above ground. They must be firmly set, with material well rammed in the hole around them, stand vertically, and in true line.

All the planking to be of white oak.

The gates and chute-doors must work easily, and be provided with fastenings as shown on plan.

WATER STATIONS.

Water stations will be built in accordance with the standard plans furnished, including:

1. A water-tank supported on an octagonal frame and covered with a weather-boarded roof, which may be circular and flat, or octagonal with inclined faces as shown on plan.
2. A pump-house as shown on plan.
3. A steam-pump and boiler complete, with necessary connections and accessories.
4. The connecting pipes from the water supply to the pump and from the pump to the tank.

Where the elevation of the water will be sufficient to supply it into the tank by gravity, the pump-house, pump, and boiler will be omitted.

WATER-TANK.

The *supporting frame* will be of white oak, and put together with hot coal-tar and lime freely applied at all joints where wood touches wood, so as to effectually close all openings. It must be painted after erection with two good coats of the same material.

The wall-plates and sills will be bolted together with ¾″ bolts running through the tenons of posts as shown. The joists will be dressed on top to a true level, and must have full bearing on the bottom of the tub throughout their whole length.

The *tub* must be of the size and shape shown, of strictly clear, white pine, staves truly jointed to the radial plane. Every piece of the bottom to be in one length, truly jointed, cut true to the proper circle, and let in the staves three quarters of an inch, the m rtise in the staves *being a full inch deep.*

The *hoops* to be of the best charcoal iron, spaced and sized as shown, each hoop being provided with a bolt adjustment as shown in detail, area of rivets in splices to be equal to that of the hoop.

The tub must be thoroughly water-tight, and provided—

1. With a double-jointed, water-tight spout and valve, properly balanced.
2. With a discharge pipe and cock.
3. With a float and outside indicator properly marked.

The *hip-roof* to be put together with a cast-iron spider-frame at the top, and wrought-iron tie-ring of 2½″ × 2½″ angle at the bottom, weighing fifteen pounds to the yard, and having a full and even bearing on top of the tub, which must be dressed level for that purpose. The man-hole at the apex to be closed with a cast-iron cover as shown.

The Pump-house must be built in accordance with the general plan furnished. The floor to be No. 2 on sills, except the space under and around the boiler, which is to be paved with brick. The coal-bunker to be lined inside with 1½-inch plank, and the roof over it to be hinged to act as a trap-door, and to be provided with inside hook and staple fastening.

The roof to be covered with shingles. The chimney-hole lined with a No. 16 galvanized-iron thimble as shown, with diameter six inches larger than that of the chimney, well secured on to the roof, and with water-tight joint.

STEAM PUMP AND BOILER.

The capacity of the pump is to be seventy-five gallons, at forty revolutions per minute, with a pressure of forty pounds steam and for a vertical rise of one hundred feet.

THE PUMP must be of simple design, strongly built, and well finished. It must have a three-inch suction and a two-and-one-half-inch discharge-opening, and be provided with air-vessel, check-valve, strainer, boiler-feeder, cocks, oil-cups, and all other necessary accessories.

THE BOILER must be of sufficient capacity to run the pump, without hard firing, at sixty revolutions per minute with a pressure of sixty pounds of steam. It must be made of the best charcoal iron, and be tested by hydraulic pressure and stamped to one hundred and fifty pounds pressure. It must be provided with safety-valve, gauge-cocks, water gauge, man-holes sufficient to render all parts of the interior easily accessible for cleaning, discharge-cock, check-valve, water-tight ashpan, and all other necessary accessories. The chimney must be sixteen feet long, and provided with a spark-arrester, damper, and drip-collar over drum as shown. The necessary connections between the pump and boiler to be complete. The material and workmanship of the entire outfit to be first-class in every particular, and to the accceptance of the Engineer.

PIPES.

The force and suction pipes must be of the best lap-welded wrought-iron pipes, tested to three hundred pounds per square inch, hydraulic pressure, thoroughly coated with coal-tar and lime inside and out, and put together with red lead at all the joints. They must be carefully laid, not less than three feet below the surface, on such grade and line as may be staked out by the Engineer, with full bearing under their entire length, and proved water-tight by trial before they are covered up.

RESERVOIR.

Where water can be obtained at a sufficient elevation to supply the tank by gravity, reservoirs shall be built if required by the Engineer, and paid for at prices bid for grading and masonry.

COAL-PLATFORM.

Must be built in accordance with plan furnished. The frame and planking to be of white oak.

ENGINE-HOUSE.

The engine-house must be built in accordance with the plan furnished, the number of stalls to be such as may be required.

The foundations will be of stone; the frame will be of pine, yellow poplar, and white oak; the sheathing and weather-boarding of yellow poplar or pine.

The floor will be *No. 2 on sills*, and on a level with the top of rails.

The walls of the pits will be of stone or brick; if of stone, the inside faces will be dressed smooth. They will be capped with white-oak sleepers as shown, extending to the walls of the turn-table. The ends of the rails on the sleepers will be curved up as shown, and backed by a 12" × 12" white-oak beam securely bolted to the sleepers.

The pits to be paved with brick, laid in cement on a good bed of mortar. The pits will be drained by the best quality of vitrified stoneware pipe ten inches in diameter, laid carefully in cement with sufficient inclination, and carried as far as necessary beyond the building to secure proper drainage. The pipe will connect with each pit by an elbow provided with a cast-iron grating.

The main rafters of the roof will be secured to the wall-plates by one-inch drift-bolts, and bolted to bolster at the other end with one-inch bolts through seasoned white-oak keys as shown. Each purlin to be fastened on main rafters by $\frac{3}{8}$" spikes and supported by knee-blocks; jack-rafters must be spiked to purlins.

Roof to have a ventilator in centre as shown, neatly finished with approved finial. Ventilator and roof to be covered with tin; each section of roof to be drained by one four-inch down-spout discharging into engine-pit through wrought-iron pipe-drains.

A smoke-funnel of No. 16 galvanized iron, and built in accordance with detail drawing, must be provided for each stall. Opening through roof for the same to be properly framed, lined with a No. 16 galvanized-iron thimble as shown, and to be entirely water-tight. Provide a connection for a seven-inch stove-pipe in each funnel.

The doors must be in accordance with detail drawings and provided with required fastenings. Frames to be of clear pine, covered with best second common ceiling stuff; end doors to have wicket-doors with good locks. All doors to fit well, work easily, and lock against a butting-post.

Windows to be box-framed, and fitted with approved locks and strong brass hook-lifts.

A $2\frac{1}{2}$" water-supply pipe to be laid in position as shown, and provided with a hydrant, valve and hose attachment as indicated on plan, for every two stalls.

TURN-TABLES.

The turn-tables to be not less than fifty feet in length, of wrought-iron, with brick or stone foundations, and walls laid in cement and capped with three thicknesses of 2" pine planks, breaking joints.

The pit to be paved with brick and drained by a 10" vitrified stoneware pipe with elbow and cast-iron grating.

The table to be well balanced, fitted with suitable lock and lever, and equal in every respect to those now in use on the completed part of the road.

SECTION-HOUSES.

Section-houses are to be built at such places as the Engineer may direct, in accordance with plans furnished.

Foundations to be of wood. The walls, partitions, and ceilings to be ceiled; brick flues to be plastered.

Floor to be No. 1. Roof to be covered with shingles and provided with four three-inch down-spouts, one at each corner of the main building. The stairway to the second floor to be fitted with substantial hand-railing, and to be ceiled to the floor of the dining-room. Provide a plain door and lock for the closet underneath.

All windows to have common frames with sliding lower sash, fitted with approved lock and strong brass hook-lifts.

Provide suitable steps for exterior doors.

TOOL-HOUSES.

Tool-houses are to be built in accordance with standard plans furnished, with wood foundations.

Floor to be No. 2 on sills. Roof to be covered with shingles. Folding-door as per detail, fitted with bolts, bar, and padlock, as shown.

CATTLE-GUARDS AND ROAD-CROSSINGS.

Cattle-guards and road-crossings must be built of white oak, in accordance with the standard plans furnished, and on solid foundations.

Cattle-guard pits must be well drained, and the superstructure kept in true line and well up to grade.

All cattle-guards must connect with adjoining fences as shown, so as to offer an effectual barrier to the passage of all kinds of stock.

FENCING.

The right of way must be fenced, where required by the Engineer, with steel-barbed wire-fencing, made of peeled red-cedar or black-locust posts, six inches in diameter, eight feet long, three feet in the ground, with earth well rammed around them, standing vertically in true line, one rod from centre to centre and joined by four or five lines (as may be required), of No. 12 double strand, twisted, steel-barbed wire, fastened in approved manner to each post, and thoroughly protected from rust by immersion in boiled linseed-oil and by two coats of approved iron-clad paint.

TELEGRAPH LINE.

A telegraph line must be built between Somerset and Boyce's Station with as many intermediate stations as may be required. The poles to be of red cedar or white oak, peeled of all bark, twenty-five feet long, not less than five inches in diameter at the small end, four feet in the ground, with material well rammed in the holes. They must set one hundred and seventy-five feet from centre to centre, on a true line parallel with and forty five feet from the centre-line of railway. When of white oak, the poles must be well charred for a length of six feet from the butt end.

Wire must be of No. 9 gauge, galvanized, properly spliced, and fastened to glass-capped insulators, firmly spiked to the poles.

Instruments to be such as are now used at stations on the completed part of the railway.

CINCINNATI SOUTHERN RAILWAY.

FOR BUILDINGS, PLATFORMS, WATER STATIONS, CATTLE-PENS, CATTLE-GUARDS, ROAD-CROSSINGS, TURN-TABLES, FENCING, AND TELEGRAPH LINE.

The undersigned hereby certify that they have personally examined the location of all structures to be built on the line of the Cincinnati Southern Railway to which they have annexed prices hereon; also, that they have carefully examined the plans and diagrams adopted for the same, and the specifications hereto annexed.

Having made such examinations, the undersigned hereby propose to the Trustees of the Cincinnati Southern Railway to complete any or all the structures, and do all the work specified according to the plans, diagrams, and specifications aforesaid, and on the acceptance of the proposal do hereby bind themselves to enter into and execute a contract for all said work and structures at the following prices:

1. Depots:—Plan A, each,	$2450 00
Plan B, each,	2145 00
Plan C, each,	1842 00
Plan D, each,	1512 00
2. Platform:—12 feet wide, per lineal foot,	1 50
6 feet wide, per lineal foot,	1 00
3. Cattle-pens:—Fence, per lineal foot,	22
Shutes, each,	25 25
Gates, each,	8 00
4. Water Stations:—Tank-frame, tank, roof, valve and spout, complete:—With Hip roof,	700 00
With Flat roof,	650 00
Pump-houses, each,	85 00
Steam-pump and boiler, complete,	700 00
Pipe in place:—1½-inch, per lineal foot,	20
2-inch, per lineal foot,	25
2½-inch, per lineal foot,	30
3-inch, per lineal foot,	40
5. Coal-platforms, per lineal foot,	5 50
6. Engine-houses:—With 3 stalls, each,	2085 00
With 4 stalls, each,	2840 00
With 5 stalls, each,	3450 00
With 6 stalls, each,	4000 00
7. Turn-tables, complete, each,	2400 00
8. Section-houses, each,	400 00
9. Tool-houses, each,	75 00
10. Cattle-guards, in place, each,	40 00
11. Road-crossings, in place, each,	25 00
12. Fencing:—One line, per mile, with 4 wires,	400 00
One line, per mile, with 5 wires,	450 00
13. Telegraph Line:—Line, per mile,	80 00
Stations, each,	45 00

The undersigned further propose to begin work within *fifteen* days from date hereof.

Signed this *26th* day of *August*, 1878.

The foregoing is a copy of the Proposals and Prices referred to in the contract of this 26th day of August, 1878.

R. G. HUSTON & CO.
RICHARD G. HUSTON.
THOMAS O'CONNER.
JOHN B. NEELY.

NORTHERN PACIFIC RAILROAD COMPANY.

GENERAL SPECIFICATIONS.*

FOUNDATIONS.

52. Foundation-pits shall be of such dimensions and excavated to such depth as the Engineer in charge of the work may deem necessary to ensure the safety and stability of the structure to be erected, and the

---

* This specification was kindly furnished for publication by Mr. J. W. Kendrick, Chief Engineer, Northern Pacific Railroad. The following sections have been omitted, however, as not distinctly falling within the scope of this book: Clearing and Grubbing, § 1 to § 6; Grading, § 7 to § 34; Tunnels, §35 to § 51; First-class Masonry, Culvert Masonry, Brick Arches, Box Culverts and Paving, § 61 to § 115; Rip-rap, Blind Drains, Abutment and Pier Cribs, § 148 to § 154; Frame Trestles, Truss Bridges, Log and Timber Culverts and Fences, § 170 to § 236.

materials so excavated shall be deposited in the embankments, unless otherwise ordered by the Engineer, and shall be considered and estimated as part of the ordinary excavation on the section.

53. Whenever required, piling or grillages composed of timber or plank shall be introduced as a part of the foundation of structures. The dimensions, quality and quantity of all materials used, and the manner in which the work shall be done, will be subject to the directions of the Engineer. Piling will be paid for by the lineal foot, measured below the cut-off, and the timber will be estimated at the price that applies to timber in structures.

54. Where piling is used for foundations, the piles must conform to the specifications under paragraph 165, and will be driven to such depth as required by the Engineer to secure a reliable foundation. Pile foundations for all masonry must be cut off below low water mark, so as to make a uniform level support for the grillage under the masonry. In case a grillage is used, its top surface must be at least 12 inches below extreme low-water.

55. In preparing foundations for trestles or other structures, care must be taken to have the bed entirely in excavation, whenever practicable, and to thoroughly tamp and solidify the soil before erecting the structure When such foundations are partially upon an embankment, they must be constructed of masonry, which will be classified as rubble or dry rubble. (See paragraphs 116 to 130.)

56. No allowance will be made for pumping or baling, unless specially provided for in the agreement. The price paid for excavation and materials used will be considered as full compensation for the same completed and delivered in the work.

57. The soil in the bottoms of foundation trenches for abutments or retaining-walls or buildings and other structures must be thoroughly tamped and brought to true and proper level before masonry or structure is commenced.

MASONRY.

58. The kind of stone to be used will be designated by the Engineer.

59. All stones must be sound, free from seams, sand-holes, and other defects.

60. All stones must be laid on their natural beds.

FIRST-CLASS RUBBLE MASONRY.

116. Rubble masonry for retaining-walls will be built of derrick stone (that is, stones of such size and weight that a derrick is required to handle them), of proper size and thickness for the dimensions of the work. They must be of fair shape, and spalled so that they will lay with good and even bearings upon the wall without the undue use of spalls or pinners. Care must be taken to secure good faces.

117. All stones must be laid with full mortar beds and joints. Exposed faces must be neatly pointed.

118. There must be a header in each course, not less than once in eight feet, so introduced between the course above and below as to make a thorough bond. The length of headers must be at least twice the width of the stretchers. All headers must be at least four feet long. When walls are five feet or less in thickness the headers must extend through them.

119. In general, no stones less than 12 inches in thickness will be allowed.

120. The walls must conform to the dimensions given by the plans.

121. Weep-holes must be left in the masonry wherever directed by the Engineer.

122. Copings must conform to the dimensions and be dressed in the manner shown by plans.

SECOND-CLASS RUBBLE MASONRY.

123. Rubble masonry for buildings, turn-tables, etc., will be composed of stones of proper size and thickness for the dimensions of the work. They must be of fair shape, and spalled so that they will lay with good and even bearings in the wall.

124. All stones shall be laid in full mortar beds and joints. All exposed faces must be neatly pointed.

125. All work must be thoroughly done and well bonded. An abundance of headers must be introduced and properly spaced, so as to make a good and substantial wall. No stone will be considered a header that does not extend through light walls.

126. The tops of all walls or piers will be finished to a true level surface with stones, the width of which is equal to the thickness of the wall.

127. No stones less than six inches in thickness are to be used; and generally the thickness must not be less than ten inches.

128. The walls must conform to the dimensions given on the plans, or must be built according to the instructions of the Engineer.

129. Water-tables and pedestal-stones must conform to the dimensions given on the plans, and must be dressed as shown therein. They must be accurately set on a bed of mortar by being tamped to place to the lines and levels shown on the plans or given by the Engineer.

DRY RUBBLE MASONRY.

130. Dry rubble masonry will be built according to the specifications for second-class rubble masonry, except that mortar will not be used.

TANK FOUNDATIONS.

131. Masonry for foundations of water-tanks will be broken range. Continuous courses will not be required.

132. No course shall be less than 12 inches in thickness.

133. Stones must have beds at least one and one-half times their thickness, and must be dressed on the upper and lower beds to three fourths of an inch.

134. All stones must be laid in full mortar beds and joints. Exposed faces must be neatly pointed.

135. In general, every third stone in each course must be a header, and shall extend through the wall.

136. No spalls will be allowed, except in small vertical openings between stretchers.

MORTAR.

137. When mortar is made with American cement it is to be composed of one part of cement to two parts of clean, coarse, sharp sand, thoroughly mixed while dry, wet to the proper consistency, and thoroughly worked.

138. It must be made on clean plank beds, and in small quantities, as required for use.

139. When made of imported cement it shall be composed of one part of cement to four parts of clean, sharp sand, or otherwise, as the Engineer may direct. It shall be mixed, wet, and worked as above specified.

140. POINTING MORTAR shall be made of equal measures of cement and clean, sharp, and fine sand, thoroughly mixed while dry, and wet to the proper consistency.

CONCRETE "A."

141. Will be made as follows: The ingredients must be hydraulic cement of the best quality, clean, coarse, sharp sand and broken stone, any piece of which shall pass through a two-and-one-half-inch ring.

142. These ingredients will be used in the proportion of one part American cement, two and one half parts sand, and five parts broken stone. The sand and cement must be thoroughly mixed on clean plank beds while dry, then wet to the proper consistency, and worked. The broken stone must then be worked into the mortar until every piece is covered. Wheel to pit and place in layers, tamping lightly until the water flushes to the surface. Finish all top surfaces level.

143. If imported cement is used the ingredients will be in the following proportions: One part cement, four parts sand, six parts broken stone, as above specified.

144. The proportions of these ingredients may be changed at the discretion of the Engineer.

145. When Concrete "A" is used in wet pits the water must be excluded by the use of canvas, side moulds of timber, or otherwise, until the cement has set.

CONCRETE "B."

146. The ingredients for the mortar are to be the same as designated for Concrete "A." The mortar is to be deposited in layers. Stones of miscellaneous sizes are then to be thrown in and rammed until entirely surrounded by mortar.

147. The top surface must be finished level at the proper height.

WELLS.

155. Wells for water stations will be 16 feet in diameter inside of the curb, which will usually be 16 inches in thickness.

156. Wells will be curbed with rubble masonry, laid in mortar (see paragraph 123 *et seq.*), or with hard, well-burned bricks, laid in cement mortar. (See paragraph 137.)

157. Wells for depots and section houses must be three feet in diameter, inside of the curb, which will usually be twelve inches thick, and composed of dry rubble masonry. (See paragraph 136.)

[illegible]

[illegible]

[illegible] approved by the Engineer. [illegible]

[illegible] in strict accordance with the standard plans.

[illegible] as the Engineer may direct.

[illegible] perfect line and surface at the completion of the work.

[illegible]

[illegible] as designated by the Engineer. They must [illegible] nor more than twelve (12) inches [illegible] nor more than twenty-two (22) inches [illegible] before they are inspected.

[illegible] at convenient points, which must be [illegible] sufficient size to keep them well up from the ground.

[illegible] the fall of a hammer weighing [illegible] penetration not to exceed [illegible] judgment of the Engineer the ground is so hard that [illegible]

[illegible]

[illegible] a great depth and piles of adequate length cannot be obtained [illegible] as far as practicable, it must be [illegible] squared and set on top of the one already [illegible] four sides and fastened together by spiking on pieces of scantling.

[illegible] for the part below the cut-off. Timber will be paid for [illegible] B. M. [illegible]

[illegible] the necessary false-work to cross streams or [illegible] are to be afterwards built in order to proceed with track-laying, [illegible] for work beyond. Such false-work will be paid for at the contract [illegible]

BUILDINGS.

237. [illegible] must be constructed according to the standard plans.

238. EXCAVATIONS. [illegible], excavating for cellars, trenches, foundations, etc., must [illegible] the plans and the directions of the Engineer and will be paid for by the cubic yard, [illegible] and at the prices that apply to grading. The price paid for excavation of [illegible] the back-filling of the same, for which no allowance shall be made.

239. DRAINS. Drains will [illegible] be of first quality of vitrified tile, with the dimensions shown by the standard plans. They must be carefully laid on a true grade, with a fall of at least one inch in 50 feet, and more if the elevation of the outlet will permit. They must be jointed with hydraulic cement, and must be scraped smooth inside as laid. They must be provided with all necessary traps, bends, and connections, and be left in perfect working order.

240. FOUNDATION-WALLS. Foundation-walls will generally be classified under the head of second-class

rubble masonry (see paragraph 129), laid with cement mortar, hydraulic lime mortar, or lime mortar, as directed by the Engineer.

241. BRICK-WORK.—Bricks used in buildings must be of standard size, well and neatly moulded and thoroughly burned. Care must be taken to exclude salmon brick, or bricks which are imperfectly burned. The stock of bricks must be assorted, and those of perfect shape, quality, and uniform color must be used in face of wall.

242. Bricks for paving and other special purposes must be selected with especial reference to the purpose for which they are intended to be used.

243. All bricks must be thoroughly wet before laying.

244. In general, bricks in the walls of buildings above the water-table, boiler-settings, and chimneys will be laid in lime mortar. (See paragraph 258.)

245. Bricks in pits or foundations, below the elevation of the water-table, and not exposed to an undue amount of moisture, will be laid in hydraulic lime mortar. (See paragraph 259.)

246. Bricks for floor arches and other masonry which is exposed to water will be laid in cement mortar. (See paragraph 260.)

247. Bricks in walls will generally be laid in common bond; five stretcher courses to one header course. The Engineer may require a more thorough bond when he deems it necessary.

248. All bricks must be laid in full mortar beds and all joints must be completely filled.

249. Particular care must be taken to secure straight, level bed-joints of moderate uniform thickness. All joints must be cut and struck as the work proceeds.

250. Arches must be turned upon proper and substantial centres, which should be slacked away as soon as the mortar has set.

251. Hollow walls must be tied together every fifth course with bricks not over three feet apart. Care must be taken to leave air-vents in such cases.

252. Anchors, hinge-castings, lookouts, nailing-strips, etc., must be properly and neatly jointed into the brick-work.

253. Where the interior of brick walls is to be lathed and plastered, build in a lath to which to nail furring-strip every fifth joint.

254. Scaffolding must be furnished by the Contracter, and must be thoroughly and strongly built.

255. Brick paving will be understood to be bricks set on edge, bedded in cement mortar and grouted.

256. Chimney flues will be constructed as shown by the plans. Especial pains must be taken to secure full mortar joints. They must be thoroughly plastered on the inside and trowelled to a smooth finish.

257. Thimbles must be provided as shown by the plans.

258. MORTAR.—Lime mortar will be composed of fresh lime and sand, in the proportion of one part of the former to about four of the latter. The proportions of lime and sand may be varied to suit the nature of the lime used, and the product must in all cases be satisfactory to the Engineer.

259. Hydraulic lime-mortar will be composed of one part of hydraulic cement, two parts of lime, and six parts of sand. The cement must be thoroughly mixed with three parts of sand in a dry state. The slacked lime must then be added gradually, the remaining five parts of sand worked into the mortar thus formed, and the whole mass worked to the proper condition for use.

260. Cement mortar will be made of hydraulic cement and sand, in the proportion of one part of cement to three parts of sand. These ingredients must be measured. They must be thoroughly mixed while dry, and then wet and worked to the proper consistency.

261. The proportion of ingredients as mentioned above may be changed by the order of the Engineer, if the mortar thus made is not satisfactory to him.

262. All mortar will be made in small quantities, as required for use, and none shall be used after it has commenced to set.

263. Cement and lime not required for immediate use must be protected from moisture; and any deterioration in its quality from this cause, and loss resulting therefrom, will be charged to the Contractor.

264. Clean, sharp sand, thoroughly screened, shall be furnished for all work.

265. Fresh water must be used for making mortar, and all mortar must be prepared on clean plank-beds.

266. PLASTER.—All lime for the rough coat shall be the best white lime, thoroughly slacked, strained through a sieve, mixed with coarse, sharp, clean sand, and plenty of properly picked winter hair.

267. The first coat of plaster must extend behind wainscoting, if any, through the floor, and must fill out all spaces between frames of timber, etc. After the first coat has dried, put on hard finish and trowel to a true and glossy surface.

268. After carpenters are through, plasterers must patch up all defects.

269. TIMBER.—Timber must be sound, free from wanes, shakes, and large, black, or unsound knots. It must be of the quality specified by the standard plans, and when this specification does not agree with the grades of the local markets, it will be understood that it must be suitable for the purpose for which it is intended.

270. All timber will be subject to the inspection and acceptance of the Engineer.

271. Timber having defects which impair its strength must be excluded from all work where it will be subjected to a considerable load.

272. Where sizes are given they will be understood to mean the dimensions of the timber as it comes from the saw, without reference to the diminution in size caused by dressing, unless an exception is noted upon the plans.

273. All timber and workmanship is subject to inspection before and after it is put into the work, and the Engineer may order any part of the structure, which in material or workmanship does not correspond with the terms of these specifications, removed, and substitution made in proper manner, at the expense of the Contractor.

274. MILL-WORK.—All material used for making window-sash, frames, and work of this description, must be made of first-quality white pine, excepting such portions of window or other frames as will not be exposed, which may be of common lumber.

275. All timber used for these purposes must be thoroughly dried and seasoned. All inferior finish shall be kiln-dried lumber, free from imperfections. Stair-railings, balusters, treads, risers, stringers, mouldings, and wainscotings must be made of material specified by the plans.

276. All finish shall be put up in the best manner, smoothed by hand, and left free from machine and tool marks.

277. Unless especially agreed to the contrary, it will be understood that interior wood-work is to be painted, unless finish is hard wood, in which case it shall be filled with oil, rubbed and finished with a hard finish.

278. When not otherwise specified, all sash will be glazed with second-quality American glass, S. S.

279. Contractor must properly protect all frames, sash, and doors, not used immediately, from the action of the rain and sun. All mill-work, except such as is required for inside work, and mouldings shall receive one priming-coat before shipping. This will not apply to the frames shipped knocked down, which will receive their priming-coat after they are fastened together and before they are put into the work.

280. All door and window frames must be carefully squared before they are put into the work, and stayed to keep them in proper position.

281. IRON.—Castings must be made of the best quality of tough gray iron, neatly moulded, free from sand-holes, flaws, or other imperfections. Particular care must be taken, especially in chord-work, to have the holes required by rods, bolts, etc., large enough to admit these without battering the threads.

282. Rod-iron must be of good quality of merchant-iron. If an enlargement of the diameter of the rods for screw-ends is called for, such enlargement is to be secured by upsetting, not by welding. An exception may be made in the case of suspension-rods for large doors and other work in which the rods are not subjected to considerable strain.

283. All turn-buckles and other forged work to be well and neatly made.

284. CARPENTER-WORK.—All framing is to be done in a neat and workmanlike manner, to give close joints, and thoroughly nailed and spiked. All joists and studding must be sized. Studding must be doubled around openings, with double headers and trusses above openings. All corners and angles must be made solid.

285. Joists must be stiffened by bridging cut in at proper intervals.

286. Roof-boards must be nailed to rafters at every intersection, to avoid warping and injury to the roof-covering.

287. Buildings which are to be plastered will be lathed with best dry pine lath. Laths will break joints every fifth lath, and shall be nailed with threepenny coarse lath-nails, leaving a three-eighths-inch crack. No vertical laths shall be put on for the purpose of piecing out.

288. In case of the omission of any essential parts upon the plans, such omissions must be supplied in workmanlike manner; and flimsy, shiftless work will not be permitted.

289. Matched flooring must be blind-nailed, and smoothed by hand.

290. Siding will be firmly nailed to each stud. Drop-siding and clapboards must be neatly jointed and blind-nailed.

291. Where floors are double, a layer of No. 2 roofing-felt must be put in between upper and lower courses.

292. The top floor must not be laid before the plastering is finished.

293. The building must be cleared of all rubbish, and swept before it is plastered. All refuse, chips shavings, etc., must be collected and disposed of by burning or otherwise; and the interior of the building, as well as the grounds around it, must be left free from all litter.

294. Hardware, locks, knobs, window-fastenings, etc., are to be neatly put into place, and must be of suitable quality and satisfactory to the Engineer.

295. PAINTING.—All woodwork that is exposed to the weather (excepting rough work) shall receive priming coat and two finishing coats, in colors corresponding to the Company's standard.

296. Body-work will be finished in dark red. Trimmings and sashes in dark green. Doors will be finished in solid body colors. No trimming paint on panels.

297. All knot-holes and cracks must be puttied, and knots or pitchy places filled with shellac before painting.

298. Interior work must be finished with two coats of paint; standard colors.

299. Shingle roofs will be finished with two coats of paint; standard colors.

WATER-TANKS.

300. Water-tanks are to be built according to the standard plans. Posts must be cut to the proper height, and sized to receive cast-iron caps. Caps must be sized to fit the casting. Timber caps should be bored to receive dowel.

301. Joists must be sized on the edges, and framed into the headers. The upper half of the joist should be left on and cut made in the header to receive it. Cut in double bridging over caps.

302. Lay tub-joists on top of level floor at right angles to grain. Joists to be sized on both edges, and to have ends cut circular one and one-half inches inside of staves of tub.

303. The edges of bottom planks are to be accurately jointed, to insure perfect contact, and be well clamped and cut to proper circle, two and one-half inches larger than small joists.

304. The floor must be well dowelled, and joints white-leaded.

305. Staves are to be carefully jointed, to secure perfect contact, and should be put together with white-lead joints, and three tiers of dowels. The chime is to be accurately fitted to the bottom. Staves are to be surfaced on both sides.

306. Put on the third band first; then commence at the bottom and put the bands in regular order. Divide the lugs equally around the tub and screw up to fair bearing.

307. Bands must be watched when filling tub to prevent breaking on account of swelling of timber.

308. Ceil as shown by plan. Dap all ceiling-joists one-half inch down on edge of tank.

309. Joists on track side to be left long enough for platform to carry pipe standard and to come out flush with outlet pipe on each side of pipe to receive weights.

310. Valve to be so placed that bolt-holes will take in two centre planks and have one-eighth-inch rubber gasket under it. The in-take pipe is to be extended up within six inches of the top of the tub, and to have a T-nipple and gate-valve, with long stem provided with T-angle above ceiling. Gate-valve to be close to bottom of tank.

311. Construct air-spaces carefully in accordance with the plans. Leave a two-by-four opening on the south side, provided with three doors, the outer one to be hinged.

312. Sheeting and battens must be in accordance with the plans.

313. Provide inside and outside ladders as shown by the plans.

PUMP-HOUSES.

314. Particular attention must be paid to the location of pump-houses, so that it will be convenient to supply them with fuel from the cars. They will be built in accordance with the standard plans.

WATER-PIPES.

315. All wrought-iron pipes with screw ends must be laid on true grade so that they can be thoroughly drained. Threads must be treated with red lead before uniting. They must be screwed together as far as practicable.

CAST-IRON PIPES.

316. Cast-iron pipes must be laid on true grade so that they can be thoroughly drained. All changes in direction are to be made with curved pipes, and connection with proper branches delivering in direction of drainage.

317. Joints in cast-iron pipes shall be made by calking in hemp packing, and shall then be run with molten lead and thoroughly calked.

318. Joints of lead pipe with iron pipe shall be made by calking in a brass ferrule and making connection between lead pipe and ferrule by a wiped joint.

319. Joints between lead pipes must be wiped.

MATERIAL.

320. Unless otherwise provided, it will be understood that the Railroad Company is to furnish to the Contractor all the material required for track, bridges, and buildings, with the exceptions hereafter noted, on board cars at point of divergence from the main line of the branch railroad to be constructed, or at points along the line of road to be constructed, but not necessarily alongside the roadbed; or, in the case of buildings and structures erected under contract, upon lines already constructed, delivery will be made on board cars at the site of such buildings or structures, or as near as practicable thereto.

321. The exceptions above referred to are the stone for rubble masonry,—and other masonry, unless otherwise specified in the contract,—gravel, concrete stone and sand for mortar, etc., logs for log culverts and log crib-work, all of which will be furnished by the Contractor, unless otherwise specified by the Contract.

322. The Contractor will be required to receive and receipt for all material immediately on arrival, and will thereafter be held responsible for its safe keeping until its incorporation in the work. Storehouses or other structures required to shelter the material will be provided by the Contractor at his own expense, and the material of the Railroad Company will not be used for this or any purpose other than that for which it is intended.

323. The Contractor will be required to handle all material at his own expense, including unloading and loading in cars, and all material must be unloaded from cars within three days after its arrival, unless special authority to the contrary is given by the Engineer.

324. Whenever cross-ties, piles, timber or other material is delivered along the line of the road, the Contractors must do the hauling required to put it in place, including loading in cars when necessary.

TRAIN SERVICE.

325. The Railroad Company will furnish the necessary engines, cars (except iron cars), and train crews required for the work of track laying, ballasting, and hauling of material, but the amount and kind to be furnished will be at the discretion of the Railroad Company. The train service will be controlled by the Engineer or such person as he may designate.

GENERAL.

326. It is distinctly understood that the quantities of work estimated are approximate only, and the Railroad Company reserves the right to have built only such kinds and quantities, and according to such plans, as the nature or economy of the work, in the opinion of the Engineer, may require.

327. The Contractor, at his own cost, must provide all wagon-roads to reach and carry on the work; he must also provide all tools of every description, and all supplies required for the prosecution of the work.

328. Any omission to disapprove of work at the time of making any monthly or other estimate will not be construed as an acceptance of any defective work, and the Contractor must remove and rebuild, or make good at his own cost, any work which the Engineer may consider to be defectively executed.

329. It is expressly understood that all work of any character, performed for the Railroad Company, under these specifications, must be satisfactory to the Engineer in charge of the work, and to the Chief Engineer.

330. The price paid for buildings, water-tanks, turn-tables, depots, section houses, and other standard structures, will be held to include the foundations, according to these plans; and it will be understood that the specifications for concrete, rubble masonry, etc., and the prices which govern such work, are intended to cover additional work of the same character which may be required, and is not shown upon the plans.

INDEX.

* Illustrated.

www.ingramcontent.com/pod-product-compliance
Lightning Source LLC
Chambersburg PA
CBHW080126041025
33595CB00019B/1511

* 9 7 8 1 1 6 9 9 7 7 7 2 3 *